INVESTMENT
CONCEPTS · ANALYSIS · STRATEGY

THIRD EDITION

Robert S. Hamada Series in Finance

INVESTMENT
CONCEPTS · ANALYSIS · STRATEGY

THIRD EDITION

ROBERT C. RADCLIFFE
University of Florida

SCOTT, FORESMAN/LITTLE, BROWN HIGHER EDUCATION
A Division of Scott, Foresman and Company
Glenview, Illinois   London, England

Credits are listed at the back of the book on pages C-1 through C-3, which constitute a legal extension of the copyright page.

Library of Congress Cataloging-in-Publication Data

Radcliffe, Robert C.
    Investment: concepts, analysis, and strategy / Robert C.
    Radcliffe. — 3rd ed.
        p.   cm.
    Includes bibliographical references.
    ISBN 0-673-46018-5
    1. Investments.   2. Investment analysis.   3. Securities.
    4. Speculation.   I. Title.
    HG4521.R26   1989
    332.63'2 — dc20

                                                    89-27499
                                                    CIP

Copyright © 1990, 1987, 1982 Scott, Foresman and Company.
All Rights Reserved.
Printed in the United States of America.

    2 3 4 5 6 RIG 94 93 92 91 90

To my parents, Robert and Doris

The objective of *Investment: Concepts • Analysis • Strategy*, Third Edition, remains the same as in previous editions: to examine how people should make portfolio investment and speculative decisions. Pure investment decisions are made in the belief that security prices are "fair," that prices are what they should be, given their risks. Investment-motivated decisions result in relatively passive trading strategies that focus on obtaining an appropriate level of portfolio risk and return. In contrast, pure speculative decisions are made in the belief that security prices might be "incorrect"— that they might provide a return either higher or lower than they should, given a security's risk. Decisions motivated by speculation result in relatively active trading strategies that focus on short- and long-run portfolio performance. Throughout the book, we examine concepts and techniques associated with each approach.

A number of methodological themes run throughout this book. Some of these include: (1) constant reference to strategies suggested by investment and speculative approaches to security selection; (2) attempts to integrate theory with pragmatic problems of application; (3) end-of-chapter problems that both review chapter content and attempt to expand the student's understanding of the material; and (4) use of actual data to illustrate techniques and concepts.

Changes in the Third Edition

The security markets have changed dramatically over the past 20 years and there is no apparent slowdown in sight. Security markets are in the process of an ongoing revolution, as evidenced by the internationalization of trading, a variety of new instruments, and improved communication abilities.

The major changes in this edition include the following:

1. *Data Analysis Problems.* Most chapters include an end-of-chapter problem which uses real data to illustrate the concepts developed in the chapter. The data is provided on computer diskette worksheets which are compatible with microcomputer programs similar to Lotus. I firmly believe that the more that students are shown real data, as opposed to hypothetical textbook examples, the more they will truly learn.

2. *Expanded Discussion of Options and Futures.* Trading volume in index options and futures has grown dramatically since the text was last revised. Because of the importance which options and futures have in portfolio hedging and arbitrage strategies, the text includes an expanded discussion of derivative securities. Options are now presented in two chapters which focus on index options and include detailed discussions of the multiperiod binomial model, synthetic securities, index arbitrages, and various realistic hedging strategies. The chapter on financial futures also includes many realistic examples of hedging and speculative strategies such as creating an index fund, portfolio insurance, and index arbitrage.

3. *Strategic Asset Allocation.* Two chapters are devoted to strategic asset allocation. The problems faced by defined benefit pension plans are discussed in more detail

than in any other investment textbook. There is an emphasis on pension funds for two reasons: (1) they present virtually all the problems which any investor must deal with, and (2) recent advances in strategic asset allocation have been focused on them.

4. *Internationalization*. Because security trading must be considered in a global context today, this new edition contains increased discussion of foreign securities. This is often difficult because the globalization of the markets is still at the stage of pioneering, and reliable return data has a short history.

5. *Recent Questions About Price Efficiency*. During the 1980s, serious questions were raised about security market efficiency. These range from questions of excess volatility and investor overreaction to questions about the January Effect. Chapter 10, which treats the efficient market hypothesis, has been expanded to include both classic studies supporting the EMH and more recent studies that seem contrary to a rationally priced market. In addition, the question of market efficiency is often integrated into other chapters when appropriate.

Text Organization

In organizing *Investment: Concepts • Analysis • Strategy*, Third Edition, I have chosen what I believe to be a rather compelling logic. Before any conceptual issues can be grasped, the student must have a general understanding of the types of securities traded in the financial market and the ways they are traded. Once such an overview has been completed, a review of concepts which underlie all security pricing and strategy decisions should be presented before serious attention can be given to individual security types. Given a strong conceptual foundation, students can then proceed to an analysis of the unique characteristics of bonds, stocks, options, futures, and other securities. Finally, various strategies of portfolio management can be evaluated. The organization of this book follows exactly such a process. It consists of four major parts: Introduction, Investment Concepts, Security Analyses, and Introduction to Strategy.

The first part, Introduction, consists of four chapters designed to provide a basic knowledge of the institutional features of security markets. Chapter 1 is a general overview of the rest of the book and presents a process of security selection, defines many important terms, and provides an overview of some critical concepts discussed later. Chapters 2 and 3 discuss institutional characteristics of the major types of securities as well as how securities are traded in the primary and secondary markets. Part 1 concludes with a discussion of United States and international stock and bond indexes as well as rate-of-return calculations. With these chapters as a background, the student should be well prepared to examine the major concepts of investment management in Part 2.

Part 2, Investment Concepts, develops and critiques a variety of the more important investment theories which underlie most security pricing and investment or speculative decisions. Chapter 5 explains why a financial market exists, the economic role of risk-free interest rates, and determinants of the risk-free interest rate. Chapter 6 extends the notion of a risk-free interest rate by discussing alternative theories of the yield curve. Chapters 7 through 9 expand on the discussion of the determination of the required return on a security by dealing with risk. These chapters start with risk faced by the individual (Chapter 7), move through the classical CAPM (Chapter 8), and conclude with criticisms and expansions of the CAPM as well as a review of APT (Chapter 9). The final concepts chapter discusses the economic logic, empirical evidence, and implications of Efficient Market Theory.

Part 3, Security Analyses, includes eight chapters dealing with individual security types. Two chapters are devoted to bonds, stocks, and options, with the first chapter in each case devoted to fundamental risk/return characteristics of the security, and the second devoted to investment and speculative trading of each security. These are followed by a chapter on financial futures and a chapter which examines securities that have recently gained in popularity: international, real estate, and investment companies.

Part 4, Introduction to Strategy, begins with the chapter titled Portfolio Management, in which the broad overview of the portfolio investment process is described. The statement of investment policy is discussed in detail and the concepts of strategic versus tactical asset allocation are presented. The next chapter, Strategic Asset Allocation, presents a number of ways in which individuals and institutions might determine their desired long-run asset allocation. Considerable attention is given to the strategic asset allocation problems faced by defined benefit pension plans. Two subsequent chapters examine speculative adjustments which might be made to the strategic asset allocation by timing (Tactical Asset Allocation) and by security selection (Company Analysis). Finally, the book concludes with a discussion of the issues involved in performance monitoring.

Supplemental Materials

A number of items are available as aids to both students and instructors. These include the following:

1. Financial Analysis Software Package. Prior to the general use of microcomputers, access to the history of security returns, investment risk, and the profits on potential trading strategies was available only to those who could afford large computer costs — scholars and institutions. Today, microcomputers have the ability to provide data to anyone who desires it.

To help such students of the security markets, a Financial Analysis Software Package is made available to instructors from Scott, Foresman/Little, Brown. This package includes two diskettes that instructors may freely copy for classroom use. One diskette contains an extensive number of "data banks." These data banks range from historical U.S. returns on various security classes to EPS, DPS, book values, and interest rates. International returns and proxies for real estate returns are also provided. These data will allow students to go beyond textbook learning into a learning based on personal discovery. The other diskette contains a wide variety of computer programs ranging from Markowitz efficient frontier packages to Black-Scholes implied standard deviations.

2. Study Guide. Students and adopters have requested that a Study Guide be available as a supplement to the third edition. This study guide is somewhat unusual when compared with other study guides. Although students who are looking for an efficient way to prepare or who are having difficulty with the material will find the Study Guide useful, its purpose is broader. Unlike introductory finance courses (in which study guides are common), investment courses tend to attract finance majors and other students who are quite serious about learning as much as possible. Thus, the Study Guide is designed with two goals in mind. First, it provides a review and test of chapter content for those who need additional aid. Second, and perhaps more important, it adds depth to the topical coverage. New material is *not* taught. However, questions and problems integrate chapter material more thoroughly than the end-of-chapter questions and problems are often able to. The Study Guide includes a series of thought questions, numerical problems, true-false questions, and multiple choice questions. Detailed solutions are provided.

3. Instructor's Manual/Test Bank. This supplement provides detailed solutions to end-of-chapter questions and problems, true-false and multiple choice test banks, computer program documentation (as noted above), and selected supplemental handouts.

Acknowledgments

Many people participated, directly or indirectly, in this project. Principal among these are my past students, whose enthusiasm, desire to learn, and encouragement are reflected on each page. In addition, I would like to acknowledge the help of the following people:

Eugene Brigham, *University of Florida*
Young Hoon Byun, *University of Florida*
Robert Brooks, *Alabama University*
Anand Desai, *University of Florida*
Gautum Dhingra, *Hewitt Associates*
Dale Domian, *Michigan State University*
Shalom Hochman, *University of Houston*
Roger Huang, *Vanderbilt University*
Mark Flannery, *University of Florida*
Miles Livingston, *University of Florida*
Andrew McCollough, *University of Florida*
Brian Maxwell, *PI Analytics, Inc.*
M.P. Narayanan, *University of Michigan*
David Nye, *University of Florida*
Thomas O'Brien, *University of Connecticut*
Richard Ogden, *PI Analytics, Inc.*

Robert Pari, *Bentley College*
Robert Penter, *Hewitt Associates*
John Pickett, *Eppler, Guerin and Turner, Inc.*
James Richardson, *University of Florida*
William Regan, *Eppler, Guerin and Turner, Inc.*
Kevin Scanlon, *University of Notre Dame*
Louis Scott, *University of Illinois at Urbana-Champaign*
Gregory Smith, *University of Florida*
Craig Tapley, *University of Florida*
Robert Wood, *Eppler, Guerin and Turner, Inc.*
William Wood, *Bridgewater College*
Soushan Wu, *National Chiao-Tung University, Taiwan*
Taiheup Yi, *University of Florida*

Special thanks also go to Barbara Long, who efficiently typed the manuscript, and to Nancy Tenney, who did a marvelous job as the copyeditor. I also appreciate the staff at Scott, Foresman/Little, Brown, who kept the project on track, in particular Bruce Kaplan, Julie Howell, and Judy Neighbor. Finally, the person who deserves my deepest thanks is my wife, Irene. Without her patience and support, this would still be a dream.

R.C.R.

Part 1   *Introduction*   1

CHAPTER 1

CHAPTER 2

CHAPTER 3

Overview of the Security Markets   64

CHAPTER 4

Market Indexes and Returns   109

Part 2 *Investment Concepts*

CHAPTER 5

The Economic Roles of Security Markets

CHAPTER 6

Term Structure

CHAPTER 7

Risk and Diversification 207

CHAPTER 8

Capital Asset Pricing Theory 265

CHAPTER 9

Capital Asset Pricing Extensions 307

CHAPTER 10

An Efficient Market 345

Part 3   *Security Analyses*

C H A P T E R 11

C H A P T E R 12

CHAPTER 13

Stock Fundamentals 478

CHAPTER 14

Stock Trading 525

C H A P T E R 15

Option Fundamentals 564

C H A P T E R 16

Option Trading 618

CHAPTER 17

Futures 676

CHAPTER 18

Other Investment Alternatives 728

Part 4   *Introduction to Strategy* 783

CHAPTER 19

Portfolio Management   784

CHAPTER 20

Strategic Asset Allocation   836

CHAPTER 23

INVESTMENT
CONCEPTS · ANALYSIS · STRATEGY

THIRD EDITION

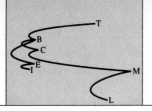

1 Introduction

"What security-selection strategy should I follow in order to achieve the highest possible returns without bearing unacceptable risk?" This is the essential question faced by all investors and speculators.

The goal of any investments text should be to help the reader develop a clear idea of the pros and cons of potential selection strategies. But such strategies can be clearly understood only after one has a sound foundation in the basic concepts and analytic techniques that apply to all securities. Consequently, this text is organized into three broad areas—concepts, analysis, and strategies.

Concepts are discussed in Part 2. The major concepts examined include (1) why financial markets and interest rates exist, (2) what security risk is and how it can be measured, and (3) how expected security returns are related to their risks. In Part 3 we analyze the critical features of specific security instruments, including (1) bonds, (2) stocks, (3) options, (4) futures, and (5) investment companies. Finally, Part 4 examines various strategies of portfolio management.

But before we can begin to address any of this material, there are certain institutional aspects that need to be reviewed. This is the purpose of the four chapters that make up Part 1. In Chapter 1, a general model of the security-selection process is presented and a number of strategic styles which we will refer to throughout the book are defined. In Chapter 2, the legal and economic characteristics of major types of security instruments are summarized. Next, the way in which security transactions take place in major U.S. markets is discussed in Chapter 3. Finally, Chapter 4 examines major security market indexes and the historical returns earned on these indexes so that we can gain a clear understanding of the rewards and risks associated with different security types.

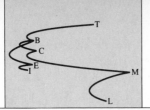

1 Overview of the Investment Process

The security markets hold a particular fascination for many people. A folklore has developed around financiers such as Drew, Fisk, Vanderbilt, and the Morgans. Market traders have developed their own unique language (*index arbitrage, fully hedged, straddled options, technical corrections,* etc.). And many people believe that with a little knowledge and luck they too can earn substantial returns.

Yet for all the psychic pleasures and possible monetary rewards that people receive from security trading, the game is played in earnest. The future welfare of individuals and families depends upon the strategies they use to select securities.

Consider the following story. At the beginning of 1980, shares of stock in Federal Express and Emery Air Freight were selling for about $8 and $16, respectively. Revenues of the two firms were about the same, and both were quite profitable. However, investment returns on the two would be quite different during the 1980s. By early 1989, shares of Federal Express had increased in value to $48, and trading in the shares was very active. A $1 investment in Federal Express made in January 1980 would have increased in value to $6 by 1989—a compound annualized return of 22%! While a significant part of the performance of Federal Express shares was due to active expansion in the United States economy, there was something clearly unique about Federal Express. For example, the average stock had an annualized return during the same time period of 16%. The saga of Emery Air Freight was exactly the opposite. Throughout the decade of the 1980s, its revenues, earnings, and dividends declined. By early 1989 its share prices had fallen to $4, and trading in the shares had virtually stopped. A $1 investment in Emery in January 1980 would have decreased in value to only 34 cents by early 1989!

Why? And what should have been done? What were the forces which could cause such price changes in each firm? Might a well-trained investor have been able to foresee the future, avoiding Emery's decline and gaining from Federal Express's increase? Was there a way for a less knowledgeable person to minimize or avoid the risks of owning Emery? In this book we examine these two basic questions about security selection: "Why?" and "What should be done?" Our goal is to gain some insights into questions such as:

Why:

- do various types of securities exist?
- do securities trade at a particular price?
- do these prices change over time?

What should be done:

- to reduce risk but still provide reasonable expected returns?
- to compensate for potential inflation?
- to reduce transaction costs and taxes?

The purpose of this chapter is to provide an overview of some of the basic concepts and approaches to security selection which are developed in later chapters. We start with a discussion of the differences between saving, investment, and speculation. A general model of the process of creating and maintaining a security portfolio is then presented. Finally, we identify the three schools of thought which claim to offer the best way to select a portfolio.

SOME DEFINITIONS

A few terms need to be defined immediately to avoid confusion about the process that we describe in general terms in this chapter and in more detail throughout the book.

Wealth: Saving Versus Consumption

At any point in time, a person has some *wealth*, which consists of the total market value (at that time) of any assets owned. As time goes by, this wealth is increased by any *income* received from job earnings or productive returns on the wealth. People will do two things with this income-enhanced wealth: (1) *consume* part or all of it and (2) *save* any portion not consumed. For example, if you start year 1 with a wealth level of $1,000 and have an income during the year of $200, then $1,200 is available during the year to be either consumed or saved. Assuming that $150 is consumed, your incremental savings during the year would be $50 and your year-end wealth and total saving would be $1,050.

Why exactly do people save? On first thought, this might appear to be a trivial question. Don't people save simply to increase their future wealth? While true in general terms, this answer is not precise enough to convey fully the true motivations for saving. The economic benefits which arise from saving are basically twofold:

1. To achieve *future consumption levels* higher than would be available if one were not to save but instead were to consume *future income levels as received*. For example, a salesperson whose income is erratic from year to year will save in years of above-average earnings in order to obtain a desired consumption level in years of depressed earnings. Similarly, we all save during our working years in order to have resources to consume in our retirement years. Saving thus allows us to obtain

consumption when we want it, independent of when income is received. *This "consumption-smoothing" motive for saving is usually associated with an "investment" strategy*.

2. To take advantage of unusually *profitable opportunities*. Occasionally an opportunity will provide potential returns which are larger than the returns available on other saving opportunities of similar risk. Undertaking such opportunities has the effect of immediately increasing a person's wealth. *This "opportunity" motive is associated with either a "speculative" or an "arbitrage" strategy*.

In sum, the ability to save provides people with two distinct benefits: the ability to separate their consumption pattern from their income pattern, and the ability to immediately increase their wealth by finding unusually profitable ventures. The first benefit is usually associated with an investment strategy and the second with a speculative or an arbitrage strategy.

Saving: Investment Versus Speculation

A distinction has traditionally been drawn between investment and speculation on the following grounds:

- Speculators accept fairly large risks, whereas investors accept only moderate-to-low risks.
- Speculators have a large portfolio turnover, whereas investors have low turnover.
- Speculators are often in and out of the market for a given security during a day (they *day trade*), whereas investors have a long-term horizon.

Given these guidelines, a gray area exists in which it is difficult to identify a particular strategy as being by its nature either speculative or an investment, and individuals may consistently switch from one approach to the other.

While there is nothing wrong with this traditional distinction, we will use the terms *investment* and *speculation* in a more precise manner. Throughout the text *investment* refers to the purchase of a security with the belief that its current market price is fair. The investor expects to earn only a *fair rate of return* commensurate with the security's risk. An investment can be in securities of high, low, or moderate risk depending upon the investor's risk tolerance and desired return. The only time investors trade is when they have excess cash, need cash for current consumption, or want tax savings.

In contrast, *speculation* refers to the purchase of a security if it is believed to be undervalued and the sale of a security if it is believed to be overvalued. The speculator expects to earn an *abnormal return* — a return above that which is fair given the security's risk. This abnormal return represents gains earned from buying undervalued securities before their prices rise to fair value or selling overvalued securities before prices fall. Speculations can occur in securities of any risk level. The speculator will trade actively if a large number of mispriced securities can be found or inactively if few mispriced securities are available.

The key difference between the speculator and the investor is information. Speculators believe they have information about a security which other market participants will soon also learn and which will cause the less well-informed people to reevaluate the worth of the security. Investors believe that all currently available information is fully impounded in the security's price. *A speculative trade is an information trade.*

This distinction is important because the speculator is effectively making a bet with the market—a bet that states, "My information is better than yours." Before entering into such a bet, the speculator should fully recognize that there are a large number of sophisticated and intelligent people with access to considerable capital who are also looking for such information. What makes the speculator's information any better than that of others? Is the information truly unique?

Consider the following example. You have just completed a thorough analysis of Techtronics Inc. and believe they will soon file for a patent on a new chemical process which should dramatically improve the company's long-run profits and dividends. Should you buy the stock in anticipation of a price increase once the earnings actually start to improve? If knowledge of the potential patent is widespread, you really don't hold any unique information. The markets will have already "discounted" the likely profit improvement into current prices. But if you believe the markets haven't fully reflected the profit potential in the stock's price, a speculative buy would be appropriate. Before trading, the wise speculator will ask, "Do I really have information that others don't, or is there something others know that I don't?"

Another term which we will have occasion to use extensively is *arbitrage*. In an arbitrage transaction a person attempts to profit from two price distortions. For example, assume AT&T common stock is traded on both the New York Stock Exchange and the American Stock Exchange. You own a seat on each exchange, so you pay no transaction costs (broker fees) to trade at either place. If AT&T is currently trading at $25 on the American and $26 on the New York, you could arbitrage by simultaneously buying at $25 and selling at $26. You could earn a $1 profit per share at no risk and with no capital commitment. Arbitrage transactions can, of course, involve much more complex trades. But their keynotes are that they entail no risk or capital commitment, and profits are gained by trading on market price imbalances.

Arbitrageurs play an important role in the operations of the security markets. By attempting to maximize their own profits, they identify and eliminate security price imbalances. The rapid trading by a large number of arbitrageurs guarantees that prices in all markets are closely interrelated and determined by similar economic factors. There is an underlying economic rationality in the markets. Speculators perform much the same function as do arbitrageurs. The principal distinction between the two is that speculation can involve more risk than a pure arbitrage transaction. Arbitrageurs tend to "cover themselves" by taking equal but opposite sides of a trade.

A SECURITY-SELECTION MODEL

A large number of savings media are available, ranging from personal business ventures to sophisticated international investment funds. This text, however, is mainly concerned with marketable securities. A *security* is a financial document which provides the owner with a specified legal claim to some part of the returns generated by a real asset. A *marketable security* is one which can be traded between two parties in a quick and inexpensive manner. People buy and sell marketable securities for a variety of reasons, but most do so with the expectation of earning a reasonable profit. Securities which are expected to provide a favorable rate of return are bought, and securities which are not expected to provide a favorable rate of return are sold. Thus, one *objective* of a security-selection model should be to *maximize the expected rate of return on one's portfolio of marketable securities.*

But there are a variety of *constraints* which people place upon their holdings. The most important of these constraints is the degree of portfolio risk. Although some opportunities might provide large expected returns, the amount of risk inherent in the opportunity might be unacceptable. As a result, any plan devised to aid in selecting securities should explicitly consider both expected returns and potential risks.

The process of security selection should consist of three separate stages, as illustrated in Figure 1-1. First, the portfolio's objective and its various constraints are

FIGURE 1-1 *Security-Selection Process*

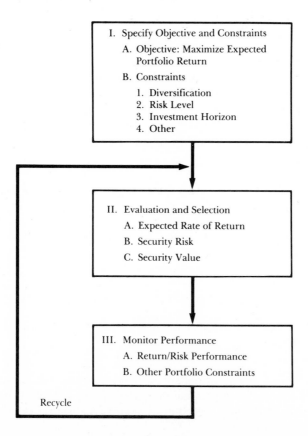

specified. Second, various securities are evaluated, and those which best meet the objective and constraints are selected. Third, the future performance of the portfolio is monitored.

Setting the Portfolio's Objective and Constraints

An ideal portfolio of securities can be determined and its performance later evaluated *only after the portfolio's objective and constraints have been developed and clearly stated in writing.* This written document is commonly referred to as a statement of investment policy. Unfortunately, many individuals and organizations give passing attention, at best, to the need for such a statement. Security selection and performance evaluation appear to involve more action and tangible outcomes, so they are often given much more attention than they deserve. Without a clear notion of what the portfolio should be designed to do, however, intelligent security choices and performance measurement are impossible. While some flexibility should be allowed, too much latitude can make the selection decisions difficult and performance evaluation impossible. Types of factors which a statement of investment policy might include are the following:

1. *Degree of diversification.* A portfolio's risk is greatly affected by the extent of the portfolio's diversification. Usually, some statement should be made about the minimum number of bonds, stocks, etc., which is acceptable. A fundamental investment concept is that diversification can significantly reduce risk without reducing expected returns.

2. *Acceptable nondiversifiable risk level.* Even with wide diversification, some risk will remain. Allowed tolerances of such nondiversifiable risk should be specified. There are a number of ways in which nondiversifiable risk can be adjusted, but the most common, as well as the most conceptually correct, is to adjust the percentage of the portfolio placed in fixed-income securities versus equities. Fixed-income securities have less nondiversifiable risk than do common stocks. Thus, the lower the stock-to-bond ratio, the lower the portfolio's nondiversifiable risk. Most investment consultants consider the stock/bond ratio to be *the* most important factor in determining long-run portfolio return and risk.

3. *Investment horizon.* A critical determinant of the portfolio's risk is the maturity of its holdings relative to when the individual intends to withdraw funds. For example, the risk inherent in a portfolio of low-dividend, high-growth stocks is considerably different for a young doctor than for a retired couple. The doctor would have little need to withdraw funds from the portfolio and could ride out temporary price declines, whereas the retired couple would plan to withdraw principal to meet living expenses and could be severely hurt by short-term price declines. Later we will see that risk is minimized when the *duration* of securities matches the *duration* of need for the funds they generate.

4. *Portfolio turnover.* Portfolio turnover is typically defined as the percentage of the portfolio market value bought (or sold) during a year. For example, if the aver-

age market value of a portfolio during a year is $1.0 million and total purchases of securities equaled $0.5 million, the turnover would be 50%. Active turnover occurs, of course, in the hopes of buying undervalued securities and selling overvalued ones. Unfortunately, the only thing sure about active turnover is that brokerage commissions increase. The degree of turnover in a portfolio is a personal matter and depends upon how well the portfolio manager can identify mispriced securities. Nonetheless, a stated maximum is wise.

5. *Nonallowable securities.* There are valid economic reasons to exclude particular types of securities from a portfolio. For example, a nontaxable charity fund should not own municipal bonds because a nontaxable fund has no need for the tax advantage which municipals provide. Similarly, an investor who has large real estate holdings might wish to exclude equity-oriented real estate investment trusts (REITs) since the addition of REITs would make the investor's total wealth overly dependent upon the real estate market.

6. *Tax considerations.* The investor's tax status is important when selecting a portfolio. Apart from particular types of trades which are used to reduce taxes, certain types of securities might be over- or underweighted. For example, individuals in high tax brackets would (all other things equal) prefer growth stocks to those providing high dividend yields. Similarly, we will see later that heavily taxed individuals would prefer low-coupon bonds to equivalent-risk high-coupon bonds.

7. *Liquidity.* The desired level of portfolio liquidity should be noted. This can be accomplished by stating a percentage of the funds to be held in short-term, highly marketable instruments as well as by specifying conditions on allowable securities (exchange on which traded, average daily volume, number of shares outstanding, etc.). The degree of liquidity is closely tied to the horizon date of when funds are needed. For example, liquidity reserves would have to be greater for a retired individual's portfolio than for individuals in the middle years of their careers.

Although this listing isn't all-inclusive, it does cover the major factors which an individual or organization must come to grips with in order to determine an optimal portfolio. In fact, a major portion of this text is devoted to the importance, the measurement, and the management of these seven factors.

Evaluation and Selection

The two most important characterisics of a security (or of a portfolio of securities) are its expected return and its perceived risk. For a given risk level, investors desire the highest expected return possible.

Single-Period Rate of Return. Rate-of-return calculations can become fairly complex when measured over a series of many time periods. These complexities are examined in later chapters. But central to any rate-of-return calculation is the notion of a *single-period rate of return.* The single-period rate of return is defined as the percentage price appreciation plus the percentage cash return (often referred to as *current yield* on a bond or *dividend yield* on a stock) during a given period. Usually, rates of return are expressed in terms of an annualized value, although quarterly, monthly, and even daily returns are also used. If R_t refers to the return during the period ending at date t, P_t and P_{t-1} refer to the security's price at dates t and $t - 1$, and C_t refers to the cash flow received at date t, then:

Single-Period Rate of Return

$$\begin{array}{cc} \text{Single-} & \text{Percentage} & \text{Percentage} \\ \text{Period} = & \text{Price} & + & \text{Cash} \\ \text{Return} & \text{Appreciation} & & \text{Return} \end{array} \qquad (1.1)$$

$$R_t = \frac{P_t - P_{t-1}}{P_{t-1}} + \frac{C_t}{P_{t-1}}$$

Equation 1.1 can be used to measure *both* historical and future expected single-period returns. When expected variables are used, the expectation operator, $E(\bullet)$, is used. For example, $E(R)$ means expected return, $E(P)$ means expected price, etc. To understand how Equation 1.1 is used, consider the following data on a stock and a bond:

Data	Description	Stock	Bond
P_0	Last year's closing price	$40	$987
C_1	This year's cash flow	$2 dividend	$50 coupon
P_1	Today's closing price	$36	$957
$E(C_2)$	Next year's expected cash flow	$2 dividend	$50 coupon
$E(P_2)$	Next year's expected closing price	$44	$1,010

Then last year's *actual rate of return* on the stock and bond would be:

$$R_1 \text{ on stock} = \frac{\$36 - \$40}{\$40} + \frac{\$2}{\$40} = -5.00\%$$

$$R_1 \text{ on bond} = \frac{\$957 - \$987}{\$987} + \frac{\$50}{\$987} = +2.03\%$$

Expected returns for the coming year would be:

$$E(R_2) \text{ on stock} = \frac{\$44 - \$36}{\$36} + \frac{\$2}{\$36} = +27.78\%$$

$$E(R_2) \text{ on bond} = \frac{\$1,010 - \$957}{\$957} + \frac{\$50}{\$957} = +10.76\%$$

It is important to recognize that this single-period return is a *market-based* measure of return in that it uses market prices and cash received. This contrasts with various *accounting-based* rates of return, which are based purely on accounting statements published by the corporation. The rate of return actually received by owners of a security is the market return. Accounting-based returns are, at best, estimates which use a large variety of "generally accepted accounting principles."

Security Risk. A detailed discussion of how investors and speculators can reduce security risk is the subject of two complete chapters. Yet an understanding of security risk is so important that we need to introduce a few concepts immediately.

First, *risk relates to potential return outcomes which may be different from expected returns*. The more diverse such outcomes, the more risky the security.

The statistic most commonly used to measure the dispersion of security returns is the standard deviation. The standard deviation can apply to either potential *future* returns (in which case we refer to it as the *ex ante* standard deviation) or to a sequence of past single-period returns (in which case we refer to it as the *ex post* standard deviation). For the present, it is sufficient to understand how the ex post standard deviation is calculated. The ex post standard deviation will be designated as σ and calculated as follows:

Ex Post Standard Deviation

$$\sigma = \sqrt{\frac{\sum_{t=1}^{N} (R_t - \bar{R})^2}{N}} \qquad (1.2)$$

where R_t = the single-period rate of return in period t, $\bar{R}$ = the average historical return in the last N periods, and N = the number of single periods over which the standard deviation is being measured. For example, assume that the common stock of Updowne Bedding provided the following sequence of returns for the past five years:

	Single-Period Rates of Returns				
Year:	1	2	3	4	5
Updowne Bedding	10%	20%	−15%	8%	2%

Then the average return would have been 5%:

$$(10 + 20 - 15 + 8 + 2) \div 5 = 5\%$$

and the ex post standard deviation would have been 11.56%:

$$\sqrt{\frac{(10-5)^2 + (20-5)^2 + (-15-5)^2 + (8-5)^2 + (2-5)^2}{5}} = 11.56\%$$

FIGURE 1-2 *Distributions of Single-Period Returns*

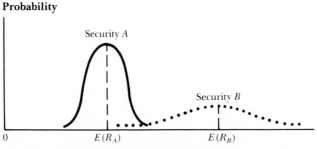

Rate of Return

The greater the standard deviation, the greater the investment risk. For example, in Figure 1-2 the standard deviation, and thus the risk, of security B is greater than that of security A. As we proceed through this book, you will gain a good understanding of how to interpret standard deviation values and what to expect from various types of securities. For now, however, the ability to calculate an ex post σ and an intuitive understanding of basic concepts are all that can be expected.

A second important concept is that *security returns are not perfectly positively correlated*. When returns on one security are lower than average, there may be significant advantages to diversification—to creating portfolios of many securities instead of only a few. The following is an extreme example of this idea.

In the standard deviation example above we found that the common stock of Updowne Bedding had a certain amount of risk, as expressed by the 11.56% ex post standard deviation of yearly returns. Now consider the stock of Falrize Electronics, which has had the following series of yearly returns:

	Single-Period Rates of Returns				
Year:	1	2	3	4	5
Falrize Electronics	0%	−10%	25%	2%	8%

The average yearly return and ex post standard deviation of Falrize Electronics are identical to those of Updowne Bedding:

$$\bar{R} = (0 - 10 + 25 + 2 + 8) \div 5 = 5\%$$

$$\sigma = \sqrt{\frac{(0-5)^2 + (-10-5)^2 + (25-5)^2 + (2-5)^2 + (8-5)^2}{5}} = 11.56\%$$

But note that the returns on the two securities move in exactly opposite directions. For example, in year 1, when Updowne has a return 5 percentage points *higher* than its 5% average, Falrize has a return 5 percentage points *lower* than its 5% average. This inverse correlation holds for each of the five years. Such a case would be extremely unusual, but the data are useful in making a very important point: when security returns are less than perfectly positively correlated, diversification can reduce risk.

In our example, it should be obvious that investment risk could have been eliminated without affecting average returns by simply investing 50% in each stock. This is shown below:

	Single-Period Rates of Returns				
Year:	1	2	3	4	5
Updowne	10%	20%	−15%	8%	2%
Falrize	0%	−10%	25%	2%	8%
50/50 Portfolio	5%	5%	5%	5%	5%

The average return remains 5%, but all risk is eliminated.

This example is artificial because it would be extremely difficult (probably impossible) to find two securities in the "real" world whose returns are perfectly inversely correlated. But *as long as security returns are not perfectly correlated, the advantages of diversification within a portfolio can be substantial.*

FIGURE 1-3 *Illustration of Random (or Naive) Diversification*

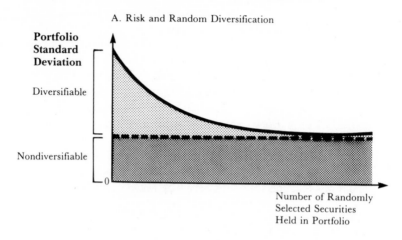

A. Risk and Random Diversification

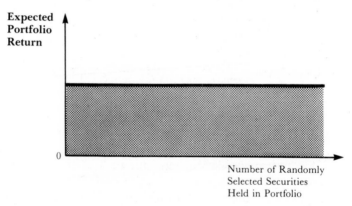

B. Expected Portfolio Return and Random Diversification

Strategies of diversification can be grouped into two categories, commonly referred to as *random* (or *naive*) *diversification strategies* and *efficient diversification strategies*. Random diversification refers to the ability to reduce portfolio risk by increasing the number of (randomly selected) securities held in a portfolio. Scholars and practitioners have demonstrated that increasing the number of securities held using a random-selection process will substantially reduce the portfolio standard deviation but have no effect upon average portfolio returns. That portion of a portfolio's risk which can be reduced by means of random diversification is known as *diversifiable risk* and is shown in panel A of Figure 1-3 as the lightly shaded area. The darker shaded area represents nondiversifiable risk. In practice, the principle of random diversification is followed by requiring diversification over a broad range of industrial classifications, forms of instruments, etc., instead of using strict random selection.

Efficient diversification relies upon mathematical programming procedures to calculate portfolios which provide the *largest expected return for a specified risk level*.

FIGURE 1-4 *Illustration of Efficient Diversification*

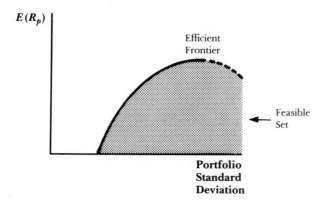

For example, the shaded area in Figure 1-4 represents the *feasible set* of risks and returns available from a given group of securities being evaluated. The solid curve along the upper boundary of the feasible set is known as the *efficient frontier* and can be calculated using a mathematical programming model. At this point we needn't get into the details of how the efficient frontier is developed. The important point is that procedures exist which allow the investor to calculate an efficient frontier once expected returns and security risks are identified. Given the investor's personal preferences for expected returns and risk, a single portfolio along the efficient frontier is selected.

Finally, return and risk are related. Larger expected returns can be obtained only by accepting larger amounts of risk. For example, Figure 1-5 illustrates the distribution of yearly rates of return on five major security categories between 1926 and 1987. Although stocks of small firms provided the largest average yearly rate of return (19.4%), such returns were clearly the most variable. Similarly, average returns on U.S. Treasury bills were the smallest (3.5%), but also the least variable.

The most widely used model to date which relates expected returns to security risks is known as the capital asset pricing model (CAPM). The CAPM states that (1) the only risk of a security which is meaningful to rational investors is its nondiversifiable risk; (2) this nondiversifiable risk is measurable by a variable known as beta (β); and (3) the beta of a security and the security's expected return are related in a linear fashion, as shown in Figure 1-6. The CAPM does suffer from various theoretical and empirical problems, but it is a powerful way in which to view the world and can be helpful in evaluating securities and monitoring investment performance.

The CAPM can be written symbolically as

Capital Asset Pricing Model
$$E(R_i) = RF + \beta_i(RP_m) \tag{1.3}$$

where $E(R_i)$ = the expected single-period return on security i; RF = the risk-free rate of interest; β_i = the beta of security i, reflecting the extent of its nondiversifiable risk; and RP_m = the risk premium demanded on the market portfolio of all assets.

FIGURE 1-5 *Historical Annual Returns on Various Security Classes (1926–1987)*

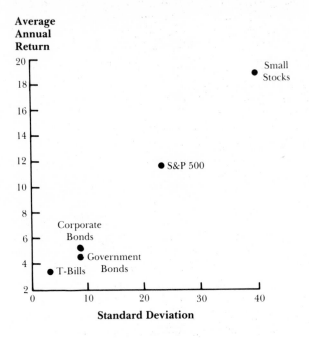

FIGURE 1-6 *Illustration of Capital Asset Pricing Model*

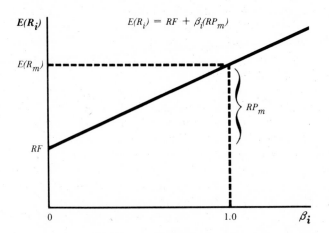

$E(R_i)$ = expected return on security i
$E(R_m)$ = expected return on the "market" portfolio of all assets
RF = risk-free rate of interest
β_i = beta of security i
RP_m = risk premium required on the market portfolio

For example, if the annual risk-free rate of interest is now 7%, the beta on the stock of ABC Corp. is 1.5, and the market risk premium is 6%, then ABC stock should be priced in the markets to yield an expected single-period return of 16%:

$$7\% + 1.5(6\%) = 16\%$$

If the current market price of ABC stock actually implies an expected annual return of 20%, the stock is undervalued and clearly should be bought. For example, the stock might now be trading at $50 per share, be expected to pay a $1 dividend during the next year, and be expected to sell for $59 one year hence. Then the expected single-period return actually implied by today's price is 20%:

$$\frac{\$59 - \$50 + \$1}{\$50} = 20\%$$

The stock would be a bargain at $50, and investors would actively purchase the stock until its current price increases to $51.72 (the price necessary to provide a fair return of 16%).

Security Valuation. To determine a security's expected single-period return, an estimate of next period's price and cash flow is needed:

$$E(R_t) = \frac{E(P_t) - P_{t-1} + E(C_t)}{P_{t-1}}$$

All security-pricing models are based upon the present values of future cash flows which the security is expected to pay to its owners. In the case of a common stock, these cash flows represent yearly cash dividends (plus an eventual liquidating dividend if the corporation is expected to cease operations at some future date). In the case of a bond, such cash flows represent yearly coupon payments plus the face value of the bond at maturity. Symbolically, the basic valuation model is written:

Basic Valuation Model
$$P_0 = \frac{CF_1}{(1 + k)} + \frac{CF_2}{(1 + k)^2} + \frac{CF_3}{(1 + k)^3} + \dots + \frac{CF_N}{(1 + k)^N} \quad (1.4)$$

where P_0 = today's fair value of the security, CF_t = the cash flow in period t, k = the required periodic return given the security's risk, and N = the last date at which a cash flow is received.

Conceptually, security valuation is quite straightforward: one need only estimate expected future cash flows plus a fair discount rate and then plug them into Equation 1.4 to obtain a value estimate. Pragmatically, however, these values can be extremely difficult to estimate.

Expected dividend flows on common stock, for example, require forecasts of future product development, sales, inflation, cost control, debt policy, taxes, etc. The list can go on almost endlessly. Similarly, to estimate a fair discount rate, one must decide what an appropriate risk premium is for the security. These topics take a full four chapters later in the text.

FIGURE 1-7 *Illustration of Performance Evaluation*

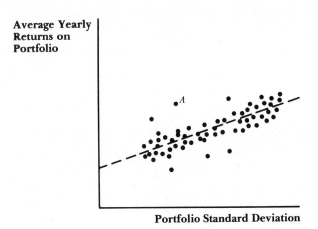

Monitoring Portfolio Performance

Finally, the performance of the portfolio must be periodically monitored and changes in strategy must be made when necessary. The most important criterion on which performance should be evaluated is the historical ability of the investment program to generate reasonable net returns for the level of risk incurred. A number of performance-measurement models have been developed. Most are based upon the CAPM. Essentially, these models relate average historical rates of return on a portfolio to an estimate of the portfolio's risk. Each portfolio's past risk/return combination is then compared with the risk/return combination on other portfolios in an attempt to find one style of security selection which *consistently* outperforms other styles. For example, in Figure 1-7 the average returns and risks of a number of hypothetical portfolios are plotted. The dashed line is a best-fit line drawn between the points (perhaps a regression line). Portfolios above the line appear to have had better performance than average, while those below the line have fared more poorly than average. Portfolio *A* had exceedingly good performance during the period examined. If it can be shown that this was consistently the case during other time intervals, the style of *A* should probably be emulated.

THREE APPROACHES TO SECURITY SELECTION

Three distinct schools of thought claim to offer the ideal way to select securities. Each differs in its preference for a speculative versus an investment strategy and in the type of analysis it uses to evaluate securities. The three approaches can be characterized as follows:

Approach	Suggested Strategy	Type of Analysis
Technical selection	Speculative	Price and trading volume charts
Fundamental selection	Mixed	Valuation of future cash flows
Efficient market selection	Investment	None — Buy and hold a widely diversified portfolio of acceptable risk

Technical Selection

Proponents of technical analysis, or technicians, believe that an examination of historical security-price and trading-volume movements can identify patterns from which future prices can be forecast. Because of their reliance upon price charting, technicians are also referred to as *chartists*. A strict technician pays no attention to a company's current earnings, financial condition, product line, patent protection, etc., believing that historical price-volume movements tell the whole story.

A basic understanding of charting can be obtained by examining the rudiments of one classic technical theory — *Dow theory*. Dow theory breaks aggregate stock price movements into three categories: (1) primary moves, (2) intermediate moves, and (3) ripples, as illustrated in Figure 1-8. Primary moves are long-term, sustained movements in one direction. A primary move with rising prices is known as a *bull market*. A primary move with falling prices is known as a *bear market*. Bull markets are said to take anywhere from two to ten years to be completed, whereas bear markets move more quickly and run their course in six months to a year.

Within any primary move are a series (often said to be three) of intermediate price moves. Intermediate moves run in the same direction as the primary move but are dis-

FIGURE 1-8 *Illustration of Dow Theory*

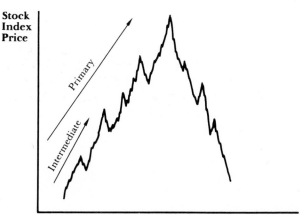

tinguished by temporary price reversals. These price reversals are often spoken of as *technical corrections* when the *market gets ahead of itself*. (The analogy is often made that primary moves are akin to ocean tides and intermediate moves to waves.) The third type of movement, ripples, represents meaningless daily price variability.

A technician will pay close attention to price reversals during intermediate moves. If the price reversal is significant, occurs on heavy trading, and is confirmed by other stock indexes, a change in the direction of the primary move may be at hand.

There are probably as many interpretations of Dow theory as there are technicians using it. This is also true for other technical trading rules, such as point-and-figure charting, head-and-shoulder movements, and relative strength. A set of precise trading rules doesn't exist, and often a technician's opinion is based on an intangible described as a *feel for the market*. Yet the heart of technical analysis lies in its total orientation to historical price and volume patterns.

As a result of extensive research conducted since the early 1960s, technical selection has been almost totally discredited. Professionals who have carefully studied the matter place little or no faith in its usefulness, yet many people still use the approach and security-trade magazines are replete with advertisements for different techniques.

Fundamental Selection

Proponents of the second approach are known as fundamentalists. It has been said that a technician is to a fundamentalist as an astrologer is to an astronomer. Fundamental analysts examine basic economic forces affecting a company in an attempt to forecast future earnings, dividends, and security risks. Given projections of potential returns and risks, fundamental analysts estimate what they believe to be the fair market value of a security. This so-called intrinsic value is then compared with the security's current market price and a buy, sell, or hold recommendation is made. Simply put, fundamentalists believe that thorough financial analysis of a security can identify mispriced securities.

The job of a *good* fundamentalist is complex, requiring unique analytic skills and training. In recent years a professional association of financial analysts and portfolio managers (known as the Financial Analysts Federation) has developed a certification program similar to the Certified Public Accountant designation. A sequence of three day-long tests is taken over a minimum three-year period. Upon successful completion, the participant is granted the designation of *Chartered Financial Analyst* (CFA). Only individuals actively involved in investment management may take the exams. The purpose of the CFA designation is to ensure high standards of professional training and ethical conduct. While the CFA designation is not a formal requirement for individuals wishing to engage in investment management, it is widely respected and is informally required for advancement in many firms.

Fundamentalists suggest a mixed investment-speculative strategy when selecting an ideal portfolio of securities. Starting from a buy-hold, pure investment-oriented portfolio which has suitable risk for the portfolio's owner, fundamentalists will suggest temporary speculative adjustments in line with their assessment of the intrinsic value of the aggregate stock and bond markets, various industries, and individual stocks or bonds. If they believe that equities as a whole are undervalued relative to bonds, they will suggest holding a larger percentage of stocks than the pure investment strategy would suggest (with an equal reduction in total bond holdings). If they believe certain industry groups are undervalued (or overvalued) in the market, they will suggest that the industry be overweighted (or underweighted) relative to the pure investment strategy. Finally, they will attempt to find individual stocks or bonds which should be over- or underweighted.

In sum, fundamentalists start from a pure investment posture and then *time* purchases and sales based upon *information* they believe they gain from fundamental analysis of aggregate markets, industries, and individual security issues.

Efficient Market Selection

The term *efficient market* does not mean a market in which trading activity is handled in a mechanically efficient manner. Instead, an efficient market is said to exist *if all known information about a security is fully reflected in its price*. The notion of a price-efficient market is a relatively new concept in investment management and, if correct, has major implications for proper investment policy.

The efficient market theory (EMT) states that fundamental analysts are so good at their jobs that all mispriced securities have been identified. Therefore, mispriced securities won't exist. The market price of a security will equal its fair intrinsic value. If this were not the case, well-informed and sophisticated fundamentalists would immediately recognize the potential profits and, through buying and selling, instantly drive the market price into equilibrium.

If the notion of an efficient market is correct, security selection turns out to be quite simple. First, define the level of risk which is acceptable for a given portfolio. Then create a combination of broadly diversified holdings of stocks and bonds which provides that risk level. Never trade simply because you believe prices are too high or too low; they aren't—they are always fair. Trade only if you have excess cash, need cash, or want tax advantages. Naturally this view is anathema to many brokers and fundamentalists (people, by the way, who rely upon trading for their livelihood). Yet considerable evidence suggests that the markets *are* amazingly efficient—much more efficient than many people believe.

SUMMARY

This text deals with the major types of marketable securities that are actively traded and examines how people decide which of these securities to include in their personal portfolios. In this first chapter we have briefly reviewed the process which should be used in the selection of any security portfolio. This process consists of three stages: (1) specifying the portfolio objective and constraints, (2) evaluating and selecting securities that meet the objective and constraints, and (3) monitoring future performance.

In practice, three basic approaches are used to select securities — technical selection, fundamental selection, and efficient market selection. Proponents of technical selection believe that security prices often move in identifiable patterns. Thus technicians rely heavily on charts of historical prices and volumes as they attempt to extrapolate any apparent trends. The procedures that technicians use have been almost totally discredited by extensive research. The securities picked through technical analysis do earn positive rates of return over the long run, but these returns are only what one would expect given the risk of the securities held. The returns are due to the risk accepted, not to the use of the technical selection approach.

In contrast to technicians, fundamentalists attempt to forecast the future cash flows which a security is expected to provide. The discounted present value of these expected cash flows represents the fundamental analyst's opinion about the intrinsic value of the security. If the actual price at which the security is trading differs from the analyst's assessment of its intrinsic value, the security is bought or sold as appropriate. Most investment professionals use a fundamental analysis approach to security selection.

Proponents of the third approach believe that any information that fundamentalists would consider important is already reflected in existing security prices. This viewpoint, referred to as the efficient market theory, suggests that securities will never be mispriced — that actual trading prices will always be identical to properly calculated fundamental intrinsic values. Extensive research has shown that while efficient market theory is an overstatement of reality, the security markets are considerably more price efficient than many people believe.

In this chapter we have also made an important distinction between the term *investment* and the term *speculation* which will be used throughout the book. Investment is used to refer to the purchase of a security with the belief that the current market price is fair. One who invests expects to earn only a fair rate of return commensurate with the security's risk. Speculation refers to the purchase (sale) of a security if it is believed to be undervalued (overvalued) in the market. Speculators trade on information which they believe is not reflected in a security's price, and they expect to earn a return in excess of what would normally be expected given the security's risk.

A NOTE ON THE ORGANIZATION OF THIS BOOK

This text is organized into four major sections. Part 1 provides a basic *introduction* and consists of this overview chapter plus reviews of various types of available securities, the mechanics of trading, and historical security returns. Part 2 develops various important *concepts*, such as why markets exist, determinants of risk-free interest rates, yield curves, risk measurement, and the relationship between risk and expected return. Part 3 presents an *analysis* of the unique risks, returns, and pricing models of various types of securities (stocks, bonds, options, futures, and other security types). And finally, Part 4 discusses alternative portfolio management *strategies*.

End-of-Chapter Questions and Problems

In any textbook, the end-of-chapter questions and problems should test students' knowledge of the material and illustrate the application of various concepts. End-of-chapter questions and problems can and should be a vital part of the learning experience.

Because the kinds of questions and problems in this text differ somewhat from those in other texts the student may have used, a brief description is needed. Our end-of-chapter questions and problems consist of three types:

1. *Review problem(s).* One or more broad review problems will be presented together with worked-out solutions.
2. *Standard questions and problems.* A number of questions and problems are presented next. An attempt has been made to order these from the easiest to the hardest. Answers to selected problems are given at the back of the book.
3. *Data analysis problems.* Because of the increasing use of computers to develop investment and speculative strategies, a number of problems and questions are presented which integrate traditional investment concepts with computer-accessed data files.

Computer Diskettes

Available from your instructor are copies of two floppy diskettes. The first diskette contains a variety of investment data sets which will be useful in conducting end-of-chapter data analysis problems and learning basic investment concepts. Examples of these data sets include the following:

1. Annual returns on U.S. money market instruments, U.S. bond indexes, U.S. stock indexes, U.S. real estate indexes, and other U.S. asset classes.
2. Annual stock returns for many foreign countries.
3. Quarterly returns on a large number of U.S. common stocks and stock/bond/ T-bill indexes.
4. Quarterly returns on a number of mutual funds.
5. Year-end prices, dividends, and earnings of the Dow Jones industrials, the S&P 400, and the S&P 500.

The data sets are stored in standard spreadsheet format and may be read using an IBM-PC compatible microcomputer. For a detailed explanation of the files on this diskette, you should first print the file labeled "README.DOC".

The second diskette contains a variety of computer programs to aid in various investment calculations.

REVIEW PROBLEM

Shown below is a data set which consists of (1) the price per share of two stocks at various quarter-ends, (2) total dividends paid on each stock during the quarter, and (3) rates of return on Treasury bills during the quarter.

| | Exxon | | IBM | | T-Bill |
Year/Qtr	Price	Dividend	Price	Dividend	Return
85/1	25.10	NA	127.00	NA	NA
85/2	26.90	0.42	123.80	1.10	1.93
85/3	25.90	0.42	123.90	1.10	1.83
85/4	27.60	0.45	155.50	1.10	1.89
86/1	27.90	0.45	151.50	1.10	1.68
86/2	30.40	0.45	146.50	1.10	1.55
86/3	33.60	0.45	134.50	1.10	1.41
86/4	35.10	0.45	120.00	1.10	1.30
87/1	42.90	0.45	150.10	1.10	1.24
87/2	46.60	0.45	162.50	1.10	1.25
87/3	48.60	0.50	150.80	1.10	1.38
87/4	38.10	0.50	115.50	1.10	1.16

a. Calculate each stock's rate of return for the quarters from 85/2 through 87/4.

b. Calculate each stock's average return.

c. Calculate each stock's ex post standard deviation.

d. Consider a portfolio consisting of 50% invested in each stock at the start of each quarter. Calculate the quarterly returns on this portfolio, its average return, and its standard deviation.

e. Is the portfolio's average return equal to the average of the two stocks' returns? Is the portfolio's standard deviation equal to the average of the two stocks' standard deviations? Why is this so?

f. Consider an equity–Treasury bill portfolio consisting of a 50% investment in the two-stock portfolio above and a 50% investment in T-bills. Calculate this revised portfolio's quarterly returns, average return, and standard deviation. Compare the results with those in part d, commenting on how these illustrate how an investor can alter a portfolio's average return and volatility by diversifying and by adjusting the stock/bond mix.

Solution

Hint: If you have access to a financial spreadsheet program, you should use it in solving this problem. The answers shown below were calculated using such a spreadsheet. Rounding differences will occur if you are not also using a spreadsheet.

a.

Year/Qtr	Exxon	IBM
85/2	8.84%	−1.65%
85/3	−2.16	0.97
85/4	8.30	26.39
86/1	2.72	−1.86
86/2	10.57	−2.57

86/3	12.01	−7.44
86/4	5.80	−9.96
87/1	23.50	26.00
87/2	9.67	8.99
87/3	5.36	−6.52
87/4	−20.58	−22.68

b. Average return   5.82%   0.88%

c. Standard deviation of Exxon:

$$\sqrt{\frac{(8.84 - 5.82)^2 + (-2.16 - 5.82)^2 + \ldots + (-20.58 - 5.82)^2}{11}} = 10.33\%$$

Standard deviation of IBM = 14.05%

d.

Year/Qtr	Exxon	IBM	50/50 Portfolio
85/2	0.5 (8.84)	+ 0.5 (−1.65) =	3.60%
85/3			−0.59
85/4			17.35
86/1			0.43
86/2			4.00
86/3			2.28
86/4			−2.08
87/1			24.75
87/2			9.33
87/3			−0.58
87/4	0.5 (−20.58)	+ 0.5 (−22.68) =	−21.63

e. Average return   3.35%
      Standard deviation   11.22%

Average of two stocks = (5.82 + 0.88)/2 = 3.35%
Average of two stocks' standard deviations = (10.33 + 14.05)/2 = 12.19%

Yes, the averages are equal. However, the standard deviations differ and the portfolio's standard deviation is smaller because of the benefits gained from diversification. Because the returns on the two stocks are not perfectly correlated, the portfolio's risk is less than the average risk inherent in the individual securities. Although the benefits gained from diversification are slight in this example, the gains are greater in real situations since more than two securities are owned and a longer holding period is used.

f.

Year/Qtr	Equity	Bills	50/50 Portfolio
85/2	0.5 (3.60)	+ 0.5 (1.93) =	2.76%
85/3			0.62
85/4			9.62
86/1			1.06
86/2			2.78
86/3			1.84
86/4			−0.39
87/1			12.99
87/2			5.29
87/3			0.40
87/4	0.5 (−21.63)	+ 0.5 (1.16) =	−10.23
Average			2.43%
Standard deviation			5.64%

Notice first that the 50/50 combination of IBM and Exxon resulted in an average return which was equal to the average of each stock's return. But the standard deviation of this 50/50 stock portfolio was not equal to the average of their standard deviations. This points out the reduction in risk which is available from diversification which has no effect on expected returns.

Also notice the reduction in both average returns and standard deviation of returns which occurs when a risk-free asset such as Treasury bills is added to a portfolio. This points out how portfolio risk and return are altered by combining risky securities with a risk-free security such as Treasury bills.

In sum, portfolio risk is altered by (1) diversification over risky securities, and (2) the mix between a risk-free security and a risky security portfolio.

The Data Analysis Problem at the end of this chapter is an expanded version of this Review Problem. You are encouraged to work the Data Analysis Problem in order to see how powerful diversification can be. Future chapters will expand upon the concepts inherent in this chapter's Data Analysis Problem.

QUESTIONS AND PROBLEMS

1. What are the two economic motives for saving a portion of one's wealth?

2. Distinguish between investment, speculation, and arbitrage.

3. Distinguish between technical, fundamental, and efficient market security-selection styles.

4. Identify a number of constraints which might be specified in a statement of portfolio objectives and constraints. Briefly indicate why each of these is appropriate.

5. When we say that returns between two securities are not perfectly correlated, what do we mean? How does this relate to the notion of portfolio diversification?

6. As a member of the board of trustees for the pension fund of a major midwestern city, you have begun to review the performance of two of the pension's investment managers. During the past year manager A was responsible for investing an average of $5 million of fund assets and placed purchase orders totaling $2 million. Manager B was responsible for $8 million of pension assets and placed $6 million in purchase orders.
   a. What was the turnover of each manager?
   b. If each manager were to continue with a similar turnover in the future, for what average number of years would each manager hold a security?
   c. What is the goal of an active portfolio turnover?
   d. Whether this goal is achieved or not, active portfolio turnover does one thing for certain. What is this?

7. Leslie Mostly inherited $100,000 last year and decided to use the money to begin a long-term investment plan. Her initial decision was to split the $100,000 into equal dollar holdings of common stocks and bonds. One year after this initial investment, her stock holdings had a market value of $55,000 and her bonds were worth $51,000. Leslie received total cash dividends on the stocks of $2,500 and total coupons on the bonds of $4,000. (This cash was *not* reinvested in the portfolio.)
   a. What was Leslie's actual return on her stocks and bonds during the past year?
   b. What was the dividend yield on the stocks and the current yield on the bonds?
   c. Why does the total return on each investment differ from its dividend yield or current yield? Which do you believe is a better measure of each investment's return during the year—the answer in part a or the answer in part b?
   d. What was Leslie's total return on her full $100,000 investment?

8. You are using the capital asset pricing model to help determine whether the common stock of XYZ Corporation offers potential speculative profits. According to a detailed report by a major brokerage firm, the stock is expected to be selling for $33 a year from now and will pay cash dividends of $1.50 per share during the year. In addition, the brokerage report indicates that the beta of XYZ stock is 1.5, the risk-free rate is 9%, and the risk premium of the market is 6%. XYZ common shares are now selling for $30.
   a. What is the expected one-year return?
   b. According to the capital asset pricing model, what is a reasonable required return?
   c. Given this information, would you purchase the stock?

9. Consider the following statements. Which is (are) likely to have been made by a technical trader? A fundamentalist? An EMT proponent?
   a. XYZ Corporation stock should be bought because its earnings growth should be higher than has recently been expected.
   b. Commitments to bonds should be increased because inflation expectations in the economy are likely to fall if the Federal Reserve continues with current policies.
   c. The Dow Jones Industrial Average is currently experiencing a selling correction and should soon resume its upward move into a third and final intermediate move.
   d. Buy and hold — trade only if you need cash or for tax purposes.
   e. Don't increase holdings of XYZ Corporation until management is able to resolve the threatened labor strike.

10. American Mutual Fund (AMF) is a *portfolio* of many securities which the general public may purchase at what is called its net asset value (NAV) (discussed in Chapter 2). The net asset value of AMF is simply a fancy name for its price. Harris Corporation is a company involved in high-technology products. The prices and dividends for each investment during a recent period are shown below.

	American Mutual Fund		*Harris Corporation*	
Year	*End-of-Year NAV*	*Dividends Paid During Year*	*End-of-Year Price*	*Dividends Paid During Year*
1975	$ 8.09	NA	$ 8.594	NA
1976	10.16	$0.62	14.750	$0.36
1977	9.51	0.81	23.312	0.45
1978	9.82	0.84	28.750	0.55
1979	10.89	0.94	32.875	0.66
1980	12.48	1.06	52.125	0.76
1981	12.37	1.02	41.125	0.84
1982	13.56	1.92	37.000	0.88
1983	15.41	1.24	40.125	0.88
1984	14.94	1.34	27.125	0.88
1985	17.74	1.42	26.125	0.88
1986	17.99	2.82	29.750	0.88
1987	17.05	1.77	26.000	0.88

NA = not applicable to question.

Yearly returns on Treasury bills for this period were:

Year:	76	77	78	79	80	81	82	83	84	85	86	87
T-Bill Returns:	5.08	5.13	7.16	10.38	11.25	14.7	10.55	8.51	10.14	7.78	6.07	5.13

   a. Calculate the single-period return for each year between 1976 and 1987 for both AMF and Harris.

   b. Calculate the average yearly return and the standard deviation of return for each. Explain why AMF's standard deviation is smaller than Harris's.

   c. Now consider a portfolio of the two stocks consisting of a 50% investment in each. Calculate the average yearly return and the standard deviation of return for this portfolio.

      Notice that the *portfolio average* return is a weighted average of the two stocks' average return. But the standard deviation of the portfolio *is not* a weighted average of the two stocks' standard deviations. What causes this result?

   d. Prepare a graph depicting the average return of each stock on the vertical axis and the standard deviation of each stock on the horizontal. Is it fair to say that investors who are averse to risk would not have wanted to own Harris stock?

   e. Calculate the average return and standard deviation for Treasury bills and plot them on the graph. Do the same for a portfolio which consists of a 50% investment in AMF and a 50% investment in T-bills.

      Connect the T-bill point, the 50/50 portfolio point, and the AMF point. This line represents (in a very general fashion) an important investment principle. What is it?

DATA ANALYSIS PROBLEM

Objectives:

- To introduce the quarterly stock return data set included on the floppy diskette.
- To review concepts of diversification and the relationship between the risk and average return earned on a security.

Answers to this problem are given in the student's workbook which accompanies this book.

1. Use a microcomputer spreadsheet program to read the data set called "QTLYSTK.WK1". Move around the data set to see the type of data which is provided and its format. Quarter-end prices as well as quarterly dividends and returns are provided on many stocks, as well as Treasury bills and a common stock index known as the Standard & Poor's 500 Index.

2. Repeat the questions asked in the Review Problem using Exxon and IBM returns.

3. Note that the last column contains quarterly returns on a portfolio which consists of an equal percentage holding of each of the stocks included on the file.

   a. Find the average quarterly return and standard deviation for this portfolio.

   b. Find the average quarterly return and standard deviation for each stock.

   c. Find the average of all the stocks' average returns as well as the average of all the stocks' standard deviations.

   d. Compare these two grand averages with the results in part a. Explain why they are the same or differ.

The concept of diversification is critical in many investment programs. After completing this Data Analysis Problem, you should begin to understand that diversification can reduce risk substantially without adversely affecting average returns.

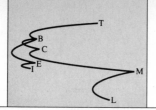

CHAPTER

2 Overview of Security Types

In this chapter we review the major types of marketable securities available for investment and speculation. The discussion is introductory. Just enough is said to give the reader a basic understanding of the institutional characteristics of each security so that the conceptual material in Part 2 can be better appreciated. More-subtle features are discussed at length in Part 3, which devotes complete chapters to various security forms.

A marketable security is a negotiable (salable) legal claim to future returns on some real asset. Life insurance policies, real estate, savings accounts, works of art, etc., are often viewed as investment or speculative vehicles. However, such "investments" are nonsalable (or salable only at a large commitment of cost and time) and will not be discussed in this text. Instead, we concentrate on negotiable security instruments such as common stocks, bonds, and mutual fund shares.

Typically, securities are classified as either *money market* instruments or *capital market* instruments. Money market instruments are normally used as short-term cash substitutes—media in which temporarily idle cash balances can be invested to earn a return. Money market instruments have short maturities (one year or less) and little default risk, and they are highly marketable. Examples include U.S. Treasury bills, commercial paper, and negotiable certificates of deposit.

Capital market instruments have longer maturities with varying degrees of risk and marketability. Examples include long-term U.S. government bonds, corporate and municipal bonds, preferred stocks, and common stocks. Capital market instruments are discussed more thoroughly later in the book. However, this is the only chapter that discusses money market instruments in any detail.

MONEY MARKET INSTRUMENTS

Individuals and organizations with temporary needs for cash sell money market securities to individuals and organizations with temporary excess cash. Transactions are large ($100 million is not uncommon) and span short intervals (overnight to one year). Large organizations participate in the money market by direct ownership of the instruments. Individuals with smaller sums of money to invest typically participate indirectly through *money market funds* (financial intermediaries that pool shareholder resources to buy money market instruments). The major money market instruments include:

1. Treasury bills
2. Other U.S. government obligations
3. Short-term municipal obligations
4. Repurchase agreements
5. Commercial paper
6. Certificates of deposit
7. Bankers' acceptances
8. Eurodollars
9. Federal funds

Treasury Bills

Treasury bills, or T-bills, are obligations sold by the U.S. Treasury to help finance federal expenditures. T-bills with three-month and six-month maturities are offered on Monday of every week, and one-year T-bills are offered every four weeks. At the time of the initial sale, an auction procedure is used in which money market banks, dealers, and other institutional investors submit competitive bids for a given dollar amount. Prices are quoted as a percentage of the T-bill's face value. For example, a bank might submit a bid of 98.275 on a $100 million issue, which, if accepted, means $98.275 million will be paid for bills having a face value of $100 million. Noncompetitive bids may also be made. When the new issue is awarded, the total face value of all noncompetitive bids is subtracted from the face value amount of bills being sold, and the remainder is distributed to competitive bidders offering the highest prices. Competitive bidders pay the price they bid, and noncompetitive bidders pay a price equal to the weighted average price of the competitive sales.

T-bills are referred to as *pure discount bonds* because they do not pay a coupon; the return to the owner comes totally from any price appreciation. As noted above, T-bill prices and discounts are stated as a percentage of face value. Discounts and percentage prices are determined using a procedure known as the *bank discount method*, assuming there are 360 days per year, according to the following formula:

Bank Discount Method

$$D = Fd\left(\frac{t}{360}\right) \qquad\qquad (2.1)$$

$$P = F - D$$

where D = the dollar discount on the $100 face value, F = the $100 face value, d = the quoted yearly discount rate, t = the number of days to maturity, and P = the price per $100 of face value.

For example, if a new three-month (91-day) bill is bought at a quoted discount of

8.55%, the price paid would be 97.83875% of face value (or $97.83875 per $100 of face value):

$$D = \$100 \times 0.0855 \times \left(\frac{91}{360}\right) = \$2.16125$$

$$P = \$100 - \$2.16125 = \$97.83875$$

It is important to recognize that the quoted discount on a T-bill is *not* the true yield to the owner. This discount represents a percentage below face value, whereas the true yield represents the percentage return on the price paid.

There are two general ways of expressing the rate of return on a T-bill. The first is based on *simple* interest and the second is based on *compound* interest. To convert from quoted discounts to effective simple interest yield to maturity, the following formula is often used:

Simple Interest T-Bill Return

$$r = \text{effective simple interest yield}$$

$$r = \frac{365 \times d}{360 - dt}$$

(2.2)

Using the formula, an 8.55% discount on a 91-day bill results in an *effective simple interest* annualized yield of 8.86%:

$$r = \frac{365 \times 0.0855}{360 - (0.0855 \times 91)} = 0.0886$$

To understand more clearly what this annualized simple interest yield of 8.86% is, consider the following. First, the bill is purchased for $97.83875 and pays back $100 91 days later. This represents a 2.209% 91-day return:

$$91\text{-day return} = \frac{\$100 - \$97.83875}{\$97.83875} = 0.02209$$

To annualize this 91-day return, it is multiplied by the number of 91-day periods there are in a 365-day year. This result is 8.86%, identical to that obtained with Equation 2.2 above:

$$0.02209 \times \frac{365}{91} = 0.0886$$

To calculate the *effective compound interest* yield, Equation 2.3 would be used where $r' = $ effective compound interest yield:

Compound Interest T-Bill Return

$$r' = \left(\frac{F}{P}\right)^{365/t} - 1.0$$

(2.3)

Using the data above, the effective annual compound yield would be 9.159%:

$$r' = \left(\frac{\$100}{\$97.83875}\right)^{365/91} - 1.0 = (1.02209)^{365/91} - 1.0 = 0.09159$$

The reason the two annualized yields vary is easy to see. During the 91-day holding period, the rate of return is clearly 2.209%. To annualize this 91-day return, the simple interest approach *multiplies* by 4.01 (the number of 91-day periods in a year), whereas the compound interest approach *compounds* this return for 4.01 periods. But which approach is the better one to use? The answer depends upon whether this is a one-time purchase or other 91-day bills will be consistently purchased in the future. If this is a one-time purchase, the simple interest approach is a realistic estimate of the equivalent annual return. However, if a policy of "rolling over" a sequence of such 91-day bills is expected to be used, then the compound interest approach should be used.

There is considerably more to know about calculating T-bill returns, but such a discussion lies beyond the scope of this book. Nonetheless, for professionals who trade T-bills in quantities of $100 million and more, such calculations are vital.

Bills may be bought with either a competitive or a noncompetitive bid at the time of initial offering by the Treasury or after the initial offering from banks and brokers who are qualified to act as government security dealers. Government security dealers provide an active secondary market in all U.S. government securities. Prices at which they are willing to buy or sell are quoted daily in the financial press. An illustration of how these quotes appear is shown below. Assume the quotes are for the close of trading on November 14, 1990.

Sample T-Bill Quotations for the Close of Trading on November 14, 1990

Maturity	Bid Discount	Asked Discount	Yield
— 1990 —			
11-23	8.16	7.98	8.11
12-27	8.06	8.00	8.19
— 1991 —			
1-10	8.35	8.29	8.51
1-14	8.53	8.47	8.71

Quotes are stated in terms of discounts. The *bid discount* is the highest price at which a dealer was willing to buy on the specified day, and the *asked discount* is the lowest price at which a dealer was willing to sell. For example, bills maturing on January 14 happened to have 61 days remaining to maturity and could be bought from a dealer at $98.565 or sold to a dealer at $98.55:

$$\text{Dealer's Selling Price} = \$100 - \$100 (\text{Discount Asked}) \times \frac{61}{360}$$

$$= \$100 - \$100 (0.0847) \frac{61}{360}$$

$$= \$98.565$$

$$\text{Dealer's Purchase Price} = \$100 - \$100 \text{ (Discount Bid)} \times \frac{61}{360}$$

$$= \$100 = \$100 \ (0.0853) \ \frac{61}{360}$$

$$= \$98.555$$

The effective annualized return on this issue is 8.71%, found by inserting the dealer's asked discount into Equation 2.2. Each T-bill usually has a face value of $1,000,000 or more. Owners are registered in Federal Research Board computers.

Other Treasury instruments similar to T-bills are also issued occasionally. Tax anticipation notes mature about a week after tax payments are due but may be tendered (turned in) on the tax date and credited against the tax bill *at par*. Since their face value maturity can be hastened by one week, the effective annualized return increases. Certificates of indebtedness are occasionally, but very rarely, issued. They differ from T-bills in that they often offer a coupon.

Other U.S. Government Obligations

The U.S. government sells many other debt obligations through either the Treasury or various federal agencies. Since most of these securities are commonly thought of as capital market instruments, they are reviewed later in the chapter. However, because of their low default risk, their high marketability, and the fact that, as time passes, many such issues have short-term maturities, they can often qualify as money market securities. For example, the Federal Home Loan Bank and other agencies sell short-term discount securities which resemble T-bills. Because of their somewhat poorer marketability and slightly greater default risk, these securities sell at yields greater than those of T-bills. Spreads of 5 to 100 basis points are common. A *basis point* represents one-hundredth of a percentage point. For example, if yields rise from 8.55% to 8.90%, they have risen 35 basis points.

Short-Term Municipal Obligations

The term *municipal* is used to refer to any politically incorporated body other than the federal government and its agencies. Examples are state, county, and city governments, school districts, and turnpike and port authorities. Municipal securities are sold with maturities ranging anywhere from a month to 30 years. The shorter-term, high-quality obligations often qualify as money market instruments.

Such securities are of four types:

1. *Tax anticipation notes* are short-term obligations sold to finance current governmental operations. As the name implies, they are sold in anticipation of near-term tax collections. They are *general obligations* (*full-faith-and-credit* obligations not

collateralized by specific physical assets) of the issuer and are repaid as soon as taxes are collected.

2. *Revenue anticipation notes* are similar to tax anticipation notes but are repaid from sources other than taxes. An example would be the revenue anticipation notes of a municipal electric system. They are referred to as *revenue obligations.*

3. *Bond anticipation notes* are sold to temporarily finance a project which will soon be refinanced with a long-term bond issue. Proceeds from such long-term issues are used to repay the bond anticipation notes.

4. *Project notes* are issued in auctions by the U.S. Department of Housing and Urban Development (HUD) to finance federally sponsored programs of local governments. Projects include neighborhood development, urban renewal, and low-cost housing. Although they are obligations of the municipality, they are guaranteed by HUD.

All of these obligations are *bearer instruments*, that is, they are assumed to be owned by the person in possession of the bond. They typically pay a coupon, and come in face value denominations of $1,000 and up.

Repurchase Agreements

Repurchase agreements (repos, or RPs) are not physical securities issued by one party to another. Instead, they are *contractual agreements* between two parties to buy and sell U.S. government securities at particular points in time. Consider the hypothetical example of First Income Securities Corporation, a dealer in U.S. government obligations. First Income Securities generates profits in three ways: by acting as a wholesaler of government securities (standing ready to buy at bid and sell at asked prices), by speculating on future changes in interest rates (buying bonds when rates are expected to fall and selling when rates are expected to rise), and by a variety of arbitrage transactions. In the course of business, the firm is likely to own government securities in amounts considerably in excess of the company's equity capital. The firm can finance this security inventory using either a bank loan or a repurchase agreement. Since repos are often cheaper, they are extensively used.

To enter into a repurchase agreement, First Income will sell a portion of the firm's government securities to, say, a city government which has temporary excess cash *and will agree to repurchase the securities at a stated price on a stated date.* Although the repo is written in a way suggesting that securities are actually sold and are later to be repurchased, in substance the municipality has given the dealer a short-term loan collateralized by U.S. government securities. The effective interest rate on the loan (return to the repo buyer) is simply the percentage difference between the sale price and the purchase price. Such a trade is often profitable to the repo seller (First Income Securities) since the interest rate paid to the repo buyer is often less than the yield on the government securities owned. For example, 181-day T-bills yielding 8.50% might be RP'd for three months at 8.40% and RP'd again for another three months at 8.40%. The repo seller would take the 10-basis-point "carry" as profit. The repo buyer would be willing to accept such a low yield because alternative investments with similar risk and scheduled maturity are unavailable. This is especially true for *overnight repos* — situations in which the lender wishes to invest for one day but can find no alternatives available other than a repurchase agreement. Dealers can thus finance large holdings of U.S. governments by continuously reentering into a sequence of many overnight repos.

Commercial Paper

Commercial paper is an *unsecured promissory note* used by financially strong manufacturing firms and finance companies. Commercial paper is generally issued on a discount basis with maturities of 270 days or less. To reduce the risk of default, commercial paper is backed with lines of credit from banks which guarantee that the issuer will have the cash necessary at maturity. Commercial paper is initially sold both directly by the issuer and through commercial paper dealers. Denominations are in amounts of $100,000 and up. While a relatively active trading market exists, many purchasers hold the paper until maturity. Commercial paper rates are close to those available on certificates of deposit and bankers' acceptances with similar maturity.

Certificates of Deposit

Negotiable certificates of deposit (CDs) are *large deposits* ($100,000 or more) *placed in commercial banks at a stated rate of interest*. Unlike other bank CDs, negotiable CDs may be bought and sold in the open market. They qualify as money market instruments since they have short maturities, have low default risk (although they are insured in part by the Federal Deposit Insurance Corporation, their risk features depend upon the issuing bank), and are reasonably marketable because of their salability in the open market. Their yields are slightly higher than those of equivalent maturity T-bills (25 to 100 basis points) because of their greater risk and poorer marketability.

Bankers' Acceptances

A bankers' acceptance is a *time draft* which the accepting bank has agreed to pay at a specified future date. Historically, most bankers' acceptances have arisen in the course of international trade. For example, a U.S. firm might wish to import shoes from a Japanese exporter. The U.S. firm will have its U.S. banker write a *letter of credit* to the Japanese exporter guaranteeing that the goods will be paid for. After receiving the letter of credit, the exporter will ship the goods and simultaneously prepare a draft on the domestic bank. This draft is taken to a Japanese bank together with supporting documentation, such as the letter of credit and shipping documents, and the Japanese bank pays the exporter. The draft is then sent to the U.S. bank, where it is "accepted." At this point a *bankers' acceptance* has been created which may be returned to the Japanese bank (if it wishes to hold the acceptance as an investment), kept by the domestic bank (if the Japanese bank wants immediate cash and the domestic bank wishes to hold it as an investment), or sold in the open market.

In effect, a bankers' acceptance is a *promissory note* which stipulates a payment amount and a date at which it will be paid. Final payment is made by the U.S. importer or by the accepting bank if the importer defaults. Acceptances are traded on a discount basis with the return to the owner consisting of the difference between the price paid and the acceptance's face value. Denominations of $100,000 or more are normal. Since both the importer and the accepting bank have agreed to pay, default risk is minimal. This low risk and a fairly active trading market allow bankers' acceptances to trade at yields only 25 to 100 basis points greater than those for T-bills with similar maturity.

Bankers' acceptances are used by borrowers who are either too small or too risky to use commercial paper. As a result, the rates are slightly above commercial paper rates. In recent years acceptances have been increasingly used to finance domestic as well as international transactions.

Eurodollars

Eurodollars are simply deposits in foreign banks *denominated in U.S. dollars*. The market initially developed in Europe, hence the term *Eurodollars*. Today the name is a misnomer since U.S. dollar–denominated deposits can be made in almost any country. Deposits are usually made for a stated time interval (six months or less) and pay a stated rate of interest. Banks receiving Eurodollar deposits use them to make loans also denominated in dollars. The Eurodollar market is a relatively recent phenomenon, growing to major international importance since the early 1960s. Today it represents a major source of financing and investment to large international organizations. Eurodollar deposits are relatively free of default risk, can be easily bought or sold, and are not subject to many of the regulations imposed by the U.S. government on deposits made in domestic U.S. banks. Because of the activities of domestic banks in the market, interest rates tend to track very closely the rates charged on domestic Fed funds.

Federal Funds

The only traders in the Federal funds market are commercial banks that are members of the Federal Reserve System. These banks are required to maintain a specified portion of their total deposits in cash, either as cash in their vaults or as cash deposited with the Federal Reserve System. Since rates of return are not paid on any required reserves maintained with the Federal Reserve, member banks attempt to maintain the smallest possible reserve position. However, since deposit increases and withdrawals cannot be predicted with complete accuracy, some banks find themselves with temporary excess reserves while others are temporarily deficient. As a result, a market has arisen which allows banks with excess reserves to lend to those with deficiencies. This market is known as the Fed funds market.

The Fed funds market is extremely active and deals with huge sums of money. Most borrowing and lending is done on an *overnight* (one-day) basis, although some *term* Fed funds are traded. Many banks rely upon brokers to bring together buyers and sellers, although some banks rely upon correspondent banks or personal knowledge. While the market is not available to non-bank borrowers or lenders, many traders believe that the overnight Fed funds rate is the base on which other money market rates rest.

FIXED-INCOME CAPITAL MARKET

Capital market securities differ from money market securities in one or more of the following ways: (1) their maturity is greater than one year, (2) their default risk is greater, and (3) their marketability is poorer. However, a clear distinction between capital market and money market instruments doesn't always exist. For example, Treasury notes and bonds which are about to mature might well be considered money market securities. The distinction between these two markets is made to add some (slightly artificial) clarity and organization to what is indeed a complex realm of securities. Capital market securities which promise to pay a fixed income include:

1. U.S. Treasury issues
2. U.S. agency issues
3. Municipal issues
4. Corporate issues

U.S. Treasury Issues

The U.S. Treasury offers two types of fixed-income securities with maturities greater than one year: Treasury notes and Treasury bonds. These are essentially identical except that *notes* have an initial maturity of ten years or less, whereas *bonds* have a maturity in excess of ten years. Both pay coupons semiannually. They are initially offered by the Treasury in competitive auctions similar to T-bill auctions except that bidders submit desired yields to maturity, as opposed to discounts, for bills. The average winning bid is then used to determine the issue's coupon (stated in eighths of a dollar) so that the securities can be sold at close to total face value.

Once issued by the Treasury, notes and bonds can be bought or sold in the same manner as T-bills—through large government security dealers. Buyers pay the dealer an asked price and sellers receive the bid price. An illustration of how note and bond quotes appear in the financial pages is shown below. Again, assume the quotes are for the close of trading on November 14, 1990.

Sample Treasury Bond and Note Quotations for the Close of Trading on November 14, 1990

Coupon Rate	Maturity	Bid Price	Asked Price	Yield
9⅞s	Nov 1990 n	100.00	100.4	6.52
13⅜s	Mar 1990 n	101.12	101.16	9.07
10⅞s	Feb 1992 n	100.15	100.19	10.37
10½s	Jan 1996 n	95.28	96.4	11.52
3½s	Feb 1996	88.17	89.17	5.84
7½s	Aug 1994–99	78.20	79.4	11.32
3s	Feb 2001	88.13	89.13	4.29
10⅜s	May 2001	92.11	92.30	11.69

The *coupon rate* represents the annual coupon paid on the bond, though coupons are actually paid semiannually. For example, the 9⅞s pay $49.375 each six months (in May and November, in this case) for a $1,000 face value. Many bond issues sold by the Treasury are callable prior to maturity. Such issues can be identified as those with two quoted maturities. For example, the 7½s are first callable in August 1994 but, if not called, mature in August 1999. *Bid* and *asked prices* appear to be in decimal form, but in reality the decimal represents *thirty-seconds of a dollar*. For example, the 10⅜s issue maturing in May 2001 can be bought from a securities dealer at 92$^{30}\!/_{32}$% of face value or sold for 92$^{11}\!/_{32}$% of face value. Finally, the *yield* column represents the yield to maturity of each issue. Using the asked price, the yield to maturity of the 10⅜s issue was 11.69%. (When callable bonds are selling at prices above face value, the yield shown is the yield to the first possible call date.)

A quick scan of the sample quotations reveals that some issues sell at yields to maturity that are substantially different from those of issues with reasonably similar maturity. The major reasons are twofold:

1. Some issues have fewer securities outstanding, which tends to result in a less active trading market and poorer marketability. Such issues must offer slightly higher yields.
2. Many of the issues receive favorable tax treatment arising out of their low coupons. Ordinary tax rates are paid on receipt of coupons, but capital gains taxes, which are often lower, are paid on differences between the discount price paid and the maturity face value when the security is held to maturity. This can result in a lower effective tax rate on low-coupon issues, which in turn results in a lower before-tax required yield. For example, the 3½s due in 1996 sold at a lower yield than issues with similar maturity simply because of the tax treatment of the low coupon.

Treasury notes and bonds are sold as registered issues, as bearer issues, and, increasingly, as *book entry issues*. As noted earlier, a registered issue specifically identifies the name of the owner, whereas bearer issues are assumed to belong to the bearer. Book entry issues are never physically distributed. Instead, records of owners are maintained by computers at the Federal Reserve, eliminating the clerical costs of physically transferring pieces of paper—the actual notes and bonds. Face value denominations range from $1,000 and up. However, most transactions are in blocks of $500 thousand to $1 million. Interest income on all U.S. Treasury securities is exempt from state and local income and property taxes.

Treasury notes and bonds have the lowest default risk and greatest marketability possible on securities of their maturity. As such they represent the foundation on which yields of other bonds having similar maturity but different risk and marketability are based.

The unprecedented volatility of interest rates in the 1970s and 1980s resulted in the introduction of many new financial instruments intended to enable investors to better cope with (or perhaps even profit from) this volatility. Among such products were CATS, TIGERS, and STRIPS. For example, in 1982, the first offering was made to the public of "Treasury Receipts" — claims to specific coupons or principal cash flows on a portfolio of U.S. Treasury securities. They were created by an investment banking firm purchasing a large pool of U.S. Treasuries and placing the securities with a custodian such as a commercial bank. The investment banker then sold legal rights to specific cash flows generated by the portfolio. Purchasers of such Treasury receipts paid an initial price and were promised a single future cash flow. In effect, the coupons and principal cash flows on the Treasuries were "stripped" and resold as zero-coupon instruments. Once sold, a secondary market in these Treasury receipts would be made by an initial underwriter.

Acronyms used to identify these Treasury receipts were novel. Two popular offerings were:

- CATS (Certificates of Accrual on Treasury Securities)
- TIGERS (Treasury Investment Growth Receipts)

People bought coupon CATS, principal CATS, and even Callable Tails (CATS with a claim to principal or coupons which could be called by the Treasury). Trading activity in such Treasury receipts reached a peak in late 1984.

In 1985, the U.S. Treasury announced the *Separate Trading of Registered Interest and Principal of Securities* — STRIPS. Under the STRIPS program, "selected Treasury Securities may be maintained in the book entry system operated by the Federal Reserve banks in a manner that permits separate trading and ownership of the interest and principal payments." Under the STRIPS program, the Treasury does not actually auction zero-coupon bonds. All sales of new bonds are conducted exactly as they have been in the past — with coupon-bearing bonds. However, once the bond is outstanding, the Federal Reserve facilitates the purchase or sale of specified coupons or principal cash flows. Trading is in $1,000 units and provided free of charge by the Fed. Initially, only six long-term Treasuries were made available for stripping, but most new bond offerings are now available. In addition, many of the new Treasury bonds are noncallable. Thus, a truly long term (up to 30 years) default-free and noncallable zero-coupon bond is available.

U.S. Agency Issues

Agency issues are not direct obligations of the Treasury. Instead, they are sold by various governmental agencies to support their financial activities. A few are backed by the full faith and credit of the United States, and many are guaranteed or supported by the Treasury. But even though agency issues don't have a direct guarantee of payment, they are considered to have top investment quality because governmental backing is implied. Major agencies selling marketable securities include the following:

1. *Federal National Mortgage Association (FNMA)*. Issues by FNMA are called *Fannie Mae issues*. FNMA is a government-sponsored corporation owned by private stockholders which exists to provide financing to the mortgage markets. Fannie Mae issues are sold without a guarantee by the U.S. government. A variety of different FNMA issues exist, ranging from short-term discount notes which qualify as money market securities to 25-year debentures. Proceeds from bond sales are used to purchase mortgages held by savings and loans, mortgage companies, insurance companies, etc.

2. *Federal Home Loan Banks (FHLB)*. There are twelve Federal Home Loan Banks which provide credit services to mortgage-granting institutions such as savings and loans, savings banks, and insurance companies. FHLB issues range in maturity from less than one year to twenty years and are not guaranteed by the U.S. government. Proceeds from bond sales are used to grant loans to FHLB members.

3. *Federal Land Banks (FLB)*. There are twelve Federal Land Banks which provide financial resources to farmers and ranchers. FLB bonds are sold with maturities ranging from eighteen months to fifteen years. They are not guaranteed by the U.S. government. Proceeds from bond sales are lent to qualifying farmers and ranchers and must be used for agricultural purposes.

4. *Federal Intermediate Credit Banks (FICB)*. Twelve Federal Intermediate Credit Banks make loans to commercial banks, agricultural credit associations, and livestock loan companies. Maturity of issues is usually nine months, although intermediate-term (two- to four-year) bonds are occasionally sold.

5. *Banks for Cooperatives*. These thirteen banks make and service loans to eligible agricultural cooperative associations. Six-month maturities are typical, but intermediate-term issues are occasionally sold.

6. *Government National Mortgage Association (GNMA)*. Issues by the GNMA are called *Ginnie Maes*. The GNMA is a wholly owned government agency within HUD and is an offshoot of the FNMA. The GNMA was organized to provide special-assistance financing to the mortgage market. This is done by either (1) buying mortgages from private lenders at prices higher than the market and selling them at market or (2) guaranteeing securities backed by pools of mortgages. In either case, the GNMA is subsidizing a special type of mortgage for which it wishes to provide assistance. Two types of securities are sold by the GNMA. *GNMA participation certificates* are backed by the full faith and credit of the U.S. government and have maturities up to 25 years. *GNMA pass-throughs* are also guaranteed by the U.S. government, and maturities run to 40 years. Pass-throughs differ from participation certificates in that pass-throughs provide *both* principal and interest repayment as the underlying mortgages being used as collateral are repaid. The principal and interest payments on the underlying mortgages are immediately passed through to the bond holder. The average life of a Ginnie Mae pass-through is about 10 years, even though stated maturity may be longer.

7. *Other Agency Obligations.* Among the other federal agencies that issue securities are the following:

Export-Import Bank
Federal Housing Administration
Tennessee Valley Authority
Farmers Home Administration
International Bank for Reconstruction and Development
Inter-American Development Bank
Small Business Administration
Student Loan Marketing Association (Sallie Maes)

Agency obligations are similar in many respects to Treasury bonds and notes. They are all virtually free of default risk, although, technically, some agencies do have a slight potential for default without the U.S. government's backing. Shorter-term agencies are actively traded and therefore have good liquidity. Longer-term issues are traded less actively than Treasuries and will command higher yields to maturity as a result. Finally, many agency obligations are exempt from state and local taxes.

Yields to maturity on a sample of U.S. Treasuries and agencies are shown in Table 2-1. Note that, regardless of the maturity class, yields on the agencies are greater than yields on the Treasuries. This reflects the agencies' slightly greater default risk and poorer marketability.

Municipal Issues

Municipal issues are bonds sold by states, counties, cities, and other political corporations. The most important feature of municipal bonds is their special tax treatment. Coupon income is totally excluded from federal income tax and is excluded from state income tax in the bond's state of origin. For example, an investor residing in Ohio would pay no income tax on coupon income received from Ohio Turnpike Authority bonds and would pay only state income tax on West Virginia Turnpike Authority

TABLE 2-1 *Yield Comparisons of U.S. Treasuries Versus U.S. Agency Obligations, December 31, 1987*

Maturity at End of Year	Treasury	FNMA	FHLB	FFC
1989	7.5%	7.82%	7.95%	8.17%
1990	8.05	8.36	8.25	8.41
1991	8.24	8.56	8.62	8.63
1992	8.43	8.74	8.77	8.90
1995	8.75	9.28	9.30	9.17
2015	9.05	9.61	—	—

FNMA = Federal National Mortgage Association
FHLB = Federal Home Loan Bank
FFC = Federal Farm Credit

bonds. Capital gains on municipal obligations are fully taxed at appropriate capital gains tax rates.

Municipal bonds are of two basic types: general obligations and revenue obligations. *General obligations (G.O.'s)* are backed by the full faith and credit of the issuer and repaid from taxes received by the issuing body. *Revenue obligations* are sold to finance a particular project and are repaid from the income earned on the project. Revenue issues do not have a claim to the tax receipts of the issuer, but instead are repaid from the revenue generated by the particular project. For example, municipal electric systems, turnpike and airport authorities, and sewage systems all issue revenue bonds.

Risk, maturity, and marketability of municipal obligations vary considerably. Usually, G.O.'s are less risky than revenues, but risks vary widely among different issuers. Maturities range from the very short-term tax anticipation notes mentioned earlier to 25-year debentures. Typically, long-term municipal issues are sold as serial bonds, as opposed to term bonds. *Serial bonds* have a predetermined series of bonds maturing each year until final maturity. *Term bonds* are repaid in full at one terminal maturity date. For example, if the city of San Francisco sells a 20-year, $50 million serial issue, it might retire $2½ million of specified bonds each year during the next 20 years. As a result, the average life of this 20-year obligation is about 10 years.

Serial bonds are used for two reasons. First, when a portion of principal is retired each year, the default risk might be lower. The municipality is forced to have capital available each year instead of waiting until maturity to come up with a large lump sum. Second, major buyers of municipals are financial institutions that like to stagger the maturity distribution of their bond portfolios over a number of years. When marketing the issue, the municipality can sell a piece of the issue with a given maturity to an institution that needs more bonds of that particular maturity. Thus, the issuer hopes that serialization will aid in the initial marketing of the bonds.

Corporate Issues

Long-term corporate debt obligations are usually term bonds with maturities of five years or more. The financial obligations of the corporate issuer are set forth in a security agreement known as an *indenture*. Indenture agreements usually specify the bond's repayment schedule, restrictions on dividend payments and liquidity, types of collateral, etc. It is the job of the *trustee* (usually a commercial bank) to ascertain that all indenture covenants are complied with. Types of information provided in the indenture include the following:

1. *Call provisions.* A call provision allows the issuer to redeem the bond by purchasing it from the holder at a specified price. Most corporate bonds are sold with a deferred call provision. Deferred call bars the issuer from calling the bond for a stipulated period (commonly five to ten years), after which time the bond is callable at stipulated prices. Call prices are initially set above face value and decline, in steps, to face value prior to maturity. Initial *call premiums* (the difference between the call price and the face value) are normally equal to one year's coupon

payment. In Chapter 8 we will see that a call provision increases an investor's uncertainty about future realized yields since the investor has no way of knowing whether or when the issue will be called. As a result, yields on callable bonds exceed those on noncallable issues.

2. *Sinking funds.* Sinking funds are annual payments made to a trustee to ensure eventual repayment of the bonds. Sinking funds may be left to accumulate as a deposit with the trustee or used to immediately retire a portion of the outstanding issue through purchase in the open market. Retirement is accomplished by calling a random set of bonds; thus, sinking fund obligations are closely related to serial bonds.

3. *Collateral provisions.* Bonds which have a legal claim to specific assets of the firm in the event of liquidation or reorganization are *secured bonds*. A *mortgage bond* is secured by a lien on real property, such as plants and buildings. Typically, mortgage bonds will be backed by a lien on a specified set of real assets, but occasionally a *blanket mortgage* is used which provides a lien on all assets of the firm. First, second, third, etc., mortgages can be placed on property with respective claims to assets during liquidation. Mortgage bonds may also be open-end, limited open-end, or closed-end. *Open-end mortgages* allow the issuer to sell additional bonds having equal claim to the mortgaged assets. Such open-end agreements will usually include an *after-acquired property clause* which requires that all future real assets purchased be added to the initial mortgage. *Limited open-end mortgages* allow new bond sales to have a lien on the same property up to a limit. This limit is normally stated as a percentage of the mortgaged debt to property cost, say 30%. Finally, a *closed-end mortgage* prohibits future debt sales with equivalent claim to the assets.

Unsecured bonds are known as *debentures*. Debenture holders are general creditors of the firm and have no legal claim to specified assets. In the event of liquidation they will be paid only after all mortgage bondholders have been reimbursed. Holders of *subordinated debentures* have a lower claim to assets than do general creditors, such as trade creditors (accounts payable).

Income bonds are repaid from the income earned on asset investments. Unlike other bonds, for which the issuer is contractually obligated to repay principal and interest regardless of current income, an income bond has no contractual commitment to pay interest and principal unless income is sufficient to do so. Revenue bonds sold by municipalities are income bonds.

Corporate bonds are often given special features which act as inducements to potential purchasers as well as cost-saving devices to the corporation in arranging future financing. Examples of such inducements are convertibility and warrants. A *convertible bond* is a debt obligation which allows the owner to tender the bond to the corporation and convert it into a given number of shares of stock. The attraction of convertibility to the bondholder is the guaranteed fixed income plus the ability to share in rapid stock price rises if they should occur. Cost savings to the issuing corporation are largely in lower yields required by investors because of the convertibility.

Bonds are often sold with warrants attached. Like a convertible provision, a bond with a warrant provides the owner with a fixed income plus the ability to share in future stock price increases. The issuing corporation hopes to save through lower required bond yields and automatic future equity sales at the exercise date. A *warrant* is a legal claim which allows the owner to buy a certain number of common shares at a specified *exercise price* any time before a specified *exercise date*. Exercise prices are initially set at levels which are expected to give the owner an eventual price break in buying the stock. For example, assume that a firm will need new equity capital two years hence. Management expects its stock price to be $70 at that time but cannot be sure of this. The firm could issue warrants with an exercise price of $60 and a maximum exercise date of two years. The $60 exercise price is set lower than the expected stock price to allow for management's uncertainty about the $70 value and to provide a potential inducement to exercise the warrant in two years. If the stock does sell for more than $60 two years hence, all warrants will be exercised. Warrant owners will get a favorable stock price and management will get the new equity financing needed.

EQUITY SECURITIES

Equity securities provide a residual claim on asset returns once all fixed-income claims have been paid. There are two basic forms of equities: preferred stock and common stock.

Preferred Stock

Preferred stock is actually a hybrid security with features of both a fixed-income obligation and a pure equity security. Similar to income bonds, preferred stocks pay a stipulated yearly cash payment only if corporate income is sufficient to do so. Preferred dividends are usually expressed as a percentage of the preferred's par value. For example, a $100 par, 6% preferred issue would pay a $6 dividend each year. If the issue is *cumulative*, any unpaid past dividends (dividends in arrears) accumulate and must eventually be paid before any dividends can be distributed to owners of common stock. Unpaid dividends on *noncumulative* preferred shares do not have to be paid. Some preferred issues are *participating*, which allows the preferred dividend to increase in a stipulated fashion as common stock dividends increase. Owners of preferred stock are usually given the right to vote for directors of the firm (and thus exert some true equity control) only if dividends have not been paid for a year or more. Preferreds also receive preferential ("preferred") treatment if the firm's assets must be liquidated, in that they have a par value claim to assets before any liquidating dividends are distributed to owners of common stock.

These features are not unique to preferred stock. They are also available on many income bonds. While an indenture agreement does not secure the preferred stock issue, such issues commonly have callability, convertibility, sinking fund, and other features found on income bonds. Because of this, many people consider preferred stock to be the economic equivalent of income bonds.

Corporate owners of preferred (and common) stocks receive a substantial tax break on any dividend income received. Bond interest income received by a corporation is fully taxed, but 85% of the dividends received by one corporation from another is excluded from taxable income. The remaining 15% is taxed at regular corporate rates. For example, if a corporation is in a 40% marginal tax bracket, the effective tax rate on preferred and common stock dividend income would be 6% (0.40×0.15). Congress has legislated this favorable tax treatment in an attempt to reduce triple taxation when one corporation owns part of another corporation. From an investment standpoint, it provides a healthy incentive for corporations with large amounts of security holdings (such as insurance companies) to heavily weight their portfolio investments toward preferred and common stock. This can result in before-tax preferred stock yields which are lower even than those of less risky corporate bond issues. Thus, preferred stocks are often unattractive to noncorporate investors.

Common Stock

The common stockholders of a corporation represent the firm's ownership. Shares of common stock sold to investors give their owners a claim to any asset returns after all debt and preferred stock obligations are fully satisfied. Common stockholders have a nonguaranteed, residual claim to asset returns. If the firm is successful, common stockholders will share in its success, and debt holders receive only their promised fixed returns. If the firm should fail, common stockholders receive liquidating dividends only after all debt holders and preferred holders have been repaid the face value of their securities.

Because of the ownership risk position which common shareholders bear, they are given two basic rights: the right to managerial control and the right to retain an initial percentage ownership. The *right to control* is provided by allowing common shareholders to vote for members of the board of directors. Normally, ownership of one share will allow one vote for each director to be elected. If you own 100 shares in a firm which is selecting three directors, you can cast 100 votes for each of the three separate positions. This procedure is referred to as *noncumulative voting*. Occasionally, *cumulative voting* is allowed to assure minority groups a voice in management. When cumulative voting is used, a vote can be cast for any one directorship equal to the number of shares owned times the number of positions available. For example, if 100 shares are owned and three directors are to be elected, 300 votes could be cast for one director's position and none for the other two. Shareholder voting occurs at annual meetings of the corporation. If a shareholder is unable to attend this meeting, a *proxy* vote can be given to another party.

The right to retain a proportionate ownership in the firm is known as the *preemptive right*. The preemptive right allows existing shareholders the first option to purchase any new share offerings of the corporation. For example, if an individual now owns 1% of the common stock of ABC Corp., he or she must be given an opportunity to buy 1% of any new common stock issues. The preemptive right is important since it limits management's ability to dilute a shareholder's percentage control through the sale of new stock to third parties. For example, consider a firm with two opposing factions known as the minority and majority groups. If the firm has cumulative voting, the minority group would be able to assure themselves of some voice in management by electing some (admittedly a minority) of the directors. But without the preemptive right, the majority could still force the minority group out of the firm by selling new stock issues only to groups of investors sympathetic with the majority view and using the proceeds to make large cash dividends. Eventually, the ownership position of the minority group would be so small that even cumulative voting wouldn't assure them a voice in the management of assets.

An illustration of how preferred and common stock price quotations appear in the financial press is shown below.

Sample Common Stock Price Quotations for the Close of Trading on November 14, 1990

52-Week				Div		Sales			
High	*Low*	*Stock*	*Dividend*	*YLD*	*P/E*	*100's*	*High*	*Low*	*Close*
87¾	61½	TBS	2.80	3.7%	10	1032	76⅜	75½	76
52¾	29	Rainbow Tractor	0.50	1.5%	•	1167	33⅝	33⅛	33¼
52¾	35⅝	Noble	3.65	8.4%	5	1520	43⅞	43⅜	43½
44½	36⅝	Noble pf	5.25	13.0%	•	9	41	41	41

The first quote is for the common stock of TBS Inc. During the previous 52 weeks, TBS had sold for as high as $87.75 and as low as $61.50. Stock trades occur in eighths of a dollar ($0.125). Thus a trade, for example, at $61.65 is impossible. The dividend shown is an annualized approximation based on the last dividend declaration. For example, if TBS had last declared a quarterly dividend of $0.70, the annual approximation would be $2.80 (4 × $0.70). The dividend yield shown here is this annualized dividend divided by the stock's current price. For example, the 3.7% TBS dividend yield is equal to $2.80 divided by the $76 closing price. The P/E statistic represents the current stock price divided by the company's latest twelve-month earnings per share. If earnings per share are negative (as for Rainbow Tractor) or not applicable (as for the Noble preferred stock), then no price/earnings ratio is shown. The total number of shares traded during the time period covered by the quotation is shown next in units of 100 shares. Since the example data are assumed to reflect a single day's trading activity, 103,200 shares of TBS were bought and sold. The next three columns indicate the stock's high, low, and closing price. (Note that preferred stocks are clearly denoted. For example, the Noble preferreds are indicated by the code *pf.*)

Common and preferred shares may be bought and sold on a formal exchange market, such as the New York Stock Exchange, or from dealers in what is known as the over-the-counter (OTC) market. These markets are discussed in Chapter 3.

Investment Company Shares

Investment companies sell common shares in the company to the public and pool the proceeds to make direct investments in debt and equity instruments. There are basically two forms of investment companies: closed-end and open-end. Since open-end firms are the more financially important of the two, our discussion here is restricted to them. Chapter 18 discusses both in depth.

Open-end investment companies are commonly referred to as *mutual funds*. Unlike a typical corporation, mutual funds sell shares to any individual wishing to own them and stand ready to buy (redeem) any shares which individuals wish to sell; hence the term *open-end*. All transactions in mutual fund shares occur between the mutual fund and the investor, not in a secondary market such as the NYSE or through dealers in the over-the-counter market. Since asset holdings are restricted to various forms of marketable securities, the total market value of the fund's assets is relatively easy to calculate. Since mutual funds are usually not allowed to use debt financing (except for normal trade payables), the market value per share of a given mutual fund is equal to the total market value of its assets (less trade payables) divided by the number of shares of stock the fund has outstanding. This value is referred to as the fund's *net asset value*. The price at which the mutual fund will buy or sell shares with the investing public is usually pegged to this net asset value.

Consider the hypothetical case of Twenty-First Centurion Fund shown in Table 2-2. All assets and liabilities are valued at their *current market values*. Subtracting the market value of liabilities from the market value of assets leaves an equity claim of $109.5 million on the assets. Since there are 4,380,000 equity shares, each share has a *net asset value* of $25. People wishing to buy new shares of the mutual fund clearly would not be willing to pay more than $25 per share. Conversely, current owners would be unwilling to sell their shares back to the fund for less than $25. As a result, all trades must transact at $25 — the net asset value.

Mutual funds follow a specified investment policy so that potential investors can pick a fund which matches their own investment objectives. Some funds, for example, hold broadly diversified portfolios of all traded stocks and bonds and trade as little as possible. These funds are referred to as *index funds*. Index funds are a phenomenon of the efficient markets hypothesis, which states that the best way to select securities is to buy a broadly diversified portfolio of securities which matches one's desired risk level and then trade only for tax reasons or if cash is needed. Other funds restrict themselves to particular types of securities: high growth, high current income, energy-related, municipal bonds, etc. *Money market funds* which invest solely in money market instruments are particularly popular during periods of high interest rates.

TABLE 2-2 *Market Value Balance Sheet of Twenty-First Centurion Fund as of November 14, 1990*

Assets	(Millions)	Liabilities and Equity	(Millions)
Cash	$ 2.1	Current liabilities	$ 0.8
Government bonds	32.5		
Corporate bonds	15.3	Equity (4,380,000 shares outstanding)	109.5
Common stocks	60.4		
		Total	$110.3
Total	$110.3		

$$\text{Net asset value per share} = \frac{\$109,500,000}{4,380,000}$$

$$= \$25$$

The most recent development within this industry is the *family of funds*. In this case, an investment advisory organization forms a number of mutual funds, each having rather narrow objectives. For example, one fund might restrict its holdings to computer technology stocks, another to electric utility stocks, another to medical technology, and another to money market instruments. Once people buy into such a family of funds, they can move their investments between the funds as they choose for a minimal transaction cost. These families of funds provide investors and speculators with improved flexibility at relatively low cost.

Mutual funds can be purchased in one of two ways: (1) directly from a securities broker, in which case a *load* (commission) is paid, or (2) directly from the mutual fund itself, in which case *no load* is paid (though there is sometimes a small transaction cost). The management of a mutual fund will decide how it wishes to market its shares, through a broker network as a load fund or directly to the public as a no-load fund. Load charges are *front-end* loads, meaning that a charge is made when the shares are initially purchased but no charge is made when they are sold. Load fees of between 7% and 9% of the fund's net asset value are normal.

The example below illustrates how mutual fund quotations appear in the financial press.

Hypothetical Mutual Fund Price Quotations for the Close of Trading on November 14, 1990

Fund Name	Net Asset Value	Offering Price	NAV Change
Acorn Fund	30.96	N.L.	−0.10
Afuture Fund	11.07	N.L.	+0.01
Alliance Capital Group			
Alliance International	10.90	11.91	+0.06
Alliance Mortgage	9.30	9.81	+0.01
Alliance Technology	16.37	17.89	−0.18

The Acorn Fund is a no-load fund (denoted by *N.L.* in the offering price column) whose net asset value of $30.96 closed $0.10 lower than on the prior trading day. The Alliance Capital Group is illustrative of a family of funds which charges a load. In the case of Alliance International, one would pay $11.91 to receive one share having a net asset value of $10.90. The $1.01 difference represents the front-end load—in this case equal to 9.27% of net asset value.

Among the potential advantages of owning mutual fund shares are that (1) extensive diversification is available by pooling the resources of many small investors and (2) asset holdings are managed by skilled professional managers.

Derivative Securities

Derivative securities do not have a direct or immediate claim on a real asset. Instead they have a claim on another security, such as a common stock or a bond, providing a claim to a real asset. As their name implies, their market value is derived from the market value of the underlying security. Two broad types of derivative securities are traded in the markets: (1) option contracts and (2) futures contracts.

Options. An *option* is a marketable security which provides for the future exchange of cash and common shares *contingent upon the option owner's desire to do so*. In the simplest type of option, a buyer is contractually allowed to purchase a given number of common shares at the stipulated price at any time on or before a stated exercise date. An option is created whenever a seller *writes* (sells) an option contract to a buyer. Option sellers are of two types: corporations and individual traders.

Corporations sell options in the legal form of warrants, rights, and convertible bonds. *Warrants* allow the owner to purchase a given number of shares of common stock at a stipulated price on or before a given date. Warrant exercise dates can extend to five years or more. Warrants are usually issued along with a debt or preferred issue in order to "sweeten" the offering. *Rights* are similar to warrants but have exercise dates from two to ten weeks in the future. Rights are created when a firm wishes to sell more stock. Since current shareholders have a preemptive right to the first purchase of new shares, they are given stock rights, which they may either exercise or sell. Stock rights represent the technical procedure through which corporations comply with the preemptive right. Warrants and rights are traded on organized exchanges, such as the American Stock Exchange, and in the OTC market. Finally, a *convertible bond* is two financial instruments in one—a straight bond with fixed-coupon and face-value repayment terms plus an option which allows the holder to redeem the bond for a specified number of common shares.

While options are often created by corporations to aid in their financing arrangements, most options are created by individual traders. Prior to 1973 option sellers and buyers were brought together by brokers in the over-the-counter market. Since 1973 an active market in options has arisen on a variety of organized exchanges, with the Chicago Board Options Exchange (CBOE) being the first and, to date, largest. These options are of two types—*calls* and *puts*. A *call option* allows the buyer to purchase 100 shares of a given stock at a specified exercise price on or before a given exercise date. A *put option* allows the buyer to sell 100 shares at a specified exercise price on or before a given exercise date.

The data below illustrate how option quotations appear in the financial press.

Hypothetical Option Price Quotations for the Close of Trading on November 14, 1990

Option on	Striking Price	Calls			Puts		
		Dec	Mar	Jun	Dec	Mar	Jun
Rainbow Tractor	30	3⅜	4⅝	5⅜	r	¹¹⁄₁₆	1⅛
33¼	35	¹⁄₁₆	1	4	1¾	2¾	4
Noble	40	4¼	r	5⅞	⅜	1⅛	1¾
43½	45	⅞	1¾	r	r	3½	r

r = not traded

Option prices are shown on two common stocks: Rainbow Tractor and Noble. (Both of these stocks were shown earlier in the common stock price quotations.) By convention, the closing price of the underlying stock on which the option is being written is shown immediately below the stock name. For example, Rainbow common shares closed at $33.25 and Noble shares at $43.50.

Let's consider the Rainbow options more closely. Both puts and calls are available on this stock at two exercise (or striking) prices, $30 and $35. The calls had exercise dates of late December, March, and June. The puts had similar exercise dates. Thus, a total of six call options and six put options are shown for Rainbow. Examine the Rainbow call option exercisable at $30. The price to buy the December/30 is $3.375. Since options are written on 100-share lots, the total purchase price would be $337.50. By paying $337.50 today, the call buyer gains the right to purchase 100 shares of Rainbow common stock at a price of $30 per share any time before the end of December.

Notice that Rainbow shares are currently selling for $33.25. Since this call allows the owner to buy the shares at $30, the call has an *immediate value* of $3.25. The extra $0.125 is the premium paid on the option in the hope that Rainbow shares might increase in price before the end of December.

The profit or loss from owning a call option consists of two components. The first represents any price gains earned when the stock is selling at values above the exercise price. The second represents a loss associated with the original option cost. For example, assume the December/30 call on Rainbow was bought for $337.50. The buyer's profit or loss at various expiration date stock prices would be:

	Price of Rainbow Tractor Common Shares				
	$20	*$25*	*$30*	*$33.375*	*$40*
Value of 100 Shares	NA	NA	$3000.00	$3337.50	$4000.00
Less Exercise Price	NA	NA	(3000.00)	(3000.00)	(3000.00)
Price Gain	—	—	$ 0.00	$ 337.50	$1000.00
Less Original Option Cost	($337.50)	($337.50)	(337.50)	(337.50)	(337.50)
Net Profit or Loss	($337.50)	($337.50)	($337.50)	$ 0.00	$ 662.50

Don't Exercise   Exercise

At prices between $30 and $33⅜ the buyer incurs a net loss, but the loss is minimized if the buyer exercises the option.[1] Note that the option is not exercised at prices below the stated exercise price. (Why pay a $30 exercise price to purchase the security when it could be acquired at a lower price in the open market?) At stock prices above the exercise price, a profit arises because the security can be acquired at a price below its traded market value. Of course, these gains are (at least) partially offset by the initial option cost.

Exchange-listed options present an important opportunity to alter the risk and po-

---

[1]In practice, options are rarely exercised. Instead, option buyers and sellers *close out* their positions by making an offsetting trade of an identical option at some time before the exercise date. Thus, the writer of a Rainbow December/30 call would make an offsetting purchase of an identical call, while the buyer of such a call would make an identical offsetting sale. The threat of actual exercise is all that is needed to ensure that the option is priced fairly.

tential profits of a portfolio. For example, the purchase of calls will generally tend to increase portfolio risk while simultaneously increasing the size of potential gains. To illustrate, let's assume that the Rainbow December/30 calls had been purchased and later exercised when the stock was selling for $40. The resulting $662.50 profit represents a 196% profit on the initial $337.50 investment. This compares with a 20% profit if the investor had simply bought the stock for $33¼: ($40 − $33¼)/$33¼. Conversely, if the stock had sold for $30 instead of $40, the option loss would be 100%, while ownership of the stock would have resulted in only a 9.8% loss. The purchase of a call can thus entail considerable risk.

Options are intriguing and, in many ways, very complex securities. A more thorough discussion will be presented in Chapters 15 and 16. For now, it is sufficient to recognize that they are useful primarily to alter a portfolio's risk level.

Futures Contracts. A futures contract is a marketable agreement which provides for the *future* exchange of assets between a buyer and a seller. The buyer of a futures contract agrees to deliver a specified amount of cash (the *futures price*) at a specified future date (the *delivery date*). The seller of a futures contract agrees to deliver a specified amount of a given asset at the future date. No cash changes hands on the date at which a futures contract is traded.[2]

Futures contracts are traded on three major classes of assets:

1. *Financial securities*, such as T-bills, GNMA bonds, Treasury bonds, and common stocks.
2. *Foreign currencies*, such as British pounds, Japanese yen, and Swiss francs.
3. *Commodities*, such as corn, cotton, gold, silver, and crude oil.

All futures trading takes place on organized securities exchanges, such as the Chicago Board of Trade and the International Monetary Market. Only financial futures are discussed in this text since they are the futures most often used in security portfolio management.

To understand what a financial future is and how it might be used in portfolio management, consider the following data on various T-bill futures:

Hypothetical T-Bill Futures Price Quotations for the Close of Trading on November 14, 1990

	(Contract = $1,000,000 of 90-day T-bills)							
	Price					*Discount*		*Open*
Contract Maturity	*Open*	*High*	*Low*	*Settle*	*Change*	*Settle*	*Change*	*Interest*
Dec 1990	91.44	91.44	91.23	91.25	−0.19	8.75	+0.19	25,631
Mar 1991	90.98	90.98	90.73	90.76	−0.22	9.24	+0.22	15,518
Jun 1991	90.50	90.50	90.33	90.34	−0.23	9.66	+0.23	3,930

---

[2]A small good-faith deposit is required by both parties to the transaction to reduce the chance that they will eventually default on the contract. This good-faith deposit is often referred to as *margin*.

Information on three different T-bill contracts is shown. For the first contract, a buyer would be obligated to pay a specified amount of cash at the end of December 1990, and the seller would be obligated to deliver $1,000,000 par of 90-day T-bills at the end of December 1990. No cash would change hands at the time the contract is agreed to by both parties on November 14. Various price and discount information is shown next to the maturity month. Note that the closing (settle) price is $91.25, which is equal to $100 minus the $8.75 discount. The convention is to show these quotations *as if* the T-bills being traded were to have a 360-day life starting at the end of December. In point of fact, however, the futures contract *actually* is on a T-bill which will have a 90-day maturity in December. The percentage of par which the buyer will have to pay in December can be found using Equation 2.1 as follows:

$$P = F - Fd\left(\frac{t}{360}\right)$$

$$= \$100 - (\$100)(0.0875)\left(\frac{90}{360}\right)$$

$$= \$100 - \$2.1875$$

$$= \$97.8125$$

On $1,000,000 of par T-bills, $978,125 will have to be paid. In the same fashion, Equations 2.2 and 2.3 would be used to calculate the buyer's effective simple interest and compound interest yields.

The final column in the price quotation shows the *open interest*—the total number of contracts which exist. Open interest will increase when a buyer and a seller trade to create a new contract. Later, when the initial buyer sells *and* the initial seller buys, open interest will fall.

To understand how futures contracts might be used by investors or speculators, it is critical to recognize what is physically happening. To review, on November 14 the buyer and seller *contract* to a *future* trade. From then until the maturity date, neither party exchanges cash or securities.[3] At the end of December, the buyer delivers cash to the seller in return for the agreed security. This is indeed a contract for the future receipt of a security.

Financial futures can be used for either *hedging* or *speculative* purposes. Hedgers use financial futures to reduce future price uncertainty. For example, in November a bank's treasurer might know that the bank will be receiving large loan repayments in late December which management has decided to reinvest in T-bills. In November, the treasurer is uncertain what T-bill yields will be when December comes. However, by purchasing a December T-bill futures contract, the treasurer can know precisely what the yield will be. Conversely, if in November, the bank's management decides that it will reduce its T-bill holdings in late December and use the proceeds for other investments, the treasurer could either wait until December to sell the T-bills (at an

---

[3]Actually, daily cash might be required from both parties by the security exchange. A discussion of this daily mark to market is best left to Chapter 17.

uncertain price today) or sell T-bill futures right now (at a known price). Buying or selling a financial future can guarantee today the price that will eventually be paid or received in the future. Thus, price uncertainty is reduced.

Not everyone, of course, believes that futures prices are always correct. Speculators estimate the price of a security at the maturity of its futures contract and buy or sell the contract as they believe appropriate. For example, consider the December T-bill contract which was trading at an 8.75% discount. A speculator who believed that, come December, 90-day T-bills would actually trade at an 8.00% discount should speculate by buying the futures. If this supposition is correct, in December the speculator will pay $978,125 for a 90-day T-bill which is selling for $980,000.[4]

The eventual impacts of such speculative trades on futures prices must, of course, be considered. Many people believe that speculative trading is, at the least, destabilizing in that it causes prices to be more volatile than they would be otherwise. Some people even believe that speculators can use their trades to manipulate prices. These fears grew dramatically during the late 1980s as large financial institutions traded in massive quantities of options, futures, stocks, and T-bills at a single point in time. In fact, many people believe that such trades were the cause of the 508-point drop in the Dow Jones Industrial Average on October 19, 1987 — "Black Monday" — and the perceived increase in stock price volatility throughout the late 1980s. Whether this is true or not is still hotly debated. However, economic theory and empirical research suggest that the existence of futures (and options) in itself does not lead to increased price volatility. Instead, any increase in price volatility is more likely to be due to two other causes: (1) the trading mechanisms set up by the various security exchanges and (2) the inability of the exchanges to efficiently process the potential demand for trading. We will return to this issue a number of times in later chapters. For now, however, we will say that, as long as security exchanges design trading procedures which can process large quantities of trades, speculative trades of futures (and options) should reduce price volatility and make price levels more realistic.

But what is meant by "more realistic"? In the case of T-bill futures, speculators attempt to forecast the price at which T-bills will actually trade when the futures mature. As a result, the T-bill futures price is best thought of as a *consensus* forecast of what the interest rate on T-bills will eventually be. Using the data above, the consensus forecast of what 90-day T-bill discounts will be as of late December is 8.75%. Similarly, the consensus forecasts of 90-day bill discounts in late March and June are 9.24% and 9.66%. The market was predicting that short-term (90-day) interest rates would continually rise over the next half-year.

Although futures contracts allow for eventual delivery of cash and some asset, actual delivery rarely occurs. The motivation behind futures trading is more to reduce the risks of future price changes than to ensure physical delivery. The buyer of a futures contract will usually sell the contract at some time before the delivery date, and the initial seller will buy back the contract before delivery. Both parties will then use

---

[4]$980,000 = \$1,000,000 - \$1,000,000 \, (0.08) \left(\dfrac{90}{360} \right).$

the profits (or losses) on their futures trading to offset unfavorable (or favorable) changes in the price of the physical asset. A more complete review of futures trading is presented in Chapter 17.

SUMMARY

This chapter has provided an introductory overview of the types of marketable securities available for investment or speculation. Most of these are discussed in more depth in later chapters.

Securities are usually classified as *money market* or *capital market* instruments. Money market securities are short-term, highly marketable, low-risk debt issues which are bought and sold as temporary cash substitutes. The money market is principally a wholesale market in which huge sums of money are traded for very short periods of time. Capital market securities have maturities greater than one year and vary considerably in risk and marketability. Capital market securities are rarely used as short-term cash substitutes. Instead, they are bought by investors for their long-run expected returns or by speculators searching for mispriced securities.

REVIEW PROBLEM #1

You are given the following price quotations on a T-bill for the close of trading on May 31 and June 30. (Note that as of June 30, this bill has a 90-day remaining life.)

T-Bill Information

	On May 31		On June 30	
Maturity	*Bid*	*Asked*	*Bid*	*Asked*
Sept 28	9.10%	9.00%	9.30%	9.25%

You are also given price quotations for the same dates on a 90-day T-bill futures contract which has a delivery date of June 30.

T-Bill Futures Contract Information

	Discount Settle Prices on	
Delivery Date	*May 31*	*June 30*
June 30	9.40%	9.25%

a. On May 31, the T-bill had a 120-day remaining life. On that day, what percentage of par value would you pay to purchase the T-bill?

b. On that day what were the effective simple interest and compound interest yields?

c. Assume you purchased the bill on May 31 and later sold it on June 30. What rate of return did you earn during this one-month period? If you were to express this return on an annualized basis, what would the return be?

d. Is there any reason why, on *June 30*, the futures contract should trade at a discount identical to the T-bill's asked discount?

e. On May 31, why would the future's discount be different from the T-bill's discount on the same date?

f. On May 31, at what price is the futures contract selling? (Use $1 million par for each contract.)

Solution

a. $P = F - Fd \dfrac{t}{360}$

$$= 100 - (100)(0.09)\left(\frac{120}{360}\right)$$

$$= 97.00$$

b. Simple interest:

$$\frac{(365)(0.09)}{360 - (0.09)(120)} = 0.09407, \text{ or } \left(\frac{100 - 97}{97}\right)\left(\frac{365}{120}\right) = 0.09407$$

Compound interest:

$$\left(\frac{100}{97}\right)^{365/120} - 1 = 0.09707$$

c. Purchase price = 97.00 from part a above.

$$\text{Selling price} \quad = 100 - 100(0.093)\left(\frac{90}{360}\right)$$

$$= 97.675$$

$$\text{One-month percentage gain} = \frac{97.675}{97.00} - 1.0$$

$$= 0.00696$$

$$= 0.696\%$$

To annualize, the simple interest should be used if this is an isolated trade.

$$(0.696\%)\left(\frac{365}{30}\right) = 8.468\%$$

If this is only one of many ongoing trades, compound interest is more reflective of the annualized return.

$$(1.00696)^{365/30} - 1.0 = 8.805\%$$

d. June 30 is the delivery date of the futures contract—the date on which the buyer has a claim to an actual 90-day bill. Thus, the future and the actual bill should trade at identical prices. If this were not the case, an investor could trade in each market and make a riskless arbitrage profit.

e. On May 31 the future has 30 days remaining before its buyer will have a claim to an actual 90-day T-bill. Thus, the futures price on May 31 is the market's consensus forecast of what a 90-day bill will trade for on June 30. This forecast of 9.40% turns out to be wrong. Nonetheless, it is the forecast as of May 31.

f. $\$1,000,000 - \$1,000,000\,(0.094)\left(\dfrac{90}{360}\right) = \$976,500.00$

REVIEW PROBLEM #2

Consider the following option quotations on General Electric common stock.

Option	Strike Price	Calls Dec	Calls Mar	Calls June	Puts Dec	Puts Mar	Puts June
General Electric	55	8¾	9	9¼	1/16	5/16	½
63¼	60	3½	4⅝	5⅝	5/16	1	1½
63¼	65	9/16	1¾	2¾	2¾	3½	4

a. How many different contracts are there here that you could trade?

b. Look at the June call exercisable at $55. Assume that you buy the call. Calculate the value of the call and your net profit or loss at the expiration date in late June for each of the following stock prices: $50, $55, $60, $65, $70, $75.

c. Again, assume that you buy the June/55 call. At what stock price would you not exercise your call at the expiration day? At what prices would you exercise? Why would you exercise even if this results in a net loss?

d. What is the expiration date break-even stock price of the June/55 call?

e. What is the immediate value of the June/55 call? Why is the option selling for a higher price?

f. Repeat parts b through e for the June/65 put.

g. Why do you suspect that the longer maturity options sell at higher prices?

h. Assume that you have $10,000 to purchase either shares of G.E. or the June/55 calls. Illustrate the greater leverage inherent in owning the calls.

i. Assume that you buy two puts and three calls, both exercisable in March at $60. In late March the price of G.E. stock is $45. What would you do with your options and what would be your net dollar profit or loss?

j. Assume that you sell one June/55 call to a buyer of the call. What will be your dollar profit or loss at the expiration date for each of the following stock prices: $50, $55, $60, $65, $70, $75? What does this show? (Compare with part b.)

Solution

a. There are a total of 18 different option contracts.

b.

Stock Price	$50	$55	$60	$65	$70	$75
Value of Call	$0.00	$0.00	$5.00	$10.00	$15.00	$20.00
Less Purchase Price	−9.25	−9.25	−9.25	−9.25	−9.25	−9.25
Net Profit	−$9.25	−$9.25	−$4.25	$0.75	$5.75	$10.75

c. $55. Don't exercise if the stock can be bought in the security market at a price lower than the exercise price. The reason is very simple; if the stock is selling in the markets at a price lower than the exercise price, why pay the exercise price to purchase it?

    Exercise should take place at the exercise date if the stock is selling for a price larger than the exercise price.

    This should be done even if the *net* profit turns out to be a loss. Again, the reason is very simple. If you do not exercise when the stock is worth more than the exercise price, your net loss is equal to the initial amount you originally paid for the option. By exercising, the loss is reduced.

d. Break-even stock price at expiration date equals the $55 exercise price plus the $9.25 original option price, or $64.25.

e. The immediate value is equal to the current stock price ($63.25) minus the exercise price ($55), or $8.25. This call option is selling at a price $1.00 higher because of the potential that the stock will sell for more than its current $63.25 on the expiration date.

f. *Part b repeated*

Stock Price	$50	$55	$60	$65	$70	$75
Value of Put	$15.00	$10.00	$5.00	$0.00	$0.00	$0.00
Less Purchase Price	−4.00	−4.00	−4.00	−4.00	−4.00	−4.00
Net Profit	$11.00	$6.00	$1.00	−$4.00	−$4.00	−$4.00

Part c repeated
Don't exercise if stock price is *above* $65.
Do exercise if stock price is *below* $65.

Part d repeated
Break-even price = $65 − $4 = $61.

Part e repeated

Exercise price	$65.00
Less stock price	−63.25
Immediate value	$ 1.75

g. Given an exercise price, the longer the maturity the larger the option's price. This is because there is a greater chance that stock prices will be higher (or lower for a put) than current stock prices.

h. *Return on the Purchase of $10,000 of Stock (158.1 shares at $63.25)*

Assumed Stock Price at Expiration:	$50	$55	$60	$65	$70	$75
Ending Value (in thousands):	$7.905	$8.696	$9.486	$10.276	$11.067	$11.858
Less Initial Value	10.000	10.000	10.000	10.000	10.000	10.000
Profit or Loss	−$2.095	−$1.304	−$0.514	$0.276	$1.067	$1.858
Rate of Return	−20.9%	−13.0%	−5.1%	2.8%	10.7%	18.6%

Return on the Purchase of $10,000 of Calls (1,081.1 calls at $9.25)

	$50	$55	$60	$65	$70	$75
Ending Value (in thousands):	$0.000	$0.000	$5.406	$10.811	$16.216	$21.622
Less Initial Value	10.000	10.000	10.000	10.000	10.000	10.000
Profit or Loss	−$10.000	−$10.000	−$4.594	$0.811	$6.216	$11.622
Rate of Return	−100.00%	−100.00%	−45.9%	8.1%	62.2%	116.2%

Note that as the stock price increases or decreases, the rate of return earned on the call ownership is more volatile than the stock returns. It is this increased volatility inherent in the call options that is referred to as their greater leverage. A similar result occurs with the ownership of puts except that stock price declines result in positive put profits.

i.

	Initial Purchase Cost	Late March Transaction	Late March Total Value
Buy 2 Puts	$ 2.000	Exercise	2(60 − 45) = $30
Buy 3 Calls	$13.875	Don't Exercise	− 0.0
	$15.875		$30.00

Net Profit = $30.00 − $15.875 = $14.125

j. Although not stressed in the text, for every buyer of an option there must be someone willing to sell (often called "write") the option. A gain (or loss) to the buyer will be a loss (or gain) to the seller.

Stock Price:	$50	$55	$60	$65	$70	$75
Option Buyer Exercises:						
You Sell	—	—	$55	$55	$55	$55
You Buy	—	—	−60	−65	−70	−75
	—	—	−$5	−$10	−$15	−$20
Original Option Value Rec'd	$9.25	$9.25	$9.25	$9.25	$9.25	$9.25
Net Profit	$9.25	$9.25	$4.25	−$0.75	−$5.75	−$10.75

Notice that the call *buyer's* profit or loss (from part b) is the call *seller's* loss or profit.

QUESTIONS AND PROBLEMS

1. Sample quotes on T-bills are shown below for two dates — January 1 and January 15. Assume the quotes represent *end-of-day* transactions and that trades could actually be made at these prices.

As of January 1

| | Discount | | |
Maturity	Bid	Asked	Yield
Jan. 15	9.00	8.70	8.851
Feb. 15	9.10	8.75	8.970
March 15	9.12	8.79	—

As of January 15

| | Discount | | |
Maturity	Bid	Asked	Yield
Feb. 15	8.80	8.70	—
March 15	8.85	8.75	9.000

a. As of January 1, at what price (percentage of par value) could you buy the January 15 bill (assume a full 14-day period)? At what price could you sell?

b. As of January 1, at what price could you buy the March 15 bill? Sell?

c. Find the missing yield values.

d. What would your dollar profit be if you buy $10 million face value of the March bill on January 1 and sell it on January 15?

e. Assume that on January 1 you buy $100 million of February bills at the 8.75% discount. This amount considerably exceeds the equity capital of your firm, and you must finance the inventory in some way. Explain how financing might be arranged and why the financing cost might be less than the 8.75% discount.

2. Two competitive bidders submit bids on $1 million of 91-day bills being offered by the U.S. Treasury. The bids differ by 1 basis point. What is the total dollar difference between each bid?

3. You are given the following T-bill quotations as of the close of trading on June 1 and June 10:

| | June 1 | | June 10 | |
T-Bill Maturity	Bid	Asked	Bid	Asked
June 30	9.00%	8.80%	9.50%	9.45%

a. At the end of June 1, how much would you have to pay to purchase $1 million in par value of the bills?

b. Note that only discount quotations are shown. What would be the price quotations for June 1 as they would appear in the financial press?

c. If you purchased some bills on June 1, what would be the simple interest and compound interest annualized yields? Why do they differ?

d. Assume you purchased the T-bill on June 1 and later sold it on June 10. What was your nine-day profit (or loss) in percentage terms? What was the cause of this profit (or loss)? What is the annualized equivalent yield?

4. The U.S. Treasury offers $2 billion in 91-day new T-bills and receives the following bids:

Discount	Competitive Bid
8.50%	$200 million
8.55	400 million
8.56	600 million
8.58	1,000 million
8.59	1,500 million
8.60	1,000 million

Discount	Noncompetitive Bid
NA	$500 million

What yield will the noncompetitive bidders receive?

5. Why might different Treasury notes or bonds sell at different yields to maturity even though their maturities are basically the same?

6. An importer must finance various planned purchases of goods. Commercial paper rates are now 7.53%, and bankers' acceptance rates are 7.68%. Why might the importer utilize the bankers' acceptance instead of commercial paper?

7. Municipalities sell a number of securities which often qualify to be called money market instruments. Identify some of these.

8. Price quotations on two mutual funds are shown below:

Fund	NAV	Offering Price
Fidelity Magellan	33.37	34.40
Price New Horizons	12.88	N.L.

a. If you invest $1,000 in each fund, how many shares would you receive of each?
b. What is the percentage front-end load on each? Explain what this is.
c. Interpret what NAV means.

9. You are given the following information on First Street Growth Fund, a mutual fund which invests mainly in high-growth stocks.

Total market value of assets	=	$500 million
Accounts payable	=	10 million
Number of shares outstanding	=	7 million

a. What is the net asset value per share?
b. If this is a no-load fund, how many shares could be acquired with $10,000?

10. You are given the following price information on the put and call options on AEP stock:

Option	Striking Price	Calls			Puts		
		Nov	Feb	May	Nov	Feb	May
AEP	15	2	2½	3	½	1	1¼
16	20	½	¾	1	3	3½	3¾

a. How many different option contracts are shown here?
b. At what price did AEP common stock close?
c. Notice that the calls with a striking price of $15 (which may be exercised any time before the end of November) are selling for $2. Can you explain why this is so?
d. Examine the November puts. Do the relative prices make sense?

e. Assume that you purchase a May put exercisable at $20 and sell the similar call. What are you hoping will happen to the price of the AEP stock?

f. Continue with the assumption of part e above. If, when the end of May arrives, AEP stock is selling for $15, what will you do with these puts and calls and what will be your net profit (or loss)?

11. You are considering the purchase of one of the following two traded options on XYZ Corporation. It is now January 1 and XYZ common is selling at $43.

Option	Exercise Price	Exercise Date	Option Price
Call on XYZ Corp.	$40	March 30	$5
Put on XYZ Corp.	$40	March 30	$2

a. If you believe quite strongly that the common stock of XYZ will be selling at $50 by March 30, what might you do?

b. Repeat part a, assuming that the March 30 price of XYZ common will be $30.

c. Complete the following table:

XYZ Common Stock Price at Expiration	Net Profit (Loss) from Buying a Call
$35	
$38	
$40	
$43	
$45	
$48	

d. Complete the following table:

XYZ Common Stock Price at Expiration	Net Profit (Loss) from Buying a Put
$35	
$38	
$40	
$43	
$45	
$48	

12. Consider the following price quotations on a 90-day T-bill futures contract:

Contract Maturity	Settle		Open Interest
	Price	Discount	
June 1986	90.34	9.66	3,930

a. Discuss how one might use this contract to hedge. Develop an example for both a purchase and a sale.

b. If you believe that interest rates on 90-day T-bills will be 10% at the end of June, what should you do?

c. Assume that you *now* own $10 million in par value of T-bills which are scheduled to mature on September 28 (90 days after June 30). If you also *sell* the future shown here, what *net* T-bill holding do you have?

d. If you purchase this contract, what price are you obligated to pay at the end of June?

e. If you purchase one unit of this contract (for the first time), what happens to the open interest?

13. Brenda Avey is the investment officer for a large life insurance company which has a marginal tax bracket of 45%. Which of the following two securities provides her with a greater promised yield to maturity?
    a. Preferred stock selling at par with a promised yield of 9.2%.
    b. Corporate bonds selling at par with a promised yield of 11.0%.

14. Two other investors are trying to decide between the preferred stock and the corporate bonds discussed in question 13. Eric Simpson is the investment officer for the local Catholic diocese, while Irene Biller is an executive with IBM, which pays taxes at a marginal rate of 60%. Which security would be expected to provide the greater returns for each organization?

15. Assume that a municipal bond and a corporate bond have identical marketability, default risk, and maturity. The municipal is selling at a 5% yield to maturity; the corporate is selling for an 8% yield to maturity.
    a. Should a person in a 30% tax bracket buy the municipal or the corporate security? (Assume the full 8% yield on the corporate is taxable at 30%.)
    b. What is the break-even tax bracket at which an investor is indifferent between the two issues?

D A T A   A N A L Y S I S   P R O B L E M

Objectives:

- To introduce the yearly returns available on various U.S. security types.
- To understand how average yearly returns and risks on these security types have differed over long time periods.

1. Use a microcomputer spreadsheet program to read the data set called "YRLYINDX.WK1". Move around the data set to see the type of data provided and its format. The data are yearly returns on various types of U.S. securities and include the following:

Security Type	Period Covered
Consumer Price Index (CPI)	1926–1988
Money Market Instruments:	
13-week Treasury bills	1926–1988
Commercial paper	1947–1988
Certificates of deposit	1947–1988
30-day bankers' acceptances	1947–1988
Fixed Income Instruments:	
Long-term Treasury bonds	1926–1988
Long-term corporate bonds	1926–1988
Preferred stock	1947–1988
Common Stock Indexes:	
Standard & Poor's 500	1926–1988
Wilshire 5000	1971–1988
Dow Jones Industrial Average	1926–1988
New York Stock Exchange Composite	1947–1988
American Stock Exchange Composite	1963–1988
Over-the-Counter Composite	1947–1988
Small Company Index	1926–1988

Many of these were discussed in this chapter; the rest are discussed in Chapter 4. We will use the Standard & Poor's 500 (S&P 500) and Small Company indexes in this problem. The S&P 500 is a stock index of 500 very large U.S. corporations. The Small Company Index is a stock index of very small U.S. corporations whose stock is traded on listed security exchanges.

2. Calculate the average annual return and standard deviation of annual returns for Treasury bills, long-term government and corporate bonds, the S&P 500, and the Small Company Index. Note: Make no adjustments for CPI; "real returns" will be examined in a later chapter.

3. Plot the average returns obtained above on a vertical axis and the standard deviations on a horizontal axis. This depicts the risk/return trade-off on a variety of different asset classes for U.S. investors having a one-year investment horizon.

4. Calculate the average and standard deviation of yearly returns for 30-day bankers' acceptances and Treasury bills over the period 1947 through 1988. Explain the differences.

APPENDIX 2A: SOURCES OF BASIC FINANCIAL INFORMATION

This appendix lists and briefly describes the major sources of security information which the *nonprofessional investor or speculator* might find useful. In addition to the listings shown, most brokerage houses distribute market letters and recommendations to customers which can be quite informative. The listing does not include sources of information which professionals would use (such as computerized data bases and academic journals). The outline first lists major newspapers, journals, and periodicals. After this, guides to industry and company data are listed. Finally, sources for particular types of securities are shown.

I. The General Financial Press

    A. Newspapers

        1. *The Wall Street Journal:* daily; review articles on current business topics and extensive market price data.

        2. *The New York Times:* daily; review articles on current business topics and extensive market price data.

        3. *Commercial and Financial Chronicle:* weekly; contains daily prices on New York, American, and Toronto exchanges plus weekly prices on regional exchanges and the OTC market.

        4. *Barron's:* weekly; articles on investment topics and extensive weekly price data.

        5. *M/G Financial Weekly:* weekly; prices, charts, and basic financial information on most actively traded securities.

        6. *Wall Street Transcript:* twice weekly; reproduces selected brokerage house reports and interviews with security analysts on a specific industry.

    B. Journals and Periodicals

        1. *Business Week:* weekly; articles on a variety of general business topics.

        2. *Financial World:* biweekly; articles on investment topics.

        3. *Forbes:* biweekly; articles on investment topics and opinions.

        4. *Finance:* monthly; review articles on current events in the financial market.

        5. *Financial Executive:* monthly; news of the Financial Executives Institute.

        6. *Fortune:* biweekly; articles on general business trends for corporate managers.

        7. *Institutional Investor:* monthly; articles of interest to managers of large institutional portfolios.

8. *Financial Analysts Journal:* bimonthly; articles of interest to practicing financial analysts.

9. *OTC Review:* monthly; analysis and discussion of stocks traded in the over-the-counter market, plus financial data.

10. *Journal of Portfolio Management:* quarterly; articles of interest to the professional portfolio manager.

II. Industry and Company Information

A. Industry Data: General Statistics

1. *Statistical Abstract of the U.S.:* industrial, social, political, and economic statistics.

2. *Business Statistics:* historical data for the U.S., updated monthly by the *Survey of Current Business.*

3. *Standard & Poor's Statistical Service:* statistics in nine major industrial groups, plus stock price averages.

4. *Basebook:* historical data by Standard Industrial Classification (SIC) number.

5. *Predicasts:* forecasts by SIC number.

6. *U.S. Industrial Outlook:* brief analysis of 200 industries.

7. *F & S Index to Corporations and Industries:* list of articles dealing with industries classified by SIC code.

8. *American Statistics Index:* guide to statistical publications of the U.S. government.

9. U.S. government publications:
   - *Census of Mineral Industries*
   - *Census of Selected Services*
   - *Census of Construction Industry*
   - *Census of Transportation*
   - *Census of Retail Trade*
   - *Census of Wholesale Trade*
   - *Annual Survey of Manufacturers*

B. Industry Data: General Information

1. *Dun & Bradstreet Key Business Ratios:* financial ratios for 125 industries.

2. *Robert Morris Associates Annual Studies:* ratios for a variety of industries.

3. *Standard & Poor's:* reports including the *Investment Advisory Service, Industry Surveys,* and *Outlook*, which provide summaries of financial data and current events.

4. *Value Line Investment Surveys:* summaries of financial data and current events.

5. *Moody's Manuals:* basic industry information and financial data.

C. Company Data

1. Corporate reports: quarterly and annual reports to shareholders by corporate management.

2. Security Prospectus: registration statement filed with the Securities and Exchange Commission (SEC) on any new security offering.

3. Required SEC Reports: monthly statement 8-K, semiannual statement 9-K, and annual statement 10-K provide information which is often more current or thorough than that reported to shareholders.

4. *Standard & Poor's Corporation Record:* historical and financial data.

5. *Standard & Poor's Analysts Handbook:* basic financial information.

6. *Standard & Poor's Stock Reports:* short reviews of financial data and forecasts.

7. *Standard & Poor's Stock Guide:* compact summary of financial information on actively traded stocks.

8. *Moody's Manuals:* historical and financial data; separate volumes deal with industrial, OTC industrial, utility, transportation, and bank-finance stocks.

9. *Value Line Investment Service:* basic financial data and projections on over 1,700 actively traded stocks.

III. Information by Type of Security

A. Money Market Instruments and Bonds

1. *Money Manager:* weekly events occurring in the short- and long-term bond markets.

2. *Weekly Bond Buyer:* weekly events occurring in the short- and long-term bond markets.

3. *Bankers Trust Credit and Capital Markets:* survey of current trends in interest rates.

4. *Moody's Bond Survey:* weekly review of events and financial data.

5. *Value Line Options and Convertibles:* financial data on convertible bonds.

6. *Moody's Bond Record:* financial data on major corporate bonds outstanding.

7. *Moody's Municipal and Government Manual:* data on U.S. government and municipal obligations.

8. *Standard & Poor's Bond Guide:* compact review of major financial data.

9. *Standard & Poor's Convertible Bond Reports:* basic information about actively traded convertible bonds.

B. Stocks: see information listed in parts IA, IB, and IIC.

C. Other Instruments

1. *Value Line Options and Convertibles:* basic information about options.

2. *Vickers Guide to Investment Company Portfolios:* general information on investment companies.

3. *Weisenberger Investment Companies:* annual background, management policy, and financial records for all U.S. and Canadian investment companies.

4. *Investment Dealers Digest Mutual Fund Directory:* semiannual statistics for mutual funds.

5. *Johnson Investment Company Charts:* data on market and various types of funds.

6. Investment Company Institute's *Mutual Fund Fact Book:* basic statistics for the industry.

7. *Commodity Yearbook:* production, prices, etc., for 100 commodities.

8. *Guide to World Commodity Markets:* information and statistics on commodity markets.

9. *Mutual Fund Values:* detailed information on mutual funds.

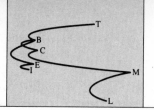
3 Overview of the Security Markets

In this chapter we review the institutional procedures used to trade stocks and bonds in the United States. Procedures unique to options, futures, and investment companies are discussed in later chapters devoted to each. This chapter is largely descriptive in nature, addressing trading procedures as they actually exist, as opposed to asking why they exist (the topic of Chapter 5).

Security transactions occur in either the *primary market* or the *secondary market*. In a primary market transaction, a buyer gives the original issuer of the security cash in exchange for ownership of the security. For example, weekly T-bill offerings by the U.S. Treasury, municipal bond sales by the state of Ohio, and common stock sales by AT&T are all primary market transactions. The key to a primary market transaction is that the original security issuer receives cash, and the public then holds a security which previously didn't exist. Subsequent to the primary offering, the security is traded between members of the public in what are referred to as secondary markets. These secondary markets include both formal exchange markets (such as the New York Stock Exchange and American Stock Exchange) and less formal markets (referred to as over-the-counter [OTC] transactions). The issuer of a security is unaffected by secondary market transactions.[1] The sale of a T-bill by a dealer in bills to a commercial bank, the sale of a municipal bond by a New York bond house to a California savings and loan association, and the sale of AT&T common stock by Ms. A to Mr. B are all secondary market transactions.

THE PRIMARY MARKET

The Investment Banker

As noted above, a primary market transaction represents the initial sale of a security by an issuer to the public. The issuer receives cash (to invest in productive assets or

---

[1]Secondary market transactions can have an indirect effect upon the original security issuer, however, because of information provided by secondary market prices. For example, the price of IBM common stock and debt can be used by IBM management to evaluate their past performance and determine the financing costs necessary to float new security offerings.

realign its capital structure), and the public receives securities (for personal investment or speculative purposes).

Figure 3-1 illustrates various decisions which a security issuer faces. First, the legal character of the issue must be determined. Second, issuers must decide whether they are willing to assume the risks of price declines during the distribution period or would rather shift these risks to some other party. Third, a formal marketing strategy must be developed. At any stage of the security offering, the issuer may decide to rely upon internal expertise or call upon the services of an investment banking firm. Investment bankers are organizations which specialize in the creation and placement of securities in the primary market and provide three basic services: (1) advice, (2) underwriting, and (3) distribution.

FIGURE 3-1 *Creation and Sale of a New Issue*

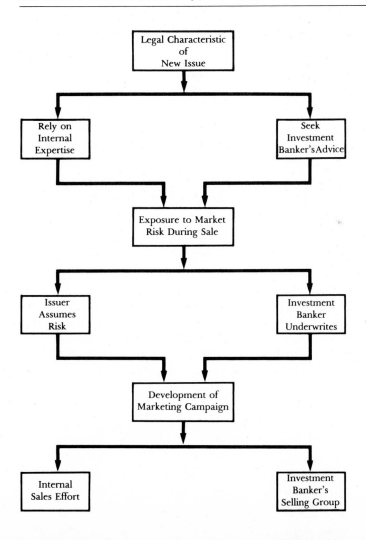

Advice. Many security issuers do not have the internal expertise or knowledge of market conditions necessary to put together a security issue. In such cases investment bankers can provide advice about the following:

1. *Type of security offering.* Given the issuer's financial structure and security market conditions, the investment banker can advise the issuer on what type of security — equity or debt — should be sold.
2. *Timing of the offering.* Given current and expected market conditions, the investment banker can suggest whether the offering should be sold immediately or delayed in hopes of a better price.
3. *Legal characteristics of the issue.* For example, if a debt issue is contemplated, the investment banker can provide advice about coupon rate, maturity, protective covenants, convertibility, call prices, etc.
4. *Price of the security.* Given suggestions about each of the above, the investment banker will suggest a price at which the security can be sold.

Issuers may elect to use only the advice services of investment bankers without using their underwriting and distribution services. In such cases a consulting fee is paid. Many issuers, of course, have the internal financial expertise to make all necessary decisions. For example, the U.S. Treasury and large corporations rarely use investment bankers for their advice services.

Underwriting. Once the type of security, date of issue, and security price have been decided upon, the issuer can proceed to sell to the public. However, if the price at which the markets would be willing to absorb the issue is set too high or if the market as a whole declines, the issuer might not receive the total dollar amount desired. For example, assume that Georgia Pacific wishes to raise $100 million in a common stock offering to support new-product expansion. Based upon a secondary market price of $27 for their existing common stock and discussions with their investment banker, management decides to sell 4 million shares at $25 per share. (The $2 price difference is used as an inducement to attract buyers and encourage fast sale.) Unfortunately, soon after the securities are offered, the price at which they are able to sell the shares actually falls to $22. This could occur either because management misjudged the price inducement necessary to attract large numbers of buyers or because all stock prices fell as a result of bad economic news. Regardless of the reason, Georgia Pacific would receive only $88 million of the desired $100 million in cash.

Investment bankers stand ready to absorb any part of the price risk that an issuer would rather not accept. This is referred to as *underwriting* an issue. Three basic degrees of underwriting are used:

1. In a *firm commitment* the banker purchases the full amount of the issue from the seller at an agreed-upon price. All market risk is shifted from the issuer to the investment banker. The banker will reoffer the securities to the general public at a higher price than that paid to the issuer. In the Georgia Pacific example, the issue might be underwritten at $24 (for 4.17 million shares to assure $100 million in cash) and reoffered at $25 to the general public. The $1 difference between what

the issuer receives and what the public pays is known as the *underwriter's spread* and represents the underwriter's compensation for assuming market risks, searching for buyers, and providing financial advice.

2. In a *stand-by agreement* the underwriter agrees to help sell the new issue for some stated time interval (usually 30 days) but will not "position the security at risk." Once the interval is passed, the underwriter purchases any unsold securities at a predetermined price. Stand-by agreements are commonly used for stock sales which are being distributed through a rights offering.

3. In a *best-efforts basis* sale, the investment banker has no obligation to purchase any of the security issue. The banker acts solely as a broker and returns any unsold securities to the issuer. A best-efforts sale is used for two types of issuers. In the first case the issuing firm demands a best-efforts sale because it is confident that the securities will be fully sold (because of the firm's size, the risk, and the market's interest in the new securities). In the second case the investment banker requires a best-efforts sale because the issuing firm is small, unestablished, and risky.

When a firm commitment is used, a *purchase group* of many investment bankers will be formed. The *lead underwriter* (or managing underwriter) conducts all negotiations with the issuer, oversees registration with the Securities and Exchange Commission (SEC), maintains accounting records, and selects other members of the purchase group. However, all members of the purchase group purchase (or "position") a part of the issue. By positioning a portion of many new issues, as opposed to positioning all of one issue, the underwriter obtains greater diversification and lower risk.

Distribution. Some issuers have the ability to market new issues directly to the general public and don't need the distribution services of an investment banker. The largest direct issuer is, of course, the U.S. government, which uses periodic competitive bid sales for Treasury and agency obligations. In addition, common stock sales using rights offerings to existing shareholders have been used increasingly by large corporations that prefer to bypass investment bankers.[2] However, most issuers don't have the extensive contacts with potential buyers that investment bankers are able to develop.

In fact, the buying syndicate itself may not have any direct contact with potential buyers. Over the years security firms have found it profitable to specialize. Some firms have concentrated on providing financial advice and underwriting services to issuers, while others have concentrated on the development of large networks of retail offices. As a result, members of the purchase group often do not have direct contact with potential buyers. To develop an effective distribution team, a *selling group*

---

[2]One interesting technique of direct placement was used by large utilities in the midwestern United States during the 1920s. Whenever these firms wanted to sell new stock or debt issues, they would have their meter readers sell them door-to-door as they went on their rounds. This novel approach disappeared when the firms were forced into bankruptcy and reorganization during the 1930s.

is usually created which consists of members of both the purchase group and selected retail brokerage houses. The final organization of a typical underwriting is shown in Figure 3-2.

The operation of the selling group is controlled by the *selling group agreement*, which (1) defines the duration of the agreement (usually 30 days), (2) specifies the split of the underwriter spread among the manager, the purchase group, and the selling group, (3) indicates accounting procedures, and (4) states that no member will sell below the offering price.

Once the underwriting syndicate has been formed, market conditions seem favorable, and all legal requirements have been met, the securities can be actively sold to the public. Prior to that time, potential buyers will have investigated the issue and perhaps even expressed interest to members of the selling group. However, actual purchase orders can't be taken until a formal "opening of the books." Some issues will have an active demand and be sold out within hours, or may even be oversubscribed. Other issues require a longer time to be distributed. During this time interval the managing underwriter is allowed to *stabilize the market* by placing orders to buy the security at a fixed price. This is the only form of security price manipulation legally allowed in the United States. Underwriters claim that market stabilization is necessary to ensure an orderly sale and offset temporary price declines. They claim that the use of price stabilizing reduces their risk exposure and thus reduces the costs to issuing firms.

FIGURE 3-2 *Purchase and Selling Groups*

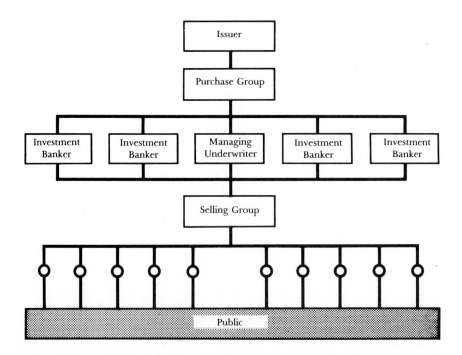

Negotiated Versus Competitive Selection. When the selling efforts of an investment banker are used, the issuer must decide whether the banker is to be selected on a *competitive* or a *negotiated* basis. In a competitive underwriting all details of the security offering (type, timing, and legal characteristics) except price are specified, and the investment banker offering the best bid price is selected. A specific time and place are set at which competitive bids are opened. Competitive bid offerings are common in municipal bond sales as well as in debt and equity sales by regulated companies. Competitive bid offerings provide the issuer the potential advantage of receiving the highest possible price because of active competition for the issue. They have the disadvantage of inflexibility because the investment banker is obligated to a firm price and is exposed to considerable market risk.

In a negotiated underwriting the issuer selects the underwriter it believes is best able to provide the unique advice, underwriting, and selling efforts necessary to the success of the particular offering. The investment banker's compensation is negotiated, as opposed to being set in a formal competitive bid. Statistical tests conducted to date suggest that competitive offerings do provide some cost advantages over negotiated underwritings. However, the cost of issuing a security is difficult to measure, and these results might well be due to inadequate cost data.[3]

Private Versus Public Placement

Private Placement. A *privately placed security* is one which is sold to fewer than 25 buyers and, as a result, needn't be registered with the SEC. While some stock issues are privately placed (often with venture capital firms), bond issues are the more predominant. As shown in Table 3-1, more than 25% of all bond issues have been privately placed.

The major advantages of private placements stem from the fact that such issues aren't registered with the SEC. As a result, a new issue can be placed quickly and without incurring the large costs of preparing a registration statement. Investment bankers might be used to find buyers, for which they are paid a finder's fee of ¼% to 1½% of the issue. But their underwriting services aren't required, thus eliminating any compensation for these services. In addition, loan covenants on privately placed bonds can be less restrictive than if the issue were sold to the general public. The issuer and buyer can "tailor fit" any required covenants, whereas a public sale might require a large number of additional covenants to attract a sufficient number of buyers.

The major disadvantage of a private placement is its lack of marketability. Because the issue is not registered with the SEC, buyers are limited in their ability to subsequently sell the issue, resulting in greater required yields.

---

[3]For example, negotiated fees will include reimbursement to the investment banker for the consulting services usually provided in such offerings. Competitive fees will not include consulting costs even though the issuer has to incur such expenses, either as internal management time or as fees paid to advising bankers. This imprecise cost measurement will make competitive fees appear lower.

TABLE 3-1 *Public and Private Placements of Corporate Issues*

Year	Total Value of Securities Issued (Millions)		Percentage of Value Privately Placed	
	Stocks	*Bonds*	*Stocks*	*Bonds*
1970	$ 7,927	$ 29,023	3.4%	16.0%
1973	10,985	20,697	8.9	37.7
1975	10,873	41,664	5.6	24.4
1977	11,961	39,872	14.1	45.6
1979	12,235	40,851	13.8	35.2
1980	22,629	56,268	3.2	20.6
1981	27,183	45,957	2.0	15.2
1982	28,093	54,836	1.6	17.6
1983	51,579	47,369	NA	NA
1984	22,628	73,357	NA	NA
1985	35,515	203,500	NA	NA
1986	68,433	355,293	9.6	22.7
1987	66,508	324,646	19.8	28.1

SOURCE: *Statistical Abstract of the United States, 1984*, U.S. Department of Commerce, and various Federal Reserve Bulletins.

Public Placement. With the few exemptions noted below, any new security issue which is sold to more than 25 buyers must be registered with the SEC. The purpose of a registration statement is to ensure that investors receive full and accurate disclosure of any information relevant to the issue. While statutes set a twenty-day waiting period between the time the registration statement is filed and the time securities may be sold to the public, in practice the SEC can shorten or lengthen the period as necessary to enable the SEC staff to review the statement for any omissions or apparent misrepresentations of fact. During periods of heavy activity, six months or more may pass before the registration is acceptable to the SEC staff. Table 3-2 provides a partial listing of the types of information required.

Before individuals are allowed to purchase a new issue, they must be given a *prospectus*. The prospectus is essentially the same as the registration statement, with certain technical information deleted.[4] SEC approval of the registration statement and prospectus does not constitute an opinion about the risks or investment merits of the security. Approval by the SEC simply means that the issuer has disclosed all facts required by law. Certain securities are exempt from registration. Major types include (1) U.S. government obligations, (2) municipal obligations, (3) commercial bank and savings and loan issues, (4) issues sold intrastate, and (5) issues sold to 25 or fewer buyers.

----

[4]Prior to approval by the SEC, a tentative version of the prospectus, known as a *red herring*, is distributed. The red herring differs from the prospectus in two minor ways. First, stamped on the front page in red (hence the term) is a statement indicating that the prospectus and registration statement have not yet received SEC approval. Second, an issue price is not shown.

TABLE 3-2 *Typical Information Required in an SEC Registration Statement*

1. General information on the issuer—location, products, and so forth
2. Purposes of issue
3. Price at which offered to the public
4. Price at which offered to any special group
5. Promoters' fees
6. Underwriting fees
7. Net proceeds to the company
8. Remuneration of any officers receiving over $25,000 annually
9. Disclosure of any unusual contracts, such as managerial profit sharing
10. Detailed capitalization statement
11. Detailed balance sheet
12. Detailed earnings statement for three preceding years
13. Names and addresses of officers, directors, and underwriters
14. Names and addresses of stockholders owning more than 10% of any class of stock
15. Pending litigation
16. Copy of underwriting agreement
17. Copy of legal opinions
18. Copy of articles of incorporation or association
19. Copies of indentures affecting new issues

Shelf Registration

In early 1982, the Securities and Exchange Commission instituted Rule 415, which has had profound implications for the way transactions take place in the primary market. Rule 415 allows issuers to preregister a security sale. The issuing firm announces its intention to sell a security, files necessary information with the SEC, and accepts competitive bids from investment bankers for the issue. Once the issue is approved by the SEC, the firm can either accept the best competitive bid or delay sale indefinitely. Generally the registration will be delayed until the issuer truly needs capital or prices are viewed to be favorable. When the sale does take place, there is no delay associated with SEC filing and approval. Thus the sale can be executed rapidly.

Issuing Costs

The costs of issuing securities consist of three components:

1. *Out-of-pocket costs* associated with internal clerical costs, management time spent putting the issue together, payments to legal counsel, payments to certified public accountants, etc.
2. The *underwriter spread*, which is the difference between the price received by the issuer and the price at which the underwriter offers it to the public.
3. A *price concession*, which is an inducement offered to the first buyer. The price concession is theoretically equal to the difference between the equilibrium price of the security and the price at which the security is offered to the public.

For example, assume ABC Corp. sells 100,000 new common shares at a time when its currently outstanding shares are selling in the secondary market for $50. To attract a large number of buyers for the new issue and to encourage quick distribution, the underwriter suggests an offering price of $48. In addition, the underwriter sets a $2 underwriter spread to compensate for the market risks of positioning the issue, to cover the costs of finding buyers, and to provide a fair profit. Net of the underwriting spread, ABC Corp. receives $46 per share. Finally, total out-of-pocket costs associated with the sale are $100,000.

Issuing costs would be as follows:

Nature of Cost	Cost per Share	Details
Out-of-Pocket Costs	$1	($100,000 ÷ 100,000 shares)
Underwriter Spread	$2	(Specified)
Price Concession	$2	($50 equilibrium − $48 offer)
Total	$5	

Little is known about the size of out-of-pocket costs since accurate data have never been compiled. Underwriter spreads range anywhere from ½% to 15% or more of the issue's offering price. The size of such spreads depends on the risks and distribution efforts faced by underwriters. For example, firm commitments on large municipal bond issues require spreads of only 1% or so during normal market conditions since underwriters are exposed to little market risk and there is an easy-to-identify and active buying market for such issues. However, small preferred stock issues from high-risk corporations can require spreads of 15% or more. Such a large spread would be due to the potential difficulty in finding buyers, the small size of the issue (most authorities believe there are clear economies of scale to underwriting), and the large price risks incurred while the securities remain in the underwriter's inventory. The split of the underwriter spread varies, but a typical split of a $2 spread on a $50 common stock would be $0.40 to the managing underwriter, $0.40 to each member of the purchase group, and the remaining $1.20 to the broker of the stock.

The costs of price concessions are difficult to measure since equilibrium security prices are difficult to estimate. These equilibrium prices represent the price at which the security would sell (under current market conditions) if it were not part of a new offering. With bonds a distinction between *seasoned* and *unseasoned* issues is often used. A seasoned bond is one which has been traded for some time (months or more), whereas an unseasoned issue is a recent offering. The yields on representative seasoned and unseasoned corporate bonds (as estimated by Moody's) are shown in Figure 3-3. Normally, unseasoned issues are sold at higher yields (lower prices) than are equivalent seasoned issues. Many people infer that this difference represents a price concession provided to buyers of a new issue. This viewpoint is not completely accepted, however. For example, Lindvall suggests that the unseasoned issues better reflect the true yields required at any point in time and that seasoned yields adjust to unseasoned yields (with a lag) — not the other way around. In sum, we simply aren't sure whether price concessions are indeed offered on new bond sales and, if so, how large they are.

FIGURE 3-3 *Yields on Corporate Bonds—Newly Issued vs. Distributed*

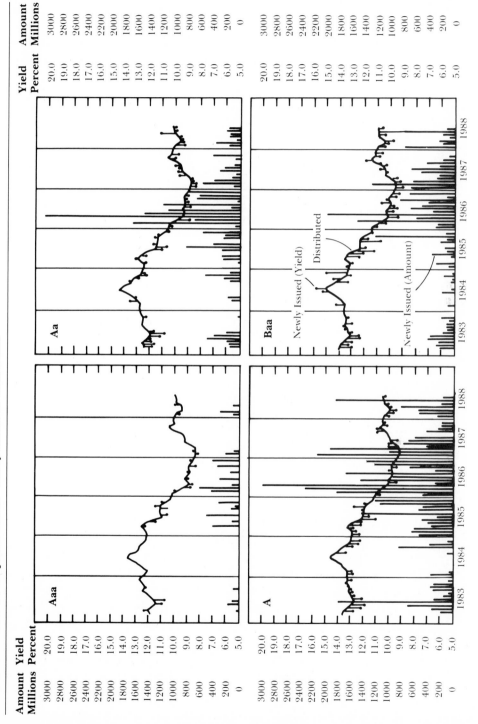

However, there do appear to be clear price concessions on *new* common stock offerings. These new offerings are referred to as initial public offerings, or IPOs. Ibbotson found that an average return of 11.4% could have been earned *in the month following* a new IPO if (1) one had purchased a broad sample of new offerings between 1960 and 1969, (2) the stocks were acquired at the offering price, and (3) the stocks were sold at the bid price at the end of the month. This 11.4% was statistically significant and represents a rather healthy one-month return. Individual security results were quite variable, however. Some IPOs provided a 70% monthly gain while others yielded a 60% loss. To receive the 11.4% average return, one would have had to participate in virtually every new offering.

Ibbotson's results confirm statistically what has been called the "new issues fad." Requests to buy into new stock offerings often exceeded the size of the offerings by a multiple of 5 to 1.[5] And Ibbotson's results have been confirmed by many other research studies. The true economic causes for price concessions on IPOs are not yet fully understood.

SECONDARY MARKETS

The New York Stock Exchange

The New York Stock Exchange (NYSE) is the largest and oldest organized security market in the United States. Formed in 1792 by a group of merchants to trade federal notes and bonds, the exchange has seen its volume grow from a few bond trades over morning coffee to more than 200 million common stock shares per day in the late 1980s. Interestingly, this supposed bastion of free enterprise was formed under a constitution which had all the characteristics of a cartel. Members of the NYSE agreed to trade only among themselves and to charge identical commission rates. These two agreements remained virtually unchanged for more than 150 years and were the fundamental cause of many changes in trading practices during the 1970s and 1980s.

Membership. The NYSE is a corporate association of about 1,500 members, each of whom has bought a *seat* (membership) and has been approved by other members. The cost of a seat is determined by the prevailing demand and supply of memberships, which are in turn a function of the future prospects for the NYSE. In the post–World War II era, seats have sold for as much as $515,000 and for as little as $35,000. Membership prices during the 1970s and 1980s dropped dramatically below the "go-go" days of the 1960s as the NYSE encountered increased competition from other mar-

---

[5]Oversubscribed issues are often allocated by brokers to favored customers. Clearly it pays to be on a broker's favored list. But perhaps one pays to be on the list by incurring large brokerage fees. In addition, underwriters offer price concessions because they don't wish to be exposed to the price risks of carrying the securities in inventory. They shift the risk to an initial buyer and in return offer what appears to be an abnormal return. These risks can be substantial. Perhaps the initial buyer receives a large return only to compensate for risks incurred.

kets and the likely elimination of many monopolistic rates. In addition to regular members who own a seat on the exchange, the NYSE allows various firms access to the trading floor by paying an annual fee.

Members are assigned particular roles, as follows:[6]

1. *Commission brokers* are partners in a brokerage firm and execute orders for their firm's clients on the floor of the exchange. Large brokerage houses will have more than one commission broker on the floor to ensure that customers' orders are rapidly executed.

2. *Floor brokers* are freelance commission brokers. They do not have direct contact with the public, but handle order overflows which the commission brokers are unable to handle. A portion of the commission broker's fee is paid to the floor broker.

3. *Registered traders* buy and sell solely for their own account. They do not handle public orders. Often called floor traders, they are speculators who attempt to buy securities experiencing a temporary influx of sell orders (which are forcing prices down) and sell securities experiencing a temporary influx of buy orders (which are forcing prices up). As a result, floor-trading operations are said to reduce price volatility and add to the market's liquidity. In recent years floor-trading memberships have been few and their trading activity negligible.

4. *Specialists* stand in the middle of every trade, both figuratively and literally. Their essential role in completing a transaction is discussed below.

Listing Requirements. Only listed securities may be traded on the NYSE floor, and until recently members were not allowed to trade listed stocks in any market other than the NYSE.[7] In early 1988 there were approximately 2,300 stocks and 3,600 bonds listed, which represented a major portion of publicly traded U.S. corporate securities. The original issuer of the security makes the decision to list or not. The major advantage claimed for listing is an improvement in security marketability. Minimum *initial listing* requirements must be satisfied, and, to remain listed, the firm must fill various *continued listing* requirements. In selecting securities to be listed, exchange officials seek firms which are national in scope and have a major standing in a growing industry. The more important listing requirements are shown in Table 3-3.

Specialist Operations. About 25% of all NYSE members act as specialists. Usually they form partnerships or corporations with other specialists to diversify risk exposure and spread administrative costs. These organizations are referred to as *special-*

---

[6]In the recent past some members acted as *odd-lot dealers*. The normal unit of trading on the NYSE is a round lot, or 100 shares. When buyers or sellers of an odd lot (a fraction of 100 shares) wished to trade, their orders were historically taken to an odd-lot dealer. The odd-lot dealer would buy (or sell) at a price equal to the next round-lot transaction on the exchange floor plus (or minus) ⅛ or ¼ dollar. Today odd-lot dealers are an extinct species. Large brokerage houses and many specialists perform the same function of assembling several odd lots into round lots, but do so at substantially reduced costs to traders.

[7]Rule 390 prevented member firms from trading listed stocks in a market other than the NYSE. This controversial practice is discussed later in the chapter.

TABLE 3-3 *New York Stock Exchange Listing Requirements*

To be listed on the New York Stock Exchange, a firm must have:
1. Earnings before taxes of at least $2.5 million in the most recent year
2. Earnings before taxes of at least $2.0 million during the two preceding years
3. Net tangible assets of at least $18 million
4. Total market value of common stock of at least $18 million
5. Publicly held shares of at least $1.1 million
6. More than 2,000 holders of 100 shares or more

ist units, and each unit is assigned a number of stocks in which it acts as specialist. For illustrative purposes, however, it is easiest to think in terms of one specialist assigned to one stock. Specialists perform two functions. First, they act as *brokers* by maintaining the *limit book*. Second, they act as *dealers* by selling and buying shares in which they are specialists.

A *limit order* is a request to buy or sell a security at a given price or better. For example, a limit order to *buy* XYZ Corp. at $75 must be transacted at $75 or less. Since limit orders are usually placed at prices "away from the market" (different from current price levels), the commission broker will leave limit orders with the specialist. The specialist records limit orders in a limit book similar to that shown in Figure 3-4. The figure shows a variety of orders to buy at prices of $30.375 or less and offers to sell at prices of $30.625 or more.[8] Requests to buy are referred to as *bid prices*, and offers to sell are called *asked prices*. None of these limit orders will trade now since the actual market price lies somewhere between the highest bid and the lowest ask. Over time, however, the price of the stock will undoubtedly increase or decrease as favorable or unfavorable news is reported. And when a price change occurs, the specialist will execute any limit orders at that price. For this service, the specialist is given a part of the commission broker's fee.

The more complex and important role of the specialist is to serve as a dealer in the stock. The NYSE uses the specialist's dealer function in an attempt to provide continuous and liquid markets. To fully understand how the specialist can provide these services, a short digression is helpful.

There are any number of ways to mechanically structure security trading activity. One method is known as a *call auction*, in which the name of each security is periodically called off (say, twice a day). At such times buyers and sellers state the price and number of shares at which they are willing to trade. The resulting trade price is that which allows the greatest number of trades. A system similar to this was used in the early history of the NYSE and is still used on various foreign exchanges. Today's procedures, however, are closer to what we might term a *continuous auction*. Buyers and sellers continuously gather at the *specialist's post* and seek to buy at the lowest price and sell at the highest price.[9]

Return to Figure 3-4 and assume that two commission brokers arrive simultaneously at the specialist's post. Commission broker A has a customer order to buy

[8]Stock prices are quoted in eighths of $1.

[9]The term *specialist's post* refers to the location on the NYSE floor where a particular stock is traded.

FIGURE 3-4 *Sample Entries from a Limit Book*

Lot	BUY	Price
3	Escher	30
6 1	Zohail Andress	1/8
4	Williams	1/4
5	Jacobson	3/8
		1/2
		5/8
		3/4
		7/8

Lot	SELL	Price
		30
		1/8
		1/4
		3/8
		1/2
3 4	Nelson Myers	5/8
4	Chance	3/4
8 2 1	Brown Goedel Bach	7/8

300 shares at the best price then possible, and commission broker B has an order to sell 300 shares. They ask the specialist, "How's the market?" And, *if the specialist decides not to trade for his own account*, he will reply, "30⅜ to ⅝." This means that the best price to sell (the bid price) is $30.375, and that the best price to buy (the asked price) is $30.625. Commission brokers A and B will recognize that they can better these prices for their customers if they trade with each other, so A will offer to buy 300 at $30.500 and B will agree to sell. But this favorable result occurred simply because the brokers were lucky enough to arrive at the specialist's post at the same moment with identical-size orders. If broker A had arrived moments earlier, the customer would have had to buy at $30.625 and broker B's customer would have had to sell at $30.375. It is exactly such situations that the specialist is designed to aid.

Acting as a *dealer* in the stock, the specialist trades at prices between the limit book's high bid and low offer. *In this role, the specialist will absorb temporary imbalances in buy and sell orders.* As compensation, the specialist hopes to earn a *jobber's turn* over time by selling at prices higher, on average, than paid.

If specialists perform their duties as the exchange desires, the public gains in three ways. First, average bid-ask spreads are narrowed by the specialist's quoting prices between the limit book prices. Second, market participants can be assured that prices will not swing erratically over short time periods, as would be the case if all orders were matched against the limit book. Finally, market participants can expect only small price changes for larger than normal orders since the specialist is supposed to stand ready to take on or dispose of larger amounts of stock. (In fact, specialists will occasionally *short sell*—a term discussed later—to meet buy orders.)

To properly fulfill their duties of providing continuous and liquid markets, specialists will often have to "go against the market" for extended periods, and their profits can be quite variable over time. The specialist has no idea whether a particular order is motivated by someone's need for (or excess of) liquidity or by special information. Against the liquidity trader, specialists profit. Against the information trader, they lose. In fact, specialist partnerships are formed in an attempt to diversify away some of the risk of dealing in single stocks. To ensure that specialists are able to provide sufficient depth of liquidity, the NYSE places minimum capital requirements on specialist units. As the volume of trading has increased over time, the minimum capital requirements have also increased.

But specialist operations have received considerable criticism. For example, a special study by the SEC suggested that the gross income per average dollar invested for an average specialist unit was about 100% per year.[10] While the NYSE has no rules barring competition between specialist units for the same stock, until the late 1970s it was a standard practice to assign only one unit per stock. The exchange rationalized the practice by stating that assigning more than one unit would fragment trading activity and cause a decline in liquidity. However, this policy was reversed in the late 1970s, and units were allowed to compete with one another. As a result, a few units did begin to compete.

But even though NYSE specialists have little direct competition on the floor of the exchange, they do face considerable competition from specialists trading similar stocks on other exchanges. As a result, in 1984 NYSE specialists substantially reduced their fees, to approximately $1.50 per round lot. More alarming, however, was the near breakdown of the specialist system and the potential bankruptcy of many specialist units which occurred in the stock market crash of October 19, 1988 – "Black Monday." We will discuss this very important event later in the chapter.

Other Exchanges

The American Stock Exchange. The American Stock Exchange (AMEX) is the only other organized stock exchange which can be considered national in scope. It is often referred to as the "Curb Exchange" because its earliest brokers traded outdoors on the curb of Wall and Broad Streets in New York City. Clerks would accept requests to trade by telephone and lean outside the office window to pass the order information on to the broker, who was standing on the street. Brokers wore bright multicolored hats so they could be recognized by the clerk, and trade information was passed by means of complex hand signals. The AMEX moved indoors in 1921 and adopted its present name in 1953. The hats are gone, but the hand signals remain. For many years there were no formal listing requirements, but today all securities traded must meet certain financial tests (similar to, but less stringent than, NYSE listing requirements).

---

[10]United States House Committee on Interstate and Foreign Commerce, Subcommittee on Commerce and Finance, *Securities Industry Study: Report and Hearings*, 92d Congress, 1st and 2d sessions, chap. 12.

In an attempt to differentiate itself and cut into the profits of the NYSE, the AMEX has been quite creative and competitive. For example, because of the less rigid listing requirements, firms traded tend to be smaller and younger than those on the NYSE. In addition, in 1976 AMEX officials requested that stocks be dually listed, that is, traded on both the NYSE and the AMEX. This was a major departure from the past, when both exchanges had agreed to forbid dual listing. (The elimination of this "New York Rule" somewhat reduced the NYSE's monopoly position and represented one more step in the development of one central market.) The AMEX originated the ADR (*American Depository Receipt*), which allows American investors to trade in foreign securities. American banks hold foreign securities in safekeeping in their foreign branches and issue claims to them (ADRs) which can be traded on American markets. Finally, the AMEX has been innovative in trading new forms of securities. They offered warrants before the NYSE would list them and began offering puts and calls early in the development of the option market. The AMEX's order execution and clearing procedures are similar to those used by the NYSE.

Regional Exchanges. A number of regional exchanges exist which provide two basic services. First, they list securities of smaller companies of only regional interest. Second, they dually list popular NYSE stocks and charge lower commissions. This second factor was a major impetus to their growth. Brokers who could not afford a seat on the NYSE could purchase a less expensive seat on a regional exchange and be able to trade the more popular NYSE stocks. Without the regional exchanges, such brokers would have had to feed their orders to NYSE member firms and give up a portion of their commissions. In addition, institutions wishing to trade large blocks of stock could trade at lower commission rates on regional exchanges than on the NYSE. Now that commission rates are no longer fixed by the NYSE, and with the growth of dual listings on the AMEX, the future of the regionals is less bright than it once was. As of 1988, the major regional stock exchanges included the Boston Stock Exchange, the Cincinnati Stock Exchange, the Midwest Stock Exchange, the Pacific Stock Exchange, and the Philadelphia Stock Exchange.

Table 3-4 shows the total dollar value of common shares sold during recent years on various stock exchanges. The value of shares traded on the NYSE clearly dominates the others.

The Over-the-Counter Market. Transactions not handled on one of the organized exchanges are called *over-the-counter (OTC) transactions*. The OTC has no central location at which all trading occurs. Instead, it is a diffuse network of brokers and dealers connected by either telephone or computer terminals. The term *over-the-counter* refers to the trading practices in the 1800s, when buyers and sellers of unlisted stocks would physically present cash or securities at a commercial bank. The bank and trader would actually trade over the counter. With the advent of telephones, the market became a telephone network between brokers and dealers. Cathode ray tubes have now been introduced in trading most OTC stocks, and the market is among the most technologically advanced in the country. Many experts believe the modern OTC market is a picture of what the future will be once organized exchanges are integrated with OTC stocks to create a single central market.

TABLE 3-4 *Market Value of Securities Sold on Various Stock Exchanges*

	Dollar Market Value of Shares (Billions)				Percentage of Total			
	NYSE	*AMEX*	*NASDAQ*	*Other*	*NYSE*	*AMEX*	*NASDAQ*	*Other*
1974	$ 99.2	$ 5.1	$ 18.7	$ 14.0	72.41%	3.72%	13.65%	10.22%
1975	133.8	5.6	21.2	17.6	75.08	3.14	11.90	9.88
1976	164.5	7.5	24.8	23.0	74.84	3.41	11.28	10.46
1977	157.3	8.5	24.7	21.4	74.23	4.01	11.66	10.10
1978	210.4	15.2	36.1	23.6	73.75	5.33	12.65	8.27
1979	251.1	20.6	44.3	28.3	72.93	5.98	12.87	8.22
1980	397.7	34.7	68.7	43.5	73.03	6.37	12.61	7.99
1981	415.9	26.4	71.1	48.4	74.03	4.70	12.66	8.62
1982	514.3	20.7	84.2	69.1	74.72	3.01	12.23	10.04
1983	815.1	31.5	188.3	110.5	71.16	2.75	16.44	9.65
1984	815.5	21.3	153.5	113.9	73.85	1.93	13.90	10.32
1985	1023.2	26.3	233.5	149.9	71.41	1.84	16.30	10.46
1986	1448.2	43.4	378.2	213.5	69.51	2.08	18.15	10.25
1987	1983.3	52.5	499.9	248.4	71.24	1.89	17.96	8.92

The securities traded in the OTC market differ considerably in size of issuer, legal nature, risk, marketability, etc. Mutual fund shares, most bank and finance stocks, most corporate bonds, and a large portion of U.S. government and municipal obligations are traded OTC. In addition, securities which are too small or unprofitable to meet the listing requirements of an organized exchange are traded OTC. (Many firms that could be listed choose not to be.) The actual size of the market is hard to determine, since any corporate issue is a candidate. All that is needed is a *market maker* in the stock who will buy or sell the stock to interested traders.

The market maker plays essentially the same dealer role for an OTC stock that the specialist does for an exchange-listed stock. (Market makers do not maintain limit books, however.) The market maker carries a trading inventory of a particular security and is willing to buy and sell with members of the general public. Market makers serve a useful purpose since the public buyer needn't spend time trying to find a public seller. The market maker is known and continuously stands ready to buy or sell. In return for this service a bid-ask spread is required. Buyers acquire securities at the higher asked price, and sellers dispose of securities at the lower bid price. Actively traded OTC securities will have as many as fifteen to twenty market makers competing for public orders. Investment bankers often make a market in the securities they underwrite, and regional brokerage houses typically make markets in local securities. However, many of the large brokerage firms enter the business simply to increase the services available to customers and increase their profits.

Brokers and dealers in OTC securities have formed a self-regulating body known as the National Association of Security Dealers (NASD), which licenses brokers and oversees trading practices. In 1971 the NASD instituted a computerized trading network known as the NASD Automated Quotation System (NASDAQ; pronounced NAZ-dak). To be included in the NASDAQ a security must have at least two market makers, have a minimum number of publicly held shares, and meet certain asset and equity capital requirements. NASDAQ is simply a "real time" information system. Current bid and ask quotations of all market makers on a security are continuously maintained through a telecommunication network. Prior to NASDAQ, a broker could obtain bid-ask quotes only by calling various dealers who made a market in the security. The best bid or ask price could take so long to find that the quote could change before the broker had time to place an order. In fact, there was no guarantee that the *best* quote had been found, since the broker often wouldn't call all market makers. So the advantages of NASDAQ are twofold: (1) it provides *current* quotations, and (2) it brings together quotes from *all* important market makers. At present there are about 5,400 stocks carried on NASDAQ.

Dealers may subscribe to one of three levels of NASDAQ services. At Level I, the broker can view on a computer terminal the highest bid and the lowest ask that market makers are currently offering on each NASDAQ stock. At Level II, *all* bid and ask quotations currently offered are shown with an identification of the market maker providing each quote. At Level III, the user has the ability to actually enter bid and ask quotes into the NASDAQ system. When a bid or ask quote has been entered into the system it is shown to all users of Levels II and III, and the dealer must be willing to trade at least one round lot (100 shares) at these prices until the dealer changes the quotations. It is important to point out, however, that NASDAQ is currently only a reporting system. Actual trades are not made through the NASDAQ computer system but by direct contact between dealers and brokers. However, the system could be easily modified to allow for the actual "crosses" between two parties directly on the system.

OTC stocks with relatively active trading volume are designated by the NASD as *National Market Issues*. All transactions in NASDAQ National Market Issues are immediately reported on the NASDAQ system. For less active issues, dealers report only total transactions at the end of a day.

In addition to OTC stocks traditionally carried on NASDAQ, there are thousands of small, thinly traded stocks whose prices had been reported only once a day on what are referred to as *Pink Sheets*. The Pink Sheets include 11,000 or more inactively traded stocks, including many "penny" stocks and stocks having only a narrow geographic interest. Beginning in 1988, the current quotes for such stocks were also made available on NASDAQ through what is called the OTC Bulletin Board. Because of the extreme thinness of trading in such stocks, prices shown on the OTC Bulletin Board should be viewed with caution.

Prior to the 1980s trading volume in the OTC market had historically been much smaller than that on formal exchange markets such as the NYSE, AMEX, or regionals. During the 1980s, however, NASDAQ made trading of OTC stocks so much easier that OTC trading volume has increased dramatically. In recent years, shares traded on NASDAQ have been approximately the same as or greater than the volume of shares traded on the NYSE.

Third and Fourth Markets. The *third market* refers to an OTC transaction in a security which is also traded on an organized exchange. The growth of the third market in the 1960s and early 1970s was due to two factors: the growth of institutional trading in large blocks of stock and minimum commission fees charged at the time by exchange members.

Throughout the 1960s large financial institutions (trust companies, pension funds, mutual funds, insurance firms, etc.) managed increasingly larger amounts of marketable securities and tended to trade more actively than they had previously. Large-block trades (transactions of 10,000 shares or more) became quite common, and a growing network of large-block dealers developed. In a typical block trade, an institution first contacts a block trader and indicates a desire to, say, sell 50,000 shares of GTE. The block trader will immediately place calls to other institutions known to have an interest in GTE (either a buying or a selling interest) and say something like, "I'm putting together a block in GTE. Want in?" So that the eventual price will be as favorable to the initial seller as possible, no statement is made about whether the original request was a buy or a sell order. Once the block trader has assembled all parties wishing to buy or sell and has negotiated an acceptable transaction price, the trade can be completed. (Normally the trader will have to position a part of the block to balance buys and sells.)

So far, so good. However, in the 1960s and early 1970s all members of the NYSE *had to* transact any NYSE listed stock on the exchange floor *at a minimum commission*. But the marginal cost of putting a block together is substantially lower than the minimum commission which was charged, so nonexchange members started to act as block traders. They could perform the same services as member firms but were not bound by exchange rules to charge abnormally high commissions. Exchange member firms attempted to overcome the excessive commissions by offering other services below cost, taking losses on the prices of securities positioned, etc. But all of these attempts were burdensome at the least and often unsuccessful. As a result, the third market flourished. By 1972 third-market trading represented about 8½% of the volume of all NYSE transactions. Since then, activity in the third market has declined significantly because the SEC decided to eliminate fixed commissions. Between 1971 and 1975, negotiated fees were slowly phased in on large-block transactions. Since May 1, 1975 (*May Day*), all commissions have been negotiated and open to full competition.

The *fourth market* refers to transactions made directly between a buyer and a seller of a large block. Brokers and dealers are totally eliminated. The *Instinet* system is a wire network somewhat similar to NASDAQ which provides current information on the number of shares subscribers are willing to buy or sell at specified prices. Transactions in the fourth market are negligible at present.

Security Orders

Basic Types. The standard unit of trading in stocks is a *round lot*, or 100 shares. Any fraction of 100 shares is referred to as an *odd lot*. Because odd-lot transactions require special servicing (assembly of many odd lots into round lots is performed either by one's broker or by the specialist), they require a larger commission per share than do round lots. The most common type of order is a *market order*, in which a customer instructs a broker to either buy or sell at the best price then available. The exact transaction price will not be known with complete certainty when the order is placed, although the eventual trade price will be quite close to prices at the moment the order is placed. The advantage of a market order is that there is no doubt that it will be executed.

A *limit order* is a request to buy or sell at a specified price or better. For example, a limit order to sell at $40 obligates the broker to sell at a price of $40 or more. As we noted earlier, most limit orders are placed at prices somewhat away from prevailing market prices and will be left with the specialist to be entered in the limit book. The disadvantage of a limit order is that the investor is not sure that the security will indeed be bought or sold. For example, assume Lois Lane believes the prospects of SMI Corp. are strong. The stock is selling at $30 per share, but, in an attempt to pick up a point or two, she places a limit order to buy at $29. If the shares of SMI Corp. immediately soar to $50, Lois will never have bought.

Finally, a *stop order* is an order which specifies a given price at which point it becomes a market order. For example, a stop order to sell at $70 will become a market order to sell the moment the stock trades at $70. There is no assurance the stop order will be filled at the stop price, but it is likely to be transacted at a price reasonably close. Stop orders to sell are commonly used to protect profits or minimize losses when one owns the related stock. Stop orders to buy are used to protect profits or minimize losses when one has previously sold the stock short (discussed later). For example, assume Lois Lane had initially placed a market order to buy a round lot of SMI and had been able to buy at $30. If the stock subsequently increased to $50, she would have an unrealized, paper profit of $20. To guard this profit, she could place a *stop-loss order* (an order to sell) at, say, $47. If the stock falls below $47, she automatically sells at about $47 and takes a realized profit of $17. If the stock continues to rise or stays at $50, the stop order is not executed.

Unless stated otherwise, all orders are assumed to be *day orders*. They must be transacted that day or they are terminated. Since market orders are almost always executed on the same day the order is placed, specification of a time period during which the order is valid is used mainly with limit and stop orders. A *good-till-canceled (GTC)* order is, of course, valid until the trader cancels it.

Some brokers will accept *discretionary orders* which allow them to buy or sell at their own discretion. The stated advantage of discretionary orders is that they allow the broker to properly time a trade. The broker is in constant contact with market prices and can (supposedly) tell when there is a temporary weakness in buying or selling conditions which provides an opportunity to trade. Such opportunities may be missed if the broker must clear all transactions with the customer before submitting an order. Most brokerage firms will *not* accept discretionary transactions, since they can lead to excessive trading and customer ill will if a trade is unsuccessful. From the customer's viewpoint discretionary transactions should be discouraged. Allowing a broker to trade discretionally is comparable to turning your checking account over to him or her.

Commissions. When the NYSE was formed in 1792, the founders agreed to two important practices which affected the structure of U.S. security markets for the next two centuries. First, they agreed to *fixed minimum commissions*; second, they agreed that they would not trade any security which was listed on the NYSE in any market other than the NYSE. The second practice eventually became known as Rule 390 and is discussed later. Since the fixed commission fees charged by brokerage firms were greater than the marginal costs of processing an order by an *efficient* broker, the practice caused a number of distortions in the markets. For example, many inefficient firms were able to remain in business and prosper. In addition, the practice of "give-ups" and payment for services in "soft dollars" became common. A give-up occurs when broker A transacts an order for a customer and receives the full commission from the customer, but then gives up a portion of the commission to broker B by transferring cash to broker B. This is done to compensate broker B for services which broker B had provided to the customer at no charge. For example, assume that the customer is a college endowment fund which has been receiving data and research information about its security portfolio from broker B. To compensate broker B, the endowment fund instructs broker A to give up to broker B, say, 50% of all commissions paid to broker A by the endowment. A "soft dollar" is similar but is an arrangement between only one broker and a customer. In this case the customer pays for services which it receives from the brokerage firm through commissions paid to the broker. For example, consider a pension fund which employs various investment managers to run its portfolio of securities. To evaluate the performance of these managers, the pension fund might employ the pension consulting division of the brokerage firm. To compensate the brokerage firm for these services, the pension fund could agree to pay, say, $10,000 in "hard dollars" (actual cash) or have the investment managers engage in security trades with the brokerage firm having commissions of, say, $20,000. A 2-to-1 ratio between soft and hard dollars is common in today's markets.

In the early 1970s, the Securities and Exchange Commission decided that all commissions should be negotiated between the broker and the customer—that is, they were to be subject to competition. Between 1971 and 1975 negotiated fees were slowly phased in on large-block transactions. And since May 1, 1975 (*May Day*), all security commissions have been negotiated rates. In practice, most brokerage firms try to set firm-wide rates that apply to particular types of transactions and customers. Thus, the customer and the broker might not actually negotiate a commission every time a trade is made. This is particularly true for a small trade. Commissions for large-block trades, however, are actively negotiated, and the customer who engages in a large block will actively shop around for the cheapest rate.

Three levels of commission rates exist: (1) full-service rates, (2) discount broker rates, and (3) rates for very large block trades. A comparison of these rates is displayed in Figure 3-5. Both full-service and discount broker rates depend on two factors: the quantity of shares traded and the price per share. The larger the quantity of shares traded and the larger the stock price, the smaller the commission fee. Most brokers will quote a total dollar commission for a given stock price and quantity of shares. For example, a full-service broker might charge $97.50 to trade 100 shares of a $40 stock. These total dollar commissions have been converted to percentage costs in Figure 3-5. For example, the $97.50 fee above represents 2.43% of the $4,000 worth of stock traded.

The term full-service is used when the broker provides more services than simply

FIGURE 3-5 *Commission Rates, Full-Service vs. Discount Brokers*

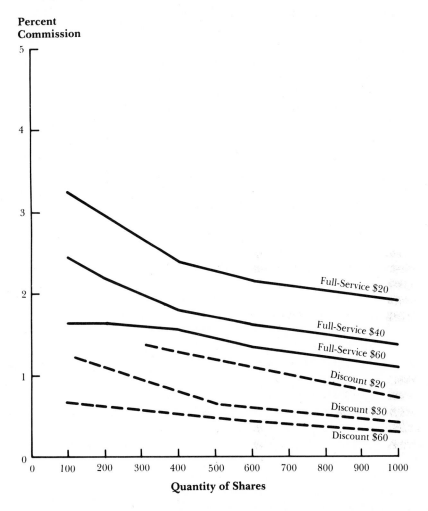

trade execution. Generally the extra service provided includes advice about long-term investment strategy and current research opinions of the brokerage firm. Commissions paid to a full-service broker can be rather sizable. For example, the purchase of 100 shares of a $20 stock would incur a commission of about 3.25%. The lowest commission that a typical customer might pay to a full-service broker will be about 1.00%. For example, the commission on 1,000 shares of a $60 stock will be about 1.1%.

Discount brokers provide only trade execution. Such brokers are particularly useful to investors who wish to develop their own investment strategy and conduct their own research. Commissions paid to discount brokers will vary considerably between firms and over time. However, discount broker commissions can usually be found which are 50% or more lower than rates charged by full-service brokers.

Finally, there is a class of security traders who engage in very large blocks and who wish trade-execution services only. An example would be investment in a stock index fund created by a bank or insurance company. Often trading as many as 200,000 shares, they have no need for research advice since they are passive investors. Such investors will shop around for the lowest commission. Commissions on large-block trades are commonly quoted in cents per share, and rates as low as 3-4 cents are possible. For a $50 stock this translates into a commission rate of 0.06% to 0.08%.

In short, commission rates are quite variable and depend on the services desired from a broker and the size of the trade.

The commissions discussed above deal with trades of listed securities. Trades of OTC securities are done on either a dealer or an agency basis. When a dealer basis is used, the broker trades the customer's securities directly with the brokerage firm itself. The brokerage firm buys or sells securities for its own account. Such dealer trades do not identify an explicit commission. Instead, the customer buys at the broker's ask price and sells at the broker's bid price. But even though an explicit commission is not identified, the broker clearly charges a fee for the transaction which is obtained through the bid-ask spread. When an agency basis trade is made, the broker arranges the trade with another brokerage firm and charges an explicit commission similar to that charged on listed stocks (although probably somewhat larger).

Execution and Clearing. At this point in our discussion it might be useful to trace through the various steps of a normal stock trade. A general flowchart of a trade *execution* is shown in Figure 3-6. Figure 3-7 shows a flowchart of the *clearing* process. There are any number of execution and clearing paths possible. We will follow a fairly common one.

Early Monday morning Clara Voigent calls her broker, Sam Lynch, and indicates that she wants to place a market order for five round lots of SMI Corp. common stock. The stock has recently been selling for about $30, and, based on an article she read in the Sunday financial press about a new patent received by SMI, Clara believes the stock is undervalued and should soon increase in value. Broker Sam will first obtain current price quotes on SMI Corp. by using a computer terminal which is tied into various exchange markets. Assume that the best quotes are available on the NYSE and are $32 bid and $32¼ ask. (Obviously, Clara wasn't the only one who read the favorable news about SMI.) This means that the highest price at which one could sell is $32 (the specialist's or limit book's highest bid) and the lowest price at which one could buy is $32¼ (the specialist's or limit book's lowest ask). Since the best prices are available on the NYSE, Sam decides to route the order to that exchange.

Next Sam needs to decide whether the order will be routed to the NYSE through the exchange's automatic execution system or through the brokerage firm's commission broker on the floor of the exchange. The automatic execution system is referred to as the *designated order turnaround* system (or *Super Dot*) and can be used to trade relatively small orders. Super Dot is an electronic order-routing system through which member firms can transmit market and limit orders in NYSE-listed securities directly to the specialist post where the securities are traded. The specialist represents the order in the auction crowd or offsets it with the limit book depending on which price is bet-

FIGURE 3-6　*Order Execution*

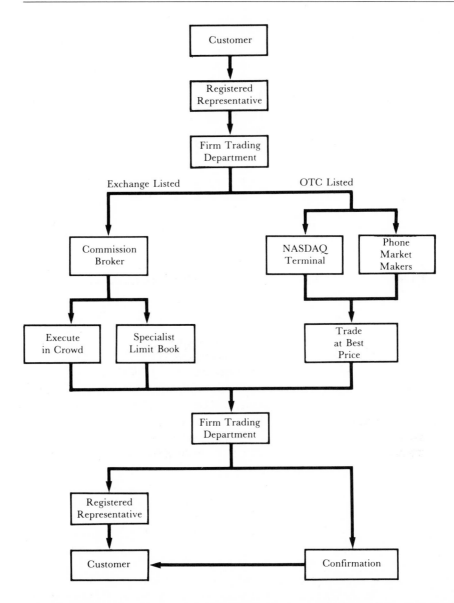

ter. As of 1988, the system could be used for up to 2,099 shares in a market order or 99,099 shares in a limit order. Super Dot is designed to allow the exchange to efficiently handle as many as 250 million shares per day. Market orders are guaranteed to be executed within three minutes. The development of Super Dot represents a major advance in security trading.

An alternative to Super Dot which is available to broker Sam would be to route the order directly to the firm's commission broker on the floor of the exchange. Let's

FIGURE 3-7 *Order Clearing Process*

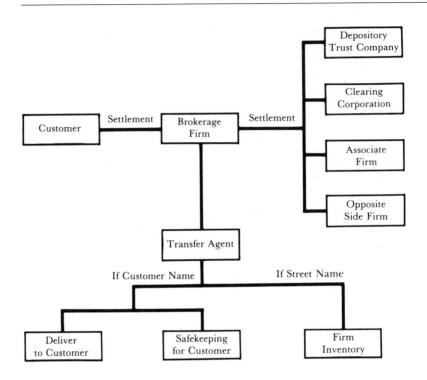

assume that Sam chooses this alternative, since it allows us to look more closely at the mechanics of a trade. Broker Sam prepares a trade ticket describing the details of the trade and transmits the ticket to his firm's trading department. An example of such a trade ticket is shown in Figure 3-8A. The trading department then communicates the order to the floor of the exchange, where the commission broker is notified. The commission broker walks to the specialist's post where SMI is traded and asks, "How's the market?" The specialist replies, "32 to ¼." Seeing no other brokers in the crowd, the commission broker indicates to the specialist "500 bought," and they exchange cards with information about the trade. The specialist's card is optically scanned by machines at the NYSE, and notice of the trade is printed on a ticker tape throughout the country. The commission broker's information card is returned to employees of the firm's trading department. They notify broker Sam and send Clara a *confirmation* of the trade in the mail. A sample confirmation is shown in Figure 3-8B. Sam calls Clara to notify her personally and everyone is happy (at least for a while).

Since Clara didn't indicate otherwise, this was a *regular way* contract, meaning that the *settlement date* will be five business days after the *trade date*. On the settlement date the brokerage firm and the customer exchange cash and securities, and the customer becomes the legal owner of the securities (or no longer the owner if securities had been sold). If Clara had desired, she could have requested a *cash contract*, which requires settlement and passing of title on the trade date. Another form of contract

FIGURE 3-8A *Sample Document of Trade Execution (Trade Ticket)*

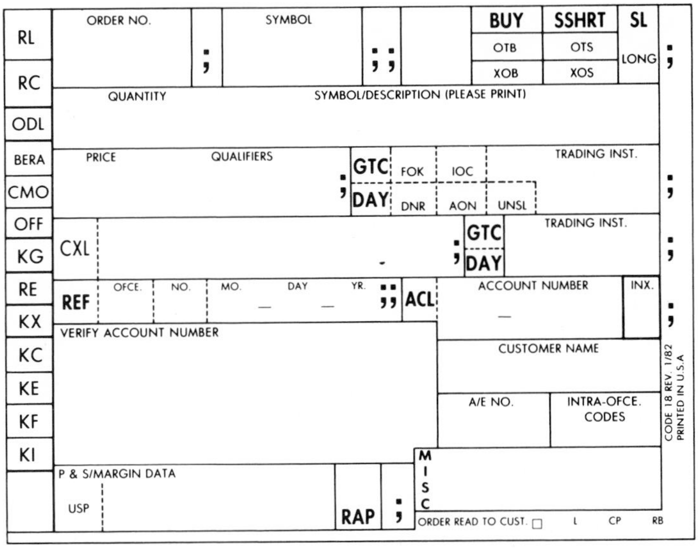

is a *seller's option*, which allows the seller to choose the settlement date.[11] Nonetheless, on the following Monday Clara is required to *deliver* to the brokerage firm $16,125 (500 × $32.25) plus commissions and taxes and, in return, be the legal owner of the stock. That same Monday, the brokerage firm will settle with the other side of the trade—in this case, the specialist.

In any trade there is a buyer who promises to deliver cash for securities and a seller who promises to deliver securities for cash. *Clearing* refers to how this process actually takes place.

Clearing consists of two steps. First, brokers to each side of the trade agree upon the number of shares traded and the price. If a disagreement occurs, it must be reconciled. Second, cash and securities are delivered to the respective sellers and buyers on the settlement date.

Clearing between firms is accomplished in one of four ways. First, the securities and cash can be physically delivered between the two firms representing the buyer and the seller. This is a time-consuming, costly, and error-prone procedure, although it is commonly used between firms in the same city. Second, small firms can use the services of larger brokerage houses to net out their purchases and sales and deliver only the required net cash and securities. Carried one step further, the services of the National Securities Clearing Corporation can be used. This organization handles trades made on the NYSE, AMEX, and OTC. Each member delivers only the net amount of securities or cash necessary to settle its accounts with the clearing corporation. Fi-

---

[11]Cash contracts and seller's options are normally used for tax purposes when title must be passed on a particular date.

FIGURE 3-8B *Sample Document of Trade Execution (Confirmation Ticket)*

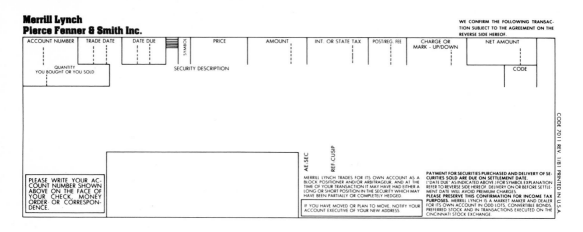

nally, the Depository Trust Company (DTC) has been organized, at which brokers and dealers may deposit large quantities of "street name" certificates on most actively traded securities. Street name refers to securities registered in the name of a brokerage firm. Customer orders are cleared simply by computer debits and credits to each firm's accounts at DTC. This reduces to a minimum the flow of paperwork required to physically move stock certificates.

The stock certificates evidencing Clara's ownership of 500 shares of SMI may be physically transferred to her name and either delivered to her or maintained by the brokerage firm in *safekeeping*. Alternatively, Clara may allow the firm to keep the securities for her in *street name*. In that case her evidence of ownership is a monthly statement from the broker indicating that she owns the shares. Clara will probably not want to be bothered with physical possession of the securities and will keep them in safekeeping or in street name. Because of the large clerical costs associated with keeping customer certificates in safekeeping, most brokerage firms will request that the certificates be held in street name. This allows the broker, for example, to maintain only one certificate in the amount of 30,000 shares for 30 customers who each own 1,000 shares. Each customer's ownership is reflected in the accounting records of the brokerage firm.[12]

Margin and Short Sales

Margin Trades. When an account is opened at a brokerage house, it will be specified as either a *cash* or a *margin* account. In a cash account the customer must fully pay for all securities bought. In a margin account a portion of the securities bought may be paid for with a loan obtained from the broker. The customer will sign a *hypothe-*

---

[12]Dividends, proxy statements, and any other literature distributed by the corporation on securities registered in street name are sent to the brokerage firm, which in turn forwards them to the customer.

cation agreement, which allows the broker to use the securities bought as collateral on a bank loan given to the broker. Thus, the broker obtains money from a bank and lends it to the customer by using a personal broker loan collateralized by the customer's securities. For this service the broker typically charges an interest rate approximately 1% higher than the rate charged by the bank.

The advantage provided by a margin account is clearly the increased leverage. For a given dollar equity capital, a larger quantity of securities can be bought. This increased leverage raises both the expected returns on an equity investment and the uncertainty about returns.

Federal law states that the Federal Reserve System may specify the *initial margin*. Regulation T allows the Federal Reserve to limit initial loans by brokers and dealers, whereas Regulation U allows it to limit security loans by commercial banks. The initial margin rate is periodically changed by the Federal Reserve as one of its policy tools for controlling economic expansions and recessions. Initial margin is usually higher for stocks than for corporate bonds. Since initial margin requirements were first set in 1934, rates have ranged between 40% and 100% for common stocks. Exchanges and brokerage firms may also specify more rigid initial margin requirements. In fact, some brokerage firms allow cash accounts only. In addition, all exchanges and brokerage firms specify a *maintenance margin* below which either more cash must be placed in the account or some securities must be sold until the account's actual margin is greater than the required maintenance margin.

Assume that in our previous example with Clara V., her broker has specified an initial margin of 60% and a maintenance margin of 35%. If Clara wishes to fully margin her purchase of SMI, she would pay broker Sam $9,675 (60% × $16,125) and borrow the remaining $6,450 from her brokerage firm. As of that date, her actual margin would exactly equal the required initial margin:[13]

$$\text{Actual Margin} = \frac{\text{Equity}}{\text{Market Value of Securities}}$$

$$= \frac{\text{Market Value of Securities} - \text{Loan Balance}}{\text{Market Value of Securities}}$$

$$= \frac{\$9,675}{\$16,125} = 60\%$$

If Clara guesses right and the price of her SMI stock increases, her actual margin will rise above the required initial margin. For example, if the stock rose to $40:

$$\text{Actual Margin} = \frac{(\$40 \times 500) - \$6,450}{\$40 \times 500}$$

$$= \frac{\$13,550}{\$20,000}$$

$$= 67.75\%$$

---

[13]For illustrative purposes we will assume Clara has only one stock in her account with broker Sam. In practice, margin is calculated by summing the value of all loans and securities held in a given account.

Clara could either withdraw the excess margin from the account or purchase more stock on margin without contributing more cash. If more shares are acquired with the excess margin, the process is referred to as *pyramiding*.

If Clara guesses wrong and the price of SMI declines, her margin will also decline. As long as the actual margin is between the required initial and maintenance margins, her account is referred to as a *restricted account*, and she would be unable to purchase new stock on margin without restoring the account to the initial margin requirement. However, as long as she doesn't purchase more stock on margin, she needn't place more equity cash into the account. If the actual margin declines below the maintenance margin, she will have to make up the deficiency (and perhaps more) by either selling securities or placing more cash into the account. If the maintenance margin is 35%, her stock value can decline to $19.85 per share before it hits the maintenance limit:

$$0.35 = \frac{(P \times 500) - \$6,450}{P \times 500}$$

$$P = \$19.85$$

At the end of each day, brokerage firms will *mark to market* their margin accounts. That is, they will calculate the actual margin in an account using closing trade prices to determine whether a margin call is needed.

To illustrate how margin might be restored if the stock falls below $19.85, assume that it falls to $15 and that broker Sam's firm requires that any margin deficiency be restored to the maintenance margin of 35%. (This will vary from firm to firm—but restoration to maintenance margin is a minimum.) In this case, Clara could bring the account into balance in a number of ways. These include the following:

1. Add new cash to the account and leave it in the form of cash.
2. Add new cash to the account and purchase more shares of SMI at $15 per share.
3. Sell shares and repay a portion of the loan.

Alternatives 1 and 2 both require a cash deposit of $2,423.08, which is used to increase her equity position—whether the equity is held in cash or securities. To illustrate the cash deposit calculation in the first alternative, we know that:

$$\frac{\text{Original Equity} + \text{New Equity}}{\text{Total Portfolio Value}} = 0.35$$

or

$$\frac{(\$15 \times 500 - \$6,450) + \text{Cash}}{\$15 \times 500 + \text{Cash}} = 0.35$$

This incremental equity of $2,423.08 could be held either as cash or as new shares of SMI Corp. (If new shares are acquired, slightly more than $2,423.08 would be required because $2,423.08 would purchase only 161.5 shares.)

If the third alternative is chosen, Clara sells shares and uses the proceeds to reduce her loan balance. In total, 300 shares would have to be sold. This is shown below, where N refers to the number of shares sold:

$$\frac{\$15(500 - N) - (\$6,450 - \$15N)}{\$15(500 - N)} = 0.35$$

$$N = 300 \text{ shares}$$

Most investors own a number of different securities. When this is true, margin calculations are not made on each security owned but on the aggregate portfolio value and aggregate debt balance. Thus if Clara owned two stocks, she might not have to post margin when SMI Corp. shares fall to $15 if the other stock has increased sufficiently in value.

Short Sales. When people buy securities, it is referred to as going *long*, and they do so in the hopes of future price increases. When people sell securities they own, it is referred to as going *short*, and they do so with the expectation prices will soon drop. When people sell a security which they *don't* own, it is referred to as *short selling*, and they do so in the hopes of buying the stock in the future at a lower price.

The mechanical process of short selling, which is actually quite simple, is displayed in Figure 3-9. Initially the short seller places an order to short sell, say, 100 shares of a stock which he or she believes is overvalued. The broker will find a willing buyer at, say, $30 per share and execute the sale. Five business days later, the broker will have to borrow shares from a *lender of shares* in order to deliver to the buyer. The lender of shares may be anyone willing to do so, but normally the broker will act as the lender by delivering securities held in "street name" for customers. The buyer receives the 100 shares, pays the $3,000 purchase price, and goes merrily on his or her way. The lender, however, will demand collateral for the shares lent, the most likely collateral being the $3,000 cash received from the buyer. Typically, the cash collateral

FIGURE 3-9 *Short Selling*

A. Origination of Short Sale

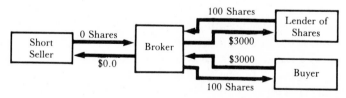

B. Covering of Short Sale

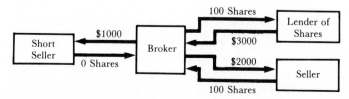

is provided "flat," that is, without any interest fee paid. If this is the case, it's quite easy to see why lenders (usually brokers) are willing to lend shares. They still have an ownership claim to the shares (through the short seller) but now have additional cash which can be invested to provide a short-term risk-free return. The share loan is a "call" loan, cancelable at any time by either party. If the lender wants the shares returned, the short seller can either find another lender or buy in the open market.

Continuing with this example, assume the share's price actually does fall to, say, $20. The short seller will cover the short by asking the broker to buy 100 shares. The new seller will receive $2,000 and give up 100 shares, which are returned to the lender of shares. In turn the lender gives the $3,000 collateral value back to the broker, who returns a $1,000 profit to the short seller.

With that basic review of short selling, we can mention a few intricacies. First, SEC rules require that all short sale transactions be specified as such. Each month the volume of short sales in various stocks is compiled and reported in the financial press. Second, the SEC requires that a short sale be made on either an "up tick" or a "zero tick" if the previously different stock price was lower. For example, assume the sequence of market transactions in a stock is:

$$20 \quad 18 \quad 18\tfrac{1}{8} \quad 18\tfrac{1}{8} \quad 18\tfrac{1}{8} \quad 18\tfrac{1}{4} \quad 17\tfrac{7}{8}$$

The first move from 20 to 18 is a down tick. The next move from 18 to 18⅛ is an up tick, and the next two moves are zero ticks. A short sale could have been transacted at 18⅛ or 18¼. The up-tick rule was created because of a concern that short sellers might start a price decline which the public would continue to feed. As the public continued to sell and further depress prices, the short sellers would cover at artificially low prices.[14]

Next, what happens to cash dividend payments? The new buyer will be carried as a shareholder of record on the corporation's books and receive payments directly from the corporation. The lender of shares (who is also an owner of the stock and deserves dividends) will be paid the dividends by the short seller. The short seller is indifferent to the dividend payment since the dividend payment loss is offset by the profit obtained by share price declines when dividends are paid. In addition, short sellers must post margin in the same amount as if they had gone long. In the example above, if the initial margin had been 50%, the short seller would have had to place equity values with the broker totaling $1,500. This is probably not a burden to the short seller because any unrestricted long securities can be used as margin. Finally, since the shares will be registered in the new buyer's name, he or she will receive all voting rights. The lender of shares will not retain any voting rights.

Short sales are a tool for sophisticated traders who know how to place stop orders to reduce risks and are able to closely follow changes in market conditions.

---

[14]Such an operation is known as a *bear raid*. *Bull raids* involve creating an initial heavy buying demand to force prices up. As the general public sees the price rise, it begins buying, thus forcing prices even higher as the bull raiders quietly sell out. Bear and bull raids are impossible in an efficient market. However, during the 1800s and early 1900s they were accepted as fact. Whether they are possible today in actively traded securities is doubtful.

THE CHANGING MARKET STRUCTURE

A fundamental change in the manner in which security orders are processed, which can best be described as revolutionary, began during the 1970s. For nearly two centuries the economic structure of the industry had been dominated by various monopolistic rules of the NYSE—in particular, (1) fixed minimum commissions, (2) an increasingly monopolistic specialist system, (3) agreements between the NYSE and AMEX not to dually list securities, and (4) member agreements to trade listed stocks only on the NYSE. Surely there was competition to NYSE trading by regional exchanges, the AMEX, and the OTC. But as long as the largest and most actively traded securities were traded on an exchange which limited membership and fixed the price of its services, such competition was ineffectual.

The factors which allowed a change in the status quo are difficult to identify fully. However, three important and interactive forces were (1) increased institutionalization of the markets, (2) an improved communication and trade execution network, and (3) the introduction and dramatic growth of stock index options and futures.

Increased Institutionalization

The term financial institution is applied to organizations such as commercial banks, insurance companies, mutual funds, and pension funds. The critical factor associated with such organizations is the size of the portfolios they control and thus the size of the trades in which they engage. Although each of these organizations trades in common stocks (commercial banks only through their trust operations), pension fund trades are clearly the most important. Pension funds represent the assets which corporations have invested in order to meet future retirement-benefit obligations to their employees. For large corporations, pension assets often exceed $1 billion and are heavily invested in stocks and bonds. With portfolios of this size, it is easy to understand the impacts their trades might have on security markets.

Perhaps the most visible effect of institutional trading is in the increased number of large-block trades. A large block is a trade in excess of 10,000 shares. Block trades in excess of 5 million shares are not uncommon, and in 1986 a 48.8-million-share block trade of Navistar International Corp. was completed.

The growth of block trading on the NYSE is displayed in Table 3-5. During the early 1970s total block trading actually grew more rapidly than shown for the NYSE because many blocks went to the third market to avoid having to pay fixed minimum commissions on the NYSE. However, once negotiated commissions came into effect, block trading on the NYSE grew to the extent that it represented 50% or more of all NYSE trading volume by the mid-1980s.

Some of the changes in the security markets which the growth of institutional trading contributed to include the following:

1. *Elimination of fixed commissions.* In order to increase transactions of block traders on the listed exchanges and reduce the growth of the third market, the ex-

TABLE 3-5 *Block Trades on the NYSE*

Year	*Average Daily Number of Block Trades*	*Shares (Thousands)*	*Percentage of Total NYSE Volume*
1965	9	48,262	3.1%
1970	60	450,908	15.4
1975	136	778,540	16.6
1980	528	3,311,132	29.2
1985	2,139	14,222,272	51.7
1986	2,631	17,811,335	49.9

changes had a strong motivation to eliminate fixed minimum commissions. Even if the SEC had not ruled minimum commissions illegal, the rapid growth of block trading would probably have led the exchanges to discontinue their use.

2. *Desire for block liquidity.* Many block trades are negotiated in what is known as the "upstairs" dealer market in a manner discussed earlier. Essentially, all parties interested in being a part of the block are contacted by a block trader over the telephone, and a price is negotiated. Often price commissions must be given by the active side of the block to induce other organizations to take the opposite side to the trade. Institutions that are motivated by information not currently discounted in the stock's price might be willing to provide such price inducements for the sake of immediate liquidity. However, institutions whose trades are not motivated by information prefer to find other means of trading which do not require such price inducements.

   Instinet as well as a computer system developed by Jefferies & Company provide a means by which such price inducements can be minimized. Institutions with a block to sell or buy submit their request to the computer system, which matches desires to trade. A subscriber to Instinet can enter a limit order in "the book" (computer) which is then available to other subscribers. The Jefferies system works more like a call market in which buyers and sellers are periodically brought together and a price is set which will trade the largest quantity of shares.

3. *Growth of futures and options.* Futures and options on aggregate stock and bond indexes were developed in the early 1980s. Positions in these instruments allow one to trade an aggregate portfolio instead of single stocks or bonds. This feature has been particularly desired by large institutions, which are often less interested in trading individual security issues than in trading aggregate portfolio positions. The use of such futures and options provides institutional investors with an inexpensive and rapid way to change their portfolio asset allocation.

4. *Globalization of financial markets.* In an attempt to broaden their diversification, pension funds have begun to purchase non-U.S. securities. To aid in this movement, the exchanges have begun to explore ways in which securities on their exchanges can be traded around the world—24 hours a day. In 1988, financial futures on U.S. Treasury bonds were the first to be traded on a 24-hour basis

across various exchanges throughout the world. And in 1989, the National Association of Security Dealers began trading in 300 OTC stocks at 4 A.M. Eastern time. The 1990s will probably strengthen trading ties between United States, Japanese, Hong Kong, and British markets.

Communication and Trade Execution

Many of the developments within the past decade were possible only because of improvements in telecommunication and computer processing. All have led to increased integration of security markets and toward the concept of a *Central Market*.

In the *Securities Acts Amendments of 1975*, Congress stated that the SEC should take actions which would rapidly move toward a Central Securities Market. Exactly how this market would work is not yet clear, but its basic functions are. Any Central Market should:

1. Allow for free entry to any individual wishing to act as a dealer in securities (that is, perform the functions now done by OTC market makers and exchange specialists).
2. Provide free access to all bid-ask quotes offered by security dealers.
3. Provide for a single source of trade quotations.

In 1975, a *Consolidated Tape* was developed to print all transactions in NYSE-listed stocks which take place on seven of the largest listed exchanges, NASDAQ, and Instinet. This information is used to publish the daily *composite stock prices* in newspapers.

In addition, listed stock exchanges make current bid and ask stock price quotations available to subscribers through the *Consolidated Quotations Services*. By using it, subscribers can quickly identify the market in which the best price is available and route a trade accordingly. This saves the time which used to be required to explore prices in each market ("shopping around") and ensures proper price execution.

Dealers now also have the ability to submit bid and ask prices through the *Intermarket Trading System (ITS)*. This is an electronic communication network which links seven listed exchanges and the NASD. Brokers representing customers as well as specialists and market makers may submit bid and ask prices and trade through the system. As of 1986, 1,278 stocks were eligible for trading on ITS, and total trades were about 5% of total NYSE stock volume.

The final step toward a true Central Market would be the creation of a single *centralized limit order book* (CLOB) which would link all markets. This has yet to be done, because many questions remain about how it should be implemented in light of the vested interests the larger exchanges have in maintaining their importance.

None of the changes in order processing instituted so far would have been possible without significant improvements in telecommunications and microcomputers.

Options and Futures Growth

The introduction and growth of trading in futures and options on aggregate stock indexes have also had profound impacts on security markets during the past decade. Stock indexes are discussed in depth in Chapter 4. These indexes can be thought of as the average price of the group of stocks included in the index. A portfolio of stocks which is *identical* to the index cannot be bought, but many portfolios are reasonably similar in makeup. Thus, when futures and options were created whose values depended on the stock indexes, investors (particularly large institutional investors) had the opportunity to take positions in both "spot" stock portfolios and similar options and futures. This opened the way for trades across the three markets (physically and legally separate stock markets, option markets, and futures markets). These trades could be used to arbitrage price differentials between the markets or to alter portfolio asset allocation. We will briefly discuss one example of arbitrage (index arbitrage) and one example of portfolio asset allocation (portfolio insurance). Details of each are presented in the chapters that discuss options and futures. Both examples are based on trades in futures only in order to keep them understandable.

Futures contracts on stock indexes can be thought of as a claim to the ownership of the stock index at the futures' delivery date. For example, if you buy an index future at $250 which is deliverable in one month, *conceptually* you have the obligation to buy one "unit" of the index for $250 in exactly one month. *Conceptually*, the contract agreement is made today and all cash and securities are delivered at the end of the month. By month-end the stock index will probably not be exactly $250. If it is higher, you have a profit. If it is lower, you have a loss. Basically you have a position in the stock index (albeit a delayed position).

Stock index futures are different from most other futures contracts, however, in a very important way. Actual delivery of cash and securities does not take place. Instead, all profits are received in cash and all losses are paid in cash. This is referred to as *cash settlement*. For example, assume that you bought a 1.0 index future for $250 and that the index turns out to be $275 at the close of trading on the future's delivery date. You would receive $25 cash profit from the futures exchange, and the person who sold the contract to you would have to pay a $25 loss to the futures exchange.

Armed with these principles, we can examine the basics of index arbitrage and portfolio insurance.

Index Arbitrage. The price of a stock index future must be closely related to the current value of the stock index itself or there will be an opportunity for arbitrage profits. The spot index price and index futures price will not be identical, but they will be closely related. For example, assume that a one-month future is trading at $250 at a time when the stock index is $200. For simplicity, assume that there will be no cash dividends on the stocks included in the index during the next month. Finally, assume that you can borrow money at a cost of 1% per month.

Well, what can you do with this information? An index arbitrage. Today you would borrow $200 and use the proceeds to invest in stocks identical to those in the index. You would also *sell* the futures for a contract price of $250. Net cash flow today is zero. A month from now you would repay your borrowings with a cash outflow of $202 ($200 × 1.01). If the stock index at that time is greater than $250 you would have a loss on the futures—but a loss which is *exactly offset* by gains on the stock which you own. Similarly, if the stock index is less than $250 your profit on the futures is *exactly offset* by your losses on the stock. This transaction is shown below for two hypothetical delivery date stock index values of 100 and 300.

	Cash Flows		
		At Delivery	
	Today	*$100*	*$300*
Today			
Issue Debt	+ $200		
Buy "Spot" Stock	− 200		
Delivery Date			
Repay Debt		− 202	− 202
Sell Stock		+ 100	+ 300
Take Profits or Losses on Futures			
($250 − $100)		+ 150	
($250 − $300)			− 50
Net Cash Flows	$ 0	+ $ 48	+ $ 48

Note that regardless of the index price, you have a guaranteed profit of $48 on no investment. This is an arbitrage—a risk-free profit with no investment.

Clearly, you and other people would continue to do this until the futures price fell to $202. And if it fell below $202, an arbitrage profit would be available by taking exactly the opposite position from that in the example.

In summary, the prices of stock index futures prices must be closely related to current stock index values. If they are not, an index arbitrage profit is available.

In the late 1980s such index arbitrages were common. In fact, on some days index arbitrage represented 20% or more of trading volume on the NYSE. Many people believe that such arbitrage has contributed to stock price volatility and decreased confidence of small investors in their ability to trade at prices not being affected by an arbitrage "program." We will return to index arbitrage in the chapters on options and futures. Index arbitrage also played a vital role on "Black Monday" (discussed below).

Portfolio Insurance. Another technique which became widely used after stock index futures (and options) had been introduced is known as portfolio insurance. Portfolio insurance is a trading strategy which (in concept) ensures a minimum portfolio value if stock prices fall but an increase in portfolio values if stock prices rise. The idea is simple. If stock prices rise, continue to hold stock and perhaps even buy more. But if prices fall, sell a certain amount of stock and place the proceeds in Treasury bills. In addition, you must have a lower stock price limit at which point you are completely out of stock and fully invested in Treasury bills. This full investment in T-bills represents the minimum portfolio value. The trading strategy is similar to using a stop loss order.

In applying this strategy, investors didn't directly sell the stock. Instead, they indirectly sold the stock by selling stock index futures. The benefits of using futures were claimed to be speed and lower transaction costs, but since positions in the stock index futures were equivalent to positions in the actual spot stock index, selling futures had the same net effect as selling spot stock.

Again, portfolio insurance guarantees a fixed minimum portfolio value if stock prices fall but allows for portfolio increases if stock prices rise. Naturally there are costs to insuring a portfolio's value. But a discussion of these must wait until we have studied more about index futures in Chapter 17.

It is easy to understand the concern that many investors felt as larger numbers of institutional investors undertook portfolio insurance programs. The programs call for a sale of stock index futures as stock prices fall. This could easily drive stock futures prices lower. Index arbitrageurs would then step in to buy futures and *sell spot stock*. Many people believe that this would drive spot stock prices down even further, triggering another wave of futures selling from the insurance programs. In short, many people believe that the implementation of portfolio insurance programs can lead to a cascading effect on declining stock prices.

Whether these concerns are valid or not, one thing is clear. The use of stock index options and futures has permanently changed the structure and interrelationships within the security markets.

BLACK MONDAY

On Monday, October 19, 1987, stock prices declined by the largest amount in history. The Dow Jones Industrial Average fell 508 points—down 22.6% in a single day of trading.

Why the decline occurred may never be known. Despite studies by a Presidential Commission, the Securities and Exchange Commission, the New York Stock Exchange, the General Accounting Office, the Senate Banking Committee, and more than six other security market organizations, no consensus opinion has emerged. Many people blame the implementation of portfolio insurance and index arbitrage, but numerous studies and economic theory suggest that these had a minor role in causing the decline. Other people suggest that security prices were severely overvalued and that negative economic news at the time caused investors to substantially reassess their opinions about stock values. Yet the negative economic news at that time was not particularly bad and in some cases not unexpected. In short, there is little agreement on why stock prices fell so precipitously.

The Prior Week

As traumatic as October 19, 1987, was, events of the prior week are often forgotten. However, during that week a number of large equity market declines occurred. These included a 95-point drop in the Dow Jones Industrial Average on Wednesday—a record point decline at that time. The decline on Wednesday has been attributed to a potential tax law change which would have adversely affected merger and acquisition activity. In addition, unfavorable trade deficits were announced, causing the value of the dollar to fall in international markets and domestic U.S. interest rates to increase.

On Thursday and Friday the Dow industrials fell an additional 58 and 108 points, respectively, as interest rates continued to rise and equity investors became more pessimistic. By Friday's close, the Dow industrials were 17% below their August 25, 1987, high—a high which represented a tripling of stock prices during the past five years. Many market professionals were concerned that the end of the five-year bull market was at hand.

Over the weekend, a number of other potentially important events occurred. The Secretary of the Treasury threatened to allow the dollar to fall further against foreign currency. If such a drop were to occur, prices of imports could increase and cause greater domestic U.S. inflation. This suggested that demanded nominal returns on all securities would increase, in turn decreasing the prices of existing securities. In addition, investors in mutual funds who were fearful that the stock market might continue to collapse placed orders to sell their shares in the funds. Although mutual funds usually maintain reserve cash positions sufficient to pay any net share redemptions without being forced to sell securities held in their portfolios, share redemptions were so large that many funds were forced to plan to sell large quantities of shares. One mutual fund organization, for example, had to sell more than 1,000 different stocks. Additional selling pressure also came from foreign investors in the U.S. equity markets who were concerned about further declines in equity prices and the value of the dollar. During the weekend, U.S. brokers received a large accumulation of foreign orders to sell stock on Monday. Finally, many portfolio insurers found that declines in stock prices during the prior week required that they sell large quantities of stock index futures on Monday. Although much futures selling had occurred under the insurance programs during the prior week, considerable demand to sell futures indexes remained.

So, going into Monday, October 19, a selling demand had accumulated from a variety of sources, and a number of negative economic news announcements were made. But nothing suggested that a 22% decline in stock prices was imminent.

Monday, October 19, 1987

An excess of sell orders immediately caused problems at the NYSE's 9:30 A.M. opening. The Dow industrials opened at 2406, down 200 points from Friday's close. This excess sell demand was so large that specialists delayed the opening of many stocks.

For example, even by 10:40 A.M., eight of the 30 Dow industrials had not begun trading because sell orders exceeded buy orders by such a large amount that the specialists were unable to determine a reasonable price at which to begin trading. In addition, all stock index futures markets opened at a deep discount from the spot stock indexes, owing at least in part to heavy futures selling by portfolio insurance programs. One index future opened at a level that was the equivalent of 70 points below the Dow industrials at that time.

Typically, index futures sell at a slight premium above the spot index. In our earlier example we determined that the futures should sell for $202 when the spot index is $200. The large futures discount suggested to many people that the futures prices were, in fact, a better statement of where the spot market should be. Thus, they began to actively sell spot stock, adding to the existing demands to sell. By late morning stock market volume was already 200 million shares (more than an average day's total volume). Although Super Dot was designed to handle a daily volume of as many as 250 million shares, it was simply unable to keep pace with the volume of orders being placed.

Early in the day, index arbitrageurs began to take advantage of the futures' price discount by selling spot stock and buying futures. This, of course, put further downward pressure on stock prices and increased the amount of trading placed into the Super Dot network. If such index arbitrage had been able to continue, spot and futures prices would have been brought into relative equilibrium with each other. This might have meant lower spot stock prices, but the markets would at least have had a better idea of what security values should really be. As long as futures and spot prices differed as much as they did, there was great uncertainty about which was the better predictor. And since trading in individual stocks was being delayed by as much as 45 to 75 minutes, many people tended to believe that the prices shown by the index futures were more accurate.

Index arbitrage virtually stopped in the late morning, however. Since trading in individual stocks was being delayed for about an hour, there was no way for the arbitrageurs to know the price at which they would trade the stock. Price certainty is critical to any well-run arbitrage. In addition, the zero-tick short sale rule prevented the arbitrageurs from selling the stock short when they needed to that morning. The withdrawal of index arbitrageurs eliminated an important market mechanism to bring futures and spot indexes into relative equilibrium.

Late in the morning, demands to buy stocks and futures improved, and prices of both rose. However, beginning with the noon hour and continuing throughout the afternoon, small investors' requests to sell intensified, and prices dropped again. Early in the afternoon, wire services indicated that the SEC chairman was considering a trading halt. This panicked many, and prices continued to drop. Although the SEC issued a statement that it was not going to institute a trading halt, this second announcement had no impact.

By mid-afternoon, the Dow industrials were down more than 300 points, and it was clear that many financial firms, particularly specialists and brokerage firms with large equity inventories, were in danger of bankruptcy. Specialists did not have the capital to purchase excess sell orders and feared huge inventory losses if they did. The same was true of OTC market makers. The result was the virtual elimination of any buying strength from specialists or market makers. A true panic set in, and the Dow industrials fell 130 points in the last thirty minutes of trading. During the day 604 million shares were traded on the NYSE, and the Dow Jones Industrial Average was down 508 points from Friday's close of 2246, a 22.6% drop in one day.

The Aftermath

The financial world was shocked. Prices of stocks around the world had fallen as dramatically as those in this country, and no one could discern any sound reason for equity values to be worth 22.6% less during the course of one day. Rumors abounded of bankrupt brokerage firms, specialist units, and individual investors who had heavily margined stock positions. The stock trading system had been so overwhelmed with orders that it had almost fallen apart. There was also the natural fear of what the rest of the week would bring. And, perhaps most important, no one knew what impacts the market crash would have on the health of the world economy.

The rest of the week did bring problems. On Tuesday, index futures trading was halted in the afternoon and spot stock prices were extremely volatile. By Thursday, however, the storm began to calm, and equity values closed slightly higher at the close of trading on Friday than they had been at Monday's close.

The Studies

As expected, numerous studies were conducted to determine what caused Black Monday. Most of these did not address the economic rationale for such a crash but focused solely on breakdowns in market mechanics. A study by the NYSE tended to blame trading in index futures. In contrast, a study by the Chicago Mercantile Exchange (on which index futures are traded) concluded that futures trading had no role in the volatility of October 19.

The most widely cited study was the Brady report, named after Nicholas Brady, chairman of the committee appointed by President Reagan to analyze the causes of the crash and make recommendations. The Brady report made five proposals:

1. One agency should be given responsibility for coordinating regulatory issues affecting all security markets. This was in reference to the fact that the Securities and Exchange Commission had regulatory power over stock and options markets whereas the Commodity Futures Trading Commission regulated futures markets.
2. A clearing system should be developed which encompasses trades in all security markets.
3. Information systems should be coordinated and disclose prices in all security markets.
4. Margin requirements should be the same for options, stock, and futures. At the time of the study, futures margins were much lower.

5. "Circuit breakers" such as price limits or coordinated trading halts should be applied to all markets.

Proposals 4 and 5 are directly aimed at portfolio insurance and index arbitrage. And in early 1988, the stock index futures markets did impose daily price limits on index futures. Whether these limits will remain is debatable.

Conclusions

We do not know and probably never will know exactly what caused the "Crash of 1987." Portfolio insurance and index arbitrage certainly hastened the price movements within the day. But whether portfolio insurance, irrational investor panic, or a rational revision of stock prices in the face of negative economic news was the cause of the sharp decline will be hotly debated for years.

What is clear is that such days are possible. Major changes in stock prices can occur in a very short time interval. Equity investors must recognize and be willing to accept the short-term risks they face. In addition, the various security markets are closely interrelated, and the options and futures markets can hasten price adjustments in stock prices.

SUMMARY

Transactions in the securities markets can arise in either the primary market, when an issue is first sold to the general public, or in the secondary markets, where members of the public trade between themselves. The major participant in placing securities in the primary market is the investment banker. Investment bankers specialize in primary offerings and are able to provide advice, underwriting, and placement services to security issuers. A consulting fee is paid when the investment banker provides only advice. But when underwriting and distribution services are also provided, the investment banker's return comes in the form of an underwriter's spread. Securities may be privately or publicly placed. Private placement can be cheaper and quicker, but public placement offers increased marketability. Most publicly placed issues must be registered with the Securities and Exchange Commission to ensure full disclosure of information about the issue.

Secondary-market transactions can occur on formal, organized exchanges or in the over-the-counter market. By far the dominant formal exchange market is the New York Stock Exchange. It lists the largest and most actively traded stocks in the United States, and their market values exceed the market values of all stocks traded OTC or on other exchanges. Transactions on the NYSE are handled on the exchange floor by a commission broker who contacts the specialist in a stock to determine existing bid-ask prices. The specialist maintains a book of untraded limit orders (from which a commission is earned if a limit order is traded), but, more important, acts as a dealer in the stock. As a dealer, the specialist absorbs temporary imbalances in the flow of buy and sell orders with the objective of providing continuity in prices over time and depth of liquidity. In the process, the specialist earns a profit from buying at lower bid prices and selling at higher asked prices. Market makers perform an equivalent role in the OTC market.

During the 1980s, major changes occurred in both the procedures used to trade securities and the profits available to exchange members. Most of these changes seem to be the result of increased institutional activity, improved communication facilities, and the introduction of options and futures.

The market crash of 1987 highlights the close interrelationship among the various security markets and the short-term risks that equity investors face. Unfortunately, the true causes of Black Monday are not known.

REVIEW PROBLEM

On Monday, July 3, you ask your broker to buy 200 shares of IBM at market, using the 50% allowed initial margin. The broker charges a commission of 2% and the brokerage firm has a 30% maintenance margin. The broker later calls you and says that the trade was executed at $70 per share. (Note that July 4 is not a business day.)

a. Why might you use a market order as opposed to a limit or stop order?

b. On what date must you pay the brokerage firm? How much must be paid?

c. Since the stock was bought on margin, below what stock price will a margin call be required?

d. If the stock falls to $40 and you intend to deposit more cash into the account to bring it back to the maintenance margin, how much cash must you deposit?

e. If the stock falls to $40 and you intend to sell stock to repay some of the debt to bring it back to the maintenance margin, how many shares must you sell?

Solution

a. A market order assures that a trade takes place at the existing best price. A limit order would be transacted only if prices are at the limit price or better. A stop order specifies a price at which the trade becomes a market order.

b. The settlement day on which cash is paid and securities received is five *business* days after the trade date. Since July 4 is a business holiday, settlement will take place on Tuesday, July 11. At that time you will pay:

Value of securities bought	
200 × $70	= $14,000
Plus commission	
$14,000 × 0.02	280
Total	$14,280
Less margin loan	
0.50 × $14,000	7,000
Net due	$ 7,280

c. Maintenance margin $= \dfrac{\text{Security Value} - \text{Loan}}{\text{Security Value}}$

$$0.30 = \dfrac{(P \times 200) - \$7,000}{P \times 200}$$

$$P = \$50$$

d. Maintenance margin $= \dfrac{\text{Security Value} - \text{Loan} + \text{Cash}}{\text{Security Value} + \text{Cash}}$

$$0.30 = \dfrac{(\$40 \times 200) - \$7,000 + \text{Cash}}{(\$40 \times 200) + \text{Cash}}$$

$$\text{Cash} = \$2,000$$

e. Maintenance margin $= \dfrac{\text{New Security Value} - \text{New Loan}}{\text{New Security Value}}$

$$0.30 = \dfrac{\$40 \times (200 - N) - (\$7,000 - \$40 \times N)}{\$40(200 - N)}$$

$$N = 116.23 \text{ shares (117 actually)}$$

QUESTIONS AND PROBLEMS

1. What are the relative advantages and disadvantages associated with negotiated and competitive underwritings?

2. How does the specialist make a profit?

3. What is an ADR?

4. Discuss the advantages and disadvantages of:
   a. Market orders
   b. Limit orders
   c. Stop orders

5. Carolina Carpets has just sold 50,000 new common shares to the public at an offering price of $70 per share. The underwriter's spread was $2.50, and management has estimated the internal management costs of selling the issue were $37,500. Immediately after the issue the price of the stock rose in the secondary markets to $72, where it has remained for the last week.
   a. Identify the various costs involved in this sale.
   b. These are costs to Carolina Carpets. Who are the recipients?
   c. If management had forced the underwriter to offer the issue at $71 per share, what would the underwriter's response likely have been?
   d. If management had used a competitive bid selection instead of a negotiated selection, would its cost have been lower?

6. Short sellers can theoretically lose an infinite amount of money but, at most, earn 100%.
   a. True or false? Explain.
   b. How might stop orders be used to reduce the risks of short selling?

7. Lawrence Carver has just opened a margin account with a local brokerage firm. The firm has a policy of 60% initial margin and 40% maintenance margin. Mr. Carver initially buys 500 shares of a stock at $40 per share on margin.
   a. What are his initial equity and loan balances?

    b. To what price may the security decline before a margin call is required?

    c. If the stock suddenly falls to $20 per share and the broker requires that the maintenance requirement be restored, how much cash must Lawrence add to his position?

    d. If the stock suddenly falls to $20 per share while Lawrence is on an annual vacation to the Middle East, how many shares must be sold to restore the maintenance margin?

  8. The manager in an underwriting syndicate will often stabilize the market for the issue by pegging prices at the offering price.

    a. Physically, how might this be done?

    b. What might be the underwriter's rationale for market stabilization?

    c. Will the underwriter always be successful in pegging prices?

    d. Various studies have shown that the market prices of new security offerings rise more in the month or two after initial public sale than would be expected given the security's risk. What does this suggest about the original selling price set by underwriters and the underwriters' ability to stabilize prices?

  9. The market value of a stock index "unit" is now $300, and two-month futures on this stock index are selling for $290. There are no dividends expected on the stock index, and the two-month risk-free rate is 2%. Illustrate the arbitrage which is possible. (Assume that you own a unit of the stock index. Thus, if you sell it, you will have full use of the proceeds — that is, you do not have to short sell the stock index.)

  10. Describe what is meant by portfolio insurance and how it is conducted. Why do many people believe that portfolio insurers were a major cause of the stock market collapse on October 19, 1987?

  11. Since the introduction of negotiated rates on both large and small stock transactions in 1975, commissions on large blocks have declined the most. Why?

  12. During the late 1980s memberships on the NYSE were trading at prices in excess of $500,000. Why would a brokerage firm pay such a large price?

DATA ANALYSIS PROBLEM

This is an interesting but relatively easy problem, so try it. You do need to recall some elementary statistics, however. The problem has the following objectives:

- To introduce the data set "QTLYINDX.WK1".
- To examine the probability that a negative return such as that created by Black Monday could have occurred given previous returns.
- To understand how a diversified portfolio would have reduced the impact of Black Monday.

  1. Use a microcomputer spreadsheet program to access the data set entitled "QTLYINDX.WK1". This data set consists of quarterly returns on the following security indexes:

Security Type	Period Covered
Money Market Securities	
Consumer Price Index	1926–1988
T-bills	1972–1988
Certificates of deposit	1972–1988
Commercial paper	1972–1988
DFA one-year bonds	1972–1988

Security Type	*Period Covered*
Fixed-Income Instruments	
Long-term Treasury bonds	1926–1988
Long-term corporate bonds	1926–1988
Long-term govt./corp. bonds	1971–1988
Intermediate-term govt./corp. bonds	1971–1988
Common Stock Indexes:	
Standard & Poor's 500	1926–1988
Wilshire 5000	1971–1988
Small Company Index	1926–1988

Move around the data set to familiarize yourself with it. In particular, find the column in which S&P 500 returns are shown.

2. Find the average quarterly return and the standard deviation of each of the quarterly returns for the Standard & Poor's 500 Index for the time interval 2603 (end of the first quarter in 1926) to 8706 (the quarter-end just prior to the quarter in which Black Monday took place). We will refer to these as:

$\bar{R}_Q$ = average quarterly return between 2603 and 8706
σ_Q = standard deviation of quarterly returns between 2603 and 8706

3. Find the return on the S&P 500 Index during the last quarter of 1987. We will refer to this as R_{8712}. Now find the number of standard deviations by which R_{8712} is away from $\bar{R}_Q$ as follows:

$$\text{Number of Standard Deviations} = (R_{8712} - \bar{R}_Q) \div \sigma_Q$$

Refer to a table of a standardized normal distribution. (There is one in Chapter 15.) Using this table and the number of standard deviations by which R_{8712} is away from $\bar{R}_Q$, estimate the probability that such a return could have occurred. (This test assumes that quarterly returns are normally distributed.)

4. What would have been your rate of return in the fourth quarter of 1987 if you had invested half your money in stocks like those in the S&P 500 and the other half in long-term governments similar to those in the Shearson Lehman Hutton long-term government index? What are the implications of this?

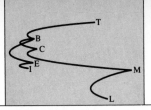

4 Market Indexes and Returns

With this chapter we conclude Part 1, which has provided an overview of security types and security markets. The purpose of this chapter is to examine various security market indexes that track historical prices and rates of return. Knowledge of how these indexes are calculated is important, since underlying each index calculation is an implied portfolio strategy. An examination of historical returns on various security types shows clearly a basic investment fact: greater returns come with greater risk.

MARKET INDEXES

"How's the market today?" This is probably the question that brokers are most often asked by their customers. But why? Why should people be so concerned about moves in aggregate security prices? One reason, of course, is that aggregate market moves have a major impact on the returns of individual stocks. Although the realized return on an individual security can be caused by a large number of economic events, a significant portion of such events affects the prices of all securities. In the capital asset pricing model, for example, a security's sensitivity to such events is captured by its market beta. Numerous studies have shown that somewhere on the order of 30% to 50% of the return variability on an individual common stock is due to aggregate market effects. In broadly diversified portfolios, market effects are even more dominant, accounting for 90% or more of the variability of portfolio returns. Second, the prices of many securities depend upon various market indexes. Examples include stock index futures and options on stock index values. Third, many people believe that the market tends to move in identifiable patterns. They believe the size and direction of current moves can be related to historical movements and used to determine whether today is a good time to buy or sell. Although considerable statistical data refute the notion that prices move in identifiable patterns, the belief remains widely accepted.

A final and more substantive reason for knowing past levels of aggregate security prices is for use as a performance criterion. How well did an actively managed portfolio perform when compared with a broadly diversified, unmanaged portfolio? As we will see in later chapters, many people would argue that *the* best portfolio of risky securities is the *market portfolio*, a portfolio that includes every risky security in the marketplace, with each security held in proportion to the percentage its total market value represents of the total market value of all securities. For example, if IBM common shares represent 5% of the market value of all risky stocks and bonds, then 5% of one's investments in risky securities should be in IBM. Other people argue that differences in tax rates, in how people are affected by inflation, in earnings expectations, in the types of real assets owned, etc., cause investors to have different optimal investment portfolios. Regardless of who is correct, some *baseline investment portfolio* which meets the needs of a particular investor can be identified. Ideally, we would like to measure the performance of an actively managed portfolio against each person's baseline investment portfolio, not against some aggregate market index which could be quite different in investment characteristics. But to do so we would have to identify each person's individual baseline investment portfolio and track it over time — certainly a difficult, time-consuming, and costly process.

The advantages of using aggregate market indexes to measure performance are twofold. First, they are convenient. One needn't spend the time and cost required to identify and track specialized baseline investment portfolios. Instead, a published index which is reasonably close in composition to that of the baseline portfolio can be used. For example, if one's baseline portfolio consists mainly of stocks in the oldest and largest U.S. corporations, the Dow Jones Industrial Average might be used to evaluate performance. Alternatively, if the baseline portfolio consists mainly of stocks in numerous small, regional firms, the NASDAQ Price Index could be used. The baseline portfolio and the market index would not perfectly match each other. However, they might be close enough to develop some judgment about how well the actively managed portfolio performed relative to a proxy for the baseline investment portfolio. Second, a *properly constructed* market index can indicate how the "average" investor and speculator did during, say, the past year. If the returns on such an index are 15% in a given year, then we could think in terms of one half of all investors and speculators earning 15% or more, and one half earning 15% or less. To do this, however, we must have a well-constructed index which covers a large number of stocks. For example, the Dow Jones Industrial Average covers only 30 so-called blue-chip stocks and certainly wouldn't reflect average market results.

A large number of common stock indexes and bond indexes are published and easily available. In the sections below we first illustrate how some of the better-known indexes are calculated and then discuss the strengths and weaknesses of using each as a proxy for baseline investment portfolios. For illustrative purposes, we use the hypothetical data shown in Table 4-1. These data assume there are a total of five common stocks available for investment, all of which are traded on the NYSE. Stocks *A*, *B*, and *C* are shares in three large firms. Stocks *D* and *E* are shares in smaller firms. Ten dates are given which we will consider to be year-ends. During years 3 to 5 and 9 to 10 an economic expansion takes place, whereas in years 6 to 8 a recession occurs. Stock prices shown in Table 4-1 tend to anticipate as well as move with these expansions and recessions.

TABLE 4-1 *Hypothetical Market Value Data*

	Year	*A**	*B*	*C*	*D*	*E*	*A**	*B*	*C*	*D*	*E*	*A**	*B*	*C*	*D*	*E*
			Per-Share Price					*Shares Outstanding*						*Total Market Value*		
	1	$50	$ 50	$50	$ 50	$ 50	100	100	100	20	20	$ 5,000	$ 5,000	$5,000	$1,000	$1,000
	2	25	50	50	50	50	200	100	100	20	20	5,000	5,000	5,000	1,000	1,000
	3	35	60	55	80	80	200	100	100	20	20	7,000	6,000	5,500	1,600	1,600
Expansion	4	21	65	60	100	100	400	100	100	20	20	8,400	6,500	6,000	2,000	2,000
	5	25	70	57	95	95	400	100	100	20	20	10,000	7,000	5,700	1,900	1,900
	6	11	70	57	90	90	800	100	100	20	20	8,800	7,000	5,700	1,800	1,800
Recession	7	14	75	60	140	140	800	100	100	20	20	11,200	7,500	6,000	2,800	2,800
	8	9	85	65	135	135	1,600	100	100	20	20	14,400	8,500	6,500	2,700	2,700
	9	18	95	73	155	155	1,600	100	100	20	20	28,800	9,500	7,300	3,100	3,100
Expansion	10	10	100	78	175	175	3,200	100	100	20	20	32,000	10,000	7,800	3,500	3,500

*Two-for-one stock split in years 2, 4, 6, 8, and 10.

Dow Jones Averages

The Dow Jones Industrial Average (DJIA) is probably the most widely quoted market index and certainly the oldest. It was first published in 1884 by Charles Dow in an attempt to gauge movements in aggregate stock prices, although it was based on the prices of only 11 stocks. Over time additional stocks were added until there were 30 by 1928. Since then a number of substitutions have been made in the stocks included in order to improve the representativeness of the index, but the total number of firms covered has remained at 30. Dow Jones also publishes a transportation index of 20 stocks, a utility index of 15 stocks, and a composite index consisting of the total 65 stocks. Each index is calculated in the same manner.

As originally conceived, the DJIA assumed that a single share was purchased and held in each of the firms making up the average. The market prices of all 30 stocks were summed and the total divided by 30. For example, assume that we wish to create a hypothetical DJIA for stocks *A*, *B*, and *C* in Table 4-1 as of year 1. Summing the prices and dividing by 3, the index value would be $50:

$$\frac{\$50 + \$50 + \$50}{3} = \$50$$

However, an adjustment to this procedure has to be made whenever a firm splits its shares or issues a stock dividend. For example, in year 2 of Table 4-1, stock *A* has a 2-for-1 stock split, and its market price per share drops to $25. It would be silly to simply sum year 2 prices and divide by 3; the index value would exhibit an artificial decline caused solely by the split. There are two ways in which one could account for such splits or stock dividends. One way is to explicitly adjust the numerator by multiplying stock *A*'s price by a *split-adjustment factor*. Following stock *A*'s 2-for-1 split in year 2, this factor would be 2.0, and the revised index would be calculated as follows:

$$\frac{(\$25 \times 2) + \$50 + 50}{3} = \$50$$

The second way is to adjust the denominator so that when an *adjusted divisor* is divided into the post-split sum of stock prices, the index doesn't change. In our example this new divisor would be 2.5 instead of the original 3.0:

$$\text{Old Index Value Prior to Split} = \frac{\text{Sum of Prices After the Split}}{\text{New Divisor}}$$

$$\$50 = \frac{\$25 + \$50 + \$50}{\text{New Divisor}}$$

$$\text{New Divisor} = \frac{\$125}{\$50} = 2.5$$

The DJIA is calculated using the adjusted-divisor approach. Any time a stock splits or issues a stock dividend of 10% or more, the divisor is recalculated. Stock dividends of less than 10% are ignored in the index calculation and treated instead as additions to reported cash dividends. These policies can have major effects upon the DJIA series, and many commentators believe they have tended to impose a downward bias on the growth of the Dow indexes. The impact of not adjusting for small stock dividend distributions is easy to see. The value decline in a share associated with small stock dividends is lost forever in the price index. For example, if an 8% stock dividend is paid on a share selling for $100 prior to the split, the resulting stock price of $92.59 ($100 ÷ 1.08) would be interpreted as a decline in the DJIA. Perhaps more important is a bias associated with adjusting the denominator. This adjustment scheme has the net effect of reducing the investment in the split shares and increasing the investment in the nonsplit shares. To see this, consider year 1 for stocks *A*, *B*, and *C*. The index value of $50 is composed of $16⅔ of each stock *A*, *B*, and *C*:

$$\$50 = \frac{\$50 + \$50 + \$50}{3}$$

$$= \$16\tfrac{2}{3} + \$16\tfrac{2}{3} + \$16\tfrac{2}{3}$$

A given percentage change in the per-share price of any security has an equal impact on the index. *Any* of the shares could fall by 10%, and the index value would decline to $48⅓. However, after the split, stock *A*'s dollar representation drops to $10, while stock *B*'s and stock *C*'s dollar representations increase to $20:

$$\$50 = \frac{\$25 + \$50 + \$50}{2.5}$$

$$= \$10 + \$20 + \$20$$

Now a given *percentage* change in the price of stock *A* has a smaller impact on the index than that of stocks *B* and *C*. *Any time a stock splits, its relative importance in the DJIA decreases and the relative importance of nonsplit stocks increases.* This is akin to an assumption that the new shares obtained in a split were sold and the proceeds were used to buy additional shares of the nonsplit stocks. If shares which undergo splits are those whose prices increase the most over time, this would result in a policy of continually selling shares of high-priced growth stocks and buying shares of low-priced growth stocks. The DJIA would be biased downward from the value which would have been obtained if the numerator-adjustment approach had been used instead. For example, if the divisor-adjustment technique is used to create a DJIA on stocks *A*, *B*, and *C* at year 10, the index would be $102.28. Alternatively, if a split-adjustment factor had been applied to the numerator, the index would have been $166.00.

The exact impact of using the divisor adjustment on current levels of the Dow is hard to determine. However, the current divisor has declined from 30 in the 1920s to about 0.7 as of early 1989. A study by Milne showed that the published divisor-adjusted value of 969 at the end of 1965 would have translated to a split-adjusted value of 1086. The manner in which splits and stock dividends are handled does seem to bias the price growth of the DJIA downward.

Another criticism of the DJIA has to do with its representativeness. Thirty large, mature (so-called blue-chip) stocks are included. Critics argue that the sample of 30 stocks cannot reasonably measure market value changes of the typical stock. In fact, studies of past price movements show that the DJIA has not been as variable as other price indexes, nor has it shown as high a growth rate.

Standard & Poor's Averages

Standard & Poor's Corporation publishes a variety of indexes which largely overcome the problems inherent in the Dow averages by including a larger and more representative number of stocks as well as by concentrating upon changes in a firm's *total market value* instead of per-share values. At present an industrial average (400 industrial firms), a utility average (40 utility firms), a transportation average (20 transportation firms), a financial average (20 firms), and a 500-stock composite index are prepared. In addition to these broad market indexes, S&P provides over 90 individual industry averages. Our discussions below assume we are speaking of the 500-stock composite index. All S&P indexes are calculated in the same manner.

To calculate an index value, the *total market value* of all stocks being examined is calculated as of a base period. At present, the base period used by S&P is the average value of 1941–43. The total market value of all firms is calculated at a future date and divided by this base-period value. The result can be thought of as a *price relative* (or wealth ratio) — the future value of investing $1 in a portfolio containing all stocks in the index *weighted in proportion to their total market values*. Finally, the price relative is multiplied by an *index number* set equal to 10.0 for the 1941–43 period. For the S&P Composite Index (the S&P 500) the calculation is as follows:

Standard & Poor's Composite Index

$$\text{S\&P Composite Index}_t = \left(\frac{\sum_{i=1}^{500} P_{it} Q_{it}}{\sum_{i=1}^{500} P_{i1} Q_{i1}} \right) \times 10 \qquad \textbf{(4.1)}$$

where P_{i1} = per-share price of stock i at the base date 1, P_{it} = per-share price of stock i at the index date t, Q_{i1} = number of shares of stock i outstanding at base date 1, and Q_{it} = number of shares of stock i outstanding at index date t.

For example, if we were to calculate the year 2 S&P index for stocks A, B, and C in Table 4-1 (using year 1 as the base date), we would first find their base date market values as follows:

$$\sum_{i=1}^{3} P_{i1}Q_{i1} = \$50(100) + \$50(100) + \$50(100) = \$15,000$$

Second, as of year 2 the *total* value of the three stocks remains unchanged at $15,000:

$$\sum_{i=1}^{3} P_{i2}Q_{i2} = \$25(200) + \$50(100) + \$50(100) = \$15,000$$

So the year 2 index value would be:

$$\frac{\$15,000}{\$15,000} \times 10 = 10$$

Using the same approach, year 10's index would be 33.20:

$$\frac{\$10(3200) + \$100(100) + \$78(100)}{\$15,000} \times 10 = 33.20$$

The S&P indexes differ from the Dow Jones indexes in three major respects. First, they include a more representative sample of the typical common stock by increasing the number of securities and by including nonindustrial, smaller firms. Nonetheless, most of the companies used are relatively large firms traded on the NYSE (exceptions are OTC-traded insurance and bank stocks), so numerous smaller OTC, AMEX, and regional stocks are excluded. The S&P indexes are dominated by the largest domestic U.S. firms. Second, a different weighting system is used. The Dow Jones indexes weight each share's relative importance according to their per-share prices. That is, a $100 stock is treated as five times more important than a $20 stock, regardless of each firm's total market value. In contrast, S&P weights each stock according to its respective total market value. We show later how these weighting schemes have important implications for performance measurement. Finally, *all* stock splits and stock dividends are automatically accounted for in the numerator of the S&P indexes because total market values are used. For example, in year 2, when stock A had a split, its price fell by 50%; but because the number of shares outstanding doubled, there was no change in the stock's total market value and no change in the S&P index.

The New York Stock Exchange Index

In 1966 the New York Stock Exchange began publishing its own market index. The index is a total-market-value-weighted index similar to the various S&P indexes. It differs from the S&P Composite Index in two respects, however. First, all stocks listed on the NYSE are included, whereas S&P includes only the largest NYSE firms (plus a few OTC firms). Second, the NYSE has a base index value of 50 as of December 31, 1965. The index value of 50 was chosen to be close to the price of an average share on that date ($53.33). In addition to the composite index of all NYSE stocks, various subindexes are also available. These include an industrial, a utility, a transportation, and a financial index.

Using the data in Table 4-1, we could differentiate the S&P index from the NYSE index by including the smaller stocks D and E in an NYSE-equivalent index. Using year 1 as the base year, the year 10 NYSE index would be 167.06:

$$\frac{\$10(3200) + \$100(100) + \$78(100) + \$175(20) + \$175(20)}{\$50(100) + \$50(100) + \$50(100) + \$50(20) + \$50(20)} \times 50 = 167.06$$

Note that between years 1 and 10 our NYSE-equivalent index grew from 50 to 167.06, or by 14.34% per year.[1] On the other hand, the S&P index grew from 10 to 33.20, or by 14.26%. The slight difference is caused by the inclusion of stocks in the NYSE index which are not in the S&P index. Over long periods of time, the actual historical growth rates of the NYSE Composite Index do tend to be slightly greater than those of the S&P Composite Index.

The AMEX Index

In 1973 the American Stock Exchange instituted a market value index similar to that of the NYSE and Standard & Poor's. Data back to 1969 were later made available. A variety of subindexes are also available by economic sector, including high technology, capital goods, consumer goods, service, retail, etc.

NASDAQ Indexes

In 1971 the National Association of Security Dealers began using its automated quotation system to determine various market value indexes on OTC stocks. Over 2,000 securities are included in its composite index. Subindexes include industrials, banks, insurance, other finance, transportation, and utilities. The indexes are similar to the S&P and NYSE indexes. The base period is February 1971, and the base index is 100. NASDAQ indexes are not available for periods prior to 1971. The only pre-1971 OTC index is an average of 35 larger OTC firms prepared by the National Quotation Bureau.

The Value Line Index

The Value Line Index was first published in 1963 and was subsequently backdated to 1961. Its base index is 100 as of June 1961. A composite index, an industrial index, a rail index, and a utility index are available. Unlike the other indexes discussed, the

---

[1] $167.06 = 50(1 + R)^9$

$(1 + R)^9 = 167.06 \div 50$

$\qquad R = \sqrt[9]{167.06 \div 50} - 1$

$\qquad R = 14.34\%$

Value Line indexes are based upon geometric means of relative price movements. First, the closing price of each stock is expressed as a ratio of the preceding day's price. These *price relatives* are then multiplied together and the Nth root of the product is found, where N refers to the number of stocks being considered. Finally, this *geometric average price relative* is multiplied by the prior day's index value to obtain today's index. Stock splits and stock dividends are handled by making an appropriate adjustment to the security's price from the prior day.

To illustrate these calculations, consider a Value Line Index based on stocks A through E in Table 4-1. The base date will again be year 1 and an index base of 100 will be used. At the end of year 2, the price relative for each stock would be 1.0. For example, adjusting for stock A's 2:1 split, its price relative would be:

$$\text{Price Relative}_A = \frac{\text{Price at Year 2}}{\text{Adjusted Price at Year 1}} = \frac{\$25}{\$25} = 1.0$$

Multiplying the five price relatives and taking the 5th root results in a geometric average relative equal to 1.0:

$$\begin{aligned}\text{Geometric Average} &= \sqrt[5]{(\text{Price Relative}_A)(\text{Price Relative}_B)\ldots(\text{Price Relative}_E)} \\ \text{Price Relative} & \end{aligned}$$

$$= \sqrt[5]{(1.0)(1.0)(1.0)(1.0)(1.0)} = 1.0$$

Of course, the Value Line Index at year 2 would remain at 100.

$$\text{Value Line Index}_t = \left(\begin{array}{c}\text{Geometric Average} \\ \text{Price Relative}\end{array}\right)_t \times (\text{Value Line Index}_{t-1})$$

$$= (1.0)(100) = 100$$

Year 3 provides a more complex situation. In that case the Value Line Index would increase to 136.45:

$$\sqrt[5]{\left(\frac{35}{25} \times \frac{60}{50} \times \frac{55}{50} \times \frac{80}{50} \times \frac{80}{50}\right)} \times 100 = (1.3645)(100) = 136.45$$

The use of this geometric averaging process has an impact upon how the Value Line series changes over time and how these changes relate to changes in other indexes. These impacts are discussed later.

Other U.S. Equity Indexes

The indexes discussed above are among the more widely known and used. Other price indexes include the following:

1. The *Wilshire 5000 Equity Index* is a value-weighted index published by Wilshire Associates. The index represents the total market value of all NYSE and AMEX stocks plus the larger OTC stocks. As its name suggests, the index consists of approximately 5,000 stocks.
2. *Moody's Composite Average* is a valued-weighted index of 200 stocks.

3. The *New York Times Industrial Average* is an index based on 25 stocks. It is calculated similarly to the DJIA, but it uses the split-adjustment factor in its numerator instead of the divisor-adjustment technique.

Stock Indexes of Non-U.S. Countries

All industrially developed countries have an exchange where local stocks and bonds
are traded. But the largest security exchanges outside the United States are the Tokyo
Stock Exchange and the London Stock Exchange. Security indexes which track values of stocks on these exchanges are the Nikkei Stock Average and the Tokyo Stock
Exchange Index for Tokyo and the Financial Times Index for London. The Nikkei
index is calculated in the same way as the Dow Jones indexes but is applied to 225
stocks. In contrast, the Tokyo Stock Exchange Index is a value-weighted index similar to the S&P indexes, applied to 1,000 issues. The *Financial Times*, a London newspaper which prepares a variety of security indexes for shares traded on the London
Stock Exchange, bases its indexes on geometric averages of stock price relatives as
Value Line does.

Perhaps the most useful international indexes are prepared by Morgan Stanley
Capital International (MSCI). MSCI creates stock indexes for more than 20 countries.
Each index consists of stocks for which a relatively liquid market exists and generally represents 60% or more of the stocks traded in a given country. The indexes are
return indexes, however, as opposed to the price indexes discussed previously in this
chapter — that is, rates of return are reported which include both price changes and
cash dividend receipts. These index returns together with other useful data are published monthly in a document entitled *Morgan Stanley Capital International Perspective*. A sample page is shown in Figure 4-1.

Unfortunately, the MSCI Perspective is not easily available to the public. However, a summary index called the Europe, Australia, Far East Index (EAFE —
pronounced E-FEE) is widely published in the financial press. Returns on this index
are available back to 1969.

Index Comparisons

Table 4-2 provides year-end values for seven major security indexes between 1960 and
1987. Figure 4-2 shows a plot of standardized index values. Each index is standardized to a level of 100 as of December 1987.

A comparison of trends and volatility in each of these indexes is difficult since the
results can depend upon the time interval selected, and, more important, none of the
indexes provides any information about dividend distributions — a major portion of
security returns. However, the figures do suggest a number of points which have been
confirmed by empirical studies using data over longer time spans. In particular:

1. Percentage price changes in each of the indexes are highly correlated with each
other, regardless of whether the percentage changes are calculated over daily,

FIGURE 4-1 *Sample Page from* **Morgan Stanley Capital International Perspective**

INTERNATIONAL STOCK MARKET TRENDS – 29 February 1988

VALUATION

PERFORMANCE

% change in stock market indices

P/BV	P/CE	P/E	Yield			this month	since 1.1.88	from high
				INTERNATIONAL INDICES (in US dollar)				
2.30	7.6	19.6	2.4	THE WORLD INDEX		5.6	8.0	-11.1
1.83	7.0	14.4	3.6	NORTH AMERICA		4.0	7.8	-21.2
2.68	8.2	25.0	1.8	EAFE (EUROPE, AUSTRALIA, FAR EAST)		6.6	8.3	-6.3
1.55	5.5	12.2	4.0	EUROPE		5.7	1.1	-19.3
4.19	14.6	49.2	0.7	PACIFIC		7.0	12.3	-2.0
4.45	15.8	54.8	0.6	FAR EAST		7.3	13.0	-0.9
				SPECIAL AREAS (in US dollar)				
2.61	8.1	23.8	1.9	THE WORLD INDEX ex USA		6.5	8.0	-7.0
1.70	6.5	13.3	3.8	THE WORLD INDEX ex JAPAN		4.4	4.7	-20.4
1.54	5.7	12.0	4.0	EAFE ex JAPAN		4.9	0.7	-22.1
1.50	8.0	11.8	3.9	PACIFIC ex JAPAN		-0.9	-2.0	-40.6
2.36	7.6	20.9	2.3	THE WORLD INDEX ex THE UK		6.2	9.0	-10.9
2.91	8.4	29.8	1.4	EAFE ex THE UK		7.7	10.0	-5.4
1.43	4.6	12.2	3.7	EUROPE ex THE UK		10.3	2.9	-20.0
				NATIONAL INDICES (in US dollar)				
1.79	4.9	12.6	5.9	BELGIUM	1	24.8	29.2	-1.5
1.50	4.4	10.6	3.5	FRANCE	2	20.8	2.2	-28.5
1.63	3.9	11.9	4.2	GERMANY	3	15.7	1.5	-27.2
1.48	3.6	9.1	2.9	NORWAY	4	8.1	6.4	-39.0
4.64	16.3	59.9	0.5	JAPAN	5	7.5	13.3	0.0
1.63	7.0	12.9	3.1	CANADA	6	6.4	4.7	-18.6
1.31	7.0	16.0	2.6	SWITZERLAND	7	5.9	-0.5	-24.0
1.55	3.8	13.2	3.0	ITALY	8	5.7	-2.7	-32.2
1.09	5.5	28.6	2.5	DENMARK	9	4.1	3.8	-7.2
1.84	7.0	14.5	3.6	USA	10	3.9	8.0	-21.1
1.03	4.2	9.7	5.2	NETHERLANDS	11	3.8	1.8	-21.1
1.96	6.9	12.1	2.5	SWEDEN	12	3.6	13.6	-17.6
1.33	8.4	15.0	2.3	FINLAND	13	1.9	-2.3	-12.6
1.99	10.0	11.3	4.1	HONGKONG	14	1.8	4.4	-38.4
1.17	4.8	16.0	3.8	SPAIN	15	0.9	4.2	-36.1
1.30	6.6	10.1	4.7	AUSTRALIA	16	0.7	-5.7	-44.8
1.60	5.7	25.3	2.6	AUSTRIA	17	0.2	-13.5	-18.1
1.77	7.3	12.1	4.5	UNITED KINGDOM	18	-0.6	-1.5	-20.9
1.52	10.9	22.7	1.7	SINGAPORE/MALAYSIA	19	-2.3	5.3	-37.9
1.08	4.9	5.5	7.5	NEW ZEALAND	20	-16.3	-19.3	-59.8

1988 range high	low	month end index					
			OTHER INDICES (in US dollar)				
101.2	93.4	100.7	FINLAND (FREE)		5.4	0.7	-0.5
115.2	98.9	113.8	SWEDEN (FREE)		3.8	13.8	-1.2
100.7	92.0	99.4	SWITZERLAND (ex REGISTERED SHARES)		6.3	-0.6	-1.3
108.4	96.7	108.4	*EAFE (FREE)		6.6	8.4	0.0
100.0	97.7	99.3	JORDAN		0.5	-0.7	-0.1
108.8	93.5	100.0	MALAYSIA		-5.0	0.0	-8.1
170.2	85.6	170.2	MEXICO		34.9	70.2	0.0
167.8	90.6	167.8	MEXICO (FREE)		28.5	67.8	0.0
134.3	100.0	134.3	THAILAND		17.1	34.3	0.0

* excludes non free shares in Finland and Sweden, and registered shares in Switzerland.

Valuation: P/BV: price to book value ratio; P/CE: price to cash earnings (earnings + depreciation) ratio; P/E: price to earnings ratio; Yield: gross dividend yield. Performance: % changes are calculated on the Morgan Stanley Capital International stock market indices-adjusted for foreign exchange fluctuations relative to the US Dollar. Performances in local currencies and exchange fluctuations are shown for each country on pages 10 to 37. Last column indicates % change from highest index level reached since 1.1.70, except for Finland and New Zealand (since 1.1.82) and other indices (since 1.1.88).

TABLE 4-2 *Major Index Price Levels Year-End Values, 1960–1987*

Year End	S&P Composite	DJIA	NYSE Composite	AMEX	Wilshire 5000	NASDAQ Composite
1987	247.08	1938	138.23	260	2417	330.47
1986	242.17	1895	138.58	263	2434	348.00
1985	211.28	1546	121.58	246	2164	324.93
1984	167.24	1211	96.38	204	1702	247.35
1983	165.34	1258	95.18	223	1723	278.60
1982	141.24	1046	81.03	170	1451	232.41
1981	122.30	875	71.11	160	1286	195.84
1980	135.76	963	77.86	174	1404	202.34
1979	107.94	838	61.95	123	1100	150.83
1978	96.11	805	53.62	75	923	117.98
1977	95.10	831	52.50	64	888	105.05
1976	107.46	1004	57.88	55	954	97.88
1975	80.19	852	47.64	42	784	77.62
1974	68.56	616	36.13	30	590	59.82
1973	97.55	850	51.82	45	862	92.19
1972	118.05	1020	64.48	64	1090	133.72
1971	102.09	890	56.43	58	949	114.12
1970	92.15	838	50.23	49	830	
1969	92.06	800	51.53	60		
1968	103.86	943	58.90			
1967	96.47	905	53.83			
1966	80.33	785	43.72			
1965	92.43	969	50.00			
1964	84.75	874	45.65			
1963	75.02	762	39.92			
1962	63.10	652	33.81			
1961	71.55	731	38.39			
1960	58.11	615	30.39			

weekly, monthly, or annual periods. The greatest correlation appears to be between the S&P Composite and the NYSE Composite. The poorest correlation appears between the NASDAQ Composite and all other indexes, but the correlation is still very high.

2. The variability of the indexes differs. The NASDAQ and AMEX indexes are the most variable, whereas the DJIA, S&P, and NYSE are reasonably similar. (Variability is usually measured as the standard deviation of percentage price changes.) Recognizing the different composition of stocks in each index, we would expect this.

3. Long-run compound annual growth rates differ. The DJIA shows the lowest growth—as one might expect, given the types of firms making up the index plus the bias introduced by the divisor-adjustment technique. Growth of the S&P and NYSE indexes is virtually identical, although the NYSE has grown slightly faster (perhaps because of the addition of smaller, more risky firms in the NYSE index). The NASDAQ and AMEX indexes have shown the greatest average annual percentage growth.

FIGURE 4-2 *Standardized Index Values (1988 = 100)*

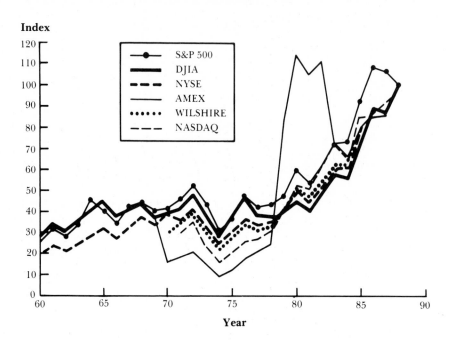

Implicit Portfolio Strategies

As noted earlier in the chapter, ideally one would wish to identify and track the return performance of some baseline investment portfolio in order to determine how well or how poorly an actively managed portfolio compares. Market indexes represent potential proxies for such baseline portfolios. In addition, if properly constructed, they can provide information about the average returns earned by all speculators and investors. None of the indexes, however, should be thought of as being the "market" portfolio of all risky securities.

A simple examination of the trends and volatility in each of the price indexes is inadequate, since none of the indexes explicitly accounts for cash dividend distributions. If any of the indexes is to be used as a proxy for the baseline equity portfolio, total rates of return will have to be calculated by adding any dividend returns to returns associated with index price changes. Yet even after dividends are accounted for, each index will perform differently because of the manner in which prices are averaged and differences in security compositions. In fact, each index corresponds to a particular type of investment strategy.

1. Returns earned on the DJIA are associated with the following buy-hold strategy:
   a. Restrict your holdings to 30 blue-chip stocks.
   b. Initially buy one share of each stock.
   c. When cash dividends are received, allocate the total receipts across all stocks in proportion to the *per-share* value of each stock.

d. When stock dividends or splits are received, sell the new shares and allocate the proceeds across all stocks in proportion to the (post-split) *per-share* value of each stock.

A number of problems are associated with actually following such a policy. First, it makes little sense to weight one's holdings ten times heavier in a $100 stock than in a $10 stock, particularly if the *total* market values of the firms are similar. Second, the policy is not *macroconsistent*; that is, not every investor could follow such a policy. Share supplies and share demands simply wouldn't balance. In addition, many people question the policy of continually switching out of stocks which split and into stocks which haven't split. Finally, not many people have a baseline stock investment portfolio which consists of only 30 blue-chip firms. Even though the DJIA is a widely followed series, it is a poor index on which to judge performance.

2. Returns on the S&P Composite are associated with the following strategy:
   a. Purchase shares in 500 of the largest domestic U.S. corporations.
   b. Weight your holdings of each based upon the total market value of each.
   c. Allocate cash dividends in the same manner — based on each firm's total market value.
   d. When stock dividends or splits are received, keep the new shares.

There are two problems associated with this type of baseline portfolio. First, it is restricted to the 500 largest domestic U.S. firms. Smaller domestic firms and all firms based outside the United States are excluded. Second, some investors may not want to weight security holdings based upon total market value. For example, IBM employees might wish to underweight IBM shares, and people in high tax brackets might wish to underweight stocks with high-dividend yields such as those of public utilities. Nonetheless, the S&P Composite is a much better performance guideline than the DJIA. The sample is more representative and splits are more reasonably handled. Most important, the S&P is macroconsistent. Every investor could follow such a policy, and shares supplied would equal shares demanded.

The NYSE, AMEX, and NASDAQ indexes follow investment guidelines identical to those of the S&P and differ only in the types of equity shares considered.

3. The Value Line Index is associated with a much different investment strategy. In particular:
   a. Select about 1,400 actively traded stocks.
   b. Initially purchase an *equal dollar amount* of each security.
   c. Each day sell off the portfolio and repurchase an equal dollar amount of shares at then-existing prices.

This policy is rather implausible. The *initial* equal dollar investment in each stock is fine (although it does make the policy macroinconsistent). The problem arises with the assumed daily rebalancing. Transaction costs would be exorbitant. Notice also that this policy requires that one sell off stocks with price increases and buy those with price decreases. While nothing is wrong with this in theory, it does mean that if the market continues to rise for a long time, the shares that rise the most are sold and those that rise the least are bought. The opposite is true in a falling market. Shares that fall the most are bought and those that fall the least are sold.

The portfolio rebalancing assumed by the Value Line Index is clearly a theoretical construct, not one that could actually be followed in practice.

BOND MARKET INDEXES

In contrast to equity market indexes, which focus upon price levels, bond market indexes focus upon rates of return earned on various categories of bonds.

The Shearson Lehman Hutton Indexes

Shearson Lehman Hutton prepares an extensive set of bond indexes of daily and monthly returns. The indexes differ from each other in two basic ways: (1) whether the issuer was the U.S. government, a corporation, or the Government National Mortgage Association and (2) the maturity of the bond issues. The following are representative of the Shearson Lehman Hutton return indexes:

1. The *Government Bond Index* includes all publicly issued, nonconvertible domestic debt of the U.S. government and its agencies. Only bonds and notes with a principal balance of $1 million or more and a maturity of one year or more are included. Flower bonds and pass-throughs are excluded.
2. The *Corporate Bond Index* includes all publicly issued, fixed-rate, nonconvertible debt of industrial, utility, and finance companies. Bonds included must have a moderate- to high-quality default rating, have a maturity of one year, and have a minimum principal value of $1 million.
3. The *Treasury Bond Index* is similar to the above two but is restricted to issues of the U.S. Treasury.
4. The *Government/Corporate Bond Index* consists of the Government Bond Index plus the Corporate Bond Index.
5. The *Mortgage-Backed Securities Index* includes all fixed-rate security issues which are backed by mortgage pools of the Government National Mortgage Association, the Federal Home Loan Mortgage Corporation, or the Federal National Mortgage Association.
6. The *Yankee Bond Index* includes all U.S. dollar–denominated bonds which are issued or fully backed by non–United States governments. Since these are sold in the United States, they are all registered with the SEC.

Information about the characteristics of these indexes is shown in Table 4-3. Probably the best index to use if one wishes to know what the return on a "typical" bond would have been is the Government/Corporate Bond Index.

TABLE 4-3 *Descriptive Characteristics of Shearson Lehman Hutton Bond Indexes as of July 31, 1988*

	Market Value (Billions)	Average Maturity	Duration*
Government Bond			
Intermediate	$ 955	3.77	3.04
Long Term	274	22.9	9.30
Total	1,229		
Corporate Bond			
Intermediate	207	5.48	4.16
Long Term	201	21.18	8.65
Total	408		
Treasury Bond Index			
Intermediate	792	3.75	3.02
Long Term	264	22.85	9.18
Total	1,056		
Government/Corporate Index			
Intermediate	1,164	4.08	3.24
Long Term	475	22.18	9.02
Total	1,639		
Mortgage Backed Securities			
GNMA	298	8.53	4.76
FNMA	118	7.61	4.45
FHLMC	185	7.22	4.35
Total	601		
Yankee Bond Index			
Intermediate	24	5.68	4.23
Long Term	27	20.36	8.61
Total	51		

*Duration is defined in Chapter 11. It is a measure of the average date at which cash flows are received which considers both par value at maturity and intermediate coupon flows.

The Salomon Brothers Index

Salomon Brothers prepares an index which is widely used to judge bond performance. This index includes all high-grade corporate bonds with a minimum maturity of twelve years. Since the index is restricted to nongovernment long-term bonds, it is not as representative of the typical bond return as the Shearson Lehman Hutton Government/Corporate Bond Index would be.

MARKET RETURNS

With the exception of bond indexes, each of the market indexes discussed so far measures historical *price levels* associated with a particular portfolio strategy. When price changes are combined with the dividends paid by each index, historical returns can be calculated. It is these returns which we examine now. One dominant fact will become obvious: Greater returns are earned only by accepting greater risks.

Return Measurement

Before we examine each index's past rates of return, we must define some basic return measures. These include the following:

1. Holding period return
2. Unit value series
3. Arithmetic average return
4. Geometric average return

The Holding Period Return. In Chapter 1 we defined the rate of return obtained during a given time period to be:

Single-Period Rate of Return

$$\frac{\text{Single-Period}}{\text{Return}} = \frac{\text{Percentage}}{\text{Price}} + \frac{\text{Percentage}}{\text{Cash}} \quad \textbf{(4.2)}$$
$$\text{Appreciation} \quad \text{Return}$$

$$R_t = \frac{P_t + P_{t-1}}{P_{t-1}} + \frac{C_t}{P_{t-1}}$$

For example, on September 30, 1987, the S&P 500 Index was $321.83. By December 31, 1987, it had declined to $247.08, and $2.2025 in dividends had been paid. Thus, the rate of return for the fourth quarter of 1987 would be calculated to be −22.54%:

$$\frac{\$247.08 - \$321.83}{\$321.83} + \frac{\$2.2025}{\$321.83} = -0.2254$$

However, an important assumption is made when the return is calculated in this fashion. It is assumed that all dividends are paid at the terminal date t. If this is not the case, then Equation 4.2 does not fairly measure the return earned. For example, on December 31, 1982, the S&P 500 was at $140.64. Between then and December 31, 1987, total dividends of $38.86 were paid. Would it then be fair to say that a five-year return of 103% was earned?[2] Clearly not, since the dividend payments were made throughout the five-year interval and, when *reinvested*, would have earned a profit which is not reflected in the 103%. If one is calculating returns for relatively short holding periods (say, one quarter), little harm might be done by assuming all dividends are received at t. But over periods of six months or more, this assumption leads to unacceptable inaccuracies.

The conceptual solution is easy to understand. Simply calculate holding period returns between all dividend-payment periods and then *link* them to find the return for the time period desired. For example, assume that the $2.2025 in dividends paid on the S&P 500 during the fourth quarter of 1987 were paid in three equal installments at the end of each month. Month-end S&P 500 prices, dividends, and monthly rates of return would be as follows:

---

[2] $\dfrac{\$247.08 - 140.64}{\$140.64} + \dfrac{\$38.86}{\$140.64} = 1.03$

	9/30/87	10/30/87	11/30/87	12/30/87
S&P 500	$321.83	$251.79	$230.30	$247.08
Dividend	NA	$0.73417	$0.73417	$0.73417
Return in Month	NA	−21.535%	−8.243%	7.605%

To link the returns we add 1.0 to each return and compound the series. Finally, 1.0 is subtracted to yield the quarter's rate of return:

$$[(0.78465)(0.91757)(1.07605)] - 1.0 = -0.2253, \text{ or } -22.53\%$$

The return of −22.53% is *slightly* different from the original return of −22.54% obtained when we assumed all dividends were paid at quarter-end. But this slight difference will increase when periods greater than a quarter are used and when returns are compounded with other returns over time.

There are two conclusions to draw. First, holding period returns might not be exactly equal to Equation 4.2 *if* dividends (or coupon interest on bonds) are paid at dates other than the terminal date. Second, rates of return which are published by various investment advisory firms on indexes such as the S&P 500 will often differ from one another as a result of differing assumptions about when dividends are paid. Some organizations go so far as to calculate daily returns and link them, whereas others assume all dividends are paid at quarter-end.

Unit Value Series. Given that you have a series of holding period returns, it is often useful to create what is known as a *unit value* series. To do so, some base number (say, 1.0) is assigned to the date preceding the first holding period return. This base number is then compounded by each period's return:

$$UV_T = 1.0(1 + R_1)(1 + R_2) \ldots (1 + R_T)$$

Unit Value
$$UV_T = 1.0\left[\prod_{t=1}^{T} (1 + R_t)\right] \tag{4.3}$$

In Table 4-4, yearly returns and a unit value series are shown for the S&P 500 Index. December 1925 is set as the base period with a unit value of 1.0. During 1926, the return on the S&P 500 was 11.61%, which results in a growth of the unit value to 1.116. During 1927 this unit value is compounded by the 1927 return of 37.48% to yield a unit value of 1.534. In short, the unit value series simply tracks the growth of an initial dollar investment.

Arithmetic Versus Geometric Averages. What was the typical yearly return on an investment in the S&P 500 between 1925 and 1987? That depends on whether we want to know the *average of the yearly returns* or the *average compound return*, which would have caused a $1.00 investment in 1925 to grow to $348.669 in 1987. They are not the same.

The average yearly return was 12.01% and is calculated as follows:

TABLE 4-4 *Unit Values and Yearly Returns of the S&P 500, 1925–1987*

Year	Unit Value	Return (%)	Year	Unit Value	Return (%)
1925	1.000	NA	1957	17.634	−10.79
1926	1.116	11.61	1958	25.282	43.37
1927	1.534	37.48	1959	28.311	11.98
1928	2.204	43.61	1960	28.441	0.46
1929	2.018	−8.41	1961	36.089	26.89
1930	1.516	−24.9	1962	32.938	−8.73
1931	0.859	−43.35	1963	40.442	22.78
1932	0.788	−8.2	1964	47.119	16.51
1933	1.214	53.97	1965	52.985	12.45
1934	1.196	−1.43	1966	47.660	−10.05
1935	1.766	47.66	1967	59.093	23.99
1936	2.366	33.92	1968	65.641	11.08
1937	1.537	−35.02	1969	60.068	−8.49
1938	2.016	31.14	1970	62.489	4.03
1939	2.007	−0.42	1971	71.437	14.32
1940	1.811	−9.78	1972	84.996	18.98
1941	1.601	−11.58	1973	72.527	−14.67
1942	1.927	20.33	1974	53.336	−26.46
1943	2.426	25.91	1975	73.183	37.21
1944	2.905	19.73	1976	90.637	23.85
1945	3.963	36.41	1977	84.129	−7.18
1946	3.643	−8.07	1978	89.657	6.57
1947	3.850	5.7	1979	106.171	18.42
1948	4.063	5.51	1980	140.582	32.41
1949	4.826	18.79	1981	133.679	−4.91
1950	6.358	31.74	1982	162.300	21.41
1951	7.885	24.02	1983	198.833	22.51
1952	9.332	18.35	1984	211.300	6.27
1953	9.240	−0.98	1985	279.275	32.17
1954	14.102	52.62	1986	331.277	18.62
1955	18.550	31.54	1987	348.669	5.25
1956	19.767	6.56			

Arithmetic Average Return

$$\bar{R} = \frac{\sum_{t=1}^{N}(R_t)}{N} \qquad (4.4)$$

$$\frac{11.61 + 37.48 + \ldots + 18.62 + 5.25}{62} = 12.01\%$$

An investor who bought a portfolio equivalent to the S&P 500 at the start of the year and sold it at the end of the year would have an average return of 12.01%. The one-year holding period is a critical assumption.

Most investment strategies, however, involve holding periods greater than one year. In that case, the investor is subject to a compounding of the sequence of returns, as shown in Table 4-4. If there is any variability in the return series, the arithmetic average $\bar{R}$ will not be the same as the average compound return, which we will refer to as $\bar{G}$. When return variability exists, $\bar{R}$ will always be larger than $\bar{G}$, and this difference grows as return variability increases.

The average compound return $\bar{G}$ is a *geometric* average of the return series and is calculated as follows:

Geometric Average Return

$$\bar{G} = \left[\prod_{t=1}^{N} (1 + R_t) \right]^{1/N} - 1.0 \qquad (4.5)$$

where N is the number of periods and the π sign stands for multiplication. Between 1925 and 1987, $\bar{G}$ was 9.9%:

$$\bar{G} = (1.1161 \times 1.3748 \times \ldots \times 1.1861 \times 1.0525)^{1/62} - 1$$

$$= 348.669^{1/62} - 1$$

$$= 0.0990, \text{ or } 9.90\%$$

To see why $\bar{R}$ and $\bar{G}$ differ, consider the following example. You invest $100 at the start of year 1. During year 1 you experience a positive 20% return. During year 2 you experience a negative 20% return. As shown in the time line below, your $100 initial value declines to $96 at the end of year 2:

	Year 1	Year 2
Return	+20%	−20%
Value $100	$120	$96

The average return, $\bar{R}$, is 0% and suggests you didn't win or lose. But you *know* the initial $100 is now worth $96; you know you lost! In contrast, the average compound return associated with an investment of $100 becoming $96 two periods later is −2.02%:

$$[(1.2)(.8)]^{1/2} - 1.0 = \left(\frac{\$96}{\$100} \right)^{1/2} - 1.0 = -0.0202$$

Why was $\bar{G}$ smaller than $\bar{R}$ in this example? Simply because the 20% decline in value was a 20% decline in both the *initial investment* of $100 and the $20 *profit* you had at the end of year 1. *A given percentage decline in value cannot be offset by an identical percentage increase in value.* This is why $\bar{G}$ will always be smaller than $\bar{R}$ if returns are not constant. $\bar{R}$ treats an $X\%$ decline as identical in impact to an $X\%$ increase. But in fact the two do not have an equal effect upon portfolio values.

Use of the Unit Value Series. The unit value series is particularly useful in calculating $\bar{G}$ values for various time periods. Recall that the unit value at any point in time is the compound growth of 1.00 from the base period to that point in time. If the unit value at date T is divided by the unit value of (say) $T - 2$, the result is the growth of 1.0 from $T - 2$ to T:

$$\frac{UV_T}{UV_{T-2}} = (1 + R_{T-1})(1 + R_T)$$

To find the compound yearly return over this two-year period, you would take the $T - (T - 2)$ root and subtract 1.0.

For example, using the data in Table 4-4, the 1-, 5-, and 10-year average compound returns earned prior to 1987 were:

1-Year Return	*5-Year Return*	*10-Year Return*
$\left(\dfrac{348.669}{331.277}\right)^{1/1} - 1.0$	$\left(\dfrac{348.669}{162.300}\right)^{1/5} - 1.0$	$\left(\dfrac{348.669}{84.129}\right)^{1/10} - 1.0$
$= 5.25\%$	$= 16.52\%$	$= 15.28\%$

By using the unit value series in this way, average compound returns can be calculated for any intermediate periods.

A Half-Century of Returns

Some market indexes have extensive histories of returns available extending back to 1926. Other indexes have return series available dating from the end of World War II. We will examine the longer series.

In Table 4-5, unit value series are presented for six major security portfolios:

1. The Europe, Australia, Far East (EAFE) Index prepared by Morgan Stanley Capital International
2. An index of returns on small stocks (smallest 20% of total share value on the NYSE and AMEX) prepared by Dimensional Fund Advisors
3. The Standard & Poor's 500 Composite Index
4. A long-term corporate bond index
5. A long-term government bond index
6. A Treasury bill index

A series of rates of return is not presented, since these unit values can be used to calculate returns for any possible time interval of a year or more. For example, the return on government bonds during 1987 was -2.66%:

$$\frac{13.330}{13.695} - 1.0 = -0.02665$$

At the bottom of Table 4-5, values of $\bar{R}$ and $\bar{G}$ are shown for this 62-year series. Over the full 1925–1987 period, stocks of small firms clearly provided the greatest long-term return. A $1 investment in January of 1925 would have grown to $1,675 if all dividends had been reinvested. This translates into an arithmetic one-year return average ($\bar{R}$) of 19.37% and a geometric average ($\bar{G}$) of 12.72%. Most equity investors, however, were more likely to have held portfolios similar to the S&P 500 and earned an $\bar{R} = 12.01\%$ and $\bar{G} = 9.90\%$. Treasury bills provided the smallest growth, with a $1 investment in 1925 growing to only $8.33 for an $\bar{R} = 3.53\%$ and a $\bar{G} = 3.48\%$. These series, of course, do not allow for the fact that transaction costs and taxes would have resulted in lower returns for investors who held portfolios of each index. Nonetheless, it is clear that over long periods of time common stocks have provided the greatest returns.

TABLE 4-5 *Unit Values of Selected Indexes, 1925-1987*

	EAFE	Small Stocks	S&P 500	Corp. Bonds	Govt. Bonds	Treasury Bills
1925		1.000	1	1	1	1
1926		0.942	1.116	1.074	1.078	1.033
1927		1.182	1.534	1.154	1.174	1.065
1928		1.813	2.204	1.186	1.175	1.099
1929		0.864	2.018	1.225	1.215	1.152
1930		0.469	1.516	1.323	1.272	1.180
1931		0.226	0.859	1.298	1.204	1.192
1932		0.218	0.788	1.439	1.407	1.204
1933		0.570	1.214	1.588	1.406	1.207
1934		0.748	1.196	1.808	1.547	1.209
1935		1.267	1.766	1.982	1.624	1.211
1936		2.168	2.366	2.115	1.746	1.213
1937		0.995	1.537	2.174	1.749	1.217
1938		1.191	2.016	2.307	1.846	1.217
1939		1.107	2.007	2.398	1.956	1.217
1940		0.972	1.811	2.480	2.075	1.217
1941		0.859	1.601	2.547	2.094	1.217
1942		1.282	1.927	2.614	2.162	1.221
1943		2.576	2.426	2.688	2.206	1.225
1944		4.117	2.905	2.815	2.268	1.229
1945		7.515	3.963	2.930	2.512	1.233
1946		6.551	3.643	2.980	2.510	1.237
1947		6.382	3.850	2.910	2.444	1.244
1948		5.965	4.063	3.031	2.526	1.254
1949		7.229	4.826	3.131	2.689	1.268
1950		10.632	6.358	3.197	2.690	1.283
1951		11.584	7.885	3.111	2.584	1.302
1952		12.094	9.332	3.221	2.614	1.324
1953		11.470	9.240	3.331	2.709	1.348
1954		18.769	14.102	3.510	2.904	1.360
1955		22.977	18.550	3.527	2.866	1.381
1956		23.724	19.767	3.287	2.707	1.415
1957		20.369	17.634	3.573	2.909	1.460
1958		34.601	25.282	3.494	2.731	1.482
1959		41.075	28.311	3.460	2.669	1.526
1960		39.325	28.441	3.774	3.037	1.567
1961		51.351	36.089	3.956	3.066	1.600
1962		45.148	32.938	4.270	3.277	1.644
1963		53.414	40.442	4.364	3.316	1.695
1964		63.301	47.119	4.572	3.433	1.754
1965		89.653	52.985	4.551	3.457	1.823
1966		85.485	47.660	4.560	3.583	1.910
1967		168.781	59.093	4.334	3.253	1.990
1968	1.000	251.416	65.641	4.446	3.245	2.094
1969	1.028	179.762	60.068	4.086	3.081	2.232
1970	0.920	161.624	62.489	4.837	3.453	2.377
1971	1.207	192.672	71.437	5.369	3.910	2.481
1972	1.661	200.321	84.996	5.759	4.132	2.577
1973	1.426	126.202	72.527	5.825	4.087	2.755
1974	1.110	94.399	53.336	5.646	4.264	2.976

TABLE 4-5 *(continued)*

	EAFE	Small Stocks	S&P 500	Corp. Bonds	Govt. Bonds	Treasury Bills
1975	1.522	159.233	73.183	6.473	4.656	3.148
1976	1.579	242.162	90.637	7.680	5.437	3.308
1977	1.885	297.713	84.129	7.812	5.401	3.478
1978	2.532	365.830	89.657	7.806	5.338	3.729
1979	2.688	531.478	106.171	7.479	5.273	4.116
1980	3.345	719.993	140.582	7.284	5.064	4.579
1981	3.311	819.857	133.679	7.214	5.159	5.253
1982	3.283	1049.498	162.300	10.373	7.241	5.806
1983	4.090	1465.834	198.833	10.860	7.291	6.317
1984	4.412	1368.063	211.300	12.640	8.424	6.935
1985	6.915	1705.428	279.275	16.546	11.032	7.471
1986	11.753	1821.397	331.277	19.649	13.695	7.925
1987	14.683	1675.867	348.669	19.334	13.330	8.331
1925–1987 Mean Annual Returns						
Arithmetic		19.37%	12.01%	5.20%	4.58%	3.53%
Geometric		12.72%	9.90%	4.89%	4.27%	3.48%
1968–1987 Mean Annual Returns						
Arithmetic	17.48%	14.11%	10.54%	8.78%	8.37%	7.57%
Geometric	15.19%	10.50%	9.19%	8.04%	7.72%	7.54%

Of course, the greater return on common stocks is accompanied by a significant cost in the form of return volatility. For example, consider the plight of people who bought the S&P 500 in 1928 when its unit value was 2.204, and had to sell in 1932, when the unit value had fallen to 0.788. Their compound return would have been a negative 23% per year! More recently, there were a number of periods lasting as long as five years during the 1970s when a return of about 0% was earned. Treasury bills, on the other hand, have shown a continual increase in value with *no* negative returns in any year.[3]

The size of this return volatility can be seen clearly in Figure 4-3. In the figure, frequency distributions of yearly returns on four of the indexes in Table 4-5 are shown. While common stocks as proxied by the S&P 500 provided average yearly returns of 12.01%, variability in returns was extensive. In one year S&P returns were as high as 54% and in another year they were as low as −43%. This is the *risk* that investors in common stocks must be willing to assume—the joy of a 54% gain and the pain of a 43% loss. In Figure 4-4, average annual returns are shown for each index together with the standard deviation of the index returns. As can be seen again, greater returns come only with greater return volatility.

---

[3]Our discussions in this chapter are limited to "nominal" returns before any loss due to inflation is considered. Inflation adjustments are treated in Chapter 5. At that time, we will see that T-bills have had years in which "real" returns were negative.

FIGURE 4-3 *Frequency Distribution of Yearly Returns*

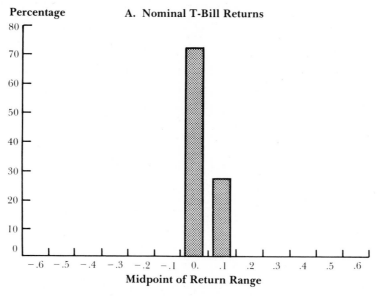

A. Nominal T-Bill Returns

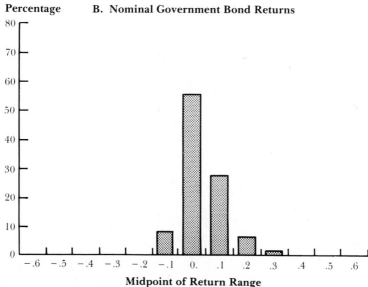

B. Nominal Government Bond Returns

SUMMARY

Security market indexes are widely used barometers of the direction of security price levels and the historical returns that could have been earned for various types of portfolios. A knowledge of how the indexes are prepared is important, because underlying

FIGURE 4-3 *(continued)*

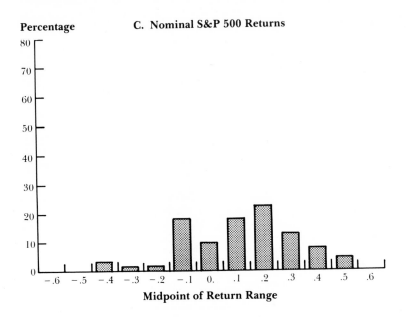

C. Nominal S&P 500 Returns

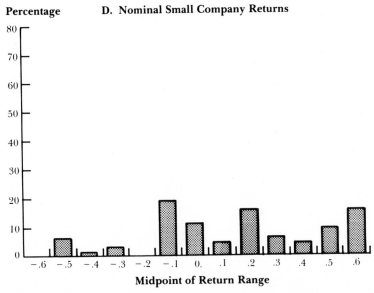

D. Nominal Small Company Returns

the calculation of each is an implicit portfolio strategy. The DJIA, for example, reflects a portfolio of 30 large-company stocks, with each stock weighted according to its price per share (a $100 stock is weighted 10 times more than a $10 stock). In comparison, the S&P 500 reflects a portfolio of 500 large-company stocks, with each stock weighted according to its *total* market value.

FIGURE 4-4 *Index Returns and Standard Deviations*

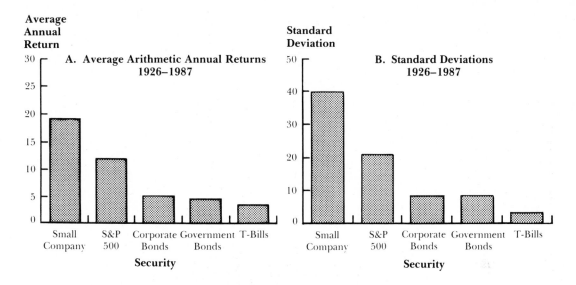

Long-run average annual returns on a portfolio of S&P 500 common stocks have been approximately 10% to 12%. Corporate bonds have provided 4% to 5% average annual returns, and Treasury bills have provided about 3.5% returns—the smallest annual average. However, with the greater returns on common stocks comes considerably greater volatility. It is not uncommon for portfolios such as the S&P 500 to have yearly returns that vary from more than +25% to less than −25%. Clearly the measurement and management of such uncertainty must comprise a large part of our discussions in later chapters.

REVIEW PROBLEMS

1. Assume that you are given the following data on three stocks (none of the stocks paid dividends):

| | | *Price* | | | *Shares Outstanding* | |
Date	*A*	*B*	*C*	*A*	*B*	*C*
0	$40	$50	$30	100	200	300
1	22*	50	28	200	200	300
2	25	55	32	200	200	300

*Two-for-one stock split on the first day of the period.

   a. Use the approach followed by Dow Jones to calculate a price index on the three stocks for each period.

   b. Now calculate a market-value-weighted index modeled after the S&P 500 Composite Index.

c. Estimate the rate of return on each index for periods 1 and 2.

d. Calculate $\bar{R}$ and $\bar{G}$ for each return series.

2. As a new employee of the Fifth National Bank Trust Department, you have been assigned to maintain the return history for a common stock portfolio managed by the trust. You have a detailed return history for four years. In addition, you have portfolio and dividend information for year 5. The trust agreement states that all dividends are distributed to the trust owner when they are received.

Annual Return on Portfolio

1	*2*	*3*	*4*
30.55%	−4.22%	19.40%	22.12%

Dividend and Portfolio Values in Year 5

	12/31	*3/31*	*6/30*	*9/30*	*10/31*	*12/31*
Dividends	—	$3M	$3M	$3M	$1M	$1M
Portfolio Value	$200M	$195M	$200M	$200M	$205M	$210M

a. Calculate the rate of return on the portfolio in the fourth quarter of year 5.

b. Calculate the rate of return on the portfolio for year 5.

c. Calculate a unit value series starting at $1 as of year 0.

d. Calculate and interpret $\bar{R}$ and $\bar{G}$ for the five-year interval. Comment on why $\bar{R}$ and $\bar{G}$ differ.

Solutions

1. a. DJIA at period 0: $\dfrac{40 + 50 + 30}{3} = 40$

DJIA at period 1: First find a new denominator:

$$\frac{20 + 50 + 30}{D} = 40$$

$$D = 2.5$$

Next find the index value:

$$\frac{22 + 50 + 28}{2.5} = 40$$

DJIA at period 2:

$$\frac{25 + 55 + 32}{2.5} = 44.80$$

b. First find the base date market value:

$$40(100) + 50(200) + 30(300) = 23,000$$

The base date index is:

$$10\left(\frac{23,000}{23,000}\right) = 10$$

S&P 500 at period 1:

$$10\left(\frac{22(200) + 50(200) + 28(300)}{23,000}\right) = 9.913$$

S&P 500 at period 2:

$$10\left(\frac{25(200) + 55(200) + 32(300)}{23,000}\right) = 11.130$$

c. Since no dividends were paid, returns on each are simply the percentage price change of each index.

Period	DJIA	S&P 500
1	0.	−0.87%
2	12.00%	12.28%

d. For DJIA:

$\bar{R} = (0 + 12.00) \div 2 \qquad\quad = 6.000\%$

$\bar{G} = [(1.0)(1.12)]^{1/2} - 1.0 \quad = 5.830\%$

For S&P 500:

$\bar{R} = (-0.87 + 12.28) \div 2 \quad = 5.705\%$

$\bar{G} = [(0.9913)(1.1228)]^{1/2} - 1 \; = 5.500\%$

$\bar{R}$ will always be greater than $\bar{G}$ when returns are variable. Average returns on the DJIA are lower than for the S&P 500 because of the weight assigned to each stock. For example, at period 0, stock C represents 25% of the DJIA but 39% ($9,000 \div 23,000$) of the S&P 500. The poor performance in period 1 and good performance in period 2 are major reasons why the S&P had greater returns. The heavier influence of stock B in the S&P 500 also had an impact.

2. a. Return from 9/30 to 10/31:

$$\frac{205 - 200 + 1}{200} = 3.00\%$$

Return from 10/31 to 12/31:

$$\frac{210 - 205 + 1}{205} = 2.93\%$$

Linked total quarter return:

$$(1.03)(1.0293) - 1.0 = 6.018\%$$

b.

Quarter	Return
1	$\dfrac{195 - 200 + 3}{200} = -1.000\%$
2	$\dfrac{200 - 195 + 3}{195} = 4.103\%$
3	$\dfrac{200 - 200 + 3}{200} = 1.500\%$
4	Part a $= 6.018\%$

Return for total year:

$$(.99)(1.04103)(1.015)(1.06018) - 1.0 = 10.90\%$$

c. *Year-End:*	*0*	*1*	*2*	*3*	*4*	*5*
Unit value	$1	1.3055	1.2504	1.493	1.8232	2.022

d. $\bar{R} = \dfrac{(30.55 - 4.22 + 19.40 + 22.12 + 10.90)}{5}$

$= 15.75\%$

$\bar{G} = [(1.3055)(.9578)(1.194)(1.2212)(1.1090)]^{1/5} - 1.0$

$= 15.121\%$

Arithmetic average returns will always be greater than compound average returns whenever the series of returns is not constant. This is due to the fact that any arithmetic return of $\pm X\%$ is assumed to have an identical impact on wealth. In fact, they do not. An $X\%$ increase in portfolio value followed by an $X\%$ decrease in portfolio value results in a smaller value than was initially available.

QUESTIONS AND PROBLEMS

1. Security market indexes have a number of possible uses. Describe these uses.

2. Returns on various security indexes are often used to judge the performance of an actively managed portfolio. What potential problems do you see in such comparisons?

3. Underlying each of the following equity indexes is an implied portfolio strategy. Identify the strategy for each.
   a. DJIA
   b. S&P 500
   c. NYSE Composite
   d. Value Line Composite

4. Use the data in Table 4-1 to calculate each year's index for the:
   a. DJIA
   b. S&P 500 Composite
   c. NYSE Composite
   d. Value Line Composite
   Use the same procedures as in the text.

5. Each of the various indexes reports not only an index price but also a dividend-per-share figure which is consistent with the way in which the index is calculated. For example, in the chapter we saw that the S&P 500 at 12/31/87 was $247.08 and that dividends paid on the index were $2.2025 during that quarter-end. Using your knowledge of how the S&P 500 is calculated, how do you suppose the $2.2025 figure was arrived at?

6. Use Table 4-5 to calculate:
   a. $\bar{G}$ for each index from its beginning date to 1987
   b. $\bar{G}$ for each index from 1962 to 1987
   c. $\bar{G}$ for each index from 1970 to 1987

7. Annual returns for the American Mutual Fund for various years are shown below:

Year	*Return*	*Year*	*Return*
1978	12.61%	1980	25.36%
1979	21.46	1981	7.76

1982	29.64	1985	30.12
1983	24.12	1986	18.43
1984	6.43	1987	4.61

  a. Prepare a unit value series.

  b. Calculate $\bar{R}$ and $\bar{G}$. Compare these with equivalent values for stock indexes shown in the chapter.

8. At the end of May, the net asset value (NAV) of the American Mutual Fund is $17.00. On June 7, you receive a $0.50 dividend which you use to purchase additional shares (no load) at the June 7 NAV of $17.30. On June 30, the NAV is $17.15. What was your one-month rate of return? Compare this with the return you would have calculated if you had assumed all dividends were received at month-end.

9. Whenever dividends are not paid, $\bar{R}$ will be equal to $\bar{G}$. True or false? Why?

10. Many people say that annualized returns over investment periods which last longer than one year are less volatile than one-year holding period returns. Let's see if this seems to be so. Calculate $\bar{G}$ values for every possible (independent) ten-year interval for the S&P 500 Index, i.e., 1987–78, 1977–68, . . . ,1937–28. Does this series appear less variable than the yearly volatility shown in Figure 4-3? Why might this be so?

DATA ANALYSIS PROBLEM

Objectives:

- To calculate $\bar{R}$ and $\bar{G}$ for selected indexes through 1988.
- To review the historical risks and average returns on various security classes.
- To examine how the length of one's investment horizon affects investment risk.

1. Access and review the contents of the YRLYINDX.WK1 data set. The following parts of this problem should be applied to at least the Treasury bill, Treasury bond, and S&P 500 data. You may perform similar calculations on other data series if you wish.

2. Copy the year identifiers in cells A26.A88 to cells A126.A188. Create a unit value series through 1988 for the following indexes (Hint: Label each column properly and enter 1.0 in cells B125.D125):
- Treasury Bills (Column B)
- Treasury Bonds (Column C)
- S&P 500 (Column D)

3. At the bottom of each column, calculate $\bar{R}$, $\bar{G}$, and the standard deviation of annual returns for each. Review and explain the results.

4. In this part we will begin to explore how an investor's time horizon affects his or her risk exposure. The calculations are somewhat complex for beginning spreadsheet users but are a useful learning exercise.

  a. First calculate the ending unit value for every possible five-year holding period, i.e., 1926–1930, 1927–1931, . . . , 1984–1988. Once this is done, calculate the geometric annualized return for each ($\bar{G}$).

  b. Now calculate the average and standard deviations of both the five-year unit value series and the $\bar{G}$ series.

  c. Repeat the process above for all possible 10-year holding periods. (Hint: Be sure to keep the summary five-year averages and standard deviations so that they can be compared with the results from the 10-year holdings.)

d. Repeat the process for all possible 20-year holding periods.

e. Complete the following tables and evaluate the results:

	Ending Wealth (Unit Value)					
	T-Bills		T-Bonds		S&P 500	
Investment Horizon	Aver.	Std. Dev.	Aver.	Std. Dev.	Aver.	Std. Dev.
1-Year						
5-Year						
10-Year						
20-Year						

	Geometric Annualized Returns ($\bar{G}$)					
	T-Bills		T-Bonds		S&P 500	
Investment Horizon	Aver.	Std. Dev.	Aver.	Std. Dev.	Aver.	Std. Dev.
1-Year						
5-Year						
10-Year						
20-Year						

5. There happens to be a bias in the calculations of the standard deviations above which makes the standard deviation imply a lower risk for longer time horizons than for a single year. What is this bias?

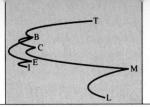

2 Investment Concepts

The purpose of the four chapters in Part 1 was to provide a broad overview of (1) the nature of the investment/speculative problem, (2) the types of securities available, (3) the markets in which they are traded, and (4) historical returns on various market indexes. Using those chapters as a foundation, we can now move into a thorough treatment of various investment concepts.

We start Part 2 by examining the major economic concepts associated with the securities markets. In Chapter 5, the economic roles which security markets and risk-free interest rates fulfill are presented. Chapter 6 expands upon the discussion of the risk-free interest rate by examining how expected future interest rates and a security's maturity can affect today's required return. Next, security risk is explicitly introduced in Chapter 7. Various quantitative measures of risk are presented, and the critical role of diversification is reviewed. Based upon these quantitative risk measures, a model is developed in Chapters 8 and 9 which attempts to tie expected security returns to the risks inherent in a security. Finally, this concepts section concludes with an examination of the investment and speculative implications of the efficient market hypothesis and the evidence which both supports and refutes this hypothesis.

The concepts presented in these six chapters provide the theoretical background from which various security media can be analyzed and portfolio strategies can be developed, as discussed in later sections of the book.

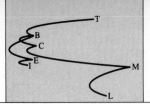

CHAPTER

5 The Economic Roles of Security Markets

In Chapters 2 and 3 we reviewed the types of securities and markets which exist today in the United States. The discussion was purely descriptive. Now we begin to ask *why* they exist as they do. Is the complex array of securities and markets simply a sophisticated game in which one person tries to win at the expense of another? Or do stocks, bonds, investment bankers, commercial bankers, mutual funds, market makers, and all the rest fulfill a needed economic role in society? And if so, what is the precise nature of this role?

Most economists believe that if people are allowed freedom of choice, they will take actions which result in the improvement of their common welfare, even though their individual actions are motivated by pure self-interest. One of these actions is the creation of efficient economic markets. As we will soon see, the major advantage which economic markets provide is something economists call *separation*. Markets which result in separation provide people with the greatest freedom of choice and allow them to pursue actions in which they have a comparative advantage relative to other people.

THE VALUE OF MARKETS

The Real Goods Market

Real goods represent tangible resources (land, grain, tractors, etc.) as well as intangible resources (technology, human skills, etc.). The advantage of having a real goods market is that people can separate how they make a living from what they consume. The Iowa farmer may use his resources to produce grain which is then swapped with other people for meat, entertainment, vacations, etc. The market for real goods allows the farmer to make decisions about his life-style which are independent (separate) from his decision about the way in which he chooses to earn a living. In the parlance of economists, the *real goods market allows us to separate our production decisions from our consumption decisions*.

Taken at face value, this separation advantage may appear meaningless, but it does have major implications for the welfare of society. First, the farmer's choice of available consumption items is improved; he needn't subsist solely on bread baked from his grain production. The expansion of available consumption products should result in greater pleasure to individuals and enhancement of the welfare of society as a whole. Second, in an attempt to increase their consumption opportunities, people will select jobs at which they have a comparative advantage. This in turn will result in a larger productive output and a higher standard of living. (People with good logic abilities will become systems analysts, and those with good manual dexterity will become surgeons.) Labor specialization will arise.

Even strict barter economies provide these advantages. However, a strict barter economy is inefficient in that individuals with grain to swap must seek out and trade directly with individuals who produce meat, entertainment, and vacations. This is clearly a time-consuming, costly, and painful way to trade. *Money* solves the problem by acting as a common medium of exchange. Money exists because it reduces the transaction costs involved in trading real goods. In all but the most aboriginal cultures, some form of money has arisen simply because it increases the efficiency of the economic system.

Even if a society has a monetized, real goods market, problems remain if there is no financial market. In particular, each economic unit is constrained in its total consumption and real saving.[1] During a given time interval, the real goods which an economic unit controls (RG_i) may be either consumed by the unit (C_i) or productively saved (RS_i).[2] Symbolically:

$$RG_i = C_i + RS_i$$

or   **(5.1)**

$$RS_i = RG_i - C_i$$

Without a financial market, there is no way for a unit to consume plus save an amount of real assets *in excess* of the real assets which it controls. As a result, members of the society with highly profitable investment opportunities available might not be able to make the full investment in real assets that they would like to. Conversely, economic units may not consume and save in real assets any amount *less than* their available resources. As a result, members of the society with unattractive investment opportunities must invest directly in real assets even if their resulting productive yields are poor. Clearly, society would be better off if the *use* of real assets could be swapped temporarily. If the use of real assets could be swapped, individuals who are able to employ real assets in the most productive manner could borrow them from individuals with an excess of resources.

---

[1]An economic unit may consist of an individual, a family, a partnership, a corporation, or a governmental body.

[2]For simplicity we assume units don't store goods at a zero yield, nor do they allow real goods to waste away. Any real goods not consumed during some time interval must necessarily be saved.

The Primary Financial Markets

A financial security is a piece of paper which provides its owner with the legal claim to some portion of the future profits on a real asset.[3] A *primary market* in financial securities makes it possible for an economic unit to consume plus invest in real assets an amount different from the unit's initial resource level. Now individuals may invest either in real assets (RI_i) or financial securities (FI_i). They may obtain the resources to do so either from the sale of financial securities (FS_i) or by real saving (RS_i)—the difference between the real goods owned by the individual and their consumption ($RG_i - C_i$).

For example, at period 0, DJ owns real resources valued at $100. With financial markets available, DJ's maximum consumption plus real investment in period 1 is no longer limited to $100. Instead, DJ can choose to consume $70, invest $50 directly in real assets, invest $20 in financial securities, and sell $40 of financial securities (borrow $40). Symbolically:

Uses of Resources			=	Sources of Resources		
Real Investment	+	Financial Investment	=	Financial Saving	+	Real Saving
RI_i	+	FI_i	=	FS_i	+	RS_i
$50	+	$20	=	$40	+	$30

The importance of primary financial markets is that individuals are no longer constrained in their real investment and consumption decisions. *The primary market separates the real investment decision from the consumption decision.* If DJ owns $100 in real goods and chooses to consume $70, he or she is no longer forced to invest $30 in real assets. Instead, any difference between investment in real goods and available resources is made up by net sales or purchases of financial securities. For example, DJ elected to make a $50 investment in real assets but had only $30 of real assets available after consuming $70 of the initial $100 available. The $20 difference ($50 - $30 = RI_i - RS_i$) was made up for by the net sale of $20 in financial securities. DJ was able to make a real investment choice which was independent (separate) from the consumption choice.

Individuals may both invest in financial assets (lend) and sell financial assets (borrow). For example, DJ lent $20 and borrowed $40. When lending occurs, one essentially passes the control of a real asset to someone else (the borrower) and receives financial securities in exchange. When borrowing occurs, one obtains the physical control of a real asset and issues a security claim to its future productive yield. DJ borrowed a net amount of $20. The real assets borrowed by issuing $20 in net financial securities were added to the direct real asset savings of $30 in order to make a real investment of $50.

As with the separation of production and consumption created by real goods mar-

---

[3]We are neglecting for the moment financial securities issued by financial intermediaries such as commercial banks and mutual funds.

kets, the advantages of separation between consumption and investment created by primary financial markets may not be immediately evident. But note that this separation means that some people in a society can be responsible for real investment decisions, and others may provide real savings without physically selecting and managing the real assets invested in. Now that a financial market exists, investments may be made in ventures offering the highest yields. *Individuals who had previously owned real assets which could be invested only at rather low yields may now lend them to more skillful entrepreneurs.* This provides two direct benefits to society: (1) increased consumption and investment freedom and (2) a higher standard of living afforded by the higher average investment yields.

Related to these benefits are two additional advantages: diversification and risk selection. Diversification over a large number of investments can substantially reduce risk without affecting expected returns.[4] When financial markets don't exist, the only way to diversify is to purchase a large number of real assets. Unfortunately, real assets are often indivisible. (It's difficult to buy a part of a lake.) Thus, smaller investors are unable to benefit much from diversification across real asset holdings. However, when primary markets are created, the claims to a real asset's returns can be broken down into smaller units. For example, $1 million required to finance a shopping center can be obtained by the sale of 10,000 common shares at $100 each. Now small investors may purchase a few shares simply for their unique diversification advantages, whereas prior to the creation of a primary market, their diversification opportunities were limited.

Individuals may also easily change their investment risk level.[5] For example, assume you are fortunate enough to inherit a large estate of diversified real assets. The estate is already well diversified across many types of real assets, so financial securities really don't offer any diversification advantages. However, the net risk of your holdings is still too great for your personal comfort. This risk could be altered by selling some of your current holdings in exchange for less risky assets. But again, this would probably be a costly and burdensome process. Alternatively, your investment risk could be reduced *without* changing real asset holdings simply by purchasing financial securities with a lower risk level. If you desired to undertake larger amounts of risk than inherent in your real assets, financial securities having a greater risk could be purchased.

In sum, financial markets play a vital role in modern societies. They increase the investment opportunities available to individuals, increase the standard of living, provide an improvement in diversification opportunities, and allow for easy shifts in investment risk levels. It is for *these* reasons that society has created financial securities—not as a game for the sophisticated to extract wealth from the naive.

While primary financial markets expand the individual's flexibility, they do not expand the flexibility of society as a whole. In the aggregate, financial borrowing must

---

[4]This is proved in Chapter 7.

[5]Arrow presents a terse (but most elegant) analysis of the economic role of securities through their ability to allocate risk.

equal financial lending. Total real investment can come only from the savings of real goods. Somehow a mechanism must automatically force real saving to equal real investment (or alternatively, financial saving to equal financial investment). This mechanism is the rate of interest. Financial savers demand a return for giving up physical control of real assets. This return comes in the form of a rate of interest required on the financial security. If everyone wanted to borrow, the rate of interest would rapidly increase to a level that would cause many people to change their minds and decide to lend instead. Interest rates adjust in response to differences in desired borrowing and lending in order to ensure that the two actually balance. Interest rates serve the same purpose as do the prices of real goods in the real goods market. Interest rates are prices which ensure an equilibrium between the supply and demand placed on the use of a real asset over time.

A Graphic Analysis

Imagine a risk-free world in which each individual is endowed with a certain amount of real assets, R_0. This world lasts for two periods, today and tomorrow (simply because we can't easily plot a three-period world). The economic choice faced by each individual is how R_0 should be consumed. How much should be consumed today, C_0, versus how much tomorrow, C_1? For the moment we will assume that resources not consumed now ($R_0 - C_0$) may be invested to provide a positive return. We designate this return as r. The consumption available next period will be greater than today's investment (I_0) by an amount equal to the productive return on the investment:

$$C_1 = (R_0 - C_0) + r(R_0 - C_0)$$
$$= I_0(1 + r)$$

In addition, we know that individuals prefer to consume as much as possible in each period but that they have some preference for immediate consumption over future consumption. Finally, a primary financial market does not exist. Later we will add a financial market to see how the optimal decision changes.

These facts can be visualized with the aid of the panels in Figure 5-1. In panel A the available *consumption opportunities* are shown as the shaded area. In period 0 the maximum possible consumption is R_0; consume all of the resource endowment today and invest nothing for consumption tomorrow. However, if part of R_0 is invested today, next period's consumption will be equal to the amount of the investment plus the production yield on the investment. As a result, the curve R_0A is not a 45° line, which would reflect simply storing resources. The consumption opportunity curve is higher by the amount of productive return. Also notice that the slope of R_0A changes at each point along the curve. This slope represents the productive rate of return, r, available from the last dollar of investment. In economic terms, r is the

FIGURE 5-1 *Consumption and Investment Without Financial Markets*

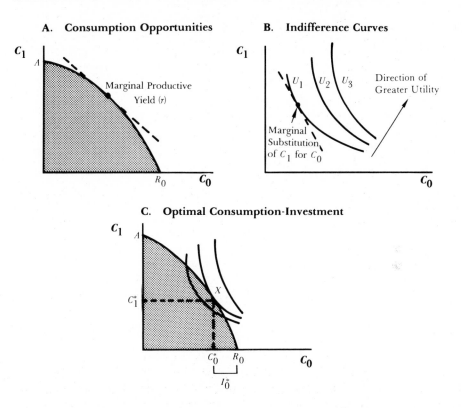

marginal return on real asset investment. The slope decreases as larger investments are made, reflecting the necessity to invest in lower-yielding projects.

Panel B illustrates the individual's preferences for consumption in each period. A series of *indifference curves* are drawn and labeled U_1, U_2, and U_3. For example, U_1 represents all combinations of C_0 and C_1 which provide identical *utility* to the consumer, that is, combinations of consumption today and tomorrow between which the individual is indifferent. The slope of an indifference curve at any point represents the amount by which consumption tomorrow must increase for the consumer to be willing to give up one unit of consumption today. Thus, the slope of the curve reflects an individual's *time preferences for consumption*. The slope increases as larger investments are made, implying that increasingly greater amounts of period 1 consumption are needed to offset continued reductions in period 0 consumption.

In panel C the consumption opportunity set is brought together with the individual's time preference schedules. Optimal consumption in period 0 will be C_0^*, and investment of I_0^* will be made. Note that at the optimal point, X, the marginal return on real asset investment (slope of the consumption opportunity line) will exactly equal the marginal increase in period 1 consumption desired (the slope of the indifference

FIGURE 5-2 *Consumption and Investment with Financial Markets*

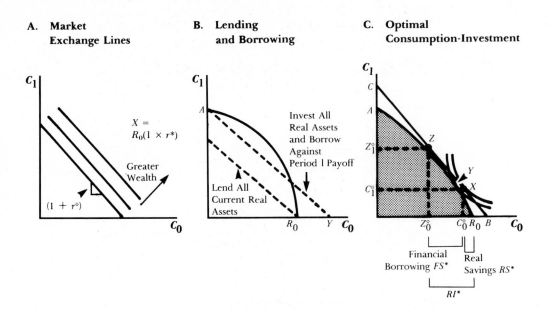

A. **Market Exchange Lines**

B. **Lending and Borrowing**

C. **Optimal Consumption-Investment**

curve). Also note that the consumption and investment decisions are not independent (separate).

Once the consumption decision is known, the investment decision is also known. Separation between consumption and investment cannot occur in a real goods market.

Now we will add a financial market, as depicted in Figure 5-2. In panel A a series of *market exchanges lines* are shown. The slope of these lines describes the equilibrium exchange between present and future consumption which has arisen in the financial markets, that is, the equilibrium interest rate on financial securities. Later in the chapter we discuss how this equilibrium interest rate, r^*, is determined. For now, however, it is enough to state that individuals may borrow or lend financial securities at the rate r^*.

In panel B the market exchange line is brought together with the consumption opportunity set. Recall that one starts at period 0 having real assets worth R_0. If one were to consume none of these assets but, instead, *lend* them by purchasing financial assets, the payoff at period 1 would be at point X. Current resources would be transferred to period 1, as shown by the lower dashed line. Obviously, this policy of lending all of R_0 is foolish—not so much because of the temporary starvation but because future consumption is less than it would have been if R_0 had been invested in *real* investments. If one wishes to invest all of R_0, the payoff from real asset investment is greater.

There are, of course, a large number of other financial and real asset choices which could be evaluated. We will look at one more before developing the optimal selection.

This example is instructive because it points out how one can use financial markets to *increase initial wealth*.

Assume that all of R_0 is invested in real assets. The payoff at period 1 would be at point A. If at period 0 one were to obtain a loan and use the payoff of A at period 1 as the loan's collateral, how much could be borrowed? The answer is the discounted present value of A, which is shown at point Y. By investing all of R_0 in real assets and borrowing against the future real asset payoff, this person can increase the total consumption possible at period 0. The financial markets can be used to increase one's wealth level.

Panel C presents the optimal solution to the question, "What portion of my wealth should I allocate to financial assets and what portion should I allocate to real assets?" The answer is amazingly simple and intuitive: Since the real and financial assets have identical risk, invest in those which provide the greatest return! Forget for the moment the question of how much to consume. The answer to the consumption question is totally *independent* of the investment question in the presence of financial markets.

Let's start at point R_0. If we are to invest \$1 of R_0, should it be in a real asset or a financial asset? Since the marginal return on the real asset (slope of consumption curve at R_0) is greater than the marginal return of financial assets (slope of the market exchange line), this first \$1 investment should be in real assets. The same is true for all investments of R_0 until we reach point Z. To the left of Z, any additional investments should be placed in financial assets since they have the greater marginal return.

But there is something even more special about point Z. By investing in real assets an amount equal to $R_0 - Z_0^*$, one *maximizes one's wealth*. For example, what is the maximum amount of consumption which can occur at period 0? The answer is at point B. This is achieved by (1) investing real assets in the amount $R_0 - Z_0^*$ and (2) obtaining a loan which is collateralized by Z_1^*. The size of this loan would be the discounted present value of Z_1^*, or $B - Z_0^*$. After making the real investments, one had Z_0^* of real assets. Adding to this the loan of $B - Z_0^*$, we can see that the most one can consume at period 0 is B. This is the current wealth of this person if *he or she invests in all real assets which have a marginal return in excess of the financial borrowing and lending rate*.

To bring this example to a close, we need to address the consumption question, "How much should be consumed at period 1?" Note that with the presence of financial markets, the original consumption possibilities curve ($R_0 - A$) no longer represents the true opportunities for consumption (except at point Z). To the right of Z, consumption opportunities are improved and obtained by investing $R_0 - Z_0^*$ in real assets and then borrowing against part (or all) of the period 1 real assets' payoffs. To the left of Z, consumption opportunities are also improved and obtained by investing first in real assets to point Z_0^* and then switching to investments in financial assets.

As displayed in panel C, the individual elects to consume at points C_0^* and C_1^*. This is obtained by (1) making an investment in real assets equal to $R_0 - Z_0^*$ and

(2) borrowing the amount $C_0^* - Z_0^*$. Of the person's initial endowment of real assets, only $R_0 - C_0^*$ is physically saved (and invested in real assets).

With the existence of financial markets, the individual has two gains: (1) increased consumption flexibility gained by separating the real investment and consumption questions and (2) an improved wealth position.

A Numerical Example

The point being made is important enough that another short example won't hurt — this time a numerical one. Assume you are faced with the situation displayed in Figure 5-3. You start with $100 of endowed real assets. To maximize your wealth, you invest in real assets until the marginal return on such investments is equal to the marginal cost of borrowing (which is the same as the marginal return on financial investments). Thus you decide to invest $40 in real assets. Doing so increases your total current wealth to $145.70. As shown on the graph, you also would like to consume goods today which will cost $90. Thus you need to borrow $30, which is available by collateralizing some of the period 1 payoffs on your real investments.

The amount you must collateralize depends, of course, on the market rate of in-

FIGURE 5-3 *A Numerical Example of Consumption and Investment with Financial Markets*

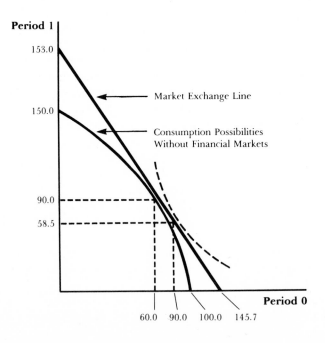

terest. The slope of the market exchange line is 153/145.70, or 1.05. Thus the equilibrium interest rate is 5%. To borrow $30, you must repay $31.50. At period 2, the $31.50 loan repayment is subtracted from the $90 payoff on your real assets, leaving $58.50 for period 2 consumption.

The data below summarize these results:

	Period 0	Period 1
Initial Endowment	$ 100.00	
Investment	(40.00)	$ 90.00
Available for Consumption	$ 60.00	90.00
Financial Transactions		
Borrow	30.00	(31.50)
Consume	$ 90.00	$ 58.50

It is possible, of course, that you may wish to consume less than $60 at period 0. In that case you would *still* invest $40 in real assets because that maximizes your wealth. However, you would then also invest in financial assets.

These examples illustrate an important point which you should not lose sight of. Financial markets create two economic benefits: (1) the income consumption flexibility gained by separating real investment decisions from consumption decisions and (2) the increased wealth gained by undertaking real investments whose returns are greater than the borrowing or lending rate on financial assets.

Brokers, Dealers, and Financial Intermediaries

The development of primary markets brings together those who want to make real investments and those who have real savings. It is an important step in the financial development of any society. But the *direct* placement of one's real savings with someone wishing to invest in real assets can be an inefficient process. The existence of money helps somewhat, since real assets can be translated into monetary equivalents so that money, instead of physical resources, is traded in the primary market. (Individuals wishing to build a plant can sell stock for money resources instead of swapping stock for concrete, labor, wood, steel, etc.) Still, there are additional improvements which can be made on the *direct* placement of resources. These improvements are provided by brokers and dealers and are associated with the following:

1. Costs of transactions
2. Differences in desired investment and financing maturities
3. Divisibility of financial securities
4. Marketability of financial securities

A broker acts as an agent for someone—typically, in arranging a security purchase or sale. A dealer takes long and short positions and trades with various market participants.

Costs of Transacting. The transaction costs of directly placing securities between lenders of funds and borrowers of funds can be large. For example, the costs to an electric power company in Alabama of directly finding buyers for a $200 million bond offering would be substantial. To float such an issue by itself, the firm would have to seek investors throughout the North American continent (at least). Conversely, the costs to an oil sheik of directly investing $200 million over a diversified group of securities would also be large. However, there are significant economies of scale to transaction costs which security brokers and dealers can obtain and which aren't available to one-time (or infrequent) borrowers and lenders.

These economies of scale arise in at least two ways. First, the average out-of-pocket cost declines as the number of transactions increases. The largest part of the cost of finding a borrower or lender is a set-up cost—a fixed cost of initially developing a network of potential traders. After one pays this set-up cost, the marginal cost of any transaction is quite small. For example, the biggest cost to Merrill Lynch (the largest security broker in the United States) of providing brokerage services is the cost of finding customers and developing an efficient communications and clearing network. Once these are in place, Merrill Lynch can execute and clear an order quite inexpensively. Therefore, it makes sense that a permanent brokerage system would be set up to bring potential borrowers and lenders of real assets together. It is a way to improve the efficiency of the primary market.

Second, there are information economies of scale. Infrequent borrowers and lenders simply don't have the knowledge of financial conditions which full-time brokers are able to provide inexpensively. For example, an Alabama power firm might have little knowledge of what impact a change in bond covenants would have on required yields, when the issue should be brought to market to avoid competing with other large primary offerings, whether the sale should be delayed in anticipation of credit loosening by the Federal Reserve, etc. Again, efficiency is best served by the creation of a brokerage system which is able to give financial advice.

Brokerage services are offered by a large variety of institutions, some of which aren't usually thought of as brokers. The most apparent are the large retail brokerage firms like Merrill Lynch, Prudential-Bache, Shearson Lehman Hutton, Kidder Peabody, Paine Webber, and many others. Investment bankers also serve a brokerage function when they distribute primary offerings, and commercial banks, as well as savings and loans, offer a form of brokerage service by bringing together borrowers and lenders. Even large CPA firms act as brokers when they find companies which would like to merge with others.

Economies of scale in transaction costs are also a reason for the existence of *dealers*. For example, the system of market makers, specialists, and block-trading houses arose because it is cheaper for society to have particular individuals carry inventories of securities to trade with the public than it would be to find the end buyer and seller in each transaction. Similarly, security underwriters are better able to absorb the risks of a new security offering than is the issuer, since a purchase group can be formed to diversify risks over many offerings. Commercial banks can carry large demand and saving deposits and reinvest them less expensively than could an individual small saver.

Maturity Differences. Dealers are often able to resolve differences in the needs of lenders and the needs of borrowers. One major difference between the two is desired investment maturity. A large number of savers prefer to lend for short time periods. For example, the large volume of demand deposits and savings accounts held in commercial banks and savings and loans are short-term investments. Borrowers, however, often prefer to enter into long-term agreements to finance the acquisition of long-term real assets. A single direct market connecting short-term lenders and long-term borrowers would work to neither party's advantage. However, dealers can step in as *financial intermediaries* to aid both sides. Although deposits with a financial intermediary would be short-term investments from the depositors' viewpoint, the intermediary can count on a continual turnover of deposits. One withdrawal would be offset by another deposit. In total, the deposits could be treated as long-term deposits and invested in long-term loans and bonds. Such services are a major function of the commercial banking and savings and loan systems.

Divisibility. While primary markets do allow one to diversify by purchasing small claims on a large real asset, dealers are able to improve on this even further. For example, assume you have $50,000 to invest. You could buy only five $10,000 T-bills, one round lot in each of 10 different stocks selling at $50 per share, etc. The amount of diversification available on such a sum of money is small. Alternatively, you could place your money with a financial intermediary (a dealer) such as a bank or a mutual fund, have it commingled with other financial investors' balances, and as a result obtain greater diversification.

Marketability. Secondary markets such as the OTC and NYSE have been developed to increase the marketability of a financial investment. Again, brokers and dealers are able to offer a service which improves the public welfare by offering easy exchange of financial asset holdings. For example, one of the important changes in financial markets during the 1980s was the increased *securitization* of the real estate mortgage market. This was done through both the investment banker community and federal mortgage agencies. We have already discussed how federal agencies such as the Government National Mortgage Association (Ginnie Mae) and the Federal National Mortgage Association (Fannie Mae) purchase pools of mortgages and the sell bond obligations to the markets collateralized by the mortgages and the government agency. These bonds are then paid off as mortgage interest and principal are received. During the 1980s, investment bankers also began to bundle pools of mortgages and use them as the collateral in public bond issues referred to as *collateralized mortgage obligations* (CMOs). Since the CMOs, GNMAs, and FNMAs are actively traded in secondary markets, they provide better marketability to investors who wish to invest in real estate mortgages than a direct mortgage loan would provide. In addition, the securitization of mortgages allows local borrowers to have access to the total national mortgage market. (They also provide local mortgage lenders with the ability to reduce their interest rate risk exposure, a topic discussed in Chapter 11.)

Equilibrium Between Markets

The creation of a broker-dealer network results in what we have called a secondary market. Individuals may now exchange real assets in the real goods market, exchange financial securities in the primary securities market, or trade financial securities in the secondary markets. Each of these markets serves a slightly different role. The real goods market allows people freedom of choice about which real goods they wish to own and increases society's standard of living by allowing people to select a career in which they have a comparative advantage. The primary securities market allows people freedom of choice about their level of consumption and increases society's standard of living by ensuring that the most productive real investments are made. The secondary securities market increases the efficiency by which people can rapidly readjust their financial investment holdings and improves diversification opportunities.

All of the markets are closely interrelated. For example, security price levels in the secondary security markets are used by potential borrowers and lenders in the primary market to determine current levels of required returns on financial securities. These signals are in turn used in the real goods markets by families, corporations, and governments when decisions are made about levels of consumption, real saving, and investment, as well as financial saving and investment. For example, if financial interest rates to a corporate borrower are negative after adjustment for expected inflation, heavy borrowing will occur to support real asset growth—even if the real assets are expected to provide low (but positive) returns. We will have occasion to return to the interactions among markets in more depth later in the chapter. Nonetheless, it should be clear that yields within each market should be identical, or major shifts in resources between markets will occur. The markets should not be segmented. The existence of speculators willing to trade between each market tends to cause yields in each to be closely related.

RISK-FREE INTEREST

The force which interrelates all financial markets is the rate of interest. This rate of interest is the borrowers' cost of obtaining capital and the return that lenders require for providing capital. Unfortunately, a single rate doesn't exist. Instead, there are a multitude of rates which vary among different security instruments. For the rest of this chapter and throughout the next four chapters, much of our attention will be spent asking why interest rates vary, *whether* current rate differences are appropriate, and, if not, what should be done. The first question is of concern to investors as we have strictly defined them, and the last two questions are asked by speculators and arbitrageurs.

Basically, the return that an individual requires from a security can be separated into two parts:

1. A risk-free rate which compensates people for the time value of money
2. A risk premium which compensates people for the risk perceived in a particular security

This is commonly written in the form of the capital asset pricing model.

Capital Asset Pricing Model

$$E(R_i) = RF + \beta_i(RP_m) \tag{5.2}$$

According to this model, security prices are set so that the expected single-period return on security i, $E(R_i)$, is equal to a risk-free rate of interest common to all securities RF, plus a risk premium unique to security i. This risk premium is equal to the relative risk perceived to be in security i, β_i (stated as "beta on security i"), multiplied by the risk premium demanded on the average security, RP_m. There are other forces which affect expected returns, and this strict version of the CAPM may not be completely accurate. However, we will use the CAPM as a pedagogic device—a model around which a variety of issues can be explored.

In the rest of this chapter we discuss the economic role, as well as the determinants, of the risk-free rate. Clearly, few things in life are certain. A perfectly risk-free security doesn't exist. Even 30-day T-bills contain some risk, not so much in the probability of default as in the uncertainty about the 30-day *real* return after inflationary losses. Thus, the types of interest rates and securities discussed in this chapter reflect a conceptual ideal rather than the rates or securities actually available in the markets. But this shouldn't detract from the importance of the concepts developed for at least two reasons. First, a large and very active market exists for securities which can *effectively* be considered risk-free. For example, many people believe U.S. Treasury and Agency obligations, high-grade corporate bonds, and high-grade municipal bonds all have such low levels of default risk that they are virtually risk-free. Second, since the required return on risky securities should conceptually contain a compensation for a risk-free return, the logical starting point in examining desired security returns is the risk-free rate.

Natural Real Rates

Among many past societies, the taking of interest was considered to be unnatural. The ancient Greeks referred to interest as *offspring*, which led Aristotle to object that the charging of interest was unnatural since money cannot have offspring. Jewish Mosaic laws forbade interest between fellow Jews. Romans were forbidden to charge interest to other Romans, and the Christian religion strongly discouraged interest taking through the Middle Ages. Saint Thomas Aquinas stated that interest constituted a payment for time, which he felt should more properly be considered a free gift of the Creator. Even in more recent times, many people considered interest to be an inherent evil—the extortion of income from the have-nots by the haves.

However, interest has existed throughout recorded history. Indeed, interest is an indispensable tool of society. Interest represents the price which a society sets on time and determines the rate at which existing and expected future resources will be consumed. This is the basic proposition of classical economists and their notion of a *natural rate of interest*.[6]

Society's Investment/Consumption Decision. Classical economists analyze interest rates in much the same way as we did earlier in the chapter when adding financial markets to a real goods market. Each economic unit makes a decision, given current interest rates, about the amount it wishes to borrow or lend. If there is a larger amount of desired borrowing than lending, interest rates will immediately increase to attract more lenders and fewer borrowers. Conversely, if there is a smaller amount of desired borrowing than lending, interest rates will immediately fall in order to attract more borrowers and discourage lending. Interest rates constitute an independent and automatic price mechanism which enforces a balance in the supply and demand for financial capital.

A more explicit way to view the role of interest is as follows. Assume that we can analyze the actions of society as a whole instead of the actions of many individual self-interested members of society — that is, that we can speak of the aggregate total.[7] This society faces a risk-free, two-period world in which it must decide how much to consume today versus tomorrow. The analysis is exactly the same as that faced by individuals in a world in which financial assets don't exist. (Question: Why can't we add a *financial market exchange line* to society's decision when in fact a financial market exists?) Panel A of Figure 5-4 displays the marginal productive yields available on investments in real assets. Yields decline as larger quantities of assets are invested, indicating diminishing returns available from real investment. Panel B plots available consumption as the shaded area and societal indifference curves as the solid curves. To achieve an optimal level of consumption, society will choose to consume C_0^* today and C_1^* tomorrow.

More important from our viewpoint, however, is that an amount of real assets equal to I_0^* will be invested in productive ventures. As a result, the marginal return on real asset investment will be r^*. Note that:

1. Interest is indeed a "natural phenomenon." It is the economic force that determines the extent to which real resources will be invested or immediately consumed.
2. The equilibrium real rate of interest is determined by an interaction between (*a*) the consumption time preferences (thriftiness) of society and (*b*) the productivity of available resources.

---

[6]Economists usually associated with classical interest theory include Irving Fisher, Alfred Marshall, John Stuart Mill, and Henry Thornton.

[7]In a way, the analysis we will use stretches the credibility of the procedure somewhat. We speak of societal indifference curves rather offhandedly, as if such things actually exist or represent an average of the society. Unfortunately, it's impossible to add together people's indifference curves. There is no way to compare the pleasure one person receives from classical music and good wine with the pleasure someone else receives from rock music and beer. Be that as it may, readers are asked to close their eyes and plunge ahead.

FIGURE 5-4 *Society's Investment-Consumption Choice*

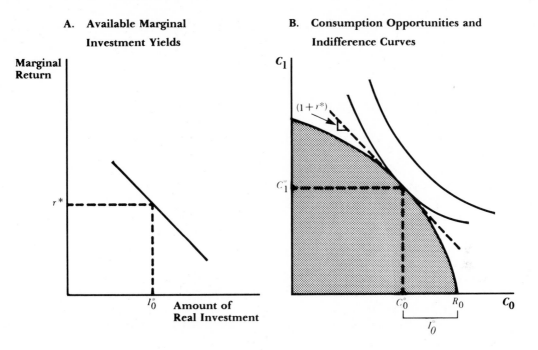

3. In a world of complete certainty, this equilibrium interest rate is set at a level such that investors' *required returns are exactly equal to the productive yields generated* from their investments. Investors will receive the return they require.

The equilibrium interest rate which arises out of classical interest theory is referred to as the *natural*, or *pure, rate*. For convenience we will refer to it symbolically as r^*.

Loanable Funds. The preceding analysis is useful because it shows explicitly that interest rates are indeed a natural phenomenon and identifies at least two fundamental forces at work in creating equilibrium levels of interest. However, this pure rate of interest was created in the market for tangible investments (tractors, lathes, farm acreage, etc.) and tangible savings (labor, land, corn, iron ore, etc.) — that is, in the *real goods market*. Unfortunately, the interest rate which arises is neither seen nor reported in the financial press. What *is* reported are the yields on U.S. Treasury obligations and other high-grade bonds. These yields are created in the *financial market* through an interaction between the demand and supply of *loanable funds*. However, the equilibrium yield in the financial market should be identical to the equilibrium yield in the real goods market.

At any point in time, society has a variety of real investment opportunities (tractors, lathes, farm acreage, etc.) whose marginal returns can be ranked in descending order, as illustrated in panel A of Figure 5-5 by the curve *RI*. This investment schedule, known as the *marginal efficiency of investment* curve, should be familiar to any

FIGURE 5-5 *Real and Financial Markets*

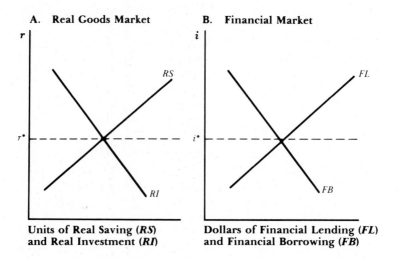

A.   Real Goods Market

B.   Financial Market

Units of Real Saving (*RS*)
and Real Investment (*RI*)

Dollars of Financial Lending (*FL*)
and Financial Borrowing (*FB*)

student of elementary economics. In addition, society owns resources (labor, land, corn, iron ore, etc.) which it is willing to devote to productive investments if reasonably compensated. Given the resources available, the level of the required compensation will depend upon society's time preferences for consumption, i.e., thriftiness. Levels of resource saving are plotted in panel A of Figure 5-5 as curve *RS*.

As before, the equilibrium rate of interest in the real goods market will be r^*, where the marginal productive return on the last unit of real investment equals the marginal required return on the last unit of real saving. This equilibrium rate r^*, is, of course, the classical economist's natural, or pure, rate. We have merely restated our earlier analysis in terms of more familiar demand and supply curves. However, in the "real" world, individuals and corporations do not physically exchange real resources. Instead, financial assets are issued by borrowers and bought by lenders. These financial assets may take the form of a loan contract with a bank, bonds, common stock, preferred stock, convertible debentures, etc. At this point the type of security really doesn't matter since we are dealing with a world of perfect certainty. All instruments are economically the same, although they may carry different legal titles. Panel B illustrates this financial borrowing (*FB*) and lending (*FL*) in the financial market. Note that the financial market is an exact image of the real goods market and that the rate of interest which prevails in the financial market (i^*) is the same as the pure rate. In equilibrium, the financial rate of interest will be equal to the pure rate. In equilibrium, $i^* = r^*$.

The Impacts of Real Economic Forces. We are now in a position to examine various forces which might affect the risk-free interest rate. (Throughout this discussion, remember that we are still examining a risk-free world from the viewpoint of the classical economist.) Classical interest theory held that only fundamental changes in the real goods market could affect equilibrium levels of interest and security prices. These fundamental changes can arise from (1) a shift in the productivity of real investment or (2) a shift in the thriftiness of society.

Consider first a shift in the marginal efficiency of capital curve. Increased productivity would shift the marginal efficiency of investment curve to the right and result in a higher r^*. Such increases could arise from either technological breakthroughs (for example, the discovery and practical application of electricity, computers, nuclear fission, and division of labor) or social changes which increase labor productivity. Reduced productivity would shift the curve back and result in a lower r^*. Such decreases could result from declines in available productive resources (oil, arable land, iron ore, etc.) or social changes which reduce labor productivity.

Figure 5-6 illustrates the impacts of an increase in productivity on the risk-free rate of interest. Assume that a major technological breakthrough occurs, causing an increase in the productive yields available from real investment. This technological breakthrough will cause a shift in the real investment curve from RI_1 to RI_2. The equilibrium pure rate will increase from r_1^* to r_2^*. Initially, however, the prevailing financial market rate will remain at i_1^*, causing a disequilibrium between real and financial markets which can't last.

The dynamic process by which the two markets adjust to a new, stable equilibrium is not fully understood by economists. However, a plausible scenario would be as follows. Initially, businesses are able to borrow funds in the financial market at a rate i_1^*. Because of technological improvement, a larger number of real investments will be profitable at this cost of capital. To enable the purchase of these newly profitable investments, businesses will sell new securities, resulting in an outward shift in the financial borrowing curve. This is represented by point 1 in panels A and B. Interest rates have not yet changed, although both real and financial investments have increased. However, savers will not readily supply additional capital without receiving a higher return. Thus, the financial market rate will rise to point 2. At this higher financial rate, real investment and security offerings will decrease to point 3. This will

FIGURE 5-6 *Equilibrium Between Real and Financial Markets*

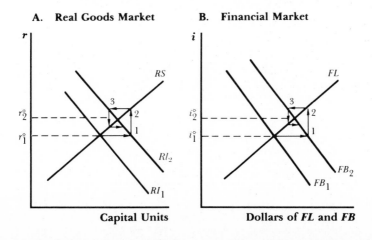

A. **Real Goods Market** B. **Financial Market**

Capital Units   **Dollars of FL and FB**

trigger a reduction in required returns on saving. Eventually the equilibrium process will reach the new, constant, real rate r_2^* and financial market rate i_2^*.

The second fundamental force which might change equilibrium interest rates would be a change in society's thriftiness. This could arise out of a sociological change in attitudes toward real saving versus immediate consumption. In addition, demographic characteristics of a population might also influence the real savings curve. For example, as a society becomes older, there is an increased propensity to spend rather than save.

The Impacts of Monetary Policy. To the classical economists, real economic factors were the sole determinants of equilibrium interest rates. Changes in the amount of money in existence could have no permanent impact on interest rates since it was believed that money would have no effect on the tangible resources available to society. Money was simply a convenient medium for exchanging real goods and services.

Consider the situation depicted in Figure 5-7. Initially, the real goods and financial markets are in equilibrium with $r_1^* = i_1^*$. One morning commercial bankers wake up to find their vaults filled with new cash. Greedy fellows that they are, they aggressively seek to lend the added cash. This action increases the supply of financial lending at all interest rates, and FL_1 shifts to FL_2. As additional loans are made, the financial market interest rate will decline from i_1^* to i_2.

At this lower financial rate, there will be an increase in the number of profitable real investment opportunities. Business will attempt to expand real investment from the initial equilibrium of RI_1^* to RI_2. At the same time, suppliers of savings will attempt to reduce their real saving from RS_1^* to RS_2. However, while businesses and consumers might wish to increase their purchases with the new money now in circulation, they will be unable to do so if the economy is at a full-employment–full-capacity level. *Attempts to purchase additional goods would simply bid prices up without affecting total output, total real saving, or total real investment.* The increase

FIGURE 5-7 *Equilibrium Between Real and Financial Markets*

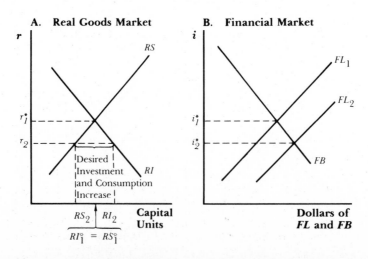

in the money supply would quickly be translated into a one-time inflation of real goods prices. For example, if the money supply had grown by 10% overnight, the prices of all real goods and services would soon increase by 10%. This inflation would decrease the actual real worth of the money supply so that the *real value* of the financial savings schedule would shift back to FL_1. As the real financial savings schedule shifts back, financial interest rates would increase until they are again in equilibrium with r_1^*.

The increase in the money supply *did* depress prevailing financial market interest rates, but only temporarily. Over time, the resultant inflation causes the money market rate to rise again to its initial equilibrium. Since classical economists were principally interested in long-run equilibrium conditions, they felt safe in saying that monetary policy has no impact on interest. Interest was essentially a "real" phenomenon in that over the long run only real, fundamental economic forces determined *RF*. This long-run average *RF* will be equal to the average r^*.

Fiscal Crowd-out. Over the years, some business leaders and economists have been concerned about the impact that government borrowing has had on market interest rates. This concern was heightened in the mid-1980s because of unusually large federal deficits. Figure 5-8 displays the relative amounts of debt which various issuers had outstanding in 1988 compared with 1972. During this sixteen-year period, the U.S. Treasury's proportion of outstanding debt had increased from 29% to over 64%, and all statistics pointed to further increases.

The argument that government borrowing increases market interest rates and crowds out individuals and organizations who would otherwise borrow is depicted in

FIGURE 5-8 *The Relative Importance of Debt Issues*

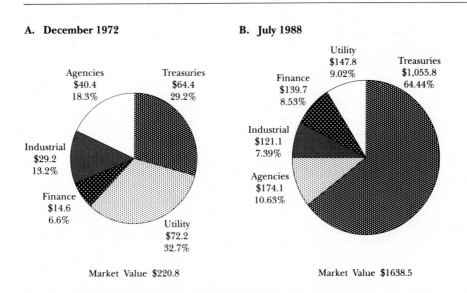

A. December 1972

Agencies $40.4 18.3%
Treasuries $64.4 29.2%
Industrial $29.2 13.2%
Finance $14.6 6.6%
Utility $72.2 32.7%

Market Value $220.8

B. July 1988

Utility $147.8 9.02%
Treasuries $1,055.8 64.44%
Finance $139.7 8.53%
Industrial $121.1 7.39%
Agencies $174.1 10.63%

Market Value $1638.5

SOURCE: Shearson Lehman Hutton, Corporate Bond Research Department.

Figure 5-9. The financial lending schedule is shown as the line *FL*. Borrowings of nongovernmental bodies for each rate of interest are shown in the financial borrowing schedule FB_1. When government borrowings are added to this, the borrowing schedule becomes FB_2. With the presence of government debt, the equilibrium interest rises from i_1 to i_2. Although total borrowing and lending increase (from $\$_1$ to $\$_2$), the rise is due solely to increased government debt and occurs at the expense of private debt. Private borrowers are crowded out of the markets because the higher rate i_2 causes them to borrow less.

How strong are the impacts of government borrowing on interest rates? We simply do not know. Many people would argue that the effects are minimal, if present at all. However, the large Treasury borrowings of the 1980s are a concern to a growing number of people who believe that the high levels of real interest rates which came at the same time as the borrowing are no mere coincidence.

Natural Nominal Rates

One of the most insightful classical economists was Irving Fisher. In 1895, at the request of the American Economic Association, Fisher undertook a detailed examination of the effect of inflation on the rate of interest. These studies were summarized

FIGURE 5-9 *An Illustration of Fiscal Crowd-out*

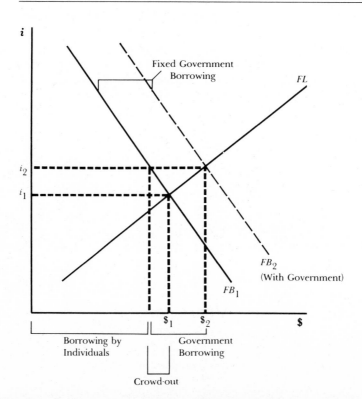

in his text, *The Theory of Interest*. In spite of its age, this is still one of the best discussions of why interest rates exist and what their inherent determinants are.

Fisher's Nominal Risk-Free Return. Fisher's analysis of interest rates is as straightforward and simple as it is important in explaining why interest rates change over time. Fisher begins with the assumption that individuals who lend money realize that what is being lent is not so much pieces of paper (cash) but control of real goods. The rate of return which lenders demand from a loan of capital represents not so much a return on money as it does an increase in their command of real goods. When a sum of money is lent, the lender wishes to receive an increase in *purchasing power* equal to the equilibrium pure rate. If lenders expect an inflation in commodity prices, they will demand a rate of return which provides compensation for both a required real rate of return and the inflation which is expected.

Suppose that both the borrower and lender know with perfect certainty that inflation during the next year will be 5%. If a *real rate* of 3% is required on a loan, the lender will charge a *nominal* rate of 8.15%. For each $1 lent today, $1.05 must be returned next period to keep the lender's purchasing power intact. If the lender requires a 3% increase in next year's purchasing power, he or she will demand a $1.0815 ($1.05 × 1.03) payment in period 2.

The relationship between the real and nominal rates of interest can be expressed symbolically. If r^* represents the equilibrium real rate of interest and I_t represents the average inflation rate expected over the next t years, then the nominal rate of interest on a security maturing in year $t(RF_t)$ would be:

Nominal Rate of Interest

$$RF_t = (1 + r^*)(1 + I_t) - 1.0$$
$$= r^* + I_t + (r^*)I_t$$

(5.3)

Assume that a Ms. Moore is attempting to determine what might be a fair rate of return on a purchase of U.S. Treasury obligations. She personally desires a real annual return of 2% per year and, after a rather thorough analysis of prevailing economic conditions, has estimated the following inflation rates:

Future Year	*Average Annual Inflation Rate Between Now and Future Year-End*
1	4%
2	5%
3	4%
4	3%
5	3%

Given these inflation expectations, Ms. Moore would determine fair nominal rates to be as follows:

Maturity Year	*Pure Rate*	*Average Yearly Inflation*	*Nominal Rate*
1	2%	4%	6.08%
2	2%	5%	7.10%
3	2%	4%	6.08%
4	2%	3%	5.06%
5	2%	3%	5.06%

Alternatively, Ms. Moore might use prevailing nominal returns on risk-free Treasury yields to forecast the market's consensus of future inflation. For example, assume she believes that other people require a real return of 2%. If prevailing yields on Treasury obligations with different maturities are as shown below, she could calculate an estimate of the marketwide consensus of inflation:[8]

Maturity Year	Yield on Treasury Bond Maturing in Year	Pure Rate	Implied Average Yearly Inflation
1	7%	2%	4.90%
2	9%	2%	6.86%
3	6%	2%	3.92%
4	5%	2%	2.94%
5	5%	2%	2.94%

Later we will see how this sort of information might be useful to speculators and arbitrageurs.

Actual Historical Real Returns. In practice, people are uncertain about future rates of inflation. Instead of using a known inflation rate in Equation 5.3, a market consensus of *expected* inflation is used. Unfortunately, there is no guarantee that the desired real rate will indeed be earned. Actual inflation might easily vary from expectations. If I_t^a refers to the actual inflation during period t, RF_t refers to the *nominal* return earned during period t, and r_t^a refers to the actual real return in period t, then we can use Equation 5.3 to show that:

Actual Real Return

$$RF_t = (1 + r_t^a)(1 + I_t^a) - 1 \qquad (5.4)$$

Rearranging Equation 5.4 to solve for the actual real return results in:

Actual Real Return

$$r_t^a = \frac{(1 + RF_t)}{(1 + I_t^a)} - 1.0 \qquad (5.5)$$

For example, if at the start of 1990 investors desire a real return of 2% and expect the inflation rate during 1990 to be 3%, they would purchase a one-year T-bill only if it yielded a nominal return of 5.06%. If the actual rate of inflation turns out to be higher — say, equal to 4% — investor's actual real return would be 1.02%:

$$\frac{1.0506}{1.04} - 1.0 = 0.0102$$

In Chapter 4 we examined unit value series of returns on various market indexes. Since each of these unit value series was developed from *actual nominal* rates of re-

---

[8]The implied average yearly inflation rates are calculated by rearranging Equation 5.3 as follows:

$$I_t = \frac{RF_t - r^*}{(1 + r^*)}$$

turn, they do not reflect the *real* returns earned on each market index. To calculate historical real returns, the nominal return unit values must be adjusted for growth in the Consumer Price Index (CPI) over time.

In Table 5-1, a CPI unit value series is presented. The unit values were calculated exactly as in Chapter 4, except that the series now is compounded at annual rates of increases in the CPI instead of at security rates of return. For example, the unit value increase in 1987 reflects a 4.25% increase in the CPI:

$$\frac{6.503}{6.238} - 1 = 0.0425$$

Similarly, the average compound annual growth in the CPI from 1925 through 1987 was 3.07%:

$$\left(\frac{6.503}{1.00}\right)^{1/62} - 1.0 = 0.0307$$

Equation 5.5 and the data in Table 5-1 can be used to calculate annual (or any period greater than a year) real returns on the various indexes discussed in Chapter 4. Of the different types of securities available, T-bills are believed to be the least risky. Figure 5-10 shows the historical record of nominal and actual real returns on T-bills since 1925. From the late 1960s until the early 1980s nominal T-bill returns increased substantially. However, after adjustment for inflation, real returns during this time interval were often negative. In the mid-1980s this trend was reversed and actual real returns were positive. As noted earlier in the chapter, a growing number of people believe this can be traced to the massive borrowings by the U.S. Treasury to finance federal deficits at that time. However, over the full 62 years covered by Figure 5-10, the average annual real Treasury bill return was only slightly greater than 0.0% (0.4%).

TABLE 5-1 *Consumer Price Index Unit Values, 1925–1987*

Year	Unit Value	Year	Unit Value	Year	Unit Value	Year	Unit Value
1925	1.000	1941	0.862	1957	1.604	1973	2.607
1926	0.985	1942	0.943	1958	1.632	1974	2.925
1927	0.965	1943	0.973	1959	1.657	1975	3.130
1928	0.955	1944	0.993	1960	1.681	1976	3.281
1929	0.957	1945	1.016	1961	1.692	1977	3.503
1930	0.900	1946	1.200	1962	1.713	1978	3.820
1931	0.814	1947	1.308	1963	1.741	1979	4.328
1932	0.730	1948	1.344	1964	1.762	1980	4.866
1933	0.734	1949	1.333	1965	1.796	1981	5.301
1934	0.749	1950	1.410	1966	1.857	1982	5.506
1935	0.771	1951	1.493	1967	1.913	1983	5.715
1936	0.780	1952	1.506	1968	2.003	1984	5.945
1937	0.805	1953	1.516	1969	2.126	1985	6.169
1938	0.782	1954	1.508	1970	2.242	1986	6.238
1939	0.779	1955	1.513	1971	2.317	1987	6.503
1940	0.786	1956	1.557	1972	2.397		

FIGURE 5-10 *Nominal and Real T-Bill Returns 1926–1987*

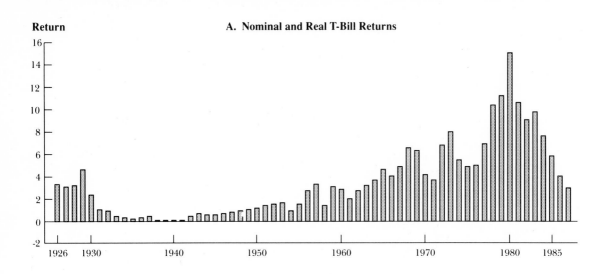

A. Nominal and Real T-Bill Returns

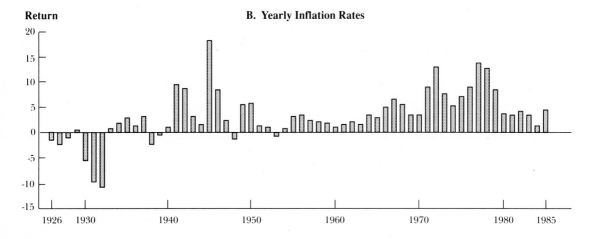

B. Yearly Inflation Rates

SUMMARY

Financial markets exist because they provide a benefit to society. Without them, the amount of total consumption and real investment available to individual economic units would be constrained. Each unit would be required to consume plus invest in real assets an amount identical to its ownership of real assets. People with few real assets or a large number of highly profitable real investment opportunities would be unable to invest as much as they desired. And people with an overabundance of assets would be forced to accept very low-yielding investments. The *primary securities market* allows people to temporarily exchange real assets for financial assets. Economic units with surpluses of real assets may lend them to borrowers who have a defi-

FIGURE 5-10 *(continued)*

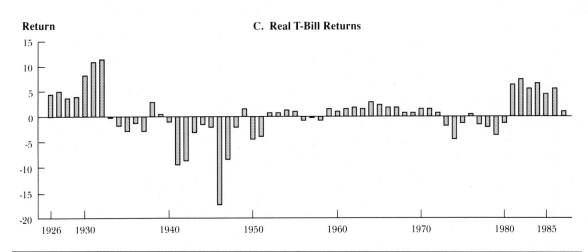

Return   **C. Real T-Bill Returns**

SOURCE: Adapted from R. Ibbotson and R. Sinquefield, *Stocks, Bonds, Bills, and Inflation: Historical Returns (1926–1978)* (Charlottesville, Va.: Financial Analysts Research Foundation, 1979), pp. 63, 64, 67. Since 1978, updated by author.

ciency. As a result, society benefits in two ways: (1) individuals have greater freedom in deciding the amounts they wish to consume and invest in real assets, and (2) the average standard of living is improved since only the most productive real assets are invested in.

To ensure an efficient exchange market for financial and real assets, a secondary market consisting of brokers and dealers exists. This secondary market is a multifaceted group of organizations, such as retail stockbrokers, large-block traders, pension funds, mutual funds, commercial banks, the NYSE, the AMEX, and the OTC.

Basically, the secondary markets (1) reduce transaction costs of matching end borrowers and lenders, (2) resolve differences between borrowers and lenders (such as maturity desires), (3) enable greater degrees of diversification by further subdividing the cost of claims on real assets, (4) allow people to easily adjust their investment risk levels, and (5) provide increased investment marketability.

The nominal risk-free rate of interest appears to be composed of a pure rate of interest (determined by society's productivity and thriftiness) plus an adjustment for expected inflation over the life of the security.

REVIEW PROBLEM

Consider the two-period investment/consumption problem in the following figure:

a. What is this person's period 0 wealth level without financial markets? With financial markets?

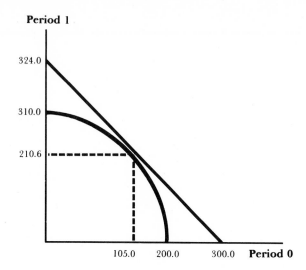

b. How much should this person invest in real assets? Why is this decision independent of the person's time preferences for consumption?

c. What is the prevailing financial rate of interest?

d. If this person wished to consume $300 at period 0, how would this be accomplished?

e. With financial markets, the consumption possibilities line increases. Why is this so?

f. Assume that this person wished to consume $150 at period 0. How would this be accomplished, and what would period 1 consumption be?

g. Assume that this person wished to consume $80 at period 0. How would this be accomplished, and what would period 1 consumption be?

Solution

a. Without financial markets, wealth would be the original endowment of $200. With financial markets, the individual is able to increase wealth by investing in real assets at a return that is greater than the financial borrowing cost. Wealth with the financial markets is $300.

b. $200 − $105 = $95. Invest the initial endowment of $200 in real assets until the marginal cost of borrowing (also the marginal return of financial investment) is equal to the marginal return on such real assets.

c. $324/$300 − 1 = 8%, the slope of the market exchange line.

d. First, invest $95 in real assets. Second, borrow against the payoff of these real investments. This loan would have a current worth of $300 − $105 = $195. Finally, consume both the loan of $195 and the remaining endowment of $105.

e. Investing $95 of the $200 endowment in real assets leaves $105 of the endowment available for consumption. If not all of this $105 is to be consumed in period 0, financial assets provide returns which are larger than the person could have obtained on real investments. If more than $105 is to be consumed, then the excess is obtained from borrowing at a financial rate which is less than the return being earned on real asset investments. (This question is designed to show that the existence of financial markets provides an economic benefit by increasing wealth and consumption opportunities.)

f.

	Period 0	Period 1	
Initial Endowment	$ 200.00		
Less Investment	(95.00)	$ 210.60	
Available for Consumption	$ 105.00	$ 210.60	
Financial Transactions			
Borrow	45.00	(48.60)	= 45 × 1.08
Consume	$ 150.00	$ 162.00	

g.

	Period 0	Period 1
Initial Endowment	$ 200.00	
Less Investment	(95.00)	$ 210.60
Available for Consumption	105.00	210.60
Financial Transactions		
Lend	25.00	27.00
Consume	$ 80.00	$ 237.60

QUESTIONS AND PROBLEMS

1. Very little was said in this chapter about the impacts of U.S. Treasury and agency borrowings, although they represent major demands of credit. Analyze the likely impacts of such borrowings on the real rate, the financial rate, the amount of total real investment, and the amount of real investment made by nongovernment units. To narrow the project somewhat, assume that (a) there is full employment, (b) there will be no inflation impacts, and (c) all borrowings are put to productive uses.

2. Indicate the likely impact of the following events (over the long run) on risk-free interest rates. Be prepared to justify opinions.
   a. Federal spending is expected to increase as a percentage of GNP and be financed with new bond sales to the public.
   b. Labor productivity declines.
   c. Technological innovations decrease relative to the past.

3. Some forecasters of long-run business and social conditions believe labor productivity will continue to decline and not be offset by new technological advances. Discuss the implications of this possibility on:
   a. Future levels of the risk-free rate
   b. Economic values of existing securities

4. While conversing with a neighbor at a Sunday afternoon barbecue, you mention your job as an arbitrageur in T-bills. Upon hearing this, the neighbor starts off on a harangue about how evil Wall Street and the securities business are: "Those big business capitalists are out to _____ the ordinary Joe. Heck, it's just a fixed roulette wheel. As far as I'm concerned, we'd be one heck of a lot better off without all them brokers and dealers!" Respond intelligently (in less than one hour).

5. Classical economists believed inflation would have no impact on the equilibrium real goods rate of interest, *r*. It turns out that this result is dependent on inflation's being "neutral,"

that is, affecting every member of society identically. Assume now, however, that there are distinct groups of people who are adversely affected, whereas other groups gain. *Now* might inflation affect *r*? Why?

6. On January 1, Jan Templeton purchased a T-bill which had 50 days remaining to maturity at a discount of 11.00%. Now that the T-bill has matured, she is attempting to estimate her real rate of return. She estimates that during this 50-day period, the inflation rate was 2% (not a yearly rate — a 50-day rate).
   a. When she bought the T-bill, what was her guaranteed nominal return? (State as both a one-year rate and a 50-day rate.)
   b. If she had expected inflation during the 50 days to be on the order of 1% (a 50-day rate), what was her expected real rate? (State as both a one-year rate and a 50-day rate.)
   c. What was her actual real return? (Again, figure both annually and for 50 days.)

7. Larry Arthurs desires to earn a 2% real return. After a thorough analysis of the economy, he develops the following estimates of future inflation rates:

End of Future Year	Average Annual Inflation Between Now and Year-End
1	12%
2	10%
3	9%

In addition, he observes the following quoted annual yields on Treasury securities:

Maturity	Annual Yield
1 year	14%
2 years	10%
3 years	12%

Develop a reasonable trading strategy that he might follow.

8. How is your answer to problem 7 dependent upon:
   a. Status of economic conditions?
   b. Degree to which arbitrage exists in the markets?
   c. Whether the money supply increase is expected by arbitrageurs or unexpected?

9. Trace the impact which an *unexpected* increase in the growth rate of M_1 would have upon both "financial market" interest rates and "real goods" interest rates. Assume this occurs at a time when employment levels are high and expected to remain high.

10. Use the data in Tables 5-1 and 4-5 to calculate the average compound annual *real* returns (real $\bar{G}$) on T-bills from 1925 to 1987.

DATA ANALYSIS PROBLEM

Objective:

• To examine the historical *real returns* earned on various security classes.

Most investors are more interested in real returns they might earn on various security classes than in nominal returns. The reason is obvious: people invest in order to be able to consume (hopefully more) in the future, and the amount they can consume is affected by inflation.

1. Access the YRLYINDX.WK1 data set and calculate real returns for each of the following security classes: T-bills, government bonds, corporate bonds, S&P 500, and small company stocks. (You may simply subtract the inflation rate each year from the security's nominal return. This will lead to slight differences from what you would get if you use Equation 5.5, but the errors are minor enough to neglect.)

2. Create a unit value series for each security class.

3. Calculate the arithmetic average annual return $(\bar{R})$, the geometric average annual return $(\bar{G})$, and the standard deviation of annual returns for each series. Evaluate the results.

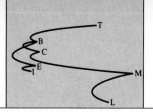

6 Term Structure

In the previous chapter we focused on the underlying determinants of the risk-free rate of interest, *RF*. In this chapter we expand that discussion to see how the maturity of a security might affect its expected return. We will see that a single risk-free rate might not exist at any point in time. Instead, various rates can exist which depend upon the maturity of the underlying security. A subscript will be added to *RF* so that we can refer to the nominal risk-free rate on a security maturing in *t* years. *RF* now becomes RF_t.

The relationship between promised security yields and security maturities is referred to as the *term structure* of interest rates. Term structures are usually displayed graphically in what is known as a *yield curve*. An example of a yield curve for U.S. Treasury securities is shown in Figure 6-1. Maturity is plotted on the horizontal axis and yield to maturity on the vertical. Yield curves are always plotted for securities with similar degrees of default risk.[1] The curve is typically an "eyeballed" best-fit line, although quantitative techniques can also be used.

Yield curves vary considerably over time in level and shape, as shown in Figure 6-2. Typically, they are low and upward sloping during periods of slack economic activity. During rapid business growth and full employment they tend to be high and somewhat downward sloping. Understanding what causes such movements in the yield curve is the overall objective of this chapter. Three basic theories are discussed:

1. *Market segmentation theory* (MST) proponents argue that people have strong preferences about the maturity structure of their financial borrowing and lending. These preferences tend to create financial asset demand and supply conditions which are *unique* to each *maturity segment* of the yield curve. Interest rates within each segment are determined largely by *current demand and supply within that segment*.

2. *Unbiased expectations theory* (UET) proponents argue that arbitrageurs will seek to profit from any yield distortions between maturity segments. They will buy in-

---

[1]Default risk refers to the probability that contractual coupon and principal payments will not be fully made. See Chapter 11 for a discussion of the determinants and impacts which default risk has on expected returns.

FIGURE 6-1 *U.S. Treasury Yield Curve*

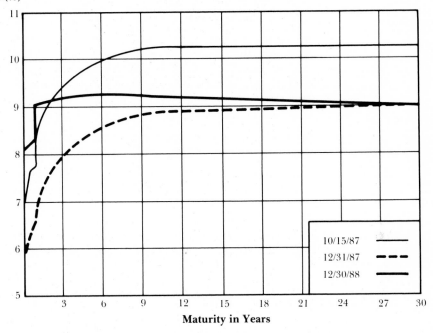

FIGURE 6-2 *Hypothetical Yield Curves at Various Stages of Economic Activity*

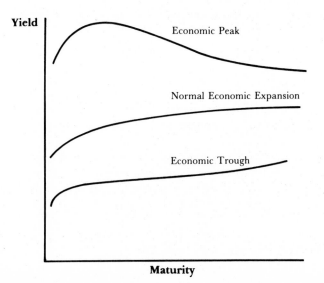

struments whose yields are currently high and simultaneously sell instruments whose yields are currently low. Their trading will cause the yields on securities of differing maturities to be closely related. According to UET, interest rates will be determined by *current as well as expected future supply and demand conditions across all market segments.*

3. *Liquidity preference theory* (LPT) proponents largely accept the conclusions reached by the UET but also believe that yields on long-term securities will typically be higher than yields on shorter-term securities. LPT proponents argue that securities with a longer term to maturity are exposed to *greater amounts of "principal risk," for which lenders will demand a compensation known as a "liquidity premium."*

The investment and speculative implications reached by each theory differ, sometimes dramatically. For example, speculative opportunities are almost nonexistent if the UET version of the yield curve is correct, whereas the MST version holds out the hope of major speculative and arbitrage opportunities. In addition, if UET is correct, the returns investors can *expect* to realize over long periods of time are unaffected by the maturity characteristics of the securities bought. According to most proponents of LPT, however, investors in long-term securities will earn greater real returns than will investors who buy a sequence of many shorter-term securities.

SOME BASIC CONCEPTS

Before we proceed with a discussion of these theories, some basic concepts need to be understood. These include the following:

1. Yield to maturity on coupon bonds
2. Bond-pricing theorems
3. Yields on pure discount bonds
4. Forward rates implied in the discount bond yield curve
5. Expected spot rates

Yields to Maturity on Coupon Bonds

The *yield to maturity* on a coupon bond is that interest rate which will discount future cash flows to the bond's current price. Since yields to maturity might be different for various maturities, we associate each yield with a given maturity as follows:

YTM_M = yield to maturity on a bond having a maturity of M years

For a bond which pays coupons at the end of each year, the YTM_M is found by solving the following equation:

$$P_0 = \frac{C}{(1 + YTM_M)^1} + \frac{C}{(1 + YTM_M)^2} + \cdots$$

**Definition
of Yield
to Maturity**

$$+ \frac{C}{(1 + YTM_M)^M} + \frac{F}{(1 + YTM_M)^M}$$

(6.1)

where P_0 = the current market price of the bond, C = the coupon payment received at each year-end, M = the number of years to maturity, and F = the par value of the bond.

To illustrate the formula's use, consider a five-year, noncallable bond which pays a 9% coupon at the end of each year and has a $1,000 face value. If the bond is currently selling at a price of $962.10, its yield to maturity is 10%:

$$\$962.10 = \frac{\$90}{(1 + YTM_5)^1} + \frac{\$90}{(1 + YTM_5)^2} + \frac{\$90}{(1 + YTM_5)^3} + \frac{\$90}{(1 + YTM_5)^4}$$

$$+ \frac{\$1,090}{(1 + YTM_5)^5}$$

$$= \frac{\$90}{1.1^1} + \frac{\$90}{1.1^2} + \frac{\$90}{1.1^3} + \frac{\$90}{1.1^4} + \frac{\$1,090}{1.1^5}$$

$$= \$81.82 + \$74.38 + \$67.62 + \$61.47 + \$676.81$$

Many readers will recognize the yield to maturity to be the same concept as the *internal rate of return* used in capital budgeting. It is a useful measure to help evaluate both historical rates of return and expected rates of return. But there are dangers in its indiscriminant use, which we will address in Chapters 11 through 14, when stock and bond investments are examined more closely.

Bond-Pricing Theorems

Equation 6.1 specifies the relationship between bond price, coupon rate, maturity, and yield to maturity from which the following five bond theorems have been developed. To illustrate each theorem, we examine the price of both 8% coupon bonds and 6% coupon bonds having one of three possible maturity dates: one year, five years, and nine years. Results are displayed in Figure 6-3.

1. *When the annual coupon rate and yield to maturity are identical, a bond will always sell at par.* In Figure 6-3 this is shown as the solid horizontal lines at the par and market values of $1,000. For example, the 8% coupon rate pays $80 each year on $1,000 face value. If investors demand an annual yield of 8%, they would be willing to pay $1,000 since the $80 coupon then represents exactly what they require.

2. *Bond prices move inversely to changes in yields to maturity.* Note in Figure 6-3 that when yields to maturity are greater than the coupon rate, the bonds sell at less

FIGURE 6-3 *Relationship Between Bond Price, Coupon Rate, Maturity, and* **YTM**

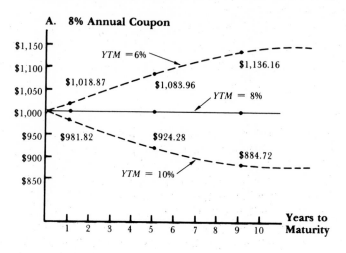

A. **8% Annual Coupon**

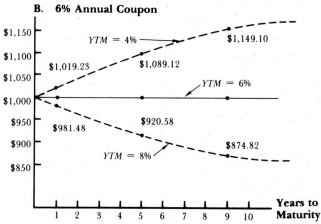

B. **6% Annual Coupon**

than par (at a discount).[2] In such cases investors expect to receive the yield to maturity from both an annual coupon and an annual price appreciation. When the yield to maturity is less than the coupon rate, prices will be greater than par (at a premium). Investors are then expecting a yearly return equal to the coupon payment minus an annual price depreciation.

3. *Long-term bonds are more price sensitive to a given change in the yield to maturity than are shorter-term bonds.* Note in panel A (the 8% coupon issue) that a change in the yield to maturity from 8% to 6% causes the one-year bond to in-

---

[2]*Discount bonds* are bonds which sell for less than par value (usually $1,000). *Premium bonds* are those which sell for more than par value. *Deep discount bonds* are bonds selling at sizable discounts, say, for $500 to $600.

crease in value from $1,000 to $1,018.87. The five-year bond increases from $1,000 to $1,083.96.

4. *While the price sensitivity of a bond increases with its maturity (theorem 3), this sensitivity increases at a decreasing rate.* Again refer to panel A and the shift in yields to maturity from 8% to 6%. Note that the one-year bond increases by $18.87, or 1.89%, whereas the five-year bond increases by $83.96, or 8.40%. The longer-term bond increased by 651 basis points more (840 − 189) than the shorter-term bond. However, the basis-point change is less between the nine-year and five-year issues. While the nine-year obligation increases by $136.16, or 13.62%, this is only a 522-basis-point improvement (1362 − 840) over the five-year bond. The longer a bond's maturity, the greater its price sensitivity. But this sensitivity increases at a decreasing rate.

5. *High-coupon bonds are less price sensitive to a given yield to maturity change than are lower-coupon bonds.* To see this, examine both panels A (8% coupon) and B (6% coupon) for bonds with a nine-year maturity. If yields to maturity are initially 6%, the 8% coupon issue sells at a premium ($1,136.16), and the 6% issue sells at par. Now assume that the yield to maturity rises to 8%. The high-coupon bond falls in price by $136.16, or 11.98%. The price of the lower-coupon bond falls by $125.18, or 12.52%. The percentage price movement is greater on the low-coupon bond. (In Chapter 11 we will see that this coupon effect is related to the effective maturity of the bond, i.e., its duration.)

These five bond theorems play an important role in the development of the various yield curve theories as well as other concepts of investing and speculating.

Yields on Pure Discount Bonds

A pure discount bond is one which does not pay any coupons but pays a single lump sum at its maturity. Since the only source of return on such bonds is price appreciation, they always trade at discounts from the lump sum to be received at maturity. For example, assume that bond 1 and bond 2 are both pure discount bonds and mature in exactly one year and two years, respectively. If the bonds have $1,000 par values and investors desire a 5% return during the next year and a 7.5% annualized return during the next two years, the bonds will trade at the following prices:

$$\text{Bond 1:} \quad \frac{\$1,000}{1.05} = \$952.381$$

$$\text{Bond 2:} \quad \frac{\$1,000}{1.075^2} = \$865.333$$

Pure discount bonds will be of particular use in this chapter, since we will be able to use their market values to calculate a structure of underlying forward rates. This is discussed immediately below. But for now it is important to understand the relationships between yields to maturity calculated for coupon-paying bonds and yields to maturity for pure discount bonds.

We will refer to the *yield to maturity on a pure discount bond* as I_M. It is calculated by solving the following equation:

Yield to Maturity on a Pure Discount Bond

$$P_0 = \frac{F}{(1 + I_M)^M} \tag{6.2a}$$

or

$$I_M = \left(\frac{F}{P_0}\right)^{1/M} - 1.0 \tag{6.2b}$$

where P_0 = the current market price of the pure discount bond, F = the bond's par value, and M = the number of years to the bond's maturity.

For example, assume that we could observe the market prices of bonds 1 and 2 above to be \$952.381 and \$865.333, respectively, but that we did not yet know their respective yields to maturity. Using Equation 6.2b, these yields would be calculated as follows:

$$\text{Bond 1:} \quad I_1 = \left(\frac{\$1,000}{\$952.381}\right)^{1/1} - 1.0 = 0.05, \text{ or } 5\%$$

$$\text{Bond 2:} \quad I_2 = \left(\frac{\$1,000}{\$865.333}\right)^{1/2} - 1.0 = 0.075, \text{ or } 7.5\%$$

Yields to maturity calculated for coupon bonds (YTM_M) will be equal to yields to maturity of discount bonds *only if the yield curve for both is flat*. This rarely (if ever) occurs. More commonly, both yield structures tend to increase as bond maturities increase. In this case, YTM_M will be somewhat lower than I_M.

The reason for this can be easily seen if we think of a coupon bond as being a series of pure discount bonds. For example, consider a two-year, 10% coupon, \$1,000 par value bond which we will refer to as bond B. This bond is really two distinct pure discount bonds. The first discount bond matures in one year at a value of \$100 and the second matures in two years at a value of \$1,100. If we use the I_M pure discount yields of $I_1 = 5\%$ and $I_2 = 7.5\%$ calculated above, investors would value these two discount bonds as follows:

Maturity	Value	
One Year	$\$100 \div 1.05$	= \$ 95.238
Two Years	$\$1,100 \div 1.075^2 =$	951.866
Total Value		\$1,047.104

Note that if bond 1 and bond 2 (the pure discount bonds) as well as bond B (the coupon bond) can be traded in the markets, then bond B must sell for \$1,047.104. If it traded at any other price, an arbitrage between the three bonds would be possible.[3] For example, if bond B could be bought for less than \$1,047.104, the arbitrage would consist of buying a certain dollar value of bond B and financing the

---

[3]This neglects potential transaction costs and differing tax characteristics of coupon versus pure discount bonds.

purchase through the sale of an equal dollar amount of bonds 1 and 2. Details of the arbitrage are beyond the scope of our present discussion. But the important point is that the coupon bond will be valued as the sum of its pure discount bond components.

Given that bond B will have a market value of $1,047.104, its yield to maturity would be calculated to be 7.38%:

$$\$1,047.104 = \frac{\$100}{1 + YTM_2} + \frac{\$1,100}{(1 + YTM_2)^2}$$

$$YTM_2 = 7.38\%$$

Note that YTM_2 is less than I_2; the yield to maturity on a coupon bond is less than the yield on a pure discount bond when the yield structure is rising. The reason is easy to see. In valuing coupon bonds such as bond B, their early cash flows are discounted at lower interest rates than later cash flows. Thus, the YTM_M implied in a coupon bond will be lower than the I_M implied on a similar maturity discount bond if the discount bond yield curve is rising.

Since the structure of yields implied in discount bond prices is not affected by such "coupon effects," it is the better measure of the annualized return which investors require for investments of a certain time period. Virtually all discussions for the rest of this chapter apply to the yields to maturity available on pure discount bonds.

Forward Rates

At a given point in time a set of (pure discount) yields to maturity exist for securities which are identical in all respects but maturity. We have defined this as the term structure of interest. Basically, each I_M reflects the rate of return which buyers are promised if they buy the bond at current prices. The term structure reflects *current*, or *spot*, rates of interest for a given maturity. Underlying any set of yields to maturity, however, is a set of other interest rates which are referred to as implied *forward rates*. These forward rates play an important role in yield curve theory and in advanced investment and speculative strategies. Symbolically, we will denote the forward rate as:

f_{Mt} = the forward rate of interest which will have an M period maturity in t years from today

For simplicity, we will think of periods as being years even though periods could conceivably be of any length. Therefore:

$f_{1,0}$ = the forward rate on one-year investments as of today, i.e., today's actual one-year *spot rate*

$f_{1,1}$ = the forward rate on one-year investments as of one year from now

$f_{1,2}$ = the forward rate on one-year investments as of two years from now

$f_{5,10}$ = the forward rate on five-year investments as of ten years from now

Forward rates are calculated using pure discount bond yields to maturity with the following equation:

Forward Rate

$$f_{Mt} = \left(\frac{(1 + I_{t+M})^{t+M}}{(1 + I_t)^t} \right)^{1/M} - 1.0 \qquad (6.3)$$

For example, assume that yields to maturity are now $I_1 = 8\%$ and $I_2 = 9\%$. This implies a forward rate on one-year investments of 10% in exactly one year from now:

$$f_{1,1} = \left(\frac{(1 + I_{1+1})^2}{1 + I_1} \right)^{1/1} - 1.0$$

$$0.10 = \left(\frac{1.09^2}{1.08^1} \right)^1 - 1.0$$

Thus an $I_2 = 9\%$ and an $I_1 = 8\%$ imply that a one-year forward rate of return equal to 10% can be "locked in" (assured) today by trading in the one-year and two-year pure discount bonds.

To illustrate how one could lock in this 10% forward return, consider the market values of discount bonds with one- and two-year maturities. Call these bond A and bond B.

$$\text{Price of } A = \frac{\$1,000}{1.08^1} = \$925.93$$

$$\text{Price of } B = \frac{\$1,000}{1.09^2} = \$841.68$$

To lock in a one-year forward rate starting at the beginning of year 2, investors would sell short the one-year bond and buy some multiple of the two-year bond. They will buy an amount of the two-year bond such that their initial investment in the two-year issue is identical to the cash received on the short sale of the one-year bond. For example, the $925.93 received from shorting the one-year bond will be used to buy 1.1 ($925.93 ÷ $841.65) two-year bonds. Thus, their net position during the first year is zero. They owe one bond A and own some multiple of bond B, which results in no actual investment during year 1. Starting in year 2, however, they continue to own bond B when bond A no longer exists. On net, they are long in bonds during period 2. Details of the trade are shown in Table 6-1 and explained as follows:

1. *At the start of period 1* sell short 1.0 of bond A. This provides immediate cash inflow of $925.93, which is used to purchase 1.1 of bond B. The net cash flow at the start of period 1 will be zero.
2. *At the end of period 1* the short sale of bond A will have to be covered. This requires a $1,000 cash outflow. The long position of 1.1 of bond B is left untouched, so the net cash flow at the end of period 1 will be negative $1,000.
3. *At the end of period 2* the 1.1 of bond B will mature and provide $1,000 cash for each full bond. A net cash inflow of $1,100 will be received.

Effectively, this process allows one to be uninvested during period 1 but assured an investment during period 2 on which a 10% yield is locked in.

TABLE 6-1 *Locking In Forward Rates*

	Cash Flows Received (Disbursed) at End of Period		
	0	*1*	*2*
1.0 Bond *A*	$ 925.93	($1,000)	—
1.1 Bond *B*	(925.93)	—	$1,100
Net Cash Flow	$0	($1,000)	$1,100
Return in Period 2 =	$\dfrac{\$1,100 - \$1,000}{\$1,000} = 10\%$		

These examples serve to emphasize four important points. First, when thinking about interest rates we should consider *existing yields* as displayed in current yield curves as well as *implied forward rates*. Interest rates consist of explicitly known spot rates as well as implied forward rates of interest.

Second, the yield to maturity on a pure discount security can be regarded as an average of many shorter-term implied forward rates. In the example above, the 9.0% yield to maturity on the two-year bond *B* is actually an average of an immediate one-year rate of 8.0% and a forward one-year rate of 10.0%. This "average" is not an arithmetic average. Instead it is a *geometric average* similar to the geometric average discussed in Chapter 4. To calculate the geometric average return, the following steps are employed:

1. Add 1.0 to each period's implied forward rate.
2. Multiply the series of values obtained in step 1.
3. Take the *M*th root of the product obtained in step 2. By taking the root of a multiplied series, one essentially gets an average of the multiplied series.
4. Finally, subtract 1.0 from the result in step 3. This step results in a geometric average rate of return. The general formula is:

Discount Bond Yield to Maturity
$$I_M = \sqrt[M]{(1 + F_{1,0})(1 + F_{1,1})(1 + F_{1,2}) \ldots (1 + F_{1,M-1})} - 1.0 \qquad (6.4)$$

Using the data for the two-year bond in our example above:
$$\sqrt[2]{(1.08)(1.1)} - 1.0 = 9.0\%$$

Equation 6.4 is the key to understanding the three yield curve theories, and we will return to it throughout this chapter as well as throughout the book. But for now it is enough to simply understand that a given I_M can be regarded as a geometric average of many implied forward rates.

Third, the mechanics of Equation 6.4 can be used by speculators to lock in implied forward rates. Speculative trading across securities of differing maturities, while motivated to earn profits, will result in a close interrelationship between yields to maturity seen in any yield curve. This is discussed more fully later in the chapter when we discuss the unbiased expectations theory.

Finally, yields to maturity on coupon bonds are only approximations of the underlying true term structure of interest rates implied by I_M values. Unfortunately, coupon bonds are much more actively traded than zero-coupon bonds. Thus, most yield curves are drawn using coupon bonds' *YTM*s.

Expected Spot Rates

Earlier we defined the spot rate of interest to be the rate of return promised on a bond if an investment is made in the bond now. Spot rates are the YTM_M and I_M yields to maturity. In addition to current spot rates of interest, speculators will develop estimates of *expected future spot rates*. We will define the expected spot rate of interest as:

$E(I_{Mt})$ = today's expectation of what the spot rate will be on pure discount bonds which will have an M period maturity in t years from now.

Speculators will compare their expected spot rate with the forward rate which can currently be obtained by trades in spot bonds and trade appropriately. In the example above, if they believe one-year bond yields will be, say, 9.2% in a year from now, the locked-in implied forward rate would provide larger yields. A policy of buying one two-year bond is expected to be more profitable than a policy of buying a sequence of two one-year bonds. Alternatively, if speculators believe one-year bond yields are going to rise substantially to, say, 10.5%, they would expect an opposite strategy to be more profitable: buy a sequence of two one-year bonds and don't buy the two-year bonds (in fact, perhaps short sell the two-year instrument).

Whenever forward rates implied by the existing yield curve differ from a person's expectation of future spot rates, a speculative trade is called for. Only when forward rates are identical to expected spot rates [f_{Mt} is equal to $E(I_{Mt})$] will there be no speculative trading. We will see later that this is the basis of UET.

Yield Curve Outliers

Ideally, yield curves should be plotted for securities which are alike in all respects other than maturity. As a practical matter this is extremely difficult. All any yield curve really controls for is default risk. But securities which have similar risks of default are often substantially different in other respects—for example, in coupon rates, marketability, and callability. Such differences often cause *outliers* on a given yield curve.

Bonds with coupon rates below current rates of interest sell at a discount. Purchasers of such low-coupon bonds expect to earn the current rate of interest by receiving both a yearly coupon payment and a yearly price appreciation as the bond approaches face value at maturity. When this text was last revised, tax rates on ordinary income (coupons) and capital gains (price changes) were equal. For much of U.S. history and in many other countries, however, the capital gains tax rate is lower. When this is the case, the *effective tax rate on low-coupon bonds is lower than the tax rate on high-coupon bonds*. As a result, before-tax yields on low-coupon bonds can be lower than those on high-coupon bonds and still provide an equivalent after-tax yield. To understand this, consider two bonds. Bond *A* is a high-coupon issue on which the typical owner pays a tax rate of 30%. Bond *B* is a lower-coupon issue which, because of favorable capital gains tax rates, has an effective tax rate of 20%. If the desired after-tax yield for both issues is 5%, the before-tax rates will vary. If BT_i refers to the before-tax yield on bond *i*, AT_i refers to the after-tax yield, and TR_i refers to the tax rate applicable to the bond, then:

After-Tax Return $$AT_i = BT_i(1 - TR_i)$$ **(6.5a)**

and

Before-Tax Return $$BT_i = AT_i \div (1 - TR_i)$$ **(6.5b)**

Using Equation 6.5b on bonds *A* and *B* results in a before-tax yield to maturity of 7.14% for bond *A* and 6.25% for bond *B*. Although both bonds provide a 5.0% after-tax yield, the high-coupon issue must sell at a higher before-tax yield since its effective tax rate is higher. This tendency for low-coupon bonds to sell at yields lower than equivalent high-coupon issues has, in the past, been the cause of many yield curve outliers.

The marketability of an issue can also affect its required yield. *Marketability* refers to the ease with which one can rapidly sell (or buy) an issue without incurring large transaction costs. To the extent that large brokerage fees or lengthy periods of time may be necessary to dispose of an issue, investors will demand compensation in the form of a higher yield. While the size of such marketability premiums is unknown, they do exist and often cause yield curve outliers.

Issue callability also presents a problem in evaluating the yield curve. Yields plotted on a yield curve represent yields the investor might earn if the security is held to maturity. Unfortunately, such yields are often meaningless for issues which are likely to be called prior to maturity. Investors will attempt to determine an expected call date and price the instrument to provide a fair yield to this expected call date.[4] Thus, plotting the yield to "stated" maturity on the yield curve can often be quite misleading.

SEGMENTED MARKETS

Market segmentation theory (MST) states that economic units which demand or supply financial resources have maturity preferences (referred to as *preferred habitats*) which effectively create a number of *somewhat* independent market segments. Conventionally, these segments are referred to as short-term (less than one year), intermediate-term (one through five years), and long-term (greater than five years). For example, on the supply side, commercial banks prefer to lend short-term, savings and loans prefer intermediate-term lending, and life insurance companies prefer long-term

---

[4]Callability is discussed in more depth in Chapters 11 and 12.

investments. On the demand side, consumer finance firms prefer to borrow short-term, retailers finance cyclical inventory and receivable growth with intermediate-term borrowing, and plant expansion is typically financed with long-term security sales. MST states that the shape and movement of the yield curve are determined by levels of current financial supply and demand within each market segment.

Maturity Preference

Why do economic units have preferred habitats? The answer is simple — to minimize risk. To minimize risk exposure, the average maturities of investments and financing should be equal.[5] This maxim holds true for all investors, whether they are John Doe, Chase Manhattan Bank, or General Motors.

Matching the maturities of sources and uses of funds makes it possible to lock in the nominal return on investment as well as its cost of financing for a given period of time. For example, assume that the nature of a firm's business necessitates making investments which have a life of N years. If the investments are financed with, say, bonds which mature before N years, the firm will have to refinance at a future, unknown rate of interest. In this case the firm is said to have exposed itself to *income* (or *refinancing*) *risk*. Net income over the next N years is less certain (because refinancing rates are unknown) than if bonds maturing in N years had been sold. If the investments are financed with, say, bonds which mature beyond N years, the firm will have to repurchase the bond in year N at an unknown market price. In this case the firm is said to have exposed itself to *principal* (or *price*) *risk*.

Consider the following numerical example. A firm is organized with the intent of investing in an asset which has a two-year life. The asset costs $100,000, is expected to provide a cash return of $10,000 in both years, and should have a salvage value at the end of year 2 of $100,000. When the asset matures in year 2, the firm will be dissolved. The firm has been presented with five alternative financing plans:

Plan	Description
A	Sequence of four 6-month loans
B	Sequence of two 1-year loans
C	One 2-year note
D	One 4-year bond
E	One 7-year bond

Finally, assume the yield curve is level, as shown in Figure 6-4, and is expected to remain unchanged during the next couple of years. Thus, interest cost and net profits are *expected* to be identical under each of the five plans. The expected investment return of 10% less the expected financing cost of 5% results in an expected net return of 5%.

However, the range of profit potential of the five financing plans differs consid-

---

[5]In Chapter 11 this statement is modified slightly to read "To minimize risk exposure, the *duration* of investments and financing should be equal." Duration is a better measure of the average date at which cash returns on an investment are repaid than the maturity date is.

FIGURE 6-4 *Illustrative Yield Curve*

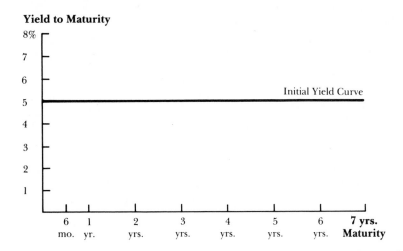

erably. Under plans A and B, a future increase (decrease) in interest rates would result in lower (higher) two-year net profits than had been expected — income risk. The opposite is true for plans D and E. Under these plans a future increase (decrease) in interest rates would result in higher (lower) two-year net profits because of the favorable (unfavorable) price at which the longer-life bonds would be repurchased in year 2 — principal risk. Only under plan C, which has a two-year maturity, will profits be insensitive to future interest rate changes. Only when the firm matches the maturities of its assets and liabilities will profit uncertainty be minimized. Figure 6-5 illustrates this conclusion graphically. In the figure interest rates are assumed to change only once — immediately after a particular plan has been adopted. Note that the further the financing maturity is from the asset maturity, the more sensitive net profits are to interest rate changes.

While this example is based on a specified asset maturity and flexible financing maturities, the opposite situation is also common. Many businesses are effectively given the maturity of financing (for example, commercial banks, which rely heavily on demand deposits, or life insurance firms, which obtain funds under long-term life insurance policies) and must arrange a suitable asset maturity.

Hedging asset and liability maturity is generally well understood and commonly practiced by financial managers. For example, a well-known life insurance actuary has recommended the following investment policy for a life insurance company in an attempt to properly match maturities:

> Sinking fund bonds should be avoided, and mortgages must be offset by longer-term assets. Bonds with high call features are to be avoided in periods of high interest rates. So-called discount, or low-coupon, bonds are especially attractive. Equities are very attractive, since they are the only long-term assets available in quantity in this country.[6]

---

[6]See Vanderhoof.

FIGURE 6-5 *Profit Sensitivity to Financing Maturity*

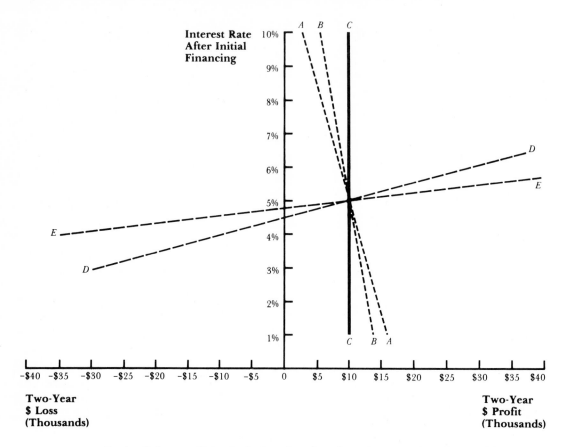

Each of these policies is designed to lengthen the maturity of asset investments to make them more consistent with expected maturity dates of the liabilities of a life insurance firm. In other industries the maturity phenomenon explains (1) commercial banks' preferences for lending short-term (liabilities are largely due on demand), (2) savings and loans' preferences for intermediate-term loans (liabilities are of intermediate duration), and (3) property-liability insurance firms' preferences for short-term, highly liquid investments (policies have a short-term life, etc.). Ways to properly match asset and liability maturities are of considerable interest to commercial banks and savings and loans, whose earnings are very sensitive to interest rate changes. In addition, a major reason for the growth in the financial futures market has been the ability to use such futures to better match the maturities of investments and liabilities. In sum, the concept of matching has gained particular importance in recent years, when interest rates have been more volatile than in the past.

Occasionally, individuals and firms will purposely mismatch their maturity structure in an attempt to take advantage of what they believe to be temporarily low or high interest rate levels. For example, during the 1970s many electric utilities financed plant expansions which had a 50-year life with short-term credit. They reasoned that interest rates were then abnormally high and would soon decline to more "normal" levels. Thus, they were willing to issue short-term debt to finance long-term plant investment in the hopes of refinancing with longer-term bonds once rates fell. In effect, the utilities were betting (speculating) that rates would fall and were willing to accept the higher risks in order to play the game. This is a classic example of financial speculation—a situation in which the financial manager attempts to take advantage of an apparent imbalance in the security markets. Unfortunately, the utilities were eventually forced to refinance their short-term debt at even higher long-term interest rates. They had misjudged the future direction of interest rates.

A somewhat opposite example occurred in the early 1980s. Yields to maturity on short-term bonds were higher than those on longer-maturity bonds. Because of this, many investment managers placed all their funds in short-term securities in the belief that the status quo would remain. They were wrong. As interest rates fell during the next few years across all maturities, those who had initially invested short-term were forced to reinvest at lower rates, while those who had invested longer-term experienced large bond price increases as rates fell. There is nothing inherently wrong with such speculation as long as speculators recognize that (1) they are indeed betting against the market, (2) they are incurring larger risks than necessary, and (3) they must be willing to accept the potentially unfavorable consequences.

Implications of MST

Market segmentation theory states that security market participants will attempt to hedge both income and principal risks. *Strictly applied*, MST suggests that this creates a level of financial supply and demand unique to each particular investment maturity range. Maturity preferences are so strong that participants in any one segment are unlikely to leave that segment for better yields within other market segments. Thus, the yield curve would be determined solely by *current demand and supply conditions within each market segment.*

Few believers in MST apply the concept in such a strict manner. While market participants may have clear maturity preferences, a certain flexibility exists which allows trading between adjacent segments. In addition, a large number of individuals who are indifferent to maturity will arbitrage rates between markets. The operations of these arbitrageurs are discussed below. Rates between various segments will thus be related to some extent. Nonetheless, proponents of MST argue that the dominant force which shifts the yield curve is a change in financial demand and supply within imprecisely defined maturity ranges. But even in this less strict version yield curves are essentially created by *current demand and supply conditions.*

To illustrate the reasoning underlying MST, we will trace its logic in explaining shifts in the yield curve during a period of economic recovery and expansion. Figure 6-6 shows yield curves for three stages of business activity. Starting with the trough of a business recession, the yield curve is reasonably flat for all but the shortest-maturity instruments. Such short-term instruments are what firms rely upon to pro-

FIGURE 6-6 *MST and the Business Cycle*

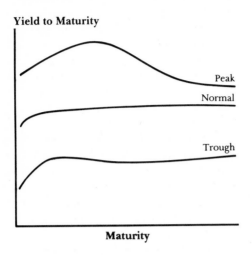

vide liquidity needs. The low level of economic activity will cause businesses to accumulate large liquidity reserves instead of reinvesting operating fund flows in unneeded inventory, receivables, and plant. The desire for increased liquidity is reinforced by businesses' attempts to guard against short-term insolvency problems which might be brought on by the recession. The net result will be a large supply of funds to the money market, causing very low short-term rates. As business activity begins to pick up, excess liquidity is spent on working capital and plant additions. In addition, total demand for credit increases across all maturity segments. This causes short-term money market rates to rise substantially while there are less dramatic rate increases across all maturity segments. Finally, as business activity moves toward the peak of the economic recovery, rates are the highest in the intermediate-maturity range in response to large demands for credit needed to support the cyclical expansion in receivable and inventory balances. According to MST, each shift in the yield curve is caused by a change in the *current* supply and demand for credit within a given maturity segment.

ARBITRAGED MARKETS

Arbitrage in a Segmented Market

In a segmented market, yields to maturity are effectively created by current supply and demand conditions within each segment. If one is able to forecast changes in *future* supply and demand, considerable opportunity for arbitrage may exist. In a market setting such as that of MST, this shouldn't be too difficult. Consider the movement of the yield curve over the course of a business cycle. If one believes in a segmented market, a repeated pattern of yield curves will exist coincident with normal business expansion and retraction. If this is so, bonds should be bought at the peak of the economic activity (to obtain large capital gains as yields eventually fall) and sold short at the trough of a recession (to gain from price declines incurred as interest rates rise and the economy expands).

To understand the possibilities for arbitrage, consider the following example. Three pure discount bonds of different maturities exist: one year, two years, and three years. We are now at date 1, a period of normal business activity. Yields to maturity on each of three bonds can be observed as prevailing market rates at date 1. These known I_M's are shown in Figure 6-7 as the solid line. Date 2 is expected to be the peak of the economic expansion, with rather high interest rates, particularly on bonds which mature two years after the start of date 2. Date 3 represents the trough of a recession with commensurately low interest rates. I_M's expected at dates 2 and 3 are shown in Figure 6-7 as the dashed lines. To complete the example, two added facts are helpful. First, we will assume that the various bonds are discount bonds, that is, they pay no intermediate coupons. The purchaser's sole return will come from capital appreciation. Second, the arbitrageurs are willing to make up to a three-year commitment at date 1. They will *not* consider the purchase of three-year bonds at date 2 or two-

FIGURE 6-7 *Yield Curves to Be Arbitraged*

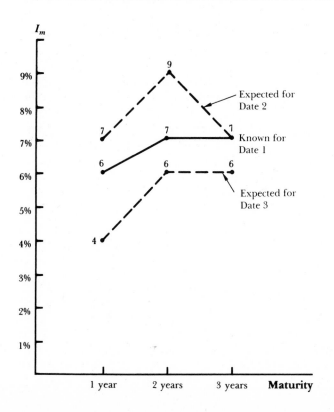

year bonds at date 3. Both of these assumptions ease the analysis considerably but do not change the essence of the conclusions.

If arbitrageurs are willing to place their money at risk for three years, they could follow any one of a number of plans. For example, they could simply buy one three-year bond at date 1. Alternatively, they could mix a sequence of three one-year bonds or a two-year bond plus a subsequent one-year bond, etc. Being indifferent to bond maturity, the arbitrageurs will select a policy which is expected to maximize their total three-year return. Table 6-2 lists the various possible strategies together with the third-year expected wealth of placing $1 into a given strategy at date 1. Clearly, a strategy of buying a one-year bond at date 1 followed by a two-year bond at date 2 will yield the largest expected profit. The lowest expected total return would be received if a sequence of three one-year bonds were purchased.

Earlier in the chapter we examined how arbitrageurs might lock in a future interest rate. This concept applies directly to this example. Note that of the four strategies in Table 6-2, those which involve purchase of a one-year bond at date 3 are ranked lowest. Arbitrageurs are capable of making larger profits in year 3 than the expected 4% one-year spot yield for that period. For example, the strategy of buying 1.07 three-year bonds at date 1 and short selling 1.0 two-year bond at date 1 will yield a 7% locked-in return during year 3. Details of this calculation are as follows:

Market Value at Start of Year 1

2-year bond	$1,000 \div 1.07^2 = \$873.44$
3-year bond	$1,000 \div 1.07^3 = \$816.29$

		Arbitrage Cash Flows at Year-End		
Strategy	*0*	*1*	*2*	*3*
Short sell 1.0 2-year bond	$873.44	—	($1,000)	—
Buy 1.07 3-year bonds	($873.44)	—		$1,070
Net cash flows	0	0	($1,000)	$1,070

7% yield in year 3

At the beginning of year 1 arbitrageurs can combine a short sale of the two-year bond and a purchase of 1.07 three-year bonds to be out of the market during years 1 and

TABLE 6-2 *Arbitrage Strategies and Profits*

Strategy	*Year 3 Expected Wealth per $1 Investment at Date 1*	*Rank*	*Details of Calculation*
A. One 3-year bond	$1.225	2	$1.07 \times 1.07 \times 1.07$
B. Three 1-year bonds	$1.180	4	$1.06 \times 1.07 \times 1.04$
C. One 2-year bond followed by a 1-year bond	$1.190	3	$1.07 \times 1.07 \times 1.04$
D. One 1-year bond followed by a 2-year bond	$1.259	1	$1.06 \times 1.09 \times 1.09$

2. At the end of year 2, they must pay $1,000 to cover the short sale. This represents the first time a net long position in the market is taken. At the end of year 3, the 1.07 three-year bonds mature and provide a $1,070 cash inflow. The purchases and sales are set up such that a 7% locked-in rate is earned during year 3.

There are a host of ways in which people can arbitrage in a segmented market. But the techniques are less important at this point in our discussion than is the idea. As long as the yield curve is determined by current demand and supply conditions, considerable arbitrage profits are available simply by making reasonable estimates of future demand and supply conditions.

Effects of a Fully Arbitraged Market

What would happen to interest rates if arbitrage were extensive? First, attempts by arbitrageurs to obtain speculative profits would eliminate all such profits. Bonds which provided large yields would be actively bought, driving their prices up and yields down. Bonds which provided insufficient yields would be actively sold, driving their prices down and yields up. Soon all possible profit opportunities would disappear. Second, long-term interest rates would be a geometric average of the current short-term spot rate and the market's consensus estimate of *expected future spot rates*. This theory of a fully arbitraged market, referred to as the *unbiased expectations theory* (UET), was initially discussed by Irving Fisher and later developed by Friedrich Lutz.

According to proponents of UET, the relationship between long- and short-term rates can be written as follows:

Future Value of $1
$$[1 + I_M]^M = [1 + I_1][1 + E(I_{11})][1 + E(I_{12})] \ldots [1 + E(I_{1M-1})] \quad \textbf{(6.6)}$$

where I_M = the yield to maturity on a pure discount bond maturing in M years, and $E(I_{1t})$ = the market's consensus forecast of expected one-year spot rates t years from today. This means, for example, that the terminal wealth expected from purchasing a 10-year pure discount bond should be the same as the *expected* terminal wealth on a sequence of 10 one-year bonds.

Expected Terminal Wealth on a 10-Year Bond		Expected Terminal Wealth on a Sequence of 10 One-Year Bonds
$[1 + I_{10}]^{10}$	$=$	$[1 + I_1][1 + E(I_{11})][1 + E(I_{12})] \ldots [1 + E(I_{19})]$

In addition, there is no particular reason to restrict the explanation to one-year forward rates. For example, the terminal wealth expected on a 10-year bond should be equal to the terminal wealth expected from first buying a six-year bond and then buying a four-year bond.

Expected Terminal Wealth on a 10-Year Bond	Expected Terminal Wealth on a 6-Year Bond Followed by a 4-Year Bond	
	6-Year Bond	4-Year Bond
$[1 + I_{10}]^{10} \quad =$	$[1 + I_6]^6 \qquad \times$	$[1 + E(I_{4,6})]^4$
	$\overbrace{[1 + I_1][1 + E(I_{11})]\dots[1 + E(I_{15})]}$	$\overbrace{[1 + E(I_{16})]\dots[1 + E(I_{19})]}$

Consider the following numerical example. Today, the start of year 1, the yield to maturity on a one-year bond is known to be 6.0%. Somehow a market consensus is developed that the expected one-year spot rate at the start of year 2 will be 6.5% and the one-year spot rate at the start of year 3 will be 7.0%:

Start of Year	Expected 1-Year Bond Rate at Start of Year	
1	6.0%	Known—today's 1-year rate
2	6.5%	Expected spot rates
3	7.0%	

By investing $1 at the start of year 1 in a one-year bond, $1.06 would be received at the end of the year. Reinvesting this $1.06 at the start of year 2 would yield $1.129 by the end of year 2 (1.06×1.065). By the end of year 3, $1.208 would be available (1.129×1.07). The terminal wealth on a three-year bond would have to equal exactly $1.208 per dollar invested or arbitrage profits would be available. Thus, $(1 + I_3)^3 = 1.208$. The *annual* yield to maturity on the three-year bond would be the geometric average of the three yearly returns:

$$\sqrt[3]{1.208} - 1.0 = 6.5\%$$

Using the same data:

- the yield to maturity of a two-year bond today would be 6.25% ($\sqrt[2]{(1.06)(1.065)} - 1.0$)
- the expected yield to maturity of a two-year bond starting at the beginning of year 2 would be 6.75% ($\sqrt[2]{(1.065)(1.07)} - 1.0$)
- the expected yield to maturity of a one-year bond starting at the beginning of year 3 would be 7.0% (by definition)

Determinants of Discount Bond Yield to Maturity

$$I_M = \sqrt[M]{[1 + I][1 + E(I_{11})][1 + E(I_{12})]\dots[1 + E(I_{1,M-1})]} - 1.0 \tag{6.7}$$

The yield to maturity on a bond maturing at the end of period M is equal to the geometric mean of expected yields on a sequence of shorter-term bonds with equal maturity.[7] For example, the following forward rates and *YTM*s are consistent with each other:

---

[7]Again, this equation is strictly true only for pure discount bonds. It is approximate for coupon obligations.

Start of Year	Expected Forward Rate	*Appropriate* YTM on a Bond Maturing at End of Year	Details
1	5%	5%	—
2	8%	6.5%	$\sqrt[2]{(1.05)(1.08)} - 1.0$
3	7%	6.66%	$\sqrt[3]{(1.05)(1.08)(1.07)} - 1.0$
4	4%	5.99%	$\sqrt[4]{(1.05)(1.08)(1.07)(1.04)} - 1.0$
5	5%	5.79%	$\sqrt[5]{(1.05)(1.08)(1.07)(1.04)(1.05)} - 1.0$

A major implication of UET is that the forward rates which are implied in the yield curve are the same as the market's consensus forecast of expected future spot rates; that is, UET states that:

$$\text{Forward Rates} = \text{Expected Spot Rates}$$

$$f_{Mt} = E(I_{Mt}) \qquad (6.8)$$

For example, if a five-year bond is currently yielding 9% to maturity and a four-year bond has an 8.7% *YTM*, then the implied one-year expected spot rate per UET at the *start* of year 5 would be 10.21%:

$$\frac{1.09^5}{1.087^4} - 1.0 = \frac{1.5386}{1.3961} - 1.0 = .1021$$

The five-year bond provides a terminal wealth of $1.5386 for each $1 initially invested. Since the four-year bond provides a terminal wealth of $1.3961, the return during the fifth year must be 10.21%, since:

$$(1.1021)(\$1.3961) = \$1.5386$$

Calculations such as these can aid speculators in determining whether prevailing interest rates are consistent with personal opinions about future interest rate levels.[8]

The investment implications of UET are at least threefold. First, if UET is strictly correct, any speculative profits that might have existed under MST will have been fully arbitraged away. Returns on the *next* speculative transaction will be zero. If UET is not strictly correct, some speculative profits will be available for the first group of speculators who act upon new information. But they must act quickly, before their information is incorporated into existing interest rates. The unbiased expectations theory is the same as the efficient market theory, but it is EMT applied to only a narrow set of securities: debt instruments.

Second, if UET is strictly correct, *the return expected for a given holding period does not depend upon the maturity of the instrument purchased.* For example, if you

---

[8]Actual applications of these ideas are difficult to implement for two reasons. First, a yield "curve" doesn't actually exist. There isn't a *continuous* set of observations between *YTM* and maturity. Instead, a number of *discrete* observations are available. When estimating implied forward rates, an approximate fitted curve is used. Second, as noted in footnote 7, this formula doesn't apply precisely to coupon obligations. Precise implied forward rates are more difficult to estimate for coupon obligations.

intend to invest for a one-year period, the return you can *expect* will be *identical* whether you (1) buy a sequence of one-month instruments, (2) buy a one-year instrument, (3) buy a 20-year instrument and sell it a year from now, or (4) choose some other approach. This is true for any desired holding period. Why? Because if it were not the case, arbitrageurs would immediately create zero-cost riskless trades with large rewards until prices were eventually pushed to levels where such profits were no longer available — to levels where the expected return for any given holding period was independent of the maturity of the securities purchased. However, while expected returns do not vary with the bond maturities selected, portfolio risk does. The concept of matching maturities of assets and liabilities is still appropriate. If UET is correct, one should simply match maturities and not worry that a strategy of holding different maturity obligations would yield higher returns.

Third, all that is known about the likely course of future interest rates is already incorporated into present yield curves. The best predictor of future interest rates is today's yield curve. Individuals using sophisticated econometric models or simple intuition will be unable to predict future interest rates any better than individuals who use today's yield curve. This doesn't mean that the yield curve is an accurate predictor of future interest rates. It only means that nothing better is available. *Forward rates of interest implicit in the yield curve are unbiased estimates of expected future spot rates.*[9]

Expected Inflation and Nominal Risk-Free Rates

According to a strict version of the unbiased expectations theory, a major determinant of a yield curve's shape is expectations of future inflation. For example, assume that a real rate of 2% is deemed to be fair during all future years. Knowing this together with expected annual future rates of inflation, one can estimate both expected spot rates and yields to maturity on bonds of varying maturities. For example, assume that you have developed the following data:

Start of Year	Desired Real Rate	+	Expected Inflation During Year	=	Expected Spot Rate	Implying a Current I_M of
1	2%		5%		7%	7.00%
2	2%		8%		10%	8.49%
3	2%		6%		8%	8.33%
4	2%		4%		6%	7.74%

---

[9]Cox, Ingersoll, and Ross have demonstrated that if the risk-free rate is stochastic (uncertain over time), logical inconsistencies exist in UET. In particular, they show that it is impossible for expected holding period returns for various maturities to be identical at the same time that forward rates are unbiased estimates of expected future spot rates. We will bypass a discussion of their argument because of its highly technical nature and because any errors which arise in UET appear to be slight.

The reader may recognize that this relationship is simply Irving Fisher's theory about the determinants of nominal risk-free rates:[10]

Nominal Risk-Free Rate $$RF_t = r^* + E(I_t) \qquad \qquad \textbf{(6.9)}$$

RF_t stands for the nominal yield to maturity on a risk-free bond that matures in t years. Economic forces within the real goods market create an expectation about future demand and supply of financial resources and result in an equilibrium real rate, r^*. To compensate investors in real dollar terms, nominal returns will allow for the average annual rate of inflation expected during the bond's life, $E(I_t)$. Since the real rate does not depend upon the bond's life, the only reason for yields to vary on bonds of similar risk is inflation expectation. If prevailing yields on 20-year Treasury bonds are 8½% and one believes the real rate is 2%, then the market's best estimate of the average inflation rate during the next 20 years is about 6½% per year. Unfortunately, no one knows the level of r^*, and estimates of it vary considerably.

UET, Yield Curves, and the Business Cycle

Market segmentation theory explains changes in the level and shape of the yield curve during the course of a business cycle as the result of changes in current demand and supply conditions within various market segments. According to UET the overall level of the yield curve shifts as a result of two forces: (1) changes in the *expectations* of future demand and supply conditions across all market segments and (2) changes in *expected* rates of inflation. During a business upswing, the yield curve will rise if market participants *revise their expectations* about future demand for and supply of funds or revise their expectations about future inflation.

LIQUIDITY PREFERENCE

Liquidity Premiums

In some respects, *liquidity preference theory* (LPT) is a refined version of the market segmentation theory. In its most general form, LPT states that borrowers and lenders have preferred maturity habitats but can be induced to trade in other maturity segments if offered an inducement to do so in the form of a higher rate of return. This yield inducement is referred to as a *liquidity premium*.

When LPT was originally developed, its proponents stated that lenders of funds (who are typically households) prefer to lend short-term, whereas borrowers (who are

---

[10]Equation 6.9 is a modified version of Equation 5.3. The interaction term between the future inflation rate and the real rate, $I_t r^*$, is dropped since its size is negligible. In addition, an expected inflation term is used instead of a known future inflation rate.

typically corporations) prefer to borrow long-term. As a result, the original proponents of liquidity preference believed lenders would demand a premium to be enticed to invest their funds long-term. Investors in long-term obligations would earn a higher yield than would investors who insisted upon short-term securities. Borrowers would have to pay a higher interest rate to borrow long-term than if they borrowed short-term.

Proponents of liquidity preference argue that the implied forward rate is actually composed of the expected spot rate plus a liquidity premium. Symbolically:

**Implied
Forward
Rate**
$$f_{Mt} = E(I_{Mt}) + l_{Mt} \qquad\qquad\textbf{(6.10)}$$

where f_{Mt} = the implied forward rate on a pure discount bond with a maturity of M years in t years from now, $E(I_{Mt})$ = the expected spot rate on a bond with a maturity of M years in t years from now, and l_{Mt} = the liquidity premium associated with a bond with a maturity of M years in t years from now.

The only difference between the LPT and UET models is whether a liquidity premium exists. For example, assume that the yields to maturity on (pure discount) bonds maturing at the end of years 5 and 6 are 8.7% and 9.0%, respectively. The implied one-year forward rate at the beginning of year 6 would be 10.5%:

$$\frac{1.09^6}{1.087^5} - 1.0 = 10.5\%$$

According to UET the expected one-year spot rate for year 6 is 10.5%. However, LPT would say that the expected spot rate is slightly lower than 10.5% by the amount of the liquidity premium.

As noted above, the early developers of liquidity preference (chiefly Hicks) believed lenders preferred to lend short-term whereas borrowers preferred to borrow long-term. As a result, all liquidity premiums would be positive and the yield curve would provide upwardly biased estimates of expected spot rates. Figure 6-8 depicts the difference between the two models for the case of constant expected spot rates. Liquidity premiums are all positive, causing implied forward rates to be greater than expected spot rates. As a result, the actual yield curve observed in the financial press will be upward sloping even though spot rates are not expected to change.

The fundamental reason that borrowers prefer to issue long-term securities and lenders prefer to buy short-term securities is based on the matching principle. If borrowers use the proceeds from a sale of securities to invest in long-term real assets but must finance with short-term borrowings, they incur an *income risk*, as noted earlier in the chapter. Conversely, if lenders (such as households) have short-term investment horizons, they incur a *principal risk* when lending long-term. Thus, lenders will demand a premium on longer-term issues to compensate for this principal risk, a premium which borrowers will be willing to pay in order not to be exposed to income risk. This premium will always be positive and will increase as the maturity of the security increases.

FIGURE 6-8 *Effects of Liquidity Premiums on Implied Forward Rates*

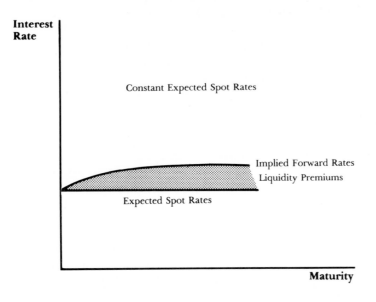

However, many people believe that liquidity premiums may not always increase with the security's maturity—that they may decrease with maturity at certain times. For example, there are times when lenders may, in fact, prefer to lend longer-term than borrowers would wish to borrow. In such a case the yield curve would have a downward bias.[11]

Liquidity Premiums and the Level of Interest Rates

The size of the liquidity premium is believed by many individuals to vary with the prevailing level of interest rates. Two schools of thought exist. The first was proposed by Hicks and suggests that liquidity premiums vary inversely with the level of interest rates. The second was proposed by Kessel and suggests a direct relationship. Hicks believed that individuals form opinions about whether yields are unusually high or low. If rates were perceived to be high and likely to decline, lenders would receive bond price increases as rates fell. At such times their principal risk wouldn't really be so much a risk as a potential for capital gains, and liquidity premiums would be quite small. If rates were unusually low and likely to increase, investors would be quite concerned about likely market value declines and would request large liquidity premiums. Hicksian liquidity premiums are illustrated in panel A of Figure 6-9.

---

[11]See Modigliani and Sutch.

Kessel, on the other hand, believes that liquidity premiums will be greatest when interest rates are perceived to be high. He reasons as follows: Short-term, low-risk securities are close substitutes for cash. They provide a way of obtaining the liquidity of cash together with a rate of return not available from cash. In periods of abnormally high interest rates, the opportunity cost of *not* holding such highly liquid instruments is large. Therefore, to induce individuals to move out of the high-yielding, short-term liquid instruments and into longer-term, less-liquid instruments, a substantial liquidity premium will be demanded. The result will be large liquidity premiums during periods of abnormally high interest rates. Conversely, when rates are abnormally low, the opportunity cost of not holding short-term instruments will not be so large. As a result, small liquidity premiums will be necessary to persuade investors to move out of short-term securities and into long-term securities. Liquidity premiums will be small during periods of low interest rates. Kessel's notions about liquidity premiums are illustrated in panel B of Figure 6-9.

Whether Kessel or Hicks is correct is an empirical question which hasn't been re-

FIGURE 6-9 *Liquidity Premiums and the Level of Interest Rates*

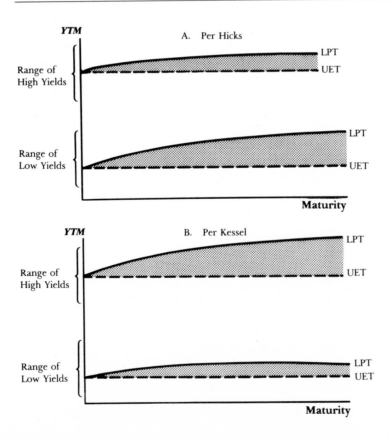

solved. But regardless of which theory is correct, most evidence suggests that if liquidity premiums do exist, they probably don't increase the yield to maturity by more than 100 basis points per annum on even the longest-term instruments.

VOLATILITY OF LONG-TERM INTEREST RATES

Both UET and LPT state that the long-term interest rate is an average of current and rationally expected future short-term rates (plus liquidity premiums in LPT). This has an important empirical implication. Since long-term rates are averages of short-term rates, the series of long-term interest rates which we observe as time passes should be less volatile than the time series of short-term rates. Long moving averages tend to smooth out the series averaged. Thus, if one were to plot the historical time series of short-term and long-term rates, the long-term rates should be much less volatile.

This simply is not the case. Although long-term rates have been somewhat less volatile than short-term rates, long-term rates have been more volatile than naive versions of either theory would imply.

Three explanations have been offered: (1) changes in desired real returns as time passes, (2) varying liquidity premiums as time passes, and (3) investor overreaction to changes in short-term rates. The first two explanations could conceivably explain the large volatility of long-term rates in the context of either UET or LPT models. In fact, even a casual observation of short-term interest rates suggests that desired real returns do change. There have been many periods in which the expected real returns on Treasury bills have been zero or negative. Similarly, there have been many periods in which large positive real returns could have been easily forecast on Treasury bills. Changing liquidity premiums are more difficult to measure. But if the large volatility in long-term rates is to be explained by changes in desired real returns and liquidity premiums, the changes in these variables must be much larger than most scholars have thought was true in the past. It is possible that long-term rates are more volatile than rational expectations models such as UET and LPT would allow.

SUMMARY

The term structure of interest rates relates the maturity of a security to the security's yield to maturity. Because of impacts that shifts in the term structure have on both actual and expected security returns, considerable attention has been given to its inherent determinants. Three theories have been developed: market segmentation theory, unbiased expectations theory, and liquidity preference theory.

Market segmentation theory states that the term structure of interest is dominated by individuals and institutions who attempt to hedge their investment risks. A hedge is created by matching the maturity of an investment with the financing maturity. Such hedging creates desires to buy or sell securities within only a narrow maturity range. As a result, the yield curve is said to be created by current levels of demand and supply in various maturity segments.

The unbiased expectations theory states that if MST is correct, then significant arbitrage profits would be available by forecasting future demand and supply conditions. Believers in UET suggest that such arbitrage will continue until profits from additional arbitrage no longer exist. At this point the yield curve will not reflect current demand and supply conditions within particular maturity segments but, instead, will reflect expectations about future demand and supply over all maturity segments. The shape of the yield curve would reflect expectations about future interest rates.

Liquidity preference theory builds upon UET by adding a liquidity premium to bonds of longer maturity. Since long-term bonds are quite price sensitive to interest rate changes, they have a principal risk which short-term lenders would prefer not to accept. To induce lenders to buy maturities which have such a risk, borrowers will have to offer a yield inducement — a liquidity premium. Liquidity premiums are believed to vary with the overall level of interest rates. However, the direction of this impact is debated.

REVIEW PROBLEMS

1. You are given the following (incomplete) data on U.S. Treasury securities. Assume a $1,000 par value for each and a coupon payment at year-end.

Security	Maturity	Coupon Rate	Price	YTM
A	2 years	10%	$982.87	—
B	4 years	10%	—	12%
C	4 years	12%	—	12%

   a. Without performing any calculations, what will be the price of C?
   b. Without performing any calculations, will the price of B be greater or less than that of C?
   c. Calculate the missing data.
   d. If interest rates rise, in what direction will the bond prices move? Which will move more, A or B? Which will move more, B or C?

2. Throughout this problem, assume that we are dealing with zero-coupon bonds. Yields to maturity on bonds having three different maturities are as follows:

Bond	Maturity	YTM
A	1 year	11.0%
B	2 years	12.0%
C	3 years	11.5%

   a. Calculate the implied one-year forward rates for the starts of years 2 and 3.
   b. Prepare a forecast of what the yield curve is *expected* to be at the start of year 2 according to UET.
   c. Calculate the implied rate on two-year bonds for the start of year 2.

d. Assume you believe that spot rates on one-year bonds will be 8% at the start of year 3. Illustrate the arbitrage you would enter into to take advantage of this.

e. Assume UET is correct and that a *real* risk-free rate of 3% per annum is required. What inflation forecasts are implicit in the yield curve?

f. Assume UET is correct. What return would you expect during the next year if you:

- Buy the one-year bond?

- Buy the three-year bond and sell in a year?

Solutions

1. a. Bond C will sell for $1,000. Bond theorem 1 states that when the annual coupon rate and yield to maturity are identical, a bond will always sell at par.

   b. Bond B will have a lower price than C because B has a lower coupon.

   c. The *YTM* of bond A is found by trial and error or with a calculator to be 11%:

$$\frac{100}{1.11} + \frac{1,100}{1.11^2} = 982.87$$

   The price of bond B will be $939.25:

$$\frac{100}{1.12} + \frac{100}{1.12^2} + \frac{100}{1.12^3} + \frac{1,100}{1.12^4} = \$939.25$$

   The price of bond C was stated to be $1,000 in part a above.

   d. Bond prices will move down — this is bond theorem 2. Bond B will fall more than bond A, according to bond theorem 3. And bond B will fall more than bond C, per bond theorem 5.

2. a.
$$f_{1,1} = \frac{1.12^2}{1.11} - 1 = \frac{\text{Accumulated wealth of \$1}}{\text{invested in two-year bond at end of year 2}} - 1$$

$$= 0.13, \text{ or } 13\%$$

$$f_{1,2} = \frac{1.115^3}{1.12^2} - 1$$

$$= 0.1051, \text{ or } 10.51\%$$

   b. In one year, the expected one-year rate is 13%, according to part a. To find the expected two-year rate, we would use Equation 6.4:

$$I_2 = [(1.13)(1.1051)]^{1/2} - 1$$

$$= 0.1175, \text{ or } 11.75\%$$

   c. Investing $1 in a three-year bond will produce a value of $1.115^3 = \$1.3862$ at the end of year 3. Investing $1 in a one-year bond will produce a value of $1.11 at the end of year 1. For $1.11 to grow to $1.3862 two years later, the average compound return (remember $\bar{G}$?) would be

$$\left[\frac{1.3862}{1.11}\right]^{1/2} - 1 = 0.1175, \text{ or } 11.75\%$$

d. Since the implied forward rate for year 3 is 10.51% (from part a above), you would want to lock in that rate instead of eventually receiving the expected spot of 8% in year 3.

	End-of-Period Cash In (Out)			
Transaction	0	1	2	3
Buy 1.0 three-year bond $1,000/1.115^3$	(721.40)	—	—	1,000
Sell short 0.9049 two-year bond at a price of $797.19 = 1,000/1.12^2$	721.40	—	(940.90)	
	0	0	(904.90)	1,000

Net Return = 10.51%

e.

	Nominal	−	Real	=	Average Yearly Inflation
1 year	11.0%	−	3.0%	=	8.0%
2 year	12.0%	−	3.0%	=	9.0%
3 year	11.5%	−	3.0%	=	8.5%

(Note that this calculation does not allow for the interaction term in the Fisher equation (Equation 5.3) in Chapter 5. This is often done because of its small numerical value.)

f. The one-year return from buying a three-year bond and selling in a year is not known with certainty but is expected to be 11.0%. Note that this 11% return expected during the next year on the current three-year bond is identical to the *known* return on current one-year bonds.

	Today	Year 1
Buy at $1,000/(1.115^3)$	(721.40)	
Sell at $1,000/(1.1175^2)$		800.76

Return = 11.00%
The 11.75% expected yield on two-year bonds at the start of year 2 comes from part c above.

QUESTIONS AND PROBLEMS

1. High-coupon bonds are less price sensitive to interest rate moves than are lower-coupon bonds. Why is this so?
2. National Aviation has three bond issues of similar risk outstanding:

Issue	Par	Maturity	Coupon	Current Price
A	$1,000	5 years	7%	$ 922.30
B	1,000	10 years	10%	1,210.40
C	1,000	10 years	4%	788.96

a. What is the yield to maturity on each of these issues?
b. Note that the yields to maturity for bonds *B* and *C* are equal. Is this likely to be the case if capital gains tax rates are lower than ordinary tax rates?
c. Without calculating prices, which of these three bonds will experience the greatest percentage price appreciation if yields to maturity fall by 100 basis points on each? Why?

    d. Between bonds *B* and *C*, which will experience the greatest percentage price appreciation if yields to maturity on each fall by 100 basis points? Why?

    e. Assume yields do drop by 100 basis points. Find the new market price of each bond.

3. Describe the rationale suggested by believers in MST for changes in the level and shape of the yield curve over the course of a classic business cycle.

4. What is an implied forward rate of interest? How can a forward rate be locked in by using existing yields on bonds of various maturities?

5. Describe why risk is reduced when investment and financing maturities are matched.

6. How does Fisher's theory of nominal interest rates fit into the UET approach to yield curves?

7. (CFA Exam Question)

Describe carefully the *immediate* effects on the money and capital markets of each of the following events. Consider each of the events independently.

    a. An increase in policy loans by life insurance companies.

    b. Revision of federal income tax laws to permit issuers to deduct dividends on preferred stocks in arriving at corporate taxable income. The 85% dividend income exclusion available to corporate investors will be unchanged.

        Note: Answer this question from the viewpoint of both MST and UET.

8. (CFA Exam Question)

    a. Draw a series of yield curves which should be in evidence on each of the following dates:

        Date 1 — Relatively stable prices and money supply

        Date 2 — Rapidly rising rates of inflation

        Date 3 — The bottom of an economic downturn

        Date 4 — The top of an expansionary cycle

    b. As an aggressive portfolio manager of a moderate-sized, taxable fund comprised solely of fixed-income securities, discuss the strategies you would employ to optimize rates of return. Assume that quality guidelines must be maintained and that you expect interest rates will:

        • Decline

        • Rise

9. (Adapted from a CFA Exam Question)

In view of the following results for investments in long-term bonds, one might question why any bond manager would want to invest in long-term bonds rather than Treasury bills. Please comment.

	Total Return 1980	1976–1980 Average
Salomon Brothers' Long-Term Bond Index	−2.6%	2.4%
U.S. Treasury Bills	11.2%	7.8%

10. The yield to maturity on a pure discount five-year bond is 8.7%. The yield to maturity on a six-year bond (of equal risk) is 9.0%. Calculate the implied one-year forward rate for the start of year 6.

11. The yield to maturity on a five-year bond is currently 8%, the yield to maturity on a six-year bond is 9%, and the yield to maturity on a seven-year bond is 9.5%.

    a. Calculate the implied forward rate on a *one*-year bond at the start of year 6.

    b. Calculate the implied forward rate on a *two*-year bond at the start of year 6.

12. If 20-year riskless bonds (say, pure discount U.S. Treasury bonds) are currently yielding 8% to maturity and similar five-year bonds are now yielding 8.5% to maturity, what is the expected rate on a 15-year bond which will *start* at the end of year 5? How might a speculator lock in this rate? Prove with calculations.

13. Assume two pure discount bonds are available. Bond X is selling a $926 and matures in one year. Bond Y is selling at $873 and matures in two years.
   a. Outline a strategy to lock in a forward rate for year 2.
   b. What return is locked in by this strategy?
   c. If you expect that in a year from now, one-year rates will be 8%, should you proceed with this transaction? If not, what should be done?
   d. What does UET say about the transaction in part c—i.e., is it valid or not? Why?

14. Assume you believe that a yearly real rate of 2% is satisfactory. You have also estimated what you believe future rates of inflation will be:

Year	Expected Inflation During the Year
1	5%
2	6%
3	7%
4	5%

Plot what you believe the yield curve for risk-free bonds should look like.

15. Assume today's yield curve is as follows:

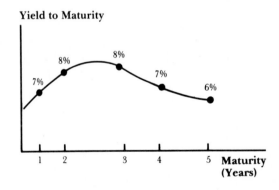

Using the concepts of UET, estimate next year's yield curve. Is this estimate likely to be very accurate? If not, does this destroy the validity of UET? If you are a believer in LPT, could you use this yield curve to predict next year's curve?

16. (CFA Exam Question)
The "Week in Bonds" column in the February 21, 1977, issue of *Barron's* included the following comment on the sale of $150 million of bonds by the investment counseling firm of Scudder, Stevens & Clark, Incorporated:

> Corporate issues also held reasonably steady in the face of an unusually large $150 million secondary sale of old company bonds by Scudder, Stevens & Clark on behalf of its private accounts such as insurance companies, pension funds, and foundations. It

represented about 10% of the total long-term bonds being managed by that investment counseling firm.

Scudder's current strategy is to "move toward shorter maturities, to include both short- and intermediate-term Treasury issues or commercial paper or other longer bonds carrying the highest coupon rates," George Johnson, its president, said. "This sale of lower-coupon long bonds isn't over yet; we would like to have even fewer, because there are good returns in other sectors of the market," he added.

Discuss the likely reasons for each of the following aspects of this strategy:
a. The sale of lower-coupon long bonds
b. The move toward shorter maturities
c. The shift from corporates to Treasury issues or commercial paper
d. The shift to other longer-term bonds carrying the highest coupon rates

DATA ANALYSIS PROBLEM

Objective:

- To examine the historical volatility of yields to maturity on both short- and long-term bonds.

Access the worksheet entitled INDEXES.WK1. In the worksheet you will find the yields to maturity at various year-ends for both short- and long-term corporate bonds. The series is maintained by the Federal Reserve System and published in a number of periodicals.

1. Plot both yield-to-maturity series with year on the horizontal axis and the two series on the vertical axis. Note that the long-term bonds display about the same volatility as the shorter-maturity bonds. Confirm this visual observation by finding the standard deviations for each series since 1935.

2. Comment on the large volatility of long-term bonds and how it creates a problem for proponents of the unbiased expectations theory.

APPENDIX 6A: EMPIRICAL TESTS

Despite numerous empirical tests of market segmentation theory, unbiased expectations theory, and liquidity preference theory, the question of which theory best describes the real world remains controversial. Most practicing investment officers subscribe to MST. Most academicians subscribe to variants of UET or LPT. Nonetheless, the weight of evidence seems to suggest:

1. Expectations about the future course of interest rates *are* impounded in existing yield curves.

2. However, such expectations about future interest rates are usually quite *inaccurate*. The market seems to find it quite difficult to forecast future spot rates.

3. Implied forward rates are, on average, larger than actual future spot rates. The fact is consistent with the existence of liquidity premiums.

4. The extent to which liquidity premiums vary with the absolute level of interest rates (Hicks versus Kessel) is debatable. Some evidence shows large li-

quidity premiums when rates are high, and other evidence shows small liquidity premiums when rates are high.

5. Evidence regarding MST is inconclusive. But, to date, none of the various studies has demonstrated a clear relationship between changes in the yield curve and changes in supply and demand within various maturity segments.

Testing Procedures

Most of the tests have examined the extent to which implied forward rates equal expectations of future spot rates. Recall that the yield curve can be used to calculate implied forward rates on, say, a one-year bond during year 3 as follows:

$$f_{1,3} = \frac{(1 + I_3)^3}{(1 - I_2)^2} - 1.0$$

If we could observe or ask market professionals what they believe the one-year spot rate would be at the start of year 3 ($S_{1,3}$), the testing procedure would be quite simple. If the implied forward rate *exactly* equaled the expected spot rate ($f_{1,3} = S_{1,3}$), UET would be correct. If the forward rate was consistently larger than the expected spot rate ($f_{1,3} - S_{1,3} > 0$), liquidity preference theory would account for the spread. If the forward rate and expected spot rates bore no clear relationship to each other, then neither UET nor LPT would be correct. In such a case if the spread between f and S was related to current demand and supply conditions, MST would be correct.

While implied forward rates can be estimated using the yield curve, expected spot rates are difficult to observe. The financial community rarely publishes estimates of future spot rates. To overcome this problem, three approaches have been used to estimate future spot rates: (1) actual spot rates, (2) error learning models, and (3) futures market rates.

Actual Spot Rates

Culbertson has examined the relationship between implied forward rates and actual future spot rates. In essence, the test involves calculating, say, the one-year

bond rate which the yield curve implies will exist two years from now and then comparing this with the one-year spot rate which actually prevails two years hence. Culbertson found wide differences between the two rates and concluded that UET was therefore not a reasonable model. While this test does examine the precision with which the market is able to predict, it does not directly test UET. Prediction errors should be anticipated as new information enters the market and causes people to reassess their expectations. Thus, it is not a valid test of UET.

Error Learning Models

An error learning model is one in which forecasts are periodically updated based upon errors made in the past. For example, assume we are interested in forecasting the one-year spot rate which we expect will prevail N years from today. In an error learning model we might say that our estimate of this rate $_0\hat{S}_{1,N}$ (where ^ denotes an estimate) would be equal to last period's estimate *plus* an adjustment for the difference between last period's estimate and today's actual one-period rate. The subscript preceding $\hat{S}$ refers to the date at which the spot rate forecast is being made. Symbolically:

$$_0\hat{S}_{1,N} = _{-1}\hat{S}_{1,N-1} + b(_0YTM_{1,0} - _{-1}\hat{S}_{1,N-1}) \quad \text{(6A.1)}$$

Expectations are revised whenever past expectations are in error. The b parameter reflects the extent to which forecasts are adjusted for past errors.

Meiselman developed and tested the error learning model in Equation 6A.1. Using corporate bond yield data for the years 1900–1954, he used regression analysis to estimate b and the extent of correlation between changes in implied forward rates and past prediction errors.

Results of his analysis are displayed in Table 6A-1. When *changes* in forward rates one year hence were examined, the model had an R^2 of 91%. That is, 91% of the variation in one-year forward rates was related to variation in predictive errors today. The R^2 fell consistently as forward rates beyond one year were examined. In addition, the regression coefficient, b (which reflects the responsiveness of forward rate changes to forecasting errors), decreased with the remoteness of the future forward rate. Meiselman inter-

TABLE 6A-1 *Meiselman's Test of the Error Learning Model*

N (in years)	Regression Coefficient b	R^2
1	0.703	91%
2	0.526	75
3	0.403	59
4	0.326	46
5	0.277	41
6	0.233	39
7	0.239	40
8	0.208	35

SOURCE: D. Meiselman, *The Term Structure of Interest Rates*, 1962.

preted the decline in both the regression parameter and the R^2 as showing that more-distant forecasts are more firmly held than nearer-term forecasts. He also concluded that these results confirmed the UET. Forecasts of future interest rates are made by market analysts and periodically updated as forecast errors are made.

Again, unfortunately, Meiselman's error learning model was not a direct test of UET. The correct procedure would be to directly relate expected spot rates with implied forward rates. Meiselman examined only implied forward rates. However, the error learning model did represent a major breakthrough in analytic techniques which would be used by most subsequent researchers.

Illustrative of the research since Meiselman is a study by Kessel. Using the error learning model, Kessel was willing to interpret the predicted forward rates as estimators of future spot rates. However, Kessel concentrated on differences between these estimated spot rates and subsequent *actual* spot rates. While actual and forecast spot rates might vary considerably over time, a consistent pattern or bias shouldn't exist if UET is correct. According to UET the average error should be zero. If, on average, the predicted spot rate is larger than the actual spot rate, then we have evidence that a liquidity premium exists.

Using Treasury bill data for the period January 1959 through March 1962, Kessel computed 14-day forward rates for six different future periods ranging from 14 to 91 days out. The average difference between forward and actual future spot rates was positive for all six series, as follows:

Future Period	Kessel's Estimate of Liquidity Premium
14 days	0.199%
28 days	0.567%
42 days	0.599%
56 days	0.444%
63 days	0.455%
91 days	0.669%

Kessel interpreted these results to represent liquidity premiums. In fact, the average errors tend to increase with maturity in the same manner that liquidity premiums should, owing to the increased market risk of longer-term bonds. Other studies in the vein of Kessel's have yielded similar results. Liquidity premiums do appear to exist.

Whether liquidity premiums are related to the absolute level of interest rates is unknown. Kessel offered evidence that suggested liquidity premiums were higher when rates were high. However, Van Horne and others have offered evidence suggesting that liquidity premiums are largest when interest rates are low.

Futures Market Rates

Since 1975, trading in financial futures has been available, and activity in the market has increased dramatically. Financial futures allow individuals to contract for the future purchase (or sale) of a financial instrument at a price and date agreed upon when the futures contract is traded. For example, today people can buy a T-bill contract which guarantees that they will be able to purchase a 30-day T-bill in exactly 60 days from now in exchange for a specified price. As such, the buyer locks in a rate of return between day 60 and day 90. Of course, an alternative to buying this 30-day T-bill futures contract would be to buy a 90-day bill and sell short a 60-day bill. Theoretically, this *forward* transaction should provide the same return as the 30-day future deliverable in 60 days. The two are identical in concept.

Do the futures rates and forward rates implied in the yield curve equal each other? Based upon research conducted to date it doesn't appear so. The reason for this isn't yet understood. Explanations largely suggest that futures and forward transactions are not really perfect substitutes. Risk differences, tax differences, and other institutional differences between the two suggest that their yields should indeed be different. In Chapter 17 we take up this problem in more depth. For now it is sufficient to say that while futures and forward rates do differ, this can be explained by institutional differences in the two types of transactions and the relative newness of the financial futures market. There is no evidence from the studies of futures rates which would suggest a segmented market, however.

Market Segmentation Tests

A limited number of market segmentation tests have also been conducted. Typically, these tests examine the relationship between the difference in the yields to maturity of long-term and short-term bonds with various measures of bond supply in each maturity range. In general, no clear relationship has been found between supply within a maturity segment and yields in that segment.

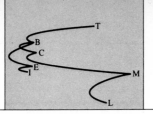

CHAPTER

7 Risk and Diversification

Without doubt, risk is one of the most striking characteristics of the security markets. An ability to understand, measure, and properly manage investment risk is fundamental to any intelligent investor or speculator. Until the mid-1960s the nature of security risk was poorly understood. Investment texts were only able to loosely define types of risk and to note that demanded returns should be commensurate with the risk inherent in a security. Since then a major revolution has occurred in our understanding of investment risk. Today reasonable approaches to risk measurement and management exist. While some major questions remain unanswered, many of the techniques have gained widespread acceptance in the financial markets.

Our discussion of security risk extends over three chapters. In this chapter we focus on risk to the single *individual*. In the two chapters which follow we expand the discussion to *all* individuals in the security markets and examine how such risk affects equilibrium security prices. Before we begin, though, a general comment is necessary.

The world is complex. It does not operate according to the strict rules of some mechanical model. Throughout the next three chapters, however, we will attempt to impose some order on the complexities which exist. This often requires that we make what appear to be extreme assumptions at various stages. For example, during most of the discussion we will be dealing with a world in which all investors have identical one-period investment horizons. This is clearly not true to reality. But the models which result from this and other assumptions provide some profound investment implications. Thus, in this chapter, which deals with risk to an individual, we will see:

1. What makes a person risk-averse.

2. How the risk in a portfolio can be reduced by diversification *without* affecting expected returns.

3. How the risk which remains after diversification can be adjusted by shifts in the portfolio's stock/bond mix.

4. How the risk of a single security should be measured. Portfolio risk and security risk are not measured in the same way.

THE SOURCE OF RISK AVERSION

At lunch one day your securities broker, Sam, offers to play the following game with you. Broker Sam will toss a coin in the air and, if heads comes up, he will give you $1. However, if tails comes up you will have to pay him $1. He says the game will be played only once. Would you play? Probably. The game is a reasonable way to pass time, offers a little adventure, and, besides, what is $1 worth these days anyway? But what if Sam offers to replay the game (only *once*, he says) with stakes of $5,000? Would you play? If you are like most people, you wouldn't. *Why?*

Although this simple game might seem rather trivial when compared with the complex decisions that investors and speculators face daily, it really isn't. The beauty of Sam's game and the questions—"Would you play?" and "Why?"—is their simplicity. They reduce to simple terms the nature of the problem faced by all speculators and investors. It turns out that if we can determine the conditions under which people are willing to speculate or invest in risky securities (play Sam's game), we are well on our way to understanding the nature of security risk and developing techniques to measure it quantitatively.

Wealth and Utility of Wealth

To explain why people make the decisions they do, economists rely upon the theory of utility maximization. In this section we examine how utility theory leads to the notion of risk aversion and how the concepts of utility theory can be useful in developing quantitative measures of security risk. Utility theory is a way of describing the relative preferences which an individual has for different wealth levels. For example, if the utility of wealth level 2 is greater than the utility of wealth level 1, we can say that wealth level 2 is preferred to wealth level 1. Utility is often described in terms of the psychological satisfaction or pleasure a person receives from a given wealth level. And economists often talk as if they can somehow calibrate the absolute level of someone's utility as consisting of so many *utils*. But thinking of utility in terms of a number of utils of pleasure and happiness is simply a convenient mental device. We cannot measure utility and say, for example, that level 2 provides twice as many utils as level 1. All we can say is that wealth level 2 is preferred to wealth level 1. In fact, we shouldn't even assign the terms *happiness, satisfaction, pleasure*, etc., to utility. Speaking very strictly, we cannot say for certain that one wealth level is more pleasurable or satisfying than another wealth level. We can say only that one wealth level is preferred to another wealth level. Again, *utility analysis is simply a way of describing the relative preferences which an individual has for different wealth levels*.

In Chapter 5 we saw that real goods markets and financial markets are created because they increase the utility which individuals receive from consumption over time. At that point we limited the discussion to a one-period, risk-free world. Individuals made choices between known levels of consumption which were available in one period, choosing a particular consumption pattern that would maximize the utility received. But the actual problem faced by individuals is different from this in at least two respects. First, people face more than a one-period world. A decision must be made about the pattern of a future consumption stream. Second, future consumption levels are uncertain. Plan as we may, there is no guarantee that the actual consumption stream will be the one expected.

Conceptually at least, utility theory can handle these difficulties. A series of consumption streams can be introduced. For example, $\tilde{C}_1, \tilde{C}_2, \tilde{C}_3, \ldots, \tilde{C}_E$ can refer to *uncertain* levels of consumption in periods $1, 2, 3, \ldots$ as well as an estate C_E left at death.

Instead of maximizing the utility of a known consumption one period hence, people will maximize the utility of a stream of unknown future consumption levels. Symbolically, this is expressed as:

Utility of Lifetime Consumption Maximize: $U(\tilde{C}_0, \tilde{C}_1, \tilde{C}_2, \tilde{C}_3, \ldots, \tilde{C}_E)$ **(7.1)**

It is at this point that we make the *first assumption* to keep the analysis tractable—that is, that *a single-period world exists*. Decisions are made today which have an uncertain outcome one period hence. This removes the multiperiod terms ($\tilde{C}_2$, $\tilde{C}_3$, etc.) from Equation 7.1 and returns us to the one-period world similar to that in Chapter 5. Now the individual wishes to maximize expected utility of consumption at the end of period 1. Since C_1 will be equal to the person's wealth at that time (W_1), the investor's goal can be stated symbolically as Equation 7.1a.

Utility of Expected-Terminal Wealth Maximize: $E[U(\tilde{C}_1)] = E[U(\tilde{W}_1)]$ **(7.1a)**

There are any number of ways in which differing wealth levels might be preferred, but most economists assume that more wealth is preferred to less. As one's wealth level increases, so does the utility attached to it. Figure 7-1 illustrates three wealth-preference orderings which all show increasing utility with wealth. The solid line represents a constant, or linear, relationship between wealth and the utility attached to it. If wealth doubles, so does utility. For each unit change in wealth, the change in utility remains constant. An incremental $1,000 provides the same amount of additional utility at an initial wealth level of $10,000 as it does at an initial wealth level of $100,000. In the parlance of economics, the solid line depicts a case of *constant marginal utility* of wealth. The dashed curve also shows an increase in utility as wealth increases but illustrates the case of *decreasing marginal utility*. An incremental $1,000 provides less utility to a person with an initial wealth of $100,000 than it would if the same person's initial wealth were $10,000. Finally, the dotted curve illustrates the case of *increasing marginal* utility. An incremental $1,000 provides more utility to a person with an initial wealth level of $100,000 than it would if the same person's initial wealth were $10,000.[1]

---

[1] There is no logical reason for these three curves to be the only possibilities. Friedman-Savage, for example, suggested that over low wealth levels people might exhibit behavior consistent with decreasing marginal utility, but after some point they begin to exhibit behavior consistent with increasing marginal utility. Friedman-Savage used such a curve to explain why people seek particular careers, as well as buy insurance and gamble at the same time.

FIGURE 7-1 *Wealth and Utility*

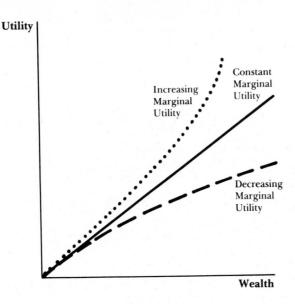

The manner in which people order wealth preferences (the shape of the utility of wealth curve) has profound implications on security pricing and risk measurement. As shown below, people who can be characterized as having constant marginal utility curves are completely indifferent to risk. People with increasing marginal utility curves are risk seekers. And people with decreasing marginal utility curves are risk-averse.

Uncertain Outcomes, Insurance, and Expected Returns

Figure 7-2 plots the utility of wealth curve for Sue Antony. Like most other people, Sue prefers more wealth to less but can be characterized as having decreasing marginal utility. An extra $1 would increase her utility but not by as much as a $1 loss would decrease her utility. Sue is a fairly well-off person with a current wealth (W_0) of $100,000, which provides a corresponding current utility of wealth (U_0).

One day Sue meets with you and your broker for lunch and Sam immediately offers to play his usual coin-tossing game. If heads comes up, Sam will pay Sue $5,000. If tails comes up, Sue will pay Sam $5,000. Sue immediately inspects the coin and says: "Nope—this is a fair coin. The odds of winning or losing are identical. Why should I expose myself to a risk without a corresponding return? *My expected utility of wealth if I decide to play the game is lower than my expected utility if I don't play.*"

To see the truth and insight of Sue's statement, refer again to Figure 7-2. Sue has two choices: to play the game or not play the game. If she elects not to play the game, her wealth remains the same and her utility remains at U_0. If she plays the game, her

FIGURE 7-2 *Utility Theory and Risk Aversion*

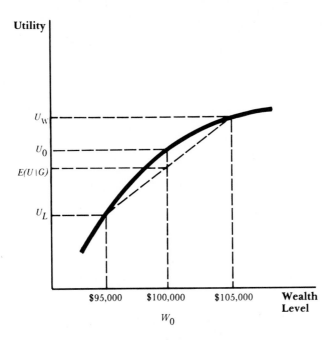

wealth will be either \$95,000 or \$105,000, with respective utilities of U_L and U_W. Thus, if she decides to play the game with a fair coin, her expected utility would be:

$$E(U \mid G) = (0.5U_L + 0.5U_W) < U_0$$

Her expected utility from playing the game is less than her current utility, so she won't play.

Given the fair gamble, the reason that expected utility is less than U_0 lies in the fact that Sue has decreasing marginal utility of wealth. The increased satisfaction obtained by a \$5,000 increase in her wealth is more than offset by the decreased satisfaction associated with a \$5,000 loss. Individuals with decreasing marginal utility are risk-averse.[2]

There are some events in life over which we have no control: we aren't given the choice to play the game or not—we are forced to play. For example, assume that most of Sue Antony's wealth is in the form of farm acreage which will either be productive during the next year or suffer little productivity if a drought occurs. Figure 7-3 plots each possibility as either wealth with productivity (W_p) or wealth with a drought (W_D) together with their respective utilities (U_p and U_D). Assume the probability of either is again 50%, so the expected wealth, $E(W)$, lies midway between W_p and W_D. Note that if Sue's wealth level were at point C with no uncertainty at all, her expected utility would be the same as it is now with her uncertain farm acre-

---

[2]Increasing marginal utility of wealth implies the person is a risk seeker, and constant marginal utility implies risk indifference.

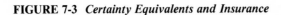

FIGURE 7-3 *Certainty Equivalents and Insurance*

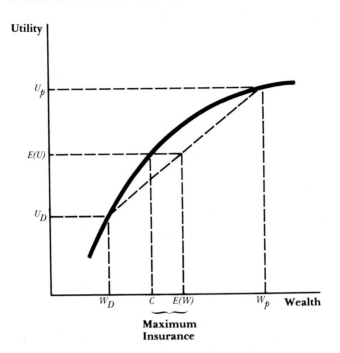

age. Point *C* is referred to as the *certainty equivalent* wealth level. Any certain wealth level greater than *C* would increase her expected utility. As a result, if Sue could *insure* herself against uncertainties (both unfavorable and favorable), the maximum she would be willing to pay is $E(W) - C$. Faced with unavoidable wealth risks, people are willing to buy insurance as long as the cost of the insurance doesn't reduce their expected utility of wealth. This is the basis of the insurance industry as well as of hedging behavior in the securities markets.

When deciding whether to buy or sell securities, however, one consciously accepts risks, and a positive expected return is required in order for the expected utility of wealth not to fall (and, one hopes, to increase). This idea is shown in Figure 7-4. We start by assuming that Sue has fully insured the risks in her wealth, resulting in a current certain wealth of *C* and corresponding utility of U_C. Now Sam offers to play the game again. If she plays, the outcomes would result in wealth levels W_L and W_W. Clearly, Sue will play only if her expected utility doesn't fall—if her expected wealth is equal to $E(W)$. Sue will demand an expected return to freely take on the chance outcome. Sam can provide this return either by changing the odds of winning and losing or by paying her to play. The form of the return is unimportant. The important fact is that Sue demands a positive expected return simply because she has a decreasing marginal utility of wealth curve.

The return which must be paid to induce people to accept the uncertain outcomes associated with securities is known as the *risk premium*. As can be seen in Figure 7-4,

FIGURE 7-4 *Security Risk and Expected Returns*

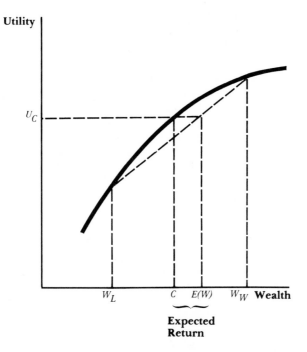

the size of the risk premium will depend upon both the risk aversion of an individual (the slope of his or her utility of wealth curve) and the size of the risk (the distribution of possible wealth levels).

MEASURING THE RISK OF A PORTFOLIO

When analyzing investment risks, we must start with the investor's total portfolio. While risks and returns on individual securities are clearly important, it is the individual's wealth level, or portfolio of *all* holdings, which is of primary concern. For example, assume that you own stock in two beer companies. If one firm improves its market share and earnings at the expense of the other, your total portfolio value might not change. The stock price increase in one firm is exactly offset by the stock price decline in the other. On net, the market value of your portfolio might remain the same.

This is a crucial point. The investor's major concern is with the risk to his or her total wealth. Individual stocks must be considered in relationship to other stocks in the portfolio and are risky only to the extent to which they add risk to the total portfolio. It is from the viewpoint of the portfolio that individual stocks are judged risky. Thus, we start our review of risk at the portfolio level.

Returning to Figure 7-4, we can see that the greater the dispersion of possible wealth outcomes, the greater the required risk premium. For example, if another risky venture were to have outcomes more widely dispersed than the W_L and W_W levels, a greater risk premium would be required. So if the investor's utility curve remains fixed, risk must be related to dispersion of possible outcomes.

For illustrative purposes, let us assume we are interested in the risk of a portfolio patterned after the S&P 500. It might or might not be the "best" portfolio to own and, in practice, people have a variety of portfolios which differ in relative degrees from the S&P 500 Index. But because it is well known and often emulated, we use it as a common illustration for the rest of this chapter. Past yearly real (after inflation) rates of return on the S&P 500 are shown in Table 7-1. We will use real returns as opposed to nominal returns since they are a better measure of changes in people's true wealth levels.

Numerous statistical measures can be used to assess the dispersion of return outcomes and, thus, proxy risk. These include the following:

1. *Range:* the high outcome less the low outcome. If the maximum possible return on a portfolio is 25% and the lowest possible return is −10%, the range would be 35%. The difficulties of using range as a risk proxy are that it doesn't consider returns between the extremes and gives no weight to the likelihood of one outcome versus another. The range of returns on the S&P 500 as shown in Table 7-1 was 91.58% and occurred between 1933 and 1937.

TABLE 7-1 *Historical Real Returns on the S&P 500 Index, 1926–1987*

Year	Real Return (%)	Year	Real Return (%)	Year	Real Return (%)
1926	13.10	1947	−3.31	1968	6.36
1927	39.57	1948	2.80	1969	−14.59
1928	44.57	1949	19.60	1970	−1.45
1929	−8.62	1950	25.95	1971	10.96
1930	−18.87	1951	18.15	1972	15.56
1931	−33.83	1952	17.46	1973	−23.45
1932	2.10	1953	−1.62	1974	−38.66
1933	53.46	1954	53.12	1975	30.20
1934	−3.46	1955	31.18	1976	19.03
1935	44.66	1956	3.70	1977	−13.95
1936	32.71	1957	−13.81	1978	−2.46
1937	−38.12	1958	41.60	1979	5.10
1938	33.92	1959	10.47	1980	20.00
1939	0.06	1960	−1.02	1981	−13.85
1940	−10.74	1961	26.22	1982	17.54
1941	−21.30	1962	−9.94	1983	18.71
1942	11.03	1963	21.12	1984	2.25
1943	22.73	1964	15.30	1985	28.40
1944	17.61	1965	10.52	1986	17.50
1945	34.16	1966	−13.40	1987	1.00
1946	−26.23	1967	20.95		

2. *Mean absolute deviation:* the average absolute difference between the possible returns on a portfolio and its expected return. Although this might be a reasonable proxy for a portfolio's risk, it is statistically quite difficult to use. In particular, there is no way of easily capturing the effects of correlation among security returns. The mean absolute deviation of S&P 500 returns was 17.6%.

3. *Probability of negative return:* the percentage of the time that returns are less than zero. While intuitively pleasing, this measure doesn't fully address all aspects of risk. For example, returns between 0 and the expected return are neglected. In addition, uncertain returns greater than the expected returns are still uncertain and should be accounted for. Finally, it is difficult to capture the effects of correlations among security returns. Of the 62 years reported in Table 7-1, there were 21 years with less than a zero return. Thus, in 34% of all years, returns on this portfolio were negative.

4. *Semivariance:* the statistical measure of variance of returns below the expected return. Semivariance does not consider uncertainty of returns larger than the expected return and also makes it difficult to capture the effects of correlations between security returns. Semivariance measures are complex equations and, since we will not be using them, we will not illustrate them. Instead, we will focus on the most commonly used measure of risk—the standard deviation.

5. *Standard deviation:* the measure of return volatility which is commonly used to measure risk. It was briefly reviewed in Chapter 1 and is examined more extensively below. On both theoretical and practical grounds, the standard deviation (or its squared value variance) seems to be the best measure of risk. First, it is a statistical measure of return dispersion (both above and below the expected return). We will use it as a measure of the dispersion of portfolio returns and risk. For example, Figure 7-5 plots the probability of a given return on the vertical axis and the level of return on the horizontal axis. The return distributions for two portfolios, *A* and *B*, are shown. Both portfolios have the same average return, but the standard deviation of returns on portfolio *B* is larger and thus *B* is more risky.

FIGURE 7-5 *Security Return Distributions*

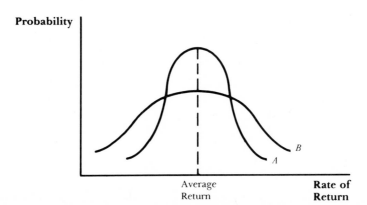

Given a choice between the two, portfolio A is clearly preferred. Second, the standard deviation is a statistical technique which can easily capture the important effects of correlation between security returns.

The standard deviation can be either calculated using actual historical return data or estimated using potential future return data. When calculated using historical returns, we speak of the *ex post* standard deviation. When calculated using future returns, we speak of the *ex ante* standard deviation. Both numbers are useful. To evaluate historical risk/return performance the ex post value is used. The ex ante standard deviation is used in determining proper investment strategy for the future.

Ex Post Standard Deviation

The ex post standard deviation of historical portfolio returns will be designated as σ_p and calculated as follows:

Ex Post Portfolio Standard Deviation
$$\sigma_p = \sqrt{\frac{\sum\limits_{t=1}^{N} (R_{pt} - \bar{R}_p)^2}{N}} \qquad (7.2)$$

where σ_p = the ex post standard deviation of portfolio returns, R_{pt} = the single-period rate of return on the portfolio during period t, $\bar{R}_p$ = the average historical return on the portfolio during the last N periods, and N = the number of periods over which the standard deviation is calculated. As noted in Chapters 1 and 4, returns in each period are calculated by adding the change in market value of the portfolio during period t to any cash dividends received during period t and dividing this total by the market value at the start of t; that is:

$$R_{pt} = \frac{MV_{pt} - MV_{pt-1} + DIV_{pt}}{MV_{pt-1}} \qquad (7.3)$$

where MV_{pt} = the market value of the portfolio at the end of period t and DIV_{pt} = the cash dividends received on the portfolio during period t.

Using the yearly return series for the S&P 500, an ex post standard deviation would be calculated as follows:

1. Calculate the average return $\bar{R}$:

$$\bar{R} = \frac{(0.131 + 0.3957 + \ldots + 0.01)}{62}$$

$$= 0.0883$$

2. Use $\bar{R}$ to calculate σ_p:

$$\sigma_p = \sqrt{\frac{(0.131 - 0.0883)^2 + (0.3957 - 0.0883)^2 + \ldots + (0.01 - 0.0883)^2}{62}}$$

$$= 0.215$$

Between 1926 and 1987 the average yearly return on a portfolio consisting of the S&P 500 was 8.83%. During this same time interval the standard deviation of returns was 21.5%. This contrasts with an $\bar{R}$ of 0.35% and a σ_p of 4.57% on Treasury bills over the same time period. The portfolio of 500 S&P Index stocks yielded 8.48% more per year, but at the cost of much larger volatility.

Ex Ante Standard Deviation

Ex post standard deviations evaluate historical volatility. Ex ante standard deviations look forward and attempt to assess potential future volatility. Ex ante standard deviations are calculated as follows:

Ex Ante Standard Deviation
$$\sigma_p = \sqrt{\sum_{s=1}^{S} P_s [R_{ps} - E(R_p)]^2} \qquad (7.4)$$

where $P_s =$ a subjective estimate of the probability of a certain "state of nature" occurring, $R_{ps} =$ the return on the portfolio in state s, $E(R_p) =$ the expected return on the portfolio, and $S =$ the number of possible states of nature. To understand its calculation, assume that after a thorough financial analysis of the economy and various individual stocks, you subjectively develop the following beliefs about the returns on a portfolio of the S&P 500 for the coming year.

Economic Conditions	Probability	S&P 500 Returns
Good	0.25	30%
Fair	0.50	15%
Poor	0.25	0%
	1.00	

Your expected return on the portfolio would be:

$$E(R_p) = 0.25(30\%) + 0.5(15\%) + 0.25(0\%) = 15\%$$

and the ex ante standard deviation would be:

$$\sigma_p = \sqrt{0.25(0.30 - 0.15)^2 + 0.5(0.15 - 0.15)^2 + 0.25(0.0 - 0.15)^2} = 10.6\%$$

When a portfolio's expected return and ex ante risk are considered with the same measures for other portfolios, an investment strategy can be explicitly developed. For example, assume you are able to continue your analysis a bit further and develop ex-

FIGURE 7-6 *Ex Ante Portfolio Risk and Return*

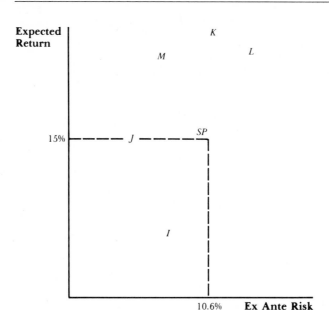

pected returns and ex ante risk measures on a host of other possible portfolio holdings. The results of the analysis are shown in Figure 7-6. Portfolio *SP* represents the first portfolio evaluated above. Clearly portfolios *J*, *K*, and *M* dominate *SP* in that they provide equivalent returns for less risk or equivalent risk for higher returns. (What can we say about portfolios *L* and *I* relative to *SP*?)

Criticisms of Standard Deviation

Criticisms of the standard deviation as an appropriate measure of risk have been numerous, ranging from the superficial to the more insightful. At the superficial level, one will hear the argument: "Standard deviation? Nonsense! No one on the Street even knows what a standard deviation is. Risk is a qualitative feel which can never be measured." True, ex ante risk assessment requires subjective judgment on the analyst's part. But this is no reason why it shouldn't be stated explicitly. Seat-of-the-pants decisions may work well in a noncomplex setting, but as alternative decisions become complex, a more sophisticated accounting system is needed. As for the comment that no one knows what the standard deviation is, there was also a time when P/E ratios, internal rates of return, burden coverage ratios, etc., were relatively sophisticated financial concepts. Since the major stock declines of the early 1970s, however, most professional investment managers have given considerable attention to risk measurement and standard deviation.

At a more substantive level, some individuals question whether portfolio standard

FIGURE 7-7 *Skewed Return Distributions*

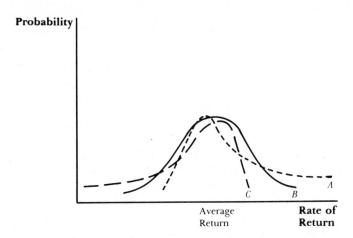

deviations by themselves are adequate measures of risk. These people believe that if rates of return are distributed in a skewed fashion, more statistical information is needed. A skewed distribution is one which is not symmetric; more observations lie in one tail of the distribution than in the other. For example, in Figure 7-7 distribution *A* is positively skewed, distribution *B* is symmetric, and distribution *C* is negatively skewed. Assuming that the expected returns and standard deviations of each distribution are equal, our theory so far says the investor would be indifferent among the three. However, if skewness does matter, then *A* would be the most preferred and *C* the least preferred.

The importance of skewness remains unresolved. For example, various studies have shown that statistical measures of skewness are quite sensitive to the time period over which data are collected. However, Arditti has presented empirical evidence suggesting that investors prefer positive skewness. In fact, simple logic suggests that future wealth must be positively skewed, since wealth cannot fall below zero but the potential for increase in one's wealth is unlimited. The potential for being at either the lower or upper wealth extremes increases as (1) more-risky securities are purchased and (2) the investment time horizon increases. But investment selection models which include the potential for skewness are quite complex and beyond the scope of this text.

It is time, then, to make our *second major assumption — the standard deviation of end-of-period portfolio returns is the proper measure of a portfolio's risk.*

Using Ex Post σ_p as an Estimate of Ex Ante σ_p. Historical data are convenient. As a result, ex post standard deviations are often used as measures of ex ante standard deviations. There is nothing wrong with using any and all information possible when forecasting the future. For this reason, historical standard deviations should be examined. But two points should be made. First, security prices are based upon expectations of the future. The standard deviation used in the determination of security prices is the ex ante value. Ex post values may be used as a convenience only. Sec-

TABLE 7-2 *Ex Post Standard Deviations of S&P 500 Real Returns for Various Time Intervals*

Interval	S&P 500 Standard Deviation
1926–1940	28.81%
1941–1955	20.10
1956–1970	15.92
1971–1987	18.70

ond, as with so many other financial variables (for example, growth rates and stock returns), the past is often a very poor predictor of the future. Standard deviations of well-diversified portfolios are fairly constant over time. But as the portfolio becomes less diversified, past σ_p and future σ_p may not be highly correlated.

As an example of how well (or how poorly) ex post σ_p predicts future σ_p, the data in Table 7-1 were broken into four intervals of about 15 years each, and the ex post standard deviation was calculated for each period. Results are displayed in Table 7-2. During the first 15-year period σ_p was 28.81%. This was certainly a poor predictor of the 20.10% σ_p which existed in the next period. Since then, however, σ_p for the S&P 500 has ranged between 15% and 20%. It is for the reader to decide whether historical standard deviations of this portfolio are reasonable predictors of the future.

DIVERSIFICATION

Diversification is the key to effective risk management. Through proper diversification, risk exposure can be minimized without affecting expected portfolio returns. We can think of diversification along two dimensions: (1) across time for a given number of securities and (2) across the number of securities for a given time period.

Diversification Across Time. Panel A in Figure 7-8 is a frequency distribution of yearly returns on our sample S&P 500 portfolio. Between 1926 and 1987 the average annual rate of return was 8.83% ($\bar{G}$). But, again, as we have noted so often before, the volatility of returns earned over a one-year time horizon was considerable. It is important to recognize, however, that this is the volatility associated with *one-year* holding periods. The volatility of return outcomes for longer holding periods is considerably less. In panel B the frequency distribution of annualized returns for all possible 10-year holding periods is shown. Notice the substantial reduction in volatility. A similar reduction in risk is shown in panel C, in which the holding period consists of all possible 25-year holding periods.

As the length of the holding period is increased, uncertainty about the average annualized compound return declines. This is shown in another way in Figure 7-9. Compound annual rates of return are shown on the vertical axis and the length of the

FIGURE 7-8 *Frequency Distributions of Annualized Returns for Various Holding Periods*

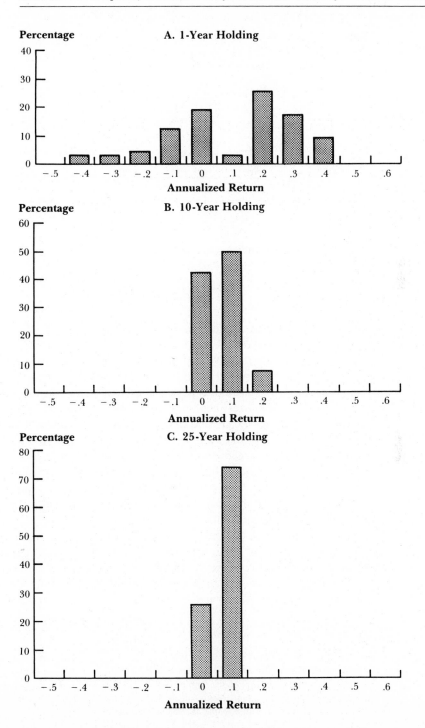

FIGURE 7-9 *Real Returns on the S&P 500 for Various Holding Periods, 1926–1987*

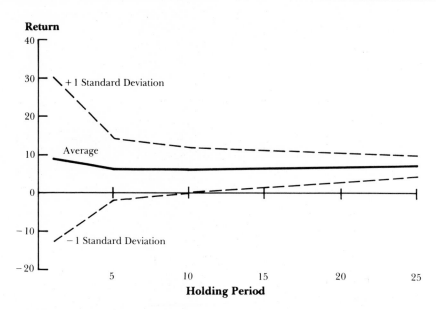

holding period is shown on the horizontal axis. The middle line plots the *average* compound annual return ($\bar{G}$) experienced for any holding period. Although $\bar{G}$ does vary a little, it is fair to say that average outcomes for holding the S&P 500 for one year are virtually identical to average outcomes for 25-year holding periods. The average annualized return one can expect to receive is *not influenced* much by the time period over which the investment is to be made. The top and bottom lines represent one standard deviation above and below the average.[3] Again, it is clear that uncertainty about average annual returns falls as the holding period increases.

Since the uncertainty related to investing in securities depends on the length of time for which the investment is to be made, the risk of owning a given portfolio is not the same for everyone. A 70-year-old retiree who purchases a portfolio such as the S&P 500 faces considerably more risk than does a 25-year-old worker who intends to hold such a portfolio until after retirement.

Why? Why does risk decline as the investment holding period increases? The answer is quite simple. The longer one holds a portfolio, the better the chance that years with poor returns will be offset by favorable years. Diversification over time works because rates of return across time are not correlated. It is this lack of correlation that is critical in any diversification strategy and is the major consideration in the next section.

---

[3]Part of the reduction in this return volatility comes from the fact that returns on each 25-year holding are not independent. For example, the first holding period covers 1926 to 1950, the second covers 1927 to 1951, etc. Note that the first and second periods have 24 years in common. This lack of true independence between returns is a major reason for the decline in the standard deviation. Nonetheless, the data do reflect the experience of all possible 25-year holding period returns from 1926 to 1987.

Diversification Across Securities. So far we have held the composition of our portfolio fixed and examined diversification over time. Now we will alter the number of securities held in the portfolio and see how this affects portfolio risk during a given holding period. We continue to use the S&P 500 Index as a reference portfolio, but now we will consider portfolios which consist of only some of the stocks included in the S&P 500.

During the five years ending December 1987, the standard deviation of real returns on our reference S&P 500 portfolio was 21.5%. But this was *not* the standard deviation of returns on the average stock in the portfolio. The average stock had a standard deviation considerably larger—equal to about 40%. If you had purchased a portfolio consisting of only some of the S&P 500 stocks, the average standard deviation was larger than if you had purchased all 500.

Naive Diversification. Naive diversification is random diversification, the purchase of a large number of securities without regard to industry classification, expected returns, etc. For example, assume you have a list of all stocks contained in the S&P 500 and attach the list to a dart board. One way to select a naively diversified portfolio would be to throw darts at the listing (assuming you are a poor dart player so that selection is indeed random). If you desire a portfolio of 20 stocks, you would throw 20 darts and invest an equal dollar amount in each (unless you're a really bad dart player and some of your tosses totally miss the board).

Figure 7-10 displays the results when such a strategy is applied to stocks contained

FIGURE 7-10 *Portfolio Risk and Naive Diversification Using Real Returns on S&P 500 Stocks, 1926–1987*

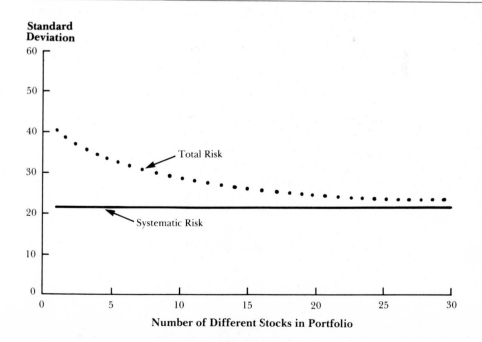

Number of Different Stocks in Portfolio

in the S&P 500. The horizontal axis shows the number of stocks in the randomly selected portfolio and the vertical axis shows the average standard deviation (of annualized return) which results from a portfolio of a given size. When only one stock is held, the portfolio standard deviation is identical to the standard deviation of the average stock which was reported above. However, as additional stocks are held, σ_p falls substantially. Reductions in σ_p caused by adding the first few stocks to the portfolio are dramatic, whereas the marginal risk reduction of adding a new stock to a larger portfolio is small. Although the marginal reduction in risk decreases as the portfolio size increases, adding one more stock to any portfolio will (on average) continue to reduce the portfolio risk.

Some care should be given to the interpretation of Figure 7-10. The reductions in risk which are shown to result from randomly increasing the number of securities are the *average* results over many computer simulations. The results are never exactly as shown. The variability is greatest when few securities are held, whereas the outcomes for large portfolios (those with more than 50 stocks) are relatively close to the curve shown. In sum, for the *average* person the results will be as shown in Figure 7-10, but any single person may experience little or no risk reduction until a large number of stocks are held.

Another way to illustrate the risk reduction associated with diversification is depicted in Figure 7-11. The data used to generate the plot were the same as those used in Figure 7-10; that is, they were actual stocks included in the S&P 500 for the 62-year interval (1926–1987). The solid line running through the middle of the figure is the average portfolio return earned for each portfolio size. As you can see, average returns are unaffected by the number of securities held. *Diversification, by itself,*

FIGURE 7-11 *Yearly Return and Naive Diversification Using S&P 500 Real Stock Returns*

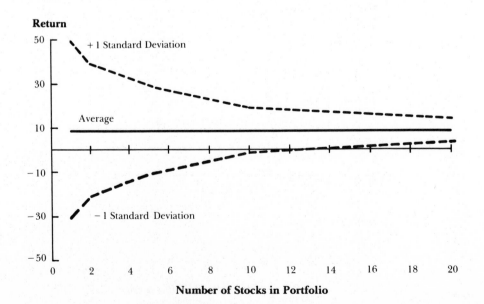

Number of Stocks in Portfolio

will not reduce past average returns or future expected returns. But the two curves surrounding the average return line represent the average plus and minus one standard deviation. Their narrowing as a portfolio grows in size shows, again, the potential risk reduction.

Systematic and Unsystematic Risk. Before we move into the mathematics of why diversification works, it is a good time to point out two concepts which will be important throughout the rest of the book and which can be seen in the results of naive diversification. These concepts are as follows:

1. Some risk cannot be eliminated by diversification. There is an underlying volatility of returns which is *systematic* to all risky securities. Diversification cannot eliminate this *systematic risk*. It can only eliminate return uncertainties which are unique to individual securities—*unsystematic risk*.

2. Individual securities have differing amounts of this nondiversifiable, systematic risk. Systematic and unsystematic risk are shown schematically in Figure 7-12.

To intelligent investors, diversifiable risk is meaningless. They will broadly diversify their portfolios to eliminate that particular type of risk. We will see in the next chapter that the only component of risk for which they will demand compensation is nondiversifiable risk. The larger a security's nondiversifiable risk, the larger the demanded return.

Unsystematic risk is often referred to as *firm-unique* risk—uncertainties about returns on one firm which can be offset by holding other firms in the portfolio. As examples of firm-unique risk, consider the following situations:

1. Firm *A* sues Firm *B* for damages incurred on a breach of contract. Clearly, if *A* wins, the market value of *B* will decline. But *B*'s loss is *A*'s gain. So a hedged (or

FIGURE 7-12 *Systematic and Unsystematic Risk*

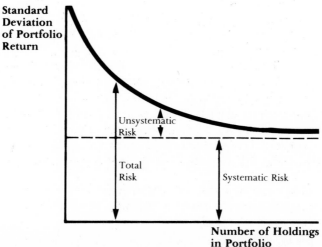

diversified) position in stocks of both *A* and *B* should eliminate any concern one might have about the lawsuit.[4]

2. Firm *C* has a labor contract due which could lead to a lengthy strike and profit declines. If Firm *C*'s lost sales are picked up by competitors, then part (or all) of the labor strike's risk can be diversified.

3. Firm *D* has a patent on a major product line which might be counteracted through research developments at competing firms. If *D* does lose its effective patent position, its profits would decline and competitors' profits would increase. Thus, the patent risk is diversifiable.

4. Regional Firm *E* is expected to have a large growth in earnings as a result of population migration into the region. But there is an uncertainty whether the in-migration will be as large as expected. This risk can be diversified by holding shares in Firm *E* as well as shares in companies operating in regions with an expected out-migration.

Systematic risk is often referred to as *market risk* — uncertainties about returns which affect all securities. Such risk cannot be eliminated by diversification but only by purchasing a risk-free security. Examples of market risk would include the following:

1. The impacts of inflation on security prices. Inflation can affect security prices in at least two ways — by changing the required risk-free rate or by changing expected future profits. While inflation will not have the same impact on all securities, its effects cannot be totally diversified away.

2. Uncertainties about long-run aggregate economic growth. Since corporate profits of all firms are dependent upon the long-run health and growth of the aggregate economy, uncertainties associated with broad economic output cannot be diversified. Factors which will affect aggregate output (and are not fully diversifiable) include population growth, labor productivity, political uncertainty, tax policy, technology, etc.

3. Changes in the market's willingness to accept risk. If average investors suddenly become more risk-averse, the return they require on their investments will increase. To provide this larger demanded return, security prices will have to fall. The opposite would occur if risk aversion declined. Thus, future changes in the market's risk aversion will affect the distribution of future security returns. This risk cannot be diversified away.

4. Interest rate changes will affect prices of all securities. Impacts of such interest rate changes are referred to as *interest rate risk* and cannot be diversified away. Interest rate risk is clearly related to each of the previous points since inflation, labor productivity, and risk aversion all affect interest rate levels.

To illustrate that securities have differing amounts of systematic risk, consider Figure 7-13. In this figure the effects of diversifying within various industries are shown

---

[4]The only way to better hedge this risk would be to own stock in each of the contending law firms.

FIGURE 7-13 *Nondiversified Risk and Different Securities Using S&P 500 Stocks, 1980–1984*

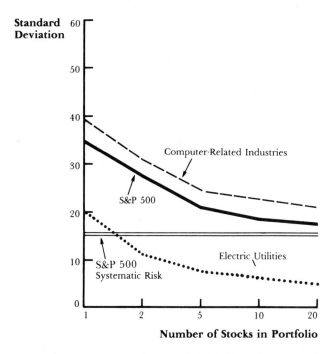

for a recent five-year period. The solid curve reflects the average outcome of naively diversifying across all stocks in the S&P 500. The dashed line represents the results of a naive diversification strategy applied to stocks in computer-related industries, whereas the dotted line reflects naive diversification across electric utilities.

Note that the risk of a single-stock portfolio in the computer industry is greater than the average for all stocks, whereas a single-stock utility portfolio is less risky. But more important than this is the amount of risk which remains undiversified in each portfolio type, as seen at the far right of each curve. The amount of systematic risk associated with the computer industry is greater than the amount for the average stock, and the amount of systematic risk for electric utilities is less than the average. The concept of this remaining systematic risk, which will differ from stock to stock, underlies most of the equilibrium security pricing models discussed in the next two chapters.

The previous examples were all developed using past returns on common stocks included in the S&P 500 Index. But the results also hold true for other types of securities, as we will see in later chapters. Diversification across bonds, mutual funds, international securities, etc., will reduce portfolio risk without reducing expected portfolio returns.

The Mathematics of Diversification. Diversification works because the standard deviation of the portfolio is *not equal* to the weighted average standard deviation of the securities which make up the portfolio. In addition to each security's σ, we must also account for the extent to which the security returns are *correlated*.

Earlier we calculated ex ante and ex post portfolio standard deviations using returns on the total portfolio. Now we will state the portfolio's standard deviation in terms of the individual securities which are held in the portfolio. Mathematically:

Security Components of σ_p

$$\sigma_p = \sqrt{\sum_{i=1}^{N} \sum_{j=1}^{N} X_i X_j \sigma_i \sigma_j r_{ij}}$$

$$= \sqrt{\sum_{i=1}^{N} X_i^2 \sigma_i^2 + \sum_{\substack{i=1 \\ i \neq j}}^{N} \sum_{j=1}^{N} X_i X_j \sigma_i \sigma_j r_{ij}}$$

(7.5)

where: σ_p = portfolio's standard deviation

σ_i = standard deviation of some security i

σ_j = standard deviation of some security j

X_i, X_j = percentage of the portfolio investment in i and j

r_{ij} = correlation coefficient which measures the correlation of returns between i and j. If i and j refer to the same security, then $r = 1.0$. Otherwise r is bounded by -1.0 and 1.0.

While Equation 7-5 will appear imposing to many students, it isn't too difficult if studied closely.[5] To understand its calculation, consider a portfolio of two stocks, A and B. In that case Equation 7.5 becomes:

$$\sigma_p = \sqrt{X_A^2 \sigma_A^2 + X_B^2 \sigma_B^2 + X_A X_B \sigma_A \sigma_B r_{AB} + X_B X_A \sigma_B \sigma_A r_{BA}}$$

$$= \sqrt{X_A^2 \sigma_A^2 + X_B^2 \sigma_B^2 + 2 X_A X_B \sigma_A \sigma_B r_{AB}}$$

Assume 40% of the portfolio is placed in security A and 60% is placed in security B. Also assume:

$$\sigma_A = 10\%$$

$$\sigma_B = 15\%$$

$$r_{AB} = +0.5$$

Then the portfolio standard deviation would be 11.5%:

$$\sqrt{(0.4^2)(0.10^2) + (0.6^2)(0.15^2) + 2(0.4)(0.6)(0.10)(0.15)(0.5)} = 0.115$$

---

[5]Equation 7.5 refers to securities i and j. This does *not* mean we are concerned with only two stocks, i and j. In fact, there are N securities being evaluated. The terms i and j are necessary since parameters for one security will have to be multiplied by parameters of other securities. For example, the standard deviation of Fox will have to be multiplied by the standard deviation of U.S. Broadcasting.

Note that this is not the same as the weighted average standard deviation of stocks held:

$$0.13 = 0.4(0.10) + 0.6(0.15) \neq 0.115$$

The correlation coefficient can have significant impacts on risk. For example, in the two-stock example above, if the correlation coefficient had been -0.5 instead of $+0.5$, the calculated portfolio standard deviation would have been 7.8% instead of 11.5%.

The most important feature of Equation 7.5 is that the portfolio standard deviation is *not* simply a weighted sum of the underlying securities' standard deviations. The relationship is more complex. Consider the situation of stock investments in both a processor of oranges and a processor of cocoa. Returns on either stock are unknown, and each has a large standard deviation of potential returns. However, returns on each stock are negatively related. When weather conditions adversely affect the profits of the orange processor, sales of hot chocolate increase and improve the profits of the cocoa processor. Good returns on one security *offset* poor returns on the other. In the context of the portfolio, an explicit allowance must be made for the extent to which returns on component securities are interrelated. This interrelationship is captured in Equation 7.5 through the correlation coefficient, r_{ij}.

The correlation coefficient (r_{ij}) is a statistical measure of the extent to which returns on two securities are related. Values of r_{ij} can range between $+1.0$ and -1.0. The panels in Figure 7-14 illustrate various degrees of correlation. In panel A returns on stocks i and j always move in the same direction. Stock i is twice as volatile as stock j and thus has the larger standard deviation. Nonetheless, returns on the stocks are perfectly correlated, $r_{ij} = +1.0$. In panel B a relationship between the returns on i and j doesn't exist. Returns on each are totally uncorrelated, $r_{ij} = 0.0$. In panel C the returns consistently move counter to each other. They are perfectly inversely correlated, $r_{ij} = -1.0$.

Security Correlation and Diversification

It is helpful to examine three extreme levels of the correlation coefficient.

1. If *perfectly negatively correlated* $(r = -1.0)$ securities are available, *proper diversification can eliminate portfolio risk*. Again, consider stocks A and B above, which had $\sigma_A = 10\%$ and $\sigma_B = 15\%$. This time assume the returns on each have perfect negative correlation. In this situation a 60% investment in A and a 40% investment in B would result in zero portfolio variance:

$$\sigma_p^2 = X_A^2 \sigma_A^2 + X_B^2 \sigma_B^2 + 2\sigma_A \sigma_B X_A X_B r_{ij}$$
$$= (0.36)(0.01) + (0.16)(0.0225) + 2(0.10)(0.15)(0.6)(0.4)(-1.0)$$
$$= 0.0$$

FIGURE 7-14 *Illustrations of Various Correlation Coefficients*

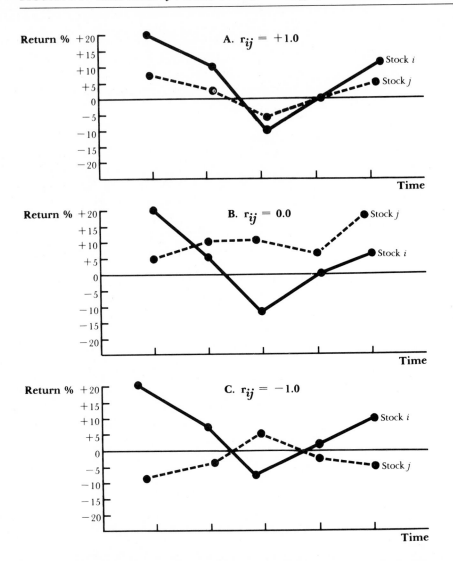

When a portfolio of the two is created (a 60/40 portfolio), unfavorable returns on one stock are offset by favorable returns on the other, so that the portfolio incurs no return volatility. Its standard deviation is zero.

Note that when $r = -1.0$, portfolio risk can be eliminated with only *two* securities. Broad diversification is not necessary. Perfect negative correlation is rarely (if ever) found in the real world, however.

2. If a large number of *uncorrelated* ($r = 0.0$) securities are available, *broad diversification can eliminate portfolio risk.* Zero correlation means that security returns

are unrelated. If one stock has a particularly large (or small) return, this has no impact at all upon other securities. *On average*, poor returns on one stock are exactly offset by the returns on all the other stocks. The key words are *on average*. Returns on two, three, four, etc., securities will tend to offset one another. But they will not do so totally. In order to ensure that portfolio risk is minimized, a large number of stocks must be held.[6]

In the real world large numbers of uncorrelated securities are difficult to find. As a practical matter it is impossible to use broad diversification to *eliminate* portfolio risk. Nonetheless, diversification can be used very effectively to *reduce* portfolio risk. Yet consider the case of commodity futures contracts. Returns which might be earned on a single futures contract are generally quite volatile; they have extremely large standard deviations. However, commodity returns are largely (not totally) uncorrelated. Thus, holding a portfolio of diversified commodity contracts can substantially reduce one's risk. Trading in a few commodities is an extremely risky venture. Trading in a large number of commodities entails much less risk.[7]

As another example, consider life insurance policies. The expected payoff date on any one policy is unknown and has an uncertainty which can be expressed as the standard deviation of years around an expected payoff date. Since the actual payoff dates of different life policies are uncorrelated, the uncertainty inherent in a large number of policies can be virtually eliminated. By holding a large number of life insurance policies, a life insurance firm can predict yearly policy payoffs with a high degree of precision. Risk is virtually eliminated through broad diversification.

3. If securities are *perfectly positively correlated* ($r = +1.0$), *diversification will provide no risk-reduction advantages.* The risk of the portfolio will be equal to the weighted average risk of the underlying securities. Regardless of the portfolio created, portfolio risk remains constant and equal to the risk of the stocks held in isolation.

Diversification does not aid in reducing portfolio risk if security returns are perfectly correlated. However, again it is unusual to find securities with perfect positive correlation in the real world. But highly correlated securities do exist in abundance. Diversification across such instruments will yield few benefits. For example, how effective would broad diversification within long-term municipal bonds be? Or how effective is diversification in numerous mortgages or diversification in common stocks of real estate developers? Perhaps not very effective.

---

[6]When two stocks (or portfolios) have a correlation of zero between their returns, a *minimum-risk* portfolio can be obtained by using the formula:

$$X_1 = \frac{\sigma_2^2}{\sigma_1^2 + \sigma_2^2}$$

$$X_2 = 1 - X_1$$

This formula does *not* yield a *zero-risk* portfolio, only a *minimum-risk* portfolio.

[7]For evidence of this point, see Dusak.

Calculating Correlation Coefficients. Correlation coefficients can be calculated using either ex post or ex ante data. The ex ante correlation coefficient for securities i and j is calculated as follows:

Ex Ante Correlation Coefficient

$$r_{ij} = \frac{\sum\limits_{s=1}^{S} P_s[R_{is} - E(R_i)][R_{js} - E(R_j)]}{\sigma_i \sigma_j} \tag{7.6}$$

where:
- σ_i = ex ante standard deviation of returns on security i
- σ_j = ex ante standard deviation of returns on security j
- R_{is} = return on security i in state s
- R_{js} = return on security j in state s
- $E(R_i)$ = expected return on security i
- $E(R_j)$ = expected return on security j
- P_s = probability of state s
- s = designation for possible outcomes where there are a total S possible states

To understand its calculation, consider the data in Table 7-3 for hypothetical stocks I and J. Returns on the stocks are believed to be related to overall economic activity. For this reason, three states of economic activity have been designated, and subjective probabilities have been assigned to each. Returns for each stock are shown for each economic state. Calculation of the correlation coefficient is performed in four steps. First, the expected return on each stock, $E(R)$, is found. Second, the standard deviation of each stock, σ, is found. Third, the numerator in Equation 7.6 is found. This is conventionally referred to as the *covariance of returns* (something we will have more to say about soon). Finally, the correlation coefficient is found by dividing the covariance of returns by the product of the two standard deviations. In the example, stocks I and J are perfectly positively correlated, $r_{ij} = +1.0$. While the standard deviations of the stocks differ, their returns move exactly in the same direction as economic conditions change.

Ex post correlation coefficients use historical returns and are calculated in much the same manner as ex ante correlation coefficients (Equation 7.6).

Ex Post Correlation Coefficient

$$r_{ij} = \frac{\sum\limits_{t=1}^{N} (R_{it} - \bar{R}_i)(R_{jt} - \bar{R}_j)/N}{\sigma_i \sigma_j} \tag{7.7}$$

where:
- R_{it}, R_{jt} = returns on securities i and j in period t, where $t = 1$ to N
- $\bar{R}_i, \bar{R}_j$ = average historical returns on i and j
- σ_i, σ_j = standard deviations of i and j returns

In Table 7-4, the correlation coefficient for the hypothetical stocks I and J is calculated. In this case, the ex post correlation coefficient is 0.725, suggesting a positive correlation between the two stocks' returns.

TABLE 7-3 *Calculation of the Ex Ante Correlation Coefficient*

State	Condition of Economy	Probability	Return on Stock	
			I	*J*
1	Good	0.2	20%	15%
2	Fair	0.6	15%	12%
3	Poor	0.2	10%	9%

Step 1: Find the expected returns:

$E(R_i) = 0.2(0.20) + 0.6(0.15) + 0.2(0.10) = 15.0\%$

$E(R_j) = 0.2(0.15) + 0.6(0.12) + 0.2(0.09) = 12\%$

Step 2: Find the ex ante standard deviations:

$\sigma_i = \sqrt{0.2(0.20 - 0.15)^2 + 0.6(0.15 - 0.15)^2 + 0.2(0.10 - 0.15)^2} = 3.16\%$

$\sigma_j = \sqrt{0.2(0.15 - 0.12)^2 + 0.6(0.12 - 0.12)^2 + 0.2(0.09 - 0.12)^2} = 1.90\%$

Step 3: Find the covariance of returns:

$$\text{Covariance} = \sum_{s=1}^{S} P_s[R_{is} - E(R_i)][R_{js} - E(R_j)]$$

$$= 0.2(0.20 - 0.15)(0.15 - 0.12) + 0.6(0.15 - 0.15)(0.12 - 0.12)$$

$$+ 0.2(0.10 - 0.15)(0.09 - 0.12)$$

$$= 0.0006$$

Step 4: Find the ex ante correlation coefficient:

$$r_{ij} = \frac{0.0006}{(0.0316)(0.0190)} = +1.0$$

Efficient Diversification

Naive diversification ensures that portfolio risk is reduced. However, it *does not guarantee that minimum risk is achieved at any level of desired return.* Efficient diversification does. Efficient diversification is a mathematical procedure which searches through a set of data provided by the security analyst to find that combination of securities which will minimize portfolio risk for a desired level of portfolio return.

The Markowitz Model

The notion of efficient diversification and the approach used in this section were originally developed by Harry M. Markowitz. In fact, Markowitz's original insights into defining and managing portfolio risk are milestones in investment literature, and he is often referred to as the father of modern portfolio theory. Markowitz suggested that the goal of the portfolio manager should be to *minimize portfolio risk for any level of expected returns* and suggested that this be accomplished by solving the following logical set of equations:

TABLE 7-4 *Calculation of the Ex Post Correlation Coefficient*

	Return on Stock				Return on Stock	
Period	*I*	*J*	*Period*		*I*	*J*
1	10%	12%	5		3%	5%
2	8%	−4%	6		12%	9%
3	−10%	−1%	7		−5%	1%
4	20%	25%	8		2%	−7%

Step 1: Find the average returns:

$$\bar{R}_i = [0.10 + 0.08 \ldots -0.05 + 0.02]/8 = 0.05$$

$$\bar{R}_j = [0.12 - 0.04 \ldots +0.01 - 0.07]/8 = 0.05$$

Step 2: Find the ex post standard deviations:

$$\sigma_i = \sqrt{[(0.10 - 0.05)^2 + (-0.08 - 0.05)^2 \ldots + (0.02 - 0.05)^2]/8} = 0.0899$$

$$\sigma_j = \sqrt{[(0.12 - 0.05)^2 + (-0.04 - 0.05)^2 \ldots + (-0.07 - 0.05)^2]/8} = 0.0963$$

Step 3: Find the covariance of returns:

$$\text{Covariance} = [(0.10 - 0.05)(0.12 - 0.05) + (0.08 - 0.05)(-0.04 - 0.05)$$
$$+ \ldots + (0.02 - 0.05)(-0.07 - 0.05)]/8 = 0.006275$$

Step 4: Find the ex post correlation coefficient:

$$r_{ij} = \frac{0.006275}{(0.0899)(0.0963)} = 0.725$$

Minimize Portfolio Risk

$$\sigma_p = \left[\sum_{i=1}^{N} X_i^2 \sigma_i^2 + \sum_{i=1}^{N} \sum_{\substack{j=1 \\ i \neq j}}^{N} X_i X_j \sigma_i \sigma_j r_{ij} \right]^{1/2} \tag{7.8a}$$

Subject to:

A Minimum Stated Expected Return

$$R^* \leq E(R_p) = \sum_{i=1}^{N} X_i E(R_i) \tag{7.8b}$$

Equation 7.8a is simply the statistical definition of the portfolio's standard deviation, which we saw earlier in Equation 7.5. This standard deviation is determined by using the percentage invested in each security (X_i), the standard deviation of each security's return (σ_i), and the amount of security correlation (r_{ij}). The term which captures security intercorrelation is called the *covariance* between two securities. Often Equation 7.8a is written with the covariance term denoted as σ_{ij} instead of as $\sigma_i \sigma_j r_{ij}$. Nonetheless, we will continue to use the approach shown above since it more explicitly captures the role of the correlation coefficient.

Equation 7.8b defines how the portfolio's expected return is calculated and states that when solving for the optimal X_i values, the resulting expected portfolio return must be equal to (or greater than) some desired level R^*. Usually, the model is solved for a number of R^* values so that one has a variety of *efficient portfolios* to choose from which differ in risk/return characteristics.

Data. To solve the set of equations, the analyst must provide data estimates on the following:

1. σ_i — standard deviations for all N securities
2. $E(R_i)$ — expected returns for all N securities
3. r_{ij} — correlation coefficients between all possible security pairs

In Table 7-5 such data are shown for seven stocks from the S&P 500. The information was developed from monthly returns over a recent five-year period. To aid in understanding the data, however, all values have been expressed as annualized values. The data are *ex post*. As such, they may not reflect ex ante beliefs about each security, beliefs which should be used in creating efficient portfolios. However, the data have the benefit of being "live." They are the *actual* statistics for each stock and provide some feel for the relative magnitude of each.

In the table, $\bar{R}$ represents the average annualized return on each stock. The σ values are annualized standard deviations of monthly returns. The diagonal in the correlation matrix is filled with 1.0s, reflecting the fact that a given security is perfectly positively correlated with itself. Only one half of the matrix is displayed since the upper half is a mirror image of the bottom half. (The correlation between IBM and Teledyne is identical to that between Teledyne and IBM.) The average correlation coefficient is equal to 0.18, typical of what one will observe when returns are measured monthly. However, there is a variability in the correlation coefficients, as evidenced by the lowest correlation of −0.12 between Campbell and Mesa, and the highest correlation of 0.36 between Exxon and IBM.

TABLE 7-5 *Historical Information on Seven Stocks from Five Years of Monthly Returns*

		Annualized	
Stock	Abbreviation	$\bar{R}$	σ
Anheuser-Busch	B	31.2%	21.8%
Campbell Soup	C	26.9	22.3
Exxon	E	20.8	20.8
IBM	I	20.2	19.4
LTV	L	5.5	41.4
Mesa Petroleum	M	17.5	51.0
Teledyne	T	35.0	39.0

			Correlation Matrix				
	B	C	E	I	L	M	T
B	1.0						
C	0.26	1.0					
E	−0.06	0.12	1.0				
I	0.11	0.29	0.36	1.0			
L	0.23	0.14	0.34	0.25	1.0		
M	−0.01	−0.12	0.50	0.12	0.26	1.0	
T	0.09	0.04	0.16	0.19	0.32	0.15	1.0

Average Correlation = 0.18

One-Stock Portfolios. As a start in selecting an efficient portfolio, let's consider holdings of a single stock. Given the foregoing discussion of diversification, we do this knowing that better portfolios must be available. But it is a logical starting point.

Figure 7-15 displays the risks and returns for each of the seven stocks. If held alone, LTV and Mesa are clearly dominated by the others. Campbell also appears to be dominated, though to a less significant degree, by a stock with less risk and greater return. If we were to stop here, it is doubtful that Campbell, LTV, or Mesa would be purchased. But this neglects the important role that diversification and security correlation play in portfolio selection. For example, Mesa and Campbell have a negative correlation equal to −0.12, which suggests that a combination of the two might reduce their combined risk to the point where they should be held.

Two-Stock Portfolios. For a two-stock portfolio consisting of, say, Mesa and Campbell, Equation 7.8a becomes:

$$\sigma_p = [X_m^2\sigma_m^2 + X_c^2\sigma_c^2 + 2(X_mX_c\sigma_m\sigma_c r_{mc})]^{1/2}$$

and Equation 7.8b becomes:

$$E(R_p) = X_mE(R_m) + X_cE(R_c)$$

But these can be further simplified by recognizing that whatever is not invested in one security is invested in the other: for example, $X_c = (1 - X_m)$. As a result, both the standard deviation and expected return can be expressed in terms of the percent invested in only one of the stocks:

FIGURE 7-15 *Portfolio Risk and Return on Single Stocks*

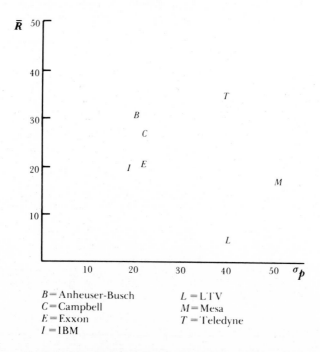

B = Anheuser-Busch   L = LTV
C = Campbell   M = Mesa
E = Exxon   T = Teledyne
I = IBM

$$\sigma_p = [X_m^2 \sigma_m^2 + (1 - X_m)^2 \sigma_c^2 + 2[X_m(1 - X_m)]\sigma_m \sigma_c r_{mc}]^{1/2} \tag{7.9a}$$

$$E(R_p) = X_m E(R_m) + (1 - X_m)E(R_c) \tag{7.9b}$$

For example, consider a 0.812 investment in Campbell and a 0.188 investment in Mesa. The standard deviation and expected return would be 19.45% and 25.13% respectively:

$$[(0.812)^2(0.223)^2 + (1.0 - 0.812)^2(0.510)^2$$

$$+ 2(0.812)(1.0 - 0.812)(0.223)(0.510)(-0.12)]^{1/2} = 0.1945$$

$$(0.812)(0.269) + (1.0 - 0.812)(0.175) = 0.2513$$

The percentages of the investments in this example were chosen with a purpose. They happen to be the percentages which lead to a *minimum variance* (or standard deviation) *portfolio*. If X_1 is invested in security 1 and $X_2 = (1 - X_1)$ is invested in stock 2, then the value of X_1 which produces the minimum possible standard deviation is found as follows:

Minimum Variance
$$X_1 = \frac{\sigma_2^2 - \sigma_1 \sigma_2 r_{1,2}}{\sigma_1^2 + \sigma_2^2 - 2\sigma_1 \sigma_2 r_{1,2}} \tag{7.10}$$

Using the Campbell-Mesa data:

$$X_c = \frac{\sigma_m^2 - \sigma_c \sigma_m r_{cm}}{\sigma_c^2 + \sigma_m^2 - 2\sigma_c \sigma_m r_{cm}}$$

$$= \frac{0.51^2 - (0.223)(0.51)(-0.12)}{0.223^2 + 0.51^2 - 2(0.223)(0.51)(-0.12)}$$

$$= 0.812$$

$$X_m = 1.0 - X_c$$

$$= 0.188$$

Equation 7.10 applies only to a two-security portfolio, but it is useful in finding what proportions in each security will lead to a minimum variance.

In Figure 7-16 risk/return curves are displayed for various two-security portfolios. Consider the Campbell-Mesa curve and note that the addition of Mesa (a stock with low expected return and high risk) to a Campbell portfolio will reduce the portfolio's risk. But this is true only up to a 0.188% investment in Mesa. Above 0.188% the portfolio's return falls *and* its risk increases. The moral of this story is twofold: (1) the addition of a stock to a portfolio can reduce risk — even a stock as "unfortunate" as Mesa — and (2) there is a limit to which the stock provides a risk-reduction benefit.

In examining Figure 7-16, note that the Campbell-Mesa combination is again dominated by other two-stock portfolios. In particular, note the significant risk reduction which can be gained by combining Anheuser-Busch and Exxon. This is due solely to the −0.06 correlation between the two stocks' returns.

FIGURE 7-16 *Portfolio Risk and Return for Two-Stock Portfolios*

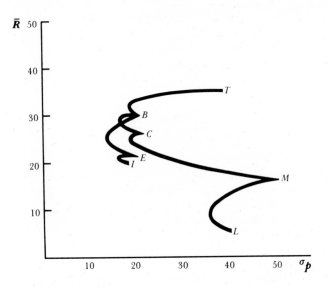

Seven-Stock Portfolios. When all seven stocks are considered together, the portfolio variance becomes more complex to calculate.[8] But its calculation follows a straightforward logic. First, the variances of each stock are weighted by X_i^2 and summed together. Second, the covariances for every possible stock combination are weighted by $X_i X_j$ and added to the summed variances.

σ_p^2 is equal to:	$\sigma_p^2 =$
Weighted Security Variances	$X_B^2 \sigma_B^2 + X_c^2 \sigma_c^2 + \ldots + X_T^2 \sigma_T^2$
Plus:	$+$
Covariance of B with all others	$2(X_B X_c \sigma_B \sigma_c r_{Bc}) + 2(X_B X_E \sigma_B \sigma_E r_{BE})$ $+ \ldots + 2(X_B X_T \sigma_B \sigma_T r_{BT})$
Plus:	$+$
Covariance of C with all others	$2(X_c X_E \sigma_c \sigma_E r_{cE}) + 2(X_c X_I \sigma_c \sigma_I r_{cI})$ $+ \ldots + 2(X_c X_T \sigma_c \sigma_T r_{cT})$
Plus:	$+$
.	.
.	.
.	.
Plus:	$+$
Covariance of m	$2(X_m X_T \sigma_m \sigma_T r_{mT})$

---

[8]Variance is used here instead of its square root, σ, to reduce the equation's complexity.

Note that each covariance between *i* and *j* is the same as between *j* and *i*. Calculating the number once and doubling it saves time.

The shaded area in Figure 7-17 illustrates the range of *feasible portfolios* from combinations of these seven stocks. Any risk/return point within the shaded area can actually be achieved by some grouping of the seven. For example, the point labeled "All" is the risk/return associated with a portfolio of all seven stocks with one seventh invested in each. It is clearly dominated by other combinations. However, all portfolios along the solid curve dominate other portfolios with equivalent risk. *These portfolios all provide the minimum risk for any expected return level.* They are referred to as *efficient portfolios*, and the curve which includes all efficient portfolios is referred to as the *efficient frontier*.

The General Case. Figure 7-18 extends our seven-stock example to the case of *N* securities. The dark-shaded area represents the seven-stock feasible set *within* the *N*-security (lighter-shaded) feasible set. When additional securities are added, the set of portfolios will increase and the efficient frontier will improve. The new feasible set and its efficient frontier were not calculated from "live" data but, instead, are hypothetical. For reference, the S&P 500 Index is shown as *SP*. The fact that the S&P 500 is not shown to be on the new efficient frontier is solely a function of the fact that the frontier shown is hypothetical. In fact, when securities such as international stocks and bonds or real estate claims are considered for investment, the efficient frontier expands even further such that a 100% investment in U.S. stocks like those on the S&P 500 is not optimal.

Markowitz made two contributions to portfolio theory. First, he suggested that an analysis such as this be done with the goal of identifying the efficient frontier. Second, he prepared a computer algorithm known as the *critical line method*, which rap-

FIGURE 7-17 *Portfolio Risk and Return for Seven Stocks*

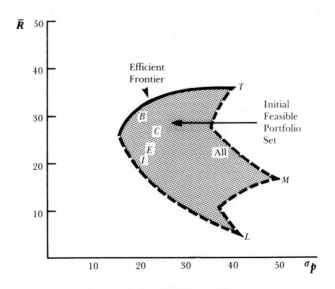

FIGURE 7-18 *Portfolio Risk and Return for N Securities*

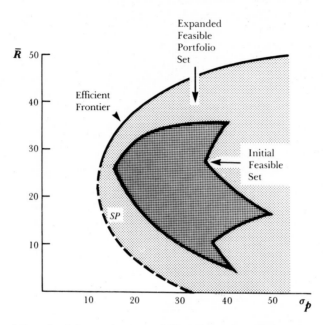

idly solved for various portfolios along the efficient frontier. A discussion of how the critical line method finds efficient portfolios is beyond this text's scope. It is sufficient to say that computer programs such as the one Markowitz developed are available to find the efficient frontier.

Implications. If one were able to develop estimates of $E(R_i)$, σ_i, and r_{ij} for all securities being considered, one could use a computer program to identify the resulting efficient frontier. Investors could then choose a single portfolio from among the resulting group which meets their personal risk and return preferences. People who are quite risk-averse would select an efficient portfolio with low risk, whereas less risk-averse people would select a *different* efficient portfolio providing greater returns. The particular portfolio of risky securities which an investor chose *would depend* upon that individual's risk aversion. Two people with identical beliefs about return distributions would create identical efficient frontiers. However, such people might then choose totally different portfolios from the frontier if their levels of risk aversion differ.

IMPACTS OF A RISK-FREE RETURN

The previous discussion was concerned solely with portfolios consisting of risky securities. No risk-free securities were considered. We now expand the set of available securities to include such a risk-free asset. When this is done:

1. No longer is there an infinite number of efficient risky portfolios from which one is selected based upon individual risk/return preferences. Instead, a single risky portfolio will dominate all others and will be selected regardless of individual risk/return preferences.
2. The individual achieves a personally suitable combination of risk and return by adjusting the percentage of the portfolio which is invested in risk-free securities.

What security is free of all risk? The typical response is that government-insured savings accounts and T-bills with maturities identical to the individual's investment period are about as risk-free as possible. But even these have a minute potential for default. And, while nominal returns might be guaranteed, *real returns* after uncertain future inflation are clearly not. Faced with this dilemma, we will do as all good economists do: we will assume the problem away. In Chapter 9 this assumption will be lifted. But to keep the analysis as straightforward as possible, we will now *assume that individuals have the opportunity to invest as well as borrow all the money they wish at a risk-free interest rate (RF)*. When the assumption is eventually removed, many major conclusions remain intact but the analysis becomes more complicated.

As before, the expected return on a portfolio which combines risk-free and risky securities is simply the weighted average of the expected returns on all securities. Assume that you plan to invest 80% of your capital in the S&P 500 reference portfolio and 20% in the risk-free security. If the expected returns on each are $E(R_{SP}) = 12\%$, $RF = 7\%$, then the expected portfolio return is 11.0%:

$$(0.20)\ 7\% + 0.80\ (12\%) = 11\%$$

In general, if $E(R_c)$ represents returns on the *combined* portfolio of risky and risk-free securities, $E(R_P)$ refers to the risky security group, and X percent is invested in the risk-free security, then:

Expected Return on Risk-Free and Risky Portfolio
$$E(R_c) = (X)RF + (1 - X)E(R_P) \qquad \textbf{(7.11)}$$

The standard deviation of a combined portfolio is simply the percentage invested in risky securities multiplied by the standard deviation of the risky securities. By definition, the variance of returns on RF is zero, and all terms in the standard deviation equation which apply to RF disappear. Using σ_p to represent the risky portfolio's standard deviation, the combined portfolio's risk is:

Standard Deviation of Risk-Free and Risky Portfolio
$$\sigma_c = (1 - X)\sigma_p \qquad \textbf{(7.12)}$$

For example, an 80/20 risky versus risk-free security mix would result in a 16% combined portfolio standard deviation if the risky securities had a 20% standard deviation:

$$0.8\ (20\%) = 16\%$$

When Equations 7.11 and 7.12 are combined, an interesting result occurs. The relationship between risk and return is linear and equal to:

Linear Risk/Return with Risk-Free Securities

$$E(R_c) = RF + \sigma_c \left[\frac{E(R_p) - RF}{\sigma_p} \right] \tag{7.13}$$

Returns expected on portfolios which combine a risk-free security with risky securities come from two sources. First, a risk-free rate is expected to be earned on *both* the risk-free security and the risky set of securities. In addition, a return is earned for bearing risk—a return equal to $[E(R_p) - RF] \div \sigma_p$ for each unit of σ_c. The number of units of σ_c risk incurred depends, of course, on the proportion of funds in the risky securities.

There is no guarantee that the expected return for bearing risk will be positive. That depends totally on the one or more risky securities being evaluated. In a moment we will return to this "risk premium" and see how it might be maximized, but first consider some examples using the following information, which is also plotted in Figure 7-19:

Security	Expected Return	σ
IBM Stock	14%	25%
Risk-Free Security	9%	0

FIGURE 7-19 *Portfolio Combinations of the Risk-Free Security with a Risky Security*

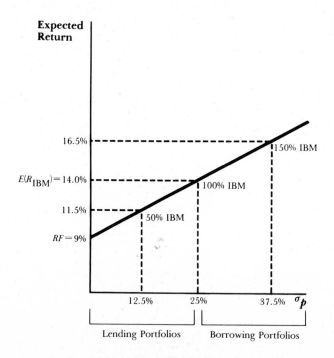

When a 100% investment is made in IBM, the portfolio return is 14%. This 14% comes from two sources: (1) a risk-free return of 9% and (2) a return for bearing risk of 14% − 9% = 5%.

When a 50% investment is made in IBM, risk is half of the 100% investment level and, thus, the return for bearing risk is also half (2.5%):

$$E(R_c) = RF + 0.5(\sigma_p)\left[\frac{E(R_p) - RF}{\sigma_p}\right]$$

$$= 9.0\% + 12.5\% \ (0.20)$$

$$= 9.0\% + 2.5\% = 11.5\%$$

Portfolios which include some amount of the risk-free security are referred to as *lending portfolios* because a portion of one's money is "lent" to borrowers at the risk-free rate. But in the same way that lending portfolios can be created which reduce expected returns and risk, *borrowing portfolios* can be created which increase risk and expected returns. Borrowing portfolios essentially use *margin* to increase the number of shares which an individual's personal equity can control.

To illustrate, assume you have $10,000 to invest and would prefer a higher return than is expected on IBM in Figure 7-19. You're also willing to accept the higher risk. Consider what would happen if you borrowed $5,000 at the risk-free rate of 9% and used the borrowing plus your personal equity to purchase $15,000 of IBM. Your expected dollar return on IBM shares would be $2,100 ($15,000 × 0.14), and after you pay $450 in interest ($5,000 × 0.09) your net dollar profit would be $1,650. On a $10,000 equity, this is a 16.5% expected return.

The same result can be obtained by using Equation 7.13, if we recognize that borrowing is simply *negative lending*:

$$E(R_c) = RF + \sigma_c\left[\frac{E(R_p) - RF}{\sigma_p}\right]$$

$$= 9\% + 1.5 \ (25\%) \ [0.2]$$

$$= 9\% + 7.5\% = 16.5\%$$

On your personal equity you earn 9%. The borrowing also earns 9%, but you must pay that to the people from whom you borrowed, so it is a wash. However, by placing $0.50 in borrowed money into the risky security for each $1.00 of your personal equity, you have magnified your risk exposure by 50%. Thus the expected risk premium increases from 5% to 7.5%. The new expected return is therefore 16.5%. But it comes only with an increase in portfolio standard deviation from 25% to 37.5% (1.5 × 25%).

The Portfolio Separation Theorem. One can combine borrowing and lending with any individual security or portfolio of securities, as displayed in Figure 7-20. In this figure, three lines are shown. The two dashed lines represent risk/return combinations on *RF* combined with IBM and on a portfolio called *O*, which lies on the efficient frontier developed earlier in this chapter. Note that the slope of each line represents

FIGURE 7-20 *Alternative Combinations of Risky Securities with a Risk-Free Security*

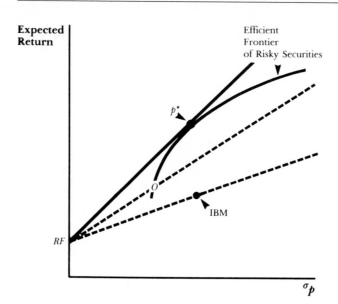

the return *expected* to be earned per unit of risk. Clearly, combinations with portfolio *O* are better than combinations with IBM since the slope of the line is greater. However, there is a single portfolio on the efficient frontier which will *maximize* the return earned for bearing risk. This is portfolio *p**, which lies on the solid line extending from *RF*.

Given the presence of a risk-free rate, two very important implications emerge:

1. *There is a single optimal portfolio of risky securities to own—regardless of the individual's risk preferences.* Different people might disagree on exactly what that optimal portfolio consists of. But for any one individual, there is only one risky portfolio which should be held.

2. *The individual can obtain a desired risk/return profile by combining this optimal risky portfolio with borrowing or lending at RF.* If the risky security portfolio contains more risk than desired, the risk can be reduced by placing a portion of the resources in risk-free securities. If the expected return is too low, the investor should borrow and invest the borrowing in the ideal risky portfolio.

A *separation* now exists between an identification of the ideal risky security portfolio (implication 1) and the selection of an appropriate risk level (implication 2). This is commonly called the *portfolio separation theorem.* The investment decision is now a two-step process: (1) identify the optimal risky security and (2) move along the borrowing-lending line to a personally acceptable risk level. Let's examine each of these steps briefly.

What does a portfolio *p** consist of? That is a matter of opinion, and opinions may vary among people who hold differing beliefs about the distributions of security returns. In the next chapter, when we add another assumption, we will be able to say more about what might be in p^*. But for now we can say only that its contents could vary from person to person. Nonetheless, for any one person, a single risky portfolio will dominate all others. Consider, for example, an investment advisory firm which provides investment counseling to less-informed clients. The firm should have a single portfolio of risky securities which it advises all its clients to purchase. The portfolio should not be changed to fit the particular needs of each client. Instead, the proportion of risk-free securities should be changed to achieve appropriate risk levels. Identification of this optimal portfolio is not an easy task, and considerable time as well as innumerable techniques are devoted to the process. Chapters 19 through 23 examine exactly this problem.

Equally important is the creation of an appropriate risk/return trade-off by borrowing or lending at RF. Investors should have a good understanding of the potential volatility of returns they are exposed to at various levels of borrowing or lending. In the professional investment community, this is often referred to as the stock/bond mix decision. Although we might not be able to identify p^*, a reasonable proxy is probably the S&P 500 Index. It is a broadly diversified portfolio which includes the majority of large U.S. corporations. In Figure 7-21 the borrowing-lending line using an assumed 0.35% real risk-free rate and historical real returns on the S&P 500 is shown. Standard deviations are shown for one-year and ten-year holding periods. The benefits of diversification over time are obvious. A tabular way of presenting the in-

FIGURE 7-21 *Borrowing-Lending Line Using Real Returns on the S&P 500, 1926–1987*

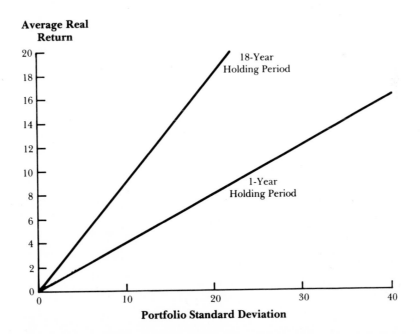

TABLE 7-6 *Asset Mix and Probable Real Yearly Returns*

Asset Mix		Probability of Annual Real Return Being Less Than or Equal to Return Shown						
*Equity**	*GIC†*	*5%*	*10%*	*25%*	*50%*	*75%*	*90%*	*95%*
0%	100%	1.0%	1.0%	1.0%	1.0%	1.0%	1.0%	1.0%
20	80	−4.5	−2.9	−0.3	2.6	5.5	8.1	9.6
40	60	−10.0	−6.9	−1.7	4.1	9.9	15.1	18.2
60	40	−15.5	−10.8	−2.9	5.7	14.3	22.2	26.8
80	20	−20.9	−14.7	−4.2	7.3	18.8	29.3	35.5
100	0	−26.5	−18.7	−5.6	8.8	23.2	36.3	44.1

*Equity based on annual (S&P 500 real returns 1926–1987).
†*Guaranteed Investment Contract* based on 1% real risk-free return.

formation in Figure 7-21 is shown in Table 7-6. Exhibits such as these are widely used by investment counselors to help clients assess the risks of various stock/bond mixes—which to academics is simply a matter of moving along the borrowing-lending line.

MEASURING SECURITY RISK

Risk and expected returns on the *total* portfolio are the two most important features of any investment or speculative strategy. And until now we have focused almost solely on the aggregate portfolio, with no mention of how an individual security's risk should be defined or measured.

A security is risky to the extent that it adds risk to the portfolio. To see how a security adds risk to the portfolio, it is helpful to refer again to Equation 7.5 and think in terms of *variance* instead of standard deviation. In such a case:

$$\sigma_p^2 = \sum_{t=1}^{N} X_i^2 \sigma_i^2 + \sum_{i=1}^{N} \sum_{\substack{j=1 \\ i \neq j}}^{N} X_i X_j \sigma_i \sigma_j r_{ij}$$

$$= \sum_{i=1}^{N} X_i^2 \sigma_i^2 + \sum_{i=1}^{N} \sum_{\substack{j=1 \\ i \neq j}}^{N} X_i X_j \text{ Covariance } (ij)$$

By a slight rearrangement of terms, we can restate this equation as:

Portfolio Risk $$\sigma_p^2 = \sum_{i=1}^{N} X_i \left[X_i \sigma_i^2 + \sum_{\substack{j=1 \\ i \neq j}}^{N} X_j \text{ Covariance } (i,j) \right]$$ **(7.14)**

Equation 7.14 is helpful because it aids in identifying each security's contribution to portfolio risk. For a given investment in security $i(X_i)$, the *total risk* associated with it can be measured by:

Total Risk of Security in Portfolio Now Held

$$= \left[X_i \sigma_i^2 + \sum_{j=1}^{N} X_j \sigma_i \sigma_j r_{ij} \right] \qquad (7.15)$$

(Note: Any summations on j implicitly assume that $j \neq i$.)

When the total risk of each security is weighted by the investment made in that security and then summed over all securities held, we have portfolio risk; that is:

Total Risk of Portfolio

$$= \sigma_p^2 = \sum_{i=1}^{N} X_i \ (\text{Total Risk of Security } i \text{ in Portfolio Now Held})$$

Following this logic, we will use Equation 7.15 as our measure of the total risk inherent in any single security.

Three important features of Equation 7.15 must be understood:

1. The total risk of a security is composed of two parts. One part relates solely to the uncertainty about returns on the security itself. This is measured as $X_i \sigma_i^2$, the first term in Equation 7.15. All other things being equal, the wider the dispersion of possible returns on a security, the larger its risk in a portfolio. The second part relates to the degree to which the returns on the security are correlated with returns on other securities now held. This is measured by the second term in Equation 7.15:

$$\sum_{j=1}^{N} X_j \sigma_i \sigma_j r_{ij}$$

All other things being equal, the larger the return correlation (r_{ij}), the larger its risk in a portfolio. Conversely, the lower the correlation, the lower its risk in a portfolio.

The fact that a security's risk is composed of these two parts is more than a simple mathematical construct. It has important investment implications. For example, assume that you are considering purchasing common stocks in country 1. After a preliminary analysis you conclude that returns on such stocks are very uncertain (they have a large σ). Continuing your search, you examine stocks of country 2. Returns on country 2 stocks are also quite uncertain. However, returns on stocks in country 1 are inversely correlated (say, $r = -1.0$) with returns on country 2. In a portfolio context, are investments in each country risky? No. Purchases of stocks in only one country would entail considerable risk. However, if a portfolio of both country's stocks is created, the marginal impact of each country's stocks on portfolio risk is small. Per Equation 7.15, the first component of security risk is positive, but the second component is negative. In the context of a portfolio of stocks from both countries, neither country is risky.

2. The *total risk* of a security depends upon the other securities held. The first component of security risk, $X_i \sigma_i^2$, does not depend upon other holdings in the portfolio. It is a risk unique to the security itself. But the covariance component of security risk *is* dependent upon other holdiings. As the percentage of investments

in other securities (X_j's), uncertainties (σ_j's), and return correlations (r_{ij}'s) change, so does a security's total risk.

Investors who have different portfolios should evaluate the risk of, say, GM differently. For one investor, GM might add significantly to portfolio risk if it were highly correlated with existing portfolio holdings. To another investor, GM might be virtually riskless if it were uncorrelated with existing portfolio holdings. There is no one measure of total security risk which can be used by all investors; it depends upon the particular portfolio held. Only when everyone holds the *same* portfolio will the risk of a given security be identical for everyone.

3. The extent to which a portfolio is diversified affects the relative importance of each component of security risk. As a portfolio becomes more diversified, *the importance of security-unique uncertainty, $X_i\sigma_i^2$, diminishes and the importance of security intercorrelations, covariance, grows.* For portfolios which are broadly diversified, security-unique risk is meaningless and security intercorrelation dominates.

Relative Security Risk

The measure of *total security risk* (per Equation 7.15) is difficult to interpret. For example, is a total security risk of 0.0058 large or small? To overcome this problem, security risks are often expressed in terms of the risk of the security *relative* to the risk of the total portfolio. Relative security risk is found by dividing total security risk by total portfolio risk:

$$\frac{\text{Relative Risk of}}{\text{Security } i} = \frac{\text{Total Risk of Security } i}{\text{Total Risk of Portfolio}}$$

Symbolically, relative security risk can be expressed as in Equation 7.16:

$$\frac{\text{Relative Risk of}}{\text{Security } i} = \frac{X_i\sigma_i^2}{\sigma_p^2} + \frac{\sum\limits_{j=1}^{N} X_j\sigma_i\sigma_j r_{ij}}{\sigma_p^2} \tag{7.16}$$

As with total security risk, relative security risk is composed of two parts, depends upon the other securities held in the portfolio, and is affected by the degree of diversification. If the relative risk measure is found to be 1.0, the security is as risky as the average security in the portfolio. If the measure is equal to 0.50, the security is half as risky as the average security held. If the measure is equal to 1.5, the security is 50% more risky.

As a practical matter, relative security risks are usually calculated only for broadly diversified portfolios. In that case the first term in Equation 7.16—$X_i\sigma_i^2/\sigma_p^2$—becomes very small (since X is very small). In a broadly diversified portfolio the relative risk of a security is approximately equal to:

$$\text{Relative Risk of Security } i \approx 0 + \frac{\sum\limits_{j} X_j \sigma_i \sigma_j r_{ij}}{\sigma_p^2} \tag{7.17}$$

$$\approx 0 + \frac{\sigma_i(\Sigma X_j \sigma_j r_{ij})}{\sigma_p^2}$$

$$\approx 0 + \frac{\sigma_i(\sigma_p r_{ip})}{\sigma_p^2}$$

$$\approx \frac{\sigma_i}{\sigma_p} r_{ip}$$

In a broadly diversified portfolio the relative risk of a single security is equal to (1) the standard deviation of its returns, (2) divided by the portfolio standard deviation, (3) multiplied by the security's correlation with portfolio returns. This measure of relative security risk is typically referred to as *beta on security i, or β_i.*[9]

Assume that you now own the S&P 500 portfolio we have used throughout the chapter and are considering the addition of a local bank, Fifth Third Bank of Cincinnati. In order to estimate its risk relative to your current portfolio, the following subjective forecasts are made:

State of Economy	Probability	Returns on	
		Portfolio	Fifth Third
Good	0.3	20%	14%
Fair	0.4	10%	9%
Poor	0.3	0%	6%

First, the standard deviation of both the S&P 500 portfolio and Fifth Third Bank's potential returns should be found. Using Equation 7.4, these will be:

$$\sigma_p = 7.75\% \qquad \sigma_{FT} = 3.13\%$$

Second, the correlation coefficient between the S&P 500 and Fifth Third returns would be found by Equation 7.6:

$$r_{pi} = 0.989$$

Finally, the beta of Fifth Third Bank *relative to your S&P 500 portfolio* can be determined:

---

[9]Beta as calculated in Equation 7.17 depends upon the portfolio of securities now held and will change as the portfolio of securities changes. Betas as reported by investment advisory firms, however, are based upon *one* reference portfolio. While the reference portfolio used varies between advisory services, typically it is some index of aggregate stock market returns, such as the Standard & Poor's Composite Index, the Dow Jones Composite Index, or the NYSE Composite Index.

$$\beta_{FT} = \frac{3.13}{7.75} \, (0.989) = 0.40$$

In the context of your portfolio, Fifth Third Bank has much less risk than the average stock now held. For another investor's portfolio this might not be the case. For example, a broadly diversified portfolio of bank stocks may have a beta of 1.0.

SUMMARY

Risk is a dominant characteristic of security investment. Individuals are said to be risk-averse if the pleasure they gain from a $1 increase in wealth is less than the pleasure they lose from a $1 reduction in wealth. By relating the concept of risk aversion to utility theory, we saw that the risk of a security depends upon the possible dispersion of its returns. In turn, the standard deviation was suggested as a reasonable way to quantitatively measure risk.

Risk inherent in the total portfolio is of more direct concern to the investor than are the risks of individual securities. While individual security risks do combine with one another to determine a portfolio's risk level, it is the total portfolio risk which is most crucial. Individual securities should be viewed as bearing a risk to the extent that adding the security to the portfolio changes the portfolio's risk.

The standard deviation of portfolio returns is not simply a weighted average of the standard deviations of the individual securities comprising the portfolio. The effects of differing levels of correlation between security returns must be accounted for. If security returns are perfectly negatively correlated (correlation coefficient $= -1.0$), diversification with only two securities can totally eliminate portfolio risk. If a large number of uncorrelated securities (correlation coefficient $= 0.0$) are available, broad diversification can virtually eliminate portfolio risk. If security returns are perfectly positively correlated (correlation coefficient $= +1.0$), diversification will provide no risk-reduction advantages. Since security returns generally have a correlation coefficient between 0.0 and $+1.0$, there are significant advantages to diversification. But in the real world portfolio risk cannot be totally eliminated. To some extent all security returns are affected by similar events, and this common component of security returns cannot be diversified away.

In a broadly diversified portfolio, the risk of any single security depends upon the standard deviation of the security's returns and the correlation of the security's returns with the returns of the portfolio. Typically, a security's risk *relative* to the risk of the diversified portfolio to which it is added is measured by beta. Beta is calculated as:

$$\beta_i = \frac{\sigma_i}{\sigma_p} \, r_{ip}$$

where β_i refers to the beta of security i, σ_i and σ_p refer to the ex ante standard deviation of returns on the security and the portfolio, respectively, and r_{ip} refers to the correlation coefficient between security *i* returns and those of the portfolio. Relative risk, or beta, will depend upon the portfolio of securities held. As a result, investors holding different portfolios will evaluate the relative risk of a given stock differently.

Perhaps the best advice which this chapter offers to both investors and speculators is to diversify. Risk-reduction advantages inherent in diversification are significant. That portion of a security's risk which is diversifiable is known as *unsystematic risk*, whereas *systematic risk* refers to the nondiversifiable portion of security risk. Contrasted with naive diversification, efficient diversification models exist which allow one to find a set of different portfolios which minimize portfolio risks for differing levels of expected returns.

REVIEW PROBLEM

You are evaluating an investment in two mutual funds whose past ten years of returns are shown below:

| Fund | Percent Return During Year | | | | | | | | | |
	1	2	3	4	5	6	7	8	9	10
FST	37	24	−7	6	18	32	−5	21	18	6
SND	32	29	−12	1	15	30	0	18	27	10

a. Calculate the standard deviation of each mutual fund's returns.

b. Calculate the correlation coefficient of the funds' returns.

c. If you had placed 50% of your money in each, what would have been the standard deviation of your portfolio and the average yearly return?

d. What percentage investment in each would have resulted in the lowest risk?

e. Assume that a yearly risk-free return of 8% was available and that you had held *only one* of the two funds. Which would have been the better to own?

f. Graph the risk and return of each fund. Given your answer to part d, what was the single efficient portfolio of the two?

g. Use part f to determine:

- How an average return of 10.8% would have been obtained
- How an average return of 17.8% would have been obtained

Solution

a. First, find the average returns:

$$\bar{R}_{FST} = (37 + 24 + \ldots + 6)/10 = 15\%$$

$$\bar{R}_{SND} = (32 + 29 + \ldots + 10)/10 = 15\%$$

Next, find the standard deviations:

$$\sigma_{FST} = \sqrt{\frac{(37 - 15)^2 + (24 - 15)^2 + \ldots + (6 - 15)^2}{10}}$$

$$= 14.0\%$$

$$\sigma_{SND} = \sqrt{\frac{(32 - 15)^2 + (29 - 15)^2 + \ldots + (10 - 15)^2}{10}}$$

$$= 14.3\%$$

b. First, find the covariance term:

$$\text{COV} = \sqrt{\frac{(37 - 15)(32 - 15) + (24 - 15)(29 - 15) + \ldots + (6 - 15)(10 - 15)}{10}}$$

$$= 187.4\%$$

Next, find the correlation coefficient:

$$r = \frac{187.4}{(14.0)(14.3)} = 0.94$$

c.
$$\sigma_p = (0.5^2)(14.0^2) + (0.5^2)(14.3^2) + 2(0.5)(0.5)(14.0)(14.3)(0.94)$$

$$= 13.9\%$$

$$E(R_p) = 0.5(15.0) + 0.5(15.0) = 15.0\%$$

d. Use the minimum variance equation (7.10) and let X stand for *FST*:

$$X_{FST} = \frac{14.3^2 - (14.0)(14.3)(0.94)}{14.0^2 + 14.3^2 - 2(14.0)(14.3)(0.94)}$$

$$= 67.6\%$$

$$X_{SND} = 32.4\%$$

e. In effect, this part asks which of the funds provided the greater return per unit of risk — the slope of the line in Figure 7-20.

For *FST*: $\dfrac{15.0 - 8.0}{14.0} = 0.5\%$ per unit of σ

For *SND*: $\dfrac{15.0 - 8.0}{14.3} = 0.49\%$ per unit of σ

They were very close, but *FST* was better.

f. Both funds had identical average returns. The minimum variance portfolio of $X_{FST} = 67.6\%$ and $X_{SND} = 32.4\%$ would also have had a 15% average return, but its risk would be lower than holding either fund in isolation. The minimum standard deviation was 13.9%.

g. Using 8% as the risk-free rate and the single efficient portfolio in part f as the optimal risky portfolio, the following risk/return relationship was available:

$$E(R_c) = RF + \sigma_c \left[\frac{E(R_p) - RF}{\sigma_p} \right]$$

where $\sigma_c = (1 - X_{RF})\sigma_p$

$$= 8.0\% + \sigma_c \left[\frac{15.0\% - 8.0\%}{13.9\%} \right]$$

$$= 8.0\% + \sigma_c [0.5036]$$

- To earn 10.8%, invest 60% risk-free and 40% in the optimal risky portfolio:

$$10.8\% = 8\% + (0.4)(13.9\%)(0.5036)$$

- To earn 17.8%, borrow 40% on your equity and invest it with your equity in the optimal risky portfolio:

$$17.8\% = 8.0\% + (X)(13.9\%)(0.5036)$$

$$17.8\% = 8.0\% + (1.4)(13.9)(0.5036)$$

QUESTIONS AND PROBLEMS

1. Explain why people are willing to purchase insurance and what determines the maximum amount of insurance they will pay for.
2. Why are people risk-averse? How does utility theory suggest that we measure risk?
3. In this chapter three major assumptions were made. What were they? Why were they required?
4. When is the standard deviation of a portfolio identical to the weighted average standard deviation of the securities held?
5. Consider the portfolio standard deviation equation below and assume that an equal dollar amount is invested in each security ($X_i = 1/N$) and that all $\sigma_i = \sigma_j$:

$$\sigma_p = \sqrt{\sum_{i=1}^{N} X_i^2 \sigma_i^2 + \sum_{\substack{i=1 \\ i \neq j}}^{N} \sum_{j=1}^{N} X_i X_j \sigma_i \sigma_j r_{ij}}$$

Show what happens to portfolio risk as N increases if:
a. $r_{ij} = -1.0$
b. $r_{ij} = +1.0$
c. $r_{ij} = 0.0$

6. "Diversification reduces risk without affecting expected portfolio returns."
a. Explain in a nonstatistical manner why the statement is correct.
b. Explain the two ways in which diversification can be gained.
7. The risk of a given security is not the same for all investors if they own different security portfolios. Why?
8. Portfolio risk can be measured by the standard deviation of its expected returns. Why should the risk of an individual security not be measured in the same way?

9. What does the portfolio separation theorem imply about proper investment policy?

10. Jake Leary has managed his own investment portfolio for the past 10 years. He feels he has had reasonable success, but because of the increasing amount of time which he must devote to his business, he is considering placing his funds with an investment management firm. Being a reasonably intelligent fellow, he calls upon you for advice. Jake initially made a $10,000 investment 10 years ago and has withdrawn all dividends and interest as received. Since then, his yearly performance has been as shown below:

	End of Year									
	1	*2*	*3*	*4*	*5*	*6*	*7*	*8*	*9*	*10*
Portfolio's Value	$11,000	$10,000	$9,000	$11,500	$13,000	$13,000	$14,000	$11,000	$14,000	$15,000
Dividends and Interest	500	500	600	600	400	600	650	600	650	650

   a. Calculate the annual rates of return he earned.
   b. Calculate the 10-year average return and standard deviation.
   c. You gather 10-year data on the following investment management firms:

	10-Year Return	
Firm	*Average*	*Std. Dev.*
A	12%	14%
B	14%	20%
C	8%	20%

   Compare Jake's performance with the performance of these three firms.

11. (CFA Exam Question)
    A stock that pays no dividends is currently selling at $100. The possible prices for which the stock might sell at the end of one year, with associated probabilities, are:

End-of-Year Price	*Probability*
$ 90	0.1
100	0.2
110	0.4
120	0.2
130	0.1

   a. Calculate the expected rate of return by year-end.
   b. Calculate the standard deviation of the expected rate of return.
   c. Describe the use of the standard deviation of the expected rate of return in making investment decisions.

12. The trust officer for First Financial Bank Corporation is evaluating three portfolio recommendations which he recently received from trust employees. To aid him in this analysis, he requested that summary information be prepared for each proposal which would relate each portfolio's returns to economic conditions for the next year. This summary information is below:

Economic Conditions	Probability	Portfolio Returns		
		Plan A	*Plan B*	*Plan C*
Exceptional	0.1	25%	15%	8%
Good	0.4	20%	13%	8%
Fair	0.4	15%	12%	7%
Poor	0.1	10%	10%	7%

Compare and contrast each of these plans.

13. Because ecological problems have recently beset Southeast Phosphorus, Inc., its board of directors have expressed an interest in diversifying the firm's product line through acquisition of another company. Southeast Phosphorus has large mining operations located on the west coast of Florida. After discussions with the firm's investment banking firm, several alternatives seem promising. These include:
    a. Southwest Tin-Mining Corporation, a tin-mining firm located in Texas.
    b. Greenfield Coal Corporation, a coal-mining firm located in Kentucky.
    c. Winn-Dixon Food Marts, a diversified food chain in Florida.
    d. Boston-Mason Foods, a diversified food chain in New England.
    e. Northwest Mining, a major competitor of Southeast Phosphorus, Inc., which mines a substitute product.

    Evaluate the extent to which each of these acquisitions might provide the greatest and least diversification to Southeast Phosphorus. Note: This is a thought question. No *single* correct answer exists; your logic is the important thing.

14. Alan Zaslow holds a well-diversified portfolio of stocks in country A. During the past 10 years returns on these stocks have averaged +8.0% per year and had a standard deviation of 7.0%. He is unsatisfied with the yearly variability of his portfolio and would like to reduce its risk without affecting overall returns. He approaches you for help in finding an appropriate diversification medium. After a lengthy review of alternatives, you conclude:

    • Future average returns and volatility of returns on his current portfolio will be the same as he has historically experienced.
    • To provide a greater degree of diversification in his portfolio, investments could be made in stocks of the following countries:

Country	Expected Return	Correlation of Returns with Country A	Standard Deviation
B	8%	+1.0	7.0%
C	8%	−1.0	7.0%
D	8%	+0.0	7.0%

    a. If Mr. Zaslow invests 50% of his funds in country B and leaves the remainder in country A, would this affect both his expected returns and his risk? Why?
    b. If Mr. Zaslow invests 50% of his funds in country C and leaves the remainder in country A, how would this affect both his expected return and his risk? Why?
    c. What should he do? Indicate precise portfolio weighting.

15. Estimates of standard deviations and correlation coefficients for three stocks are:

Stock	σ_i	Correlation with		
		1	2	3
1	8%	1.0		
2	10%	0.5	1.0	
3	12%	0.5	−1.0	1.0

a. If equal investments are made in stocks 1 and 2, what is the standard deviation of the portfolio?

b. If equal investments are made in all three stocks, what is the standard deviation of the portfolio?

c. What percentage of investment in stocks 1 and 3 will minimize portfolio risk? Hint: A little calculus is necessary here.

d. What percentage of investment in stocks 2 and 3 will minimize portfolio risk? Why? Hint: Calculus is *not* necessary to answer this question.

16. Consider a portfolio of three stocks. Calculate the total risk of each stock and the total risk of the portfolio.

Stock	Portfolio Investment	σ_i	Correlation with		
			A	B	C
A	0.25	10%	1.0		
B	0.40	12%	0.3	1.0	
C	0.35	15%	0.4	0.6	1.0

Notice that stock *C* has the largest total risk. Why is this? Do any characteristics of stocks *A* and *B* affect the total risk of stock *C* in this portfolio?

17. Two investors are considering the addition of stock in Samson Bodybuilders, a high-growth chain of franchise operations, to their respective portfolios. Ms. D. Lilah owns a broadly diversified portfolio of stocks in health-related businesses. Mr. C. St. Sanes owns a broadly diversified portfolio of communication stocks. Relevant statistical information is shown below:

	Ms. D. Lilah	Mr. C. St. Sanes	Samson
Standard Deviation	11%	16%	20%
Correlations			
Ms. D.	1.0		
Mr. C.	0.7	1.0	
Samson	0.8	0.2	1.0

What is the measure of the relative risk of Samson Bodybuilders stock (beta) to each of these investors?

18. Historical data are given below on six stocks, calculated in the same manner as were the data for the seven stocks discussed in the chapter. Assume that these represent your ex ante expectations.

Stock	ID	Annualized 1980–1984	
		Return	Standard Deviation
Amsted	A	7%	30%
Bethlehem Steel	B	4	34
Duke Power	D	26	18

Hewlett-Packard	*H*	21%	31%
Lilly	*L*	10	20
Mobil	*M*	10	32

Correlation Matrix

	A	*B*	*D*	*H*	*L*	*M*
A	1.0					
B	0.5	1.0				
D	−0.1	0.2	1.0			
H	0.4	0.5	0.0	1.0		
L	0.5	0.3	0.0	0.3	1.0	
M	0.4	0.2	0.0	0.2	0.2	1.0

a. Plot each on risk/return axes. *Neglecting* any consideration of security correlation, does one stock dominate the others?

b. Consider an investment in Lilly and Mobil. Is there a single combination of the two which beats all others? What is the standard deviation and return of this combination?

c. Calculate the minimum variance portfolio between a combination of Duke, Lilly, and Mobil. Plot it on the graph from part a. If these are the only securities to be held, identify the efficient frontier.

d. Plot various two-stock portfolios and use these to *estimate* the feasible portfolio set of these six portfolios.

e. Note that Duke Power (an electric utility) has the lowest correlation with the other firms. Why might this be the case?

f. If the risk-free rate is 8.0%, what securities appear to be in the single optimal *portfolio*?

g. These data are restricted to six stocks. When more are considered, how is the conclusion to part f likely to change? Why?

h. Given the conclusion in part f, how would one:

- Achieve a standard deviation of 14%?

- Achieve an expected return of 36%?

19. Use the data in problem 18 to calculate the standard deviations of a portfolio of all six stocks with an equal percentage holding in each.

DATA ANALYSIS PROBLEMS

Objectives:

- To illustrate the benefits of naive diversification
- To illustrate a basic asset allocation study

Problem 1: Naive Diversification

In this problem, we will examine various aspects of naive diversification. Access the QTLYSTK.WK1 data set. Since we will be using only the quarterly returns on each stock, you will find it useful to delete all rows with stock price and dividend data. (Do not save the altered data set under the name QTLYSTK.WK1 or you will lose the deleted data.)

1. At the bottom of each return series column, calculate the average and the standard deviation of each stock quarterly return.

2. Find the grand average of both numbers above. Interpret what these grand averages represent.

3. In a blank column to the far right of the data, calculate what the quarterly returns would have been on a portfolio which consisted of an equal percentage investment in each stock. Do this for all quarters. (Hint: If you have deleted all price and dividend data, and assuming 25 stocks, this is easily accomplished by a calculation similar to the following: @SUM(B5..Z5)/25.)

4. Find the average and the standard deviation of this equally weighted portfolio quarterly return. Contrast these values with those obtained in part 2. Interpret the results.

5. Select any five of the stocks and create portfolio returns on equally weighted combinations of the five. Repeat part 4 and interpret the results.

6. Now select another five stocks and redo part 5. Note that you do not obtain exactly the same mean and standard deviation as for the five-stock portfolio in part 5. What is the implication?

Problem 2: Efficient Diversification

In this problem, we will calculate an ex post efficient frontier using various security *classes* (indexes) instead of single securities. In practice, this is referred to as an asset allocation study. Asset allocation is discussed in Appendix 7B. You might wish to read this appendix before doing this problem.

1. Access the YRLYINDX.WK1 data set. In blank columns to the right of the data, calculate yearly real returns for the following asset classes by subtracting CPI from the asset's nominal return. Do this for 1926 through 1988. Classes to use: T-bills, govt. bonds, corp. bonds, S&P 500, small companies.

2. Find the average and standard deviation of each asset class's real annual returns.

3. Find the correlation coefficients for each possible pair of asset classes. (Hint: The regression capability of your worksheet program will calculate an R^2 value between each return series pair. This is simply the correlation coefficient squared. Therefore you can use the square root of R^2 as the correlation coefficient.)

4. Create an ASCII "input data set" which will be read by the efficient frontier program "ASSETALL" as follows:
   a. In a blank area of the worksheet, type in the data which are read by ASSETALL. The format of these data is described in Appendix 7B. (Hint: A "return increment" of 1.0 would be satisfactory.)
   b. "Print" the data to a disk file. Call this printed data file INPUT.PRN.

5. Leave the spreadsheet and be sure the active diskette or disk drive is the same as the one on which you have the ASSETALL program. To run ASSETALL, simply enter the word ASSETALL.

   Follow the directions. In this example, you should request that a *short sale constrained* efficient frontier be calculated. The input data set which is requested will INPUT.PRN if you labeled it such in part 4b. You might wish to call the output data set which is requested A:OUTPUT.EF, B:OUTPUT.EF, or C:OUTPUT.EF depending on where you have sufficient storage space.

6. Once the efficient frontier is calculated, choose the option "Exit to DOS." Use the DOS print command to print the output efficient frontier data. For example, if saved on the C: drive, "print C:OUTPUT.EF".

7. This is the ex post efficient frontier of these five asset classes. Interpret the results.

8. What changes in this process might you make if you wished to calculate an ex ante frontier for a large portfolio, say, $500 million of pension fund assets?

APPENDIX 7A: THE SINGLE-INDEX MODEL

The Markowitz model requires that analysts supply estimates of securities' (1) expected returns, (2) standard deviations, and (3) correlation coefficients. Most analysts could probably provide estimates of expected security returns if forced to, but security standard deviations would be much more difficult to obtain. Analysts have typically not been trained to think in terms of a standard deviation. But again, if pressured, they could probably provide opinions. Estimates of correlation coefficients are another matter. Not only are analysts unaccustomed to thinking in terms of return correlations, but they usually follow a fairly narrow group of securities and would be unable to provide reasonable estimates of correlations between securities they follow versus securities they don't follow.

To illustrate the large number of inputs needed to use the Markowitz model, think of a case in which 200 stocks are being considered as possible holdings. Input requirements would be calculated as follows:

Input Variable	Inputs Required	In General for N Securities
Expected returns	200	N
Standard deviations	200	N
Correlation coefficients	19,900	$N(N-1) \div 2$
	20,300	$N(N+3) \div 2$

The Markowitz model is inconvenient to use principally because of the large number of correlation coefficients which must be estimated. Obtaining the needed inputs for the Markowitz model is clearly a formidable task. As a result, a simplified version known as the *single-index portfolio model* has been developed. The single-index model attempts to eliminate this problem by relating returns on each security, *not* to returns on *all other securities*, but instead to

returns on *one common index*. Typically, a broad index of common stock returns such as the S&P 500 is used. We'll call this the *market index*.

The single-index model assumes the following relationship between individual security returns and returns on the market index:

$$\tilde{R}_{it} = A_i + \beta_i \tilde{R}_{mt} + \tilde{E}_{it} \qquad \text{(7A.1)}$$

Figure 7A-1 presents a graphic view of the relationship. The random return, $\tilde{R}_{it}$, on any security i during period t is composed of:

1. A constant periodic return, A_i, which is unique to security i. This constant return is earned regardless of the level of market returns.

2. A return which is sensitive to random market index returns. This is equal to $\beta_i \tilde{R}_{mt}$. β_i is the slope of the line in Figure 7A-1 and indicates the expected increase in security return for a 1 percent increase in market return. If β_i is 0.8, a 10% market return will result in an 8% stock return (over and above A_i). $\tilde{R}_{mt}$ is the random percentage market return in period t.

3. A random residual error, $\tilde{E}_{it}$. The residual error is the difference between the actual return, $\tilde{R}_{it}$, and the return expected given market returns, $A_i + \beta_i \tilde{R}_{mt}$. For example, if $A_i = 3.5\%$, $\beta_i = 1.2$, $\tilde{R}_{mt} = 10\%$, and $R_{it} = 17.5\%$, the residual error is $+2.0\%$. This is found by subtracting the expected return of 15.5% ($3.5\% + 1.2 \times 10\%$) from the actual return of 17.5%.

The benefit of decomposing security returns in this manner lies in the ease of calculating individual security correlation coefficients, r_{ij}. This can be done using the following formula:

$$r_{ij} = \frac{\beta_i \beta_j \sigma_m^2}{\sigma_i \sigma_j} \qquad \text{(7A.2)}$$

Equation 7A.2 is correct only if the random residual error terms for security i, $\tilde{E}_i$, are uncorrelated with

FIGURE 7A-1 *Relationship Between Security and Market Returns; Single-Index Portfolio Model*

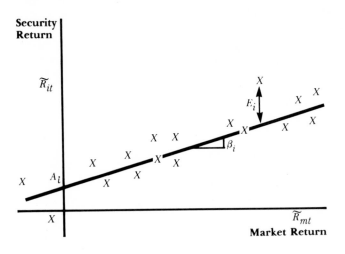

the random residual error terms for security j, $\tilde{E}_j$. This simply means that any comovement which might exist between the returns on two securities is completely captured by their relationship with a common index. For example, assume that the analyst is evaluating three securities. He or she is able to estimate standard deviations for each, betas for each, and the market's standard deviation as follows:

Security	Beta	Standard Deviation
1	0.8	10%
2	0.5	15%
3	1.3	10%
Market index	1.0	8%

Then correlation coefficients are easily found:

Correlation	Value	Details
$r_{1,2}$	0.17	= (0.8 × 0.5 × 64) ÷ (10 × 15)
$r_{1,3}$	0.67	= (0.8 × 1.3 × 64) ÷ (10 × 10)
$r_{2,3}$	0.28	= (0.5 × 1.3 × 64) ÷ (15 × 10)

Correlations between two securities are not estimated directly, but indirectly through their mutual relationship with one common index. In the full Markowitz model analysts needed to estimate $[N(N-1) \div 2]$ explicit correlation coefficients. In the single-index model, estimates of one β for each security, one standard deviation for each stock, and the market's standard deviation are all that are required. Thus, only $2N + 1$ inputs are required to find correlation coeffi-

cients. Figure 7A-2 plots the number of correlation inputs necessary under both models.

Because of its relative simplicity, the single-index model has been used more extensively than the full Markowitz method. But the single-index model is no more than a simplified approximation to the full Markowitz approach. It is totally dependent upon the accuracy of Equation 7A.2, and this accuracy depends upon various statistical characteristics of the single-index model. Most important among these is the requirement that the residual errors (E_j, E_i) between various securities be uncorrelated with each other. All correlation between security returns must be captured by the β term, the correlation with the market index. In practice, Equation 7A.2 does provide reasonable estimates of security correlations, and the single-index model appears to be a fairly accurate approximation of the Markowitz model.

For example, the betas of IBM and Exxon happen to be 0.77377 and 0.8932, respectively. Using σ on the S&P 500 of 14.8% as the market index, and the data in Table 7-4, the *implied* correlation between the two stocks is:

$$\frac{\beta_I \beta_E \sigma_m^2}{\sigma_I \sigma_E} = \frac{(0.7737)(0.8932)(0.148^2)}{(0.194)(0.208)} = 0.375$$

The actual correlation coefficient between the two was 0.36.

Before we leave the single-index model, it is useful to point out how Equation 7A.1 relates to the con-

FIGURE 7A-2 *Number of Correlation Inputs Required for Efficient Diversification Models*

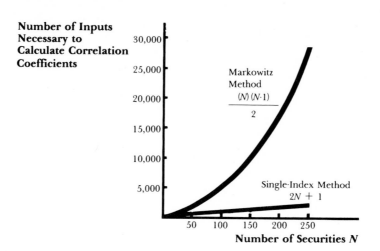

cepts of systematic and unsystematic risk. If security returns are indeed created as Equation 7A.1 suggests (a constant + sensitivity to random market returns + a random residual term), then it can be shown that the total risk of a security's return can be decomposed into two parts, as shown in Equation 7A.3:

$$\text{Total Risk} = \frac{\text{Systematic}}{\text{Risk}} + \frac{\text{Unsystematic}}{\text{Risk}} \qquad \textbf{(7A.3)}$$

$$\sigma_i^2 = \beta_i^2 \sigma_m^2 + \sigma_{ri}^2$$

where σ_i^2 = the variance of returns on security i, β_i = the beta of i (or sensitivity of i's returns to market returns), σ_m^2 = the variance of returns expected on the market index being used, and σ_{ri}^2 = the variance of security i's random residual return.

The variance of returns on a security is determined by two factors. The first relates to how sensitive a security's returns are to events which affect all securities. This sensitivity is captured by beta. The uncer-

tainty associated with such aggregate economic events is captured by the perceived variance of market returns. This portion of total security risk cannot be diversified since it reflects events which affect all securities. The second factor accounts for uncertainty about a security's returns which are not related in any systematic way to other securities. This part of a security's return is totally independent of returns on other securities. As a result, these residual returns tend to net out across a large number of securities. They offset each other and can be diversified away.

Finally, the beta of this single-index model, the beta used in the chapter to measure a security's risk relative to a diversified portfolio, and the beta developed in the next chapter are closely related to one another. In fact, if the theory of Chapter 8 is correct, the three betas measure exactly the same thing and should be identical. However, each is developed for different purposes.

APPENDIX 7B: ASSET ALLOCATION

The concept of an efficient frontier was illustrated in the chapter using a variety of individual stocks. In practical applications, however, efficient frontiers are usually found using a variety of aggregate *asset classes*. In this appendix, we review how this is done.

An Ex Post Efficient Frontier

In Table 7B-1, summary data are presented on five major U.S. security classes. The data represent real rates of return over the time interval 1926–1987. Al-

TABLE 7B-1 *Historical Real Return Information, 1926–1987*

	Asset Class				
	Treasury Bills	*Govt. Bonds*	*Corp. Bonds*	*S&P 500*	*Small Company*
Average	0.35%	1.40%	2.02%	8.83%	16.19%
Standard Deviation	4.57%	10.41%	10.34%	21.50%	39.83%
Correlation Coefficient Matrix:					
T-Bills	1.000				
Govt. Bonds	0.614	1.000			
Corp. Bonds	0.597	0.953	1.000		
S&P 500	0.132	0.224	0.292	1.000	
Small Companies	0.040	0.032	0.123	0.812	1.000

though some investors would be interested in nominal returns, most are more concerned about real increases in their wealth. Thus, only real returns are analyzed here.

Average annual real returns ranged from as low as 0.35% on Treasury bills to 16.19% for an index of small companies traded on the NYSE and AMEX. Of course, greater average returns came at the cost of greater return volatility. For example, the standard deviation of yearly real Treasury bill returns was only 4.57%, whereas the Small Company Index had a standard deviation of about 40%.

Correlation coefficients ranged from close to 0.0 to almost 1.0. The true equity indexes (S&P 500 and Small Company) were highly correlated with each other ($r = 0.812$) but only moderately correlated with the fixed-income and money market securities.

A variety of computer programs are available which can use the data in Table 7B-1 to find a *historical* efficient frontier for individuals having a one-year investment horizon. Such a program is included on the diskette provided with this text. The program is called ASSETALL.

ASSETALL has a number of features which you might wish to explore by following its menu of selections. The most critical, however, is the selection of either a short-sale constrained frontier or a no-short-sale constrained portfolio. The short-sale constrained alternative calculates an optimal risk/return portfolio in which the investment in each asset class is zero or greater. As its name implies, no asset class may be

sold short. Since this is a common restriction for most large institutional investors, we will use it here.

Input Data. ASSETALL reads an input data set from a microcomputer which is then used to calculate the efficient frontier. The data set must be an ASCII file. For the data in Table 7B-1, this input data set would look as follows:

```
5           1.0
0.35        1.40    2.02    8.83    16.19
4.57        10.41   10.34   21.50   39.83

T-Bills
1.0

Govt.
0.614       1.0

Corp.
0.597       0.953   1.0

S&P 500
0.132       0.224   0.292   1.0

Small
0.04        0.032   0.122   0.812   1.0
```

The meaning of most of these data is clear when they are compared with Table 7B-1. The first line does require a brief explanation, however. The first number represents the number of securities for which you are providing data—5 in our example. The second

FIGURE 7B-1 *Illustration of a Historical Efficient Frontier Based on Yearly Real Returns, 1926–1987*

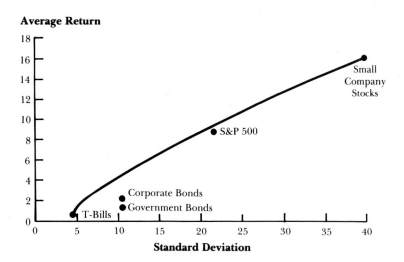

identifies the "return increment" to be used in finding optimal portfolios. By specifying 1.0, we have told ASSETALL to provide optimal portfolios which have average returns (or expected returns when using ex ante data) which differ by 1.0 percentage points.

Note: A complete description of the ASSETALL computer package is available in the Student Workbook and Instructor's Manual for this text. However, except for the input data set shown above, it is menu driven and requires little training. It can be executed by placing the diskette which contains the ASSET-ALL.COM files into drive A: and entering the word "ASSETALL".

The Historical Frontier. The efficient frontier which results from the data in Table 7B-1 is shown in Figure 7B-1 and Table 7B-2. Look at the lowest-risk portfolio and notice that it provides a slightly greater return than 100% invested in Treasury bills but at lower risk. This is the benefit created by diversification.

Ex Ante Efficient Frontiers

Practical asset allocation studies differ from the example above in two major ways. First, additional asset classes are used, such as real estate and international

TABLE 7B-2 *Composition of Selected Optimal Portfolios*

Portfolio	Average Return	Standard Deviation	Percentage Invested in Each Asset Class				
			T-Bills	Govt.	Corp.	S&P 500	Small Co.
1	0.51%	4.55%	99.42	—	—	1.29	0.29
2	1.00	4.70	93.97	—	—	4.18	1.85
3	5.00	11.50	37.61	—	25.96	21.16	15.28
4	8.00	18.08	—	—	40.91	32.53	26.56
5	9.50	21.66	—	—	27.39	38.17	34.43
6	12.00	30.62	—	—	—	43.36	56.64
7	16.19	39.83	—	—	—	—	100.00

FIGURE 7B-2 *Improvement in Efficient Frontier with Addition of Asset Classes*

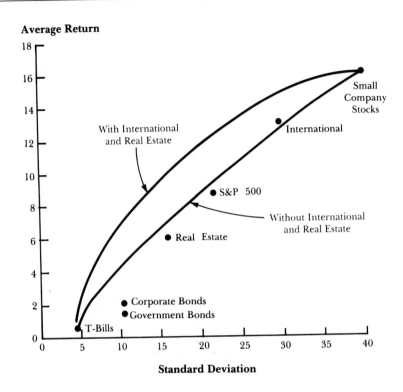

return indexes. Second, the input data should reflect the analyst's estimate of future expected returns, standard deviations, and correlation coefficients. Both of these topics are discussed in Chapter 20. As you might imagine, developing estimates of the various input variables is a difficult task.

But it is clear that the addition of additional asset classes typically expands the feasible set of risk/return combinations and moves the efficient frontier to the left. To illustrate this, two additional asset classes were added to the five used above and the efficient frontier was calculated again. The same data were used on the original five. Data on the two new classes consisted of:

	Real Estate	*International Stocks*
Average	6.0%	13.0%
Std. Dev.	15.85%	29.82%

Correlation Coefficients with:

	T-Bills	*Govt.*	*Corp.*	*S&P 500*	*Small*	*R.E.*	*Intl.*
Real Est.	0.10	0.10	0.10	0.10	0.10	1.0	0.10
Intl.	0.00	0.00	0.00	0.10	0.30	0.1	1.0

Reliable historical return data on real estate and international stocks are available for only a short period of time. Therefore, estimates such as these are almost totally subjective, but they are probably reasonable.

The expanded efficient frontier obtained by adding these two asset classes is shown in Figure 7B-2. Although the results do depend on input assumptions, typically the optimal combinations of risk and return improve as additional asset classes are used. Diversification works!

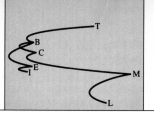

CHAPTER

8 Capital Asset Pricing Theory

In the previous chapter we concentrated on how individual investors and speculators can determine the single portfolio of risky securities which is optimal to them and how this portfolio can be combined with lending at the risk-free rate or borrowing in order to achieve a preferred risk/return trade-off. In this chapter we extend the discussion to the market in general and examine the following question: If all investors pursued optimal portfolio selection, how would this affect equilibrium security prices and expected returns?

The equilibrium model which results is known as the *capital asset pricing model*. Embodied in this model are two fundamental relationships. Since there is often confusion between the two, we will state each immediately.

The first relationship, known as the *capital market line*, specifies the return one should expect to receive on a *portfolio*. If the portfolio provides this expected return, it is an *efficient portfolio* and should be purchased. If the portfolio provides a lower return, it should not be held. The capital market line is written symbolically as:

Capital Market Line $$E(R_p) = RF + \sigma_p \left[\frac{RP_M}{\sigma_M} \right]$$ **(8.1)**

The return you should expect to receive on any portfolio is equal to a risk-free rate earned for delaying consumption plus a risk premium earned for bearing risk inherent in the portfolio. (We will delay any discussion of this risk premium until it can be examined closely.) It is important to remember that the capital market line treats the relationship between expected returns on *efficient portfolios* and the risks of such portfolios.

The second relationship, known as the *security market line*, is broader and is able to treat individual securities as well as portfolios. It expresses the return which should be expected in terms of a risk-free rate and the relative risk of the security (or portfolio). The security market line is written symbolically as:

Security Market Line $$E(R_i) = RF + \beta_i [RP_M]$$ **(8.2)**

As with the capital market line, there is a risk-free and a risk component. But the security market line expresses the risk premium differently and treats *any* security i, while Equation 8.1 treats efficient portfolios only. As one would expect, the security

265

market line is the more widely used because of its greater generality. But it can only be understood in the context of the capital market line.

In the standard capital asset pricing model which is developed in this chapter, a single portfolio of risky securities emerges which all investors should hold in combination with borrowing or lending. This portfolio is referred to as the *market portfolio* and consists of *all risky securities in existence, with relative holdings of each dependent on each security's total market value.* The critical role of the market portfolio is, without doubt, the central conclusion of this theory. From the optimality of the market portfolio come both the capital market line and security market line. From it also come a variety of investment and speculative implications which have had major impacts on portfolio strategies within the last decade. The dominance of this market portfolio, however, is simply a logical consequence of the various assumptions made. After reviewing its development, the reader will probably sit back and say, "Of course, it makes perfect sense—if the assumptions are correct." In this chapter these assumptions are treated as abstractions of reality which are needed in order to develop a simple relationship between equilibrium risk and return. Although none of them is strictly true, we will wait until the next chapter to examine the empirical accuracy of the model and the effects of lifting each assumption.

THE CAPITAL MARKET LINE

Assumptions

The intent of this chapter is to develop a model which explains security prices when the market is at equilibrium. *Equilibrium exists when prices are at levels which provide no incentive for speculative trading.* At equilibrium the quantity of shares desired for sale by investors (nonspeculators) is equal to the quantity desired for purchase by investors.

If the price of a given security is lower than its equilibrium level, an *excess demand* will arise and speculators will bid up prices until the excess demand is removed. Similarly, if prices are greater than equilibrium, speculators will create an *excess supply* and force prices down by their selling. The point at which price levels attract no information trading is what we consider equilibrium.

If prices are set at equilibrium, trades between buyers and sellers will continue to occur. Individuals (and organizations) who have excess cash and wish to invest come to the market with bids to buy, while individuals (and organizations) who need cash come to the market with offers to sell. However, at equilibrium, no one is offering to buy or sell out of a belief that existing prices are wrong: no one trades with a *speculative* motive, and no one trades because he or she has unique information not yet available to other participants. *For the market to be truly at equilibrium, all buyers and sellers must have the same information.* If they don't, then by definition the market cannot yet be at equilibrium.

Equilibrium prices will change with the passage of time, as world events occur and provide new information about the prospects of the firms which originally issued the securities. And, if events are dramatic, equilibrium price changes will also be dramatic. Hence there is nothing particularly inconsistent about having significant gyrations in security prices over time and a market which is always at equilibrium. The large price movements might simply reflect continuous and occasionally large adjustments to equilibrium levels necessary as new information unfolds. In contrast, many people would argue that actual market prices are never at equilibrium but, instead, are constantly chasing (but never finding) the changing equilibrium levels. Which theory is correct really doesn't matter here. We are interested only in equilibrium pricing, not actual prices. To begin to understand what creates an actual price we must first understand the forces which create an equilibrium price. Only then can we look for differences between actual and equilibrium prices.

At this point we can summarize and state our first assumption: *Equilibrium prices exist only when speculative (information) trading is zero.* For security markets to be at equilibrium we must *assume that all market participants currently have identical information*—they have *homogeneous expectations* about the future.

This assumption of homogeneous expectations is often stated another way: All participants have equal and costless access to information. If new information is released to a select few people, or even released to different groups at different times, prices would be set by the speculative trades of the people or groups who first receive the information. But, again, an equilibrium exists only when all investors have common information.

Next, we will *assume that there are no impediments to achieving exactly the portfolio that one wishes.* In other words, the markets are *frictionless.* Among the principal impediments which might exist are the following:

1. Transaction costs. Brokerage fees and bid-ask spread fees are assumed to be zero, so that all purchases and sales desired will be transacted.
2. Security indivisibility. We will assume that all securities are infinitely divisible. Investors can take any position they wish. If an individual's optimal decision is to own 115.37 shares of AT&T, it is assumed possible.
3. Taxes. We will assume that taxes are zero.[1]
4. Trading price impacts. We will assume that the trading actions of the individual investor do not affect price levels. Your decision, or that of another investor, to trade does not, in isolation from all other trades, affect prices. Only the aggregate of all trades causes prices to move to equilibrium.

Finally, we will carry forward the three assumptions of Chapter 7 regarding how the individual chooses an optimal security portfolio:

1. *A one-period world exists for all investors.*
2. *Investors seek to maximize the expected utility of end-of-period wealth, and this utility is determined by expected returns and the standard deviation of returns.*
3. *People may borrow or lend at a constant risk-free interest rate.*

---

[1] The critical tax impact occurs when capital gains and ordinary tax rates vary. To some extent, we will see the effects of this in the next chapter. For now, it is simplest to assume away all taxes.

In summary:

1. Decisions are made in a one-period world.
2. Expected returns and standard deviation of portfolio returns determine an individual's utility.
3. A risk-free security exists in which all investors can borrow or lend.
4. Expectations are homogeneous.
5. No impediments exist to obtaining a desired portfolio:

   • There are no transaction costs.
   • There are no taxes.
   • Securities are perfectly divisible.
   • Trading by the single individual does not affect prices.

Some of these assumptions are relatively easy to accept. Others require a more heroic effort. But they are all necessary to develop a simple formulation of market equilibrium which we can tinker with later.

Market Equilibrium

Given these assumptions, we are ready to examine what a state of market equilibrium would imply about the measurement of risk, the risk/return trade-off, and security price levels. The analysis, fortunately, is quite easy to understand and is depicted in Figure 8-1.

Consider the situation faced by the individual shown in the figure. The individual first evaluates the expected returns and risks available on various portfolio combinations and, from this, is able to identify the efficient frontier of risky portfolios. Next, the optimal risky portfolio is found by determining which portfolio will provide the largest risk premium when it is held in combination with the risk-free security. This optimal risky portfolio is denoted as portfolio M.

Now consider the situation faced by another individual. It is identical. Since investors have homogeneous expectations, each will arrive at the same conclusion—that portfolio M is *the* optimal risky portfolio. People will differ in the amount of risk they wish their portfolios to contain, but risk can be adjusted by altering the amount of lending and borrowing. Portfolio M is never changed. It is the only portfolio of risky securities which people wish to hold.

Well, what if some security exists which is not in M? It won't be owned—not by anyone. Instead, it will be used as wallpaper in family dens, displayed in investment classes to illustrate a great story, etc. Conversely, any security which exists and is held in a portfolio is in M. Portfolio M consists of *all* owned securities.

Portfolio M is called the *market portfolio*, and its existence as the optimal efficient portfolio for all investors is the single most important implication of this standard version of the capital asset pricing model. Not surprisingly, this implication has come under attack from academicians and practitioners alike. Much of Chapter 9 will be

FIGURE 8-1 *Efficient Frontier and Borrowing-Lending Line Available to All Market Participants*

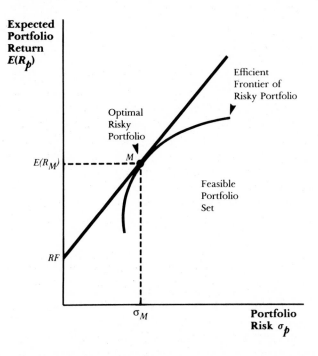

devoted to such criticisms. But, for now, we will accept this result and see what develops from it.

Optimal X_i Holdings. The investment process consists of two steps: (1) identifying the optimal risky portfolio (the percentage to invest in each available risky security— X_i) and (2) borrowing or lending to achieve the desired risk/return trade-off. The capital asset pricing model states that the market portfolio is the optimal risky portfolio. And since all investors wish to hold this same portfolio, it should be no surprise that the *percentage of a risky portfolio held in security i is equal to the total market value of security i as a percent of the total market values of all securities.*

Proportion of Risky Portfolio Held in *i*
$$X_i^* = \frac{P_i N_i}{\sum\limits_{i=1}^{T} P_i N_i}$$
(8.3)

where: X_i^* = optimal percentage of the *risky portfolio* (i.e., excluding borrowing-lending) held in security *i*

P_i = market price of security *i*

N_i = quantity of security *i* outstanding

T = total number of securities outstanding

For example, assume there are only three risky securities available:

Security	Price	Units Outstanding	Total Value	Percentage of Total
1	$ 30	200	$ 6,000	30%
2	50	200	10,000	50
3	1,000	4	4,000	20
			$20,000	100%

The total market value of these securities is $20,000. Since the securities are held by various market participants, the total wealth of these participants devoted to risky securities is also $20,000. But since they all wish to have the same percentage holdings of each, the percentage which any one person will invest in a given security *must be equal* to the security's percentage of the total value of all risky securities. Thus, everyone will place 30% of their risky portfolio in security 1, 50% in security 2, and 20% in security 3. If this were not the case, the markets would not clear. One or more investors would remain wanting to buy or sell a specific holding.

Why the Market Portfolio? Given our assumptions, it is perfectly reasonable that the market portfolio is optimal. Securities differ only in expected returns and standard deviations of returns. As we saw in Chapter 7, diversification by itself has no effect on expected portfolio returns. For example, if the addition of another security reduces expected returns below the desired level, an investor can borrow to achieve the desired return but still obtain the risk-reduction advantages of the increased diversification. The market portfolio is in essence the most diversified portfolio available. Once it is held, there is no way to further diversify away risk.

Consider Figure 8-2, which schematically shows all risky securities in the world within a large circle. A few of the individual securities are illustrated by the small boxes. Gains or losses in value incurred by particular securities are depicted by arrows showing where the gain or loss came from and went to. Security 1, for example, incurs two losses of value, one which is passed to security 2 and one which is not passed to another asset but simply leaves the system. *Gains and losses to individual securities which are passed on to other securities and remain within the system can be diversified away by holding a portfolio of all securities. These are unsystematic risks. Gains or losses to the total system are nondiversifiable systematic risks.*

Simply stated, the market portfolio is the most broadly diversified portfolio available. Any portfolio with fewer securities or a dissimilar percentage of investments in each security is not adequately diversified.

The CML Equation. The capital market line (CML) states the equilibrium relationship which exists between the returns which should be expected on efficient portfolios of securities and the risks of such portfolios. For reference, look back to Figure 8-1. The CML is the borrowing-lending line extending from *RF* through portfolio *M*.

FIGURE 8-2 *The Market of All Risky Assets (Diversifiable and Nondiversifiable)*

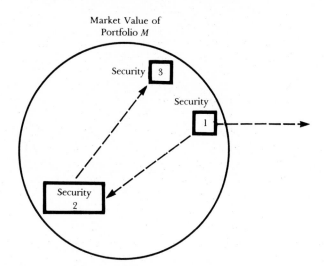

In equilibrium, the return expected on a *portfolio* of securities must be at least equal to Equation 8.4a or the portfolio is inefficient and will not be held. As you might expect, in equilibrium, the only portfolios which meet the criterion are combinations of *RF* and the market portfolio.

Capital Market Line Equation

$$E(R_p) = RF + \sigma_p \left[\frac{E(R_M) - RF}{\sigma_M} \right] \qquad \textbf{(8.4a)}$$

where: $E(R_M)$ = expected return on the market portfolio

σ_M = standard deviation of the market portfolio's return

First, one should expect a risk-free return simply for delaying the consumption of the portfolio's worth. Second, a risk premium should be expected which is determined by two things: (1) the total risk of the portfolio (σ_p) and (2) the best risk-related return per unit of σ available in the market. Since the market portfolio dominates all other risky portfolios in equilibrium, it provides the best risk-related return per unit of σ.

In Equation 8.4a, the term $E(R_M) - RF$ is a measure of the risk premium which is expected to be earned above the risk-free rate for bearing the market portfolio's risk. We refer to it as RP_M. If $E(R_M)$ equals 16% and the risk-free rate is 10%, then $RP_M = 6\%$. You should recognize, however, that the term $E(R_M) - RF$ does not create the percentage risk premium available to market participants. Instead, it is RP_M in combination with RF which creates $E(R_M)$. The term $E(R_M) - RF$ is simply a measurement of RP_M. To avoid any confusion about what is a measurement term and what is a determinant, it is useful to restate the CML as follows:

FIGURE 8-3 *The Capital Market Line*

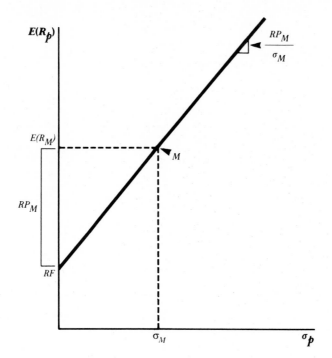

$$E(R_p) = RF + \sigma_p \left[\frac{RP_M}{\sigma_M} \right] \qquad\qquad \textbf{(8.4b)}$$

In Figure 8-3 a plot of the CML is shown.

For illustration, assume that $RF = 10\%$, $RP_M = 6\%$, and $\sigma_M = 20\%$. Then the return on a portfolio which is half as risky as the market portfolio should provide an expected return of 13%:

$$E(R_p) = 10\% + 10\% \left[\frac{6\%}{20\%} \right]$$

$$= 13\%$$

A combination of 50% in the market portfolio and 50% in the risk-free security would provide exactly this 13% expected return. Other portfolios with $\sigma_p = 10\%$ should be judged against the 13%. If the other portfolio has a higher expected return, it should be aggressively purchased. If the other portfolio has a lower expected return, it should not be bought.

If the markets are in equilibrium, however, it would be impossible to find another portfolio with $\sigma = 10\%$ and $E(R_p)$ greater than 13%. The only portfolio capable of both $\sigma_p = 10\%$ and $E(R_p) = 13\%$ is a 50/50 combination of M and RF. All other portfolios are inefficient—dominated by the extensive diversification gains of the market portfolio.

Determinants of RP_M. Recall from Chapter 5 how RF is determined. It is not a number handed to society by a financial dictator. Instead, the risk-free rate is determined by market participants themselves as a function of their time preferences for consumption and the marginal productivity of capital. The risk premium is also determined in the marketplace and is a function of society's risk aversion and the marginal returns available from risky assets. To illustrate the process, consider the three panels of Figure 8-4. In panel A, the risk-free rate is removed. The dashed lines are societal indifference curves reflecting the marginal increases in expected returns for the marginal change in risk which is necessary to maintain a given utility. (Think of these indifference curves as an average across all members of society.) The ideal portfolio is denoted as M. Now move to panel B, in which a risk-free rate is introduced. Suddenly M no longer is efficient and M_2 is held in its place. To achieve its desired risk/return level, society will attempt to borrow at RF and will place both equity and borrowings in M_2 in order to be at the optimal point B. But society cannot borrow from itself. The sum of all individual borrowing and individual lending *must* be zero. It is impossible for society to be at point B. However, attempts to purchase M_2 will force the prices of M_2 up and its expected return down. Similarly, lack of demand for M will cause its expected returns to rise as its prices fall. Equilibrium will finally result when the optimal risky portfolio M is consistent with zero net borrowing and lending, as shown in panel C.

There are two important points to recognize in this illustration. First, the risk premium is not forced on society by risks and expected returns associated with risky assets. Instead, it is the interaction of *available* risk/return trade-offs with society's risk *preferences* which determines the risk premium. Second, any such equilibrium must also be consistent with zero net lending and borrowing.

FIGURE 8-4 *Determination of the Risk Premium*

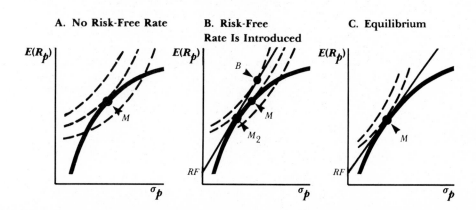

TABLE 8-1 *Market Value of Various Asset Types*

	Market Value (Billions)	*Percent U.S. Total*	*Percent World Total*
Domestic United States:			
Equities	$1,380.6	29.7%	
Debt	1,111.7	23.9	
Real Estate	2,161.3	46.4	
Total U.S.	$4,653.6	100.0%	62.5%
Non–United States:			
Equities	1,049.3	—	
Debt	1,748.3	—	
Real Estate	NA	—	
Total Non–U.S.	$2,797.6	—	37.5
Total	$7,451.2	—	100.0%

The Market Portfolio

In theory, the market portfolio consists of all risky assets. These would include U.S. equities, U.S. bonds, U.S. real estate, non–U.S. equities, non–U.S. bonds, pork belly commodities, Chinese oil paintings, etc. In practice, the market portfolio cannot actually be held or even identified. Market frictions make trading with certain countries impossible and with others very costly.[2] But the crude data which are available suggest some interesting implications.

Table 8-1 provides a recent estimate of what the market portfolio might consist of. In the far right column the value of non–U.S. assets is estimated to be 37.5% of the world total. This figure is obviously understated because estimates of real estate values outside the U.S. are not available and because the debt and equity values are only for major international security exchanges. But, even if we are unable to obtain accurate figures on non–U.S. values, it should be clear that a large part of portfolio *M* consists of non–U.S. assets — that international diversification is necessary to obtain the broadest diversification possible. We will return to this in Chapter 18 when international diversification is examined.

Next, consider only the information shown on domestic U.S. assets. Real estate dominates holdings of either equity or debt. To diversify broadly over only U.S. assets, an individual's portfolio should contain almost one half its value in real estate.[3] And of the debt and equity securities available, an approximately equal commitment

---

[2]Imagine the reaction if a person were to visit Moscow and ask to purchase an interest in Siberian timberland because he or she wished to hold the market portfolio.

[3]In fact, a large part of most people's wealth consists of the equity they have in their homes and land. If the value of these are highly correlated with other real assets, this equity ownership in homes and land probably achieves much of the diversification suggested in real estate.

should be made to each. The data in Table 8-1 are very imprecise. But they do suggest the important roles which international securities and real estate should play in the creation of a well-diversified portfolio. In fact, increased attention has recently been focused on exactly these two asset categories, and most large portfolios (pension funds in particular) have substantially increased investments in each.

THE SECURITY MARKET LINE

The CML specifies the equilibrium relationship between expected return and risk for *efficient portfolios*. It cannot be used to evaluate the equilibrium expected return on a single security because σ_i is not a proper measure of a security's true risk. The risk of a security depends upon the portfolio to which it is added and must reflect the covariability of the security's returns with other assets in the portfolio.

In this section we examine how the risk of a single security should be measured when the markets are in equilibrium. The analysis is similar to that in Chapter 7, where we evaluated the risk of a single security to one individual. The principal difference here is that we know what the optimal risky asset portfolio is—the market portfolio. The model which is developed is known as the *security market line* (SML).

Beta: A Security's Nondiversifiable Risk

The standard deviation of the market portfolio is:

Market Portfolio Risk
$$\sigma_M = \left[\sum_{i=1}^{N} X_i^2 \sigma_i^2 + \sum_{\substack{i=1 \\ i \neq j}}^{N} \sum_{j=1}^{N} X_i X_j \sigma_i \sigma_j r_{ij} \right]^{1/2} \tag{8.5a}$$

where there are N different risky assets available. As before, σ_M is a function of each security's variance of returns (σ_i^2) and covariances with other securities ($\sigma_i \sigma_j r_{ij}$). Actually, the variance term can also be thought of as a covariance term—the covariance of the security with itself. If this is done, Equation 8.5a can be written as

Market Portfolio Risk
$$\sigma_M = \left[\sum_{i=1}^{N} \sum_{j=1}^{N} X_i X_j \sigma_i \sigma_j r_{ij} \right]^{1/2} \tag{8.5b}$$

Now, let's pull out of this equation only those terms associated with, say, security 8, so we can look more closely at how it affects σ_M:

Security 8's Terms in σ_M
$$[X_8 X_1 \sigma_8 \sigma_1 r_{8,1} + X_1 X_8 \sigma_1 \sigma_8 r_{1,8}$$
$$+ X_8^2 \sigma_8^2 + \dots$$
$$+ 2X_8 X_9 \sigma_8 \sigma_9 r_{8,9} + \dots$$
$$+ 2X_8 X_N \sigma_8 \sigma_N r_{8N}] \tag{8.6}$$

Look at the first line. Here the weighted covariances between 8 and 1, as well as between 1 and 8, are shown. Since they are equal, all such future covariances are multiplied by 2—for example, on lines 3 and 4. The second line displays the covariance of 8 with itself. The final line treats the covariance of 8 with the last security N.

The equation may look complex, but its economic interpretation is straightforward. Equation 8.6 is simply:[4]

$$2X_8 \text{ [covariance of 8 with the market portfolio]} = 2X_8[\sigma_8\sigma_M r_{8M}]$$

If this is the case, then the risk of the market portfolio is simply the sum of many such covariance terms for each security. Symbolically:

Market Portfolio
Risk
$$\sigma_M = [2X_1(\sigma_1\sigma_M r_{1M}) + \ldots + 2X_8(\sigma_8\sigma_M r_{8M}) \\ + \ldots + 2X_N(\sigma_N\sigma_M r_{NM})]^{1/2} \tag{8.7}$$

Finally, we can examine how changes in holdings of security 8 affect the risk of the market portfolio. This is done by taking the derivative of σ_M with respect to X_8:

Changes in σ_M for a
Small Change in X_8
$$\frac{\partial \sigma_M}{\partial X_8} = \frac{\sigma_8\sigma_M r_{8M}}{\sigma_M} = \sigma_8 r_{8M} \tag{8.8}$$

The risk which security 8 provides to the market portfolio as X_8 changes slightly is its nondiversifiable uncertainty. *Only that portion of its risk which is correlated with the market is important.* For example, in Chapter 7 the standard deviation for Campbell was 22% and for IBM it was 19%. Campbell clearly has the more volatile returns. But assume that $r_{CM} = 0.25$ and $r_{IM} = 0.60$. Then which stock is really the riskier? As shown below, Campbell's contribution to portfolio M's standard deviation is less than IBM's:

Stock	σ_i	×	r_{iM}	=	Nondiversifiable Risk to M
Campbell	22%		0.25		5.5%
IBM	19%		0.60		11.4%

In general, we can say that *the risk of security i is the nondiversifiable risk which it adds to portfolio M* as small changes are made in X_i:

Risk of Security i
in Equilibrium
$$= \frac{\text{Nondiversifiable}}{\text{Standard Deviation}} = \sigma_i r_{iM} \tag{8.9}$$

A more commonly used security-risk measure is the amount of nondiversifiable risk inherent in the security *relative* to the risk of the market portfolio. This relative risk measure is known as *beta* and is equal to:

Beta of Security i
$$\beta_i = \frac{\sigma_i}{\sigma_M}(r_{iM}) \tag{8.10}$$

---

[4]This is not strictly true since only one $X_8^2\sigma_8^2$ term is shown in Equation 8.6. Given the large number of securities in M, this is certainly a negligible error.

Dividing σ_i by σ_M provides a measure of how volatile the security is in relation to the volatility of the market portfolio. Multiplying by the correlation coefficient determines how much of this relative volatility should be counted. If the security is perfectly correlated with the market portfolio, then all of the relative volatility counts. None of it can be eliminated in M by diversification. If the correlation is zero, then none of the volatility counts. All of it can be eliminated by diversification when combined with M.

The Betas of M and RF. The risk of the market portfolio relative to itself is, of course, 1.0:

$$\beta_M = \frac{\sigma_M}{\sigma_M}\,(r_{MM}) = 1.0$$

Any security with a beta equal to 1.0 has the same amount of nondiversifiable risk as in the market portfolio. When added to M, risk will not change. So the return which should be expected on a security with a beta of 1.0 should be the same as $E(R_M)$.

The risk of the risk-free rate is by definition equal to zero and it will have a beta of zero:

$$\beta_{RF} = \frac{0.0}{\sigma_M}\,(0.0) = 0.0$$

Similarly, other securities which have a beta of 0.0 should be priced to provide an expected return equal to the risk-free rate. That does not mean that zero-beta securities will *actually* return RF. They may not if they have a positive σ. But as long as they are uncorrelated with M, all such volatility can be diversified away in M. And if all such uncertainty can be eliminated, their *expected* return should be equal to RF.

The Expected Return on Individual Securities (SML)

The capital market line expressed the expected return on a portfolio in terms of the standard deviation of the portfolio:

CML $$E(R_p) = RF + \sigma_p\left[\frac{RP_M}{\sigma_M}\right] \qquad \textbf{(8.11a)}$$

For each unit of σ, a risk premium equal to $RP_M \div \sigma_M$ is required.

Now that we have a measure of the nondiversifiable risk of the security, we can apply the CML logic to it also. For example, let $RF = 10\%$, $RP_M = 6\%$, and $\sigma_M = 20\%$. In the earlier illustration, recall that IBM contributed an 11.4% standard deviation to the market portfolio and Campbell contributed 5.5%. The equilibrium which should be expected on each is:

FIGURE 8-5   *The Security Market Line*

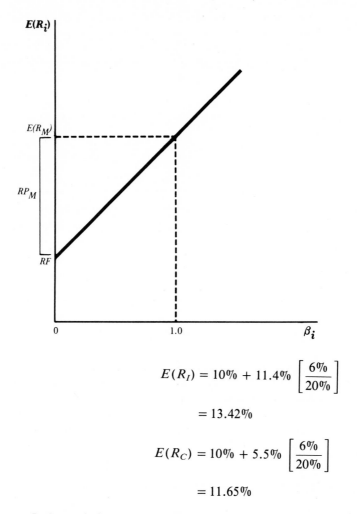

$$E(R_I) = 10\% + 11.4\% \left[\frac{6\%}{20\%} \right]$$

$$= 13.42\%$$

$$E(R_C) = 10\% + 5.5\% \left[\frac{6\%}{20\%} \right]$$

$$= 11.65\%$$

In general, for any security *i*:

$$E(R_i) = RF + \sigma_i r_{iM} \left[\frac{RP_M}{\sigma_M} \right]$$

The Security Market Line

$$= RF + \frac{\sigma_i r_{iM}}{\sigma_M} [RP_M] \qquad \textbf{(8.11b)}$$

$$= RF + \beta_i [RP_M]$$

Equation 8.11b is known as the *security market line* and is depicted graphically in Figure 8-5.

Using the IBM and Campbell data again, the betas on each would be:

$$\beta_I = \frac{\sigma_I}{\sigma_M} r_{IM} = \frac{19\%}{20\%} (0.60) = 0.570$$

$$\beta_C = \frac{\sigma_C}{\sigma_M} r_{CM} = \frac{22\%}{20\%} (0.25) = 0.257$$

Placing these betas into the SML, the expected returns on each would be the same as those found when the CML was used:

$$E(R_i) = RF + \beta_i[RP_M]$$

$$E(R_I) = 10\% + 0.570 \ [6\%] = 13.42\%$$

$$E(R_C) = 10\% + 0.275 \ [6\%] = 11.65\%$$

The SML Versus the CML. Let's consider some applications of both the SML and CML and, in the process, remove any confusion about when to use which one. We use the following data on two portfolios and a single stock:

Security	σ	r_{iM}	Beta	$\dfrac{E(P_1 + D_1)}{P_0} - 1.0$
Portfolio *MRF*	10%	1.0	0.5	13.0%
Portfolio *AMF*	20%	0.9	0.9	15.4%
Exxon Common Stock	20%	0.5	0.5	13.0%
Market Portfolio	20%	1.0	1.0	16.0
RF	0	0.0	0.0	10.0

The column on the far right indicates the return which is expected on each. This might or might not be equal to the equilibrium expected return; we will find out only after we have analyzed each.

Consider holding any of these three as your *total portfolio*. In that case you would apply the CML, since it identifies expected returns which are available on efficient portfolios of all possible risk levels:

CML	$E(R_p) = RF + \sigma_p \left[\dfrac{RP_M}{\sigma_M}\right]$
Portfolio *MRF*	$13.0\% = 10.0\% + 10.0\% \ (0.3)$
Portfolio *AMF*	$16.0\% = 10.0\% + 20.0\% \ (0.3)$
Exxon Stock	$16.0\% = 10.0\% + 20.0\% \ (0.3)$

Returns which should be expected on each (if they represent your total portfolio) are shown above and in Figure 8-6. Only portfolio *MRF* can be bought at a current price, P_0, and later receive an expected dividend $E(D_1)$ and price $E(P_1)$ which provide a satisfactory return. Only portfolio *MRF* is efficient. Portfolio *AMF* is expected to provide a 15.4% return, whereas an efficient portfolio with a standard deviation similar to that of *AMF*($\sigma = 20\%$) is expected to provide a 16.0% return. Clearly *AMF* is not an efficient portfolio. Exxon is even worse, providing an expected return of 13.0% when a similar-risk *portfolio* would provide 16.0%.

If the market *is in equilibrium*, this is not a surprising conclusion. Look at the cor-

FIGURE 8-6 *CML Example*

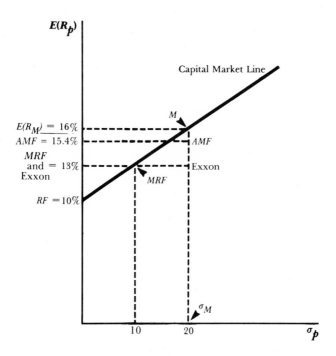

relation coefficient on each. Portfolio *MRF* is perfectly correlated with the market portfolio. It has no unsystematic, diversifiable risk. In fact, you may have guessed what *MRF* really is. There is only one way in which such a perfectly diversified portfolio can be constructed — by placing a portion of the portfolio in the market portfolio and then lending or borrowing at *RF*. Portfolio *MRF* is a 50/50 combination of *M* and *RF*. The other two investments, however, have correlations with portfolio *M* of less than 1.0. Each has some unsystematic, diversifiable risk. If the market is at equilibrium, such investments simply would not qualify as efficient portfolios because they would not be satisfactorily diversified.

Now let's look at these three investments again, not as total portfolios but as individual securities which are to be placed into a portfolio containing many other securities (*M*, of course). To evaluate the return which should be expected on a security if it is to be a part of a much larger portfolio, the SML is used:

SML	$E(R_i) = $	RF	$+$	$\beta_i[RP_M]$
Portfolio *MRF*	13.0%	$= 10.0\%$	$+$	$0.5\ (6.0\%)$
Portfolio *AMF*	15.4%	$= 10.0\%$	$+$	$0.9\ (6.0\%)$
Exxon Stock	13.0%	$= 10.0\%$	$+$	$0.5\ (6.0\%)$

In this context each investment is fairly priced. As shown above and in Figure 8-7, each is expected to provide a return equal to what equilibrium conditions sug-

FIGURE 8-7 *SML Example*

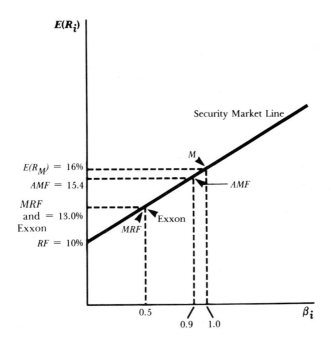

gest should be earned. Notice that the SML is able to identify the fair expected returns on an efficient portfolio such as *MRF*. Even though the SML is intended to evaluate single securities, it may also be used on portfolios. In fact, Exxon is a relatively diversified corporation and could be easily thought of as a portfolio composed of each of its business lines. The SML, however, asks only whether the security or portfolio is fairly priced. It does not indicate whether the investment is an efficient portfolio. To determine whether a portfolio is efficient, the CML must be used.

Portfolio Betas

There are two ways of calculating the beta of a portfolio: (1) at the portfolio level or (2) at the component security level. At the portfolio level, the beta is simply:

Portfolio Beta $$\beta_p = \frac{\sigma_p}{\sigma_M} \, r_{pM} \tag{8.12}$$

The standard deviation of portfolio returns is divided by the standard deviation of the market portfolio to find the amount of uncertainty in the portfolio relative to *M*. This value is then multiplied by the correlation between *p* and *M* to determine what portion of the relative uncertainty will not be diversified away when *p* is held together with *M*. If the correlation coefficient and standard deviations are *ex ante* measures, this is a proper way of measuring β_p. Such an ex ante beta measures subjective beliefs about the portfolio's relative nondiversifiable risk. However, ex post measures are commonly used as proxies for ex ante data, in which case standard deviations and correlation coefficients of the portfolio's historical returns are used to estimate beta.

There are two possible biases in such a beta estimate:

1. The past can be a poor predictor of the future. Estimates will depend to a large degree on the time period chosen, and all such estimates are often inaccurate predictors.

2. If the composition of the portfolio (the X_i values) has changed over time, the beta associated with current holdings will not be the beta calculated from the past returns of different holdings. The beta measured will not be the beta for the current portfolio.

The first bias is discussed in some depth in Appendix 8A, and, as it turns out, there is no totally satisfactory resolution to the problem. The second bias, however, is easily overcome.

The beta of a portfolio is a weighted average of the betas on the securities which make up the portfolio:[5]

Portfolio Beta
$$\beta_p = \sum_{i=1}^{N} \beta_i X_i \qquad (8.13)$$

For example, the beta of a portfolio consisting of the following securities is 1.0:

Security	X_i	β_i	Product
A	0.25	1.5	0.375
B	0.25	1.0	0.250
C	0.25	1.2	0.300
D	0.25	0.3	0.075
			1.000

The bias in a beta estimate that may arise if a portfolio's composition has changed over time can be easily overcome if the beta on each constituent security is estimated and then averaged.

POTENTIAL USES OF THE CAPM

The theory we have been discussing is the classic version of what is known as the theory of capital asset pricing, or the capital asset pricing model (CAPM). In Chapter 9, extensions are made to it which remove its various assumptions. But now is an ap-

---

[5]Remember, this is not true of the portfolio's standard deviation. The fact that σ_p is not a weighted average of all σ_i drives all the discussion of Chapters 7 through 9.

propriate time to review some of its implications and see how they might be used in practice. Three major topics are examined:

1. Analysis of security *pricing*
2. Development of an ideal investment *strategy*
3. Evaluation of a portfolio's *performance*

Pricing

Our discussion of the capital asset pricing model has said very little so far about prices. The discussion has revolved almost completely around risk and expected returns. It didn't have to—we could have developed an equilibrium model of prices which parallels our model of risk and return. Concentrating on risk and expected return was simply a convenient way to approach the problem. Nonetheless, it is a security's price which is transacted in the markets and which determines whether speculative opportunities exist.

The equilibrium price should provide no opportunity for speculative profits. It should be set at such a level that *expected returns from buying the security are identical to those available on an efficient portfolio of equivalent nondiversifiable risk.* For example, if $RF = 10\%$, $RP_M = 6\%$, and the beta of a stock $= 0.7$, then the stock should be priced to provide an expected return of 14.2%:

$$E(R_i) = RF + \beta_i(RP_M)$$

$$14.2\% = 10.0\% + 0.7\ (6.0\%)$$

If this security is trading at a price lower than equilibrium, then a speculative profit is possible and excess demand will exist until the price is forced up to equilibrium. If the security is trading at a higher than equilibrium price, speculators will sell (short sell if there are no restrictions on doing so) until the price is at equilibrium. In short, expected return from owning the security should be:

**Equilibrium
Required Return** $$E(R_i) = RF + \beta_i(RP_M) \tag{8.14}$$

The return which will actually be earned consists of any increases (or decreases) in the security's price plus any cash payoff, such as dividends on a stock or coupons on a bond. In the case of a stock:

**Actual Security
Return** $$R_{i1} = \frac{P_{i1} - P_{i0} + D_{i1}}{P_{i0}} \tag{8.15}$$

where: P_{i1} = price of security i at the end of period 1

P_{i0} = price of i at the beginning of period 1

D_{i1} = dividends received during period 1

For the security to be priced at equilibrium, the expected outcome of Equation 8.15 should be equal to the fair return expressed in Equation 8.14:

Equilibrium Required Return = Expected Security Return

**Equilibrium
Market
Returns**

$$RF + \beta_i(RP_M) = \frac{E(P_{i1}) - P_{i0} + E(D_{i1})}{P_{i0}} \qquad (8.16)$$

Rearranging this quite logical statement and letting P_{i0}^* represent the equilibrium price of i, we see that this equilibrium price is simply the present value of the expected end-of-period price and dividend discount at a return appropriate for its level of non-diversifiable risk:

**Equilibrium
Security Price**

$$P_{i0}^* = \frac{E(P_{i1}) + E(D_{i1})}{1.0 + RF + \beta_i(RP_M)} \qquad (8.17)$$

For example, let's compute the equilibrium price of Exxon stock given the following data:

$$RP_M = 6\% \qquad \beta_X = 0.5 \qquad E(P_{X1}) = \$52.70$$

$$RF = 10\% \qquad E(D_X) = \$\ 3.80$$

According to the SML, one should expect a 13.0% return on any investment in a security having the amount of nondiversifiable risk present in Exxon shares:

$$10.0\% + 0.5\ (6.0\%) = 13.0\%$$

Since the expected price at the end of the period (say, one year) is $52.70 and the expected dividend is $3.80, the equilibrium price must be $50.00:

$$\frac{\$52.70 + \$3.80}{1.13} = \$50.00$$

The equilibrium pricing formula stated in Equation 8.17 strictly applies to a single-period world that meets all the assumptions made at the start of the chapter. There is no warranty on its validity when it is used in other situations. In practice, however, the principal features of the model are used widely. Security analysts forecast expected future dividends and prices on a stock and discount them to the present using a discount rate generated from the SML. A detailed illustration of how this is done is delayed to Chapter 22, where we have the opportunity to explore the process of security analysis in some depth.

Strategy

The implications for portfolio strategy which arise from the CAPM are quite reasonable and, even if not *strictly* true, they provide clear guidance. At the center of this theory is the market portfolio. It is *the* single optimal portfolio of risky assets—the only portfolio of risky assets that should be held. In theory, this makes sense; in practice, it is impossible to achieve. But even if the market portfolio cannot actually be held, one should not discard the principle of broad diversification. For example, an easy way to own 100 to 200 stocks with a very small equity investment is to purchase three or four mutual funds which hold distinctly different types of stocks. In addition, holdings such as real estate and international securities represent major asset classes which are too often neglected.

The optimal investment in a security depends upon the market value of that security relative to the market value of all securities. For example, if IBM's common stock represents 4.37% of all U.S. equity value, then 4.37% of an individual's U.S. common stock portfolio should be in IBM. Again, this principle is difficult to carry out in practice. However, index funds are designed to be identical to various broad stock indexes (such as the S&P 500). As such, they represent a good way to obtain proper weightings. But even well-run index funds are unable to maintain precisely the same percentages in the fund as in the index. Differences are small, but they do exist. Barring the use of such an index fund, some reasonable relationship between the total value of an issue and its weighting in the portfolio should be maintained. An investor certainly shouldn't place twice as much of his or her money in a small computer firm such as Storage Technology as in a massive firm such as IBM. In such a case much potential for diversification would be lost.

After a portfolio is broadly diversified (even if not in M), one can adjust the borrowing-lending mix to achieve a preferred risk/return level. Lending portfolios can be created by purchasing U.S. Treasury securities, and borrowing portfolios can be created by using margin. As we will see in Chapters 15 through 17, options and financial futures also provide a number of ways to alter a portfolio's risk level and move along the borrowing-lending line. Finally, we should always remember that greater expected returns come only with greater uncertainty.

Performance Evaluation

Concepts of the CAPM have been increasingly used by investors and speculators to evaluate the performance of one style of management against others. In fact, a number of investment-counseling services offer services which provide comparisons of performance based in large measure on the CAPM.[6] Although these performance measures are typically used to evaluate the risk/return performance of large investment firms, such as mutual funds, bank trust departments, and pension funds, they could also be used by individuals to measure their personal performance, to evaluate the buy-sell selections of security analysts, etc. Three basic performance models have been suggested to date: (1) the Sharpe model, (2) the Treynor model, and (3) the Jensen model.

---

[6]Among the better-known performance services are those offered by SEI, Merrill Lynch, Shearson Lehman Hutton, Wilshire Associates, and Frank Russell Company.

The Sharpe Performance Index. Using the concepts of the capital market line, Sharpe suggested that historical performance be calculated as "the return earned for bearing risk per unit of *total* risk." Symbolically, the Sharpe index (referred to as S_p) is calculated as follows:

Sharpe Performance Index

$$S_p = \frac{\bar{R}_p - \overline{RF}}{\sigma_p} \qquad (8.18)$$

The return for bearing risk is shown in the numerator as the average portfolio return, $\bar{R}_p$, minus the average risk-free rate $\overline{RF}$. Total risk (both diversifiable and nondiversifiable) is measured in the denominator by the standard deviation of past portfolio returns (σ_p). For example, Table 8-2 presents the historical returns earned by a hypothetical mutual fund. The Sharpe index for the sample fund would be:

$$\frac{4.00\% - 2.29\%}{11.23\%} = 0.152$$

TABLE 8-2 *Sample Fund Data*

Period*	Beginning T-Bill Rate†	Return on Fund‡	Excess Fund Return	Return on S&P 500	Excess S&P 500 Return
1	2.0%	18.0%	16.0%	17.0%	15.0%
2	2.0	9.0	7.0	12.0	10.0
3	3.0	12.0	9.0	10.0	7.0
4	3.5	(15.0)	(18.5)	(16.0)	(19.5)
5	3.0	(5.0)	(8.0)	(4.0)	(7.0)
6	3.0	12.0	9.0	14.0	11.0
7	2.0	20.0	18.0	16.0	14.0
8	1.5	(10.0)	(11.5)	(8.0)	(9.5)
9	1.5	(8.0)	(9.5)	(5.0)	(6.5)
10	2.0	2.0	0.0	(2.0)	(4.0)
11	2.0	(1.0)	(3.0)	1.0	(1.0)
12	2.0	14.0	12.0	13.0	11.0
Average	2.29%	4.00%	1.71%	4.00%	1.71%
σ	0.63%	11.23%	11.32%	10.52%	10.63%
$r_{FM} = 0.97$		Alpha = −0.07			

$$\text{Beta on Fund} = \left(\frac{11.32}{10.63}\right)0.97 = 1.03$$

$$\text{Beta on S\&P} = 1.0$$

*Each period is assumed to be three months in length.
†Stated in terms of a quarterly rate; e.g., if the annual rate is 8.24%, the quarterly rate is 2% since 1.02^4 equals 1.0824.
‡Calculated as the change in the net asset value plus all dividend receipts divided by net asset value at the beginning of the period.

The Sharpe performance index for the mutual fund should be compared with that of other funds as well as that of the aggregate market. The larger a particular fund's Sharpe index relative to the market and other funds, the better its performance. Again using Table 8-2 data, the Sharpe index for the S&P 500 stocks would be 0.163 [(4.00 − 2.29) ÷ 10.52], suggesting that the illustrated fund performed slightly worse than an unmanaged portfolio of all S&P 500 stocks. A given value of the Sharpe index is meaningless by itself. It must be related to other funds and to the aggregate market.

The Treynor Performance Index. Treynor chose to treat only the nondiversifiable market risk of an investment and developed the following performance index (referred to as T_p):

Treynor Performance Index
$$T_p = \frac{\bar{R}_p - \bar{RF}}{\beta_p}$$
(8.19)

The Treynor index treats only that portion of a portfolio's (or a security's) historical risk which is important to investors as estimated by β_p and neglects any diversifiable risk. As such it is a general performance measure which can be used regardless of any other securities an investor might own or the extent of diversification in the portfolio being evaluated. This nondiversifiable past risk is measured as β_p, the historical beta of the investment's returns. Like S_p, T_p is a relative measure and must be compared with the values of other funds as well as the aggregate market in order to determine how well an investment actually fared. Using Table 8-2 data, the sample fund had a Treynor index value of:

$$\frac{4.00\% - 2.29\%}{1.03} = 1.66\%$$

compared with a market performance of:

$$\frac{4.00\% - 2.29\%}{1.0} = 1.71\%$$

The fund was able to provide a 1.66% quarterly rate of return per unit of beta, whereas the market portfolio provided 1.71%.[7]

Performance rankings obtained by the Sharpe and Treynor indexes are usually very similar. When they differ, it is because some funds are not perfectly diversified. To see this, recall that beta is measured as:

$$\beta_p = \frac{\sigma_p}{\sigma_m} r_{pm}$$

where r_{pm} is the historical correlation coefficient between the portfolio and market returns. Thus we could restate the Treynor index as:

[7]The beta in this example was calculated on "excess returns," i.e., returns above the T-bill return.

$$T_p = \frac{(\bar{R}_p - \bar{RF})}{\sigma_p} \left(\frac{\sigma_m}{r_{pm}} \right)$$

$$= \left(\frac{\text{Sharpe}}{\text{Index}} \right) \left(\frac{\sigma_m}{r_{pm}} \right)$$

The Treynor index is equal to the Sharpe index multiplied by the standard deviation of market returns and divided by the correlation coefficient. If investments being evaluated are *perfectly diversified* ($r_{pm} = 1.0$), the Treynor index is equal to the Sharpe index multiplied by the market's standard deviation (a constant), and rankings obtained using either approach will be identical. If investments being evaluated *aren't perfectly diversified* ($r_{pm} < 1.0$), performance rankings using S_p might be different from those using T_p.

Which of the two measures is the better? This depends on the nature of the investments being evaluated. If the investments being evaluated represent *all* of an individual's security portfolio, the Sharpe measure is probably more meaningful. In this case the total risk (both systematic and unsystematic) of the investments is the *same* as the risk being borne by the individual. However, if the investments being evaluated represent only a fraction of the individual's security portfolio, the Treynor measure might be more appropriate. In this case only the *nondiversifiable*, systematic risks of the investments represent risk to the owner.

The Jensen Performance Index. Like Treynor, Jensen relied directly on the CAPM to develop an estimate of investment performance. However, unlike Treynor's *relative* measure of performance, Jensen's *alpha* is an absolute measure which estimates the constant periodic return which an investment was able to earn above (or below) a buy-hold strategy with equal systematic risk.

Jensen begins with the one-period security market line, which states that the expected return on an investment during period t is equal to the prevailing risk-free rate plus a risk premium (equal to the portfolio's beta multiplied by the market risk premium). That is:

SML for a Portfolio
$$E(R_{pt}) = RF_t + \beta_p[E(R_{mt}) - RF_t] \qquad (8.20)$$

As long as investors aren't fooled into consistently over- or underestimating realized returns, the historical counterpart to this expectational model would be:

Market Model for a Portfolio
$$\tilde{R}_{pt} = R\tilde{F}_t + \beta_p[\tilde{R}_{mt} - R\tilde{F}_t] + \tilde{E}_{pt} \qquad (8.21)$$

Each of the returns in Equation 8.21 is an actual realized return during some time interval—say, a month, a quarter, or a year. The value of β_p is the historical estimate of beta and is assumed to remain constant during the time period being examined. The term $(\tilde{R}_{mt} - R\tilde{F}_t)$ represents the earned risk premium on the market portfolio during period t and can, of course, be negative. Finally, the $\tilde{E}_{pt}$ term reflects portfolio returns which are unrelated to market returns. The more completely diversified a portfolio, the smaller the nonmarket-related returns in any period.

Jensen then expresses Equation 8.21 in excess-return form by subtracting RF_t from both sides. This allows him to concentrate upon returns earned solely for bearing risk and results in Equation 8.22:

Excess Return Regression in Equilibrium

$$(\tilde{R}_{pt} - R\tilde{F}_t) = \beta_p[\tilde{R}_{mt} - R\tilde{F}_t] + \tilde{E}_{pt} \qquad \textbf{(8.22)}$$

If the CAPM is correct and speculators neither win nor lose in their efforts to find mispriced securities and call market turns, then Equation 8.22 will describe the return series on *all* security holdings. However, if some speculators consistently win and others consistently lose, portfolio returns would be better described as follows:

Jensen's Alpha

$$(\tilde{R}_{pt} - R\tilde{F}_t) = \alpha_p + \beta_p[\tilde{R}_{mt} - R\tilde{F}_t] + \tilde{E}_{pt} \qquad \textbf{(8.23)}$$

In this model the portfolio alpha, α_p, represents the constant periodic return which the portfolio manager is able to earn above (or below, if negative) an unmanaged portfolio having identical market risk. Jensen suggested that statistical regression procedures could be used to estimate α_p and β_p values in Equation 8.23. If the estimated alpha values were positive and statistically significant, the fund would have outperformed a passive buy-hold strategy. If the alpha values were negative and statistically significant, the fund would have underperformed a buy-hold strategy.

To understand how the Jensen approach works, consider the hypothetical-return diagram in Figure 8-8. Excess returns are plotted for three mutual funds (A, B, and C) against corresponding excess returns on the market. Assume that when these returns are used to estimate the regression in Equation 8.23 we find:

$$\text{Fund } A: \quad (\tilde{R}_{At} - R\tilde{F}_t) = -2.0\% + 1.0(\tilde{R}_{mt} - R\tilde{F}_t)$$
$$(3.0\%) \ (0.2)$$
$$\text{Fund } B: \quad (\tilde{R}_{Bt} - R\tilde{F}_t) = +4.0\% + 1.2(\tilde{R}_{mt} - R\tilde{F}_t)$$
$$(1.0\%) \ (0.1)$$
$$\text{Fund } C: \quad (\tilde{R}_{Ct} - R\tilde{F}_t) = -3.0\% + 0.5(\tilde{R}_{mt} - R\tilde{F}_t)$$
$$(1.0\%) \ (0.1)$$

Note: Values below the regression parameters represent standard deviations of each term.

Each of the funds had different systematic risk levels. Fund B had the highest systematic risk, with a beta of 1.2, and fund C had the lowest. Extracting the effects which each fund's systematic risk had upon its periodic excess returns, we are left with alpha—the constant rate of return. Alpha for fund A is a negative 2.0%. But the standard deviation of 3% implies that this estimate of fund A's alpha is not statistically different from zero.[8] Fund A has provided a set of returns with risk and return characteristics similar to those from buying and holding an unmanaged portfolio with a beta of 1.0. Fund B, on the other hand, has a statistically significant and positive alpha. Exclusive of its systematic risk, fund B has been able to provide a constant peri-

FIGURE 8-8 *Illustration of Jensen's Alpha*

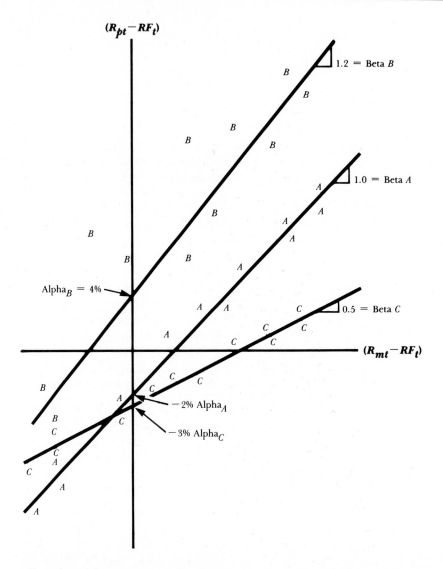

odic return 4.0 percentage points higher than available from an unchanged portfolio. It has outperformed the market. Finally, fund *C* has a significant and negative alpha. Adjusting for its risk, we find that fund *C* has underperformed the unmanaged portfolio by 3% per period.[8]

---

[8]Throughout the book we will use 1.96 standard deviations away from zero (or some other hypothesized value) as our criterion of statistical significance. This is common practice and involves a confidence level of 95%.

The Jensen and Treynor measures can be shown to be virtually identical, each approaching performance measurement from a slightly different angle. The advantages of the Jensen index are twofold. First, it yields an absolute performance measure which is easy to interpret (e.g., a constant periodic excess return of 4.0 percentage points better than an unmanaged portfolio). Second, the performance measure can be determined to be statistically significant or insignificant. We will discuss these and other performance measures further in Chapter 23.

SUMMARY

For the security market to be in a state of equilibrium, prices must be at levels which induce no speculative trading—the demand by investors to buy exactly equals the supply by other investors. If this is true, investors and potential speculators have *homogeneous expectations* of the future. The purpose of this chapter was to examine how securities would be priced under such equilibrium conditions. However, to develop a manageable model of equilibrium, a variety of assumptions had to be made. First, we assumed a *one-period world* in which risk-averse individuals could determine the expected end-of-period utility by knowing the *expected return and standard deviation of portfolio returns*. Next, we assumed a *frictionless market*, a market in which brokerage fees, taxes, etc., would not impede trading. Finally, we assumed that all individuals could borrow or lend at a *risk-free rate*.

The model which results from these assumptions is known as the *capital asset pricing model*. Embodied in this model are two fundamental economic relationships: (1) the CML, which specifies what the expected return on an *efficient portfolio* should be in terms of the portfolio's standard deviation, and (2) the SML, which specifies what the expected return on any *security or portfolio* should be in terms of its *nondiversifiable risk*. The single efficient portfolio of risky assets which drives the CML and the SML is the *market portfolio*, a portfolio consisting of all risky assets available, with each held in proportion to its total market value.

Under the CAPM's assumptions, this is a perfectly reasonable outcome. The market portfolio is the *most widely diversified portfolio available*. Any other portfolio will suffer in comparison because the risk it contains could be eliminated simply by costless diversification. If the diversification across an additional security reduces the return, the return can be restored by borrowing at *RF*. As first discussed in Chapter 7, the selection of the best risky portfolio is separate from the selection of an appropriate risk/reward level. First, diversify as broadly as possible (buy the market portfolio). Then borrow or lend at *RF* to achieve the risk/return preference of the individual investor.

The CML and SML have gained wide use within the professional investment community. Security analysts use the theory in *pricing* stocks, portfolio managers develop proper portfolio *strategies* around its principles, and consultants use it to evaluate a portfolio's performance. Most such pragmatic applications require estimates of a security's beta. Obtaining such beta estimates is discussed in Appendix 8A.

REVIEW PROBLEM #1

As a financial consultant to a pension fund, you are preparing a presentation on the various aspects of the theory of risk and expected return discussed in this chapter. The following questions review certain major features of this theory.

a. What is meant by market equilibrium and what assumptions are used in its development?

b. Assume there are three major classes of risky securities available, as follows:

Security Class	Total Market	σ	RE	E	D	Total
				Correlation with		
Real Estate	$10,000	20%	1.0			0.65
Equity	6,000	30%	0.3	1.0		0.60
Debt	4,000	15%	0.3	0.3	1.0	0.30

What is the market portfolio? How much of its risky assets should the pension invest in each security type? What is the σ of such a portfolio?

c. If $RF = 8.0\%$ and $RP_M = 5.0\%$, what are the CML and SML equations?

d. One member of the pension fund's board of trustees has stated that their investment portfolio should have a long-run expected return of 12%. In theory, how would this be obtained?

e. An assistant believes that the beta of Textron common stock is 1.2. What should Textron stock be expected to earn to qualify for a purchase?

f. The local representative of a common stock mutual fund has been pressing the pension fund's trustees to invest solely in the fund. One reason which the representative offers is that the fund has a beta of 1.0 and thus its risk is the same as the market portfolio's risk. Comment.

Solution

a. The security market is in equilibrium if prices are at levels which attract no speculative trading. In this case people have common beliefs about the future. Assumptions used in the model are the following:

(1) We live in a one-period world.
(2) $E(R_p)$ and σ_p are all that matter.
(3) Everyone may borrow or lend at RF.
(4) All investors have homogeneous expectations.
(5) Markets are frictionless.

b. Given these assumptions, and for the markets to clear, the optimal market portfolio is:

Security	X^*
Real Estate	0.50
Equity	0.30
Debt	0.20

$$\sigma_p = [(0.5)^2(20)^2 + (0.3)^2(30)^2 + (0.2)^2(15)^2 + 2(0.3)(0.5)(0.3)(20)(30)$$
$$+ 2(0.3)(0.5)(0.2)(20)(15) + 2(0.3)(0.3)(0.2)(30)(15)]^{1/2}$$
$$= 16.7\%$$

c. CML equation:

$$E(R_p) = 8.0\% + \sigma_p \left(\frac{5.0\%}{16.7\%} \right)$$

SML equation:

$$E(R_i) = 8.0\% + \beta_i [5.0\%]$$

d. For each σ_p of an efficient portfolio, a return of 0.3% is earned above the 8% risk-free rate. Thus, to have an expected return of 12.0%, σ_p must be $(12 - 8) \div 0.3$, or 13.33%:

$$8.0\% + 13.33\% \ [0.30] = 12.0\%$$

Efficient portfolios would be combinations of portfolio M and RF. To get a $\sigma_p = 13.33\%$ when $\sigma_M = 16.7\%$, they should invest 80% of the portfolio in the market portfolio:

$$\frac{13.33}{16.7} = 0.80$$

The remaining 20% would be placed in risk-free securities.

e. $E(R_T) = 8.0\% + 1.2 \ [5.0\%]$ (the SML)

$\qquad = 14.0\%$

f. The mutual fund's beta may be 1.0, but this only says that the fund has nondiversifiable (systematic) risk identical to that of the market portfolio. However, unless the mutual fund's percentages of holdings are identical to the percentage weights of the market portfolio, the fund still has some diversifiable (unsystematic) risk and should not be held as the pension's only investment.

REVIEW PROBLEM #2

On page 294 is a plot of expected returns and standard deviations of four securities. Point M represents the market portfolio. Points X, Y, and Z can be thought of as individual securities or portfolios of securities.

a. Does a risk/return diagram such as this one imply that the security markets are in equilibrium or disequilibrium according to CAPM?

b. Write the CML and SML equations underlying this diagram.

c. What are the betas of each security?

d. What is the beta of a portfolio consisting of a 1/3 investment in X, Y, and Z? What should be the expected return on this portfolio?

e. Stocks Y and Z are equally risky since they have the same standard deviation. True or false? Why?

f. Another security not shown here is stock A. It has a beta of 0.7 and an expected return of 8.0%. Would you buy or short sell this stock? Is the market in equilibrium? If not, how would equilibrium be achieved?

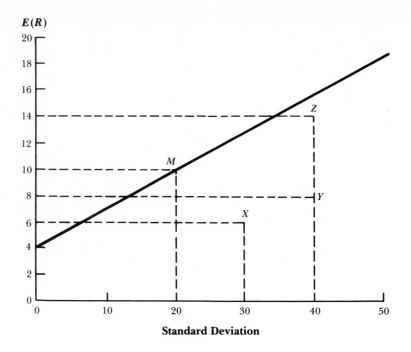

Standard Deviation

Solution

a. The diagram implies a CAPM equilibrium since no security "beats" the market portfolio.

b. CML: $E(R_p) = 4\% + \sigma_p \left(\dfrac{10\% - 4\%}{20} \right)$

   SML: $E(R_i) = 4\% + \beta_i (10\% - 4\%)$

c.

Security	Beta	Calculation
X	0.3333	$6 = 4 + \beta_X (6)$
Y	0.6666	$8 = 4 + \beta_Y (6)$
Z	1.6666	$14 = 4 + \beta_Z (6)$

d. $\beta_p = 1/3\ (0.33) + 1/3\ (0.66) + 1/3\ (1.66)$

   $= 0.888$

$E(R_p) = 4\% + 0.888\ (6\%)$

   $= 9.3\%$

e. False. Z is riskier as evidenced by the higher expected return, which implies a larger beta.

f. The expected return which you should require is 8.2%:

$$E(R_i) = 4\% + 0.7\ (6\%)$$

$$= 8.2\%$$

Since it is priced to return only 8.0%, the stock should be "underweighted" or perhaps even sold short. Eventually its price will fall as you and others sell until an 8.2% return is actually expected.

QUESTIONS AND PROBLEMS

1. If the correlation coefficient between the returns on a portfolio and the market portfolio is 1.0, this is an efficient portfolio. True or false? Why?

2. A broadly diversified portfolio of commodities (corn, tin, gold, comic books, etc.) has a zero correlation with the market portfolio. It will therefore provide a return equal to the risk-free rate. True or false? Why?

3. In equilibrium, all investors have homogeneous expectations. What does this mean and why is it a necessary condition for equilibrium?

4. How would an index fund help an investor to purchase the market portfolio?

5. After a thorough analysis of both the aggregate stock market and the stock of XYZ, Inc., you develop the following opinions:

Economic Conditions	Likely Return		Probability
	Aggregate Market	XYZ	
Good	16%	20%	0.4
Fair	12%	13%	0.4
Poor	3%	-5%	0.2

At present the risk-free rate is equal to 7%. Would an investment in XYZ be wise?

6. Assume that the risk-free rate of interest is 8%, the market has an estimated risk premium of 6%, and the market's standard deviation of returns is 10%. Calculate the variance (or standard deviation) of returns for each portfolio below.
   Portfolio 1: 30% risk-free bonds, 70% the market
   Portfolio 2: diversified portfolio with beta = 1.5

7. The policy committee of Investor's Diversified Corporation (IDC) recently used reports from various security analysts to develop inputs for the single-index model. Output derived from the single-index model consisted of the following efficient portfolios:

Portfolio	Expected Return	Standard Deviation
1	8%	3%
2	10%	6%
3	13%	8%
4	17%	13%
5	20%	18%

   a. If the prevailing risk-free rate is 6%, which portfolio is the best?

   b. Assume that the policy committee would like to earn an expected 10% with a standard deviation of 4%. Is this feasible?

   c. If a standard deviation of 12% were acceptable, what would the expected portfolio return be and how would IDC achieve it?

8. Consider the following information on three securities. Which has the greatest systematic risk? Which has the smallest?

Security	σ_i	r_{iM}
1	σ_1	r_{1M}
2	$\sigma_2 = \sigma_1$	$r_{2M} > r_{1M}$
3	$\sigma_3 > \sigma_1$	$r_{3M} = r_{1M}$

9. You expect the stock of Firm X to sell for $70 a year from now and to pay a $4 dividend. If the stock's correlation with portfolio M is -0.3, $\sigma_X = 40.0\%$, $\sigma_M = 20.0\%$, $RF = 5\%$, and $RP_M = 5.0\%$, what should the stock be selling for? Explain this result.

10. Note: This question requires knowledge of Appendix 8A. Using five years of monthly returns, the following regression statistics were generated using the market model and a broad common stock index:

Security	A_i	σ_i	r_{il}
Mesa Petroleum	−0.21	14.7%	0.48
Anheuser-Busch	0.15	6.3%	0.25
Teledyne	0.01	11.3%	0.51
XYZ Mutual Fund	0.20	5.2%	0.95
Index	0.00	4.3%	1.00

a. Calculate an estimate of β for each.
b. Do you think the market model betas during the next five-year period will be the same, higher, or lower?
c. Assuming that the index used is the market portfolio, that $RP_M = 7.0\%$, and that $RF = 9.0\%$, calculate the equilibrium expected return on each.
d. Assume that each security is the only holding of the portfolio. Calculate required expected returns and explain why these are not the same as the answer to part c.
e. Calculate the beta of a portfolio consisting of an equal investment in each stock.

11. Note: This question requires knowledge of Appendix 8A. You are given the following estimates of stock i's and stock j's characteristic lines plus estimates of each stock's standard deviation of returns:

$$(\tilde{R}_{it} - R\tilde{F}_t) = 1\% + 1.5\ (\tilde{R}_{Mt} - R\tilde{F}_t)$$

$$(\tilde{R}_{jt} - R\tilde{F}_t) = 4\% + 1.0\ (\tilde{R}_{Mt} - R\tilde{F}_t)$$

$$\sigma(\tilde{R}_{it} - R\tilde{F}_t) = 20\%;\ \sigma(\tilde{R}_{jt} - R\tilde{F}_t) = 10\%$$

a. One-year T-bills are now yielding 8%. If the market portfolio is *expected* to return 13% during the year, what is the expected return on each stock as of the beginning of the year?
b. The year goes by and the market portfolio *actually* provides a 10% rate of return during the year. Given this, what is your expectation of the return earned on each stock during the year?
c. If stock i actually returned 15% and stock j actually returned 11%, what was the residual error return for each stock?
d. Why might a residual error return arise, and what is its role in diversification?
e. If the standard deviation of stock i's residual error term is 10%, what is your best estimate of the standard deviation of excess returns—i.e., $\sigma(\tilde{R}_{Mt} - R\tilde{F}_t)$—on the market portfolio?

12. Management of a mutual fund has considered three alternative strategies:

Plan	% Investment in		T-Bonds	Beta of Stocks	Portfolio
	T-Bonds	Stocks			
1	0.0	100	0	1.0	?
2	20	80	0	1.0	?
3	30	70	0	1.0	?

a. Which is the most risky strategy?

b. If $RF = 7\%$ and the expected return under plan 1 is 14%, what is the market risk premium?

c. Management believes that this risk premium is too low and that the market will soon adjust it upward. Given this, which plan might management wish to pursue?

d. Would this be a speculative or an investment strategy?

13. Suppose you have gathered quarterly data on the net returns of four mutual funds and related them to equivalent market returns (S&P 500) and 90-day T-bill returns via the following regression model:

$$(\tilde{R}_{pt} - R\tilde{F}_t) = \alpha_p + \beta_p(\tilde{R}_{mt} - R\tilde{F}_t) + \tilde{E}_{pt}$$

	α_p		β_p			Std. Dev.
Fund	Coefficient	Std. Dev.	Coefficient	Std. Dev.	R^2	E_{pt}
1	0.98%	1.00%	0.80	0.05	95%	12%
2	2.18%	1.50%	1.30	0.15	80%	23%
3	2.18%	0.75%	1.20	0.12	90%	18%
4	−0.04%	0.50%	1.02	0.08	97%	14.4%

a. Which fund's returns were the most closely correlated to market returns?

b. Which fund had the most market risk?

c. Which fund had the most total risk?

d. Rank these funds in terms of the Jensen performance measure.

e. Which funds statistically outperformed or underperformed the market? Use 95% confidence levels.

f. Restate the alpha values in terms of their annualized equivalents.

14. Note: This question requires knowledge of Appendix 8A. The table below provides two years of monthly returns on Campbell Soup, Teledyne, the DFA Small Company Portfolio, and the Wilshire 5000 Common Stock Index. Use the Wilshire 5000 as the market index.

Period	Campbell	Tele	DFA	W5000	Period	Campbell	Tele	DFA	W5000
1	−1.9	14.6	6.3	4.2	13	4.2	1.7	−0.1	−1.6
2	−4.8	4.6	7.1	3.2	14	−6.1	−3.5	−6.5	−3.9
3	4.5	−5.5	5.2	3.6	15	2.7	1.5	1.7	1.4
4	−2.3	−1.3	7.7	7.4	16	0.5	−6.6	−0.1	0.3
5	8.3	4.4	8.7	1.3	17	−7.0	29.7	−5.2	−5.3
6	4.6	7.9	3.5	3.9	18	11.1	19.1	3.0	2.4
7	−1.4	−2.1	−0.9	−3.2	19	−2.5	8.0	−4.2	−1.9
8	8.0	−1.6	−2.0	0.6	20	3.1	6.8	10.0	11.3
9	0.9	2.9	1.3	1.6	21	9.2	2.6	0.3	0.6
10	7.2	0.1	−5.7	−2.6	22	3.4	−3.5	−2.2	0.0
11	2.3	0.8	5.2	2.8	23	−2.5	−4.1	−3.4	−1.1
12	3.4	2.5	−1.4	−1.1	24	2.2	−6.7	1.5	2.4

a. Use the market model to estimate the A_i and b_i terms.

b. Notice that DFA tracks the W5000 much more closely than do the two stocks. Why?

c. Estimate the systematic and unsystematic risk of each.
    (Hint: $\sigma_i^2 = \beta_i^2 \sigma_1^2 + \sigma_E^2$)

d. If $RF = 11\%$ and $RP_M = 6\%$, estimate the equilibrium expected returns on each.

e. Assume that the W5000 is a good estimate of the market portfolio. If each of these securities were to be held as the only risky asset in a portfolio, calculate the return which should be expected. Why does this differ from the estimated returns in part d?

f. Why is the Wilshire 5000 not a good representation of the market portfolio?

DATA ANALYSIS PROBLEM

Objective:

- To calculate estimated betas using the market model described in Appendix 8A

1. Access the QTLYSTK.WK1 data set. Since this problem does not use stock prices or dividends you might wish to delete them temporarily. (Be careful not to save the altered data set under the name QTLYSTK.WK1 or you will lose the price and dividend data.)

2. Use the regression feature of your spreadsheet program to run market model regressions for each stock. Use the S&P 500 returns as the proxy for the market portfolio.

3. In a blank column to the right of the stock returns data, calculate the quarterly returns on an equally weighted portfolio of all the stocks. Find the market model beta estimate of this portfolio and compare it with the average of the individual stock betas.

APPENDIX 8A: ESTIMATING BETA

In theory, beta represents the nondiversifiable, systematic risk of an individual security or portfolio of securities. It reflects a risk for which a return should be expected. Theory treats it as a subjective estimate made by each individual of what the future might hold. It is, indeed, an *ex ante* opinion of likely systematic risk during the next period of time.

In practice, it is rare that subjective statements of beta are made. Instead, estimates based on historical returns are used. In this section, we examine how these historical estimates of the true beta are prepared. Since the techniques provide only estimates of the true beta, we must be careful to differentiate between the two. Theoretical beta will continue to be represented as β_i. Estimates of β_i will be represented as b_i.

When we move from the theoretical concept of β_i to a real-world estimate, we encounter a variety of very serious problems. For example, the world simply does not consist of one period. Should beta be estimated over a time period that consists of the past month, the past five years, or the past twenty years? Should beta be estimated using daily, weekly, monthly, quarterly, etc., returns? How should changes in the product line of a firm be factored in? How does one estimate the

beta of a bond whose life is continually changing and thus will be less sensitive to systematic economic shocks?

The list of problems associated with estimates of β_i based on historical data is long. And many of these problems remain unresolved. Yet β_i values are commonplace today and the techniques used to develop them should be understood.

The Market Model

The market model (MM) is an *equation* which relates the return on security i during time period t to the return on some index during the same time period. The market model equation is written as:

Market Model $\tilde{R}_{it} = A_i + b_i(\tilde{R}_{It}) + \tilde{E}_{it}$ **(8A.1)**

$\tilde{R}_{it}$ represents the volatile return (hence the tilde) on security i during period t. It is equal to the sum of three components. First, a constant return is earned in each period regardless of the return on the index. This is A_i, referred to as *alpha*. Next, the security is said to have a sensitivity to the return on the index during

FIGURE 8A-1 *The Market Model*

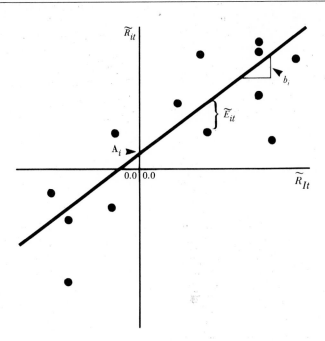

that period. The index return is denoted as $\tilde{R}_{It}$, and the sensitivity of security i to the index is b_i. (This, of course, is the estimate of β_i.) Finally, there is a difference between what the actual return on security i is and what the first two terms suggest the return should have been. This difference is the error term, $\tilde{E}_{it}$.

Figure 8A-1 is a graphical representation of this market model. When the index has a zero return, the security is expected to have a rate of return of A_i (on average). As the index has a positive or negative return, the extent to which security i tends to share in this return depends on the slope of the line—b_i. During any period of time, however, the security's return might not be exactly equal to the constant A_i plus its sensitivity (b_i) times the index return $(\tilde{R}_{It})$. Events that have no effect on the index return might have an effect on the security's return. On average, the A_i and b_i times $\tilde{R}_{It}$ will capture the *security's return*, but errors will occur. These errors are the $\tilde{E}_{it}$ values.

For example, assume that you are given the following market model data on IBM for a recent calendar quarter:

$$A_{IBM} = 2.0\% \qquad R_{IBM,t} = 12.0\%$$

$$b_{IBM} = 0.7\% \qquad R_{I,t} = 10.0\%$$

The data are displayed in Figure 8A-2. If the index had a return of 0.0%, the expected return on IBM would be 2.0%. However, the index had a 10.0% return. The b_{IBM} of 0.7 indicates that a 10% index return is *expected* to result in a 7.0% return on IBM above the constant 2.0%. Adding the 2.0% and 7.0% results in an *expected return of 9.0%*. However, IBM's actual return was 12%. The difference between the actual 12.0% and the expected 9.0% is the error during this time period—3.0%. On average, these error terms will be zero because of the way in which A_i and b_i are statistically estimated.

The Market Model Versus the SML. Compare the market model (Equation 8A.1) and the security market line (from Equation 8.11b):

Market Model	$\tilde{R}_{it} = A_i + b_i(\tilde{R}_{It}) + \tilde{E}_{it}$	**(8A.1 above)**
Security Market Line	$E(R_i) = RF + \beta_i(RP_M)$	**(8.11b above)**

They look suspiciously similar—obviously not a coincidence since b_i is intended to be an estimate of β_i.

FIGURE 8A-2 *Sample Market Model for IBM*

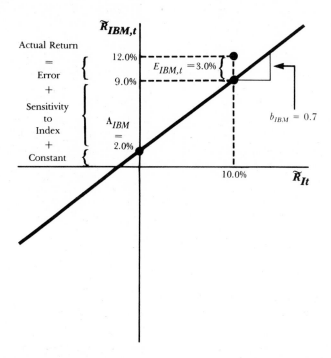

But are they the same? The answer is maybe. There are two principal differences between them—(1) alpha in the MM versus the risk-free rate in the SML and (2) the index in the MM versus the market portfolio in the SML.

We can see these differences more clearly if we restate the SML in a way which has β_i multiplied by the $E(R_M)$:

Restatement of SML

$$E(R_i) = RF(1 - \beta_i) + \beta_i[E(R_M)]$$

(8A.2)

The average security has a β_i of 1.0. Thus, when Equation 8A.2 is applied to the average security, $E(R_i) = E(R_M)$—which makes common sense. But, more important, the $RF(1 - \beta_i)$ term is zero. For the market model to be a good representation of the SML, the average A_i should also be zero. If this is not true: (1) the market might be in a state of disequilibrium, (2) the index used in the MM as a proxy for portfolio M might be substantially biased, or (3) the SML might simply be a poor description of real security markets.

The key, of course, is to start off with an index

which is a good proxy of the market portfolio. In practice, the market model is usually applied only to common stocks and the index is usually a broad stock index, such as the S&P 500, the NYSE index, or some other value-weighted index.[9] Whether such market models fairly capture the essence of the SML is a hotly debated topic which we will return to in the next chapter. No one doubts that the market indexes used are wrong; the question is, *how* wrong are they?

Beta Estimates. The A_i and b_i parameters in the MM are calculated by regressing the security's historical returns against the returns on some index. In our examples, we will use the S&P 500. In Table 8A-1, monthly returns for a recent five-year interval are shown for two stocks (IBM and LTV) and for the

---

[9]Bonds present a problem since the life of a bond constantly gets shorter as time passes. If the historical returns on a bond are regressed against some index, the b_i is an average for the time period. Other assets, such as real estate, present an even more fundamental problem—reliable historical returns don't exist.

TABLE 8A-1 *Monthly Returns for LTV, IBM, and the S&P 500*

R_{LTV}	R_{IBM}	R_{SP500}
0.00000	−0.06215	−0.004380
−0.18367	−0.12205	−0.088949
0.15000	−0.01570	0.041140
−0.09783	0.02478	0.046571
−0.03614	0.06095	0.040992
0.30000	0.11064	0.065039
−0.10577	0.01701	0.005835
0.11828	−0.02099	0.037915
0.02885	0.03899	0.016021
0.28037	0.03542	0.102377
0.18248	−0.00367	−0.022630
0.04321	−0.05157	−0.045743
0.05325	0.01142	0.013277
0.11798	−0.02918	0.048069
−0.03025	−0.06012	−0.023456
0.05699	0.01680	−0.001657
−0.19608	−0.01489	0.002489
0.04878	−0.03024	−0.002514
−0.17442	−0.00249	−0.062099
−0.16197	−0.01814	−0.040068
0.14286	−0.04850	0.049148
0.08088	0.07495	0.036590
−0.10884	0.04358	−0.016700
0.00000	0.11868	−0.017544
−0.07634	−0.01399	−0.060548
−0.08333	−0.03434	0.004597
0.01818	0.07531	0.040014
−0.09821	−0.02942	−0.039162
−0.11881	−0.01423	−0.004559
−0.11364	0.08247	−0.022991
0.08974	0.08739	0.115977
−0.15294	0.04078	0.022090
0.09859	0.08859	0.110364
0.16026	0.09371	0.036123
0.01111	0.11272	0.027501
0.12088	0.02727	0.033134
0.11765	0.00996	0.018995
0.02193	0.02778	0.044644
0.03448	0.14988	0.074922
0.10833	−0.04103	−0.012346
−0.05639	0.08090	0.046247
−0.12000	0.00104	−0.033014
0.15455	0.00062	0.011319
−0.01969	0.06172	0.021046
−0.03226	−0.00099	−0.015174
0.15417	−0.06647	0.017426
0.06522	0.03940	0.001983
−0.02721	−0.06455	−0.009216
−0.07343	−0.02563	−0.038859
0.05303	0.03401	0.024959

TABLE 8A-1 *(continued)*

R_{LTV}	R_{IBM}	R_{SP500}
−0.03597	−0.00219	0.005465
−0.22015	−0.04440	−0.059356
−0.08654	−0.01856	0.030223
−0.12632	0.04728	−0.016451
0.16265	0.12731	0.106332
−0.01042	0.00404	0.007679
−0.18947	0.01187	−0.000060
0.00000	−0.02307	−0.015112
0.02597	0.01129	0.022375

Average		
0.45%	1.54%	1.15%

Standard Deviation		
11.95%	5.59%	4.27%

Correlation with R_{SP500}		
0.61	0.59	1.00

S&P 500. In Figure 8A-3, the returns on each stock are plotted against the returns on the S&P 500. The two lines are referred to as *characteristic lines* and represent the best-fit regression lines for each stock. Consider the characteristic line for IBM. It intercepts the vertical axis at 0.6%. This is the regression estimate of A_i for IBM. The slope of the line is equal to 0.77. This is the regression estimate of b_i for IBM. In sum, the characteristic line and market model for IBM are:

IBM
Characteristic $E(R_{IBM}) = 0.6\% + 0.77\ (R_{SP500,t})$
Line

$$(8A.3)$$

IBM
Market $\tilde{R}_{IBM,t} = 0.6\% + 0.77\ (\tilde{R}_{SP500}) + \tilde{E}_{IBM}$
Model

$$(8A.4)$$

IBM's beta is estimated to be 0.77, implying that IBM has less nondiversifiable risk than does the S&P 500. If the risk-free rate is equal to 10% and the risk premium on the market portfolio is 6%, the equilibrium return which one should expect to earn on a share of IBM is 14.6%:

$$E(R_{IBM}) = RF + 0.77\ (RP_M)$$

$$14.6\% = 10\% + 0.77\ (6\%)$$

In contrast, LTV's characteristic line has a slope much greater than IBM's, indicating that it has a larger amount of nondiversifiable risk. Its *b* of 1.7 suggests

FIGURE 8A-3 *Characteristic Line Example, Monthly Returns for a Five-Year Period*

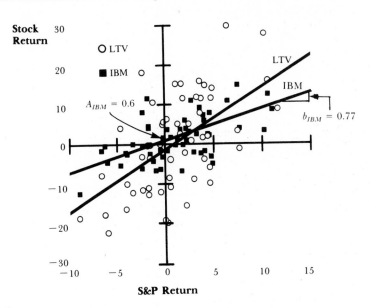

that LTV has 70% more systematic risk than the aver-age stock and its equilibrium expected return should be 20.2%:

$$10\% + 1.7\ (6\%) = 20.2\%$$

The regression procedure calculates b values using an equation similar to Equation 8.10, which specified a security's true β_i. Specifically:

Regression Estimate of b $\qquad b_i = \dfrac{\sigma_i}{\sigma_I}\ (r_{iI})\qquad$ **(8A.5)**

where: σ_i = standard deviation of security i's his-torical returns

σ_I = standard deviation of the index's histor-ical return

r_{iI} = historical correlation between i and I

For example, in Table 8A-1, the standard deviations and correlation coefficients are shown for LTV, IBM, and the S&P 500. Using these, the b values for IBM and LTV are:

$$b_{IBM} = \frac{5.59}{4.27}\ (0.59) \qquad b_{LTV} = \frac{11.95}{4.27}\ (0.61)$$

$$= 0.77 \qquad\qquad = 1.71$$

Beta estimates such as these are available from any number of sources. The major brokerage houses, banks, and investment advisory firms are all very will-ing to sell their b values. To calculate the regression equation, all one needs is access to historical returns and a computer package. The b values obtained from each source will be somewhat different, since each b supplier has its own unique way of calculating the characteristic line. For example, different indexes are used. Some use excess returns (the return in period t less the T-bill return in t). Some use daily returns, others monthly, etc. And many provide "adjusted" b values—something we discuss in a moment. Most of the estimates, however, are reasonably similar.

To illustrate, Table 8A-2 presents b values created by the author for various stocks in the S&P 500. The index used to generate these b values was not the S&P 500 but, instead, an index with more than 500 stocks, including many firms smaller than those in the S&P 500.[10] Also shown is the b of the S&P 500. Note that b_{SP500} is slightly less than 1.0, implying that the aver-

---

[10]These b values were calculated using excess monthly returns for a five-year period. The index was the Center for Research in Security Prices value-weighted market index.

TABLE 8A-2 *Illustrative Betas*

Company	Beta
Middle South Utilities	0.299470
Philadelphia Electric Co	0.421063
Chemical New York Corp	0.628447
Goodyear Tire & Rubber Co	0.924434
Niagara Mohawk Power	0.357685
Public Service Elec & Ga	0.334671
Texas Utilities Co	0.241467
Pacific Gas & Electric	0.145618
Southern Co	0.365085
Central & South West Cor	0.282447
Duke Power Co	0.094342
Dana Corp	0.678298
Sear, Roebuck & Co	0.859260
Southern Calif Edison Co	0.253661
Eastman Kodak Co	0.505859
Exxon Corp	0.835662
Beatrice Co	0.438998
Philip Morris Inc	0.587872
Burroughs Corp	0.90162
Georgia-Pacific Corp	1.17036
Honeywell Inc	1.15948
Bankers Trust New York Co	0.92745
Gould Inc	1.21621
Borg-Warner Corp	0.95609
Allied Corp	1.09718
McDonnell Douglas Corp	1.28652
American General Corp	1.02937
American Cyanamid Co	0.89943
Revlon Inc	0.84249
Black & Decker Corp	1.13096
RCA Corp	0.79101
CBS Inc	0.85176
Warner-Lambert Co	0.98033
American Express	0.85300
Kaufman & Broad Inc	2.14235
Federal Paper Board Co	1.06923
National Gypsum Co	1.39210
Grumman Corp	1.48491
Teledyne Inc	1.76380
Wang Laboratories-Cl B	2.22450
Apple Computer Inc	1.50000
General Dynamics Corp	1.30829
Prime Computer	2.40101
Tandy Corp	1.77792
Tonka Corp	1.09149
Lowe's Cos	1.20000
Searle (G. D.) & Co	1.02811
Lockheed Corp	1.57955
Macmillan Inc	1.10984
Wendy's International In	1.05000

TABLE 8A-2 *(continued)*

Company	Beta
Handleman Co	1.03977
Toys R Us Inc	1.20000
Cullinet Software Inc	1.80000
Hasbro Bradley Inds	1.39715
S&P 500	0.94000

age stock in the S&P 500 has slightly less systematic risk than the average stock included in this broader index.

Diversifiable Versus Nondiversifiable Risk. The returns plotted in Figure 8A-3 can be used to illustrate again the difference between diversifiable and nondiversifiable risk. Notice that rarely does the return plot exactly on the characteristic line. An error almost always exists. It is these error terms which are diversified away. As long as the error for stock i (E_{it}) is *not correlated* with the error on all other stocks j (E_{jt}), the errors will go to zero when all the stocks are combined. If the error terms are correlated, either we have a poor index proxy of portfolio M or the CAPM is wrong. These are points which are examined more closely in the next chapter.

Portfolio Characteristic Lines. Historical beta values can be calculated for portfolios in the same fashion as they are for individual securities. The major difference is that the error terms of portfolio returns are closer to the characteristic line. This, of course, is due to the fact that the diversifiable error terms of single securities cancel out in the portfolio.

For example, in Figure 8A-4, quarterly returns for LTV and a portfolio known as the DFA Small Company Portfolio are plotted against the S&P 500. This DFA portfolio consists of a large number (in the hundreds) of small stocks. Note that the b of the DFA portfolio is substantially greater than 1.0. The systematic risks of small firms are quite large. Note also that the error terms for this portfolio are much smaller than they are for a single stock such as LTV.

What Is Alpha? Little has been said yet about what the A_i term is supposed to be. If the market is in

FIGURE 8A-4 *Characteristic Lines for LTV Stock and the DFA Portfolio*

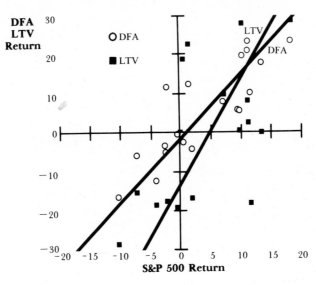

equilibrium and if a suitable index has been used, then alpha should be:

Equilibrium Alpha $\qquad A_i = RF(1 - \beta_i) \qquad$ **(8A.6)**

If $\beta_i = 0$, the security should have an alpha equal to the risk-free return. As β_i increases, the value of alpha should decline.

When the market model is used, however, A_i values are found which differ from the equilibrium prediction of what they should be. For example, in Figure 8A-3, $b_{IBM} = 0.77$ and $A_{IBM} = 0.6$. During the five-year period for which these estimates were made, the average monthly return on T-bills was about 0.9%. Thus, the equilibrium prediction for IBM's alpha would be 0.2:

$$0.9\,(1 - 0.77) = 0.2$$

The actual A_i was higher.

Presuming that the index used in the MM is satisfactory and that the CAPM is a reasonable predictor of reality, differences in the actual A_i and its equilibrium equivalent are thought of as abnormal returns. In the case of IBM, the 0.4% (0.6 − 0.2) difference would reflect greater risk-adjusted performance than is available on the average stock. On an annualized basis this translates to about a 5.0% greater return on IBM than other stocks of equivalent risk yielded.

The difference between the actual A_i and its equilibrium equivalent is simply Jensen's alpha discussed earlier. It is a widely used measure of historical performance. Unfortunately, it is a poor predictor of future performance.

THE ACCURACY OF BETA ESTIMATES

The market model provides estimates of historical b values. How good are these at forecasting future b values? Evidence developed to date suggests two major conclusions:

1. Beta estimates of single stocks are poor predictors of future b values. Predictability improves if beta is estimated for a portfolio, and this predictability

increases as the number of securities held in the portfolio increases.

2. Beta estimates tend to move towards 1.0. If b is found to be less than 1.0 during a given time interval, chances are that it will increase in the next time period. Conversely, if b is greater than 1.0, chances are that it will fall.

Predictability

A classic study of how well a past *b* predicts the future *b* was conducted by Blume. He used the market model on monthly returns for nonoverlapping seven-year intervals to calculate *b* on portfolios consisting of from 1 stock to 50 stocks. Then for each portfolio size, he examined the correlation between an initial period's *b* and the subsequent period's *b*. Both the correlation coefficient, *r*, and its squared value, R^2, were calculated. We will discuss only the R^2 measure since its meaning is easiest to understand. In the context of Blume's study, R^2 is the percentage of variability in the subsequent period's *b* explained by the variability in the initial period's *b*. If R^2 is 100%, then the subsequent *b* values are perfectly predicted. If $R^2 = 30\%$, then only 30% of the variability is predicted.

Blume's results are shown in Table 8A-3. For single securities, *b* is a poor predictor. Only 36% of the subsequent period's variability in *b* is explained by the variability in the initial period. For portfolios, however, the predictability improves markedly. For a 10-stock portfolio, R^2 is 85%, and by the time 50 stocks are held, R^2 is 96%. This is because estimation errors on single-stock *b* values are uncorrelated with each other and thus disappear in portfolios. The conclusion is obvious. The market model beta for a single stock is a highly questionable estimate of the stock's true systematic risk. Beta estimates of portfolios are more trustworthy.

Betas Tend to Move to 1.0. Studies have also shown that betas estimated in one period tend to be closer to

TABLE 8A-3 *Predictability of b Values*

Number of Securities in Portfolio	R^2
1	36%
2	53%
4	71%
7	77%
10	85%
20	95%
50	96%

SOURCE: M. Blume, "Betas and Their Regression Tendencies," *Journal of Finance* 10, no. 3 (June 1975): 785–96.
R^2 = Percentage of variability of *b* in a subsequent period explained by variability of *b* in the initial period.

1.0 in the subsequent period. Again using some of Blume's results, Table 8A-4 shows the estimated betas on six portfolios for two time periods. The portfolios are arranged from the smallest beta to the largest. Note that there is a definite trend for low betas in the initial period to have higher betas in the subsequent period, and for high beta portfolios in the initial period to have a smaller *b* in the subsequent period.

Whether this tendency is due to economic forces which cause companies with extreme beta estimates to either increase or decrease their risk or whether it is due to statistical aberrations is not known. However, it *is* a well-documented fact.

Adjustments to Market Model Betas. Given the small predictive content of market model betas for individual stocks, a variety of methods have been suggested to improve forecasting accuracy. Three of the more popular methods include the following:

1. Arbitrarily adjusting toward 1.0
2. Adjusting on the basis of Bayesian statistics
3. Relating betas to fundamental characteristics of the individual stocks

Recognizing that market model beta estimates in one time interval tend to move towards 1.0 in the next time interval, many organizations adjust calculated market model betas towards 1.0. A variety of methods are used which vary in sophistication. For example, one could use the relatively naive procedure of saying that the predicted beta will be some fraction, say halfway, between the market model estimate and 1.0. For example, a market model estimate of 1.8 would be stated as a predicted beta of 1.4, and an estimate of 0.5 would be predicted as 0.75. In his original study, Blume used a more sophisticated approach

TABLE 8A-4 *Beta Estimates Move Toward 1.0*

Portfolio	Initial 7/54–6/61	Subsequent 7/61–6/68
1	0.39	0.62
2	0.61	0.71
3	0.81	0.86
4	0.99	0.91
5	1.14	1.00
7	1.34	1.17

SOURCE: M. Blume, "On the Assessment of Risk," *Journal of Finance* 6, no. 1 (March 1971): 1–10.

and found that his market model betas in a second time period were related to those in a prior time period as follows:

$$b_{i2} = 0.343 + 0.677 b_{i1}$$

There is no guarantee, however, that such relationships will remain stable over time.

Another approach, first suggested by Vasichek, is based on Bayesian statistics. First, market model estimates are calculated for a large number of stocks. Among the output will be the following statistics:

b_i = estimate of beta for stock i

$\sigma(b_i)$ = standard deviation of stock i's beta

$\bar{b}$ = the average of all betas calculated

σ_{all} = the standard deviation of the sample betas

Vasichek suggested that a revised beta, b_i^*, be calculated for each stock as follows:

Vasichek Beta Adjustment

$$b_i^* = b_i \frac{\sigma_{all}^2}{\sigma_{all}^2 + \sigma(b_i)^2} + \bar{b} \frac{\sigma(b_i)^2}{\sigma_{all}^2 + \sigma(b_i)^2}$$

(8A.7)

To illustrate, assume we have just calculated the following for five stock beta estimates:

	Stock				
	1	2	3	4	5
b_i	0.8	0.9	1.0	1.1	1.2
$\sigma(b_i)$	0.1	0.1	0.2	0.2	0.4

$\bar{b}$ = average of the betas

= 1.0

σ_{all} = standard deviation of the sample betas

= 0.1414

Consider stock 5 with an estimated beta of 1.2. Using Equation 8A.7, the Bayesian predicted beta would be 1.02:

$$b_5^* = 1.2 \frac{0.1414^2}{0.1414^2 + 0.4^2} + 1.0 \frac{0.4^2}{0.1414^2 + 0.4^2}$$

$$= 1.2(0.11108) + 1.0(0.88892) = 1.02$$

Note that the two weighting terms add to 1.0. Note also that as $\sigma(b_i)$ becomes larger, the weight given to b_i becomes smaller and the weight given to $\bar{b}$ greater.

Other researchers have suggested that we try to explain future betas not only in terms of past beta estimates but also in terms of fundamental characteristics of the stocks. Such betas, which have come to be known as *fundamental betas*, are widely used. To illustrate, assume that we have calculated market model betas on a large number of stocks in periods 1 and 2. In addition, we have information about certain fundamental characteristics of the stocks. Our data consist of the following for each stock:

b_{i1}, b_{i2} = beta estimate for stock in periods 1 and 2

IND_i = a measure of the firm's industry

LEV_i = a measure of the firm's financial leverage

VOL_i = a measure of past profit volatility

Then the following regression could be run in order to determine the importance of each variable in predicting b_{i2}:

$$b_{i2} = a_0 + a_1(b_{i1}) + a_2(IND_i) + a_3(LEV_i)$$

$$+ a_4(VOL_i) + e_i$$

The estimated regression parameters could then be used to predict betas on stocks not in our sample or to predict future betas, given b_{i2} and a firm's current fundamental characteristics.

There are a variety of statistical procedures which would be better than regression analysis. But the basic concept of what is meant by "fundamental betas" should be clear.

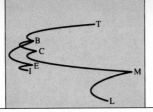

9 Capital Asset Pricing Extensions

The capital asset pricing model has two major attractions: (1) its simplicity and (2) its implications. It is not strictly true, of course; it cannot be, given its assumptions. But the extent to which both its simplicity and its implications should be rejected is largely an empirical question. If the model predicts actual security returns in a reasonable fashion, it should not be rejected until a better predictive model is developed.

In this chapter we examine: (1) alternative versions of the CAPM as various assumptions are lifted, (2) a competing pricing model known as arbitrage pricing theory (APT), and (3) empirical tests of both the CAPM and APT. In many respects, the empirical tests have shown results consistent with the standard theory or alternative versions of the theory. However, serious empirical questions remain. In fact, a strong case can be made that neither the CAPM nor APT is empirically testable.

EXTENSIONS OF THE THEORY

In this section we examine the removal of the following CAPM assumptions:

1. Risk-free borrowing and lending
2. Homogeneous expectations
3. Taxes equal to zero
4. Frictionless markets
5. Divisibility of assets
6. Single-period model

Risk-Free Borrowing and Lending

One assumption of the CAPM is that a single, risk-free asset is available to all investors. Indeed, the existence of the risk-free asset has profound effects on the relationship between expected returns and risk. Fischer Black has reformulated capital market

FIGURE 9-1 *The CML with No Riskless Asset*

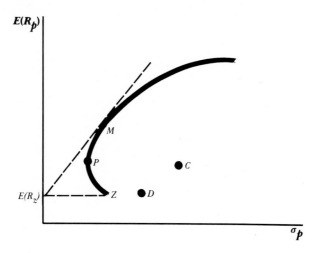

theory under the assumption that *RF* doesn't exist. His analysis is illustrated in Figure 9-1.

The efficient frontier of risky securities is shown as the solid line, and the market portfolio is designated as *M*. While a risk-free security doesn't exist, there should exist one or more portfolios whose returns are uncorrelated with *M*. Such a portfolio is referred to as a *zero-beta portfolio* since it has a zero beta relative to the market portfolio. Portfolios *Z, D,* and *C* are meant to identify different zero-beta portfolios. Black showed that investors, faced with the lack of a riskless asset, would combine portfolio *M* with one of these zero-beta portfolios. In particular, the zero-beta portfolio with the lowest *total* risk will be selected. *Without a risk-free asset, the best alternative available is to select a portfolio which is uncorrelated with market returns and has the lowest standard deviation possible.* In Figure 9-1, *Z* is the minimum-variance, zero-beta portfolio.

In this case the CML is no longer linear but a curve extending from point *P* through *M*. The SML, however, retains its linearity. Figure 9-2 shows how the SML would look when a minimum-variance, zero-beta portfolio is used. Mathematically, it is expressed as:

Zero-Beta CAPM

$$E(R_i) = E(R_Z) + \beta_i[E(R_m) - E(R_Z)]$$
$$= E(R_Z) + \beta_i[RP_m]$$

(9.1)

where $E(R_Z)$ reflects the expected return on the lowest-risk, zero-beta portfolio. The only difference between Equation 9.1 and the original form of the CAPM is that a constant risk-free rate doesn't exist. Investors will now buy or sell portfolio *Z* in combination with *M* to achieve desired levels of risk and return. In all other respects the two models are identical.

When we review various empirical tests of the CAPM later in the chapter, we will find that empirical estimates of historical risk-free rates estimated in the studies are

FIGURE 9-2 *The Zero-Beta CAPM*

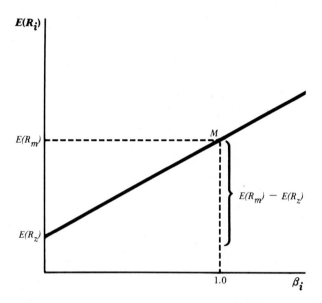

much larger, on average, than historical risk-free returns, and that these estimates vary considerably over time. The zero-beta version of the CAPM is often used as the explanation. The $E(R_Z)$ term may change from period to period as the minimum-variance zero-beta portfolio changes. And actual return outcomes on this portfolio will be distributed around $E(R_Z)$. In sum, the $E(R_Z)$ term would imply results similar to those provided by the empirical tests. This does not mean the zero-beta model is correct—it means only that the two are consistent.

There is a pragmatic difficulty in using the zero-beta CAPM to estimate equilibrium expected returns which does not exist with the standard CAPM. Instead of using, say, Treasury bills to measure the one-month risk-free rate, one must provide an estimate of $E(R_Z)$. This is a difficult task. Ideally, one should use ex ante data on all securities available to find the minimum-variance zero-beta portfolio. Not only is this impossible, since data on all securities are not available, but it would be very costly if one used a reasonable subset of all securities as a proxy. Similarly, historical estimates of $E(R_Z)$ are of questionable value since they are so variable over time. While the zero-beta model does explain the empirical problems which emerge with the standard CAPM, its practical implementation is difficult.

Homogeneous Expectations

The CAPM developed in Chapter 8 was based on the assumption that all individuals have identical beliefs about the future—that is, they have homogeneous expectations about expected security returns, standard deviations, and covariances. This would occur only if everyone had costless access to information about securities and

FIGURE 9-3 *Portfolio Choice with Heterogeneous Expectations*

received new information at the same time. In reality, there is a cost associated with obtaining information, and new information is available to some people before it is to others.[1] In reality, people have heterogeneous expectations.

To see what this implies about market equilibrium and the CAPM, consider Figure 9-3, which shows efficient frontiers for two people. Investor 1 and investor 2 have identical beliefs about bond risk and expected returns but differ in their expectations about stock returns. As a result, two different efficient frontiers exist, and each investor will identify a different optimal portfolio of risky assets to hold in combination with borrowing or lending at RF. This optimal risky asset portfolio is P_1^* for investor 1 and P_2^* for investor 2.

In equilibrium, security prices must be at levels which allow the markets to clear (that is, the demand for securities is equal to the supply outstanding). Let's *assume* that this is the case in Figure 9-3. Prices are at levels which result in equal demand and supply. No one looks at a market price and decides to trade any further; everyone is quite satisfied with the portfolio he or she owns. However, investors 1 and 2 still disagree with each other because they hold different information.[2] The principal impacts of a situation such as this are as follows:

---

[1]For example, consider the cost of this book and your dollar opportunity cost of reading it instead of selling hamburgers or lying on the beach.

[2]In Chapter 8, an equilibrium was stated to exist only when everyone has identical information. At this point we are looking at an equilibrium which is less perfect. Since people have differing expectations, they realize they have different information. In a perfect market they could find the information held by others and adjust prices. In this less than perfect market, they are constrained from finding such information.

1. The market portfolio does not play the critical role which it does with homogeneous expectations. While some people might perceive it to be the optimal risky asset portfolio, many others will not and will hold a subset of the market. None of them will be wrong. Given the information available to each person, each selects what he or she perceives to be the ideal risky asset portfolio.

2. Each person will still use borrowing and lending to achieve his or her desired risk/return level.

3. The portfolios which people hold will be the result of both pure investment decisions (the price of the security is fair) and speculative decisions (the price is not fair). In fact, some people will short sell a security when they believe its fair price is less than its actual market price. Under the standard CAPM, everyone agrees that expected returns are positive and directly related to nondiversifiable risk. As a result no one would short sell under the standard CAPM. Whether any individual will be able to consistently "win" on his or her speculative positions is the subject of the next chapter.

4. Since people might hold different portfolios, each would evaluate the beta of a given security differently. The b values developed from a market model equation should be based upon an index which is equivalent to each person's optimal portfolio.

5. Each person will have a personal equivalent of the CML and SML equations. An aggregate CML and SML across the total market would also exist, but (a) it would be a complex weighted average of each individual's CML and SML, and (b) it would no longer be a description of how any one person should price an asset.

In summary, a linear relationship between risk and return remains. But it varies between people and might be negative for some. In addition, diversification will be much less, and this beta will differ from the beta suggested by the standard CAPM.

Taxes Equal to Zero

Another assumption of the CAPM is that there are no taxes. The existence of taxes will not seriously violate the analytic results of the model as long as *a single tax rate* exists which is applied to all forms of income as well as to all individuals. Neglecting other assumptions, the addition of a common tax rate results in both a pretax and a posttax CAPM where all terms in the posttax version (except beta) are equal to the pretax version multiplied by (1 − tax rate). Problems with taxes arise when (1) there are different tax rates for ordinary income and for capital gains, and (2) tax rates vary among individuals.

Ordinary Taxes Versus Capital Gains Taxes. For the moment let's leave all other assumptions of the CAPM unchanged, but allow for the existence of a capital gains tax rate which is less than the ordinary tax rate. Brennan was the first to show that this would result in a revised version of the CAPM, as follows:

CAPM and Taxes
$$E(R_i) = RF + \beta_i[RP_M] - T(D_M - RF) + T(D_i - RF) \qquad (9.2)$$

where T = a positive coefficient which accounts for the impact of different ordinary and capital gains rates, D_M = the dividend yield on the market portfolio, and D_i = the dividend yield on stock i. The expected return is now a function of the dividend yield on a stock (or the current yield on a bond); the larger the dividend yield, the greater the before-tax return must be. If the dividend yield is the same as the market and $\beta_i = 1.0$, then $E(R_i) = E(R_M)$.

The investment implications of this model make common sense. Pretax expected returns will be a function of the security's beta, its dividend yield, and a term (T) which accounts for the differential rates and the wealth of people affected by each tax rate. Individuals still hold widely diversified portfolios but not necessarily the market portfolio. Instead, investors with tax rates lower than the weighted average rate should hold relatively more securities having a high dividend yield and fewer securities with low dividend yields. Pension funds and endowments (which pay no tax) can earn greater pretax and posttax returns by molding their diversified portfolios to higher-cash-yielding securities. Conversely, individuals in a high tax bracket should emphasize low-cash-yielding securities.

Varying Tax Rates. Now consider the case in which capital gains tax rates and ordinary rates are identical, but rates vary among individuals. In that case each individual will perceive different after-tax expected returns and risks. Even though individuals may have homogeneous expectations about pretax returns, they will have heterogeneous expectations of posttax returns (the only thing that matters). In short, the addition of varying tax rates among people results in a world of heterogeneous expectations. Investors with different tax rates will (1) have different SMLs, (2) hold different portfolios of risky assets, and (3) perceive security risks differently.

In the earliest empirical tests of whether dividend yields (and thus tax rates) affect required security returns, Black and Scholes concluded that "it is not possible to demonstrate that the expected returns on high (dividend) yield stocks differ from the expected returns on low (dividend) yield common stocks either before or after taxes."[3] However, Litzenberger and Ramaswamy extended the after-tax CAPM to include a progressive tax scheme and found empirically significant tax effects. They conclude: "The data indicate that for every dollar increase in return in the form of dividends, investors require an additional 23 cents in before-tax return."[4]

Frictionless Markets

A frictionless market is a market in which there is nothing to constrain the investor from selecting any portfolio desired. Besides taxes, transaction costs and costly access to information are the most common types of friction which exist. When these

---

[3]F. Black and M. Scholes, "The Effects of Dividend Yield and Dividend Policy on Common Stock Prices and Returns," *Journal of Financial Economics* 1 (May 1974): 1.

[4]R. Litzenberger and K. Ramaswamy, "The Effect of Personal Taxes and Dividends on Capital Asset Prices," *Journal of Financial Economics* 7 (June 1979): 190.

are considered, we return again to a world of heterogeneous expectations. We won't refer again to the implications of such a model. They are exactly as discussed in the previous section on taxes.

Divisibility of Assets

The assumption that persons can hold any percentage of their wealth in a given asset might at first appear to be harmless. A half-share of AT&T cannot, of course, be owned. But in the context of most portfolios, a half-share is virtually meaningless. Similar to a share of AT&T, all the real assets and security claims to real assets which we have examined can be considered to be (almost) perfectly divisible. But there is an asset which we all own which cannot be sold, an asset which must be held in its total—human capital. In the context of the CAPM, how do a person's innate abilities affect optimal security holdings? Does a person who is a marvelous computer designer hold the same proportion of computer-related stocks in her portfolio as does a person who is a marvelous piano tuner? It is doubtful. The addition of human capital as an asset which should be considered together with more traditional notions of risky assets changes the implications of the CAPM substantially. It also adds further common sense to the model's investment implications. Unfortunately this comes with a loss in the usefulness of market model b_i values.

In a model which lifts no other assumptions, Mayers examined equilibrium security pricing when human capital is treated as a valuable but nonmarketable asset. He obtained a relationship which looks very much like the standard SML:

CAPM with Nonmarketable Assets

$$E(R_i) = RF + \beta_i'[E(RP_M)] \tag{9.3}$$

Two terms differ from the standard—β_i' and RP_M. Both terms now refer not to a market of financial securities and real tangible assets, but to a market which also includes the total value of human capital. For example, β_i' is equal to:

Beta with Human Capital as an Asset

$$\beta_i' = \frac{\mathrm{cov}(R_i R_M) + \dfrac{V_H}{V_M}\,\mathrm{cov}(R_i R_H)}{\sigma_M^2 + \dfrac{V_H}{V_M}\,\mathrm{cov}(R_M R_H)} \tag{9.4}$$

In the equation, V_H refers to the total value of human capital in society. It is clearly not measurable, but it might be very important in determining proper investment strategies. The term V_M is the total value of all financial securities and real tangible assets which we have previously called the market portfolio. If the value of human capital is zero, Equation 9.4 is identical to that of the standard notion of beta.

However, if human capital has a positive value, then two new forces affect a security's nondiversifiable risk. The first of these is the covariance between returns on the security and returns on human capital—$\mathrm{cov}(R_i R_H)$. The larger this covariance, the greater a security's systematic risk. Any asset or security which has a positive correlation between its returns and the returns on human capital is more risky than the CAPM suggests. This term captures the nondiversifiable risk of a security not included in the standard CAPM. The second term is in the denominator of Equation 9.4 and represents the covariance between the traditional market portfolio and human capital returns. It is basically an adjustment to the total risk associated with tangible and intangible assets.

There are potential problems with this model. For example, what causes the market portfolio to have any value at all if it is not human capital? Certainly without the existence of humans there would be no market portfolio to even consider. Yet the notion of an indivisible, nontradable asset does suggest some reasonable conclusions. For example, what diversification does the pension fund of a computer manufacturer gain from investing in computer companies to the degree the standard CAPM suggests? Since employees' returns on their human capital are already heavily invested in the computer industry, doesn't a market portfolio of risky securities overweight holdings of computer firms? The pensions of many corporations, in fact, often have large common stock holdings of the firm itself. Is such a strategy a reasonably diversified one for the beneficiaries of the pension, whose future income is already so closely tied to the future of the corporation? A perfect example occurred a few years ago when the New York City pension plans were asked to help the city out of a fiscal crisis by purchasing securities issued by the city. There is no doubt that this would have provided welcome relief to New York's fiscal problems. But employees of the pension already had a large investment in the city (their jobs) which would have been substantially increased by the pensions' investment in the city itself. This was not the road to reasonable diversification.

We all have human capital which cannot be traded away—it is ours and ours alone. Thus, the ideal portfolio of marketable securities will differ for each of us. If a person is a chemical engineer, the value of his human capital is directly tied to the productivity of chemical firms, and his holdings of such securities should be less than those of other people in order to achieve satisfactory diversification. The principle of diversification should consider intangible asset returns as well as the returns of tangible real assets and securities.

Single-Period Model

The last assumption we remove is the first we made—that is, that decisions are made in a one-period world. The reason for leaving it to the last is that a satisfactory understanding of multiperiod effects on the model is not yet available. Although extensive research has been conducted, this is an extremely difficult problem and we know only a little of the answer yet.

One thing we do know is that the single-period model can be applied to a multiperiod world if certain conditions are true (or assumed away). Fama has shown that these conditions are the following:

1. People's *consumption preferences* are independent of future events. For example, your preference for mystery books over college texts remains unaffected by the level of the Dow Jones Industrial Average a year from now. Or your preference for South African diamonds over pearls remains unaffected by political events in South Africa.

2. People act as if future *consumption opportunities* are independent of future events. For example, you believe the opportunity to consume mystery books will be independent of the level of the Dow industrials a year from now. Or that the opportunity to consume South African diamonds is independent of political events in South Africa.

3. People act as if the distributions of future *asset returns* are determinable at the start of the year and are independent of future events. For example, the potential returns which you assess today on an investment in a college text will be the same as the assessment you would make a year from now, even though the Dow may have fallen 50%. Or the potential returns you assess today on an investment in South African diamonds will be the same as the assessment you would make a year from now, regardless of political events in South Africa.

Basically, these conditions say that future events will not cause people to change their decisions. If decisions today are independent of the future, it is logical that a one-period model is quite satisfactory in explaining portfolio choice. In reality, these conditions probably hold only over short time intervals at best. One would be hard pressed to say that the tastes and opportunities of an infant are independent of world events as the infant proceeds through life.

In an early multiperiod model in which investors face a world with many possible "states of nature," Merton found that more than one optimal portfolio existed, as opposed to the single optimal market portfolio of a one-period CAPM. Thus, there might be many betas associated with a given stock. The number of such optimal portfolios (and relevant betas) was equal to the number of possible states of nature that might arise. However, in a further expansion of Merton's multiperiod model, Breeden concluded that only one beta is needed when betas are measured relative to changes in the aggregate real consumption rate.

The mathematics of such models lie beyond the scope of this text. Thus we will not review their logic here. However, they are all based on assumptions similar to those used in the classic CAPM. In addition, however, they assume that investors have a time-additive, state-independent utility of consumption. This simply means that (*a*) total utility of consumption over one's lifetime is equal to the sum of the utility of consumption at all points in time, and (*b*) a person's utility function is not related to the state of the world. Again, these are probably very restrictive assumptions. Unfortunately, a model which truly captures the multiperiod nature of investment and consumption decisions is yet to be developed.

EMPIRICAL EVIDENCE

The Nature of the Tests

Clearly, the CAPM rests upon a number of assumptions which are not strictly true in the real world. This does not mean, however, that the model is totally without merit. Its validity can be assessed only by examining how well it predicts real-world phenomena. This is an empirical question.

The CAPM is an ex ante model. Individuals develop subjective judgments about (1) the risk-free rate, (2) the beta of a security, and (3) the appropriate market risk premium. While people may not go through such an explicit mental process, perhaps they act as if they do. Tests of the CAPM are always tests of the SML:

Security Market Line

$$E(R_i) = RF + \beta_i[RP_M] \qquad (9.5)$$

This is an ex ante relationship. People develop (common) beliefs about what the systematic risk of security i (β_i) will be in the future and are faced with a future expected risk premium.

Unfortunately, in testing the model we can't look into investors' minds to see whether this is the relationship they use to determine equilibrium expected returns. For example, investors might be totally blind to the importance of security covariance and price a security's standard deviation instead of its covariance to the market. But it is doubtful that serious tests of ex ante pricing could be performed; at least none have been conducted to date. Instead we rely upon history. Do past security returns tell a story which is consistent with the CAPM? In particular, is the average historical return earned on security i ($\bar{R_i}$) equal to (1) the average historical risk-free rate ($\overline{RF}$) plus (2) a risk premium which is equal to the security's estimated historical beta (b_i) multiplied by the average historical risk premium earned on the market ($\overline{RP_M}$)?

The Historical Test

$$\bar{R_i} = \overline{RF} + b_i[\overline{RP_M}] \qquad (9.6)$$

Compare this statement of how securities should have behaved in the past (if the CAPM is valid) with the ex ante SML in Equation 9.5. They have very similar terms, but the SML terms are *expectations* of the future, whereas the statistical tests rely on *averages* of the past.

Equation 9.6 is justified as the historical equivalent of the SML based on simple logic. Over long time intervals, *expectations will be equal to average outcomes*. People are rational enough to recognize when they are consistently over- or underestimating returns or betas. If they find such a bias, they will adjust their expectations until observed outcomes average what they expect them to. If this is true: (1) average historical returns will reflect past expectations of returns, (2) average historical systematic risk will reflect past expectations of systematic risk, and (3) average historical risk premiums will reflect past expectations of risk premiums. Equation 9.6 is the historical counterpart to the SML.

The difficulty of using Equation 9.6 to test the SML is not in its logic; the difficulty lies instead in its implementation. In particular, how are the b values estimated and what index is used to measure the market portfolio? Empirical tests which attempt to determine whether Equation 9.6 supports the CAPM are actually testing whether:

1. The b values are true estimates of historical betas.
2. The index used to measure historical risk premiums is the market portfolio.
3. The CAPM is correct.

If any of these fails, the test as a whole will fail. As we will see below, considerable attention has been given to beta estimates. Unfortunately, equal care hasn't been given to the index. In fact, there is some question whether the theory will ever be truly testable since the market portfolio is impossible to identify.

Empirical tests of the SML examine the following regression equation equivalent of Equation 9.6:

Regression Test of SML

$$\bar{R}_i = \alpha_0 + \alpha_1 b_i \tag{9.7}$$

where the known quantities are:

$\bar{R}_i$ = the average single-period return on security i during some past time interval

b_i = the estimated historical beta for security i

and the statistically estimated values should be:

α_0 = the average risk-free rate which prevailed during the testing period, $\overline{RF}$

α_1 = the market risk premium earned during the testing period, $\bar{R}_m - \overline{RF}$

Regardless of the means of testing the CAPM, there are a number of implications of the theory which statistical tests should support or question:

1. The intercept term in Equation 9.7 should not be significantly different from the average risk-free rate during the testing period. Occasionally, empirical tests are performed on excess returns, where the risk-free rate which prevailed during a particular period is subtracted from both the left- and right-hand sides of Equation 9.7. In this case α_0 should not be statistically different from zero.
2. The relationship between $\bar{R}_i$ and b_i should be linear.
3. The term α_1 should be positive and equal to $(\bar{R}_m - \overline{RF})$, the earned risk premium.
4. Beta should be the only factor related to average historic returns. Variables such as a security's diversifiable risk should be statistically insignificant.

Tests on Individual Stocks

Douglas examined the relationship between average security returns and various risk measures on a sample of more than 600 stocks for various time intervals between 1926 and 1960. Using different five-year intervals he calculated (1) each stock's average quarterly rate of return, (2) the variance of each stock's quarterly rate of return, and (3) the covariance of the stock's return with the quarterly returns of an index of all 600 stocks. Using these values, he then estimated the following regression equation for each five-year period:

Douglas Single-Stock Test

$$(1 + \bar{R}_i) = \alpha_0 + \alpha_1(\sigma_i^2) + \alpha_2(\sigma_{ij}) + e_i \tag{9.8}$$

where $\bar{R}_i$ = the average quarterly return on stock i during the five-year period, σ_i^2 = the variance of i's quarterly return, σ_{ij} = the covariance between i's return and the index of all the 600 stocks during the five-year period, and e_i = random estimation errors.

His results for each five-year period are displayed in Table 9-1. The α_0 regression coefficient should reflect one plus the quarterly risk-free rate. While his estimates were perhaps slightly higher than quarterly values of $1 + RF$, they weren't the major concern raised by his results. His estimates of α_1 reflect the impact of a security's *total* risk on average returns. Per the CAPM, α_1 values should be zero. But most are positive and statistically significant, with 95% confidence or better, contrary to the CAPM. Estimates of α_2, on the other hand, should reflect the earned price of risk: $(R_m - RF) \div \sigma_m$. Yet most of these values are statistically insignificant. In a related study of individual stock returns and betas, Lintner found similar results.

But both the Douglas and Lintner studies appear to suffer from various statistical weaknesses which *might* explain their anomalous results. In a subsequent study Miller and Scholes reviewed these statistical problems and concluded that the *empirical* relationship between average security returns and unsystematic risk could be due to (1) measurement errors incurred in estimating individual stock betas, (2) the fact that estimated betas and unsystematic risks are highly correlated, and (3) a skewness which was present in the distribution of observed stock returns. While Miller and Scholes don't reject the implications of the Douglas and Lintner studies, they suggest that the statistical problems encountered when *individual stocks* are used might be the reason for the discouraging results. To date we have no strong evidence that returns on individual securities do, or do not, conform to the CAPM.

Tests on Portfolios

Because of these statistical problems, most tests since then have concentrated upon *portfolios* of securities.

TABLE 9-1 *Douglas Test of CAPM*

		$(1 + \bar{R}_i) = \alpha_0 + \alpha_1(\sigma_i^2) + \alpha_2(\sigma_{ij})$			
	α_0	α_1		α_2	
Period	*Coefficient*	*Coefficient*	*T-Value*	*Coefficient*	*T-Value*
1926–31	0.99	0.15	2.14	0.63	0.72
1931–36	1.03	0.18	6.00	0.17	0.81
1936–41	0.99	0.39	2.60	−0.30	−0.54
1941–46	1.04	0.69	4.93	1.19	1.43
1946–51	1.01	0.08	0.38	0.66	0.53
1951–56	1.02	−0.21	−0.68	−3.51	−1.99
1956–60	1.03	1.13	4.18	−3.21	−2.08

SOURCE: G. Douglas, "Risk in the Equity Markets: An Empirical Appraisal of Market Efficiency," *Yale Economic Essays* 9, no. 1 (1969).

FIGURE 9-4 *Black, Jensen, and Scholes Study*

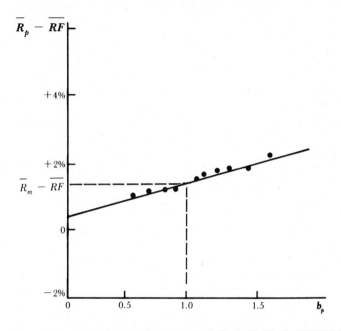

SOURCE: F. Black, M. Jensen, and M. Scholes, "The Capital Asset Pricing Model: Some Empirical Tests," in *Studies in the Theory of Capital Markets* (New York: Praeger, 1972).

The Black, Jensen, and Scholes Study. Black, Jensen, and Scholes used all NYSE stocks for the period 1931–1965 to form 10 portfolios of different beta levels. Then average monthly "excess returns" on each portfolio were regressed against the portfolio's beta. For example, let's say we have identified 10 different portfolios for each month between 1931 and 1965. During a given month the return on each portfolio is calculated and the 30-day risk-free rate (which existed at the start of the month) is subtracted. This results in a monthly series of excess returns for each portfolio. The average of each series is then calculated, and this average is regressed against the portfolio betas.

Results of the Black, Jensen, and Scholes study are displayed in Figure 9-4 and shown below:

$$\frac{\text{Monthly}}{\text{Average}} \frac{\text{Excess}}{\text{Return}} = \alpha_0 + \alpha_1 \text{ (portfolio beta)}$$

$$(\bar{R}_p - \bar{RF}) = 0.359\% + 1.08\% \ (b_p)$$

$$(T\text{-value}) \qquad (6.53) \qquad (20.77)$$

These results conform with the CAPM in that a clear linear relationship exists between average excess returns and beta. They do not conform with the version of the

FIGURE 9-5 *Black, Jensen, and Scholes Results*

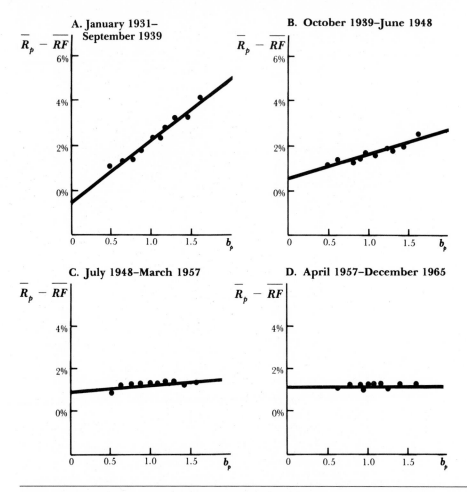

SOURCE: F. Black, M. Jensen, and M. Scholes, "The Capital Asset Pricing Model: Some Empirical Tests," in *Studies in the Theory of Capital Markets* (New York: Praeger, 1972).

traditional CAPM in which a known risk-free rate exists. Recall that the portfolio returns are excess returns. If the 30-day T-bill rate had been the risk-free rate, the intercept term should have been zero. However, the intercept term of 0.359% implies that the return on a portfolio with zero systematic risk is not *RF* but something larger. This evidence is contrary to the traditional CAPM. As a result, Black developed a zero-beta CAPM theory which is discussed below.

Black, Jensen, and Scholes also examined the same regression for various time intervals. Results are shown in Figure 9-5. Again, a linear relationship exists, but the intercept term is usually greater than zero and changes in each period. The slope isn't always positive, implying that there are lengthy time intervals during which beta and average returns are negatively related.

The Fama and MacBeth Study. Fama and MacBeth extended the work of Black, Jensen, and Scholes in two ways. First, they examined the relationship between portfolio returns and betas for each month between January 1935 and June 1968. Second, they examined the impacts of two additional factors: beta squared and unsystematic risk.

The return-generating model which they examined was:

Fama-MacBeth Regression

$$\underbrace{\begin{array}{c}\text{Return}\\\text{in}\\\text{Month } t\end{array}}_{R_{pt}} = \text{Constant} + \underbrace{\begin{array}{c}\text{Beta}\\\text{Effect}\end{array}}_{} + \underbrace{\begin{array}{c}\text{Beta}\\\text{Squared}\\\text{Effect}\end{array}}_{} + \underbrace{\begin{array}{c}\text{Unsystematic}\\\text{Risk}\\\text{Effect}\end{array}}_{} \quad \textbf{(9.9)}$$

$$R_{pt} = \alpha_{0t} + \alpha_{1t}(\beta_{pt-1}) + \alpha_{2t}(\beta_{pt-1})^2 + \alpha_3(\sigma_{pt-1})$$

where R_{pt} is the return on a portfolio in month t, β_{pt-1} is the estimated portfolio beta in the prior month, $(\beta_{pt-1})^2$ is the beta squared, and σ_{pt-1} is the average unsystematic risk of the stocks in a portfolio in the prior month. When this equation was estimated for each month between January 1935 and June 1968, there was considerable variability in each of the regression coefficients. We will discuss only the *average monthly* results, as shown in Table 9-2.

The intercept term, α_0, was 0.2% per month. When annualized, this represents a rate of return of 2.4% per year. While this was not too far from the average 30-day T-bill return during the same time interval, the term wasn't statistically different from zero on average and showed considerable month-to-month variability. The estimate of the market risk premium, α_1, was usually statistically significant, as we would expect if the CAPM is correct. The two remaining terms, which were testing for nonlinearity and effects of unsystematic risk, appeared to be unrelated to portfolio returns.

TABLE 9-2 *Fama-MacBeth Test of CAPM*

$$\tilde{R}_{pt} = \alpha_{0t} + \alpha_{1t}(\tilde{B}_{pt-1}) + \alpha_{2t}(\tilde{B}_{pt-1})^2 + \alpha_3(\tilde{\sigma}_{pt-1})$$

Parameter	Average Monthly Value	Number of Standard Deviations from 0.0
α_0	0.0020	0.55
α_1	0.0114	1.85
α_2	0.0114	−0.86
α_3	0.0516	1.11

SOURCE: Reprinted from "Risk, Return and Equilibrium: Empirical Tests," *Journal of Political Economy*, May–June 1973, pp. 622–23, by E. Fama and R. MacBeth, by permission of The University of Chicago Press. © 1973 by the University of Chicago. All rights reserved.

Conclusion. Numerous other studies have empirically tested the CAPM. On net, the evidence suggests that:

1. The intercept term is generally larger than the risk-free rate. This indicates that some revised version of the CAPM is needed.
2. The relationship implied in the CAPM holds best for lengthy time spans, as opposed to short intervals of five years or so.
3. Beta is the only measure of risk which is empirically related to average returns. Whenever unsystematic risk appears to be important, it can be explained by statistical weaknesses in the data used.
4. The relationship between beta and average returns is linear.

What Is the Market Portfolio?

In theory, the market portfolio M consists of all risky assets. Since these include stocks, bonds, futures contracts, real estate, human capital, etc., portfolio M is impossible to identify. In fact, aggregate common stock returns are difficult enough to determine. While a large number of stocks are included in indexes such as the S&P Composite and the NYSE Composite, literally thousands of OTC stocks are excluded.

Typically, people have compromised by assuming that the returns on the broad stock market indexes are highly correlated with returns on the true portfolio M. The appropriateness of this compromise and, in fact, the testability of any version of the CAPM have come under sharp attack, however, in a breakthrough article by Roll. The results of Roll's critique of the CAPM are profound, but they can be summarized as follows:

1. Tests of the CAPM are in reality tests of the market portfolio's mean variance efficiency.
2. The market portfolio consists of all risky assets, which can never be totally observed. Thus, the CAPM (that is, the efficiency of M) is untestable.
3. As long as the proxy used for M is mean-variance efficient (sits on the efficient frontier) *ex post*, then the betas calculated against this proxy and average security returns will *mathematically* be linearly related to the proxy portfolio's risk and return. The linearity observed in most of the empirical research between security betas and average returns is a mathematical tautology. Its only economic meaning is that the proxy portfolio was mean-variance efficient. But this efficiency of the proxy does not prove the efficiency of the market portfolio or the validity of the CAPM.
4. If the proxy used for M is not *ex post* mean-variance efficient, the empirical results have no meaning whatsoever, and any form of relationship might be found between average security returns and beta (approximately linear, curvilinear, residual error risk found to be significant, etc.).
5. Models which attempt to evaluate investment performance via the CAPM are inappropriate.

Roll's critique of the CAPM elegantly expressed what many people had previously stated more informally but without such force and economic rigor. Because of the potential significance of these arguments to existing financial theory, modern investment management techniques, and performance evaluation, we must examine the ideas more thoroughly. The fact that the mean-variance efficiency of the market portfolio is the single testable hypothesis of the CAPM is easy to understand intuitively. For example, in a world in which a risk-free security exists, the CAPM is based upon all individuals electing to hold only one portfolio of *risky assets*. This portfolio must be M—the market portfolio of all risky assets. Tests of CAPM are inherently tests of portfolio M's mean-variance efficiency. But it is clear that researchers will never be able to completely identify what portfolio M consists of. As a result, the CAPM is untestable.

Roll's third and fourth conclusions are more difficult to understand, and their mathematical proof lies beyond the scope of this book. Nonetheless, we must understand the meaning of the conclusion to appreciate the true status of empirical tests of the CAPM. Assume that there are an unidentifiably large number of risky assets available. To proxy these assets, we examine the historical returns on, say, 1,000 observable common stocks. In calculating individual stock betas, we measure a stock's ex post standard deviation (σ_i), the standard deviation of ex post returns on *some* portfolio (σ_p), and the ex post correlation coefficient between the stock's and the portfolio's return (r_{ip}). Beta is then measured as beta = $(\sigma_i r_{ip})/\sigma_p$. An infinite number of reference portfolios could be created using the 1,000 stocks. Of such possible reference portfolios, some will be ex post efficient (in that they provide the lowest variance of returns for a given mean return) and others will not be efficient. If we happen to use *any* of the ex post efficient portfolios, then the following precise mathematical relationship will exist:

Estimated SML $$\bar{R}_i = RF + \beta_i[\bar{R}_p - RF] \tag{9.10}$$

While this is the empirical version of the CAPM tested, Roll showed that the relationship is purely mathematical. There is no economic content to it. Studies which have found a linear relationship offer no proof at all that the CAPM is correct. If an empirical test finds a linear relationship, it simply means that the researcher was fortunate enough to have chosen an ex post mean-variance efficient portfolio as a market proxy. If the researcher does not find a linear relationship between historic beta and mean security returns, nothing can be concluded at all. Either the researcher used an inefficient portfolio as the market proxy, or the CAPM is invalid. But it is impossible to distinguish between the explanations.

Roll's fifth conclusion can be illustrated with the use of Figure 9-6. Assume the CAPM is true. The dashed lines represent the actual efficient set of risky real assets and the true capital asset pricing line. However, individuals wishing to evaluate investment performance use a market portfolio proxy, say, the Standard & Poor's Composite Index. If the researchers are lucky, the S&P Composite will represent one of the many available efficient portfolios. Since the composite index is assumed to be efficient, a linear relationship will exist between return and beta risk, shown as the solid SML line.

FIGURE 9-6 *Effects of Roll's Comments on Performance Evaluation*

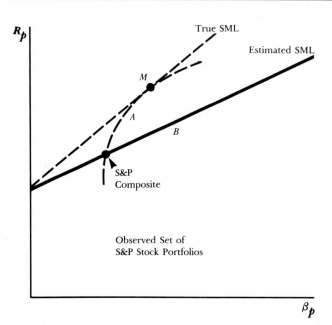

With this as background, what is to be concluded about the performance of mutual funds *A* and *B*? While *A* appeared to outperform the market, all it really did was outperform combinations of borrowing and lending portfolios of the S&P. Its apparent good performance is meaningless. Roll's observation is intuitively quite simple. If the market portfolio is *the* best set of risky assets to hold, no other portfolio can ever beat it. If some investment or speculative strategies seem to "beat the market," then either the CAPM is wrong (in which case it shouldn't be used to evaluate performance), or a poor market proxy was used (in which case, again, it shouldn't be used).

In conclusion, Roll's observations have raised fundamental questions about the CAPM's truth, testability, and use in evaluating investment performance.

Conclusions

As initially developed, the capital asset pricing model was built on a variety of assumptions. These included the following:

1. Selection decisions are based on investor preferences—utility curves. It was assumed this implied that expected portfolio returns and standard deviations of portfolio returns were the only variables of importance to the investor.

2. All investors have a common risk-free rate at which they may invest or borrow unlimited amounts.

3. Information is costless, because all investors have the same beliefs; their expectations of the future are homogeneous.

4. Taxes are zero.

5. There are no impediments to trading such as brokerage fees; that is, frictionless markets exist.

6. Securities may be traded in any quantity including fractional units.

7. Decisions are based on the distribution of terminal wealth at a single future date.

Since the CAPM's original development, a large body of literature has been created which deals with these assumptions. The models discussed above provide a flavor of the results. In most cases the market portfolio continues to play a critical role, in that it usually remains the optimal portfolio of risky assets that an individual should hold. In addition, expected returns are linearly related to systematic market risk. Usually, such systematic risks can be captured by a single-beta model, but a variety of so-called multibeta models have been developed.

ARBITRAGE PRICING THEORY

The various models reviewed above are all descendants of the original CAPM. Although they have removed many of the classic CAPM assumptions, they are all based on assumptions about the preferences investors have for different distributions of wealth—that is, they are all built on the *utility* an investor places on a given distribution of wealth. Given a particular utility function, the models have been able to develop appropriate measures of portfolio risk.

In the early 1970s Stephen Ross offered an alternative model of security pricing known as *arbitrage pricing theory* (APT). In its final form, APT may appear to be similar to CAPM, but it is actually a completely different species. Whereas the CAPM is built on utility theory, APT says nothing about investor preference. Instead, it is built on the economic principle that identical goods should sell at identical prices.

In this section we will develop the basic theory and implications of APT. A word of warning is necessary before we begin, however. The final APT model can look deceptively similar to the CAPM. In fact, the two theories *can* lead to the same investment implications. But the theories are based on completely different logical developments and *do not necessarily* result in the same investment implications. As we develop the logic of APT, you will probably understand it better if you put the CAPM out of your thoughts for a while and focus solely on what APT suggests. After this new theory is fully developed, you can then recall your knowledge of CAPM and directly compare the two models. APT is a theory which competes with CAPM—it is not an extension. It is another way to view the world.

Theory of Arbitrage

The Law of One Price. A basic principle of economics is that two goods which are perfect substitutes for each other must be priced identically. If not, arbitrage transactions will occur until the prices of the goods are identical. For example, consider two grocery stores located next to each other and the price of grade A eggs in each. What would happen if store 1 were to sell the eggs for $1.00 a dozen and store 2 were to sell them for $2.00 a dozen? Some enterprising person would stand outside store 2 and take orders to sell eggs for (say) $1.50. Then, each time she received an order, she would immediately buy eggs for $1.00 from store 1. On each order, she would earn a $0.50 arbitrage profit. Of course, the arbitrage would continue until the price of eggs in each store was identical. At that point the arbitrageur would look for other price discrepancies.

We defined arbitrage back in Chapter 1, but it is useful to review the definition in the context of the egg example. First, note that our arbitrageur made no investment. She bought eggs only when she made a sale. True arbitrage involves no capital commitment. Second, note that the arbitrageur had no risk. The purchase and sale prices were known. True arbitrage involves no risk. In short, an arbitrage transaction results in a risk-free profit with no capital commitment. It is the potential for such arbitrage profits between securities which drives the arbitrage pricing theory.

The formal arbitrage pricing theory is a development of the 1970s, but arbitrage transactions have existed since humans developed the most primitive economies. Today arbitrage in the security markets is extensive. A large number of people earn a living by selling gold in one country and simultaneously buying it in another, by purchasing Treasury bills from one bank and simultaneously selling them to another (remember bid-ask spreads), by purchasing shares of IBM on one stock exchange and simultaneously selling them on another, etc. Arbitrage operations are possible as long as prices of perfect substitutes are different.[5]

The end result of arbitrage is that two perfect substitutes must sell for the same price. This is known as the law of one price. Without calling it such, we have, in fact, made use of this principle when developing the standard CAPM. For example, the expected return on securities with the same betas must be identical in equilibrium.

Determinants of Security Returns. Proponents of APT state that returns on securities are due to a variety of events which cause investors to reassess (neglecting interest and dividends) what the value of a security should be. For example, inflation rates, food production, and population growth and redistribution affect the investment worth of all securities to varying degrees. Other events, such as labor strikes in the airline industry or clothing fads, affect a subset of all securities. Finally, certain events have an effect on only a single security. APT expresses this belief as follows:

---

[5]As we will see in Chapters 15–17, the potential for arbitrage profits is also the force which is responsible for market prices of security options and futures contracts.

APT
Realized
Returns

$$\tilde{R}_{it} = a_{0t} + b_{i1}\tilde{F}_{1t} + b_{i2}\tilde{F}_{2t} + b_{i3}\tilde{F}_{3t} \ldots b_{iN}\tilde{F}_{Nt} + \tilde{e}_{it}$$

$$= a_{0t} + \sum_{K=1}^{N} b_{iK}\tilde{F}_{Kt} + \tilde{e}_{it} \qquad \text{(9.11)}$$

The $\tilde{F}_{Kt}$ terms are referred to as *factors*—events in period t which affect all securities or subsets of securities. For example, $\tilde{F}_{1t}$ might represent real growth of GNP in the United States during year t and thus take on a value of, say, 4.0%. The notion that these factors can influence the returns on either all securities or only particular subsets of securities is important and something we will have more to say about later. The b_{iK} terms represent the return sensitivity of security i to the level of factor K. The a_{0t} term is the return that is expected in period t on all securities when the value of all factors is zero. Finally, the $\tilde{e}_{it}$ term represents the return which is unique to security i in period t.

Two of these variables have symbols similar to CAPM variables (b_{iK} and $\tilde{e}_{it}$), and to a degree they measure somewhat similar forces. But they should not be confused with CAPM betas or residual errors. One of the b_{iK} APT variables *might* represent the sensitivity of a security's returns to returns on the market portfolio, but then again it *might not*. APT is silent as to what the factors are. The factors might be found via statistical tests, but knowledge of the factors is unimportant in the development of this theory. In addition, in APT $\tilde{e}_{it}$ reflects returns unique to security i, whereas in CAPM it is simply a return which is uncorrelated with the market portfolio.

It is important to note that Equation 9.11 is a *linear* equation. None of the terms are raised to an exponent (other than 1.0), and their cumulative effects are summed. This is not done for simplicity—it is a logical consequence of the theory and a major empirical implication. We show why this is so below.

Equation 9.11 can be used to state the *expected return* on a security as follows:

APT
Expected
Returns

$$E(R_{it}) = a_{0t} + b_{i1}\bar{F}_{1t} + b_{i2}\bar{F}_{2t} + \ldots + b_{iN}\bar{F}_{N}$$

$$= a_{0t} + \sum_{K=1}^{N} b_{iK}\bar{F}_{Kt} \qquad \text{(9.12)}$$

where $\bar{F}_{Kt}$ denotes the expected value of factor K in period t. This relationship is then used to re-express the actual *realized return* in period t as follows:

APT
Realized
Return

$$\tilde{R}_{it} = a_{0t} + b_{i1}(\bar{F}_{1t} + \tilde{f}_{1t}) + b_{i2}(\bar{F}_{2t} + \tilde{f}_{2t}) \ldots$$

$$+ b_{iN}(\bar{F}_{Nt} + \tilde{f}_{Nt}) + \tilde{e}_{it}$$

$$= a_{0t} + b_{i1}\bar{F}_{1t} + b_{i2}\bar{F}_{2t} \ldots + b_{iN}\bar{F}_{Nt} \qquad \text{(9.13)}$$

$$+ b_{i1}\tilde{f}_{1t} + b_{i2}\tilde{f}_{2t} \ldots + b_{iN}\tilde{f}_{Nt} + \tilde{e}_{it}$$

$$= E(R_{it}) + (b_{i1}\tilde{f}_{1t} + b_{i2}\tilde{f}_{2t} \ldots b_{iN}\tilde{f}_{Nt}) + \tilde{e}_{it}$$

where the $\tilde{f}_{Kt}$ terms represent the *unexpected outcome* of a given factor in period t. For example, assume factor 1 reflects real growth in U.S. GNP. If expected GNP growth is 4.0% but actual growth turns out to be 3.5%, then $\tilde{f}_{1t}$ would be -0.5%.

The last line of Equation 9.13 says that the realized return is composed of two parts: the return which is expected and an unexpected return. The unexpected return is also composed of two parts: return sensitivity to unexpected factor outcomes and to unexpected security-unique events.

Effects of Arbitrage

According to APT, Equation 9.13 is not simply a convenient way to approximate the process by which security returns are generated. The theory of arbitrage pricing implies that Equation 9.13 must be true! If disequilibriums in security market prices are fully arbitraged, then security returns will be generated by exactly such a linear model.

To ensure that all possible arbitrages are in fact conducted, APT makes the following three assumptions:

1. Short selling is unrestricted and short sellers have full use of cash proceeds. If limits are placed on the amount one could short sell or if the cash inflow from short sales cannot be used to finance an offsetting purchase, then complete arbitrage of mispriced securities might not be possible.
2. There are no costs to trading. If transaction costs such as brokerage fees must be paid, the arbitrage of a mispriced security is limited.
3. There are a sufficient number of securities available such that security-unique risk (the uncertainty about e_{it}) can be eliminated by holding a well-diversified portfolio. If the "idiosyncratic" risk can be eliminated, then the only uncertainties which must be dealt with are uncertainties about factor outcomes.

Given these assumptions, Equations 9.11 through 9.13 must be true.

This is best illustrated if we consider a one-factor world. In such a world, APT states that expected and realized returns should be generated by the following relationship:

One-Factor Expected Return	$E(R_{it}) = a_{0t} + b_{i1}\bar{F}_{1t}$	**(9.14a)**
One-Factor Realized Return	$\tilde{R}_{it} = E(R_{it}) + b_{i1}\tilde{f}_{1t} + \tilde{e}_{it}$	**(9.14b)**

Let's begin the analysis of why this should be so by first assuming that it is not. Consider the three securities shown in Figure 9-7. Clearly their expected returns are not linearly related to their factor sensitivities.

Consistent with APT assumptions, we will assume that each security is actually a well-diversified portfolio such that all firm-unique risk is zero. That is, the variance of each e_{it} term is zero.

An arbitrage consists of a transaction guaranteeing a risk-free profit with no capital commitment. Given the data shown in Figure 9-7, there is a clear arbitrage available. This consists of buying portfolio B and financing the purchase by short selling a combination of A and C having a factor sensitivity identical to that of B.

FIGURE 9-7 *Illustration of One-Factor Expected Returns*

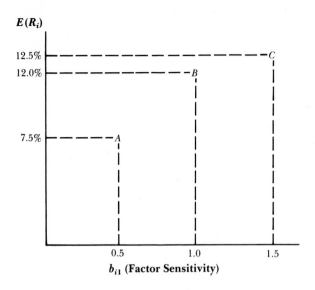

Security B has a factor sensitivity of 1.0 and an expected return of 12%. If we were to invest 50% in A and 50% in C, the net factor sensitivity would also be 1.0, but the expected return would only be 10%. In terms of factor pricing we could think of the relationships as follows:

For Securities A and C_0:

$$E(R_{it}) = 5\% + b_{i1} \, (5\%)$$

For Security B:

$$E(R_{it}) = 7\% + b_{i1} \, (5\%)$$

It is this extra 2% constant return which will provide the arbitrage profit.

To illustrate the arbitrage, assume we decide to buy $100,000 of portfolio B. To finance the purchase, portfolios A and B would be short sold in an aggregate amount of $100,000. Since we want the factor risk of the A and C portfolios to exactly off-set the 1.0 risk of B, 50% of the $100,000 would be obtained from A and the re-maining 50% from C. This is shown below, where X_A represents the fraction of portfolio A:

$$1.0 = X_A 0.5 + (1 - X_A) 1.5$$

$$X_A = 0.50$$

Potential outcomes of this transaction are shown in Table 9-3. Three possible unex-pected factor outcomes are shown ($f = -5\%$, 0%, and $+5\%$) in order to prove that a known profit is indeed guaranteed. The profit of $2,000 represents the 2.0% greater constant return available on portfolio B. Of course, anyone seeing the situation

TABLE 9-3 *One-Factor Arbitrage Outcome*

	Today		End of Period		
	$	Factor Risk	Low $(f_{1t} = 5\%)$	Expected $(f_{1t} = 0)$	High $(f_{1t} = 5\%)$
Buy Portfolio *B*	−100,000	+1.0	+107,000	+112,000	+117,000
Sell Portfolio *A*, *C*					
Portfolio *A*	+50,000	−0.25	−52,500	−53,750	−55,000
Portfolio *C*	+50,000	−0.75	−52,500	−56,250	−60,000
Net	0.0	0.0	2,000	2,000	2,000

Low Calculations:

$$100,000 + 100,000 \ [12\% + 1.0 \ (-5\%)] \ = 107,000$$
$$50,000 + \ \ 50,000 \ [7.5\% + 0.5 \ (-5\%)] \ = \ \ 52,500$$
$$50,000 + \ \ 50,000 \ [12.5\% + 1.5 \ (-5\%)] = \ \ 52,500$$

High Calculations:

$$100,000 + 100,000 \ [12\% + 1.0 \ (5\%)] \ = 117,000$$
$$50,000 + \ \ 50,000 \ [7.5\% + 0.5 \ (5\%)] \ = \ \ 55,000$$
$$50,000 + \ \ 50,000 \ [12.5\% + 1.5 \ (5\%)] = \ \ 60,000$$

depicted in Figure 9-7 would jump at such an arbitrage. As a result of many such trades, the prices of the securities would adjust until the relationship between each security's expected return and its sensitivity to the factor *is linear*.

This notion is reinforced in Figure 9-8, where expected returns on securities are related to the single common factor by a strange wavy curve. Clearly, there are a large number of potential arbitrages available in the world depicted in the curve. The important point, however, is that these arbitrage transactions will finally result in a linear relationship between expected returns and factor sensitivities such as that shown by the dashed line.

Factor Portfolios. Let's now consider a world in which there are two factors which affect the returns on all securities. In this case, APT states that expected and realized returns would be generated by the following relationships:

Two-Factor Expected Return

$$E(R_{it}) = a_{0t} + b_{i1}\bar{F}_{1t} + b_{i2}\bar{F}_{2t} \tag{9.15a}$$

Two-Factor Realized Return

$$\tilde{R}_{it} = E(R_{it}) + b_{it}\tilde{f}_{1t} + b_{i2}\tilde{f}_{2t} + \tilde{e}_{it} \tag{9.15b}$$

In this case, expected returns are related to expected factor outcomes by a hyperplane such as that shown in Figure 9-9. In this case, of course, the expected return on a security (such as *X* shown in the figure) will depend on the security's sensitivity to both factors.

If there are two factors, any arbitrage must result in zero factor sensitivity for both factor 1 and factor 2. This can be done by selecting proper percentage holdings of the

FIGURE 9-8 *General Illustration of One-Factor Expected Returns*

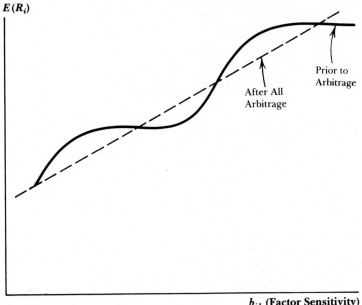

various portfolios available. For example, assume that three well-diversified portfolios have factor sensitivities as shown below:

Security Portfolio	Factor Sensitivities		Expected Return
	b_{i1}	b_{i2}	
W	0.80	0.40	7.6%
X	0.40	0.80	7.2%
Y	1.20	0.00	8.0%
Z	0.00	1.20	8.0%

Is there an arbitrage possible in this case?

If expected returns on either factor are not linearly related to factor sensitivity, then an arbitrage is possible. Let's consider factor 1 first. We do this by eliminating all factor 2 risk. Notice that portfolios W and X could be combined in a manner which would result in zero factor 2 sensitivity. This would consist of either:

For a Net Cash Inflow:	*For a Net Cash Outflow:*
Purchase \$1 of X	Sell \$1 of X
Sell Short \$2 of W	Buy \$2 of W

Letting X_i refer to the percentage of your net investment in security i, the resulting factor 1 and factor 2 sensitivities would be:

$$b_{pK} = (X_X \times b_{XK}) + (X_W \times b_{WK})$$

FIGURE 9-9 *Relationship of Expected Returns to Expected Factor Outcomes*

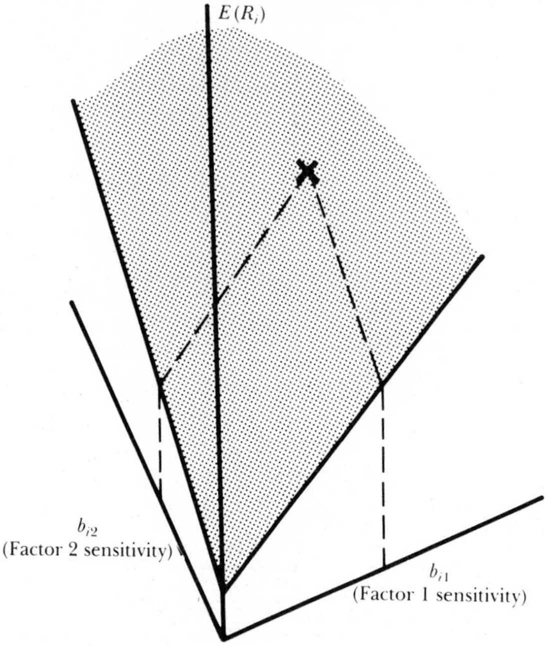

Factor	For a Net Cash Inflow:	For a Net Cash Outflow:
1	$b_{p1} = (1.0 \times 0.40) + (-2.0 \times 0.80)$ $= -1.2$	$b_{p1} = (-1.0 \times 0.40) + (2.0 \times 0.80)$ $= +1.2$
2	$b_{p2} = (1.0 \times 0.80) + (-2.0 \times 0.40)$ $= 0.0$	$b_{p2} = (-1.0 \times 0.8) + (2.0 \times 0.40)$ $= 0.0$

And the resulting expected returns would be:

$$E(R_{pt}) = X_X \times E(R_{Xt}) + X_W \times E(R_{Wt})$$

For a Net Cash Inflow:	For a Net Cash Outflow:
$E(R_{pt}) = (1.0 \times 7.2) + (-2.0 \times 7.6)$ $= -8.0\%$	$E(R_{pt}) = (-1.0 \times 7.2) + (2.0 \times 7.6)$ $= +8.0\%$

In short, when W and X are combined to have zero factor 2 sensitivity, they provide an expected return of either $+8.0\%$ or -8.0% depending on whether there is an initial cash outflow or inflow. Similarly, factor 1 sensitivity of this portfolio is either $+1.2$ or -1.2. Since the expected return and factor sensitivity of portfolio Y are also $+8.0\%$ and $+1.2$, it is clear that there is no arbitrage available on factor 1.

In contrast, an arbitrage is available on factor 2. In this case, factor 1 risk is eliminated by trading \$2 of X and \$1 of W in an opposite position. The results are summarized below:

For a Net Cash Inflow:		
Sell $2 X	*Plus*	*Buy $1 W*
$b_{p1} = (-2 \times 0.4)$ $= 0.0$	$+$	(1×0.8)
$b_{p2} = (-2 \times 0.8)$ $= -1.2$	$+$	(1×0.4)
$E(R_{pt}) = (-2 \times 7.2)$ $= -6.8$	$+$	(1×7.6)

For a Net Cash Outflow:		
Buy $2 X	*Plus*	*Sell $1 W*
$b_{p1} = (2 \times 0.4)$ $= 0.0$	$+$	(-1×0.08)
$b_{p2} = (2 \times 0.8)$ $= +1.2$	$+$	(-1×0.04)
$E(R_{pt}) = (2 \times 7.2)$ $= +6.8$	$+$	(-1×7.6)

Since portfolio Z has identical factor 2 risk but a greater expected return, the arbitrage would consist of:

	Cash	*Factor 2* *Sensitivity*
Buy $1 Portfolio Z	$-\$1$	$+1.2$
Sell Portfolio of W and X	$+\ 1$	-1.2
Net	$\$0$	0.0

This example serves to point out three important ideas. First, arbitrageurs can create portfolios which focus on individual factors — portfolios which are insensitive to all other factor outcomes. Therefore, they can arbitrage mispricing within each possible factor and ensure that a linear relationship exists between expected returns and the various factors. Second, investors can create portfolios which have factor sensitivities that meet their unique needs. For example, assume that an oil factor exists and that you are investing pension assets for an oil firm. By proper selection, a portfolio could be created which hedges (to various degrees) the risk to employees of a decline in the oil business. Finally, this example points out the relationship between the factor sensitivity of a total portfolio and the sensitivities of the securities held. The sensitivity of the total portfolio to a given factor is simply a weighted average of the factor sensitivity of each security held.

Symbolically:

Portfolio Sensitivity to Factor K

$$b_{pK} = \sum_{i=1}^{M} X_i b_{iK} \qquad (9.16)$$

where X_i = the percentage invested in security i and b_{iK} = the sensitivity of security i to factor K.

Priced Factors. The proponents of arbitrage pricing theory believe that expected returns on a security are determined by a constant return associated with all securities plus sensitivities to various economic events, or factors. Earlier we expressed this in Equation 9.12 as follows:

APT Expected Returns

$$E(R_{1t}) = a_{0t} + b_{i1} \bar{F}_{1t} + b_{i2} \bar{F}_{2t} + \ldots + b_{iN} \bar{F}_{Nt}$$

The relationship must be linear and must hold for all securities and portfolios, or arbitrage profits will be available.

Note that the expected return consists of a risk-free return plus a number of terms which could be thought of as risk premiums. A risk-free rate is available since it is (theoretically) possible to create a portfolio which has no net exposure to factor uncertainties and no residual security risk. The risk-free rate might change over time. But within any single period a known risk-free rate will apply to all securities. The more interesting terms are the factors and security sensitivities.

In our earlier discussion we thought of F_{1t} as being, say, the expected real growth of GNP. The F_{1t} could take on a value of, say, 4%, and b_{i1} might be 3.0. Similarly, F_{2t} might reflect changes in the level of employment with $F_{2t} = 200,000$ and $b_{i2} = 0.00003$. If these are the only two factors used in determining what the expected return on a security should be, they are referred to as *priced factors*. A priced factor is an uncertain economic event which affects the expected return that investors will require.

Earlier we classified the types of events which could affect a security's return into three groups:

1. Events affecting all securities
2. Events affecting a subset of all securities
3. Events affecting only a single security

Clearly, events that affect only a single security can essentially be diversified away. Thus they will not be priced factors—investors will not require compensation for bearing such uncertainties. Similarly, it is clear that events which affect the returns of all securities *will* be priced—investors will demand compensation for bearing their uncertainties. The difficulty arises with events which affect subsets of all securities. APT is mute on whether such factors will be priced. The conceptual answer is probably that it depends on whether such uncertainties can be diversified away. Economic events whose uncertainties can be eliminated through reasonable diversification should not be factors which investors price. The pragmatic answer given by proponents of APT is that they don't know—that only empirical studies can determine what factors are in fact priced.

Let's assume that two factors are priced and that we know the following:

	Factor 1	*Factor 2*
Type of event	GNP Growth	Employment Change
Expected F_{Kt}	4.0%	200,000
Security A's b_{iK}	3.0	0.00003
Current risk-free rate of interest = 4%		

In this case the expected return on security A would be 22%:

$$= 4.0\% + 3.0\ (4.0\%) + 0.00003\ (200,000)$$

$$= 4.0\% + 12.0\% \quad + 6.0\%$$

$$= 22.0\%$$

The two values of 12% and 6% associated with the priced factors are thought of as risk premiums. When this is done, the factor sensitivity terms are standardized in a way that makes the average sensitivity = 1.0. The b_{iK} values we have discussed are divided by the average b_{iK} values across all securities.

Assume that the average b_{iK} values in the example above are:

$$b_{i1} \text{ average} = 2.0$$

$$b_{i2} \text{ average} = 0.00004$$

Then the expected return on security A could be expressed as:

$$E(R_{At}) = 4.0\% + \frac{3.0}{2.0} \ (4.0\% \times 2.0) + \frac{0.00003}{0.00004} \ (200{,}000 \times 0.00004)$$

$$= 4.0\% + 1.5 \ (8\%) + 0.75 \ (8\%)$$

$$= 22.0\%$$

After this standardization, the APT is usually expressed as:

APT Expected Returns
$$E(R_{1t}) = a_{0t} + b_{i1}\lambda_{1t} + b_{i2}\lambda_{2t} + \ldots + b_{iN}\lambda_{Nt} \qquad (9.17)$$

where the average b_{iK} term is now 1.0 and the λ_{Kt} terms are thought of as the risk premium associated with each priced factor.

APT and the CAPM

You should now recall your knowledge of the CAPM so that we can compare and contrast the two theories.

The theories are similar in a number of respects. Both express the expected return on a security as the sum of a risk-free rate plus a risk premium. Both imply broad diversification. And if there is only one priced factor, b_{i1} of APT is the same as beta$_i$ of the CAPM, and λ_{1t} is the same as the risk premium on the market portfolio.

They differ, however, in their fundamental assumptions. Whereas the CAPM is based on utility theory, APT is based on the economic principle of arbitrage. Although a one-factor model might look suspiciously like the CAPM's security market line, or multifactor models like multibeta CAPM models, they are in fact different species. APT does not assume that investors care only about expected returns and standard deviations of returns. The theory also says nothing about the optimality of the market portfolio.

Tests of APT

Because of Roll's suggestion that the CAPM is logically untestable, most recent empirical research has explored the validity of APT. These tests can be classified into two types: (1) tests in which the researcher does not hypothesize any specific type or number of factors but, instead, extracts statistically significant factors from historical returns and (2) tests of whether explicitly defined potential factors are related to security returns. We shall refer to the first class of tests as *unspecified factor* tests and the second class as *specified factor* tests.

Unspecified Factor Tests. In these tests, the researcher begins the study with no preconceived idea as to how many priced factors exist or what any such factors might represent. Instead, a statistical procedure known as factor analysis is used to extract whatever statistically significant factors might be present in a sample of security returns.

Factor analysis is a complex statistical procedure which was developed much before and independent of the development of APT. It takes observations on a large number of variables and tries to identify one or more statistically significant underlying forces which could have created the variables observed. For example, assume that you collect the following observations on a sample of people: height, weight, age, hair color, and hair length. If factor analysis is used, a single important factor related to height, weight, and hair length would emerge. Age and hair color would be unrelated to the factor and unexplained by the model. The factor analysis procedure would not be able to identify what the single factor is a proxy for—even though you could logically deduce that it is a gender factor.

When applied to security returns, a time series of returns on a sample of securities is used. Factor analysis then finds various underlying factors which best explain the covariance of returns within the sample. The number of factors found depends on the statistical significance desired by the researcher and the particular version of factor analysis employed. (There are many.)

In essence, the procedure uses a large number of return observations on many securities to determine whether the returns can be explained by a few common forces. If all security returns are what we have called firm-unique returns, then no common factors would be found. If the CAPM is correct, a number of common factors might be found, but only one priced factor.

After a set of common factors is found, a factor sensitivity is found for each stock and each factor. We will define these as:

$$\hat{b}_{iK} = \text{the sensitivity of security } i \text{ to common factor } K$$

Although these $\hat{b}_{iK}$ values are statistical estimates of our earlier b_{iK} terms, their units can differ considerably.

To examine which of the factors are priced by investors, a cross-sectional regression similar to the following is performed:

Factor Regression
$$\bar{R}_i + a_0 + a_1\hat{b}_{i1} + a_2\hat{b}_{i2} + \ldots + a_N\hat{b}_{iN} + e_i \qquad \textbf{(9.18)}$$

where $\bar{R}_i$ = the average return on security i, b_{iK} = the estimated factor sensitivities, and e_i = an unexplained error term. The regression parameters which are estimated include the constant return term a_0 and the slope coefficients a_1 through a_N.

If a particular factor is priced by investors, the slope term associated with the factor should be statistically significant. For example, if factor 1 is a priced factor, a_1

will be statistically different from 0.0. Alternatively, if a factor is found for which investors do not require compensation in the form of higher (or lower) expected returns, the a_K regression estimate will not be statistically different from zero.

In the earliest version of this test, Roll and Ross used a sample of daily returns on 42 portfolios of 30 stocks each. They suggested that at least three but no more than six common priced factors appeared to exist in their sample. Other studies have found similar results. But these studies are not without critics, as we shall discuss below.

Specified Factor Tests. One of the principal difficulties with the approach above is that the procedure does not suggest what the priced factors represent. Therefore, a number of researchers have hypothesized a variety of possible factors which might be priced and have developed tests to see whether they are. For example, Fogler, John, and Tipton tested a model in which they claim that three factors (returns on a stock market proxy, changes in interest rates, and changes in bond default rates) are related to individual stock returns. In addition, Oldfield and Rogalski investigated aggregate stock returns and Treasury bill returns as common factors.

The most complete test of a specified factor model to date was conducted by Chen, Roll, and Ross. They suggested that a large portion of the covariances between securities can be explained by unanticipated changes in four variables:

1. The difference between long-term and short-term Treasury yields to maturity
2. Inflation rates
3. The difference between yields to maturity of BB-rated bonds and Treasuries
4. Growth of industrial production

Is APT Testable?

Serious questions remain, however, whether APT can ever be empirically tested. Studies by Dhrymes, Friend, and Gultekin provided evidence that the number of common factors found in an unspecified factor test increased as: (1) the number of securities in the sample increased, and (2) the length of the time period sampled increased. Roll and Ross responded that this would be expected. As additional securities or returns are collected, additional common factors might emerge. For example, as the sample size increases, firms from a number of new industries might be included which share a common factor. Roll and Ross point out that it is the number of priced factors which is important, not the total number of factors.

Perhaps the most telling criticism of APT was made by Shanken. His argument goes as follows. Assume that APT *does* apply to the underlying economic structure of the economy. There are certain basic economic industries each of which is sensitive to various factors that are priced by investors. Individual firms then create portfolios of these basic industries. When firms create such asset portfolios, they alter the level of factor risk inherent in their securities. For example, assume that two underlying priced factors exist. Firm A might invest in the underlying economic industries in a way that eliminates all of factor 2. Thus, if APT researchers sample firms similar to firm A, they will conclude that factor 2 doesn't exist. The returns which are examined on securities can mask or exacerbate the underlying factor risks in the economy.

This could be a particular problem if firms are constantly changing the nature of their asset portfolios, as in the case of mutual funds. No one would suggest obtaining empirical estimates of common priced factors from mutual fund returns, since the security holdings of the funds are constantly changing. The problem is less severe at the individual stock level since firms do not shift asset mixes as rapidly as mutual funds do. Nonetheless, the problem remains.

Stationarity of Risk Premiums

Underlying all of the CAPM and APT tests was an unstated assumption: the return-generating process is stationary. By this we mean that the covariances between the returns of any two securities don't change and that the market risk premium doesn't change.

Research into this stationarity assumption is in its infancy, but a number of studies suggest that it is a problem. For example, consider Figure 9-10, in which estimates of monthly standard deviations of the S&P 500 are shown. There is considerable variability in this risk proxy—enough to suggest that investors might change whatever risk premiums they require.

A recent study by French, Schwert, and Stambaugh indicates that this may be the case. When changes in estimates of stock price volatility were related to returns on the S&P 500 during a given month, these researchers found evidence that the expected market risk premium is positively related to the predicted volatility of stock returns.

If investors' perceptions of risk and their required risk premiums are continuously changing over time, tests of various asset pricing models will be difficult. At present, we must be open-minded and continue to explore. We do seem to know two things: (1) return variability and required returns are directly related, and (2) diversification reduces return variability.

SUMMARY

In summary, should we say that the standard CAPM is supported by historical evidence and is robust enough that its major conclusions remain even when various assumptions are removed? A strong case can be made for responding no to the question. Empirical tests found returns on portfolios with zero systematic risk to be much larger than the risk-free rate approximation. And the empirical observation that average historical portfolio returns are linearly related to b_i values and unrelated to other potential measures of risk has been shown by Roll to be due (most likely) to the luck of the researchers in choosing an ex post efficient portfolio as their index. In fact, Roll has argued that since tests of the CAPM are no more than tests of the mean-variance efficiency of an unobservable market portfolio, the model is untestable.

In addition, when constraints are lifted, severe damage is done to the simplicity,

FIGURE 9-10 *Estimated Monthly Standard Deviations of the S&P 500*

**Estimated Monthly
Standard Deviation**

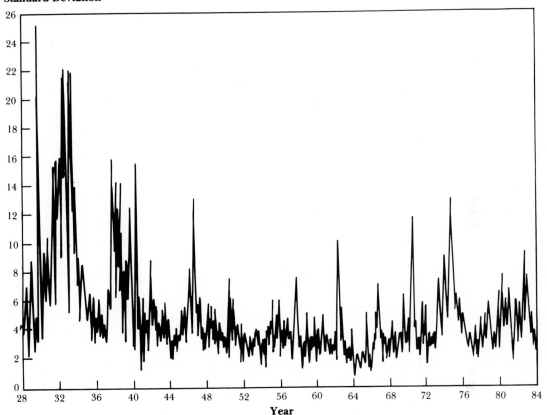

Year

implications, and pragmatic value of CAPM theory. The recognition of differential tax rates implies that the market portfolio is not optimal but that portfolios should be molded to the unique tax situation of a particular individual. This makes common sense, but it also means that there is no single beta which is appropriate for all people and that a single SML does not exist. The same is true when people have heterogeneous expectations, pay costs to transact or obtain information, and have differing human capital correlation with the market portfolio of financial securities. Finally, for the CAPM to be true in a multiperiod world, some onerous assumptions must be made which essentially say that future decisions are unaffected by future events. Clearly, the standard CAPM is wrong.

But is the theory so wrong that it should be discarded, its implications forgotten, and investment texts shortened? The answer to the first two questions, at least, is no. The CAPM presents many insights which don't totally disappear when various assumptions are removed. People should diversify broadly even if this doesn't result in owning the market portfolio. Expected returns will be related to a beta that is unique to each person's portfolio but that is reasonably similar between people if they diversify broadly. The risk of the portfolio is adjusted by combining a person's optimal risky asset portfolio with borrowing and lending. In sum, most of the model's investment implications remain. The CAPM is similar to the concept of perfect competition in economics—it is not a perfect reflection of reality, but it is the best place to start.

An alternative pricing model, the arbitrage pricing theory, is built on the economic principle that perfect substitutes must have the same price or arbitrage profits will be available. Through the action of arbitrage, prices reach an equilibrium. The APT is appealing in that it allows for heterogeneous expectations, says nothing about people's utility curves, does not require the use of the market portfolio, and can result in a pricing equation identical to the SML. However, the theory is not clear about exactly which factors are important to pricing securities, and empirical quests for these factors have been largely unsuccessful.

So what should we do? If the reader has taken to heart one major theme of this book, the answer is clear. Diversify—use all reasonable approaches available. Each approach provides its own description of security pricing and portfolio choice. All look at the same question from different angles and, if taken together, provide a better perspective on equilibrium security pricing and optimal portfolio choice.

REVIEW PROBLEM

The purposes of the problem are (1) to review how various risk measures are calculated, (2) to review efficient portfolio selection and the CML/SML relationships, and (3) to review Roll's observations about the CAPM.

Assume you have a risk-free rate available equal to 2%. In addition, you have identified two portfolios of stocks which had the following returns over the past five years:

	1	2	3	4	5
Portfolio 1	10.0%	0.0%	10.0%	20.0%	10.0%
Portfolio 2	15.0%	2.5%	15.0%	2.5%	15.0%

a. Calculate the following measures:

$\bar{R}_p$ for $p = 1, 2$

σ_p for $p = 1, 2$

r_{12}

b. What is the minimum variance portfolio and what is its standard deviation? (Hint: Look at Equation 7.10.)

c. Given a risk-free rate of 2%, what is the *single* ex post efficient portfolio of risky securities?

d. As noted, portfolios 1 and 2 consist of more than one stock. Portfolio 1 is smaller and consists of stocks A and B. The correlation coefficient between A's and B's returns is 0.0. Also $\sigma_B = 2\sigma_A$, $\sigma_A = 7.0711\%$, and $\bar{R}_A = \bar{R}_B = 10.0\%$. What then are the optimal X_A and X_B holdings in portfolio 1?

e. Portfolio 1 has a correlation with the single ex post efficient portfolio of about 0.70. Since stocks A and B are uncorrelated with each other, will they also have individual correlations with the efficient portfolio equal to 0.70?

f. What is the beta of portfolio 1?

g. Use the beta of portfolio 1 to calculate the correlation of stocks A and B with the efficient frontier (the single ex post efficient portfolio). Calculate the beta estimate for stocks 1 and 2. (Assume the correlation coefficients are identical.)

h. If you were to calculate market model estimates of the characteristic lines for stocks A and B (using as the index the single ex post efficient portfolio), what would you arrive at?

i. Assume you calculated many such market model beta estimates and called them b_i. You then regress the average return on each stock (R_i) against these b_i values and get:

$$\bar{R}_i = 2.0\% + 8.0\%\ b_i \qquad R^2 = 100.0\%$$

Does the linear relationship which perfectly fits the data confirm that the CAPM is correct?

Solution

a. $\bar{R}_1 = (10.0 + 0.0 + 10.0 + 20.0 + 10.0) \div 5 = 10.0\%$

$\bar{R}_2 = (15.0 + 2.5 + 15.0 + 2.5 + 15.0) \div 5 = 10.0\%$

$$\sigma_1 = \left[\frac{(10.0 - 10.0)^2 + \ldots + (10.0 - 10.0)^2}{5} \right]^{1/2} = 6.3246$$

$$\sigma_2 = \left[\frac{(15.0 - 10.0)^2 + \ldots + (15.0 - 10.0)^2}{5} \right]^{1/2} = 6.1237$$

$$r_{12} = \left[\frac{(10.0 - 10.0)(15.0 - 10.0) + \ldots + (10.0 - 10.0)(15.0 - 10.0)}{5} \right] \times \frac{1}{(6.32)(6.12)}$$

$= 0.0$

b. $\text{minimum } X_1 = \dfrac{\sigma_2^2 - \sigma_1\sigma_2 r_{12}}{\sigma_1^2 + \sigma_2^2 - 2\sigma_1\sigma_2 r_{12}}$

$= \dfrac{6.1237^2 - 0.0}{6.3246^2 + 6.1237^2 - 2(0.0)}$

$= 0.484$

$X_2 = 1 - X_1 = 0.516$

$\sigma_{min} = [(0.484^2)(6.3246^2) + (0.516^2)(6.1237^2)]^{1/2}$

$= 4.4\%$

c. Since portfolios 1 and 2 have the same average return, the minimum variance portfolio from part b above is the *single* ex post efficient portfolio of risky securities.

$$\text{CML:} \quad E(R_p) = 2.0\% + \sigma_p \left(\frac{10.0\% - 2.0\%}{4.4\%} \right)$$

$$\text{SML:} \quad E(R_i) = 2.0\% + B_i (10.0\% - 2.0\%)$$

d. Since $r_{AB} = 0$ and $\bar{R}_A$ and $\bar{R}_B$, the minimum variance combination of the two is optimal.

$$X_A = \frac{(2 \times 7.0711)^2 - 0.0}{7.0711^2 + (2 \times 7.0711)^2 - 0.0}$$

$$X_A = 0.80$$

$$X_B = 1 - X_A = 0.20$$

e. No. This would be the case only if stocks A and B were perfectly correlated with each other. Otherwise, some of their volatility will be diversified away in the portfolio combination of the two and the portfolio will be more highly correlated with the market portfolio (our ex post single efficient portfolio of risky securities 1 and 2). Portfolios are more correlated with the market portfolio than single stocks.

f.
$$B_1 = \frac{6.3246}{4.4}(0.70) = 1.006$$

g. $B_1 = 1.006 = X_A B_A + X_B B_B$

$$= 0.8\frac{7.0711}{4.4}r + 0.2\frac{14.1422}{4.4}r$$

Therefore $r = 0$.

$$B_A = \frac{7.0722}{4.4}(0.52) + 0.836$$

$$B_B = \frac{14.1422}{4.4}(0.52) = 1.671$$

h. $\tilde{R}_{At} = 1.64\% + 0.836(\tilde{R}_{mt}) + \tilde{E}_{At}$

$\tilde{R}_{Bt} = -6.71 + 1.671(\tilde{R}_{mt}) + \tilde{E}_{Bt}$

Beta estimates should be the same as in part g. Alpha estimates are plugged so that average return on the stocks is 10% and average return on the market is also 10%.

i. No. We have here the problem noted by Roll. Whenever an ex post efficient portfolio is used to estimate market model betas, the relationship between the average return on each stock and its market model beta must be linear and perfectly fit the data. The relationship is mathematical only and simply says you used an ex post efficient portfolio. It does not confirm the CAPM.

QUESTIONS AND PROBLEMS

1. What is a minimum-variance, zero-beta portfolio? Why do we even need to consider such a thing? How does it fit with empirical results on the CAPM?

2. Why would people have heterogeneous expectations? Are any implications and economic relationships of the standard CAPM preserved when people have heterogeneous expectations?

3. Consider a world in which capital gains tax rates are lower than ordinary rates but all people face the same rates. How does this affect equilibrium pretax expected returns? If you were counseling a college endowment fund (which pays no taxes), what advice would you give in such a world?

4. Assume that people pay different tax rates. What are the equilibrium risk/return consequences of this and how would it affect the investment advice you give?

5. The one-period CAPM can be applied to a multiperiod world if certain conditions are met. What are these?

6. You are an adviser to the Chicago Transit Authority's pension fund board of trustees. For these trustees, what are the implications of Mayers' analysis of human capital in a CAPM context?

7. The SML states that:

$$E(R_i) = RF + \beta_i[RP_M]$$

Empirical tests of this relationship examine a regression of historical average returns on a beta estimate:

$$\bar{R}_i = \alpha_0 + \alpha_1 b_i$$

a. What is the logic in using the empirical equation as a test of the theory?
b. How are b_i values obtained? Do you see any potential problems in determining appropriate b_i values?
c. If the theory is supported, what should α_0 and α_1 turn out to be?

8. A number of researchers have tested non-CAPM versions of historical returns on single stocks, such as:

$$\bar{R}_i = \alpha_0 + \alpha_1(\sigma_i^2) + \alpha_2(b_i)$$

If α_1 turns out to be positive and statistically significant, is this contrary to CAPM? How might the test, when applied to single stocks, be biased? How does a test using portfolios of securities overcome some of these biases?

9. What were the major conclusions of the Black, Jensen, and Scholes and Fama and Mac-Beth studies of CAPM?

10. What are the major implications of Roll's critique of the CAPM?

11. Stocks 1 and 2 are affected by three factors, as shown below. Factors 2 and 3 are unique to each stock. Expected values of each are $E(F_1) = 3.0\%$, $E(F_2) = 0.0\%$, and $E(F_3) = 0.0\%$. Neither stock pays a dividend, and they are now selling at prices $P_1 = \$40$ and $P_2 = \$10$. You expect their prices in a year to be $E(P_1) = \$45$ and $E(P_2) = \$10.70$.

$$\tilde{R}_1 = 6.0(\tilde{F}_1) + 0.3(\tilde{F}_2) + 0.0(\tilde{F}_3)$$
$$\tilde{R}_2 = 1.5(\tilde{F}_1) + 0.0(\tilde{F}_2) + 0.4(\tilde{F}_3)$$

a. What do factors 2 and 3 reflect? In the context of a broadly diversified portfolio, should the 0.3 and 0.4 be positive, as they are shown?
b. Neglecting F_2 and F_3, create a riskless arbitrage.
c. Relate the return equations above to the CAPM.

12. In what ways is APT different from the CAPM?

13. Stocks X and Y are affected by three factors, as indicated below:

$$\tilde{R}_X = 3(\tilde{\phi}_1) - 1.0(\tilde{\phi}_2) + 0.0(\tilde{\phi}_3)$$
$$\tilde{R}_Y = 1.5(\tilde{\phi}_1) + 0.0(\tilde{\phi}_2) + 0.3(\tilde{\phi}_3)$$

The factors ϕ_2 and ϕ_3 are security-unique factors, and ϕ_1 is a common factor. Stock X is now selling for $\$50$ and stock Y is selling for $\$25$. Neither pays a dividend. You (and other arbitrageurs) expect that stock X will be selling for $58 in one year and stock Y will be selling for $26. Expected ϕ_1 is 4.0.

a. Create a riskless arbitrage between the two.

b. Logically, why are ϕ_2 and ϕ_3 unimportant?

c. What price levels of X and Y would no longer provide an arbitrage profit?

d. If actual ϕ_1 is 6.0, ϕ_2 is 2.0, and ϕ_3 is 4.0, what is the realized return on each?

14. You are given the factor sensitivities on four well-diversified stock portfolios. Both factors 1 and 2 are priced factors.

Portfolio	b_{i1}	b_{i2}	$E(R_i)$
A	0.4	0.6	7.8%
B	6.0	0.4	8.2%
C	1.0	0.0	9.0%
D	0.0	1.0	8.0%

a. What is meant by a "priced" factor?

b. Find the percentage to invest in A and B such that the combination has:
   − zero factor 2 risk
   − zero factor 1 risk

c. Is portfolio C correctly valued?

d. What is the relationship between factor 1 and expected returns in the following:

$$E(R_i) = a_0 + b_{i1}\bar{F}_{1t}$$

e. Is portfolio D correctly valued?

f. What is your best estimate of the following relationship:

$$E(R_i) = a_0 + b_{i1}\bar{F}_{1t} + b_{i2}\bar{F}_{2t}$$

g. Create an arbitrage using A, B, and D in which $100,000 of D is traded. Show the end-of-period value of this arbitrage for the following actual outcomes of factor 2:

$$\begin{array}{lll} \text{Low:} & F_2 = 0 \\ \text{Expected:} & F_2 = 3 \\ \text{High:} & F_2 = 6 \end{array}$$

h. Why is a risk-free rate available in this model?

i. Why must a fully arbitraged APT model be linear?

15. What are the difficulties associated with testing APT?

16. What is the difference between a specified factor model and an unspecified factor model?

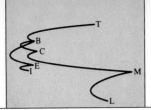

10 An Efficient Market

A common theme throughout this section has been that people seek abnormal profits—profits that are larger than investors should expect, given the risks they bear. A second theme has been that such attempts must eventually eliminate these abnormal profits. In a competitive world, security prices will move to levels which provide only a fair return for the risk accepted.

Efficient market theory (EMT) states that the security market is a *fair game*: the odds of having a future return greater than should be expected given a security's risk are the same as the odds of having a lower return than should be expected—50%. There is no way to use the information available at a given point in time in order to earn an abnormal return. Positive returns will be expected, of course, because securities contain risk for which a risk premium will be earned. However, long-run abnormal returns will be zero.

Few ideas have caused more controversy or hold more profound trading implications than the concept of an efficient securities market. No longer is it taken for granted that active speculation can result in higher long-run rates of return than are available from a passive investment strategy. In an efficient security market, a passive strategy of buying and holding is wiser than active speculation since transaction costs are lower and diversification is more easily achieved.

Although the EMT has caused a major revolution in investment management, it is highly controversial. While active security selection can be intellectually challenging and emotionally exciting, the "game" is played in deadly earnest. People's careers and savings are at stake. To many technicians and fundamentalists, persons who espouse the efficient market theory are ignorant of the facts of life. They believe that such investment strategies are likely to prevent people from earning all they might from their investments (as well as cause many technicians and fundamentalists to lose their jobs). To many proponents of an efficient market, technicians and fundamentalists are either charlatans or naive optimists whose policies would needlessly drain investors' savings. Because of this controversy and its profound implications, we will review a broad range of empirical studies.

Empirical studies of efficient markets can be thought of as belonging to one of two eras. During the 1960s and 1970s, virtually all tests of EMT were supportive. To the extent that potential inefficiencies were present in the tests, they were not pursued.

The concept of an efficient market was a logical and clearly important new theory. And most empirical evidence suggested that it was, indeed, a powerful theory. Beginning in the 1980s, a number of studies began to appear which indicated that either security markets were not as efficient as scholars previously believed or that our understanding of asset pricing models and market efficiency had to be considerably broadened. Empirical tests from both eras are presented here in order to provide a complete taste of the development of EMT.

THE CONCEPT OF AN EFFICIENT MARKET

Why?

Security prices are determined by expectations of future economic profits, risks, and interest rates. In developing such expectations, individuals assess any information which is available at that time. For example, when deciding whether IBM common stock is fairly priced, one would review international economic conditions, competition, the state of computer technology, patents, market saturation, management expertise, antitrust legislation, inflation, etc. While the list of relevant information is almost endless, the point is that such information is crucial to making a pricing decision. It is in this sense that we can say that security prices might fully reflect all relevant information. *A securities market in which market prices fully reflect all known information is called efficient.*

Paradoxically, security markets can be efficient only if a large number of people disagree with the EMT and attempt to find ways of earning speculative profits. To make a speculative profit, an individual must hold unique information about a security which other market participants are unaware of. As soon as new information is obtained, speculators who have the information will immediately trade. If the speculators discover favorable information, they will attempt to purchase the security before others become aware of it and bid the price up. If speculators discover unfavorable information, they will immediately sell. As a result, profit-maximizing speculators will attempt to obtain information before other market participants. This results in a race for new information and, *at the extreme*, all information will be reflected in security prices as soon as it becomes available.

The term *price efficient* is used to indicate that security markets are efficient in processing information.[1] Prices will not adjust to new information with a *lag* but, instead, instantaneously. Four conditions are necessary to have such an efficiently priced market:

---

[1]A *price-efficient* market is different from an *institutionally efficient* market. The latter refers to the ease, speed, and cost with which investors in real goods are able to obtain financial resources from real goods savers.

1. Information is costless and available to all market participants at the same point in time. (People have *homogeneous expectations*.)

2. There are no transaction costs, taxes, or other barriers to trading. (The markets are *frictionless*.)

3. Prices are not affected by the trading of a single person or institution. (People are *price takers*.)

4. All individuals are rational maximizers of expected utility.

Clearly, all four conditions are not *strictly* true. Information is *provided* to some individuals (corporate directors) before others, and some individuals (security analysts) might be more adept at *creating* new information by interrelating a complex set of previously available information. But if this is true, amateur investors (who tend to receive information last and are least able to analyze it) would hire well-informed professionals to provide them with the information and to manage their portfolios. In this way amateur investors would be capable of indirectly trading on information as soon as it becomes known. The second condition is clearly untrue since transaction costs, taxes, and legal investment restrictions do exist. Yet transaction costs are relatively minor and wouldn't lead to the major price distortions which many fundamentalists and technicians believe exist. The effects of taxes and legal restrictions on trading activities (such as margin requirements) are less clear.

Because these criteria aren't strictly true in the "real" world, a distinction is made between a *perfectly efficient* and an *economically efficient* market. A perfectly efficient market is one in which prices *always* reflect all known information, prices adjust instantaneously to new information, and speculative profits are simply a matter of luck. In an economically efficient market, prices might not adjust instantaneously to information, but, over the long run, speculative profits can't be earned after transaction costs such as brokerage commissions and taxes are paid.

This point has been elegantly examined in a paper by Grossman and Stiglitz titled "On the Impossibility of Informationally Efficient Markets." In a world in which information is costly to obtain, security prices must offer a profit incentive to compensate individuals for their costs incurred in searching for new information. If prices are always "correct," no one will have a profit incentive to search for new information. This would, of course, quickly lead to a situation in which new information is not discovered and reflected in prices. In the Grossman and Stiglitz analysis, actual security prices reflect the information of informed traders plus a random "noise term." This noise term is, on average, zero—so security prices do, on average, fully reflect the information held by informed traders. However, there is variability in the noise term, meaning that individual securities might be over- or undervalued. The size of such price distortions depends on a number of factors, including the number of informed traders. Their number will increase until the marginal profits available from being an informed trader are equal to the training and search costs required to become informed. Thus, security price inefficiencies will be large enough to support a profession of informed traders, but informed trader profits should be only large enough to offset their costs of being informed. Again, the security market might not be perfectly efficient but, instead, economically efficient.

So What?

From a philosophic standpoint, an efficient capital market is a crucial component of any capitalistic society. With an efficient capital market, security prices provide accurate signals for capital allocation. Security prices of high-risk industries will be set so that high rates of returns will be both demanded *and* expected. Security prices of low-profit industries will be low and discourage further investment. Conversely, industries which fulfill an important public need will have potentially high profits, resulting in high security prices and an influx of needed capital. Thus, an efficiently priced security market properly assesses the future of particular industries and allocates capital as needed. When firms sell securities, they expect to receive fair prices. When investors purchase securities, they expect to pay fair prices.

Second, in an efficient security market, speculative profits are, *on average*, nonexistent. Because security prices reflect all known information, mispriced securities are impossible to find. Speculators who believe they have identified such a mispriced security are actually missing a crucial bit of information. Over time speculative trading does nothing but reduce the speculator's wealth as transaction costs and taxes are incurred which are not offset by speculative profits. Occasionally, some speculators will "luck out" and earn substantial profits. But this is not due to any permanent insight or ability on their part. Instead, such profits are due solely to chance and would be available to passive investors as well. For every lucky speculator there is an equally unlucky speculator. Speculation is a zero-sum game.

Since speculative profits are, on average, not available, *investing* yields a larger return for any risk level. An investment strategy consists of (1) selecting an acceptable portfolio risk level, (2) broadly diversifying, and (3) never trading simply because one believes prevailing prices are too high or too low. Investors trade only when they have a cash deficiency or excess and to take advantage of various tax laws.

An additional implication of an efficient market is that the demand curve for a security should be perfectly elastic. This is illustrated in Figure 10-1.[2] Since all investors hold the same information, they will all agree upon the same fair market price. Investors are said to have homogeneous expectations. In Figure 10-1 the fair market price of the security (given available information) is $50. At prices above $50 an in-

---

[2]*Elasticity* is an economic term relating the sensitivity of changes in one variable to changes in another. Typically, it relates the percentage change in quantity (demanded or supplied) to the percentage change in price. A demand elasticity of 1.0 means that a given percentage change, say, in price will lead to the same percentage change in quantity demanded. Perfectly inelastic demand means that any percentage change in price will have no effect on quantity demanded. Perfectly elastic demand means that a small percentage change in price will produce an infinite percentage change in quantity.

FIGURE 10-1 *Demand and Supply of Shares Given Homogeneous Expectations*

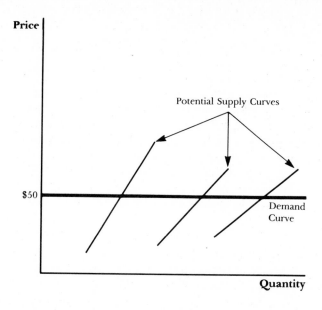

finite number of shares would be offered, and at prices below $50 no shares would be offered. Thus, $50 would be the only market price in existence until new information entered the market. Since investors have common beliefs, shifts in the supply curve would have no impact upon prices. For example, if a corporation decided to issue additional common shares, stock prices should not be affected. Any additional shares would be absorbed at existing prices.[3] In addition, large block purchases and sales of stock by financial institutions should have no effect on share prices.

Included in the set of available information are historical security prices and volume. If prices fully reflect all known historical information, such price and volume data would be reflected in existing security prices. Technical strategies would be useless. To the extent that historical security price patterns might have aided security selection in the past, the information will be accounted for in today's prices and will then be of no marginal use. Empirical tests of the usefulness of technical analysis are referred to as *weak-form* tests of the EMT.

A more stringent requirement of the EMT is that when a new piece of information becomes publicly available, it is instantaneously accounted for in prices. For example, if a firm announces larger operating cash flows than had been anticipated, the informational value of the announcement will be immediately reflected in stock prices. A lag in the price adjustment (which would allow speculators to trade profit-

---

[3]This assumes, of course, that new information is not associated with the new share issue. There is a clear distinction between impacts of the share sale itself and impacts of information related to the sale.

ably) would not exist. Similarly, if the Federal Reserve were to increase the money supply growth rate by more than had been expected, stock prices would rise instantaneously. Empirical tests which examine how accurately security prices adjust to new information are referred to as *semistrong-form* tests.

Finally, if information is costlessly available to all market participants, no one group of individuals will have a monopoly on information (to use for speculative profits). Groups which are often perceived to hold better information include security analysts, professional portfolio managers, stock exchange specialists, and corporate insiders. The EMT states that long-run rates of return for these groups will be no better than those for a passive investor who accepts equivalent investment risk. Empirical studies which test for the possibility of a monopoly on information are referred to as *strong-form* tests.

EMT and Asset Pricing Models

The end result of both the capital asset pricing model (CAPM) and arbitrage pricing theory (APT) is a price-efficient securities market—a market in which expected returns are directly related to the risks inherent in a security which cannot be eliminated by diversification. For both the CAPM and APT to be true, security prices must be efficient prices. But the reverse is not necessary. An efficient market could exist without the CAPM or APT as the model underlying security prices. The relationship between the CAPM and EMT (or APT and EMT) runs one way. Both the CAPM and APT imply an efficient market, but an efficient market does not imply either the CAPM or APT.

Empirical tests of EMT often require estimates of expected security returns in order to see whether a particular trading rule or group of investors can consistently earn returns in excess of an expected fair return. For example, are the returns earned by corporate insiders consistently higher than should be expected—that is, are they higher more than 50% of the time? If one were to buy stocks that rise 5% above a previous low price and sell stocks that fall 5% below a previous high price, would the returns be consistently higher than should be expected? If one buys a market index portfolio on Monday and sells it on Friday, would the returns earned be consistently higher than should be expected? There are innumerable questions such as these which require an estimate of expected security returns. In such cases the CAPM is often used. But it has been used because it was the best model of expected returns available at the time. Its use does not mean that an efficiently priced market is also a market in which the CAPM prevails. Arbitrage pricing theory, in fact, has been increasingly used to test various implications of EMT.

Finally, it is important to recognize that whenever the CAPM or APT is used to test for market efficiency, the test is actually a joint test—a test of market efficiency and a test of the pricing model used. In many situations where market inefficiencies are presumably found, it is difficult to tell whether such inefficiencies really exist or whether the risk/return model used is incorrect.

USEFULNESS OF HISTORICAL PRICES: WEAK-FORM TESTS

If security markets are efficient, prices will reflect all known information. As a result, prices will change only as new information arrives. But, by definition, new information must be random. If information flows followed an identifiable trend, this trend would become known and thus be reflected in current prices. Thus, "new" information must be random. And since new information enters randomly and prices react instantaneously to the information, *changes in stock prices will be random*.

In an efficient market, security prices follow what is referred to as a *random walk*. By this we mean that price changes over time are random. A price rise on day 0 doesn't increase or decrease the odds of a price rise or fall on day 1, day 2, etc. Price changes on any particular day are uncorrelated with historical price changes. If security prices do, indeed, follow a random walk, technical trading rules are useless. For example:

1. Cycles won't exist. Blue Mondays, summer rallies, etc., are a figment of someone's overactive imagination.
2. Charting price patterns such as head-and-shoulder moves, inverted saucers, and rising pennants is of no value in predicting future prices.
3. Trading rules such as odd-lot behavior, moving averages, and relative strength are not roads to riches for anyone but stockbrokers.

Clearly, the concept of random walk is anathema to technicians.

Who is correct, random walkers or technicians? The question can't be answered by attacking the underlying assumptions or logic of either approach. While good conversation might take place over a glass of beer, such a conversation would quickly degenerate into a series of opinionated statements and convince no one. The only reasonable way to answer the question is to see which approach best describes the "real" world.

Statistical tests which examine the usefulness of historical prices to predict future prices are of two basic types: (1) tests which examine the correlation between price changes and (2) tests which examine the profitability of various technical trading rules.

Early Tests of Security Price Randomness

When people speak of randomness in security prices, they actually mean randomness in *percentage price changes*. No one argues that *prices* of a stock are not correlated from one day to the next. They are. Nor do people argue that dollar price changes between two days are uncorrelated with previous dollar price changes. They are too. The question is whether relative (or percentage) price changes are related over time. The correlation which exists between price levels or dollar price changes exists solely because of the *level* of a stock's price and is economically meaningless.

The first known test of the random walk hypothesis was performed by a French mathematician, Bachelier, about 1900. Although he successfully showed that stock prices could be characterized as following a random walk, his work lay dormant for more than fifty years. In 1953 Kendall examined the correlation of weekly changes in nineteen British security price indices as well as spot prices for cotton and wheat. In his analysis of the data, Kendall (rather dramatically) suggested:

> The series looks like a wandering one, almost as if once a week the Demon of chance drew a random number from a symmetrical population of fixed dispersion and added it to the current price to determine the next week's price.

Since Kendall, a large number of tests of the random walk hypothesis have been performed. We will review the classic study by Fama.

Fama examined daily returns for each of the 30 Dow Jones industrials during a time period beginning at the end of 1957 and extending through September 1962. Using these data, he performed a variety of statistical tests. First, correlation coefficients were calculated for daily returns on each of the 30 Dow industrials. For each company ten different correlations were found. The first correlation related the return on day 0 with the return on day 1, the second correlated day 0 with day 2, the third correlated day 0 with day 3, etc. That is, returns on any particular day were correlated with each of the prior ten days' returns.

Results of these tests are displayed in Table 10-1. The 30 Dow Jones industrials are listed together with correlation coefficients which Fama obtained for each of the ten different lags. Wherever the calculated correlation coefficient is statistically different from 0.0, it is denoted with an asterisk. In such cases Fama was able to say (with 95% confidence) that the interday correlation between returns was *not* equal to zero. But such cases were rare and the level of correlation was small. For example, look at the one-day lag for Alcoa. The correlation of 0.118, while statistically different from zero, means that about 1.4% ($R^2 = 0.118^2 = 1.4\%$) of the next day's return can be explained by the prior day's returns—not very helpful! It is hard to believe that such a slight "statistically significant" correlation in daily returns could provide a road to riches via technical analysis!

In addition to the daily return correlations, Fama calculated correlations for returns using time intervals greater than a day. Returns were calculated over four-, nine-, and sixteen-day intervals and then correlated with prior four-, nine-, and sixteen-day returns. Again, few correlations were statistically different from zero and, in such cases, the correlation was small enough to be of no probable use to traders who rely upon clear trends.

Many other studies similar to Fama's were conducted during the 1960s and 1970s. On the whole, these studies indicated that:

1. Short-term security returns are generally unrelated to prior returns. This is true not only for the United States but also for many other countries.

2. In those cases where a significant correlation does exist between past and present returns, the size of the correlation is so slight that it is doubtful that profitable trading rules could be developed.

TABLE 10-1 *Fama's Correlations of Daily Returns on DJIA for Lags of 1 to 10 Days*

| | Number of Days' Lag | | | | | | | | | | |
Stock	1	2	3	4	5	6	7	8	9	10	T
Allied Chemical	0.017	−0.042	0.007	−0.001	0.027	0.004	−0.017	−0.026	−0.017	−0.007	1223
Alcoa	.118*	.038	−.014	.022	−.022	.009	.017	.007	−.001	−.033	1190
American Can	−.087*	−.024	.034	−.065*	−.017	−.006	.015	.025	−.047	−.040	1219
AT&T	−.039	−.097*	.000	.026	.005	−.005	.002	.027	−.014	.007	1219
American Tobacco	.111*	−.109*	−.060*	−.065*	.007	−.010	.011	.046	.039	.041	1283
Anaconda	.067*	−.061*	−.047	−.002	.000	−.038	.009	.016	−.014	−.056	1193
Bethlehem Steel	.013	−.065*	.009	.021	−.053	−.098*	−.010	.004	−.002	−.021	1200
Chrysler	.012	−.066*	−.016	−.007	−.015	.009	.037	.056*	−.044	.021	1692
Du Pont	.013	−.033	.060*	.027	−.002	−.047	.020	.011	−.034	.001	1243
Eastman Kodak	.025	.014	−.031	.005	−.022	.012	.007	.006	.008	.002	1238
General Electric	.011	−.038	−.021	.031	−.001	.000	−.008	.014	−.002	.010	1693
General Foods	.061*	−.003	.045	.002	−.015	−.052	−.006	−.014	−.024	−.017	−1408
General Motors	−.004	−.056*	−.037	−.008	−.038	−.006	.019	.006	−.016	.009	1446
Goodyear	−.123*	.017	−.044	.043	−.002	−.003	.035	.014	−.015	.007	1162
Int'l. Harvester	−.017	−.029	−.031	.037	−.052	−.021	−.001	.003	−.046	−.016	1200
International Nickel	.096*	−.033	−.019	.020	.027	.059*	−.038	−.008	−.016	.034	1243
International Paper	.046	−.011	−.058*	.053*	.049	−.003	−.025	−.019	−.003	−.021	1447
Johns Manville	.006	−.038	−.027	−.023	−.029	−.080*	.040	.018	−.037	.029	1205
Owens Illinois	−.021	−.084*	−.047	.068*	.086*	−.040	.011	−.040	.067*	−.043	1237
Procter and Gamble	.099*	−.009	−.008	.009	−.015	.022	.012	−.012	−.022	−.021	1447
Sears	.097*	.026	.028	.025	.005	−.054	−.006	−.010	−.008	−.009	1236
Standard Oil/Calif.	.025	−.030	−.051*	−.025	−.047	−.034	−.010	.072*	−.049*	−.035	1693
Standard Oil (N.J.)	.008	−.116*	.016	.014	−.047	−.018	−.022	−.026	−.073*	.081*	1156
Swift and Co.	−.004	−.015	−.010	.012	.057*	.012	−.043	.014	.012	.001	1446
Texaco	.094*	−.049	−.024	−.018	−.017	−.009	.031	.032	−.013	.008	1159
Union Carbide	.107*	−.012	.040	.046	−.036	−.034	.003	−.008	−.054	−.037	1118
United Aircraft	.014	−.033	−.022	−.047	−.067*	−.053	.046	.037	.015	−.019	1200
U.S. Steel	.040	−.074*	.014	.011	−.012	−.021	.041	.037	−.021	−.044	1200
Westinghouse	−.027	−.022	−.036	−.003	.000	−.054*	−.020	.013	−.014	.008	1448
Woolworth	.028	−.016	.015	.014	.007	−.039	.013	.003	−.088*	−.008	1445

*Sample autocorrelation is at least two standard deviations to the left or to the right of its expected value under the hypothesis that the true autocorrelation is zero.

SOURCE: Reprinted from "The Behavior of Stock Market Prices," *Journal of Business*, vol. 38, January 1965, pp. 34–105, by E. Fama, by permission of The University of Chicago Press. © 1965 by The University of Chicago. All rights reserved.

3. A minor tendency seems to exist toward positive correlation. But this can be explained by realizing that stocks contain risk and will, on average, yield positive returns. The slight positive correlation in returns simply reflects long-run positive returns on stocks. When returns are adjusted for such a risk impact, they show no correlation.

4. A "large return" day tends to be followed by another "large return" day. But there is no relationship with the *direction* of the subsequent return. That is, given a large price drop on day 0, the price change on day 1 is also likely to be large—but the direction unknown.

5. Tests on T-bill and futures prices suggest they, too, follow a random walk.

Recent Developments in Random Walk

During the past decade a number of studies have reexamined many investment theories which had grown to become almost academic dogma — with results which are disquieting to many investment scholars. This is certainly true of the notion of random walk. These recent random walk studies can be grouped into two categories: (1) studies of *return correlations* and (2) studies of *return patterns*.

Return Correlations. Studies conducted of the random walk hypothesis during the 1960s and 1970s focused primarily on short-term returns (daily, monthly, etc.) of individual securities. For example, the Fama study discussed above used daily returns on each of the DJIA stocks. Recent studies, however, have focused more on return correlations of aggregate portfolios using returns calculated over longer time intervals (one-year returns, two-year returns, etc.).

An example of such studies is one conducted by Fama and French in 1988. The heart of their test is consistent of the following regression equation:

Fama-French Regression

$$R(t, t + T) = a + b \times R(t - T, t) \qquad (10.1)$$

where $R(t, t + T)$ = the return on a portfolio over the time interval starting at t and ending at $t + T$, and $R(t - T, t)$ = the portfolio return over the time interval starting at $t - T$ and ending at t. Values of T ranged from one to twelve years. Returns were calculated for a value-weighted portfolio of all NYSE stocks, an equally weighted portfolio of all NYSE stocks, and five portfolios of NYSE stocks which differed in firm size. Firm size is defined as price per share multiplied by number of shares outstanding. Data included the period 1926–1986.

If long-term portfolio returns are correlated, the slope coefficient b should be statistically significant. And if returns tend to cycle between better than expected and worse than expected, b should be negative.

The slope coefficients they found are displayed in Figure 10-2. The number of years over which a return is calculated is shown as T on the horizontal axis. For example, if a time series of two-year returns is used, the value of T is 2. Note that there is no relationship in the sequences of one-year rates of return — the value of b is close to 0.0 for all portfolios examined. However, as the time interval over which a rate of return is calculated is increased, the slope term becomes negative. Although not shown in the figure, most of the values at $T = 3$ are statistically significant. Also note that portfolios dominated by smaller stocks (quintiles 1–3 and the equally weighted portfolio) showed the strongest relationship between past and future returns.

Fama and French noted that the results of their study are consistent with the hypothesis that stock prices have both "permanent" and "temporary" components. The permanent component is identical to the concept of an efficiently priced security — the price it would trade for if all information were reflected in its price. The temporary component is some amount above or below its permanent component. If the temporary component is, say, greater than the permanent component, prices will fall

FIGURE 10-2 *Slope Coefficients of Returns in Adjacent Years*

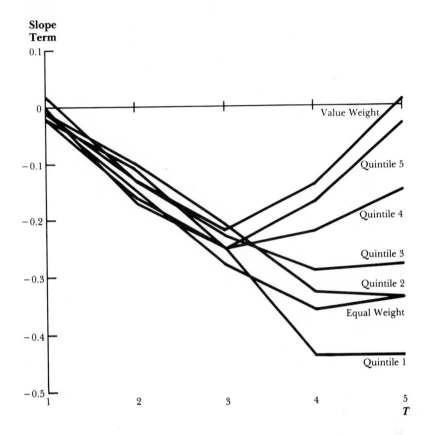

to the permanent component level some time during the next few years. Thus the study is consistent with models in which prices take long swings away from fundamental values.

But Fama and French also point out that their results are consistent with equilibrium models in which risk premiums required by investors change over time. If market risk premiums increase and decrease over time, security prices will react by decreasing and increasing. This could be the true reason for their results. The notion of a constantly changing equity risk premium is a common theme arising from recent investment research. We will have more to say about it throughout this chapter.

In another recent study, Lo and MacKinlay present even more disturbing evidence to proponents of the random walk hypothesis. Concentrating on correlations of weekly returns on various portfolios formed by firm size, they found that the serial correlation of returns could be as large as 30%. In addition, the correlation was positive, meaning that the "temporary component" hypothesis suggested by Fama and French could not explain these data.

Return Patterns. If the random walk hypothesis is valid, there should not be any consistent patterns in security returns. While early tests of random walk did not detect any strong evidence that return patterns exist, more recent studies have found persuasive evidence of systematic patterns in stock returns. These patterns are referred to as:

1. The January Effect
2. The Monthly Effect
3. The Weekly Effect
4. The Daily Effect

The *January Effect* refers to the fact that stock returns in January are greater than returns in other months. This is particularly true for stocks of relatively small firms. In a study conducted by Keim, portfolios of small firms *always* had January returns greater than portfolios of large firms during the period 1963–1979. Previous to the Keim study, it was well known that portfolios of small stocks tended to have greater yearly returns than portfolios of large stocks, even when adjusted for estimated CAPM betas or APT factors. But the startling evidence of Keim showed that nearly 50% of this excess return comes in the *first five days of January*!

Figure 10-3 is based on the Keim study. Months of the year are shown on the horizontal axis. The vertical axis represents the average difference between excess returns on a portfolio of the smallest 10% of NYSE and AMEX stocks and excess returns on a portfolio of the largest 10% of NYSE and AMEX stocks. During January the average difference was +0.714%. The average difference for all months excluding January was 0.102%. When annualized, these figures translate to yearly returns of about 8.9% and 1.2%, respectively.

Clearly something unusual is happening to small stocks in January. What this might be is still unknown. The major explanation offered to date is known as the *tax selling hypothesis*.

The folklore underlying the tax selling hypothesis is that, late in the year, individuals sell stocks which have declined in value during the year in order to realize a capital loss for tax purposes. Proceeds from the sales are then reinvested in early January, and the buying pressure causes the prices of such stocks to rise. Since stocks with small capitalization are likely to be heavily weighted in the small stock portfolios, returns on such portfolios would tend to exhibit the greatest returns in January. While some empirical evidence supports this view, much does not. For example, in Keim's study, small firms which hadn't experienced price declines in the previous year still incurred large positive returns in January. In addition, the January Effect is worldwide, observed even in countries in which there are no capital gains taxes and countries in which the taxable year does not end in December. Also, why should people who sell low-priced securities in order to realize a capital loss wait until January of the next year to reinvest?

A difference has also been found in the pattern of returns during any month which is referred to as the *Monthly Effect*. Ariel found that during the period 1963–1981, returns in the first half of any month (on an equally weighted market index) were

FIGURE 10-3 *The January Effect, 1963–1979*

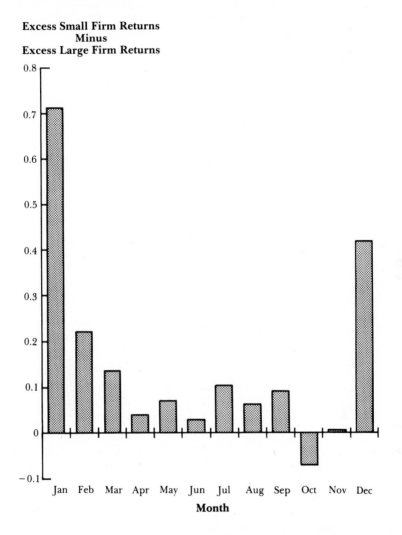

much greater than during the second half of the month. During this 19-year period, the annualized return during the first half of any month was 51.1% versus a 0.0% return during the second half of the month. Even when January returns were removed, Ariel found statistically significant average returns in each half of the month. Why this occurs is, again, unexplained.

The *Weekly Effect* refers to the unusual behavior of stock returns on Monday versus other days of the week. Much evidence shows that Monday stock returns are substantially lower, on average, than those on other days of the week. Logic would suggest that, if daily stock returns are positive over long sampling periods and if stock returns arise from a continuous accumulation of new information, the Monday returns should be three times as large as on other trading days. This simply isn't the case.

For example, Smirlock and Stark calculated daily returns in three ways: (1) from the closing price on trading day t to the closing price on trading day $t + 1$, (2) from the closing price on day 1 to the opening price on day $t + 1$, and (3) from the opening price on day $t + 1$ to the closing price on day $t + 1$. A summary of their results is shown in Figure 10-4. Regardless of the method of return calculation, the average Monday return is substantially negative. Other studies document this day-of-the-week effect back to 1928 in the United States and to many international stock indexes.

Finally, a *Daily Effect* has also been found: stock prices tend to increase dramatically in the last 15 minutes of trading, regardless of the day of the week. In a study by Harris, which used transactions data for all NYSE stocks during the period between December 1981 and January 1983, he found that stock prices rose in the last 15 minutes of trading 90% of the time.

FIGURE 10-4 *Close to Close, Close to Open, and Open to Close Daily Returns for DJIA, 1963–1983*

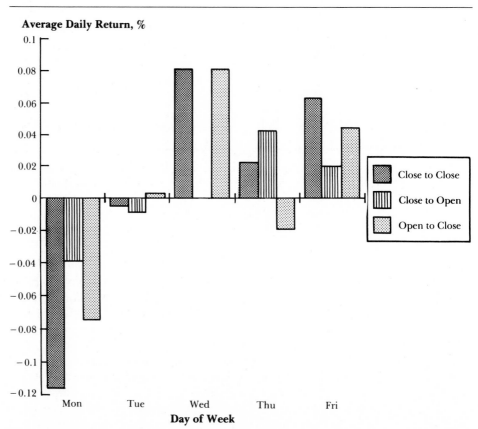

Does the Market Follow a Random Walk? The theory of efficient markets and its implication that stock prices should follow a random walk are well entrenched in scholarly thought. Although many researchers now believe that the evidence accumulated to date requires a rejection of the random walk hypothesis, other scholars aren't yet ready to concede. They point out that if one were to look hard enough at any theory, apparent violations of the theory could be found. For example, assume that students in an investment course were each to flip a coin at the start of the day and use the outcome to predict stock price changes that day. In a very large class, a few of the students will show an ability to predict with startling degrees of statistical significance. The same could be true of empirical studies. When a large number of different studies are conducted on basically random stock returns, some of the studies will (by pure chance) find evidence that contradicts the theory. Other scholars have pointed out that random walk is not required in a very broad interpretation of efficient market theory, but such interpretations exclude the CAPM or APT and have not yet been developed. Probably the most serious question which must be addressed is the small-firm effect in early January. So, is the random walk hypothesis right or wrong? We simply don't know!

Tests of Trading Rules

In an efficient market the prices of all securities fully reflect all known information about the security. No speculator should be able to *use* existing information to earn excess risk-adjusted profits on a *consistent basis* after all transaction costs and taxes are considered. If you believe you have found an under- or overvalued security, it simply means you don't have all the information which is known about the security. One implication of this is that trading rules will not beat passive buy-hold strategies having similar risk.

A trading rule is exactly what its name implies: a rule that specifies when a given security will be bought or sold. In practice, a large number of trading rules have been developed, and many are widely used today. A great deal of research has gone into testing the usefulness of such rules. On the whole, this research suggests that trading rules which practitioners have used in the past do not work. However, many of the studies performed during the past decade have uncovered price anomalies which might provide excess trading-rule profits. Some of these were discussed above in the context of seasonal return patterns and long-term return correlations. Other anomalies are discussed below.

There are four criteria which any trading rule must meet before it can be declared a winner:

1. It must be based only on information known at the date that the rule is implemented.
2. Returns must be calculated after all transaction costs and taxes.
3. Returns must be compared against an equivalent-risk passive buy-hold strategy.
4. Excess risk-adjusted returns must be earned consistently over a long time period.

We will look at two types of trading rules. The first consists of trading strategies suggested and used in the past by practitioners. The results have been largely negative. But care should be taken in interpreting these results, since it is doubtful that the discoverer of a profitable rule would have actually proclaimed it to the public. Once known to all speculators, its value would probably disappear. Thus, there is a bias against finding such a rule. Rules of the second type arise from recent scholarly research.

Classic Studies of Practitioner Rules

Three practitioner trading rules are examined here: (1) filter trading rules, (2) moving average rules, and (3) relative strength rules. Although many other studies have been conducted of similar rules, the three discussed here should give you a good flavor of both the types of strategies and their performances.

Filter Trading Rules. A filter trading rule consists of the following decision criteria:

> If the security price moves up by $X\%$ above a prior low, buy and hold until the price falls by $Y\%$ below a previous high, at which time simultaneously sell and go short.

Such a rule is close to the spirit of many chartist policies and is easily testable. Alexander, as well as Fama and Blume, has examined the profitability of such a rule. In a 1961 study Alexander concluded:

> In fact, at this point I should advise any reader who is interested only in practical results, and who is not a floor trader and so must pay commissions, to turn to other sources on how to beat buy and hold.

Since the Fama and Blume study included several features not present in Alexander's study, we will concentrate upon their results. They tested the profitability of 24 potential filters ranging in size from 0.5% to 50% on each of the 30 Dow Jones industrials. Average results for each of these filters are shown in Table 10-2. Note that:

1. Average security returns *before* commissions (column 1) varied, depending upon the filter. The most profitable filter appears to be the smallest (0.5%). Thus, it seems that some slight positive correlation within security returns did exist which an extremely small filter could capture to yield positive returns. (Recall the slight positive correlation noted in Table 10-1.)
2. Average security returns *after* commissions were usually negative or quite small. This is consistent with the belief that security markets are not perfectly efficient but are economically efficient.

TABLE 10-2 *Annual Returns for Various Filters Averaged over All Companies*

| Filter | Average Return per Security | | Breakdown of Average Return per Security Before Commissions | | Number of Profitable Securities per Filter (5) | Total Transactions (6) |
	Before Commissions (1)	After Commissions (2)	Long (3)	Short (4)		
0.005	0.1152	−1.0359	0.2089	0.0097	27/30	12,514
.010	.0547	−.7494	.1111	−.0518	20/30	8,660
.015	.0277	−.5614	.1143	−.0813	17/30	6,270
.020	.0023	−.4515	.0872	−.1131	16/30	4,784
.025	−.0156	−.3732	.0702	−.1378	13/30	3,750
.030	−.0169	−.3049	.0683	−.1413	14/30	2,994
.035	−.0081	−.2438	.0734	−.1317	13/30	2,438
.040	.0008	−.1950	.0779	−.1330	14/30	2,013
.045	−.0117	−.1813	.0635	−.1484	14/30	1,720
.050	−.0188	−.1662	.0567	−.1600	13/30	1,484
.060	.0128	−.0939	.0800	−.1189	18/30	1,071
.070	.0083	−.0744	.0706	−.1338	16/30	828
.080	.0167	−.0495	.0758	−.1267	15/30	653
.090	.0193	−.0358	.0765	−.1155	17/30	539
.100	.0298	−.0143	.0818	−.1002	19/30	435
.120	.0528	.0231	.0958	−.0881	21/30	289
.140	.0391	.0142	.0853	−.1108	19/30	224
.160	.0421	.0230	.0835	−.1709	17/30	172
.180	.0360	.0196	.0725	−.1620	17/30	139
.200	.0428	.0298	.0718	−.1583	20/30	110
.250	.0269	.0171	.0609	−.1955	15/29	73
.300	−.0054	−.0142	.0182	−.2264	12/26	51
.400	−.0273	−.0347	−.0095	−.0965	7/16	21
.500	−.2142	−.2295	−.0466	−.1676	0/4	4

SOURCE: Reprinted from "Filter Rules and Stock-Market Trading," *Journal of Business*, Special Supplement, January 1966, pp. 226–41, by E. Fama and M. Blume, by permission of The University of Chicago Press. © 1966 by The University of Chicago. All rights reserved.

3. Columns 3 and 4 decompose the before-commission returns into respective long and short positions. Clearly, someone who wishes to use a filter trading rule should think twice about short selling. Returns on short positions were disastrous.

In sum, the slight positive correlation which may exist in short-term security returns did not lead to a profitable filter trading rule. The extremely low filter necessary to capture such correlations required extremely large commission fees. Given this evidence, Fama and Blume saw no point in examining the *consistency* of nonexistent profits or adjusting for *equivalent risk levels*. The only people who might be enriched by using filtering techniques of this sort would be brokers. Speculators would quickly go bankrupt.

Moving Average Rules. Although filter rules are close in spirit to the principles suggested by technicians, they are not widely used in practice. However, the use of moving averages is broadly acclaimed.[4] The moving average rule is:

> If the stock's price moves above its moving average by $X\%$, buy it and hold until the price moves $Y\%$ below its moving average and then sell short.

Often 5% filters and a 200-day moving average are suggested by technicians. Such a rule has been tested by various researchers—with mixed but essentially unfavorable news for technicians. For example, in one study by Seelenfreund, Parker, and Van Horne, daily prices between 1960 and 1966 were obtained for 30 randomly selected NYSE stocks. Initially, $1,000 was assumed either to be invested via a buy-hold strategy in each of the 30 stocks or to be speculated with by following a moving average rule. Various filters (0%, 2%, 5%, 10%, and 15%) and moving averages (100-day, 150-day, and 200-day) were used.

Results are displayed in Table 10-3. Rarely did a moving average filter yield larger profits than the buy-hold strategy—before or after commission fees. In fairness to the moving average rule, however, a number of adjustments in the methodology might have yielded better results. First, there is no guarantee that risks inherent in the buy-hold strategy are equivalent to those in the trading strategy. Using the moving average strategy, one is periodically "out of the market" and, thus, will incur no market risk. Using the buy-hold strategy, one is constantly invested in the market and exposed to market risk. Conceptually, buy-hold returns *should* have been higher because of risk exposure. Second, when the moving average strategy requires that one be out of the market, cash is assumed to be held. Superior results might be available if, on such occasions, a diversified portfolio of stocks were held instead of cash. In fact, other studies have suggested moving averages may yield better results than those shown in Table 10-3. The question remains unresolved, but no one has presented results which are clearly in favor of a moving average rule.

Relative Strength. A stock's relative strength is usually defined as the ratio of its current price to some aggregate market index. For example, if Techtronics Corporation is selling for $40 and the S&P Composite is at $100, Techtronics' relative strength would be 0.40. As with most technical indicators, however, any number of variants to the basic indicator are used in practice. One variant of relative strength which has been claimed to have good success was initially developed and tested by Robert A. Levy. He calculated a stock's relative strength at a point in time as the ratio of its current market price to a moving average of the same stock's price over the prior 26 weeks. The following technical trading rule was then tested. First, rank all securities from the highest to the lowest relative strengths. Initially purchase an equal dollar amount of all stocks in the top $X\%$ of the ranking. This $X\%$ is known as the *cast-in range*. In a subsequent period prepare a new relative strength ranking. If one of

---

[4]A moving average of N periods is calculated by adding closing prices for each of the prior N periods and dividing by N.

TABLE 10-3 *Average Compound Rates of Return with Exponential Smoothing (Smoothing Factor α = 0.01)*

	Long Position Only			Long and Short Positions			
Stock	Before Brokerage Commissions	After Brokerage Commissions	Number of Transactions	Before Brokerage Commissions	After Brokerage Commissions	Number of Transactions	Buy and Hold
American Bank Note	0.086	0.080	4	0.061	0.054	7	0.128
American Potash & Chemical	.093	.081	7	.126	.109	13	.032
Braniff Airways	.602	.588	6	.544	.526	11	.684
California Packing	.101	.093	5	.086	.075	9	.131
Cessna Aircraft	.158	.152	4	.218	.208	7	.100
Chock Full O'Nuts	.049	.045	3	.112	.106	5	−.057
City Stores	.086	.077	6	.047	.034	11	.051
Consolidated Foods	.073	.058	8	−.065	−.083	15	.198
Crane Company	.131	.125	4	.087	.080	7	.167
Gardner Denver	.106	.095	7	.045	.029	13	.152
Granby Mining	.147	.137	6	−.024	−.034	11	.313
Harshaw Chemical	.117	.111	4	.105	.097	7	.133
Hoffman Electronics	.020	.014	4	.064	.056	7	−.022
International Harvester	.143	.133	6	.089	.076	11	.201
Johnson & Johnson	.185	.173	7	.142	.124	13	.218
Marathon Oil	.078	.067	7	.010	−.005	13	.126
Marquette Cement	.002	−.006	5	.090	.078	9	−.114
National General	.067	.065	2	.067	.065	3	.094
Packard Bell	.016	.014	2	.016	.014	3	.008
Poor & Company	.117	.115	2	.117	.115	3	.121
Rayonier	.164	.158	4	.147	.139	7	.194
Rohr Corporation	.237	.228	5	.264	.251	9	.240
George D. Roper	.186	.173	7	.131	.114	13	.230
Scott Paper	.056	.044	7	.075	.058	13	.035
Sunbeam	.119	.107	7	.078	.062	13	.160
Tidewater Oil	.102	.172	6	.102	.089	11	.227
Timken Roller Bearing	.114	.107	5	.092	.083	9	.144
United Fruit	.082	.080	2	.082	.080	3	.134
Welbilt	−.043	−.048	4	−.038	−.045	7	−.048
West Virginia Pulp and Paper	.049	.043	4	.052	.044	7	.069

Source: A. Seelenfreund, G. G. C. Parker, and J. Van Horne, "Stock Price Behavior and Trading," *Journal of Financial and Quantitative Analysis* (September 1968): 263–81.

the stocks in the portfolio has a new relative strength ranking which is *below* the top $Y\%$ ranked securities, sell the stock and use the proceeds to purchase stocks now in the top $X\%$. The $Y\%$ is known as the *cast-out range*.

Results of such a trading rule are displayed in Table 10-4. The example consisted of weekly price data on a sample of 200 NYSE stocks for the period October 1960 through October 1965. (All data are shown after brokerage commissions and before taxes.) During this time period a buy-hold strategy would have netted an average yearly return of 13.4% across the 200 stocks. Using a 10% cast-in range, some of the cast-out ranges did not provide a higher return than buy-hold. But others did. For

TABLE 10-4 *Net Returns from Levy's 10% Cast-In Rule*

Cast-Out Percentage	Net Annual Return	Four-Week Returns	
		Average*	Standard Deviation
10.0%	−3.2%	−0.19%	4.87%
25.0	11.1	0.86	4.90
50.0	16.3	1.22	4.39
75.0	19.1	1.41	4.41
80.0	20.0	NA	4.60
90.0	17.8	1.35	4.55
97.5	13.2	1.05	3.50
Buy-Hold	13.4%	1.02%	3.50%

*Arithmetic average.

Source: M. Jensen, "Random Walks: Reality or Myth," *Financial Analysts Journal* 23, no. 6 (November–December 1967): 79.

example, the 80% cast-out range showed a yearly return of 20.0%. Levy took the profits from these winning cast-out ranges as proof that technical trading can, indeed, beat buy-hold.

However, there are three major problems in drawing this conclusion. First, the risk associated with the relative strength criteria should be compared with that for the buy-hold strategy. When this was done, it was clear that buy-hold had less volatility of monthly rates of return than did the trading rule portfolios. This larger trading portfolio risk was probably due to both the selection of high-beta stocks (using Levy's definition of relative strength can result in the selection of high betas) and the lack of diversification in the trading portfolio. Second, no adjustment has been made for the larger taxes which would have to be paid using the trading rule. By actively trading, one is continually *realizing* capital gains which would be taxed, whereas capital gains under buy-hold are unrealized, resulting in deferral of taxes. Third, the rule must be shown to work consistently over a variety of time periods. Basically, all Levy did was "mechanically mine" his data until a trading rule was found which would have worked during the time period being examined. Of the 68 variations of his basic rule, he was bound to find some which appeared to beat buy-hold. When Jensen and Bennington applied Levy's relative strength criteria to other time intervals and risk-adjusted the results, they found the technique was inconsistent and on the whole inferior to a buy-hold strategy.

Recent Evidence of the Potential of Trading Rules

Earlier in the chapter we noted a number of apparent contradictions to the concept of an efficient market. One of these was the large excess CAPM returns on portfolios of small stocks. Although other contradictions to EMT have been found which suggest potentially profitable trading rules, the small-firm effect is the one most thoroughly documented to date. Because of its importance we will review it at some length.

The Small-Firm–P/E Effect. Prior to the late 1970s a number of studies had suggested that stocks with a low price-to-earnings ratio (P/E) outperformed those with high P/Es. However, a rigorous study of this possibility in the context of the CAPM was not conducted until 1977 when Basu used a standard market model approach to the question. Basu sampled an average of 500 stocks over the years 1956–1969. For each year, the stock's P/E was calculated and then placed in one of five P/E groups. Monthly returns were then calculated on each group (portfolio) assuming an equal investment in each stock in the group. This was done using a buy-and-hold strategy for the next twelve months. Market model estimates were then obtained for each group's monthly returns over the full fourteen-year period.

The results are summarized in Table 10-5. Portfolio A was the highest P/E group and portfolio E the lowest. Average annual returns were lowest for the high P/E firms and greatest for the low P/E firms. P/E and average returns were inversely related. This could make sense, of course, if the low P/E stocks had the greatest systematic risk. But the table shows that this was not the case. Low P/E stocks had the lowest estimated betas. Strange . . .

Basu then simulated returns which various types of investors might realistically have expected by holding portfolio E (low P/E) in excess of those from a portfolio having a similar beta but no constraint upon P/E. Taxes, transaction costs, and even search costs to identify portfolio E were considered. Depending upon the type of investor (e.g., taxed versus nontaxed), *excess* annual returns of between 0.5% and 3.5% were still earned on the low P/E group. Clearly, this evidence contradicted EMT.

In 1981 Reinganum confirmed Basu's finding but suggested that perhaps it really wasn't a low P/E causing the excess returns but instead a "small-firm effect." When Reinganum compared excess daily returns on portfolios of stocks having different total market capitalization (price per share times shares outstanding), he found results similar to Basu's. Low-capitalization stocks outperformed high-capitalization stocks.

A flurry of research and debate then arose. Which was more dominant — P/E or

TABLE 10-5 *Portfolio Performance by P/E Group*

	Group					
	A	A^*	B	C	D	E
Median P/E	35.8	30.5	19.1	15.0	12.8	9.8
Average Annual Rate of Return	9.34%	9.55%	9.28%	11.65%	13.55%	16.30%
Estimated Beta	1.11	1.05	1.04	0.97	0.94	0.99

A^* contains the highest P/E quintile stocks in A but excludes those with negative earnings.

SOURCE: From Basu's "Investment Performance of Common Stocks in Relation to Their Price-Earnings Ratios: A Test of the Efficient Market Hypothesis," *Journal of Finance* 32 (June 1977): 667.

market capitalization? And why do these results arise? Is the market inefficient or is the market model simply missing something? Let's examine each of these points in turn.

P/E Versus Small-Firm Effect. The basic problem in determining which, if either, of these two variables is the more important in causing excess returns is that P/E and market capitalization (MC) are highly correlated. Small firms tend to have low P/Es, and large firms tend to have higher P/Es. Some way had to be found to control for this before the effects of each could be separated.

Basu offered a reasonable approach. First, create five P/E groups based upon the stock's P/E at the start of the year. Call these PE1 through PE5, with PE1 referring to the lowest P/E group. Then create five MC groups based upon each stock's market capitalization. Call these MC1 through MC5, with MC1 referring to the lowest market capitalization group. These P/E and MC portfolios will be highly correlated with each other. To remove this correlation, create a new (randomized) PE1 group called PE1* by selecting the lowest P/E quintile stocks in each of the five MC groups. This way PE1* has broad market capitalization coverage but still consists of low P/E stocks. Repeat the process to create PE2* through PE5*. In each case the result will be a group of stocks with the P/E levels desired but which have a broad distribution of market capitalization. To create market capitalization groups which are culled of any P/E effect, exactly the same process is followed. To create MC1*, select the lowest-capitalization stocks from each of the five P/E groups, and so forth.

Results of such nonrandomized and randomized portfolios are displayed in Table 10-6. The top half shows data on nonrandomized portfolios. The three left-hand columns give the results when various nonrandomized MC portfolios are selected; the three right-hand columns give the results for nonrandomized P/E portfolios. In both cases, the correlation between P/E and MC is obvious. Low-capitalization firms tend to have low P/E ratios. The bottom half shows results for the randomized groupings. When portfolios are selected according to Basu's rule, the correlation disappears. In particular, market capitalization is independent of P/E when the selection criterion is P/E, and, conversely, P/E is independent of MC when the selection criterion is MC.

Basu used these randomized portfolios to examine the separate effects of the P/E ratio and market capitalization on excess monthly market model returns. Some results are displayed in Table 10-7. Look first at the MC results. Low-capitalization stocks had the largest estimated betas and high-capitalization stocks had the smallest betas. Average monthly excess returns were slightly greater for low-cap stocks, and there was a tendency for the excess return to fall as market capitalization rose. The T-statistic measures how far each return was from 0.0%. At normal confidence levels (90% or 95% confidence), none of these excess returns was statistically different from zero. Now look at the randomized P/E groups. Although these average excess returns are not always statistically different from zero (PE1* is most bothersome), they are larger overall than calculated for the MC groups.

These numbers are not inconsequential. For example, the compound annualized excess returns on PE1* and PE5* are 3.17% and −2.37%. It is not surprising that these results have excited much of the professional investment community. During

TABLE 10-6 *Effects of Randomizing P/E and MC Portfolios*

			Nonrandomized Portfolio		
	Median			*Median*	
Portfolio	*MC*	*P/E*	*Portfolio*	*P/E*	*MC*
MC1	30.3	10.0	PE1	7.1	74.2
MC2	81.6	10.6	PE2	10.3	135.6
MC3	177.1	11.8	PE3	12.5	187.5
MC4	414.9	12.8	PE4	15.8	257.6
MC5	1,163.8	13.9	PE5	25.6	338.7
			Randomized Portfolio		
	Median			*Median*	
Portfolio	*MC*	*P/E*	*Portfolio*	*P/E*	*MC*
MC1*	32.7	11.6	PE1*	7.6	176.9
MC2*	94.0	11.6	PE2*	9.7	174.4
MC3*	189.4	11.6	PE3*	11.9	171.2
MC4*	414.8	11.9	PE4*	14.9	176.4
MC5*	1,082.3	11.7	PE5*	23.8	180.9

SOURCE: Adapted from S. Basu, "The Relationship Between Earnings Yield, Market Value, and Return for NYSE Common Stocks: Further Evidence," *Journal of Financial Economics* 12, no. 1 (1983).

the mid-1980s numerous portfolios have been created, in large part, upon results such as these. Some of these portfolios focus on low P/E stocks whereas others focus on low-capitalization stocks. An example of a portfolio oriented toward low-cap stocks was used in the end-of-chapter problems of Chapter 8 — a portfolio known as the DFA Small Company Portfolio.

There is no doubt that low P/E and low-capitalization stocks have large excess

TABLE 10-7 *Performance of Randomized MC and P/E Portfolios*

Portfolio	*Estimated Beta*	*Average Monthly Excess Return*	*T-Statistic*
MC1*	1.19	0.15%	1.61
MC2*	1.03	−0.02	−0.39
MC3*	0.94	−0.08	−1.36
MC4*	0.86	−0.04	−0.53
MC5*	0.71	−0.09	−0.90
PE1*	0.93	0.26%	3.30
PE2*	0.90	0.12	1.73
PE3*	0.91	−0.10	−1.63
PE4*	0.94	−0.18	−2.24
PE5*	1.04	−0.20	−1.59

SOURCE: Adapted from S. Basu, "The Relationship Between Earnings Yield, Market Value, and Return for NYSE Common Stocks: Further Evidence," *Journal of Financial Economics* 12, no. 1 (1983).

returns when tested with the standard market model. Whether P/E or MC is the dominant source of these returns is debatable, although Basu's results favor P/E. But why these excess returns exist is the question we turn to now.

Do These Excess Returns Indicate a Market Inefficiency? The tests reported above and others like them used *market model* estimates of the CAPM to test the *efficient market theory*. The results which were obtained could be due to error in any combination of these basic components. To date, questions have been raised about the following four issues:

1. Stability of results over time
2. Beta measurement
3. Transaction costs
4. Tax selling

Many of these issues were examined when it was believed that market capitalization dominated the P/E effect. As a result, tests of each issue were often carried out using only the capitalization variable.

First, there is a question of how consistent these excess returns were. If there was instability over time (one period with positive excess returns and another with negative excess returns), the results could be solely a function of the time period which the tests examined. A study by Philip Brown, Kleidon, and Marsh suggested that this might, in fact, be the case. Using Reinganum's data over the period 1967–1979, they found that the small-firm effect varied over time and appeared to be nothing more than a random walk.

Second, a question arose over how betas were estimated. Many of the studies calculated beta estimates using daily returns. But this can introduce a strong bias for stocks that are infrequently traded, as is the case with low-capitalization firms. For example, consider two stocks which have identical returns from day to day. Both should have the same variance of return and beta estimate. However, if one of the stocks were actually traded (say) every other day, its return series would have a smaller variance and beta estimate. Returns on days of no trading would be measured as zero and returns on trading days would measure the net result of two days of true returns.

To illustrate the size of this potential bias, Roll compared the returns on a portfolio which emphasized small-capitalization stocks with those of the S&P 500 Index. His results are shown in Table 10-8. The far left column identifies the time interval used to measure each portfolio's return. The time intervals range from daily to every 126 days. The next column is the average annualized excess return on the small-firm portfolio over that of the S&P 500. This ranges between 12.2% and 12.56% — certainly an attractive return if it is not offset by equivalent increases in risk. The last two columns show what happens to the risk of the small-firm portfolio relative to the S&P 500 as the return interval increases. The result is astounding. Consider beta estimates. When returns are measured daily, the small-firm portfolio is 12% *less* risky than the S&P 500. However, when returns are measured every 126 days, the small-firm portfolio is 48% *more* risky.

It was evidence such as this that led to a totally new area of research dealing with

TABLE 10-8 *Roll's Comparison of Small-Firm Portfolio Returns with Returns on the S&P 500*

Interval over Which Returns Are Calculated	Annualized Excess Return over S&P 500	$b_S \div b_{SP}$	$\sigma_S^2 \div \sigma_{SP}^2$
1 day	12.56%	0.88	1.05
5 days	12.53	1.06	1.56
10 days	12.53	1.16	1.90
21 days	12.63	1.25	2.16
42 days	12.63	1.36	2.73
63 days	12.30	1.39	2.72
126 days	12.20	1.48	3.17

b_S = Estimated beta of small-firm portfolio
b_{SP} = Estimated beta of S&P 500 portfolio
σ_S^2 = Variance of returns of small-firm portfolio
σ_{SP}^2 = Variance of returns of S&P 500 portfolio

SOURCE: R. Roll, "A Possible Explanation of the Small-Firm Effect," *Journal of Finance* 36 (September 1981): 879–88.

how betas should be estimated for infrequently traded stocks. We will overcome any urge to detour into that area in order to stick with the main story which is unfolding. (It is sufficient to say that there are now such things as Scholes-Williams and Dimson beta-estimation procedures which might not have been developed if Basu had not raised the P/E controversy a few years before.) But what happens to the excess returns on small stocks when better techniques are used to estimate beta? They fall, but they do not disappear. When beta estimates are adjusted for infrequent trading in small-capitalization stocks, excess returns are about 50% of what had been previously observed. But they are still sizable and contrary to the CAPM and EMT.

A third issue was raised by Stoll and Whaley, who argued that transaction costs for small-capitalization stocks were larger than for other stocks. In particular, the bid-ask spread is greater for small-capitalization stocks. After adjusting for brokers' commissions and the costs associated with buying at the asked price and selling at the bid, they concluded that the excess returns disappeared; in fact, they became negative. This suggests that although the market might not be perfectly efficient, it is economically efficient.

There are two potential problems with the Stoll and Whaley results. First, people often trade *not* at the bid and ask prices, but *between* them. This would lessen the impact of transaction costs and perhaps return to a situation of positive excess returns. Because it is hard to tell, this may be a minor point. But, more important, Stoll and Whaley's results do not explain the existence of the January Effect.

The basic question of why there are excess market model returns on low P/E and small firms is unanswered. There is some evidence that is consistent with a tax-loss price-pressure effect. Why it is not arbitraged away can (at least partly) be explained by the existence of transaction costs large enough to make arbitrage trades unprofitable. Whether a buy-hold strategy applied to low P/E or small-capitalization stocks will be a way of beating the market in the future is unclear.

PRICE ADJUSTMENT TO NEW INFORMATION

In a perfectly efficient security market, prices adjust instantaneously to new information. For example, if Texas Instruments announces it has a patent on a new transistor which is both cheaper to produce and longer-lived than existing transistors, the price of its stock should increase immediately to a new equilibrium level. If its price adjusts with a lag or overadjusts, speculative profits would be available. This is illustrated in Figure 10-5, where price is plotted against time. Period 1 represents the date of a favorable announcement by the firm. Prior to date 1 investors believe that the company's long-run dividend growth will be a constant 6% per year and that a return on equity of 13% would be fair. Given these beliefs, together with last period's dividend payment of $4.62 per share, the stock sells for $70 per share [$70 = (4.62 × 1.06) ÷ (0.13 − 0.06)]. At date 1 the firm announces that a new product line should increase its long-run growth in dividends to 7% per year without adversely affecting the firm's risk. If the EMT is correct, the stock price should increase to $82.40 at date 1 (immediately after the announcement) and remain there until further new information arrives. The path of EMT prices is shown by the solid line. However, if market participants do not immediately recognize the importance of the firm's announcement, a lag in price adjustment will occur, as illustrated by the dashed line. Clearly, if a lagged response to new information exists, speculative profits would be available and equal to $82.40 − $70.00. Alternatively, prices might consistently over-

FIGURE 10-5 *Immediate vs. Lagged Price Adjustment*

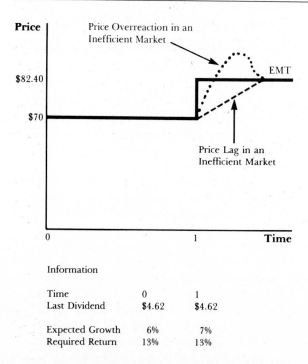

Information		
Time	0	1
Last Dividend	$4.62	$4.62
Expected Growth	6%	7%
Required Return	13%	13%

react to the announcement, as shown by the dotted curve which initially rises above the equilibrium price. In this case speculators could also earn profits on any over-reaction.

Empirical tests of the semistrong-form EMT are fewer in number than weak-form tests largely because it is difficult to identify with precision the dates at which a particular type of information becomes known. Still, a number of rigorous tests have been conducted. Since most of these tests rely upon a complex statistical methodology associated with the CAPM, we will first discuss this methodology. Once this methodology is understood, we will turn to the price effects of various types of corporate announcements and other market events.

The Methodology As Applied to Stock Splits

A stock split is simply an increase (or a decrease for a reverse split) in the number of shares which a corporation has outstanding. In a 2-for-1 split, shareholders would receive two new shares for each old share. Stock dividends are small stock splits, typically cases where ¼ or fewer new shares are received for each initial share held. Because a split has no effect on a firm's investments or financial structure, it should also have no effect upon the firm's total market value. Individual share prices would decline, of course, but total firm value would remain unchanged. Stock splits represent a fairly easy event on which to test the semistrong-form EMT because the announcement of data can be reasonably determined and because we know what the effect of the announcement should be. Moreover, they provide a good introduction to how one might conduct a semistrong-form test.

In the best-known test of stock splits, Fama, Fisher, Jensen, and Roll (FFJR) examined 940 splits on the NYSE between 1927 and 1959. Virtually all splits greater than 5:4 were examined. FFJR hypothesized that splits themselves provide no new information about a firm. Price movements to levels other than those suggested by the split should be related to more fundamental information, such as cash dividend announcements. For example, an $80 stock which undergoes a 2:1 split should provide the investor with a zero return on the split date; that is:

$$R_t = \frac{P_t - P_{t-1} + D_t}{P_{t-1}} = \frac{(\$40 \times 2) - \$80 + \$0}{\$80} = 0.0$$

Note that the split price ($40) is adjusted for the total number of shares owned after the split date. If a positive (or negative) return were found on the split date which was not associated with more fundamental company news, then security prices would be reacting to the split, and evidence of market inefficiency would be found.

According to the CAPM, stock returns are affected by both aggregate-market and company-unique information. Thus, if one is attempting to identify the impact of a firm-unique event, the market-related part of returns must be controlled for. Unadjusted, raw stock returns at the date of a split should not be used. For example, if a security's return on a split date were +5.0%, this could be due to favorable market information affecting all stocks, favorable company information, or both. In an attempt to isolate that part of a security's return which was unique to company events alone, FFJR examined "residual errors" from the market model; that is:

$$\underset{\tilde{R}_t}{\underset{\text{on Day } t}{\text{Raw Return}}} = \underset{a}{\underset{\text{Daily Return}}{\text{Constant Average}}} + \underset{b(\widetilde{RM}_t)}{\underset{\text{to Market Moves}}{\text{Return Due}}} + \underset{\tilde{e}_t}{\underset{\text{to Firm News}}{\text{Return Due}}} \quad \textbf{(10.2)}$$

where $\tilde{R}_t$ = the return on stock in period t, a = the constant average return, b = the beta estimate of the stock, $\widetilde{RM}_t$ = the return on the aggregate market portfolio during period t, and $\tilde{e}_t$ = the residual error in period t, the portion of the raw return due to firm-unique events. Estimates of a and b can be developed using a regression equation relating a stock's historical returns to historical market returns. Using regression estimates of the a's and b's, FFJR calculated the e_t values for each stock split during the 29 months prior to and 30 months following each split.

Two additional steps were taken before the data were analyzed. First, an *average firm-unique return* (AR) was found for each month surrounding the split, as follows:

Average Market Model Residual in Month t

$$AR_t = \frac{\sum\limits_{i=1}^{N} e_{i,t}}{N} \quad \textbf{(10.3)}$$

where AR_t = average firm-unique return for month t (any of the 29 months before or 30 months after the split), $e_{i,t}$ = firm-unique return on stock i during month t, and N = number of splits examined in a given month.

Second, a *cumulative average firm-unique return* (CAR) was found for each month by summing all average firm-unique returns through a particular month. Mathematically:

Cumulative Market Model Residual in Month t

$$CAR_t = \sum\limits_{K=-29}^{t} AR_K \quad \textbf{(10.4)}$$

To empirically evaluate the price impact of a split, either the AR_t or the CAR_t values may be examined. Conventionally, the cumulative average return is discussed the most.

Figure 10-6 presents a plot of CAR for each of the 60 months surrounding a split. Month 0 represents the month in which the split occurred. An examination of the figure suggests that:

1. Stocks that split appear to have had a dramatic increase in price during the 29 months prior to the split. This is reflected in the substantial growth in CAR prior to the split date. However, these price increases cannot be attributed to the eventual split, since rarely was a split announced more than four months prior to the effective date of the split.

2. After the split date, the CAR is remarkably stable. This implies that from the split date forward, firm-unique returns were zero. The split had no immediate or long-run impact on security prices.

FIGURE 10-6 *Stock Price Movement Around Stock Splits*

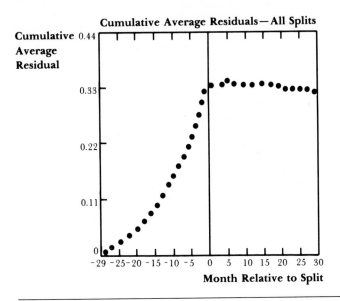

SOURCE: E. Fama, L. Fisher, M. Jensen, and R. Roll, "The Adjustment of Stock Prices to New Information," *International Economic Review* (February 1969). Copyright © 1969.

Results displayed in Figure 10-6 suggest the market is efficient in that splits, by themselves, had no observable effect on security prices. In addition, FFJR examined how more fundamental economic news provided at the date of the split would affect stock prices. To do this, they segregated the split stocks into two groups: one in which cash dividends were reduced and the other in which cash dividends were increased. They hypothesized that a change in cash dividend payments would provide indirect information about the firm's future prospects and that market prices would adjust rapidly to the new information.

Results for each of these groups are displayed in Figure 10-7. When *CAR*s are grouped according to this more fundamental economic news, the series behaves differently. Companies which increased cash dividends had a positive growth in *CAR* after the split (prices continued to rise with the favorable news). For stocks in the "decreases" group, security prices fell. In sum, splits by themselves appear to have had no impact upon stock prices. But when real information is provided coincident with the split, prices adjust in the direction expected.

The FFJR study was the first in a series of studies which relied upon a methodology suggested by the capital asset pricing model. Refinements have been made to the procedure, but the basic methodology remains unchanged. Even if you believe that empirical tests of the CAPM and Roll's comments have cast doubts on the model's validity, there is little disagreement that aggregate market returns must be controlled for when firm-unique events are being examined. For example, a market factor can

FIGURE 10-7 *Stock Price Movement Around Stock Splits Incurring Dividend Policy Changes*

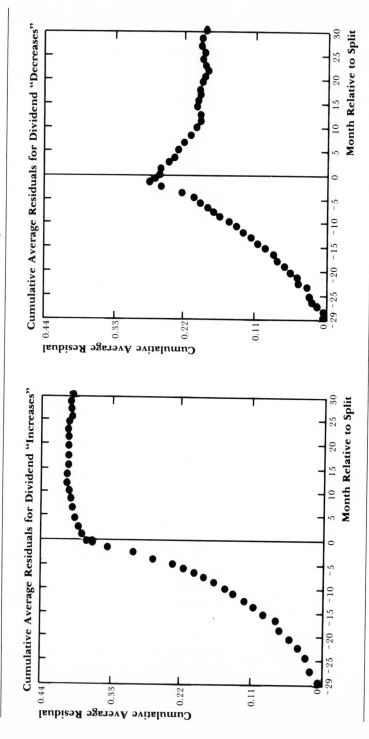

Source: E. Fama, L. Fisher, M. Jensen, and R. Roll, "The Adjustment of Stock Prices to New Information," *International Economic Review* (February 1969). Copyright © 1969.

play a dominant role in the arbitrage pricing model—the major alternative to the CAPM. Examination of average and cumulative firm-unique returns derived from a market model similar to Equation 10.2 is one of the best techniques we have at present to evaluate the price effects which are firm-unique.

Information Announcements Made by Corporations

Major sources of new information are the periodic public announcements made by corporate officers and the firm's yearly financial statements. In recent years researchers have begun to examine the effects which such corporate announcements have on stock prices. This section reviews the major conclusions reached to date.

Earnings Announcements. Early studies examining the behavior of stock prices during the weeks surrounding an earnings announcement all indicated that the announcements possessed informational content and that the value of the information was rapidly reflected in share prices. The real question, however, is not whether earnings announcements do or don't have an informational value but, instead, what impacts *expected versus unexpected* earnings announcements have on stock prices. Corporate earnings announcements may or may not represent new information to investors. To the extent that announced earnings are what investors expect, stock prices should have already discounted the announced earnings level. However, to the extent that announced earnings are unexpected, a price adjustment would be necessary. If markets are efficient, the adjustment would be virtually instantaneous. If they are inefficient, a lag would exist and signal the possibility of speculative profits.

This issue was recognized by Ball and Brown, who used data for 261 firms for the period 1946–1966 to examine stock price impacts of unexpected earnings announcements. They were able to identify each announcement as either "favorable" or "unfavorable." Favorable announcements were cases in which reported earnings were greater than predicted by a naive mechanical forecasting model. Unfavorable announcements were cases in which reported earnings were lower than predicted. For each group, Brown and Ball calculated *CAR*s for the twelve months prior to and six months following an announcement. Results are displayed in Figure 10-8. Note first that the market accurately anticipates favorable or unfavorable earnings reports, and prices are adjusted accordingly. The *CAR* rises throughout the year for favorable earnings and falls for unfavorable earnings. This is evidence that the market is capable of forecasting company earnings (more accurately than Brown and Ball's prediction model) and adjusting stock prices accordingly. Second, a portion of the favorable (or unfavorable) announcements were not completely anticipated, and prices continued to adjust after the split. While postannouncement price adjustments were not instantaneous, they were fairly small and might not have been large enough to offset various transaction costs (commissions and search costs). Brown and Ball concluded that no more than 10–15% of the information in annual earnings reports is not anticipated by the market.

An improvement in the mechanical forecasting procedure used by Ball and Brown

FIGURE 10-8 *Stock Price Movement Around "Abnormal" Earnings*

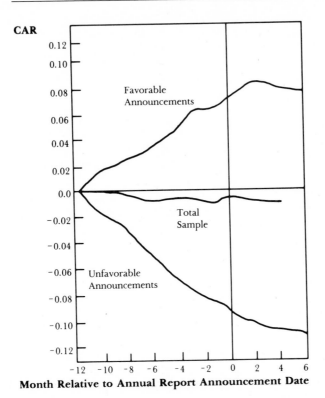

Month Relative to Annual Report Announcement Date

SOURCE: R. Ball and P. Brown, "An Empirical Evaluation of Accounting Income Numbers," *Journal of Accounting Research* 6 (Autumn 1968): 169.

was developed by Brown and Kennelly. Classifying announcements as providing "good," "bad," or "indifferent" news, they found results similar to those found by Ball and Brown. However, some researchers have found evidence of a persistent lag in price adjustments. For example, Brown used daily return data and observed a continued positive trend in prices of stocks issuing a favorable earnings report and a continued negative trend for unfavorable reports which lasted for more than 60 days after the announcement. Joy, Litzenberger, and McEnally used weekly price data around quarterly earnings reports and found that: (1) stocks issuing expected earnings levels exhibited no distinct trend, (2) stocks issuing unexpectedly poor earnings showed an almost immediate price adjustment, but, most important, (3) stocks issuing unexpectedly good earnings exhibited an adjustment that continued over 26 weeks following the announcement.

In a more recent study Rendleman, Jones, and Latane categorized the size of unexpected earnings into ten groups. To do this they calculated a measure of standardized unexpected earnings (*SUE*), as follows:

**Standardized
Unexpected
Earnings**

$$SUE = \frac{EPS - E(EPS)}{SEE}$$ **(10.5)**

where *EPS* represents the earnings per share announced for a given quarter, $E(EPS)$ is their estimate of *EPS* based on a regression analysis of the firm's historical earnings, and *SEE* is the standard error of the estimate (the standard deviation of the error term in the regression). Data were obtained from quarterly earnings announcements made by approximately 1,000 firms during the period 1972–1980. *SUE* was calculated for each firm for a given quarter and, based on its value, the firm was placed into one of ten groups. This was done for all quarters. Finally, *CAR* was calculated for each group starting 20 days before the announcement through 90 days after the announcement.

   Average results are shown in Figure 10-9. Note that immediately prior to the announcement day, security returns moved exactly in the direction one would expect. Firms with positive values of *SUE* had positive returns in excess of what the market model would suggest and firms with negative values of *SUE* had returns lower than

FIGURE 10-9 *Recent Evidence on Unexpected Earnings*

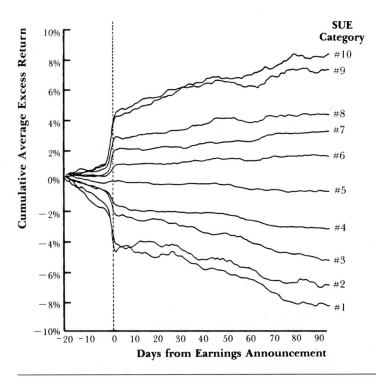

SOURCE: R. Rendleman, C. Jones, and H. Latane, "Empirical Anomalies Based on Unexpected Earnings and Importance of the Risk Adjustments," *Journal of Financial Economics* 3 (November 1982): 285.

expected. This is consistent with the rapid price adjustment which EMT implies. The results are not consistent with EMT, however, if the announcement was "leaked" to some individuals, as the slight preannouncement moves in *CAR* tend to suggest. More important, however, are the continued movements in *CAR* over the 90 days after the announcement. For EMT to be strictly true, all price adjustments should occur at the date of the announcement. Yet the *CAR* values after the announcement date are large enough to cover transaction costs and leave a tidy speculative profit. Either the market model did not adequately capture the expected returns on these securities or we have a violation of semistrong-form efficiency.

In sum, prices do appear to adjust to unexpected announcements. But the speed of this adjustment process is questionable. There is evidence that a lag exists which might provide speculative profits — particularly if the speculator doesn't have to pay large brokerage fees.

Management Forecasts. Although it is not common practice, corporate management will occasionally issue *forecasts* of the firm's earnings per share before the firm issues a formal financial report. One of the early studies of the price effects of such announcements was by Foster. He suggested that a management forecast has information content if the forecast differs from the market's prior expectation of *EPS*. Using a mechanical model to develop the market's expected *EPS* and a sample of 68 management forecasts, Foster concluded that any information content inherent in the announcement was reflected in stock prices within two days. More recent studies have not been so conclusive. All show that market prices do tend to anticipate favorable and unfavorable announcements and that, therefore (barring information leaks by management), the markets are pricing much of the same information which management uses in its earnings forecasts. However, after the announcement day some studies show stable *CAR* values, whereas others show a continued drift in *CAR* — particularly for unfavorable announcements.

Accounting Changes. Firms will occasionally change the accounting techniques they use to compute balance sheets and income statements. In some cases these changes can have a real effect upon the cash flows available to stockholders. For example, a switch from FIFO to LIFO inventory valuation can substantially reduce the firm's tax bill and result in greater cash flows. Such changes are referred to as *real changes*. Other accounting changes have no impact upon cash flows and are known as *cosmetic changes*. Real changes should affect stock prices, whereas cosmetic changes should have no effect.

Summaries of the results of two studies are shown in Figure 10-10. Panel A shows the cumulative residual error values for stocks which switched from FIFO to LIFO and vice versa. The firms which switched to LIFO had an increase in share prices of about 5% during the year preceding the switch. This is consistent with the belief that shareholders discount cash flows, not reported earnings, and that cash flows would be higher under LIFO.

Results for firms switching from LIFO to FIFO were similar. Theoretically, their *CAR* values should fall because of lower expected cash flow levels. Sunder found evidence of this occurring. More recent work by Abdel-Khalik and McKeown suggests that there may be much more to the LIFO-FIFO switching than simply the tax bene-

FIGURE 10-10 *Cumulative Average Residual Errors for Accounting Changes*

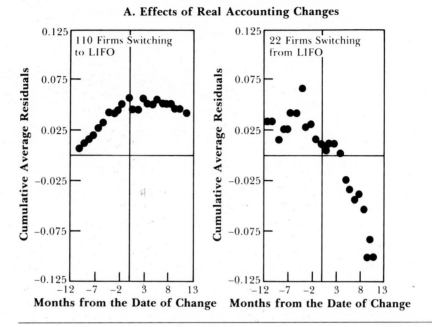

A. Effects of Real Accounting Changes

SOURCE: S. Sunder, "Relationship Between Accounting Changes and Stock Prices: Problems of Measurement and Some Empirical Evidence," *Journal of Accounting Research* (Supplement 1973): 1–45.

fits gained or lost. Their work suggests that management uses the switch to signal other information. Nonetheless, the evidence to date indicates that the market does discount *real* accounting changes, although the length of time it takes prices to adjust may again not fully support the EMT.

Panel B of Figure 10-10 shows the cumulative residual errors obtained by Kaplan and Roll for two types of cosmetic accounting changes. The top plot treats changes from accelerated depreciation to straight-line depreciation for shareholder reports. While such a depreciation switchback would increase earnings, cash flows would be unaffected. Note that the residual errors are all negative. The stocks of firms making the switch are, in general, doing worse than the market. Yet there is no evidence that the switch had any lasting effect on share prices. The bottom plot treats changes from deferral of the investment tax credit to immediate flow-through. Again, such changes would increase reported earnings in the year of the change but have no effect upon cash flows. The plot shows an increase in *CAR* immediately following the change to flow-through followed by a reversal starting around week 10.

There are two ways to interpret these results. First, it is hard to determine whether such changes are statistically significant. They could well be due to chance. Second, they could reflect a temporary fooling of market participants. But if the market is, indeed, temporarily fooled, no one could profit from it unless he or she could trade at very low transaction costs, because the average size of the move was less than 3%.

Many other studies of how changes in accounting statements affect security prices

FIGURE 10-10 *(continued)*

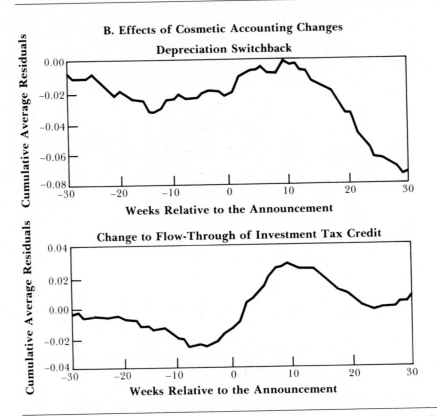

B. Effects of Cosmetic Accounting Changes

Depreciation Switchback

Weeks Relative to the Announcement

Change to Flow-Through of Investment Tax Credit

Weeks Relative to the Announcement

SOURCE: Reprinted from "Investor Evaluation of Accounting Information: Some Empirical Evidence," *Journal of Business* 45, no. 2 (April 1972): 225–57, by R. Kaplan and R. Roll, by permission of The University of Chicago Press. © 1972 by The University of Chicago. All rights reserved.

have been conducted. On the whole they indicate that the market is rational enough to see through cosmetic changes and able to use changes which imply real information. For example, the use of pooling accounting doesn't seem to affect stock prices. And the imposition of FAS 8, dealing with foreign currency translation, doesn't seem to have resulted in unusual (positive or negative) returns. However, hard conclusions are difficult to reach since so many factors are interrelated.

Large Block Trades. Additional evidence that security markets are best characterized by the EMT is provided in tests of large block trades. Block trades are extremely large purchases or (more generally) sales of stock. *Barron's* classifies a trade of 20,000 shares or more as a block, but trades of 50,000 shares or more are quite common.

Recall that the EMT states that investors have homogeneous beliefs. If this is true, the demand curve for a security would be perfectly elastic, and changes in the supply of a stock should have no impact upon prices. While prices might change at the date of an increase or decrease in the number of shares offered for sale, the price change would not be due to supply changes per se but to information which arrives at the same time. In one study Scholes examined firm-unique returns associated with large secondary offerings and found that such block sales are, on average, coincident with a 1% or 2% fall in firm-unique returns. Since Scholes found no relation between the size of the trade and the price decline, and no subsequent price improvement, he concluded that the price decline was not due to the block sale but was due instead to a simultaneous piece of unfavorable information which caused a permanently lower equilibrium stock price. Scholes's data are consistent both with an immediate price adjustment to new information and with homogeneous expectations.

In another study Kraus and Stoll examined large block trades occurring on the NYSE but did not include secondary offerings. Their results were slightly different from Scholes's. Figure 10-11 plots the pattern of prices which they observed during the day of a block sale. As the block is "overhanging" the market (potential buyers are being sought), price begins to decline below prior-day levels. Eventually the block is sold at a price near the day's low (down 1.86% from the opening price). After the trade, price begins to recover but never reaches the day's opening price (down 1.148% from opening). Kraus and Stoll believe these results imply two types of block trade effects: a liquidity impact and an information impact. The liquidity impact represents the difference between the block trade price and the end-of-day price. This liquidity

FIGURE 10-11 *Intraday Price Impacts of Large Block Sales*

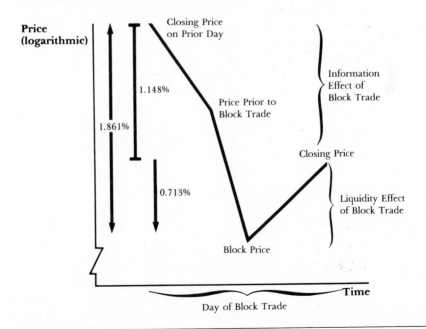

SOURCE: A. Kraus and H. Stoll, "Price Impacts of Block Trading on the New York Stock Exchange," *Journal of Finance* 27, no. 3 (June 1972): 569–88.

impact is thought to be a price inducement paid to attract buyers. The information impact is the difference between the end-of-day price and the opening price and reflects the effect of negative information inherent in the fact that someone wished to dispose of such a large holding. The information impact is consistent with the EMT, but the liquidity impact is not. Nonetheless, liquidity impacts were quite small (on average about 0.7%) and clearly not indicative of gross market inefficiencies or the source of potentially large speculative profits (especially after commissions). In fact, most market professionals and academicians now believe the markets are very efficient in absorbing large block transactions.

New Issues. According to the efficient market theory, the prices at which new security offerings are sold to the public should, on average, be equal to their equilibrium levels. There should not be a persistent undervaluing of new shares, since corporate issuers will insist that their underwriters obtain the best price possible. Similarly, a persistent overvaluation shouldn't exist, as buyers wish to pay the lowest price possible. If investors have homogeneous beliefs, new issue prices should be equal to their equilibrium values. Ibbotson has investigated the historical price behavior of new issues during the first 60 months of a new issue's life and found mixed results. Based upon Ibbotson's data, initial purchasers of new issues appear to receive approximately an 11–12% abnormal return during the first month the security is held. However, by the third month new issue prices appear to have reached equilibrium levels.

The statistically significant abnormal returns during the first couple of months of a new issue's life have to be disturbing to strict proponents of the EMT. Initial purchasers appear to be given a price inducement to accept the new offering. Yet when viewed from the perspective of a technician or of many fundamentalists, who believe that gross inequities remain in the markets for lengthy periods of time, the results must be even more disturbing. From their viewpoint the apparent inefficiency found by Ibbotson isn't nearly as large as other inefficiencies they believe are commonplace, and it is eliminated within a couple of months. We should also note that Ibbotson's results were based upon the CAPM and might not adequately reflect the total risk taken on by first-time purchasers of new issues. In fact, Ibbotson's results suggest continuing decreases in beta risk during the first 60 months of an issue's life. There may well have been a large, unmeasurable risk associated with the first couple of months which could reasonably explain the apparent 11–12% abnormal performance. But until we gain a better understanding of such risks, the results are contrary to semistrong-form efficiency.

Other Studies. Many other studies of semistrong-form efficiency have been conducted. Some of the more representative are the following:

1. *Money supply growth.* Studies by Rozeff, by Cooper, and by Rogalski and Vinso all suggest that money supply growth directly affects stock prices. However, anticipated changes in the growth rates are reflected in prices before the change, and unexpected changes are almost instantaneously reflected in prices.
2. *Dividend change.* Both Watts and Pettit have modeled dividend changes and shown that prices tend to anticipate such changes.

3. *Stock recommendations.* Davies and Canes analyzed price impacts of favorable and unfavorable stock recommendations as reported in the "Heard on the Street" column published in the *Wall Street Journal*. The information seems to have an immediate effect on prices in the direction expected.

4. *Options.* Chiras and Manaster have presented evidence that temporary disequilibriums exist between options and stock prices which can provide abnormal returns to nonexchange members.

Questions About Semistrong-Form Efficiency

Just as empirical tests began to appear in the 1980s questioning weak-form efficiency, other tests appeared questioning the validity of semistrong-form efficiency. Although a number of studies in the classic efficiency vein had hinted at such inefficiencies, interpretation of the studies was in large part made consistent with the theory of efficient markets. For example, even though many studies had shown that stock prices adjust to unexpected earnings announcements with a clear lag, many scholars focused on the market's ability to properly anticipate favorable or unfavorable announcements and adjust stock prices prior to the formal announcement. Any postannouncement lag did little to shake their faith in a basically efficient market.

Two types of studies, both based on market overreactions, called this faith in EMT into doubt. The first type of study focused on aggregate stock index prices and suggested that returns on market indexes have been much more volatile than they should have been. The second focused on individual stocks and suggested that market participants overreact to news events involving individual companies. As new research is developed, the jury is still out on both questions. (But regardless of the final decision, our understanding of investment returns is clearly expanding!)

Is the Stock Market Too Volatile? In June of 1981 a study of the first type was published by Shiller. The telling part of Shiller's study consisted of two figures, shown as Figures 10-12 and 10-13. Figure 10-12 is based on the Standard & Poor's Composite Stock Index, and Figure 10-13 is based on the Dow Jones Industrial Average. In each figure, two lines are displayed, one denoting a variable labeled P and the other a variable labeled P^*. The P variable represents the "detrended" value of the *actual* "real" (adjusted for inflation) security index. This detrended value was found by dividing the actual "real" index price by a long-run exponential growth factor for the index. Use of such detrended indexes makes it easier to examine price departures from the long-run growth of the index. If yearly changes in the index had been constant, P would have plotted as a horizontal line across the figure.

The value of P^* is the detrended value of what the real index should have been *if investors had perfectly forecast future real dividend payments.* (Since dividends beyond 1979 were unknown, Shiller made reasonable future growth assumptions based on past growth rates.) In other words:

$$P^* = \sum_{t=1}^{N} \frac{D_t}{(1 + K)^t} + \sum_{t=N+1}^{\infty} \frac{E(D_t)}{(1 + K)^t}$$

FIGURE 10-12 *Shiller's Detrended Estimates of a Perfect Foresight Stock Index Versus Actual Index (S&P Composite)*

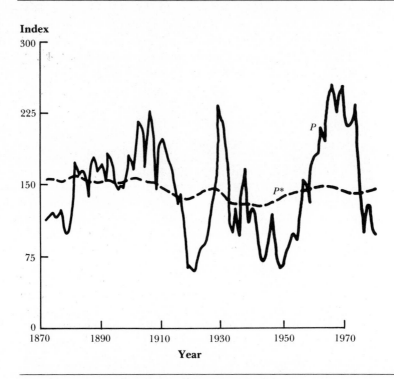

SOURCE: R. Shiller, "Do Stock Prices Move Too Much to Be Justified by Subsequent Changes in Dividend?" *The American Economic Review* 71, no. 3 (June 1981).

where D_t is equal to the actual real dividend paid in years $t = 1$ to N, N is the last year in which Shiller could observe an actual dividend, and $E(D_t)$ is equal to the expected real dividend in year t based on past dividend growth rates. The variable K is a *constant* discount rate—a point that becomes important soon.

The variable P^* can be thought of as a moving average of future dividends with each dividend weighted by the discount factor. Since P^* values close to each other have a large number of common dividend payments, the moving average will be fairly smooth. While real dividends did vary over the sample period, they did not vary long enough or far enough to cause large movements in P^*.

Efficient market theory does not suggest that $P = P^*$. Instead, it says that $P = E(P^*)$—that today's prices are equal to the market's current expectation of what P^* should be. At any point in time, the market will make an error in the assessment of what P_t^* should be. Defining this error as u_t, the error will be $u_t = P_t^* - P_t$. Stated in terms of what the *true* equilibrium index value should be, the relationship is $P_t^* = P_t + u_t$. Forecast errors u_t must be uncorrelated with actual forecasts (P_t). If they are not, a given P_t would indicate the relative size of the error (u_t), and a better estimate

FIGURE 10-13 *Shiller's Detrended Estimates of a Perfect Foresight Stock Index Versus Actual Index (DJIA)*

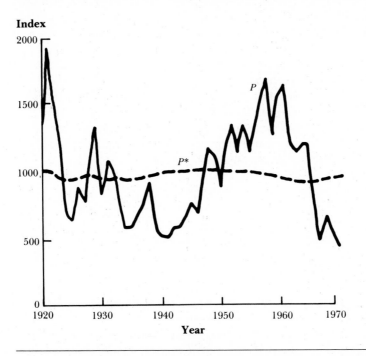

SOURCE: R. Shiller, "Do Stock Prices Move Too Much to Be Justified by Subsequent Changes in Dividend?" *The American Economic Review* 71, no. 3 (June 1981).

of $E(P_t^*)$ would be made and reflected in changes in P_t values. Since u_t and P_t are uncorrelated, the following relationship must be true:

$$P_t^* = E(P_t^*) + u_t$$

$$= P_t + u_t$$

$$\text{(10.6a)}$$

$$\text{Variance } (P^*) = \text{Variance } (P) + \text{Variance } (u)$$

$$\text{Variance } (P^*) \geq \text{Variance } (P)$$

$$\text{(10.6b)}$$

$$\sigma(P^*) \geq \sigma(P)$$

$$\text{(10.6c)}$$

It is Equation 10.6c on which Shiller "hangs his hat." The equation states that the standard deviation of actual market prices must be less than (or equal to) the standard deviation of perfect foresight index values. Although the Shiller paper focuses on whether this relationship can be rejected with statistical significance, his fundamental point can be most easily observed in Figures 10-12 and 10-13. A review of the statistical arguments lies beyond the scope of this text.

Figures 10-12 and 10-13 both suggest that actual security prices depart substantially from what a perfect foresight model would have been—that is, P is more volatile than it should be, given the volatility of P^*. Clearly such departures could have resulted from market uncertainties about future dividend growth. But the growth of dividends on each index has been remarkably steady over time. Regardless of economic recessions and depressions or economic booms, aggregate dividend increases have been relatively stable from year to year.

So, given the relatively steady growth in dividends over time, why should aggregate security prices differ so dramatically from perfect foresight prices? This is exactly the question Shiller asked. To quote him: "Clearly the stock market decline beginning in 1929 and ending in 1932 could not be rationalized in terms of subsequent dividends!" Basically, Shiller's conclusion is that stock prices are more volatile than they should be given the observable volatility of the underlying dividend stream.

Stunned by this startlingly simple but powerful shot at efficient markets, scholars began to investigate models of speculative bubbles, fads, intergenerational models, etc. At present, the principal explanation offered for Shiller's results is that market participants change the risk premium which they require for investing in stock—that is, the discount rate applied to future dividends changes. The P^* index values in Shiller's study are based on a single discount factor, meaning that the market risk premium is assumed constant. However, if K changes over time, P^* might, in fact, be much more volatile.

Many recent studies suggest that market risk premiums do change and that they tend to move with business cycles. For example, a study by Fama and French indicates that the expected returns on both bonds and stocks are inversely related to economic conditions. When the economy is growing at very low rates or is in recession, default premiums on bonds and market risk premiums on stocks increase. Conversely, when the economy is near a peak, default and market risk premiums decline.

Why this occurs is yet unknown. It could be due to changes in risk aversion or in risk assessment, or a combination of the two. Changes in risk aversion could occur if wealth levels rise and fall with business cycles. The same is true of risk assessment if investors perceive greater risk during economic downturns and smaller risk in periods of rapid economic growth.

In short, risk premiums do appear to change over time and, at least partially, can explain Shiller's results.

Do Individual Stocks Overreact? Research in experimental psychology indicates that most people tend to overreact to unexpected and dramatic news events. This has led a number of researchers to ask whether stock investors also overreact to news events. As is true with most investment research, the issue is not resolved, but some fairly strong evidence has been presented in favor of market overreaction.

For example, a study by DeBondt and Thaler examined stocks which had experienced large positive or negative market model excess returns over periods up to five years. Stocks having large negative excess returns were placed into a "loser" portfolio, and stocks having large positive excess returns were placed into a "winner" portfolio. Monthly returns on NYSE stocks over the period 1926–1982 were used.

Their principal results are displayed in Figure 10-14. Cumulative excess returns on

FIGURE 10-14 *The Performance of Past Winner and Loser Portfolios*

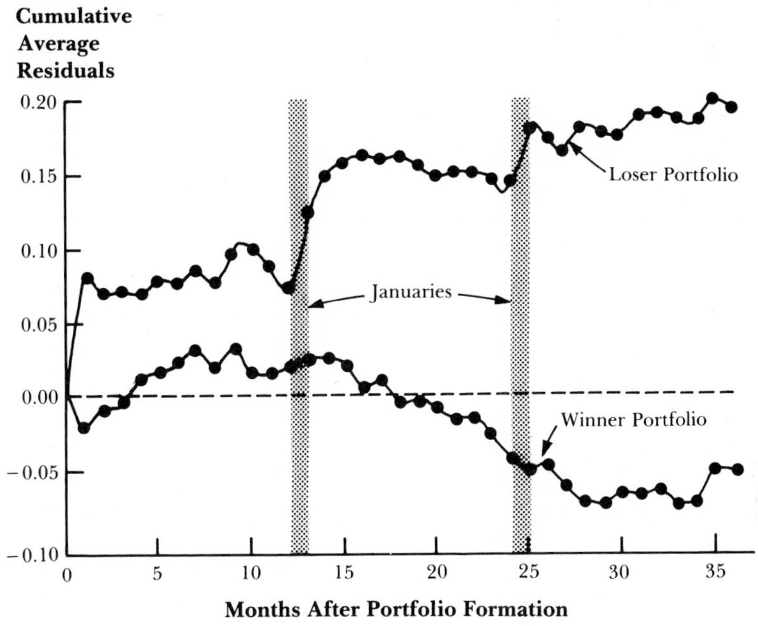

SOURCE: W. DeBondt and R. Thaler, "Does the Stock Market Overreact?" *Journal of Finance* 11, no. 3 (July 1985).

portfolios of 35 "winners" and 35 "losers" are shown for the 36 months following portfolio formation. Loser portfolios outperformed the market by 19.6% 36 months after formation. Winner portfolios underperformed the market by 5.0% — resulting in a difference between the two of 24.6%!

Note that most of the loser portfolio returns come in jumps. As one might expect, these jumps occur in January — that is, much of the superior loser performance can be traced to the January Effect.

MONOPOLISTIC ACCESS TO INFORMATION: STRONG-FORM TESTS

The strong-form version of EMT states that all individuals have exactly the same set of information. No one has a monopoly on relevant information. Because certain groups — security analysts, portfolio managers, and corporate insiders — are often said to have the best knowledge about particular stocks, empirical tests of strong-form market efficiency have focused on their performance relative to a buy-hold strategy.

Security Analysts

Security analysts are the epitome of market professionals. Trained in sophisticated analytic techniques and devoting full-time efforts to evaluating the investment worth of a narrow list of stocks, they should be capable of identifying mispriced securities if anyone can. However, this doesn't always seem to be the case.

Diefenbach examined the usefulness of research recommendations made by security analysts to institutional clients. Generally such reports are not available to the public at large. Diefenbach collected all research recommendations received by an investment firm between November 1967 and May 1969. The subsequent market performance of each stock recommended for purchase or sale was then measured over the following 52 weeks and compared with the performance of the Standard & Poor's Industrial Index. His results showed that buy recommendations outnumbered sell recommendations by a 26:1 margin. On average, the buy recommendations *fell* in price by −0.3%, and only 47% of the recommendations had a price rise greater than the S&P industrials. Clearly, the analyst's buy recommendations did not, on aggregate, beat a passive strategy of buy-hold. Some analysts were able to considerably outperform the S&P 425. But when Diefenbach examined the consistency with which such analysts were able to provide superior performance, he concluded that chance alone could have done as well. There was no obvious consistency in superior performance.

Sell recommendations yielded a different story. While there were very few sell recommendations, such recommendations typically were more accurate. In total, 74% of the sell recommendations fell in price by more than the S&P industrials. Only one analyst suffered the indignity of having the majority of his sell recommendations *outperform* the S&P during the next year.

In another study Logue and Tuttle examined the performance of recommendations that analysts made to the general public. Using virtually every recommendation made by six major brokerage firms during the period July 1970 through June 1971, they subjectively classified each recommendation as a "buy," a "qualified buy," a "hold," a "qualified sell," or a "sell." Regardless of how long an investor waited for the average recommendation to pay off, it did not. The average stock recommendation seems to have fared no better or worse than would the purchase of a randomly selected stock. Logue and Tuttle did observe some tendency for greater returns on sell recommendations (as did Diefenbach) and better performance by some firms. Still, they concluded that an investor who routinely follows the advice of his or her brokerage firm would, on balance, do as well by randomly selecting securities.

But there is hope. In both the Diefenbach and the Logue and Tuttle studies some analysts were found who consistently outperformed the market. While their performances could have been matters of chance, they may have reflected a clear ability to find mispriced stocks. For example, Groth, Lewellen, Schlarbaum, and Lease found positive excess returns in the month in which analysts for one brokerage house made buy or sell recommendations. Although the recommendation could have been caused by price movements during the month of recommendation, excess market model returns in subsequent months remained positive (although smaller). In addition, studies by Black as well as by Copeland and Mayers suggest that Value Line recommendations consistently beat buy-hold strategies of equivalent risk. More recently, a study by Bjerring, Kakonishola, and Versmaelen found the recommendations of a large Canadian brokerage house to have significantly positive abnormal return after transaction costs. In sum, evidence that security analysts are able to predict better than by chance does exist, but the ability does not seem to be common throughout the profession.

Portfolio Managers

Two advantages are cited in support of professional portfolio management: that pooling many investors' funds leads to increased diversification and that professionally managed funds will provide greater returns than will unmanaged funds. According to EMT, only the first reason is valid.

Various studies examining the historical performance of professionally managed portfolios are reviewed in Chapter 19. None of these find evidence of consistently superior performance. For example, in Jensen's comprehensive study of mutual fund returns between 1955 and 1964, the average fund performed more poorly than a buy-hold procedure of equivalent risk. And funds which were superior to buy-hold in one period were usually poorer performers in the subsequent period. Funds which remained superior in both periods could have done so simply by chance. There is little evidence that professional portfolio management is capable of consistently beating passive buy-hold strategies.

Corporate Insiders

Corporate insiders are defined as directors, officers, and major shareholders. Because of their intimate knowledge of corporate events, they may be privy to inside information from which speculative profits could be earned.

To test whether insiders do possess and exploit special information, Jaffe examined insider trades on 200 NYSE stocks at different dates between 1962 and 1968. Cumulative average residual returns were calculated at three dates subsequent to an insider trade (one, two, and eight months) in an attempt to examine both short- and long-run stock price movements. Results of his test are displayed in Table 10-9.

The *CAR*s for the total sample were not particularly large. But returns for the first and second months after the trade were large enough not to have arisen by chance. By the end of the second month, insiders had earned a firm-unique return of 1.18%. This translates into an annualized return of 7.3%. When Jaffe split the sample into large versus small insider trades (column 2 of Table 10-9), the returns were not much different from the total sample. But when *CAR*s were examined for stocks having an intensive number of inside purchases or sales, larger profits were found. As shown in column 3, the two-month *CAR* was 2.09%. This translates into an annualized yield of 13.1%. Jaffe's study seems to provide evidence that insiders had access to privileged information and profited from it.

Trades by insiders are reported by law in the "Official Summary of Insiders Trad-

TABLE 10-9 *Insider Trading Profits*

	Cumulative Average Return (CAR)		
Months After Trade	*(1)* *Total* *Sample*	*(2)* *Large* *Transactions*	*(3)* *Intensive* *Trading*
1 month	0.0060*	0.0062*	0.0098*
2 months	0.0118*	0.0134*	0.0209*
8 months	0.0136	0.0184	0.0507*

*Found to be statistically different from zero at 95%, i.e., not arising out of chance.

SOURCE: Reprinted from "Special Information and Insider Trading," *Journal of Business* 47, no. 3 (July 1974): 410–28, by J. Jaffe, by permission of The University of Chicago Press. © 1974 by The University of Chicago. All rights reserved.

ing" by the SEC. Might noninsiders use this data, which is typically available two months after an insider trade, to earn speculative profits? When *CAR*s of intensively traded insider stocks were examined *after* publication of the official summary, Jaffe found that speculative profits were available. But, after transaction costs, such profits amounted to a mere 2.5%. Still, this evidence is contrary to strong-form and semi-strong-form EMT. Whether such abnormal returns will continue in the future is uncertain.

STRATEGY IN AN EFFICIENT MARKET

The evidence presented in this chapter indicates that the markets are certainly *not perfectly efficient*. However, for many people with little knowledge, high search costs, and large transaction costs, the markets are probably close to being economically efficient. Such people might be wise to consider themselves as operating in an efficient market and to develop reasonable investment strategies. If they wish to speculate, it should be with a limited portion of their portfolio.

Reasonable trading strategies in an efficient market include the following:

1. *Diversify.* Purchase shares in no-load stock and bond funds which have a policy of minimal trading activity. An ideal stock fund would be an index fund.
2. *Select a suitable market risk level.* Examine the historical volatility of the aggregate market portfolio and use this to subjectively determine an acceptable stock/bond mix. Highly risk-averse people should invest more heavily in bonds, whereas aggressive investors may use the leverage inherent in margin and options.
3. *Don't try to time.* Simply buy and hold until the portfolio is to be liquidated. Trade when excess cash is needed or available. Don't try to find mispriced securities.
4. *Keep tax considerations in mind.* For example, zero-tax pension funds should be placed in high-coupon bonds because such bonds have higher before-tax yields. Although the stock evidence is less clear, it does seem that high-dividend-yield stocks also sell at high before-tax expected yields. Some care should be taken, how-

ever, that these tax considerations don't excessively reduce portfolio diversification. Finally, year-end tax swaps should be used to reduce taxes.

5. *Consider marketability.* The portfolio should provide the degree of marketability which might be needed to meet unexpected cash needs.

SUMMARY

An efficient securities market is the consequence of intense competition for information. Individuals seeking speculative profits will search out any information which will aid in identifying mispriced securities. And, at the extreme, all such information will be reflected in existing prices.

A perfectly efficient market is one in which market prices are exactly equal to current intrinsic values. The conditions necessary for a perfectly efficient market are the following: (1) information must be provided freely and instantaneously to all market participants, (2) there must be no costs associated with trading, (3) actions taken by a single individual cannot affect prices, and (4) people maximize expected utility. Since the first two requirements are not strictly true, we differentiate between a perfectly efficient market and an economically efficient market. In an economically efficient market, prices may vary from true intrinsic worth, but long-run speculative profits are not available after transaction costs. In such a market a passive strategy of *investing* will yield larger long-run returns than will a speculative strategy.

The extent to which security markets can be characterized as being economically efficient can be tested only by examining empirical data. To date, such empirical evidence indicates that:

1. Short-term security returns appear to follow a random walk. Many cycles, trends, and patterns which seem to exist are simply figments of an overactive imagination. Thus, technical trading rules that rely upon historical price charts are useless to both the speculator and the investor. Yet long-term security returns might not be totally random, and a number of return patterns have been found. Of particular interest is the January Effect.

2. New information is reflected in security prices with little time lag. In fact, market prices often adjust before an actual announcement. There is some evidence, however, that the postannouncement price adjustment can extend over a month or more and that speculative profits may be available if one pays small transaction costs.

3. Many groups of market professionals who should be able to generate speculative profits appear unable to do so. For example, the performance of security analysts and mutual funds has not consistently beaten a buy-hold strategy.

4. Some individuals do appear to have a monopoly on information. Corporate insiders and some security analysts have been able to outperform buy-hold.

It appears that markets are *not strictly efficient*. But for all practical purposes, it is wiser to approach security selection from the viewpoint of EMT than to assume that gross mispricing exists.

REVIEW PROBLEM

In this problem you will use market model estimates of residual returns on two stocks to determine whether the announcement of an unexpected cash dividend had any impact on the security values and whether a lag occurred in any such adjustment.

Market returns are shown below for 12 periods before the announcement ($T = -12$ to -1), the date of the announcement ($T = 0$), and 12 periods after the announcement ($T = 1$ to 12).

	Before Announcement				*After Announcement*		
			Rates of Return				
T	*Stock 1*	*Stock 2*	*Market*	*T*	*Stock 1*	*Stock 2*	*Market*
−12	3	5	2	0	−11.776	−21.12	−15
−11	2	4	2	1	6.41	10.338	6
−10	14	15	11	2	2.08	2.848	1
−9	−20	−35	−24	3	6.41	10.338	6
−8	9	16	10	4	−2.25	−4.642	−4
−7	6	9	6	5	−5.714	−10.634	−8
−6	5	11	6	6	0.714	1.05	0
−5	0	6	3	7	−1.884	−3.444	−3
−4	10	14	8	8	5.044	8.54	5
−3	17	32	21	9	−6.214	−10.934	−8
−2	0	−4	−1	10	−1.884	−3.444	−3
−1	5	13	5	11	11.106	19.026	12
				12	11.972	20.524	13

a. Estimate the following market model regressions for each stock using the returns for $T = -12$ to $T = -1$:

$$\tilde{R}_t = a + b(\widetilde{RM}_t) + \tilde{e}_t$$

b. The results of step a should yield the following:

$$R_1 = 0.714 + 0.866 \ (RM)$$

$$R_2 = 1.050 + 1.498 \ (RM)$$

Use these two models to estimate residual errors for days $T = 0$ to $T = +12$.

c. Compute the average residual for each day in the postannouncement period as well as the cumulative average residual.

d. Comment on whether these results are consistent with EMT.

Solution

a. The market model regressions are shown in step b above.

b through d.

T	*Stock 1*	*Stock 2*	*AR*	*CAR*
0	0.5	0.3	0.4	0.4
1	0.5	0.3	0.4	0.8
2	0.5	0.3	0.4	1.2

3	0.5	0.3	0.4	1.6
4	0.5	0.3	0.4	2
5	0.5	0.3	0.4	2.4
6	0	0	0	2.4
7	0	0	0	2.4
8	0	0	0	2.4
9	0	0	0	2.4
10	0	0	0	2.4
11	0	0	0	2.4
12	0	0	0	2.4

This is inconsistent with EMT in that a lag occurs in the adjustment of stock prices. By the end of day $T = 5$ a 2.4% cumulative excess return is earned.

QUESTIONS AND PROBLEMS

1. What are the four conditions which would lead to a perfectly efficient market?

2. What is the difference between a perfectly efficient and economically efficient security market? How does the study by Grossman and Stiglitz fit into an economically efficient market?

3. Discuss what is meant by weak-form, semistrong-form, and strong-form efficiency.

4. Why does a perfectly efficient market imply a perfectly horizontal demand curve for a security?

5. If the security markets are in fact strong-form efficient, should anyone decide to become a security analyst or active portfolio manager? What would the impact of such a decision be on strong-form efficiency?

6. "For the CAPM to be correct, the security markets must be efficient." "For the security markets to be efficient, the CAPM must be correct." Evaluate these statements.

7. "The concept of a random walk in stock prices is bizarre and implies totally irrational behavior by the investing public. Nothing could be further from the truth than random walk. Prices are related to fundamental economic worth." Comment.

8. Technicians often say that trading conditions change in the market such that a rule that works during one period might not work during another period. They believe trading rules shouldn't be inflexible but, instead, should be adjusted as new market conditions arise. Comment.

9. a. "Speculation is a zero-sum game across the market at any point in time as well as for any single speculator over time." How is this statement related to EMT?

   b. For the markets to be efficient, speculators must trade on any price disequilibriums. If speculators earn profits from doing so, is this inconsistent with market efficiency?

10. Consider the following situations and indicate in each case whether the concept of market efficiency is violated.

    a. A friend tells you that the concept of market efficiency is clearly invalid, offering as proof the fact that during the past three years she has considerably beaten the market averages. Returns on her portfolio in each year were 15%, 18%, and 25%, whereas the market returns were only 12%, 15%, and 18%.

    b. A financial consulting firm has just announced a newly designed complex computer program which would have generated consistent (risk-adjusted) excess returns after all transaction costs and taxes if it had been used during the last ten years.

c. Ten years ago a financial consulting firm began to use a complex computer program to analyze financial reports. Since the introduction of this technique the firm has consistently earned (risk-adjusted) excess returns after all transaction costs and taxes.

d. During the past five years most people have earned positive average returns. However, some people have earned considerably more than others.

e. You have correlated the percentage change in gold prices from day 0 to day 1 (as of 9:00 A.M. each day) with the percentage change in the NYSE Composite Index during day 1 (percentage change from 10:00 A.M. to 4:00 P.M.). You find a statistically significant correlation coefficient of negative 0.45.

f. A research study finds that firms switching from expensing R&D expenditures to capitalizing them have positive and statistically significant CAR levels which increase steadily for five months. Beyond five months the CAR steadily returns to zero.

g. Trading activity by corporate insiders results in permanent and statistically significant CAR levels.

11. A large portion of the empirical studies rely upon a methodology suggested by the capital asset pricing model. Do you find any logical inconsistency in using the CAPM to test for inefficiencies in the market? How is this concern at least partially resolved by the arbitrage pricing model?

12. Why is the estimated beta of an infrequently traded stock biased downwards from its true beta? Provide an illustration.

13. Price-to-book-value ratios of the S&P industrials are used by many people to determine a portfolio's stock/bond mix: the larger the ratio, the smaller the percentage held in stock, and vice versa. How might this be tested?

14. How might you test the following hypothesis: Low price-to-book-ratio stocks outperform the high price-to-book stocks. Integrate your answer with the discussion of the small-firm–P/E effect in the chapter.

15. (CFA Exam Question)
The efficient market theory has major implications for the practice of portfolio management. One obvious implication is the determination of superior analysts. Another is how to carry out the management of portfolios, assuming no access to superior analysts. Assume that none of the analysts to whom you have access is superior. List and discuss five of the specific investment practices you should implement for your clients.

16. (CFA Exam Question)
In recent years several major financial institutions have developed index funds and offered these to pension accounts and others.
a. Give the justification used for investing in these index funds, which simply attempt to replicate the market.
b. Indicate whether this justification is consistent with the efficient market theory.

17. Recent empirical tests of the efficient market theory have uncovered a number of results suggesting that inefficiencies may exist.
a. List and briefly discuss those presented in the chapter.
b. Assume that you wish to defend EMT in light of these apparent inconsistencies. How would you do so?

18. Recent empirical evidence suggests that expected stock returns change over time—that risk premiums are inversely related to the business cycle.

a. Why might risk premiums change in such a manner?

b. How does this partly explain the larger than expected volatility in aggregate stock prices (such as the S&P Composite) which Shiller found?

c. If market risk premiums do change over time, should an investor's asset allocation (where the assets are on, say, the CAPM borrowing-lending line) be constant?

DATA ANALYSIS PROBLEM

Objective:

- To demonstrate that returns on common stocks in year t are virtually uncorrelated with returns in year $t + 1$—i.e., the random walk hypothesis appears to be true for common stocks.

Access the data worksheet YRLYSTK.WK1 and select one (or more) common stock indexes.

1. Insert a blank column beside each stock return series you select. Copy the return series into this blank column. But the new series should either lead or lag the original series. For example, the S&P 500 returns in 1927 should be next to an entry for the returns on the S&P 500 in 1928.

2. Make note of the columns and rows which have nonzero entries.

3. In a blank part of the worksheet, regress the returns in one column against the returns in the other. It does not matter which column is the y (dependent) or x (independent) variable. We are only interested in the R-square value from the regression.

4. The square root of R-square is the correlation coefficient. Calculate this correlation coefficient of "returns in year t versus returns in year $t + 1$." Is this consistent or inconsistent with random walk?

5. Does this mean that the random walk hypothesis is correct? Why?

P A R T

3 Security Analyses

The purpose of Part 3 is to review various types of security media in depth. Bonds are treated in two chapters, as are stocks and options. The first chapter in each case is devoted to a discussion of certain fundamental concepts *relative to the instrument. The second chapter is devoted to* investment and speculative trading procedures. *Following these are chapters which treat futures and other securities.*

The eight chapters which comprise this section rely heavily on the basic security market concepts and theories introduced in Part 2. For example, the various theories of the term structure of interest rates play a crucial role in bond investment and speculative procedures, have an impact upon required equity returns, and must be understood in order to understand the pricing of financial futures contracts. Similarly, the measurement of security risk, the use of diversification, and the concept of the CAPM are fundamental to an understanding of the role of bonds in an investment portfolio, the valuation of common stocks, and the measurement of mutual fund performance.

CHAPTER

11 Bond Fundamentals

In Chapter 2 various institutional features of bonds were discussed. We turn now to a more complete analysis of bond investment and speculation. In this chapter we discuss a variety of topics which are fundamental to an understanding of all fixed-income securities, including (1) the place of bonds in an investment or speculative program, (2) bond valuation, and (3) measurement of bond risks and returns. In the next chapter these ideas are used to illustrate typical bond speculation and investment policies.

WHY BONDS?

Bonds represent a major portion of the market value of actively traded securities, and historical bond returns have often exceeded common stock returns. Yet bonds have historically had an image of being dull—of offering a limited, fixed income with little chance for price appreciation, and of interest chiefly to "little old ladies sitting in a bank vault clipping coupons." For too many people, stocks are where the action is. This perception is unfortunate, since bonds can provide significant investment and speculative opportunities.

As an investment vehicle bonds can be used to manage portfolio (1) diversification, (2) systematic risk, (3) maturity, (4) liquidity, and (5) tax characteristics.

Portfolio Diversification

Bonds can expand the risk/return opportunities available to individuals. For example, between 1926 and 1987 average nominal yearly returns and standard deviations on a broad index of common stocks and a broad index of United States government bonds were as follows:

	1926 Through 1987	
	S&P 500 Stocks	Government Bonds
Average Yearly Return	12.01%	4.57%
Standard Deviation	20.88	8.46

During this time period the average annual risk-free rate (proxied by T-bill returns) was about 3.5%.

The stock portfolio provided an 8.51% risk premium (12.01% − 3.50%) for bearing a 20.88% standard deviation. This translates into a 0.408% risk premium for each unit of standard deviation (8.51% ÷ 20.88%). The government bond index provided only a 0.126% risk premium for each unit of standard deviation [(4.57% − 3.50%) ÷ 8.46%]. If possible investments were restricted to combinations of the risk-free security and only *one* of these two risky portfolios, the stock portfolio would clearly be best.

However, if returns on stocks and bonds were not perfectly correlated, it might have been advantageous to create a portfolio of both stocks and bonds. In fact, this would have been the case. From 1926 to 1987, the correlation coefficient between returns on the S&P 500 and the government bond index was 10.57%. Though we will not show the proof here, such a correlation applied to the other results in a single optimal portfolio consisting of a 66% investment in the S&P 500 and a 34% investment in government bonds. Combining such a stock/bond portfolio with the risk-free security would have provided a risk premium per unit of standard deviation of 0.42% − a better result than provided by combinations of stocks with *RF* or bonds with *RF*.

These results are shown graphically in Figure 11-1. The solid lines represent various risk and return combinations available from borrowing or lending at the risk-free rate in combination with holding one of the three risky security portfolios. The mixed stock and bond portfolio provides the greatest return for any risk level.

Portfolio selection should be based upon expectations of the future. Thus, the 66%

FIGURE 11-1 *Bonds as an Investment*

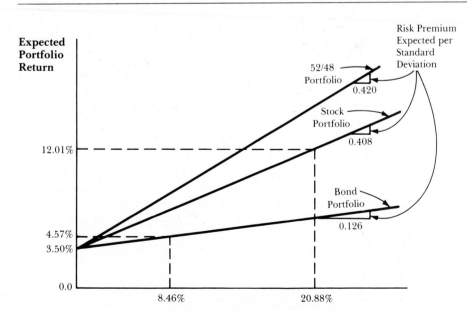

stock/34% bond optimal portfolio of this example should be applied to current portfolios only if you believe that the past is a fair predictor of the future. But the example does point out one potential advantage of using bonds—diversification.

Conceptually, bonds provide a means of obtaining additional diversification in otherwise all-stock portfolios. Economic events which tend to increase stock prices often depress bond prices, and vice versa. By holding both stocks and bonds the investor is better able to diversify away such risks. In fact, according to the traditional version of the CAPM, investors should hold bonds and stocks in proportion to the aggregate market values of each. At the end of 1987, bonds represented about 45% of actively traded securities. Based on the traditional CAPM, then, 45% of an investor's commitment to risky securities should be in bonds. If the CAPM is not strictly true (and empirical evidence was offered in Chapter 9 which suggests that it isn't), percentage bond holdings will vary among investors depending upon individual tax brackets, current income needs, perceptions of the future, etc. Nonetheless, bonds might provide significant diversification advantages.

Portfolio Risk Adjustment

In addition to taking advantage of the diversification opportunities that bonds offer, investors can change the level of systematic risk to which they are exposed simply by changing their stock/bond mix. We will see later in the chapter that betas calculated on bonds typically are much lower than betas calculated on common stocks. As a result, people who are exposed to more market risk than they find acceptable can reduce this risk by placing a larger percentage of their capital in bonds and less in stocks.

Portfolio Investment Horizon

Different investors have different investment horizons. For example, young people might plan to maintain their security portfolios over a 20- to 30-year time period, whereas retired individuals might plan to invest for only five to ten years. As we saw in Chapter 6 (and as discussed at length below), the risk of a portfolio is minimized when the maturity of its investments is identical to the maturity date when cash is needed. High-dividend-yield, low-price-growth common stocks have a shorter effective maturity than low-dividend-yield, high-price-growth stocks, since the average date at which cash is received is earlier. The effective maturity date of stocks does vary. Nonetheless, the maturity flexibility offered by common stocks is narrow when compared with that of bonds. Since bonds are available with a life as short as one day or as long as 30 years, they are good vehicles through which the maturity date of investments and cash needs can be matched.[1]

---

[1] For the present we will use the terms *maturity date* and *effective maturity date* rather loosely. However, later in the chapter we will see that the best way to evaluate a security's effective maturity is through a measure known as *duration*.

Portfolio Liquidity and Tax Features

A large number of bond issues are actively traded at low transaction costs. Investors who need the ability to sell rapidly without affecting existing market prices or paying large commissions can use such bonds to increase their portfolio liquidity. In addition, some bonds have unique tax features (municipal obligations, in particular) which allow investors to better manage their after-tax rates of return.

Bonds can also be used as a speculative medium. For example, in Chapter 6 we discussed how arbitrage transactions could lead to significant profits if the bond market is divided into various maturity segments. In that case speculators will develop forecasts of future interest rates and go long in bonds which are expected to exhibit lower required yields in the near future and go short in bonds which are expected to exhibit increases in required yields. Such a speculative transaction is known as a *rate anticipation swap*. A variety of other possible speculative swaps (for example, yield pick-up swaps, quality swaps, and tax swaps) are discussed at length in the next chapter.

BOND VALUATION

Basic Valuation Formulas

Valuation can entail a number of complexities which are best left alone for a while so that we can concentrate on fundamental principles. Two of these complexities are the potential for default and the potential for early retirement by call. So, until stated otherwise, we will assume that all instruments discussed have no default risk and are noncallable. This is really not a very limiting assumption, since there are numerous bonds outstanding which are virtually default-free and noncallable.

Finding a Bond's Price

The worth of a bond is the present value of all future cash flows paid to the bondholder. These cash flows may consist of two components: periodic coupon payments and par value at maturity. While some bonds pay only par value at maturity (for example, T-bills and commercial paper are *zero-coupon*, or pure discount, bonds), most pay coupons. We shall use the following symbology:

$f_{1,t}$ = forward rate of interest on a one-year bond t years from now

C = periodic dollar coupon payment

M = number of periods remaining in the bond's life

F = face (or par) value at maturity

P_0 = present worth of the bond

The value of P_0 is equal to:

Price of a Bond

$$P_0 = \frac{C}{(1+f_{1,0})} + \frac{C}{(1+f_{1,0})(1+f_{1,1})} + \frac{C}{(1+f_{1,0})(1+f_{1,1})(1+f_{1,2})}$$

$$+ \ldots + \frac{C}{(1+f_{1,0})\ldots(1+f_{1,M-1})} + \frac{F}{(1+f_{1,0})\ldots(1+f_{1,M-1})}$$

$$\text{(11.1)}$$

For example, a $1,000 face-value bond which pays an annual coupon of $80, has a three-year remaining life, and on which the one-year forward rates are 9.0%, 8.0%, and 7.0% during each of the next three years would be worth $998.76:

$$\frac{\$80}{(1.09)} + \frac{\$80}{(1.09)(1.08)} + \frac{\$80}{(1.09)(1.08)(1.07)} + \frac{\$1,000}{(1.09)(1.08)(1.07)} = \$998.76$$

Look at each term individually. The $80 coupon received after one year has a present worth of $73.39 ($80 ÷ 1.09). If one-year yields are expected to be 8% during the second year, then the $80 payment at the *end* of year 2 is worth $74.07 at the *start* of year 2 ($80 ÷ 1.08). This $74.07 value is then discounted at the 9% rate required during year 1 to find its present worth of $67.95 ($74.07 ÷ 1.09). Continuing with this process for the year 3 coupon and face-value payment and then adding the resulting present values together results in a current value for the bond of $998.76.[2]

In practice, bond prices are *not* calculated using forward rates unique to each period during which a cash receipt is paid. Instead, a geometric average of the forward rates is determined, and this single discount rate, known as the *yield to maturity* (*YTM*), is used to discount all cash flows.[3] In Chapter 6 we saw that this average can be approximated as a geometric average as follows:

Yield to Maturity $YTM_M = \sqrt[M]{(1+f_{1,0})(1+f_{1,1})\ldots(1+f_{1,M-1})} - 1.0$ **(11.2)**

where the yield to maturity on a bond maturing in period M is designated as YTM_M. Using the three forward rates above (9%, 8%, and 7%), Equation 11.2 implies that the *YTM* on a three-year bond would be 8.00%:

$$\sqrt[3]{(1.09)(1.08)(1.07)} - 1.0 = 8.00\%$$

Equation 11.2, however, is only a close approximation of the actual *YTM*, providing the exact *YTM* only for zero-coupon bonds. When a coupon is paid, the actual *YTM* differs slightly. For example, if we solved the following equation for YTM_3, we would find the actual *YTM* to be 8.05%:

---

[2]This decomposition of forward rates is based largely upon the unbiased expectations theory discussed in Chapter 6.

[3]Most bond traders do not think in terms of forward rates applicable to each future period, but instead think in terms of a single yield to maturity. However, as we saw in Chapter 6, these *YTM*s can be used to determine an underlying sequence of many implied forward rates. In theory, these implied forward rates should equal the expected spot rates (plus a possible liquidity premium).

$$\$998.76 = \frac{\$80}{1 + YTM_3} + \frac{\$80}{(1 + YTM_3)^2} + \frac{\$1,080}{(1 + YTM_3)^3}$$

$$YTM_3 = 8.05\%$$

The 5 basis-point difference is minor, however, and we will continue to say that Equation 11.2 represents the manner in which yields to maturity are related to expected forward rates.

Throughout the rest of the book we will usually think of a bond's price as being the present value of all future coupon and principal payments when discounted at a *single* discount rate — the yield to maturity:

Yield to Maturity $$P_0 = \sum_{t=1}^{M} \frac{C}{(1 + YTM_M)^t} + \frac{F}{(1 + YTM_M)^M}$$ **(11.3)**

Consider another example. An analyst wishes to determine the worth of a five-year bond which will pay a $95 coupon at the end of each year and has a par value of $1,000. Similar risk issues are now selling at a *YTM* of 10.25%. Using Equation 11.3, the present worth of this bond would be $971.75:

$$\frac{\$95}{1.1025} + \frac{\$95}{1.1025^2} + \frac{\$95}{1.1025^3} + \frac{\$95}{1.1025^4} + \frac{\$1,095}{1.1025^5} = \$971.75$$

Finding Yields to Maturity

Often the existing market price of a bond will be known and the *YTM* unknown. In such cases Equation 11.3 can be solved to find YTM_M given existing prices instead of the other way around. For example, if the current price of a four-year bond with a $1,000 face value and 10% coupon is $950.00, its *YTM* is found by solving the following equation:

$$\frac{\$100}{1 + YTM_4} + \frac{\$100}{(1 + YTM_4)^2} + \frac{\$100}{(1 + YTM_4)^3} + \frac{\$1,100}{(1 + YTM_4)^4} = \$950.00$$

The value of YTM_4 can be determined by iteratively trying different discount rates until one is found which discounts the future cash flows back to a present worth of $950.00. Alternatively, a preprogrammed calculator could be used. In addition, extensive bond-pricing tables are available which allow users to quickly estimate prices or *YTM*s. Regardless of the approach used, the *YTM* on this instrument would be 11.63%.

Semiannual Interest

Most coupon bonds quote the coupon payments as if they were paid once a year, but interest is actually paid semiannually. For example, a 7% coupon, four-year bond which pays interest semiannually will provide a sequence of eight coupon payments of \$35 each six months plus \$1,000 at the end of four years. To value such a bond, we must think in terms of *six-month periods* instead of yearly periods. If the stated annual yield to maturity is 8%, the bond's present worth would be \$966.33:

$$\frac{\$35}{1.04} + \frac{\$35}{1.04^2} + \frac{\$35}{1.04^3} + \cdots + \frac{\$35}{1.04^8} + \frac{\$1,000}{1.04^8} = \$966.33$$

When semiannual coupon payments are made, (1) the number of periods to maturity is doubled, (2) the coupon payment is half the quoted annual rate, and (3) the discount rate is half the stated annual yield to maturity. If quarterly (or even more frequent) payments are made, adjustments similar to those involved with semiannual interest should be made.

Notice that while a stated annual *YTM* of 8% is used, the *effective YTM* is higher. The investor starts out with, say, a \$1 investment on which 4 cents is earned at the end of six months. This balance of \$1.04 then earns an additional 4% during the second six months. So by year-end, \$1.0816 is available for each \$1 invested. The effective yield is 8.16% even though the market-quoted yield is 8%.

Value at Noninterest Dates. Equation 11.3 assumes that we are finding a bond's value immediately after an interest payment date and that a full period (six months or one year, depending on coupon-payment dates) remains until the next cash receipt. Bond trades, of course, are only rarely made at a coupon-payment date. When trades occur at other times, accrued interest must be accounted for. The procedure used to do this consists of the following steps:

1. Calculate the value of the bond at the next interest-payment date, assuming interest has just been paid.
2. Add the next interest payment to this amount. The sum will represent the bond's value immediately prior to the next interest payment.
3. Find the present worth of this amount.
4. Subtract the interest which has accrued on the bond since the last interest-payment date.

Consider a 10% coupon issue which matures in 10 years and 2 months. Interest is paid semiannually and investors require a quoted 8% annual *YTM*.

1. As of the next interest date, the bond will have 10 years of life remaining and should sell at:

$$\sum_{t=1}^{20} \frac{\$50}{1.04^t} + \frac{\$1,000}{1.04^{20}} = \$1,135.92$$

2. Adding the \$50 interest payment to be received at that time, the total value of the cash plus the security value will be \$1,185.92.
3. Two months prior to this date, this sum will be worth \$1,170.52:

$$\frac{\$1,185.92}{1.04^{2/6}} = \$1,170.52$$

4. But a portion of the next interest payment belongs to the owner for the prior four months. This accrued interest of $33.33 (50 × 4/6) is subtracted from the above value to find the adjusted true value of the bond today, $1,137.19.

This procedure can be expressed in equation form and solved by computer for either price or *YTM*. Bond traders and brokerage houses use exactly such a procedure when calculating prices or yields.

Yield to Call. When a bond is likely to be called by the issuer prior to maturity, the *YTM* can be a misleading figure. In such cases the investor should calculate an *expected yield to call date*. Equation 11.3 would be modified by estimating the *expected* call date and considering coupon payments up to that date plus the call price of the bond.

Because considerable uncertainty exists about the expected call date, most bond houses calculate and publish a *yield to first call* return. Instead of using an expected date of call, the first possible call date is used. In this case Equation 11.3 is modified as follows:

Yield to Call
$$P_0 = \sum_{t=1}^{C} \frac{C}{(1 + YTM_C)^t} + \frac{CALL}{(1 + YTM_C)^C} \tag{11.4}$$

where *CALL* is the dollar payment which would be made at the first call date, *C* is the number of periods until call, and YTM_C is the yield to first call.

Bond Price Theorems

In Chapter 6 five bond price theorems were presented. Because of their importance, they are listed again here.

1. When a bond's coupon rate equals the investor's required *YTM*, the bond's value will be equal to par regardless of maturity.
2. Bond values move inversely to changes in required *YTM*.
3. Long-term bonds are more price sensitive to a given interest rate change than are shorter-term bonds.
4. While price sensitivity increases with maturity, it increases at a decreasing rate.
5. High-coupon bonds are less price sensitive than lower-coupon bonds to a given interest rate change.

REALIZED BOND RETURNS AND RISK

Yield to maturity is a *promised* rate of return which, as we shall soon see, will actually be earned only under very restricted assumptions. In this section we develop the notion of a *realized bond return*, discuss why it differs from promised *YTM*, and show how it can be used to evaluate a bond's risk.

The Horizon Date and Realized Returns

Securities are bought to be sold. When an investor purchases a security, it is with the hopes of earning a fair rate of return up to some terminal *horizon date*, at which time the security will be sold to provide cash for current consumption. For example, college students may need cash in a few years to support graduate education. A husband and wife may be investing to provide cash during retirement ten to fifteen years away, and insurance firms will invest to provide cash to service expected future insurance claims. All of these investors have a horizon date in mind at which time they expect to sell their securities.[4] Speculators also have a terminal horizon date at which they expect to conclude a given security transaction. The concept of horizon date (*HD*) is crucial to an understanding of bond yields, risks, and trading strategies.

Consider the situation of Continental Casualty Corporation, a medium-sized casualty insurance firm. CCC has just begun to offer a new type of insurance policy which is expected to require cash to meet insured losses three years after each new policy is signed. Thus, *HD* equals three years. All insurance premiums are paid when the policy is signed, and these proceeds are invested in bonds. In a sense, CCC is indifferent to intermediate yearly returns on its bond investments. The important consideration is the amount of net profit available in year 3 after all insurance losses are paid. For example, assume that each policy provides CCC with a $1,000 premium at the start of year 1 which may be invested for three years, at which time the investments will have to be sold to pay expected insurance losses of, say, $1,225. If the investment of $1,000 grows to a value greater than $1,225 by the end of year 3, the firm will have earned a profit. If the $1,000 investment grows to only $1,225 (or less), the firm will just break even (or incur losses). The *sequence* of yearly rates of return on CCC's bond investments is of little importance. Instead, the firm is interested in the terminal worth of its investments at the end of year 3 — the horizon date.

Consider the following three alternative sequences of yearly returns:

Series	Return During Year		
	1	*2*	*3*
A	6.10%	5.00%	10.00%
B	20.00%	−10.00%	13.40%
C	9.00%	4.00%	8.07%

In each case a $1,000 investment grows to exactly $1,225 by the end of year 3:

Series	Horizon Date Value		Details
A	$1,225	=	$1,000 (1.061 × 1.05 × 1.1)
B	1,225	=	1,000 (1.20 × 0.9 × 1.134)
C	1,225	=	1,000 (1.09 × 1.04 × 1.0807)

---

[4]Clearly, most individuals will have a *number* of horizon dates in mind. For example, a retired couple may intend to sell a portion of their security portfolio at the start of each year to meet that year's consumption needs. For simplicity's sake, however, we will restrict our discussion to a single date.

Even though each series has a different *sequence* of yearly returns, CCC should be indifferent among them. Each provides the same terminal wealth. Expressed in the form of a rate of return, each series provides the same average *annual realized rate of return*. The *annual realized return* on a bond investment will be denoted as *ARR* and represents the constant annual discount rate which will discount the horizon date value of a bond investment back to the initial dollar investment made. Mathematically:

$$\text{Initial Investment Value} = \frac{\text{Horizon Date Investment Value}}{(1 + ARR)^{HD}} \qquad \textbf{(11.5)}$$

or

Annual Realized Return $\qquad ARR = \sqrt[HD]{\dfrac{\text{Horizon Date Investment Value}}{\text{Initial Investment Value}}} - 1.0 \qquad \textbf{(11.6)}$

where *HD* represents the number of years to the horizon date. In the CCC example the *ARR* would be 7.0% regardless of which series of yearly returns is earned:

$$\sqrt[3]{\frac{\$1,225}{\$1,000}} - 1.0 = 7.0\%$$

Determinants of *ARR*

The annual realized return on a bond investment is determined by the size of the investment's horizon-date dollar value. Anything that can change the *HD* value will change the *ARR*. Factors that can change this *HD* value include:

1. Changes in the general level of interest rates affecting:
   a. The bond's *HD* market value
   b. Earnings on the reinvestment of coupons
2. Characteristics of the individual bond investment, including:
   a. The bond's coupon rate
   b. The bond's potential default
   c. The bond's potential call

As an illustration, start by assuming that a 9% noncallable, four-year, default-free bond could be bought today for $1,000. Since the bond is selling at par, its promised *YTM* is equal to 9% – the coupon rate. Also assume that the yield curve is flat, the bond is held for three years, and the level of interest rates remains unchanged at 9%. What will the *ARR* be? To determine this, we need to know what the year 3 *HD* value will be. This value consists of the following components: the market value of the bond, the receipt of all coupons, and the receipt of interest earned on reinvestment of coupons.

The market value of the bond will be $1,000 at the end of year 3 since interest rates don't change. In total, $270 in coupons will have been received (three years times $90 per year). Finally, $25 in *interest earned on interest* will have been received: two years' interest on the first $90 coupon payment ($90 \times 1.09^2 - $90) plus one year's interest on the second coupon ($90 \times 1.09 - $90). Thus, the investment value at the end of year 3 will sum to $1,295:

Component	HD Value
Market Value of Bond	$1,000
Receipt of Coupons	270
Interest on Interest	25
Total	$1,295

The *ARR* will equal 9.0%:

$$\sqrt[3]{\frac{\$1,295}{\$1,000}} - 1.0 = 9.0\%$$

In this case the *ARR* does equal the promised *YTM*. But this occurs only because the following conditions are met: (1) *interest rates in the economy don't change* from 9%, resulting in a constant market value of $1,000 and reinvestment of coupons at a rate equal to the promised *YTM*; (2) the bond *does not default*; and (3) the bond *isn't called*.

Now let's change one assumption—the level of interest rates. Assume that immediately after the bond is bought at par, the level of interest rates increases to 10% and remains there. At the end of year 3 the $1,000 investment will be worth $1,288.81:

Component	HD Value	Details
Market Value of Bond	$ 990.91	($1,090 ÷ 1.1)
Receipt of Coupons	270.00	
Interest on Interest	27.90	[$90(1.10^2) - $90] + [$90(1.10) - $90]
Total	$1,288.81	

Now the *ARR* will be 8.82%:

$$\sqrt[3]{\frac{\$1,288.81}{\$1,000.00}} - 1.0 = 8.82\%$$

Anything that might alter a bond investment's *HD* value will affect its *ARR* and cause the *ARR* to be different from the promised *YTM*. If the yield curve shifts, both market values and interest earned on interest are affected (as in the example above). If the bond defaults on a portion of its promised cash flows, all three components of *HD* value would be affected. Total coupon receipts would fall, interest on interest would be lower, and the bond price would probably decline, reflecting an added default risk. Finally, if the bond were called, coupons and interest on interest would be affected because new bonds would have to be bought, probably at a lower coupon and reinvestment rate.

Measuring Uncertainty of Realized Returns

Individuals should be more concerned about the dispersion of potential horizon date *ARR*s than with the volatility of the sequence of periodic returns which make up the realized returns. Let's return again to the Continental Casualty Corporation example and assume the firm has $100,000 to invest for a three-year period and is evaluating potential yearly rates of return which it might earn during this time period. To simplify matters, management believes that one of three yearly return series will occur. These are:[5]

Series	Probability	Return During Year			Geometric Average Annual Realized Return
		1	*2*	*3*	
A	0.3	6%	5%	10%	7%
B	0.4	10%	5%	6%	7%
C	0.3	5%	10%	6%	7%
Total	1.0				

Clearly, each of these return series is volatile — *from year to year*. But each series provides an average annual realized return of 7%. Regardless of which volatile series actually occurs, *there is no uncertainty* about the three-year realized return and the *HD* cash flow.

The standard deviation of realized returns for a given horizon date is a better measure of a bond's risk than the standard deviation of intermediate yearly returns. To understand how the standard deviation of realized returns is calculated, assume that $1,000 is invested in a 10%, 10-year bond. The desired holding period is three years, and the yield curve for bonds of equivalent default risk is now flat with a promised *YTM* of 10% for all maturities. In addition, there is a 30% chance that immediately after the bond is purchased, the yield curve will rise by 1% and remain there. There is also a 30% chance that it will decline by 1%. This is depicted in Figure 11-2.

To calculate potential realized returns, we must first determine the various investment values which might occur at *HD*. As before, these cash values consist of three components: (1) market value of the bond at the end of year 3, (2) total coupon payments received prior to the horizon date, and (3) interest earned on interest from coupon reinvestment. First, the price of the bond at the end of year 3 will depend on yields to maturity as of the horizon date, as follows:

---

[5]These *yearly* returns are calculated in the normal manner:

$$R_t = \frac{MV_t - MV_{t-1} + C_t}{MV_{t-1}}$$

where *MV* refers to the market value at a given date and *C* refers to any cash flows. The idea of interest on interest is explicitly considered since all cash flows are assumed to be reinvested.

FIGURE 11-2 *Holding Period Risk and Yield Curve Uncertainty*

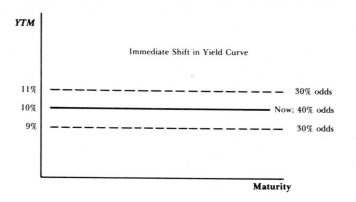

$$\text{End of Year 3}$$

Level of Yield Curve	Price of Bond	=	Present Value of Coupons			+	Present Value of Par
9%	$1,050.30	=	$\dfrac{\$100}{1.09} + \dfrac{\$100}{1.09^2} + \ldots +$		$\dfrac{\$100}{1.09^7}$	+	$\dfrac{\$1,000}{1.09^7}$
10%	$1,000.00	=	$\dfrac{\$100}{1.1} + \dfrac{\$100}{1.1^2} + \ldots +$		$\dfrac{\$100}{1.1^7}$	+	$\dfrac{\$1,000}{1.1^7}$
11%	$ 952.88	=	$\dfrac{\$100}{1.11} + \dfrac{\$100}{1.11^2} + \ldots +$		$\dfrac{\$100}{1.11^7}$	+	$\dfrac{\$1,000}{1.11^7}$

Second, as long as the bond *does not default* on any coupon payment and *is not called*, total coupon receipts will be $300 ($100 at the end of years 1, 2, and 3). Finally, interest earned on reinvestment of coupons will depend upon possible shifts in the yield curve, as follows:

Level of Yield Curve	Interest on Coupons	=	First-Year Coupon	+	Second-Year Coupon	–	Total Coupons
9%	$27.81	=	$100(1.09^2)	+	$100(1.09)	–	$200
10%	$31.00	=	$100(1.1^2)	+	$100(1.1)	–	$200
11%	$34.21	=	$100(1.11^2)	+	$100(1.11)	–	$200

In sum, end-of-year-3 investment values would be:

Level of Yield Curve	HD Cash Value	=	Market Value of Bond	+	Coupon	–	Interest on Coupons
9%	$1,378.11	=	$1,050.30	+	$300.00	+	$27.81
10%	$1,331.00	=	$1,000.00	+	$300.00	+	$31.00
11%	$1,287.09	=	$ 952.88	+	$300.00	+	$34.21

This would provide realized returns of:

Level of Yield Curve	Probability	Realized Yield to Horizon Period
9%	0.3	11.28%
10%	0.4	10.00%
11%	0.3	8.78%

The expected realized return is 10.02%. The standard deviation of *ARR* would be 0.97% and is caused by uncertainty about future bond prices and interest on interest.[6]

Buying a 10-year bond and holding it to the three-year horizon date is only one of many strategies which might be followed. Others include: (1) buy a 10-year bond, sell it at the end of year 1, reinvest in a new 10-year bond, sell it at the end of year 2, etc.; (2) buy a three-year bond and hold it until it matures; (3) buy a three-year bond, sell it after a year, purchase another new three-year bond, etc. According to the unbiased expectations theory, *expected* realized returns under any of these strategies would be identical. Transactions by speculators would force yields on bonds of differing maturities to levels where expected profits from all trading strategies are equal. Believers in market segmentation theory and liquidity preference theory disagree, of course, and believe that expected returns will vary between each strategy. Regardless of which theory is correct concerning *expected* realized returns, there is no doubt that the *risks* associated with each strategy differ. This is discussed in the next section.

Determinants of Bond Risk

Anything that influences the distribution of realized horizon date returns also affects bond risk. Uncertainty about *ARR* is usually attributed to one of four factors: (1) default risk, (2) call risk, (3) reinvestment rate risk, and (4) price risk.

Default Risk. If the issuer of a bond is unable to make all coupon and principal payments as promised, realized yields will be less than promised. The greater the uncertainty about default, the greater the uncertainty about realized returns which might be available at some horizon date. Default risk is discussed in the next section of this chapter.

Call Risk. Issuers are often allowed to retire a bond issue prior to scheduled maturity. As a result, investors are uncertain that coupon and principal payments will be made as scheduled in the indenture agreement. Call risk is also discussed later in the chapter.

---

[6] $\sqrt{0.3(0.1128 - 0.1002)^2 + 0.4(0.1000 - 0.1002)^2 + 0.3(0.0878 - 0.1002)^2} = 0.97\%$

Reinvestment Rate Risk. Uncertainty about possible shifts in the yield curve creates an uncertainty about future returns from coupon reinvestment. If future reinvestment rates are different from a bond's promised *YTM*, its realized *YTM* will not equal its promised yield. The same is true for yields to horizon dates. If reinvestment rates between now and a future horizon date are uncertain, realized returns as of that horizon date will also be uncertain.

Price Risk. Bond prices are inversely related to required rates of return. If required returns increase, bond prices fall, and vice versa. The only date at which a bond's price is certain is at maturity (barring default or call). As a result, price risk exists whenever an individual's horizon date and a bond's maturity differ.

IMMUNIZATION

Default and call risks cannot be eliminated, and required bond yields must be adjusted for the relative degrees of each. However, reinvestment rate and price risk *can* be virtually eliminated by selecting appropriate bond lives. Reinvestment rate risk and price risk both arise from uncertainty about future interest rates. In fact, both risks are aspects of a more basic risk: *interest rate risk*. But note that changes in interest rates work in opposite directions on reinvestment and price risks. If interest rates increase, reinvestment income *increases* whereas bond prices *decline*. Conversely, a reduction in interest rates causes reinvestment income to *decline* and bond prices to *increase*. Since the two forces move in opposite directions, it is possible for the favorable impacts of one to exactly offset the unfavorable impacts of the other. This is the basic concept behind strategies which *immunize* a portfolio against interest rate risk. The fact that reinvestment rate risk and price risk can offset each other by proper selection of a bond's maturity has only recently been fully understood. Because of its growing importance in both investment theory and practice, we will spend considerable time with the concept in this chapter and the next.

Consider the following situation. You are the investment adviser for Anne Curat. Anne has just come to you with $100,000 which she wishes to invest for *exactly* 4.24 years. She states that the investment must be in default-free, noncallable bonds. Anne will pay you a commission based upon how close her realized *HD* return is to what you initially promise. After a quick survey you believe the following opportunities are available to her:

Bond	Coupon	Maturity	Promised YTM	Current Price
A	0%	4.24 years	9%	$ 693.92
B	9	2.00	9	1,000.00
C	9	20.00	9	1,000.00
D	9	5.00	9	1,000.00

In addition, the yield curve is now flat and is expected to stay flat.

If interest rates don't change between now and 4.24 years from now, you really

TABLE 11-1 *Bond Values in 4.24 Years Considering Reinvestment and Price Risks*

Interest Rate	Price at Horizon Date*	+	Total† Coupons	+	Interest on Intermediate Cash Flows	=	Horizon Date Cash Value	Realized Returns
Bond B:								
7%	$1,016	+	$320	+	$44	=	$1,380	7.89%
9%	1,021	+	360	+	60	=	1,441	9.00%
11%	1,025	+	400	+	78	=	1,503	10.09%
Bond C:								
7%	1,208	+	360	+	46	=	1,614	11.95%
9%	1,021	+	360	+	60	=	1,441	9.00%
11%	874	+	360	+	75	=	1,309	6.56%
Bond D:								
7%	1,035	+	360	+	46	=	1,441	9.00%
9%	1,021	+	360	+	60	=	1,441	9.00%
11%	1,006	+	360	+	75	=	1,441	9.00%

*Includes interest accrued in year 5.
†Coupons are paid annually.

don't have a problem; each of the four bonds would provide a 9% realized return. But since interest rates may well change, you are somewhat uncertain about each bond's realized return over the 4.24-year period. Indeed, you foresee the possibility that immediately after the $100,000 is invested, interest rates may rise to 11% or fall to 7%. What should you do? First, promise Anne a 9% realized yield and then consider each bond in turn.

Bond *A* is a zero-coupon bond maturing in exactly 4.24 years. Since all of its yield comes in the form of price appreciation, it is not exposed to price or reinvestment risk. Its realized return will be 9%, regardless of future shifts in the yield curve.[7] Bonds *B*, *C*, and *D* will each be exposed to varying degrees of price and reinvestment rate risk. Bond *B* has a maturity much shorter than the 4.24-year *HD* and will be exposed to considerable reinvestment rate risk. When bond *B* matures in two years, a new bond will have to be bought at a *YTM* which is currently uncertain. Bond *C* matures after the horizon date and will be exposed to considerable price risk since its market value in 4.24 years will depend upon yields at that date, which are currently uncertain. Bond *D* matures slightly after the horizon date and will be exposed about equally to both reinvestment rate and price risks.

This can be seen in Table 11-1, where *HD* cash values are calculated for each bond and for each possible shift in the yield curve. Realized yields for bonds *B* and *C* are clearly uncertain. If the yield curve falls to 7%, realized yields on *B* will be less than

[7]Year 4.24 Investment Value $= \$100,000 \times \dfrac{\$1,000}{\$693.92} = \$144,108.83$

$$ARR = \sqrt[4.24]{\$144,108.83/\$100,000} - .10 = 9.00\%$$

9% because of lower reinvestment rates, and they will be higher than 9% for C since its price increases more than enough to offset lower reinvestment rates. If the yield curve increases to 11%, the opposite will occur. Bond B will have a return greater than 9% because of improved reinvestment rates, and C will have a lower return because its price decline more than offsets larger interest on interest.

Notice the curious results for bond D. Regardless of shifts in the yield curve, it provides a 9% realized yield. Why? The answer lies in the fact that D's reinvestment rate and price risks exactly *offset* each other. *The coupon rate and maturity of bond* D *were selected so that the "average date" of its cash flows is exactly 4.24 years hence.* While D repays principal of $1,000 at the end of five years, cash is received in the form of $90 coupons at each year-end. The average date at which a dollar of cash is received on bond D is 4.24 years. Economically, bond D is equivalent to a 4.24-year, zero-coupon bond.

Duration

The "average date" at which cash is received is known as a bond's *duration*. The most widely used measure of duration is referred to as D and is calculated as follows:

$$D = \sum_{t=1}^{M} \left[\frac{t \times PV_t}{\sum_{t=1}^{M} PV_t} \right] \qquad (11.7)$$

where D = the duration of a bond, t = a given year number, M = the number of years to maturity, PV_t = the present value of cash flows received in year t, and ΣPV_t = the present value of all cash flows (the bond's price). Bond D's duration is shown below. First, the present value of each year's cash flows is found using the bond's promised *YTM* as the discount rate. These are then stated as a percentage of the total present value. Finally, these percentages are multiplied by the year number in which the cash flow is received and summed.

Year	Cash Flow	Present Value	Percentage of Total	Year Number	Product
1	$ 90	$ 82.57	8.257%	1	0.0826
2	90	75.75	7.575	2	0.1515
3	90	69.50	6.950	3	0.2085
4	90	63.76	6.376	4	0.2550
5	1,090	708.42	70.842	5	3.5421
		$1,000.00		$D =$	4.2397 years

A Simple Approach to Calculating D. The calculation of D in Equation 11.7 may appear quite imposing. But the logic behind it is really very simple. To illustrate this, consider again the cash flow data on the five-year, 9% coupon bond discussed above. This bond promises to pay $90 at each year-end plus $1,090 at its maturity in five years. Now, consider this to be not one bond, *but a portfolio of five distinctly different bonds.* The first bond in this portfolio matures in one year and pays $90. The second bond matures in two years and has one cash payment equal to $90 at its maturity, etc. Finally, the last bond matures in five years and pays a single cash flow of $1,090 at its maturity. In short, our original bond is now considered to be a portfolio of *five different zero-coupon bonds.*

What is the duration of each of these zero-coupon bonds? Since each provides cash at one date only (its maturity), *the duration of each is identical to its maturity.* The duration of the one-year $90 bond is one year, the duration of the two-year $90 bond is two years, etc. We are just about ready to calculate the duration of this portfolio of five bonds. But to do so we must know that *the duration of a portfolio is equal to the weighted average duration of the bonds held in the portfolio*; that is:

Duration of a Portfolio

$$D_P = \sum_{i=1}^{N} X_i D_i \qquad \text{(11.8)}$$

where D_P represents the portfolio's duration, D_i represents the duration of i, and X_i is the percentage of the portfolio invested in bond i.

Look again at the duration calculation for the original five-year, 9% coupon bond which we are now considering to be a portfolio of five zero-coupon bonds. The dollar investment made in the one-year zero-coupon bond is $82.57 — the present value of $90 received in one year. The dollar investment made in the two-year zero-coupon bond is $75.75 — the present value of its $90 maturity cash payment in two years, etc. The total value of this portfolio is $1,000. Thus, X_1 is equal to 8.26%, X_2 is equal to 7.58%, . . . , and X_5 is equal to 70.84%. We can now use Equation 11.8 to calculate the portfolio's duration:

$$D_P = X_1 D_1 + X_2 D_2 + X_3 D_3 + X_4 D_4 + X_5 D_5$$

$$= 0.08257(1) + 0.07575(2) + 0.06950(3) + 0.06376(4) + 0.70842(5)$$

$$= 4.2397 \text{ years}$$

The number and types of calculations we have just used to find the bond's duration are identical to those in Equation 11.7. But we have employed a convenient mental device which allows us to calculate a bond's duration without having to memorize Equation 11.7. All we have to do is consider a coupon bond to be a portfolio of many zero-coupon securities and recognize that the duration of a portfolio is the weighted average of the duration of the securities held in the portfolio.

Minimizing Bond Risk. Figure 11-3 illustrates the relationship between a bond's total risk and its duration based on the investor's horizon date. Inherent default and call risks are unaffected by duration or the investor's *HD*. However, reinvestment and price risks are. Whenever a bond's duration is shorter than the *HD*, uncertainty about future reinvestment rates dominates price risks and a *net reinvestment rate risk* exists. Whenever a bond's duration is longer than the *HD*, uncertainty about future price levels dominates reinvestment risks and a *net price risk* exists. However, these two risks exactly offset each other when the duration equals the *HD*.

FIGURE 11-3 *Duration, Horizon Date, and Bond Risks*

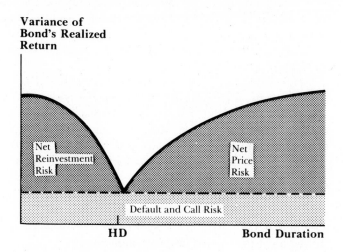

Bond immunization does work in practice. For example, Fisher and Weil examined the standard deviation of bond returns for three different horizon dates (5 years, 10 years, and 20 years) using two alternative investment strategies. In strategy 1 a bond portfolio with a 20-year maturity was constantly held. At the start of each year, 20-year bonds were bought, and the old bonds (which would then have a 19-year maturity) were sold. In strategy 2 they constantly held bonds with a maturity equal to the desired *HD*. Their data consisted of yearly returns on long-term, high-grade corporate bonds between 1925 and 1968.[8] If bond immunization works, the standard deviation of actual realized returns from expected realized returns should be lower in strategy 2. Results are shown below.

| | Standard Deviation of Differences Between Expected Versus Actual Horizon Date Investment Value | |
Length of Horizon Date	*Strategy 1*	*Strategy 2*
5 years	0.115	0.0026
10	0.174	0.0120
20	0.182	0.0290

SOURCE: Reprinted from "Coping with the Risk of Interest-Rate Fluctuations: Returns to Bondholders from Naive and Optimal Strategies," *Journal of Business* 44, no. 3 (October 1971) by L. Fisher and R. Weil, by permission of The University of Chicago Press. © 1971 by The University of Chicago. All rights reserved.

The values represent the standard deviation of differences between expected and actual *HD* wealth assuming an initial portfolio value of $1. Clearly, the duration strategy provided the smallest variation in *HD* wealth.

---

[8]Since a bond's maturity is not the same as its duration (except for zero-coupon bonds), Fisher and Weil's test was only an approximation of the duration strategy.

DEFAULT RISK

Expected Versus Promised Yields

Default risk is the possibility that *promised* coupon and par values of a bond will not be paid. For example, in the early 1980s, the Washington Public Power Supply defaulted on bonds which had been sold to finance nuclear power plants in the state of Washington. Although each WPPS (as in WHOOPS) bond *had promised* very specific coupon and eventual par value payments to owners, it was clear that investors had to expect much less.

The WPPS bonds are a recent and dramatic example showing that *promised* yields to maturity can be different from *expected* yields to maturity. In early 1985, one issue of these bonds promised to pay annual coupons of $160 through 1991. At prices quoted in January 1985 of $730, this represented a *promised YTM* of 24½%. But it was clear that WPPS would not be able to meet its promised obligation and that expected returns were much lower.

We saw earlier that promised yields to maturity will differ from expected yields if interest rates change over time or if the security is not held to maturity. This difference between expected and promised returns was due to interest rate risk. We saw also that this interest rate risk could be eliminated by immunizing the bond portfolio—setting its duration equal to the desired horizon date. The impacts of default risk, unfortunately, cannot be eliminated. The potential for default has two possible effects on a bond's price. First, it causes expected future cash flows to be less than promised. Second, it can increase the bond's systematic risk and thus increase the return which should be expected from owning it.

For example, consider a U.S. government bond with a $1,000 par value, 10% coupon, and two-year maturity. Such a bond would be (virtually) devoid of default risk because of the government's ability to print money in order to pay off the bond. If the risk-free rate is 10%, this bond would be priced to provide an expected risk-free return—at $1,000:

$$\frac{\$100}{1.10} + \frac{\$1,100}{1.10^2} = \$1,000$$

If the investor has properly immunized by setting the bond portfolio's duration equal to the horizon date, there will be no interest rate risk or default risk on this bond. Thus, its expected return will equal the promised *YTM* and both will equal *RF*.

The addition of default risk, however, causes the *expected* future cash flows to be less than promised. If investors expected a $90 coupon instead of the $100 promised coupon, this impact of potential default would result in a price of $982.64:

$$\frac{\$90}{1.10} + \frac{\$1,090}{1.10^2} = \$982.64$$

In addition, if the potential for default is nondiversifiable, the return required on the bond would be greater than the risk-free rate. For example, assume that this bond has a beta of 0.3 and that $RP_M = 6\%$. Then a fair expected return of 11.8% [10% + 0.3(6.0%)] would be used to discount the bond's *expected* cash flows. Adding this possibility of nondiversifiable default risk to the lower expected cash flows results in a bond price of $952.55:

$$\frac{\$90}{1.118} + \frac{\$1,090}{1.118^2} = \$952.55$$

In sum, default risk will reduce a bond's price by (1) causing expected cash flows to be less than promised and (2) requiring a return in excess of *RF* if the default risk is nondiversifiable.

Yields to maturity on bonds that have default risk overstate the bond's true expected return. For example, the bond discussed above would have a market price of $952.55. Using the *promised* series of cash payments, its promised yield to maturity is 12.84%:

$$\frac{\$100}{1.1284} + \frac{\$1,100}{1.1284^2} = \$952.55$$

But its *expected* yearly return is only 11.8%. The extent to which promised and expected yields to maturity differ depends, of course, on the amount of default risk inherent in the bond and the extent to which this risk is nondiversifiable. Across the market of all bond issues, this bias inherent in *YTM* is small, but in particular cases it can be substantial.

To date, little solid evidence has been developed about the systematic risk of bonds and their betas. We do know that bond betas appear to be small—less than 0.3 in most cases. Unfortunately, the calculation of bond betas involves a host of problems which don't exist (or are glossed over) with equity beta estimates. For example, beta estimates are made using returns calculated over time intervals which might vary from the investor's horizon date. Calculating bond betas using monthly returns makes a five-year duration bond appear to be more risky than a one-year duration bond, since the five-year bond is more sensitive to interest rate changes. However, to a person who has a five-year horizon date, the five-year duration bond is clearly less risky. In addition, historical bond beta estimates are biased because the life of a bond is constantly changing during the period over which its beta is estimated.

Historical Experience

The few studies dealing with historical default rates have concluded exactly what we would expect: Default rates are much higher during periods of economic recession and depression than during normal periods. For example, Atkinson examined average yearly *corporate* default rates for various time intervals between 1900 and 1965. The default rate was defined as the par value of bonds going into default during a given year divided by the total par value of nondefaulted bonds at the start of the year. His

TABLE 11-2 *Corporate Default Rates*

Period	Percentage of Initial Par Value Defaulting*
1900–1943	1.70%
1944–65	0.10
1900–1909	0.90
1910–19	2.00
1920–29	1.00
1930–39	3.20
1940–49	0.40
1950–59	0.04
1960–65	0.03

*Average per year.

SOURCE: T. R. Atkinson, *Trends in Corporate Bond Quality* (New York: National Bureau of Economic Research, 1967).

results are shown in Table 11-2.[9] Clearly, the greatest default rates occurred between 1910 and 1919 and between 1930 and 1939. Default experience during the rapid economic growth since 1940 has been quite small, associated with particular industries faced with technological competition.

Hempel examined *municipal* bond defaults during depressionary periods and found:

Years of Depression	Average Yearly Rate of Default on Par
1837–43	8.5%
1873–79	4.1
1893–99	1.7
1929–37	1.9

Default risk appears to be related to broad economic shocks, such as economic recessions and depressions, which affect all security returns. Thus, at least a portion of default risk is systematic and nondiversifiable.

Rating Agencies

The default risks of most actively traded bonds are rated by various independent organizations. Standard & Poor's and Moody's are the largest of these rating agencies, concentrating upon corporate and municipal issues. Fitch's is a smaller organization which concentrates upon institutional issues. These ratings reflect each agency's opin-

---

[9]The default rates in Table 11-2 are stated as percentages of par value. Thus, they overstate the actual loss rate because most bonds which default will be selling below par. And even if a bond defaults, the owners typically receive some compensation.

TABLE 11-3 *Ratings of Bonds' Default Risks*

Moody's	Standard & Poor's	Definition*
Aaa	AAA	The highest rating assigned. Capacity to pay interest and principal extremely strong.
Aa	AA	Very strong capacity to pay interest and principal. Differ from highest-rated issues only in small degree.
A	A	Strong capacity to repay interest and principal but may be susceptible to adverse changes in economic conditions.
Baa	BBB	Adequate protection to repay interest and principal but more likely to have weakened capacity in periods of adverse economic conditions.
Ba	BB	Some speculation with respect to repayment capacity. Have some quality and protection characteristics, but major uncertainties exist.
B	B	Moderate default risk.
Caa	CCC	High default risk. May be in default or in severe danger of default.
Ca	CC	Highly speculative and likely to be in default.
C		For Moody's, the lowest-rated bonds. Can be regarded as having extremely poor prospects of ever attaining any real investment standing.
	C	For S&P, income bond on which interest is not being paid.
	D	In default. Payment of interest and/or principal in arrears.

*Adapted from Standard & Poor's *Bond Guide* and Moody's *Bond Record*.

ion about an issue's potential default, *not* its relative investment merits. Table 11-3 presents a summary of the ratings used by Moody's and S&P.

Not only do the ratings provide an opinion about the default risk of an issue, but they are often used to define allowable bond purchases for some investors. For example, the Comptroller of the Currency has stated that bank investments must be *investment grade*. Historically, the comptroller has defined investment grade to include bonds rated in the top four rankings. In addition, *legal lists* of approved bonds are used in some states to identify bonds which regulated savings banks, trust companies, and insurance companies may purchase. These legal lists rely upon ratings by Moody's and Standard & Poor's. Rating designations in addition to those shown in Table 11-3 are sometimes used to more accurately reflect an agency's opinion. For example, Standard & Poor's will occasionally indicate a (+) or (−) on ratings between AA and BB. Moody's will apply A1 and Baa1 to the better-quality *municipals* within the A and Baa categories. Nonrated issues are designated NR.

To evaluate a bond's potential for default, rating agencies rely upon a committee analysis of the issuer's *ability* to repay, *willingness* to repay, and *protective provisions* for an issue. Ratings given by Moody's and S&P for a particular issue will usually be identical. When a difference does exist, it will be no larger than one grade and reflects the relative strength or weakness of each agency's opinion.

The Historical Accuracy of Ratings

With rare exceptions, the ratings assigned by S&P and Moody's have closely followed actual historical default rates. In a thorough study of corporate bonds issued between 1900 and 1943, Hickman examined by rating category the proportion of bonds which defaulted. Nine rating categories were used, with the following results:

Rating Category	Comparable S&P Rating	Percent of Par Value Defaulting Prior to Maturity
I	AAA	6%
II	AA	6
III	A	13
IV	BBB	19
V–IX	Below BBB	42

SOURCE: W. B. Hickman, *Corporate Bond Quality and Investor Experience* (Princeton, NJ: Princeton University Press, 1958).

The two highest-rated categories experienced similar and relatively low default rates. As the ratings decreased, the default rate increased.

Hickman also examined the actual *realized YTM*s on bonds of each rating and compared them with *promised* yields. If investors properly assess future rates of default, the difference between promised and realized yields should reflect the expected default rates. For each bond he calculated a realized annual return based upon buying the bond at its issue price, receiving the sequence of coupons actually paid, and obtaining the terminal value of the bond when it reached maturity, defaulted, or was called. Results of this analysis are shown in Table 11-4. Surprisingly, Hickman found that realized *YTM*s exceeded promised *YTM*s. This occurred because, during the period he studied, interest rates fell, resulting in a large number of bonds being called as issuers took advantage of lower rates. When the original issues were called, investors received a call premium above par and thus a higher realized return than promised. Consequently, Hickman's realized yields were unduly influenced by interest rate movements during his study period.

To correct for this, Fraine and Mills substituted promised yields for realized yields

TABLE 11-4 *Realized YTM by Rating*

Rating Category	Average Promised YTM	Realized YTM	
		Hickman	Fraine/Mills
I	4.5%	5.1%	4.3
II	4.6	5.0	4.3
III	4.9	5.0	4.3
IV	5.4	5.7	4.5
V–IX	9.5	8.6	NA

SOURCES: W. B. Hickman, *Corporate Bond Quality and Investor Experience* (Princeton, NJ: Princeton University Press, 1958); H. Fraine and R. Mills, "The Effect of Defaults and Credit Deterioration on Yields of Corporate Bonds," *Journal of Finance* 16, no. 3 (September 1961).

whenever realized yields were larger. Their results are shown in the rightmost column of Table 11-4. When modified by Fraine and Mills, promised yields exceeded realized yields, and the difference increased for the lower default ratings.

Default, Yield Spreads, and Term Structure

Yield Spreads. Yield spreads are often calculated for bonds of equivalent maturity. For example, if two bonds with 10-year maturities are selling at promised *YTM*s of 8% and 9.5%, respectively, the yield spread between the two is 150 basis points. Yield spreads are created by:

1. Differences in *expected default rates*. Bonds that have greater chances for default will certainly sell at greater promised *YTM*s.
2. Differences in *systematic risk*. Bonds whose potential realized returns are more sensitive to broad economic shocks will have larger promised *YTM*s.
3. Differences in *call provisions*. As discussed later, callable bonds will sell at higher promised *YTM*s than will equivalent noncallable issues.
4. Differences in *coupon rates*. Bonds with low coupons are taxed at effectively lower tax rates and will thus sell at lower before-tax promised *YTM*s.
5. Differences in *marketability*. The more marketable a bond, the lower the required *YTM*.

Yield spreads are typically charted over some historical time period for bonds of equivalent maturity but different default ratings. For example, Table 11-5 presents yield spreads between Treasury bonds and two long-term corporate bond series, AAA and BBB. While differences in systematic risk, call, and coupon effects may not be constant over time, these are usually neglected, and changes in yield spreads are attributed to changes in default risk. A priori, we might expect yield spreads to increase during economic recessions and decrease during active business expansion. During recessions yield spreads might increase as a result of (1) investors' becoming more risk-averse and thus requiring larger default premiums, *and* (2) increased probability of default. The opposite would be true for an economic expansion. There is evidence (although mixed) that this does occur. In Table 11-5 yield spreads between corporate AAA and Treasury bonds moved somewhat with the business cycle. Consistent with the fact that AAAs contain small amounts of default risk, these movements were slight. Yield spreads on BBB versus Treasury bonds exhibit a more dramatic sensitivity to business cycles.

Term Structure. Yield curves for bonds that have greater default risk will lie above those of less risky bonds. Figure 11-4 presents hypothetical yield curves for default-free Treasury obligations as well as A and B grade corporates. How is the size of the default-risk premium related to a bond's maturity? This question is not fully resolved.

TABLE 11-5 *Yields and Yield Spreads*

Year	Treasury	Corporate		AAA − Treasuries	BBB − Treasuries
		AAA	BAA		
1950	2.32	2.62	3.24	0.30	0.92
51	2.57	2.86	3.41	0.29	0.84
52	2.68	2.96	3.52	0.28	0.84
53	2.93	3.20	3.74	0.27	0.81
54*	2.53	2.90	3.51	0.37	0.98
55	2.80	3.06	3.53	0.26	0.73
56	3.05	3.36	3.88	0.31	0.83
57*	3.47	3.89	4.71	0.42	1.24
58	3.43	3.79	4.73	0.36	1.30
59	4.07	4.38	5.05	0.31	0.98
1960*	4.01	4.41	5.19	0.40	1.18
61	3.90	4.35	5.08	0.45	1.18
62	3.95	4.33	5.02	0.38	1.07
63	4.00	4.26	4.86	0.26	0.86
64	4.15	4.40	4.83	0.25	0.68
65	4.21	4.49	4.87	0.28	0.66
66	4.66	5.13	5.67	0.47	1.01
67*	4.85	5.51	6.23	0.66	1.38
68*	5.25	6.18	6.94	0.93	1.69
69	6.10	7.03	7.81	0.93	1.71
1970*	6.59	8.04	9.11	1.45	2.52
71	5.74	7.39	6.56	1.65	2.82
72	5.63	7.21	8.16	1.58	2.53
73	6.30	7.44	8.24	1.14	1.94
74*	6.99	8.57	9.50	1.58	2.51
75*	6.98	8.83	10.39	1.85	3.41
76	6.82	8.48	9.67	1.66	2.85
77	7.06	8.02	8.97	0.96	1.91
78	7.89	8.73	9.45	0.84	1.56
79	8.74	9.63	10.69	0.89	1.95
1980*	10.81	11.94	13.67	1.13	2.86
81*	13.72	14.23	16.55	0.51	2.83
82*	10.54	11.83	14.14	1.29	3.60
83	11.83	12.57	13.75	0.74	1.92
84	11.50	12.13	13.40	0.63	1.92
85	8.67	9.91	11.22	1.24	2.55
86	7.05	8.36	9.98	1.31	2.93
87	8.41	9.25	10.56	0.84	2.15

*Recessionary periods.

SOURCE: Various Federal Reserve Bulletins.

Johnson has presented reasonably strong support for the belief that default-risk premiums *increase as maturity increases* for bonds of *moderate to low* default risk (A grades) while default-risk premiums *decrease as maturity increases* for bonds of *high* default risk (B and lower grades). His explanation is that the chance of default

FIGURE 11-4 *Term Structure and Default Risk*

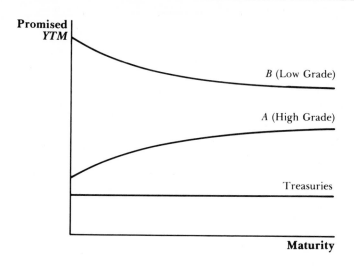

for low-risk issues increases with maturity, since time alone can allow for many unforeseen, adverse events to arise. However, longer maturities on high-risk bonds might allow the issuers to find ways out of their present financial crises.

Statistical Determinants of Yield Spreads

Fisher studied yield spreads between 366 corporate and Treasury bonds of equivalent maturity. His purpose was to examine the relative effects of three default-risk proxies and one marketability proxy on the size of the corporate yield spreads. Table 11-6 summarizes a portion of his results. Probability of default was estimated by (1) *EV*, earnings variability; (2) *SOL*, the number of years since the firm had defaulted on any debt obligations; and (3) *ED*, the ratio of the firm's equity market value to its debt par value. Marketability was measured by *BMV*, the total market value of bonds in the public's hands. Log values of each variable were used in the regression analysis. As a result, regression coefficients reflect the *percentage changes* in yield spreads for a *percentage change* in each variable. For example, the estimated coefficient on the equity-debt ratio of −0.537 implies that a 1% increase in this ratio (all other things remaining constant) leads to a 0.537% decline in yield spreads. Similarly, a 1% increase in the number of bonds outstanding seemed to result in a 0.275% decline in yield spreads. Fisher's results are important because each explanatory variable was highly significant, and the model was able to explain about 75% of the variability in yield spreads.

A number of other studies have examined bond yield spreads with essentially the same results. A large portion of the differences in bond yields can be explained by both theory and empirical evidence as due to the differential risks and marketability of the bonds.

TABLE 11-6 *Fisher's Study of Corporate Bonds*

$$\log(\text{yield spread}) = \alpha_0 + b_1 \log(EV) + b_2 \log(SOL) + b_3 \log(ED) + b_4 \log(BMV)$$

Variable	Regression Coefficient	t-Value
α_0 (constant)	0.987	—
EV	0.307	9.59
SOL	−0.253	7.03
ED	−0.537	17.32
BMV	−0.275	13.10

$R^2 = 75.0\%$

EV = a measure of earnings variability calculated as the standard deviation of the prior 9 years' earnings divided by average earnings.

SOL = the number of years since the firm was last in default on a debt obligation.

ED = the total market value of equity divided by the total par value of bonds. This is a financial leverage ratio.

BMV = the total market value of the bonds owned by the public.

SOURCE: L. Fisher, "Determinants of Risk Premiums on Corporate Bonds," *Journal of Political Economy* 67, no. 3 (June 1959): 217–37.

Price Impacts of Rating Changes

The most widely known measures of bond default risk are the quality ratings provided by organizations such as Moody's, Standard & Poor's, and Fitch's. As we've already seen, bond yield spreads are directly related to the amount of default risk implied by these ratings. But do investors and speculators rely on the rating services as the *unique* source of information about a bond's default risk? That is, are the rating agencies better able to discern the default risk inherent in a bond than are investors and speculators?

The answer to this question depends upon the amount of information held by the rating services versus the amount of information held by bond market participants. If the rating services have better access to historical data or are better at forecasting future data, then their ratings provide a new and unique source of information to the markets. However, if they have access to the same historical data as everyone else and are unable to forecast any better than bond investors and speculators, then their ratings do not have unique informational value. In fact, it is quite possible that the ratings may not even reflect all the information which is available to bond traders at a given point in time. Changes in ratings might lag information flows to bond market participants. Bond issuers typically contract with the various rating agencies to rate a new issue and continually update the rating throughout the bond's life. For this service, the issuers pay a one-time fee to the rating agencies selected. Subsequent to the initial rating and sale, the bond will be periodically reviewed to determine whether a change in rating is necessary. Approximately one half of all corporate issues are reviewed quarterly or annually, and the other one half have no set review period. So it is possible that changes in a bond's default risk might accumulate for some period of time before the rating agencies will issue a revised rating.

To investigate whether changes in default ratings have any impact upon bond prices, Weinstein examined monthly rates of return on a sample of corporate bonds for the period July 1962 through July 1974. Control portfolios were created for each default grade, and a series of monthly returns on these control portfolios were calculated. Next, a sequence of "risk-adjusted returns" was calculated for each bond which had a rating change by subtracting the bond's return in a given month from the return on the control portfolio having a similar initial default grade. For example, if bond 1 had been downgraded from a double-A-grade to a single-A-grade during a given month, its monthly return would be subtracted from the double-A-grade control portfolio's monthly return. Such risk-adjusted returns were calculated during the month of the rating change, for the prior 19 months, and for the subsequent 6 months.

Accumulating these risk-adjusted returns for bonds which underwent a rating change suggested the following:

1. There was some evidence that bond prices had adjusted to changing default conditions 6 to 18 months *before* the rating change.
2. During the 6 months prior to the rating change, there appeared to be no price impacts.
3. During the rating-change month, the price impact was negligible, if one even existed.
4. During the 6-month period after the rating change, there were no noticeable price impacts.

This evidence suggests that while default ratings do reflect the underlying default risk of a bond, they do so with some lag. Investors and speculators recognize the changing default risks and incorporate these changes into bond prices before the rating agencies announce their changes. Thus, ratings don't appear to have unique informational value.

CALL AND TAXES

Call Impacts on Yields

Virtually all corporate bonds and a large percentage of municipal bonds may be retired prior to formal maturity by exercise of a call provision. Issuers will call an issue if the present value of future coupon savings associated with refunding the issue offsets the costs of doing so. To the investor the effects of a call are twofold. First, the realized return during the time span for which the bond has been held will be larger than promised because principal repayment occurs earlier than anticipated and because a call premium is typically received. Second, when the bond is called, reinvestment of the call proceeds must be made at a lower rate of return than available on the original issue. On net, the second effect offsets the first, and the realized return over the horizon date is lower than if the issue had not been called.

Assume you bought a 10-year, triple-A, 10% coupon bond in 1985 at a promised *and* expected *YTM* of 10% (no default risk). You anticipate holding the bond for the full 10 years and do not expect a change in the yield curve from 10%. Since coupons are expected to be reinvested at 10%, a 10% realized return is expected. For five years you are correct, but at the start of year 6 the yield curve drops dramatically, and the issuer calls each bond at a price of $1,050. At that date the best yield available on five-year bonds of equivalent risk is 6%.

Your realized return on the initial issue for the five years it was held will be a fine 10.67%:

$$ARR = \sqrt[5]{\frac{\$1,660.51}{\$1,000}} - 1.0 = 10.67\%$$

where:

$$\frac{\text{Year 5}}{\text{Investment Value}} = \text{Call Price} + \frac{\text{Total Coupons}}{\text{Received}} + \frac{\text{Interest on}}{\text{Interest}}$$

$$\$1,660.51 \quad = \quad \$1,050 \quad + \quad \$500 \quad + \quad \$110.51$$

However, if the yield curve does not change from 6%, your realized return between years 6 and 10 will be 6%. During the full 10 years your average annual realized return will be about 8.31%:

$$\sqrt[10]{(1.1067^5)(1.06^5)} - 1.0 = 8.31\%$$

The low reinvestment rate available after the call causes your *10-year realized yield* to be less than promised. Naturally, investors do not like the call privilege and will request larger promised yields if call is likely.

Jen and Wert examined the difference between promised and actual realized *YTMs* for high-grade utility bonds between 1956 and 1964. Figure 11-5 illustrates their results. Promised *YTMs* in the primary offering are plotted on the horizontal axis. Actual realized yields were calculated following the procedure used above and are shown on the vertical axis. The dashed line is a 45° line representing equality between promised and actual realized *YTMs*. As expected, realized yields on issues with initially large *YTMs* were less than initially promised.

The fact that realized yields are often less than promised yields on callable bonds does not mean that such bonds are poor investments. As with their view of default risk, investors recognize that realized yields may be less than promised, and they adjust prices downward so that they expect to receive a fair return. To date, research on callable bonds suggests that:

1. Callable bonds sell at higher promised yields than noncallable issues.
2. Immediately callable bonds sell at higher promised yields than bonds which have a deferred call.
3. The yield spread between callable and noncallable bonds widens during periods of high interest rates.
4. The yield spread between callable and noncallable bonds increases with the bonds' maturities.

FIGURE 11-5 *Promised Versus Actual YTM on Callable Bonds*

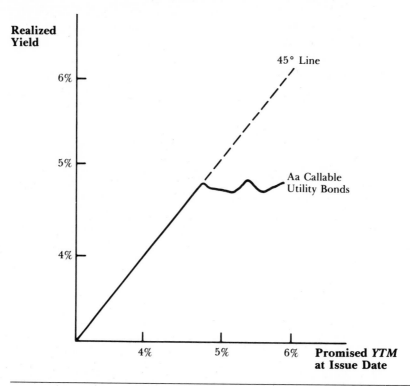

Source: F. Jen and J. Wert, "The Effect of Call Risk on Corporate Bond Yield," *The Journal of Finance* 4 (December 1967): 646.

When people buy a callable bond, they are in effect placing a bet with the issuer. The issuer will develop expectations of future interest rate decreases and be willing to pay a higher call premium as long as the future interest savings associated with a call are expected to offset the call expense. Investors, on the other hand, are betting that the call premiums are more than adequate to offset a possible call resulting in a reinvestment at a low interest rate. Who's won the game in the past? We don't know.

When buying a callable bond, investors should examine the level to which interest rates must fall before the issue would be called. For example, assume Cadiz Pedro, Inc., sells a 20-year, 9% coupon bond at par. The issue is first callable at the end of five years at a price of $1,100. If Cadiz does call the bond at the end of year 5, it will incur a cash outflow of $1,100 per bond and save $90 per year for 15 years plus $1,000 15 years hence (in year 20). The internal rate of return on this call would be 7.84%:

$$\frac{\$90}{1.0784} + \frac{\$90}{1.0784^2} + \cdots + \frac{\$90}{1.0784^{15}} + \frac{\$1,000}{1.0784^{15}} = \$1,100$$

If interest rates are expected to be 7.84% or lower by the end of year 5, the issue might well be called.[10]

One way to control against call risk would be to purchase low-coupon, deep-discount bonds. Even though interest rates may decline, prices of these issues are unlikely to rise to their stated call prices. However, before-tax yields on deep-discount bonds are often lower than equivalent-risk, high-coupon bonds. This is caused by the different ways in which returns on low- and high-coupon bonds are taxed.

Tax Impacts on Yields

Coupon income on corporate bonds is taxed at the investor's ordinary tax rate. Long-term capital gains and losses are often taxed at lower capital gains rates. To understand the effects which differences in ordinary and long-term capital gains rates can have on before-tax bond yields, consider the following scenario. Investors are attempting to value two bonds of identical risk. Bond L matures in five years and pays a $30 yearly coupon. Bond H matures in five years and pays a $100 yearly coupon.[11] Given the risks of the bond, investors wish to receive an after-tax return of 5% on each. Their average ordinary and capital gains tax rates are 50% and 25%, respectively.

To price each bond, future *after-tax* cash flows should be discounted at the demanded after-tax return of 5%. Prices of bonds L and H would be:

$$P_L = \sum_{t=1}^{5} \frac{30(1 - 0.5)}{1.05^t} + \frac{1,000 - (1,000 - P_L)(0.25)}{1.05^5}$$

$$= \$811.53$$

$$P_H = \sum_{t=1}^{5} \frac{100(1 - 0.5)}{1.05^t} + \frac{1,000 - (1,000 - P_H)(0.25)}{1.05^5}$$

$$= \$1,000$$

The price of L would, of course, be lower since its coupons are lower.

Given these prices, what is the before-tax yield to maturity on each? Using before-tax cash flows, we would find the before-tax YTM on L to be 7.68% and on H to be 10%.[12] The low-coupon issue will sell at a lower before-tax YTM since its *effective* tax rate is lower.

---

[10] Actually, yields will have to be somewhat below 7.84%, since calling the issue entails additional costs for the issuer (underwriter fees, accounting costs, etc.).

[11] We will neglect the obvious differences in each bond's duration in order to keep the example as simple as possible.

[12]
$$\$811.53 = \sum_{t=1}^{5} \frac{30}{1.0768^t} + \frac{1,000}{1.0768^5}$$

$$\$1,000 = \sum_{t=1}^{5} \frac{100}{1.1^t} + \frac{1,000}{1.1^5}$$

To determine whether a person should be in low- or high-coupon bonds which are otherwise identical, the *after-tax* return on each should be calculated. For example, using the data above, individuals with marginal tax rates higher than 50% would prefer the low-coupon bond, and individuals with lower tax rates (or even zero rates, such as endowment funds and charities) would select the higher-coupon issue.

When this text was last revised, the ordinary and capital gains tax rates were identical. However, historically the capital gains rate has been lower than the ordinary rate.

SUMMARY

This chapter has developed a number of fundamental bond price and return relationships. Conceptually, the value of a bond is equal to the present value of all future coupons and principal payments discounted at forward rates appropriate to the period during which the cash payment is received. In practice, however, a single discount rate known as the promised yield to maturity is used to discount all cash flows. It is important to recognize that this yield to maturity is a promised yield. Annual realized yields may be different if (1) interest rates change, (2) the bond defaults on a portion of its promised coupon or principal value, or (3) the bond is called prior to scheduled maturity.

Uncertainty about annual realized returns, *ARR*, which is caused by possible changes in the level of interest rates, can be largely eliminated by immunizing bond investments. Immunization consists of selecting bonds with a duration equal to the investor's planned horizon date. By properly immunizing the bond portfolio, gains (or losses) caused by reinvestment of coupon receipts at higher (or lower) future rates of interest are offset by losses (or gains) caused by changes in the bond's market value.

Default risk and call risk can be reduced by selecting instruments with little chance of default or call, as well as by diversifying over a variety of different bonds. But default and call risk cannot be eliminated. The level of default risk is estimated by professional rating agencies such as Standard & Poor's and Moody's, who assign default quality rankings to the more actively traded issues. Historically, default rates have been closely related to the quality ratings these firms assign. Call risk can be judged by estimating the level to which interest rates must fall before the issuer would find it profitable to call the issue.

REVIEW PROBLEM

You are considering the purchase of the following bond:

Maturity	Coupon	Par
3 years	11% (annual)	$1,000

a. If you require a *YTM* of 13% on bonds of equivalent risk and maturity, what do you believe is a fair market price?

b. If the bond is selling for a price of $975.98, what is its *promised YTM*?

c. You actually expect the bond to provide a final payment of $1,050 in year 3 instead of the promised $1,110 (par plus coupon). Using the bond's market price of $975.98, what is your expected annual return? If the return on three-year risk-free securities is equal to 10.0%, why might this bond sell at a higher expected return?

d. Why is the expected return different from the yield to maturity calculated in part b?

e. What is the duration of this bond? (Neglect its default risk and use a *YTM* of 12%.)

f. Investor A has a horizon date of 4.0 years. Neglecting default and call, why is the bond risky to investor A?

g. Investor B has a horizon date of 2.0 years. Neglecting default and call risk, why is this bond risky to investor B?

Solution

a.
$$\frac{\$110}{1.13} + \frac{\$110}{1.13^2} + \frac{\$1,110}{1.13^3} = \$952.78$$

b. By calculator or by trial and error, *YTM* is found to be 12.0%:

$$\frac{\$110}{1.12} + \frac{\$110}{1.12^2} + \frac{\$1,110}{1.12^3} = \$975.98$$

c. Again by calculator or by trial and error, the *expected* return is 10.16%:

$$\frac{\$110}{1.1016} + \frac{\$110}{1.1016^2} + \frac{\$1,050}{1.1016^3} = \$975.98$$

If the default risk on this bond is systematic (nondiversifiable), a risk premium above the risk-free rate of 10% will be required.

d. The yield to maturity is the return which is expected only if all promised payments are indeed expected. If this is not the case, *YTM* will be an upwardly biased measure of the true expected return.

e. We will solve this by considering the bond to be a portfolio of three zero-coupon bonds:

Bond	Duration	Value	X_i	Weighted Duration
1	1 year	$ 98.21*	10.06%	0.1006 = (1 × 0.1006)
2	2 year	87.69†	8.99	0.1796 = (2 × 0.0899)
3	3 year	790.08‡	80.95	2.4285 = (3 × 0.8095)
		$975.98	100.00%	2.7087 years

*$110 ÷ 1.12 = $98.21
†$110 ÷ 1.12² = $87.69
‡$1,110 ÷ 1.12³ = $790.08

f. Investor A faces net reinvestment risk since the average date at which cash is to be received (2.7 years) is sooner than the date when cash is needed (4.0 years). The portfolio will have to be reinvested at unknown future interest rates.

g. Investor B faces a price risk since cash is needed in 2.0 years but the portfolio matures (on average) in 2.7 years. To obtain this cash, the portfolio will have to be sold at unknown future prices.

QUESTIONS AND PROBLEMS

1. Data Corporation has three bonds outstanding which are each rated AA by Standard & Poor's:
   - An 8% annual coupon issue due in 5 years
   - A 5% annual coupon issue due in 20 years
   - An 8% annual coupon issue due in 20 years

   At present, yields to maturity are 10% on 5-year AA issues and 8% on 20-year issues.
   a. Find the price of each bond.
   b. You expect that the Federal Reserve will begin to tighten credit and force yields up by 50 basis points (across all maturities) in the very near future. Price the bonds as if the YTM increase were to occur immediately.
   c. Rank the bonds in order of sensitivity to the interest rate change and explain the economic reason for this ranking.

2. The Thomas Company's bonds have three years remaining to maturity. A 7% coupon is paid annually on $1,000 par value. What is the promised YTM if the bonds are selling at $880? At $1,083?

3. Suppose FMC sold a bond issue with a 10-year maturity ($1,000 par value) which paid a 10% coupon rate semiannually.
   a. Two years after the bonds are issued, promised YTMs on such bonds are 8%. At what price would the bonds sell?
   b. If two years after the bonds are issued, promised YTMs are 12%, at what price would the bonds sell?
   c. In each case above, what is the *effective* promised YTM given that coupons are paid semiannually?

4. The current yield curve for A-quality bonds is flat at a promised YTM of 10%. You buy a 10-year, 9% annual coupon issue. Immediately the yield curve falls to 8% and remains there until you sell at the end of three years. Assuming all coupon receipts are reinvested, what is your ARR? Why is it not equal to the 10% promised YTM? What type of risk was most important in this situation?

5. The yield curve for A-quality bonds is flat at a promised yield to maturity of 10%. You decide to buy a sequence of three one-year bonds (selecting bonds selling at par—that is, with coupon rates equal to the then-existing promised YTM). Immediately after you buy the first one-year bond, the yield curve falls to 8% and remains there. By the end of year 3, what is your ARR? Why is it not equal to 10%? What type of risk was most important in this situation?

6. Consider the following four bonds:

Bond	Annual Coupon	Maturity	YTM
1	4%	4 years	8%
2	6	4	8
3	6	5	8
4	0	3¾	8

a. Calculate D (duration) for each.

b. Explain (economically—not mathematically) why some of the values differ.

7. Assume that you have fully immunized your bond portfolio by setting the investment duration, D, equal to your planned horizon date (HD). For example, $D = HD = 4$ years. If interest rates don't change in the future, will you plan to sell the bonds at the planned horizon date or at the scheduled maturity date? Why?

8. What happens to the value of D if YTMs rise? If they fall? Assuming your HD is fixed in time and you wish to be fully immunized, will you have to rebalance the bonds held in your portfolio (sell some and buy others) in order to remain immunized against further interest rate changes?

9. Under what conditions might promised YTMs be different from ARRs actually earned?

10. (CFA Exam Question)

In *Inside the Yield Book*, Homer and Leibowitz state, "For most long-term bonds, the 'interest-on-interest' is a surprisingly important part of the total compound return to the bondholder: typically over half." The following three available corporate bonds are being considered for purchase:

- An 8% noncallable 20-year bond priced at 100
- A 5% noncallable 20-year bond with 17 years remaining to maturity, priced at 72⅜
- A 9½% noncallable 20-year bond with 19 years remaining to maturity, priced at 114½

All three issues have a YTM of approximately 8%. Assume that the bond selected will be held to maturity and that interest is to be reinvested in a growing tax-free pension account.

a. Which security would be most attractive if it is presumed that interest rates will decline steadily for the next two decades to a level of approximately 4%? Explain and justify.

b. Which security would be most attractive if interest rates were to increase steadily for the next two decades to a level of approximately 10%? Explain and justify.

c. As the fiduciary of a college endowment fund that must distribute all income (tax-free), which security would you select? Explain and justify.

11. (CFA Exam Question)

The trustees of the Farnsworth Pension Fund, which is expected to have a long-term positive net cash flow, are considering the purchase of one of two noncallable bonds. As indicated below, these bonds are identical in every aspect except coupon (and resulting price).

	Bond A	Bond B
Par	$1,000.00	$1,000.00
Coupon	10.00%	5.00%
Market price	100	68⅞
Length to maturity	10 years	10 years
Yield to maturity	10.00%	10.00%
Current yield	10.00%	7.26%
Present value of $1,000 in 10 years	$ 377.00	$ 377.00
Present value of 20 semiannual coupons	$ 623.00	$ 311.00
Present value of bond	$1,000.00	$ 688.00

a. Discuss the two bonds in terms of the certainty of achieving a specific realized compound yield.

b. Discuss how your answer to part a would be affected if you expect interest rates to rise.

c. Discuss how your answer to part a would be affected if you expect interest rates to fall.

12. (CFA Exam Question)

Three bond portfolios display the following schedules:

Maturities	A	B	C
Under 1 year	5%	30%	7%
Over 1 and under 3 years	0	30	9
Over 3 and under 5 years	0	30	9
Over 5 and under 10 years	0	10	15
Over 10 and under 15 years	30	0	15
Over 15 and under 20 years	30	0	15
Over 20 and under 25 years	30	0	15
Over 25 years	5	0	15
Total	100%	100%	100%

What outlook for changes in the level of interest is indicated by each portfolio?

13. (CFA Exam Question)

Which would be more attractive to an investor in a 55% ordinary tax bracket (25% capital gains)? Assume that each instrument has equivalent features regarding maturity, credit soundness, call protection, etc. Assume a 10-year maturity.

a. A taxable bond selling at 100 with an 8% coupon

b. A tax-free bond selling at 100 with a 6% coupon

c. A taxable bond selling at 80 with a 7% coupon

14. (CFA Exam Question)

The Ancient Brotherhood of Railroad Firemen has a pension fund with a book value of $100 million. Additions to the portfolio are currently being made from annual net cash inflow. The fund has been managed for many years by a committee of the brotherhood. None of the committee members has had any formal training or experience in either security analysis or portfolio management. They have relied largely on security salespeople for advice.

The committee now recognizes that the members of the Ancient Brotherhood of Railroad Firemen are in a profession that will die with them. In five years the majority of the brotherhood will have retired, and most will have died within twenty-five years. In view of these circumstances, the committee feels that the portfolio is not as well structured as it should be and has approached you to seek your help as a professional investment counselor.

The percentage structure of the portfolio at market value is now:

15%	recently issued long-term premium bonds with 10-year call protection
10%	medium-term bonds
15%	tax-free municipal bonds
15%	growth stocks
15%	cyclical stocks — principally companies mining or producing natural resources considered to be in scarce supply
15%	preferred stocks
5%	short-term notes
10%	residential real estate mortgage loans — average maturity of 15 years
100%	

Comment on the suitability of this portfolio given the circumstances of the brotherhood. Suggest portfolio changes you think are appropriate.

15. National Products, Inc., has just issued a 10-year bond at par which pays an annual coupon of 12%. The issue is first callable at $1,120 per bond any time after the first four years of the bond's life. In answering the following questions, assume that neither you nor NPI will incur any transaction costs in future bond transactions.
    a. If NPI does call the bond at the *start* of year 5, what is the internal rate of return earned by the firm?
    b. If you expect that *YTMs* on six-year bonds will be 8% at the *start* of year 5, do you expect NPI to call the issue?
    c. Assume that the yield curve is flat and remains constant at 12% during years 1, 2, 3, and 4. At the start of year 5, however, the yield curve drops to 8%. NPI calls the bond issue and you use the proceeds to reinvest in a new six-year bond at par. Subsequently, yields remain at 8%. What is your 10-year *ARR*?

16. Consider a bond which has a low coupon compared with currently issued obligations.
    a. Compared to currently issued bonds having the same maturity and default risk, which would have the shorter duration? Why?
    b. Which would sell at lower before-tax promised *YTMs*? Why?
    c. Which would have the lower probability of call? Why?

17. You are thinking about buying an 8% coupon issue which matures in 5¼ years. Interest is paid semiannually, and investors require a 12% *YTM*. What price will you pay to purchase the issue?

18. (CFA Exam Question)
    In June 1982, when the yield to maturity (*YTM*) on long-term bonds was about 14%, many observers were projecting an eventual decline in rates. It was not unusual to hear customers urge their portfolio managers to lock in these high rates by buying some new issues with the high coupons. You recognize that it is not really possible to lock in such returns for coupon bonds because of the potential reinvestment rate problem if rates decline. Assuming the following expectations for a five-year bond bought at par, *compute* the total realized compound yield (without taxes) for the bond below.

    Coupon: 14% (Assume annual interest payments at end of each year.)
    Maturity: 5 years
    One-year reinvestment rates during:

    Years 2, 3 = 10%
    Years 4, 5 = 8%

19. (CFA Exam Question)
    As the portfolio manager for a large pension fund, you are offered the following bonds:

	Coupon	Maturity	Price	Call Price	Yield to Maturity
Edgar Corporation (new issue)	14.00%	2002	$101¾	$114	13.75%
Edgar Corporation (new issue)	6.00	2002	48⅛	103	13.60
Edgar Corporation (1972 issue)	6.00	2002	48⅞	103	13.40

    Assuming that you expect a decline in interest rates over the next three years, *identify* and *justify* which of these bonds you would select.

20. (CFA Exam Question)
    a. Assume a $10,000 par value zero-coupon bond with a term-to-maturity at issue of 10 years and a market yield of 8%.
    (1) *Determine* the duration of the bond.

      (2) *Calculate* the initial issue price of the bond at a market yield of 8%, assuming semi-annual compounding.

      (3) Twelve months after issue, this bond is selling to yield 12%. *Calculate* its then-current market price. *Calculate* your pretax rate of return, assuming you owned this bond during the 12-month period.

  b. Assume a 10% coupon bond with a duration (*D*) of eight years, semiannual payments, and a market rate of 8%.

      (1) *Determine* the duration of the bond.

      (2) *Calculate* the percentage change in price for the bond, assuming market rates decline by 2 percentage points (200 basis points).

CHAPTER

12 Bond Trading

This chapter is a direct continuation of the previous one. Chapter 11 surveyed various bond concepts which must be understood in order to develop reasoned speculative and investment programs. In this chapter we use the concepts to suggest various types of speculative and investment trading strategies. The chapter is divided into four major sections. Because of its important role in developing strategies, the concept of duration is discussed first. The next section examines basic bond investment policies and the important role of immunization. The third section presents some typical speculative transactions, and the fourth section combines investment and speculative strategies into what is known as contingent immunization.

DURATION

Duration has important uses for both the speculator and the investor. Speculators can use a bond's duration to quickly estimate the percentage change in a bond's price for a given change in interest rates, thus bypassing the more complex and time-consuming process of finding a bond's present value at various interest rates. Investors can also use duration to minimize the extent to which they are exposed to interest rate risk. When bonds have a duration equal to the desired horizon date, the reinvestment rate and price risks associated with changing interest rates offset each other. A rise in interest rates would cause losses due to bond price declines. However, if duration equals the expected selling date, the now larger reinvestment income would exactly offset these price losses. Alternatively, interest rate declines would cause lower reinvestment income as well as higher offsetting prices.

Calculation

Duration is the weighted average date at which cash is to be received. There are a number of ways in which this weighted average might be calculated. The formula for D given in Chapter 11, originally developed by Macauley, uses as weights the present value of each year's cash flow as a percentage of the bond's price. The present value of each year's cash flow is calculated using the bond's promised *YTM*; that is:

$$D = \sum_{t=1}^{M} t \, \frac{PV_t}{\sum_{t=1}^{M} PV_t} \qquad\qquad (12.1)$$

where t = a given year number, M = the number of years to maturity, and PV_t = the present value of cash received in year t found by using the bond's promised YTM. For example, the duration of a three-year, 10% coupon bond selling for a promised YTM of 12% would be 2.73 years:

Year	Cash Flow	Present Value	Percentage of Total	Year Number	Product
1	$ 100	$ 89.29	9.38%	1	0.0938
2	100	79.72	8.37	2	0.1674
3	1,100	782.96	82.25	3	2.4675
		$951.97	100.00%		
				$D =$	2.7287 years

By using a single YTM discount rate to find D, we are implicitly assuming certain things about the shape and potential change in the yield curve. In particular, we assume that the yield curve is flat and that if the yield curve changes, it moves up or down a constant number of basis points over all maturities. The measure of D does not allow for rising or falling yield curves or different yield changes in the short versus long ends of the curve. Clearly, this is unrealistic. As a result, various other duration measures have been developed. Two such duration measures are discussed in Appendix 12A. However, for most practical problems D closely approximates the other estimates. Throughout the rest of this chapter we will rely upon D as our measure of bond duration.

Use of Duration

Portfolio Duration. If a certain amount of money will be needed at a known future date, interest rate risk can be *virtually* eliminated by selecting bonds with an equivalent duration. If a husband and wife are saving to have cash available in 10 years to help their children with college expenses, bonds having an average duration of 10 years would reduce their risk exposure.

Normally, a single horizon date will not exist. Pension funds, life insurance companies, college endowments, retired people, etc., will all have to sell securities to have cash available at a series of future dates. However, the concept of duration applies to *both* assets and liabilities. One need only calculate the duration of cash needs (liabilities) and select bond investments with similar durations to minimize interest rate risks. For example, if the liabilities of a pension fund have an average duration of 18 years, bond investments with a duration of 18 years would minimize reinvestment and price risks. The economic logic behind this policy is not difficult to understand. Say you need $1,000 at the end of years 3, 4, and 5. One policy to eliminate interest rate risk would be to buy three different zero-coupon bonds which mature at the end of years 3, 4, and 5. No coupons would be received, so you would not be exposed to reinvestment risks. Each bond will pay $1,000 at maturity, so you are exposed to no price risk. Duration simply translates a coupon bond into an equivalent zero-coupon bond.

Duration is *additive*, which means that the duration of a portfolio of bonds is the weighted average of each individual bond's duration. Symbolically:

Duration of a Bond Portfolio

$$D_p = \sum_{i=1}^{N} X_i D_i \qquad (12.2)$$

where D_p refers to the portfolio's duration, X_i is the percentage of funds placed in bond i, D_i is the duration of bond i, and there are N bonds held. For example, assume that an equal investment is made in five bonds with the following durations:

Bond	Duration	Percentage of Total	Duration Times Percentage
1	4 years	20%	0.8 years
2	7	20	1.4
3	10	20	2.0
4	15	20	3.0
5	20	20	4.0
		100%	11.2 years = Duration of portfolio

The duration of this portfolio would be 11.2 years.

As a practical matter it is probably wise to diversify broadly over a large number of bonds to achieve some average portfolio duration. As we will see later, doing so allows one to diversify away unsystematic default and call risks. In addition, this diversification overcomes some of the errors in D associated with the assumptions of a flat yield curve and parallel shifts in the yield curve.

Bond Price Changes. While not exact, the following relationship exists between percentage bond price changes, duration, and changes in a bond's *YTM*:

$$\frac{\% \text{ Change in}}{\text{Bond Prices}} \approx -D \left[\frac{\% \text{ Change in}}{(1 + YTM)} \right] \qquad (12.3)$$

For example, assume that the *YTM* on a bond is expected to decline from 11% to 10% in the near future. If the bond has a four-year duration, the expected price increase is (about) 3.6%:

$$-4 \left(\frac{1.10 - 1.11}{1.11} \right) = 3.6\%$$

Speculators needn't examine maturity and coupon effects separately, since both are included in the duration measure. If interest rates are expected to fall across all maturities, buy bonds with a long duration. If yields are expected to change by different amounts in each duration range, buy bonds with a duration which will provide the largest return per Equation 12.3.

Since duration is able to capture the sensitivity of bond price changes to changes in interest rates, duration should be closely related to bond betas. In fact, a number of researchers have developed this tie mathematically. Assuming that all investors have the same single-period time horizon (say, one month or one year), we define the following terms:

D_{it} = duration of bond i at date t

D_{mt} = duration of the "aggregate market portfolio" at date t

r_{im} = correlation coefficient between the change in the YTM of bond i and the change in the expected return on the aggregate market portfolio

σ_i = standard deviation of the changes in the YTM of bond i

σ_m = standard deviation of the changes in the expected return on the aggregate market portfolio

B_{it} = beta on bond i at date t

Then we have:

Bond Beta
$$B_{it} = \left(\frac{D_{it}}{D_{mt}}\right)\left(\frac{\sigma_i}{\sigma_m}\right)(r_{im}) \qquad \textbf{(12.4)}$$

For example, assume that $\sigma_i = 3\%$, $\sigma_m = 5\%$, $r_{im} = 0.5$, the duration of the market portfolio is ten years, and the duration of a bond is five years. Then this bond's beta would be 0.15:

$$\left(\frac{5 \text{ years}}{10 \text{ years}}\right)\left(\frac{3\%}{5\%}\right)(0.5) = 0.15$$

The bond beta relationship of Equation 12.4 points out a number of things which have been observed by researchers attempting to estimate bond betas. These include the following:

1. Bonds with short-term maturities have low betas. This is expected from Equation 12.4 since short-maturity bonds have short durations.
2. Bonds with high coupons have lower betas than lower-coupon issues. Again Equation 12.4 suggests this, since bonds with high coupons have (effectively) shorter cash flow lives — duration.
3. Bond betas change over time — they are unique to a given date t. As time passes, the number of periods to maturity declines and thus duration and beta decline.

Rebalancing. Any time the level of interest rates changes, a bond's duration will change. For example, earlier we calculated that the duration of a three-year, 10% coupon bond selling at a YTM of 12% would be 2.73 years. If interest rates suddenly fell to 8%, the bond's new D value would be 2.74 years. Although the change in D in this example appears small, much larger differences would be obtained if a bond with a longer maturity had been used. The important point, however, is that duration is inversely related to the level of interest rates. If YTMs rise, D falls. If YTMs fall, D increases.

An investor with a 2.73-year horizon date could immunize against interest rate risks by holding the 10% coupon, three-year issue when rates are 12%. If rates do fall to

8%, the gain in the value of the bond's price (expected 2.73 years hence) will exactly offset the lower returns available from coupon reinvestments. The investor would be immunized against this first shock to interest rate levels. However, once this shock has occurred, the duration of all bonds held will change. The portfolio will have to be *rebalanced*.

Conceptually, every time interest rates increase, the duration of a bond portfolio is shortened. To remain immunized, the portfolio should be rebalanced by purchasing bonds with a longer duration than the portfolio would then have. For example, if the investor's *HD* is 5.0 years, bonds with an initial weighted average duration of 5.0 years would be held. If interest rates were to rise suddenly, the investor would gain enough from higher-coupon reinvestment returns to exactly offset the decrease in bond prices expected at the horizon date. However, after the rate increase there would be a mismatch between the *HD* and the *now* shorter-term *D* value. In order to remain immunized, the investor would have to decrease percentage holdings of shorter-duration securities and increase holdings of longer-duration bonds.

Exactly the opposite situation would occur if interest rates fell. In that case the investor would be immunized against a *single* shock to rates by having price gains offset coupon reinvestment losses. However, unless the portfolio is rebalanced after the change, *D* would be longer than *HD*, and the investor would be exposed to interest rate risk. To remain immunized, the investor should increase holdings of shorter-duration instruments and reduce holdings of long-duration instruments. Of course, it is impractical to continually rebalance the bond portfolio for every change in interest rates; the transaction costs would be phenomenal. In practice, many portfolio managers rebalance yearly. While this doesn't eliminate interest rate risk, it does keep transaction costs to a reasonable level.

BOND INVESTMENT POLICIES

By our definition of investment versus speculation, investors accept security prices as fair—that is, priced so that the expected return is commensurate with the risk. Investors rely upon active trading by speculators to seek out and trade in mispriced securities in order to ensure that gross distortions among security prices will not exist. While some speculative profits might exist, they are small and not worth the cost to the investor of finding them.

Passive Management

The ideal investment policy is often referred to as "passive," but this doesn't mean the investor sits on the sidelines. In fact, investors must pay close attention to the status of their bond portfolios to ensure that they continue to meet their personal objectives. For example, an investor who wishes to hold only high-grade, four-year-duration bonds must periodically keep track of each security's default rating and duration. If market conditions change sufficiently to cause the portfolio's default risk to increase or its duration to differ from four years, the investor should rebalance. The term *passive* is used simply to distinguish investment policies from the more "active" trading associated with speculators. Investors do not passively accept changing market conditions if these changes result in portfolio holdings which are inconsistent with their portfolio objectives.

As noted in Chapter 1, investors should first clearly state the objectives which the bond portfolio is expected to fulfill. Only after an explicit listing of precise objectives can the appropriate bond holdings be determined and monitored over time. The following seven factors are important to any investment program.

Default Risk. An acceptable level of default risk should be specified (usually in terms of an agency rating) and purchases limited to these quality grades or better. Since default risks on individual bonds are likely to change, a diversified portfolio of bonds of given quality should be held. Simply holding a few bonds rated, say, single-A exposes the investor to more default risk than necessary.

Interest Rate Risk. Bond portfolios with a weighted average duration about equal to the investor's expected horizon date will limit reinvestment and price risks caused by potential shifts in the yield curve. In line with the diversification concept, different durations might be held which will average out to the desired duration, as opposed to buying only bonds of a specified duration. The duration of bonds in passive investment portfolios should not be shortened or lengthened in response to *possible* increases or decreases in interest rates. However, the portfolio should be periodically rebalanced in order to remain immunized once *actual* rates have changed.

Call Risk. The possibility of call should be examined. If noncallable bonds or callable bonds with a deferred call date beyond one's horizon date are available, they are strong candidates for purchase. In addition, low-coupon issues whose prices aren't likely to rise enough to be subject to call are also viable candidates. Callable bonds will provide higher promised *YTM*s than noncallable bonds and maybe equivalent realized yields, but the presence of a call feature makes the duration of a bond uncertain.

Marketability. The marketability of the bonds should be suited to the investor's possible needs for immediate cash. Given the large number of actively traded and highly marketable bonds, there is really no need for most individuals to seek the slightly higher yields on less-marketable instruments. On the other hand, institutional portfolios with long-term investment horizons and well-defined cash needs can more easily afford to own less-marketable issues.

Taxes. Investors should select instruments which will increase after-tax yields. For individuals and institutions in low tax brackets this might mean high-coupon bonds. For high-tax-bracket portfolios, low-coupon and municipal securities are likely to provide larger after-tax returns. U.S. government issues are exempt from most city and state income taxes. In addition, year-end tax swaps can be used. Tax swaps are discussed later in the chapter.

Current Yield. Some portfolios have a particular need for large current yields. For example, many endowment funds are limited to spending current yield (coupon and dividend income) and may not reduce principal in order to meet expenses. If given a choice between two bonds yielding a promised 8% to maturity which are identical in all respects except for coupon, the high-coupon issue might be preferred.

Selection of Specialized Instruments. Occasionally, investors can find particular types of bonds which exactly fit their objectives but also provide an extra advantage. One example is what is referred to as a *cushion bond*. A cushion bond is one which pays a coupon much larger than prevailing market rates of interest and thus sells at a premium. However, the size of the premium is limited somewhat by the bond's call price. For example, a seven-year, 12% coupon issue would normally sell for $1,208.27 when market interest rates are 8%. If the bond is callable at $1,100, this call price would tend to curb any price increases above $1,100 so that the bond might sell for, say, only $1,175. At this price the bond's promised *YTM* would be 8.57% — higher than the 8% yields on equivalent default-risk bonds. Of course, the risk of a cushion bond is its possible call. If the investor buys at $1,175 and the issuer immediately calls it at $1,100, a 6.4% *loss* would be incurred ($75 ÷ $1,175). Other examples of bonds which could provide a plus include *index bonds*, which have coupon payments indexed to the rate of inflation, and *flower bonds*, which are Treasury issues that may be bought at a discount from par but credited against federal estate taxes at par.

Expected Investment Returns

What level of investment returns should be expected from bond investment policies? This is a difficult question to answer. For example, do we mean nominal returns before taxes, real returns before taxes, or real returns after taxes? At this point we will restrict our discussion to expected nominal returns before taxes. In this case expected long-run bond investment returns are determined by four factors: (1) the level of the yield curve when the investment is made and changes in the level over time, (2) the duration of the bond portfolio relative to the planned horizon date, (3) whether the yield curve is best explained by UET, LPT, or MST, and (4) the default or call risk inherent in the bond investments.

To see the effects of these four factors, we will first consider expected returns when an investor owns a fully immunized portfolio of bonds and the yield curve is assumed to be explained by the unbiased expectations theory. We will assume that the yield curve prevailing when the investment is made is as shown in Figure 12-1. The investor is assumed to have a four-year horizon date. For ease of calculation all bonds are default- and call-free and are pure discount bonds. Later we will lift the default- and call-free assumptions.

FIGURE 12-1 *Illustration of Expected Returns*

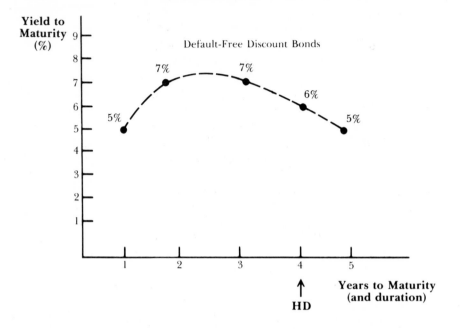

The annual realized return (ARR) earned during the four-year horizon period is the geometric average of the returns earned during years 1, 2, 3, and 4. Because we have assumed that our investor is fully immunized, the return earned in a given year is simply the percentage price change on an initial four-year bond during the year in which the return is being calculated. The price at the end of any year is simply the present value of the $1,000 face value at maturity discounted at the yield to maturity then prevailing for bonds of that maturity.

Consider the return during year 1 on an initial four-year discount bond. Its initial price is simply the present value of $1,000 discounted for four periods at a 6% *YTM*, or $792.09:

$$\frac{\$1,000}{1.06^4} = \$792.09$$

Its expected price at the end of year 1 is a little more difficult to figure since we need to estimate the level of the yield curve at the end of year 1. Given that we have assumed the UET holds, we can find *expected* future yield curves by calculating implied forward rates in today's yield curve as follows:[1]

---

[1] Forward rates were found as follows:

$$F_{1t} = \frac{(1 + YTM_t)^t}{(1 + YTM_{t-1})^{t-1}}$$

	At Initial Purchase			After One Year	
Maturity	YTM	Forward Rate	Expected YTM[2]		Details
1 year	5.00%	5.00%	9.04%		
2 years	7.00	9.04	8.01	$=$	$\sqrt[2]{(1.0904)(1.07)} - 1.0$
3 years	7.00	7.00	6.33	$=$	$\sqrt[3]{(1.0904)(1.07)(1.0306)} - 1.0$
4 years	6.00	3.06	5.00	$=$	$\sqrt[4]{(1.0904)(1.07)(1.0306)(1.0109)} - 1.0$
5 years	5.00	1.09	N/A		

According to UET the implied forward rates represent today's expectation of future spot rates. Thus, we can use the implied forward rates to calculate an expected future yield curve. Today's one-year implied forward rate of 9.04% for the start of year 2 is the expected one-year spot rate for one year from now. Using the one-year forward rates for years 2 and 3, we can estimate what the YTM on a two-year bond might be in exactly one year. In sum, we can estimate future yield curves using the existing yield curve. (Again, this procedure is appropriate *only* if UET is correct.)

Returning to the example, the price of the original four-year bond *after* a year has passed will be equal to the present value of $1,000 discounted for three years at the three-year YTM—$831.82:

$$\frac{\$1,000}{1.0633^3} = \$831.82$$

Therefore, its expected return during year 1 would be 5.00% [($831.82 − $792.09) ÷ $792.09]. The first year's return on the four-year bond is not expected to be its quoted YTM, but instead the same as the yield on a one-year bond. In fact, *if UET is used to describe the yield curve, the returns on bonds of any maturity are expected to have a return during year 1 equal to the yield on a one-year bond—5%. The expected return during any given year is the same for all maturities.*

We could continue with this numerical example to show expected returns on the initial four-year bond during years 2, 3, and 4. But the previous calculations should be adequate to show that the expected return during any future year is the same as the forward rate for that year. These results are displayed in Figure 12-2. The vertical axis plots the expected return, and the horizontal axis plots the value of duration minus horizon date. This value of $D - HD$ reflects the extent to which the portfolio is immunized. Negative values reflect net reinvestment rate risks, and positive values reflect net price risks.

What is the expected ARR on the purchase of a four-year bond? Simply the geometric average annual return during its four-year life:

$$\sqrt[4]{(1.05)(1.0904)(1.07)(1.0306)} - 1.0 = 6\%$$

---

[2]The expected YTMs are off slightly from the detailed calculations because of roundings in the implied forward rates.

FIGURE 12-2 *Expected Returns in Each Future Period*

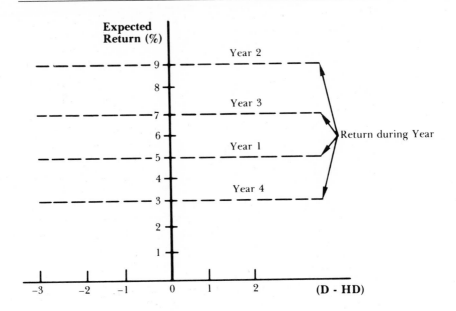

If UET is correct and default-free bonds are purchased, the *expected* return over some *HD* is simply the level of yields for bonds at that maturity as shown on the yield curve. The expected return during any one year may be different from this quoted *YTM*, but on average the *YTM* is expected to be earned. In fact, regardless of the maturity selected, the four-year expected yield is still 6% — that is, a sequence of four one-year bonds or two two-year bonds is expected to yield 6%. Such is the result of UET.

In summary, the nominal return before taxes which one can expect over a given time interval is simply the prevailing level of yields to maturity on bonds of that duration if:

1. *The unbiased expectations theory is correct.* If LPT is correct, most economists believe long-term bonds will provide an annual return, at most, 1% higher than short-term bonds provide. If MST is correct, there is no way for the investor to develop forecasts of expected returns without making explicit forecasts of future yield curves.

2. *The bonds have zero default and call risk.* If the bonds contain some default or call risk, expected returns will be somewhat less than the promised *YTM*s.

3. *The yield curve does not change or the investor is fully immunized.* Yield curves do change dramatically in very short time intervals. For example, Figure 12-3 plots yield curves for U.S. government issues for five dates during an eight-month interval. Clearly, the yield curve has been quite volatile. The only way investors

FIGURE 12-3 *U.S. Treasury Yield Curve*

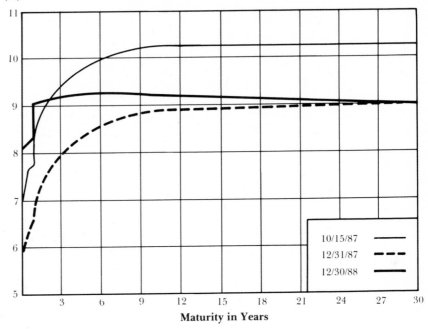

could have offset this volatility and been virtually assured the yield they expected when bonds were initially bought would be to fully immunize their holdings: set $D = HD$.

Passive Bond-Risk Management

Passive bond-risk management is based in large part on the concept of the unbiased expectations theory. UET states that the return one can *expect to earn* between the initial investment date and some future horizon date is unaffected by the duration of the securities purchased. Bonds which are equivalent in default risk and call features provide the same expected future returns regardless of their duration. However, UET does not claim that uncertainty about future returns is independent of the bonds' duration. In short, the bond portfolio which is chosen will affect risk but will not affect expected returns.

In this section we look more closely at bond-risk management. Benefits of diversification are first reviewed. Then two practical approaches to minimizing interest rate risk are discussed: immunized portfolios and dedicated portfolios.

Bond Diversification. Whenever the returns on securities are not perfectly correlated, diversification across the securities will reduce portfolio risk. To illustrate the potential advantages inherent in corporate bond diversification, McEnally and Boardman collected monthly rates of return for 515 corporate bonds rated Baa or better from December 1972 through June 1976. They then simulated the results which would have been obtained by holding portfolios with different numbers of bonds. Each portfolio's risk was measured by the variance of that portfolio's monthly return during the full time period examined. Portfolios were constrained to consist of only one quality rating (Aaa, Aa, A, or Baa), and the number of bonds allowed in each portfolio ranged from 1 to 40. Their results are displayed in Figure 12-4.

The reduction in bond portfolio risk made possible by increasing the number of bonds held is dramatic and is achieved quite rapidly. While McEnally and Board-

FIGURE 12-4 *Naive Bond Diversification*

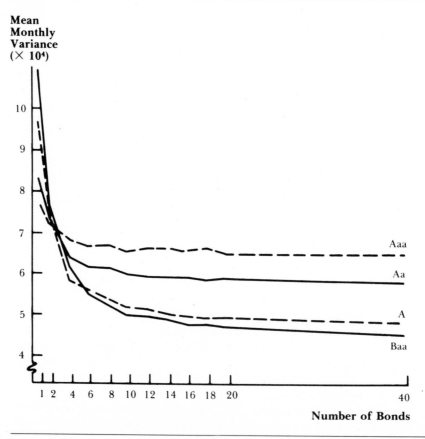

SOURCE: R. McEnally and C. Boardman, "Aspects of Corporate Bond Portfolio Diversification," *The Journal of Financial Research*, Spring 1979.

man showed that benefits associated with common stock diversification are even greater, the reduction in bond risk is still substantial. One interesting characteristic of these results is that portfolios of the lowest-quality bonds (Baa) had the least total risk when the portfolio was broadly diversified. At first this might seem counterintuitive, since quality rankings are supposed to be measures of default risk. But consider two groups of bonds. Group Aaa has virtually no default risk. As a result, returns on these bonds are a function only of changes in general market rates of interest. They are all affected by the same set of economic events, and thus their returns are highly correlated with each other. This high correlation reduces the potential benefits of diversification. The second group, group Baa, are bonds with considerable default risk. Prices of these bonds are influenced by the general level of interest rates in the same manner as group Aaa, but in addition their prices are affected by events unique to their individual companies and industries. As a result, returns on group Baa bonds are not highly correlated, and diversification can substantially reduce bond risks. In fact, we will see that speculators trading on expected changes in interest rate levels will restrict their trading to high-quality securities which move only with changes in general interest rate levels. They will not trade in lower-quality issues to pick up profits on forecasted yield curve changes since too many extraneous factors can affect the prices of low-quality bonds.

Immunized Portfolios. We have discussed the concept of bond portfolio immunization at some length in this and the previous chapter. Most of our examples, however, have related to "bullet" immunization—the immunization of a single future horizon date. At this point we will examine how immunization can be applied to a series of horizon dates and identify some of the practical problems associated with the use of immunization.

Assume that you are the administrator of a pension fund. The fund will have payment obligations of two types: (1) future benefit payments to current employees and (2) current and future benefit payments to retired employees ("retired lives"). Immunized portfolios are widely used to fund the pension's retired-life portion but are less used for active employees. This is because retired-life benefit payments can be projected more accurately and because benefits to current employees are real-dollar liabilities (tied to inflation through salary growth). Real-dollar liabilities *cannot* be immunized.

Table 12-1 gives hypothetical actuarial projections of the total benefits which will be paid to retired lives. Instead of a single horizon date to be immunized, a series of many horizon dates exists. Each could be immunized separately, of course, but it would be easier and cheaper if they could all be immunized at one time. This is really very simple to do. Instead of using the series of many horizon dates, a single weighted average horizon date is calculated in exactly the same way that a bond's duration is calculated.

For example, let's assume that interest rates are 10% for all maturities. In order to fund the $5 million due at the end of year 1, $4,545,454.54 in zero-coupon, one-year duration bonds would have to be bought ($5 million ÷ 1.10). Similarly, to fund the $5 million due at the end of year 2, $4,132,231.41 would have to be bought ($5

TABLE 12-1 *Hypothetical Pension Fund — Total Benefits Paid to Retired Lives*

End of Year	Pension Obligation	End of Year	Pension Obligation
1	$5 million	6	$3 million
2	5	7	3
3	4	8	2
4	4	9	1
5	4	10	0

million $\div 1.10^2$). Continuing with the other liabilities, a total investment of $21.47 million would be required. The duration of these liabilities is calculated below in the same fashion that the duration of a bond is calculated.

Year	Current Funding Requirement	Percentage of Total	Weighted Average Liability Duration
1	$ 4.54 million	21.15%	0.2115
2	4.13	19.24	0.3847
3	3.01	14.02	0.4206
4	2.73	12.72	0.5086
5	2.48	11.55	0.5776
6	1.69	7.87	0.4723
7	1.54	7.17	0.5021
8	0.93	4.33	0.3465
9	0.42	1.96	0.1761
10	0.00	—	—
Total	$21.47 million	100.00%	3.6000 years

The weighted average duration of these liabilities is 3.6 years. To immunize this liability series, $21.47 million must be invested in bonds which have a portfolio duration equal to 3.6 years. In theory this could be done by purchasing $21.47 million of one bond with a 3.6-year duration. However, theory doesn't allow for transaction costs associated with the periodic rebalancing necessary as interest rates change. Nor does it allow for the fact that yield curves are not flat and don't shift in a parallel fashion over time, as assumed by *D*. Thus, it is rare in practice to find a single bond purchased for immunization. Instead, a large number of bonds are purchased with varying durations. To be considered for selection, these bonds must have good marketability (to reduce transaction costs) and little default and call risk (to assure that the bonds' calculated duration is reasonably accurate).

Dedicated Portfolios. A dedicated bond investment portfolio is one which will provide coupon payments and maturing principal amounts *exactly* when required to meet liabilities (desired cash receipts). A dedicated portfolio is an immunized portfolio, but a very special type of immunization occurs. Recall from our pension example that a single bond with a 3.6-year duration would be sufficient to immunize the pension's liability stream. If one wished to purchase two bonds, one with a three-year duration and one with a four-year duration, then 40% would be invested in the three-year bond and 60% in the four-year bond. This combination also results in a portfolio duration of 3.6 years. Many other combinations resulting in a 3.6-year duration are possible, of course. A dedicated portfolio simply carries these possible combinations to the limit. In a dedicated portfolio, rebalancing is theoretically unnecessary. Scheduled coupons and maturing principal amounts exactly match the cash needs.

To determine the composition of a dedicated portfolio, one must first develop a list of suitable holdings. Naturally, bonds with significant default risk will be excluded, since they may not provide cash flows when required. However, some default risk may be acceptable in view of the greater expected returns. In addition, noncallable bonds are desirable. Unfortunately, there are few noncallable bonds with long-term durations. Call risk can be minimized by purchasing low-coupon bonds which are selling at prices so low that they are never likely to reach the bond's call price. But again, there is a trade-off. Such low-priced bonds often have high default risk (thus the low price) and are often priced for their strong tax advantages (something many organizations using dedicated portfolios really don't need). In short, when a list of viable purchase candidates is developed, there is often a trade-off between expected return and the accuracy of the cash matching.

Once a list of purchase candidates is determined, a linear programming problem is solved which minimizes total cash outflow to purchase securities subject to the cash needs being met:

$$\text{Minimize Portfolio Cost} = X_1 P_1 + X_2 P_2 + X_3 P_3 + \ldots + X_N P_N$$

Subject to:

$$CF_t \le X_1 CF_{1t} + X_2 CF_{2t} + X_3 CF_{3t} + \ldots + X_N CF_{Nt}$$

$$CF_{t+1} \le X_1 CF_{1t+1} + X_2 CF_{2t+1} + X_3 CF_{3t+1} + \ldots + X_N CF_{Nt+1}$$

$$\vdots$$

$$CF_T \le X_1 CF_{1T} + X_2 CF_{2T} + X_3 CF_{3T} + \ldots + X_N CF_{NT}$$

where: P_i = price to purchase bond i

CF_t = cash flow required at date t

CF_{it} = cash flow provided at date t by bond i

X_i = number of bond i's purchased

Periodically (often once a year) this linear programming model is rerun in the hopes of finding a new set of bonds which will match cash with the desired horizon dates but cost less than the current market value of the bonds held. If such a set is available, the current portfolio is sold and the revised portfolio purchased. Any excess funds are returned to the portfolio owners to deal with as they please.

Dedicated portfolios have a number of advantages over more classic immunization techniques. First, they are easier to understand. Exact cash matching as a means of immunization against interest rate risk is a much easier concept to follow than the reinvestment and price risk offsets associated with normal immunization. Second, a rebalancing is not necessary every time interest rates change, as is necessary with normal immunization. In addition, if a good cash match is in fact possible, a more accurate forecast of future returns is possible. One need not worry about D's assumption of a flat yield curve with parallel shifts over time. Finally, the procedure can result in a larger number of bonds being held and thus a greater amount of diversification than might be obtained by standard immunization.

Dedicated portfolios do have their costs, however. Most of these relate to reduced flexibility. In particular, many bond managers desire to trade bonds in an attempt to pick up abnormal profits through quality swaps and other speculative trades discussed in the next section. In a dedicated portfolio, the bond manager faces more constraints on available trading opportunities.

Effects of Calls

In early 1986, investors became increasingly convinced that rapid inflation had been licked for some years into the future. Federal Reserve monetary policies had been steadily reducing inflation over the prior four years and, in early 1986, oil prices fell dramatically as world demand for oil declined and OPEC unraveled. The result was a dramatic decrease in interest rates across all maturities. By mid-1986, 30-day Treasury bills were selling at a *YTM* of less than 6.0% and 30-year Treasury bonds were selling at a *YTM* of 7.2%. Just six months earlier these yields had been 8.5% and 11.5%, respectively. The resulting increases in bond prices were equally dramatic. Many long-term bonds experienced returns during the year prior to March 31, 1986, of 45% or more. But not all was rosy—particularly for people who owned callable bonds.

Many people bought long-term bonds in the early 1980s with the belief that they would be getting high coupon earnings for many years to come. Unfortunately, they had given too little attention to their bonds' call provisions. As interest rates plummeted, large numbers of call announcements appeared in the financial press. One advisory firm estimated that there were more than 330 calls by taxable corporations during 1986. And potential municipal bond calls were impossible to estimate, owing to the large number of bond issues outstanding (about 53,000 different issues in 1986).

As a result, most of the price increases in bonds came in the U.S. Treasury market, because Treasury bonds are not callable until five years before maturity. Investment portfolios with large holdings of Treasuries increased substantially in value. But portfolios of corporate and municipal bonds had their returns limited by the call provisions on these bonds.

Besides affecting the returns on actively managed bond portfolios, these calls were an embarrassment to many professionals who had supposedly created fully immunized bond portfolios. When bonds held in such portfolios were called, all aspects of immunization were lost. It was foolhardy to try to immunize using callable bonds.

BOND SPECULATION

Overview

A wide variety of market participants speculate in bonds. At one extreme are individuals and institutions that prefer to follow a basic investment policy over the long run but are willing to enter into occasional short-term speculations. For example, the manager of a commercial bank's secondary reserve position keeps investments short-term in order to hedge (immunize) against possible short-term liquidity demands. But if the manager firmly believes long-term rates are going to fall in the near future, he or she might lengthen the portfolio's duration to take full advantage of the expected capital gains caused by the lower rates. At the other extreme are a host of speculators and arbitrageurs who specialize in one narrow area of bond trading. For example, there are speculators who trade in nothing but T-bills, in bankers' acceptances, in commercial paper, in financial futures, etc. Usually such narrow speculation occurs in short-term money market instruments. In between these two extremes are managers of fixed-income portfolios designed to fulfill certain specified investment objectives (default risk, tax characteristics, duration, etc.). These managers will actively take part in a host of speculative techniques in order to improve portfolio returns while still meeting their portfolios' stated objectives over the long run. In this section we will review the types of transactions which such middle-ground, mixed investment-speculative managers might undertake.

While speculation in fixed-income securities has always existed, the extent of its use increased during the late 1970s and early 1980s. Before then, bond yields and prices had been reasonably stable, and the bond market was considered a place for conservative investors to earn reasonably guaranteed returns. However, during the 1970s interest rates and bond prices were quite volatile, and the bond market began to attract individuals who hoped to earn substantial profits by accurately forecasting future price levels. In addition, the increased availability of computers allowed speculators to model expected profit opportunities from alternative future yield curve scenarios. Added to this, improvements in communications networks provided current price quotes so that speculators could take immediate advantage of any temporary price imbalances.

There are numerous ways to speculate in bonds. We will present only one general way of doing so. But regardless of the techniques used, there are certain keys to successful bond speculation. These include the following:

1. *Fast access to new information.* Speculators must have early access to economic and political news so that they can trade before bond prices change in reaction to the new information.

2. *Liquidity.* Because speculators must be able to trade quickly on new information without affecting market prices, they prefer to trade in bonds with large active markets.

3. *Interest rate sensitivity*. Most bond speculation revolves around forecasts of future interest rates. For this reason, speculators prefer to trade largely in instruments whose prices are influenced by changes in the general level of interest rates, as opposed to those for which default and call risks are important. Most speculation is done in high-quality corporate and municipal bonds or U.S. government issues.

One way to order the process of bond speculation is shown in Figure 12-5. Initially, a set of investment objectives are specified which are used to determine the ideal bond investment portfolio. We will use Leibowitz's term for this ideal investment portfolio and refer to it as the *baseline portfolio*. The baseline portfolio will be fully immunized, having a portfolio duration equal to the planned horizon date. In addition, the baseline portfolio should consist of bonds having appropriate default risk, call protection, tax characteristics, marketability, and other features necessary to fulfill the portfolio's stated objectives. After the baseline portfolio has been determined (but not yet bought), the manager of the portfolio will forecast future levels of the yield curve and alter the portfolio's duration in hopes of improving upon the next period's return. If interest rates are expected to rise, duration will be shortened in order to reduce expected price losses and improve reinvestment income. If interest rates are expected to fall, duration will be lengthened in order to reduce expected losses from lower reinvestment income and improve expected price gains. The portfolio is not fully immunized and thus is subject to interest rate risk. But the manager might judge the risks well worth taking for the extra returns expected. After the portfolio's duration is set, the manager will examine individual bonds and purchase those offering the greatest yields but still meeting the portfolio's long-run objectives. (Later in the chapter we will discuss how this is done when bond swaps are examined.) Finally, the manager will constantly monitor the portfolio's performance, new economic and political news, and prices of bonds which might be substituted (swapped) for those now held.

We will now consider two important steps in analyzing future yield curves and potential bond swaps.

Trading on Yield Curve Shifts

Theoretically, if a fully immunized bond portfolio is maintained, the *ARR* between the time at which the portfolio is acquired and the *HD* at which the portfolio is sold should be equal to the portfolio's promised *YTM* when initially bought.[3] For example, panel A in Figure 12-6 plots as the solid line a hypothetical yield curve for pure discount bonds which have no call or default risks. If the horizon date is 10 years and a portfolio of bonds with a 10-year duration is initially bought, then the expected *ARR* over the next 10 years is 10%. However, as we just saw, the expected returns

---

[3]In practice, of course, this statement neglects the impossibility of complete immunization and the existence of default and call risks.

FIGURE 12-5 *The Process of Bond Speculation*

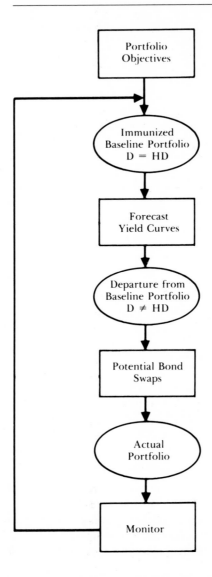

during any *single* year are expected to be different from this geometric average *ARR*.[4] For example, during year 1 the expected return would be 8% *if* the yield curve shifts through time as the unbiased expectations theory suggests it should. This first-year expected return is plotted as the solid line in panel B. The one-year return is shown

---

[4]Expected single-period returns will be the same as the expected *ARR* only if the yield curve is flat. Why?

FIGURE 12-6 *Yields on Discount Bonds with No Default or Call Risk*

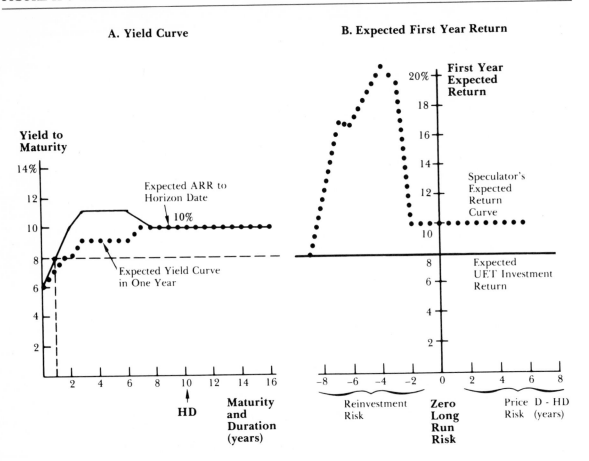

A. Yield Curve

B. Expected First Year Return

on the vertical axis, and the difference between the duration of the portfolio selected and the horizon date is shown on the horizontal axis. When duration is equal to the horizon date ($D - HD = 0$), the portfolio is fully immunized against interest rate risks. When duration is less than the *HD*, the portfolio is exposed to net interest rate reinvestment risk. When duration is greater than the *HD*, the portfolio is exposed to net interest rate price risk.

Assuming the *HD* is 10 years, the baseline portfolio should have a duration of 10 years. However, the speculator will forecast future levels of the yield curve and temporarily change the portfolio's duration in an attempt to pick up yearly returns greater than expected from the immunized baseline portfolio. For example, if the dotted curve in panel A of Figure 12-6 reflects the speculator's estimate of the yield curve level in exactly one year, this would result in the one-year rates of return as shown in panel B by the dotted curve. Details of the revised one-year expected returns are shown in Table 12-2.

In Table 12-2 three sets of columnar data are shown. The first set of columns rep-

TABLE 12-2 *Calculation of Revised Expected Returns*

Initial Period			After One Year			One-Year Return	
						Original	
Maturity	Yield	Price	Maturity	Yield	Price	Maturity	Return*
1 year	8%	$925.93	1 year	7%	$934.58	1 year	8.0%
2	10	826.45	2	8	857.33	2	13.1
3	11	731.19	3	9	772.18	3	17.3
4	11	658.87	4	9	708.42	4	17.2
5	11	593.45	5	9	649.93	5	19.4
6	11	534.64	6	9	596.27	6	21.6
7	10.5	497.12	7	10	513.16	7	19.9
8	10	466.51	8	10	466.51	8	10.0
9	10	424.09	9	10	424.09	9	10.0
10	10	385.54	10	10	385.54	10	10.0
11	10	350.49	11	10	350.49	11	10.0
12	10	318.63	12	10	318.63	12	10.0
13	10	289.66	13	10	289.66	13	10.0
14	10	263.33	14	10	263.33	14	10.0
15	10	239.39	15	10	239.39	15	10.0
16	10	217.63	16	10	217.63	16	10.0

*Return $= \dfrac{P_t - P_{t-1}}{P_{t-1}}$

resents yields and pure discount bond prices for the initial yield curve shown as the solid line in panel A of Figure 12-6. The second set of columns represents the speculator's forecast of what the yield curve and pure discount bond prices will be one year hence. The third set of columns shows the one-year rates of return which the speculator expects will be earned by initially purchasing bonds of any particular maturity. For example, assume that a six-year bond is initially bought at a *YTM* of 11% and a price of $534.64. After one full year has passed, the bond will have a five-year maturity. Because the speculator believes five-year instruments will offer *YTM*s of 9% and sell at $649.93, the one-year return on this bond will be 21.6%:

$$\frac{\$649.93 - \$534.64}{\$534.64} = 21.6\%$$

From the speculator's perspective, expected one-year returns are shown by the dotted curve in panel B of Figure 12-6. If the baseline portfolio is held, the speculator expects a 10% one-year return. However, by shortening the portfolio's duration, the speculator can expect a return as high as 21%. Of course, when the portfolio's duration is set below (or above) that of the baseline portfolio, interest rate risk is incurred. The portfolio manager must decide whether the added expected return is worth the risk.

The speculator might forecast an infinite number of yield curve patterns and resulting single-period returns. While an attempt might be made to match the baseline portfolio over time, temporary departures will be made in hopes of improving the sequence of single-period returns. If the speculator is successful, the horizon date *ARR* will be higher.

To further examine this single-period yield curve analysis, consider Figure 12-7. Three yield curve forecasts are assumed to have been made. In the optimistic scenario the yield curve drops substantially, causing positive returns on all bond maturities except those of the longest duration. In the pessimistic scenario the yield curve rises and results in losses on all but the shortest-duration bonds. Finally, the expected yield curve shift will result in large single-period returns on intermediate-term bonds but lower returns on short- and long-duration bonds. If the manager moves into bonds with a duration somewhat less than a fully immunized position, say, point *A*, the expected (and optimistic) single-period returns are much better than expected from holding bonds with $D = HD$. And even if the pessimistic scenario occurs, losses are small. In addition, bonds at point *A* could be combined with bonds at point *B* to obtain a weighted-average duration shown by the dashed line. In fact, point *Z* is a combination of *A* and *B* which will fully immunize the portfolio and result in higher expected single-period returns than available from owning bonds which individually have a duration equal to the horizon date.

FIGURE 12-7 *Single-Period Return Forecasts*

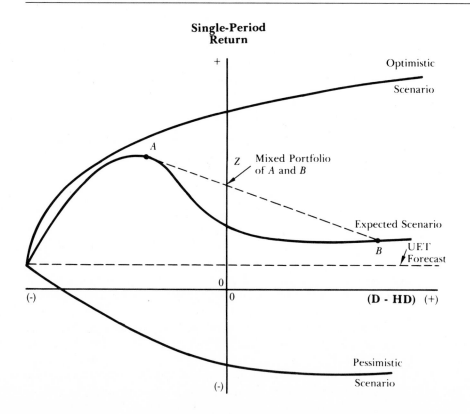

Bond Swaps

Once a weighted portfolio duration has been determined, the speculator can begin to select particular bonds. Although our discussion has been worded to imply that this is the first time the bond portfolio has been set up, in practice speculators make modifications to existing portfolios. For this reason, the techniques used to decide which bonds to purchase or sell are known as *bond swaps*. We will review a few of these bond swaps using the data shown in Table 12-3. The table shows two types of bonds—bonds now owned and potential replacements. Bonds which are now owned are designated by a single letter (*Q, R, S,* etc.), and potential replacements are designated by double letters (*QQ, RR, SS,* etc.).

Rate Anticipation Swap. If a speculator believes interest rates will soon fall (and that this has not yet been fully recognized in current prices), bonds should be bought in hopes of capital gains. To maximize price appreciation, *long-term, low-coupon issues* should be acquired. Stated differently, bonds with short durations should be replaced by equivalent-risk, long-duration bonds. For example, consider bond *Q*, which is now owned, and bond *QQ*, which might be used to replace it. If promised *YTM*s on both bonds are expected to fall reasonably soon from 12% to 10%, the approximate percentage price increase in each would be:

Bond	Actual Percentage Price Increase	$\approx$	$-D\left[\dfrac{Percentage}{Increase\ in\ (1\ +\ YTM)}\right]$
Q	12.29	$\approx$	$-6.33(-0.0179) = 11.33$
QQ	17.04	$\approx$	$-8.48(-0.0179) = 15.18$

Now consider bonds *R* and *RR*. Bond *R* has a longer maturity but a higher coupon than *RR*. What should be done in this case if rates are expected to decline? Select *RR*, since its lower coupon offsets its shorter maturity, resulting in a longer duration than *R* has. If one expects rates to rise but is forced to hold some bond investments, holding bonds with short durations will minimize expected price losses.

Yield Pickup Swap. Occasionally two identical bonds will sell at temporarily different prices and *YTM*s. For example, bonds *S* and *SS* are identical in all respects except that *S* is now selling at $1,000 to yield 10.0% to maturity, while *SS* is selling at $996.83 to yield 10.1% to maturity. A yield pickup swap could involve selling *S* and buying *SS*. Price imbalances like this could be due to temporary abnormal buying or selling in one of the issues. In addition, new issues often sell at price discounts from equivalent seasoned issues. Care should be taken, however, that the two securities are indeed perfect substitutes. Minor yield differences could be due to slight default-risk differentials, differences in call features, or differences in marketability.

Quality Swaps. If the economy is currently at a peak of business expansion and headed into a recession, one might well expect both a decline in all interest rates and a widening in yield spreads between bonds of differing default risk. The trading strat-

TABLE 12-3 *Bond Swap Data*

Bonds	Default Rating	Years to Maturity	Annual Coupon	Years to Duration*	Current Price	Promised YTM
Now Owned						
Q	AA	10	12%	6.33	$1,000.00	12.0%
R	AA	15	12	7.63	1,000.00	12.0
S	AA	4	10	3.49	1,000.00	10.0
T	BBB	10	13	6.13	1,000.00	13.0
U	BBB	10	13	6.13	1,000.00	13.0
V	AA	10	5	7.57	646.65	11.0
W	AA	5	6	4.41	848.35	10.0
Potential Replacement						
QQ	AA	15	7%	8.48	$ 659.46	12.0%
RR	AA	13	5	8.61	550.35	12.0
SS	AA	4	10	3.49	996.83	10.1
TT	AA	10	14.25	6.13	1,127.07	12.0
UU	AAA	10	11	6.54	1,000.00	11.0
VV	AA	14.67	12	7.57	1,000.00	12.0
WW	AA	5	6	4.41	848.35	10.0

*Calculated as D_1.

egy in this case would be to buy *long-duration, high-quality bonds*, since yields on these issues would decline the most. Yields on lower-quality issues would also fall in sympathy with all rates. But increased default-risk spreads would partially offset such declines. For example, bonds *T* and *TT* have similar long durations, but *TT* is of better quality. If rates are expected to decline and yield spreads to widen, bond *TT* would be preferable.

Quality swaps are possible even if one doesn't expect overall rates to move dramatically. For example, bonds *U* and *UU* have a 2% yield spread which reflects default-quality differences between the two. If the trader believes this spread will widen, bond *U* should be short sold and *UU* bought. Although the speculator might not know which of the two bond prices will adjust, being short in *U* and long in *UU* will cover any possible outcome. In fact, if the short and long positions are based upon each bond's duration, there should be only minimal risk in the transaction. Many bond traders evaluate the appropriateness of current yield spreads by examining trends in historic averages.

Tax Swaps. A variety of tax swaps exist; we will discuss two. The first of these involves trading based upon coupon rates. Consider bonds *V* and *VV*, which are identical except for coupons. (Their maturities differ, but they have equal durations.) Notice that the *YTM* of *V* is lower than that of the equivalent-duration, higher-coupon issue, *VV*. This simply reflects the fact that effective tax rates on low-coupon bonds are lower than on higher-coupon issues; thus their before-tax yields may be lower. Assume, for simplicity, that you are in a 50% tax bracket. Should you swap

VV for *V*? The answer, of course, depends upon the after-tax *YTM* on each. In fact, the after-tax yield is 6.85% on *V* and 6.00% on *VV*. Clearly, *V* should be held.[5]

A second type of tax swap involves selling a bond now owned at a taxable loss to obtain an immediate tax advantage and reinvesting *both* the sale proceeds and the tax savings. Assume you had originally bought bond *W* at $1,000. Since its current price is $848.35, you could sell it with a *realized* tax loss of $151.65. If your capital gains rate is 30%, taking this loss will allow you to reduce taxes by $45.50 (0.30 × $151.65). You could immediately reinvest the sale proceeds of $848.35 in bond *WW* and be in the same situation except that you *now* have $45.50 in tax savings which can also be reinvested. Of course, you will pay $45.50 in capital gains when bond *WW* matures, but in the meantime, you have had free use of $45.50 to invest for larger total returns. To be allowed this form of tax swap, bonds *W* and *WW* must be legally different issues. For example, bond *V* couldn't be sold to realize a taxable loss and then immediately repurchased. The IRS considers a sale and repurchase of the same security to be a "wash sale" and will disallow the taxable loss.

COMBINED ACTIVE-PASSIVE STRATEGIES

It would be rare to find a fixed-income-portfolio manager who is unable to offer evidence that he or she can beat a passive immunized strategy. If the managers are allowed the freedom to pick the time period and the data for comparison, they will surely find something to place their ability in a good light.

How well active management actually works is questionable. For example, consider Figure 12-8. Each bar represents the compound annual rate of return over the five-year period ending in the year shown. For each year, three bars are shown. The leftmost bar represents returns on an immunized five-year portfolio held in government securities, the middle bar represents the average results of bank fixed-income managers as published by Frank Russell Company, and the rightmost bar represents the return on the Salomon Brothers High Grade Index. Based on a five-year horizon date, it is clear that immunization procedures would have fared better on the whole than either the average bank manager or the Salomon Brothers index. This is not a truly fair test, in that the investor's horizon might have been different from five years and

---

[5]The after-tax *YTM*s are found by calculating the discount rate which will discount all *after-tax* cash flows to the initial bond price. For bond *V*:

$$\$646 = \sum_{t=1}^{10} \frac{\$50(1 - 0.5)}{1.0685^t} + \frac{\$1,000 - (\$1,000 - \$646)(0.25)}{1.0685^{10}}$$

For bond *VV*:

$$\$1,000 = \sum_{t=1}^{14.67} \frac{\$120(1 - 0.5)}{1.06^t} + \frac{\$1,000 - (\$1,000 - \$1,000)(0.25)}{1.06^{10}}$$

This assumes a 25% capital gains tax in the maturity year.

FIGURE 12-8 *Historical Returns for Ten Five-Year Periods Ending in December, 1973–82*

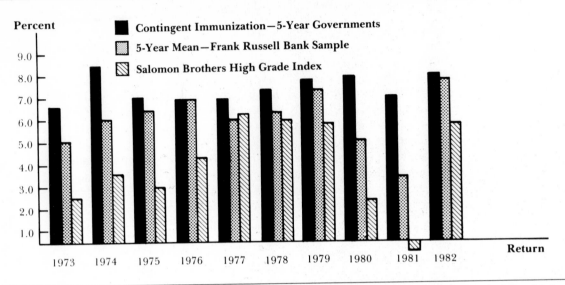

SOURCE: K. Meyer, "Managing Bond Portfolios with Combination Active/Passive Strategies," in *Techniques for Managing Bond Portfolios*, ed. D. Tuttle (Charlottesville, Va.: Institute of Chartered Financial Analysts, 1983), p. 83.

the holdings of the banks and the Salomon index did not have a five-year duration. But it does raise a serious question about the value of active bond management.

Passive immunization strategies seem to have grown out of two events of the 1970s: (1) increased bond risk exposure caused by the unprecedented volatility of interest rates and (2) a concern that active bond management really doesn't work. In response to these concerns, immunization strategies were developed and marketed by all major bond managers. Immunization techniques had the advantage of virtually eliminating interest rate risk and providing (what appeared to be) high expected returns. But once in place, these immunization strategies had the disadvantage (to their marketers) of eliminating the need for active management. The use of immunization considerably narrowed the product line of bond managers and, thus, endangered many jobs.

It should come as no surprise, then, that a new, "improved" version of immunization was presented, a version which limits the risk exposure associated with active bond management but still allows a role for active management. This is commonly referred to as *contingent immunization.*

Contingent Immunization

Contingent immunization is really a very simple notion. The owner of a bond portfolio and the manager agree to a *minimum return* which will be earned or exceeded over some future time period (commonly five years). The manager is then free to actively speculate with the portfolio until enough of its value has been lost that the only way to guarantee the minimum return is immediate immunization. Contingent immunization provides downside risk protection on the bond portfolio's return.

As an example, assume that contingent immunization is to be used to manage $10 million starting on January 1, 1990. At that date, the portfolio's owner and the manager agree to two basic objectives:

1. The minimum compound annual return will be 9.55%.
2. This 9.55% will be calculated over the next five years.

Note that the return in any one year could be much less than 9.55% because the agreement calls for an *average* compound return of 9.55% over the next five years. Both parties realize that the minimum portfolio value after five years will be $15.78 million ($10 million $\times$ 1.0955^5).

Also assume that on January 1, 1990, the annual return available on default- and call-free government bonds with a five-year duration is 11.3%. The difference between the 11.3% which could be earned if the $10 million were to be fully immunized and the 9.55% guarantee is a margin of safety given to the portfolio manager to induce active trading. The portfolio owner is willing to accept the 175-basis-point difference in the hope that the manager's active management will result in a compound return greater than the 11.3% return of a passive immunized strategy.

The portfolio manager could conceptually approach active trading in one of two ways. In the first case, he or she could take a portion of the $10 million and immunize it so that it will be worth the guaranteed $15.78 million in five years. In total, $9.24 million would be necessary:

$$\frac{\$10,000,000(1.0955^5)}{1.113^5} = \$9,238,173$$

The remaining $761,827 could then be actively managed and, perhaps, even totally lost. It is unlikely that this procedure would be used, but it does point out again the margin of safety given to the manager.

Alternatively, the manager could begin to actively trade the portfolio. At the end of each day, the new fully immunized return which is then available would be calculated and compared with the portfolio's value at that time. If the portfolio's value compounded at that return is greater than the guaranteed $15.78 million promised for December 31, 1994, the manager continues to have a margin of safety. For example, assume that one year later the return available from immunizing four-year-duration government bonds has risen to 12%. If the portfolio has a value in excess of $10.03 million, a margin of safety still exists:

$$\frac{\$10,000,000(1.0955^5)}{1.12^4} = \$10,027,437$$

If the portfolio has a value equal to $10.03 million, it must be immediately immunized. (If its value is less than $10.03 million, it is time to fire the manager and the firm's computer programmers.)

Contingent immunization is a risk-reduction technique. It places bounds on the risks accepted in an active bond-management program. Given the volatility of interest rates in the 1970s and 1980s and the risks associated with an unencumbered active management strategy, it is a valuable risk-reduction tool. However, there is no magic underlying its procedures. There is no reason to expect contingent immunization to result in greater returns than those available from a truly immunized strategy unless bond managers are, indeed, able to predict future bond prices. And, if they are able to do so, why limit their abilities to generating excess returns? Contingent immunization is a strategy which lies between passive bond selection and unencumbered active bond management.

SUMMARY

This chapter has illustrated how the fundamental concepts of bond pricing and returns as discussed in Chapter 11 can be applied to bond investment management and speculation. Crucial to both styles of trading is the concept of duration and the matching of duration with a planned horizon date to minimize interest rate risk exposure. While immunization will not completely eliminate interest rate risk, it can reduce it substantially.

Investment portfolios in bonds should (1) contain only bonds of an appropriate default risk, (2) be immunized against interest rate risk, (3) be reasonably well protected against unforeseen calls, (4) have good marketability, and (5) include instruments which will increase after-tax yields. Bond diversification can reduce the variability of single-period rates of return, particularly in lower-default quality grades.

Bond speculation can be profitable if the speculator is able to consistently predict future bond prices. Bond speculation can be thought of as taking place at two levels. At the first level, yield curves forecast for some future date are used to calculate potential single-period returns on bonds of different durations. These are then evaluated to see whether the returns expected by departing from a fully immunized portfolio are worth the risks incurred. At the second level, individual bonds are examined to see whether a bond swap would be profitable. Swaps examined in this chapter included (1) rate anticipation swaps, (2) yield pickup swaps, (3) quality swaps, and (4) tax swaps.

Historical evidence and logic suggest that active bond management will not, on average, result in larger returns than are available from passive immunization strategies. A market in which there are so many traders with equal access to information should set prices fairly, as efficient market theory suggests.

Contingent immunization is a recent approach to integrating a passive immunization strategy with a more active strategy. It sets limits on the amount of downside risk associated with an actively managed bond portfolio. Whether contingent immunization provides greater value than a fully immunized portfolio depends on whether active bond management works.

REVIEW PROBLEM

The yield curve on U.S. Treasury obligations is shown below:

Maturity	YTM	Maturity	YTM
1 year	10%	5 year	11%
2 year	10	6 year	10
3 year	11	7 year	10
4 year	12	8 year	10

a. Under what conditions would the maturity of various Treasury bonds be identical to their duration?

b. Assume that each is a zero-coupon bond. Forecast next year's yield curve based on UET.

c. You are the financial vice-president for a casualty insurance firm and have estimated that the firm will have to pay $7 million in damage claims in exactly one year and $10 million in exactly two years. How could you immunize these liabilities today?

d. If you do immunize as in part c, will you earn 10% with certainty?

e. If you were to place some of your money in one-year and three-year bonds *today*, what percentage should each represent in order to be immunized? And for one-year and two-year bonds?

   Your economic staff has forecast the following yield curve for one year hence (other years are not needed):

Maturity in One Year	YTM
1	12%
2	5%

f. According to UET, which strategy will provide the greater expected return during the next year?

   • Immunize over one-year and two-year bonds

   • Immunize over one-year and three-year bonds

g. According to your economic staff, which strategy provides the greatest expected returns during the next year?

   • Immunize over one-year and two-year bonds

   • Immunize over one-year and three-year bonds

Solution

a. Maturity and duration would be identical if each security pays no cash prior to its maturity date, that is, if all are zero-coupon bonds.

b. One year from now each *YTM* will be what it is today less the contribution of today's one-year spot rate. *YTM*s for one year hence are:

Maturity in One Year	YTM
1	$(1.10^2 \div 1.1) - 1.0 \quad = 10.00\%$
2	$(1.11^3 \div 1.1)^{1/2} - 1.0 = 11.50$
3	$(1.12^4 \div 1.1)^{1/3} - 1.0 = 12.67$
4	$(1.11^5 \div 1.1)^{1/4} - 1.0 = 11.25$
5	$(1.10^6 \div 1.1)^{1/5} - 1.0 = 10.00$
6	$(1.10^7 \div 1.1)^{1/6} - 1.0 = 10.00$
7	$(1.10^8 \div 1.1)^{1/7} - 1.0 = 10.00$

c.

End of Year	Liability	Present Value at 10%	Percent of Total	Weighted Duration
1	$ 7.00 million	$ 6,363,636	43.50%	0.4350
2	10.00	8,264,463	56.50	1.1300
		$14,628,099	100.00%	1.5650

An investment of $14.63 million will have to be made in a bond portfolio having a duration of 1.565 years. This could be a single bond, multiple bonds, or even a perfect cash-matched dedicated portfolio.

d. Not necessarily. For any immunization other than a cash-matched dedicated portfolio, three things must be true: (1) you must be able to rebalance at zero transaction costs every time interest rates change, (2) the yield curve must be flat, and (3) all shifts in the yield curve must be parallel. In reality only the flat yield curve is present in this example. Such problems will not be present for a cash-matched dedicated portfolio.

e. From part c, D must be 1.565 years. Let X_i be the percentage to invest in bonds with duration (maturity in this question) equal to i.

For X_1 and X_3:

$$1.565 = X_1(1.0) + (1 - X_1)(3.0)$$

$$X_1 = 71.75\% \text{ and } X_3 = 28.25\%$$

For X_1 and X_2:

$$1.565 = X_1(1.0) + (1 - X_1)(2.0)$$

$$X_1 = 43.5\% \text{ and } X_2 = 56.5\%$$

f. According to UET, expected returns are the same for any maturity strategy. Only risk is affected by differing duration strategies. However, both alternatives in part e have identical durations. Thus, UET would imply that both strategies have the same expected return and the same risk. They are identical.

g. The yield curve which your staff projects is different from what UET implied in part b. Using the forecasts of your staff, the returns on each duration strategy would be:

Strategy $X_1 = 43.5\%$ and $X_2 = 56.54\%$

Return in the next year on a current two-year bond:

$$P_0 = \$1,000 \div 1.10^2 = \$826.45$$

$$E(P_1) = \$1,000 \div 1.12 = \$892.86$$

$$E(R) = \frac{892.86}{826.45} - 1.0 = 8.04\%$$

$$E(R_P) = 0.435\,(10\%) + 0.5654\,(8.04\%)$$

$$= 8.89\%$$

Strategy $X_1 = 71.75\%$ and $X_3 = 28.25\%$

Return in the next year on a current three-year bond:

$$P_0 = \$1,000 \div 1.11^3 = \$731.19$$

$$E(P_1) = \$1,000 \div 1.05^2 = \$907.03$$

$$E(R) = \frac{907.03}{731.19} - 1.0 = 24.05\%$$

$$E(R_P) = 0.7175\,(10\%) + 0.2825\,(24.05\%)$$

$$= 13.97\%$$

The strategy of immunizing over the one-year and three-year bonds provides the greatest expected return.

QUESTIONS AND PROBLEMS

1. Laurie Marcus is employed as a corporate bond arbitrageur for a large broker-dealer firm. On September 1, she notices two bonds which are quite similar in nature but which are selling at different promised yields to maturity. Each bond has identical call terms, default risk, and maturity. Bond A is a 10-year, 8% coupon (paid $40 each August 30 and February 30), selling at a promised *YTM* of 8%. Bond B is a 10-year, 8% coupon (also with the same semiannual dates), selling at a promised *YTM* of 7.8%.
   a. What is the market price of each bond?
   b. Which of the two bonds might she buy, and why? Might she wish to sell short one of the bonds and go long on some of the other? Why?
   c. Assume she buys one bond A and one bond B on September 1. In exactly one year she sells both bonds at par. What is her realized return on each? (Assume coupon reinvestment at 8%.)

2. You are evaluating two 15-year U.S. Treasury bonds. Treasury bond A is selling at par to yield 7½% *YTM*. Treasury bond B has a much lower coupon rate than does bond A and is selling at a *YTM* of only 6½%.
   a. Why might the lower-coupon issue be selling at the lower *YTM*?
   b. Although a 100-basis-point spread exists between the two bonds, you notice that the normal spread is 75 basis points. Given that you believe the spread will again return to 75 basis points, which bond would you buy and which would you sell? Why not simply buy (or sell) only one of the bonds?
   c. Is this arbitrage of buying one bond and selling the other riskless?

3. How does the coupon rate on a bond affect its:
   a. Price volatility?
   b. Duration?
   c. After-tax return?

4. What is the value of D for a four-year bond which pays a $40 coupon each six months? Assume YTM is a 10% stated annual rate.

5. The duration of a bond portfolio is 7.3 years and the average YTM of bonds held is 12%. Estimate the percentage increase in the portfolio's value if YTMs fall to 11%.

6. The duration measure D makes some very specific assumptions about the nature of yield curves. What are these?

7. The bond investment officer of Pacific Insurance Corp. is evaluating the firm's current portfolio holdings and finds the following:

Bond Category	Total Market Value	Duration (D)	Yields to Maturity	
			Current	Expected
A	$ 50 million	1 year	9%	10%
B	$100	3 years	9	10
C	$ 50	5 years	9	10
D	$100	7 years	9	10
E	$200	12 years	9	10

a. What is the bond portfolio's duration?

b. If the expected YTMs are estimates for one month hence, what is the approximate percentage gain or loss in the portfolio's market value during the next month?

c. If the firm has specified a horizon date of 7.4 years, should the bond manager be worried about the expected price losses and shift into the shorter-duration bonds?

d. Assume the manager elects to maintain this immunized position. If interest rates do rise to 10%, what adjustments will have to be made in the portfolio in order for it to remain immunized?

8. Itex Corp. has a 15-year, 12% coupon (annual) issue outstanding which is now selling at $1,125. The bond is callable at $1,100. Itex also has a similar default-risk bond outstanding with a 15-year maturity and 10% coupon which is selling at par.

a. Why is the 12% coupon issue a cushion bond?

b. What is the promised YTM on the issue?

c. What advantages does a cushion bond offer?

d. What are the disadvantages of a cushion bond?

9. You have gathered the following data on a variety of bonds which are candidates for various *investment* portfolios:

Bond	Moody's Quality Rating	D	Annual Coupon	YTM	Call Price	Current Price
1	Aa	3.7 years	9.00%	9.00%	$1,090	$1,000
2	Aa	3.5	13.00	9.27	1,100	1,120
3	Baa	10.0	10.00	10.50	1,150	980
4	A	10.0	10.00	9.30	1,150	1,075
5	A	15.0	5.00	9.00	1,050	770
6	Baa	7.0	11.00	10.50	1,200	1,027
7	A	7.0	3.00	7.00	1,050	700

Evaluate the appropriateness of each bond for each of the following investment portfolios:

a. A charitable organization which has yearly contribution campaigns. While the organization would like to use all contributions to fund current research as well as to help families with current difficulties, the directors are somewhat concerned about yearly volatility in total contributions to the fund. As a result, the directors would like to maintain an average investment life of four to five years.

b. A pension fund for employees in a young and growing company. Expected retirement benefits will not begin to any major degree for at least another 20 years.

c. A pension fund for employees of a large midwestern city. A large proportion of the workers will be retiring within the next five years although their benefits are likely to be paid largely between years 5 through 10.

d. A doctor in a high income tax bracket who plans to retire within the next year and live off his extensive investments.

10. (CFA Exam Question)

A pension fund sponsor has established a simplified baseline portfolio to serve as a benchmark for the fixed-income portfolio. By mutual agreement with the sponsor, the manager retains complete discretion to implement strategic changes in the composition of the actual fixed-income portfolio. For example, if she is bearish on bonds, she may hold as much of the portfolio in short maturities as she considers advantageous. The fund's baseline portfolio is shown below:

	Maturity	*Percent*
Short Term	Up to 1 year	10%
Intermediate Term	One to 10 years	40
Long Term	More than 10 years	50
Total Baseline Portfolio		100%

a. Briefly discuss the steps involved in determining the composition of a baseline portfolio.

b. If the manager retains complete discretion to alter the composition of the actual portfolio (as in this case), discuss the probable impact of the baseline portfolio on the manager's investment strategy.

c. Given this baseline portfolio, describe the procedure for measuring the manager's actual performance.

d. Suppose that at a particular point in time, the average maturity of the portfolio increases from 10 years to 11 years. At the same time, the duration of the portfolio declines.

(1) Explain how this could happen.

(2) Other things being equal, explain what an increase in average maturity but a decline in duration would suggest about the riskiness of the portfolio.

11. You are the manager of a $50 million fixed-income portfolio which is run under a strategy of contingent immunization. The plan calls for a four-year horizon and a minimum return of 10%. Currently, immunized returns available on four-year-duration bonds are 11.5%.

a. How much could you lose on the first day and still be able to provide the 10% minimum return?

b. A year goes by and the value of the portfolio is now $60 million. At that time, immunized returns on three-year-duration bonds are 11.0%. Do you need to immunize?

c. If interest rates rise, this could be favorable or unfavorable to you. Explain why.

d. At the end of four years the value of the portfolio has grown from $50 million to $87 million. Have you provided any value to the portfolio?

e. Why do people use contingent immunization instead of simply allowing fixed-income managers full discretion over the portfolio they manage?

12. (CFA Exam Question)

The ability to immunize is very desirable for bond portfolio managers in some instances.

a. Discuss the components of interest rate risk—i.e., assuming a change in interest rates over time, explain the two risks faced by the holder of a bond.

b. Define immunization and discuss why a bond manager would immunize his or her portfolio.

c. Explain why a duration-matching strategy is a superior technique to a maturity-matching strategy for the minimization of interest rate risk.

d. Explain in specific terms how you would use a zero-coupon bond to immunize a bond portfolio. Discuss why a zero-coupon bond is an ideal instrument in this regard.

e. Explain how contingent immunization, another bond-portfolio-management technique, differs from classical immunization. Discuss why a bond portfolio manager would engage in contingent immunization.

13. A friend of yours is the administrator of a college endowment fund which is designed to pay the expenses of a unique program at the college. Expenses of the program will be $1 million each year for seven years. After seven years the program will have been outmoded by new technology and will be disbanded. Interest rates on default- and call-free bonds are 12% for all maturities. Present various immunization strategies ranging from the purchase of one bond to the creation of a dedicated portfolio. Provide calculations and a discussion of the pros and cons of each approach.

14. The current yield curve on U.S. Treasury obligations is shown below. Assume all are pure discount bonds. If you wish to maintain an average portfolio duration of six years but are willing to temporarily depart from it, use this information to develop a number of possible speculations.

Maturity	YTM	Maturity	YTM
1 year	8.0%	6 years	8.5%
2	9.0	7	8.0
3	9.5	8	7.0
4	9.0	9	7.0
5	8.5	10	7.0

You have reason to believe that the yield curve by the *end of the coming year will be*:

Maturity	YTM	Maturity	YTM
1 year	7.0%	6 years	8.0%
2	8.0	7	8.0
3	8.0	8	7.0
4	8.0	9	7.0
5	8.0	10	7.0

15. You are given the following current yield curve on U.S. Treasuries. Assume for all calculations that all are pure discount bonds.

Maturity	YTM	Maturity	YTM
1 year	8.0%	6 years	8.5%
2	9.0	7	8.0
3	9.5	8	7.0
4	9.0	9	7.0
5	8.5	10	7.0

    a. What is the duration of each of these pure discount bonds?

    b. Assume your *HD* is four years and you want to buy only bonds with maturity in years 1 and 6. What percentage investment should be made in each to assure a fully immunized portfolio?

    c. Using the notion of UET, calculate next year's expected yield curve.

    d. If you bought the five-year bonds and held them to maturity, what is your expected *ARR*? (Assume you believe in UET.)

    e. If you bought the five-year bonds and sold them in exactly one year, what is your expected return? Why is this different from the *ARR* found in part d? (Again, assume UET.)

16. (CFA Exam Question)

As senior investment officer for the Street Insurance Company, you have been asked by the president to justify the increased turnover rate in the debt portfolio over the past year. You have been given the following examples of transactions which were executed by your staff. Describe the bond-portfolio-management methods illustrated by the transactions.

Month	*Rating*	*Issue*	*Price*	*Yield*
January	Sold: Aaa	Standard Oil of California 7% due 4/1/96	91¼	7.83%
	Bought:	U.S. Treasury bonds 7% due 5/15/98	92	7.72%
June	Sold:	U.S. Treasury bonds 7% due 5/15/98	97	7.26%
	Bought: Aaa	Standard Oil of California 7% due 4/1/96	94	7.57%
July	Sold: Aaa/AA	Pacific Telephone & Telegraph 7⅝% due 6/1/09	100	7.625%
	Bought: Aa/AA	Illinois Power 7⅝% due 6/1/03	99¾	7.65%
October	Sold: Aa/AA	Illinois Power 7⅝% due 6/1/03	99	7.71%
	Bought: Aaa/AA	Pacific Telephone & Telegraph 7⅝% due 6/1/09	98¾	7.73%
March	Sold: Aaa	General Electric 7½% due 3/1/96	105	7.07%
	Bought: Aaa	Short-term investments		

17. (CFA Exam Question)

You are an investment adviser who specializes in the management of bond portfolios for a broad spectrum of institutional investors. The following probabilistic matrix of expected economic and bond market conditions is being used by your firm to guide the selection of bonds for client portfolios.

Economic and Bond Market Expectations, 1982–84

Probability of Occurrence	10.0%	25.0%	40.0%	20.0%	5.0%
Average Annual Rate					
Inflation	12.0%	9.0%	7.5%	5.0%	−5.0%
Real GNP Growth	3.0%	2.0%	2.5%	3.5%	.0%
Average Annual Yield					
Money Market Instruments	20.0%	15.0%	10.0%	8.5%	5.0%
Long Bonds, New Issue, Corporate (Aa)	18.0%	14.0%	10.5%	10.0%	6.0%

Current Yield Levels

Money Market Instruments	12%
Long Bonds, New Issue, Corporate (Aa)	14%

Given the above matrix and the bond alternatives listed below, select and justify the bonds you would emphasize in the portfolio of:

a. An endowment fund that needs investment income to balance its budget
b. A pension fund for which the median age of the employees covered is 33
c. A casualty insurance company experiencing underwriting losses

Bond Investment Alternatives

Issue	Coupon	Maturity	Yield to Maturity
Treasury Bonds and Notes (noncallable)			
	8⅞ %	June 1983	12.80%
	16	Sept. 1983	13.70
	11¾	Nov. 1985	13.30
	13¾	May 1986	13.65
Industrial Bonds (callable 10 years from date of issue)			
Aa Rated	14½%	Dec. 1991	14.50%
Aa Rated	9⅞	June 2004	14.10
Aa Rated (new issue)	0	June 1992	13.90
Baa Rated	16	March 1986	16.00
Baa Rated	9⅞	August 1999	16.90
Utility Bonds (callable 5 years from date of issue)			
Aa Rated	15 %	Dec. 1991	15.00%
Aa Rated	8¾	August 2000	14.40
Aa Rated	16⅛	April 2021	16.10
Baa Rated	18¼	Oct. 1989	17.25
Baa Rated	15¼	Sept. 2010	17.70
Municipal (Tax-Exempt) Bonds (callable 15 years from date of issue)			
Aa Rated	11 %	March 1995	11.50%
Aa Rated	7⅜	July 1990	11.75
Baa Rated	13	Feb. 2002	14.00
Baa Rated	6⅝	Jan. 1984	9.75

18. Consider the following bond data:

Bond	Default Rating	Years to Maturity	Annual Coupon	D	Current Price	Promised YTM
1	Aa	10	13%	—	$1,000.00	13.0%
2	Baa	13	4	—	415.80	14.0
3	A	8	9	7.3	—	13.2
4	Aa	5	10	4.5	—	13.0
11	Baa	10	10	—	791.31	14.0
12	Baa	15	8	—	631.47	14.0
13	A	10	11	7.1	—	13.2
14	B	7	10	4.5	—	14.5

a. Is the duration of bond 11 shorter or longer than the duration of bond 12?
b. Assume you believe the yield spread between Aa and Baa bonds should be 75 basis

points (0.75%), as opposed to the 100 basis points shown between bonds 1 and 2. Develop an arbitrage strategy between the two.

c. You are considering the addition of either bond 2 or bond 12 to the portfolio of a high-tax-bracket client whose investment characteristics include a desire for moderate-to-low default risk and moderate duration. Select either 2 or 12 and justify your choice.

d. The yield curve is now flat and is expected to drop as we begin to enter a recession. Between bonds 3 and 13, which would a speculator buy?

e. The yield curve is now flat and you expect it to drop as we enter a recession. However, yields on high-default-risk bonds won't drop as dramatically as low-default-risk bonds because of an increase in risk premiums. Between bonds 4 and 14, which might you buy?

f. Consider only bond 14. If the *YTM* on this bond were to move downward to 12.0% (tomorrow morning), by about what percentage would its price be expected to rise?

19. (CFA Exam Question)
Bicentennial University was founded in 1975 to open its doors on July 4, 1976. At the time it was founded, it was endowed with a large contribution to be invested entirely in bonds. The investment guidelines of this endowment fund state the following:

> The fund may acquire only U.S. Treasury and agency bonds and corporate bonds rated Aa or higher. While the fund may not engage in arbitrage swaps or other short-term trading techniques, the investment policy may take cognizance of changing interest rate patterns both in the broad sense and in terms of various sectors of the bond market. It is suggested that some attention be given to balance among maturities to avoid overconcentration in any one part of the maturity scale.

At the time the fund was established, economists noted that the U.S. government was borrowing very heavily to finance a substantial debt, but expectations were that this deficit would begin to shrink in size over the subsequent six months. Corporations, because of the recession, had substantially lightened their borrowings after largely restoring liquidity, and this was expected to continue for at least the next six months and perhaps longer. At such time as the economy again began to build steam, economists generally expected corporate borrowing to accelerate—perhaps in a year or so. Federal Reserve policy was rather easy and accommodating in an effort to stimulate the economy and encourage recovery from the recession. At the time the Bicentennial University Bond Endowment Fund received its cash investment, interest rates were approximately as follows:

Short-term U.S. Treasuries, Certificates of Deposit, and Commercial Paper	5.5–6%
1- to 2-year Treasuries	7%
5- to 10-year Treasuries	8%
5- to 10-year Federal Agencies	8.15%
5- to 10-year Industrial and Utility Bonds (Aa)	8.15–8.40%
Long-term Treasuries (over 15 years)	8.5%
Long-term Industrials (Aa over 15 years)	9%
Long-term Utilities (Aa over 15 years)	9.5%

Outline in broad terms an investment policy for the Bicentennial University Bond Endowment Fund, keeping in mind a 12- to 18-month objective and taking account of the circumstances described above. Justify your answer.

20. (Note: This question draws upon material in Appendix 12A.) You have been asked to estimate duration measures D_1 and D_2 for a five-year U.S. Treasury note which pays $70 coupons annually. The current Treasury yield curve is shown as:

Maturity	*YTM*
1 year	8.0%
2	9.0
3	9.0
4	8.5
5	8.0

a. Calculate D_1 and D_2.
b. In this case why is D_2 the better measure of duration?
c. D_2 is not, however, a precise duration measure. Why?

21. (CFA Exam Question)
Active bond management, as contrasted with a passive buy-and-hold strategy, has gained increased acceptance as investors have attempted to maximize the total return on the bond portfolios under their management. The following bond swaps could have been made in recent years as investors attempted to increase the total returns on their portfolios. From the information presented, identify the reason(s) investors may have made each swap.

	Action		*Call*	*Price*	*YTM*
(a)	Sell:	Baa-1 Georgia Pwr. 1st Mtg. 11⅝% due 2000	108.24	75⅝	15.71%
	Buy:	Baa-1 Georgia Pwr. 1st Mtg. 7⅜% due 2001	105.20	51⅛	15.39
(b)	Sell:	Aaa Amer. Tel. & Tel. Notes 13¼% due 1991	101.50	96⅛	14.02
	Buy:	U.S. Treasury Notes 14¼% due 1991	NC	102⅕	13.83
(c)	Sell:	Aa-1 Chase Manhattan Notes Zero Coupon due 1992	NC	25¼	14.37
	Buy:	Aa-1 Chase Manhattan Notes Float Rate due 2009	103.90	90¼	–
(d)	Sell:	A-1 Texas Oil & Gas 1st Mtg. 8¼% due 1997	105.75	60	15.09
	Buy:	U.S. Treasury Bond 8¼% due 2005	NC	65.60	12.98
(e)	Sell:	A-1 K Mart Convertible Deb 6% due 1999	103.90	62¾	10.83
	Buy:	A-2 Lucky Stores S.F. Deb 11¾% due 2005	109.86	73	16.26

APPENDIX 12A: TWO ADDITIONAL DURATION MEASURES

Bond duration measure D uses a bond's promised yield to maturity as *the* single discount rate applied to all cash flows. By using this measure, however, we are implicitly making two assumptions about yield curves: (1) that the yield curve is flat, and (2) that changes in yields which occur are identical for all maturities. We will now refer to this measure of duration as D_1.

The duration measure known as D_2 removes the first assumption of a flat yield curve. Using D_2, yield curves may be rising or falling, depending upon the levels of implied forward rates. If forward rates are increasing (e.g., $F_{1,1} < F_{1,2} < F_{1,3}$, etc.), the yield curve will also be increasing. If forward rates are declining (e.g., $F_{1,1} > F_{1,2} > F_{1,3}$, etc.), the yield curve will be declining.

In many respects D_2 is similar to D_1. The present value of each year's cash flow is found and expressed as a percentage of the bond's price. These percentages are then multiplied by the year number in which a cash flow is received. The sum of these products is D_2. However, D_2 differs from D_1 in the manner in which the present value of each period's cash flow is calculated. Where D_1 uses the *single YTM* as the discount rate:

$$PV_t \text{ in } D_1 = \frac{CF_t}{(1 + YTM)^t}$$

D_2 uses the product of implied one-period forward rates up through the date of the cash flow. That is:

$$PV_t \text{ in } D_2 = \frac{CF_t}{(1 + F_{1,1})(1 + F_{1,2})\ldots(1 + F_{1,t})}$$

$$(12A.1)$$

where the $F_{1,n}$ terms represent one-year implied forward rates as of the start of period n. For example, if $F_{1,5}$ equals 10%, the one-year forward rate of interest as of the start of year 5 is 10%.

Table 12A-1 illustrates the calculation of D_1 and D_2 for a 10% coupon, four-year-maturity bond. The bond is now selling at $1,004.84, which represents a 9.85% promised YTM. Underlying this YTM are a series of implied one-year forward rates. Currently one-year money is assumed to earn 8%. The implied rates during years 2 and 3 are given as 10%, and during year 4 the implied rate is given as 12%. Using the single YTM, we find that D_1 equals 3.4881 years. Using the individual forward rates, we find that D_2 equals 3.4799.

However, D_2 still retains the second assumption inherent in D_1, namely, that yields change by the same number of basis points regardless of the security's maturity. D_2 does allow yields on three-year bonds to be 8% when yields on 10-year bonds are 10%. But if three-year yields decline by 50 basis points

TABLE 12A-1 Calculation of D₁ and D₂ 10% Coupon, Four-Year Maturity

D_1

Year t	Cash Flow t	Discount Rate t	PV_t	Percent of Total	×	Year Number	=	Product
1	$ 100	1.0985	$ 91.04	9.06%	×	1	=	0.0906
2	100	$(1.0985)^2$	82.88	8.25	×	2	=	0.1650
3	100	$(1.0985)^3$	75.45	7.51	×	3	=	0.2253
4	1,100	$(1.0985)^4$	755.47	75.18	×	4	=	3.0072
			$1,004.84*	100%				
						D_1	=	3.4881 years

D_2

Year	1-Year Forward Rate	Cash Flow t	Discount Rate t	PV_t	Percent of Total	×	Year Number	=	Product
1	0.08	$ 100	1.08	$ 92.59	9.21%	×	1	=	0.0921
2	0.10	100	(1.08)(1.1)	84.17	8.38	×	2	=	0.1676
3	0.10	100	$(1.08)(1.1^2)$	76.52	7.62	×	3	=	0.2286
4	0.12	1,100	$(1.08)(1.1^2)(1.12)$	751.56	74.79	×	4	=	2.9916
				$1,004.84*	100%				
							D_2	=	3.4799 years

*Off slightly due to rounding.

to 7.5%, then the yields on the 10-year issue must also drop by 50 basis points to 9.5%. The yield curve is required to move in parallel shifts for D_2 to be the precise measure of duration. These parallel shifts are referred to as *additive changes* in yields.

The duration measure D_3 amends this additive-change assumption in D_2 to allow for *multiplicative changes* in yields. In this case all yields are expected to change by a given percentage. For example, a 20% increase in three-year yields from 8% to 9.6% must also result in a 20% increase in 10-year yields from 10% to 12%. We will not show an example of how D_3 is calculated.

D_2 and D_3 are somewhat better approximations of how the yield curve actually changes in the real world than is D_1. However, they too are not completely ac-

curate. In fact, no one knows exactly how changes in the yield curve can be best modeled. All known duration measures are approximations. There is no way to *completely* eliminate all reinvestment and interest rate risk with coupon bonds. Fortunately, the values obtained using any of the techniques are quite close, and matching each with a planned horizon date will reduce interest rate risks substantially. Table 12A-2 provides estimates of D_1, D_2, and D_3 as prepared by Bierwag and Kaufman. Both a 5% and a 10% coupon are examined. In addition, a rising yield curve and a declining yield curve (top and bottom halves of the table) are examined. Entries in the table are calculated duration measures. For example, under a rising yield curve scenario a 5%, 15-year bond has duration measures for D_1, D_2, and D_3 of 10.23, 10.00, and 10.36

TABLE 12A-2 *Duration Estimates Using D_1, D_2, and D_3*

Term to Maturity (years)	Zero Coupon Holding Period Yield (%)	5% Coupon			10% Coupon		
		D_1	D_2	D_3	D_1	D_2	D_3
A. Upward Sloping Yield Curve							
1	6.10	0.99	0.99	0.99	0.98	0.98	0.98
2	6.20	1.93	1.93	1.93	1.87	1.87	1.87
3	6.30	2.82	2.82	2.82	2.68	2.68	2.68
4	6.40	3.67	3.66	3.67	3.43	3.43	3.45
5	6.50	4.47	4.46	4.48	4.13	4.12	4.16
6	6.60	5.22	5.22	5.25	4.77	4.76	4.81
7	6.70	5.94	5.92	5.99	5.37	5.35	5.42
8	6.80	6.61	6.59	6.66	5.93	5.90	6.00
9	6.90	7.24	7.20	7.31	6.45	6.40	6.53
10	7.00	7.83	7.78	7.92	6.93	6.86	7.03
11	7.10	8.38	8.31	8.48	7.39	7.29	7.49
12	7.20	8.90	8.79	9.01	7.81	7.69	7.92
13	7.30	9.37	9.24	9.49	8.21	8.05	8.32
14	7.40	9.82	9.64	9.95	8.58	8.38	8.69
15	7.50	10.23	10.00	10.36	8.92	8.68	9.04
16	7.60	10.60	10.32	10.73	9.25	8.95	9.35
17	7.70	10.95	10.60	11.07	9.56	9.20	9.65
18	7.80	11.26	10.85	11.37	9.84	9.42	9.91
19	7.90	11.56	11.06	11.64	10.11	9.62	10.15
20	8.00	11.82	11.24	11.87	10.36	9.80	10.37
21	8.10	12.06	11.39	12.08	10.60	9.95	10.57
22	8.20	12.28	11.52	12.25	10.82	10.10	10.75
23	8.30	12.47	11.61	12.40	11.03	10.22	10.91
24	8.40	12.65	11.68	12.52	11.23	10.33	11.06
25	8.50	12.81	11.74	12.61	11.41	10.42	11.18

TABLE 12A-2 *(continued)*

Term to Maturity (years)	Zero Coupon Holding Period Yield (%)	Duration in Years					
		5% Coupon			10% Coupon		
		D_1	D_2	D_3	D_1	D_2	D_3
B. Downward Sloping Yield Curve							
1	8.50	0.99	0.99	0.99	0.98	0.98	0.98
2	8.40	1.93	1.93	1.93	1.86	1.86	1.87
3	8.30	2.81	2.81	2.81	2.67	2.67	2.67
4	8.20	3.65	3.65	3.65	3.41	3.41	3.41
5	8.10	4.44	4.44	4.43	4.09	4.10	4.06
6	8.00	5.18	5.19	5.16	4.71	4.72	4.68
7	7.90	5.88	5.89	5.84	5.29	5.31	5.24
8	7.80	6.53	6.55	6.47	5.82	5.85	5.76
9	7.70	7.14	7.17	7.06	6.31	6.36	6.23
10	7.60	7.71	7.76	7.61	6.77	6.84	6.67
11	7.50	8.24	8.31	8.12	7.20	7.29	7.08
12	7.40	8.73	8.83	8.59	7.60	7.72	7.46
13	7.30	9.19	9.33	9.01	7.97	8.13	7.82
14	7.20	9.62	9.80	9.43	8.32	8.52	8.16
15	7.10	10.02	10.24	9.81	8.64	8.89	8.48
16	7.00	10.39	10.67	10.15	8.95	9.25	8.77
17	6.90	10.74	11.08	10.49	9.24	9.60	9.06
18	6.80	11.06	11.47	10.80	9.51	9.94	9.33
19	6.70	11.37	11.85	11.08	9.77	10.27	9.60
20	6.60	11.65	12.22	11.37	10.01	10.59	9.84
21	6.50	11.91	12.57	11.62	10.24	10.91	10.08
22	6.40	12.15	12.92	11.86	10.46	11.22	10.31
23	6.30	12.38	13.26	12.08	10.66	11.53	10.52
24	6.20	12.59	13.59	12.30	10.86	11.83	10.74
25	6.10	12.79	13.91	12.51	11.04	12.13	10.94

SOURCE: Reprinted from "Coping with the Risk of Interest Rate Fluctuations: A Note," *Journal of Business*, July 1977, by G. O. Bierwag and G. G. Kaufman, by permission of The University of Chicago Press. © 1977 by the University of Chicago. All rights reserved.

years, respectively. While the values differ, they are all very close. Other researchers have shown that D_1, D_2, and D_3 will vary from each other in amounts that might be worrisome mainly for high-coupon, long-life (say, 50 years) bonds.

More important than the imprecision inherent in these measures of duration are the uncertainties caused by possible call or default. Anything which would interrupt the scheduled flow of future cash payments will alter a bond's duration. This is certainly true of early retirement via a bond call or the delay of cash receipts via default on scheduled coupon payments. Again, a bond's actual duration is not known with complete accuracy. But, as noted before, using duration as a measure is a reasonable way to minimize interest rate risks.

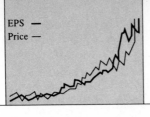

CHAPTER

13 Stock Fundamentals

Common stocks differ from bonds in two fundamental respects: risk and maturity. Bondholders receive a claim to a promised stream of cash flows up to some fixed maturity date, whereas common stockholders receive a claim to an infinite sequence of unknown residual earnings (earnings of the firm after all bond claims are satisfied). In principle, both instruments can be evaluated on the same basis, that is, on how well they fit the duration, tax, risk, marketability, and other objectives of the total portfolio. In practice, however, the increased risk and maturity characteristics of stocks cause a variety of problems which require close analysis but which are relatively unimportant to bonds. For example, valuation models, analyses of equity risk premiums, and analyses of earnings growth are crucial to stock selection but of lesser importance to bond selection. Conversely, a large number of concepts which are crucial to bond selection are relatively unimportant to stock selection. For example, duration, yield curve shifts, and detailed arbitrage techniques are fundamental to bond trading but are of lesser importance to stock trading. Although a common set of principles applies to both bonds and stocks, their risk and maturity differences require that we stress the principles differently.

When bond selection was discussed in Chapters 11 and 12, a clear distinction was made between expected realized returns, promised yields to maturity, and actual realized returns. The same ideas apply to common stock selection, although the conventional terminology is somewhat different, and common stocks are usually evaluated over a single period (one month, one year, etc.), as opposed to over a planned horizon date.[1] Individuals will *purchase* a stock if their *required return is less than (or equal to) their expected return* on the stock. Conversely, they will *sell* a stock if their *required return exceeds* the stock's *expected return*. Once the buy or sell decision is made, a single-period *actual return* is realized which may be different from that expected or required.

---

[1] Theoretically, the single period can be thought of as the time interval between now and the horizon date. If, for example, the horizon date is two years away, two years would be used as the single period. In practice, however, stock returns are usually evaluated over time intervals shorter than typical horizon dates.

FIGURE 13-1 *Required Versus Expected Returns*

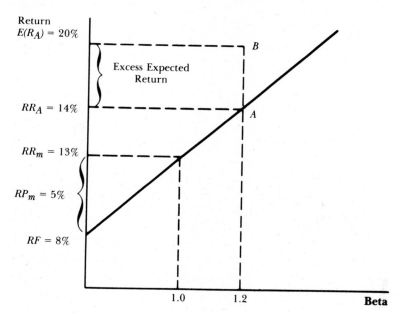

RR_A = Required return on Achilles Corp.

RR_m = Required return on aggregate market

The required rate of return should fairly compensate investors for both delaying immediate consumption and accepting the risk inherent in the security. In terms of the traditional capital asset pricing model, this can be expressed as:

**Security Market
Line (SML)**
$$RR_i = RF + \beta_i(RP_m) \tag{13.1}$$

where RR_i refers to the required single-period return on stock i, RF is the current risk-free rate of interest (compensation for delaying consumption), β_i is the amount of nondiversifiable risk in stock i relative to the aggregate market portfolio, and RP_m is the risk premium required on a stock of average risk. Assume that you have completed an analysis of Achilles Corporation and believe the stock has 20% more nondiversifiable risk than the average stock (implying a beta of 1.2). If the risk-free rate is now 8% and you believe a 5% risk premium on an average stock is fair, your required yearly return will be 14% [8% + 1.2(5%)]. This is shown in Figure 13-1 as point A.

Single-period expected returns on a stock are composed of an expected dividend yield plus an expected capital gains yield. Mathematically:

Single Period
Expected Return

$$E(R_t) = \frac{D_t}{P_{t-1}} + \frac{P_t - P_{t-1}}{P_{t-1}}$$

(13.2)

where $E(R_t)$ refers to the expected return during period t, D_t is the expected dividend to be paid at the end of period t, and P_t (or P_{t-1}) is the price of the stock at the end of period t (or $t - 1$). For example, assume that Achilles Corporation is now selling on the NYSE at $40. You expect that a year from now a $2 dividend will be paid and the stock will be selling for $46. As a result, your expected return is composed of a 5% dividend yield plus a 15% capital gain yield, a total expected return of 20%:

$$\$2/\$40 + \frac{\$46 - \$40}{\$40} = 0.2$$

This is plotted in Figure 13-1 as point B.

Any difference between expected and required returns is referred to as an expected *excess return*. Excess returns represent *pure* profit, a profit earned above that required to compensate for the stock's risk. According to the efficient market theory, excess returns will not exist. Individuals will buy or sell the stock until its price is set so that expected returns equal required returns. However, if the markets are not perfectly efficient, excess returns such as the difference between points A and B in Figure 13-1 might be possible.

Actual returns are calculated in the same manner as expected returns, except that actual dividends and prices are used instead of expected values. For example, if Achilles *actually* pays a dividend of $2.10 and sells for $43 at year-end, the actual return would be 12.75%:

$$\frac{\$2.10}{\$40} + \frac{\$43 - \$40}{\$40} = 0.1275$$

Throughout this chapter and the next we examine various aspects of common stock selection. As with the two bond chapters, this chapter concentrates on fundamental stock concepts; the next chapter focuses more directly upon stock trading. Two broad topics are discussed in this chapter: (1) stock valuation and (2) stock returns. Because of the pivotal role that stock prices play in determining returns, valuation is taken up first.

VALUATION

Market Clearing Prices

The market price of a stock, like that of all other economic goods, is a function of supply and demand. At a given point in time the available supply of the stock is fixed and equal to the quantity sold by the issuer. This is illustrated by the vertical line S

in Figure 13-2. Total demand to own the stock depends upon the price at which it could be bought. At high prices only the most optimistic individuals would be willing to hold the security in their portfolios, and demand would be small. At low prices demand would increase. Any time there are differences of opinion about any stock's (or any security's) future prospects, a downward-sloping demand curve, such as that shown in Figure 13-2, would result.

As shown in Figure 13-2, the equilibrium price of the stock is P^*. At P^*, total desire to own the stock equals the outstanding supply. At higher prices investors desire to hold fewer shares than are actually available, and attempts by investors and speculators to sell shares will drive prices down to P^*. At prices lower than P^* attempts to buy shares will drive prices up.

Figure 13-2 is useful in making four points:

1. Investors need not all agree about the proper value of a security. Forecasts of future prospects will differ among investors when they hold different information about the security. This is important to recognize, since the discussion of market value in this chapter is addressed largely to the single investor's assessment of a stock's value within his or her portfolio. Our aim is not so much to establish P^* as it is to determine the price a particular investor would be willing to pay. We will refer to this price as its *intrinsic* or *fair value*.

2. The equilibrium clearing price represents a market consensus about the intrinsic value of the security. This equilibrium price should soon be established as the

FIGURE 13-2 *Security Price Determination*

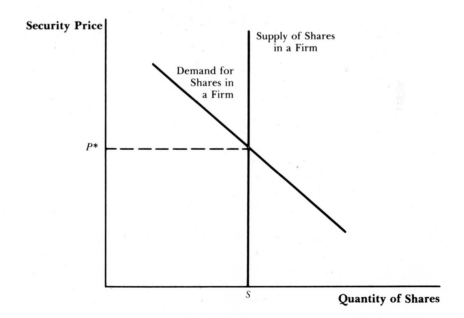

prevailing market price for buying or selling on a security exchange. If the existing market price varied from P^* (by more than the broker's commission), trading activity would rapidly force the market price into equilibrium.

3. The slope of the demand curve is determined by the extent to which investors have similar beliefs about a security's prospects. When a diversity of opinions exists, the demand curve will be downward sloping, and changes in supply will affect prices. When there is complete agreement, the demand curve is horizontal; regardless of supply, only one price will prevail.[2] The extent to which individuals assign similar values to a security depends upon the information they hold. If all investors hold the same information, the demand curve is horizontal. If information is not costless and not available to everyone, a downward-sloping demand curve would result.

4. Equilibrium prices, and thus market trading prices, will change only when (*a*) new information enters the market to cause a shift in the demand curve or (*b*) the quantity supplied changes (assuming investors have diverse opinions).

As noted, the focus of this section is on how an individual investor might assign a value to a given stock. This value estimate may differ from existing trading prices if the investor holds either more or less information about the security than does the market average. Wise investors will attempt to determine *why* their value estimates differ from market prices. Is it because they have better information or poorer information?

General Approaches to Valuation

Historically, at least six approaches to assessing the value of a security have been used. These are:

1. Par value
2. Book value
3. Liquidation value
4. Replacement value
5. Substitution value
6. Present value

To help illustrate the meaning and usefulness of each approach, a recent balance sheet of Anheuser-Busch, Inc., is shown in Table 13-1.

Par Value. The par value (or stated value) of stock is specified in the firm's corporate charter. Par value is simply a legal definition which has no economic impact upon the

---

[2]Assumptions of homogeneous expectations and a perfectly elastic demand curve are used in the traditional version of the CAPM.

TABLE 13-1 *Anheuser-Busch, Inc., Consolidated Balance Sheet, December 31, 1986*

Assets	(millions)	Liabilities and Equity	(millions)
Cash and Marketable Securities	$ 69.4	Accounts Payable	$ 491.7
Accounts Receivable	373.0	Wage and Salaries	180.0
Inventories	427.8	Other Current Liabilities	343.9
Other Current Assets	150.4		
Total	1,020.6	Total	1,015.6
		Long-Term Debt	1,126.8
Gross Plant and Equipment	6,099.3	Deferred Taxes	1,090.8
Accumulated Depreciation	1,671.7	Convertible Preferred	286.9
Net Plant	4,427.6	Shareholder Equity	
Other Assets	385.6	Common Stock ($1 Par)	295.3
		Capital in Excess of Par	6.1
		Retained Earnings	2,472.2
		Foreign Currency Adj.	0.9
		Treasury Stock	(460.8)
		Total	2,313.7
	$5,833.8		$5,833.8

firm. The fact that Anheuser-Busch common stock had a $1 par value is useful to know only because it occasionally aids in calculating the number of common shares outstanding. Dividing Anheuser-Busch's common stock dollar balance of $295.3 million by the $1 par shows the firm had 295.3 million shares outstanding. Many firms issue stock without designating a par or stated value.

Book Value. The total book value of a security is the dollar amount recorded on the firm's balance sheet. For example, the book value of Anheuser-Busch's common equity was $2,313.7 million. To find book value per share, total book value is simply divided by the number of shares outstanding. Anheuser-Busch had 295.3 million common shares outstanding and thus had a book value per share of $7.84 ($2,313.7/ 295.3).

As a general rule, book value is a poor indicator of the value of a stock for at least three reasons. First, it is historical in nature rather than future-oriented. In the case of Anheuser-Busch, a large percentage of its land, plant, and equipment are recorded in historical, original-cost dollars and may bear little relationship to current, inflated prices. The replacement value of its assets is surely larger than recorded book values. Second, comparability of reported book values between companies is a significant problem. Two companies may be identical in all respects except for their accounting procedures. For example, LIFO versus FIFO inventory valuation, straight-line versus declining balance depreciation, capitalizing versus expensing R&D, etc., are all generally accepted accounting principles which can lead to significantly different book values among firms.[3] Finally, book value reflects solely the original dollar investment made by a security holder. If this investment earns a return higher (or lower) than investors currently require, the current intrinsic worth should be higher (or lower) than the initial investment.

Liquidation Value. The liquidation value of a security represents the cash a security holder would receive if the firm discontinued operations, sold its assets, and distributed the net proceeds to security holders in order of legal priority. Liquidation is, by definition, the last action a firm would ever take, and thus liquidation value represents the *minimum* value of a security. Because corporate liquidations are rare and asset liquidation values are difficult to assess, liquidation value is typically not calculated. Even if a security's liquidation value were known, the assets of a firm are generally worth more as a going concern than in liquidation. If they are not, the firm should be liquidated.

Replacement Value. Replacement value represents a security's claim to the current reproduction value of the firm's assets. It differs from liquidation value in that liquidation value applies to the net selling value of assets, whereas replacement value applies to the cost required to reproduce existing asset productivity at today's prices. If there were no transaction costs associated with liquidating a firm (attorney fees, selling commissions, disassembly costs, etc.), liquidation and replacement values should be equal. However, such costs do exist, and replacement value exceeds liquidation value.

The problem with using replacement value as a measure of a stock's worth is twofold and is similar to that of using liquidation value. First, replacement value is difficult to determine. For example, in Anheuser-Busch's Form 10-K (an annual update of financial information provided to the SEC), management took four pages to discuss the difficulties of calculating replacement value and the dangers of its use. Only one-half page was needed to present their results. Nonetheless, if Anheuser-Busch's replacement value estimates were accurate, the replacement value of the firm's assets would have been much larger than reported book value.[4] Second, a stock bears an economic value to the extent that future cash flows are expected. These cash flows might be totally unrelated to the asset's replacement value. For example, if the tastes of American consumers suddenly switched from beer to wine, the replacement value

---

[3]There are situations in which book value is a good estimate of a security's value. For example, public utility commissions in various states follow a policy of increasing (or decreasing) customer rates whenever the market price of the stock is below (or above) book value per share. If commissions actively pursue this policy of setting market value ÷ book value ratios equal to 1.0, market prices should be very close to book values. In addition, for some firms the recorded book value is a reasonable approximation of the asset's replacement value. For example, short-term bank loans and demand deposits are probably recorded at values close to their true values.

[4]Quoting from Anheuser-Busch's Form 10-K: "Development of replacement cost information represents experimentation in financial reporting. . . . Since individual companies will develop replacement cost information differently, the data will not necessarily be comparable between companies."

of Anheuser-Busch's breweries would mean little in assessing the value of the firm's common stock.

Substitution Value. Substitution value reflects the value of a security when compared with that of substitute securities. An example will best illustrate this procedure. Assume that we wish to assign a value to the common stock of ABC Corporation. The company's product line is shown below:

Product	Total Dollar Earnings
A	$10 million
B	7 million
C	3 million
	$20 million

If we could find three different firms each of which, respectively, sells only product A, B, or C, then we should be able to create a portfolio of the three which would exactly duplicate ABC Corporation. The total market value of the portfolio of the three firms would equal the substitution value of ABC Corporation. Assume that we find three such firms, and observe:

Firm	Traded Market Value	÷	Total Dollar Earnings	=	Market Value Per $ Earnings
AAA Corp.	$500 million	÷	$50 million	=	$10
BBB Corp.	$600 million	÷	$40 million	=	$15
CCC Corp.	$ 8 million	÷	$ 1 million	=	$ 8

Knowing this, we could estimate a substitution value for ABC Corporation as follows:

Product	Market Value Per $ Earnings	×	ABC Corp. Total Dollar Earnings	=	Substitution Value
A	$10	×	$10 million	=	$100 million
B	$15	×	7 million	=	$105 million
C	$ 8	×	3 million	=	$ 24 million
					$229 million

The substitution value of ABC would equal $229 million.

For a firm like Anheuser-Busch, one would probably divide its product line into beer production and distribution, tourist entertainment (Busch Gardens), and baking supplies (e.g., yeast production and distribution). Substitution value is a fairly common approach to valuation. For example, whenever brokers or security analysts compare the price/earnings ratio of one firm against another, they are using a substitution value concept.

There are two problems with using substitution value. First, it neglects any economies (or diseconomies) of scale which might arise when products A and B are produced together as opposed to separately. Second, and more important, is the practical problem of identifying comparable firms. Management talent, patents and copyrights, geographic areas, etc., all cause considerable differences in firms even though their product lines appear identical. Substitution value estimates are imperfect at best.

Present Value. The basis of the present-value approach was discussed in Chapter 11 when the bond valuation model was presented. According to the present-value model, the current worth of a security is equal to the present value of the future economic benefits which the security holder expects to receive. A variety of present-value models exist. We will concentrate upon the most commonly used version, known as the *dividend valuation model.*

To illustrate the dividend valuation model, we will calculate the equity value of Midwest Machinery, Inc. Midwest's current financial statements are shown in Table 13-2.

The Dividend Valuation Model

The most commonly used approach to valuing common stock is to find the present value of expected future dividends. After an analysis of the future prospects and risks of a firm, the analyst estimates the dividends *per share* expected to be paid in each future year as well as an appropriate rate of return to be earned in each future year. If we define D_t as the dividend per share expected to be received at the end of year t, N as the number of years during which dividends will be paid, and K_t as the required return for year t, then the value of the stock would be:

General Dividend Valuation Model

$$P_0 = \frac{D_1}{1 + K_1} + \frac{D_2}{(1 + K_1)(1 + K_2)}$$

$$+ \ldots + \frac{D_N}{(1 + K_1)(1 + K_2)\ldots(1 + K_N)}$$

(13.3)

Since common stock has an infinite legal life, N could be infinity. However, if investors expect that the firm's assets will eventually be liquidated, N would be equal to the number of periods until expected liquidation.

To demonstrate the application of Equation 13.3, assume that a business venture is formed to harvest timber from a large tract of land. Timber cutting is expected to last three years and to provide dividends per share of $2, $3, and $25 at the end of years 1, 2, and 3, respectively. At the end of year 3 the land is to be sold and the corporation dissolved. After an analysis of expected risk-free rates and risks associated with the project, the investor determines that a return of 9%, 10%, and 12% in each respective year would be necessary. Given this information, the value of each share would be $22.95:

$$\frac{\$2}{1.09} + \frac{\$3}{(1.09)(1.10)} + \frac{\$25}{(1.09)(1.10)(1.12)} = \$22.95$$

TABLE 13-2 *Midwest Machinery Financial Statements, End of Year 0*

Assets	(millions)	Liabilities and Equity		(millions)
Current Assets	$ 20	Current Liabilities	(8%)	$ 10
		Long-Term Debt	(8%)	30
		Total Debt		$ 40
Gross Plant	$150	Common Stock ($1 Par)		2
Accumulated Depreciation	⟨70⟩	Paid-in Surplus		10
		Retained Profits		48
Net Plant	$ 80			
		Total Equity		$ 60
Total Assets	$100			
		Total Liabilities and Equity		$100

	(millions)
Sales	$200.0
Cost of Goods Sold	120.0
Gross Profit	$ 80.0
Selling, General, and Administration	50.0
Depreciation	10.0
Net Operating Income	20.0
Interest	3.2
Net Income Before Tax	16.8
Taxes (50%)	8.4
Net Income	$ 8.4
Total Dividends Paid	$ 8.4

Clearly, the dividend model is analogous to bond valuation models. The difference lies solely in the difficulties of specifying the inputs—the uncertainty about future dividends and the appropriate discount rate. Reasonable estimates of the level and timing of future dividends can be made only after the analyst has developed well-informed opinions about future national and international economic events, determinants of industry growth, probable firm market share, cost control, financing policies, etc. Developing such opinions can be a major task.

Required returns are also difficult to specify. If the assumptions of the CAPM are reasonably valid, it could be used. On that basis, the required return in year t would be equal to:

$$K_{et} = RF_t + \beta_t(RP_{mt})$$

where K_{et} = required equity return in year t, RF_t = risk-free rate available in year t, β_t = the beta of the stock expected for year t, and RP_{mt} = the market risk premium during year t. Differences in any of these return determinants from year to year would cause differences in individual K_{et}'s. Again, these variables are extremely difficult to estimate with any reasonable confidence.

In practice, professional analysts generally apply a *single discount rate* to all cash flows rather than a rate unique to each year. In this case the dividend model becomes:

Dividend Valuation with a Single Discount Rate

$$P_0 = \frac{D_1}{1 + K_e} + \frac{D_2}{(1 + K_e)^2} + \cdots + \frac{D_N}{(1 + K_e)^N}$$

$$= \sum_{t=1}^{N} \frac{D_t}{(1 + K_e)^t}$$

(13.4)

Security Market Line

and K_e is estimated from:

$$K_e = RF + \beta_e(RP_m)$$

(13.5)

The risk-free rate used is the expected yield to maturity on a risk-free security maturing in year N. Beta and the market risk premiums are assumed to be constant over time. The subscript e is used to designate an equity variable. K_e represents the cost of equity capital and β_e represents the beta of equity capital (as opposed to the cost and beta of debt capital or firm assets).

Capital Gains Versus Dividends. If the average stockholder were asked why a particular stock had been purchased, the answer would most likely be, "For its return—for the dividends and capital gains I expect to receive," and (neglecting risk) the answer is correct. But if capital gains are part of the returns which an investor values, why don't they appear in Equation 13.4? They do, although not explicitly.

Consider the situation in which a shareholder expects to sell shares at the end of year 2. The value of the stock at the end of period 0 would be equal to the present value of any dividends expected during years 1 and 2 plus the present value of the expected stock price at the end of year 2:

$$P_0 = \frac{D_1}{1 + K_e} + \frac{D_2}{(1 + K_e)^2} + \frac{P_2}{(1 + K_e)^2}$$

Yet the expected price at the end of year 2 should be equal to the present value (at the end of year 2) of dividends expected to be paid after year 2:

$$P_2 = \frac{D_3}{1 + K_e} + \frac{D_4}{(1 + K_e)^2} + \cdots$$

Thus, P_0 *is* determined by both future dividends and future selling prices. But since *all future selling prices must reflect future expected dividends*, the base determinant of existing stock prices is expected future dividends.

Constant Growth Model. If the dividends paid by a firm are expected to grow at a *constant growth rate to infinity*, Equation 13.4 can be considerably simplified. Defining G as this expected constant growth rate, Equation 13.4 reduces to:

Constant Dividend Growth Model

$$P_0 = \frac{D_1}{K_e - G}$$

$$= \frac{D_0(1 + G)}{K_e - G}$$

(13.6)

For example, consider the data on Midwest Machinery. Assume that after a thorough analysis of Midwest, an analyst concludes:

1. $RF = 8\%$
2. $RP_m = 5\%$
3. Beta of Midwest $= 1.2$
4. Long-run growth in dividends *per share* $= 5.6\%$
5. Expected dividend next year $= \$2.52$

Given these data, a required return of 14% is necessary [8% + 1.2(5%)], and the analyst would assess the value of Midwest to be $30 per share:

$$\frac{\$2.52}{0.14 - 0.056} = \$30$$

Firms which are expected to pay dividends that will grow at a constant rate to infinity clearly do not exist. Yet some firms do have reasonably stable dividend growths over relatively long time periods. In such cases Equation 13.6 provides a good approximation of the security's worth.

It is instructive to examine the composition of a stock's expected returns when the constant growth model is valid. Investors develop estimations of G and K_e and then determine a market price, P_0, so that the required return is expected to be earned. By rearranging Equation 13.6 we can see that, during each year, this expected return comes in two forms: an expected dividend yield and a growth in stock price. If the investor's required return equals the expected return, then:

Equilibrium	$\dfrac{\text{Required Yearly}}{\text{Return}}$	$=$	$\dfrac{\text{Expected}}{\text{Dividend Yield}}$	$+$	$\dfrac{\text{Expected Growth}}{\text{in Stock Price}}$	
Between						
Required and						**(13.7)**
Expected Returns	K_e	$=$	$\dfrac{D_1}{P_0}$	$+$	G	

For example, a stock which is selling for $25 and last paid a $0.92 dividend that is expected to grow over the long run at a constant rate of 9% per year is providing an expected return of 13%:

$$\frac{\$0.92(1.09)}{\$25} + 0.09 = 0.13$$

Whether the 13% is an appropriate return to expect on such an investment depends upon one's perceptions of the risk-free rate, the stock's beta, and the market risk premium.

In the case of Midwest Machinery, if its shares were now trading at $50, the analyst would not recommend a purchase. At a market price of $50 the expected return is 10.64% when a 14% return should be required:

$$\text{Expected Return} = \frac{D_1}{P_0} + G = \frac{\$2.52}{\$50} + 0.056 = 0.1064$$

As initially presented in Equation 13.6, G was defined as the dividend growth rate, but G also indicates the rate of growth in the stock's price. When a stock is priced via Equation 13.6, the best estimates of what K_e and G will be in the future are current estimates. Certainly they will change. But the best *estimates* of both, say five years hence, are the estimates made now, at period 0. Thus, the best estimation of the denominator in future years is today's denominator. The only term for which an expected change can be forecast is next period's dividend. Each year the numerator is expected to grow at a rate G. As a result, stock price is also *expected* to grow at rate G.

Consider another example. Assume that an analyst believes dividends paid on the Dow Jones Industrial Average (DJIA) will grow at a fairly constant rate over the long run. The analyst also believes the Dows are *properly valued* today at a current market price of $2,000. If the long-term, risk-free rate is 8%, the market risk premium is 6%, the beta of the DJIA is 1.0, and next year's expected dividend yield on the DJIA is 5%, what is the estimated value of the DJIA one year hence? First, a required rate of return of 14% is necessary (14% = 8% + 1.0 × 6%). Next, since the constant growth model applies, 5% of this required return will come in the form of an expected dividend yield, with the remaining 9% coming from yearly price growth. Thus, the DJIA is expected to be 9% higher, or $2,180, one year hence.

The constant growth model is appropriate whenever G is assumed constant to infinity, regardless of whether G is greater than zero, less than zero, or equal to zero. When G is exactly zero, Equation 13.6 reduces to an equation which is used to evaluate a perpetuity:

Value with Zero Growth
$$P_0 = \frac{D}{K_e}$$
(13.8)

When growth is negative, large dividend yields will be required to offset yearly price losses in order to earn required returns.

Nonconstant Growth. Few stocks can reasonably meet the assumption of constant dividend growth. Young, developing firms are likely to pay no dividends early in their lives as all profits are retained in the business to support necessary asset expansion. (An example would be IBM during the early years of computer development.) Once such firms are well established and can institute dividend payments, the payments are likely to grow at a faster yearly rate than the firm is capable of sustaining over the long run. Finally, even mature firms are likely to have erratic dividend growth rates as the profits of the firm respond to normal business cycles.

For most of these situations, a *nonconstant growth* model would be appropriate. When using the nonconstant growth model, a future date is expected to eventually arrive beyond which the constant growth model can be used but before which dividends are expected to grow at yearly rates different from this longer-run constant rate. Working through an example will help make this clearer. Consider the stock of a department store in a city which is experiencing rapid population growth. Last year's dividend was equal to $1. During the next three years this dividend is expected to grow at 12% per year owing to a combination of population growth and lack of competi-

TABLE 13-3 *Illustration of Nonconstant Growth Model*

Future Year	Yearly Growth	Expected Dividend	Present Value at 15%
1	12%	$1.12	$ 0.97
2	12	1.25	.95
3	12	1.40	.92
4	7	1.50	.86
5	7	1.61	.80
6	7	1.72	.74
7	7	1.84	.69
8	7	1.97	.64

Total of Years 1–8 $ 6.57

Plus present value of price at end of year 8:

a. Price at end of year 8:

$$P_8 = \frac{D_8(1 + G)}{K - G}$$

$$= \frac{\$1.97(1.03)}{0.15 - 0.03}$$

$$= \$16.91$$

b. Present value at period 0:

$$\frac{\$16.91}{1.15^8} = \qquad\qquad \$ 5.53$$

Total Value at Period 0 $12.10

tion. Subsequently, growth will equal the population growth of 7% a year for another five years as competition from scheduled new store openings takes hold. Finally, as population growth slows, a long-run constant dividend growth of 3% per year is expected. What is the intrinsic value of this security if the required return is 15%?

The solution is shown in Table 13-3. First, expected yearly dividends are calculated for each of the next eight years (the years of abnormal growth). These are then discounted at a 15% required return to find their respective present values. In total, the present value of the first eight years' dividends is equal to $6.57. Beyond year 8 the constant growth model can be used. The value of a share at the end of year 8 would be equal to year 9's dividend divided by $K_e - G$. This year 8 share value is $16.91. To express this future price in terms of its present value, the $16.91 is discounted at the 15% required return for eight periods to get $5.53. The value today of all dividends expected beyond year 8 is $5.53. Summing the present value of dividends between now and the end of year 8 ($6.57) with the present value of dividends beyond year 8 ($5.53), the value of the share is $12.10.

The general formula applied to nonconstant growth firms is:

Nonconstant Dividend Growth Valuation

$$P_0 = \sum_{t=1}^{T} \frac{D_0(1 + G_1)(1 + G_2)\ldots(1 + G_T)}{(1 + K_e)^t}$$

$$+ \frac{D_T(1 + G)}{K_e - G} \times \frac{1}{(1 + K_e)^T}$$

(13.9)

where G_t represents the growth rate in any year of abnormal growth t, T is the last date of abnormal growth, and G is the long-run constant growth rate after year T.

Determinants of G. Sustainable growth in dividends per share, whether constant or not, is directly related to two fundamental factors: the rate of return on equity investments and the percentage of earnings retained in the business. Symbolically:

Sustainable Growth $$G = ROE \times B$$ (13.10)

where B is the retention ratio (percentage of net income retained in the business) and ROE is the return on equity invested in the firm.

To illustrate this relationship, consider Midwest Machinery again. Assume that with the existing assets and capital structure, the firm could continue to earn net income equal to $8.4 million. Additions to plant needed to replace deteriorating equipment would be exactly covered by yearly depreciation provisions, and all income would be paid as dividends. Now assume that the board of directors suddenly decides to start retaining 40% of future earnings on which a 14% rate of return can be earned. If this policy is implemented immediately, the $8.4 million net income will be apportioned between $3.36 million in retained equity (0.4 retention × $8.4 income) and $5.04 million in dividends. Since 2 million shares are outstanding, present dividends per share will be $2.52 ($5.04 ÷ 2). Total equity will increase by the $3.36 million to $63.36 million. At a return on equity of 14%, next year's net income will be $8.87 million (0.14 × $63.36), and dividends per share will be $2.66 [($8.87 × 0.6) ÷ 2.0]. As a result of this retention policy, dividends will grow from $2.52 this year to $2.66 next year, a growth rate of 5.6%:

$$G = ROE \times B$$

$$= 14\% \times 0.4 = 5.6\%$$

The return on equity can also be separated into its individual components.[5] Analytically, ROE is a function of three factors:

1. *Asset efficiency* — the extent to which management can generate sales from a given asset base. Asset efficiency is measured by the asset-turnover ratio: sales ÷ assets.
2. *Expense control* — the extent to which management can increase net income after taxes from a given sales base. Expense control is measured by the after-tax profit margin: net income ÷ sales.

_____

[5]ROE is the accounting rate of return on the book value of equity. It is not the market rate of return which the shareholder actually receives. Although market returns and accounting returns are related, many factors influence market returns which do not affect accounting returns (at least not immediately). For example, changes in RF, RP_m, beta, expected dividend growth, etc., all affect stock prices and thus actual market returns but have no direct effect upon ROE.

3. *Debt utilization*—the extent to which management relies upon debt financing to support a given level of assets. Debt utilization is measured by the ratio: total assets ÷ total equity.

When these terms are multiplied, individual terms cancel to yield the return on equity:

Return on Equity

$$ROE = \frac{\text{Assets}}{\text{Efficiency}} \times \frac{\text{Expense}}{\text{Control}} \times \frac{\text{Debt}}{\text{Utilization}}$$ **(13.11)**

Determinants of Return on Equity

$$\frac{\text{Net Income}}{\text{Equity}} = \frac{\text{Sales}}{\text{Assets}} \times \frac{\text{Net Income}}{\text{Sales}} \times \frac{\text{Assets}}{\text{Equity}}$$

A decomposition similar to this one is often helpful when analyzing historical or potential changes in equity returns. In the case of Midwest Machinery the 14% *ROE* is composed of an asset efficiency ratio of 2.0 ($2 in sales generated for each dollar of assets), an expense control ratio of 4.2% ($0.042 of profits per $1 of sales), and a debt utilization measure of 1.67 ($1.67 in assets for each $1 of equity).

Growth Stocks

To most laymen the term *growth stock* simply means a stock whose price is expected to increase at a faster rate than the average. For many years this definition was also common within the professional analyst community. However, as understanding of the determinants of stock values has developed, a more precise definition has arisen. *A growth stock is one for which the available returns on investments are greater than investors' required returns.*

A true growth situation has major implications for the value of the firm. This can be understood by examining the constant dividend growth model:

$$P_0 = \frac{D_1}{K_e - G} = \frac{D_1}{K_e - (B \times ROE)}$$

Next year's dividend per share will be equal to next year's earnings per share less any earnings retained in the business. Next year's earnings per share will equal per share book value (*BV*) times the accounting return on equity. Thus the constant dividend growth model can be expressed as follows:

$$P_0 = \frac{(BV \times ROE)(1 - B)}{K_e - (B \times ROE)} = BV \times \left[\frac{ROE(1 - B)}{K_e - (B \times ROE)} \right]$$ **(13.12)**

Note how the relationship between accounting returns on equity (*ROE*), desired investment return (*K_e*), and the retention rate (*B*) affects the value of a stock. Of course, *ROE* can be greater than, equal to, or less than *K_e*. This can be expressed symbolically by stating:

$$ROE = K_e + C$$ **(13.13)**

TABLE 13-4 *Relationship Between P_0, K_e, ROE, and B*

Firm	Book Value Per Share	K_e	ROE	Price for Various B		
				B = 0.3	B = 0.5	B = 0.8
NRML	$50	12%	12%	$50.00	$50.00	$ 50.00
GRTH	50	12	14	62.82	70.00	175.00
NGRT	50	12	10	38.89	35.71	25.00

where C is a "constant" representing some difference between *ROE* and K_e. Substituting Equation 13.13 into 13.12 results in:

Market Price Versus Book Value
$$P_0 = BV\left[\frac{K_e(1 - B) + C(1 - B)}{K_e(1 - B) - CB}\right] \qquad (13.14)$$

If *ROE* (returns earned) equals K_e (returns demanded), the stock's price is *not* affected by the payout ratio and will be equal to the book value per share. This was the case for Midwest Machinery. While future dividends are expected to grow, the value of the stock was equal to its book value. However, when *ROE* exceeds K_e (C is positive), the stock price will be larger than its book value and will increase as the retention rate increases. Finally, when *ROE* is less than K_e (C is negative), stock prices will be less than book value and will decrease as the retention rate increases.[6]

These relationships are illustrated in Table 13-4 for three firms. Firm NRML represents a normal firm in which competitive pressures have forced *ROE* to equal K_e. Note that regardless of the retention rate, the stock price of NRML is the same as the stock's book value. Firm GRTH represents a typical growth situation in which *ROE* exceeds K_e. In this case the stock price increases as the retention rate increases. Finally, Firm NGRT is a negative-growth situation with K_e greater than *ROE*. As NGRT retains larger portions of income, its price falls.

The simple fact that a stock is a "growth" stock doesn't necessarily mean it is a good buy. Growth stocks may sell at their intrinsic values and should be bought for their investment merits rather than for their speculative potential. If one is searching for mispriced securities, growth stocks should provide no more candidates than normal- or declining-growth stocks. A good analyst will recognize a growth situation for what it is and look closely at why the firm's *ROE* exceeds K_e as well as how long this might persist. For example, in the early 1970s the price of Levitz Furniture common shares rose dramatically, largely because Levitz's *ROE* was considerably greater than K_e, and the firm was rapidly expanding. Unfortunately, analysts grossly misestimated how long it would take before competition forced Levitz's *ROE* to decline to K_e. As analysts began to recognize the considerable competition which Levitz faced and revised their estimates of future *ROE*s downward, Levitz common share prices dropped precipitously.

---

[6]This is true only if the firm restricts new investment to equal retained profit plus new debt in an amount that maintains a target capital structure.

The Price/Earnings Ratio

The price/earnings ratio of a stock is equal to the stock's current market price divided by some measure of earnings per share; that is:

$$P/E \text{ Ratio} = \frac{\text{Market Price}}{\text{Earnings per Share}} \qquad (13.15)$$

As such, the P/E ratio indicates the dollar price being paid for each $1 of a firm's earnings. P/E ratios are widely used by professional analysts as a measure of the relative prices of different stocks.

The stock's current market price is easy to determine, since it is probably reported in the financial press. Earnings per share (*EPS*), however, are more difficult to determine. The easiest earnings figure to use would be the latest *EPS* as shown on the company's financial statements. In fact, P/E ratios reported in the financial press are typically calculated using such latest reported *EPS* numbers. However, people buy a stock not for its past earnings but, instead, for its expected future earnings. As a result, many security analysts will report P/E ratios based upon next year's expected *EPS*. Even then a problem can arise when comparing P/E ratios among firms if some of the firms are expected to have abnormally high *EPS* next year whereas others are expected to have an abnormally poor year. To correct for such an unusual situation, many analysts calculate the P/E ratio based upon an estimate of *normalized* earnings per share. Normalized *EPS* can be estimated either by a purely subjective guess or by using sophisticated statistical models. Regardless of how normalized earnings are calculated, they are meant to reflect the normal level of the firm's earnings exclusive of any temporary effects caused by the state of the business cycle, seasonal conditions in the industry, or unusual events affecting the firm.

Conceptually, the P/E ratio is determined by three factors: (1) investors' required returns, (2) expected earnings retention rate, and (3) expected returns on equity. Again, the easiest way to demonstrate this is to use the constant dividend growth model:

$$P_0 = \frac{D_1}{K_e - G}$$

Defining E_1 as next year's expected earnings per share and using other terms as we have previously, the constant growth price model can be rearranged into a P/E ratio model as follows:

Determinants of P/E Ratio

$$P_0 = \frac{E_1 \times (1 - B)}{K - (ROE \times B)}$$

$$P_0/E_1 = \frac{E_1(1 - B) \div E_1}{K - (ROE \times B)} = \frac{1 - B}{K - (ROE \times B)} \qquad (13.16)$$

Equation 13.16 states that if dividends are expected to grow at a constant growth rate, the P/E ratio is theoretically equal to the stock's expected dividend payout ratio $(1 - B)$ divided by the difference between the required return and the expected growth rate ($ROE \times B$). In the case of Midwest Machinery, we have been assuming an expected payout ratio of 60%, a required return of 14%, and an expected constant *ROE* of 14%. This would imply a thoretical P/E ratio of 7.14:

$$\frac{0.60}{0.14 - 0.14(0.4)} = 7.1429$$

In other words, we should be willing to pay $7.14 for each $1 of Midwest's earnings per share expected next year. Since we had earlier assumed an earnings per share next year of $4.20 ($8.4 million net income ÷ 2.0 million shares), this implies a stock price of $30.00:

Estimated Current Stock Value	=	Theoretical P/E Ratio	×	Expected Earnings Next Year
P_0	=	P_0/E_1	×	E_1
$30	=	7.1429	×	$4.20

Figure 13-3 shows the P/E levels for the Standard & Poor's Composite Index. Price/earnings ratios are shown for each year-end from 1926 through 1987. To mea-

FIGURE 13-3 *Price/Earnings Ratios for the S&P 500, 1926–1987*

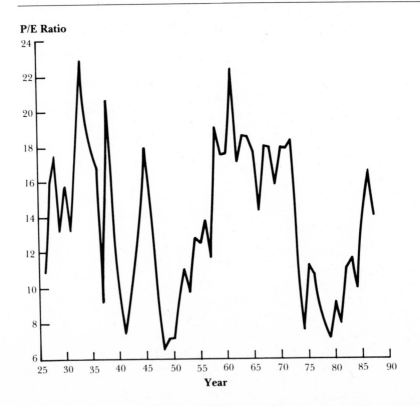

sure earnings per share, Standard & Poor's used reported earnings during the year for which a P/E ratio is shown (E_0 instead of E_1). As can be seen, aggregate market P/E ratios have been quite volatile. Unfortunately, many people simply look at today's P/E ratio, compare it with historical values, and then conclude that the market (or a single stock) is either overvalued or undervalued. For example, at the end of 1979 P/E ratios were at their lowest point for a number of years, and this persuaded many people that the market was undervalued. The market may, or may not, have been undervalued in late 1979, but a simple comparison of historical averages to current P/E ratios isn't adequate information on which to make such a decision. P/E ratios *should* change over time in response to changes in expected payout ratios, expected corporate returns on equity, and required returns. In 1979, for example, a good case could be made for the P/E ratio in Figure 13-3 to be the reported 7.3. For example, assuming that in 1979 the long-term risk-free rate was 10% and the market risk premium was 5%, the required return on the average stock would have been 15% per year. Also assuming a long-run *ROE* of 16.0% and a dividend payout ratio of 40%, long-run dividend growth would be 9.6% per year [16.0% $(1 - 0.4)$]. Thus the fair P/E ratio for the market index would have been about 7.4:

$$\frac{0.4}{0.15 - 0.096} = 7.4$$

In no way should this assumed growth or required return be taken as an accurate depiction of the market's expectations in 1979. The purpose of the example is simply to show that reasonable predictions are consistent with the 1979 P/E level. P/E ratios change over time in response to changes in the market's perceptions of future payout ratios, required returns, and expected growth rates.

Abnormal Growth. When a firm's dividends per share are expected to grow for a number of years at a faster (or slower) rate than expected in the long run, variants of Equation 13.16 can be used. We will illustrate only one abnormal growth model in which yearly growth will be G^* through year T and G thereafter. In this case the current price/earnings ratio is a multiple of the expected P/E ratio at the end of year T:

Abnormal Growth P/E Ratio

$$P_0/E_1 = \left(\frac{P_T}{E_{T+1}}\right)\left(\frac{1 + DY + G^*}{1 + K_e}\right)^T$$

$$= \left(\frac{1 - B}{K_e - G}\right)\left(\frac{1 + DY + G^*}{1 + K_e}\right)^T \qquad \textbf{(13.17)}$$

where T = the last year during which abnormal growth occurs, B = the long-run retention ratio expected after year T, DY = the stock's current dividend yield, G^* = the abnormal dividend growth rate through year T, G = the constant dividend growth rate after year T, and K_e = required equity return.

For example, consider a stock on which the required return is 12%. Abnormal dividend growth of 10% per year will continue for 10 years, after which the growth rate will fall to 7%. The retention ratio after year T is expected to be 50%, and the current dividend yield is 5%. Thus, the P/E ratio *at the end of year T* is expected to be:

$$P_T/E_{T+1} = \frac{1.0 - 0.5}{0.12 - 0.07}$$

$$= 10.0$$

The current P/E ratio would be:

$$P_0/E_1 = 10.0 \left(\frac{1.0 + 0.05 + 0.1}{1.12}\right)^{10}$$

$$= 10(1.30)$$

$$= 13.0$$

Sometimes security analysts will rearrange Equation 13.17 to solve for T instead of today's intrinsic P/E ratio. For example, assume that we have all the information above except for the duration period T. We expect that eventually the actual P/E ratio will be 10, we observe a current actual P/E of 13, and we estimate $G^* = 10\%$, $DY = 5\%$, and $K_e = 12\%$. In that case:

$$P_0/E_1 = P_T/E_{T+1} \left(\frac{1 + DY + G^*}{1 + K_e}\right)^T$$

$$\frac{P_0/E_1}{P_T/E_{T+1}} = \left(\frac{1 + DY + G^*}{1 + K_e}\right)^T \qquad \textbf{(13.18)}$$

$$\ln\left(\frac{P_0/E_1}{P_T/E_{T+1}}\right) = T \times \ln\left(\frac{1 + DY + G^*}{1 + K_e}\right)$$

and

$$T = \ln\left(\frac{P_0/E_1}{P_T/E_{T+1}}\right) \div \ln\left(\frac{1 + DY + G^*}{1 + K_e}\right)$$

Using the above data:

$$T = \ln\left(\frac{13}{10}\right) \div \ln\left(\frac{1.15}{1.12}\right)$$

$$= 0.2624 \div 0.0264 = 10.0 \text{ years}$$

OTHER VALUATION APPROACHES

The discussion above was based on a model which says that a share of stock is worth the present value of future dividends expected to be paid on the share. This makes perfect sense—the only way a share of stock can improve the owner's ability to consume is to pay dividends. A common stock is not like a painting, a record, or a book. It isn't bought for the enjoyment gained from looking at it, listening to it, or reading it on a rainy evening. A stock is bought for the future consumption opportunities it provides. And these can come only from the dividends it provides. Without the potential for future dividends, a stock is worth nothing.

Other valuation models exist in which dividends are not explicitly seen in an equation. We will examine three of these: (1) earnings valuation, (2) cash flow valuation and (3) investment opportunities valuation. However, all of these approaches are simply rearrangements of the basic dividend model. The role of dividends as the source of stock value never disappears.

Earnings Valuation

Underlying any ongoing stream of dividends are the earnings of the firm. These earnings, by definition, belong to the equity shareholders, so why can't we simply express the value of a share of common stock in terms of the earnings per share that the firm is expected to generate? We can. But in doing so an important point must be recognized: *Any earnings which are retained within the firm (not paid as dividends) are additional investments made by shareholders in the firm and should also be valued.*

For example, let's return to the Midwest Machinery example. To review, we are at the start of year 1. During year 0, Midwest earned $8.4 million on 2 million shares, or $4.20 per share. Since none of these earnings were retained in year 0, earnings per share will also be $4.20 in year 1. However, during year 1 Midwest intends to begin retaining 40% of all profits in the firm. This would result in retained profits of $1.68 per share and dividends per share of $2.52 in year 1. Beyond year 1 the retained profits will generate an expected *ROE* of 14% and result in a sustainable growth rate of 5.6%. Finally, investors require a return of 14%. Placing this information into the constant dividend growth model, each share of Midwest is worth $30:

$$P_0 = \frac{D_1}{K - G} = \frac{\$2.52}{0.14 - 0.056} = \$30$$

Now consider the valuation of the expected earnings which each share has a claim to. In particular, consider the $4.20 earnings per share (*EPS*) for year 1. All of this $4.20 belongs to the shareholder even though the firm will retain some of it. So why not simply find its present value? It does belong to the shareholder, so why not value it? And looking beyond year 1, all subsequent *EPS* also belong to the shareholder. So why not find their present values and say that the stock is worth the sum of the present values of all future *EPS*?

The answer is very simple. When a firm's management retains a portion of a shareholder's *EPS*, it is the same as the shareholder's being paid all *EPS* in dividends and then *reinvesting* the earnings retained. When Midwest Machinery pays dividends per share of $2.52 on earnings per share of $4.20, it is the same as paying the full $4.20 in dividends and having the shareholder immediately reinvest $1.68 in the firm. Retention of profits represents new investment by the equity owners.

It is perfectly correct to value the earnings per share of a stock as long as the reinvestment of earnings is also valued. The worth of a share of common stock is equal to the present value of all future expected earnings per share less the present value of all future investments per share:

General Earnings Valuation Model

$$P_0 = \sum_{t=1}^{N} \frac{EPS_t}{(1 + K_e)^t} - \sum_{t=1}^{N} \frac{IPS_t}{(1 + K_e)^t}$$

(13.19)

$$P_0 = \sum_{t=1}^{N} \frac{EPS_t - IPS_t}{(1 + K_e)^t}$$

where: EPS_t = the expected earnings per share in year t

IPS_t = the expected investment per share in year t

This equation values the expected future earnings-per-share stream which legally belongs to the shareholder. But it also values expected future investments made by the shareholder in order to generate the *EPS* stream.

Constant Growth Earnings Valuation. The general earnings valuation model shown in Equation 13.19 can be simplified considerably if future growth is expected to be constant. Again using G as this expected constant growth rate, Equation 13.19 reduces to:

Constant Growth Earnings Model

$$P_0 = \frac{EPS_1 - IPS_1}{K_e - G}$$

(13.20)

Applied to the Midwest Machinery example:

$$P_0 = \frac{\$4.20 - \$1.68}{0.14 - 0.056}$$

$$= \$30$$

Note that the dividend valuation model and the earnings valuation model are identical. The dividend model focuses upon net cash flows received by the investor (dividends), whereas the earnings model explicitly accounts for both the legal ownership of *EPS* and the incremental future reinvestment of earnings.

A Special Case. If the return that investors require (K_e) is identical to the return earned on owners' investments in the firm (ROE), the worth of a stock is simply the capitalized value of next year's earnings per share:

Value When $K_e = ROE$

$$P_0 = \frac{EPS_1}{K_e}$$

(13.21)

In fact, that is exactly the case for Midwest Machinery. Investors require a return of 14% and the firm is expected to generate a 14% *ROE* on any equity investment made in the firm. Thus, Equation 13.21 can be used to value the shares of Midwest:

$$P_0 = \frac{\$4.20}{0.14}$$

$$= \$30$$

When $ROE = K_e$, the retention of profits will have no impact on a stock's value. For example, if Midwest retains $1.00 at period 0, the dollar will grow to $1.14 one year later. But when this $1.14 is discounted back to its period 0 present value at 14%, it is worth exactly $1.00. *When* ROE = K$_e$, *retained earnings are invested in assets which have a zero net present value.*

Equation 13.21 would usually apply to firms in highly competitive, mature industries, such as food distribution, paper products, and public utilities.[7] It would not apply to developing industries, such as computer technology, or industries in decline, such as typewriter manufacturing. As a practical matter, it is wise to always use Equation 13.19 or Equation 13.20, since they apply to all firms.

Cash Flow Valuation

In principle, the worth of any asset is the present value of all future *cash flows* generated from the asset. In the calculation of accounting earnings per share there are a number of expenses which are no more than accounting entries. Depreciation, amortization of patents, goodwill, bad debt allowances, and many other "accounting expenses" involve no cash outflow during the year in which they are reported. Shouldn't they be added back to reported earnings per share in order to more fairly represent the cash flows generated from business operations?

Many analysts, in fact, do add such noncash expenses to earnings per share and compute the value of cash flows per share generated by the firm. This is referred to as a *cash flow valuation model*. First, expected cash flows from operations for year t (CF_t) are calculated as follows:

**Cash Flow
per Share**
$$CF_t = EPS_t + \frac{NCE_t}{N_t} \qquad \textbf{(13.22)}$$

where NCE_t refers to total noncash expenses expected in year t and N_t refers to the number of shares expected to be outstanding in year t. In addition, the investment per share (IPS_t) used in the earnings valuation model must be adjusted from a *net* investment to a *gross* investment. It was implicit in the earnings model that depreciation (and other noncash expenses) would be reinvested in the firm. However, if we wish to treat such items explicitly as cash available to equity holders, we must also explicitly recognize that such cash flows are in fact reinvested. The expected gross investment per share for year t (GPS_t) is calculated as:

**Gross Investment
per Share**
$$GPS_t = IPS_t + \frac{NCE_t}{N_t} \qquad \textbf{(13.23)}$$

Using these two adjustments, the cash flow valuation model is:

**General Cash Flow
Valuation Model**
$$P_0 = \sum_{t=1}^{N} \frac{CF_t - GPS_t}{(1 + K_e)^t} \qquad \textbf{(13.24)}$$

---

[7]Public utilities face indirect competition through regulatory authorities. A principal objective of most regulatory agencies is to set consumer prices at a level where ROE will be equal to K_e.

As you might imagine, a constant growth equivalent model can also be applied to this cash flow approach. We will not formally define it since it should be obvious given the two previous constant growth models. But let's illustrate its application to Midwest Machinery. First, expected cash flow for year 1 is found to be $9.20:

$$CF_1 = EPS_1 + (NCE_1 \div N_1)$$

$$= \$4.20 + (\$10.0 \div 2.0) = \$9.20$$

Second, expected gross reinvestment is $6.68:

$$GPS_1 = IPS_1 + (NCE_1 \div N_1)$$

$$= \$1.68 + (\$10.0 \div 2.0) = \$6.68$$

Thus, the stock is worth $30 using the cash flow valuation model:

$$\frac{\$9.20 - \$6.68}{0.14 - 0.056} = \$30$$

The dividend and cash flow models yield the same price, of course, because they both show the net cash which is received by shareholders—dividends. The only difference is cosmetic, in that the cash flow version explicitly shows cash flows available from operations and cash flows reinvested in the firm.

Investment Opportunities Valuation

The investment opportunities model separates the value of a share into two components: (1) the value of the existing assets and (2) the value of future investment opportunities. As an example, let's consider a competitor of Midwest Machinery—Western Machinery Corporation—which is identical to Midwest in all respects except in the return its equity holders require. Assume that the value of K_e for Western Machinery is 12%. As a result, the per share value of the stock will be:

$$P_0 = \frac{D_1}{K_e - G} = \frac{\$2.52}{0.12 - 0.056} = \$39.375$$

Let's take a close look at why the stock is selling for $39.375. First, the earnings per share of the firm are $4.20. To help make the example less complex, we will assume that accounting depreciation is equal to the actual economic depreciation of the firm's assets. Thus, management could pay all earnings of the firm as dividends to shareholders and not deplete the economic productivity of the assets. The existing assets are capable of providing a perpetual stream of dividends equal to current earnings per share. The present value of this perpetual dividend flow available from existing assets is $35:

$$\frac{EPS}{K_e} = \frac{\$4.20}{0.12} = \$35$$

Without retaining any profits, the existing assets can generate cash flows which have a current worth of $35 per share.

However, the management of Western Machinery does intend to make future investments in the firm. For example, at the end of the current year each shareholder will be asked to invest an incremental $1.68 (the retained profits per share). When this $1.68 is invested at 14%, it will yield an expected perpetual cash flow of $0.2352 ($1.68 × 0.14). Discounted at 12%, this perpetual cash flow stream will be worth $1.96 (0.2352 ÷ 0.12) at the end of the year. But the shareholder has been asked to pay $1.68 for the new assets, so the end-of-year expected *net present value* of these new investments will be $0.28 ($1.96 − $1.68).

The same type of analysis could be applied to all future years. Management will ask shareholders to invest in new assets which generate positive net present values. These net present values won't be forthcoming until future years, but there is no reason why their current present values should not be added to the stock's price. When the company is expected to maintain a constant retention of profits (B) and be able to invest at a constant return on new investment (ROE^*), the stock can be valued as follows:

Constant Growth Investment Opportunities Model

$$\underset{\substack{\text{Price} \\ \text{Per} \\ \text{Share}}}{\underbrace{P_0}} = \underset{\substack{\text{Value of} \\ \text{Existing} \\ \text{Assets} \\ \frac{EPS_0}{K_e}}}{} + \underset{\substack{\text{Value of Future} \\ \text{Investment Opportunities} \\ \frac{B(EPS_0)}{K - (ROE^*)B} \left[\frac{ROE^* - K}{K} \right]}}{} \qquad \textbf{(13.25)}$$

When applied to Western Machinery:

$$P_0 = \frac{\$4.20}{0.12} + \frac{0.4(\$4.20)}{0.12 - 0.056} \times \frac{0.14 - 0.12}{0.12}$$

The current stock value of $39.375 consists of a $35.00 value placed on existing assets plus a $4.375 value associated with today's worth of the expected future profitability of new investments.

Equation 13.25 is the constant growth version of the investment opportunities model. When ROE^* and B values are expected to change over time, the more general model shown below should be used.

General Investment Opportunities Model

$$P_0 = \frac{EPS_0}{K_e} + \sum_{t=1}^{\infty} \frac{B_t EPS_t (ROE^* - K_e)}{K_e} \left(\frac{1}{1 + K_e} \right)^t \qquad \textbf{(13.26)}$$

Again, the results obtained under each valuation model will be identical. They all value expected dividend flows. However, each focuses on a different approach to dividend valuation, and each approach can provide useful insights. For example, the investment opportunities model separates the value of existing assets from the value of future investment opportunities. If a large part of a stock's worth is associated with future opportunities, the security analyst would certainly wish to place an emphasis on technological developments and potential competition within the industry.

ESTIMATING EXPECTED RETURNS

Each of the valuation models introduced thus far is used to estimate a fair market price. Based on a forecast pattern of expected dividends and a statement of what the fair return (K_e) should be, a fair price is calculated and compared with the actual market price. Many analysts, however, turn the process around and use the actual market price together with expected future dividends to calculate the *expected return*.

For example, assume you are analyzing Pacific Telesis common shares at a time when the shares are trading at $70. After analysis of potential future dividend growth, you conclude that next year's dividends per share will be $6.00 and that future growth is likely to be constant at about 8% per year. Given this information, you can estimate the expected long-run rate of return from owning the stock by solving for K_e in the constant dividend valuation equation:

$$P_0 = \frac{D_1}{K_e - G}$$

$$\$70 = \frac{\$6.00}{K_e - 0.08}$$

$$K_e = 16.57\%$$

Given your forecast of future dividends, the purchase of Pacific Telesis at $70 provides an expected return of 16½%. Whether this is satisfactory or not depends upon the firm's beta, prevailing risk-free rates, and the slope of the SML.

For most stocks, the constant growth model does not apply, and some version of a nonconstant growth model is required. Most investment advisory organizations which estimate expected returns instead of fair prices require that the analyst forecast dividends yearly to some specified future period, say, year T. The analyst is then asked to estimate sustainable growth beyond year T in the standard fashion ($G = B \times ROE$). Finally, this information is used together with the stock's actual market price to infer what the expected long-run return should be.

To illustrate, we will use some data published by Value Line. Among other things, Value Line publishes:

1. The dividends per share which it expects next year (D_1)
2. The dividends per share which it expects four years from now (D_4)
3. The retention rate and return on equity which it expects four years from now (B_4 and ROE_4)
4. The stock's current price (P_0)

Using D_4 and D_1, intermediate dividends D_2 and D_3 can be estimated. And assuming that B_4 and ROE_4 reflect a long-run stable situation after year 4, they can be used to calculate sustainable growth after year 4. Finally, K_e can be found by finding the interest rate which will discount expected dividends to today's price:

$$P_0 = \sum_{t=1}^{4} \frac{D_t}{(1 + K_e)^t} + \frac{D_4(1 + G)}{K_e - G} \frac{1}{(1 + K_e)^4}$$

Consider information provided in a recent Value Line forecast on Hewlett-Packard. Shares of HP were selling for $48 in late 1988. Value Line provided the following projections:

$$D_{1989} = \$0.26$$

$$D_{1992} = \$0.40$$

$$B_{1992} = 93\%$$

$$ROE_{1992} = 14\%$$

The compound annual expected growth in dividends per share between 1989 and 1992 is 15.44%:

$$(0.40 \div 0.26)^{1/3} - 1 = 0.1544$$

This is used to calculate D_{1990} and D_{1991}:

$$D_{1990} = \$0.26(1.1544) \qquad D_{1991} = \$0.26(1.1544)^2$$

$$= \$0.30 \qquad\qquad\qquad = \$0.35$$

Next, sustainable growth beyond 1992 is estimated as:

$$G = B \times ROE$$

$$= 0.93 \times 14\% = 13.0\%$$

Finally, the dividend equation from which K_e is found can be expressed as:

$$\frac{\$0.26}{1 + K_e} + \frac{\$0.30}{(1 + K_e)^2} + \frac{\$0.35}{(1 + K_e)^3} + \frac{\$0.40}{(1 + K_e)^4} + \frac{\$0.40(1.13)}{K_e - 0.13} \times \frac{1}{(1 + K_e)^4} = \$48$$

To solve for K_e, a trial-and-error procedure must be used. A first estimate of K_e is arbitrarily chosen and used to estimate the constant growth price which would prevail at the end of year 4. This price and the four dividends are then discounted at K_e to see whether they equal today's $48 price. If not, an adjustment is needed in K_e. Table 13-5 shows the prices obtained at various K_e interest rates. Since 13.60% yields a price close to the $48 price of HP, we will use it as our estimate of Value Line's expected return on Hewlett-Packard.

Once such expected returns are obtained on many stocks, each is plotted against the stock's estimated beta to obtain an estimate of the current security market line. Stocks with above-average expected returns for a given estimated beta level are believed to be ideal purchase candidates. Conversely, stocks with lower-than-average expected returns for a given estimated beta level are believed to be candidates for sale. An example of an estimated security market line is shown in Figure 13-4. Each point on the figure comes from data provided in a Value Line survey. Expected returns were calculated using the nonconstant growth approach used in our Hewlett-Packard analysis. Stocks plotted are primarily those in the DJIA, but a few others were chosen to add some variability to the beta estimates. The risk-free rate on long-term Treasuries was about 9.5%. Stocks which plot above the estimated SML are purchase candidates. Stocks which plot below the estimated SML are sell candidates.

TABLE 13-5 *Calculation of Expected Returns on Hewlett-Packard Stock*

	1989–1992 Growth 15.44%					
	Dividends					
	1989	*1990*	*1991*	*1992*	*1992 Value*	
Cash Flow	$0.26	$0.30	$0.35	$0.40	$0.45208/(K − 0.1302)$	
K	*Present Value of Future Cash Flow*				*1992 Price*	*1988 Price*
14.00%	0.23	0.23	0.23	0.24	$27.31 =	$28.24
13.75	0.23	0.23	0.24	0.24	36.99 =	37.93
13.60	0.23	0.23	0.24	0.24	46.80 =	47.74
13.50	0.23	0.23	0.24	0.24	56.75 =	57.69

Note: The values above are rounded. All sums are calculated to the sixth decimal place.

FIGURE 13-4 *Security Market Line, December 1984*

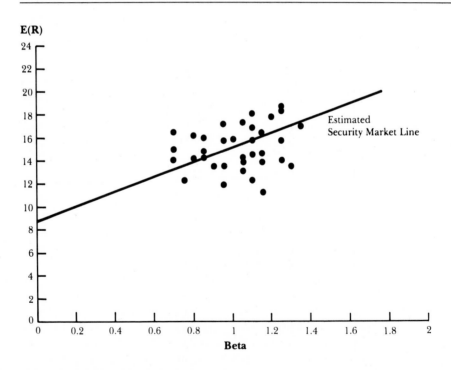

DETERMINANTS OF HISTORICAL RETURNS

Historical stock returns are logically composed of two parts: the first reflects *expected* returns, and the second reflects returns (or losses) associated with *unexpected* price changes or dividend changes. For example, suppose the constant dividend model is used to evaluate the worth of a stock which is expected to pay a $3.00 dividend next year, has an expected dividend growth rate of 8%, and has a required return of 14%. On the basis of these data, the fair value of the stock would be $50:

$$\frac{\$3}{0.14 - 0.08} = \$50$$

If the stock is, in fact, selling for $50, the expected return will be identical to its required return (14%) and be composed of a 6% dividend yield and an 8% expected growth in the stock's price. Now, assume that after one year the stock is actually selling for $56 (as opposed to the expected price of $54) and pays a $3.20 dividend. The actual return would be 18.4%. Decomposing this realized return into its expected and unexpected components, we would find:

$$\frac{\text{Realized}}{\text{Return}} = \text{Expected Return} + \text{Unexpected Return}$$

$$18.4\% = \frac{\$54.00 - \$50.00}{\$50.00} + \frac{\$3.00}{\$50.00} + \frac{\$56.00 - \$54.00}{\$50.00} + \frac{\$3.20 - \$3.00}{\$50.00}$$

$$18.4\% = 14\% + 4.4\%$$

Over long periods of time average unexpected returns should be zero. If they are not, people would soon recognize that the stocks are consistently providing higher (or lower) returns than expected, and they would adjust prices up (or down) until speculative profits were no longer available. However, during any single period of time unexpected returns can be quite large. These unexpected returns could be caused by one of two factors: (1) changes in the required return which is used to discount expected dividends or (2) changes in the expected future dividends of the firm. Each of these factors is discussed below.

Changes in Required Returns

If expected dividend growth doesn't change, an increase in required returns should drive stock prices down. Conversely, a reduction in K_e should result in higher stock prices. We will use the CAPM as a means of discussing changes in required returns.

The Risk-Free Rate. Nominal risk-free rates were discussed at length in Chapters 5 and 6. Although economists are not in complete agreement about the determinants of RF, there is a wide consensus that nominal rates are composed of a pure, real rate r^*, an expected inflation premium $E(I)$, and short-term Federal Reserve policy impacts:

$$RF = r^* + E(I) + \text{Fed Impacts} \qquad (13.27)$$

To date, studies attempting to examine changes in r^* tend to suggest that the real rate of interest is reasonably stable over time. However, inflation expectations are quite variable and can cause major changes in the nominal risk-free rate of interest.

Market Risk Premiums. All other things held constant, an increase in market risk premiums will result in higher required returns and lower actual returns for all stocks. Market risk premiums reflect both investors' risk aversion and the amount of risk perceived in the market. A change in either will cause RP_m to change.

We noted in Chapter 10 that a number of tests of efficient market theory suggest that market risk premiums might change over time with business conditions. Estimates of market risk premiums have been obtained using three different approaches. First, a historical *earned* risk premium can be calculated by subtracting the average risk-free return earned ($\overline{RF}$) from average market returns earned ($\overline{R}_m$) during some past period. Estimates of $\overline{RF}$ have been calculated using both high-grade short-term and high-grade long-term bonds. For example, using average returns on short-term T-bills, an annual risk premium of about 8.5% was earned between 1926 and 1987. Using long-term government bonds to proxy RF, an earned risk premium of about 7.4% was earned. However, *earned* risk premiums are sensitive to the data used, may not truly reflect investors' expectations, and can't accurately address changes in RP_m which occur over time.

A second approach used to estimate risk premiums relies upon direct investor surveys. Such a study was conducted by Charles Benore of Paine Webber Mitchell Hutchins. Benore surveyed various institutional portfolio managers and asked them to complete the following:

> Assume that a double-A, long-term utility bond currently yields about 9½%; the utility common stock for the same company would be attractive to you relative to the bond if its expected total return is at least _____ %.

Figure 13-5 presents the frequency distribution of responses. The weighted average risk premium was 4.9%. Of course, Benore's study is restricted to high-quality utility stocks which typically have estimated betas of 0.6 to 0.8, but it is suggestive of the risk premiums for stocks in general.

The third approach estimates risk premiums from actual market data. For example, Brigham, Shome, and Vinson have used Value Line forecasts of future dividends and existing market prices to estimate the expected returns on each of the 30 DJIA stocks at a given point in time. The procedure they use is similar to the one we used in examining Value Line's estimate of Hewlett-Packard's expected return in late 1988. Brigham, Shome, and Vinson average the expected returns and subtract an estimate of the risk-free rate (a long-term Treasury rate) to estimate the risk premium for the DJIA prevailing on that date.

Results of their study for the years 1966–1983 are shown in Figure 13-6. Their estimated risk premium shows no tendency to rise or fall over the full period, but there is considerable variability over time. The largest estimate was 6.92% in late 1974 and the smallest was 3.75% in 1983. The average over the full 19-year period was 5.59%. It is important to remember that their estimates apply to a set of 30 large U.S. companies whose average beta is certainly less than 1.0 (about 0.8 to 0.9). Therefore the risk premium on the average stock should be somewhat larger.

Figure 13-7 combines levels of long-term Treasury yields to maturity, with the Brigham, Shome, and Vinson (BSV) risk-premium estimates to show expected returns on the DJIA since the mid-1960s. Volatility in the risk premium did contribute to the

FIGURE 13-5 *Survey of Utility Stock Risk Premiums*

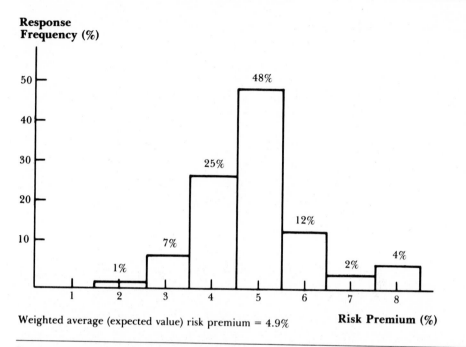

Weighted average (expected value) risk premium = 4.9%

SOURCE: Charles Benore, Paine Webber Mitchell Hutchins, Inc., "A Survey of Investor Attitudes Toward the Electric Power Industry," September 25, 1979.

volatility of this series, but it was dominated by volatility in the risk-free rate (caused largely by volatility in inflation expectations).

At the start of this section we noted that two economic factors cause actual returns to be different from expected: (1) changes in required returns and (2) changes in expected future earnings and dividends. The impact of changes in required returns can be seen using the BSV data. For example, given constant earnings and dividend expectations, changes from year to year in the BSV expected returns should be negatively correlated with actual market returns. An increase in expected future returns could come only if prices fall (resulting in a lower than expected actual return); a reduction in expected returns would cause prices to rise (resulting in a higher than expected return).

The extent to which changes in expected returns generated realized returns can be seen in Figure 13-8. Actual returns on the S&P 500 Index are shown on the vertical axis for the period 1966 through 1983. Year-to-year changes in expected returns are shown on the horizontal axis. With a few (dramatic) exceptions, reductions in required returns are associated with positive stock market returns and increases in required returns are associated with negative returns. The exceptions represent changes in perceptions of future earnings growth offsetting the effect of changes in required returns.

FIGURE 13-6 *Estimated Risk Premium of the DJIA*

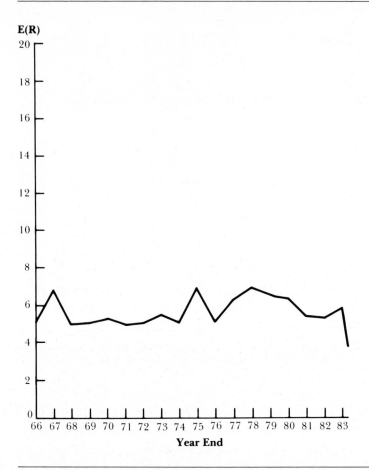

SOURCE: Adapted from Brigham, Shome, and Vinson, "The Risk Premium Approach to Measuring a Utility's Cost of Equity," *Financial Management Journal* (Spring 1985): 33–45.

Beta. If other things remain the same, an increase in a stock's beta will increase its required return and result in a lower stock price and lower actual return. Whereas changes in *RF* affect the prices of all securities, changes in beta affect the price of only that stock. The beta of a stock is determined by two basic factors: the degree of non-diversifiable business risk inherent in the firm's assets and the degree of debt utilization. Any time a firm's product line or debt-to-equity ratio changes, its stock beta is likely to change.

The beta of a firm's assets is a weighted average of the beta of each asset:

$$\beta_A = \sum_{a=1}^{N} X_a \beta_a$$

(13.28)

FIGURE 13-7 *Expected Returns for the DJIA*

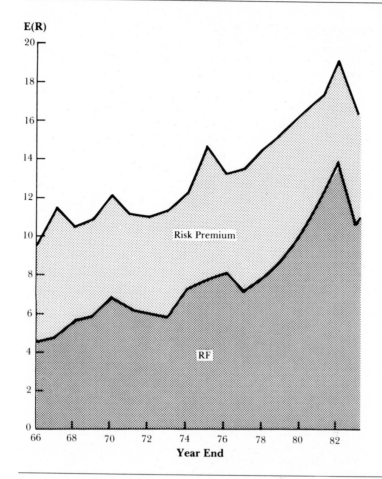

SOURCE: Adapted from Brigham, Shome, and Vinson, "The Risk Premium Approach to Measuring a Utility's Cost of Equity," *Financial Management Journal* (Spring 1985): 33–45.

where β_A = the beta of the firm's total assets, X_a = the percentage of the firm's asset value committed to asset a, β_a = the beta of asset a, and N = the number of assets held.

The beta of a single asset is equal to:

$$\beta_a = \left(\frac{\sigma_a}{\sigma_m}\right) r_{am} \tag{13.29}$$

where σ_a = the perceived standard deviation of returns on asset a, σ_m = the perceived standard deviation of returns on the market portfolio, and r_{am} = the correlation coefficient of returns on asset a versus the market.

FIGURE 13-8 *S&P 500 Return Versus Changes in the DJIA's E(R), 1966–1983*

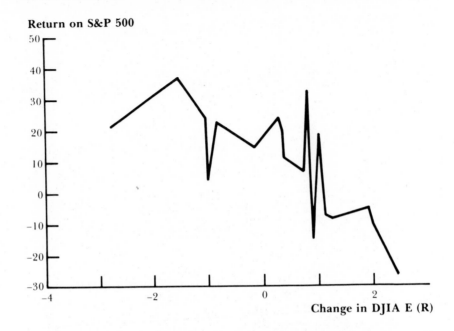

For example, assume that the management of Conglomatron, Inc., is considering the acquisition of Data Files Corporation. Relevant data on both companies are shown below:

	Conglomatron	Data Files
Current Market Value of Assets	$100 million	$50 million
Standard Deviation of Asset Returns	20%	30%
Standard Deviation of Market Returns	10%	10%
Correlation of Asset Returns with Market	0.7	0.2

Then the asset beta for each firm would be:

$$\beta_C = (20\%/10\%)(0.7) = 1.4$$

$$\beta_D = (30\%/10\%)(0.2) = 0.6$$

and the beta of the merged firms would be:

$$\beta_{Merged} = \frac{\$100}{\$100 + \$50}\,(1.4) + \frac{\$50}{\$100 + \$50}\,(0.6) = 1.13$$

Would the price of Conglomatron stock rise after the merger *since its beta is lower*? In an efficiently priced market it would *not*. In an efficiently priced market the $50 million value of Data Files already reflects its beta. Its value of $50 million is expected to provide exactly the return necessary for a beta of 0.6.

Continuing with the example, the *equity* beta of Conglomatron will be influenced by its use of financial leverage. Specifically, the equity beta is equal to:

**Equity Beta
as a Function
of Asset Beta**

$$\beta_E = \beta_A[1 + (D/E)(1 - T)] \qquad (13.30)$$

where β_E = the beta of the common stock, β_A = the beta of the assets, D/E = the target debt-to-equity ratio, and T = the corporate tax rate.

For example, if Conglomatron does acquire Data Files, has a marginal tax rate of 50%, and finances with 50% debt and 50% equity, its equity beta would be 1.69:

$$\beta_E = 1.13[1 + (1.0)(1 - 0.5)] = 1.69$$

Hamada has investigated the relative importance of debt financing to equity betas and found that, on average, debt financing causes equity betas to be 24% higher than asset betas.[8]

Earnings Growth

Growth of corporate earnings and stock prices are intimately related. Over the *long run* there is a close correspondence between the two. For example, in Figure 13-9 the level of the S&P Composite Index is plotted together with its earnings per share between 1927 and 1987. Clearly, over the long run, market price levels increase with earnings. And in the *short run*, unexpected changes in earnings can have dramatic effects on stock prices. To see this, examine Figure 13-10, which displays the results of the study by Ball and Brown discussed in Chapter 10. Ball and Brown set out to evaluate the impacts which an *unexpected* change in earnings had upon stock prices. Using a variety of statistical procedures, they identified firms which reported earnings higher than, the same as, or lower than expected. They then measured the price movement of the stock for twelve months prior to and six months after the earnings announcement. Price movements due to the stock's beta and market returns were eliminated in an attempt to examine price movements in response to earnings announcements only. In Figure 13-10 stocks with unexpected favorable earnings announcements show significant price growth. Stocks with unexpected unfavorable announcements decrease in value. Unexpected earnings changes *do* affect stock prices.

Note that most of a stock's price adjustment occurs *before* the announcement date. In order to capture possible gains, you must be able to predict unexpected earnings announcements earlier than the average person. Clearly, somebody was able to forecast some of the so-called unexpected earnings, or the prices in Figure 13-10 would not have adjusted as soon as they did.

---

[8]Equation 13.30 was developed by Hamada and assumes that the only impact which debt has on the value of a firm arises out of the tax deductibility of debt interest expense. Since this belief is open to serious question, so too is Equation 13.30. However, no one seriously questions the notion that increased reliance on debt financing increases equity betas. The only question is the precise nature of the relationship.

FIGURE 13-9 *Price Level and Earnings of the S&P 500 Index*

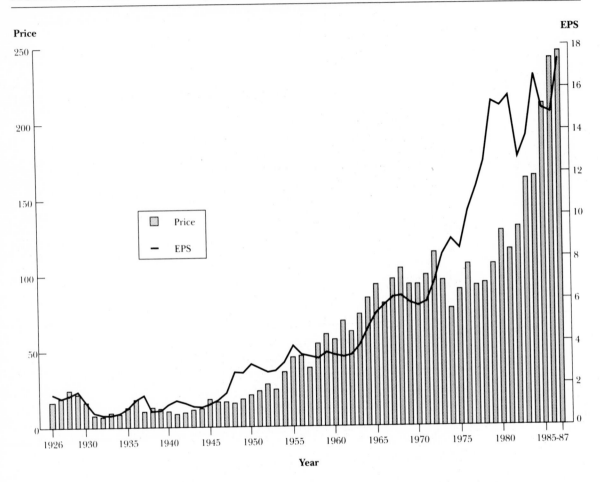

However, earnings and growth rate predictions are more difficult to develop than one might believe. For example, historical growth rates are very poor predictors of future growth. Many investors believe a company's earnings will show a fairly predictable long-run growth consistent with its industry and managerial talent which will be temporarily interrupted by easily forecastable changes in national output. This doesn't seem to be true. A large body of research suggests that historical growth rates are only slightly related to future growth. This was first noted by Little in a paper appropriately titled "Higgledy Piggledy Growth." Little reported that successive changes in earnings per share of British firms were statistically uncorrelated. Numerous studies flowed from "Higgledy Piggledy," most confirming the results. For example, Brealey studied 700 U.S. firms between 1951 and 1963 and found correlations of earnings changes to be close to zero. Brealey performed four different tests. First, earnings changes in one year were correlated with the subsequent year's change. The average correlation coefficient across all firms was −0.06. Second, earnings changes in one

FIGURE 13-10 *Price Impacts of Unfavorable and Favorable Earnings Reports*

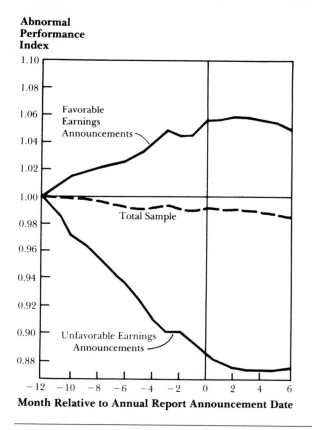

Month Relative to Annual Report Announcement Date

SOURCE: Adapted from R. Ball and P. Brown, "An Empirical Evaluation of Accounting Income Numbers," *Journal of Accounting Research* (Autumn 1968): 169.

year were correlated with changes two years in the future. The average correlation coefficient across all firms was −0.06. Third, industries were created and the correlation coefficient was calculated for adjacent years' earnings changes; the result was −0.03. Finally, industry changes were correlated with changes two years hence, and the result was −0.05. Brealey could find little hope of estimating future earnings from the past. This does not mean people are unable to forecast earnings with any reasonable degree of accuracy. But such accurate forecasts must draw upon information beyond simple historical trends.

How have security analysts fared in their earnings predictions? The answer is debatable, but some evidence suggests not so well. The best-known study of security analysts' forecasts was conducted by Cragg and Malkiel. Their study was based upon earnings forecasts for 185 corporations made by five financial institutions. Each forecast was an average annual earnings growth rate expected over the next five years. First, Cragg and Malkiel compared these forecasts with various measures of historical growth. They found that over half the variation in forecasted growth was associated with historical growth. Even though historical growth is an extremely poor predictor of the future, a large part of the analysts' forecasts relied upon this past growth. Still, the analysts did consider other factors, since past growth was not totally related to their forecasts. Second, Cragg and Malkiel examined how close the analysts' forecasts were to actual future growth. The average correlation coefficient between actual and forecast growth for the five institutions was 0.35 — not a particularly stellar performance. While one institution did show a relatively high degree of accuracy (correlation = 0.7), the authors pointed out that this institution concentrated on large, relatively mature firms whose earnings are likely to be quite stable and predictable.

Commonalities in Actual Returns

In Chapter 8 we said that a stock's return could be separated into three parts: (1) a constant rate of return which is earned regardless of random economic events which affect the firm, (2) a sensitivity to economic events affecting all stocks, which is captured by beta, and (3) returns which are unique to the firm and have no effect on other stocks. But is there more to it than this? Are stock returns related to each other in ways other than covariability with an aggregate market portfolio? The answer seems to be yes.

For years, market professionals have said that a stock's return is influenced by a sensitivity to aggregate market moves, industry conditions, and firm-unique events. The first statistical evidence supporting this was prepared by King, who selected 63 NYSE stocks and calculated their monthly percentage price changes between 1927 and 1960. Using a multivariate statistical procedure, he was able to group the securities into different industries and calculate the percentage of variation in returns due to market effects, industry effects, and effects unique to each stock. The statistical methodology selected industries based upon how closely returns on securities were correlated *after* effects of the aggregate market had been removed. King did not specify industries — he allowed the computer to select those stocks that seemed to group together best. However, interestingly, these statistically created industries were essentially identical to the industry classifications used by the Securities and Exchange Commission (SEC). King's study suggested that common industrial classifications are indeed reasonable. Given the diversification of product lines by many firms in recent years, this is a little surprising.

Table 13-6 reports the percentage of return variability which was due to the aggregate market, to industry groupings, and to each stock. These results suggest that:

1. The importance of a market-wide effect upon individual security returns was less apparent in more recent years (1952–1960) than prior to the 1950s (1927–1952). The reason for this remains unclear. It could be due to fundamental changes in economic variability, increased disclosure by firms, etc.
2. Industry-related factors contributed about 12% to the inherent variability of stock returns. This was true throughout the 1927–1960 period examined.
3. Market and industry effects vary considerably by industry.

TABLE 13-6 *Results of the King Study*

| | Proportion of Return Variability Due to | | | | | |
| | 1952–1960 | | | 1927–1952 | | |
	Market Effects	*Industry Effects*	*Stock Effects*	*Market Effects*	*Industry Effects*	*Stock Effects*
Tobacco Industry	9%	17%	74%	36%	15%	49%
Oil Industry	37	20	43	54	19	27
Metals Industry	46	8	46	63	9	28
Railroad Industry	47	8	45	63	11	26
Utilities Industry	23	14	63	47	13	40
Retail Trade	23	8	69	48	11	41
Overall	31	12	51	52	13	35

SOURCE: Adapted from B. King, "Market and Industry Factors in Stock Price Behavior," *Journal of Business* 39 (January 1966): 139–90.

In a follow-up study Farrell selected 100 stocks from a large number of *different* SEC industry classifications. Monthly price changes from 1961 through 1969 were examined using a statistical procedure similar to King's. After removing market-wide effects, this procedure yielded four different groups. The stocks in each group tended not to follow normal industry designations. Instead, they resulted in what Farrell chose to call (1) growth stocks, (2) stable stocks, (3) cyclical stocks, and (4) the only clear industry grouping—oil stocks. Percentages of each stock's variability explained by the market and each pseudo-industry were similar to those found by King. The market explained about 30%, and each pseudo-industry explained between 10% and 30%.

The King and Farrell studies are interesting because they show that stock returns are related in ways other than a common market effect. These relationships seem to be related to industrial classifications as well as "types" of stock (growth, stable, etc.). This does *not* violate the assumptions of the CAPM if industry or security-type returns are uncorrelated with those of other industries and types, but the results are more consistent with APT. Broad diversification is still the ruling order. However, diversification must be more carefully handled. Simply holding a large number of stocks within a few industries or within a given security type, such as growth stocks, will not achieve the full benefits of diversification. To ensure that a portfolio has eliminated all diversifiable risk, a large number of stocks from different industries and different security types should be held.

SUMMARY

The most widely used stock valuation model is known as the dividend valuation model, in which the intrinsic worth of a stock is estimated by discounting all future *expected dividends per share* at a return which depends upon the stock's risk. If dividends are expected to grow at a constant rate for an indefinite period of time, the general dividend model reduces to the constant dividend growth model. This model states that the intrinsic worth of a stock (P_0) is:

$$P_0 = \frac{D_0(1 + G)}{K_e - G}$$

where D_0 refers to the *per share* dividends just paid, G refers to the expected constant growth rate, and K_e refers to the required return on an equity investment. A nonconstant growth variant of this basic model allows for a number of years during which dividends per share grow at different rates but assumes that, after some point in the future, the best estimate of dividend growth is a constant rate.

A growth stock was defined as a stock for which the shareholders' required return is less than the return a company is actually able to provide. Whenever a firm is able to earn a larger rate of return on shareholder investments than shareholders require, shareholders will prefer the firm to retain a larger portion (perhaps all) of the firm's earnings since this will increase the expected future dividend stream as well as the stock's intrinsic worth. Alternatively, if required returns are equal to the marginal returns the firm is able to earn on new shareholder investment, shareholders will be indifferent to the level of profit retention in the firm.

Valuation models which focus upon characteristics other than dividends have been developed. For example, models may be based on earnings per share, cash flow per share, or a firm's investment opportunities. Each of these, however, is no more than a variant of the basic dividend model. Without the prospect of future dividends, a stock is worth nothing.

Actual returns earned, of course, will rarely be identical to expected returns. A change in the real rate of interest, inflation expectations, required market risk premiums, and stock betas all result in a new equilibrium required and a stock price other than expected. Similarly, changes in expectations of earnings and, thus, dividends will also result in stock prices other than expected.

REVIEW PROBLEM #1

Here is some financial and stock market information about a hypothetical firm called Data Control.

Data Control, Inc.
Financial Statements for the Year Ended December 1990

Assets	(millions)	Liabilities and Equity	(millions)
Current Assets	$1,300	Debt	$1,200
Net Plant	1,500	Equity	1,600
Total Assets	$2,800		$2,800

	(millions)
Sales	$4,800
Cash Expenses	4,110
Depreciation	150

Net Operating Income	540
Interest	100
Net Income Pretax	440
Tax	(200)
Net Income	$ 240
Dividends Paid	$ 144

Market Information as of December 1990

Common Shares Outstanding	40 million
Price Per Share	$47.70
Risk-Free Rate	9%
Expected Return on the Market	14%
Estimated Beta	1.20

a. Calculate what the required return on Data Control should be using the security market line.

b. Calculate the sustainable growth rate (G) which would exist if the financial relationships shown in the balance sheet and income statements were to remain constant over time.

c. What is the fair market price of Data Control? (Use the dividend valuation model.)

d. Use the constant earnings and cash flow models to determine the stock's fair value.

e. Would you buy this stock? Why or why not?

f. What would a firm believer in efficient market theory say about your decision in part e?

g. Assume that Data Control's beta is really 1.0. Now what should the stock sell for?

Solution

a. K_e $= RF + B(RP_m)$
$= 9\% + 1.2(14\% - 9\%)$
$= 15\%$

b. G $= B \times ROE$
$6\% = 0.4 \times 15\%$
$B = \dfrac{240 - 144}{240} = 0.40$
$ROE = \dfrac{240}{1600} = 0.15$

c. The constant growth model can be used here since the retention rate and ROE are expected to remain constant:

$$P_0 = \frac{D_0(1 + G)}{K_e - G} = \frac{3.60\,(1.06)}{0.15 - 0.06}$$

$$= 42.40$$

d. Constant earnings valuation model:

$$P_0 = \frac{(EPS_0 - IPS_0)(1 + G)}{K_e - G}$$

$$= \frac{(6.00 - 2.40)(1.06)}{0.15 - 0.06}$$

$$= 42.40$$

$$EPS_0 = 240 \div 40 = 6.00$$

$$IPS_0 = (240 - 144) \div 40 = 2.40$$

Constant cash flow valuation model:

$$P_0 = \frac{(CF_0 - GPS_0)(1 + G)}{K_e - G}$$

$$= \frac{(9.75 - 6.15)(1.06)}{0.15 - 0.06}$$

$$= \$42.40$$

$$CF_0 = EPS_0 + (\text{Deprec.} \div 40)$$

$$= 6.00 + (150 \div 40) = 9.75$$

$$GPS_0 = IPS_0 + (\text{Deprec.} \div 40)$$

$$= 2.40 + (150 \div 40) = 6.15$$

e. Given this information, the stock is worth $42.40. Since it is selling for $47.70, it is over-priced and you should not purchase it. In fact, if you really believe the $42.40 price, you might short sell it.

f. "You must have missed some important information. The market price of $47.70 totally reflects all information available to the markets on the stock."

g. The required return would be 14%:

$$9\% + 1.0(14\% - 9\%) = 14\%$$

And the fair price would be $47.70:

$$\frac{\$3.60(1.06)}{0.14 - 0.06} = \$47.70$$

If the true beta is 1.0, the stock is fairly priced in the markets.

REVIEW PROBLEM #2

You have gathered the following data on five stocks which are assumed to have constant dividend growth. In addition, data are given on a sixth stock which is not expected to have constant growth.

Stock	1	2	3	4	5
Price	$111.11	$62.50	$125.00	$31.25	$11.76
D_1	$ 4.00	$ 3.00	$ 5.00	$ 1.00	$ 0.40
G	8%	8%	10%	12%	13%
Beta	0.6	0.8	1.0	1.2	1.4

Stock 6:

Last Dividend = $0.20
(Just Paid)

Growth in Dividends:
  Years 1-5   = 20%
  Year 6 Plus =   5%
  Beta   = 1.6

a. Calculate the expected returns on stocks 1 through 5.

b. Use this information to specify the security market line.

c. What should stock 6 be selling for today?

Solution

a. In the constant growth model:

$$P_0 = D_1/(K - G)$$

Therefore:

$$K = D_1/P_0 + G$$

Using this relationship for stocks 1 through 5:

$$K_1 = 4.00/111.11 + 0.08 = 11.6\%$$
$$K_2 = 3.00/62.50 \ + 0.08 = 12.8\%$$
$$K_3 = 5.00/125.00 + 0.10 = 14.0\%$$
$$K_4 = 1.00/31.25 \ + 0.12 = 15.2\%$$
$$K_5 = 0.40/11.76 \ + 0.13 = 16.4\%$$

b. A graph of the K values above against the betas of each indicates the following SML relationship:

$$K = 8\% + beta \ (6\%)$$

c. The price at which stock 6 should trade can be calculated as follows:

$$K_6 = 8\% + 1.6(6\%) = 17.6\%$$

Year	Div.	Price	Present Value at 17.6%
1	0.2400	—	0.2041
2	0.2880	—	0.2082
3	0.3456	—	0.2123
4	0.4147	—	0.2168
5	0.4977	—	0.2213
5	—	4.1475*	1.8439
		Total	2.9066

$$*P_6 = \frac{0.4977(1.05)}{0.176 - 0.05}$$

$$= 4.147$$

Stock 6 should sell for $2.91. If it is trading for more than $2.91, it is not providing a return commensurate with its (CAPM) risk and thus should not be purchased. If it is trading for less than $2.91, it should be bought.

QUESTIONS AND PROBLEMS

1. Discuss the relative pros and cons of using the following approaches to estimate a security's value:
   a. Par value
   b. Book value
   c. Liquidation value
   d. Replacement value
   e. Substitution value
   f. Present value

2. Why is it wrong to say that the worth of a stock is the present value of expected future earnings per share on that stock?

3. A friend of yours has just completed a computer program which estimates the *total* dividends which a firm is expected to pay and finds the present value of these at the discount rate of your choosing. The friend calls the result "Total Equity Value" and divides this by the number of shares now outstanding to calculate today's per-share value. Where is your friend's grand effort in error?

4. (CFA Exam Question)
   You have made a very preliminary analysis of three common stocks with the information set forth below. All three stocks have the same investment grade or quality. Assume that the same important numerical financial ratios and relationships which currently exist (such as price/earnings ratio, payout ratio, dividend yield, etc.) will extend into the future, with small cyclical variations, for as far as you can see. For the investments being considered, you require a rate of return of 10% a year. Based solely on the information given in this problem:
   a. Which, if any, of the stocks meet your requirements? Show your calculations.
   b. Which one of the three stocks is most attractive for purchase?

	Stock		
	A	*B*	*C*
Return on Total Assets	10%	8%	12%
Return on Stockholders' Equity	14%	12%	15%
Estimated Earnings per Share in Current Year	$2.00	$1.65	$1.45
Estimated Dividend per Share in Current Year	$1.00	$1.00	$1.00
Current Market Price	27	25	23

5. Dividends per share of Jacques's Jackets were $2.54 ten years ago. The latest dividend (just paid) was $5.00. The stock has a beta of 1.5. The risk-free rate is 6%, and the market risk premium is 4%.
   a. If future dividend growth is expected to be identical to historical growth, what should the market value of JJ stock be?
   b. If JJ stock is selling at the price found in part a, what are next year's expected dividend yield and capital appreciation yield?

6. Historically, RR Corporation has retained 60% of its profits in the business. This is expected to continue. Future asset returns (*ROA*) are expected to be 10%, and the debt-to-equity ratio will remain constant at 25%. The risk-free rate is 8%, RP_m can be taken as 5%, and beta is about 1.3. The present dividend (just paid) was $2.50, and the stock is selling at $45. Should you buy or sell the stock?

7. You have been requested to estimate a fair market price for a new stock offering. Long-run growth will be constant, and the following data apply:

Last Year's Dividend per Share	$3
Last Year's Earnings per Share	$4
After-Tax Profit Margin	2%
Debt-to-Equity Ratio	100%
Asset Turnover	4 times
RF	8%
RP_m	6%
Beta	1.5

  a. Estimate the firm's return on equity.
  b. Estimate the firm's expected dividend growth.
  c. Estimate the fair value of the stock.

8. First Arizona Bancgroup dividends are expected to grow with population, personal income, and inflation at about 8% (forever). The stock is selling at $40 and beta is 0.90. RF is 8% and RP_m is 5%. What is the implied growth rate in the stock's price if next year's dividend will be $2.00? Would you buy or sell the stock?

9. The common shares of GEB Resources are currently being traded on the OTC at $35 per share. A dividend of $2.00 was just paid. You expect this dividend per share to grow at a constant rate of 6%. What must your required return be if you believe the $35 price is reasonable?

10. Hulu Huup, Inc., has introduced a new line of huups to be used only by consenting adults. In evaluating the company, you believe earnings and dividends will grow at a rate of 20% for the next three years, after which the growth rate will fall to −5%. If the beta of HH is 2.0, the risk-free rate is 6%, and the market risk premium is 6%:
  a. Calculate the current fair value of the stock today if the last dividend (D_0) was $3.
  b. Calculate the value of the stock at the end of year 3 and at the end of year 4.
  c. If your projections hold true, what will the dividend yield be during year 3? Why is it so large compared with the required return?

11. Use the constant growth dividend valuation model to explain the economic forces which determine the price/earnings ratio of a broad stock market index. Obtain estimates of each of these as of the date you work this problem and compare the resulting P/E ratio with the actual P/E of the S&P 500.

12. A ratio which is widely used to gauge the level of the stock market is known as the price-to-book ratio (P/B ratio). It is calculated by dividing the market price of an individual stock (or a market index) by the accounting book value of the stock (or the index).
  a. Use the constant growth model to show what economic forces determine the P/B ratio.
  b. Under what conditions will the ratio be greater than 1.0?

13. Under what conditions will a stock's market value be the same as its accounting book value? Explain why.

14. Consider the following information about stocks *A* and *B*:

	Stock A	*Stock B*
Expected Dividends Next Year	$1.00	$2.33
Expected Constant *ROE*	20%	20%
Expected Retention Rate	70%	30%
Required Return on Securities of Equivalent Risk	20%	20%

a. Which stock is more sensitive to changes in risk premiums and growth expectations?

b. Is either a true growth stock?

15. Many portfolio managers claim to be growth-stock managers. When asked what this means, they often respond, "We purchase stocks which are expected to have greater than average price growth over the coming decade."

a. Is this a fair definition of a true growth stock? Why?

b. Would you expect true growth-stock managers to have larger portfolio *returns* than managers who purchase more income-oriented stocks?

c. Would you expect true growth-stock managers to have better *risk/return performance* than managers who purchase more income-oriented stocks?

16. A past issue of Value Line published the following estimates for DuPont:

$$\text{Beta} = 1.15 \qquad\qquad b_{1985} = 60\%$$
$$D_{1985} = \$3.10 \qquad\qquad ROE_{1985} = 15\%$$
$$D_{1988} = \$4.00$$

a. The stock was selling for $49. Estimate the expected returns from purchasing at $49 and receiving the dividend stream projected by Value Line.

b. The risk-free rate (long-term Treasuries) on this date was 11.5%. Using a market risk premium of 6%, what do you conclude about the purchase of DuPont shares?

c. What would a staunch believer in EMT say about your conclusion in part b?

17. South Central Bank Corporation is a Florida bank holding company with loans and deposits of $500,000,000 which are expected to grow at close to the local population estimates of 4% per year. Because of the continued emphasis the bank wishes to place on both wholesale (business) banking and its traditional retail business, its yield spread is expected to remain around 4%. Last year this yield spread (return on loans less cost of funds) provided a *net* interest income of $20,000,000. Expenses and taxes are expected to be 70% of net interest income. Earnings are now $6,000,000, or $5.00 per share. Dividend payout is, and will remain, about 50%. A fair return on South Central's stock would be 13.5%.

a. What is a share of South Central worth today?

b. If the stock is selling at $30, would you suggest it to either a retired couple or a young surgeon? (Select only one.)

CHAPTER

14 Stock Trading

The extent to which people should actively manage their common stock portfolios by using various forms of speculation and arbitrage or passively manage their portfolios by using a buy-hold strategy depends upon two factors: their philosophy about how the market actually works and their knowledge.

Philosophically, one might believe that actual prices can be unrelated to a security's inherent intrinsic value for extended time intervals. Temporary periods of overoptimism and pessimism might drive prices above or below their economic worth. Fads might arise and cause excessively high P/E ratios in some industries as other industries fall from favor and sell at depressed P/Es. Heavy trading by financial institutions in particular types of stocks could drive prices up if the institutions were buying and drive prices down if they were selling. If institutions restricted their portfolio holdings to particular types of stocks, a *two-tier* market might arise with stocks favored by the institutions selling at higher average P/E ratios than those not so favored. If the stock market is affected by such forces, then the trading profits available to a speculator could be quite handsome.

At the other philosophic extreme, one might believe that actual market prices always reflect the stock's fair economic worth. Prices would change over time, of course, but these price changes would simply reflect the market's ever changing assessment of the worth of the stock in light of new information. Prices would rise when market participants become more optimistic about the future and fall when they become more pessimistic. But such optimism and pessimism are caused by the market's best available expectations of future cash dividends, not by temporary fads. Prices of stocks in some industries will rise, and in others they will fall. The explanation is not to be found in temporary fads but, instead, in the above- (or below-) average earnings and risk prospects of that industry. If stock prices in such industries do eventually reverse themselves, it is not because a fad has run its course. It would be due, instead, to new information which has become available and caused a revision of the industry's earnings and risk prospects. In sum, this view of the world is that of a strict belief in the efficient market theory (EMT). Proponents of this sort of security market would follow a passive, buy-hold investment policy.

The extent of one's knowledge will also affect the trading strategy employed. For example, someone with little training in stock valuation (and with no desire to obtain the training) might be best advised to use a passive style. Even if the person doesn't believe in the strict version of the EMT, the marginal speculative profits available from obtaining the training may not be worth the large dollar and time costs necessary to obtain it.[1]

Conversely, people with unique skills might employ them to earn speculative profits. But if these potential profits are large, there will be considerable competition among such experts. As a result, of those experts who obtain new information, the fastest have a better chance of earning larger profits. The importance of obtaining new information rapidly has caused a high degree of specialization. At its broadest level this specialization takes the form of trying to earn speculative profits by (1) calling turns in the aggregate market or (2) attempting to find individual under- and overpriced securities. For example, some investment advisers admit they are unable to analyze specific companies but, instead, claim to be able to forecast future turns in the level of aggregate stock prices. Other investment advisers make no pretense about being able to time the market, but claim to be capable of finding individual under- or overvalued stocks.

Throughout the rest of this chapter we review the basic policies and procedures followed by both stock *investors* and stock *speculators*. To some degree the material is an overview of topics covered in more depth later in the book. For example, the discussion on stock speculation in this chapter is expanded upon in Chapters 20 through 22. Nonetheless, it is useful to develop a broad perspective at this point.

STOCK INVESTMENT POLICY

An Efficiently Priced Market

The concept of an efficiently priced security market is the foundation on which all stock investment rules are developed. Because of its importance, it is useful to review efficient market theory again. First, proponents of the efficient market theory believe the fair value of a stock is determined by expectations—expectations of future economic profits, risks, and interest rates. For example, assume that we are valuing the common shares of Dow Chemical Company and believe the constant dividend growth model applies. To assess the firm's fair value, we would estimate Dow's expected dividend growth rate and determine a required return given the perceived risk of owning the stock plus existing risk-free interest rates. Perhaps our estimates result in a dividend growth of 8%, a required return of 14%, and a current dividend of $1.45. We would believe the fair value of Dow stock should be $26.10:

$$\frac{\$1.45(1.08)}{0.14 - 0.08} = \$26.10$$

---

[1]People with little knowledge of the security markets could, of course, buy the services of experts (brokers, investment advisers, security analysts, etc.). But without the training themselves how are they to know who the experts are?

This belief that prices are related to underlying economic values immediately separates EMTers from strict technicians, who believe that the potential stream of future earnings and risks have no effect upon market prices.

Second, securities which are not selling at their perceived fair values will be bought or sold until actual market prices are identical to their perceived fair values. For example, if Dow is actually trading at $30, speculators will immediately sell the issue until its price is driven to $26.10. Because the profits from such speculation could conceivably be quite large, there will be considerable competition among speculators. This competition should cause rapid price adjustment to fair values. It won't take weeks for the price to fall from $30 to $26.10. Theoretically, the adjustment should be instantaneous. It is at this point that the fundamentalists and those believing in EMT separate. Fundamentalists believe a substantial lag can exist in price adjustments to new information. EMTers believe the market is more efficient in adjusting price levels.

Third, the intensive competition among speculators will ultimately result in everyone's having the same set of information. Since speculative profits will be available from obtaining new information more rapidly than others do, there would be considerable competition for new information. In the extreme this would result in everyone's obtaining new information at the same time. This doesn't mean that every market participant needs to physically receive each piece of information. Instead, it can be obtained indirectly by employing experts who receive it directly and then pass it on to clients. If everyone receives the same set of information, each will have common expectations and estimates of fair stock values. The demand curve for any stock will be perfectly elastic. That is, stock prices will be unaffected by temporary imbalances between desire to buy versus desire to sell a stock in the secondary market. If desire to buy a stock at a single point in time exceeds desire to sell, then an infinitesimally higher price would attract a flood of potential sellers.

Finally, prices will change as new information becomes available (not because of temporary demand/supply conditions). For example, if Dow announces a new product line which the market believes will cause dividend growth rates to increase to 8.5% but have no effect upon risk, the stock's price will increase instantaneously to $28.60:

$$\frac{\$1.45(1.085)}{0.14 - 0.085} = \$28.60$$

New information is by definition unexpected or random. If information about the earnings prospects and risks of a firm becomes available to the market with an observable trend (for example, a piece of good news is normally followed by three other good announcements), this trend will be already discounted in today's prices. The only types of news events which will affect prices are those which are unexpected. For example, if the Federal Reserve announces an increase in the growth rate of money, the announcement would have no effect upon prices if it had already been expected by speculators. However, if the money growth rate had been higher or lower than expected, security prices might change.

The notion of a perfectly priced market is based upon a number of assumptions which probably aren't strictly true in the real world. For example, it takes some time for new information to be made available to most market participants. As a result, a lag in price adjustments to new information might occur. Panel A in Figure 14-1 illustrates this effect. At dates 1 and 2 new information enters the market (unfavorable news on date 1 and favorable news on date 2). According to a strict interpretation of EMT, prices would adjust instantaneously, as shown by the solid line. However, if a lag occurs in the distribution of the information, prices would adjust

FIGURE 14-1 *Strict EMT Versus Economic EMT*

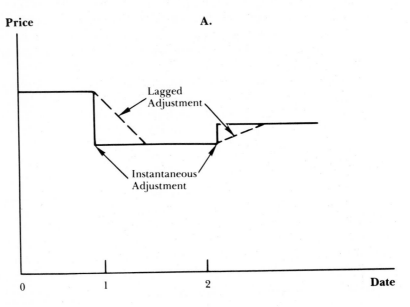

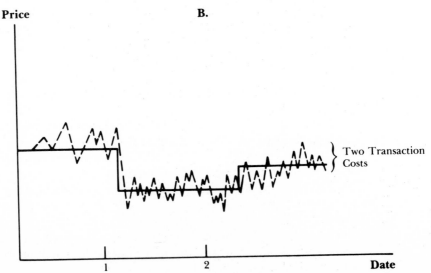

as shown by the dashed line. The existence, length, and potential for profiting on such lags were discussed in Chapter 10, when various empirical studies were reviewed.

Another assumption of a strict interpretation of EMT is that transaction costs do not exist. In practice, however, transaction costs do exist and can lead to market prices which differ from intrinsic values. Panel B of Figure 14-1 shows the effect of transaction costs on prices when lags to new information don't exist. As long as market prices don't depart from intrinsic values by more than two transaction costs (a purchase plus a sale), speculation will be unprofitable. Even people who own seats on the organized exchanges incur transaction costs. Although they do not pay brokers' commissions, they do incur clerical trading costs, opportunity time costs, and risk costs of overweighting or underweighting a particular stock in their portfolios. Similar to transaction costs are tax impacts. Individuals who own a stock on which they have an unrealized capital gain would be inclined not to sell it if prices rose somewhat above intrinsic values, because taxes would have to be paid immediately on now *realized* gains. (Of course, nontaxed organizations, such as pension funds, would not have to worry about differences in realized versus unrealized capital gains.)

In a *strict* EMT world, stock prices would not depart from their estimated fair economic values, and there would be no profits available from additional speculation. The best trading strategy would be to buy and hold. In a world with small transaction costs and tax *imperfections*, prices might depart from their fair values. However, after subtracting transaction costs and taxes from any gross trading profits, the best strategy would still be to buy and hold. While the markets would not be strictly efficient, they would still be what is referred to as *economically efficient*.

Trading in an Economically Efficient Market

In an economically efficient market, prices may depart slightly from intrinsic values. However, no trading strategy would be able to beat a simple buy-hold policy after all transaction costs, taxes, and risks are considered. If there were a system which could beat the buy-hold strategy, it would soon be discovered and used so actively that it would no longer work. For example, assume we knew that stock prices consistently seemed to be low on Mondays and high on Fridays. If this is true, we should actively buy on Monday and sell on Friday. But as we do so along with other people, prices would become higher on Monday and lower on Friday until the rule no longer worked. Such profitable trading rules must self-destruct.[2] Prices might still be lower on Monday than on Friday, but after all transaction costs, taxes, and risk considerations, the rule would not be profitable.

A stock *investment* portfolio should be tailored to the portfolio's stated goals and should consider the following factors:

---

[2]The argument is often made that a profitable trading rule will not self-destruct if it is kept secret. This is possible. But remember that there are a large number of very sophisticated people looking for profitable trading rules. The rule may not remain secret for long. In addition, it is likely to be more profitable for someone who possesses a profitable rule to sell it to others than to trade on it alone with a small amount of capital.

TABLE 14-1 *S&P Composite Weightings by Economic Sector*

	Percentage of Index Value		
Sector	*1980*	*1984*	*1988*
Consumer Spending	23.3%	24.3%	30.3%
Energy	25.2	15.3	11.8
Capital Spending	18.0	20.0	18.2
Financial/Interest Sensitive	15.9	18.0	20.6
Basic Industry	11.5	7.3	8.1
Consumer Durable	2.1	5.8	5.4
Transportation	2.0	2.4	2.6
Miscellaneous	2.0	6.9	3.0
	100.0%	100.0%	100.0%

SOURCE: *Portfolio Strategy*, Goldman Sachs Research, Goldman Sachs & Company, September 1980, January 1985, and January 1989.

Diversification. The most important rule for investors to follow is to diversify. This can be accomplished quite simply in a number of ways. For example, shares of a well-diversified mutual fund could be bought. Or stock investments could be spread across a large number of different industries. Perhaps the best way to diversify would be to purchase an index fund. Ideally, the index fund's assets would mirror the aggregate market portfolio. According to the traditional version of the CAPM, the best portfolio of risky investments is the market portfolio, which we've referred to as portfolio *M*. If, for example, the common shares of American Telephone & Telegraph represent 3.0% of all stocks traded in the stock market, then 3.0% of one's stock portfolio should be in AT&T. Since the market portfolio of all stocks can't be precisely defined, various market proxies such as the Standard & Poor's Composite Index are used. There are also a number of ways of classifying the shares in, say, the S&P Composite. Two standard ways are shown in Tables 14-1 and 14-2. Table 14-1 shows the percentage market value weightings of various economic sectors in the S&P Composite, while Table 14-2 shows the percentage market value weightings of a variety of different industry classifications. Of course, it would be quite expensive to set up such a diverse portfolio, and the required initial investment would be large. Index funds have been developed to overcome such obstacles.

Risk Level. Once a well-diversified portfolio has been created, its total risk should be set at a level consistent with its objectives. As with the creation of effective diversification, there are a number of ways in which this could be done. Per the CAPM, the mix of risky stocks and (nominally) risk-free bonds should be altered. If the investor wishes a portfolio risk level which is 20% less risky than the aggregate market, then 80% of the portfolio would be placed in a broadly diversified group of common stocks and the remainder in risk-free securities. Depending upon the portfolio's expected horizon date, these risk-free securities would vary only in terms of duration. T-bills, T-notes, T-bonds, commercial paper, repurchase agreements, and other high-quality paper can be used as the risk-free portion. In practice, high-quality

TABLE 14-2 *S&P Composite Weightings by Selected Industries*

	Percentage of Index Value		
Sector	*1980*	*1984*	*1988*
Oils	19.45%	13.39%	10.71%
Office and Business Equipment	6.71	8.51	5.85
Telephone	5.41	4.39	5.75
Drugs	3.93	4.26	6.26
Electric Power	3.38	4.73	4.61
Chemicals	3.34	2.12	3.94
Foods	2.42	3.46	3.49
Automobiles	2.39	3.08	2.84
Banks	2.13	2.21	3.30
Machinery	2.06	1.07	1.52
Aerospace	1.98	2.40	1.92
Electronics	1.94	1.34	1.03
Natural Gas	1.69	1.29	0.91
Tobacco	1.42	1.72	2.76
Beverage	1.16	1.52	2.39

SOURCE: *Portfolio Strategy*, Goldman Sachs Research, Goldman Sachs & Company, September 1980, January 1985, and January 1989.

corporate bonds, municipal bonds, low- or high-coupon issues, etc., are used to alter the bond/stock mix and still take advantage of tax laws and duration and liquidity requirements.

Another way of achieving the desired portfolio risk level is to restrict portfolio holdings to common stocks with a specified average risk level. For example, if a beta of 0.8 is desired, only stocks with a beta of, say, between 0.7 and 0.9 are held. The advantage of this is that the number of securities held is limited (cutting down brokerage fees). The disadvantage is that the extent of diversification is limited.

Closely related to beta rankings are the quality rankings assigned to stocks by various investment advisory services. The best-known rankings are those used by Standard & Poor's. To develop the ratings, Standard & Poor's uses a computerized scoring system based upon a stock's earnings and dividend record for the most recent ten years and assigns the following quality ratings:

A+	Highest	B+	Average	C	Lowest
A	High	B	Below Average	D	In Reorganization
A−	Above Average	B−	Lower		

The ratings are designed to provide information about total diversifiable and nondiversifiable risk in stock. They should not be confused with bond ratings, which address default risk characteristics only.

A number of empirical studies have examined the extent to which the S&P stock-quality ratings are related to a stock's beta coefficient and future rates of return. Table 14-3 presents the results of one such study conducted by Haugen. Using 806 New York Stock Exchange common stocks rated by S&P in 1956, Haugen related the quality rating as of that date to various risk measures and average monthly rates of re-

TABLE 14-3 *Stock-Quality Ratings and Subsequent Risk and Return*

(1) 1956 Quality Rating	(2) Beta	(3) Return Standard Deviation	(4) (5) Number of Stocks		(6) Survival Rate	(7) Arithmetic Average Return
			Start	*End*		
A+	0.77	0.0014	102	81	0.79	0.008
A	0.78	0.0014	149	111	0.74	0.009
A−	0.80	0.0014	130	92	0.71	0.010
B+	0.94	0.0019	198	106	0.54	0.010
B	1.13	0.0028	93	51	0.55	0.012
B−	1.21	0.0033	74	31	0.42	0.011
C	1.38	0.0046	60	22	0.37	0.012

SOURCE: R. Haugen, "Do Common Stock Quality Ratings Predict Risk?" *Financial Analysts Journal* (March–April 1979): 68–73.

turn between 1956 and 1971. Beta levels as shown in column 2 increase consistently from 0.77 for stocks rated A+ to 1.38 for stocks rated C. Standard deviations also increase as quality ratings are poorer. Columns 4, 5, and 6 provide some information on the survival rate of stocks in each quality rating. For example, of the 102 firms rated A+ in 1956, 81 were still being traded in 1971. Haugen referred to this as a survival rate of 79%. Survival rates decreased as quality ratings declined. However, as Haugen pointed out, mergers into other firms accounted for much of the nonsurvival rate. The survival rate is not a good bankruptcy estimate. Finally, arithmetic average monthly rates of return were largest for the stocks with the lowest quality ratings.

Timing. Because, according to EMT, stock prices are always equal to their intrinsic values (or no further away than the size of a buy-sell transaction cost), investment timing is really no problem. Buy when excess cash is temporarily available and sell when cash is needed. Over any investment time horizon this simple buy-hold strategy would be expected to yield larger returns for a given risk level than would attempts to time purchases and sales in anticipation of future price moves. Market prices are presumed to always be fair, and speculative attempts at timing would lead only to the larger transaction costs associated with active trading and the possibly greater risks associated with less than full diversification. The empirical evidence in support of and in conflict with the efficient market theory was presented in Chapter 10. While some evidence runs counter to the EMT, a large body of research suggests that the efficient market model is a better depiction of reality than many people might believe.

Investment Horizon and Duration. As noted earlier, the fundamental concepts underlying proper bond selection and stock selection are the same. Only the relative emphases given to particular ideas differ. This is true of horizon date analysis. Bond investment techniques are able to deal rather explicitly with duration principles, since a reasonably certain series of cash flows and discount rates can be specified. In common stock investment, on the other hand, both the cash flow series and the appropriate discount rate are more uncertain, resulting in only approximate duration values. Nonetheless, common stock investment should also consider duration.

The measurement of a stock's duration depends upon the expected sequence of future cash flows to be received by existing shareholders. If the constant dividend growth model applies, Boquist, Racette, and Schlarbaum have derived the formula for a stock's duration, D_i, to be:

$$D_i = \frac{1.0}{K_i - G_i} \tag{14.1}$$

for the case of continuously compounded dividend growth.[3] For example, if the required return on a stock is 14% and expected (continuous) dividend growth is 8%, the stock's expected duration is 16⅔ years. Two comments about this duration measure are appropriate. First, in the constant growth case, D_i is simply the reciprocal of the stock's expected dividend yield. In our example the 14% required return is expected to be earned by the receipt of an 8% capital gains yield plus a 6% dividend yield. Dividing the dividend yield into 1.0 results in the expected duration (1.0 ÷ 0.06 = 16⅔). Second, the expected duration measure can be quite sensitive to small changes in either expected growth or required returns. In the example, a change in growth expectations from 8% to 10% results in a change in expected D_i from 16⅔ years to 25 years. Nonetheless, common stock duration should be considered. The stock portfolio of a young investor who does not plan to withdraw any capital from the portfolio until retirement some 30–40 years away may be weighted heavily toward high-growth, low-dividend-yield stocks. Individuals with retirement needs within the next 5–10 years would stress higher dividend yields and lower growth components.

If stock duration is to be stressed, care should be taken to assure adequate diversification. If only high-dividend-yield stocks are selected, there is the danger that considerable diversifiable risk remains in the portfolio. Firms which pay high dividend yields tend to be affected by similar types of economic events. The same is true for low-dividend-yield stocks. Probably the best way of obtaining the desired level of duration is to mix short-duration, risk-free securities with an investment in the market portfolio. For example, assume that Bill Williams intends to retire soon and has an investment horizon date of, say, 10 years (the weighted average date at which cash will be needed). Also assume he intends to proxy the market portfolio by investments in an index fund which holds value-weighted holdings in the S&P Composite Index. If the S&P dividend yield is 5% (and the constant growth model applies), its expected duration is 20 years. In addition, one-year T-bills could be bought. To obtain the desired 10-year duration, 47.4% of his investment could be placed in the index fund and the other 52.6% in T-bills. This is found by letting X represent the percentage of funds placed in one-year T-bills, letting $(1 - X)$ represent the percentage placed in the 20-year S&P Composite, and solving the following equation:

---

[3]For discrete compounding:

$$D_i = \frac{1 + K_i}{K_i - G_i}$$

$$10 \text{ years} = X(1 \text{ year}) + (1 - X)(20 \text{ years})$$

or

$$10 \text{ years} = 0.526(1 \text{ year}) + (0.474)(20 \text{ years})$$

This portfolio would provide both the desired duration and rather extensive diversification.

This example may have suggested to many readers that there is a relationship between the beta of a stock and its duration. In fact, this was seen in Chapter 12, when bond betas and duration were discussed. Symbolically, if D_{it} = the duration on stock i at date t, D_{mt} = the duration on the market portfolio at date t, σ_i = the standard deviation of the instantaneous changes in required returns on stock i, σ_m = the standard deviation of the instantaneous changes in required returns on the market portfolio, and r_{im} = the correlation coefficient between changes in required returns on stock i and the market portfolio, then:

$$\text{Beta}_i = \left[\frac{D_{it}}{D_{mt}} \right] \left[\frac{\sigma_i \times r_{im}}{\sigma_m} \right] \tag{14.2}$$

Equation 14.2 shows clearly that firms with low dividend yields and high growth have higher degrees of nondiversifiable risk than do equivalent firms with higher dividend yields and lower growth. A stock's expected growth rate and its beta are positively correlated.

Tax Factors. Returns on common stocks arise from both yearly dividend yields, which are taxed at ordinary tax rates, and capital gains, which are often taxed at the lower capital gains rate. When the capital gains tax rate is lower than the ordinary tax rate, many practitioners tailor a stock portfolio's mix of dividend yield and growth components to the tax characteristics of its owner. The procedure is similar to that used on high-coupon versus low-coupon bonds. For example, consider two stocks which have identical risks and therefore identical after-tax required returns. The before-tax expected returns may vary, however, if the dividend-yield/price-growth mix is different. Returns on the firm with the larger price growth rate would be taxed at an effectively lower rate and therefore would sell at lower before-tax required and expected returns. Individuals in higher-than-average tax brackets would purchase stocks with high growth rates in order to minimize taxes and maximize after-tax returns. Individuals in lower-than-average tax brackets (or zero brackets for charitable organizations and pension funds) would purchase the high-dividend-yield stocks.

To economists who have studied this problem, however, the impact of taxes upon before- and after-tax returns is not quite so clear. It is beyond the scope of this text to get into all the arguments about dividend policy. However, we can note that there is some empirical evidence by Litzenberger and Ramaswamy which suggests that low-dividend-yield stocks do sell at lower before-tax expected returns. This is in contradiction to other evidence by Black and Scholes, which suggested that the dividend-yield effects are negligible or nonexistent. Both theoretically and empirically the question remains unresolved. In practice, stock portfolios can be designed with an eye to reducing tax liabilities, but considerable care should be taken to ensure that this doesn't leave the portfolio with large amounts of potentially diversifiable risk.

Year-end tax swaps can be used in the investment portfolio to delay tax payments in the same way they are used in bond portfolios. For example, assume that you own a portfolio of stocks which is diversified by having one stock from each of the various S&P industry categories. Perhaps one of these stocks is shares in Dow Chemical which were bought at $35 but are now selling at $25. You could sell Dow for a *realized* taxable loss of $10 and immediately reinvest the $25 proceeds in a close substitute for Dow—say, Union Carbide. This swap leaves you with a $25 investment in the chemical industry but allows you to take an immediate tax savings on the $10 realized loss. If your capital gains tax bracket is 25%, you save $2.50 in taxes, which can be invested. Eventually, this $2.50 tax refund will have to be repaid to the government when Union Carbide shares are sold. But you receive the interest earnings on the $2.50 until Union Carbide is indeed sold.

Marketability. Finally, a portfolio's marketability should fit its stated marketability objectives. Normally, this does not present a problem to small- and medium-sized portfolios, since a large number of common stocks exist which can be sold quickly and at low transaction costs in the secondary markets. In addition, the use of money market instruments can increase portfolio marketability. For very large portfolios (say, a $5 billion pension fund) marketability can present a larger problem, however. In such cases the portfolio must be invested in a large number of different stocks, each having a reasonable block trading market.

STOCK SPECULATION

Overview

Pure investment portfolios are rare. Instead most individuals and institutions develop some notion of what their investment portfolio should be and then alter it to take advantage of what they perceive to be temporary pricing anomalies within the market. While there are numerous ways in which this is done in actual practice, a logical process to create speculative stock portfolios is shown in Figure 14-2. In most respects this process is identical to the process of bond speculation discussed in Chapter 12. First, long-run portfolio objectives are specified and a baseline investment portfolio is designed (but not actually bought) which should meet these objectives. For example, the pure investment portfolio for a $20 million pension fund might be characterized as follows:

1. Maintain a beta of 0.5 by placing half of all funds in high-coupon, long-term Treasury bonds and the other half in common stocks.
2. The common stock portfolio will be broadly diversified by owning shares in the three largest firms of each S&P industry.

FIGURE 14-2 *The Process of Stock Speculation*

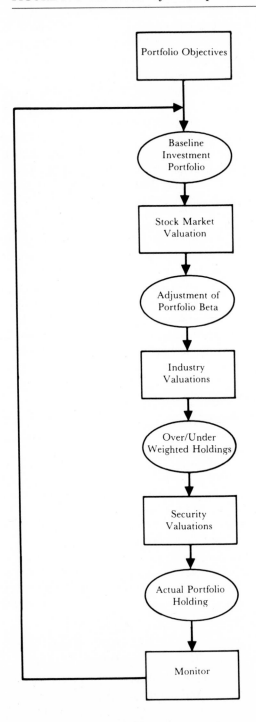

3. The percentage investment in each industry will be equal to the percentage which that industry represents of the S&P Composite Index.

Once the investment portfolio is determined, it can be altered in ways which its manager hopes will improve the fund's long-run risk/return performance. This can be done by attempting to "time the market" by periodically adjusting the stock/bond mix, by identifying industries which are under- or overvalued and adjusting the industry weightings in the portfolio to reflect the extent of this price discrepancy, and finally by identifying individual securities which are under- or overvalued and adjusting the actual mix of securities held in each industry accordingly. For example, assume a portfolio manager believes that the stock market is currently undervalued and likely to rise dramatically during the next year. To take advantage of this, the stock/bond mix would be changed to increase the portfolio's current beta. In addition, if the manager believes that consumer durable stocks are priced much lower than they should be, but electric power shares are overpriced, then he or she would overweight the consumer durable industry and underweight electric power shares. Finally, the actual stocks held within each industry would be determined, based upon which appear to be the most undervalued. Each of these steps is discussed at length in Chapters 20 through 22.

For the rest of this chapter we will examine stock speculation procedures using two stocks as examples: Dow Chemical and Union Carbide. The data and procedure used are similar to those in a question asked on a past Chartered Financial Analysts exam. The discussion does not include an analysis of market timing and includes only a little industry analysis. However, it is a good overview of the steps required in the analysis of a single stock.

Dow Chemical and Union Carbide

At the end of 1984 Union Carbide Corporation was the third-largest U.S. chemical producer, and Dow Chemical Company was the second-largest. The product mixes of both companies are basically similar, although some differences exist. Union Carbide produces ethylene, which is subsequently used in producing many of its chemical and plastic products. Final industrial products include thermoplastics, industrial gases, and ferroalloys. Consumer products include Prestone auto products, insect repellents, Linde jewelry, Glad disposable containers, and Eveready batteries. In 1984 3% of revenues were spent on research, and international operations accounted for 31% of the firm's revenue. Revenues and operating income were classified as follows:

	Revenues	Operating Income
Chemicals and Plastics	52%	40%
Gases, Metals, and Carbons	26	28
Consumer Products	22	32
	100%	100%

Dow Chemical produces organic and inorganic chemicals, magnesium, pesticides, and pharmaceuticals. Consumer products include Saran Wrap and styrofoam. In 1984 4% of revenues were spent on research, and international operations accounted for 52% of sales. Revenues and operating income were classified as follows:

	Revenues	Operating Income
Chemicals	45%	30%
Plastics	37	78
Bioproducts and Consumer Items	18	−8
	100%	100%

Based on various statistical data for several years ending in 1984, the CFA exam asked test-takers to:

1. Characterize the historical growth and stability of the physical volume of chemical shipments.
2. Determine which of the firms historically had the greater return on equity (ROE) and specify why.
3. Determine which of the firms had the greater liquidity and financial flexibility.
4. Estimate the growth rate of dividends which each firm is likely to sustain.
5. Determine which of the two companies should be added to a pension fund portfolio and explain why.

Historical Growth

An understanding of the historical growth pattern of an industry is important because it can point out various potentials and risks which might be experienced again in the future. Table 14-4 presents various information on chemical industry sales and general economic statistics. There are any number of ways in which these statistics could be evaluated, many discussed in Chapter 21. Among the more important techniques is regression analysis, in which one variable is statistically related to another.[4] One variable is referred to as the *dependent* variable and is said to be explained by the *independent* variable. For example, chemical industry sales could be treated as the dependent variable and related to an independent variable such as *GNP* as follows:

$$\widetilde{RS}_t = a + b(\overline{GNP}_t) + \tilde{e}_t \qquad (14.3)$$

where $\widetilde{RS}_t$ is the real value of chemical industry sales in year t (the third column in Table 14-4); GNP_t = real GNP in year t (the fourth column in Table 14-4), and $\tilde{e}_t$ = a random error term in year t representing the difference between the actual value of $\widetilde{RS}_t$ and the value of $\widetilde{RS}_t$ estimated by the statistical model. The a term is a statis-

---

[4]Regression analysis is treated more thoroughly in Chapter 21. For now we will simply indicate the nature of its potential use in a security analysis.

TABLE 14-4 *Chemical and Allied Product Shipments Compared to Gross National Product, 1970–1982*

| | | Wholesale Price Index | | | |
| | | Billions of 1972 Dollars | | Wholesale Price Index 1972 = 100 | |
Year	Chemical Shipments (Billions of Current $)	Chemical Shipments	GNP	Chemical	All Industrial Commodities
1982	172.8	61.6	1480	280.5	264.9
1981	180.5	65.4	1512	276.2	257.9
1980	162.5	65.0	1475	250.0	232.8
1979	147.7	69.2	1479	213.4	200.5
1978	129.9	68.1	1439	290.8	177.6
1977	118.2	63.9	1370	185.0	165.5
1976	104.1	57.9	1298	179.6	154.7
1975	90.4	52.0	1234	173.9	145.5
1974	83.6	59.33	1248	140.9	130.5
1973	65.0	61.6	1255	105.6	106.8
1972	57.3	57.3	1186	100.0	100.0
1971	50.9	50.9	1122	100.0	96.7
1970	48.5	49.4	1086	98.1	93.3

SOURCES: *Predicasts Basebook*, published annually by Predicasts, Inc., Cleveland, Ohio: 1984, p. 329; 1983, p. 344; *Survey of Current Business*, United States Department of Commerce, various editions.

tical estimate of real industry sales when real *GNP* is zero. In this particular model we would expect it to be zero since there could not be any chemical sales without some positive level of *GNP*. However, if real industry sales are not linearly related to real *GNP* and we use data for a relatively small number of years, a positive or negative *intercept term* (*a*) might be obtained. The *b* term is a regression coefficient which estimates the change in the dependent variable for each unit change in the independent variable and is often referred to as the *slope* of the regression line. Besides estimates of the intercept and slope terms, a variety of additional statistical information is given. At this point only the value of R^2 is used. R^2 is defined as the percentage of variation in the dependent variable explained by variation in the independent variable.

If Equation 14.3 were estimated using least-squares regression analysis on the data in Table 14-4, the results would be:

$$\widetilde{RS}_t = \$8.66 + 0.037\ (\widetilde{GNP}_t) + \tilde{e}_t$$

$$R^2 = 78.55\%$$

In other words, when *GNP* is zero, real industry sales are estimated to be $8.66 billion. For each dollar change in real *GNP*, real industry sales are estimated to increase by $0.037. This can be interpreted to mean that real chemical industry sales are estimated to be 3.7% of real *GNP*.

This regression and three others are displayed in Table 14-5. The second regres-

TABLE 14-5 *Industry Regression Results*

Regression Number	Model Estimates	R^2
1	Real Industry Sales = 8.66 + 0.037 (Real GNP)	78.55%
2	ln(Real Sales) = 3.90 + 0.0214 (Time)	58.42%
3	ln(Real GNP) = 6.98 + 0.028 (Time)	94.24%
4	% Change in Real Sales = −4.91 + 2.49 (% Change Real GNP)	75.81%

sion relates the natural log values of real industry sales to time. Such regressions are discussed more fully in Chapter 21. But for now we can say that when the natural log of a variable is regressed against time, the slope term represents the average compound growth rate of the variable. For example, regression 2 in Table 14-5 indicates a compound growth in real industry sales of 2.14%. Regression 3 indicates a compound growth in real *GNP* of 2.8% over the same thirteen-year time interval. As indicated by the higher R^2 on real *GNP* in regression 3, *GNP* growth was more stable than the growth of the chemical industry. Regression 4 relates percentage change in real industry sales to percentage changes in real *GNP*. The slope term of 2.49 is interpreted to mean that for each percentage point change in real *GNP*, real industry sales change by 2.49 percentage points. For example, if real *GNP* increases (or decreases) by 4.0% in one year, real industry sales are estimated to increase (or decrease) by 9.96% (2.49 × 4.0%). This is a measure of how sensitive industry sales are to changes in aggregate economic output. The larger the slope term in regression 4, the larger the beta of the stocks of such firms would be expected to be.

An analysis of both Tables 14-4 and 14-5 suggests the following important points:

1. Real *GNP* had been increasing about 2.8% per year. In contrast, real industry shipments had been increasing by 2.14%. Over this time period, industry sales were a declining portion of *GNP*.

2. More important, however, is the sensitivity of industry sales to changes in *GNP*. This sensitivity suggests that the stocks of firms in the industry will have betas in excess of 1.0.

3. Most of the differences in the price levels of chemical goods compared with those of all other industrial goods occurred in 1974 and 1975. This can be traced to the heavy dependence which chemical firms have on oil and to the oil embargo which occurred in the mid-1970s.

Historical *ROE*

Table 14-6 provides data relevant to each firm's *ROE* for the 10 years ending in 1984. Looking first at the *ROE* figures, two things are apparent. First, over the 10-year period, Dow usually had a larger return on equity than did Union Carbide. The average *ROE* for Dow was 15.1%, whereas the average *ROE* for Union Carbide was

TABLE 14-6 *Dow and Union Carbide Profitability Ratios, 1975–1984*

	Return on Equity		Return on Assets		Long-Term Debt to Equity		Asset Turnover		Net Profit Margin	
	Dow	UC	Dow	UC	Dow	UC	Dow	UC	Dow	UC
1984 (est.)	10.0%	7.7%	6.8%	5.3%	48%	46%	1.5	1.3	4.6%	4.1%
1983	5.8	4.3	3.7	2.9	56	48	1.4	1.2	2.7	2.4
1982	4.4	6.1	2.6	4.2	69	47	1.2	1.2	2.1	3.4
1981	11.5	12.5	6.4	8.9	81	40	1.3	1.4	4.8	6.4
1980	18.1	14.2	10.2	10.2	78	39	1.3	1.5	7.6	6.7
1979	20.1	13.9	11.2	9.6	79	44	1.3	1.6	8.5	6.1
1978	16.9	10.9	9.1	7.7	86	41	1.1	1.5	8.4	5.0
1977	17.8	11.5	10.1	7.8	76	47	1.1	1.4	8.9	5.5
1976	21.4	14.5	13.0	9.5	65	52	1.2	1.4	10.8	7.0
1975	25.1	13.9	15.3	9.5	64	46	1.2	0.8	12.6	6.7
Average	15.1	10.9	8.8	7.6	70	45	1.3	1.3	7.1	5.3

Source: Various issues of Value Line Investment Survey, 1978–1985 (New York: Arnold Bernhard & Co.).

10.9%. But before concluding that Dow was, for the period studied, a much better-managed firm, we need to understand why this was the case. Second, both firms had recently had declining *ROE*s—much lower than in the late 1970s. The cause of this must also be understood in order to develop sound predictions of future equity returns.

Let's consider the first question: Why did Dow rather consistently have the larger *ROE*? As shown in the prior chapter, a firm's return on equity is determined by the returns on its asset investments and the amount of debt used by the firm:

$$\frac{\text{Return on}}{\text{Equity}} = \frac{\text{Return on}}{\text{Assets}} \times \frac{\text{Total Assets}}{\text{Equity}}$$

$$ROE = \frac{\text{Income}}{\text{Assets}} \times \frac{\text{Assets}}{\text{Equity}}$$

Using the average values for the 10-year period:[5]

Firm	ROE	=	ROA	×	Debt Use
Dow	15.1%	=	8.8%	×	1.70
UC	10.9%	=	7.6%	×	1.45

A large part of Dow's greater *ROE* came from its greater use of debt. For every $1 of equity, Dow used $0.70 in debt, while Union Carbide used only $0.45 in debt. Dow

[5]The equations are slightly wrong because of rounding. Also note that Table 14-6 does not show the ratio *TA/E* but, instead, the ratio of long-term debt to equity. In practice it is common to exclude current liabilities and not deal with actual total assets, but to use total assets less current liabilities instead. Once this is done the ratio *TA/E* is equal to long-term debt-to-equity ratio plus 1.0.

did have a slightly larger return on its asset investment, but the major reason for its greater *ROE* was its greater use of debt.

There is nothing particularly wrong with this. But it does mean that Dow probably had a larger beta than did Union Carbide. And much of the larger *ROE* earned by Dow was due simply to increased leverage, as opposed to significantly better management. If Union Carbide had used the same amount of debt as Dow, its average *ROE* would have been much closer to Dow's.

Why did Dow have the (somewhat) greater return on assets? This can be at least partly answered by looking at the determinants of *ROA*—the revenues generated on each dollar of assets and the income available on each dollar of revenues:

$$ROA = \frac{Sales}{Assets} \times \frac{Income}{Sales}$$

Again, using the average values for the 10-year period:

Firm	ROA	=	Asset Turnover	×	Net Profit Margin
Dow	8.8%	=	1.3%	×	7.1
UC	7.6%	=	1.3%	×	5.3

Note: Equations do not balance due to rounding.

Dow had the larger average *ROA* solely because of its better profit margin. Whether this was the result of better control of expenses by Dow's management or the nature of each firm's product line cannot be determined by the data available. It is, however, a question that any serious stock analyst would pursue.

Summarizing to this point, Dow's larger *ROE* was due primarily to its greater use of financial leverage. The somewhat larger net profit margins might or might not have been due to better management.

Let's turn now to the decline in *ROE*s of both firms. A review of Table 14-6 suggests that this was due in large measure to decreasing profit margins in both firms (and probably over the chemical industry as a whole). Profit margins will fall if (1) prices decline, (2) variable expenses increase, or (3) unit sales decrease, causing fixed costs not to be covered as well. Variable expenses include labor, marketing, advertising, and raw materials. Of these, all would have been constant (or growing with inflation) except raw material costs. A major raw material cost for these firms would be for oil and energy, whose prices decreased in the early 1980s. Clearly, declining oil prices would not cause the net profit margin to decline. However, heavy competition in selling prices and declining unit sales did occur during the economic recession of the early 1980s. As economic activity grew at a slow rate, rising per-unit fixed costs (lower capacity utilization) and increased price competition cut deeply into profit margins. By 1984 these pressures were almost totally removed domestically. But the industry faced a new problem—the value of the U.S. dollar relative to foreign currencies.

In 1983 and 1984, the U.S. dollar was trading at historic peaks in relation to foreign currencies. This made it (1) costly for foreigners to purchase U.S. goods, (2) inexpensive for U.S. firms to purchase foreign goods, and (3) unprofitable for U.S.

firms to convert sales made in foreign countries to U.S. dollars. All of these resulted in decreased U.S. dollar sales for chemical firms such as Dow and Union Carbide which made a large portion of their sales in international markets.

In sum, the declines in profit margins were the principal cause of lower *ROE*s. The declines were caused by low unit sales in a recession and the subsequent increase in the value of the U.S. dollar. Neither of these conditions was likely to be permanent. Economic activity, in fact, did improve later in the 1980s and, over time, the value of the dollar was expected to decline. Thus, we could predict that the low net profit margins of each firm would improve during the next few years. From our perspective of trying to value the stock of each firm, it is clear that a constant growth model would probably be inaccurate.

Liquidity and Financial Flexibility

Table 14-7 includes two ratios which are commonly used to evaluate a firm's ability to meet both its short-term and long-term debt obligations.

The current ratio is simply the current assets of a firm divided by its current liabilities. It reflects the amount of short-term asset liquidity which a firm has. For example, at the end of 1984, Union Carbide had $1.90 of current assets for each $1.00 of current liabilities, whereas Dow had only $1.40 of current assets per $1.00 of current liabilities. Although we should not conclude that Dow had insufficient liquidity, it is clear that Union Carbide was the more liquid of the two firms. This was true for all years shown in Table 14-7.

The times interest earned ratio reflects the number of times operating income was able to cover interest expenses. Since interest is paid before any federal income taxes,

TABLE 14-7 *Liquidity, Debt, and Dividend Information for Dow and Union Carbide*

	Current Ratio		Times Interest Earned Before Tax		Dividend Payout Ratio		Dividends Per Share	
	Dow	UC	Dow	UC	Dow	UC	Dow	UC
1984	1.4	1.9	2.4	2.6	68%	62%	$1.80	$3.40
1983	1.4	1.8	1.9	1.3	120	113	1.80	3.40
1982	1.8	2.0	1.5	2.3	158	76	1.80	3.40
1981	1.7	2.2	2.3	5.2	61	35	1.80	3.30
1980	1.6	2.2	3.7	6.4	38	31	1.65	3.10
1979	1.4	2.2	4.6	6.2	35	34	1.50	2.90
1978	1.6	2.0	4.4	5.0	41	46	1.25	2.80
1977	1.5	2.2	4.9	5.0	38	46	1.15	2.80
1976	1.4	2.3	6.5	7.1	29	35	0.95	2.50
1975	1.5	2.5	8.6	8.5	23	38	0.75	2.40
Average	1.53	2.13	4.08	4.96	61%	52%		

SOURCE: Calculated using data in each company's annual report.

the times interest earned ratio is usually calculated using pretax income. For example, consider the following income statement of a firm:

Net Sales	$1,000
Cost of Goods Sold	600
Gross Profit	$ 400
Operating Expenses	300
Net Operating Income	$ 100
Interest Expense	20
Net Taxable Income	$ 80
Taxes	40
Net Income	$ 40

The times interest earned ratio would be 5.0:

$$\frac{\$100}{\$20} = 5.0$$

Looking at the times interest earned ratios in Table 14-7, it is clear that both firms experienced a rather dramatic decrease in their abilities to pay interest expenses from operating income over the prior decade. Although not shown here, these ratios are substantially lower than those for a typical manufacturing firm. Both firms needed to improve their times interest earned ratios through a combination of increased profit margins and reduced debt costs. In short, the financial flexibility of both firms had been decreasing and needed improvement.

Estimated Dividend Growth

Both firms were suffering from temporary pressures on earnings. Because of this, neither firm had increased its dividend in the last three years. How long such pressures would last before *ROE* and growth prospects would be more in line with a normal relationship was uncertain. But it could be expected that future dividends would increase as the value of the U.S. dollar declined, allowing profit margins to improve. The growth in dividends over the next few years would probably be larger than the growth rate after the industry was fully recovered. Given the data available to us, any specific forecasts would be totally arbitrary. Instead, we will use the forecasts provided by Value Line analysts. In late 1984, Value Line published the following predictions:

	Dividends per Share		*In 1988*	
	1985	1988	*ROE*	*B*
Dow	$1.80	$3.00	18.5%	55%
Union Carbide	$3.60	$6.40	16.5%	60%

Using this information we could either (1) estimate K_e and calculate an equilibrium market price for each firm, or (2) use the actual market price of each firm and calculate the expected long-run return. We will do both.

Equilibrium Prices. In late 1984, the long-term risk-free rate could be proxied by the yields on U.S. Treasuries as about 12%. Although the risk premium was unknown, we will use a value of 6%. Betas for each stock are estimated from the characteristic lines shown in Figures 14-3 and 14-4. Each characteristic line was determined by regressing monthly returns on each stock against the monthly returns on the S&P 500 Index for the five-year period ended December 1984. Results were:

	Using Monthly Returns	
	Standard Deviation	Correlation With S&P 500
S&P 500	4.27	1.00
Dow Chemical	7.83	0.68
Union Carbide	7.18	0.50

$$\tilde{R}_{Dt} = -0.010 + 1.25\,(\tilde{R}_{SPt}) + \tilde{e}_{Dt}$$

$$\tilde{R}_{UCt} = -0.005 + 0.84\,(\tilde{R}_{SPt}) + \tilde{e}_{UCt}$$

These market model beta estimates can be used to determine the return which should be expected for securities having similar amounts of systematic risk:

$$E(R_D) = 12\% + 1.25(6\%)$$

$$= 19.50\%$$

$$E(R_{UC}) = 12\% + 0.84(6\%)$$

$$= 17.04\%$$

Finally, an equilibrium price for each is calculated by discounting future expected dividends at each stock's equilibrium expected return. Calculations are shown in Table 14-8. Note that year 4 has two cash flows: one representing the dividend in year 4 and the other representing the expected market price of each stock using the constant growth model and estimates of sustainable growth based upon Value Line's projections of ROEs and retention rates.

The estimated equilibrium prices and actual market prices are:

	Estimated Equilibrium	Actual Market
Dow Chemical	$23.38	$30.00
Union Carbide	$65.46	$50.00

Based on this analysis, Dow Chemical shares appear to be overvalued in the market and Union Carbide shares undervalued.

Expected Return. As an alternative to using K_e to estimate price, we can use the actual market price to estimate expected returns. This is done by solving for K_e in the two equations on pages 546 and 547:

FIGURE 14-3   *Dow Returns Versus the S&P 500 for the 60 Months Ended December 1984*

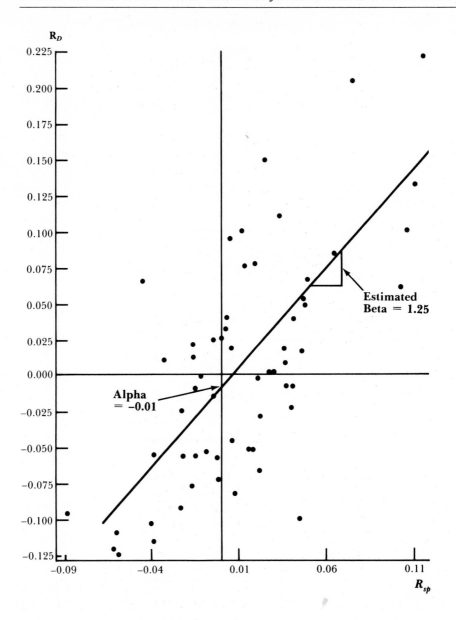

Dow Chemical's Expected Return

$$\$30 = \frac{\$1.80}{(1 + K_e)} + \dots + \frac{\$3.00}{(1 + K_e)^4} + \frac{\$3.00(1.102)}{K_e - 0.099} \frac{1}{(1 + K_e)^4}$$

$$K_e = 17.33\%$$

FIGURE 14-4 *UC Returns Versus the S&P 500 for the 60 Months Ended December 1984*

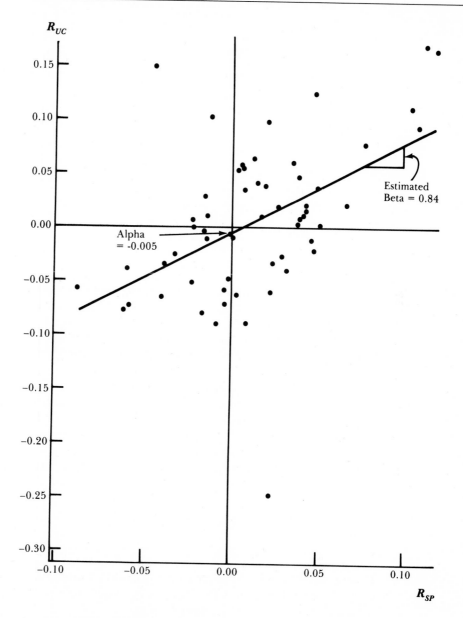

Union Carbide's Expected Return

$$\$50 = \frac{\$3.60}{(1 + K_e)} + \cdots + \frac{\$6.40}{(1 + K_e)^4} + \frac{\$6.40(1.099)}{K_e - 0.099} \; \frac{1}{(1 + K_e)^4}$$

$$K_e = 19.25\%$$

TABLE 14-8 *Calculation of Dow and Carbide Equilibrium Prices*

| | Dow Chemical | | Union Carbide | |
Year	Cash Flow	Present Value*	Cash Flow	Present Value†
Dividend 1	$ 1.80	$ 1.51	$ 3.60	$ 3.08
Dividend 2	2.13	1.49	4.36	3.18
Dividend 3	2.53	1.48	5.28	3.29
Dividend 4	3.00	1.47	6.40	3.41
Ending Price	35.55‡	17.43	98.51§	52.50
Total		$23.38		$65.46

*Discounted at 19.50%.

†Discounted at 17.04%.

$$‡P_4 = \frac{\$3.00(1.102)}{0.195 - 0.102} = \$35.55.$$

$$§P_4 = \frac{\$6.40(1.099)}{0.1704 - 0.099} = \$98.51.$$

These expected returns would then be compared with each stock's beta estimate and the security market line, as in Figure 14-5. Usually, many other stocks will also be plotted so that the slope of the SML can be determined. However, we will use $RF = 12\%$ and $RP_M = 6\%$ as estimates of what would be obtained if many stocks had been evaluated. Since Union Carbide plots above the SML it represents a good purchase candidate, and since Dow plots below the SML it should be sold.

Using both the equilibrium price approach and the expected return approach, Union Carbide is the better stock to purchase. However, this assumes that our input data properly reflect all known information about each stock. They probably don't. A more thorough analysis is really needed before a truly informed opinion can be offered. The purpose of this example, however, was not so much to determine whether either stock should be purchased or sold as it was to illustrate the process of stock analysis. Details of a thorough security analysis are treated in depth in Chapter 21.

Bhopal

The analysis presented above was prepared in late 1984 using estimates of year-end 1984 financial statements. In early December 1984, however, an accident at a Union Carbide chemical plant in India killed almost 2,000 people. The Bhopal disaster completely altered the future of Union Carbide.

On December 4, 1984, the press announced that a deadly gas, methyl isocyanate, had leaked from a Union Carbide plant in Bhopal, India. Early reports indicated that about 400 people were killed, but the number soon increased to 2,000. On December 5, 1984, investors who were concerned about Union Carbide's legal liabilities sold more than 6 million shares (close to one-tenth of all common shares outstanding) and

FIGURE 14-5 *Dow–Union Carbide Security Market Line*

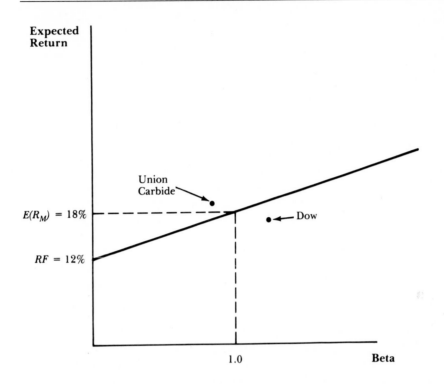

prices fell from $50 to $32. For the next five months, new disclosures continually questioned the size of the company's potential legal liability to Indian residents (some reports suggested it would be the largest and most lucrative civil legal case in history) and cited numerous safety violations in U.S. chemical plants. On January 18, Moody's Investors Service lowered ratings on various Union Carbide bond obligations and, throughout early 1985, the stock price traded between $36 and $40.

In late 1985, however, GAF Corporation announced an offer to acquire Union Carbide. By January of 1986, the GAF offer had been increased to $78 per share and the share prices of Union Carbide rose accordingly. Management of Union Carbide engaged in an active defensive strategy to fend off GAF's "hostile" takeover attempt. The strategy included three plans of action:

1. Long-term debt was increased and the proceeds were used to repurchase common shares at $85 per share. This caused long-term debt to double, and total equity to fall by 79%.

2. Many agricultural, chemical, and metal product lines were sold in order to provide cash for debt service and increase future profitability.

3. A work force reduction was initiated, together with cuts in overhead costs.

It is clear that Union Carbide's direction was altered dramatically by two unpredictable events—the Bhopal disaster and the fight with GAF. Such are the risks associated with stock valuation.

SUMMARY

Stock investment and speculation can be approached, conceptually, in much the same manner as bond investment and speculation. In fact, stock selection decisions should be closely interrelated with bond decisions. Basic decisions about a portfolio's beta and duration, extent of diversification, use of tax swaps, orientation towards growth versus current income, etc., all require mixed stock/bond decisions.

Stock *investment* portfolios should (1) be broadly diversified, (2) be combined with nominally risk-free securities to obtain a desired nondiversifiable risk level, (3) not attempt to time the market or find mispriced securities, (4) be mixed with bonds to achieve an appropriate duration and marketability, and (5) be traded only for potential gains from tax swaps. The basic model used to justify such a buy-hold investment portfolio is the efficient market theory. While a strict version of EMT is unsupported by empirical evidence, the evidence does suggest that, after considering the taxes, transaction costs, and risks involved in various speculative strategies, a buy-hold strategy beats a speculative strategy more often than most people realize. Details of the empirical studies were presented in Chapter 10.

Stock speculation can take place at three levels: (1) timing aggregate market moves, (2) finding overvalued and undervalued industries, and (3) finding overvalued and undervalued stocks within an industry. Individual speculators usually specialize in one level. Market timers increase the stock-to-bond mix (and thus the portfolio's beta) if they expect unusually good aggregate market returns. If stock market prices are expected to fall, they will increase the commitment to short-term bonds and reduce the stock portion. Industry analysts will overweight industries which are expected to show good performance and underweight those with expected poor performance. This is in contrast to a market-weighted portfolio in which the percentage holdings of each industry correspond to the percentage of an industry's total market value compared to the total market value of all stocks. Stock analysts will do much the same thing for individual stocks.

REVIEW PROBLEM

Table 14-A provides information on Du Pont, the largest U.S. chemical producer. Its products include nylon, polyesters, commodity chemicals, and plastic products. In 1981, Du Pont acquired Conoco Oil. The company's foreign sales are 31% of revenue.

a. Evaluate Du Pont's historical *ROE* in comparison with those of Dow and Union Carbide.

b. Evaluate Du Pont's liquidity and long-term debt use.

TABLE 14-A *Information on Du Pont*

Year	Revenues (millions)	Long-Term Debt (millions)	Equity (millions)	Book Value	EPS	DPS	Current Ratio	Times Interest Earned
				Per-Share Information				
1977	$ 9,435	$1,290	$ 4,317	$28.37	$ 3.69	$1.92	2.6	6.8
1979	12,572	1,104	5,312	35.07	6.42	2.75	2.6	11.7
1981	22,810	7,330	10,458	43.60	5.81	2.75	2.0	4.6
1983	35,378	4,733	11,472	47.03	4.47	2.50	1.8	5.3
1984 (est.)	36,000	4,600	12,280	50.25	6.10	2.90	–	–
1985 (est.)	39,000	4,600	13,200	54.00	6.90	3.10	–	–
1988 (est.)	50,000	5,500	16,000	65.00	10.00	4.00	–	–

Note: All information except for the current ratio and times interest earned extracted from the November 9, 1984, Value Line Investment Survey, published by Arnold Bernhard & Co. The current ratio and times interest earned were calculated from annual reports of E. I. du Pont de Nemours & Company.

c. Do you think Du Pont stock can be valued using the constant growth model? Value Line estimates of Du Pont's dividends in 1985 and 1988 were $3.10 and $4.00, respectively. Value Line also predicted an *ROE* and retention rate of 15% and 60% for 1988. The price per share was about $49 in late 1984.

d. The characteristic line for Du Pont (calculated using monthly returns for the five years ended December 1984) was:

$$\tilde{R}_{DPt} = -0.004 + 1.15\,(\tilde{R}_{SPt}) + \tilde{e}_t$$

Calculate the equilibrium price of Du Pont shares.

e. Calculate the expected return on Du Pont shares and compare it with the SML in Figure 14-5.

Solution

a.

Year	Dow	UC	Du Pont[1]	=	Asset Turn[2]	×	Profit Margin[3]	×	Debt Use[4]
			Return on Equity						
1977	17.8%	11.5%	13.0%	=	1.68	×	5.95%	×	1.30
1979	20.1	13.9	18.3	=	1.96	×	7.72	×	1.21
1981	11.5	12.5	13.3	=	1.28	×	6.11	×	1.70
1983	5.8	4.3	9.5	=	2.18	×	3.09	×	1.41
1984	10.0	7.7	12.1	=	2.13	×	4.15	×	1.37

[1] EPS ÷ Book Value per Share.
[2] Revenue ÷ (Long-Term Debt + Equity).
[3] Plugged to have equation balance. Data not given.
[4] (Long-Term Debt + Equity) ÷ Equity.

Important points:

• Du Pont's *ROE* has moved with the industry. However, during the 1980s Du Pont's *ROE* was consistently better than Dow's and Union Carbide's.

- When Du Pont's asset turnover shown above is compared with Dow's and Union Carbide's in Table 14-6, Du Pont is consistently better. This explains some of Du Pont's larger *ROE*.
- Du Pont's net profit margin is not out of line with that of Dow and Union Carbide. The worst year for Du Pont (1983) was also the worst year for both Dow and Union Carbide.
- Du Pont clearly uses less debt than either Dow or Union Carbide. The large debt increase in 1981 (associated with the acquisition of Conoco) is being reduced.

In sum, Du Pont had the largest *ROE* because of its assets turnover and net profit margin, i.e., its return on assets.

b. The current ratio of Du Pont is similar to, if not better than, Union Carbide's. The firm does not appear to have a liquidity problem.

The times interest earned ratio is better than either Dow's or Union Carbide's. However, there was a dramatic drop in 1981, the year in which Conoco Oil was acquired. The improvement in 1983 together with the reductions in debt mentioned above indicate that Du Pont intends to improve its financial flexibility in the future.

c. The following annual dividend growth rates are implied by the Value Line forecasts.

Period	Growth	Calculation
1984–1985	6.9%	$(3.1 \div 2.9) - 1.0$
1984–1988	8.4%	$(4.0 \div 2.9)^{1/4} - 1.0$
Beyond 1988	9.0%	$15\% (0.60)$

The constant growth model is not strictly correct. Whether it is used or not depends upon the desired accuracy. We will use both constant growth (at 9%) and non-constant growth approaches below.

d. B = 1.15 (from characteristic line)
RF = 12% (from chapter)
RP_m = 6% (from chapter)
K = 12% + 1.15 (6%)
= 18.9%

Constant Growth Model Price:

$$\frac{\$2.90(1.09)}{0.189 - 0.09} = \$31.93$$

Non-Constant Growth Price

Year	Dividend	Pres. Value	Growth Assumption
1985	$ 3.10	$ 2.61	Value Line Estimate
1986	3.37	2.38	Compound Growth from $3.10 to 4.00 in 3 years
1987	3.67	2.18	
1988	4.00	2.00	Value Line Estimate
Beyond 1988	44.04	22.04	Sustainable Growth of 9%
		$13.21	

$$44.04 = \frac{4.00(1.09)}{0.189 - 0.09}$$

Conclusion: In both cases the market price of Du Pont shares appears to be overvalued.

e. Using the constant growth model, the expected return is:

$$E(R) = Dividend\ Yield + Growth$$

$$15.45\% = \frac{\$2.90(1.09)}{\$49} + 0.09$$

The required return in Figure 14-5 (and calculated above) is 18.9%.

QUESTIONS AND PROBLEMS

1. Identify the characteristics of a pure investment portfolio for the following accounts:
   a. A $20.0 million pension fund which will not have to pay large retirement benefits for another 20 years. Employees are factory workers and clerical staff for a young high-technology firm. Most employees own no stocks or bonds of their own.
   b. A 45-year-old lawyer with a successful practice. The lawyer is in a high tax bracket, won't need the funds until retirement, and is willing to accept above-average risk. $200,000 is to be invested. No other investments are held.
   c. A 60-year-old machinist with a portfolio worth $80,000, an average tax bracket, and a desire for less than average risk. Major retirement income will come from a diversified pension fund.
   d. A young family with two children not yet in school. Both parents have promising careers as CPAs and are willing to accept moderate risk. At present they have $10,000 to invest and expect that at least that amount will be available for new investment every year.

2. You are given the following data on six common stocks and asked to evaluate the appropriateness of adding each to the investment portfolio of: (a) a $20.0 million pension fund, (b) a 45-year-old lawyer willing to accept moderate to high risk who is in a high tax bracket, (c) a 60-year-old machinist who will accept average risk, (d) a young family with two children not yet in school with both parents professionally employed and willing to accept moderate risk.

Stock	Expected Long-Run ROE	Expected Dividend Payout	Current Dividend	Current Stock Price	Beta	G	$K_e = 8\% + \beta(5\%)$
1	15.0%	0.3	$3.00	$66.30	1.5	10.5%	15.5%
2	15.0	0.7	1.50	22.40	0.7	4.5	11.5
3	20.0	0.5	1.00	36.67	1.0	10.0	13.0
4	10.0	0.9	5.00	36.07	1.4	1.0	15.0
5	12.0	0.7	2.50	37.54	0.5	3.6	10.5
6	20.0	0.3	0.30	17.10	1.6	14.0	16.0

3. You are evaluating three stocks and are curious about how sensitive their prices are to changes in required returns. Stocks *A* and *B* are expected to provide constant dividend growth rates, although their individual risks and growths differ as follows:

	A	*B*
Required Return	14%	12%
Expected Constant Dividend Growth	9%	6%

Stock *C* has the same required return as *B* but is expected to have an abnormal dividend growth of 10% for 6 years, after which the growth rate is expected to be constant at 6% per year.

a. Which of the stocks has the longest duration?

b. Which stock would have the highest beta?

4. In this chapter's Dow–Union Carbide example, our analysis resulted in the conclusion that Dow's stock was overpriced and Union Carbide's underpriced. But the example was intended to illustrate the major steps in any stock analysis and made no claims for accuracy. If you were to undertake a more complete analysis of each firm, what would you do to improve upon the analysis shown in the chapter?

5. (CFA Exam Question)

The household products industry consists primarily of consumer nondurables such as cleaning agents and personal care items which are sold through grocery, drug, and other retail stores. According to one investment advisory service, industry sales approached $20 billion during 1982. The Procter & Gamble Company (PG) and the Clorox Company (CLX) accounted for a large share of this volume.

PG is the nation's leading producer of soaps and detergents (Tide, Cheer) and also holds major market positions in other consumer lines, such as toothpaste (Crest), disposable diapers (Pampers), and dessert mixes (Duncan Hines). The company's $12 billion in annual sales can be broken into the following segments: laundry and cleaning products (47%), personal care products (39%), food products (10%), and other products (4%).

CLX was a subsidiary of PG before being divested following a Federal Trade Commission order in 1967. At that time the company's only product was Clorox liquid bleach. Now as a separate entity, CLX has been engaged in a determined diversification effort. In the past year, for example, the company paid $123 million to purchase the operations of Olympic paints and stains. On a pro forma basis, this business constituted approximately 10% of the nearly $900 million in sales realized by CLX in 1982.

In addition to using acquisitions, both PG and CLX have attempted to enhance their growth by pursuing international markets and by making substantial commitments to research and development. In the fiscal year ended June 30, 1982, these activities were as follows:

	PG	CLX
Foreign Sales (in millions)	$3,737.0	$90.0
Percent of Total Sales	31.2%	10.4%
R&D Outlays (in millions)	$ 286.0	$16.0
Percent of Total Sales	2.4%	1.8%

Despite difficult economic conditions, both PG and CLX had profit increases in 1982 ranging from 14% to 16%. Gains of similar magnitude are generally expected by the investment community in the current year. It appears that the stable nature of their consumer product lines, strong finances, and lower raw materials costs are providing the basis for continuing profit increases in this environment.

The Value Line Investment Survey projects the following annual rates of growth for each company over the next five years:

	PG	CLX
Sales Per Share	10.0%	12.5%
Earnings Per Share	11.5%	15.0%
Dividends Per Share	10.0%	11.5%

TABLE 14-B *The Economy, the Industry, the Companies*

	U.S. GNP			Household Products Industry			Company Sales*			
							PG		CLX	
Year	Current $ (billions)	Constant $ (billions)	GNP Price Index (1972 = 100)	Current $ (millions)	Constant $ (millions)	Consumer Price Index (1967 = 100)	Current $ (millions)	Constant $† (millions)	Current $ (millions)	Constant $† (millions)
1982	3058	1476	207.2	19,100	6607	289.1	11,994	4149	867	300
1981	2938	1503	195.5	18,514	6797	272.4	11,416	4191	714	262
1980	2633	1474	178.6	17,641	7148	246.8	10,772	4365	637	258
1979	2418	1479	163.4	15,412	7089	217.4	9,329	4291	565	260
1978	2164	1439	150.4	14,426	7383	195.4	8,100	4145	466	238
1977	1918	1370	140.1	12,764	7033	181.5	7,284	4013	422	233
1976	1718	1298	132.3	11,570	6786	170.5	6,513	3820	380	223
1975	1549	1232	125.8	10,317	6400	161.2	6,082	3773	333	207

Compound Annual Growth Rate (1975–1982)

10.7%	2.7%		9.6%	0.3%		11.1%	1.7%	14.4%	4.6%	

Standard Deviation (1975–1982)

2.0%	2.3%		3.6%	3.8%		3.5%	2.2%	3.6%	4.1%	

*Results from continuing operations.
†Series represents current dollar sales deflated by the U.S. consumer price index.
SOURCES: *Economic Report of the President*, 1983; the Value Line Investment Survey; annual reports of the Procter & Gamble Company and the Clorox Company.

a. Based on the data provided in Table 14-B, compare the economy, the household products industry, PG, and CLX in terms of growth and stability. Show comparisons in current dollar and constant dollar terms. State your conclusions and discuss any problems in the comparisons.

b. Return on shareholders' equity can be defined as a function of turnover, leverage, pretax profit margin, and income tax rate. Using each of these component ratios, as provided in Tables 14-C and 14-D, calculate the net return on common equity for PG and CLX for the two individual years 1977 and 1982. Identify the component ratios which account for differences in the level and trend of return on equity between PG and CLX in these two years.

c. Considering qualitative as well as quantitative factors, select either PG or CLX as the stock you would prefer for one of your core holdings in a long-term pension fund portfolio. Support your selection with four significant reasons. Base your answer on the background information provided and the data in Tables 14-B, 14-C, 14-D, 14-E, 14-F, and 14-G, as well as the following:

	Per Common Share*	
	PG	CLX
Current Price (January 6, 1983)	$115.00	$23.75
1982 Price Range – High	$118.25	$24.75
– Low	$ 77.75	$10.62
1982 Actual Earnings	$ 9.39	$ 1.90

1983 Estimated Earnings	$ 10.60	$ 2.30
Indicated Annual Dividend	$ 4.20	$ 0.89
Book Value	$ 50.35	$11.75

*Not adjusted for share splits made subsequent to 1982.

TABLE 14-C *Selected Financial Ratios*

Fiscal Year	Dividends ÷ Net Earnings		Net Sales ÷ Total Assets		Quick Assets ÷ Current Liabilities		Net Earnings ÷ Common Equity	
	PG	CLX	PG	CLX	PG	CLX	PG	CLX
1982	43.7%	45.3%	1.60×	1.61×	0.75×	1.15×	18.7%	16.0%
1981	47.0	48.8	1.64	1.72	0.80	1.21	17.3	15.3
1980	43.9	53.5	1.64	1.70	0.81	1.32	17.8	14.4
1979	44.6	53.9	1.65	1.69	0.93	1.41	17.8	13.9
1978	43.8	45.9	1.63	1.33	1.14	1.01	17.5	16.0
1977	43.1	37.8	1.62	1.35	1.22	1.30	17.5	18.7
1976	42.3	39.1	1.59	1.38	1.35	1.23	17.0	19.8
1975	47.2	57.8	1.66	1.26	1.32	0.97	15.7	14.9

Averages

Fiscal Year	Dividends ÷ Net Earnings		Net Sales ÷ Total Assets		Quick Assets ÷ Current Liabilities		Net Earnings ÷ Common Equity	
	PG	CLX	PG	CLX	PG	CLX	PG	CLX
1979-82	44.8%	50.4%	1.63×	1.68×	0.82×	1.27×	17.9%	14.9%
1975-78	44.1	45.2	1.63	1.33	1.26	1.13	16.9	17.4
1975-82	44.5	47.8	1.63	1.51	1.04	1.20	17.4	16.1

TABLE 14-D *Selected Financial Ratios*

Fiscal Year	Net Earnings ÷ Pretax Earnings		Pretax Earnings ÷ Net Sales		Total Assets ÷ Common Equity		Net Earnings ÷ Total Assets	
	PG	CLX	PG	CLX	PG	CLX	PG	CLX
1982	55.4%	56.0%	11.7%	9.3%	1.80×	1.92×	10.4%	8.4%
1981	56.3	55.0	10.4	9.7	1.80	1.67	9.6	9.2
1980	59.4	53.2	10.0	9.8	1.82	1.62	9.8	8.9
1979	56.4	53.6	10.9	9.7	1.75	1.57	10.2	8.8
1978	53.3	51.0	11.8	12.9	1.71	1.82	10.2	8.8
1977	53.1	50.5	11.9	15.0	1.71	1.82	10.3	10.3
1976	54.2	50.3	11.3	15.6	1.74	1.83	9.8	10.8
1975	53.4	50.3	10.2	12.0	1.72	1.96	9.1	7.6

Averages

Fiscal Year	Net Earnings ÷ Pretax Earnings		Pretax Earnings ÷ Net Sales		Total Assets ÷ Common Equity		Net Earnings ÷ Total Assets	
	PG	CLX	PG	CLX	PG	CLX	PG	CLX
1979-82	56.9%	54.5%	10.8%	9.6%	1.79×	1.70×	10.0	8.8%
1975-78	53.5	50.5	11.3	13.9	1.72	1.86	9.9	9.4
1975-82	55.2	52.5	11.0	11.8	1.76	1.78	9.9	9.1

d. As a cross-check on the decision made in response to part c, you consult the security market line (SML) analysis provided by a large investment advisory firm. At year-end 1982, their SML is plotted as shown in the graph in Figure 14-A, with PG and CLX located as shown. Discuss the significance of the SML in terms of its level and slope and indi-

TABLE 14-E *Market Valuations and Other Common Stock Data*

Year	Average Annual Price-Earnings Ratio		Average Annual Dividend Yield		Earnings per Common Share*		Dividends per Common Share*	
	PG	CLX	PG	CLX	PG	CLX	PG	CLX
1982	8.4×	6.3×	5.2%	7.2%	$9.39	$1.90	$4.10	$0.86
1981	8.9	6.7	5.3	7.3	8.08	1.66	3.80	0.81
1980	9.5	7.0	4.6	7.6	7.74	1.44	3.40	0.77
1979	12.1	7.1	3.7	6.0	6.95	1.30	3.10	0.70
1978	13.3	8.6	3.3	4.7	6.17	1.35	2.70	0.62
1977	15.7	8.3	2.7	4.5	5.57	1.43	2.40	0.54
1976	18.3	9.7	2.3	4.4	4.85	1.33	2.05	0.52
1975	21.9	9.0	2.1	6.1	4.03	0.90	1.90	0.52

Averages					Compound Annual Growth			
1979–82	9.7×	6.8×	4.7%	7.0%				
1975–78	17.3	8.9	2.6	4.9				
1975–82	13.5	7.8	3.7	6.0	12.1%	7.8%	12.2%	8.6%

*Per-share data not adjusted for share splits made subsequent to 1982.
SOURCES: Corporate annual reports and the Value Line Investment Survey, November 5, 1982.

TABLE 14-F *Selected Financial Statistics for the Procter & Gamble Company*

	Fiscal Year							
	1982	1981	1980	1979	1978	1977	1976	1975
Operations (in $ millions)								
Sales	11,994	11,416	10,772	9,329	8,100	7,284	6,513	6,082
Depreciation	267	237	196	170	139	125	112	97
Interest	95	98	97	66	55	53	53	39
Income Taxes	622	518	438	443	446	406	337	288
Net Earnings	777	668	640	575	510	460	400	332
Financial Position (in $ millions)								
Cash	578	616	477	619	723	745	795	528
Receivables	851	775	879	694	606	536	436	465
Current Assets	3,113	3,052	3,008	2,693	2,475	2,342	2,129	1,829
Total Assets	7,510	6,961	6,553	5,664	4,984	4,487	4,103	3,653
Current Liabilities	1,912	1,730	1,670	1,410	1,168	1,048	914	754
Long-Term Debt	846	846	835	642	574	533	566	558
Common Equity	4,164	3,863	3,603	3,229	2,915	2,624	2,357	2,118

FIGURE 14-A *Security Market Line, December 31, 1982*

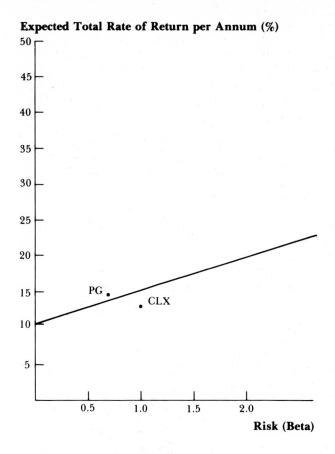

Expected Total Rate of Return per Annum (%)

cate whether the plots of PG and CLX in Figure 14-A either confirm or refute your recommendation made in response to part c.

6. (CFA Exam Question)

The Coca-Cola Company (KO) and PepsiCo, Inc. (PEP) are the leading companies in the worldwide market for soft drinks and snack foods.

KO is the world's largest soft-drink company. Principal products in terms of sales volume are Coca-Cola, Tab, Sprite, Hi-C, and Minute Maid Orange Juice. In 1982, KO acquired Columbia Pictures for $692 million in cash and stock in order to capitalize on what its management sees as "enormous opportunities in the passive leisure-time industry." In 1983, KO disposed of Wine Spectrum (Taylor Wine Company and the Monterey Vineyard). Soft drinks provide about 72% of KO's annual net sales, food products 16%, and entertainment 12%.

PEP is the world's largest producer of snack foods and the second largest factor in the soft-drink market behind KO. Snack foods (Frito-Lay) and food service (Pizza Hut and Taco Bell) represent about 50% of PEP's annual sales volume, with soft drinks (Pepsi, Diet Pepsi, Teem) accounting for an additional 39%.

TABLE 14-G *Selected Financial Statistics for the Clorox Company*

	Fiscal Year							
	1982	*1981*	*1980*	*1979*	*1978*	*1977*	*1976*	*1975*
Operations (in $ millions)								
Sales	867.1	714.0	637.4	565.4	465.8	422.1	379.7	331.1
Depreciation	15.5	12.7	10.3	9.2	6.4	5.2	4.8	4.4
Interest	13.7	5.0	4.3	3.6	1.5	1.9	2.3	3.5
Income Taxes	35.5	31.2	29.2	25.5	29.5	31.4	29.4	19.9
Net Earnings	45.1	38.1	33.2	29.5	30.7	32.0	29.8	20.2
Financial Position (in $ millions)								
Cash	65.6	62.0	64.5	47.8	13.2	43.7	22.4	14.4
Receivables	90.1	72.2	57.5	55.6	89.9	65.6	56.5	52.7
Current Assets	234.1	224.7	201.1	175.8	190.3	177.2	146.0	136.2
Total Assets	539.6	416.0	374.4	334.7	350.3	311.6	275.1	265.2
Current Liabilities	135.2	110.6	92.5	73.4	101.6	83.8	64.3	68.9
Long-Term Debt	100.4	38.4	37.2	38.8	46.7	48.5	54.1	60.0
Common Equity	281.4	249.6	230.6	213.2	192.3	171.0	150.8	135.3

Since 1976 the number of gallons of soft drinks sold in the United States has grown at an annual rate of 3.7%. During this period the annual increase in gallons sold in the United States was 4.6% for KO and 6.4% for PEP. Some analysts predict that despite the introduction of soft drinks with greater appeal to an older population, unit growth in the U.S. will slow as the 13- to 24-year-old age group declines in relative importance.

KO and PEP have diversified their product offerings and have sought out foreign markets where the population is younger on average and the growth is faster than in the U.S. The geographical distribution of net operating revenues is approximately as follows:

Estimated 1983 Net Operating Revenues

	KO	*PEP*
U.S. and Puerto Rico	58%	77%
Europe and Africa	18	8
Canada and Pacific	16	4
Latin America	8	11
	100%	100%

Because of the strong U.S. dollar, high inflation rates in Latin markets, and price controls in Mexico, 1983 was a difficult year for KO and PEP. Many analysts believe that earnings for each of these companies will increase considerably in 1984 as price controls are relaxed in Mexico and foreign economies improve.

a. Base your answer to this question solely on the foregoing information and the data in Table 14-H.

(1) Compare the economy, the food and beverage industry, KO, and PEP in terms of growth and stability for the period 1976–1983. Show comparisons in current dollars

and constant dollars, identifying those trends that are useful for making investment decisions.

(2) List four conclusions you can draw from the comparisons.

(3) List three problems in using the data to draw useful investment conclusions.

TABLE 14-H *The Economy, the Industry, the Companies*

| | U.S. GNP | | | Food and Beverage Industry | | | | Company Sales* | | | |
| | | | | | | Prod. Index (1967 = 100) | | KO | | PEP | |
Year	Current $ (billions)	Constant $ (billions)	GNP Price Index (1972 = 100)	Current $ (billions)	Consumer Price Index (1967 = 100)	Food	Beverage	Current $ (millions)	Constant $ (millions)†	Current $ (millions)	Constant $ (millions)†
1983 (est.)	$3,304	$1,536	215.2	$417	298.6	155.9	199.7	$6,820	$2,284	$7,700	$2,579
1982	3,073	1,485	206.9	397	289.1	151.0	193.7	6,249	2,162	7,499	2,594
1981	2,954	1,514	195.1	376	272.4	152.0	197.1	5,889	2,162	7,027	2,580
1980	2,632	1,475	178.4	345	246.8	149.6	193.4	5,621	2,278	5,975	2,421
1979	2,418	1,479	163.4	312	217.4	147.4	189.5	4,689	2,157	5,089	2,341
1978	2,164	1,439	150.4	276	195.4	142.7	180.1	4,095	2,096	4,300	2,201
1977	1,918	1,370	140.0	250	181.5	138.8	168.1	3,394	1,870	3,649	2,010
1976	1,718	1,298	132.3	231	170.5	132.9	156.9	2,989	1,753	3,109	1,823

Compound Annual Growth Rate (1976–1983)

| | 9.8% | 2.4% | 7.2% | 8.8% | 8.3% | 2.3% | 3.5% | 12.5% | 3.8% | 13.8% | 5.1% |

Standard Deviation (1976–1983)

| | 3.2% | 2.7% | 2.0% | 2.8% | 3.5% | 1.6% | 3.2% | 6.3% | 5.4% | 6.5% | 4.2% |

*Results from continuing operations—no adjustments made for sale of Wine Spectrum by KO in 1983.
†Series represents current dollar sales deflated by the U.S. consumer price index.
SOURCES: *Economic Indicators*, November 1983; corporate annual reports.

TABLE 14-I *Selected Financial Ratios*

| | EBIT ÷ Assets | | Total Assets ÷ Common Equity | | Net Earnings ÷ Pretax Earnings | | Net Sales ÷ Total Assets | |
Fiscal Year	KO	PEP	KO	PEP	KO	PEP	KO	PEP
1983 (est.)	21.1%	14.7%	1.78×	2.56×	56.0%	58.0%	1.33×	1.75×
1982	23.7	16.9	1.68	2.57	55.0	57.2	1.47	1.82
1981	24.3	17.7	1.60	2.53	55.4	58.5	1.69	1.89
1980	24.3	18.3	1.59	2.39	55.1	56.5	1.77	1.90
1979	26.2	18.5	1.51	2.20	55.4	59.8	1.70	1.92
1978	27.8	19.8	1.46	2.13	54.4	56.1	1.69	1.89
1977	27.9	20.1	1.41	2.31	54.0	55.4	1.59	1.83
1976	28.3	16.9	1.39	2.55	53.4	54.4	1.57	1.77

Averages

1980–83	23.3%	16.9%	1.66×	2.51×	55.4%	57.5%	1.57×	1.84×
1976–79	27.6	18.8	1.44	2.30	54.3	56.4	1.64	1.85
1976–83	25.4	17.9	1.55	2.41	54.8	57.0	1.60	1.85

Note: Average of beginning- and end-of-year assets and equity used where applicable in computing ratios.

b. Base your answer to this question on the ratios provided in Tables 14-I and 14-J and the company data in Tables 14-L and 14-M. Return on stockholders' equity is a prime measure of management's performance and can be calculated using turnover, leverage, pretax profit margin, and income tax rate. Utilizing these ratios:

TABLE 14-J *Selected Financial Ratios*

Fiscal Year	Pretax Earnings ÷ Net Sales		Net Earnings ÷ Total Assets		Net Earnings ÷ Common Equity		Dividends ÷ Net Earnings	
	KO	PEP	KO	PEP	KO	PEP	KO	PEP
1983 (est.)	14.8%	6.4%	11.0%	6.5%	19.6%	16.6%	64.6%	53.1%
1982	14.9	7.1	12.1	7.4	20.3	18.9	62.8	48.9
1981	13.7	7.2	12.8	8.0	20.6	20.3	59.5	44.1
1980	13.1	7.7	12.8	8.3	20.3	19.8	63.2	44.1
1979	15.2	8.2	14.3	9.4	21.6	20.8	57.6	40.9
1978	16.2	9.2	14.9	9.8	21.8	20.9	57.4	40.6
1977	17.5	9.7	15.1	9.9	21.3	22.8	57.5	38.6
1976	18.0	9.6	15.1	9.2	21.1	23.4	55.7	35.4
Averages								
1980–83	14.1%	7.1%	12.2%	7.6%	20.2%	18.9%	62.5%	47.6%
1976–79	16.7	9.2	14.9	9.6	21.4	22.0	57.1	38.9
1976–83	15.4	8.1	13.5	8.6	20.8	20.4	59.8	43.2

Note: Average of beginning- and end-of-year assets and equity used where applicable in computing ratios.

TABLE 14-K *Market Valuations and Other Common Stock Data*

Fiscal Year	Average Annual Price/ Earnings Ratio		Average Annual Dividend Yield		Earnings per Common Share		Dividends per Common Share	
	KO	PEP	KO	PEP	KO*	PEP†	KO	PEP
1983 (est.)	12.4×	11.9×	5.2%	4.4%	$4.15	$3.05	$2.68	$1.62
1982	9.6	12.1	6.5	4.1	3.95	3.23	2.48	1.58
1981	9.6	9.4	6.7	4.2	3.90	3.22	2.32	1.42
1980	9.7	7.7	6.5	5.1	3.42	2.86	2.16	1.26
1979	11.4	8.8	5.1	4.4	3.40	2.70	1.96	1.11
1978	13.7	11.6	4.2	3.5	3.03	2.40	1.74	0.98
1977	14.3	11.5	4.0	3.3	2.68	2.14	1.54	0.83
1976	17.7	13.9	3.1	2.5	2.38	1.79	1.33	0.63
Averages								
1980–83	10.3×	10.3×	6.2%	4.5%				
1976–79	14.3	11.4	4.1	3.4				
1976–83	12.3	10.9	5.2	3.9	8.3%	7.9%	10.5%	14.4%

*Includes results of Columbia Pictures from June 30, 1982.
†Amounts for 1978–81 restated to reflect overstatement of net income aggregating $92.1 million.
Sources: Corporate annual reports and the Value Line Investment Survey, December 2, 1983.

(1) Calculate the net return on average common equity for KO and PEP for the two years 1977 and 1983.

(2) Identify the ratios that account for the level and trend of return on equity for each company in these two years.

TABLE 14-L *Selected Financial Statistics for the Coca-Cola Company*

	Fiscal Year							
	1983 (est.)	*1982*	*1981*	*1980*	*1979*	*1978*	*1977*	*1976*
Operations (in $ millions)								
Sales	6,820.0	6,249.0	5,889.0	5,621.0	4,689.0	4,095.0	3,394.0	2,989.0
Depreciation	180.0	148.9	136.9	131.0	110.0	91.0	80.0	70.0
Interest	73.0	74.6	38.3	35.1	10.7	7.8	NA	NA
Income Taxes	444.0	419.8	360.2	330.4	318.0	303.0	273.0	251.0
Net Earnings	565.0	512.2	447.0	406.0	395.0	361.0	321.0	288.0
Financial Position (in $ millions)								
Cash	616.4	311.0	393.0	289.0	209.0	369.0	418.0	403.0
Receivables	831.3	751.8	483.5	523.1	435.1	338.3	279.9	237.3
Current Assets	2,444.2	2,076.6	1,636.2	1,622.3	1,305.6	1,236.6	1,103.5	1,027.3
Total Assets	5,331.0	4,923.3	3,564.8	3,406.0	2,938.0	2,582.8	2,254.5	2,007.0
Current Liabilities	1,702.7	1,326.8	1,006.3	1,061.6	884.2	744.0	596.3	506.4
Long-Term Debt	475.0	462.3	137.3	133.2	31.0	15.2	15.3	11.0
Common Equity	2,990.0	2,778.7	2,270.8	2,074.7	1,918.7	1,739.6	1,578.0	1,434.0

TABLE 14-M *Selected Financial Statistics for PepsiCo, Inc.**

	Fiscal Year							
	1983 (est.)	*1982*	*1981*	*1980*	*1979*	*1978*	*1977*	*1976*
Operations (in $ millions)								
Sales	7,700.0	7,499.0	7,027.0	5,975.0	5,089.0	4,300.0	3,649.0	3,109.0
Depreciation	260.0	230.4	205.5	172.9	142.1	117.0	93.7	79.1
Interest	156.0	166.2	149.7	114.7	73.1	52.0	46.0	45.0
Income Taxes	206.0	226.8	210.8	200.8	168.2	174.3	158.3	135.3
Net Earnings	285.0	303.7†	297.5	260.7	250.4	223.0	196.7	161.7
Financial Position (in $ millions)								
Cash & Equivalents	397.3	280.3	239.0	232.0	205.0	167.0	256.0	231.0
Receivables	785.7	746.1	741.4	596.7	557.2	433.6	374.4	324.5
Current Assets	1,739.4	1,590.6	1,762.5	1,326.5	1,201.4	1,010.5	997.0	903.7
Total Assets	4,588.9	4,197.5	4,040.0	3,399.9	2,888.9	2,416.8	2,130.3	1,853.6
Current Liabilities	1,440.0	1,345.6	1,430.7	1,005.3	843.6	650.7	574.5	478.9
Long-Term Debt	786.7	864.2	816.1	781.7	619.0	479.1	427.9	278.6
Common Equity	1,786.3	1,650.5	1,556.3	1,381.0	1,247.0	1,165.0	971.9	753.0

*Amounts for 1978–1981 restated to reflect overstatement of net income aggregating $92.1 million.
†Before unusual charge of $79.4 million.

c. When the annual net sales of KO and PEP were regressed against GNP for the years 1973–1983, a high degree of correlation was found to exist. The regression equation, standard error of estimate, and coefficient of correlation for each company are listed below:

	KO	PEP
Coefficient of Correlation	.996	.997
Standard Error of Estimate ($ millions)	$158.1	$166.1
Regression Equation	−966.76 + 2.36 (GNP)	−2053.81 + 3.02 (GNP)
1983 Sales ($ millions)	$6,820	$7,700

Assuming that current dollar GNP increases 8% per annum to $4,850 billion in 1988, calculate the projected sales for each company in that year. Calculate the annual sales growth projected for KO and PEP and compare these projections to the growth of earnings implied by each company's return on equity as calculated in part b.

d. As a portfolio manager for a pension fund with a long time horizon, you are considering either KO or PEP as an addition to the portfolio.

(1) Calculate the implied total return for both KO and PEP.

(2) Calculate the SML-based expected return for both KO and PEP using the security market line data shown below.

(3) Discuss the implications of the calculations in parts d(1) and d(2) for choosing either KO or PEP.

(4) Select either KO or PEP for the portfolio. Give three well-supported reasons for your choice.

	Per Common Share	
	KO	PEP
Stock Price (Jan. 16, 1984)	$51¾	$36⅞
1984 Estimated Earnings	$4.80	$3.55
Indicated Dividend	$2.90	$1.71
Price Range (1983)—High	$57½	$40¼
—Low	$45½	$32⅝
Book Value	$23.85	$20.95
Value Line Beta	.80	.95

Other Market Data	
Risk-Free Return	9.0%
Expected Market Return	14.0%

15 Option Fundamentals

In Chapters 11 through 14 we examined securities that have a direct claim to a firm's earnings: debt instruments, which receive a promised fixed amount of earnings, and equity instruments, which receive residual earnings after all debt holders have been paid. In this chapter we examine securities that have an indirect claim to earnings: options on a direct-claim security. An option is an agreement between two individuals. One individual is given the legal right to buy (or sell) a specified asset at a specified price on or before a specified date. Acquiring this right does not mean being *required* to buy (or sell)—the individual does so at his or her "option." As compensation, a nonreimbursable fee is paid to the individual who sells the right.

The recent growth in option trading and in the types of options available has been phenomenal. Prior to 1973 all option trading occurred in the OTC market, and volume was negligible. In 1973, the first listed exchange trading took place as a trial in options on only sixteen common stocks. The result was so successful that by the late 1980s options were being traded on a wide variety of assets and on many exchanges worldwide. Today exchange-listed options are available on individual stocks, many debt instruments, broad stock indexes, foreign currencies, and even stock index futures. Clearly, these options must present opportunities to market participants which are not available from traditional debt and equity instruments.

Two chapters are devoted to security options. In this chapter, the basic character and valuation of puts and calls is explained. In Chapter 16, various hedging, speculation, and arbitrage procedures are discussed. The chapters focus on stock options, although most of the principles apply to options on other types of underlying assets as well.

PUTS AND CALLS: INSTITUTIONAL FEATURES

Stock options come in two basic types: puts and calls. A put is an option to *sell* a given number of shares of a particular stock at a specified price on or before a given date. Puts are purchased by buyers and sold by writers. For example, a 90-day put on IBM at $120 allows the option buyer to sell a share of IBM at $120 any time during the next 90 days.

A call is an option to *buy* a given number of shares of a particular stock at a specified price on or before a given date. For example, a 90-day call on IBM at $120 allows the option buyer to purchase a share of IBM at $120 any time during the next 90 days.

Definitions

To understand put and call valuation, the following terminology is necessary:

1. *Option premium.* The price paid by the option buyer and received by the option seller—the *writer.* Stock options are usually written on 100 shares of stock, so the option premium on a call is the price a call buyer pays to be able to buy 100 shares of a specified stock at a specified price. The option premium on a put is the price paid by a buyer to be able to sell 100 shares of a specified stock by a specified date.

2. *Exercise (or striking) price.* The per-share price at which the common stock underlying the option may be bought (a call) or sold (a put). A given stock may have a variety of different options available on it, each having a different exercise price.

3. *Expiration date.* The last date at which an option can be exercised. In the financial press, the expiration date is indicated by a particular month. The expiration date for common stocks is the Saturday following the third Friday of the expiration month.

4. *European versus American options.* European options may be exercised only at the expiration date. American options may be exercised any time on or before the expiration date. In a sense, an American option is a sequence of many European options.

5. *Naked versus covered options.* The writer of a call option may be required to sell the stock. If the call is sold on a stock the writer does not own, the call is said to be a *naked call.* If the call is sold on a stock now owned, the call is *covered.* Put sales may also be naked or covered depending on the writer's position in the underlying stock.

6. *In-, out-of-, and near-the-money.* If the underlying stock's price is higher than a call's exercise price, the call is said to be *in-the-money.* The call has a recognizable, immediate value. If the stock price is substantially lower than the exercise price, the call option is said to be *out-of-the-money.* The value of the call does not arise from the current stock price but from possible future stock prices. *Near-the-money* refers to cases in which the exercise price is only slightly more than existing stock prices. In-, out-of-, and near-the-money also apply to put options, but the definitions are reversed.

Table 15-1 illustrates price quotations for IBM puts and calls. At the close of trading, IBM common shares were trading at $123. Thus, April IBM calls with an exercise price of $110 were in-the-money and traded at a price of $15.875 per share. Since calls are bought and sold in 100-share lots, one IBM $110 call exercisable on or before the Saturday following the third Friday in April would have a cost of $1,587.50. Individuals who thought IBM shares would increase in value could have bought 100

TABLE 15-1 *IBM Put and Call Quotations on December 31*
(IBM Stock Close = $123)

Exercise Price	Calls			Puts		
	January	*April*	*July*	*January*	*April*	*July*
$110	13⅝	15⅞	18½	⅛	⅞	1⅜
$120	4⅜	7¾	10	⅞	3⅛	4⅛
$130	⅝	2⅞	5¼	6⅞	8¼	8¾

shares of the stock outright at a cost of $12,300.00 or one call exercisable at $110 expiring in late April at a cost of $1,587.50. Note that: (1) the more distant the expiration date, the larger the call premium, and (2) the higher the exercise price, the lower the call premium. Later we will discuss why this is so.

Put options were also available on IBM. For example, one could have bought the right to sell 100 shares of IBM at a price of $110 on or before late April for a premium of $87.50.

It is important to understand the cash flows associated with buying and writing both types of options. Consider trades in the IBM April $110 calls first. Today will be referred to as day zero.

For each 1.0 call purchased, buyers will have to pay $1,587.50 to call writers *on day zero*. This option premium is an immediate cash outflow to the buyer and an immediate cash inflow to the writer. Let's assume that time passes such that we are now at the expiration date and the buyer of the call hasn't yet exercised the option. (For most stock call options there is a logical reason not to exercise prior to the expiration date. Later we discuss why.) Let's assume that the price of IBM shares has increased in value to $140. Since the option is about to expire, call buyers will be forced to decide whether they will exercise or not. Given that the stock is worth $140 versus an exercise price of $110, call buyers will exercise. For each 1.0 call, the buyer will have a cash outflow of $11,000 ($100 × 110 shares) and receives shares worth $14,000 ($140 × 100). The call writer will deliver 100 shares and receive a cash inflow of $11,000.[1] These cash flows are summarized below:

Cash Flows in Call Trade Example

	Day 0	Expiration Date
Buyer of 1 Call:		
Pay Premium	−$1,587.50	
Pay Exercise Price		−$11,000
Writer of 1 Call:		
Receive Premium	+$1,587.50	
Receive Exercise Price		+$11,000

[1]This example results in a net profit to the buyer of 1.0 call equal to $1,412.50 ($3,000 − $1,587.50) and a net loss to the writer of $1,412.50. Profit and loss outcomes are discussed later. For now, we focus solely on cash flows associated simply with buying and later exercising the options.

Now consider the case of April $110 put options. At day zero the market quote of ⅞ translates to a price of $87.50 for a put on 100 shares. At day zero, the $87.50 will be a cash outflow to the buyer and an inflow to the writer. If the expiration date arrives and IBM is selling for $140, the buyer will not exercise. (Why sell the stock at the put exercise price of $110 when stock could be sold in the open market for $140!) Thus, there will be no cash flows at the expiration date in our example.

Cash Flows in Put Trade Example

	Day 0	Expiration Date
Buyer of 1 Put:		
Pay Premium	−$87.50	
No Exercise		−
Writer of 1 Put:		
Receive Premium	+$87.50	
No Exercise		−

The data in Table 15-1 apply to options on the shares of individual firms—shares of IBM in the example. Put and call options are also available for *stock indexes*, which track the value of a portfolio of many stocks. In fact, by the late 1980s options on the S&P 100 Index were the most actively traded type of option contract. Options on stock indexes can be thought of as options on specific stock portfolios and (with one important difference) can be analyzed in the same manner as options on individual companies.

The only important difference between options on individual shares and options on stock indexes relates to exercise. If the buyer of an IBM call exercises the call, the call buyer pays the exercise price, receives IBM shares, and earns a profit equal to the difference between the share's market value and the exercise price. Actual delivery of shares takes place at exercise. However, because of the difficulty of creating stock portfolios which are identical to a stock index, physical delivery does not take place with stock index options. Instead, the writer pays the buyer the dollar value of the buyer's profit.

Illustrative price quotations on the S&P 100 Index are shown in Table 15-2. The S&P 100 Index was constructed by the Chicago Board Options Exchange to closely resemble the S&P 500. It consists of 100 different stocks instead of 500 in order to make it easier to create stock portfolios that mimic the index. This is particularly important in that it facilitates the process of arbitrage when actual market prices of options differ from their theoretically correct values.

TABLE 15-2 *S&P 100 Index Quotations (S&P 100 Index Close = $238.26)*

Exercise Price	Calls			Puts		
	January	February	March	January	February	March
$230	11½	16½	18½	4⅜	8⅞	12½
$240	5¼	10⅜	13¾	8½	13	15
$250	1¹¹⁄₁₆	6¼	9	14⅝	17¾	20

The purchase of a 1.0 call (or put) is conceptually the right to buy (sell) 100 "units" of the S&P 100 Index. This is similar to the purchase of a 1.0 call (put) on an individual stock where the purchaser has a right to buy (sell) one round lot of the shares. For example, if you were to purchase 1.0 of the January $240 calls shown in Table 15-2, you would pay a $525 call premium to the writer. This gives you the right to purchase 100 units of the S&P 100 Index at an exercise price of $24,000 ($240 × 100). Given that the current spot value of one S&P 100 Index unit is now $23,826 ($238.26 × 100), this call is an in-the-money call.

As with options on individual shares, it is important to understand the cash flows associated with buying or writing options on stock indexes. Assume, for example, that trades are made in 1.0 of the January $240 calls and puts. Also assume that the value of the S&P 100 Index is $200 on the expiration date. This would result in the following cash flows:

Cash Flows of 1.0 S&P 100 Call

	Day 0	*Expiration Date*
Buyer of 1 Call:		
Pay Premium ($5¼ × 100)	−$525	
No Exercise		—
Writer of 1 Call:		
Receive Premium	+$525	
No Exercise		—

Cash Flows of 1.0 S&P 100 Put

	Day 0	*Expiration Date*
Buyer of 1 Put:		
Pay Premium ($8¼ × 100)	−$850	
Exercise [($240 − $200) × 100]		+$4,000
Writer of 1 Put:		
Receive Premium	+$850	
Exercise		−$4,000

Option premiums initially paid by the buyer to the writer are simply the quoted option price times 100. At the expiration date the stock index is $200. Thus the call owner, who has the right to buy the index at $240 per "unit" when the index is worth only $200, has no incentive to exercise. In contrast, the put owner has the (conceptual) right to sell at $240 something worth $200 in the market. The $40 profit per index unit will be paid by the writer to the buyer when the buyer states a wish to exercise. Note, again, that profits, not the physical index, are delivered at expiration on stock index options.

Although the S&P 100 Index options are the most popular, a variety of other stock index options are also actively traded. These include the following:

1. *S&P 500 Index.* Traded on the CBOE, these options are valued at 500 times the option quote (versus 100 for the S&P 100 options).
2. *Major Market Index.* These are options on an index of 20 stocks and are traded on the American Stock Exchange. The index is an equally weighted index which is highly correlated with the Dow Jones Industrial Average. Since it is an equally

weighted index of only 20 stocks, stock portfolios can be easily created that mimic the index.

3. *NYSE Index*. Obviously these are options on the NYSE Index and are traded on the NYSE. Each unit represents 100 times the price quote.

A number of other less popular stock index options are also traded. However, the S&P 100 options are, by far, the most actively traded.

The History of Puts and Calls

Instruments similar to puts and calls have existed throughout history. For example, during the middle 1880s traders in New York gathered in what were known as "bucketshops" to place bets upon future prices of some common stocks. While these bets did not constitute a claim to the underlying stock, they *were* side bets on a security's future price and had payoffs similar to those for options. In more recent years formal puts and calls could be purchased or sold in the over-the-counter market through brokers who were members of the Put and Call Dealers and Brokers Association. Individuals who wished to buy a call on a particular stock would contact a member of the association, who would then contact other members in an attempt to find a potential seller. Terms such as exercise price, exercise date, option premium, etc., would then be negotiated between the buyer and seller.

Option trading changed dramatically in 1973 when the first *organized* option exchange was formed: the Chicago Board Options Exchange (CBOE). Since then option trading has been one of the most dynamic segments of the securities industry. By the end of 1989, options were traded on five domestic U.S. exchanges: the CBOE, the American Stock Exchange, the Pacific Stock Exchange, the Philadelphia Exchange, and the NYSE, as well as on many international markets. The availability of organized exchanges provided significant advantages over OTC option trading:

1. *Standardization of contract*. Specified exercise dates and exercise prices are now available. Prior to the formation of organized exchanges a large variety of exercise prices and dates were used.
2. *Liquidity*. Organized exchanges in standardized contracts allow the individual to buy or sell whenever desired. Previously, contracts had to be closed directly with the initial buyer or seller.
3. *Disclosure and surveillance rules*. Organized markets maintain relatively strict trading, disclosure, and surveillance procedures.
4. *Guaranteed clearing*. Each option exchange has an easy-to-use and formal means of bringing buyers and sellers together. In addition, the option *clearing corporations* guarantee delivery of underlying shares and cash. When trades occurred on the OTC, there was greater uncertainty about stock and cash delivery when an option was exercised.
5. *Lower transaction costs*. Brokerage fees for options traded on organized exchanges are substantially less than required in OTC trading. This is due to the ease of matching the other side to a trade, increased trading activity, and the institution of exchange clearing corporations which have taken over many brokerage duties from the OTC.

During the 1980s, options on stock indexes were offered by various exchanges and quickly began to dominate option trading. Not only do stock index options allow speculators to bet on movements in aggregate stock prices but, more important, they provide a cheap and fast means of adjusting the market risk of an investor's total portfolio.

Other Types of Listed Options

In Chapters 15 and 16 the discussion of option contracts is limited to stock options: options on stocks of individual firms or portfolios of stocks (as proxied by stock indexes). Listed options are also available, however, on three other types of assets: (1) debt securities, (2) commodities, and (3) foreign currencies. Usually such options are not on the underlying asset itself but on a futures contract on the underlying asset. Since "options on futures" cannot be understood until we have a good understanding of futures contracts, discussion of them is delayed until Chapter 17.

Why Options Exist

Since their introduction, trading volume of exchange-listed stock options has grown tremendously. But why? What does a stock option offer that is not available in traditional forms of direct equity ownership? Has the dramatic growth in options trading simply been the result of security brokers "pushing" options for large brokerage fees on options trades? Perhaps — option brokerage fees are larger than fees for other securities. But it is more likely that options provide something that direct ownership claims in stocks do not. In truth, scholars are not completely sure about what has caused the growth of options trading. However, if people are reasonably rational, there must be more to the phenomenon than large brokerage fees. Three basic explanations have been offered to suggest why option trading has become as important as it is:

1. *Improved borrowing and lending rates.* We will see later how options can be combined with stock positions to create a risk-free portfolio. A long position in this stock-option portfolio provides a risk-free rate of interest. A short position results in borrowing at a risk-free rate. If investors are otherwise unable to lend or borrow at the risk-free rate, they will naturally prefer to use options to do so. This is not simply theory. Many investment organizations use option positions as a source of borrowing to finance their security inventories because using options is less expensive than obtaining brokers' loans from commercial banks.

2. *Increased use of margin.* Margin requirements affect stock trading in three ways. First, there is a limit on the amount one can borrow on a long stock position — typically 50% of the stock's value. Second, when a stock is sold short, the seller does not have access to the proceeds from the sale. Instead, the proceeds are used as collateral and given to the lender of shares, who can then invest the proceeds at a risk-free return. Returns on the proceeds benefit the lender of shares — not the short seller. Third, in any short sale a performance bond (margin) must be given

in addition to the collateral. This performance bond could be risk-free securities owned by the short seller. In that case any earnings on the performance bond belong to the short seller and, thus, the short seller is not harmed by this requirement. However, small investors often provide a cash performance bond and thus are hurt economically by this requirement.

Options provide ways to get around these margin restrictions. Some of the techniques are too complicated to discuss in this text. But it is easy to see how people can overcome the restriction on the amount of margin leverage. Consider the IBM call options in Table 15-1 which have an exercise price of $130 and an expiration date of July. If you have $10,000 to invest, you can buy 19 calls ($10,000 ÷ $525), which have a claim on 1,900 shares of IBM (19 × 100). Alternatively, you could use your $10,000 plus $10,000 in borrowing (at a cost, say, of 10% per year) to purchase 163 actual shares ($20,000 ÷ $123) of IBM. Borrowing $10,000 is the limit available under margin rules. Now, let's assume that when July comes, the shares of IBM stock are worth $170. The rate of return on each investment is:

Option Position	*Stock Position*
$$R = \frac{\text{Ending Value}}{\text{Investment}} - 1.0$$	$$R = \frac{\text{Ending Value}}{\text{Investment}} - 1.0$$
$$= \frac{\text{Option Value}}{\text{Investment}} - 1.0$$	$$= \frac{\text{Stock Value} - \text{Interest}}{\text{Investment}} - 1.0$$
$$= \frac{1,900(\$170 - \$130)}{\$10,000} - 1.0$$	$$= \frac{163(\$170) - 0.1(\$10,000)^{7/12}}{\$10,000} - 1.0$$
$$= 660\%$$	$$= 171\%$$

Both returns are glorious, but that is not our point. The point is that the option provided a greater return because there was greater financial leverage inherent in the call option than in a 50% marginal stock position. Later we will be able to state explicitly the degree of financial leverage inherent in any given option. For now, it is sufficient to say that many options provide greater leverage than is available on fully margined stock investments.

3. *Reduced transaction costs.* Brokerage fees on a single call option are generally higher than they are on a round-lot stock purchase. But it is unfair to conclude from this that options cannot provide a means of reducing transaction costs. Transaction costs should not be evaluated at the single-trade level but, instead, at the level of total trades made on a portfolio over time. There are many portfolio strategies for which options will be cheaper to trade than stocks and bonds.

For example, assume you are the manager of a $100 million pension portfolio which is currently invested equally in stocks and bonds. Trustees of the pension have just instructed you to adjust the stock/bond mix to 80/20 as soon as possible. If you were to actively begin buying stocks and selling bonds, you might not get the best price available, since your transactions might affect market prices. A slower and more orderly readjustment might result in lower transaction costs. Options could be used in this case to immediately obtain an effective 80/20 stock/bond mix with lower transaction costs. The purchase of certain call options could increase the portfolio's effective stock commitment right away. As actual stock holdings are increased slowly over time, the call option position would be eliminated.

There are many other situations in which option trading could be less costly than stock and bond trading. Short-term strategies that require active trading between stocks and bonds will often be less costly if options are used. Longer-term, buy-hold strategies are cheaper if options are *not* used.

All of the advantages claimed for options which are not available from stock and bond combinations have a common theme. The introduction of options makes available certain return and risk combinations that are impossible to obtain when only debt and equity securities are used. In the parlance of economics, options add *completeness* to the markets.

Trading Mechanics

When a broker receives a customer's request to buy or sell a specific option, the trade is transmitted to the appropriate exchange floor. At present there are five U.S. exchanges on which stock options are traded. A "runner" conveys the order to a *floor broker* who represents the brokerage firm. The floor broker takes the order to the post at which the option is traded and attempts to obtain the best price possible through an *open outcry* system. The matching trade will be with either another floor broker, a market maker, or an *order book official*. The market makers play the same role on the option exchanges as they do on stock exchanges—they are members of the exchange who provide liquidity by trading for their own account. Order book officials are employees of the exchange who handle public limit orders; they do not trade for themselves.

Once a trade occurs, the *Option Clearing Corporation* (OCC) is notified. The Option Clearing Corporation was formed by the various option exchanges and is the sole organization responsible for clearing all option trades (stock and non-stock). The brokerage firm representing the buyer must pay for the option by 9:00 A.M. (Central Time) on the first business day following the trade. Note that this is not the same as for trades in stocks, which have five business days between trade and settlement dates. The purchaser's cash payment is then transferred to the option writer's brokerage firm, and the OCC creates a long position for the buyer and a short position for the writer in its computer.

Subsequent to the initial trade the buyer or the writer can close out his or her position by making an offsetting trade in the same option. When the OCC sees that an account has an identical long and short option position, the two positions are eliminated.

When buyers wish to exercise, their broker notifies the OCC. The OCC then assigns the exercise to an option writer who still has an open short position in the option. If a call on an individual stock is exercised, the brokerage firm representing the call owner delivers cash to the firm representing the writer in return for the securities. When a put is exercised, the securities are delivered in return for cash. Both are conducted on the *exercise settlement date*, which is five business days after OCC is notified of the desire to exercise.

Margins. No borrowing is allowed on naked option purchases. Writers of options with no offsetting position in the stock must deposit the dollar amount of the *current* premium plus an additional percentage of the current premium into a margin account. This extra percentage depends on how far the option is in- or out-of-the-money as well as on the requirements of the brokerage firm the writer deals with. Since the writer's margin depends on each day's option premium, it is effectively *marked to market* each day.

Most option traders do not maintain naked option positions but, instead, have positions in other securities which offset the option position risk to some degree. Margin requirements in such cases are too complex to review here. However, traders should become familiar with the margin rules their brokers have specified.

Taxes. Taxation of option profits depends on whether the option is: (1) exercised, (2) held to expiration but not exercised, or (3) sold prior to expiration.

Consider first an exercised call (puts are exactly the reverse). When buyers exercise calls, for tax purposes they have bought the stock at a price equal to the exercise price plus the original call premium paid plus any commissions or other costs involved in buying and exercising the call. Writers who have calls exercised against them have sold the stock at a price equal to the exercise price plus the original premium received less any commissions or other costs involved in writing the call. The date at which the option was initially traded or the period of time it was held is unimportant for tax purposes. The stock is assumed to be bought by the call owner and sold by the call writer on the exercise date.

When calls (or puts) are never exercised, the premium lost by the buyer is treated as a capital loss. Whether this capital loss will be a short-term or long-term loss depends on how long the option was held. However, the option writer's gain in such cases is always treated as a short-term capital gain.

When buyers of an option close out their positions by subsequent sales, the difference between the two option premiums is treated as a capital gain or loss, short- or long-term depending on the holding period. When writers close out their positions by subsequent purchases, their profit or loss is always considered a short-term capital gain or loss.[2]

Commissions. Broker commissions are paid whenever an option is traded or exercised. The size of option commissions differs between brokerage firms. When compared with stock commissions, the commission on a given dollar value of options will almost always be greater than the commission on *the same dollar value* of stock. However, such a comparison fails to take certain important differences into account. For example, option prices are always less than the prices of the stocks on which the options are written. Thus, a given dollar amount will purchase a larger quantity of

---

[2]If option writing is part of the taxpayer's normal business activity, then gains and losses are taxed as ordinary income.

options, resulting in greater transaction costs to the broker. In addition, a given dollar investment in options represents a very different investment from the same investment in stocks. For example, we will see soon that a call option is simply a leveraged ownership of the stock. Investing $X in calls usually results in substantially different risks and expected returns than $X invested in stocks. In short, it is very difficult to compare commissions on options with stock commissions.

Regulation. Historically, different segments of the financial markets have been regulated by different governmental organizations. For example, the Federal Reserve has principal control over commercial banks having a national charter, the Commodity Futures Trading Commission has regulatory responsibility for futures markets, and the Securities and Exchange Commission is responsible for the stock and bond markets. When originally developed, listed stock options were made the responsibility of the SEC.

Black Monday, however, served to point out the extent to which all security markets are interrelated and the importance of being able to rapidly coordinate actions by the various regulatory authorities. In fact, after the Brady Commission had completed its study of the events surrounding Black Monday, the Commission recommended that a single federal agency be given oversight over all security markets. Although this suggestion has met with considerable controversy, there is no doubt that the debate over how the options, futures, and equity markets should be regulated will continue.

EXPIRATION DATE OUTCOMES

We turn now to a consideration of how options should be valued. There are two general classes of valuation models which arise: (1) models which focus on expiration date payoffs, and (2) models which focus on payoffs during the next instant in time. Both approaches have their unique advantages and disadvantages. For example, continuous-time models yield precise and logical values of either a call or a put, but at the cost of mathematical complexity. In contrast, valuation models based on expiration date payoffs are mathematically easier to understand but only allow us to determine what the difference should be between the price of a call and the price of a put with similar terms — one option cannot be valued in isolation from the other. Our discussion will start simple and build as we proceed. A fundamental concept is the expiration date payoff from an option position.

Investment Value at Expiration Date

The term *expiration date* is used here to refer to the instant in time before the option's life ends. Trades can still be made in the stock and options. And enough time remains to exercise if we wish. But any value inherent in the option comes solely from the fact that expiration date stock prices are different from the option's exercise price.

The term *investment value* is also being used with care. It refers to the market value of a particular security portfolio. If the portfolio consists of the ownership of one call, the portfolio's investment value will be the same as the call price. But in many cases we wish to examine portfolios of various option and stock combinations. Thus, investment value can refer to the value of individual securities or portfolios of the securities.

Four types of securities are considered: (1) a call option, (2) a similar put option, (3) the individual stock or stock index on which the options can be exercised, and (4) a zero-coupon risk-free security which matures at the option's expiration date. The following symbols are used:

P_c = market price of the call
P_p = market price of the put
P_x = exercise price of both options
P_s = market price of the stock (or stock index)
P_{RF} = market price of the risk-free security

To illustrate the results numerically, assume that the put and call are both exercisable at \$250 and that the risk-free security pays off \$250 at expiration.[3] Although actual option trades provide claims to 100 units of the stock, it is less cumbersome to analyze the options on a per-share basis.

Finally, the options being evaluated here are European options since, strictly speaking, American options might be exercised prior to the expiration date. This usually turns out to be a relatively unimportant point. But to keep the arguments as clean as possible, we are technically evaluating only European options.

Investment Value of One Call. The panels in Figure 15-1 depict the expiration date investment value of positions in one call. Panel A represents the investment value of being long (owning) the call, and panel B represents the investment value of being short (writing) the call.

If the stock is worth more than the call's exercise price, the call will have a value equal to the stock price minus the exercise price. If this is the case, the call owner will capture this value either by selling the call for this amount or by exercising. In contrast, if the stock is worth less than the call's exercise price, the option will die worthless.

These statements are not only intuitively obvious — they *must* be true. If they are not, then large *arbitrage profits* are possible. For example, assume that the stock's price is \$300. As shown in panel A the call option should be trading for \$50. For the sake of argument, assume that option market participants are irrational enough to let the actual option price be \$40. The arbitrage which is available in this case consists of:

---

[3] Although it is unusual to observe individual stock prices close to \$250, stock indexes such as the S&P 100 Index have recently traded near this level. Given the importance of such stock index options, the value of \$250 is realistic. The \$250 par value on the risk-free securities is identical to the exercise price simply for convenience. In the examples below, the \$250 par allows us to trade in 1.0 units of the risk-free security. More realistic examples are presented in the next chapter, at which time multiple Treasury bills are traded.

FIGURE 15-1 *Investment Values of One Call at Expiration Date*

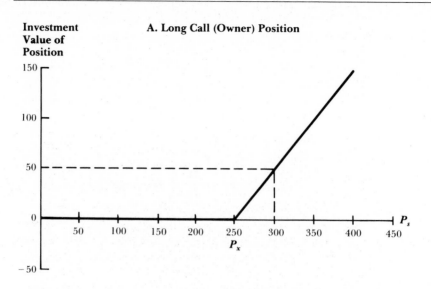

A. Long Call (Owner) Position

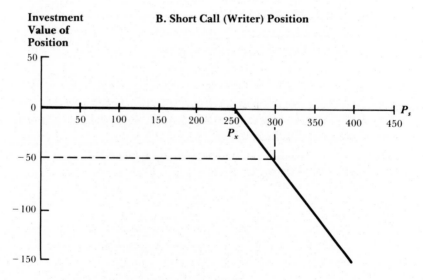

B. Short Call (Writer) Position

Transaction	Cash Flow
1. Buy call at market price	−$ 40
2. Exercise call to obtain stock	−250
3. Sell stock at market price	+300
Net (at no risk and no investment)	$ 10

An arbitrage is a transaction between two securities which involves no net cash invest-ment and results in a known risk-free cash inflow. This is exactly the case in our example—for no cash investment an immediate cash inflow of $10 is received. Clearly, such arbitrages would quickly force the option's price to $50. If the call price rose above $50, an opposite arbitrage would be conducted.

These results are commonly written symbolically as:

Call Value at Expiration
$$P_c = \max(0, P_s - P_x) \tag{15.1}$$

The price of a call at the expiration date will be the maximum of zero or the stock price minus the call's exercise price.

Note that the call writer experiences expiration date investment values which are exactly opposite to those of the call buyer. Although it might seem strange that someone would take a position they know will lead to no value or negative value, remember that the writer received the call premium. If the call premium is large enough, the writer would be willing to accept such potential payoffs.

Investment Value of One Put. The panels in Figure 15-2 depict the expiration date value of long and short positions in one put. Note that the value of owning the put increases as the value of the stock falls. This is because the put provides the owner with a guaranteed selling price. The owner of a put actually benefits from stock price declines.

The value of a put at its expiration date is expressed symbolically as:

Put Value at Expiration
$$P_p = \max(0, P_x - P_s) \tag{15.2}$$

The price of a put at the expiration date will be the maximum of zero or the put's exercise price minus the stock price.

Investment Value of One Stock or One T-Bill. Although naked positions in calls and puts such as those shown in Figures 15-1 and 15-2 can be taken, it is more common to have offsetting positions in other securities. There are many reasons for doing so, the most important being to limit the investor's risk. Two other reasons are illustrated immediately below. But in order to illustrate how the investment values of different portfolio positions combine, the expiration date value of buying or short selling one stock or one risk-free asset such as a Treasury bill must be understood.

Actually, such positions are easier to understand than the naked option positions shown above. Consider the panels of Figure 15-3. In panel A the expiration date investment values of being long or short one share of stock are shown. Remember, these are not profits from buying or shorting the stock. Instead, they are the market values of each position on the expiration date. For example, if the stock is worth $250, a long position in one share is worth +$250 and a short position is worth −$250. In panel B the expiration date investment values of being long or short one T-bill are shown. Since the par value of the T-bill is assumed to be $250 and the T-bill matures on the options' expiration date, a long position will result in a cash inflow of $250,

FIGURE 15-2 *Investment Values of One Put at Expiration Date*

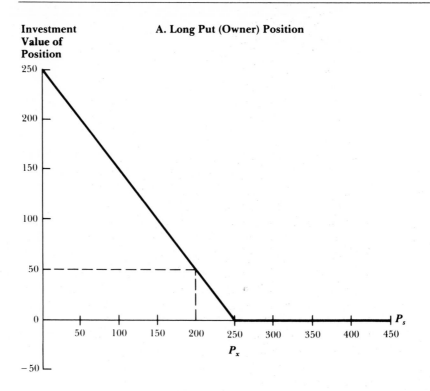

and a short position will require a cash outflow of $250. These T-bill cash flows are independent of the stock price.

Armed with a knowledge of the expiration date investment values of these four basic securities, we can begin to develop an understanding of option *strategy and valuation*. The option strategy illustrated below is known as *portfolio insurance*. Many other strategies are possible, of course, but portfolio insurance is a particularly intriguing one. The valuation implications illustrated below indicate that the value of any one of these four asset types should be the same as the value of a portfolio of the other three. This concept is known as the *put-call parity* model.

Portfolio Insurance. Consider the expiration date investment value of a portfolio which consists of a long position in 1.0 stock and 1.0 put as shown in panel A of Figure 15-4. The stock investment values are shown as the open circles, the put investment value is shown as the dashed line, and the investment value of the portfolio of both is shown as the solid line. Note that when the stock price exceeds the put's exercise price, the put is worthless and all of the portfolio's value comes from the stock. However, when the stock's value is less than the put's exercise price, the put has a positive value which exactly offsets stock price declines below $250. For example, if the stock is worth $125, the put will also be worth $125; thus the total portfolio will be

FIGURE 15-2 *(continued)*

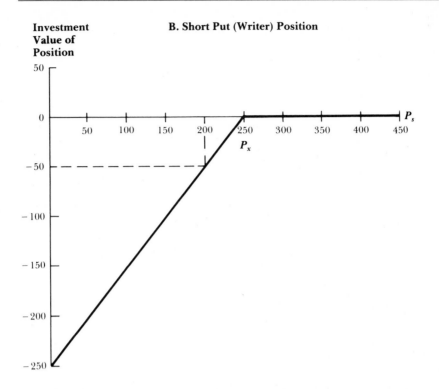

B. Short Put (Writer) Position

Investment
Value of
Position

valued at $250. When a put is purchased on a long stock position the result is a minimum portfolio "floor value." This is referred to as *portfolio insurance.*

This result should be intuitively obvious. Since the ownership of a put guarantees the price at which an investor can sell the stock, the combination of the two will never be worth less than this guaranteed price—the put's exercise price.

In panel B another way to obtain portfolio insurance is shown. In this case, the portfolio consists of a long position in 1.0 T-bill and 1.0 call. Since the T-bill will be worth $250 regardless of the stock price, the portfolio will again be worth at least $250. In addition, if the stock rises above the call's exercise price, the call will also have a positive investment value. Again, we have an insured portfolio floor with the opportunity for the portfolio to increase in value when the stock trades at more than the call's exercise price.

The insured portfolios illustrated in Figure 15-4 serve to make three important points. First, it is the ability to use option positions together with other securities in order to create unusual investment strategies which has attracted many investors to options. Second, even though an insured portfolio seems ideal (a known minimum value if the stock declines but increased values as the stock rises), it comes at a cost— the option premium paid to purchase either the put or the call. Both of these points are discussed in detail in the next chapter when option strategies are examined. Third,

FIGURE 15-3 *Investment Values of Stock and T-Bills at Expiration Date*

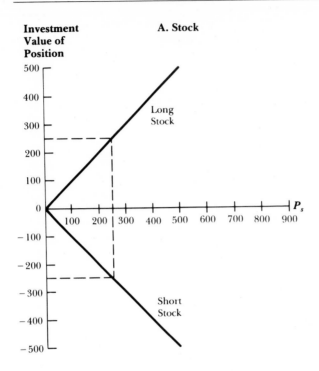

note that there are two portfolios which consist of very different securities but which *are economically the same* since they have the same expiration date outcomes. Since the two portfolios provide the same final outcomes, the total value of each must be identical, both at the expiration date and at all prior trades; that is:

$$\frac{\text{Cost to Purchase}}{\text{1.0 stock and 1.0 put}} = \frac{\text{Cost to Purchase}}{\text{1.0 T-bill and 1.0 call}}$$

This is the basic idea underlying the put-call parity valuation model.

One Asset Is a Combination of the Other Three. The put-call parity valuation model is based on the following fact: expiration date investment values for any one of these four assets (European calls, European puts, stock, or T-bills) can be exactly replicated by an appropriate combination of the other three.

This point is illustrated graphically in Figure 15-5. Each of the four panels illustrates how one of the asset's expiration date investment values is simply the sum of the other three. Portfolios of the other three are not randomly chosen! They are unique. In addition, the quantity of each asset position is not random. For each 1.0

FIGURE 15-3 *(continued)*

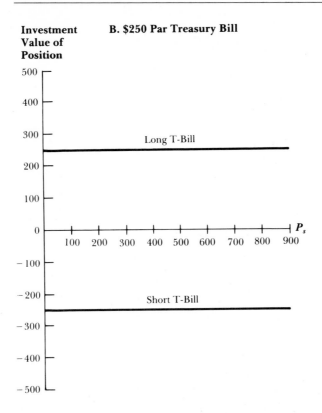

Investment Value of Position

B. $250 Par Treasury Bill

of one asset, a position of 1.0 in the other assets is taken. This 1:1 relationship becomes very important later in the chapter, when it is discussed as the "hedge ratio."

Consider panel A, in which a call option's expiration-date investment is shown to be the same as a portfolio consisting of: buy 1.0 stock, buy 1.0 put, short sell 1.0 T-bill. At a stock price equal to P_x, the stock is worth +$250, the put is worthless, and the short T-bill requires a cash outflow of −$250; that is, the portfolio value is zero, the same as that of a call. At stock prices greater than P_x, the put is worthless and the portfolio is worth the stock price less $250 ($P_s$ − $250); that is, the same as a call with an exercise price of $250. Finally, at stock prices below P_x, the long put and long stock together create a known value of $250. (Recall the portfolio insurance example above.) But this is exactly offset by the cash outflow of $250 on the short T-bill position; that is, at prices below P_x, the value of the portfolio is zero, the same as that of a call. At all stock prices, this portfolio (long 1.0 stock, long 1.0 put, short 1.0 T-bill) provides the same outcomes as a long call position. It is a call!

An evaluation of panels B and C is left as a useful exercise to the reader. However, in both cases the conclusion is the same: expiration date investment values on any one

FIGURE 15-4 *Investment Value at Expiration Date—Portfolio Insurance*

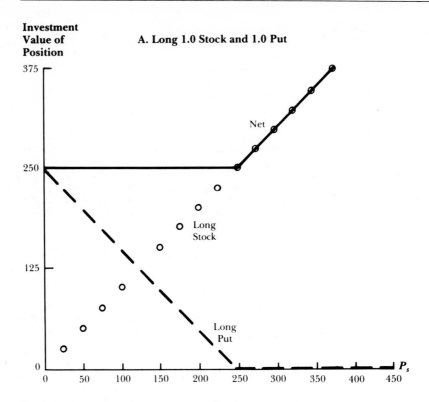

of these four assets can be exactly replicated by an appropriate combination of the other three.

Panel D, however, is particularly interesting in that it shows how a T-bill position can be replicated. Since we can easily observe market prices of T-bills, we can also easily determine what that value of this replicating portfolio should be.

A T-bill is replicated by: 1.0 long stock, 1.0 long put, and 1.0 short call position. If the stock's value is equal to P_x ($250), the put and call investment values are zero. Thus, the portfolio is worth $250—identical to the T-bill payoffs. At higher stock prices, gains from the stock are offset by losses on the short calls; that is, at higher stock prices than P_x the portfolio continues to be worth $250, identical to the T-bill payoff. When stock prices are less than P_x, the put offsets stock price declines, and the portfolio value remains at $250; that is, at stock prices lower than P_x, the portfolio's payoff is identical to that of a T-bill. *This portfolio is a perfect substitute for a Treasury bill!*

Each of the plots in Figure 15-5 is based on the most fundamental option valuation model which exists: the put-call parity model. We turn now to a formal statement of this model.

FIGURE 15-4 *(continued)*

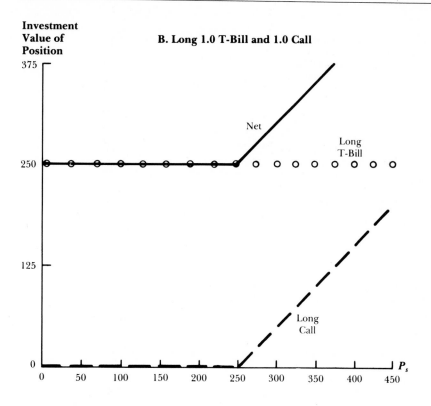

Put-Call Parity

In the absence of cash dividends, transaction costs, and taxes, a distinct relationship should exist between premiums on European puts and calls. To see this, we will define:

P_x = the exercise price on both the put and the call

P_s = the price of the stock at the exercise date

P_p = the current premium on a put for one share of stock

P_c = the current premium on a call for one share of stock

RF = the risk-free rate of interest on a bond with duration identical to the exercise date

T = the number of periods until the expiration date

As above, we will consider a covered portfolio of one stock, one put, and one written call. At the exercise date, P_s will either be less than, greater than, or equal to P_x.

FIGURE 15-5 *One Asset Is a Unique Combination of the Other Three at the Expiration Date*

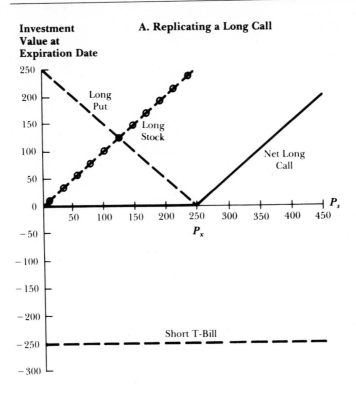

As shown above, the value of this covered portfolio will be P_x, regardless of what P_s is at the exercise date; that is:

	Stock Price at Expiration	
	Less Than Exercise Price	*Greater Than (or Equal to) Exercise Price*
Value of Stock Bought	P_s	P_s
Value of Put Bought	$P_x - P_s$	0
Value of Call Sold	0	$-(P_s - P_x)$
Net	P_x	P_x

Since the value of the covered portfolio at exercise is riskless and equal to P_x, the *present value* of the covered portfolio should be equal to P_x discounted at the risk-free rate:

Put-Call Parity Model

$$P_s + P_p - P_c = \frac{P_x}{(1 + RF)^T}$$

(15.3)

FIGURE 15-5 *(continued)*

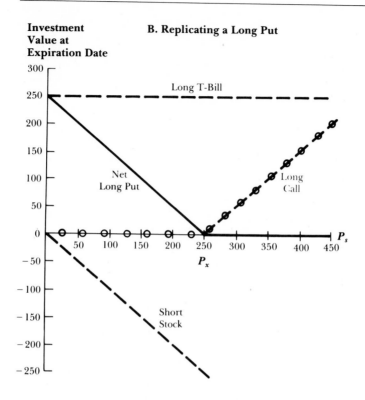

Alternatively, the difference between the call and put price should be:

Call Minus Put

$$P_c - P_p = P_s - \frac{P_x}{(1 + RF)^T}$$ **(15.4)**

Note that Equation 15.4 cannot be used to find the value of, say, a call unless the value of its equivalent put is known. It is a relative valuation model. Nonetheless, it is based on reasonable assumptions.

Earlier in the chapter, illustrative put and call prices were presented for options on the S&P 100 Index. Information about two of these options is summarized here:

Options	*T*	P_x	*Price*
Call on S&P 100 Index	1 month	$240	$5.25
Put on S&P 100 Index	1 month	$240	$8.50

Value of S&P 100 Index = $238.26

At the time of these price quotes, the one-month risk-free rate was 0.28%. According to put-call parity, the call option should be trading for $1.07 less than the put:

FIGURE 15-5 *(continued)*

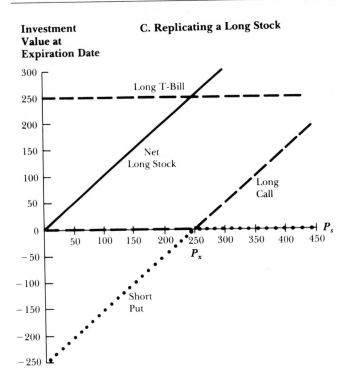

C. Replicating a Long Stock

$$P_c - P_p = \$238.26 - (\$240/1.0028)$$

$$= -\$1.07$$

Since the call was actually trading for $3.25 less than the put, the put-call parity model was not working. Why this was so is unclear. If we look at the assumptions underlying the theory, they could not explain such a large difference. Transaction costs, for example, certainly would not be large enough to explain the difference. Dividends also would be too small to be the cause. And many investors such as pension funds and endowment funds are not taxed and could have taken advantage of the price discrepancy through arbitrage transactions.

Illustrative Arbitrage. Realistic arbitrages are examined in the next chapter. However, it is useful to illustrate the basics of an option arbitrage now. The example above indicated that $P_c - P_p$ was more negative than it should be. We can't say which option is mispriced. But we can say that their relative prices were wrong.

The arbitrage (based on a single unit of the S&P 100 Index) is shown in Table 15-3. Since the call is selling for less than it should relative to the put, one would buy 1.0 call and sell 1.0 put. To make this portfolio risk-free, a short position in the stock would be taken. (Recall Equation 15.3.) The net effect of these positions is a known

FIGURE 15-5 *(continued)*

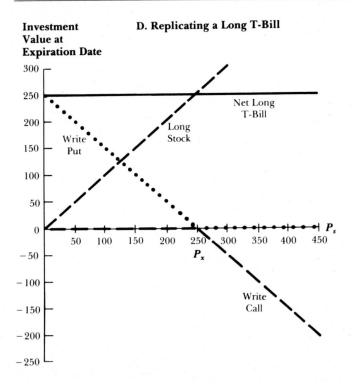

Investment Value at Expiration Date

D. Replicating a Long T-Bill

cash inflow today and a known cash outflow at the expiration date. In Table 15-3, two possible expiration date stock index values are shown, and for both the portfolio payoffs are identical—that is, a long position in 1.0 call and short positions in 1.0 put and 1.0 stock index unit are the same as short selling 1.0 T-bills currently worth $241.51. To make this into an arbitrage (in which no net position is taken), the position inflow of $241.51 is used to purchase actual T-bills. The result is a $0.0 dollar cash flow at day 0 and a +$2.19 cash inflow at the expiration date.

Exactly why the put would have been overvalued relative to the call in this example is unknown. The price quotes used, however, were as of the end of 1987, soon after Black Monday. Perhaps investors were, in fact, paying more for insurance against market declines (the put) than they should have. In general, though, arbitrage profits based on the put-call parity model are small.

The put-call parity model was originally outlined by Hans Stoll and later expanded by Robert Merton. To date, three major empirical tests of the model have been conducted. Stoll, as well as Gould and Galai, used OTC put and call price quotations and found that the put-call parity model described the real-world option prices fairly accurately. While some anomalies were found, their sizes were small. Arbitraging between puts and calls would have provided positive average profits only if no transaction costs were paid. Profits from trading between puts and calls were available only

TABLE 15-3 *Stock Index Arbitrage Based on Put-Call Parity*

		Cash Flow at Date	
		Expiration	
Transaction	0	$P_s = 200$	$P_s = 280$
Buy 1.0 Call ($P_x = 240$)	−$ 5.25	$ 0.00	+$ 40.00
Sell 1.0 Put ($P_x = 240$)	+ 8.50	− 40.00	0.00
Sell 1.0 Stock	+ 238.26	− 200.00	− 280.00
Portfolio	+ 241.51	− 240.00	− 240.00
Buy T-bills	− 241.51	+ 242.19*	+ 242.19*
Net	$ 0.00	$ 2.19	+$ 2.19

*242.19 = 241.51 × 1.0028, where 0.28% is the one-month risk-free return.

to exchange members, not to the general public. A more recent study by Klemkosky and Resnick examined exchange-listed American options and found results consistent with the parity model. However, they also found a small degree of inefficiency which they ascribed to overpriced calls.

The True Nature of a Call Option

At the beginning of this chapter, we gave a legal definition of a call. Such a definition is important, of course, since it determines the profit profiles associated with calls. But it does not adequately describe what a call really is. A call is actually a portfolio of three different securities: (1) a long position in a stock, (2) the sale of debt to partially finance the stock, and (3) the purchase of an insurance policy in the form of a put. To see this more clearly, the put-call parity model can be rearranged to show the determinants of a call's price as follows:

Value of a Call
$$P_c = P_s - \frac{P_x}{(1 + RF)^T} + P_p \tag{15.5}$$

The worth of a call is equal to (*a*) the cost associated with buying the stock, (*b*) less a loan having a maturity value equal to the option's exercise price discounted to its current worth at a risk-free rate, (*c*) plus the cost of a put.

The concept is really very simple. Say you want to purchase a single share of Digital Equipment Corporation at a price of $200. To help finance the purchase you visit a local banker and ask for a loan which matures in exactly a year and has a par value of $150.[4] The banker knows you well and trusts that you will most likely pay off the loan. But she has a little concern that, if DEC stock is selling for less than $150 when

---

[4]This would be impossible in practice since margin restrictions would allow the banker to lend no more than 50% of the stock's value. But this is exactly one of the beauties of options—they can provide leverage in excess of margin restrictions.

the loan is due, you will give the share to the bank, disappear, and leave them with a loss. For this reason, the banker will demand some insurance that you will not default. You could place a call to Lloyd's of London to see if they'd insure you, but the most obvious insurance would be the purchase of a put exercisable at $150. If this insurance (put) is bought and given to the bank, their loan is free of any risk. If DEC sells for more than $150 in a year, you will be able to pay off the loan. If DEC sells for less than $150—at, say, $130—the bank can collect its $150 by selling the put for $20 and the stock for $130. As a result, your loan is free of risk and the bank will lend to you at a risk-free rate of interest. Assuming that RF is 10% and that the put costs $5, you are able to control DEC shares at a cost of:

$$P_c = P_s - \frac{P_x}{(1 + RF)^T} + P_p$$

$$\$68.63 = \$200 - \frac{\$150}{1.10} + \$5$$

You now have a call option on DEC shares. If the stock is selling for more than $150, you will exercise your claim to the shares by paying off the loan (the exercise price). If the shares are less than $150, you will not exercise your option to own them.

There are two important points in this discussion. First, a call option is nothing more than a leveraged position in an underlying asset. Second, you can *create* a call option on any asset—a stock, a portfolio of stocks, a restaurant, etc. If puts are not traded on the asset, then it is time to visit with the local insurance agent. We will return to this later in the chapter.

Synthetic Calls. An artificial or synthetic call can be created on any asset. Given the discussion so far, we can create a synthetic call which will have *expiration date* payoffs identical to those for a traded call. Later in the chapter we will see how synthetic calls can be created which have the same payoffs as a traded call during the *next instant in time.*

Assume that you wish to buy a call option on a piece of land. When you approach the landowners, they say they are not willing to sell you a call on the land but are willing to sell the land for $100,000. To create a synthetic call you could: (1) purchase the land for $100,000, (2) obtain a loan from a bank at a risk-free rate, and (3) purchase insurance that promises to pay the banker if you default on the loan (thus the banker lends to you at a risk-free interest rate). Such insurance policies can be obtained (at a price). Assume that the loan is due in 12 months and has a par value of $80,000, no intermediate interest payments, and an annual interest rate of 8%. Also assume that the insurance policy costs you $1,000.

The combination of these three assets (the land, the loan, and the insurance) is a call option on the land for which you paid $26,925.93:

Land	−	Loan	+ Insurance	
$100,000	−	$80,000/1.08 +	$1,000	= $26,925.93

FIGURE 15-6 *Net Profit at Expiration Date, Naked Call and Put Positions*

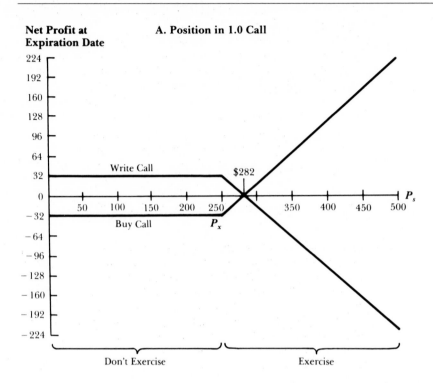

The call has an expiration date of one year and an exercise price of $80,000. At year-end, you will pay off the loan (exercise the option) if the land is worth more than $80,000. If the land is worth less than $80,000, you will default on the loan (not exercise) and let the bank take the land and whatever insurance payment is needed to make up the full $80,000.

Option Profits

The previous discussions have focused on expiration date investment values of various security positions; they have not examined the net profit from the positions. Expiration date net profits look very similar to investment value payoffs except that: (1) payoffs to option buyers are reduced by the amount of the option premium paid, and (2) payoffs to writers are increased by the amount of the option premium received.

Net profits for various portfolios are displayed in Figures 15-6 and 15-7. Data underlying the figures are as follows:

FIGURE 15-6 *(continued)*

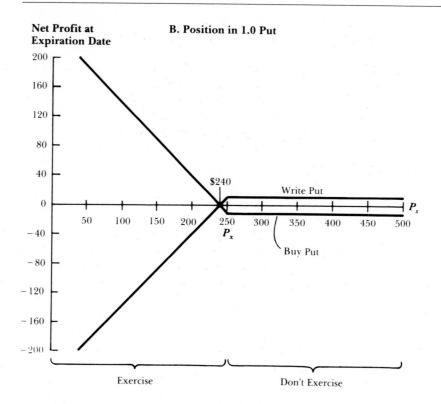

**Net Profit at
Expiration Date**   **B. Position in 1.0 Put**

Value at Initial	
Trade Date	

$$P_s = \$250$$
$$P_c = \$\ 32$$
$$P_p = \$\ 10$$
$$P_x = \$250 \quad \text{(for both options)}$$
$$P_{T\text{-}bill} = \$227.27 \quad \text{(discounted at 10\%)}$$

In Figure 15-6 net profits are shown for naked option positions. In the case of a call, the option writer profits if the stock is trading below P_x on the expiration date. The option buyer has a net positive profit only if the stock price is greater than the exercise price plus the initial call premium paid. Note, however, that the call buyer will exercise any time the stock is trading for more than P_x (at the expiration date) even if a net loss exists. If a net loss exists when P_s is greater than P_x, it can be minimized by the exercise. The initial option premium paid is a sunk cost and should not affect the decision to exercise.

In Figure 15-7, net profits on two portfolios of securities are shown. In panel **A**, an insured portfolio will incur a net loss whenever P_s is less than P_x. But the loss

FIGURE 15-7 *Net Profit at Expiration Date, Portfolio Combination*

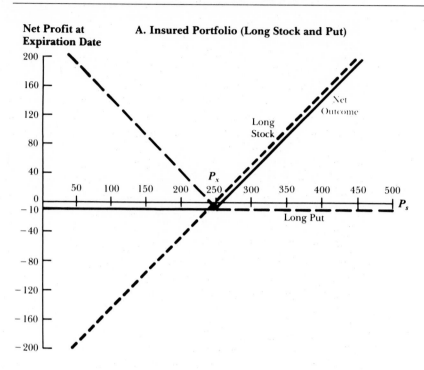

may not be as large as if the stock were held alone. As the stock price becomes greater than P_x, the portfolio value also increases. But it is always worth less than a full stock investment by the dollar amount paid for the put. In panel B, the net profits from a portfolio which replicates a call are shown. The solid line representing the net effect is identical to the naked long call position shown in panel A in Figure 15-6.

Minimum Option Values

The put-call parity model values one option relative to the other. It does not value either option independent of the other. Thus, if a put is not traded, the value of a call cannot be determined, and vice versa. However, a *minimum* option value can be found.

In this calculation we will deal with both European and American options. However, for simplicity, the options are on stocks which do not pay cash dividends. In addition, we neglect any impacts of transaction costs and taxes.

There are two minimum option values which can be calculated. We will refer to them as the *hard floor* and the *soft floor* prices. The American option has both floors. The European option can logically have only the soft floor. These floor values are illustrated in Figure 15-8 for both a call and a put. Both options have an exercise price

FIGURE 15-7 *(continued)*

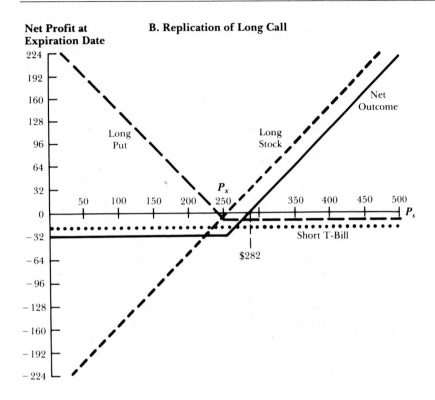

Net Profit at Expiration Date

B. Replication of Long Call

of $250. In addition, it is assumed that they expire in exactly six months and that the annual risk-free rate is 10%.

The logic of the hard floor of a call is obvious. If the stock is now selling for less than P_x, the option's value cannot be negative. Call owners, after all, are not forced to exercise at P_x —they have the *option* to do so. If the stock is now selling for more than P_x, then an American option must be worth *at least* $P_s - P_x$, the current stock price minus the exercise price. Consider a current stock price of $300 shown in panel A. The hard floor value is $50. If an American call were to sell for less than $50, an instantaneous arbitrage profit would be available. Say that the call premium is only $40. You could buy the American call (−$40), exercise it to obtain the stock (−$250), and immediately sell the stock (+$300). The result would be a net cash inflow of $10 at no risk. As you and others profit from this arbitrage, the price of the call will soon be driven to $50. Symbolically, the hard floor value of a call option is:

Hard Floor of a Call $\qquad\qquad P_c \geq \max(0, P_s - P_x)$ $\qquad\qquad$ **(15.6)**

The logic behind the soft floor relies on the principle of dominance. If portfolio *A* provides identical investment values as portfolio *B* for some states of nature but larger investment values in all other states, then portfolio *A* is said to dominate port-

FIGURE 15-8 *Hard and Soft Option Floors*

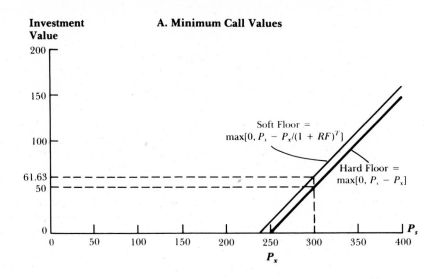

A. Minimum Call Values

Soft Floor $= \max[0, P_s - P_x/(1 + RF)^T]$

Hard Floor $= \max[0, P_s - P_x]$

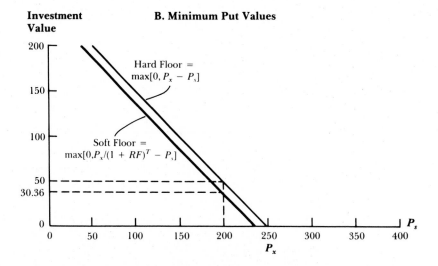

B. Minimum Put Values

Hard Floor $= \max[0, P_x - P_s]$

Soft Floor $= \max[0, P_x/(1 + RF)^T - P_s]$

folio *B*. If portfolio *A* dominates portfolio *B*, then the current market value of portfolio *A* must be at least equal to and perhaps greater than that of portfolio *B*.

Now, consider two portfolios. Portfolio *A* consists of the ownership of 1.0 call and a T-bill (which matures at the call's expiration date and has a par value equal to the call's exercise price). Note that if the stock is worth less than P_x on the expiration date, the call position will be worthless and the portfolio's investment value will come solely from the T-bill payoff—P_x. If the stock is worth more than P_x, the proceeds from the T-bill will be used to pay the exercise price and, thus, the portfolio would evolve into one share of the stock. Portfolio B consists solely of one share of the stock.

Portfolio A has exactly the same expiration date investment values as portfolio B when P_s is greater than P_x. However, at stock prices below P_x, portfolio A dominates portfolio B. This is shown symbolically as follows:

	Initial Market Value	$ Expiration Date Investment Value	
		$P_s \leq P_x$	$P_s > P_x$
Portfolio A:			
Buy 1.0 Call	$-P_c$	—	$+(P_s - P_x)$
Invest Risk-Free to Payoff P_x	$-P_x/(1 + RF)^T$	$+P_x$	$+P_x$
Net	$-P_c - P_x/(1 + RF)^T$	$+P_x$	$+P_s$
Portfolio B:			
Buy 1.0 Stock	$-P_s$	P_s	P_s

↑
Portfolio A dominates B here

Since portfolio A dominates B, the initial market value of A must be equal to or greater than the initial market value of B:

$$P_c + P_x/(1 + RF)^T \geq P_s \qquad (15.7)$$

And since the call's price cannot be negative, the soft floor value is given by:

Soft Floor of a Call $\qquad P_c \geq \max[0, P_s - P_x/(1 + RF)^T] \qquad (15.8)$

For our six-month call option when the annual risk-free rate is 10%, the soft floor would be \$61.63—that is, \$11.63 greater than the hard floor:

$$\$300 - 250/1.10^{0.5} = \$61.63$$

A logic similar to that used above can also be applied to put options. Without detailing the process, the floors on a put should be:

Hard Floor on a Put $\qquad P_p \geq \max(0, P_x - P_s) \qquad (15.9)$

Soft Floor on a Put $\qquad P_p \geq \max[0, P_x/(1 + RF)^T - P_s] \qquad (15.10)$

CONTINUOUS-TIME VALUATION

The put-call parity valuation model works because we are able to combine the stock, call, and put in a manner which is risk-free *at the expiration date*. Since we can observe the market prices of the risk-free asset and the stock, we can infer what the call value should be relative to the put. Symbolically:

$$\underset{\text{Stock \& Option Portfolio}}{\text{Value of Risk-Free}} = \underset{\text{Asset with Payoff} = P_x}{\text{Value of Risk-Free}}$$

$$\underset{\underset{\text{Known}}{\uparrow}}{P_s - P_c + P_p} = \underset{\underset{\text{Known}}{\uparrow} \quad \underset{\text{Known}}{\uparrow}}{P_x/(1 + RF)^T}$$

But this risk-free position is possible only if both options are available. An explicit valuation of one option, without knowledge of the other option price, was not possible.

It turns out that, if we shift our attention from investment values at the expiration date to investment values in the next instant in time, the put is not required to value the call or the call to value the put. A continuous-time risk-free position is possible using only two assets: the call and stock or the put and stock.

In this section we examine these very important continuous-time valuation models. Two approaches are reviewed: (1) the binomial model and (2) the Black-Scholes model.

The Binomial Model

The binomial model is a continuous-time model "in the limit." We will see what "in the limit" means soon. But for now it is sufficient to note that it is called the binomial model because it assumes that during the next "period of time" stock prices will go to *only one of two values.* Although this assumption might seem to be a strange one on which to develop a practical valuation model, it really isn't if we think of a "period of time" as being very short and of the eventual expiration date as being many periods from now. Our discussion of the binomial model proceeds in two stages. In the first, the mechanics of a single-period binomial valuation is discussed. In the second, the single-period approach is extended to multiple periods.

Single-Period Binomial Model. Suppose one-period call options are available on shares of Unique Corporation. Each option is exercisable at $40, and Unique shares are now selling at $50. The firm owes its name to the fact that at the option's expiration date its shares will be selling at one of only two possible prices—either $62.50 or $37.50. What should the call option sell for?

To answer this, remember that if we could form a portfolio of the stock and option which results in a risk-free expiration date outcome, we could value the option. That is, the stock's price and the price of the risk-free portfolio are observable, so we can infer what the call option value must be.

In the put-call parity model a risk-free position was obtained by trading in 1.0 units of each asset (for example: buy 1.0 stock, buy 1.0 put, write 1.0 call). In the current situation this 1:1 *hedge ratio* is no longer valid.

Note that the stock prices could be either $62.50 or $37.50, a price range of $25. In contrast, the call will be worth either $22.50 ($62.50 − $40) or $0, a price range of $22.50. Since the stock price is more variable, the hedge ratio will be less than 1.0. For our stock position to exactly offset a short position in 1.0 call, we should buy less than 1.0 share. It turns out that the risk-free hedge ratio is simply:

$$\begin{array}{c} \text{Risk-Free} \\ \text{Binomial} \\ \text{Hedge Ratio} \end{array} = \frac{\text{End-of-Period Range of Option Prices}}{\text{Expiration Date Range of Stock Prices}} \qquad \textbf{(15.11)}$$

In our example, the hedge ratio is 0.90 ($22.50/$25).

Calculations show that a portfolio of 0.90 shares long and 1.0 call short is indeed risk-free. This portfolio replicates a T-bill having a par value of $33.75:

Using a Call and Stock to Replicate a Risk-Free Position

		Expiration Date	
	Today	*$P_s = \$37.50$*	*$P_s = \$62.50$*
Buy 0.90 Stock	−$45.00	+$33.75	+$56.25
Write 1.0 Call	+ P_c	−	−$22.50
	−$45.00 + P_c	+$33.75	+$33.75

Assuming that the one-period risk-free rate is 10%, the current price of the call should be $14.32:

$$P_c = 0.90(\$50) - \frac{\$33.75}{1.1}$$

$$= \$14.32$$

Look closely at the equation above and compare it mentally with the put-call parity equation for the value of a call (Equation 15.5). Three things are different. First, the hedge ratio of 0.9 is multiplied by the stock price. Although a hedge ratio is not explicitly shown in the put-call parity equation, a hedge ratio implicitly exists and is equal to 1.0. In this respect, the two models are similar; only the value of the risk-free hedge ratio changes. Next, the second term in the put-call parity model is the discounted present value of P_x. In the binomial equation above, the second term could be thought of as being the present value of P_x multiplied by a second type of hedge ratio. In the binomial example above, this second hedge ratio is 0.84375, since $0.84375 \times \$40 = \$33.75$. In the put-call parity approach, this second hedge ratio is implicitly 1.0. Again, the two models are essentially the same, except that they use different values of the hedge ratio. The third difference between them is that no puts are needed in the binomial model. This is the only fundamental difference between the two models.

The fact that a put is not required in the binomial model is due solely to the assumption that only two stock prices would exist at the expiration date. With only two possible outcomes, two assets are sufficient to create a risk-free portfolio. If three or more outcomes are possible, then more than two assets are needed to value the call. In the context of a multiperiod binomial model, however, this problem tends to disappear.

Look again at the binomial call price in our example:

$$P_c = 0.90(\$50) - \frac{\$33.75}{1.1}$$

What this really says is that you can replicate the outcomes of the call option with a portfolio of stock and cash! In this case, 0.90 shares of stock would initially be purchased and risk-free debt worth $33.75/1.1 would be issued. The fact that such a portfolio is identical to the call is shown below:

Using Stock and Debt to Replicate a Call Position

	Today	Expiration Date	
		$P_s = \$37.50$	$P_s = \$62.50$
Buy 0.90 Stock	−$45.00	+$33.75	+$56.25
Issue Debt	+$30.68	−$33.75	−$33.75
	−$14.32	−$ 0.0	$22.50

Similarly, the stock position could be replicated with a portfolio of the call and T-bills. *Any one asset can be replicated by holding appropriate quantities of the other two.*

Given the logic of the single-period binomial approach, what should a put be worth in our illustration above if it is also exercisable at $40? Since the range of stock prices at the expiration date is $25 and the put's range is $2.50 ($2.50 − 0), the risk-free hedge ratio is 0.10 ($2.50/$25)—that is, 0.1 share of stock should be bought for each 1.0 put bought. This results in the following risk-free portfolio:

Using a Put and Stock to Replicate a Risk-Free Position

	Today	Expiration Date	
		$P_s = \$37.50$	$P_s = \$62.50$
Buy 0.10 Stock	−$5.00	+$3.75	+$6.25
Buy 1.0 Put	$-P_p$	+$2.50	−
	$-\$5.00 - P_p$	−$6.25	$6.25

$$P_p = \frac{\$6.25}{1.1} - \$5.00$$

$$= \$0.68$$

Multiperiod Binomial Valuation. The principles underlying the binomial model can be extended to value an option which has an expiration date more than one period from now. Although there is no limit on the number of periods between "now" and the option's expiration, the basic approach can be illustrated with a two-period example.

Consider a stock which is now trading for $50. During any period of time the stock will either increase or decrease by 25%. Thus, over the course of two periods, the stock price will follow one of the branches shown in panel A of Figure 15-9. The assumption of *equal percentage price changes* within a given period and across all time periods is made solely for convenience. The binomial approach does not require it.

FIGURE 15-9 *Prices of Stock and Calls During the Next Two Periods*

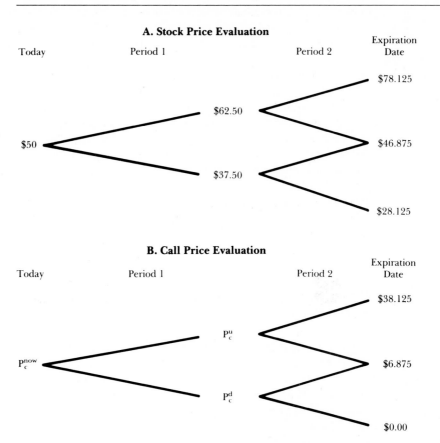

A. Stock Price Evaluation

Today   Period 1   Period 2   Expiration Date

$50

$62.50

$37.50

$78.125

$46.875

$28.125

B. Call Price Evaluation

Today   Period 1   Period 2   Expiration Date

P_c^{now}

P_c^u

P_c^d

$38.125

$6.875

$0.00

Note that this stock is identical to the stock used in the previous example. A call is available on this stock which has an exercise price of $40 and an expiration date at the end of period 2. Again, this is the call used in the single-period example, but it now has two periods to expiration. If the risk-free rate is constant and equal to 10% per period, what should the call trade for today?

Well, let's see what we know about the call. The situation is depicted in panel B of Figure 15-9. We definitely know the expiration date values for each of the three possible expiration date stock prices. For example, if the stock goes up by 25% in both periods, the stock will be worth $78.125 at the end of period 2. Therefore the call will be worth $38.125, given its exercise price of $40. What we don't know (yet) are the potential call values at the end of period 1 or, of course, what the call value should be today. Call values at the end of period 1 will clearly depend on possible expiration date stock prices. These end-of-period-1 call values are denoted as:

P_c^u = price of call given that the stock went up in period 1

P_c^d = price of call given that the stock went down in period 1

Can you determine what P_c^u and P_c^d should be? Certainly. In both cases, there is only one period remaining, so the single-period binomial approach can be used. We will calculate P_c^u and P_c^d in a moment. But remember that when this is done, a portfolio of the stock and call is created which replicates a risk-free security. The portfolio is risk-free because a risk-free hedge ratio is calculated as the range of possible end-of-period call prices divided by the range of possible stock prices. This hedge ratio represents the number of stocks to purchase for each 1.0 call written.

If this is true for the last period of the option's life, why shouldn't it be true for all other periods? It is! *In any period, a risk-free portfolio can be created based on that period's end-of-period stock prices and call prices.* Therefore, to calculate what today's option price should be, we value the options when they have only one period remaining in their life and then "roll back" to today.

Results of this process are shown in Table 15-4. Three steps are used. In the first, P_c^u is found using the single-period approach. As shown, the risk-free hedge ratio is 1.0 stock per 1.0 call, and the call price should be \$26.136. In the second step, P_c^d is found in a similar manner. Note that the hedge ratio in this case is 0.366⅔ because the call's expiration date values are not as variable as the stock's. Thus, fewer shares are held in order to make the hedged portfolio risk-free.

In the final step, P_c is calculated. Note that the hedge ratio in this case depends on the *period 1 stock prices and period 1 call prices* found in steps 1 and 2. At the beginning of period 1, the risk-free hedge ratio is 0.87044, and the call should trade for \$17.825.

Obviously, when the binomial model is extended to a multiperiod case, the calculations can be tedious. Thus, most people rely on computer programs to solve for proper option prices. But the principle that a risk-free combination of the stock and option can be achieved within each period remains. As the stock's price changes over time, the hedge ratio also changes, so the stock position will have to be rebalanced. But the ability to constantly have a risk-free portfolio means that the option's price can always be solved for.

The Black-Scholes Model

Assume that an option has an expiration date T months from now. In applying the binomial model we divide the time between today and T into N equal-length periods each having a time of $t = T/N$. For example, if $T = 3$ months and $N = 3$, each period is a month; if $N = 90$, each period is a day, etc. *In the limit* as N approaches infinity, the length of any period approaches zero and the binomial model truly becomes a continuous-time model.

Fischer Black and Myron Scholes were the first researchers to identify an option pricing model based on continuous time. Their insights were groundbreaking. Like the capital asset pricing model, arbitrage pricing theory, and the efficient market hypothesis, the Black-Scholes model revolutionized financial theory and practice. Improvements have been and will continue to be made to their original model. Yet its fundamental importance remains.

TABLE 15-4 *Two-Period Binomial Valuation Example*

1. Find P_c^u:
   a. Hedge ratio = ($38.125 − $6.875)/($78.125 − $46.875)
      = 1.0
   b. Value of call in risk-free replicating portfolio:

	Period 1	End of Period 2 $P_s = \$46.875$	End of Period 2 $P_s = \$78.125$
Buy 1.0 Stock	−$62.50	+$46.875	+$78.125
Write 1.0 Call	+P_c^u	−6.875	−38.125
	−$62.50 + P_c^u	$40.00	$40.00

   $P_c^u = \$62.50 − \$40/1.1$

   $= \$26.136$

2. Find P_c^d:
   a. Hedge ratio = ($6.875 − $0)/($46.875 − $28.125)
      = 0.366⅔
   b. Value of call in risk-free replicating portfolio:

	Period 1	End of Period 2 $P_s = \$28.125$	End of Period 2 $P_s = \$46.875$
Buy 0.366⅔ Stock	−$13.75	+$10.3125	+$17.1875
Write 1.0 Call	+P_c^d	−0.0	−6.875
	−$13.75 + P_c^d	$10.3125	$10.3125

   $P_c^d = \$13.75 − \$10.3125/1.1$

   $= \$4.375$

3. Find P_c:
   a. Hedge ratio = ($26.136 − $4.375)/($62.50 − $37.50)
      = 0.87044
   b. Value of call in risk-free replicating portfolio:

	Period 1	End of Period 1 $P_s = \$37.50$	End of Period 1 $P_s = \$62.50$
Buy 0.87044 Stock	−$43.522	+$32.6415	+$54.4025
Write 1.0 Call	+P_c	−4.375	−26.1360
	−$43.522 + P_c	$28.2665	$28.2665

   $P_c = \$43.522 − \$28.2665/1.1$

   $= \$17.825$

Assumptions. The Black-Scholes model is based on the following assumptions:

1. A constant risk-free rate of interest exists at which people can borrow or lend any amount of money.
2. There are no transaction costs.
3. Stock may be short sold without restrictions.
4. The standard deviation of the stock's return is constant.
5. The stock pays no dividends.
6. Stock prices follow a continuous diffusion process.
7. Continuous rates of return are normally distributed.

Since the last two assumptions have not been used previously in the book, a short explanation is appropriate.

The panels in Figure 15-10 illustrate various possible stock price movements over time. In panel A, there are various time intervals in which the stock *cannot* be traded—that is, prices do not trade in "continuous time." In addition, there are numerous jumps in prices, either from one moment to the next or between two adjacent trading periods. This is known as a jump process. In panel B, prices trade in continuous time but have a variety of price jumps. The price might be $40 one moment and $50 the next. Trades at all prices between $40 and $50 do not occur. This is a continuous-time jump process. The stock price model which Black-Scholes assumed is shown in panel C. There is a continuous set of possible trade prices. Even though a trade might not occur at a particular point in time, a trade is possible at a known price. In addition, there are no price jumps. When the stock moves from $40 to $50, trades (or possible trades) occur at all intermediate prices. This makes it a diffusion process. Although a continuous-time diffusion process is a simplification of reality, the model works well in practice.

The assumption that continuous-time returns are *normally distributed* was also made for ease of analysis. Assume that the price of a stock is $40 at the start of a day and $50 at the end. Assuming no dividend, there are two ways of expressing the rate of return during the day:

Discrete End-of-Day Compound Return	$R = (\$50/\$40) - 1.0$ $= 25.00\%$
Continuous Compound Return	$r = \ln(\$50/\$40)$ $= 22.31\%$

The discrete compound return assumes that the return during a period is provided at the end of the period—a one-time return. The continuous compound return assumes that returns are continuously generated over time.

The assumption that continuous returns are normally distributed is illustrated in Figure 15-11. In panel A the distribution of continuous returns is shown as a normal bell-shaped distribution. By making this assumption, however, we are saying that future stock price levels are *not* normally distributed. If continuous returns are normally distributed, then future stock prices are "log-normally" distributed. That is, if you

FIGURE 15-10 *Potential Stock Price Movements*

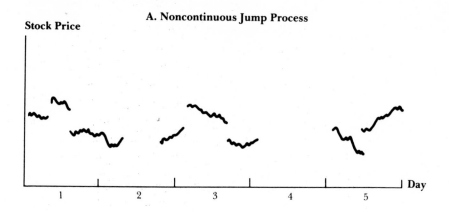

A. Noncontinuous Jump Process

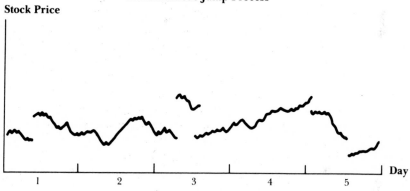

B. Continuous Jump Process

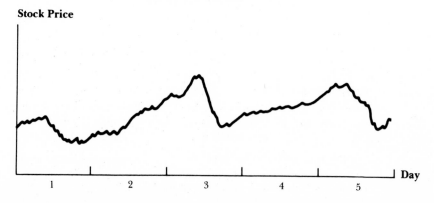

C. Continuous Diffusion Process

FIGURE 15-11 *Distributions of Continuous Returns and Stock Prices*

A. Normal Continuous Returns

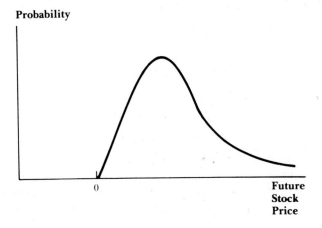

plot a frequency distribution of the log natural of the future prices, the distribution would be a normal distribution. But if you plot a frequency distribution of the actual prices, the distribution would be skewed to the right, as shown in panel B. Actually, such a distribution makes sense. Even if a large number of negative stock returns arise, the minimum stock price is zero. However, there is no upward bound on stock prices arising from a large number of positive stock returns.

Call Valuation. Black and Scholes demonstrated that under these assumptions, risk-free hedge portfolios can be created in continuous time. This would require that a *European* call price be:[5]

---

[5]The Black-Scholes model applies strictly to European call options. If an American option will *never* be exercised before the expiration date, the model would apply. However, if there is uncertainty about early exercise, the Black-Scholes model is an approximation of the true option value.

Black-Scholes Option Model

$$P_c = P_s[N_{d1}] - \frac{P_x}{e^{(RF)(T)}}[N_{d2}] \tag{15.12}$$

where:

$$d_1 = \frac{\ln\left[\dfrac{P_s}{P_x}\right] + T\left[RF + \dfrac{\sigma^2}{2}\right]}{\sigma\sqrt{T}}$$

$$d_2 = \frac{\ln\left[\dfrac{P_s}{P_x}\right] + T\left[RF - \dfrac{\sigma^2}{2}\right]}{\sigma\sqrt{T}}$$

$$= d_1 - \sigma\sqrt{T}$$

and where P_c = the value of the call, P_s = the current price of the stock, P_x = the exercise price of the call, $e = 2.7183$, RF = the *continuously* compounded annual risk-free rate, σ = the standard deviation of the *continuously* compounded annual rate of return on the stock, $\ln$ = the natural log of the bracketed number, T = the time remaining to expiration on an annual basis, and N_{d1} and N_{d2} = the value of the cumulative normal distribution at d_1 and d_2.

To illustrate how Equation 15.12 is used, we will value a call option on XYZ stock. Assume you *know* that:

$$P_s = \$68.125$$
$$P_x = \$60.0$$
$$RF = 0.1325 \text{ per year}$$
$$T = 2 \text{ months}$$

In addition, you have *estimated* the continuous annual standard deviation of returns on XYZ to be 0.4472 ($\sigma^2 = 0.2$). First, d_1 and d_2 would be:

$$d_1 = \frac{\ln\left[\dfrac{68.125}{60.0}\right] + \dfrac{2}{12}\left[0.1325 + \dfrac{0.2}{2}\right]}{0.4472\sqrt{2/12}} = 0.91$$

$$d_2 = \frac{\ln\left[\dfrac{68.125}{60.0}\right] + \dfrac{2}{12}\left[0.1325 - \dfrac{0.2}{2}\right]}{0.4472\sqrt{2/12}} = 0.72$$

Second, the value of N_{d1} and N_{d2} must be found. These represent the cumulative probability of the normal standard distribution from $-\infty$ to d_1 and from $-\infty$ to d_2, respectively. This is illustrated in Figure 15-12. Consider first d_1. The cumulative probability below the zero mean of the standard normal distribution is 50%. The value of d_1 is 0.91, meaning it is 0.91 standard deviation above the zero mean. If we refer to Table 15-5, which provides the cumulative probabilities of various standard deviations, we find that a standard deviation of 0.91 corresponds to a cumulative probability of 0.3186. In total, N_{d1} would be $0.5 + 0.3186 = 0.8186$. Using a simi-

FIGURE 15-12 *The Normal Density Function*

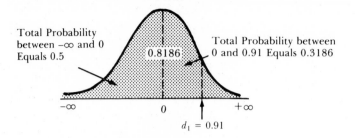

Total Probability
between −∞ and 0
Equals 0.5

0.8186

Total Probability between
0 and 0.91 Equals 0.3186

−∞   0   +∞

$d_1 = 0.91$

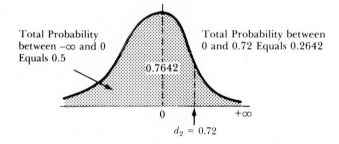

Total Probability
between −∞ and 0
Equals 0.5

0.7642

Total Probability between
0 and 0.72 Equals 0.2642

0   +∞

$d_2 = 0.72$

lar procedure for d_2 equal to 0.72 provides an $N_{d2} = 0.7642$. Finally, we can calculate the call option's price by substituting into Equation 15.12:

$$P_c = \$68.125(0.8186) - \frac{\$60}{2.7183^{(0.1325)(0.16667)}} (0.7642)$$

$$= \$10.92$$

Comparison of Three Models. We now have three call valuation models: the Black-Scholes model, the binomial model, and the put-call parity model. They are summarized below:

	Call Value	=	Value of Long Position in Asset	−	Value of Short Position in Debt	+	Cost of Insurance
Black-Scholes	P_c	=	$(N_{d1})P_s$	−	$(N_{d2}) \dfrac{P_x}{e^{RF \times T}}$	+	0
Binomial	P_c	=	$(HR_1)P_s$	−	$(HR_2) \dfrac{P_x}{(1 + RF)^T}$	+	0
Put-Call Parity	P_c	=	$(1.0)P_s$	−	$(1.0) \dfrac{P_x}{(1 + RF)^T}$	+	$(1.0)P_p$

Before we analyze their similarities, two housekeeping chores are needed. First, even though we did not formally express the binomial model in terms of the two hedge ratios, HR_1 and HR_2, we did note that they exist. Their precise calculation need not be

TABLE 15-5 *Areas of a Standard Normal Distribution*

An entry in the table is the proportion under the entire curve which is between $d = 0$ and a positive value of d. Areas for negative values of d are obtained by symmetry.

d	.00	.01	.02	.03	.04	.05	.06	.07	.08	.09
0.0	.0000	.0040	.0080	.0120	.0160	.0199	.0239	.0279	.0319	.0359
0.1	.0398	.0438	.0478	.0517	.0557	.0596	.0636	.0675	.0714	.0753
0.2	.0793	.0832	.0871	.0910	.0948	.0987	.1026	.1064	.1103	.1141
0.3	.1179	.1217	.1255	.1293	.1331	.1368	.1406	.1443	.1480	.1517
0.4	.1554	.1591	.1628	.1664	.1700	.1736	.1772	.1808	.1844	.1879
0.5	.1915	.1950	.1985	.2019	.2054	.2088	.2123	.2157	.2190	.2224
0.6	.2257	.2291	.2324	.2357	.2389	.2422	.2454	.2486	.2517	.2549
0.7	.2580	.2611	.2642	.2673	.2703	.2734	.2764	.2794	.2823	.2852
0.8	.2881	.2910	.2939	.2967	.2995	.3023	.3051	.3078	.3106	.3133
0.9	.3195	.3186	.3212	.3238	.3264	.3289	.3315	.3340	.3365	.3389
1.0	.3413	.3438	.3461	.3485	.3508	.3531	.3554	.3577	.3599	.3621
1.1	.3643	.3665	.3686	.3708	.3729	.3749	.3770	.3790	.3810	.3830
1.2	.3849	.3869	.3888	.3907	.3925	.3944	.3962	.3980	.3997	.4015
1.3	.4032	.4049	.4066	.4082	.4099	.4115	.4131	.4147	.4162	.4177
1.4	.4192	.4207	.4222	.4236	.4251	.4265	.4279	.4292	.4306	.4319
1.5	.4332	.4345	.4357	.4370	.4382	.4394	.4406	.4418	.4429	.4441
1.6	.4452	.4463	.4474	.4484	.4495	.4505	.4515	.4525	.4535	.4545
1.7	.4554	.4564	.4573	.4582	.4591	.4599	.4608	.4616	.4625	.4633
1.8	.4641	.4649	.4656	.4664	.4671	.4678	.4686	.4693	.4699	.4706
1.9	.4713	.4719	.4726	.4732	.4738	.4744	.4750	.4756	.4761	.4767
2.0	.4772	.4778	.4783	.4788	.4793	.4798	.4803	.4808	.4812	.4817
2.1	.4821	.4826	.4830	.4834	.4838	.4842	.4846	.4850	.4854	.4857
2.2	.4861	.4864	.4868	.4871	.4875	.4878	.4881	.4884	.4887	.4890
2.3	.4893	.4896	.4898	.4901	.4904	.4906	.4909	.4911	.4913	.4916
2.4	.4918	.4920	.4922	.4925	.4927	.4929	.4931	.4932	.4934	.4936
2.5	.4938	.4940	.4941	.4943	.4945	.4946	.4948	.4949	.4951	.4952
2.6	.4953	.4955	.4956	.4957	.4959	.4960	.4961	.4962	.4963	.4964
2.7	.4965	.4966	.4967	.4968	.4969	.4970	.4971	.4972	.4973	.4974
2.8	.4974	.4975	.4976	.4977	.4977	.4978	.4979	.4979	.4980	.4981
2.9	.4981	.4982	.4982	.4983	.4984	.4984	.4985	.4985	.4986	.4986
3.0	.4987	.4987	.4987	.4988	.4988	.4989	.4989	.4989	.4990	.4990

developed here. Second, the term *RF* (risk-free rate of interest) has been attached to both a discrete end-of-period compound rate and a continuously compounded rate. The two are different. For example, if $1 at the start of a year grows risk-free to $1.10 by the end of the year, the discrete rate is 10% and the continuous rate is 9.53% (log natural of $1.10/$1.00).

Notice how similar the models are! True, the continuous-time models do not require the presence of a put in order to obtain risk-free stock and call option positions, but otherwise they are very much alike. They all say that a call option is a leveraged position in the underlying asset—that is, a call can be replicated by an appropriate long position in the underlying asset (stock in our case) and an appropriate short position in risk-free securities (having a par value equal to P_x and maturity equal to the option's expiration date). The "appropriate" position is defined by the hedge ratio. For put-call parity, the hedge is always $1:1:1$ (stock, debt, put). For Black-Scholes, the call is replicated by owning N_{d1} shares of stock and selling N_{d2} units of risk-free debt (each with a par value of P_x). For example, in our illustration of how one should find the value of a call using the Black-Scholes model, we found:

$$P_c = (0.8186)P_s - 0.7642\, P_x / e^{RF \times T}$$

This call was the same thing as buying 0.81862 shares of the actual stock and issuing 0.7642 units of risk-free debt.

Determinants of Call Prices. The Black-Scholes option pricing model can be used in a variety of ways. Most important, perhaps, is its ability to explicitly indicate the various factors which determine call premiums. These are:

1. *Current stock price.* The higher the stock's price, the greater the call premium.
2. *Exercise price.* The higher the exercise price, the lower the call premium.
3. *Time to expiration.* The longer the time to expiration, the greater the possibility that the stock will eventually sell above the call's exercise price and thus the greater the call premium.
4. *Variance of stock returns.* The more variable the future returns on a stock, the greater the possibility the stock will eventually sell above the call's exercise price and thus the greater the call premium.
5. *Risk-free rate.* The greater the risk-free rate, the greater the call's value. This relationship is not as intuitively clear as the others. Remember that calls will be priced in accordance with their ability to create a riskless future payoff. When this future certain cash flow is discounted to obtain *present worths* of a mixed stock-and-call portfolio, higher discount rates yield lower present values. Since the mixed portfolio consists of owning stock and writing calls, a lower present worth can be obtained only by higher call premiums.

Note that the value of a call is *not a "direct" function of expected future stock prices.* This point is true for each of the call valuation models developed in this chapter. In none of them is the call price directly affected by possible future stock prices. Only *current stock prices* are needed to value the call. The reason is simple. Calls are valued based on the fact that they can be mixed with stock positions to create a risk-free portfolio. If the value of the long stock position and short call position is not the same as the value of equivalent risk-free debt, arbitrage profits are possible.

The call price is, of course, affected *indirectly* by expected future stock prices in that possible future prices determine today's stock price. The important point, however, is that investors do not need to predict future stock prices in order to value a call.

Dividend Adjustments. Cash dividends have three possible impacts on call valuation. First, if the dividends are large enough, the calls might be exercised early. We discuss this in the next chapter. If this is possible, a call valuation model does exist but it is quite complex.[6] Second, if dividends are unknown, risk-free hedge portfolios cannot be formed. For these reasons, the calls cannot be valued without relying on investor preference models such as the capital asset pricing model. Both of these problems are relatively minor for most call options, however.

The third case consists of known cash dividends which are not large enough to threaten an early exercise. If this is true, a relatively simple adjustment can be made to the Black-Scholes model. Let D_t represent a known cash dividend to be paid on day t from now. There may be one or more D_t values, but only those paid during the option's life are considered. The Black-Scholes model can still be used, but now with an adjusted stock price P_s^*:

Dividend Adjusted Stock Price

$$P_s^* = P_s - \sum_{t=1}^{T} D_t / e^{RF \times t}$$ **(15.13)**

For example, in our previous illustration the current stock price was \$68.125. If known cash dividends equal to \$2.00 are to be paid exactly one and two months from now:

$$P_s^* = \$68.125 - \$2.00 / e^{0.1325(0.08333)} - \$2.00 / e^{0.1325(0.16666)}$$

$$= \$64.19$$

This stock value would be used in the model in place of P_s.

Put Valuation. The valuation of a European put can be found by inserting the Black-Scholes call price into the put-call parity model. The result is:

European Put Value

$$P_p = -P_s N_{-d1} + \frac{P_x}{e^{RF \times T}} N_{-d2}$$ **(15.14)**

Note that the cumulative normal density function is evaluated at negative d_1 and d_2 values.

Assume that the stock price is \$40, the put exercise price is \$40, the expiration date is four months, the continuous risk-free interest rate is 12%, and the standard deviation of continuously compound stock returns is 30% per year:

$$d_1 = \frac{\ln\left(\dfrac{\$40}{40}\right) + 0.12(\frac{1}{3} + 0.09/2)}{0.3\sqrt{\frac{1}{3}}}$$

$$= 0.26$$

$$N_{-d1} = 0.3974$$

$$d_2 = 0.26 - 0.3\sqrt{\tfrac{1}{3}}$$

$$= 0.09$$

---

[6]See Roll (1977), Geske (1979), and Whaley (1981).

$$N_{-d2} = 0.4641$$

$$P_p = -\$40(0.3974) + \frac{\$40}{e^{(0.12)(1/3)}}(0.4641)$$

$$= \$1.94$$

The pricing of American puts is more difficult because of problems that potential early exercise presents. Models which can approximate the value of American puts exist but are beyond the scope of this book.

Empirical Evidence

As you might expect, there have been a large number of empirical studies of the Black-Scholes model. Two basic questions have been examined: (1) Can the model be used to earn abnormal returns? (2) Are there any persistent differences between actual call prices and those predicted by the model?

To see whether abnormal returns might be earned by using the model, researchers compare theoretical prices with market prices. If the call is overvalued, a short position is taken in the call. If it is undervalued, a long position is taken. Of the five variables needed to value calls on non–dividend-paying stocks, only the standard deviation of annualized returns is unknown. To estimate this term, some researchers use past variability of stock returns. However, a more common practice is to calculate a weighted average implied standard deviation (*WISD*) for the stock. For each call option (on a given stock on a given date), the researcher solves for the standard deviation which will yield the call's actual market price. These implied standard deviations are then averaged (for a given stock for that day). Finally, theoretical prices for the calls on a given stock are calculated using the *WISD* for each call. By properly weighting the holdings, the portfolios of simulated purchases and sales are designed to have virtually no risk. (We discuss how this is done in Chapter 16.)

In studies of this type, Trippi as well as Chiras and Manaster found that abnormal returns appeared to be available when positions in substantially mispriced calls were taken. When transaction costs were considered, the profits remained but were considerably reduced.

However, most empirical studies have been aimed at testing the robustness of the Black-Scholes model itself. These tests examine whether persistent pricing biases exist within the model. To date, the following observations have been made:

1. The Black-Scholes model accurately predicts market prices of at-the-money calls which expire in more than two months and pay no dividends.
2. The model is less successful for deep in-the-money or out-of-the-money calls.
3. Calls with an expiration of less than one month are significantly mispriced.
4. Calls on stocks with unusually high or low volatility are often mispriced.

Earlier in the text the comment was made that, although security pricing and trading may be an enjoyable intellectual and psychological process, the game is played in earnest. There is a strong profit motive to find option pricing models which work better than those used by others. As a result, much of the research on option modeling is being conducted today within the large investment trading firms.

One model bias in particular has been investigated in some detail. This is the "exercise price bias." The Black-Scholes model tends to misprice deep in-the-money and out-of-the-money calls. For example, a study by MacBeth and Merville found that the model overvalued out-of-the-money calls and undervalued in-the-money calls. Their results can be seen in Figure 15-13. The vertical axis represents the percentage difference between actual market prices and those obtained by the Black-Scholes equation. Theoretical prices were found using the implied standard deviation of the call which was the least in-the-money. The horizontal axis represents how deep in- or out-of-the-money the call was.

FIGURE 15-13 *Exercise Price Bias of Black-Scholes Model*

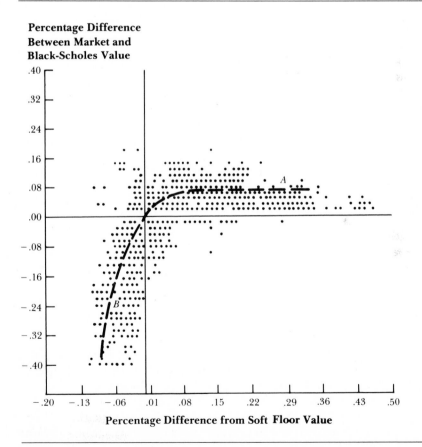

Percentage Difference
Between Market and
Black-Scholes Value

Percentage Difference from Soft Floor Value

SOURCE: Adapted from J. MacBeth and L. Merville, "Tests of the Black-Scholes and Cox Call Option Valuation Models," *Journal of Finance*, May 1976.

Consider call option A. This is a deep in-the-money option which is selling for about 8% more than the Black-Scholes equation suggests it should. For call A and other in-the-money options, the Black-Scholes equation undervalues the options. The opposite is true for call option B. This is an out-of-the-money call which is selling for about 40% less than the model predicts. For call B and other out-of-the-money calls, the Black-Scholes equation overvalues the options.

Whether this exercise price bias is consistent over time is debatable. In a study by Rubinstein which matched option prices with stock prices at exact points in time (instead of using daily closing prices), an exercise price bias was usually present, but the direction depended on the time interval examined. Rubinstein suggested that the biases observed could be related to changes in macroeconomic forces such as the levels of stock prices, market volatility, and interest rates.

Constant Elasticity of Variance Models. Considerable empirical evidence exists showing that the standard deviation of returns is inversely correlated with the level of a stock's price. High-priced stocks tend to have smaller return standard deviations than low-priced stocks. This suggests that the standard deviation used in the Black-Scholes model might not be constant but, instead, tied to the level of stock prices. As the stock's price varies over time, the standard deviation also changes.

One way to handle this was initially suggested by Cox and is referred to as the constant elasticity of variance (CEV) model. The CEV model relates the standard deviation to stock price as follows:

CEV Standard Deviation
$$\sigma^* = \sigma(P_s)^{a-1.0} \tag{15.15}$$

where σ^* is the standard deviation used in the Black-Scholes model, σ is a constant, P_s is the current stock price, and a is some number between 0 and 1. When a equals 1, the CEV model is identical to the one proposed by Black and Scholes.

This model owes its name to the fact that the elasticity of variance with respect to stock prices is constant. A demonstration of this fact is unimportant here. Instead, the important point is that the Black-Scholes model is only a special case of a more general model.

SUMMARY

A *call* option allows its owner to purchase a given stock at a specified exercise price on or before a specified expiration date. A *put* allows its owner to sell a given stock at a specified exercise price on or before a specified expiration date. *European* options may be exercised only at the expiration date, whereas *American* options may be exercised any time on or before the expiration date. Since 1973, American puts and calls have been traded on various organized exchanges, and trading volume has increased dramatically.

The key to valuing options is to recognize that they can be combined with the underlying stock to create a riskless, perfectly hedged position. Because of this, options are valued in the context of the riskless hedge. Black and Scholes were among the first to recognize this point and use it to develop a general *option pricing model*. While the option pricing model is mathematically complex, it explicitly identifies those factors which determine an option's value, and it is actively used by market professionals to identify over- or undervalued options. The five factors which determine call option premiums are:

1. *Current stock price.* The higher the stock's price, the larger the call premium.
2. *Exercise price.* The higher the exercise price, the smaller the call premium.
3. *Time to expiration.* The longer the period to expiration, the larger the call premium.
4. *Variance of stock returns.* The larger the variance of the stock's returns, the larger the call premium.
5. *Risk-free rate.* The larger the risk-free rate, the larger the call premium.

Only one of the five factors is not known with certainty: the variance of the stock's returns.

REVIEW PROBLEM

Consider the following options on a single stock:

	Calls		Put C
	A	B	
Months to Expiration	3	9	3
Continuous Yearly RF	10.00%	10.00%	10.00%
Discrete Yearly RF	10.52%	10.52%	10.52%
Std. Dev. Stock Returns	40%	40%	40%
Exercise Price	$55	$55	$55
Option Price	$2.56	–	$6.20
Stock Price	$50	$50	$50
Cash Dividend	$0	$0	$0

a. Why should call B sell for more than call A?

b. Is the put-call parity model working for options A and C?

c. How would you trade call A, the stock, and T-bills in order to replicate the expiration date outcomes of put C?

d. What is the hard floor and soft floor of call A?

e. Calculate the Black-Scholes values of call A and call B.

f. Interpret what N_{d1} and N_{d2} mean.

Solution

a. Call B has the longer time to expiration. There is a greater chance that the call will be exercised at a positive value.

b. $P_c - P_p = P_s - P_x/(1 + RF)^T$ in theory

$$= \$50 - \$55/(1.1052^{0.25}) = -\$3.64$$

Actual difference $= \$2.56 - \$6.20 = -\$3.64$

Therefore, put-call parity is working.

c. Buy 1.0 call A, sell short 1.0 stock, buy debt now worth $\$55/(1.1052^{0.25})$.

d. Hard floor $= \max(0, \$50 - \$55) = \$0$

   Soft floor $= \max(0, \$50 - \$55/(1.1052^{0.25}) = \$0$

e. *Call A Data*

$$d_1 = \frac{\ln\left(\dfrac{50}{55}\right) + 0.25\left(0.10 + \dfrac{0.4^2}{2}\right)}{0.4\sqrt{0.25}} = -0.25$$

$$d_2 = \frac{\ln\left(\dfrac{50}{55}\right) + 0.25\left(0.10 - \dfrac{0.4^2}{2}\right)}{0.4\sqrt{0.25}} = -0.45$$

$N_{d1} = 0.5 - 0.0987 = 0.4013$

$N_{d2} = 0.5 - 0.1736 = 0.3264$

$$P_c = \$50(0.4013) - \frac{\$55}{e^{(0.1)(0.25)}}(0.3264)$$

$$= \$2.56$$

Call B Data

$$d_1 = \frac{\ln\left(\dfrac{50}{55}\right) + 0.75\left(0.1 + \dfrac{0.4^2}{2}\right)}{0.4\sqrt{0.75}} = 0.11$$

$d_2 = d_1 - \sigma\sqrt{T} = -0.23$

$N_{d1} = 0.5 + 0.0438 = 0.5438$

$N_{d2} = 0.5 - 0.091 = 0.409$

$$P_c = \$50(0.5438) - \frac{\$55}{e^{(0.1)(0.75)}}(0.409)$$

$$= \$6.32$$

f. To replicate the instantaneous payoffs of the call, one should buy N_{d1} shares and issue N_{d2} units of debt which is now worth $P_x/e^{RF \times T}$.

QUESTIONS AND PROBLEMS

1. A call and put exist on the same stock. Each is exercisable at $50. They trade now for:

$$P_s = \$45 \qquad P_c = \$8 \qquad P_p = \$1$$

   Calculate the expiration cash flow, investment value, and net profit from:
   a. Buy 1.0 call
   b. Write 1.0 call
   c. Buy 1.0 put
   d. Write 1.0 put

   Do this for expiration date stock prices of $40, $45, $50, $55, and $60.

2. What is the important difference between options on individual stocks and options on stock indexes?

3. Trading in listed stock options provides a number of advantages over over-the-counter options. What are these advantages?

4. What economic reasons have been offered for the existence of options?

5. Assume that call options on Xerox are to expire today. They have an exercise price of $70, the stock is trading at $65, and the option is selling for $8. What is the arbitrage?

6. Consider the following put and call options:

	Call	Put
Market Price	$ 7	$ 2
Exercise Price	$70	$70
Exercise Date	4 mo.	4 mo.
Risk-Free Rate = 10% annualized (discrete compound)		
Stock Price = $75		

   a. What is the hard floor minimum value for each option?
   b. Is put-call parity working?
   c. What is the arbitrage based on put-call parity?
   d. What is the soft floor minimum value?
   e. Given that the call is selling for less than its minimum value, what market transaction could you conduct to benefit from this? Note: Do *not* use the put in your transaction.

7. You are given the following information:

$$P_s = \$74 \qquad P_p = \$5.09 \qquad P_x = \$65$$

$$RF = 10\% \qquad \text{Expiration} = 1 \text{ year}$$

   Assume that the stock pays no dividends and that the risk-free rate will remain constant.
   a. What should be the price of a call also exercisable at $65 with an expiration date of one year?
   b. How could you develop a portfolio of these securities which will have a payoff in one year which is identical to being long the stock? Short the stock? (You may not buy or sell the stock.)
   c. How could you develop a portfolio of these securities which will have a payoff in one year which is identical to writing one put? (Again, you may not trade the put.)

d. Underlying these calculations is the economic definition of what a call and a put really are. What does a call consist of? What does a put consist of?

8. You wish to purchase a call option on a local warehouse having an expiration date of one year and an exercise price of $1 million. The warehouse owner will not sell you such an option but is willing to sell the warehouse for $1.1 million. The current risk-free interest rate is 9% per year, and insurance on a one-year, $1 million loan would be $10,000. How could you create a synthetic call option on the warehouse?

9. An analysis of Hylough Corporation suggests that in one year the price of its common shares will be either $80 or $50. They currently sell for $60. An option that expires in one year with an exercise price of $60 can be bought for $10.23. What is the one-year risk-free rate?

10. (CFA Exam Question)
You are considering the sale of a call option with an exercise price of $100 and one year to expiration. The underlying stock pays no dividends, its current price is $100, and you believe it has a 50% chance of increasing to $120 and a 50% chance of decreasing to $80. The risk-free rate of interest is 10%.
   a. Describe the specific steps involved in applying the binomial option pricing model to calculate the call option's value.
   b. Compare the binomial option pricing model to the Black-Scholes option pricing model.

11. The value of a stock index is now $100. At the end of any future period the stock index will be either 20% greater than its beginning price or $16\frac{2}{3}$% lower. A European put is available on the stock index. It is exercisable at $100 and has an expiration date at the end of three periods from now—i.e., after the third stock return.
   a. Trace out the price pattern of the stock index for three periods.
   b. What the the potential expiration date values of the put?
   c. Calculate the intermediate values of the put as well as what the put should be worth today.
   d. Assume you buy 1.0 put and 1.0 stock. Trace through the value of this portfolio over future periods.

12. Consider the information provided below:

	Options on ABC Stock				
	Call Options				Put Option
	A	B	C	D	E
Current Market Price of:					
Option	$16.12	$10.62	$ 8.31	$10.50	$ 7.25
Stock	$80	$80	$80	$80	$80
Option Information:					
Exercise Price	$70	$80	$90	$90	$70
Months to Expiration	3	3	3	6	3
Market Information:					
Continuous Yearly RF	12%	12%	12%	12%	12%
Expected Cash Dividends	0	0	0	0	0
Std. Dev. of Stock Returns	60%	60%	60%	60%	60%

a. Calculate the Black-Scholes value of each option.

b. Note that call A and put E have identical terms. Use the put-call parity model to value the put, given the Black-Scholes value of call A. Comment on why the put's value is the same as found in part a.

c. Interpret what the terms N_{d1} and N_{d2} mean for call A and put E.

13. What are the underlying assumptions of the Black-Scholes model, and why are they needed?

14. Assume that you are given the following information on a stock and its calls:

$$P_s = \$65$$
$$P_x = \$60$$
$$RF = 12\% \text{ (continuous annual)}$$
$$\sigma = 40\% \text{ (annual)}$$
$$\text{Maturity} = 6 \text{ months}$$

You also know with certainty that the stock will pay a $1 dividend in exactly three months, followed by a $1 dividend just before the option's expiration date in six months.

a. What should be the price of this call?

b. Without performing any calculations, if you had neglected to consider the dividend payments, would you have estimated the price to be the same, greater, or less than in part a? Why?

15. All other things being equal, a $1 increase in a call option's exercise price will lead to a $1 decrease in the call option's value. True or false? Why?

16. Consider the following events and indicate how each would affect call and put price. Use (+) to indicate an increase, (−) to indicate a decrease, (0) to indicate no effect, and (?) to indicate indeterminant results. Be prepared to justify each choice. Consider each event in isolation from the others.

	Effect on	
	Call Price	*Put Price*
a. Inflation expectations increase and cause required returns on Treasury obligations to increase.		
b. The company pays a large stock dividend.		
c. The company pays a large cash dividend.		
d. Investors become more risk-averse.		
e. A company suffers an unexpected and severe labor strike.		
f. The beta of the stock increases.		
g. The firm increases its debt-to-equity ratio.		
h. The expected return on the stock increases, but its risk doesn't.		
i. The expected return on the stock increases, but its risk does also, causing the stock price to remain constant.		
j. Time passes.		

CHAPTER

16 Option Trading

In this chapter, we examine how the principles of option valuation can be used in investment and speculative strategies. These strategies focus primarily on stock options, since they are currently the options most widely used in portfolio management. In addition, a variety of other option forms (rights, warrants, and convertibles) are discussed. Finally, we show how securities such as debt and equity can also be thought of as option combinations.

CALCULATING BLACK-SCHOLES PRICES

Assume that you observe the following year-end prices:[1]

Illustrative December 31 Price Quotes

	Options on the S&P 100		Options on IBM Stock		
	Call A	*Put A*	*Call X*	*Call Y*	*Put X*
Exercise Price	$240	$240	$110	$120	$110
Exercise Date	March	March	April	April	April
Option Price	$13.75	$15.00	$11.25	$6.25	$4.50
Current Price of Underlying Stock	S&P 100 Spot Index = $238.26		IBM Stock Price = $115.625		

Are these values consistent with the Black-Scholes equation?

According to the dividend-adjusted Black-Scholes model, the calls and puts should be a function of six variables:

1. P_s = current stock price
2. P_x = option exercise price
3. T = time to expiration
4. D_t = cash dividends paid on day t

---

[1] All data in this example are actual market data. Price quotations are as of December 31, 1987.

5. RF = constant, continuously compounded risk-free rate

6. σ = standard deviation of the stock's continuously compounded return

Three of these variables are directly observable: P_s, P_x, and T. Although T may be expressed in any unit of time you wish, it is commonly thought of as a fraction of one year, since RF and σ are usually expressed as annualized equivalents. The other three variables must be either calculated or estimated.

Cash Dividends

Cash dividends are relatively easy to estimate. In the case of a single stock such as IBM, one can forecast one or more cash dividends during the option's life based on a historical pattern. In many cases, management will have publicly announced any dividends which will be paid during the option's life. For example, assume we can forecast that IBM stock will go ex-dividend in exactly one month and that the cash dividend will be $1.10. Dividends on stock indexes can also be reasonably predicted for short time horizons based on simple extrapolations of the past. Dividends on stock indexes, however, occur in a continuous fashion instead of at identifiable single dates. Although a call valuation model for continuous dividend payments does exist, we will assume that all dividends are paid halfway through the S&P 100 option's life. Assume that the dividend yield on the S&P 500 Index (during the stock index option's life) is 0.91%. This suggests that dividends on the March S&P 100 options would be $2.168:[2]

S&P 100 Spot Price	$238.26
Dividend Yield	× 0.0091
	$2.168166

Risk-Free Interest

The best proxy for the risk-free rate is the return on a Treasury bill with a maturity equal to the option's expiration.[3] The price at which a T-bill is traded depends on whether one buys at the dealer's *asked discount* or sells at the dealer's *bid discount*. For convenience we will average the two discounts.

Assume that on December 31, the average of the bid-ask discounts on a Treasury bill maturing in late March was 5.68%. Thus, the average trade price of one T-bill would be:

$$\text{Price} = 100 - 100(0.0568)/(90/360)$$

$$= 98.58\% \text{ of par}$$

---

[2]Although dividends on each of the 100 stocks underlying the index could be forecast, this procedure is faster and cheaper. Any errors are likely to be small. In practice, however, precise estimates are required when large dollar quantities are traded.

[3]If the T-bill rate which applies to any intermediate dividend payments is different, then it should be applied to such cash flows.

The discrete and continuous three-month returns associated with this price are:

$$RF_{\text{discrete}} = (100/98.58) - 1.0$$

$$= 1.44\%$$

$$RF_{\text{continuous}} = \ln(1 + RF_{\text{discrete}})$$

$$= \ln(1.0144)$$

$$= 1.43\%$$

This 1.43% three-month continuous rate needs to be expressed as an annualized rate, given that we have chosen to consider a value of $T = 1.0$ to represent one year. This can be done in two ways:

$$RF_{\text{continuous}} = \ln[(100/\$98.58)^4]$$

$$= 5.721\%$$

or

$$RF_{\text{continuous}} = \ln(100/\$98.58) \times 4$$

$$= 5.721\%$$

The two approaches are mathematically identical.

We will use this 5.721% continuous risk-free rate for all dividends and options in our examples. In practice, however, if discounts vary with different Treasury bill maturities, then a variety of discount rates should be used.

Standard Deviation

The standard deviation term σ in the Black-Scholes equation represents the standard deviation of continuous compound price returns and is assumed to be constant over the option's life. Since it is not directly observable, it is the toughest variable to estimate. There are two general ways to handle the problem. We illustrate the first using the S&P 100 options and the second using the IBM options.

Ex Post Standard Deviation. In the first approach, one looks to the past to estimate what σ might be during the option's life. The choice of the time period chosen will, of course, affect the estimate. If the return-generating process is stationary, statistical theory suggests that the number of return observations should be as large as feasible in order to reduce biases in the results. Unfortunately, there is no reason to believe that the volatility of stocks and stock indexes remains constant over time. The analysis of past standard deviation is, at best, an approximation of what the future holds.

In Table 16-1, quarterly returns on the S&P 500 Index are shown. Since the S&P 100 Index was designed by the CBOE to closely emulate the larger S&P 500 Index, volatility of the larger index should be a good proxy for the other. A 10-year time period ending December 31, 1987, was arbitrarily selected for illustrative purposes. In

TABLE 16-1 *Discrete and Continuous Quarterly Returns on the S&P 500, 1978–1987*

	Quarterly Returns			Quarterly Returns	
Quarter-End	*Discrete*	*Continuous*	*Quarter-End*	*Discrete*	*Continuous*
March 78	−4.93	−5.06	June 83	11.10	10.53
June 78	8.50	8.16	September 83	−0.10	−0.10
September 78	8.66	8.31	December 83	0.40	0.40
December 78	−4.93	−5.06	March 84	−2.40	−2.43
March 79	7.08	6.84	June 84	−2.61	−2.64
June 79	2.72	2.68	September 84	9.68	9.24
September 79	7.54	7.27	December 84	1.76	1.74
December 79	0.13	0.13	March 85	9.18	8.78
March 80	−4.07	−4.16	June 85	7.34	7.08
June 80	13.41	12.58	September 85	−4.10	−4.19
September 80	11.20	10.62	December 85	17.19	15.86
December 80	9.46	9.04	March 86	14.02	13.12
March 81	1.32	1.31	June 86	5.85	5.69
June 81	−2.31	−2.34	September 86	5.61	5.46
September 81	−10.22	−10.78	December 86	−6.94	−7.19
December 81	7.01	6.78	March 87	21.35	19.35
March 82	−7.23	−7.50	June 87	5.00	4.88
June 82	−0.62	−0.62	September 87	−22.50	−25.49
September 82	11.46	10.85	December 87	6.58	6.37
December 82	18.14	16.67	Average	3.97	3.54
March 83	10.02	9.55	Std. Dev.	8.50	8.56

practice, you would probably wish to try a variety of time intervals to see whether one predicts better than others.

The second and third columns represent the discrete quarterly return, R_t, and the continuous quarterly return, r_t. Again, the continuous return is calculated as:

Continuous Return
$$r_t = \ln(1 + R_t) \tag{16.1}$$

It is the standard deviation of the r_t series which we wish to estimate. First, the average continuous return, m, is found. It is then used to find an *unbiased* estimate of σ:

Mean Continuous Return
$$m = \frac{\left(\sum_{t=1}^{N} r_t \right)}{N} \tag{16.2}$$

Unbiased Estimate of σ
$$\sigma = \left[\frac{\sum_{t=1}^{N} (r_t - m)^2}{N - 1} \right]^{1/2} \tag{16.3}$$

Note that $N - 1$ is used in this equation instead of N. In large samples this results in unbiased estimates of σ. The mean and standard deviation shown in Table 16-1 are:

$$m = 3.54\% \text{ per quarter}$$

$$\sigma = 8.56\% \text{ per quarter}$$

Since *RF* and *T* are being expressed as annualized returns, we need to convert the 8.56% quarterly standard deviation to an annualized equivalent. Although we will not show the mathematical proof here, when one is dealing with a series of continuous returns drawn from a stationary distribution and uncorrelated with each other over time, then:

Multiperiod Standard Deviation of Continuous Returns σ for T period $= \sqrt{T} \times \sigma$ for 1 period   **(16.4)**

Therefore, the annualized standard deviation based on the historical S&P 500 continuous returns would be 17.12%:

$$\sigma_{\text{annual}} = \sqrt{4} \times 8.56\%$$

$$= 17.12\%$$

Standard deviation estimates obtained in this fashion will depend on the time period chosen and will change over time. For example, the results of a study by French, Schwert, and Stambaugh are shown in Figure 16-1. They estimated *monthly* standard deviations using all daily returns within a month for all months between 1928 and 1984. Months are shown on the horizontal axis, and the estimated *monthly* σ is shown on the vertical. To express these estimates as annualized equivalents, you should multiply the estimate by $\sqrt{12}$. The variability of σ estimates is obvious.

Implied Standard Deviation. The second approach uses the actual call prices to infer the standard deviation that is currently being priced in the call — that is, P_c and all other terms are used to calculate the *implied standard deviation* (*ISD*) of the call. When this is done for the IBM calls:

$$ISD \text{ for Call } x = 29.55\%$$

$$ISD \text{ for Call } y = 32.85\%$$

Once the *ISD* values are found for each call, a *weighted implied standard deviation* (*WISD*) is calculated. The simplest way to calculate the *WISD* is to treat each *ISD* equally. If there are *N* calls outstanding and σ_i is the *ISD* for call *i*, then:

Equally Weighted WISD $$WISD = \left(\sum_{i=1}^{N} \sigma_i \right) \Big/ N$$ **(16.5)**

Using the two *ISD*s on IBM calls, the *WISD* would be (29.55% + 32.85%)/2 = 31.20%.

A variety of weighting procedures are used in practice. Some underweight options deep in- or out-of-the-money. Others weight by the sensitivity of the option price to changes in the standard deviation. But regardless of the approach taken, *WISD* values

FIGURE 16-1 *Estimates of Monthly Standard Deviation of the S&P 500*

**Estimated Monthly
Standard Deviation**

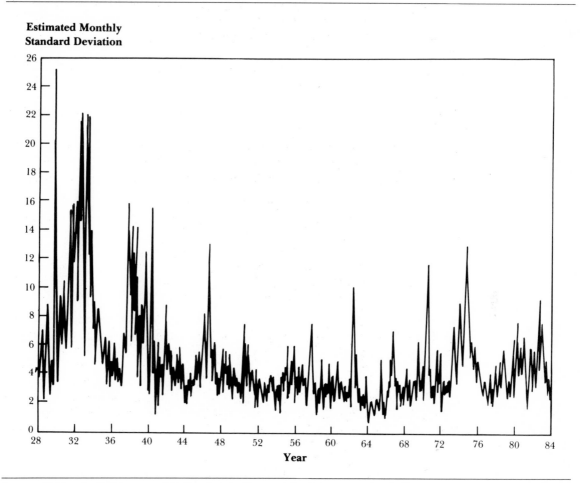

Source: K. French, G. Schwert, and R. Stambaugh, "Expected Stock Returns and Volatility," *Journal of Financial Economics* 19 (1987).

appear to be better predictors of actual future price volatility than estimates based on historical price changes.

There is one particularly interesting use of the *ISD* which deserves mention. When applied to the S&P 100 (or other index options), calculated implied standard deviations indicate the consensus market opinion about changes in equity market risk. For example, consider Figure 16-2, in which the *ISD* is plotted for each quarter-end during the period 1983–88. Each observation is the *ISD* of the S&P 100 call option which is closest to being at-the-money. During most of this period, the implied standard deviation of the S&P 100 ranged between 15% and 20%. However, in the month in which Black Monday occurred, market risk rose dramatically.

FIGURE 16-2 *Implied Standard Deviation of S&P Index Options*

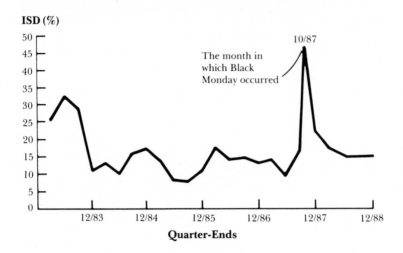

S&P 100 Call and Put Price Estimates

Using the estimate of σ based on historical data and the dividend-adjusted Black-Scholes model, the theoretical value of the S&P 100 calls would be calculated as follows:

$$T = \tfrac{3}{12} = 0.25$$

$$P_s^* = \$238.26 - \frac{\$2.168}{e^{0.05721(0.125)}}$$

$$= \$236.11$$

$$d_1 = \frac{\ln\left(\dfrac{236.11}{240.00}\right) + 0.25(0.05721 + 0.1712^2/2)}{0.1712\sqrt{0.25}}$$

$$= 0.019$$

$$d_2 = d_1 - \sigma\sqrt{t}$$

$$= 0.019 - 0.1712\sqrt{0.25}$$

$$= -0.067$$

$$N_{d1} = 0.508 \qquad D_{d2} = 0.4721$$

$$P_{call}^{SP100} = \$236.11(0.508) - \frac{\$240}{e^{(0.05721)(0.25)}}(0.4721)$$

$$= \$8.25$$

Clearly, one of two things must be true. Either the standard deviation estimate used is too small or the market price of the call is too high.

To value the put we will use the following dividend-adjusted version of put-call parity (again assuming dividends are received halfway through the option's remaining life):[4]

<table>
<tr><td align="center">*Value of Risk-Free*
Portfolio Today</td><td align="center">*Value of Risk-Free*
Portfolio at Expiration Date</td></tr>
<tr><td align="center">$P_s + P_P - P_c$</td><td align="center">$P_x + (D)e^{RF \times (T/2)}$</td></tr>
</table>

implying that:

Dividend Adjusted Put-Call Parity

$$P_P = P_c - P_s + \frac{P_x + (D)e^{RF \times (T/2)}}{e^{RF \times T}} \qquad (16.6)$$

Assume that we wish to know if the put is properly valued *relative* to the call. In this case, we should use the call's actual market price instead of its theoretical price.[5] Substituting in the appropriate values, we find that if the call is $13.75, the put should be selling for $14.23:

$$= \$13.75 - \$238.26 + \frac{\$240 + 2.168\,e^{0.05721(0.125)}}{e^{0.05721(0.25)}}$$

$$= \$14.23$$

Given that the put's market price is $15, it is *overvalued* relative to the call's price. Later in the chapter we will examine an *index arbitrage* which could be conducted in this case.

IBM Call and Put Price Estimates

Using the *WISD* and the $1.10 dividend to be paid in one month, the theoretical value of the IBM call X should be:

$$T = \tfrac{4}{12} = \tfrac{1}{3}$$

$$P_s^* = \$115.625 - \frac{\$1.10}{e^{0.05721(1/12)}}$$

$$= \$114.53$$

---

[4]The put-call parity model used here has been adjusted to account for the receipt of the $2.168 dividend halfway through the option's life. This model was derived in the Chapter 15 problems.

[5]If the theoretical price were used and resulted in a theoretical put price different from the actual market price, we wouldn't know if this was due to an inaccurate theoretical call price or a mispriced put. Because of our uncertainty about the theoretical call price, it is best to ask: Given the call's market price, is the put fairly valued?

$$d_1 = \frac{\ln\left(\dfrac{114.53}{110}\right) + \frac{1}{3}(0.05721 + 0.312^2/2)}{0.312\sqrt{\frac{1}{3}}}$$

$$= 0.42$$

$$d_2 = d_1 - \sigma\sqrt{T}$$

$$= 0.42 - 0.312\sqrt{\tfrac{1}{3}}$$

$$= 0.24$$

$$N_{d1} = 0.6628 \qquad N_{d2} = 0.5948$$

$$P_{\text{Call } X} = \$114.53(0.6628) - \frac{\$110}{e^{(0.05721)(1/3)}}(0.5948)$$

$$= \$11.72$$

Thus the theoretical price is very close to its actual market price of $\$11.25$.[6]

Using call X's actual market price and a dividend-adjusted put-call parity equation, the market price of the put should be $\$4.64$:

$$P_P = P_c - P_s + \frac{P_x + D \times e^{(RF \times 3/4T)}}{e^{RF \times T}}$$

$$= \$11.25 - \$115.625 + \frac{\$110 + 1.1 \times e^{(0.05721 \times 3/12)}}{e^{(0.05721 \times 1/3)}}$$

$$= \$4.64$$

Like the IBM call, the market price of the put ($\$4.50$) is very close to its theoretical value.

TRADES BASED ON EXERCISE DATE PAYOFFS

As we saw in Chapter 15, option payoffs can be evaluated at two points in time: on the expiration date of the option or at the next moment in time. In this section various hedging and speculative strategies which focus on an option's expiration date will be examined. Continuous-time hedging and speculation are discussed in the next section.

Hedging Strategies

To hedge usually means to take a position which offsets some type of risk. When applied to options, this risk is the uncertainty about the value (or rate of return) of the underlying security on which the option is written. A hedge is not conducted in the

---

[6]This should not be surprising given the manner in which σ was estimated.

expectation of abnormal profits. Instead, the hedge simply alters the risk inherent in owning the underlying asset.

Portfolio Insurance. An insured portfolio has a minimum floor value if the underlying asset declines beyond some point but increases in value if the asset increases in value. Based on the put-call parity model an insured portfolio can be created with options in one of two ways:

1. Buy 1.0 put for each 1.0 share owned.
2. Buy T-bills having a par value equal to the desired minimum portfolio value and calls with any remaining funds.

Although the concept of portfolio insurance could be applied to each of the individual stocks in a portfolio, it is usually cheaper to trade in stock index options which are similar to the holdings of the aggregate stock portfolio. Thus, if one owns an equally weighted portfolio of stocks similar to the Dow Jones industrials, an index option on the American Stock Exchange's Major Market Index might be traded. Similarly, if a value-weighted portfolio of many large capitalization stocks is owned, index options on the S&P 100, S&P 500, or NYSE might be better. Throughout our examples of portfolio insurance, we will use the price quotes shown earlier in the chapter for S&P 100 options. In review:

$$P_{SP100} = \$238.26 \qquad P_c = \$13.75 \qquad RF = 5.721\%$$
$$P_x = \$240.00 \qquad P_p = \$15.00 \qquad T = 3 \text{ months}$$

Portfolio Insurance with Puts. Assume that you have $10 million in cash that you wish to invest in equities similar to those included in the S&P 100 Index. You know that in 1½ months the stocks will pay a 0.91% dividend yield which you intend to reinvest at a risk-free return of 5.721% (continuous annual rate) for another 1½ months. You also believe that the value of the stocks will rise on average during the next three months, but obviously their values could also decline substantially. If you are very sensitive to declines in the value of your portfolio during the next three months, you could either: (1) invest most of the $10 million in risk-free securities such as three-month T-bills with the residual in equities or (2) place the majority of the $10 million in stocks but insure a minimum portfolio value by purchasing puts—in effect, buying insurance.

To guarantee a *fixed* minimum floor, you should purchase 1.0 put for each 1.0 "unit" of the stock index you own. Since S&P 100 puts with a $240 exercise price are *quoted* at $15, the cost of one put is really $1,500. The actual (or spot) S&P 100 Index doesn't really trade in the market, but, if it did, each unit would be quoted at $238.26. Since each put is on 100 units of the index, the cost of buying a unit of the spot S&P 100 Index would be $23,826 (if it actually traded). Since we need a 1:1 relationship between the long put and long stock position, the number of puts and stock would be identical and equal to 394.85:

$$N(\$1,500 + \$23,826) = \$10 \text{ million}$$
$$N = 394.8511411$$

Here N equals the quantity of stock index units and puts purchased. Although fractional shares and puts cannot actually be traded, we will assume that they can be in order to see that a truly insured portfolio is conceptually possible. The initial investment consists of:

$$\begin{array}{ll}
\text{Stock } (N \times \$23,826) = & \$\ 9,407,723 \\
\text{Puts } \ (N \times \$1,500) \ = & \underline{592,277} \\
& \$10,000,000
\end{array}$$

The expiration date value of this portfolio for various S&P 100 Index values is shown in Table 16-2. Dividends will be received in 1½ months and be reinvested at the risk-free rate to provide a known value of $86,225 at the expiration date. The long put position will, of course, have a positive value only if the S&P 100 Index is below $P_x = \$240$ on the expiration date. Note that, if this does occur, the increased put value exactly offsets the decreased stock value. Below $P_x = \$240$, the put and stock values move in a 1-for-1 inverse relationship (hence the 1.0-for-1.0 hedge ratio!). The minimum value of this insured portfolio is:

Minimum PortfolioValue:

Guaranteed Stock Value	
(394.8511411 units at $24,000/unit)	$9,476,427
Guaranteed Dividend Value	86,225
Total	$9,562,652

Any time the S&P 100 Index closes at less than $240 you are guaranteed that your portfolio's value is $9,562,652. But if the stock index increase in value above $240, your insured portfolio also increases in value.

Naturally, there is a cost—one has to pay $592,277 to buy the puts. This represents almost 6% of the portfolio's initial value. To many investors this would represent a rather sizable outlay to insure the portfolio's minimum value three months from now. And if one were to continuously "roll over" the hedge, there would soon be no port-

TABLE 16-2 *Portfolio Insurance Illustration Long Stock and Long Puts*

S&P 100 Index at Expiration Date (P_s)	Reinvested Dividends[1]	Put Value[2]	Stock Value[3]	Portfolio Value
$200	$86,225	$1,579,404	$ 7,897,023	$ 9,562,652
$220	86,225	789,702	8,686,725	9,562,652
$238.26	86,225	68,704	9,407,723	9,562,652
$240	86,225	0	9,476,427	9,562,652
$260	86,225	0	10,266,130	10,352,355
$280	86,225	0	11,055,832	11,142,056

[1]$(0.91\% \times 9,407,723)e^{(0.05721 \times 0.125)} = \$86,225.$

[2]$((\$240 - P_s) \times 100) \times 394.8511411$ (or $0.00 if $P_s > \$240$).

[3]$(P_s \times \$100) \times 394.8511411.$

folio value left to insure! But some investors might be so concerned with short-term losses in the portfolio's worth that they would be willing to pay the cost.

The cost of the portfolio insurance has both direct and opportunity cost components. The direct cost is the $592,277 spent on the puts. The opportunity costs consist of lost dividends and potential lost stock price appreciation on the $592,277. The lost dividend is constant for all spot prices and equal to $5,428:

$$(\$592,277 \times 0.91\%)\, e^{(0.05721 \times 0.125)} = \$5,428$$

The opportunity cost due to potential spot price appreciation applies to spot prices greater than $240 and increases directly with spot prices above $240. This price appreciation opportunity cost can be calculated as follows:

Units of Spot Which Could Be Purchased at $23,826

100% Stock Portfolio:	$10,000,000/$23,826 =	419.7095610
Insured Portfolio:	$ 9,407,723/$23,826 =	−394.8511411
(off slightly because of rounding)		

Increased Spot Units in 100% Stock   24.8584199

Price Appreciation
Opportunity Cost = (24.8584199 × 100) (P_s − $238.26)

  = 2,485.84199 (P_s − $238.26)
  for $P_s > 240$ at expiration

To illustrate the impact of the put costs, consider the following two expiration date spot prices: $240 and $280.

Value of 100% Stock:	$P_s = \$240$	$P_s = \$280$
Stock: $10,000,000 × P_s/238.26	$10,073,029	$11,751,868
Dividends: ($10,000,000 × 0.91%)$e^{(0.05721)(0.125)}$	91,653	91,653
	$10,164,682	$11,843,521
Value of Insured Portfolio:		
From Table 16-2	−9,562,652	−11,142,056
Excess from 100% Stock	$ 602,030	$ 701,465

The components of the portfolio value differences are:

	$P_s = \$240$	$P_s = \$280$
Direct Cost of Puts	$592,277	$592,277
Opportunity Costs:		
Dividends	5,428	5,428
Price Appreciation (24.8584199 × 100) (P_s − $238.26)	4,325	103,760
	$602,030	$701,465

The expiration date investment values of a 100% stock investment and the insured portfolio are shown in Figure 16-3. The cost of an insured portfolio is visually clear. For the insured portfolio to be worth more than a 100% stock position, the stock

FIGURE 16-3 *Portfolio Insurance, Long Puts and Long Stock*

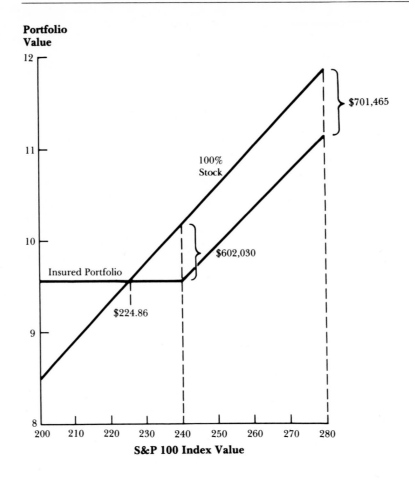

must fall by an amount which exceeds the direct cost of the puts ($592,277) and the lost dividends ($5,428). This would occur at spot S&P 100 prices of $224.86 or less:

$$\frac{\text{Exercise Price} \;-\; \text{Cost Per Unit}}{\$240 \;-\; \dfrac{(\$592,277 + \$5,428)}{(394.8511411 \times 100)}} = \$224.86$$

Neglecting dividends, the insured portfolio value is determined by the exercise price of the put options chosen. If a lower exercise price is selected, then the floor value is also lower. (This, of course, results in lower direct and opportunity costs.) Investors have as many minimum portfolio values as there are put exercise prices.

Note that the expiration date *insured* floor is not adjusted by changing the quantity of puts owned. To obtain a guaranteed floor value (at the expiration date), the hedger must own 1.0 put for each 1.0 unit of the stock index owned. The impacts of

FIGURE 16-4 *Impacts of Different Put Positions*

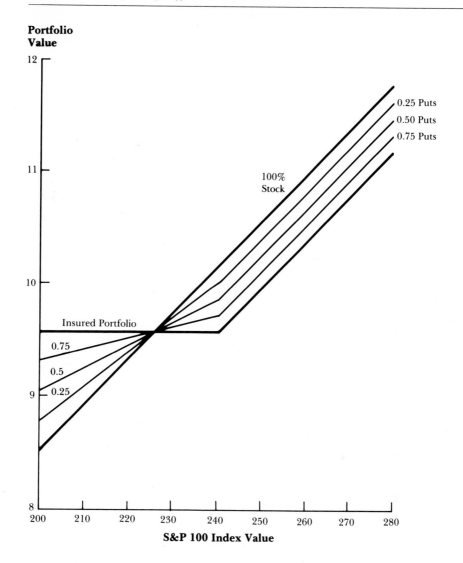

owning fewer than 1.0 put unit of the spot good are illustrated in Figure 16-4. As fewer puts are held, the insured floor is increasingly lost, but investment values at stock index values greater than $240 are improved.

The costs of portfolio insurance can be large, and they increase as spot index values increase above the put's exercise price. During the middle to late 1980s, however, portfolio insurance was the rage—particularly with corporate pension sponsors facing financial distress. The way in which they insured their pension portfolios was usually not with puts, but the procedure they used had (about) the same outcomes. The process they used is discussed later in this chapter and in Chapter 17.

TABLE 16-3 *Portfolio Insurance Illustration, Long Calls and Long T-Bills*

S&P 100 Index at Expiration Date	T-Bill Value[1]	Call Value[2]	Portfolio Value
$200	$9,562,651	0	$ 9,562,652
$220	$9,562,651	0	$ 9,562,652
$238.26	$9,562,651	0	$ 9,562,652
$240	$9,562,651	0	$ 9,562,652
$260	$9,562,651	$ 833,657	$10,396,308
$280	$9,562,651	$1,667,313	$11,229,964

[1]$9.562651 \times \$1,000,000 = \$9,562,651$.

[2]$416.8283636 \times (P_s - \$240) \times 100$ if $P_s > \$240$.

Portfolio Insurance with Calls. Portfolio insurance can also be obtained by buying calls and T-bills. Again, assume that you have $10 million in cash to invest. In order to directly compare a "call/T-bill" strategy with the "stock/put" results above, assume that you wish to have a minimum portfolio value identical to that in the stock/put example—$9,562,652.

This means that you need to purchase 9.562652 T-bills, each having a par value of $1 million.[7] Since the current price of a three-month T-bill was earlier found to be 98.58% of par, a total of $9,426,861 will have to be spent on the Treasury bills:

$$0.9858 \times \$9,562,652 = \$9,426,861$$

This would leave $573,139 to purchase calls on the S&P 100 Index, or a total of 416.83 calls:

Dollar Investment
in S&P 100 Calls = $10,000,000 − $9,426,861

= $573,139

Number of
S&P 100 Calls = $573,139/($13.75 × 100)

= 416.8283636

In Table 16-3 the expiration date investment values of this call/T-bill portfolio are shown. The minimum portfolio value is $9,562,652, simply because we bought enough T-bills to achieve this level. And at spot S&P 100 values above $P_x = \$240$ the portfolio increases in value because of investment value payoffs on the long calls. This is a portfolio with a minimum floor value which also participates with increases in the index above $240.

Similar to portfolio insurance gained with a long put–long stock position, this insurance has both direct costs and opportunity costs. But note that in our example the use of calls instead of puts results in lower opportunity costs. For example, Table 16-2 shows that at an index of $280 the total portfolio is worth $11.142 million if puts and

---

[7]Again, fractional trades are allowed for illustrative purposes.

the spot index are bought. However, Table 16-3 indicates that the portfolio would be worth $11.229 million if calls and T-bills are bought.

Why? The answer can be traced back to the put-call parity equation examined early in the chapter. At that point, we found that the theoretical put value was $14.23 versus an actual market price of $15. The put was overvalued relative to the call. Therefore, strategies which involve purchasing the calls would dominate equivalent strategies using long put positions.

Portfolio Insurance on Other Assets. Minimum portfolio values can be obtained on any security or commodity on which options are traded. For example, assume you own 10 Treasury bonds. You could create a minimum future floor value on the portfolio by purchasing 10 puts on T-bonds at the desired exercise price and expiration date. Alternatively, you could emulate the expiration date payoffs of such a portfolio by purchasing calls on T-bonds and T-bills.

Portfolio insurance can even be obtained on assets which do not have traded puts or calls by creating synthetic option positions. This is illustrated later in the chapter.

Call Overwriting. A common practice among many investors is a technique known as call overwriting. This is simply writing calls on stocks which are owned in the portfolio. The benefit of call overwriting is that it increases the immediate cash inflow to the portfolio. The cost is that it limits portfolio price appreciation.

Assume you own 100 shares of IBM stock and that the calls are those shown on the first page of this chapter:

Stock Price = $115.625	Call X Exercise = $110.00
Call X Price = $11.25	Call X Expiration Date = 4 months

The effects of writing 1.0 call for each share owned are shown in Table 16-4 and Figure 16-5. Note that the immediate value of the portfolio increases by the amount of the call premium—$1,125. Investing this cash inflow in T-bills also tends to increase the expiration date value of the portfolio. But by writing the calls you have stated your willingness to sell the stock to a call buyer at a fixed price of $110 even if the stock is worth more at the expiration date.

Return Distributions. Most of our expiration date option analyses have examined *investment values* at that date. Another approach is to examine the *return distributions* which exist. For example, consider the panels in Figure 16-6. In panel A, the expiration date investment value in IBM call X is shown. In panel B, an assumed probability distribution is shown for the price of IBM stock at the expiration date.[8] The expected stock price of $122 indicates that the expected call price will be $12. Given a current call price of $11.25, this translates into an expected return of 6.7% on a naked call position.

In Figure 16-7, the hypothetical *return distributions* for a four-month ownership

---

[8]The IBM stock price distribution was approximated using an expected annualized return of 15% and the *WISD* of 31.2% calculated earlier. Four-month equivalents of both were used in developing panel B.

TABLE 16-4   *Call Overwriting, Initial and Expiration Date Values*

At Date of Overwriting Program	
Stock Value	+$11,562.50
Call Premium	+1,125.00
	$12,687.50

At Expiration Date (in Four Months)

	Known Values				
Stock Price	Premium[1]	Dividend[2]	Calls	Stock	Total
$ 90	$1,146.66	$111.58	$ 0	$ 9,000	$10,258.24
$100	$1,146.66	$111.58	$ 0	$10,000	$11,258.24
$110	$1,146.66	$111.58	$ 0	$11,000	$12,258.24
$115.625	$1,146.66	$111.58	−$ 562.5	$11,562.5	$12,258.24
$120	$1,146.66	$111.58	−$1,000	$12,000	$12,258.24
$130	$1,146.66	$111.58	−$2,000	$13,000	$12,258.24
$140	$1,146.66	$111.58	−$3,000	$14,000	$12,258.24

[1]$1,125 \times e^{0.05721 \times 4/12} = \$1,146.66.$

[2]$(100 \times \$1.10) \, e^{0.05721 \times 3/12} = \$111.58.$

of either the stock or the call are shown. The stock's return distribution is approximately a normal distribution. In contrast, the call's return distribution is highly skewed to the right.

When options are added to an otherwise 100% stock portfolio, the portfolio return distribution shifts. The nature of these shifts can be seen in Figure 16-8. In panel A, various mixes of long stocks and written calls are shown. As before when no calls are written, the return distribution is a normal bell-shaped distribution. However, as calls are written on the stocks, the distribution tends to move to the right (because of the call premiums which are received) but is truncated at lower returns (because of the inability to gain from any stock price appreciation). Panel B shows that the opposite is true when puts are purchased. The distribution moves to the left (reflecting the cost of the puts) but is truncated at greater returns than a 100% stock position (reflecting the insurance feature of the put).

When options are used in a portfolio, they tend to cause skewed return distributions. Because performance monitoring techniques based on the CAPM assume normal return distributions, this can cause serious biases if one is using options in a portfolio and simultaneously evaluating the portfolio's performance with CAPM measures.

Speculation

Speculative strategies attempt to take advantage of disequilibrium prices (perceived or real). We will look at three types of speculative strategies:

FIGURE 16-5 *Call Overwriting*

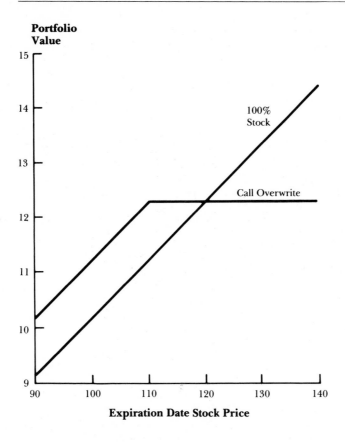

1. Index arbitrage
2. Creation of forwards
3. Strips, straps, etc.

Index Arbitrage. The term index arbitrage is applied to the speculative transaction which can be conducted when the prices of derivative securities (options and futures) are not in line with current prices of a stock index. In a strict arbitrage, there is a zero-risk cash inflow with no required cash outflow.

To illustrate an index arbitrage, we will use the S&P 100 Index calls and puts reviewed earlier. On December 31, the S&P 100 Index closed at $238.26. A call on the index selling for $13.75 was exercisable in three months at $240. An equivalent put sold for $15. Finally, the continuous risk-free interest rate was 5.721% (annualized), and a known dividend of $2.168 was to be paid in 1½ months on the index.

From these data, we conclude that the put is overvalued relative to the call. Since we cannot be sure which of the two options is mispriced (they both could be), we will

FIGURE 16-6 *IBM Call Return Distribution*

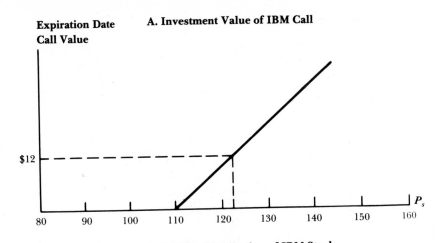

A. Investment Value of IBM Call

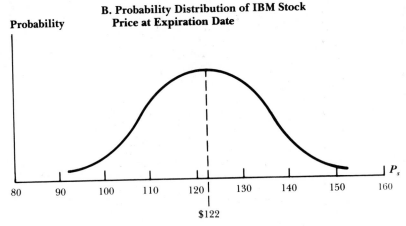

B. Probability Distribution of IBM Stock Price at Expiration Date

take offsetting positions in both. Since the put is overvalued relative to the call, the put will be sold and the call purchased.

However, a short put and long call position involves a fair degree of risk. If the stock index falls in value, we lose on the call. If the index rises in value, we win on the put. To offset this risk, a short position in the underlying stock index is taken. We know from put-call parity that if all positions are taken in a 1.0-to-1.0 relationship, the expiration date value of the portfolio is risk-free.

But even though we now have a risk-free portfolio, the transaction is not a pure arbitrage since there is a net cash outflow required at the expiration date. A pure arbitrage will have only one positive and risk-free cash flow. To make the transaction into a true index arbitrage we must buy T-bills today which have an expiration date payoff sufficient to pay the (risk-free) cash required in the put, call, and stock portfolio.

FIGURE 16-7 *IBM Stock and Call Return Distributions*

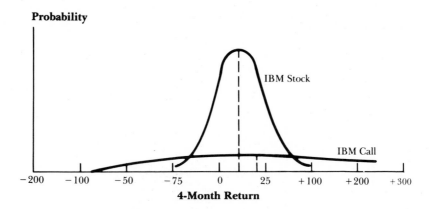

To illustrate such an arbitrage, assume that there are no transaction costs and that we can trade in fractional quantities of the assets. Also, all dividends paid on the short sale of the stock are financed initially with the purchase of T-bills.

In Table 16-5, the results of this transaction are shown for an initial trade in 500 puts and calls. Two possible expiration date values are used for the S&P 100 Index ($200 and $250) in order to show that outcomes from the arbitrage are, in fact, insensitive to eventual index values. First, 500 puts are sold and 500 calls bought to take advantage of the price disequilibrium:

1. Sell 500 puts:

Net Inflow = (500 × 100) × $15 = +$750,000
Expiration Date Value = −(500 × 100) × ($240 − $200) = −$2,000,000

TABLE 16-5 *Illustration of a Stock Index Arbitrage*

	Today	1½	S&P 100 = $200	S&P 100 = $250
1. Sell 500 Puts	+$ 750,000		−$ 2,000,000	$ 0
2. Buy 500 Calls	− 687,500		0	+ 500,000
Risky Option Portfolio	+$ 62,500		−$ 2,000,000	+$ 500,000
3. Sell 500 Units of S&P 100	+ 11,913,000	−$108,400	−$10,000,000	−$12,500,000
	+$11,975,500	−$108,400	−$12,000,000	−$12,000,000
4. Buy Treasury Bills				
a. Finance Dividends	− 107,627	+$108,400		
b. Finance $12 Million	− 11,829,591		+$12,000,000	+$12,000,000
Net	+$ 38,282	$ 0	$ 0	$ 0

FIGURE 16-8 *Hypothetical Stock-Option Return Distribution*

A. Writing Calls on a Stock Portfolio

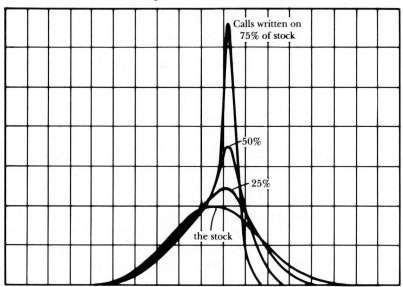

B. Buying Puts on a Stock Position

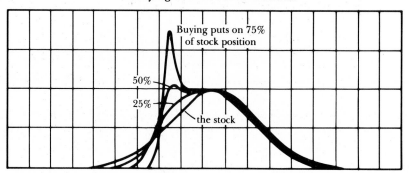

2. Buy 500 calls:

> Net Outflow = (500 × 100) × \$13.75 = \$687,500
> Expiration Date Value = (500 × 100) × (\$250 − \$240) = +\$500,000

Stocks are then added in order to make the portfolio risk-free. Note that this will be a short position in stocks requiring the payment of a cash dividend in 1½ months.

3. Sell 500 units of S&P 100 Index:

> Net Inflow = (500 × 100) × \$238.26 = \$11,913,000
> Dividend   = (500 × 100) × \$2.168 = \$108,400

Expiration Date Value:
$$= -(500 \times 100) \times \$200 = -\$10,000,000$$
$$= -(500 \times 100) \times \$250 = -\$12,500,000$$

Note that all cash flows are known today. The transaction provides an immediate cash inflow of $11,975,500. In return, $108,400 must be paid in 1½ months and $12,000,000 at the option's expiration. This is identical to obtaining a risk-free loan!

To make it a pure arbitrage, T-bills are used to finance all future cash outflows:

4. a. To finance dividends on the short stock position:

$$\$108,400/e^{(0.05721 \times 0.125)} = \$107,627$$

b. To finance expiration date payment:

$$\$12,000,000/e^{(0.05721 \times 0.25)} = \$11,829,591$$

The arbitrage profit from this transaction is $38,282 — received today!

Some comments about such arbitrages are necessary. First, the profit is large simply because the trades were large; index arbitrages are usually conducted only by large institutions. Second, transaction costs and the inability to trade in fractional units of the assets will reduce the profit and increase risk exposure. However, many large institutions pay very small commissions and are able to trade in quantities large enough to minimize risk. In addition, all trades must be executed instantaneously at known asset prices. If the price of an asset changes by the time that the trade is expected, all arbitrage profits can disappear. That is why the NYSE's *designated order turnaround* (DOT) system is critical to successful index arbitrage.

Note that large positions in the stock index must be taken — either long or short. But since the index itself is not traded, how is this done? There are three things that could be done. First, one could actually buy or sell all shares in the index in appropriate quantities such that the stock position mirrors the index. This is most easily done with options on the Major Market Index since it consists of only 20 stocks which are equally weighted. Second, one could create a "basket" of stocks which closely track the index. Finally, one could trade in an index equivalent in the financial futures market. Financial futures are the topic of Chapter 17.

Creating a Forward Contract. An intriguing aspect of options is that they can be combined to create payoffs identical to those for other securities. One such security is a forward contract. A forward contract is an agreement today between two parties for the future trade of a specified asset at a specified price on a future specified date. No cash is exchanged prior to the forward's delivery date. Forwards are very similar to futures contracts and are discussed in Chapter 17.

Consider the following position in IBM options which have identical exercise prices and expiration dates: buy 1.0 call, write 1.0 put, and sell enough T-bills to finance the net cash outflow. The net effect of this is a forward contract to buy the shares.

Using the data on IBM call X and put X, and two assumed expiration date stock prices, the following *cash flows* (note: not investment values) would take place:

		Cash Flow When $P_x = \$110$	
		Expiration Date	
	Today	$P_s = \$90$	$P_s = \$130$
Buy Call	−$11.25	—	−$110.00
Write Put	+ 4.50	− 110.00	—
Sell T-Bill	+ 6.75	− 6.88	− 6.88
Net	$ 0.00	−$116.88	−$116.88

Today there would be no cash investment, since you used a trade in T-bills to assure this.

If the stock eventually trades for $90 the call will be worth zero, but the short put position requires that you buy the stock for $110. Note that we are not tracing the investment value of the put position ($90 − $110) but the gross cash flow. Given the T-bill repayment of $6.88:

$$6.75\,e^{(0.05721 \times 1/3)} = \$6.88$$

your net cash flow will be $116.88; and you will be the proud owner of one share of IBM stock.

If the stock eventually trades for $130, you will pay $110 to exercise the call, the put will die worthless, and $6.88 will be paid on the T-bill position. Again, you are the owner of the stock at a price of $116.88.

In short, options can be used with T-bills to create forward contracts in the underlying assets. If you believe that the price of IBM in April (the options' expiration date) will be higher than $116.88, you might wish to purchase such a forward contract. Alternatively, if futures contracts exist on the underlying assets, the futures should be selling at a price close to the forward price available on the options. If not, an arbitrage profit is possible.

Combinations of Put and Call Options

The variety of option contracts which can be mixed together is mind-boggling. We will briefly examine four common forms. Figure 16-9 depicts profit and loss possibilities for many of these.

A *straddle* is a put and call on the same security with identical expiration dates and striking prices. A straddle may be either purchased (a put and a call are bought) or sold (a put and a call are written). Panel A in Figure 16-9 illustrates both types. Purchasers are betting on great stock price variability to earn a profit, while sellers are counting on small stock price variability to earn a profit. But neither is forecasting a move in the stock's price in one direction to be more probable than a move in the opposite direction. For example, a straddle purchaser believes that by the expiration date, the underlying stock's price will be substantially different from today but assigns equal probability to a price increase or decrease. For the purchaser to break even, the stock's price must increase or decrease by an amount equal to the premium on both the put and the call.

FIGURE 16-9 *Straddles, Strips, and Straps Values at Exercise Date*

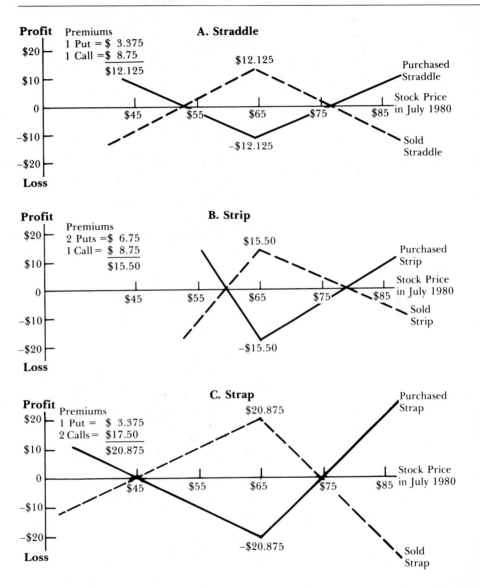

A *strip* is two puts and one call on the same security with identical expiration dates and striking prices. A purchased strip is similar to a purchased straddle, but the purchaser believes the probability of a price decline is greater than the probability of a price increase. A strip which is sold is just the opposite. These are illustrated in panel B of Figure 16-9. For the purchaser to break even, the stock price must increase or decrease by an amount that will cover the premium paid on two puts and one call. The break-even point for stock price declines is half that for stock price increases since two puts are owned for each call, causing the purchaser's profits to be more sensitive to price declines.

A *strap* is two calls and one put. It is similar to a strip except that purchasers believe the odds of a stock price increase exceed those of a price decline. Panel C in Figure 16-9 illustrates the profit potential to a buyer or seller of a strap.

A *spread* involves buying an option and selling an equivalent option which differs in only one respect. A *money spread* consists of buying an option at one striking price and selling an option at a different striking price. Both options would be on the same stock and have identical maturities. A *time spread* involves buying and selling options similar in all respects except for expiration dates. A *butterfly spread* involves buying, say, an option exercisable at $50 with a six-month expiration and selling $50 exercise options (on the same stock) with three-month and nine-month maturities. Butterfly spreads can also be created which have a single expiration date but are spread across exercise prices.

Option spreading is a widely used technique, and more detailed examples of such spreads should aid in understanding the potential risks and rewards involved in option trading. Table 16-6 presents information which is assumed to be known or estimated on the call options of Digital Equipment. We will use this information to illustrate a variety of possible spreads. There are two ways in which we might examine potential spreads. The first evaluates potential profits at the expiration date, and the second utilizes the Black-Scholes model to determine short-term riskless arbitrage positions.

In Table 16-6 call options *A* and *B* are identical except for exercise prices. Since option *A* is exercisable at $70 and option *B* at $80, a money spread could be created by purchasing one and selling the other. For the sake of argument consider the purchase of *A* at $10.20 and the sale of *B* at $3.63 for a net purchase price of $6.57 ($10.20 − $3.63). Net profit/loss positions are shown in Figure 16-10 as the solid line. Note that gains and losses to the spread differ for stock price levels (at expiration) between $70 and $80. For example, if the stock is worth less than $70 at expiration, the short position in option *B* expires worthless, resulting in a profit equal to the initial

TABLE 16-6 *Option Spread Data*

	A	B	C
Months to Exercise	2.5	2.5	8.5
Risk-Free Rate	8.88%	8.88%	9.17%
Current Stock Price	$78.63	$78.63	$78.63
Exercise Price	$70.00	$80.00	$80.00
Call Premium			
-Actual	$10.20	$ 3.63	$ 8.50
-Per OPM	$10.51	$ 3.51	$ 9.00
Expected Cash Dividend	$ 0.0	$ 0.0	$ 0.0
N_{d1}	0.879	0.524	0.629
Transaction	Buy	Sell	Buy

                Money Spread   *Time Spread*

FIGURE 16-10 *Spreads*

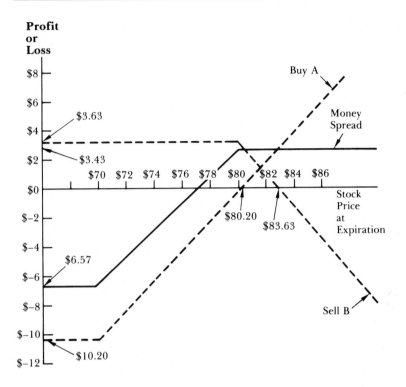

premium of $3.63. (An option to buy at $80 something selling for less than $70 won't be exercised.) Offsetting this, however, is the $10.20 loss incurred on the purchase price of option *A*. (As before, call option *A* won't be exercised at a price of $70 if the stock is actually selling for less than $70.) On net, a maximum loss of $6.57 is possible. At the other extreme, if the stock sells for more than $80 at expiration, a maximum gain of $3.43 is possible. For example, assume the stock sells for $82 at expiration and we neglect the initial cost of the spread for a minute. Option *B* (which was sold) will be exercised and result in a $2 loss. However, option *A* (which was bought) will also be exercised at a profit of $12. On net, a $10 profit is earned before any allowance for the costs of entering into the spread. Once this investment cost is deducted, a net profit of $3.43 is earned ($10 − $6.57). In summary, losses on this money spread would be limited to the initial investment of $6.57 if the stock price is below $70 since neither option is exercised. Gains would be limited to $3.43 — the difference between the exercise prices ($10) of both options which are exercised less the $6.57 investment cost.

At prices between $70 and $80, option *A* will be exercised and option *B* will expire worthless. The break-even price of $76.57 will provide an exercise profit exactly equal to the initial investment cost. If a person believes stock prices are more likely to be above $76.57 at the expiration date than below $76.57, a money spread such as this would make sense.

TRADES BASED ON CONTINUOUS TIME

In the previous section, we reviewed a variety of hedging and speculative strategies based on an option's value at its expiration date. Such strategies are usually based on applications of the put-call parity model. In this section, we use the Black-Scholes model to illustrate continuous-time option strategies. A continuous-time strategy is one which is constantly rebalanced so that the stock/option position has the desired short-term return payoffs—usually risk-free. In practice, continuous rebalancing can be quite costly, so investors and speculators will rebalance daily or weekly.

Early Exercise

Now that we are no longer focusing on expiration date payoffs, we need to deal with the possibility of early exercise. If transaction costs to trade the stock are large, it might be less costly to exercise an option than to trade the stock. However, this is extremely unlikely. In the more realistic case of small (or no) transaction costs, three principles of early exercise exist:

1. Call options on stocks which pay no cash dividends should never be exercised before the expiration date.
2. Call options on stocks which pay a large cash dividend might be exercised immediately before the dividend is paid.
3. Put options might always be exercised.

Call Options on Stocks with No Cash Dividend. Consider an American call option which is exercisable at $50 any time during the next three months. The stock is selling for $55 and will not pay any cash dividends during the option's life. The option is trading for $7.

This $7 call price can be thought of as consisting of two components, an immediate in-the-money value and a time value:

Immediate Call Value	$5
Time Value	2
Call's Market Price	$7

Assume that you own the option but would prefer to own the stock. Should you exercise the option today in order to obtain the stock? No! If you are, in fact, foolish enough to exercise, you would pay the exercise price of $50 to be the owner of the stock. Alternatively, you could sell the option for $7 and use the proceeds together with only $48 to buy the stock in the open market. Clearly, the better alternative is to sell the option, since it results in a smaller out-of-pocket cash flow.

If we exercise any call on a non-dividend stock prior to its expiration date, we throw away the time value inherent in the option. The only time that one should exercise a call on a stock which pays no cash dividends is when the call's time value is zero. This will occur only at the call's expiration date.

Since American calls on stocks which will not pay cash dividends should never be prematurely exercised, such American calls will be worth the same as equivalent European calls — that is, the Black-Scholes model can be used to value such American calls.

Call Options on Stocks with Large Cash Dividends. When large cash dividends are to be paid, it is possible that early exercise is optimal. For example, consider the situation of the call option above but now assume that a $15 cash dividend will be paid tomorrow. This is illustrated in Figure 16-11. On the day before the stock goes ex-dividend, the stock is selling for $55 and the call for $7. Assuming that the $7 call price is a proper price according to the Black-Scholes model, the call must trade for this amount or arbitrage profits would be available. Tomorrow, however, the stock will go ex-dividend and drop in value to about $40. As a result, the call's value will also fall — to a new Black-Scholes value of, say, $3.

Should you exercise this call? Yes — but only very late on the day prior to the ex-dividend date. By exercising you capture the call's immediate value of $5 ($55 − $50). If you do not exercise, you will be left with a call which is worth only $3 tomorrow. In short, if the call's immediate value ($P_s - P_x$) is greater than the value of the call once the stock goes ex-dividend, you should exercise immediately before the ex-dividend date.

Note that the exercise takes place just before the ex-dividend date. At any prior time, the call will have a time value (albeit small) which you should not lose through premature exercise.

A revised version of the Black-Scholes model has been developed by Roll as well as Cox, Ross, and Rubinstein which takes into account the potential for early exer-

FIGURE 16-11 *Call Values Before and After Ex-Dividend Date*

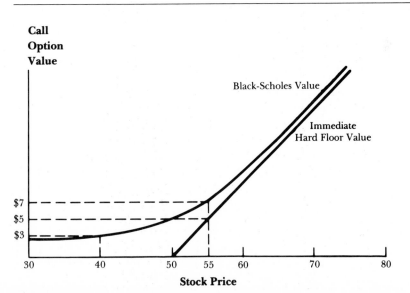

cise of an American call.[9] A reasonable approximation consists of calculating two Black-Scholes call values. The first would use the stated expiration date together with any intermediate cash dividends. The second would use the early exercise date as the option's life. The larger of the two call values should be its fair market price.

Put Options. There are always situations in which early exercise of a put is better than non-exercise, even if the stock does not pay cash dividends. To understand why, we return to the put-call parity model for *European* options:

Put-Call Parity
$$P_c - P_P = P_s - P_x/(1 + RF)^T \qquad (16.7a)$$
$$P_c = P_s - P_x/(1 + RF)^T + P_P \qquad (16.7b)$$

Since the price of the call must be less than (or equal to) the stock price, we can say:

$$P_s \geq P_c \qquad (16.7c)$$

and

$$P_s \geq P_s - P_x/(1 + RF)^T + P_P \qquad (16.7d)$$

Canceling the P_s terms in Equation 16.7d, we can say that the price of a European put will always be equal to or less than the present value of the exercise price.

European Put Price Bound
$$P_P \leq P_x/(1 + RF)^T \qquad (16.8)$$

Equation 16.8 makes perfect sense. The most that a put option can be worth is its exercise price (when $P_s = \$0$). But since this cannot be collected on a European put until the expiration date, the maximum current put value will be the present value of P_x.

Now consider this relationship as shown in panel A of Figure 16-12. Three European put value lines are shown representing the option: (1) at its expiration date, (2) one month prior to expiration, and (3) two months prior to expiration. Note that at high stock prices the put is worth more "alive" than "dead"—it has a positive time value. However, at low stock prices the European put can actually have a negative time value. The option owner would prefer to exercise today but cannot, since the option is European. At stock prices to the left of points 1 and 2, the put owner would prefer to own an American put since it could be *immediately* exercised.

Because early exercise of a put might be desirable, American puts must be worth more than European puts. This is illustrated in panel B of Figure 16-12. Unfortunately, models that identify points such as 1 and 2 in panel A and calculate American put values are very complex. Valuation models of American puts are beyond the scope of the book.[10]

---

[9]See R. Roll, "An Analytic Valuation Formula for Unprotected American Call Options on Stocks with Known Dividends," *Journal of Finance* 5 (1977), and Cox, Ross, and Rubinstein, "Option Pricing: A Simplified Approach," *Journal of Financial Economics,* September 1979.

[10]See Parkinson, Brennan, and Schwartz as well as Cox, Ross, and Rubinstein for numerical techniques used to value American puts which might be prematurely exercised.

FIGURE 16-12 *The Value of American and European Puts*

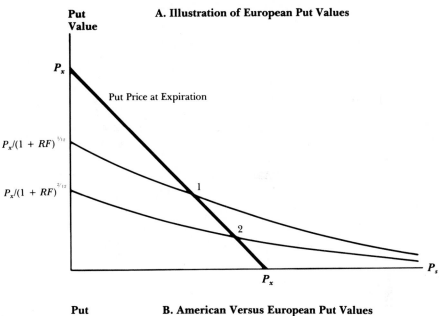

A. Illustration of European Put Values

Put
Value

P_x

Put Price at Expiration

$P_x/(1 + RF)^{1/12}$

$P_x/(1 + RF)^{2/12}$

1

2

P_x

P_s

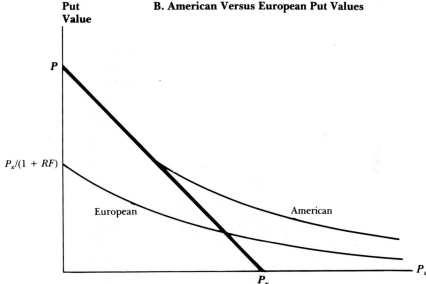

B. American Versus European Put Values

Put
Value

P

$P_x/(1 + RF)$

European

American

P_x

P_s

Hedging Strategies

Continuous-time option strategies can be used to alter the risk exposure of a portfolio. Before examples of such strategies are shown, however, we need to review the importance of the N_{d1} term in the Black-Scholes model and see how the (instantaneous) beta of a call can be calculated.

FIGURE 16-13 *Hedging and Option Prices*

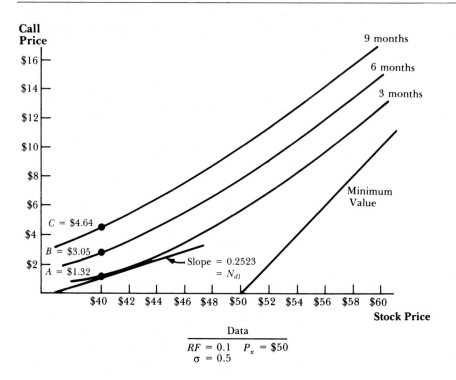

Data

$RF = 0.1 \quad P_x = \$50$
$\sigma = 0.5$

Importance of N_{d1}. Figure 16-13 plots Black-Scholes call premiums versus stock prices for options exercisable at $50 when the standard deviation of stock returns is 0.5, the risk-free rate is 10%, and three exercise dates are assumed (three, six, and nine months). As we saw earlier, call premiums increase with the stock's price and expiration date. Assuming that the stock is currently selling at $40, the options would be worth $1.32, $3.05, and $4.64, respectively, as illustrated by points A, B, and C in the figure.

Also shown in Figure 16-13 is a line drawn tangent to point A. The slope of this line is important since it represents the change in the value of the call premium for a very small change in the stock's price. The slope at A is 0.2523, meaning that if the stock price changes from $40 by approximately $0.01, the option premium will move in the same direction by an amount equal to $0.002523.

Another way to view point A is to say that if one share of the stock is bought and one call option is sold, only 74.77% (100% − 25.23%) of the future price variability remains. Alternatively, we could sell 3.96 options (1 ÷ 0.2523) for each share bought and eliminate *all* price uncertainty. The change in the option's price for a small change in the stock's price is known as the *hedge ratio. The hedge ratio indicates the number of shares which should be bought for each call sold in order to eliminate price risk. N_{d1} is this hedge ratio.* In the same manner, 1.0 ÷ hedge ratio indicates the number of options which should be sold for each share bought.

The hedge ratio is easily calculated by using the Black-Scholes option model value of N_{d1}. N_{d1} is the hedge ratio which will protect against small price changes. For example, assume you buy one share of the stock in Figure 16-13 for $40 and sell 3.96 of the A options at $1.32 per option. As a result, your investment is $34.77 ($40 − 3.96 × $1.32). If the stock's price immediately falls to $39.50, the option would now sell for approximately $1.19. Your equity investment remains constant:

Value of Stock	$39.50
Value of 3.96 Calls	(4.73) (3.96 × $1.19)
Equity Value	$34.77

While the stock decreased $0.50, you gained $0.50 through reduced call values.

These hedges are appropriate, however, for only short time intervals and small changes in stock prices. Any time N_{d1} changes, the hedge ratio should also be revised. The hedge ratio will change with changes in the stock price (P_s), risk-free rate (RF), stock return price variance (σ^2), and time to expiration (T). Ideally, hedges should be continuously changed. As a practical matter, instantaneous hedges are impossible.

Risk-free positions can also be accomplished using only the options themselves. Assume that a stock has two calls available which differ in either expiration date or striking price. If N_{d1} for the first option is 0.4, then 2.5 of this option should be sold for each share bought to create a riskless hedge. If N_{d1} for the second option is 0.5, then 2.0 of this option would be sold for each share bought. Alternatively, you could buy 1.25 (0.5/0.4) of the first option for each 1.0 of the second option sold. Or 0.8 of the second should be bought (0.4/0.5) for each 1.0 of the first sold. Options can be combined to yield riskless hedges. But again, such hedges are riskless only for an instant in time.

Call Betas. Recall that in any portfolio of securities the portfolio's expected return is a weighted average of the expected return on each individual security. If the portfolio being considered is a perfectly hedged portfolio consisting of stock and a written call, then:

Expected Return on a Hedged Portfolio
$$E(R_H) = X_s E(R_s) + X_c E(R_c) \tag{16.9}$$

where $E(R_H)$ = the expected return on the hedged portfolio, X_s = the percentage of capital committed to the stock, $E(R_s)$ = the expected return on the stock, X_c = the percentage of capital committed to the call, and $E(R_c)$ = the expected return on the call.

In the Black-Scholes model, N_{d1} indicates the number of shares which should be bought for each call option written. Denoting P_s as the current price of the stock, the amount of money invested in stock per option written is ($N_{d1} \times P_s$). Letting P_c equal the call premium, the *net* amount of money invested in this perfectly hedged portfolio would be ($N_{d1} \times P_s - P_c$), and the percentage invested in stock would be:

$$X_s = \frac{N_{d1} P_s}{N_{d1} P_s - P_c}$$

The amount invested in calls would be:

$$X_c = 1 - X_s$$

In a risk-free portfolio the amount invested in stock exceeds the net amount invested, $X_s > 1.0$, and the amount invested in calls is negative, $X_c < 0.0$.

Because the portfolio is riskless, its expected return should equal the risk-free rate, RF. As a result, the expected return on a call option would be found as follows:

$$RF = X_s E(R_s) + (1 - X_s) E(R_c)$$

$$E(R_c) = \frac{RF}{1 - X_s} - \frac{X_s}{1 - X_s} E(R_s)$$

Expected Return on a Call

$$E(R_c) = RF + N_{d1} \frac{P_s}{P_c} [E(R_s) - RF] \qquad (16.10)$$

For example, if RF is 1% on a four-month T-bill (about 4% annually), the expected return on the stock is 3% (about 12.5% annually), the stock and call are selling for $50 and $5, respectively, and the hedge ratio N_{d1} is 0.25, then the expected return on *one* call option would be:

$$E(R_c) = 1\% + 0.25 \left[\frac{\$50}{\$5}\right] (3\% - 1\%)$$

$$= 6\%$$

While options can provide significant leverage potential if not placed in covered portfolios, they also contain more risk than is inherent in the underlying stock. All of this additional risk is market-related, nondiversifiable risk and can be captured by relating the option beta to the stock beta. Analytically, if β_c refers to the call option beta and β_s refers to the stock beta, then

Beta of a Call

$$\beta_c = \left[N_{d1} \frac{P_s}{P_c}\right] \beta_s \qquad (16.11)$$

Using data from the prior example and assuming the stock beta is 1.0, the call option beta would be 2.5.

The economic intuition underlying the betas of a call is relatively straightforward. For a cost of P_c you control an asset which is worth P_s—that is, you have "leveraged up" your investment by effectively borrowing $P_s - P_c$. Both your investment of P_c and your borrowing of $P_s - P_c$ are invested in the stock. Given that the stock has a beta of β_s, the beta of your leveraged position is $(P_s/P_c) \times \beta_s$.[11] But the call does not move dollar-for-dollar with the stock. Instead, for each $1 change in the stock price the call price changes by N_{d1} dollars (approximately). To reflect this fact, we multiply the leveraged beta position by N_{d1}.

---

[11]This is similar to moving along the security market line by borrowing (or lending) at the risk-free rate.

Adjusting a Portfolio's Systematic Risk. Assume that you own $10 million of stock which is very similar to the S&P 100 Index. Since your spot stock portfolio is similar to the index on which the S&P 100 calls are traded, you can use the calls to adjust the (instantaneous) beta risk of your aggregate portfolio.

Early in the chapter we calculated the following values for such an S&P 100 call:

S&P 100 Call Information

T = ¼ year	P_s = $238.26
RF = 5.721%	P_c = $ 13.75
σ = 17.12%	P_x = $240.00

$$N_{d1} = 0.508$$

We will assume that the beta of the S&P 100 Index is 1.0. Thus the beta of this call would be 8.8:

$$(\$238.26/\$13.75) \times 0.508 = 8.802624$$

As a first example of how calls can be used to adjust systematic risk, assume that we wish to continue to own the $10 million in stock but want to trade enough calls so that our net portfolio beta is 0.0. This would, of course, mean that we would sell calls on the S&P 100 Index. When the calls are sold, a call premium will be received. Assume that the call premium is invested in Treasury bills.

We first calculate the dollar value of calls which will result in a portfolio beta of 0.0. Define this dollar call position as $Call:

$$beta_p = (\% \text{ in stock})(beta_s) + (\% \text{ in calls})(beta_c) + (\% \text{ in T-bill})(beta_{TB})$$

$$0.0 = \frac{\$10,000,000}{\$10,000,000}(1.0) + \frac{\$Call}{\$10,000,000} \times 8.802624 + \frac{\$Call}{\$10,000,000} \times 0.0$$

$$\$Call = -\$1,136,025$$

The negative sign on $Call simply confirms that we should *sell* calls. A positive sign would have implied call purchases. Thus, if we sell $1,136,025 worth of S&P 100 calls and invest the proceeds in Treasury bills, the (instantaneous) beta of the total portfolio will be 0.0. Since each call is valued at $1,375 ($13.75 × 100), we need to sell 826.2 calls:

$$\$1,136,025/\$1,375 = 826.2$$

The calculations above are based on the relationship between the beta of a call and the beta of the underlying asset. We can also use our understanding of N_{d1} to determine the call position which will perfectly offset our stock risk. In this example the value of N_{d1} is 0.508, which implies that we should sell 1.97 calls for each unit of the S&P 100 Index that we own:

$$1.0/0.508 = 1.968504$$

The question then is: "How many units of the S&P 100 Index do we own?"

Since the S&P 100 Index has a current *spot* value of $238.26 and each S&P 100 option is a claim to 100 times the spot value, our $10 million in stock is the equivalent of 419.7 index units:

$$\$10,000,000/(\$238.26 \times 100) = 419.70956$$

Thus, we should sell 826.2 calls in order to obtain an instantaneously risk-free position:

$$419.70956 \times 1.968504 = 826.2$$

The answer is the same regardless of the technique used.

The example above was presented for illustrative purposes only. In actual cases, investors would rarely use the call options to obtain a completely risk-free position. Instead, options are used to temporarily alter a portfolio's systematic risk by a more moderate amount. For example, assume that you have $10 million invested in Treasury bills and stocks which are similar to those in the S&P 100 Index. Your desired T-bill/stock mix is 20/80, but the actual current mix is 40/60—that is, your desired portfolio beta is 0.8 but the actual current beta is only 0.6. The situation is depicted below:

		Investment	
Asset Class	*Beta*	*Actual*	*Desired*
Treasury Bills	0.0	$ 4,000,000	$ 2,000,000
S&P 100 Stocks	1.0	6,000,000	8,000,000
		$10,000,000	$10,000,000
Portfolio Beta		0.6	0.8

In this case, we wish to increase the systematic risk of the portfolio with call options. Thus, we should *purchase* calls using part of the T-bill investment to pay for them. Again, letting $Call represent the dollar call position, the quantity of calls to purchase would be:

$$0.8 = \frac{\$6,000,000}{\$10,000,000}(1.0) + \frac{\$Call}{\$10,000,000}(8.802624) + \frac{\$4,000,000 - \$Call}{\$10,000,000}(0.0)$$

$$\$Call = +\$227,205$$

$$\# \text{ of Calls} = \$227,205/(\$13.75 \times 100)$$

$$= 165.24$$

We should purchase 165.24 calls and pay for them with $227,205 of T-bills.

In the two examples above, we used call options on a stock index to adjust the instantaneous systematic risk of the portfolio. Three comments about such trades are appropriate. First, the results apply to only a moment in time. As time passes, as stock prices move, etc., the option's beta value will also shift. Therefore, one should select calls which do not experience major changes in their betas with slight changes in other variables. This usually means that options close to expiration (say, one month or less) should not be used. Second, the options can be used to adjust a portfolio's risk level only if the spot stock which is owned is similar to the index on which the options are written. For example, if the spot stock portfolio consisted of an equal weighting of 25 large industrial stocks, calls on the Major Market Index would be more effective than S&P 100 calls.

Finally, note that each of the stock/option/T-bill positions could have been obtained simply by trading in the spot stock and T-bills. In the first example, we could have obtained a zero beta by selling the $10 million in stock to buy $10 million in T-bills. In the second example, we could have sold $2 million in T-bills and invested the proceeds in stocks. Whether to trade the options or the spot securities depends on which is cheaper. Certainly this means that the brokerage costs of each should be evaluated. But other, less quantifiable, costs need to be evaluated. For example, a *rapid* purchase or sale of sizable dollar amounts of stock can affect the stock's spot price or may simply not be possible. A trade in the options might be accomplished more rapidly and at small market price impacts. In addition, large institutions such as pension funds typically employ many investment managers to manage the institution's investments in each security class. For example, a $1 billion pension fund might employ, say, 20 managers to invest the pension's position in equities, five managers to invest in bonds, and two managers to invest in money market securities such as Treasury bills. If the aggregate portfolio's asset allocation is to be modified, it might be faster and more cheaply accomplished by trading options than by transferring funds from certain managers to other managers.[12]

It is this ability to temporarily adjust a portfolio's risk level without disturbing the underlying spot investments which has caused the rapid growth of trading in stock index options.

Dynamic Replication of Portfolio Insurance. Earlier in the chapter, we reviewed how one could insure a minimum portfolio value by either: (1) purchasing stock similar to a stock index and purchasing puts on the stock index, or (2) purchasing calls on a stock index plus Treasury bills. There are, however, a number of problems with the use of listed options in insuring a portfolio floor. These include the following:

1. The stock portfolio might be quite different in composition from any stock index on which options are traded.
2. The listed options might not have an exercise date identical to the date at which an insured portfolio is desired. For example, a floor value five years hence could not be obtained with listed options.
3. Listed options in the United States are American options, and thus some degree of risk is incurred from the potential of early exercise.
4. There are maximum position limits for listed puts.

---

[12]Investment managers are typically compensated by charging a percentage of the market value of securities managed. For example, an annual fee of 0.75% of asset value would be common for an equity manager. For this reason, managers will fight and delay acting on any requests that they return funds which they manage to the portfolio owner.

As a result, many portfolio insurance programs do not actually use listed puts or calls. Instead, they rely on the principles of option theory to create *synthetic or artificial* option positions. This is done by dynamic asset allocation between stocks and Treasury bills.[13]

The logic underlying the approach is easy to understand. An initial position is taken in a stock portfolio and Treasury bills. The exact mix is left solely to the discretion of the portfolio owner. Any T-bills initially owned or purchased in the future should have a maturity date identical to the date at which the portfolio is to have an insured floor. The maturity date of the T-bill defines the expiration date of the put option which is dynamically replicated. If the value of the underlying stock *increases* during a given interval of time, a portion of the T-bills are sold and the proceeds are invested in additional stock. If the value of the underlying stock *decreases* during a given interval of time, a portion of the stock is sold and the proceeds are invested in T-bills. In fact, a lower limit is set on the stock value such that, if the stock falls below this limit, 100% of the portfolio has been transferred to T-bills. In short, a trading strategy is used which dynamically (meaning adjusted over time) replicates the outcomes of trading in listed options.

To illustrate the mechanics of dynamic option replication, we will use the binomial valuation model and data from a paper written by Thomas O'Brien. When applied in practice, the Black-Scholes model is used. However, the principles and calculations of dynamic option replication are much easier to see in the binomial approach.

Panels A–C of Figure 16-14 present the basic situation. The stock portfolio is now worth $100. During any future period the value of the stock could increase by 20% or decrease by 16⅔%. Under the assumption that we wish to have an insured portfolio at the end of period 3, the potential stock price evolution is shown for three future dates. In panel B, the values of a put option are shown. The put has an expiration date at the end of period 3 and an exercise price of $100 and is valued using a 2% risk-free rate per period. The put values are calculated using the multiperiod binomial approach discussed in Chapter 15. In panel C, the outcomes of a portfolio consisting of 1.0 long stock and 1.0 long put are shown. An initial investment of $110.48 is required to purchase both the stock and the put. This combination has a $100 minimum floor value at the end of period 3. But if the stock is worth more than $100 at that time, the portfolio (partially) shares in the price increase.

Now assume that we wish to start with $110.48 and replicate the outcomes of panel C by proper combinations of stock and T-bills instead of purchasing the puts. We wish to conduct a trading strategy which synthetically replicates a long stock/long put position.

Another way of thinking about this replication portfolio is that we intend to take positions in the stock and T-bills which replicate a long call/T-bill portfolio. The proportions allocated to the stock and riskless asset change every period.

---

[13]If portfolio insurance longer than one year is used, U.S. Treasury strips would be used in place of T-bills.

FIGURE 16-14 *Binomial Valuation Results*

A. Stock Price Evolution

Period: 0   1   2   3

172.80

144.00

120.00   120.00

$100.00   100.00

83.33   83.33

69.44

57.87

B. Put Price Evolution
$P_x = \$100$ RF = 2%

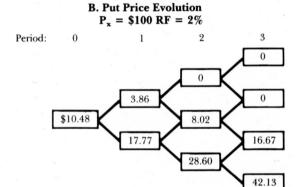

Period: 0   1   2   3

0

0

3.86   0

$10.48   8.02

17.77   16.67

28.60

42.13

C. Insured Portfolio
(Long Stock and Long Put)

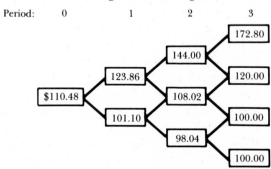

Period: 0   1   2   3

172.80

144.00

123.86   120.00

$110.48   108.02

101.10   100.00

98.04

100.00

SOURCE: T. O'Brien, "The Mechanics of Portfolio Insurance," *Journal of Portfolio Management*, Spring 1988.

FIGURE 16-15 *Hedge Ratios: Number of Stock Units to Own at Each Possible Stock Price*

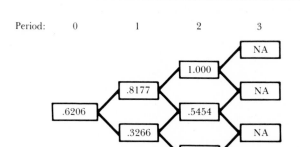

Source: T. O'Brien, "The Mechanics of Portfolio Insurance," *Journal of Portfolio Management*, Spring 1988.

In Figure 16-15, call option hedge ratios are shown. For example, at period 0 the hedge ratio of 0.6206 means that, if we wish to replicate a call during period 1, we should invest in 0.6206 *units* of the stock and place the remaining capital in T-bills. This is the call hedge ratio discussed in Chapter 15. If the Black-Scholes model were being used, it would be the value of N_{d1}.

In Figure 16-16 the net results of the replication portfolios are shown. At date 0, the stock is worth $100. We purchase 0.6206 units of the stock for $62.06 and place the remaining capital in T-bills.

At the end of period 1 the T-bills will have increased in value by 2% to $49.39, and the per unit stock value will be either $120 or $83.33. Thus, our portfolio will be worth either $123.86 or $101.10. If the stock has increased to $120, the new hedge ratio is 0.8177. Thus we would want to own $98.12 (0.8177 × $120) of stock. This requires that we sell $23.65 of T-bills (to increase the stock investment from 0.6206 × $120 to $98.12). That is, if the stock increases in value we buy more stock.

If the stock had decreased to $83.33, the hedge ratio would have fallen to 0.3266 and we would sell $24.50 in stock to buy T-bills.

Each of the other blocks in Figure 16-16 is evaluated in much the same fashion. If the stock increases in value during the period, we buy more stock and finance the purchase with the sale of T-bills. If the stock decreases in value, we sell stock and buy T-bills. Note that the final results in period 3 are identical to the long stock/long put position in panel C of Figure 16-13. The dynamic trading strategy replicates an option position.

The costs of this replication must be clearly understood. They are identical to the costs of using listed puts. First, there is the direct cost of the puts—the $10.48 at date 0. Second, there is the opportunity cost if the stock increases in value. For example, if the stock is worth $172.80 at the end of period 3, our insured portfolio is worth

FIGURE 16-16 *Dynamic Replication of Insured Portfolio*

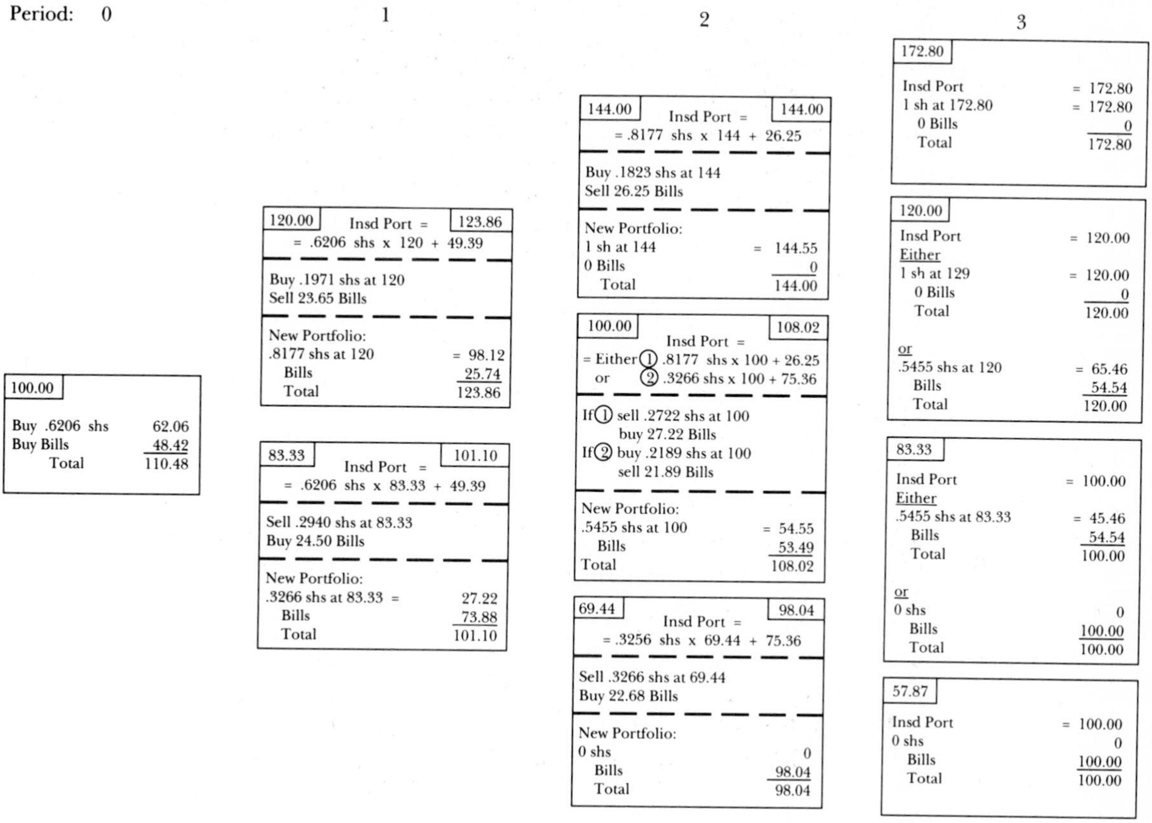

Period: 0   1   2   3

172.80	
Insd Port	= 172.80
1 sh at 172.80	= 172.80
0 Bills	0
Total	172.80

144.00	Insd Port =	144.00

= .8177 shs x 144 + 26.25

Buy .1823 shs at 144
Sell 26.25 Bills

New Portfolio:
1 sh at 144   = 144.55
0 Bills   0
Total   144.00

120.00	Insd Port =	123.86

= .6206 shs x 120 + 49.39

Buy .1971 shs at 120
Sell 23.65 Bills

New Portfolio:
.8177 shs at 120   = 98.12
Bills   25.74
Total   123.86

120.00	
Insd Port	= 120.00
Either	
1 sh at 129	= 120.00
0 Bills	0
Total	120.00

or
.5455 shs at 120   = 65.46
Bills   54.54
Total   120.00

100.00	Insd Port =	108.02

= Either ① .8177 shs x 100 + 26.25
or   ② .3266 shs x 100 + 75.36

If ① sell .2722 shs at 100
     buy 27.22 Bills
If ② buy .2189 shs at 100
     sell 21.89 Bills

New Portfolio:
.5455 shs at 100   = 54.55
Bills   53.49
Total   108.02

100.00	

Buy .6206 shs   62.06
Buy Bills   48.42
Total   110.48

83.33	Insd Port =	101.10

= .6206 shs x 83.33 + 49.39

Sell .2940 shs at 83.33
Buy 24.50 Bills

New Portfolio:
.3266 shs at 83.33 =   27.22
Bills   73.88
Total   101.10

83.33	
Insd Port	= 100.00
Either	
.5455 shs at 83.33	= 45.46
Bills	54.54
Total	100.00

or
0 shs   0
Bills   100.00
Total   100.00

69.44	Insd Port =	98.04

= .3256 shs x 69.44 + 75.36

Sell .3266 shs at 69.44
Buy 22.68 Bills

New Portfolio:
0 shs   0
Bills   98.04
Total   98.04

57.87	
Insd Port	= 100.00
0 shs	0
Bills	100.00
Total	100.00

SOURCE: T. O'Brien, "The Mechanics of Portfolio Insurance," *Journal of Portfolio Management*, Spring 1988.

$172.80. Yet if we had initially invested all $110.48 in stock, it would have grown to $190.91 ($110.48 × $172.8/$100).

The purpose of this example is to show how investors can obtain portfolio insurance using a dynamic trading strategy instead of listed options. In practice, Black-Scholes N_{d1} values are used as the hedge ratios. In addition, the spot stock is often not traded; instead, stock index futures are used. We return to this in the next chapter.

Speculative Strategies

Continuous-time models can also be used in speculative strategies to take advantage of mispriced options. Two speculative techniques are reviewed here.

Incorrect Call Prices. Earlier in this chapter we applied the Black-Scholes model to valuation of calls on the S&P 100 Index. As an estimate of the index's standard deviation of returns, we used an ex post sigma value which indicated that the S&P 100 calls should be trading for $8.25 versus an actual market price of $13.75. Clearly we could have erred in assuming that the ex post standard deviation should be used to value the call. But assume that, after careful thought, we continue to believe that the ex post sigma estimate is reasonable and that the call is overvalued.

Given this assumption, there is a risk-free speculative opportunity which involves selling the S&P 100 call and buying a portfolio identical to the S&P 100 Index. Given the calculated N_{d1} value of 0.508, we should sell 1.9685 (1.0/0.508) calls for each unit of the S&P 100 Index purchased. This would result in an instantaneously risk-free position with expected returns in excess of the risk-free rate.

Assume that on the day after the trade the stock index remains at 238.26 and that the call option decreases to our $8.25 estimate of its fair value. Cash flows on this speculation would be:

	Day 0	Day + 1
Buy Stock Index	−$238.26	+$238.26
Sell 1.9685 Calls	+ 27.07	− 16.24 (1.9685 × $8.25)
Net	−$211.19	$222.02

If our estimate of $N_{d1} = 0.508$ is correct, the position created on day 0 will be risk-free. If the call price adjusts to its fair value on day 1, the daily return on the speculation will be 5.13%. If the call's price does not adjust to its fair value on day 1, the stock/option position would be rebalanced to keep it risk-free until the call price does adjust to its fair value. At the latest, the call value must be equal to its fair value on the call's expiration date.

Incorrect ISD Values. The price of a call will depend on the standard deviation of the underlying stock returns which market participants access. This standard deviation should be identical for calls on a given stock with a given expiration date. If the implied standard deviation is different for two call options which differ only in exercise prices, a speculative profit is possible.

For example, consider the call options on IBM stock examined earlier in the chapter. The standard deviations implied by the market prices of two IBM calls and their N_{d1} values were:

IBM Call Option	Implied Std. Dev.	N_{d1}
Call X	29.55%	0.6628
Call Y	32.85%	0.4761

The options had identical exercise dates and should, therefore, have identical implied standard deviations.

Call Y, however, had a larger implied standard deviation than call X. Although we cannot say which, if either, implied standard deviation is correct, we can say that call Y is overvalued relative to call X since call Y has the greater implied standard deviation. To take advantage of this, call Y should be sold and call X purchased.

Given their respective N_{d1} values, a risk-free position would consist of 1.5088 (1.0/0.6628) of call X bought per 2.1004 (1.0/0.4751) of call Y sold. For each 1.0 of call X bought, 1.3920 of call Y should be sold.

SPECIAL STOCK OPTION FORMS

Our discussion of options on the stock of a given firm or on stock indexes has focused on options created in the secondary markets. Such options are created by an option writer to meet the needs of an option buyer. Exercise of such options affects only the writer and the buyer, not the firm on which the options are traded. They are secondary market transactions only.

However, firms also issue options on their securities. Such options are referred to as warrants, rights, and convertibles. They differ from exchange-listed options in that their exercise has direct impact on the financial condition of the firm. Their exercise affects the cash flow of the issuing firm, its outstanding shares, and, in the case of convertible bonds, its debt-to-equity ratio. Because of these effects, options sold by firms to the public are much harder to value.

Warrants and Rights

Warrants and rights are options which are issued by a corporation. Warrants are typically offered as "sweeteners" to bond or preferred stock issues and have expiration dates between three and five years. Rights are issued to facilitate new common stock offerings and have maturities of less than three months. In theory, the value of warrants and rights should reflect both their option value and the increased value of a firm's assets once the warrants or rights are exercised. In practice, however, the option pricing model typically yields reasonable estimates of a warrant's or right's value. Warrants are typically protected against stock splits and stock dividends, but not against cash dividends. Rights have no dividend protection because of their short-term nature.

Convertible Securities

Institutional Features. A convertible security is a bond or preferred stock which may be converted at the owner's discretion into a prescribed number of the firm's common shares. As with put and call options, a terminology has developed around convertibles which must be understood before their investment value can be examined. The *conversion ratio* indicates the number of shares obtained when each bond (or preferred share) is tendered for conversion. A conversion ratio of 20:1 on a bond means 20 shares of common will be received for each bond converted. A conversion ratio of 2:1 on a preferred share will provide two common shares for each preferred. The *conversion price* of a security is the bond's (or preferred's) par value divided by the conversion ratio. For example, a conversion price of $50 per share on a 1,000 par bond implies a conversion ratio of 20:1. Clearly, the extent of the conversion privilege can be stated in terms of either the conversion ratio or the conversion price. Conversion terms of many bonds provide for an increase in the conversion price over time. For example, a bond may not be convertible for the first five years of its life, have a conversion price of $100 during years 6 through 10, $110 for the subsequent five years, etc. Conversion prices are usually adjusted for stock splits or stock dividends. They are not protected against cash dividend payments.

Three identifiable values can be attached to convertibles. These are illustrated in panel A of Figure 16-17. *Conversion value* is the security's value as stock. For example, if a bond is convertible into 20 shares of a stock now selling for $35, its conversion value would currently be $700. If the stock is expected to grow at a constant 8% rate each year, future conversion values would be as shown in the figure. *Straight-*

FIGURE 16-17 *Conversion, Straight-Debt, and Convertible Bond Values*

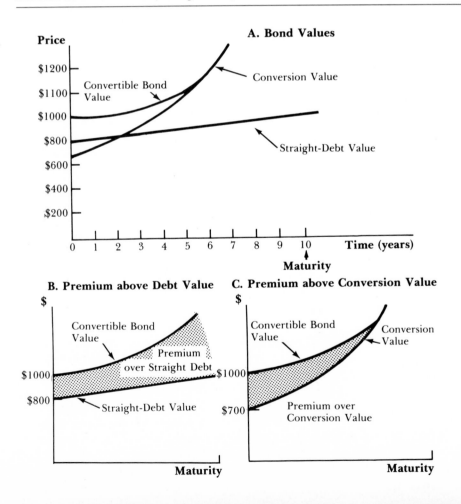

debt value is the security's value as a nonconvertible bond. If the instrument pays a 7% coupon, has a maturity of 10 years, and bonds of identical default risk and maturity are currently selling at promised yields to maturity of 10%, its initial straight-debt value will be $815.62. Assuming that promised yields to maturity on straight debt do not change over the bond's life, the straight-debt value should increase steadily to $1,000 at maturity in year 10.

At any point in time, the *minimum* value of the convertible will be the larger of either its straight-debt or its conversion value. However, actual *convertible bond values* are always greater than straight-debt or conversion values. Panel A of Figure 16-17 shows an initial convertible bond value of $1,000 which increases over time.

Convertibles invariably sell at premiums over both their straight-debt and conversion values. To illustrate, premiums above straight-debt value are shown in panel B of Figure 16-17, and premiums above conversion value are shown in panel C. Note that the two premiums are inversely related. At low conversion values, the premium over conversion value is large, but the premium over straight-debt value is small. At high conversion values, the premium over conversion value is small, and the premium over debt value is large. The reason for this is clear once we understand why premiums exist.

Convertible Premiums. Purchasers of a convertible security receive two distinct legal rights to the future cash flows of a firm. The first is the right to fixed yearly coupons (or preferred dividends) plus par value when the security matures, is called, or is converted. This legal right has a present worth which represents the straight-debt value. The second right allows the security owner to acquire a specified number of common shares at any time during the convertible's life by tendering the bond. This legal right has a present worth equal to the value of one call on the stock times the conversion ratio.[14]

For example, assume you know the following information about a convertible bond:

Convertible Bond Characteristics

Straight Bond Information		*Stock Information*	
Yearly Coupon	$70	Current Stock Price	$40
Maturity Date	10 years	Yearly Std. Dev. of Stock Return	50%
Known Call Date	3 years	Conversion Price	$50
Call Price	$1,070		
Quality Rating	Baa		

Market Information

10-Year Risk-Free Rate	8%
3-Year Risk-Free Rate	9%
10-Year Baa Rate	11%
3-Year Baa Rate	12%

---

[14]A general theory of convertible bond pricing has not yet been fully developed. This discussion illustrates only that the convertible premium is essentially the value of a call option on the stock. However, it neglects the impacts conversion will have on a firm's capital structure and the price of its common stock.

The value of the bond as straight debt would equal $929.73:

$$\sum_{t=1}^{3} \frac{\$70}{1.12^t} + \frac{\$1,070}{1.12^3} = \$929.73$$

Note that a three-year maturity, a call price of $1,070, and discount rates for three-year Baa bonds are used since the bond *will* be called in three years. Next, the value of a call on one share could be approximated using the Black-Scholes option model as:

$$P_c = \$40(0.6879) - \frac{\$50}{2.718^{0.09(3)}}(0.3520)$$

$$= \$14.08$$

where:

$$d_1 = \frac{\ln\left[\dfrac{40}{50}\right] + 3\left(0.09 + \dfrac{0.25}{2}\right)}{0.5\sqrt{3}} = 0.49$$

$$d_2 = \frac{\ln\left[\dfrac{40}{50}\right] + 3\left(0.09 - \dfrac{0.25}{2}\right)}{0.5\sqrt{3}} = 0.38$$

$$N_{d1} = 0.6879$$

$$N_{d2} = 0.3520$$

Each call would be worth about $14.08. Since each bond provides 20 calls, the conversion premium of the bond should be worth $281.60 ($14.08 × 20). In total, the convertible bond would be worth its debt value plus its conversion premium value, or $1,211.33 ($929.73 + $281.60).

Figure 16-18 depicts the theoretical relationship between conversion premiums and conversion values. At very *low* conversion values, the premium will be small since there is only a small likelihood the bond will ever be worth anything other than its straight-debt value. The convertible bond will sell at a slight premium, however, since there is some small probability that conversion value will eventually exceed debt value. At *high* conversion values, the premium will be large. There are two reasons for this. First, the convertible has a clear immediate value as stock (an in-the-money option). Second, if some time remains before the bond is expected to be converted, there is a value associated with potential future stock price increases.

In principle, convertible premiums can be determined by the option pricing model. In practice, this is quite hard to do and may yield inaccurate results. Difficulties are caused mainly by (1) not knowing when the bonds will be converted (the exercise date), (2) not knowing the impact that changes in the firm's capital structure will have on stock prices, and (3) the fact that the Black-Scholes model does not adequately handle stocks which pay cash dividends. To date, a precise model of convertible bond values has not been developed.

FIGURE 16-18 *Conversion Premiums*

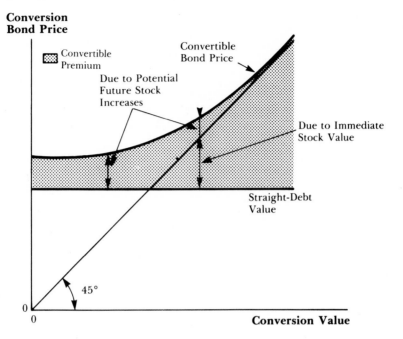

Nonetheless, the option pricing model is helpful in explaining the relative size of convertible premiums. Specifically:

1. The higher the current *stock price*, the larger the conversion premium.
2. The more distant the expected *exercise date* (which is the date when the corporation is expected to call the bonds), the larger the conversion premium.
3. The more *variable the stock returns*, the larger the conversion premium.
4. The greater the *risk-free rate*, the larger the conversion premium.
5. The smaller the *cash dividends* paid by a firm, the larger the conversion premium.

The existence of convertible bond premiums is often attributed to the fact that convertible owners are able to share in the potential price growth of the common stock but incur lower downside risk because of the convertible's minimum value as straight debt. This is quite true. As the conversion value of the bond increases, so will its market price. And if the conversion value should decline precipitously, the convertible will always retain its straight-debt characteristics. Thus owners of a convertible bond receive the best of both its stock and bond characteristics but few of its bad features. To obtain these relative advantages, buyers are willing to pay a premium. This premium will be large if stock price growth is favorable, and considerable downside risk protection is achieved by having a bond floor not much below existing prices. As the conversion value moves to levels substantially above the straight-debt floor, downside risk protection diminishes and premiums disappear.

This explanation of convertible premiums is essentially identical to that offered from the option pricing model. The potential to share in stock price growth is equivalent to the option value which arises from what we have labeled potential appreciation value. And the downside risk protection is equivalent to the fact that losses from owning a call option are limited. The choice of which explanation is better is a matter of personal taste and convenience. However, the option pricing model explicitly recognizes convertibles for what they are—complex call options on common stock—and it identifies those factors which affect the size of convertible premiums.

The size of convertible premiums can be affected by a number of other factors. For one thing, convertible securities can be attractive to individuals who believe a stock will increase in value and are willing to trade on margin. At many times in the past, margin requirements on stock have been higher than on convertibles. Some people say that the increased borrowing power available on convertibles has increased the demand for them and forced their prices up. Whether this is, in fact, true is debatable. Recently, margin requirements on stocks and convertibles have been identical, thus eliminating any possible influence on convertible prices.

The purchase of convertibles can often entail lower transaction costs than the purchase of a like amount of stock. If the investor would pay $100 in brokerage fees to buy, say, 20 shares of stock but only $90 to buy a convertible which is exchangeable into 20 shares, the premium would rise by $10 per bond to offset the cost differential. Finally, many institutional investors are restricted by custom or regulation from investing in common stock. They are able to sidestep such constraints and indirectly purchase stock by acquiring convertibles.

As with put and call options, owners of a convertible bond will typically not convert voluntarily. Instead, they will be *forced* to convert when the corporation calls the bonds at a price substantially below existing conversion values. For example, assume that a corporation has convertible bonds outstanding which are now callable at $1,070 but with a conversion value of $1,200. If the firm wishes to reduce its debt and increase its equity, it would call the bonds. Owners of the convertibles would clearly convert since conversion provides a value of $1,200 where the call provides only $1,070.

Convertible investors would convert *voluntarily* only if dividend yields began to exceed coupon yields. For example, assume the convertible is selling at $1,210 when its conversion value is $1,200. The convertible is *effectively* stock and will rise and fall almost one-for-one with the stock. It is exposed to the same price risk as the stock. If coupon payments are $50, the bond's current yield would be 4.13% ($50 ÷ $1,210). If total dividend receipts received upon conversion would be $80, the dividend yield would be 6.61% ($80 ÷ $1,210). The investor is exposed to identical price risks and *price* returns with either the convertible or the stock. But, since dividend yields are larger, a higher return would be earned if the investor voluntarily converted.

Convertible Trading. Owners of a convertible acquire two securities in one: a fixed-income bond plus call options on the common stock. To determine the appropriateness of a convertible, the terms of each should be examined.

Fixed-Income Features. Chapter 12 indicated various factors which should be examined when acquiring a fixed-income security, including (1) default risk, (2) interest rate risk, (3) call risk, (4) marketability, (5) current yield, and (6) taxes. Each of these also applies to the fixed-return component of a convertible. Investors in convertibles must realize that the conversion value of the instrument *might* eventually be worthless. If so, they will be left with a bond (or preferred) which should fit the needs of their bond portfolio. Default risk should not be any greater than allowed on a straight bond issue. Duration of the bond (if not called) should be close to the investor's horizon date needs in order to reduce interest rate risk exposure. The bond should have reasonably active trading volume if there is a possibility of temporary cash needs. And coupons should be selected to minimize taxes. In short, the bond component of a convertible should fit well with the needs that the investor's bond portfolio is designed to provide. *Convertible Features.* Convertibles are perceived by many investors to be an ideal security, one which provides stable cash income, downside risk protection in the form of the straight-debt value, and the possibility of price increases if the firm fares well. This is true. But as we noted, a price is paid for these advantages in the form of a convertible premium. Individuals should carefully evaluate the size of convertible premiums over straight-debt or conversion values since this is the price they pay to obtain the convertible privilege.

While precise valuation models don't yet exist to determine the fair premium, an intuitive approach similar to the following might be helpful.

Consider the data shown in Table 16-7, which has supposedly been developed after a thorough analysis of firms *A, B, C,* and *D*. Convertible *A* is effectively selling as a straight bond. Its premium over debt value is 2.8% while its premium over stock value is 50%. The company is not expected to force conversion; its expected exercise date is the stated maturity of 10 years. Since the stock price is expected to grow by 3% per year, the expected conversion value won't exceed debt value in year 10. This is probably caused by the large cash dividend payout (70%), which tends to depress future stock price growth. However, there is an uncertainty associated with future price growth ($\sigma = 10\%$) which provides the impetus for a small conversion premium. *Investors* should judge this issue largely on its bond merits and recognize that little is being gained (or paid) for the convertible privilege. *Speculators* should buy or sell the issue depending upon their personal predictions of stock price variance versus their

TABLE 16-7 *Illustrative Convertible Bond Data*

	Current Value of			% Premium over		Expected			
Bond	Convertible Bond	Straight Debt	Conversion Value	Debt	Stock	Call Date	Stock Growth	Dividend Payout	Return Std. Dev.
A	$ 900	$875	$ 600	2.8%	50.0%	10 yrs. (maturity)	3%	70%	10%
B	1,200	875	1,100	37.1%	9.1%	2 yrs.	8%	20%	30%
C	1,006	875	845	15.0%	19.0%	4 yrs.	9%	20%	40%
D	1,006	875	845	15.0%	19.0%	3 yrs.	9%	20%	35%

assessment of what the rest of the market believes. If they believe that future price variability will be greater than the market's assessment, they should buy the issue. If they believe that future price variability will be less, they should sell.

Bond B is dramatically different and sells essentially as a stock issue. Using option terminology, bond B is in-the-money. The 9.1% premium over conversion value reflects the 30% standard deviation of stock price returns and the expected two-year remaining life. This bond is selling as stock and should be evaluated as such. Its bond features are less meaningful, and potential investors in B should ask whether this stock has the risk and tax characteristics appropriate to their stock portfolio. The potential advantage of owning B lies in the fact that if the bond is exercised in two years, its conversion value is expected to be $1,283 ($1,100 \times 1.08^2$). The risks lie in potential call before two years and the lack of any downside risk protection if the stock price should decline dramatically.

Bonds C and D are convertibles in the truest sense of the word. They have reasonable chracteristics of both the bond and the stock. But look at the data and decide which you would buy. Since the expected call date on C is longer and the standard deviation of price returns larger, C's option value should be higher than D's. It is not. Buy C and sell D. It is exactly such comparisons that one should make when evaluating the relative premiums of convertible bonds. Unfortunately, in the real world the information isn't so clear.

Other Securities as Options

Many securities can be thought of as a combination of options and other more elementary securities. For example, put-call parity implies that the payoffs of a common stock are the same as the ownership of both risk-free debt and call options together with the sale of put options. Many people now consider options to be the building blocks used in creating more complex security forms. In fact, *any security which has some degree of limited liability has an option attached to it.* That is what an option is — a limited-liability claim. In order to truly understand and value more complex security forms, we must recognize the options which are attached to them.

Equity as a Call Option on Firm Assets. The owners of a firm's equity effectively own a call option on the firm's assets which they have bought from the firm's debt holders. If the value of firm assets (P_s) is greater than a maturing debt payment (P_x), the equity holders will pay the promised debt claim. In this case, the equity will be worth the difference between the asset value and the debt repayment ($P_s - P_x$). If the value of firm assets is less than the maturity debt payment, the equity owners will default on the debt. In this case, the equity value will be zero. But it will not be negative, since equity has limited liability.

The call features of equity can be best seen in a simple example. Let's say that the assets of a corporation are currently financed with debt and equity. The equity holders have *promised* to pay the debt holders $50 million in exactly one year. In a moment

FIGURE 16-19 *Firm Equity as a Call Option*

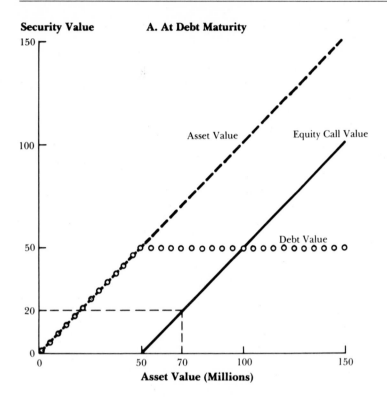

we will consider the impacts of intermediate coupon payments. But for now, assume that the only debt obligation is the $50 million par value due at year-end.

The call option character of the firm's equity can be seen in Figure 16-19. In panel A, the values of firm assets, debt, and equity are shown at the maturity date of the debt. If the assets are worth more than the promised debt repayment of $50 million, the equity holders will pay the debt holders and have a claim to any excess asset value. For example, if the assets are worth $70 million, the debt will be repaid and the equity will be worth $20 million. However, if the assets are worth less than $50 million, equity holders will default on their debt promise and turn all assets over to the debt holders. The equity is clearly a call option in this case with $T =$ one year and $P_x =$ $50 million.

In panel B, the situation one year prior to the debt maturity is shown. At an asset value of $70 million, the equity value would be *more* than its hard floor value of $20 million because of the time value inherent in the option. Assuming a 10% continuous risk-free rate and a standard deviation of asset returns of 50%, the equity call value would be about $28. Thus the debt would be worth $42 ($70 − $28).

Note that the debt holders face default risk and thus value the bonds lower than

FIGURE 16-19 *(continued)*

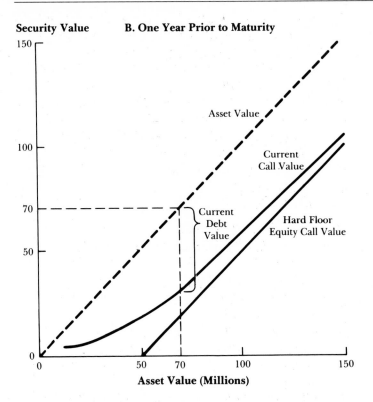

they would if no default were present. At a risk-free rate of 10%, the $50 million par due in one year would be worth $45.24:

$$50/e^{0.1} = \$45.24$$

Because of the potential for default, however, the bonds are worth only $42.

Note also that, prior to the debt's maturity, equity holders could take actions which effectively transfer wealth from the bond holders to the equity holders. For example, the value of assets might remain at $70 million but, if equity holders place the assets into more risky ventures, the standard deviation of asset returns would increase and the equity call value would also increase. By accepting more-risky projects, the equity holders increase the default risk of bond holders. The resulting decrease in bond values would be captured by equity holders as an increase in stock value. Dividend distributions can have the same effect. The slope of the equity call value curve (N_{d1}) is less than 1.0. Thus, a $1 dividend reduces the value of firm assets by $1, but the value of equity declines by less than $1. The net difference represents the gain to shareholders of a $1 dividend. Dividend distributions increase the potential for default and thus transfer value from bond holders to equity holders.

To guard against such wealth transfers, bond holders specify various types of bond covenants. For example, the amount of dividends which can be paid and the conditions under which they can be paid (positive earnings, for example) are legally agreed to in the bond indenture. Other covenants attempt to control the asset risk exposure of investment and production decisions or collateralize the debt with specific assets which have relatively little risk.

Bond Default Premiums. The ownership of debt with the potential for default clearly has option characteristics. In the example above, a risky debt position can be viewed as consisting of: (1) the ownership of firm assets and (2) the sale of a call option to equity owners with P_x equal to the par value of the bond and T equal to the maturity date of the bond. If the asset value of the firm at the debt's maturity is less than P_x, the debt holder's value will be the asset value. If the firm's asset value is greater than P_x, the call owners will exercise their option to purchase the assets and the debt holder will be left with a maximum value of P_x.

An alternative way to view debt with the potential for default is as (1) the ownership of risk-free debt and (2) the sale of a put on the value of the firm's assets. Under this view, the bond holders always receive the payment from the risk-free securities but lose on the puts they have written if the value of firm assets falls below P_x.

Regardless of the viewpoint chosen, risky debt has option positions:

$$\frac{\text{Risky}}{\text{Debt}} = \frac{\text{Asset}}{\text{Ownership}} + \frac{\text{Write Call}}{\text{on Assets}}$$

or

$$= \frac{\text{Ownership of}}{\text{Risk-Free Debt}} + \frac{\text{Write Put}}{\text{on Assets}}$$

This has led many analysts to evaluate bond default premiums in the context of option theory. For example, in panel B of Figure 16-19, if firm assets are worth $70 million one year before the $50 par on debt is due, the equity would be worth $28 million. The remaining $42 million of asset value would be assigned to debt holders, implying a continuous return of 17.4%. Given the risk-free rate of 10%, this implies that a 7.4% default premium is demanded by bond holders.

Other Options on Bonds. Most bonds pay periodic coupons prior to a par value balloon payment at maturity. In this case, each coupon payment can be thought of as an option to purchase another option. For example, if equity holders elect to pay the first interest installment, they have exercised their option to stay in business and (possibly) make future interest and principal payments. If any of the payments are not made, debt holders seize the firm's assets, and equity holders have no remaining value in the firm. Thus, a coupon bond can be thought of as a *compound option*.

Callable bonds have another option—a call option that bond holders have sold to equity holders which gives equity holders the right to buy the bonds at a predetermined price prior to the bonds' maturity. Since the call premium received by the bond holder is part of the price paid by the bond holder, its price is *less than* what would have been paid if the bond had been call-free. For example, assume that a call-free bond is worth $1,000 and that management is willing to pay $50 for a call option which specifies the price at which it can repurchase the bonds. The buyer of a callable bond would then pay $950 for the bonds: $1,000 for the non-callable bond equivalent less the $50 call premium.

SUMMARY

The existence of exchange-traded options has multiplied the ways in which investors can alter portfolio risk and engage in speculative strategies. Perhaps the most useful aspect of trading in options is their use in adjusting the systematic (beta) risk of a portfolio. Underlying positions in stocks, bonds, Treasury bills, etc., need not be disturbed. Instead, option positions are taken on top of the spot security positions to temporarily increase or decrease the aggregate portfolio risk. This explains the trading dominance of stock index options such as those on the S&P 100.

Trading in stock index options has caused the spot stock market, T-bill market, and option market to become more interrelated. If prices between the markets are not in equilibrium, large speculative profits can be obtained through index arbitrage.

Option trading has had a profound impact on the types of strategies available to investors and speculators and has enabled us to better understand the valuation of many other securities.

REVIEW PROBLEM

Assume that new *European* option contracts are created on a stock index of 250 over-the-counter stocks. This hypothetical index is referred to as the OTC 250, and each option is a claim to a trade on the quoted price of the spot index *times 250*. It is June 30 and you have gathered the following information about the options:

Current Spot Price of OTC 250	= $120
Expected Cash Dividends on OTC 250	= $0
Current Discount Rate on 180-Day T-bills	= 7.74%
Options on the OTC 250:	

	Call	Put
Exercise Price	$100	$100
Exercise Date	6 months	6 months
Estimated Std. Dev.	30%	30%
Current Market Price	$28	$2

a. Calculate the yearly continuous and discrete risk-free rates implied in the T-bill discounts.

b. Calculate the Black-Scholes price for the call.

c. Given that the actual market price is different from the Black-Scholes price, what does this suggest about the implied standard deviation actually being priced by market participants?

d. Is the put-call parity model working properly in current market prices?

e. You are the manager of a $100 million portfolio of stocks which is very similar to the OTC 250 index. If you were to use the puts to insure a floor value of the stocks in six months:
  (1) How many puts should you buy? (You will sell some of the stock to pay for the puts.)
  (2) What is the minimum portfolio value?
  (3) Briefly discuss the cost of this portfolio insurance.

f. You could have also created an insured portfolio by investing the $100 million in calls and T-bills. Given the answer to part d, would this be better than using puts?

g. Given that put-call parity is not working, there is an index arbitrage possible. Illustrate this arbitrage. Assume you trade in $25 million worth of spot OTC 250. Show the expiration date payoffs for spot values of the OTC 250 at that time of $100 and $140.

h. Why did the problem specify that the options be European options?

Solution

a. T-bill price $= 100 - 100(0.0774)(180/360)$

$$= 96.13$$

6-month return $= (100/96.13) - 1 = 4.025798\%$

$(1 + 365\text{-day discrete return}) = 1.04025798^{365/180} = 1.0833$

365-day continuous return $= \ln(1.0833) = 0.08$

b.
$$d_1 = \frac{\ln(120/100) + (180/365)(0.08 + 0.3^2/2)}{0.3\sqrt{(180/365)}}$$

$$= 1.16$$

$d_2 = 0.95$

$N_{d1} = 0.8770 \qquad N_{d2} = 0.8289$

$$P_c = \$120(0.8770) - \frac{100}{e^{0.08(180/365)}}(0.8289)$$

$$= \$25.56$$

c. The implied standard deviation in the market price of $28 is *greater* than the 0.3 used in part b.

d. $P_c - P_c = \$120 - 100/e^{0.08(180/365)}$

$$= \$23.87$$

Since the actual call price is $26 greater than that of the put, the call is overvalued relative to the put.

e. (1) $N =$ number of puts and units of stock to hold

$N(\$2 \times 250 + \$120 \times 250) = \$100,000,000$

$N = 3,278.6885$

(2) $3,278.6885 \times (\$100 \times 250) = \$81,967,213.13$

(3) There are two costs. First is the direct cost of buying the puts ($3,278.6885 \times \$2 \times 250 = \$1,639,344$). Second is the opportunity cost if the stock increases in value, since the full $100 million is not invested in the stock.

f. No. The call is overvalued. You would prefer strategies which do not involve purchasing the calls.

g.

	Today	Expiration Date $100	Expiration Date $140
Buy 833⅓ Stock Units*	−$25,000,000	$20,833,333	$29,166,666
Buy 833⅓ Puts	− 416,666	—	—
Sell 833⅓ Calls	+ 5,833,333	—	− 8,333,333
Total	−$19,583,333	$20,833,333	$20,833,333
Sell T-bills**	+ 19,583,333	− 20,371,379	− 20,371,379
Net	$0	+ $461,954	+ $461,954

*Units = $25,000,000/(\$120 \times 250) = 833⅓$
**$19,583,333 \times e^{0.08(180/365)} = \$20,371,379$

h. We needed to be sure that early exercise does not occur. Since no dividends are to be paid, there would be no danger of early exercise for American calls. However, there is always the potential that American puts would be exercised if the OTC 250 fell significantly.

QUESTIONS AND PROBLEMS

1. You have been given the following series of monthly returns on a stock. The returns are discrete returns. Calculate the ex post estimate of the Black-Scholes standard deviation.

1	2	3	4	5	6	7	8	9	10	11	12
5%	15	2	−8	1	−4	20	5	−8	10	8	0

2. You have calculated the implied standard deviations on two call options. They differ only in exercise price. (They are on the same stock and have identical expiration dates.) What is the instantaneous risk-free speculation which is possible?

	Call A	Call B
ISD	40%	50%
N_{d1}	0.8	0.6

3. You have a portfolio of 50 stocks which looks very similar to the S&P 100 Index. You wish to take a position in puts which will insure a minimum portfolio floor value. You could trade in puts on the S&P 100 Index or trade a put on each of the 50 stocks held. Which alternative would be cheaper?

4. In the Review Problem, all net cash flows occur at the expiration date of the options. Is there any way to obtain these net inflows when the arbitrage is initiated? What amount would be received?

5. Assume that a dividend of D dollars will be paid on the expiration date of a put and call option. Derive the put-call parity model for this case.

6. The market value of a portfolio which you manage is $30 million. You have been asked to use either puts or calls in a portfolio insurance program. Since the portfolio is similar to the S&P 100 Index, you intend to use S&P 100 Index options. Relevant data are:

Current Spot Value of S&P 100	= $300
Current (discrete) Risk-Free Rate	10% per year
Dividend Yield on S&P 100	2% per year

(Assume they are paid in exactly six months from now)

Option Information:	Call	Put
Current Price	$35	$5
Exercise Price	$280	$280
Expiration Date	6 months	6 months
Option Type	Euro	Euro

a. Is put-call parity working?

b. Illustrate the expiration date values of an insured portfolio using the puts. Do this for S&P 100 values of $200, $250, $300, and $350.

c. Use the calls together with T-bills to create an insured portfolio which has the same minimum floor value as in part b. Calculate its values for S&P 100 values of $200, $250, $300, and $350. Compare the results with those obtained for part b and explain why they are different.

d. Using the puts, at what S&P 100 Index value are you better off with the insured portfolio than with a 100% stock position?

7. Why are portfolio return distributions skewed when options are used in a portfolio (and held to expiration)? What are the implications of this?

8. Use the data from question 6 to illustrate the outcomes of an index arbitrage. Trade in stock worth $10 million.

9. Consider the following information:

	Call	Put
Exercise Price	$100	$100
Exercise Date	3 months	3 months
RF = 12% discrete		

Illustrate a trade with these assets which results in a three-month forward contract on the underlying common stock.

10. Index arbitrages will involve the purchase or sale of a stock index such as the S&P 100. As a practical matter, how is this accomplished?

11. Why is the efficient operation of the NYSE's designated order turnaround system so important to the conduct of index arbitrage?

12. What are some of the critical differences between trades based on expiration date values versus continuous-time values?

13. What are the conditions under which an American call or put would be exercised early?

14. A local broker has advised the trustees of a charitable organization to sell calls on stocks held in the organization's portfolio in order to increase the portfolio's cash yield. Comment.

15. How does the use of options in a portfolio affect the portfolio's stock/bond mix?

16. (CFA Exam Question)

EverSafe Insurance Company holds 10,000 shares of Exxon at a cost of $80 per share in the pension account of one of its clients. As portfolio manager for the account you expect the shares to rise gradually over the next six to nine months. The following Exxon call options are quoted on the CBOE:

	Expiration		
Exercise Price	*3 months*	*6 months*	*9 months*
70	12	13	14½
80	2½	6½	8
90	NA	2½	4½

The current price of Exxon shares is 81. State the rationale for and implications of writing call options that expire in nine months with an exercise price of $80.

17. Explain the economic intuition underlying what the beta of a call is:

$$beta_c = beta_s \times (P_s/P_c) \times N_{d1}$$

18. You are the manager of a $100 million portfolio which is now invested as follows: $50 million in stock similar to the S&P 100 and $50 million in T-bills. Relevant data on S&P 100 calls include:

Price of S&P 100 Spot Index = $250
Price of S&P 100 Call   = $15
N_{d1} of Call   = 0.75
Beta of S&P 100 Spot Index = 1.0

How many calls would you trade to change the portfolio's instantaneous beta to:
a. 0.0
b. 1.0
c. 0.6

19. Why would people use call options to adjust the systematic risk of a portfolio instead of actually adjusting the spot assets held?

20. Assume that you wish to create an insured portfolio value. How would you do it with a program of dynamic option replication? Why might you use a dynamic replication instead of trading in listed puts or calls?

21. Explain why premiums over the conversion value of convertible bonds might disappear. Use the concepts of the option pricing model.

22. Why do convertible bonds sell at a lower promised yield to maturity than do nonconvertible bonds which are otherwise identical?

23. The market value of the assets of a corporation is currently $130 million. The firm has on issue a debt outstanding which has a par value of $100 million and a due date of exactly one year. No intermediate interest payments are required. The risk-free (continuous) rate is 12% and the standard deviation of returns on the firm's assets is 70%.
a. What should be today's equity and debt value?
b. What is the default premium being required by debt holders?
c. By how much would shareholders gain if a $20 million dividend is paid?
d. In terms of option theory, what is the position of a debt holder if default risk is possible?

DATA ANALYSIS PROBLEM

Objective:

- To use the Black-Scholes call valuation model on current option prices to evaluate whether any speculative opportunities appear to exist.

1. From a recent financial newspaper, find the closing prices for S&P 100 calls which have the same expiration dates but differing exercise prices. (Choose a call expiration date which is at least one month from today.) In addition, find the average of the bid and ask discounts on T-bills which mature approximately when your call options expire.
2. Calculate the annualized continuous risk-free rate implicit in the T-bill discount.
3. Access the OPMISD.WK1 data set and review the instructions. Basically, this data set does two things: (1) it calculates Black-Scholes call prices if you specify all variables including the stock's standard deviation, and (2) it calculates the ISD if you specify all variables including the call price.
4. Follow the instructions in order to estimate the implied standard deviations for each call option.

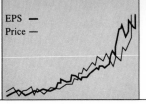

CHAPTER

17 Futures

Most economic transactions occur in what is known as the spot (or cash) market and require *immediate* delivery of cash for some real asset. Often, however, individuals don't have an immediate need for the asset but know that at some future date the asset will have to be purchased or sold. For example, an electric utility has both current and future needs for coal or oil, a flour manufacturer has current and future needs for wheat, and a pension portfolio manager will eventually need to buy new Treasury obligations. Whenever such future requirements exist, three alternatives are available: (1) buy the asset now and store it until needed, (2) wait to buy the asset at a future date at then-existing *spot* market prices, or (3) enter into a *forward contract* with another party which stipulates that the asset will be delivered on a specified date and at a specified price. The risks and costs of these three alternatives are considerably different. In the first, substantial storage costs are incurred. In the second, there is uncertainty about future prices. In the third, the buyer of the forward contract incurs no storage costs and shifts all price risk to the seller.

A *futures contract is a marketable forward contract*. While all assets may have forward contracts written on them, few are amenable to organized futures trading. To assure a viable futures trading market, the asset should:

1. Be standardized
2. Have an active demand
3. Be storable
4. Be valuable in proportion to bulk

An active futures market in automobiles, Rembrandt paintings, lettuce, or foam rubber would be impossible to develop since each fails to meet one or more of these criteria. However, a variety of commodities and financial instruments do meet these requirements and are actively traded in the futures market.

The basic motivation behind futures trading is to reduce price risk — uncertainty about future spot prices. A farmer who will harvest wheat in September could sell September wheat futures and be assured of a fixed price per bushel. Conversely, a baker who will need wheat in September could buy September wheat futures and also be assured of a fixed price. Without futures markets, the wheat producer and the user each face uncertain (but opposite) price risks. With the existence of futures markets, the two parties are able to reduce their risks by *hedging*.

Conceptually, futures markets could consist solely of hedgers if each hedger desiring to buy is exactly offset by a hedger desiring to sell. As a practical matter, hedging demand and supply at any given moment won't exactly offset each other. This excess demand or supply for hedging is absorbed by *speculators* who attempt to earn a profit from buying futures when prices are temporarily low and selling when prices are temporarily high. Speculators are invaluable to the effective functioning of a futures market. They stand ready to absorb price risk, provide trading liquidity, reduce price variability over time, and force futures prices to be related to expected future spot prices.

INSTITUTIONAL FEATURES

General Types of Futures Contracts

The origin of futures trading is usually traced to twelfth-century Europe and the rapid expansion of trade fairs in northern Italy and Flanders. Although most transactions were of a spot nature (cash and commodity swapped on the spot), negotiable *lettres de faire* were also used, which specified the future delivery of goods. Over time, the center of commercial trading moved to London, and dealers on the various London exchanges performed the services of speculators. In the United States, futures trading developed in the middle 1800s in Chicago and New York with the founding of the Chicago Board of Trade, the New York Produce Exchange, and the New York Coffee Exchange. At the end of 1984, there were twelve U.S. futures exchanges which traded in the following types of futures:

1. Agricultural commodities
2. Metallurgical commodities
3. Foreign currencies
4. Financial instruments
   a. Short-term debt obligations
   b. Intermediate- to long-term debt obligations
   c. Stock indexes
   d. Options on stock index futures

Prior to the mid-1970s, futures contracts on financial instruments did not exist, and virtually all trading was in agricultural and metallurgical commodities. By the late 1980s, however, more than 50% of all trading on the major futures exchanges was in financial futures. Given the nature of this book, we will focus our attention solely on financial futures.

Some Definitions

Much of the terminology associated with futures trading is similar to that of other securities. However, some terms are unique to futures, and it is best that we start with a look at them. As an example, Table 17-1 provides hypothetical price quotations on a variety of T-bill futures as of December 31, 19xx.

1. *Contract specification.* Buyers and sellers must know exactly what they are trading. As a result, great care is taken to define precisely the nature and terms of each futures contract. The T-bill contract shown in Table 17-1 trades on the International Monetary Market and is for $1 million in face value of U.S. Treasury bills having a maturity *as of the date of delivery* of 90 days. Specification of this particular contract is quite easy. As we will see later, specifications of other contracts can often be quite complex and can have important implications for the value of the contract.

2. *Maturity, or date of delivery.* The maturity, or date of delivery, is the date a which contract buyers must deliver cash and sellers must deliver securities that meet the contract specifications. Financial futures are always available for a variety of different delivery dates. Three different delivery months are shown in Table 17-1: March, June, and September. The actual date of delivery varies by kind of financial instrument. T-bill futures, for example, are deliverable on the Thursday following the third Monday of the delivery month. This particular delivery date was chosen because it coincides well with new T-bill sales by the U.S. Treasury, thus assuring that there will be a large number of 90-day bills available at that time. Delivery dates on other financial futures are not as precise. For example, T-bond contracts are deliverable any time during the month of delivery, with the precise day chosen by the seller.

3. *Futures price.* For each delivery date, four futures prices are given (see Table 17-1). They are the price at which trading opened, the high and low for the day, and the settle price. Usually the settle price will be the last trading price for the day. However, if trading activity in the given contract was small or nonexistent towards the end of the day, a settlement committee will establish the settle price. The futures price is not the price which would actually be paid for a contract. It is only an in-

TABLE 17-1 *Sample T-Bill Futures Information, December 31, 19xx, Traded on the International Monetary Market. Contract Specification: $1,000,000 Face Value of 90-Day Treasury Bills*

Delivery Dates	Futures Prices				Open Interest
	Open	*High*	*Low*	*Settle*	
March	91.67	91.72	91.60	91.65	27,067
June	91.21	91.22	91.12	91.16	8,017
September	90.75	90.79	90.69	90.72	1,762

dex of a contract's value (which is easily interpreted by people who trade actively). The T-bill prices shown in Table 17-1, for example, are *discount prices* based on a 360-day Treasury bill. The actual T-bill contracted for, however, has a 90-day maturity. Thus a conversion is necessary to determine the actual contract price. We will explain these conversions later, when we discuss each financial contract in depth.

4. *Open interest.* Open interest refers to the number of long (or short) contract positions which are outstanding. When a contract with a new delivery date is created, open interest will be zero before any trades occur. If the first trade is for five contracts, open interest will increase to five. If a new buyer purchases a contract from a person who had previously bought and is now closing out his or her position by selling, open interest will not change. If both parties to a trade are closing out previous positions, open interest will fall by the number of contracts they trade. Open interest is meant to reflect the activity and liquidity of a given contract. As of December 31, 19xx, there were 27,067 open contracts on T-bills deliverable in March.

5. *Delivery point.* Actual delivery under a contract is rare. Most positions are closed out by offsetting trades prior to the delivery date. However, if delivery of cash and securities on a financial future actually does take place, the delivery point is at the futures exchange or by wire transfer to the exchange. This contrasts with delivery of agricultural and metallurgical contracts, which takes place at various places away from the exchange. The place of delivery is important in pricing commodity futures but of no importance for financial futures.

6. *Margin.* Theoretically, no cash or securities change hands until the delivery date. The futures contract is, after all, a contract for *future* trading. However, to help ensure that the parties to the contract do not default on their obligation, a good faith deposit, or *margin*, must be given to the broker. The margin could be cash, a letter of credit, or short-term U.S. Treasury securities. Margin requirements are set by the exchange and vary among contracts. More rigid margin requirements may be set by a brokerage house if it wishes. Margins on the major financial futures will be specified when they are discussed later in the chapter.

Types of Financial Futures

The first financial future, traded in October 1975, was offered by the Chicago Board of Trade (CBT) on GNMA certificates. Since then, both the variety of contracts and trading activity have grown rapidly. Instruments which did not even exist a decade ago are now used as a matter of course by many individuals in their daily investment or speculative activities.

Many kinds of contracts have been offered, and many more are currently being developed. Many of the new types of contracts offered in the past did not develop active trading volume, and this will certainly be true for many of the new contracts now being developed. In some cases, weak trading performance was due to poor contract design, but it is also likely that the trading public has simply been unable to keep pace with the potential uses of new financial products.[1] Whether activity will improve in the less successful contracts remains to be seen. Some will probably disappear, while others will gain activity as people learn more about their potential.

Nonetheless, many contracts have been clear successes. These can be categorized into four basic groups. The first consists of contracts written on high-grade, short-term debt obligations such as Treasury bills, certificates of deposit, and Eurodollars.[2] These are currently traded exclusively on the International Monetary Market (IMM), a division of the Chicago Mercantile Exchange (CME). The second group of successful contracts are those in intermediate- to long-term U.S. government-backed obligations. These include T-note and T-bond contracts traded on the Chicago Board of Trade (CBT). Futures contracts on stock indexes represent the third group. These very successful contracts have been trading only since 1982, when the Kansas City Board of Trade offered contracts on the Value Line Composite Index. However, because of the way the Value Line Composite Index is calculated, this contract has not been nearly as successful as contracts on the S&P 500 Composite (traded on the CBT), the NYSE Composite (traded on the New York Futures Exchange—NYFE), and the Major Market Index, which is designed to emulate the Dow Jones Industrial Average (traded on the CBT).[3] The most recent development—and certainly the most complex—is option contracts written on financial futures. These options are currently written on many types of financial futures.

These four types of financial futures differ considerably in (1) their contract specifications, (2) their equilibrium pricing relationships, and (3) their role in investment and speculative strategies. For this reason, a separate section of this chapter is devoted to each.

Futures Versus Forward Contracts

Assume that it is July 1 and you are the investment officer of a commercial bank. Typically, the bank has a large demand for consumer loans between July and December as customers request loans for summer vacations and year-end holiday purchases. However, early in the new year, loan repayments are expected to exceed new loan requests. As a result, at the start of the new year, excess cash will be available which you have been told to invest in six-month T-bills until the cycle repeats itself the next summer.

---

[1]When financial futures were first offered, they were hailed by the brokerage community as a source of revenue. However, as different and more complex contracts have been offered, many brokerage firms have complained that they simply cannot keep pace with the knowledge required to trade the contracts.

[2]See Chapter 2 for a discussion of each of these.

[3]The problem with the Value Line Composite is that it is impossible to hold an actual stock portfolio similar to it. (See Chapter 4.) This reduces its potential for both arbitrage and hedging.

You have three basic alternatives:

1. Wait until January and invest excess funds at the T-bill rates available at that time. The advantage of this approach is that the bank can use the funds in the meantime for consumer loans. The disadvantage is the uncertainty about what return will be available when you actually invest. If rates turn out to be less than you expect, the earnings of both your department and the bank will be lower than budgeted. This could affect both the price of the bank's common stock and, perhaps, your job. By waiting to invest, you assume a risk.

2. Buy T-bills now which mature in a year, which will involve no risk to you or the bank. But this alternative is self-defeating in that money will not be available for consumer lending. The bank's earnings will certainly be less than expected and you will certainly lose your job.

3. Arrange today—on July 1—for the purchase of T-bills at the start of the new year. Not only will funds be available for consumer loans in the meantime, but you will also be sure of the investment return on T-bills when they are purchased.

The third alternative is clearly the best. When the new year comes, T-bill rates may be higher than you contracted for, and, in hindsight, you may be sorry you entered into the agreement. But, then, rates may also be lower than you contracted for and you'll look very smart indeed. If debt markets are reasonably rational (as unbiased expectations theory and efficient market theory suggest), the odds of higher or lower rates are identical—50%. So from the perspective of July 1, the best decision is to eliminate future uncertainty by arranging for the future purchase of T-bills on January 1 at a specified price.

There are three ways of doing this. First, you could enter into a contractual agreement with another party stating that you will deliver a certain amount of cash to them on January 1 and that they will deliver a certain quantity of six-month T-bills to you. This known as a *forward contract*. Forward contracts are widely used in practice. Mortgage brokers, for example, constantly create new mortgage loans which they contract to sell to another party at a future date at a stipulated price.

The second approach is to create an *artificial forward contract* by purchasing 12-month T-bills and short selling an equivalent present worth of six-month T-bills. As we saw in Chapter 6, this results in a zero position from today through month 6 and a long position (with a known return) from the start of month 7 through month 12.

The choice between these two forward contract alternatives depends in part on which provides the greater return. Neglecting default on the first, they have identical risk. But the returns on each are likely to be very similar. After all, how do you think the person you contract with under the first alternative determines the T-bill return he or she is willing to offer? Clearly, that person is also looking at the returns available on an artificial forward contract. Expected returns on the actual forward contract and the artificial contract must be very close.

The third approach would be to purchase a six-month T-bill *futures contract* with a delivery date of early January.[4] Such a contract would also guarantee a fixed return on a six-month T-bill exactly when you desire it.

There are, however, some important differences between forward contracts and futures contracts. Some are minor. Others are not.

Default Risk. The first difference between forward and futures contracts is the potential for default under the forward contract. If you are careful in selecting the partner with whom you forward contract, the probability of default may be small, but it does exist. There is no guarantee that the other party will indeed honor the contract. The exchanges on which futures are traded, however, pride themselves on the fact that no customer has lost money through default by the other party to a contract. The exchanges have large insurance reserves to reimburse defaults by buyers or sellers. Yet this default concern is also virtually nonexistent if you create an artificial forward contract. The U.S. Treasury will default on its obligations only after all others in the country have done so. The default risk of artificial forward contracts is negligible. Default risk for a standard forward contract, however, does exist.

Marketability. A standard forward contract is not marketable. The only way to get out of it would be to renegotiate with the other party to the contract, or, if they are unwilling to renegotiate, to enter into an offsetting contract with still another party. In both cases, you are likely to be in the weaker bargaining position. In addition, there could be substantial time and cost associated with renegotiation. Futures contracts, however, are continuously traded on organized exchanges. You can get out of a futures contract simply by calling your broker. Yet, as is the case with default risk, much of this concern can be eliminated by the use of artificial forward contracts. The instruments which we used to create artificial forward contracts are as actively traded as futures contracts on such instruments, if not more so.

Transaction Costs. Transaction costs include cash expenses as well as the opportunity cost of time spent in finding a party to trade with. Both of these can be substantial when a standard forward contract is used. In comparison, the transaction costs of entering into or closing out a futures contract or an artificial forward contract are considerably less.

Marking to the Market. In both a standard forward contract and an artificially created forward contract, the only time that cash is paid is at the maturity date. This is not the case for a futures contract. A futures contract requires both an initial cash margin and subsequent cash inflows or outflows associated with a process called *marking to the market*. Margin is usually very small, and it can be met by cash, letters of credit, or short-term U.S. Treasury instruments. If letters of credit are used,

---

[4]In practice, this is impossible since there are no such T-bill futures. As an example, we can overlook this problem. But the inability to truly match the desired purchase or sale date with an equivalent financial future is a problem which must be examined, and we will do so later in the chapter.

no cash is actually paid. If U.S. Treasuries are used, the owner still has a claim to the earnings on the securities. Thus, margin does not represent an incremental cash outflow to the person who has bought or sold a futures contract. The process of marking to the market, however, will usually result in a series of cash inflows and outflows before the contract's maturity. This is a major difference between futures and forward contracts.

As an example, assume that it is January 1 and you wish to purchase either a forward or a futures contract on 90-day T-bills with a maturity date of late March. After investigating each, you discover that they have identical terms. Specifically, the price of a 90-day T-bill with a par value of $1,000,000 and a delivery in late March is $980,000. If you were to purchase the forward contract, the only date at which cash would trade hands would be in late March, when you pay the $980,000 to receive the T-bills. However, if you were to purchase the futures contract, an *initial* margin of $2,000 would have to be posted. Since this can be in the form of either a letter of credit or short-term Treasuries, the margin does not represent an incremental cash outflow to you. In addition to the initial margin, a *maintenance margin* level will be specified. For the T-bill futures the maintenance margin is $1,500 per $1 million contract. If your cumulative losses cause the value of your initial margin to fall below the maintenance margin, you will have to pay additional *cash* (not Treasuries or letters of credit) in order to restore the account to the initial margin level.

For example, assume that on January 2 this futures contract settles at a dollar value of $979,750.[5] You have suffered a loss of $250 and the value of your margin will be $1,750 ($2,000 − $250). Since this is greater than the required maintenance margin of $1,500, you will not be called on to provide additional cash. Now assume that on January 3, the futures contract settles at a dollar value of $978,500. The loss on this day of $1,250 ($978,500 − $979,750) reduces the value of your margin account from yesterday's value of $1,750 to $500. Thus, you will have to provide your broker with $1,500 in *cash* to restore the margin to the initial requirement of $2,000.

In order to reduce paperwork for both the broker and the trader, the trader will provide a cash deposit that is larger than the required initial margin. The broker then will invest any funds not required to meet margin calls in money market instruments. In addition, the trader's account will be credited for any daily *profits* that occur on the futures. For example, if your T-bill contract settles at a value of $980,000 on January 4, the $1,500 profit earned since the prior day ($980,000 − $978,500) will be credited to your money market account.

A fundamental difference between futures contracts and forward contracts is this daily settlement procedure of marking to the market. With forward contracts, all profits and losses are taken on one day—the maturity date. With futures contracts, profits and losses are realized daily. The sum of the daily profits and losses on a future will be identical to the single profit or loss on the forward contract. However, the timing of the cash flow will be different. In a way, *a futures contract is a series of many one-day forward contracts.*

---

[5]The word *settle* is used for futures contracts instead of *close* since it is this price at which all margin accounts will be *settled*. As noted earlier, this may or may not be the last trading price.

Contract Specifications. Forward contracts may be created on any security or good. Artificial forward contracts may be created on a variety of securities, depending on the spot instruments which exist. Futures contracts, however, can only be traded on futures instruments listed on an exchange. This can be important. For example, assume you are the treasurer of GTE and know that you will have to borrow on March 15 in order to pay scheduled quarterly income taxes. To help assure a borrowing rate, you might wish to sell a T-bill future maturing on March 15. Unfortunately, such a futures contract does not exist. There are contracts maturing later in March that can guarantee you a late March trading price. But if you were to sell one of these with the intention of offsetting it on March 15, you would not know the March 15 price and would not be able to eliminate your uncertainty. In contrast, you could enter into a standard forward contract with an investment banker or create an artificial forward contract with the terms you desire. Forward contracts have considerably greater flexibility.

Other Potential Differences. Two final points should be made. First, many people think that artificial forward contracts are too complex. They would rather trade the more easily understood future. This is a matter of opinion. A second and, perhaps, more important difference between the two is that many organizations are prohibited from short selling. As a result, they cannot create an artificial forward contract and must rely on either a standard forward commitment or a financial future.

In Table 17-2 is a summary of the advantages and disadvantages of each type of forward commitment. Futures contracts exist for exactly the same reason that options exist. They create risk/return combinations which are not available (or are available only at greater cost) from combinations of other securities or legal contracts.

Trading Procedures

Trading procedures for financial futures are similar in many respects to those for other securities. But some differences do exist which are worth noting. In addition, by following a trade from its origination to its conclusion we can see how futures play an important role in risk reduction. Our illustration will use the price quotations for March T-bills shown in Table 17-1.

Assume that it is January 1. The weather has been terrible but you are in good spirits because you plan to take a vacation to Fort Lauderdale in late March. To finance the trip, you will have to borrow some money. That's OK since you are sure that you will be able to repay the loan later in the year. Unknown to you, a corporate treasurer in New York is considering how to invest $9,791,250 which is expected to be available from a government contract in late March. Both of you have just read about T-bill futures and have decided to try them out for their supposed ability to reduce uncertainty about future interest rates.

The Transaction. Simultaneously you each call your brokers. Since the treasurer intends to buy 90-day Treasury bills with the $9,791,250 when the money arrives in late

TABLE 17-2 *Advantages and Disadvantages of Forward Versus Futures Contracts*

Standard Forward Contract

Advantages	Disadvantages
1. Available contract specifications	1. Default potential
2. No mark to market	2. Lack of marketability
	3. Large transaction costs

Artificial Forward Contract

Advantages	Disadvantages
1. Available contract specifications	1. Complexity
2. No default potential	
3. Very marketable	
4. Small transaction costs	
5. No mark to market	

Futures Contract

Advantages	Disadvantages
1. Lack of complexity	1. Rigid contract specifications
2. No default potential	2. Marked to market
3. Very marketable	
4. Small transaction costs	

March, she places an order to purchase March T-bill futures. Since you intend to borrow in late March, you place an order to sell March T-bill futures. The types of orders available are essentially similar to stock orders (market, stop, limit, etc.). The minimum contract size is $1 million, so you place an order to sell one contract and the treasurer buys ten. Each broker immediately contacts a representative of his or her firm on the floor of the International Monetary Market (the only futures market in T-bills). This representative, known as a *pit broker*, would go to the *trading pit* where T-bill futures are traded and use hand signals together with an *open outcry* to identify another side to the trade and a price agreeable to both. The opposite side might be another hedger, a speculator, or a floor trader known as a *scalper.* The scalper is a speculator who is a member of the futures exchange and thus doesn't pay commissions. Assume both you and the treasurer transact at a price equal to $91.65.

Each of you would be notified by your respective brokers that the trade had been executed and that the price was $91.65 per contract. Neither of you would know with whom you traded, since the exchange's *clearing corporation* will step in and act as the person who bought from you and the person who sold to the treasurer. Having the exchange act as the buyer and seller once a trade occurs minimizes the risk of eventual default. If the person who bought from you does default, the exchange absorbs the loss. The treasurer and you will have to post $2,000 of initial margin per contract.

At this point you have a contract to sell $1 million of par value 90-day Treasury bills in late March at the contract price of $91.65. This $91.65 is a discount price based on a 360-day T-bill. It is not the actual percentage of par which will be paid. To calculate the actual price, exactly the same procedures would be used that were presented in Chapter 2 when we discussed spot Treasury bills. First, the *annualized discount* is found by subtracting the stated price from $100:

$$\text{Annualized Discount} = \$100 - \$91.65$$

$$= 8.35\%$$

Next, the 90-day discount is found by multiplying the annualized discount by the fraction of a 360-day period which the T-bill will be outstanding:

$$\text{90-Day Discount} = \frac{90}{360} \times 8.35$$

$$= 2.0875\%$$

The 90-day price is equal to $100 minus this discount, or $97.9125. Since you sold one contract and the treasurer bought ten, in late March:

You will receive $979,125 ($1 million × 97.9125%).[6]

The treasurer will pay $9,791,250 ($10 million × 97.9125%).

The Hedge. Let's see exactly what each of you has. The treasurer has the contractual ability to pay $9,791,250 in late March for ten Treasury bills which will mature exactly 90 days later for $10 million. The 90-day and annualized simple interest return on these (future) T-bills are:

$$\text{90-Day Return} = \frac{\$10,000,000}{\$9,791,250} - 1.0$$

$$= 2.132\%$$

$$\begin{array}{l} \text{Simple Interest} \\ \text{Annualized Return} \end{array} = 2.132\% \times \frac{365}{90}$$

$$= 8.65\%$$

You have one contract with exactly the opposite terms. You will receive cash and deliver T-bills. The receipt of cash is essentially the borrowing of money at an annualized cost to you of 8.65%. (We will see in a moment where you will get the T-bills to deliver.)

All you will need to worry about until the contracts mature is the margin calls that may arise as the contracts are marked to the market. Because margin calls add unnecessary complexities to the example, we will ignore the daily mark-to-market aspect of futures.

Your contracts mature late in March, at which time cash and securities are to be delivered. Rarely will a contract remain open and actual delivery take place. Most

---

[6]This is going to be a *great* vacation if you plan to spend $980,000!

people will take their profits or losses by making an offsetting trade. However, it is possible to hold the contract open and demand actual delivery. It is this possibility which is critical in determining what a futures price will be prior to the maturity date.

Let's assume that immediately before the T-bill contract matures, the treasurer enters an offsetting trade by selling ten contracts. You, however, do not close out your position and insist on receiving the $979,125 in cash. Also assume that the discount on actual 90-day T-bills has increased from 8.35% when you initially traded to 9.00% at the contract's maturity. Because the contract is now maturing, *it must sell at exactly the same price as spot 90-day Treasuries*. The two instruments are perfect substitutes.

The treasurer had initially bought ten contracts worth $9,791,250. However, since then the discount yield has risen and caused a decrease in the value of the contract. At its maturity, contracts on $10 million par value securities will sell for:

$$\$10,000,000 - \$10,000,000 \times .09 \times \frac{90}{360} = \$9,775,000$$

When the treasurer sells the futures, she will incur a loss of $16,250:

$$\frac{\text{Treasurer's}}{\text{Profit (Loss)}} = \frac{\text{Selling}}{\text{Price}} - \frac{\text{Purchase}}{\text{Price}}$$

$$(\$16,250) \quad = \$9,775,000 - \$9,791,250$$

However, the purchase price of 90-day spot T-bills has also declined. When the loss on the futures contract is added to the cost of buying actual T-bills, the treasurer will still pay $9,791,250 — exactly what she contracted for when she initially purchased the futures contract:

Purchase Price of $10 million 90-Day T-Bills at 9% Discount	$9,775,000
Plus Futures Loss	16,250
Net Price Paid	$9,791,250

Now, how about your situation? You have decided to leave your contract open and to actually deliver $1 million in par value 90-day T-bills in return for $979,125 in cash. The easiest way to find a T-bill to deliver would be to purchase it in the spot market. Let's assume that you can borrow from a commercial bank at the prevailing risk-free rate of 9%. (This is probably wrong. We will see what happens in a moment if you cannot borrow at *RF*.) The price of a 90-day T-bill is $97.75.[7] If you borrowed $977,500 and used it to buy T-bills, the cash inflow from the loan would be exactly offset by the cost of the T-bills. You could then deliver on your contract and receive the $979,125 in cash which the contract promised. Ninety days later the loan would mature and you would pay $1,000,000. The 90-day and annualized simple interest cost to you are exactly what you had contracted for back on January 1:

---

[7] $97.75 = \$100 - [(\$100 \times 0.09)(90/360)]$.

	Your Cash Inflows (Outflows)		
	January	*March*	*June*
Futures Transactions			
Sell Futures	–	–	
Deliver on Contract		$979,125	
Loan Transactions			
Borrow at 9%		977,500	
Repay Loan			−$1,000,000
Spot T-Bill Transactions			
Buy 9% T-Bill		− 977,500	
Net	$0.0	$979,125	−$1,000,000

$$\text{90-Day Interest Rate}$$
$$= \frac{\$1,000,000}{\$979,125} - 1.0$$
$$= 2.132\%$$

$$\text{Annualized Simple Interest Cost} = 2.132\% \times \frac{365}{90}$$

$$= 8.65\%$$

HEDGING

In our example, both you and the corporate treasurer eventually received exactly what was contracted for on January 1. You received a loan in late March which cost 2.132% over 90 days, and the treasurer made an investment in late March which had a 2.132% 90-day return. You both were able to eliminate interest rate uncertainty by properly hedging your future needs. The reason this is possible is really quite simple. *Any increases or decreases in spot market prices caused by changes in interest rates were exactly offset by profits or losses on the futures transaction.* For example, when late March came, you had to borrow at prevailing interest rates of 9%. This meant that the most you could get on the $1 million loan was $977,500. However, when the profit on the futures contract of $1,625 ($979,125 − $977,500) is added to the loan proceeds, you had a cash total of $979,125 — exactly what you contracted for in the futures. The treasurer faced the opposite situation. Losses on the futures, when added to the investment in spot T-bills, created a return identical to that offered in January on the futures.

Two Types of Hedges

Futures contracts can be used to hedge two types of positions:

1. Future cash flows
2. Current portfolio holdings

The foregoing example illustrated the first type. The treasurer was able to guarantee the interest rate at which *future cash inflows* would be invested, and you were able to guarantee the interest rate at which *future cash outflows* would be financed. As we will see later in the chapter when various contracts are discussed, this is a major benefit of futures. A pension fund, for example, can guarantee today the rate of return at which future cash inflows will be invested. Similarly, a corporation which plans to borrow at a known date can guarantee today the rate of return it will have to finance at. When futures are used to hedge future cash flows, a locked-in future position is obtained.[8]

The second type of hedge is not on future cash flows but, instead, on existing security holdings. For example, assume that you are the investments officer for a major commercial bank and have a large inventory of 180-day T-bills which you plan to sell in exactly 90 days from now. If you do not employ a futures or forward contract but, instead, continue to hold the inventory to the end of the 90-day period, you will be uncertain about the price at which the T-bills can be sold. But if you sell a futures contract today on 90-day T-bills with a maturity of three months from now, you will have locked in the eventual sales price. This future sale will leave you with a long position for days 1 to 90 and both a long and a short position (which net to a zero position) for days 91 to 180.

Why not simply sell the 180-day T-bills and buy 90-day T-bills? This would result in exactly the same position and may be accomplished at lower brokerage fees. It would also be less complex. The question is a good one. Too often financial futures are suggested for situations which are more easily handled by trading in spot instruments. However, there are occasions when you would be unable to sell a spot instrument. For example, consider the case of an investment banking firm which has purchased a new bond issue of IBM. The firm plans to sell the bonds to the public as rapidly as possible, but as long as some remain in inventory, the firm is exposed to the risk that they might decline in value if interest rates rise. By selling a financial future on bonds similar to IBM's (U.S. Treasury bonds are a very close substitute), much of this risk is eliminated. If interest rates do rise, the value of the IBM inventory declines, but this is offset by gains on the futures contracts.[9]

Criteria for a Perfect Hedge

All of our examples so far have been perfect hedges. A perfect hedge exists when all risk can be eliminated. Perfect hedges are possible to create in practice, but they are more the exception than the rule. In order to create a perfect hedge, three things must be true:

---

[8]A guaranteed interest rate is possible only if a *perfect hedge* is possible. This is discussed in the next section.

[9]This situation did actually occur when IBM sold its first large bond issue in the late 1970s. Immediately after IBM's investment bankers purchased the bonds, interest rates rose dramatically. Firms which had not covered their long position in the IBM bonds with short positions in futures suffered tremendous losses. Those who had properly hedged were heroes!

1. The future's maturity must be identical to the date at which one wishes to trade in the spot market. For example, if money available to the treasurer in our earlier illustration isn't going to be received until April 15, the hedge we created would not totally eliminate interest rate uncertainty. An uncertainty about changes in rates between late March and mid-April would still exist.
2. The size of the contract traded must be identical to the amount of cash one wishes to borrow or lend. For example, if you had really planned to borrow only $1,000 for your vacation, the trade on $1 million in T-bills simply wouldn't eliminate your interest rate risk. Uncertainty caused by the mismatching of the size of the futures contract and your needs would still exist.
3. The instrument on which the future is written must be identical to the security one wishes to eventually trade. For example, it is doubtful that you could borrow at the same rate as the U.S. Treasury. Uncertainty about changes in the spread between your borrowing rate and T-bill yields would still exist.

Perfect hedges are rare. However, the closer the futures contract specifications are to a person's needs, the more the hedge can reduce risk.

Optimal Hedges. When a futures contract's specifications are not identical to the instrument which is being hedged, risk will still remain. However, it can be minimized. Consider a portfolio of two securities: a futures contract and the spot market instrument being hedged. When the hedge is entered into, there is uncertainty about the maturity-date futures price (σ_F) plus uncertainty about the value of the spot instrument (σ_S). In addition, there will be a correlation between the maturity-date prices of the two securities (r_{FS}). If Q_S refers to the quantity of the spot instrument you wish to hedge, we can use the risk concepts discussed in Chapter 7 to find that amount of the futures contract (Q_F^*) which will lead to a minimum variance portfolio. This value of Q_F^* is:[10]

Optimal Hedge
$$Q_F^* = Q_S \frac{\sigma_S}{\sigma_F} r_{FS}$$
(17.1)

---

[10]The variance of the hedged portfolio's value at the maturity date would be:

$$\sigma^2 = Q_S^2 \sigma_S^2 + Q_F^2 \sigma_F^2 - 2Q_S Q_F \sigma_S \sigma_F r_{SF}$$

The negative sign on the last term is caused by the fact that futures and spot returns will be negatively related.

To find quantity Q_F^* which minimizes this variance, the variance equation is differentiated with respect to Q_F set equal to zero and solved for the value of Q_F^*:

$$\frac{\partial \sigma^2}{\partial Q_F} = 2Q_F \sigma_F^2 - 2Q_S \sigma_S \sigma_S r_{SF}$$

$$0 = Q_F(2\sigma_F^2) - 2Q_S \sigma_S \sigma_F r_{SF}$$

$$Q_F = \frac{2Q_S \sigma_S \sigma_F r_{SF}}{2\sigma_F^2}$$

$$= Q_S \frac{\sigma_S}{\sigma_F} r_{SF}$$

In our earlier example, the treasurer wished to purchase $9,791,250 of 90-day Treasury bills in late March. Since the futures and spot T-bill prices would have to be identical at that time, $\sigma_S = \sigma_F$ and $r_{FS} = 1.0$. Thus the optimal value of T-bill futures would be:

$$Q_F^* = \$9,791,250(1.0)(1.0)$$

$$= \$9,791,250$$

Each bill future had a per-unit contract value of $979,125. Thus exactly ten contracts would be purchased and all risk would be eliminated.

But what if the cash available to invest were $15,000,000 and would not be available until mid-April? In that case, subjective estimates of σ_S, σ_F, and r_{SF} would have to be made. If a sufficient history is available on both the spot and futures instruments, one could estimate each by using historical data. But many financial futures do not have an extensive price history on which reliable estimates can be based. The spot instrument being hedged is a 90-day T-bill to be purchased in mid-April. Most likely the uncertainty about its price (σ_S) is close, if not identical, to the uncertainty about 90-day T-bill prices at the end of March (σ_F). But the correlation coefficient between the two instruments will not be 1.0. The correlation will be large, however— say, 0.90. As a result, a value of $15,000,000 in spot T-bills implies that a total value of $13,500,000 in March T-bill futures should be bought:

$$\$15,000,000 \,(1.0)(.9) = \$13,500,000$$

Each future was selling at a per-contract value of $979,125. Thus 13.79 futures contracts would provide a minimum risk portfolio. Because fractions of a contract cannot be purchased, either 13 or 14 contracts would be purchased. Risk would be reduced, but not eliminated.

Equation 17.1, as well as simple logic, suggests that the closer the financial future contract specifications are to the spot instrument being hedged, the better the hedge will be. In general, one should attempt to find contracts which:

1. Provide a security with maturity and risk characteristics similar to those of the spot instrument being hedged
2. Mature close to the date at which the spot instrument is to be bought or sold
3. Have a contract value which can closely hedge the total dollar value of spot instruments to be bought or sold

Basis and Basis Risk. The *basis* of a futures contract is equal to the futures price minus the spot price:

$$\text{Basis} = \text{Futures Price} - \text{Spot Price}$$

Typically, futures prices exceed spot prices, resulting in a positive basis. For example, on December 31, 19xx, 90-day T-bill futures maturing in March of the next year had a contract value of $97.913 per $100 of par value T-bills. The purchase price of an equivalent spot T-bill was $95.975 per $100 of par value T-bills. Thus, the basis between the futures and spot was $1.94 ($97.913 − $95.975). Similarly, S&P 500

March futures settled at \$170.2 and the spot S&P 500 Index closed at \$167.24. Thus, the basis in the March stock futures was \$2.96 (\$170.2 − \$167.24).

A basis exists because of the *carrying costs* inherent in a spot instrument. *Carrying costs* are the costs of holding a commodity or financial asset in inventory. For example, assume you now hold a spot T-bill which matures in *180 days*. The market value of this T-bill is now \$95.975 per \$100 par. If you intend to hold this T-bill for three months and then sell it, you will require that the expected selling price be sufficient to cover all costs which you incurred while holding the T-bill inventory. For a T-bill the only carrying cost would be a risk-free return on your investment. (For agricultural and metallurgical commodities, carrying costs such as insurance and storage would be incurred.)

Assume that the three-month risk-free return is now 2.02%. Compounding the current spot T-bill's value at this rate results in the price at which you should expect to sell in three months:

$$\frac{\text{Expected Spot Selling}}{\text{Price in 3 Months}} = \frac{\text{Current}}{\text{Spot Price}} \times \frac{\text{3-Month}}{\text{Carrying Cost}}$$

$$\$97.913 \quad = \quad \$95.975 \quad \times \quad 1.0202$$

But notice that this expected selling price should also be the current market price of a 90-day T-bill future deliverable three months from now. In three months, the future and your (currently 180-day) spot T-bill will be perfect substitutes.

If market prices are in equilibrium, the carrying costs associated with owning the spot instrument should be equal to the basis on the futures contract. If the two are different, abnormal profits are available by taking opposite positions in the spot and futures. For example, if the three-month risk-free rate in our example had actually been 1.0% instead of 2.02%, one should buy the 180-day spot T-bill and simultaneously sell the futures. This would lock in a 90-day risk-free return of 2.02% when other 90-day risk-free assets are yielding only 1%. But the net result of many people's doing this would cause prices to change until abnormal profits no longer existed and the basis would be identical to the carrying costs of owning the spot instrument.

Now let's examine the relationship between the basis and the risk inherent in a hedged position. The basic motivation of any hedge is to increase the certainty of a future (not *futures*) trading price. This future trading price can be stated in terms of the *initial basis* when the hedge is first taken and the *cover basis* when the hedge is offset (that is, covered):

$$\frac{\text{Realized Future}}{\text{Trading Price}} = \frac{\text{Initial}}{\text{Spot Price}} + \frac{\text{Initial}}{\text{Basis}} - \frac{\text{Cover}}{\text{Basis}}$$

$$P_N \quad = \quad S_O \quad + \quad (F_{TO} - S_O) - (F_{TN} - S_N) \tag{17.2}$$

In the equation, N refers to the date at which the hedge is *lifted* (covered) by offsetting trades in the futures and spot markets.

When the hedge is created on day 0, everything is known except for the cover basis. If the spot security and futures contract are on identical instruments (say, 90-day T-bills), then the cover basis will have to be zero and the future trading price to be realized will be known with certainty. A perfect hedge is available. However, if the cover basis is not known with certainty, a perfect hedge will not be possible. The cover basis will be unknown in two cases: (1) if the cover date is different from the futures contract's delivery date, or (2) if the spot security is different from the security underlying the futures contract. Both of these risks were discussed earlier. Hedged positions are risky to the extent that there is uncertainty about the cover date basis.

FUTURES ON SHORT-TERM DEBT

Contracts Available

During the past decade numerous futures have been offered on short-term, high-grade financial instruments. Many of these have not been successful and are no longer available. As of 1989 all trading in these instruments was on the International Monetary Market (IMM), a division of the Chicago Mercantile Exchange. Two contracts were widely traded: (1) T-bills and (2) Eurodollar deposits. Basic information on each is shown in Table 17-3.

T-Bill Futures

All of our previous examples have been on T-bill futures because they are the most easily understood of all financial futures, and they are widely used. The only active T-bill futures contracts are written on 90-day bills.

   To understand various trading strategies available in T-bill futures, it is important to recall a few T-bill pricing relationships. First, T-bills trade at discounts to par value and receive no coupons; they are pure discount bonds. Second, the percentage discount is not the same as the annualized bond equivalent yield. Instead, the quoted discount rate represents the percentage below par at which the bill is bought, not the percentage return on actual money invested. In addition, when calculating the actual dollar discount at which a bill is traded, the Federal Reserve assumes there are 360 days per year. Assume that at the close of trading on July 30 a T-bill maturing on August 28 could be bought at a quoted discount of 7.13%. Since the bill has a remaining life of 29 days and prices are determined using 360 days per year, the discount would be $0.5744 per $100, giving a purchase price equal to 99.4256% of face value:

$$\frac{\text{Dollar Discount}}{\text{per \$100 Face}} = \text{Face Value} \times \text{Quoted Discount} \times \frac{\text{Days Remaining}}{360}$$

$$\$0.5744 = \$100 \times 0.0713 \times \frac{29}{360}$$

$$\frac{\text{Purchase Price}}{\$100 \text{ Face}} = \text{Face Value} - \text{Dollar Discount}$$

$$\$99.4256 = \$100 - \$0.5744$$

TABLE 17-3 *Summary of Contract Specifications: Three-Month Eurodollar Time Deposit and 90-Day Treasury Bill*

Specifications	Three-Month Eurodollar Time Deposit		90-Day U.S. Treasury Bill	
Size	*$1,000,000*		*$1,000,000*	
Contract Grade	1) Cash settlement		1) Treasury bills with 91 days to maturity	
Yields	Add-on		Discount	
Hours	7:30 A.M.–2:00 P.M.		8:00 A.M.–2:00 P.M.	
Months Traded	Mar, Jun, Sep, Dec, & Spot Month		Jan, Mar, Apr, Jun, Jul, Sep, Oct, Dec	
Clearing House Symbol	ED		T1	
Ticker Symbol	ED		TB	
Minimum Fluctuation in Price	.01 (1 basis pt)($25/pt)		.01 (1 basis pt)($25/pt)	
Limit Move	1.00 (100 basis pts)($2,500) No spot month limit		.60 (60 basis pts)($1,500)	
Last Day of Trading	2nd London business day before 3rd Wednesday		2nd day following 3rd weekly Treasury bill auction in contract month. (Effective with Jun '83 contract, the day before the first delivery day)	
Delivery Date	Last day of trading		1st Thursday after 3rd weekly bill auction in the delivery month	
Minimum Margins	I $2,000	M $1,500	I $2,000	M $1,500
CD T-Bill Spread			I $ 500	M $ 400
Eurodollar/CD Spread	I $ 500	M $ 400		
Eurodollar/T-Bill Spread	I $ 700	M $ 600	I $ 700	M $ 60
Spread Margins	I $ 400	M $ 200	I $ 400	M $ 200
Delivery Month Margins	I $2,000	M $1,500	I $2,000	M $1,500
Delivery Month Spread Margins	I $ 400	M $ 200	I $ 400	M $ 200

SOURCE: Copyright 1984, Chicago Mercantile Exchange.

For each $99.4256, one could receive $100 29 days hence. This implies a simple interest bond yield of about 7.27%:

$$\frac{\text{Simple Interest}}{\text{Yield}} = \frac{\text{Face Value}}{\text{Purchase Price}} - 1.0 \times \frac{365}{\text{Days Remaining}}$$

$$= \frac{\$100}{\$99.4256} - 1.0 \times \frac{365}{29}$$

$$7.27\% = 0.5777\% \times \frac{365}{29}$$

Finally, if the bills deliverable under a futures contract are assumed to have a 90-day maturity, a change in the quoted discount of one basis point represents a $25 change in the value of a $1 million face value futures contract:

$$\$1,000,000 \times 0.01\% \times \frac{90}{360} = \$25$$

For example, if a bill contract is purchased at a discount of 5.20%, the delivery price contracted for would be $987,000:

$$\text{Delivery Price} = \frac{\text{Face Value}}{\text{of Contract}} - \left(\frac{\text{Discount in}}{\text{Basis Points}} \times \frac{\text{Amount Change per Basis Point}}{\text{per \$1 Million Face Value}} \right)$$

$$= \$1,000,000 - (520 \times \$25)$$

$$\$987,000 = \$1,000,000 - \$13,000$$

If a person buys a 90-day T-bill future at a 5.20% discount and later sells it at a 5.10% discount, a $250 profit would have been earned:

Profit = $25 [Interest Basis Points at Purchase − Interest Basis Points at Sale]

$250 = $25   (520   −   510)

or

Profit =   Selling Price   −   Purchase Price

$250 =   [$1 million − ($25 × 510)]   −   [$1 million − ($25 × 520)]

Alternatively, if the future had been bought at a 5.20% discount and sold at a 5.30% discount, a $250 loss would have been incurred. This $25 price impact for each 1-basis-point change in a $1 million 90-day T-bill future is quite helpful in quickly pricing T-bill futures contracts and figuring trading gains and losses.

Section A in Table 17-4 shows hypothetical discounts and actual prices for various 90-day bill futures at the close of trading on June 30, 19X1. Section B shows hypothetical discounts and actual prices for cash bills of various maturities on the same day. We will use this information to illustrate a variety of hedging and speculative transactions. While the examples clearly don't exhaust all possible combinations, they do provide a general sense of the types of trades which speculators and hedgers can enter into.

TABLE 17-4 *90-Day T-Bill Futures and Cash Prices as of June 30, 19X1*

A. 90-Day T-Bill Futures Prices

	6/30/X1		
Delivery Date	Actual Price	Discount	Bond Yield
September 19X1	97.87	8.52%	8.82%
December 19X1	97.84	8.64	8.95
March 19X2	97.80	8.80	9.12
June 19X2	97.75	9.02	9.36
September 19X2	97.69	9.22	9.58
December 19X2	97.65	9.42	9.76
March 19X3	97.59	9.64	10.02
June 19X3	97.55	9.82	10.18

B. Spot T-Bill Prices

		6/30/X1		
Maturity	Days After June 30	Actual Price	Discount	Bond Yield
September 23, 19X1	86	97.86	8.97%	9.28%
December 22, 19X1	176	95.78	8.63%	9.13%

Basic Long Hedge. If an organization's cash flow projections show that in the near future a large sum of excess cash will be temporarily available, T-bill futures can be used to lock in a future interest rate at which the excess cash can be invested. For example, assume it is now June 30, 19X1, and $20 million in cash will be available to invest for a 90-day period as of middle to late September 19X1. As a long hedge a September T-bill futures contract would be bought on June 30. When the $20 million cash actually becomes available (say, on September 23), the futures contract would be sold and physical T-bills bought.

Ideally, the $20 million cash would become available and the futures position would be closed exactly on the futures delivery date. This would mean that spot and futures rates on the bills would be identical (cover basis = $0), resulting in an actual yield on the cash bills equal to the yield at which the initial futures were bought. For example, assume that on June 30, bill futures were bought at an 8.52% discount and that by September 23, 90-day spot bill rates had fallen to discounts of 8.00%. The net transaction would be as follows:

Futures	Discount Rate	Price per $10-Million T-Bills	Bond Yield
Bought 90-Day Futures on 6/30/X1	8.52%	−$9,787,000	8.82%
Sold 90-Day Futures on 9/23/X1	8.00	9,800,000	8.28
Profit	0.52%	13,000	0.54%
Spot			
Buy 90-Day T-Bill on 9/23/X1	8.00	− 9,800,000	8.28%
Net Result	8.52%	−$9,787,000	8.82%

Although discounts available on spot bills fell to 8.00%, the futures hedger was actually able to lock in an 8.52% discount because of the profits earned on the futures transactions. This profit of $13,000 was composed of a 52-basis-point change in 90-day futures rates at $25 per basis point ($1,300 = 52 × $25) times ten contracts. This allowed the hedger to pay only $9,787,000 in out-of-pocket cash for bills selling for $9,800,000.

This perfect hedge worked because the cover basis was zero. The 90-day futures sold at the same discount as did the spot bill. If the hedge had been placed in futures deliverable at dates different from when cash would become available for spot investment (for example, by buying December futures in the above example), the cover basis would most likely be different from zero.

In this example there is another way to lock in a 90-day rate on June 30 for money which would become available on September 23. Instead of trading in futures, one could lock in a *forward rate* in the cash market. Note that the time difference between the September 23 and December 22 spot bills is exactly 90 days. If one were to buy a December 22 bill and short sell some September 23 bills, there would be no cash position until September 23. But once the short sale is closed on September 23, a 90-day long position would be held. Details are shown in Table 17-5. On June 30, December 22 spot bills are bought for $957,800. To come up with the cash, the 0.9787 September 23 bill is sold short. As a result, there is no cash position between June 30 and September 23. However, on September 23 the short position is covered at a cost of $1,000,000 *per bill*, or $978,700 in cash outflow, since the 0.9787 September bill was short. On December 22 the long position matures and provides $1,000,000. In net, $978,700 is invested on September 23 for a $1 million cash return 90 days later. This represents a return of 2.18% for 90 days: a *discount return* of 8.52% or a *bond equivalent* return of 8.82%.

TABLE 17-5 *Creation of 90-Day Forward Rate as of June 30, 19X1*

	Cash Flows — In (Out)		
	June 30	*September 23*	*December 22*
Buy Dec. 22 Spot Bill	$957,800		$1,000,000
Short Sell 0.9787 Sept. 23 Bill*	− 957,800	−$978,700	
	$ 0	−$978,700	$1,000,000

Annualized Return:
Discount = 8.52%†
Bond Yield = 8.82%‡

* $\dfrac{\text{Dec. Bill Price}}{\text{Sept. Bill Price}} = \dfrac{95.78}{97.86} = 0.9787$

† $\dfrac{\$1,000,000 - \$978,700}{\$1,000,000} \times \dfrac{360}{90} = 8.52\%$

‡ $\dfrac{\$1,000,000 - \$978,700}{\$978,700} \times \dfrac{365}{90} = 8.82\%$

Speculation. According to Table 17-5, a bill future now exists which requires that the buyer pay $978,700 in the third week of September 19X1. In return, the buyer will receive 90-day T-bills with a total face value of $1 million. This future is said to sell at a discount of 8.52%, although the effective annual bond yield is actually about 8.82%. If a speculator expected that 90-day cash bills would *actually* be selling at discounts greater than 8.52% towards the end of September 19X1, the futures contract should be sold. The speculator's belief that bill rates will rise might rest on any one of a number of reasons, for example, a belief that investors will revise upward their expectations of inflation, unexpectedly tight Federal Reserve policy, or unusually large new Treasury sales in late September. But regardless of the reason, the speculator would sell in anticipation of lower cash bill prices in the delivery month than contracted for in the bill future.

Assume that on June 30 the speculator sells one September 19X1 bill contract. At that time the normal margin associated with futures trading will have to be posted and a brokerage commission paid. In September the speculator may either hold the contract open for delivery or cover the initial sale by purchasing the same contract just prior to the delivery date. Since the futures contract should sell at the same discount as an equivalent cash bill at delivery, the profits or losses from either strategy would be the same. If the speculator had guessed right and 90-day T-bill discounts rise to, say, 9.00%, a profit of $1,200 would have been earned (9.00% − 8.52%, or 48 basis points × $25 per basis point). However, the speculator has gambled that bill discounts won't fall. If they do, the speculator would be stuck with having to deliver an 8.52% discount bill when the cash bill actually available at that time yielded less. For example, if bill discounts actually fell by 48 basis points because of a temporary easing of credit by the Fed, a $1,200 loss would have been incurred.

Arbitrage. Arbitrage transactions can be accomplished by going long and short between both bills and futures. For example, we saw above that a 90-day investment return starting on September 23 could be obtained either by buying a 90-day bill future deliverable in September *or* by short selling some spot bills maturing on September 23 and simultaneously buying December 22 spot bills. As the example was originally designed, one would have been indifferent between the two approaches since each was expected to provide the same return. However, if the September future had been selling at 8.30% (with no changes in spot prices), an arbitrage consisting of selling the September future and creating a long September forward position should be entered into. Whenever futures rates are different from implied forward rates in the spot market, a profitable arbitrage opportunity exists (at least before transaction costs).

Consider another potential arbitrage. Suppose 90-day and one-year spot bills are selling at 8.80% and 9.00%, respectively. If the following 90-day futures are also available, what sort of arbitrage opportunity exists?

Delivery Month	90-Day Bill Discount
3 months	8.85%
6 months	8.90%
9 months	8.70%

A one-year investment in bills could be obtained either by buying a one-year spot bill at 9.00% or by purchasing a three-month spot bill plus a *strip* of each of the 90-day futures at an average discount *less* than 9.00%. Clearly, the one-year spot bill would provide the higher expected return. In fact, an arbitrage consisting of going long the one-year spot bill plus short the three-month bill and each future would provide a nearly riskless profit.

The Valuation of T-Bill Futures. There are two related ways of valuing a T-bill future. Neither treats the impacts of daily marking to market, but they do provide a good estimate of what the future should sell for. As we review each method, it will be clear that neither is new to you. The basics of the first method were presented earlier in this chapter and the second was introduced as early as Chapter 6.

Consider the spot T-bills shown in Table 17-4. On June 30, a T-bill maturing on December 22 is selling for 95.78% of par. If you were to buy it and hold it until September 23, it would then have a maturity of 90 days. Thus, its price on September 23 should be identical to the price at delivery of the 90-day futures. But the expected price of this December 22 spot bill is easily calculated. If you are to invest $95.78 on June 30 in a risk-free security and hold the investment until September 23, you would demand a risk-free rate of return. Since the September 23 spot T-bill is selling for $97.86, the risk-free return associated with the June to September period is:

$$\frac{\$100}{\$97.86} - 1 = 2.187\%$$

Thus the expected price of the December 22 spot T-bill should be $97.87 on September 23:

$$\$95.78 \,(1.02187) = \$97.87$$

It turns out that the September futures are priced correctly. If they had been trading at a value different from the expected value of the spot instrument, arbitrage profits would have been available. In general, if F_{Tt} refers to the price of a T-bill futures contract with a delivery at date T quoted at date t, and $S_{T+90,t}$ refers to the date t spot price of an instrument which *will be a perfect substitute* for the futures on date T, then:

Futures Price Determined by Current Spot Prices $$F_{Tt} = S_{T+90,t}(1 + RF_{T-t}) \qquad (17.3)$$

The spot instrument chosen must be a perfect substitute for the futures at date T. In addition, the risk-free rate used should apply to the period from t to T.

The approach illustrated above is known as the *cost of carry* model. Let's now review an alternative way to value T-bill futures which is known as the *forward rate* model. This alternative approach to valuing the T-bill future states that the return which the future will provide must be the same as that available in the forward market. For example, a 90-day forward rate can be obtained by purchasing the December 23 spot issue and short selling an equal dollar value of the September 23 issue. The cash flows of this artificial forward contract are:

	June	*September*	*December*
Buy 1.0 December	−$95.78	—	$100
Short 95.78 ÷ 97.86 Sept.	95.78	−$97.87	—
Net	$ 0.	−$97.87	$100.00

$$90\text{-Day Return} = \frac{100}{97.87} - 1$$

$$= 2.176\%$$

In fact, this is exactly the 90-day return promised on the September futures — it is selling for $97.87.

In general, the futures price F_{Tt} should be identical to the forward contract price available on day t:

**Future Price Equals
Forward Price**

$$F_{Tt} = FC_{Tt} = \frac{S_{T+90,t}}{S_{Tt}} \qquad (17.4)$$

where FC_{Tt} = the forward contract price on day t for a perfect substitute of the futures instrument deliverable on date T

Eurodollar Deposit Contracts. For a variety of reasons, returns on Eurodollar deposits tend to be 1 to 2 percentage points greater than equivalent maturity CDs.[11] The Eurodollar deposit contract also has a principal value of $1 million. It is priced using the add-on method, similar to CDs. But an important difference between this contract and others we have discussed is delivery. Delivery takes place on the last trading date and is done by a cash settlement, as opposed to actual delivery of the instruments. This cash settlement price is determined by the IMM and is based on a complex polling of various banks which are active in the three-month Eurodollar deposit market. Essentially, the price is an average of rates offered by various banks at the close of the contract's last trading day.

FUTURES ON INTERMEDIATE- AND LONG-TERM DEBT

The most actively traded futures on intermediate- to long-term debt securities are all traded on the Chicago Board of Trade (CBT). Contract specifications on two of these are shown in Table 17-6. The contracts are not identical, but they are similar in most features. Because T-bond contracts are more actively traded than T-note contracts, we will restrict our discussion to them.

---

[11]In large part this is due to differences in marketability and default risk. In addition, foreign banks do not face the reserve requirements on U.S. dollars that domestic banks do. As a result they are able to offer slightly higher yields.

TABLE 17-6 *Contract Specifications on Intermediate- to Long-Term Debt Futures*

	U.S. Treasury Notes	U.S. Treasury Bonds
Trading Unit	$100,000 face value 8% coupon or equivalent	$100,000 face value 8% coupon or equivalent
Deliverable Grade	6½- to 10-year Treasury note	Treasury bond not callable for 15 years
Delivery Method	Federal Reserve book entry wire system. Invoice is adjusted for maturity (or call) and coupon.	
Delivery Date	Any day in the delivery month	
Daily Price Limit	$3,000	$3,000
Initial Margin	$ 900	$2,000
Maintenance Margin	$ 600	$1,500

U.S. Treasury Bond Futures

Each contract is on $100,000 of par value U.S. Treasury bonds having a maturity (or call, if callable) of at least 15 years and an *assumed* coupon of 8%. Prices are quoted in thirty-seconds of a dollar. Thus a price of 71-02 represents a price quote of 71$\frac{2}{32}$, or $71,062.50, on a single $100,000 par contract. Each point ($\frac{1}{32}$) represents a value of $31.25 per contract.

Delivery. The price of any futures contract depends on the price at which the deliverable security is expected to sell on the delivery date. For T-bill contracts the deliverable instrument is easily identified. The deliverable instrument on a T-bond contract is not so easy to identify. Because of its critical importance in determining T-bond futures prices, we must look a little closer at T-bond delivery.

Delivery can take place at any time during the maturity month and is initiated by the short side. Once the short has declared an intention to deliver, the clearing corporation matches the short with the oldest outstanding long position, and securities and cash are exchanged two business days later. This uncertainty about the precise date of delivery causes a risk to the futures purchaser which cannot be hedged.

The second aspect of delivery which creates a risk is that the bonds which are deliverable are not precisely defined. Any U.S. Treasury bond with a maturity in excess of 15 years (or a call date longer than 15 years, if it is callable) will qualify. This means that a wide range of coupons and maturities will qualify for delivery. Recognizing that the value of each bond is affected by its maturity and coupon, the clearing corporation has extensive tables which attempt to adjust for such differences. These tables are used to convert the contractual trade price to an actual invoice price which the purchaser of the future will pay. This adjustment factor is called the *delivery factor*. Yet the tables are unable to precisely price each of the many alternative bonds available for delivery. There will always be a few bonds which are the *cheapest to deliver*. As a result, active participants in the market will constantly evaluate the cheapest bonds to deliver and base the futures price on their expected value in the month of delivery.

Potential Use in Portfolio Management. Throughout this chapter most of the examples of how futures might be used have dealt with the hedging of specific cash flow needs or specific security holdings. Implicit in these are speculative and arbitrage trades which could occur if market prices are not in equilibrium. Many of the same techniques also apply to T-bond futures. However, T-bond futures can also be used to manage aggregate bond portfolio risk. It is this potential role that we will examine.

Assume that you are the manager of a $1 billion pension fund which has a policy of maintaining an asset mix of 50% equities, 40% bonds, and 10% cash. Since the relative performance of each of these security types varies over time, the actual market value mix will often depart from this desired mix. Assume that the bonds currently have a market value of $440 million — $40 million more than desired. There are two ways in which the bond position can be restored to $400 million: (1) sell $40 million in spot bonds and allocate it to stocks and cash as appropriate or (2) sell T-bond futures.[12]

As we saw in Chapter 12, the duration of a bond portfolio (D_p) is a measure of how sensitive the value of the portfolio is to a change in interest rates. Specifically:

$$\text{\% Change in Bond Prices} = -D_p \times \left[\frac{\text{\% Change in}}{(1 + YTM)} \right] \tag{17.5}$$

An alternative way of expressing this relationship is:

$$\text{\% Change in Bond Prices} = -D_p \left(\frac{YTM_t - YTM_{t-1}}{1 + YTM_{t-1}} \right) \tag{17.6}$$

Assume that the duration of your portfolio is four years. Thus, a 100-basis-point increase in, say, an existing YTM of 10% will cause a 3.64% decrease in your bond portfolio's value, or a dollar loss of $16.0 million:

$$-4 \left(\frac{0.11 - 0.10\%}{1.10} \right) = 3.64\%$$

$$-0.0364 \times \$440 \text{ million} = -\$16.0 \text{ million}$$

This $16.0 million is called the *dollar duration* of the portfolio. Since the negative sign on D_p is unnecessary, it will be dropped:

$$\text{Dollar Duration} = D_p \left(\frac{YTM_t - YTM_{t-1}}{1 + YTM_{t-1}} \right) \times \text{Bond Portfolio Value} \tag{17.7}$$

Note that if you actually had $400 million invested in bonds, the dollar duration would be $14.55 million (0.0364 × $400). T-bond futures can be sold in an amount

---

[12]This example is based on one presented by Goldman Sachs in their publication *Asset Allocation Using Futures Contracts*, February 1985.

that would adjust the actual dollar duration from $16.0 million to $14.55 million—that is, decrease it by $1.45 million.

To calculate the duration of the T-bond future, we must first determine which T-bond is the cheapest to deliver. Assume this cheapest-to-deliver bond has a duration of 6.24 years. Since each contract is a claim on $100,000 worth of an 8% T-bond, the dollar duration of such a T-bond future is:

$$6.24 \left(\frac{0.11 - 0.10}{1.10} \right) \times \$100,000 = \$5,672.73$$

Unfortunately, the bond which is cheapest to deliver does not have an 8% coupon. Thus we must adjust this 8% coupon bond's dollar duration into the actual deliverable bond's dollar duration. Mechanically, this is done by dividing the 8% coupon result by a *delivery factor* provided in CBT's tables. Assume the delivery factor for this bond is 0.9883. Thus, the dollar duration of the cheapest to deliver T-bond future is:

$$\frac{\text{Dollar Duration}}{\text{T-Bond Future}} = \frac{\text{Duration of Deliverable Bond}}{\text{Delivery Factor}} \left(\frac{YTM_t - YTM_{t-1}}{1 + YTM_{t-1}} \right) \times \$100,000$$

$$\$5,739.88 = \frac{6.24}{0.9883} \left(\frac{0.11 - 0.10}{1.10} \right) \times \$100,000$$

So we finally arrive. To reduce the bond portfolio's dollar duration by $1.45 million, you would sell 253 T-bond futures:

$$\frac{\$1,450,000}{\$5,739.88} = 253 \text{ T-bond futures}$$

There is no doubt that this is a tedious calculation. The logic, however, is correct, and the calculations can be easily programmed on any microcomputer and many calculators. The use of T-bonds to alter bond portfolio risk is actually much easier and perhaps cheaper than direct sale or purchase of spot bond instruments.

FUTURES ON EQUITY INDEXES

In 1982, stock index futures began trading on various exchanges. The first contract was based on the Value Line Composite. By 1989 four contracts were being actively traded:

1. NYSE Index contracts on the New York Futures Exchange (NYFE—a division of the NYSE)
2. S&P 500 Index contracts on the Chicago Mercantile Exchange
3. Value Line Index contracts on the Kansas City Board of Trade
4. Major Market Index contracts on the Chicago Board of Trade (designed to emulate the Dow Jones Industrial Average)

TABLE 17-7 *Contract Specifications of Major Stock Index Futures*

	NYSE Index	S&P 500 Index	Major Market Index	Value Line Index
Size	$500 times index value	$500 times index value	$250 times index value	$500 times index value
Delivery	Mark to market on closing index value on maturity date			
Delivery Date	Last day of trading in the delivery month	Third Thursday of maturity month	Third Friday of maturity month	
Months Traded	March, June, September, December	March, June, September, December	All Months	March, June, September, December
Minimum Price Change	$25	$25	$12.50	$5
Margin (For Hedging) Initial Maintenance	$1,500 $ 750	$2,500 $1,500		$2,500 $1,500

Contract specifications for each of these are shown in Table 17-7. Because the S&P 500 contract is similar to the others our discussion revolves around it.

The S&P 500 Contract

The S&P 500 Index future is quoted in terms of the value of the S&P 500 Composite Index, but the actual dollar value of each contract is 500 times the quoted value. For example, if the contract's settle price is $170, the contract's value is $85,000 ($170 × 500). Minimum price moves are 0.05, or $25. If you bought the contract at $170 and later sold at $160, your loss would be $5,000.

As with other futures contracts, no cash payment is made at the date of the trade except for a good-faith deposit (margin). The values of daily portfolio positions are marked to market. Contracts are available with settlement dates in March, June, September, and December. Delivery (settlement) occurs on the third Thursday of the maturity month. Brokerage commissions are charged once and allow both a buy and a sell.

A unique feature of stock index futures is that physical delivery of the underlying asset never occurs. Instead, the contract requires that, at maturity, all profits be paid to the customer by the clearing corporation and that all losses be paid to the clearing corporation by the customer. Because of daily marking to market, virtually all of the profits and losses will have already been distributed.

Pricing. Refined valuation models which fully take into account daily marking to market and other risk features of these contracts are not reviewed here. However, a simple arbitrage valuation model is used in practice and provides prices reasonably close to those observed.

Assume that you purchase a stock portfolio at date *t* which is identical to one "unit" of the S&P 500 Index. The value of this spot portfolio is S_t. You know that you intend to sell the portfolio at date T. Its price at date T (S_T) is, of course, unknown to you today. But the dividends you will receive between t and T (D_T) are reasonably predictable. Let's assume they are known with certainty and will all be paid on date T. Given this information, you could guarantee the price at which you will sell the spot portfolio by selling one futures contract at a price of $F_{T,t}$. The cash inflows and outflows which would result are:

	Date	
	t	T
At Date t:		
Buy Spot Portfolio	$-S_t$	
Sell Future		F_{Tt}
At Date T:		
Sell Spot Portfolio		S_T
Buy Future		$-F_{TT}$
Collect Dividends		D_T
Net	$-S_t$	$F_{Tt} + D_T$

Two things should be recognized. First, at its maturity, the value of the futures contract must be equal to the spot index value at that time ($S_T = F_{TT}$). That is, after all, how the index contract is legally written. As a result, the S_T and F_{TT} cancel each other out. Second, note that once S_T and F_{TT} cancel, every cash flow is known with certainty. S_t is the current spot index value, D_T is the known dividend, and F_{Tt} is the known futures price at which you trade. For an investment of S_t a *known* payoff of $F_{Tt} + D_T$ is available. To eliminate the potential for arbitrage, a risk-free rate must equate the two cash flows. Letting RF refer to the risk-free rate available over the period t to T:

Arbitrage Spot and Index Future Relationship
$$S_t = \frac{F_{Tt} + D_T}{1 + RF} \qquad (17.8)$$

Restating this in terms of the futures price:

Arbitraged Stock Index Futures Price
$$F_{Tt} = S_t(1 + RF) - D_T \qquad (17.9)$$

This arbitrage pricing model says that the value of the future is the certainty equivalent value of owning the spot index less the dividends which will be earned on the spot index which are not available on the futures contract.

To illustrate Equation 17.9, assume that the following current spot information is known:

Spot Price of the S&P 500 Index	= $250
Annual (discrete) Risk-Free Rate	= 9%
Annual Dividend Yield of the S&P 500 Index	= 4%

Then a three-month contract on the S&P 500 should trade for $252.94:[13]

$$\$250(1.09)^{0.25} - 0.01 \times \$250 = \$252.94$$

Hedging Strategies

As was true with stock index option hedging strategies, futures hedging using stock index futures is designed to alter the systematic risk exposure of a portfolio. If index futures are purchased, systematic market risk is increased. If index futures are sold, systematic market risk decreases. Trading in stock index futures has no impact on a portfolio's diversifiable, non-market risk. Thus, for the futures contract to be a good hedging vehicle, it should be on a stock index which is similar in makeup to the spot equities which are owned.

Three of the more common hedging uses of stock index futures are discussed here:

1. Adjusting portfolio betas
2. Creating index portfolios
3. Use in portfolio insurance programs

The examples use the hypothetical data on an S&P 500 future presented above. The spot S&P 500 Index is $250, the annual risk-free rate is 9%, and the spot stock index will pay a $2.50 dividend in exactly three months. We will assume that a futures contract is available on the S&P 500 which is deliverable in three months and which is now trading in the market for $252.94.[14]

Adjusting Portfolio Betas. Assume that you are the administrator of a $100 million pension fund. An investment committee which sets investment strategy has a desired T-bill/equity mix of 40/60. The investment committee has also stated that the beta of the equity portfolio should be equal to 1.0 (relative to the S&P 500 Index). A number of professional managers have been employed to run portions of the pension fund in the hopes that their unique skills can provide long-run returns in excess of what the fund would earn if it were to fully "index" the portfolio.

Because of recent moves in stock prices and purchases by the managers, the present portfolio differs from the investment committee's stated objectives. At present the equity portfolio represents $70 million of the $100 million portfolio. And the average beta of stocks held by portfolio managers is 1.0. The situation is summarized below:

	Actual		Desired	
Asset	Dollars	Beta	Dollars	Beta
T-bills	$ 30 million	0.00	$ 40 million	0.00
Equity	70 million	1.0	60 million	1.00
Portfolio	$100 million	0.7	$100 million	0.60

---

[13]This assumes that all dividends are paid on the futures' delivery date.

[14]This market price is identical to the futures' theoretically correct value. If actual market prices differ from theoretical values, some of the hedging advantages of the contract are reduced. In practice, arbitrage maintains a close relationship between theoretical and market prices.

You could achieve the desired position by actually trading in the spot securities — by selling $10 million of stock and insisting that the equity managers increase their betas. But this could be costly, confusing, and time-consuming. Alternatively, you could trade in S&P 500 futures to achieve the desired position *without* disturbing the underlying spot portfolio.

The critical question, however, is not whether stock futures can do the job, but how many contracts should be traded.

Well, consider the present situation. Since the $70 million equity position has a beta of 1.0, it is similar to owning 560 "units" of the S&P 500 Index:

$$\frac{\$70,000,000}{\$250 \times 500} = 560$$

If the beta on the $70 million had been only 0.9, only 504 units of the index would effectively be owned:

$$560 \times 0.9 = 504$$

Stated more formally, the number of effective units of a stock index which is owned can be stated as:

$$\frac{\text{Actual Units of}}{\text{Stock Index Owned}} = \left(\frac{\$ \text{ Value of Actual Equity Portfolio}}{\$ \text{ Value of the Spot Index Unit}}\right)\left(\frac{\text{Beta of}}{\text{Actual Portfolio}}\right)$$

$$Q_t = \left(\frac{EMV_t}{S_t \times I}\right)(B_t) \qquad\qquad \text{(17.10)}$$

where Q_t equals the effective number of index units owned at date t, EMV_t equals the equity market value at date t, S_t equals the quoted spot index at t, I is an adjustment factor unique to each futures contract (for example, 500 for the S&P 500 futures), and B_t is the equity portfolio beta at date t.

Applied to our situation:

$$Q_t = \frac{\$70,000,000}{\$250 \times 500}(1.0)$$

$$= 560$$

We can use the same logic to calculate the *desired* units of the index we wish to own. In this case, let us represent desired values with an asterisk:

$$\frac{\text{Desired Units of}}{\text{Stock Index}} = \left(\frac{\$ \text{ Value of Desired Equity Portfolio}}{\$ \text{ Value of the Spot Index Unit}}\right)\left(\frac{\text{Beta of}}{\text{Desired Portfolio}}\right)$$

$$Q_t^* = \left(\frac{EMV_t^*}{S_t \times I}\right)(B_t^*) \qquad\qquad \text{(17.11)}$$

In our example, the desired number of units of the spot index is 480:

$$\left(\frac{\$60,000,000}{\$250 \times 500}\right)(1.0) = 480$$

Therefore, the quantity of stock index futures to trade (T_t) is simply the difference between the two:

Optimal Stock Index Futures to Adjust Systematic Risk

$$
\begin{aligned}
T_t &= Q_t^* - Q_t \\
&= 480 - 560 \\
&= -80
\end{aligned}
\qquad\qquad \textbf{(17.12)}
$$

Equity contracts should be traded. The negative sign implies that they should be sold.

Would it work? Would the actual portfolio position together with a short position in 80 S&P 500 futures provide exactly the same future payoffs as (costlessly) adjusting the spot portfolio to the desired position? Probably not, since stock index futures transactions can only adjust systematic risks. Thus, if the spot equity portfolio is not perfectly correlated with the stock index, futures will not provide the same delivery date payoffs. *But if the spot portfolio is perfectly correlated with the stock index, trades in futures will provide exactly the desired outcome.* This is shown in Table 17-8.

In the table, two spot values are shown for the S&P 500 Index at the future's delivery date—$200 and $300. For each, the portfolio value of the desired spot position is the same as the actual spot position combined with 80 futures sold.[15]

The use of stock index futures will not usually work as neatly in practice as it did in the example above, for four major reasons:

1. The spot equity portfolio will not be identical to the contract traded. Thus, the portfolio's value will not exactly track changes in the index.
2. At the date the contract is held, the spot index will be different from the contracts index $(S_t \neq F_{Tt})$. This difference is known as the basis of the contract. If the contract is expected to be offset before the maturity date, the size of the basis will be unknown and a risk will be incurred. The basis risk of stock hedging can be substantial. If the contract is to be held to maturity, there will be no basis risk.
3. Uncertain future dividends make it impossible to use futures to exactly duplicate a spot stock portfolio.
4. Fractional contracts cannot be traded.

Nonetheless, stock futures can play an important role in temporarily altering a portfolio's stock mix. This is a major reason for the growth of trading in stock futures.

Creating Index Portfolios. An index portfolio is a portfolio of securities which will have a return equal to (or close to) the return on a given security index. The underlying index could be a U.S. common stock index such as the S&P 500, a U.S. bond index such as the Shearson Lehman Hutton Government/Corporate Bond Index, or international stocks in the Europe, Australia, Far East Index. Index portfolios are held in order to obtain broad diversification within a given asset class and in the belief that active investment managers cannot provide greater risk-adjusted performance.

Prior to the introduction of stock index futures, index portfolios were created by actual purchases of the spot securities in weights similar to the index. For example,

---

[15]The 182 difference is due to rounding of the futures' theoretical price.

TABLE 17-8 *Adjusting Systematic Risk with Futures*

	Portfolio Value of Desired Position	
	Spot Index in Three Months	
	$200	*$300*
T-Bills:		
$40,000,000 \times 1.09^{0.25}$	$40,871,127	$ 40,871,127
Equity:		
Dividends		
$60,000,000 \times 0.01$	600,000	600,000
Value		
$60,000,000 (200/250)$	48,000,000	
$60,000,000 (300/250)$		72,000,000
Total	$89,471,127	$113,471,127

	Portfolio Value of Current Spot and Future Position	
	Spot Index in Three Months	
	$200	*$300*
T-Bills:		
$30,000,000 \times 1.09^{0.25}$	$30,653,345	$ 30,653,345
Equity:		
Dividends		
$70,000,000 \times 0.01$	700,000	700,000
Value		
$70,000,000 (200/250)$	56,000,000	
$70,000,000 (300/250)$		84,000,000
Net Prior to Futures	$87,353,345	$115,353,345
Futures		
Sell		
80 (252.94×500)	10,117,600	10,117,600
Buy		
80 (200×500)	−8,000,000	
80 (300×500)		−12,000,000
Futures Profit or Loss	2,117,600	− 1,882,400
Total	$89,470,945	$113,470,945

if an S&P 500 Index portfolio were to be formed, long positions in 500 stocks would ideally be taken with each held in proportions similar to their current weightings in the index. In practice, however, returns on spot index portfolios often do not totally emulate the underlying index. Transaction costs and the inability to maintain identical security weightings both cause return differences.

Stock index futures offer a cheap alternative to creating an indexed position in common stocks. This is done by: (1) purchasing Treasury bills having a maturity date equal to the stock index futures delivery date and (2) purchasing a proper quantity of index futures. If the stock index future is purchased at a price equal to its theoretical value, the net position will provide a return *identical* to the underlying index return.

To demonstrate this idea conceptually, let S_t be the quoted value of the spot stock index at day t, RF the risk-free rate over the life of a given futures contract, D the value of known dividends paid on day T, and T the delivery date of the stock index future. The index portfolio transaction is summarized below:

At day 0, Treasury bills are purchased in a dollar amount equal to the current spot price of the index—S_0. This investment will be worth $S_0(1 + RF)$ at the future delivery date. Also on day 0 a long position in 1.0 future contract is taken. This conceptually obligates you to cash outflow on the delivery date equal to $S_0(1 + RF) - D$, the future's theoretical value. But since the T-bill has a cash inflow at that time equal to $S_0(1 + RF)$, the net of the two cash flows is a positive cash flow equal to the spot index dividend of D. Finally, to obtain a cash inflow equal to the spot index value on day T, you sell the futures contract (initially bought on day 0) at the end of day T. At that time, the value of the future must be identical to the value of the spot index.

		Cash Flows	
Today	0	Futures Delivery	
Buy T-Bills	$-S_0$		
Buy 1.0 Futures		$-F_{T0} = -[S_0(1 + RF) - D]$	
Net		$+D$	
Delivery Date			
Sell the Future Above		$+F_{TT} = S_T$	
Total	$-S_0$	$S_T + D$	

The net effect of this transaction is that you spend S_0 on day 0 and receive $S_T + D$ at the delivery date. Your return is identical to the actual returns on the index!

To illustrate, assume you have $10 million in cash and wish it to earn a return identical to that of the S&P 500 Index. It is December 31, and the following spot and futures information is available.

Spot S&P 500 Index	= $250.00
Dividend to Be Paid in Three Months	= $ 2.50
Futures Price on S&P 500 Deliverable in Three Months	= $252.94
Three-Month Risk-Free Rate	= 2.17782%

The index portfolio transactions are summarized below for two possible spot prices at the delivery date.

	March Delivery Date	
	$S_T = \$200$	$S_T = \$300$
Return on Stock Index	$\dfrac{200 - 250 + 2.50}{250}$	$\dfrac{300 - 250 + 2.50}{250}$
	$= -19.00\%$	$= 21.00\%$

Today	0	$S_T = \$200$	$S_T = \$300$
Purchase T-Bills	−$10,000,000	+$10,217,782	+$10,217,782
Buy 80 Futures			
$10,000,000/(\$250 \times 500)$	−	− 10,117,600	− 10,117,600
Delivery Date			
Sell 80 Futures		+ 8,000,000	+ 12,000,000
Total	−$10,000,000	+$ 8,100,182	+$12,100,182
Rate of Return		−19.00%	+21.00%

Such a procedure appears to work well in practice. For example, past quarterly returns on the S&P 500 Index and three-month futures positions identical to those in the example shown above are shown in Table 17-9. Quarterly returns on the actual S&P 500 are quite close to those on the futures indexed portfolios.

Use in Portfolio Insurance Programs. In Chapters 15 and 16, the concept and application of portfolio insurance were discussed. A minimum portfolio value can be insured by trading listed put and call options or by using a trading strategy which dynamically replicates the payoffs of the options. Dynamic replication requires that stock be sold when its value declines and bought when its value increases. Because of costs associated with actually trading in the spot stock, stock index futures are commonly used.[16] For example, if the trading strategy calls for the sale of $10,000,000 in spot stock, futures with a claim to $10,000,000 of the stock index are sold instead. Clearly, for this procedure to work, the actual stock held must be reasonably similar to the stock index on which the futures are traded.

Speculative Strategies

If the futures contract is traded at values different from those implied by Equation 17.9, speculative profits are possible. The most widely known speculation is an index arbitrage.

Index Arbitrage. In our illustration above, the S&P 500 futures have a theoretical value equal to $252.94. If actual futures prices are lower, an index arbitrage consisting of buying the futures and selling the spot S&P 500 Index could be conducted. If actual futures prices are higher, then exactly the opposite positions would be taken. In addition, trades would take place in T-bills in order to finance any initial cash outflow or invest any initial cash inflows.

Assume that the index futures, theoretically worth $252.94, could actually be traded for $255. The index arbitrage consists of selling the futures and buying the spot

---

[16]The costs of trading the spot stock include brokerage fees, price impacts, and delays in trading. During the late 1980s when portfolio insurance was active, these costs were lower if stock index futures were used.

TABLE 17-9 *S&P 500 Index Returns and Returns on Indexed Futures Portfolios*

	Quarterly Rate of Return on:		
Quarter-end	Theoretical Futures[1]	Actual Futures[2]	S&P 500
6/88	6.51%	7.04%	6.51%
3/88	5.69	6.36	5.69
12/87	−22.54	−22.77	−22.54
9/87	6.58	7.51	6.58
6/87	4.95	5.84	4.95
3/87	21.31	21.93	21.31
12/86	5.59	6.28	5.59
9/86	−6.96	−6.89	−6.96
6/86	5.85	5.67	5.85
3/86	14.02	14.19	14.02
12/85	17.12	17.37	17.12
9/85	−4.07	−4.34	−4.07
6/85	7.27	6.74	7.27
3/85	9.17	8.14	9.17
12/84	1.82	0.83	1.82
9/84	9.64	9.85	9.64
6/84	−2.01	−2.52	−2.01
3/84	−3.00	−3.30	−3.00
12/83	0.38	0.22	0.38
9/83	−0.17	−0.17	−0.17
6/83	11.04	12.78	11.04
3/83	9.99	9.94	9.99
12/82	18.22	19.62	18.22

[1]The return which would have been earned if the three-month futures had been trading at their theoretically correct values at the start of each quarter.

[2]The return based on actual market prices of the futures at the start of each quarter.

Note: Transaction costs and mark-to-market are not included.

to offset the risk inherent in a short futures position. To finance the spot purchase, T-bills would be sold short.

In Table 17-10 an index arbitrage is illustrated in which $50 million of spot stock (which is very similar to the S&P 500) is bought at date 0. Since the spot index is $250 at that time, the $50 million spot position represents an ownership of 400 units of the S&P 500 stock index:

$$\$10,000,000/(\$25 \times 500) = 400$$

To offset the equity risk of this long position, 400 futures contracts on the S&P 500 Index are sold. The delivery date value of this position is known and equal to $51 million:

$$400(\$255 \times 500) = \$51,000,000$$

Finally, $50 million of three-month Treasury bills are sold to provide the financing of the spot stock purchase. Thus, there is no net cash flow at date 0.

At the index futures' delivery date, dividends on the spot stock are received and

TABLE 17-10 *Illustration of an Index Arbitrage*

		Delivery Date	
Today	*0*	$S_T = \$200$	$S_T = \$300$
Buy Stock Portfolio	−$50,000,000		
Sell 400 Futures at $255		+$51,000,000	+$51,000,000
Sell T-Bills	+ 50,000,000		
Delivery Date			
Dividends Received		+$ 500,000	+$ 500,000
Sell Stock Portfolio		+ 40,000,000	+ 60,000,000
Buy 400 Futures		− 40,000,000	− 60,000,000
T-Bills Mature		− 51,088,909	− 51,088,909
Net	$0	+$ 411,091	+$ 411,091

Calculations:

$50,000,000/(\$250 \times 500) = 400$
$400(\$255 \times 500)$ $= \$51,000,000$
$400(\$2.50 \times 500)$ $= \$ 500,000$
$50,000,000(\$200/\$250)$ $= \$40,000,000$
$50,000,000(\$300/\$250)$ $= \$60,000,000$
$50,000,000(1.09)^{0.25}$ $= \$51,088,909$

all positions are unwound: the stock is sold at prevailing prices, the futures are bought at identical prices, and the short Treasury bill position is paid off.

Note that this transaction involves only two unknown future cash flows: the delivery date values of the spot stock and the futures. But these two values must exactly offset each other, since the price of a futures contract must be equal to the spot good near the close of trading on the future's delivery date.

Triple Witching Hour. The potential for large arbitrage profits should keep the market price of index futures very close to the theoretical price shown in Equation 17.9. In fact, large institutions have set up computer-based systems which constantly monitor prevailing futures, spot, and Treasury bill prices to determine whether a profitable arbitrage is available. If so, the computer system generates trade orders to the spot, futures, and Treasury bill markets. Such trades are variants of what is called a *program trade.*[17] As a result, market prices rarely move outside a transaction cost bound around the theoretical futures price.

There are two features of index arbitrage which have had dramatic impacts on the delivery date volatility of common stocks. First, the trades are risk-free solely because the futures price *must* be equal to the spot index value at the moment of delivery — the futures exchange defines the futures price to be so at that time. Therefore, ar-

---

[17]A program trade is a large purchase or sale of many securities at virtually the same moment in time. When NYSE stocks are included in the "program," the designated order turnaround system is used to ensure simultaneous transactions.

bitrageurs will maintain their spot stock and futures positions for as long as they can on the delivery date, usually until the last hour or two. Second, settlement of the futures is in cash. Delivery of spot stock indexes is not allowed. Therefore, in order to unwind an index arbitrage position, any stock position must be closed directly on the stock exchange floor. If the original arbitrage position had consisted of being long stock, large quantities of stock will have to be sold late in the day of the futures delivery. If stock had originally been sold in the arbitrage, large quantities of stock will have to be purchased.

These two features of the arbitrage have had dramatic impacts on stock prices during the futures' delivery date. If the programs required large stock sales, the value of the Dow Jones Industrial Average would fall by 30 to 50 points in the last hour of trading. The opposite occurred if the programs required stock purchases. Arbitrageurs were indifferent to such large price savings in spot stock, since, whatever they lost on their spot stock transactions, they simultaneously won on their futures position. For example, assume that in closing out the arbitrage, large stock sales forced spot prices down. At the same time, however, index futures were being bought. Thus, the arbitrageur was not affected by such price savings.

But the general investing public was harmed. For example, public traders who happened to trade during the last hour of the delivery date often traded at prices substantially different from true equilibrium levels. In addition, the public perception grew that the stock market had become more volatile, solely because of the actions of index arbitrageurs.

This problem was particularly severe when index future delivery dates coincided with expiration dates on stock index options. In this case, arbitrages between the spot index, futures on the index, *and* options on the index were being closed out, resulting in abnormally large spot stock trading. Because three stock index positions were being traded at the same time, this time came to be known as the "triple witching hour."

Black Monday. Many people have blamed portfolio insurance and index arbitrage for Black Monday—October 19, 1987, when the Dow Jones Industrial Average fell by 508 points, 22.6% in one day. Though it is doubtful that they were the sole cause of such a massive price decline, they probably played a role.

The events surrounding Black Monday are discussed in Chapter 3 and will not be reviewed at length here. But some discussion is necessary. In the week prior to Monday, October 19, 1987, stock prices had fallen substantially. This meant that many portfolio insurers had to move out of stock and into Treasury bills by selling stock index futures. At the opening of trading on that Monday, stock futures were trading at sizable discounts from the spot stock indexes. This gap created a profit potential for index arbitrageurs, who began to sell spot stock and buy futures. This, of course, added to the downward pressure on spot stock values and *perhaps* created the need for additional sales of futures by portfolio insurers.

Whether the two forces caused a cascading decline in stock prices is debatable. It is clear, however, that they added to the volume of orders being placed and contributed to the virtual "meltdown" of the trading system. The NYSE's designated order turnaround system simply could not handle the volume of public and arbitrage orders being placed, and large delays occurred between the time at which a market order was placed and the time at which it was transacted. Since index arbitrage requires simultaneous trading between futures and spot stock, it became impossible to conduct an arbitrage. By noon, most index arbitrageurs had stopped their activities, thereby removing an economic force which would bring spot and futures prices into relative equilibrium.

OPTIONS ON FINANCIAL FUTURES

Recently option contracts on financial futures have been introduced and have gained wide public acceptance. An option on a financial future is exactly what its name implies—you buy (or write) a put or a call option on a financial futures contract. Why the underlying asset is a futures contract on some index as opposed to the actual spot index is discussed in a moment. First, we should look more closely at the terms of the major contracts.

Major Types of Options on Financial Futures

In Table 17-11 are shown contract specifications of three major options on financial futures. Prices of these options as of December 31, 19XX, are shown in Table 17-12.

Consider first the options on T-bond futures with an exercise price of $70 and a futures maturity of June. The underlying security on this option is a T-bond *future* on $100,000 of 8% coupon Treasury bonds. The option has an exercise date one month before the future's contract maturity. Thus, the option must be exercised before the end of May. The call buyer pays $2^{1}\!\%_{4}$% of the $100,000 contract value, or

TABLE 17-11 *Contract Specifications of Options on Financial Futures*

	Underlying Financial Future		
	Treasury Bonds	*S&P 500 Index*	*NYSE Index*
Exchange Listing	Chicago Board of Trade	Chicago Mercantile Exchange	New York Futures Exchange
Trading Unit	$100,000 Par Value of T-Bond Futures	One S&P Index Futures Contract	One NYSE Index Futures Contract
Option Premium	$\frac{1}{64}$ of 1% of a $100,000 Futures Contract	$500 Times Price Quotation	$500 Times Price Quotation
Maturity Date of Futures	March, June, September, December	March, June, September, December	March, June, September, December
Exercise Date of Options	One Month Prior to Maturity of Futures Contract	Last Trading Day of Underlying Index Futures	Last Trading Day of Underlying Index Futures

TABLE 17-12 *Prices of Options on Futures Contracts*

Options	Exercise Price	Call Exercise Dates			Put Exercise Dates		
		March	*June*	*September*	*March*	*June*	*September*
T-Bond	70	1-50	2-10	2-30	0-47	2-63	N/A
T-Bond	72	0-50	1-23	1-45	1-46	4-24	N/A
T-Bond	74	0-18	0-51	1-07	3-14	N/A	N/A
S&P 500	170	3.95	7.65	N/A	3.75	4.65	N/A
S&P 500	175	2.10	5.15	7.30	6.90	7.15	N/A
NYSE	98	2.50	4.55	6.10	2.05	2.50	2.60
NYSE	100	1.65	3.50	5.05	3.20	3.35	3.40

$2,156.25, for this call on the future. For this payment, the call buyer may exercise the option at any time before the end of May and buy the June T-bond future at $70,000.

Next, consider the call options on an NYSE futures contract with maturity in September. This option has two exercise prices, $98 and $100. The option with a $98 exercise price provides the call (put) buyer with the right to purchase (sell) a *futures contract on the NYSE Index* at $98 any time between now and the exercise date. The exercise date is the same as the delivery date of the futures contract. For this right, the call buyer pays a premium of $3,050 (6.10 × $500) and the put buyer pays $1,300 (2.60 × $500). The terms on the S&P 500 contract are similar, except the underlying instrument is a futures contract on the S&P 500 Index.

Options Versus Futures

Options and futures are distinctly different securities.[18] When held alone, they have quite different payoffs. For example, the purchase of a call option results in unlimited profits if the asset's price increases but limited losses if the price falls. The purchase of a financial future, however, results in both unlimited profits and unlimited losses. For the loss protection which an option provides, the buyer pays a price at the date of purchase in the form of a premium. No such premium is demanded on a financial future because a future provides no downside risk protection. Futures require a cash payment only at maturity (ignoring mark to market) and in an amount equal to the spot price which is expected to prevail at maturity.

As an example, assume you are the manager of a common stock portfolio which is currently worth $10 million and is very similar to the NYSE Composite Index. During the past year, the average NYSE stock has had a return greater than you had expected and you would like to protect the profits earned on your portfolio. You can

---

[18]They can be combined with other common stock and debt to duplicate each other, as seen earlier in this chapter. In their "raw" form, however, they are different securities.

FIGURE 17-1 *Protection of Portfolio Value with Futures and Options*

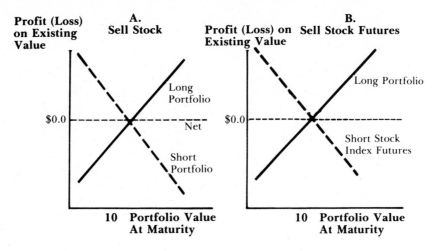

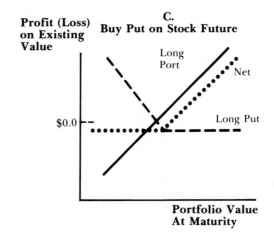

do this by: (1) selling the stocks, (2) selling a futures contract on the stocks, or (3) buying puts on the portfolio. The outcomes of each strategy are shown in Figure 17-1. Panel A depicts the first alternative—simply sell the stock. The net position would be zero. As stock prices rise or fall you would be unaffected because you don't own any stock.

Panel B depicts the outcomes if you sell stock index futures contracts against the portfolio.[19] The economic effect of being long the portfolio and short the futures is identical to selling the stock outright. Your net stock position is zero, so changes in

----

[19]The correct number of futures to sell can be calculated using Equation 17.12.

stock prices have no effect on your wealth. Selling the stock outright and selling stock futures are, economically, the same thing. (The primary reason to use the futures alternative is that it might reduce transaction costs associated with the rapid sale of stock.)

The use of options, however, will always leave you with a position in the securities and some future payoff. For example, panel C shows that a long stock portfolio position combined with a long put position (on an equivalent portfolio) results in a limited loss and unlimited potential gain. The purchase of the put provides insurance against declines in the portfolio's value.

We could evaluate a wide variety of option combinations with the portfolio. The results, however, would be identical to those given in Chapter 16, so there is no need to do so again. If we were to repeat our analysis, however, an important difference between the use of options and the use of financial futures would emerge: Options provide a larger number of potential payoff patterns to choose from. Futures result in only two possible outcomes: the claim to stock is either increased or decreased.

Why Options on Futures Exist

Option contracts are available on actual spot securities such as the S&P 500 Index, the NYSE Index, and Treasury bonds. So why create options on futures contracts for each? What is gained by having the underlying security a futures contract instead of the spot security? Three principal reasons have been offered:

1. *Delivery is eased.* Using a futures contract as the security underlying the option eases delivery in two ways. First, the quantity of futures is unlimited. If you are forced to deliver a T-bond future as the writer of a call, for example, you could simply *create* a new T-bond future by purchasing one in the futures market. In contrast, the supply of actual spot T-bonds is limited. Second, there is a greater certainty about what is being delivered when a future is used. (This is true only for T-bonds.) The deliverable instrument is a future on a $100,000 par 8% long-term Treasury bond. When the spot security is deliverable, one could receive any number of different types of coupons or maturities.
2. *Price accuracy.* Options on futures and the futures themselves are traded almost side by side on the same exchanges. Thus, the option prices can continuously reflect existing futures prices. In contrast, spot securities are traded in other markets and their prices are available with a slight lag.
3. *Flexibility.* The option on a future provides the opportunity to acquire the future without incurring an incremental transaction cost.

The relative importance of each of these reasons depends on the type of securities being traded. For example, ease of delivery is quite important for T-bond contracts. As a result, options on T-bond futures are more widely used than are options on spot T-bonds. However, ease of delivery is less important for stock index option contracts.

As a result, options on stock index futures are used less than are options on the spot stock indexes.

SPOT INSTRUMENTS ON AGGREGATE STOCK INDEXES

Throughout the 1980s it became clear that large institutions were more interested in trading aggregate portfolios than individual stocks. The important question had changed from "What stocks should I trade?" to "What asset classes should I trade?"

In 1989 new forms of securities were created—spot instruments which represented a claim to an aggregate stock index. These securities have the potential to revolutionize how the public invests and speculates. Prior to their introduction, one could emulate the returns on an aggregate stock index either by buying all stocks in the index or by buying futures (or options) on the index. The first alternative can be costly and difficult to maintain (particularly the reinvestment of dividends in proper proportions). And many investors are prohibited from using futures and options or are unfamiliar with how they can be used.

Index Participations

The first new form of security is called an *index participation* (IP). Two stock exchanges currently offer IPs: the AMEX and the Philadelphia Stock Exchange. An index participation is an exchange-traded security which gives the buyer the equivalent of a long position in the stocks of an entire stock index. To eliminate the opportunity for arbitrage profits, the value of an IP is very closely tied to the underlying value of the stock index on which the IP is based. Each trade in an IP has both a buyer and a seller. The buyer has an ownership position in the index. The seller has a short position in the index. Each quarter, dividends are paid to buyers by the sellers.

IPs are currently available on the S&P 500 Index and two proxies for the Dow Jones Industrial Average (the Major Market Index offered by AMEX and the Blue Chip Index offered by the Philadelphia Exchange). In our examples, we will speak only of the S&P 500 IPs. Trades in the other two are virtually equivalent.

IPs on the S&P 500 Index are quoted in dollars in decimal format. Price quotes are equal to 1/10th the quoted value of the underlying index. A single trading unit represents 100 IPs. As an illustration, assume that the S&P 500 Index is currently 301. The quoted price of one IP would be $30.10 and the purchase of one round lot would cost $3,010.00 (plus brokerage fees). Purchasers of IPs may also use margin of up to 50% as with the purchase of any common stock.

Buyers may hold the security for as long as they wish and receive dividends at each quarter-end. There are three ways in which a long position can be closed. First, one could simply sell the security in the secondary market. The sale price might not be exactly identical to 1/10th the S&P 500 Index at that time, but it will be very close. Second, one day each quarter is designated as the *cash-out* day (the third Friday of the last month of a calendar quarter). On this cash-out day, IP owners may receive a cash value based on the value of the S&P 500 at its opening. Finally, owners of large blocks of IPs (500 units for the S&P 500 IP) may actually receive the physical delivery of the 500 stocks in the index. Since fractional shares cannot be delivered, a cash value is also provided to make up for the difference in the value of securities delivered and the value of the IPs.

Stock Exchange Portfolios

At the date this text was last revised, the NYSE had just announced its intention to offer a product which would compete with IPs. However, pending SEC approval, the NYSE was unable to provide much information about the security. The NYSE's security is to be called the *stock exchange portfolio* (SEP) and is actually more a service than a new security. The purchaser of an SEP will actually receive the 500 stocks underlying the S&P 500 Index, and his or her brokerage account will actually be credited with the securities. In the same manner, the seller of an SEP will have the securities deducted from his or her brokerage account. Thus, an SEP is more a way of trading the S&P 500 than it is a security. But if approved by the SEC, this new investment form should reduce the costs of index arbitrage and portfolio hedging.

SUMMARY

Futures contracts on financial instruments are a phenomenon of the 1980s. At present, active markets exist on:

1. Short-term debt instruments, such as T-bills, CDs, and Eurodollar deposits
2. Long-term debt instruments, such as T-bonds, T-notes, and GNMAs
3. Stock indexes, such as the NYSE and S&P 500

Options on various futures have also been recently offered.

Individuals who go long a financial futures contract are legally obligated to buy the security at a stipulated price in a stipulated month. Individuals who go short a contract are required to deliver the security at the stipulated price in the stipulated month. Physical delivery rarely occurs, however, since long and short positions are usually offset before the contract's maturity date.

The basic purpose of financial futures is to reduce price risk by hedging one's physical security position with an opposite futures position. A perfect hedge which eliminates all risk is difficult to achieve in practice, but risk can be substantially reduced by selecting futures which (1) mature close to when cash is needed or will be available, (2) have a contract value similar to the amount being hedged, and (3) have a deliverable security similar to the security you intend to buy or sell.

Financial futures are one more tool with which the risk and return position of a portfolio can be managed. They open up a variety of new ways to speculate and can easily alter the market risk exposure of a portfolio (the stock/bond mix). However, similar to options, they are complex instruments and should be used only after they are well understood.

REVIEW PROBLEMS

1. You are given the following price quotations on spot T-bills as well as on T-bill and CD futures. Assume the futures mature on the last day of the month and ignore marking to market.

T-Bill Spot Price Quotations

Maturity	Life	Discount
March 30	30 days	10.00%
June 30	120 days	11.00%

Futures Price Quotations

Security	Maturity	Contract	Discount
T-Bill Future	March 30	$1 million – 90 day spot	11.80%
CD Future	March 30	$1 million – 90 day spot	12.50%

   a. Find the market price for $1,000,000 in par value of each T-bill instrument.
   b. Do you think the T-bill future is fairly priced?
   c. How can you create a riskless arbitrage?
   d. The treasurer of a corporation will need to sell $50 million of 90-day commercial paper in middle June and is considering a hedge in either T-bill futures or CD futures. Use the following estimates to determine which contract should be traded and the optimal number of contracts to trade:

	Standard Deviation of Instrument 15 Days Before Contract Maturity	Correlation with		
		Commercial Paper	T-Bills	CDs
Commercial Paper	5.0	1.00		
T-Bill Future	5.0	.90	1.00	
CD Future	5.0	.95	.85	1.00

2. You are the administrator of a portfolio worth $500 million. Over the long run you would like to maintain a cash/bond/stock mix of 5%/30%/65%. Owing to recent movements in the markets the present mix is 5%/40%/55%. You plan to adjust this mix to that desired by using financial futures. Assume that interest rates are now 10%.
   a. Your bonds have a duration equal to what you would like to maintain, $D_1 = 5$ years. The cheapest-to-deliver T-bond has a duration of 8.2 years and a delivery factor of 0.975. How many T-bond futures should you buy or sell?
   b. The beta of your stock portfolio is close to 1.2 and that of the NYSE is close to 1.0. If you wish to maintain the 1.2 beta, how many NYSE futures should you buy or sell? Assume the spot NYSE is trading at $120 and futures on the NYSE are $130.

Solutions

1. a. March 30 Spot T-Bill $= \$1 \text{ million} \left[1 - 1(0.1) \dfrac{30}{360} \right]$

$\qquad\qquad\qquad\quad = \$991,666.67$

$\quad$ June 30 Spot T-Bill $= \$1 \text{ million} \left[1 - 1(0.11) \dfrac{120}{360} \right]$

$\qquad\qquad\qquad\quad = \$963,333.33$

$\quad$ T-Bill Future $\qquad = \$1 \text{ million} \left[1 - 1(0.118) \dfrac{90}{360} \right]$

$\qquad\qquad\qquad\quad = \$970,500$

(or $1 million − $25 per basis point × 1180 basis points)

b. The return on the 90-day T-bill which could be delivered on the future should be identical to the return on a forward contract created with spot T-bills. Forward contract (90-day) yield:

	Today	March 30	June 30
Buy 1.0 June 30	−$963,333.33	−	$1,000,000
Short Equivalent March 30 ($963,333 ÷ 991,666)	963,333.33	−$971,428.56	−
Net	$ 0.0	$971,428.56	$1,000,000

$\qquad\qquad\qquad\qquad\qquad$ 90-day return $= 2.94\%$

Futures contract (90-day) yield:

$$\frac{\text{Sell}}{\text{Buy}} - 1.0 = \frac{1,000,000}{\$970,500} - 1 = 3.04\%$$

One or more of the following must be true: (1) the future is underpriced, (2) the June 30 spot is overpriced, (3) the March 30 spot is underpriced.

c. A riskless arbitrage would be:

	Today	Today	March 30
Buy 1.0 Future		$ 0.0	−$970,500.00
Sell 1.0 June 30 Spot		$963,333.33	
Buy 0.971428 March 30 Spot		− 963,333.33	971,428.56
On March 30			
Sell Future at Any Price (say, $1)			1.00
Buy June 30 Spot *at the Same Price*			−1.00
Net Cash Flow		$ 0.0	$ 928.56

You have no capital invested, no risk, and a known dollar profit.

d. Since commercial paper and CDs are more highly correlated, the hedge should be on CD futures (note that the standard deviations are all equal):

$$Q_F^* = \$50 \text{ million} \left(\frac{5}{5}\right) 0.95$$

$$= \$47.5 \text{ million}$$

Each contract is on \$1 million of CDs. Thus either 47 or 48 contracts would be purchased.

2. a. First you intend to *sell* futures which are the equivalent of \$50 million in five-year duration bonds. The dollar duration of this would be:

$$5 \left(\frac{.11 - .1}{1.1}\right) (\$50 \text{ million}) = \$2.27 \text{ million}$$

Next, the dollar duration of a single T-bond futures contract is:

$$\frac{8.2}{0.975} (\$100,000) \left(\frac{.11 - .1}{1.1}\right) = \$7,645.69$$

The number of T-bond contracts which is equivalent to \$2.27 million in dollar duration is:

$$\frac{\$2,270,000}{\$7,645.69} = 297$$

b. You would *buy* stock futures which are the equivalent of \$50 million in stock with a beta of 1.2. This would be:

$$\frac{\$50,000,000}{120 \times \$500} \times 1.2 = 1,000 \text{ contracts}$$

QUESTIONS AND PROBLEMS

1. How does a futures contract differ from an option contract, both legally and economically?
2. What is the difference between a futures contract and a forward contract?
3. What advantages can you see to the futures exchanges' stepping in once a trade has occurred and becoming the buyer to the seller and the seller to the buyer?
4. It is January 1, and a 90-day T-bill future maturing in June is trading at an 8.85% (360-day) discount. You buy five contracts.
   a. What are you now legally obligated to do under the contract?
   b. How much margin must you provide?
   c. At what discount will you be required to provide cash in order to restore the initial margin?
   d. If you sell two weeks later at a discount of 8.95%, what is your dollar profit or loss?
   e. If you are considering holding to maturity and selling five contracts at that time (instead of taking delivery), what is your expected profit if the markets are in equilibrium?
   f. As of January 1, what is the dollar duration of your position?
5. It is now March 1. You buy a September T-bond future selling at \$95.25 to yield 8.57%. On June 1 you cover the long future by selling at \$99.25 (8.09% yield) and simultaneously buy spot T-bonds at \$99.75. What is your net purchase price?

6. A commercial bank officer expects that the bank will be issuing $500 million worth of 90-day certificates of deposit in March. It is now January 1, and 90-day CD futures maturing in March are quoted at a 9.70% discount.

   a. What is the implied hedge which is available? Illustrate why (in concept) this hedge would eliminate uncertainty about financing costs to the bank.

   b. In practice, risk would not be eliminated. Why?

7. A commercial bank now has $500 million of 90-day certificates of deposit outstanding. When these mature, they will probably be rolled over into new CDs if the bank pays the competitive rates which will exist at that time. It is now January 1, and 90-day CD futures maturing in March are quoted at a 9.70% discount.

   a. What is the implied hedge?

   b. Compare the situation with that in question 6. How are these situations different?

8. Thirty-day and 60-day spot T-bills are now selling for $99.25 and $98.50, respectively. In addition, you observe that the price of a 30-day T-bill future which matures in 30 days is $99. Create an arbitrage which will take advantage of any price imbalances.

9. Spot and futures prices are shown below for the close of trading on January 1:

Spot T-Bill Instruments

Maturity	Quoted Discount
90 days	8.0%
180 days	8.2%
270 days	8.4%
360 days	8.6%

Futures on 90-Day T-Bills

Maturity	Quoted Discount
Current	?
90 days	8.0%
180 days	9.0%
270 days	?

   a. What should the discount be on the futures which are currently maturing?

   b. If the markets are now in equilibrium, what should be the discount on the 270-day futures? (Ignore marking to market.)

   c. Why did part b require that marking to market be ignored?

   d. Again, ignore marking to market. Create an arbitrage on the 90- and 180-day futures.

10. Why should a perfect hedge work?

11. What is the importance of delivery in futures pricing? Contrast the delivery features of futures on T-bills, T-bonds, and stock indexes.

12. On December 30, T-bond futures maturing exactly two years later were quoted at 67-24.

    a. Interpret this price quote.

    b. Why is the price so low? These are, after all, default- and call-free U.S. Treasury obligations.

    c. In deciding what price is actually paid for any T-bonds actually delivered, the clearing corporation divides the price quotation by a delivery factor which is generally less than 1.0. Why do they do this, and why do you suppose it is less than 1.0?

13. It is now January 1, and you hold $5 million par value of corporate bonds with a market value of $4,893,750. You sell 50 T-bond contracts at $1,025 per bond. By March 15 the

basis (between the future and the average corporate bond value) has changed from $46.25 to $51.25. If you simultaneously sell spot and buy futures, what is your net selling price? What is your gain or loss on the initial corporate bond value?

14. People hedge in financial futures to reduce price risk. What must happen to the hedge basis during the life of a hedge in order for the hedge to be perfect, i.e., to eliminate all price risk? What features of a financial future should one look at in order to reduce price risks as much as possible?

15. You are short financial futures and long securities. Do you want the basis to increase or decrease?

16. The basis spread between December and June T-bond futures is now 7 basis points (December price less June price). During the next month you expect this to widen. Create a spread between the two contracts.

17. The optimal hedge as shown in Equation 17.1 requires estimates of σ_S, σ_F, and r_{FS}. Assume you are hedging with a contract that has a good history available. How might you statistically estimate each term?

18. Assume that you intend to borrow $100 million in mid-February. It is now January 1, and 90-day T-bill futures maturing at the end of March are quoted at an 8.0% discount. Assume you have statistically estimated the following:

- Standard deviation of futures prices = $2
- Standard deviation of your borrowing price = $3
- Correlation between S and $F = 0.7$

What is the optimal hedge?

19. Outline a basic trading strategy for each of the cases presented below. You may buy or sell any of the financial futures contracts discussed in the chapter. Be sure to specify the contract's maturity month.

a. It is January 1, and the treasurer of a life insurance company maintains large holdings of U.S. Treasury bills, as follows:

1-month maturity	$1.5 million
3-month maturity	0.7 million
6-month maturity	1.0 million
1-year maturity	2.0 million

The treasurer wishes to hold these bills in order to protect the firm from temporary liquidity needs, but wishes to protect against losses in value if interest rates rise.

b. The investment adviser to a college endowment fund has been told that in early June a major contribution of $500,000 will be received. Believing that rates are now at a peak, the adviser will be investing the contribution in T-bonds.

c. In early March a mutual fund manager has a large position in intermediate- and long-term corporate bonds. He is forecasting a rise in interest rates.

d. The situation is the same as in part c, except the manager is forecasting a decline in interest rates.

e. A real estate investment trust buys mortgages from local financial institutions and then packages them for resale to the market. It is February 15, and the package should be ready for sale by middle August.

f. The treasurer of a corporation estimates that on May 15, $10 million in commercial paper will have to be sold to finance seasonal working capital needs. The treasurer believes that by May commercial paper rates will be higher than existing rates on June financial futures.

g. The situation is the same as in part f, except the treasurer believes June futures rates are higher than will exist in May.

20. What does dollar duration measure?

21. It is January 1. The duration of your bond portfolio as measured by D_1 is 6.0 years, its market value is $700 million, and its yield to maturity is 10%. Assume that D_1 for the cheapest-to-deliver T-bond is 6.5 years and has a delivery factor of 0.90.
  a. How many futures contracts would you buy or sell to increase the effective value of the portfolio to $800 million with $D_1 = 6.0$ years?
  b. How many futures contracts would you buy or sell to leave the market value at $700 million but reduce its duration to four years?
  c. In either case above, what factors might cause the holding you take on to be wrong?
  d. Ignoring part c, what would you do when the futures mature?

22. Hedges of a stock portfolio using stock index futures work best if the portfolio is similar to the underlying futures index. Why is this so?

23. Stock index futures can increase or decrease a portfolio's systematic *market* risk. They cannot hedge unsystematic risks. Why?

24. You are the administrator of a stock portfolio which is now worth $1 billion and has a beta of 1.1. You would like to reduce the beta to 1.0 and reduce the equity claim to $900 million. Futures prices of the NYSE index contract are 115.
  a. How could you accomplish your goal with futures?
  b. Actually, you have many maturity dates to choose from. How might you decide which to use?
  c. What would you do when the futures mature?
  d. Why might this not work out the way you wish?

25. On December 31, six-month T-bills were priced to provide a six-month return of 4.28%. (This is the effective return, not the discount.) At the same time, the S&P 500 Index closed at $167.24, and the futures contract on the S&P 500 with a June maturity closed at $173.00. Dividends expected on the S&P 500 between January and June of the next year were $3.70. Was the future priced according to the arbitrage valuation model?

26. A general model for valuing stock index futures is not currently available. However, an arbitrage model is often used to approximate the value of a stock index future.
  a. What is the arbitrage which is conducted?
  b. Is the current futures price equal to the expected value of the index when the contract matures?
  c. What is the role of dividends in this model?
  d. What problems does the model assume away?

27. Today is June 30, and you observe the following market data:

S&P 500 Index:	
Current price	$300.00
Dividend to be paid in 3 months	$ 3.00
Treasury Bills:	
Quoted discount on 3-month 90-day bill	8.00%
S&P 500 Index Future	
Quoted price of a future with a	
3-month (90-day) delivery date	$324.00

a. Is the future properly priced?

b. Illustrate the index arbitrage which could be conducted. (Trade in spot stock now worth $100 million and assume you can trade fractional units.)

c. You manage a $500 million portfolio of equities and Treasury bills. At present, $250 million of equities with a beta of 1.1 are held. You would prefer that the portfolio effectively have $300 million of equity and that the equity beta be 1.0. How many futures could you trade to achieve this outcome without trading the spot equity?

d. Will the futures/spot position taken in part c result in the same portfolio values in three months as an adjustment of the spot portfolio to your desired mix? Illustrate for S&P 500 values of $280 and $320. Explain any difference.

28. On January 1 you are evaluating how various options on T-bonds, futures on T-bonds, and options on T-bond futures might be used on a $100 million bond portfolio. The portfolio includes non-Treasury issues, but they are all high-grade long-term corporates. December 31 closing prices were:

Options on Spot T-Bonds			*Premium*	
Underlying Issue	Strike Price	Expiration	Call	Put
$100,000 12% T-Bonds Due 8/2013	104	March	1.02	2.20

Options on T-Bond Futures			*Premium*	
Underlying Issue	Strike Price	Futures Maturity	Call	Put
$100,000 T-Bond Future	70	March	1-50	0-47

T-Bond Futures		
Underlying Issue	Settle Price	Maturity
$100,000 T-Bonds	$71\frac{2}{32}$	March

Illustrate how these contracts could be used in the following situations and explain the risks you face in each case.

a. You intend to sell the bonds in March and invest the proceeds in stocks.

b. You are worried about large interest rate increases and would like to limit the possible losses if this were to occur.

c. You are unsure which way interest rates will move but are confident that they will move substantially.

d. You don't believe interest rates will move much in either direction but think that they are just as likely to increase as to decrease.

e. You intend to invest an additional $100 million in March in similar bonds.

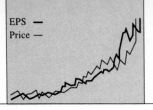

CHAPTER

18 Other Investment Alternatives

This chapter concludes our analysis of various marketable securities with a discussion of (1) investment companies, (2) international investment, and (3) real estate investment. Investment company securities have been actively used for decades in the management of small to medium-size portfolios. They are relatively easy to understand, and they can be acquired as easily as any common stock. International and real estate securities, however, have only recently gained serious attention by the U.S. investment community. Their potential role in portfolio management is more complex, and they are more difficult to trade. As such, they are likely candidates for large portfolios. Because investment companies are the most actively used, most of this chapter will be devoted to them.

Each of these three investment alternatives provides the same potential advantage when added to a portfolio—diversification. Managers of investment companies as well as proponents of real estate and international securities often claim that such securities can provide abnormal risk-adjusted returns. Whether this is true or not is not clear. Numerous statistical tests of investment company returns suggest that chance alone can explain the ex post good and bad performers. Yet most of these tests are based on the suspect capital asset pricing model. Rigorous tests of international and real estate performance haven't been conducted to date because a trustworthy return history is lacking. So we simply do not know whether these securities can, in fact, provide abnormal returns. Nonetheless, we do know that they can provide substantial reductions in portfolio risk through increased diversification.

INVESTMENT COMPANIES

Shares of investment companies differ from other securities in two major respects:

1. The amount of *diversifiable risk is often minimal.* Funds provided by investment company shareholders are pooled and reinvested in numerous individual securities, each of which would have considerable diversifiable risk if held in isolation. When held in a large portfolio, much of this diversifiable risk is offset among the securities held. As a result, investment companies can offer an easy way to diversify.

2. The assets of an investment company represent pools of marketable securities which are *managed according to specified objectives*. As a result, individuals can match their unique investment objectives with those of the investment company and, they hope, gain better performance under professional management than they would obtain on their own.

Assume that ABC Fund has just been formed with the specific objectives of maximizing capital growth while incurring moderate risk. The fund would issue its own common shares and use the proceeds to purchase securities which the management adviser believes will best meet the fund's stated objectives. Assume that 2 million common shares are sold at $10 per share. To meet the risk objective, the $20 million proceeds might be invested in a combination of stocks and bonds having an average beta of about 1.0. To meet the capital growth objective, management would attempt to identify corporations with low dividend payouts and potentially large equity returns. Individuals who might find the shares of ABC Fund attractive could be characterized as having a moderate to high tax bracket, small current income needs, few other security holdings, and little or no knowledge about security selection. In sum, ABC Fund can provide something not available from a *direct* investment in common stocks, bonds, options, futures, etc., in that it is a well-diversified pool of securities which are professionally managed according to a specified objective.

Organizational Forms

The Investment Company Act of 1940 defined three types of investment companies:

1. Face-amount certificate companies
2. Unit investment trusts
3. Managed investment companies

Face-Amount Certificate Companies. Face-amount certificate companies are the least common. They specify a fixed dollar amount which each certificate holder will receive at maturity and are therefore essentially debt obligations.

Unit Investment Trusts. Unit investment trusts are *unmanaged, fixed* security portfolios. The sponsor of a unit trust purchases a large number of securities and places them under the physical control of an independent trustee. In return, the trustee provides the sponsor with claims to the securities known as *redeemable trust certificates*. The trust certificates are then sold to the general public at a price equal to their *net asset value* plus a small markup. Net asset value equals the net market value of the fund's assets divided by the number of shares which the fund has outstanding. For example, a brokerage firm might sponsor a unit trust by purchasing $100 million of various short-term money market instruments and placing them in the safekeeping of a local bank. The bank would then issue, say, 10 million trust certificates, each having a net asset value of $10. The brokerage firm would in turn offer the certificates to the public at, say, $10.10. The extra $0.10, referred to as the *load*, compensates the sponsor for expenses and provides a fair profit. After the initial sale the sponsor will make a market in the certificates by buying from those who wish to sell and using the repurchased certificates to sell to those who wish to buy. The package of securities underlying a unit trust certificate is (except in very rare cases) kept unchanged. Any interest, dividends, and principal repayments are distributed immediately to certificate holders. Normally, trust assets are debt instruments with fixed lives, so that the trust goes out of existence as the bonds are repaid. Unit trust certificates generally have claims to short-term money market instruments, tax-exempt municipal obligations, and, less frequently, long-term corporate bonds.

Unit trusts were particularly important prior to the Tax Reform Act of 1976, when they were the only way of legally packaging a diversified set of municipal bonds and passing the income on to the fundholder tax-free. Since the 1976 Tax Reform Act, managed investment companies are also allowed to distribute municipal bond income as tax-free income.

Managed Investment Companies. Managed investment companies differ from unit trusts in that an investment adviser is hired by the company's board of directors to *actively manage* the fund's assets. While the fund's board of directors will specify an overall objective which the fund's portfolio holdings should fulfill, most advisers have broad discretionary powers over which securities are held and how often the portfolio is turned over. Legally, the fund's board of directors selects the investment adviser. In reality, it's the investment adviser who creates the fund and selects the board of directors.

Investment advisory firms often manage a variety of different funds, each with its own unique investment objective. This provides potential advantages to both the investment adviser and the investor in the fund. The adviser can appeal to a wider clientele of potential investors, which should result in a larger dollar amount of funds being managed. In turn, the adviser's gross income is increased since advisory fees are based in part on the dollar amount of funds being managed. Investors gain in three possible ways: (1) by being able to select a fund which most closely meets their needs, (2) by being allowed to exchange shares in one fund for those of another fund at reduced costs if both funds are managed by the same adviser, and (3) by lower management fees created by the economies of scale inherent in managing larger sums of money which are (at least partially) passed on to owners.

Open-End Funds

Open-end investment companies (commonly referred to as *mutual funds*) account for the largest portion of the business, representing about 90% of all investment company assets at the end of 1988. Open-end companies stand ready to buy or sell shares in the fund whenever the public desires. Share transactions are *not* made between an owner who wishes to sell and a potential owner who wishes to buy, as is the case with other types of securities. Instead, buyers purchase shares directly from the fund and sellers *redeem* their shares by selling directly to the fund. The total number of shares outstanding will vary from day to day: hence the term *open-end*.

All share redemptions and sales are priced at the mutual fund's net asset value. For example, consider the balance sheet of XYZ Fund:

	$ Million
Market Value of Security Portfolio	$550.0
Cash	40.0
Receivables	35.0
Market Value of Assets	$625.0
Current Liabilities	($20.0)
Equity Market Value	$605.0

If 20 million shares are outstanding, net asset value would be $30.25 ($605.0 ÷ 20). Net asset value is calculated twice each day and is based upon the latest offering prices of securities held in the portfolio. Purchases and sales of mutual fund shares are cleared at the first net asset value calculated after the purchase or sale request.

The open-end feature of these funds requires that the management adviser maintain considerable investment liquidity and be sensitive to changes in investors' objectives. On any one day share redemptions may exceed new share sales, in which case the fund may need to sell large blocks of portfolio assets to provide the necessary cash. The portfolio must also be liquid enough to meet extended periods of net redemptions caused by investors' disenchantment with past performance or future prospects. Throughout the 1960s and the early 1970s, purchases of mutual fund shares by the public exceeded redemptions. However, the industry encountered large *net* redemptions in almost every year from 1971 to 1980. This period of sustained net redemptions not only caused mutual funds to restrict portfolio holdings to highly marketable securities, but also changed the types of products offered by the industry and the industry's marketing strategy. As shown in Figure 18-1, net purchases of non–money market mutual funds increased during the 1980s as the stock market increased in value.

Money Market Funds. A dramatic example of how the industry reacted to changing conditions in the 1970s was the creation of money market funds in 1973. The classic mutual fund had previously invested primarily in long-term instruments. However, in the mid-1970s the industry was faced with major declines in net asset values, large net redemptions, and high interest rates. To reattract investment funds, money market funds were created for the purpose of investing in short-term, low-risk, and highly marketable money market instruments. Portfolio securities generally consist of Treasury bills, negotiable certificates of deposit, prime commercial paper, etc. During periods of high interest rates money market funds are especially popular among conservative investors who would otherwise invest in saving accounts or certificates of deposit offered by banks and savings and loan associations. Since a ceiling was placed on the interest rate which banks and savings and loans could pay on deposits, money market funds were quite attractive during periods when money market yields exceeded this ceiling. At the end of 1974 there were 15 money market funds managing $1.7 billion in assets. Four years later, 61 funds existed and managed $10.9 billion in assets.

FIGURE 18-1 *Sales and Redemptions of Mutual Funds*

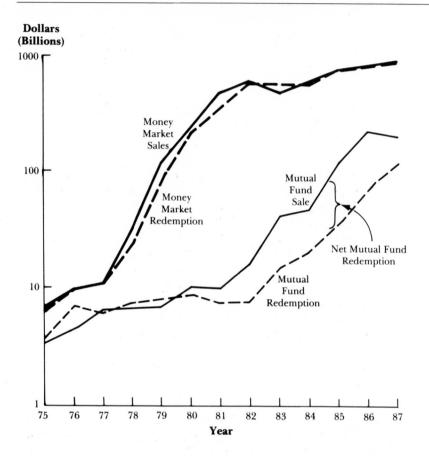

Some money market funds have arrangements with a bank which allow investors in the fund to write checks on their investment holdings. The bank simply clears the check by redeeming a required number of the investor's shares in the fund. Restrictions are usually placed on the minimum size of the check.

Load Versus No-Load Funds. The load on a mutual fund share is the commission paid to acquire the share. When an individual buys a load fund, a price equal to the share's net asset value plus a load is paid. Typically, commissions are not paid when the share is redeemed (thus the term *front-end load*). A typical load is *stated* to be 8.5% (although a few *low-load* mutual funds have stated loads of 4% or less). The *effective* load is higher than the stated load, however. For example, if you invest $10,000 in an 8.5% load fund, the broker takes a load commission of $850 and you actually acquire $9,150 in shares. While the stated load is 8.5%, the effective load is 9.3% ($850 ÷ $9,150). Shares in load funds are sold exclusively by brokers or other marketing organizations. The load represents compensation to the broker for services provided to the customer in selecting an appropriate fund and clearing the transaction. However, even when the load is averaged over both the initial purchase and the eventual sale, load charges are larger than brokerage fees on a normal stock purchase and sale.

No-load mutual funds are bought and sold at net asset value without a commission. A few charge a redemption fee of 0.5% to cover clerical costs and discourage redemption, but usually no transaction costs are paid. No-load funds are not available from brokers (for obvious reasons) and must be bought directly from the fund itself. No-load mutual funds can be identified in the financial press by the letters N.L. listed beside the net asset value quotation. In addition, they advertise extensively and have formed an industry association which provides basic fund information.

The historical performance of the average load fund does not appear to be any different from that of no-load funds, even before the load fee is considered. As investors began to recognize this in the mid-1970s, the demand for load fund shares dropped, and many funds changed their status from load to no-load. The only apparent advantage associated with load funds seems to be that a broker provides advice about which funds best meet the investor's objectives.

Closed-End Funds

In contrast to open-end funds, a *closed-end* fund does not stand ready to buy or sell shares in the fund. Instead, transactions in closed-end shares occur between two market participants trading in the secondary markets, just as for any other common stock. The only time a closed-end fund is directly affected by market transactions is when the shares are initially offered to the public in the primary offering. Brokerage fees identical to those of other common stocks are paid at purchase and sale.

The investment objectives and management styles of closed-end funds are similar to those of open-end funds. However, closed-end funds *do not* sell at net asset value, although the funds do calculate net asset value twice a day. A closed-end fund's prices are affected by supply-and-demand conditions for its shares prevailing at any one time. Closed-end shares may sell at a premium above net asset value or, more commonly, at a discount from net asset value. Figure 18-2 shows average discounts and premiums on eight closed-end investment companies from 1981 through 1986.

No one is really sure why closed-end funds sell at prices other than net asset value. Some people believe the market evaluates the management of a fund and pays a corresponding premium or discount. Funds managed by advisers who are expected to perform poorly are hypothesized to sell at discounts. While net asset value may be worth $50, management is expected to lose, say, $5 of this value through excessive brokerage fees and bad decisions. Thus, the shares are effectively worth $45. Some evidence that substantial discounts from net asset value are related to poor performance does, in fact, exist. Other people believe that a *mutual fund's* net asset value overstates its true after-tax worth to owners. It is said that when people buy a mutual fund, they are buying a tax liability. A large part of a mutual fund's net asset value can represent unrealized capital gains on which taxes will have to be paid by the investor when the management adviser sells the securities, resulting in a realized gain. Since net asset value doesn't account for this potential tax liability, it overstates the

FIGURE 18-2 *Discounts or Premiums on Closed-End Stocks*

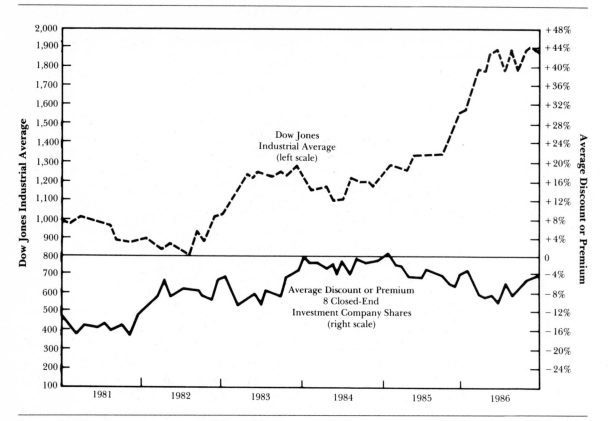

Source: Reprinted by permission from the *Wiesenberger Investment Companies Service*, 1987 Edition, copyright © 1987, Warren, Gorham, and Lamont, New York, p. 20.

fund's true worth. The discount associated with closed-end funds could represent the average value of this tax impact.[1] Others say that the net asset value of the fund cannot be properly measured if some assets are not highly marketable.

Regardless of why discounts and premiums exist, they are a fact of life. And since the size of a discount or premium changes over time, an additional risk to that inherent in the fund's security portfolio is added to ownership of closed-end companies. While some of this risk can be diversified by holding many closed-end funds, much of it is nondiversifiable.

If a closed-end fund is selling at a discount, why doesn't the investment adviser simply repurchase the fund's shares and sell its assets? For example, a fund with net asset value of $50 which is selling at $45 could sell $50 in securities and repurchase

---

[1]Of course, this argument is unable to explain the existence of premiums over net asset values.

a share at $45. The $5 difference would benefit remaining shareholders. While this makes economic sense and a number of closed-end funds have indeed liquidated assets, it is a rare occurrence. The repurchase of shares and sale of assets lowers total asset value, and since most management advisers are compensated based on a percentage (usually 0.5%) of the total assets being managed, their income would fall. In addition, if this strategy were carried to its legitimate end, the fund would be totally liquidated and the adviser out of a job.

Investment Strategies

Stated Objectives. Virtually all investment funds have an explicitly stated investment objective. This objective suggests the types of risks which the fund will incur, the split between current income and capital growth, industries or securities in which the fund intends to concentrate, portfolio turnover, etc. While these may change over long periods of time, or management may temporarily take security positions which are contrary to the stated objective, the fund's objective provides information which is quite helpful to potential investors.

Objectives of most funds can be categorized as follows:

1. *Aggressive growth:* Common stock funds stressing capital growth and minimal current income. Portfolio risk is above average. Portfolio turnover is usually high.
2. *Growth:* Less growth and portfolio risk than with aggressive growth funds.
3. *Growth and income:* An equal commitment to current income and capital appreciation. Such a fund may have lower portfolio turnover than growth funds. Some bonds will often be held, and portfolio risk is equal to or slightly less than that in the aggregate stock market.
4. *Balanced:* Approximately equal proportions of equity and fixed-income securities, with commensurately lower risk. The focus is more on current income than on capital appreciation.
5. *Income:* Largely high-yield, fixed-income securities. Bond funds, money market funds, and many unit trusts fall into this category.

Table 18-1 illustrates the percentage of mutual fund assets managed according to each of these objectives. Growth funds and growth and income funds clearly dominate the industry. However, income fund assets grew rapidly in the late 1970s as interest rates reached historical peaks and investors appeared to become more conservative.

Investment Policies

Most investment companies attempt to follow a consistent investment policy. For example, some funds choose to provide as much diversification as possible in order to appeal to investors with few other security holdings. The Investment Company Act

TABLE 18-1 *Stated Mutual Fund Investment Objectives*

	Percentage of Total Mutual Fund Assets					
Year	Aggressive Growth	Growth	Growth and Income	Balanced	Income	Other
1971	5.3%	37.8%	37.8%	12.7%	6.4%	0.0%
1972	5.8	33.8	41.6	12.2	6.5	0.1
1973	5.2	33.8	40.6	13.0	7.4	0.0
1974	4.4	32.2	40.5	13.5	9.4	0.0
1975	4.7	32.5	39.6	12.1	11.1	0.0
1976	4.6	29.0	38.2	10.3	16.4	1.5
1977	4.9	25.8	35.8	9.1	18.7	5.7
1978	5.1	25.3	33.8	8.2	20.7	6.9
1979	6.1	26.5	33.7	6.9	25.7	1.1
1980	8.0	28.7	33.4	5.8	22.9	1.2
1981	9.0	27.5	33.0	5.1	24.4	1.0
1982	12.5	24.7	28.6	4.0	29.2	1.0
1983	16.5	22.8	26.0	2.7	30.5	1.5
1984	10.3	19.5	23.0	2.1	38.5	6.6
1985	7.9	13.9	17.8	1.6	52.5	6.3
1986	5.8	10.2	13.2	1.8	62.6	6.4
1987	6.0	10.6	14.1	2.0	60.0	7.3

of 1940 defines a *diversified* investment company as one with 75% or more of its assets meeting the following two criteria: (1) security holdings of any one issuer may not represent more than 5% of the fund's total portfolio value, and (2) holdings of any one security may not represent more than 10% of the issue outstanding. Funds not meeting these criteria are known as *nondiversified* investment companies. Nondiversified funds attempt to appeal to individuals with numerous other security holdings and provide expertise in one narrow area.

Typical of nondiversified funds are *idea funds* (energy funds, ecology funds, etc.), *industry funds* (chemical funds, gold funds, etc.), and funds which hold the securities of only one *country*. These specialized funds have not been particularly successful in attracting capital over the long run and tend to come and go with various security fads.

Exchange funds and *hedge funds* are interesting historical devices which have declined in importance. Prior to recent tax law changes, people holding securities on which they had earned substantial unrealized capital gains could dispose of the securities (perhaps to achieve more diversification) without paying taxes by swapping them for the shares of an exchange fund. Taxes were paid only when the exchange fund shares were sold. Hedge funds were created to use convertibles, options, short sales, bank borrowing, etc., to actively manipulate the risk position of the portfolio. Contrary to their name, most hedge funds did not reduce risk but, instead, increased portfolio risk through financial leverage.

Real estate investment trusts (REITs) are similar to standard closed-end investment companies except they are limited to investments in real estate–related assets and make considerable use of borrowing to finance asset holdings.[2] There are three major types of REITs. *Mortgage trusts* invest in packages of mortgages on commercial and residential property as well as in construction and development loans to real estate developers. During the middle 1970s many of the loans made by mortgage trusts defaulted, resulting in insufficient cash flow to meet their own debt obligations. When their stock prices dropped precipitously, many firms elected to switch their legal status to standard real estate companies, and some went bankrupt. *Equity trusts* take an equity interest in commercial property, such as shopping centers, office buildings, etc. They, too, suffered from many of the problems associated with mortgage trusts but, on the whole, fared better. Finally, *hybrid trusts* represent combinations of both equity and mortgage trust assets.

Most REITs were initially formed by large banks and insurance companies with a background in real estate lending and investment. Unfortunately, the types of assets in which they invested provided little diversification to protect against shocks within the economy, and many trusts were poorly managed. REITs represent a reasonable way to enter the real estate market, but because of the amount of their inherent diversifiable risk they should represent only a portion of a person's total investment portfolio.

Index Funds

As shown later in this chapter, the historical performance of the average investment company hasn't equaled that of even the broad market indexes such as the S&P 500. And those few firms that do perform well in one time period seem to be unable to do so consistently. This evidence, combined with a growing understanding of efficient market theory, has led to the creation of various *index funds*.

Index funds are designed to provide broad diversification and keep expenses to a minimum. No attempts are made to forecast general market moves or identify relatively under- or overvalued securities. As a result, the expenses of maintaining a large security analysis and portfolio management staff are eliminated along with the brokerage fees and selection errors incurred in active portfolio management. The prospects of the First Index Investment Trust, for example, described the trust as follows:

> First Index Investment Trust (the "Trust") is a new open-end investment trust designed as an "index fund" and is the first of its kind to be offered to the public. The Trust's investment objective is to provide investment results that correspond to the price and yield per-

---

[2]While extensive use of financial leverage was common among investment companies prior to the 1950s, few open- or closed-end funds currently use debt other than normal trade payables. Mutual funds are restricted by law in the amount of debt they may use, and closed-end funds usually choose not to employ financial leverage. REITs are an exception.

formance of publicly traded common stocks, as represented by the Standard & Poor's 500 Composite Stock Price Index.

The number of index funds currently available is limited, although more will undoubtedly be offered. Indexing is a more common practice within commercial bank trust departments and corporate pension funds than in investment companies.

COSTS AND BENEFITS

Costs

There are five explicit costs to owning investment company shares and a sixth cost that is less identifiable, but perhaps more important. The identifiable costs include the following:

1. *Load fee:* the commission paid when mutual fund shares are acquired through a broker. As noted earlier, a typical load is effectively around 9% and is paid front-end. No-load funds are available by direct correspondence with the fund. Closed-end fund transactions occur at normal stock brokerage fees.

2. *Advisory fee:* yearly payment to the fund's management adviser. Payment is made from fund assets and represents compensation for security analysis and portfolio management services. A typical fee is 0.5% of asset market value annually. Occasionally the advisory fee is reduced according to a predetermined schedule as assets increase. Basing the fee on total asset value supposedly provides an inducement to the adviser to increase portfolio values by performing well. However, it has also provided an inducement to increase assets by active marketing campaigns to sell new shares. A few funds base advisory fees on how the fund's performance compares with the performance of a market index such as the S&P 500.

3. *Administrative expenses:* salaries and wages of fund personnel, rental expenses, legal and accounting fees, etc., paid from fund assets. Administrative expenses are usually less than 0.5% of asset value per year.

4. *Transaction costs:* brokerage fees paid on security transactions. While the brokerage commission paid on any one trade is relatively small, transaction costs can be important if the adviser turns over the portfolio rapidly.[3] Portfolio turnover varies widely, with some funds purchasing or selling as little as 20% of portfolio value in a year and others having more than 100% turnover. In addition to brokerage fees, large block purchases and sales cause temporary price pressure on market prices. An average price pressure cost is about 1% of the security's value.

---

[3]Turnover is generally measured as the percentage of total asset value bought or sold during a year. If average asset values are $10 million, and $6 million worth of securities are bought or sold, the turnover is 60%.

5. *Marketing costs.* Organizations which sell mutual funds to the public incur various marketing costs. If the fund charges a load, all such costs are part of the load. A recent regulatory change allows the distributor of no-load funds to charge a fee against the fund's assets in order to compensate the distributor for marketing costs. Such mutual funds are known as *12b-1 plans*. The fee is usually about 0.2 to 0.3% of assets.

Individuals considering the purchase of shares in an investment company should be familiar with the relative size of these expenses for the funds they are interested in. The largest costs are often the load and transaction costs.

The final cost involves *possible security losses from active portfolio management*. Assume that at period 0 you had bought a well-diversified portfolio of securities having a beta of 1.0 and a market value of $10,000.[4] During the next five years you reinvested all dividend receipts but otherwise didn't trade. At the end of five years this buy-hold, passive strategy resulted in a portfolio worth $16,105.10, representing a realized yearly return of 10%.[5] Your friend Argus Trisstyler followed a different strategy. He invested $10,000 in XYZ Special Selection Fund, a no-load fund with a beta of 1.0. This fund followed a policy of actively turning over the portfolio and overweighting its holdings in industries which the investment adviser believed would outperform other stocks. Argus also reinvested all dividends. But after five years he found that the value of his portfolio (even *before* advisory fees, administrative expenses, and transaction costs were deducted) was $14,025.52. *Before expenses*, management of XYZ has been able to provide a realized return of only 7% per year although the market risk of the portfolio was identical to yours. We will label this 3% yearly loss *active management costs*.

This example was contrived, of course, to lead to a loss resulting from active management costs. If it had been prepared by investment advisers, they no doubt would have changed it to yield an active management *gain*. Whether active management (speculation) of investment company portfolios leads to consistent gains or losses is an empirical question to be discussed in detail later. However, at this point we should make a number of points:

1. In an economically inefficient market, some managers might be able to consistently earn higher returns from active management than from passive management. These gains may or may not be sufficient to cover transaction costs, administrative expenses, and management fees. Other managers will consistently earn lower returns from active management (until net redemptions force them out of business).

2. In an economically efficient market active management gains will be impossible if the portfolio is well diversified. The performance of a diversified portfolio which

---

[4]Perhaps $10,000 worth of an S&P index fund.

[5]
$$\sqrt[5]{\frac{16,105.10}{10,000}} - 1.0 = 10\%.$$

is actively managed will be identical to one with passive management before any expenses are deducted. The only thing active management can do in an efficient market is to increase transaction and administrative costs, resulting in lower net returns to fundholders.

3. In an economically efficient market, active management losses will always exist if the portfolio is not well diversified. Consistent trading gains are unavailable in an efficient market. By seeking such nonexistent gains through overweighting some industries or securities, a larger diversifiable risk exposure is incurred than necessary.

Benefits

Taxes. Investment companies do not pay federal income taxes on any interest income, dividend income, or realized capital gains distributed to shareholders as long as they are classified as a *regulated investment company* according to the Internal Revenue Code. To be classified as such, they must meet the following conditions:

1. 90% of all income is a result of security market transactions.

2. 90% of all interest and dividend income is distributed to shareholders. (Note that this does not refer to realized capital gains.)

3. Fund assets are diversified. At least 50% of the portfolio must (*a*) not have more than 5% of the fund's assets invested in the securities of any one issuer, and (*b*) not have a position in a security representing 25% or more of the security's total market value.

If classified as a regulated investment company, the fund will pay corporate taxes only on interest and dividend income retained by the firm. As a practical matter, all interest and dividend income (net of operating costs) is distributed to shareholders, who then pay taxes at their individual ordinary tax rates. Realized capital gains may be distributed to shareholders or retained in the fund. If the capital gains are distributed, shareholders pay taxes at their appropriate rates. If the capital gains are retained, the fund pays a tax equal to the maximum possible capital gains rate and reports this tax to shareholders, who can then claim a tax refund if their personal tax rate would have been lower. Shareholders are usually given the option of taking interest, dividend, and net realized capital gains in the form of either cash or additional shares in the fund.

Care should be taken to examine tax ramifications when an investment company is being selected. All other things being equal, the investor would prefer that the fund *delay realization* of its capital gains for as long as possible. To illustrate this, assume that you are considering the purchase of two funds which have identical investment objectives, risks, and net asset values. Data on each are shown below:

	Hyturn Fund	Loturn Fund
Net Asset Value	$50	$50
Composition:		
Cost Value	$30	$30
Capital Gains:		
— Realized	8	0
— Unrealized	8	16
Subtotal	$16	$16
Dividends and Interest	4	4
Total	$50	$50

Both funds have a $50 net asset value, but the composition of this value differs. Loturn Fund shows a $16 capital gain, all of which is unrealized gain on which shareholders will not have to pay a capital gains tax. Hyturn Fund shows an identical capital gain of $16 but chose to sell many of the securities on which a capital gain had arisen and thus has a realized capital gain of $8. If shareholders reinvest all dividends received in either of the funds, their investment will remain $50. Hyturn will distribute $12 in dividends (dividend interest income plus realized capital gains), which reduces its net asset value to $38. But by reinvesting the $12 dividend, a shareholder in Hyturn still has $50 committed to the market. Loturn will pay $4 in dividends (dividend and interest income), which will reduce its net asset value to $46. By reinvesting the $4 dividend, the shareholder in Loturn has $50 committed to the market. However, the net wealth position of each shareholder will differ, since Hyturn shareholders are forced to pay capital gains taxes, but Loturn shareholders are not. Assuming ordinary tax rates are 40% and capital gains are 20%:

	Hyturn Shareholders	Loturn Shareholders
Total Investment After Dividend Reinvestment	$50.00	$50.00
Taxes Paid:		
Interest and Dividend Income	(1.60)	(1.60)
Capital Gain Dividends	(1.60)	(0.00)
Net Wealth	$46.80	$48.40

Loturn shareholders, of course, will eventually have to pay taxes on the fund's capital gains since they cannot remain unrealized forever. But why pay earlier than necessary, as with Hyturn? Paying taxes should be delayed as long as possible. In sum, funds *with high turnovers not only incur larger transaction costs, they can also increase the shareholder's tax burden.*[6]

---

[6]Note, however, that even a purchase of Loturn involves a tax liability. The investor pays $50 in net asset value for something which is really worth $48.40 ($50 − $1.60) after taxes.

Investment Company Services. Most investment companies offer a variety of services to shareholders. Some of these include the following:

1. *Security custody.* The investment adviser will arrange for a bank or brokerage house to maintain physical custody of portfolio securities and ensure that all interest and dividends are received when paid by the issuing firm. This frees the shareholder from such chores. While a custody fee is charged to the fund, it will be lower than what shareholders would pay if they personally managed their own portfolios.

2. *Fund swaps.* Investment advisers often act as advisers to a variety of funds, each with a different investment objective. Holders of one fund are usually allowed to swap shares of one fund for another at reduced load charges or redemption fees.

3. *Checking accounts.* Money market funds often have arrangements with a bank that allow shareholders to write checks against their share balances. As noted earlier, each check must be written for a minimum amount. However, this provides the liquidity advantages of a checking account together with high current income on share balances.

4. *Accumulation plans.* Three forms of accumulation plans are available. The simplest involves *automatic reinvestment* of all dividend distributions in shares of the fund.

   Voluntary plans specify periodic new investments in the fund of some minimum amount. The fund mails the investor a "gentle" reminder just prior to the investment date. Some funds will also arrange to transfer fixed amounts from the investor's bank at prespecified dates. Investors are not legally committed to such deposits, but many seem to appreciate the discipline which such plans impose.

   Contractual accumulation plans specify fixed dollar amounts to be deposited at fixed dates (usually monthly) over extended periods of time. If the contractual plan is on a load fund, a large portion of the early payments goes to cover the *total* load on all future purchases, and few new shares accumulate. While the investor is not legally obligated to make payments, early withdrawal from such a plan can leave the investor with very few shares and large brokerage fees. Contractual plans in load funds may be more of a disservice than a service.[7]

5. *Withdrawal plans.* Some funds will arrange for the shareholder to automatically withdraw a fixed dollar amount or fixed percentage of asset value each month. This allows people with fixed cash needs and little concern about depleting capital values a guaranteed cash inflow.

---

[7]Under the 1970 amendments to the Investment Company Act of 1940, the customer's load under a contractual plan can be determined in one of two ways. Under the first type, a 50% front-end load may be charged. But if the plan is canceled within 18 months, all net asset value and commissions in excess of 15% of total payments to date are reimbursed to the shareholder. Under the second type, the "spread load" plan, the load is spread over the first 48 monthly payments and the average may not exceed 16% of the total payments.

6. *Keogh plans.* Special accounts are available which satisfy all federal requirements for individual retirement accounts (IRAs) and Keogh plans. These plans provide a tax shelter on income received prior to withdrawals from the account at retirement.

Fit of Fund and Investor Objectives. Investment companies provide an easy way for individuals to create portfolios which best meet their personal investment objectives. There are basically two dimensions to a fund's stated objective: one relates to tax considerations and the other to risk. Individuals in *high tax brackets* might prefer growth-oriented funds with low turnover in order to minimize taxes, whereas retirees and others in *lower tax brackets* might prefer income funds. Individuals with *high risk tolerance* might select an aggressive growth fund, whereas individuals *more concerned with risk* would be more comfortable with a balanced fund. How well do stated objectives actually mirror the tax and risk dimensions which shareholders will experience? Unfortunately, there is no empirical evidence regarding tax impacts. However, a large body of research shows that stated objectives are closely related to a fund's actual risk exposure.

Fund risk exposure can be measured as either the *total risk* (standard deviation) of the fund's returns or as the nondiversifiable *market risk* (beta). In Figure 18-3, both standard deviation and market model beta estimates are shown for various mutual fund objectives. The data were developed by the author and cover 255 mutual funds with ten years of quarterly returns ending December 1984. Panel A provides information about the standard deviation of each mutual fund category. The two ends of each bar represent the average for a given group plus or minus two standard deviations. Thus, the range of each bar is about 95% of all funds in a given category. The line through the middle of each bar is the average for the particular group. In panel B, similar information is shown for beta estimates. On the whole, both total risk and systematic risk are related to stated fund objectives. The overlap which exists between groups simply reflects the imprecision of many of the fund's objectives.

Diversification. One of the major benefits of owning shares in an investment company is the potential for broad diversification resulting from the large number of securities held by the fund. A portfolio is completely diversified if all its risk is determined by nondiversifiable market risk. If part of a portfolio's excess returns are unrelated to excess market returns, a diversifiable risk exists.

On the whole, mutual funds do provide good diversification. For example, when the excess quarterly returns (quarterly return minus 90-day T-bill return) of the 255 mutual funds were regressed against excess returns on the S&P 500, the average R^2 was 84%. A value of 100% would mean that all unsystematic risk had been diversified away. The maximum R^2 was 97.5% and the minimum was 37% (an income fund with few stocks). Investors considering investment companies for their diversification can find a large number of funds that will provide extensive diversification. But if diversification is the goal and only one mutual fund will be held, it is proba-

FIGURE 18-3 *Relationship of Risks to Fund Objectives Based on Returns for the Ten Years Ending December 1984*

A. Objectives and Standard Deviations of Returns

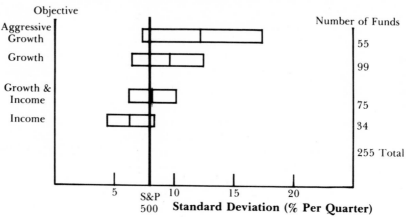

B. Objectives and Betas

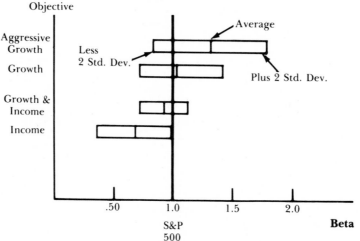

bly best to stay away from closed-end funds, REITs, and mutual funds which concentrate assets in certain industries.

Active Portfolio Management. One of the advantages often claimed for ownership of investment company shares is that portfolio assets are actively managed by well-trained professionals. There is little doubt that the staffs of most management advisory firms have considerable educational training and investment experience. However, as we noted above, a question does exist whether this training and experience will actually provide better performance than that available from an unmanaged portfolio. The historical performance of management advisers is discussed below.

PERFORMANCE MEASUREMENT

The Issues

Returns on the shares of a managed investment company are calculated in the same manner as returns on any other marketable security. Share price appreciation during some time interval is added to any dividends received, and this total is divided by the share price at the beginning of the period. For example, assume that on September 30 Windsor Fund had a net asset value of $12.87 per share. By December the fund has paid $0.98 in dividends and is selling at a net asset value of $12.65. Thus, Windsor Fund's return during the quarter was 5.9%:

$$\frac{12.65 - 12.87 + 0.98}{12.87} = 5.9\%$$

Assume a return of, say, 1.8% on the S&P Composite during the same quarter. The question is: Did Windsor Fund outperform the market in this quarter?

There is no doubt that Windsor Fund had a higher return than would have been provided by a passive, unmanaged position in the S&P Composite. But this doesn't necessarily mean that Windsor Fund's management was able to outperform the market. While realized security returns are important, they are only one aspect of performance evaluation. In addition, we should consider the following:

1. *Risk*. Any performance measure must explicitly incorporate an allowance for the amount of risk incurred. Instead of thinking about return earned on an investment, we should think about *return earned per unit of risk*.

2. *Consistency*. The risk/return performance of a managed portfolio should consistently beat that of an unmanaged portfolio. During any one year, a managed account could provide a higher return per unit of risk than an unmanaged account owing to management skill or pure luck. Only by examining the consistency of a fund's performance can we decide whether skill or luck caused a given year's performance.

3. *Expenses*. Portfolio managers may have sufficient skill to identify mispriced securities or call turns in the market, but unless these gains are large enough to offset the expenses associated with owning investment company shares, passive management would provide larger net returns.

Risk/Return Measurement

As a product of much of the theoretical and empirical research on the capital asset pricing model, three models have been developed to aid in examining the historical risk/return performance of actively managed portfolios. These were discussed at length in Chapter 8. The Sharpe performance index divided the average return earned for bearing risk by the standard deviation of historical returns; that is:

$$S_p = \frac{\bar{R}_p - \overline{RF}}{\sigma_p} \tag{18.1}$$

where S_p refers to the Sharpe performance index for portfolio p, $\bar{R}_p$ is the average historical return on portfolio p, $\overline{RF}$ is the average risk-free rate, and σ_p is the standard deviation of portfolio p returns. The Sharpe measure includes both diversifiable and nondiversifiable risk in the denominator. S_p for a given fund is related to other funds as well as to some aggregate market index in order to determine the relative performance ranking of each.

The Treynor performance index (T_p) is calculated in much the same manner as Sharpe's except that only the nondiversifiable risk of the portfolio as proxied by beta (B_p) is used:

$$T_p = \frac{\bar{R}_p - \overline{RF}}{B_p} \tag{18.2}$$

Like the S_p measure, the Treynor performance index is a relative measure which must be compared with values for other funds and an aggregate market index.

Finally, the Jensen performance index tests for a statistically significant and positive constant rate of return. This constant, nonmarket-related return is known as alpha and is estimated by empirically testing the following regression equation:

$$\widetilde{ER}_{pt} = A_p + B_p(\widetilde{ER}_{mt}) + \tilde{E}_{pt} \tag{18.3}$$

Excess portfolio returns ($\widetilde{ER}_{pt}$ = the portfolio return in period t minus the risk-free rate in t) are related to excess market returns. Jensen stated that portfolios with positive and statistically significant A_p values could be said to have outperformed the market; they were able to earn a *constant* rate of return above that available from an investment in a combination of risk-free securities and the market portfolio having the same beta. Conversely, funds with a negative and statistically significant alpha could be said to have underperformed the market. Funds with alphas not significantly different from zero performed equal to the market.

Most empirical tests of investment company performance have relied upon one of these three models or slight variants of them.

Historical Performance

Many studies examining these three performance measures have been conducted, but most are more than ten years old. So, instead of reviewing rather dated past studies, we will examine the performance of the 255 mutual funds mentioned earlier using ten years of quarterly data ending December 1984. Each of the performance measures requires that a market portfolio proxy be used for comparison. We will use two market proxies: (1) the S&P 500 Index and (2) the Wilshire 5000 Index. The S&P 500 is a widely used market proxy. However, it overweights large-capitalization stocks listed on the NYSE. The Wilshire 5000 covers a larger number of companies and thus has a broad representation of OTC and smaller-capitalization stocks. The Wilshire 5000 better represents the pool of stocks from which mutual funds select. Quarterly T-bill returns will be used as the risk-free rate.

Table 18-2 presents basic statistics on 70 of the 255 funds, using the S&P 500 as the market proxy. The first three columns are the calculated Jensen, Sharpe, and

TABLE 18-2 *Mutual Fund Performance Numbers for the Ten Years Ending December 1984*

Name of Fund	Jensen	Sharpe	Treynor	Beta	MER	SER
ABT GROWTH & INCOME TR.	−0.003508	0.098776	0.0112445	0.66197	0.0074436	0.075358
†ACORN FUND	0.018371	0.347439	0.0318067	1.20361	0.0382829	0.110186
AFFILIATED FUND	0.006207	0.272737	0.0231284	0.94250	0.0217985	0.079925
AFUTURE FUND	0.007713	0.252365	0.0233115	1.13961	0.0265659	0.105268
ALPHA FUND	0.000239	0.181663	0.0167750	1.03053	0.0172872	0.095160
†AMCAP FUND	0.020163	0.361365	0.0334398	1.19329	0.0399033	0.110424
†AMER. CAPITAL COMSTOCK	0.023993	0.417110	0.0375898	1.13997	0.0428513	0.102734
AMER. CAPITAL ENTERPRISE	0.006531	0.240998	0.0218816	1.22334	0.0267687	0.111074
AMERICAN BALANCED FUND	0.001617	0.213470	0.0190404	0.64739	0.0123265	0.057743
AMERICAN CAPITAL HARBOR	0.007704	0.280031	0.0258138	0.83107	0.0214530	0.076609
†AMERICAN CAPITAL PACE FD	0.030286	0.477352	0.0478004	0.96891	0.0463145	0.097024
*AMERICAN GROWTH FUND	0.012993	0.325438	0.0313124	0.87976	0.0275473	0.084647
AMERICAN HERITAGE FUND	−0.004419	0.142692	0.0137071	1.55796	0.0213551	0.149659
AMERICAN INVESTORS FUND	−0.011347	0.084974	0.0085089	1.41233	0.0120173	0.141424
†AMERICAN MUTUAL FUND	0.012169	0.371239	0.0312682	0.82643	0.0258410	0.069608
AMERICAN NATIONAL GROWTH	0.012556	0.276027	0.0263932	1.27470	0.0336434	0.121884
AXE-HOUGHTON FUND B	−0.000816	0.167848	0.0153940	0.70973	0.0109256	0.065092
AXE-HOUGHTON STOCK FUND	−0.007451	0.109871	0.0102052	1.17565	0.0119977	0.109199
BABSON GROWTH FUND	−0.010488	0.074945	0.0062441	1.01831	0.0063585	0.084842
BEACON GROWTH FUND	−0.009888	0.044115	0.0038331	0.77797	0.0029821	0.067597
BEACON HILL MUTUAL FUND	−0.005131	0.116873	0.0101452	0.80202	0.0081367	0.069620
BLC GROWTH FUND	0.000653	0.197581	0.0170992	1.17398	0.0200741	0.101599
BOSTON CO. CAP. APPREC.	−0.002764	0.160700	0.0137788	1.00001	0.0137790	0.085744
BOSTON FOUNDATION FUND	0.003578	0.244654	0.0218460	0.67468	0.0147391	0.060245
BULL & BEAR CAP GROWTH	0.005952	0.235315	0.0211458	1.29321	0.0273460	0.116210
BULL & BEAR EQUITY INC.	0.002519	0.223346	0.0197417	0.78741	0.0155449	0.069600
BULLOCK FUND	0.000213	0.203553	0.0167687	0.94518	0.0158495	0.077864
CANADIAN FUND	−0.007395	0.068694	0.0071027	0.78337	0.0055641	0.080998
CENTURY SHARES TRUST	0.004151	0.196861	0.0213600	0.86178	0.0184075	0.093505
*CHARTER FUND	0.015228	0.339063	0.0332434	0.91182	0.0303120	0.089399
CHEMICAL FUND	−0.009924	0.079340	0.0067352	1.01188	0.0068152	0.085899
CIGNA GROWTH FUND	−0.001639	0.182087	0.0150570	1.10258	0.0166015	0.091173
COLONIAL GROWTH SHARES	−0.002434	0.163747	0.0141299	1.00859	0.0142512	0.087032
*COLUMBIA GROWTH FUND	0.010603	0.291002	0.0251355	1.23397	0.0310165	0.106585
COMMERCE INCOME SHARES	−0.001426	0.158948	0.0146081	0.73690	0.0107647	0.067725
COMPANION FUND	−0.000160	0.197715	0.0163976	1.10063	0.0180478	0.091282

TABLE 18-2 *(continued)*

Name of Fund	Jensen	Sharpe	Treynor	Beta	MER	SER
COMPOSITE BOND & STOCK	−0.000765	0.174419	0.0155382	0.76105	0.0118254	0.067799
STATE STREET INV. CORP.	0.001619	0.210058	0.0181429	1.01221	0.0183643	0.087425
STEADMAN AMERICAN INDUS.	−0.022383	−0.062740	−0.0060171	0.99212	−0.0059698	0.095150
STEADMAN ASSOCIATED	−0.009980	−0.002140	−0.0002088	0.59574	−0.0001244	0.058113
STEADMAN INVESTMENT	−0.015428	−0.032991	−0.0031823	0.78214	−0.0024891	0.075445
STEADMAN OCEANOGRAPHIC	−0.016722	−0.052094	−0.0062884	0.73238	−0.0046055	0.088408
STEIN R&F CAPITAL OPPOR.	0.007437	0.233675	0.0220531	1.34982	0.0297676	0.127389
STEIN R&F STOCK	−0.004296	0.148462	0.0130091	1.21550	0.0158127	0.106510
STEIN R&F TOTAL RETURN	−0.007861	0.098358	0.0082539	0.94835	0.0078276	0.079583
STRATTON GROWTH FUND	0.003645	0.220505	0.0195719	1.20344	0.0235536	0.106817
SURVEYOR FUND	−0.003240	0.151097	0.0135577	1.08520	0.0147128	0.097373
TECHNOLOGY FUND	0.004556	0.235507	0.0207144	1.09226	0.0226256	0.096072
†TEMPLETON GROWTH FUND	0.015951	0.369359	0.0333490	0.94914	0.0316528	0.085697
TUDOR FUND	0.015021	0.309426	0.0295538	1.15453	0.0341206	0.110271
†TWENTIETH CENTURY GROWTH	0.030766	0.362727	0.0363331	1.55461	0.0564837	0.155720
†TWENTIETH CENTURY SELECT	0.029804	0.419716	0.0397527	1.28412	0.0510470	0.121623
UNIFIED MUTUAL SHARES	−0.000405	0.188072	0.0161119	0.93958	0.0151383	0.080492
UNITED ACCUMULATIVE FUND	0.003771	0.247104	0.0205348	0.94469	0.0193991	0.078506
UNITED CONTL. INCOME FD.	0.003893	0.240167	0.0214417	0.79472	0.0170403	0.070952
UNITED INCOME FUND	0.000682	0.198886	0.0173193	0.87904	0.0152243	0.076548
UNITED INTL. GROWTH FUND	0.003770	0.235330	0.0207723	0.89145	0.0185175	0.078687
UNITED RETIREMENT SHARES	−0.000854	0.172457	0.0154858	0.80717	0.0124996	0.072480
UNITED SCIENCE & ENERGY	−0.002325	0.163033	0.0142061	0.99472	0.0141311	0.086677
†UNITED VANGUARD FUND	0.015014	0.328436	0.0295730	1.15227	0.0340760	0.103752
USAA MUTUAL FD GROWTH	−0.008631	0.105369	0.0090974	1.15914	0.0105452	0.100079
VALUE LINE FUND	0.009753	0.251644	0.0248054	1.18039	0.0292801	0.116355
*VALUE LINE LEVER. GROWTH	0.026257	0.358980	0.0372405	1.26863	0.0472445	0.131608
VANCE, SANDERS SPECIAL	0.013092	0.298181	0.0274755	1.19757	0.0329038	0.110348
WALL STREET FUND	−0.008854	0.098076	0.0082223	1.06403	0.0087488	0.089205
†WASH. MUTUAL INVESTORS	0.009620	0.318182	0.0271492	0.90702	0.0246248	0.077392
*WEINGARTEN EQUITY FUND	0.016811	0.314177	0.0289891	1.35069	0.0391553	0.124628
WELLESLEY INCOME FUND	0.003395	0.212447	0.0237500	0.47115	0.0111899	0.052671
WELLINGTON FUND	0.000911	0.207135	0.0177626	0.74744	0.0132764	0.064096
†WINDSOR FUND	0.019435	0.400601	0.0355007	1.02518	0.0363947	0.090850

Treynor performance numbers. The last three columns are the estimated beta, mean excess return (*MER*), and standard deviation of excess returns (*SER*). Funds with a Jensen alpha which is statistically different from zero at a 90% confidence level are noted with a single asterisk. Funds which are statistically different from zero at a 95% confidence level are noted with a dagger.

Table 18-3 presents a summary of the tests' results. Examine the Sharpe performance measure first. The average mutual fund earned a quarterly excess return of 0.2177% for each unit of standard deviation. When compared with the S&P 500 value of 0.2042%, it would appear that the funds did slightly better on average than a buy-hold strategy. But, as noted above, the S&P 500 Index is probably not a fair representation of the securities from which mutual funds select. In fact, when S&P 500 returns are regressed against broader indexes, the estimated beta of the S&P 500 is

TABLE 18-3 *Summary of Sharpe-Treynor-Jensen Performance Measures Using 255 Mutual Funds for the Ten Years Ending December 1984*

Sharpe Excess Return to Total Risk: S_p

Average	0.2177%	Maximum	0.5115%
S&P 500	0.2042%	Minimum	−0.0735%
Wilshire 5000	0.2355%	95% of all observations	0.0191%–0.4162%

Treynor Excess Return to Market Risk: T_p

Average (with S&P 500)	1.98%	Maximum	5.00%
Average (with Wilshire)	2.13%	Minimum	−0.85%
S&P 500	1.65%	95% of all observations	0.10%–3.86%
Wilshire 5000	2.06%		

Jensen's Alpha

Using the S&P 500 as the market proxy:

Average Alpha	0.38%	
Number of Funds Which Were:		
Significantly Positive	33	(greater than 1.96 σ from 0.0)
Not Different from 0.0%	222	
Significantly Negative	0	(less than 1.96 σ from 0.0)
Total	255	

Using the Wilshire 5000 as the market proxy:

Average Alpha	0.05%	
Number of Funds Which Were:		
Significantly Positive	18	(greater than 1.96 σ from 0.0)
Not Different from 0.0%	210	
Significantly Negative	27	(less than 1.96 σ from 0.0)
Total	255	

slightly less than 1.0 (about 0.9). So the observation that mutual funds outperform the S&P 500 should come as no surprise; many mutual funds select from a broader universe of stocks than the S&P 500. When the average Sharpe measure for mutual funds (0.2177%) is compared against the Wilshire 5000 Index (0.2355%), the mutual funds perform more poorly on average. Our first conclusion must be that *performance results depend on the market index used*.

When the Treynor performance measure is used, the mutual funds seem to beat both market proxies. The average excess return relative to the estimated beta is 1.98% when beta is estimated using the S&P 500. This compares with a 1.65% value for the S&P 500. Mutual funds again beat the S&P 500. In fact, the same thing happens when the Wilshire 5000 is used as the market proxy. The average fund had a Treynor measure of 2.13% versus 2.06% for the market proxy. But note that the difference between average mutual fund results and those of each index is small. In the case of the S&P 500, the 0.33% difference (1.98% − 1.65%) translates into a 1.3% per annum excess return (1.0033^4 − 1.0). In the case of the Wilshire 5000, the difference translates into a 0.3% per annum excess. Clearly the differences are slight. In fact, they could be due simply to chance and to the time period selected. What we really need to know is not whether a difference existed, but whether the difference is due to chance or is in fact statistically significant. Our second conclusion must be that *to mean anything, performance results of mutual funds should be statistically different from a reasonable market proxy.*

Next, consider Jensen's alpha, which measures the constant return in excess of the risk-free rate which a manager earns once the systematic risk of the portfolio has been accounted for. A major advantage of this technique is that it allows us to determine whether good or bad performance was statistically significant. For example, when Windsor Fund's excess quarterly returns are regressed against the excess returns on the Wilshire 5000, the following estimates are obtained:[8]

$$\widetilde{ER}_{W,t} = 1.63\% + 0.94(\widetilde{ER}_{WS,t}) + \tilde{E}_{W,t} \quad R^2 = 83.97$$
$$\quad\quad (0.60) \quad\quad (0.07)$$

The estimated beta is 0.94, the R^2 is 83.9%, and Jensen's alpha is 1.63%. In parentheses under the regression parameters are the standard deviations of each regression estimate. In order to test whether alpha is statistically different from zero, a Z statistic is calculated as follows:

$$Z = \frac{\text{Alpha Estimate} - 0.0}{\text{Standard Deviation of Alpha}}$$

$$= \frac{1.63 - 0.0}{0.60} = 2.72$$

When the calculated Z is greater than 1.96, we can say with 95% confidence that the fund outperformed the market index. Conversely, when the calculated Z is a negative 1.96, we can say with 95% confidence that the fund underperformed the market index. In Windsor Fund's case, the calculated Z of 2.72 suggests that the fund *did* statistically outperform the market index as proxied by the Wilshire 5000.

Summary statistics on Jensen's alpha are shown in Table 18-3. When the S&P 500 is used as the market proxy, 33 out of the 255 funds had statistically significant positive performance. None had significant negative performance. Since we are using a 95% confidence level, 5% of all funds can be expected to show statistically significant performance even if the true alpha is 0.0. Thus, by chance alone, we would have expected to find 13 funds (255 × 0.05) with significant positive alphas and 13 with significant negative alphas. The results appear to be better than this. But, again, the S&P 500 is probably a poor market proxy.

When alphas are calculated on the Wilshire 5000, the number of funds with significant positive performance falls to 18, and 22 funds emerge as statistical underperformers.

Remember, we are dealing with 255 mutual funds. Of these, 210 were unable to outperform a passive buy-hold strategy consisting of holding T-bills and an index

---

[8]Using the ten years of data ending December 1984.

TABLE 18-4 *Correlation Between Performance Measures Using S&P 500 or Wilshire 5000 as Market Proxy*

	Jensen	Sharpe	Treynor
Jensen	1.00		
Sharpe	0.95	1.00	
Treynor	0.96	0.99	1.00

fund similar to the Wilshire 5000.[9] Another 27 had significant negative performance. Only 18 of the funds provided significant excess returns. Thus our third conclusion must be that *the overwhelming number of mutual funds do not statistically outperform a reasonable proxy of the market portfolio.*

We saw in Chapter 8 that these three performance measures will be highly correlated with each other if a fund's returns are highly correlated with the market index proxy. This is the case with our example. As shown in Table 18-4, the correlation coefficients between the various performance indexes range from 95% to 99%. When dealing with diversified portfolios such as these, relative rankings are virtually unaffected by the measurement index used. (Remember, though, that the Jensen alpha lends itself to testing statistical significance.)

One last question remains: Is there any consistency in performance over time? If there is, then people should invest in the funds which have done well historically. If there is not, then historical performance should not be a criterion for selecting future holdings. In examining the question, we will use Jensen's alpha as the performance measure and the Wilshire 5000 as the market proxy.

Figure 18-4 is a plot of the performance of each fund in two different periods—the first and second five-year intervals of the ten years examined above. For each period, Jensen's alpha was measured and its value in the first five-year period was plotted against its value in the second five-year period. The vertical and horizontal lines drawn in the figure separate the funds into four groups:

	Estimated Alpha in		Performance Interpretation	
Group	Period 1	Period 2	Period 1	Period 2
1	>0.0	>0.0	Good	Good
2	>0.0	≤0.0	Good	Bad
3	≤0.0	>0.0	Bad	Good
4	≤0.0	≤0.0	Bad	Bad

If consistency in performance exists, we would expect a predominance of points in group 1 (good-good) and group 4 (bad-bad). Visually, this does not appear to be the case—the pattern is virtually random.

The transition of funds from period 1 groups into period 2 groups is shown on page 752:

[9]In truth, no such fund exists, so a passive strategy such as this was not feasible. Nonetheless, the evidence on the ability of mutual funds to beat the market remains valid.

FIGURE 18-4 *Jensen Performance in Periods 1 and 2*

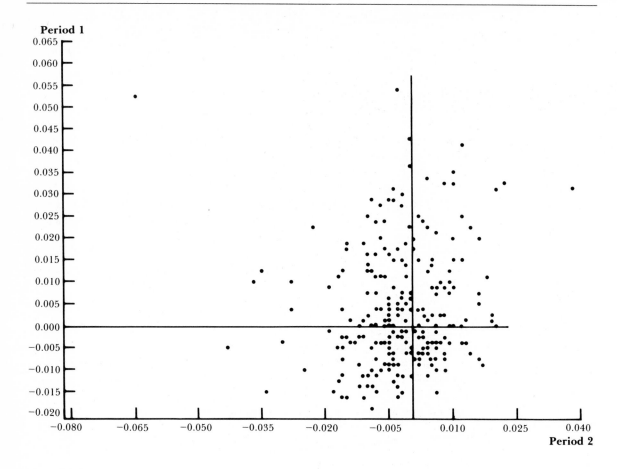

	Period 1		Period 2		
Group	*Number*		*Group*	*Expected by Chance*	*Actual*
Good	132		Good	66	60
			Bad	66	72
Bad	123		Good	61.5	45
			Bad	61.5	78
Total	255			255	255

On average, good (or poor) performance in one period is not followed by good (or poor) performance in the next period. So our fourth conclusion must be that *there appears to be no consistency in performance from period to period.*

Problems with Performance Indexes

As expected, the empirical performance studies have come under sharp attack from professional portfolio managers. While much of this criticism has come from people unfamiliar with capital market theory, some important questions have been raised by knowledgeable practitioners and academicians. Basically, the problems are the following:

1. Is portfolio *variance* a reasonable total proxy? Arditti has shown, for example, that if investors also consider skewness of returns to be important, then investment companies have fared better than suggested by studies relying solely upon variance of returns.

2. Are the historical *betas* used to evaluate performance properly calculated? Conceptually, beta should be calculated using returns on an aggregate wealth portfolio of all risky assets. Such a portfolio would include common stocks as well as bonds, real estate, precious metals, nonmarketable human resources, etc. The S&P or Wilshire indexes are (at best) convenient, but perhaps inadequate, proxies for the market portfolio.

3. Is the single-period CAPM an appropriate model on which to evaluate performance? Recent research suggests that, when the traditional CAPM is expanded, a single market-related beta is insufficient to explain excess returns. Instead, various forms of multifactor models might be necessary.[10]

There *are* problems associated with the Sharpe, Treynor, and Jensen measures. However, no rigorous study has yet shown consistent abnormal performance by mutual funds.

INTERNATIONAL INVESTMENT

Foreign investment can be accomplished in two ways:

1. *Direct investment*—the purchase of securities issued by a foreign corporation or government

2. *Indirect investment*—the purchase of securities issued by a domestic corporation which makes real asset investments in a foreign country

Both direct and indirect foreign investment have been common practice among European investors for decades. However, until the late 1970s, virtually all foreign investment by U.S. residents was made indirectly through U.S.-domiciled multinational corporations. Only recently have U.S. investors begun to take a serious look at investing nontrivial portions of their portfolios directly in foreign securities.

---

[10]R. Roll, "Ambiguity When Performance Is Measured by the Securities Market Line," *Journal of Finance* 33 (September 1978): 1051–69.

In this section we will examine why direct international investment is appealing to a growing number of U.S. investors, how it can be accomplished, and what some of the dangers of doing so are.

The World Market Portfolio

If one takes the standard capital asset pricing model to its limit, the single optimal portfolio of risky assets which all investors should hold consists of all risky assets in the world. This, of course, is absurd. Political restrictions placed on capital flows into and out of many countries, the lack of liquid security markets in all but the most developed countries, substantial differences in the availability of information, differing tax rates, etc., all do severe damage to the CAPM in a worldwide context.

Nonetheless, an examination of the total value of marketable assets within the more developed countries does suggest that the principle of diversification may still be quite valid. Figure 18-5 presents an estimate of the *world market wealth* portfolio as of the end of 1984. The data are centered on marketable assets traded in only the more developed countries, and most of the asset values are approximations. But even if a sizable allowance is made for estimation errors, it is clear that much of this wealth is non-U.S. wealth. Figure 18-6 focuses on the 1984 value of traded debt and equity securities. These values are more accurate than those in Figure 18-5.[11]

Both figures underestimate the actual value of marketable assets in countries with developed capital markets and say nothing about less developed countries. Although more accurate data would be nice to have, the figures do suggest that U.S. investors who limit their security holdings to U.S. securities *could* be severely limiting the amount of diversification available to their portfolios. If returns on marketable securities in non-U.S. countries are highly correlated with U.S. market returns, the gains available from international diversification would be slight. However, if the returns are not highly correlated, the gains from diversification could be sizable.

International Diversification

One of the classic studies examining the potential for international diversification was performed by Solnik in the mid-1970s. Solnik examined the results of the naive diversification strategy that would result if a U.S. investor had randomly selected securities from two different groups. The first group consisted solely of U.S. stocks. The second group consisted of both U.S. and European stocks. Stock returns were calculated weekly for the period 1966–71.

Results are shown in Figure 18-7. As we saw in Chapter 7, naive diversification does reduce portfolio risk up to some limit which we have referred to as nondiversifiable market risk. This happens whether one is dealing with returns on U.S. domestic

---

[11]Unfortunately, more recent estimates of the world market portfolio are not available.

FIGURE 18-5 *Estimate of Total World Wealth, 1984*

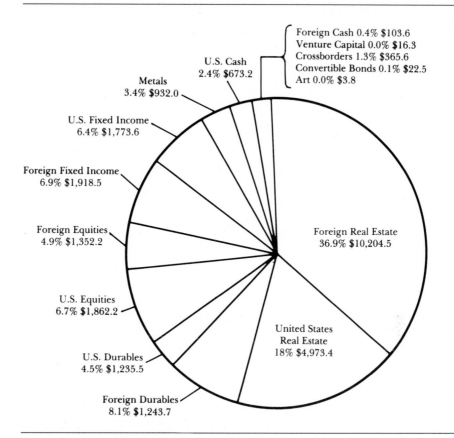

Foreign Cash 0.4% $103.6
Venture Capital 0.0% $16.3
Crossborders 1.3% $365.6
Convertible Bonds 0.1% $22.5
Art 0.0% $3.8

U.S. Cash
2.4% $673.2

Metals
3.4% $932.0

U.S. Fixed Income
6.4% $1,773.6

Foreign Fixed Income
6.9% $1,918.5

Foreign Equities
4.9% $1,352.2

U.S. Equities
6.7% $1,862.2

U.S. Durables
4.5% $1,235.5

Foreign Durables
8.1% $1,243.7

Foreign Real Estate
36.9% $10,204.5

United States
Real Estate
18% $4,973.4

SOURCE: R. Ibbotson, L. Siegel, and K. Love, "World Wealth: Market Values and Returns," *Journal of Portfolio Management*, Fall 1985.

stocks or returns on both U.S. and international securities. The important implication of Figure 18-7 is that the nondiversifiable risk of internationally diversified portfolios was considerably lower than that of portfolios restricted to U.S. securities.

Domestic and Exchange Rate Returns. Solnik's results have been confirmed in numerous other studies. There is no doubt that (in the past) broad international diversification would result in lower nondiversifiable risk than would a portfolio limited to domestic U.S. securities. But the risks and returns associated with a foreign investment are more complex than those of an investment in one's own country. When one buys a foreign security, two things affect its risk and expected return:

1. The risk and expected return inherent in the *security itself*. (We will call this *domestic* risk and return.)

FIGURE 18-6 *Estimated World Investable Wealth, 1984*

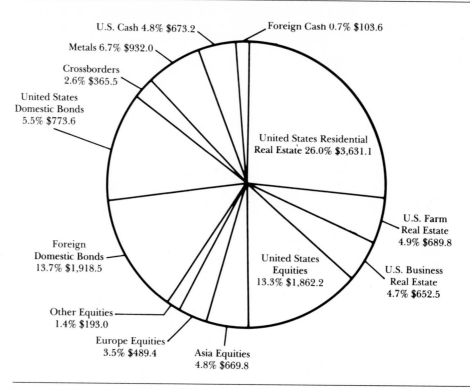

U.S. Cash 4.8% $673.2

Foreign Cash 0.7% $103.6

Metals 6.7% $932.0

Crossborders 2.6% $365.5

United States Domestic Bonds 5.5% $773.6

United States Residential Real Estate 26.0% $3,631.1

U.S. Farm Real Estate 4.9% $689.8

Foreign Domestic Bonds 13.7% $1,918.5

United States Equities 13.3% $1,862.2

U.S. Business Real Estate 4.7% $652.5

Other Equities 1.4% $193.0

Europe Equities 3.5% $489.4

Asia Equities 4.8% $669.8

SOURCE: R. Ibbotson, L. Siegel, and K. Love, "World Wealth: Market Values and Returns," *Journal of Portfolio Management*, Fall 1985.

2. The risk and return inherent in the *currency of the country* in which the security is traded. (We will call this *exchange rate* risk and return.)

To illustrate, consider two companies which are identical in all respects except for their country of origin: Tuff Truck, Inc. (TT), which is a U.S. firm, and Lloyd's Lorry, Ltd. (LL), a British firm. At the beginning of the year, shares of TT trade on the New York Stock Exchange for $50 and shares of LL trade on the London Stock Exchange for £50. By the end of the year, TT sells for $60 and has paid a $1 dividend; LL sells for £60 and has paid a £1 dividend. Thus the return a U.S. resident earns on TT is 22%, and the return a British resident earns on LL is also 22%. However, the return a U.S. resident would have earned on LL (and the return a British resident would have earned on TT) is not necessarily 22%. When a foreign investment is made, the return on the investment is composed of a return on the underlying security as well as a return on the foreign currency. When you buy a foreign security, you buy both the *security and the currency* in which the security is denominated.

To continue with the example, assume that at the start of the year it takes $1.50

FIGURE 18-7 *Naive Domestic U.S. Diversification Versus Naive International Diversification*

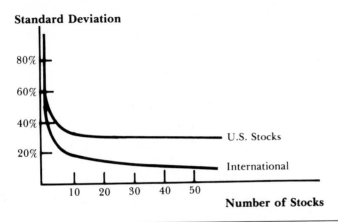

SOURCE: B. Solnik, "Why Not Diversify Internationally Rather Than Domestically?" *Financial Analysts Journal* (July/August 1974): 48–54.

to buy one British pound note—the exchange rate is $1.50 per £. To purchase shares in Lloyd's Lorry at £50, a U.S. resident would have to pay $1.50 per £, or $75. At the end of the year the investor would have a claim to £60 in share value and £1 in dividends. Let's say that the exchange rate at that time is $1.20 per £. If the share value and dividends are reclaimed to the United States, the U.S. resident would receive only $73.20 (£61 at $1.20 per £). As a result, the U.S. investor's return on the British security is a negative 2.4%:

$$\frac{\$73.20}{\$75.00} - 1.0 = -0.024$$

The investment in LL provided a positive return, but this was offset by the investment losses on the British pound.

In order to calculate the return on an investment in foreign security i, the domestic return on security i must be compounded by the return on the foreign currency. In our example, each $1 U.S. investment in LL resulted in a +22% return, as $1 grew to $1.22. However, each $1 U.S. investment in the foreign currency resulted in a −20% return, as $1 fell to $0.80. Compounding the 1.22 by the 0.80 results in an end-of-year value of $0.976 for each $1 investment at the beginning of the year:

$$\$1(1.22)(0.80) = \$0.976$$

This, of course, represents a 2.4% loss.

In general, if R_i^f represents the return on foreign security i, R_i^d represents the domestic return (the return on the security in the country in which it is issued) on security i, and R_x represents the return on the exchange of currency:

Return on Foreign Investment

$$(1 + R_i^f) = (1 + R_i^d)(1 + R_x)$$

and

$$R_i^f = (1 + R_i^d)(1 + R_x) - 1.0$$

(18.4)

For example, if we apply this equation to the British resident's return on Tuff Truck, a return of +52.50% was earned:

$$(1.22)(1.25) - 1 = 0.5250$$

where

$$R_x = \frac{\text{Ending Exchange Rate}}{\text{Beginning Exchange Rate}} - 1 = \frac{\$1.50 \text{ per pound}}{\$1.20 \text{ per pound}} - 1$$

$$= 25\%$$

Ex Post Foreign Returns. Table 18-5 provides information about the annualized returns and risks which U.S. investors would have experienced if they had invested in the security indexes of various countries for the ten-year period ending with 1980. The data should not be used as forecasts of what should be expected in the future. Instead, they are shown solely to illustrate how changes in foreign exchange rates can affect returns on foreign investments.

TABLE 18-5 *Ex Post Average Annual Returns and Standard Deviations for U.S. Investors (December 1970–December 1980)*

Stocks of Country	Average Annual Return			Standard Deviation of Returns		
	Domestic	Exchange	Total US	Domestic	Exchange	Total US
Germany	4.14%	6.65%	11.07%	13.87%	11.87%	18.39%
Belgium	7.12	4.97	12.44	13.28	11.02	18.76
Denmark	11.41	2.49	14.18	15.41	10.28	17.65
France	7.79	2.16	10.12	22.00	10.24	25.81
Italy	6.64	−4.22	2.14	24.21	8.58	26.51
Norway	8.05	3.58	11.92	28.61	8.89	29.92
Netherlands	7.02	5.79	13.22	16.37	10.97	18.91
United Kingdom	12.93	−0.12	12.79	28.94	8.84	31.61
Sweden	8.52	1.84	10.52	15.05	8.89	18.06
Switzerland	2.67	9.63	12.56	16.80	14.67	21.40
Spain	0.76	−1.29	−0.54	16.71	9.10	20.26
Australia	10.86	0.53	11.45	24.62	9.15	27.15
Japan	13.80	6.68	21.40	16.39	10.42	19.55
Hong Kong	26.05	−0.41	25.53	47.95	5.63	45.80
Singapore	22.69	−4.69	16.94	35.82	6.52	36.03
Canada	14.85	−1.88	12.69	18.92	4.16	20.29
United States	6.78	0.00	6.78	16.00	0.00	16.00

SOURCE: B. Solnik and B. Noetzlin, "Optimal International Asset Allocation," *Journal of Portfolio Management* (Fall 1982): 11–21.

The first three columns of data show average annual domestic returns, exchange rate returns, and total foreign returns to U.S. residents. For example, consider the data for Germany. The average annual return on an index of German stocks which a resident of Germany would have earned was 4.14%. U.S. residents purchasing German stocks would also have earned this 4.14%. But in addition, U.S. residents who purchased German stocks had to purchase German currency to do so. The average annual return on this currency investment was 6.65%. When the domestic return is compounded by the exchange rate return, U.S. investors earned an average 11.07% return per year. In contrast, consider a German resident's investment in U.S. stocks. These stocks provided an average annual domestic return of 6.78% to both U.S. and German owners. But the German investor would have suffered a 6.65% exchange rate loss. On net, a German investor in U.S. stocks would have had a −0.3% average annual return.[12]

The last three columns in Table 18-5 show the annualized standard deviation of domestic returns, exchange rate returns, and total foreign returns to U.S. investors. Note that the standard deviation of total foreign returns is not the sum of domestic and exchange rate standard deviations. This happens because domestic and exchange rate returns are not perfectly correlated.

Two important implications can be drawn from Table 18-5:

1. The *average return* on foreign investment in a given country is often substantially affected by average exchange rate returns.

2. The *volatility of returns* on foreign investment in a given country is often substantially affected by volatility of exchange rates.

Exchange rates play an important role in the risks and returns on foreign investment.

EAFE Indexes. Historical information on the total market value and returns of securities in various nations of the world is difficult to develop, particularly if one wishes to include real estate and bond information. International security markets are not as well developed as those in the United States. However, Morgan Stanley Capital International (MSCI) has recently tracked *common stock values* in most of the more industrially developed countries. The index of countries which they use is known as the EAFE Index (the Europe, Australia, and Far East Index). Figure 18-8 illustrates the relative market value of stocks in the EAFE countries and the United States as of December 1970 and November 1988. In Table 18-6, the market value and percentage weighting by country are shown for November 1988. Clearly, Japan equity values dominated the United States by late 1988.

Historical U.S. dollar returns on the EAFE Index are shown in Table 18-7. Note the returns in 1985 (of 56.73%) and 1986 (of 69.97%). These drew the attention of many investors and caused many U.S. residents and institutions to begin to increase

---

[12] $R_{US}^f = (1.0678)(1 - 0.0665) - 1.0$

$\quad = -0.3\%$

FIGURE 18-8 *Share of Global Stock Market Capitalization*

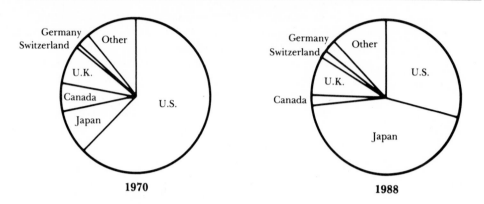

1970   1988

TABLE 18-6 *Total Equity Capitalization in EAFE Index, November 1988*

	Equity Capital[1]	% of World	% of EAFE
Australia	$ 135,460.0	1.6%	2.3%
Austria	8,514.9	0.1	0.1
Belgium	56,929.0	0.7	1.0
Canada	238,054.9	2.7	NA
Denmark	26,104.2	0.3	0.4
Finland	23,394.6	0.3	0.4
France	214,883.0	2.5	3.6
Germany	233,612.0	2.7	3.9
Hong Kong	72,984.3	0.8	1.2
Italy	135,061.7	1.6	2.3
Japan	3,857,966.2	44.5	64.6
Netherlands	83,726.4	1.0	1.4
New Zealand	13,922.3	0.2	0.2
Norway	15,105.2	0.2	0.3
Singapore/Malaysia	41,206.8	0.5	0.7
Spain	88,883.8	1.0	1.5
Sweden	84,766.8	1.0	1.4
Switzerland	148,407.7	1.7	2.5
United Kingdom	733,411.1	8.5	12.3
USA	2,445,239.2	28.2	NA
South Africa Gold	16,570.4	0.2	NA
Total: The World Index	$8,674,204.5	100.0%	100.0%
Total: EAFE			$5,974,340.2

[1]Stated in U.S. dollars.

their commitment to international equities. However, such returns were largely caused by declines in the value of the U.S. dollar. Investors who had security holdings denominated in foreign currencies won! Again, we see the critical role which the currency exchange rate can play.

TABLE 18-7 *Yearly Returns on EAFE Index (in U.S. Dollars)*

Year	EAFE Return	Year	EAFE Return
1969	2.78	1979	6.16
1970	−10.49	1980	24.44
1971	31.19	1981	−1.04
1972	37.65	1982	−0.83
1973	−14.18	1983	24.57
1974	−22.12	1984	7.88
1975	37.03	1985	56.73
1976	3.79	1986	69.97
1977	19.38	1987	24.93
1978	34.32	1988	28.60

Note: EAFE does not include the United States.

Exchange Rate Theory

A large body of theory and empirical testing has examined various aspects of currency exchange rates. Although much of it lies beyond the scope of this book, we should examine some fundamentals of the classic theory integrating international exchange.

Our concern is with three basic questions about exchange rates. First, what causes the existing (or spot) exchange rate between two countries? Second, what causes this exchange rate to change over time? Third, is there any way in which exchange rate risk can be hedged? The answer to each of these questions is clearly important to anyone considering the diversification of a portfolio using international securities.

Spot Exchange Rates. The equilibrium spot exchange rate between two countries is determined by the quantity of money circulating in each country. For example, consider two countries which produce only one commodity, say, rice. Country A issues money denominated in units called Azz, and country B issues money denominated in units called Bzz. The rice production and money units outstanding for each country are:

	Country A	Country B
Rice Production	100,000 lbs	200,000 lbs
Money Units in Circulation	100,000 Azz	400,000 Bzz
Local Price of Rice	1 Azz/lb	2 Bzz/lb

The equilibrium exchange rate must be .05 Azz per 1.0 Bzz (or 2 Bzz per 1.0 Azz). If this were not the case, arbitrage transactions would be possible. For example, if the current exchange rate were 1.0 Azz per 1.0 Bzz, country A's currency would be overvalued relative to country B's. A person in country B with 10,000 Bzz of currency could buy rice in either country. If the rice were bought in the domestic market, 5,000 pounds could be acquired (10,000 Bzz ÷ 2 Bzz per lb). If the rice were bought in the foreign market from country A, the 10,000 Bzz would first be converted to 10,000 Azz (that is, a 1:1 exchange rate) and then 10,000 pounds of rice would be bought in country A. Knowing this, people in country B would rapidly bid up the number of Bzz units they are willing to pay for an Azz until the exchange rate reached 2 Bzz per 1.0 Azz.

Reality, of course, is considerably more complex. Countries produce a tremendous variety of goods, political restrictions are imposed on the import and export of goods, etc. But the basic variable which determines the level of a current exchange rate is the quantity of money circulating in each country.

To express the determinants of the current exchange ratio symbolically, let:

$X_0^{d/f}$ = the exchange rate between one unit of domestic currency and one unit of foreign currency at period 0 (e.g., $X_0^{A/B} = 0.5$ and $X_0^{B/A} = 2.0$)

P_0^d = the price per unit of output at period 0 of domestic production (e.g., $P_0^A =$ 1 Azz and $P_0^B = 2$ Bzz)

P_0^f = the price per unit of output at period 0 of foreign production (e.g., $P_0^B =$ 2 Bzz and $P_0^A = 0.5$ Azz)

The spot exchange rate is:

Spot Exchange Rate
$$X_0^{d/f} = \frac{P_0^d}{P_0^f}$$
(18.5)

Changes in Exchange Rates. Changes in exchange rates are caused by relative inflation rates in two countries. To continue with our example, assume that, one year later, rice production in each country is unchanged but that there are now 120,000 units of Azz circulating and 420,000 units of Bzz. The unit price of rice in country A will now be 1.20 Azz (120,000 Azz ÷ 100,000 lbs), and the unit price in country B will be 2.10 Bzz (420,000 Bzz ÷ 200,000 lbs). Thus, the new equilibrium exchange rate will be 0.57 Azz per 1.0 Bzz (or 1.75 Bzz per 1.0 Azz).

The exchange rate changed because the countries experienced differing rates of inflation. Inflation in country A was 20%, and in country B it was 5%. Because inflation was more rapid in country A, the value of its currency fell relative to country B's.

The relationship which exists between past and future exchange rates is referred to as the *purchasing power parity model* and is written symbolically as:

Purchasing Power Parity
$$X_1^{d/f} = X_0^{d/f} \left(\frac{1 + I_1^d}{1 + I_1^f} \right)$$
(18.6)

where: $X_1^{d/f}$ = the number of domestic current units necessary to acquire 1.0 unit of foreign currency at date 1

I_1^d = the domestic inflation rate during period 1

I_1^f = the foreign inflation rate during period 1

In practice, the purchasing power parity model often will not explain short-term movements in exchange rates.[13] However, there is little doubt that the major force causing shifts in exchange rates is relative inflation rates between countries.

---

[13]For a summary of how well the model works, see Bergstrand, "Selected Views of Exchange Rate Determination After Floating," *New England Economic Review* (May–June 1983): 14–29.

Hedging Exchange Rate Risk and Forward Exchange Rates. There are three ways in which the exchange rate risk associated with international investment can be hedged.

The first involves the maintenance of offsetting positions in both the currency and commodities of a foreign country. For example, assume that you are a U.S. investor. You have purchased shares of a British stock index worth $15,000 when the exchange rate is $1.50 per British pound. In addition, you plan to visit Britain in three months and spend the $15,000. If the exchange drops to $1.20, your £10,000 investment will be worth only $12,000 ($1.20 × £10,000). But this investment loss is offset by your commodity gain—the $12,000 still purchases £10,000 of British goods. By being long the currency and short British goods, your risk is eliminated.

In reality, a hedge such as this is usually unreasonable. It is hard to imagine, for example, a pension fund both investing in British pounds and intending to spend dollars on British commodities.

A second approach is more viable and should be followed by anyone who is serious about international investment—diversify over many countries. The exchange rate risk incurred when investments are made in a single foreign country can be substantial. However, if exchange rate returns are uncorrelated, much of the risk (depending on the number of countries available) can be eliminated. For example, Table 18-8 presents the correlation coefficients of exchange rate returns between various countries from the perspective of a U.S. investor. The data apply to the ten-year period ending in 1980. Consider the correlation of 0.94 in exchange rate returns on investments in Belgium and Austria. Clearly, a U.S. investor would not have obtained much reduction of exchange rate risk by diversifying foreign investments across these two countries. However, diversification of exchange rate risk would have worked if investments had been made in Canada and Austria, because the correlation between their exchange rate returns is −0.09. The economies of many countries are so closely integrated that diversification of foreign investment among them will not reduce exchange rate risk. However, there are many countries for which the correlation is quite

TABLE 18-8 *Correlation Coefficients of Exchange Rate Returns, Various Countries, 1970–1980*

	Aus	Bel	Can	Den	Fra	Ger	Ita	Jap	Net	Spa	Swe	Swi	UK
Austria	1.00												
Belgium	0.94	1.00											
Canada	−0.09	−0.13	1.00										
Denmark	0.83	0.87	−0.09	1.00									
France	0.11	0.03	−0.02	0.05	1.00								
Germany	0.95	0.91	−0.12	0.83	−0.01	1.00							
Italy	0.04	0.10	−0.11	0.06	−0.02	0.11	1.00						
Japan	0.15	0.23	−0.54	0.24	−0.34	0.22	−0.05	1.00					
Netherlands	0.96	0.94	−0.16	0.88	−0.05	0.95	0.10	0.24	1.00				
Spain	0.43	0.38	0.07	0.62	0.36	0.46	0.55	−0.13	0.49	1.00			
Sweden	0.60	0.64	0.29	0.72	0.46	0.53	−0.01	−0.20	0.63	0.00	1.00		
Switzerland	0.90	0.90	−0.30	0.79	0.07	0.84	0.10	0.33	0.88	0.14	0.44	1.00	
United Kingdom	0.21	0.20	−0.29	0.11	−0.01	0.23	0.42	0.28	0.18	0.25	−0.07	0.22	1.0

SOURCE: Calculated from information provided in Ibbotson, Carr, and Robinson, "International Equity and Bond Returns," *Financial Analysts Journal* (July/August 1982): 2–24.

small and in which diversification will reduce exchange rate risk. A number of other studies have also shown that exchange rate returns are often close to zero. Much, although not all, exchange rate risk can be eliminated by broad diversification among countries.

The third approach is to hedge by trading in currency futures and forward markets. For example, currency futures are currently traded on the International Monetary Market for British pounds, Canadian dollars, Japanese yen, Swiss francs, and German marks. If forward contracts on other currencies are needed, they can be bought or sold through a variety of organizations active in international finance.

The price of a forward or futures contract in a foreign currency is set in exactly the same way as are the prices of other financial investments; that is:

$$\text{Forward Price} = \text{Expected Future Spot Price}$$

We saw earlier that spot exchange rates change with changes in the relative inflation rates of two countries. Thus, expected future spot prices are determined by *expected* inflation rates. Symbolically:

Forward Exchange Rate

$$F_{Tt}^{d/f} = X_t^{d/f} \frac{1 + E(I_{Tt}^d)}{1 + E(I_{Tt}^f)} \tag{18.7}$$

where: $F_{Tt}^{d/f}$ = the futures price of the domestic currency which matures at date T quoted on date t

$X_t^{d/f}$ = the spot exchange rate at date t

$E(I_{Tt}^d)$ = the expected domestic inflation between dates t and T as of date t

$E(I_{Tt}^f)$ = the expected foreign inflation between dates t and T as of date t

Interest Rate Parity. If capital is allowed to flow between countries at zero cost and if taxes are identical in all countries, the expected *real rate of return* for a given risk level should be identical in all countries. If this were not the case, capital would flow from the country with the lower expected real returns to the country with the larger real returns until the two real returns are equal.

Nominal expected returns would differ between countries if the countries have different expected rates of inflation. For example, if the real risk-free rate is the same in two countries, the relationship between nominal risk-free rates should be:

Nominal Risk-Free Rate Relationship

$$\frac{1 + RF^d}{1 + RF^f} = \frac{1 + E(I^d)}{1 + E(I^f)} \tag{18.8}$$

For example, in late 1988 the spot rate between U.S. dollars and British pounds was \$1.844 per pound, and the six-month forward rate was \$1.8125 per pound. Thus, according to the forward/spot relationship shown in Equation 18.7, the ratio of six-month U.S. to British inflation should be:

$$F_{T0}^{d/f} / X_0^{d/f} = \frac{1 + E(I^d)}{1 + E(I^f)}$$

$$\$1.8125 / \$1.844 = 0.9829$$

At that time, the six-month return on U.S. Treasury bills was 4.22%. This implies that the six-month nominal risk-free rate in Britain should have been 6.03%:

$$\frac{1.0422}{1 + RF^f} = 0.9829$$

$$RF^f = (1.0422/0.9829) - 1.0$$

$$= 6.03\%$$

What should you have done if the British nominal rate of return had been higher, say, equal to 8.00%? Invest in British risk-free assets and sell British pound forwards (buy U.S. dollar forwards) to guarantee the dollar value of your investment. For example, $100,000,000 U.S. dollars would have provided 54,229,934 pounds at the exchange rate of $1.844 per pound. Invested in Britain for six months, this would have yielded 58,568,329 pounds. If pound forward contracts had been sold at $1.8125 per pound, the 58,568,329 pounds could have been converted into $106,155,096. Your nominally risk-free U.S. dollar return would have exceeded the Treasury bill return of 4.22% by a sizable amount. Only at a nominally risk-free return of 6.03% in Britain would you be indifferent between U.S. and foreign investment.

Forward and Futures Currency Hedges. In the example above we were able to engage in a hedge with forward contracts which created a guaranteed U.S. dollar return. Unfortunately, if we had invested in nominally risk-free securities which had a maturity beyond the delivery date of existing forwards and futures, a risk-free hedge would not have been possible. We would have to be exposed to exchange rate risk. Similarly, if we had invested in risky foreign securities, we could not have eliminated exchange rate risk since we would have an uncertainty about the quantity of the foreign currency which is to be returned to the United States. Both of these problems reduce the effectiveness of forward and futures hedges. As a result, U.S. investors who invest in risky international securities for long time periods can not rely on forwards and futures to reduce exchange rate risk. Instead, they must rely on time and country diversification.

Ways to Invest Internationally

International investment can be undertaken by indirect or direct investment. Indirect investment consists of purchasing the shares of a U.S. company which does a significant amount of business in foreign countries—a multinational corporation. Since the shares of such firms are listed on major U.S. stock exchanges, they can be traded rapidly and at low cost. In addition, multinationals are able to make asset investments in many countries which would not allow direct portfolio investments. The major difficulty in using U.S.-based multinationals as a vehicle for international diversification is that they do not provide diversification advantages as large as can be obtained by direct investment.

The easiest form of direct investment is the purchase of an investment fund which specializes in foreign securities. Owing to the recent interest in international investing (particularly by pension funds), the number of such international investment funds has grown rapidly. Small investors may choose from mutual funds specializing in international securities. Large investors can also choose from a variety of commingled funds offered by U.S. banks and insurance companies as well as commingled funds incorporated and managed outside the United States. Commingled funds are similar to mutual funds but are offered by banks and insurance funds and are not traded in the secondary security market. Purchase of a share in such investment companies can be accomplished quickly and at low cost. Substantial exchange rate risk remains, however, unless the fund is diversified over numerous countries or the investor creates hedge positions in the forward currency markets.

Finally, the securities of a foreign corporation or government could be directly acquired. Many of the larger foreign corporations are traded on U.S. exchange markets through ADRs, and many brokerage firms have access to foreign exchange markets.[14] The major disadvantages of this approach are that (1) the number of securities traded on U.S. markets is limited, (2) foreign markets often do not have the depth of trading necessary to easily absorb large transactions without affecting prices, and (3) the individual investor is likely to have poor (or at least untimely) information about the securities.

Difficulties of International Investment

International investment is not a panacea. It is simply an added tool which can be used in portfolio management. But there are dangers that must be recognized.

Many investment managers sell their services based on historical performance. We saw earlier that the performance of domestic U.S. mutual funds does not appear very impressive. The risk-adjusted returns which they have earned could as easily have been obtained by a passive buy-hold strategy. The same applies to managers of foreign securities. Although the evidence on their performance is sparse, there is serious doubt that they should be able to generate abnormal risk-adjusted returns. The benefit of international investment is additional diversification, not abnormal performance. When a manager is selected, attention should be given to how broadly his or her holdings are diversified. In addition, portfolio returns associated with exchange rate returns should be discounted since they will probably not be the same in the future.

Increased diversification is probably the sole reason to invest internationally. But to obtain this diversification gain, one must have security positions in many countries. Placing funds only in British, German, and Japanese firms is inadequate. Unfortunately, there are at present no easy ways to purchase ownership positions of stock indexes in a large number of countries.

Monitoring costs are also high. Information about the financial condition and future prospects of U.S. corporations is widely circulated and available at little cost. In

---

[14]An ADR is an American depository receipt. See Chapter 2.

contrast, public information about many foreign corporations is considerably less and, in many countries, insider information is extensive. Thus the monitoring costs necessary to remain informed about the securities can be great. In addition, the time and transaction costs associated with hedging exchange rate risk must be considered.

Finally, one must be willing to accept the political risks associated with investment in a foreign country. Political risk refers to constraints placed on the return of both the initial investment and the earnings from the investment. Such constraints can range from taxation of profits and withdrawal of capital to complete expropriation of the investment. Over relatively short time periods, political risks are predictable enough that severe losses can be avoided. However, over extended periods of ten to twenty years, political risk is hard to avoid. Certainly, the risks associated with individual countries can be continuously monitored and one can hope to withdraw an investment from a country before significant losses occur. But this increases monitoring costs, and it is doubtful that political risk can be totally avoided.

REAL ESTATE EQUITY INVESTMENT

The last form of investment which we will examine is real estate. Ownership claims to real estate returns, like all other securities, can be debt claims, equity claims, or combinations of debt and equity. Debt claims consist of direct ownership of mortgages or indirect ownership of mortgage pools such as GNMAs. These debt claims can be evaluated in the same manner as any other short- to intermediate-term debt instrument. Once default risk, coupon, and maturity are considered, they are perfect substitutes for other types of debt claims. For this reason, we will not discuss mortgages or mortgage-backed securities in this section but will focus, instead, on equity claims.

Investment texts have traditionally said little (if anything) about the use of real estate equity in a security portfolio. This is understandable. In the past, a principal advantage associated with real estate has been its favorable tax treatment. This meant that only a small portion of all investment portfolios would have found real estate to be a viable holding—portfolios owned by people in high marginal tax brackets. In addition, a market in which real estate equity could be easily traded did not exist. Thus, it was costly to acquire or dispose of a given equity claim.[15] Finally, very little was known about the returns earned on real estate equity and how they might complement traditional stock/bond portfolios. Today, none of these concerns can be completely dismissed. Yet recent developments have reduced the tax features of real estate, increased its marketability, and shown that a real estate equity position can play an important role in portfolio strategy.

Real estate seems to provide two distinct advantages to a traditional stock/bond portfolio.[16] The first is our old friend diversification. Although truly accurate corre-

---

[15]The exception is real estate investment trusts.

[16]For the remainder of the chapter, the term *real estate* should be interpreted as *real estate equity*.

lations between real estate returns and stock (or bond) returns covering extended periods of time are not available, most people who have examined the matter believe that real estate is sufficiently uncorrelated with stock (and bond) returns that it can improve portfolio diversification. The second advantage is that real estate can provide an inflation hedge. During the 1970s and 1980s, changes in the value of land and tangible property were positively correlated with rates of inflation. In contrast, stocks and intermediate- to long-term bond returns appeared to be negatively correlated with inflation.

Yet real estate investment, like international investment, has its unique characteristics and dangers which must be considered seriously by anyone thinking about adding it to a stock/bond portfolio.

Characteristics of Real Estate Investment

When you buy a share of common stock, you are actually buying a portfolio of three distinct assets: (1) the talent of the firm's employees, (2) the tangible property used by the employees, and (3) the land on which the tangible property is located. Usually the largest portion of this portfolio will be the employees' talent, but it is important to recognize that investment in a common stock does involve an investment in real estate.

Nonetheless, a large amount of real estate is not controlled by companies traded in the secondary stock markets. Figure 18-9, for example, displays an estimate of the relative market values of real estate, equities, bonds, and cash equivalents as of the end of 1980. At that time, real estate represented about 60% of the total. Of this, about 70% was associated with the value of residential housing, 12% was business real estate, and 18% was farm-related. When the value of residential real estate is deducted, business and farm real estate represented about 35% of all market value. Although the purchase of common stock does involve an investment in real estate, the proportion of a share's value which real estate represents is small compared to the importance of real estate in the total economy. This suggests that for a portfolio to be truly diversified, investment in real estate equity is needed.

As noted earlier, real estate investment comes in two broad categories: land and tangible property. The important investment characteristics of the two are both similar and dissimilar. For example, they are similar in that neither is very marketable and both are valued in large part by their particular location. They are dissimilar in that each is taxed differently and land has an infinite life (duration), whereas, in comparison, tangible property has a much shorter life. Thus, as we review the characteristics of real estate investment which make it different from common stock investment, we should be careful to distinguish between land and tangible property.

Five major investment characteristics set equity ownership of real estate apart from equity ownership of a traded common stock.[17] First, stocks are actively traded in a

---

[17]The sequence in which we discuss these differences does not imply their order of importance.

FIGURE 18-9 *Estimated U.S. Capital Value, 1984*

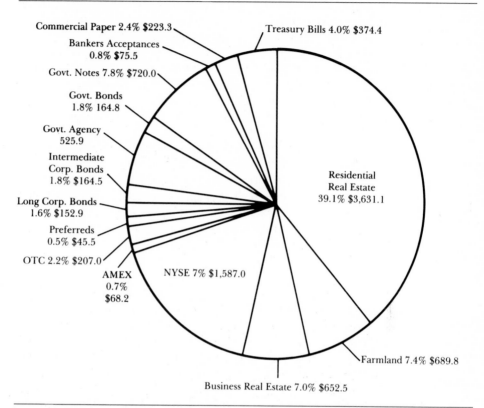

SOURCE: R. Ibbotson, L. Siegel, and K. Love, "World Wealth: Market Values and Returns," *Journal of Portfolio Management*, Fall 1985.

market which has almost instantaneous and free access to information. As a result, the market prices of stock are "fair" in the sense that prices fully reflect all information available. Buyers purchase at fair prices. Sellers sell at fair prices. In contrast, information about real estate is costly to develop and, thus, trading prices may not be equilibrium prices. More analysis must go into the purchase (or sale) of real estate. This means, for example, that the selection of a real estate portfolio manager can significantly affect the risk/return performance of the real estate holdings. The stock market appears to be priced efficiently, so it is doubtful that a stock investment manager can consistently earn abnormal returns. However, the real estate market is generally thought to be inefficiently priced, so it is possible that a real estate investment manager can consistently earn abnormal returns (either positive or negative).

Second, stock prices have a continuous price history which is determined by the consensus of a large number of market participants. Thus, an accurate rate of return can be determined and ex post risk and average returns can be calculated precisely.

In contrast, real estate prices are set by no more than a few appraisers. At the time a real estate trade actually occurs, this isn't really a problem. The buyer and seller have clearly agreed on the market value of the asset, regardless of appraised values. It is when prices are set by appraisal value *between* trade days that problems arise in the calculation of returns. Because of the nature of the appraisal process, there is a tendency to "smooth" the price of a property. As a result, returns on real estate appear to be much less volatile than they would be if the returns were measured on actual market transactions. This is a significant problem in comparing the relative risks and returns of stocks versus real estate. At present, a truly reliable real estate return series has not been developed.

Third, *direct* investment in real estate is much less marketable than direct investment in common stock. The legal fees, accounting fees, brokerage fees, and price concessions associated with an attempt to rapidly buy or sell property can be substantial. For some investors, such as property casualty firms or retirees, these costs are unacceptable. Other investors, such as pension funds and life insurance firms, have little need for immediate liquidity. In an attempt to overcome this problem, the real estate industry has attempted to develop various types of *marketable indirect* claims to real estate. These are discussed later in the chapter. They are more marketable than direct ownership of property, but they are still less marketable than the typical common stock and are often traded at appraised value instead of true market value.

The maturity (or duration) of real estate depends on the type of property purchased. For example, the purchase of a convenience store on land which is leased probably has a maturity of between five and ten years. However, the purchase of farmland in Iowa has an infinite maturity. Care must be taken so that when real estate is added to a portfolio it does not misalign the desired maturity (duration) distribution.

Perhaps the most important difference between real estate and the common stock of a business that is unrelated to real estate is the manner in which each is taxed. Land cannot be depreciated for tax purposes. Thus, there are no tax advantages associated with its ownership. Tangible property, however, can often be depreciated for tax purposes at a rate much faster than the true economic depreciation of the property. Over the life of the property, total depreciation cannot exceed the property's cost. Yet in the early years of the property's life, tax-deductible depreciation will usually be greater than economic depreciation. This means that a relatively young property will be priced, in part, for the tax advantages it provides. This price will be attractive only to individuals who pay taxes at a high enough rate to take advantage of the tax shields. For example, a charitable organization which pays no taxes would find the price of such young property to be too high. However, as the tax advantages associated with accelerated depreciation are used up, the property would become more attractive to individuals and organizations which do not pay taxes and less attractive to those needing tax shields.

The detailed tax aspects of real estate investing are complex and certainly beyond the scope of this text. Nonetheless, it is important to remember that taxation affects the value of tangible property and determines what type of investor should own it at each stage in its life.

Real Estate Equity Returns

Historical Estimates of Return and Risk. Virtually all real estate return series are estimates based on an *appraisal of market values and cash flows*. With very rare exceptions, they are not calculated using actual market-value trading prices. Over long time periods, actual average real estate returns probably are close to those estimated by appraisal techniques. However, return estimates for specific years can be in substantial error. In particular, the smoothing inherent in appraisal techniques creates a less volatile series of estimated returns than if returns were calculated using actual trade prices. As a result, the standard deviations of estimated real estate returns and their correlation coefficients with other assets are biased downward. In sum, long-run *average return* estimates are probably reasonable approximations, but long-run *risk estimates* are probably much lower than they should be.

A number of these estimates are shown in Table 18-9. Instead of listing returns for each year, a unit value series is presented.[18] The Ibbotson and Siegel unit values are based on a variety of estimations, including sample appraisals, changes in the Consumer Price Index, construction costs, etc. The Miles and McCue estimates are based on cash flows and appraisals on properties held by a large life insurance firm.

The EAI returns are average returns on a large number of commingled real estate equity funds tracked by Evaluation Associates Incorporated. The PRISA returns are those on one commingled fund, the "Prudential Real Estate Separate Account A."

In Table 18-10 the Ibbotson and Siegel data are compared with returns on common stocks over equivalent time periods. Note that the average returns on the real estate estimates are slightly lower than the average common stock returns. Nonetheless, the two are reasonably similar, and other studies have suggested that average real estate returns may be greater than average common stock returns.[19] On the whole, it appears that real estate provides a return approximately equal to that of common stock. The dramatic differences in Table 18-10 are not between average returns, but between standard deviations. The total stock standard deviation of annual returns is 17.52%, while the total real estate standard deviation is 3.71%. During the same time period the standard deviation of T-bill returns was 3.32%.

Certainly real estate cannot be expected to provide long-run returns similar to those of common stock but be only as risky as Treasury bills. The markets are not that inefficient. The problem, of course, lies in the smoothed manner in which real estate returns are calculated. Unless returns are calculated on *actual trade* prices, risk and correlation measures simply cannot be trusted.

One study has evaluated real estate returns using actual trade prices. Unfortunately, the time period covered is not very lengthy. Using quarterly returns on ac-

---

[18]See Chapter 4 for a discussion of unit values. The return in year t is calculated as:

$$R_t = (UV_t \div UV_{t-1}) - 1.0$$

where UV refers to the unit value at the end of year t or $t - 1$.

[19]For example, the geometric mean return of the Miles-McCue data in Table 18-9 is 13.1% compared with a return on the S&P 500 during the same period of 7.9%.

TABLE 18-9 *Historical Estimates of Real Estate Returns Unit Value Indexes*

Year	Ibbotson and Siegel			Miles and McCue*	EAI	PRISA
	Total	Business	Farm	Residential		
1946	1.000		1.000	1.000			
1947	1.108		1.163	1.082			
1948	1.223		1.316	1.183			
1949	1.256		1.389	1.200			
1950	1.384		1.693	1.269			
1951	1.566		1.998	1.413			
1952	1.657		2.139	1.458			
1953	1.707		2.160	1.544			
1954	1.793		2.314	1.610			
1955	1.864		2.452	1.663			
1956	1.958		2.642	1.732			
1957	2.085		2.847	1.836			
1958	2.216		3.211	1.911			
1959	2.301	1.000	3.366	1.977			
1960	2.395	1.025	3.503	2.063			
1961	2.525	1.053	3.822	2.160			
1962	2.653	1.087	4.166	2.251			
1963	2.829	1.314	4.573	2.386			
1964	2.829	1.134	4.573	2.386			
1965	2.983	1.168	4.920	2.509			
1966	3.189	1.216	5.542	2.649			
1967	3.401	1.276	6.220	2.789			
1968	3.643	1.358	6.860	2.964			
1969	4.318	1.595	7.998	3.533			
1970	4.782	1.754	8.619	3.946			
1971	5.231	2.026	9.628	4.249			
1972	5.698	2.218	11.451	4.518			
1973	6.362	2.383	15.440	4.815	1.000		
1974	7.239	2.576	18.557	5.451	1.081		
1975	8.212	2.804	21.993	6.160	1.150		
1976	9.008	3.029	26.291	6.611	1.217	1.000	1.000
1977	10.006	3.301	29.270	7.363	1.347	1.117	1.095
1978	11.483	3.703	34.421	8.410	1.518	1.266	1.231
1979	13.619	4.240	41.202	10.001	1.902	1.478	1.489
1980	15.436	4.724	45.516	11.447	2.288	1.746	1.867
1981	16.182	5.360	46.003	11.942	2.673	2.094	2.306
1982	17.452	5.917	43.988	13.210		2.509	2.697
1983						2.836	2.840
1984						3.230	3.159
1985						3.656	3.614
1986						4.084	3.939
1987							4.184
1988							4.200

SOURCES: Ibbotson and Siegel, "Real Estate Returns: A Comparison with Other Investments," *AREUEA Journal* 12, no. 3 (1984): 239; Miles and McCue, "Commercial Real Estate Returns," *AREUEA Journal* 12, no. 3 (1984): 364.

*Equally weighted average of industrial, office, retail, residential, and motel returns. Fiscal year returns and September 30 of each year.

TABLE 18-10 *Comparison of Estimated Annual Real Estate Returns with Annual Common Stock Returns*

	Arithmetic Mean	Geometric Mean	Standard Deviation
Common Stocks			
NYSE Index	12.25%	10.90%	17.16%
AMEX Index (1960–82)	9.33	6.66	23.30
OTC Index	15.17	13.05	21.41
Total	12.42	11.00	17.52
Real Estate			
Farms	11.32	11.09	7.21
Residential Housing	7.50	7.43	3.89
Business (1960–82)	8.10	8.03	3.78
Total	8.33	8.27	3.71

SOURCE: Ibbotson and Siegel, "Real Estate Returns: A Comparison with Other Investments," *AREUEA Journal* 12, no. 3 (1984): 228.

tual real estate trade prices between 1973 and 1978, Hoag found that the standard deviation of real estate was 8.61% versus 10.38% for the S&P 500. Again, the time period he used was very short, but his estimates suggest that real estate is more risky than appraisal techniques imply.

Diversifiable Risk and Inflation Protection. Although historical real estate return series are not as accurate as we would wish and bias downward the true volatility of real estate market values, they are the best measurements we have at present. In addition, a number of open-end real estate funds are now available for which net asset value is determined by periodic appraisals. Buyers and sellers trade with the fund at appraised net asset value. Thus, even if the appraisals do not truly represent market values, people trading in such funds would have experienced a return history similar to that in Table 18-9.

A principal reason for adding real estate to a stock/bond portfolio is diversification. The lower the correlation is between real estate returns and the returns on stocks and bonds, the greater the diversification potential. Table 18-11 shows historical correlation coefficients between annual real estate returns and returns on (1) the S&P 500, (2) long-term corporate bonds, and (3) U.S. Treasury bills. The correlation between stock and bonds is approximately zero. If this holds true in the future, real estate will be a good diversification tool.

In addition, Miles and McCue examined how various classes of commercial real estate are correlated with the S&P 500 as opposed to an aggregate index such as that used in Table 18-11.[20] They found that the correlation of each class was also close to

---

[20]Classes included industrial, office, retail, residential, and motel.

TABLE 18-11 *Correlation Coefficients Between Asset Returns*

	Real Estate	S&P 500	Long-Term Corporate Bonds	Treasury Bills	Inflation
Real Estate	1.00				
S&P 500	−0.06	1.00			
Long-Term Corporate Bonds	−0.06	0.14	1.00		
Treasury Bills	0.44	−0.25	0.15	1.00	
Inflation	0.85	−0.27	−0.19	0.70	1.00

0.0. Thus, the low correlation between real estate returns and common stock returns seems to be pervasive throughout different types of real estate. To ensure as much diversification as possible, one should diversify broadly across all types of real estate. No single class should be over- or underweighted because of its unusual correlation with stock returns.

Many people believe that in addition to providing diversification, real estate will act as an inflation hedge. Based on the return series which are available, this seems to be true. For example, the correlation estimate between real estate returns and inflation rates is shown in Table 18-11 to be 0.85. The greater the inflation rate, the greater the real estate returns. And the smaller the inflation rate, the smaller the real estate returns. The only other security having a similar correlation with inflation is Treasury bills. Both stocks and bonds had a negative correlation with inflation.[21]

Participation in Real Estate Equity

Equity ownership of real estate can be accomplished by *direct or indirect ownership*. Direct ownership means that one is the sole proprietor or a partner in the asset. Indirect ownership means that one has bought shares in a firm which owns real estate. We will discuss only indirect ownership since indirect claims are marketable and offer an easy way to gain broad diversification across a large number of real estate properties. There are, at present, two major ways of obtaining an indirect security claim to real estate: (1) REITs and (2) CREFs.

Real estate investment trusts (REITs) are similar to closed-end investment companies. Shares are sold to the public in a primary offering and leveraged with borrowings to purchase real estate assets. There are three general types of REITs: (1) *equity* funds which invest solely in real estate equity ownership positions, (2) *mortgage* funds which invest solely in various forms of mortgages, and (3) *hybrid* funds which combine equity and mortgage positions. REITs may be purchased in the secondary markets through a stockbroker. They represent the only way that small investors can

---

[21]These correlations are based on one-year time intervals. The correlation between inflation and each asset's long-run return is not well documented.

participate by an indirect security claim in real estate equity. Unfortunately, they were very poorly managed during the 1970s, and many firms went bankrupt. Because of their use of financial leverage, large investors such as pension funds rarely use them.

A commingled real estate fund (CREF) obtains funds from a variety of pension funds and invests the proceeds in a diversified real estate portfolio. CREFs are available only to pension funds and are offered by banks, insurance firms, and real estate advisory organizations. A CREF may be either open- or closed-end, similar to stock investment companies. Open-end CREFs usually calculate the appraised value of assets monthly and use these to define the fund's net asset value. Since shares may be bought or sold at this net asset value, CREFs provide a degree of liquidity for pension funds. However, the sponsor can set conditions under which withdrawal of investments may occur. This allows the sponsor sufficient leeway to obtain cash for share redemptions without having to sell assets in a forced liquidation. But it also limits the true liquidity of the pension fund's investment, particularly if a large number of pension funds attempt to redeem their shares at about the same time.

SUMMARY

Investment companies are financial intermediaries which pool the resources of individual investors and reinvest in a portfolio of marketable securities. Investment company shares can offer two major advantages over other security media: (1) broad diversification and (2) management with a stated objective in mind. Two broad classes of investment company shares exist. Open-end funds (also known as mutual funds) stand ready to buy or sell shares in the fund directly from the investor and manage the bulk of investment company assets. Closed-end fund shares are bought and sold through the organized security markets in the same manner as other common stocks. Mutual fund shares are traded through a broker at net asset value plus a front-end load if the fund is known as a load fund, or directly from the fund at net asset value if the fund is no-load. Closed-end funds rarely trade at net asset value. Instead, their prices are created by demand-and-supply conditions for their shares, and they usually sell at substantial discounts from net asset value.

Perhaps the single largest advantage offered by investment company shares is the ability to easily own a portion of a well-diversified portfolio. Although exceptions exist, most funds are broadly diversified, and their risk exposure remains reasonably constant over time.

While most funds claim that better performance can be obtained through active professional management than through a passive buy-hold strategy, the empirical evidence based on the CAPM is often contrary. When each of the three major performance measures (the Sharpe, Treynor, and Jensen indexes) is used to evaluate past performance, the results suggest that (net of all expenses) active management at best merely matches a passive strategy. Random chance can explain the few funds which appear to have had consistent above-average performance.

International investment has recently gained the interest of large portfolio managers, primarily for its increased diversification possibilities. However, international investment has an added dimension which is not associated with investments made in one's own country—exchange rate risk. Exchange rate risk can be partially eliminated by broad diversification across a large number of countries and by hedging in the forward or futures markets. As a practical matter, however, exchange rate risk cannot be totally eliminated.

Real estate equity investment also offers the chance for broader diversification than is available in traditional portfolios of stocks and bonds. However, various characteristics of real estate set it apart from stocks and bonds and deserve careful attention before an investment decision is made. For example: (1) real estate is much less marketable, (2) prices are often set by unique tax advantages that would not be availble to many investors, (3) the selection of a real estate portfolio manager can have substantial effects on returns, and (4) the duration associated with an investment in land can shift the total portfolio's duration. In addition, a reliable history of real estate returns is not available, making it difficult to judge how much diversification potential there really is.

REVIEW PROBLEMS

1. In the chapter, the performance of 255 mutual funds over the period 1975–1984 was examined. Statistics on two of these funds are shown below. (Standard deviations of the regression parameters are shown in brackets below each estimate.)

	AMF	Putnam Investors
Average Excess Quarterly Return	2.58%	1.64%
Standard Deviation of Excess Quarterly Returns	6.96%	9.36%

$$\widetilde{ER}_{AMF,t} = 0.96\% + 0.75\,[\widetilde{ER}_{WS,t}] + \tilde{E}_{AMF,t} \qquad R^2 = 92.7\%$$
$$\qquad\qquad (0.31)\quad (0.03)$$

$$\widetilde{ER}_{PI,t} = -0.49\% + 1.00\,[\widetilde{ER}_{WS,t}] + \tilde{E}_{PI,t} \qquad R^2 = 88.9\%$$
$$\qquad\qquad (0.51)\quad (0.06)$$

a. Calculate the Sharpe, Treynor, and Jensen performance measures for each fund.
b. Did either of these funds statistically outperform the market? (Use 95% confidence levels.)
c. Which of the funds was more diversified?
d. Which of the funds had a greater systematic risk?

2. You are a U.S. resident thinking about investing $100,000 in German stocks. The exchange rate is currently $0.30 per mark. You expect that the German stocks will earn 15% for German residents. You also expect that the inflation rate over the next year will be 9% in Germany and 6% in the United States.
a. If you do not hedge your investment, what is your expected one-year return? What part is due to domestic expected returns and what part is due to exchange rate returns?
b. Given this information, what do you think the one-year forward rate should be?

c. Assume the one-year forward rate is exactly what you calculated in part b. What hedge would you make to offset exchange rate risk?

d. Assume that the German stocks do provide a domestic return of 15%, but that the exchange rate in a year is $0.40 per mark. If you hedged, what is your return?

e. Why may this hedge not work?

Solutions

1. a.

	American Mutual Fund	*Putnam Investors*
Sharpe	2.58% ÷ 6.96% = 0.3707	1.64% ÷ 9.36% = 0.1752
Treynor	2.58% ÷ 0.75 = 3.44%	1.64% ÷ 1.00 = 1.64%
Jensen's Alpha	0.96%	−0.49%

In each case, AMF had the better risk-adjusted performance.

b.

	American Mutual Fund	*Putnam Investors*
Calculated Z on Alpha	0.96 ÷ 0.31 = 3.10	−0.49 ÷ 0.51 = −0.96

Using $Z = 1.96$ for a 95% confidence level, AMF had a statistically significant positive performance. The 0.96% per quarter translates to 3.9% $(1.0096^4 - 1.0)$ per year. Putnam Investors had a negative estimated alpha but it is not statistically different from 0.0.

c. American Mutual Fund was the more diversified as evidenced by the 92.7% R^2.

d. Putnam Investors had a systematic risk equal to that of the Wilshire 5000 since its estimated beta was 1.0. This is greater than AMF's estimated beta of 0.75.

2. a. Dollar and deutsche mark (DM) flows are:

Today			*One Year Later*	
Invest Dollars	$100,000		$111,834	Receive Dollars
Buy DM at $0.30/DM		15% →		Sell DM at $0.2917*
Invest DM	333,333 DM	Return	383,333 DM	Receive DM

*Expected Spot Rate $= (\$0.30)\left(\dfrac{1.06}{1.09}\right) = \$0.2917$

Expected Return on Dollar Investment $= \dfrac{\$111,834}{\$100,000} - 1.0 = 11.834\%$

Domestic Return $= 15\%$

Exchange Rate Return $= \dfrac{0.2917}{0.300} - 1.0 = -2.752\%$

$R^f = (1.15)(0.9725) - 1.0 = 11.834\%$

Note that by not hedging, your *expected* return is equal to the compounding of the 15% domestic return and the −2.75% exchange rate loss. However, since you are uncertain about the exchange rate in one year from now, you are also uncertain about the exchange rate return.

    b. The forward rate should be the expected spot rate of \$0.2917/DM.

    c. Sell futures (or forward) contracts on 383,333 DM at a price of \$0.2917/DM. This will lock in the expected return of 11.834%. (This is lower than the 15% domestic German return, but recall that inflation in Germany is expected to be greater by about 3 percentage points. Thus, equilibrium returns on German stocks should be about 3 percentage points higher than the returns on domestic U.S. stocks. Given the lower U.S. inflation rate, the 11.83% might be fair.)

    d. You have sold futures contracts on 383,333 DM at \$0.2917/DM. If the exchange rate in a year is \$0.400/DM, the 383,333 DM received in a year from now can be translated back to \$153,333, for a gain of \$41,499 more than expected. But this is exactly offset by a \$41,499 loss on the futures [(0.2917 − 0.4) × 383,333]. Thus, your return is exactly what was expected — 11.83%. Given the hedge there is no uncertainty in your expected return *associated with exchange rates*.

    e. The hedge might not work:
        (1) if contracts in 383,333 DM units are unavailable.
        (2) if the contracts mature on dates other than those on which you intend to translate marks into dollars.
        (3) if the domestic German return is not 15%.

QUESTIONS AND PROBLEMS

  1. Give your reaction to the following statement from the dual-purpose Hemisphere Fund's 1967 annual report:

    The concern of diversification is a meaningful one in the mutual fund industry, particularly in a dual fund, but overdiversification can be harmful. It is our view that the more companies in a portfolio, the more average the investment performance. We think that a portfolio's assets should be divided so that a significant amount of these assets are in relatively few well-chosen companies. Otherwise the impact of good ideas is greatly reduced.

  2. What do the various performance studies of investment companies suggest about the correctness of efficient market theory?

  3. Relative to managed investment companies, what may be the advantages and disadvantages of a unit investment trust?

  4. To evaluate the historical performance of McMaster Fund, you collect the following data:

	Percentage Return in Year							
	1	*2*	*3*	*4*	*5*	*6*	*7*	*8*
McMaster Fund	17.2	2.6	−33.9	−32.5	19.7	31.0	14.5	17.3
S&P 500	14.3	19.0	−14.8	−26.5	37.3	24.1	− 7.2	6.6
DJIA	9.8	18.5	−13.5	−23.7	44.9	22.9	−12.9	2.8
One-Year T-Bills	7.0	6.0	7.5	8.0	8.5	8.5	9.0	8.5

    a. Calculate S_p and T_p using both the DJIA and the S&P 500 as the market proxy.
    b. Plot McMaster returns against the S&P 500 and visually estimate alpha.
    c. Using this plot, estimate McMaster Fund's beta.

5. Historical information on fund *A* and fund *B* is given below, assuming that an initial investment of $10,000 is made in each.

Fund A	1	2	3	4
Net Asset Value — Start of Year	$10,000	$12,000	$10,000	$10,500
Interest and Dividends Received	4,000	3,500	4,000	4,000
Realized and Unrealized Capital Gains	4,000	(1,500)	2,000	3,000
Net Asset Value Before Dividend Distributions	$18,000	$14,000	$16,000	$17,500
Income Dividend Distributions	(4,000)	(3,500)	(4,000)	(4,000)
Realized Capital Gain Distributions	(2,000)	(500)	(1,500)	(2,000)
Net Asset Value — End of Year	$12,000	$10,000	$10,500	$11,500

Fund B	1	2	3	4
Net Asset Value — Start of Year	$10,000	$13,000	$11,250	$12,500
Interest and Dividends Received	4,000	3,500	4,000	4,000
Realized and Unrealized Capital Gains	4,000	(1,500)	2,000	3,000
Net Asset Value Before Dividend Distributions	$18,000	$15,000	$17,250	$19,500
Income Dividend Distributions	(4,000)	(3,500)	(4,000)	(4,000)
Realized Capital Gain Distributions	(1,000)	(250)	(750)	(1,000)
Net Asset Value — End of Year	$13,000	$11,250	$12,500	$14,500

a. Calculate the yearly rates of return on each and compare them.
b. Which fund did better?
c. Assuming you are in a 40% ordinary income tax bracket, a 20% long-term capital gains bracket, and all distributed capital gains are long term, which fund performed better? Why?

6. Consider the following information on six funds and six individuals. Try to match various funds with the situation facing each individual.

Fund	Objective	Beta	R²	Load Fund
			Return Information	
A	Maximum Capital Gains	1.2	70%	No
B	Maximum Capital Gains	1.2	95%	Yes
C	Capital Gains	1.0	90%	No
D	Moderate Growth and Income	0.9	95%	No
E	Income	0.6	85%	Yes
F	Index to S&P 500	1.0	99%	No

Individual	Tax Bracket	Age	Ability to Accept Risk	Trading Activity	Other Security Holdings
1	Moderate	30	Moderate	Active	Few
2	High	35	High	Inactive	Few
3	High	35	High	Active	Many
4	Low	65	Low	Inactive	Few
5	Moderate	20	Moderate	Active	Few
6	Moderate	20	Moderate	Inactive	Many

7. Suppose you have gathered quarterly data on the net returns of four funds and related them to equivalent market returns (S&P 500) and 90-day T-bill returns via the following regression model:

$$\widetilde{ER}_{pt} = a_p + b_p(\widetilde{ER}_{mt}) + \tilde{E}_{pt}$$

Fund	a_p Coefficient	a_p Std. Dev.	b_p Coefficient	b_p Std. Dev.	R^2
1	0.98%	1.00%	0.80	0.05	95%
2	2.18%	1.50%	1.30	0.15	80%
3	2.18%	0.75%	1.20	0.12	90%
4	−0.04%	0.50%	1.02	0.08	97%

a. Which funds' returns were most closely related to market returns?
b. Which fund had the most market risk?
c. Which fund had the most total risk?
d. Rank these funds in terms of the Jensen performance measure.
e. Which funds statistically outperformed or underperformed the market? (Use 95% confidence levels.)
f. Restate the alpha values in terms of their annualized equivalents.

8. The following regressions and data come from the tests of mutual fund performance discussed in the chapter.

	Excess Return Regressions					Excess Quarterly Returns	
$\widetilde{ER}_{F,t}$ =	a	+	b	× $(\widetilde{ER}_{WS,t})$	R^2	Mean	Std. Dev.
Acorn	1.40%		1.13		83.1%	3.82%	11.02%
	(.74)		(0.08)				
Chemical	−1.31		0.93		92.7%	0.68%	8.59%
	(0.38)		(0.04)				
Evergreen	2.09		1.33		81.3%	4.93%	13.03%
	(0.93)		(0.10)				
Hartwell	0.44		1.58		71.3%	4.10%	13.41%
	(1.46)		(0.16)				
Scudder	− .61		0.54		54.2%	0.55%	6.54%
	(0.73)		(0.08)				

a. Assume that you now own shares of Acorn and your broker is suggesting that you sell them and buy shares of Hartwell. The broker's rationale is that the average return on Hartwell has been much better than for Acorn. Without getting into questions of consistency of performance over time, respond.
b. Which of these funds would you classify as aggressive growth? Which are low-risk funds?
c. Calculate S_p, T_p, and alpha.
d. Which funds have statistically outperformed and underperformed the market? (Use a 95% confidence level.)
e. Assume you are a believer in efficient market theory. A friend has asked which of the funds (one or more) should be bought if he wishes to obtain a market risk exposure of 1.0. What is your suggestion?

9. The current spot rate between U.S. dollars and British pounds is $1.25/£. The nominal risk-free rate in the U.S. is 8.15%, and the real risk-free rate of interest is 3%.
   a. What is the expected U.S. inflation rate?
   b. If the one-year forward rate is $1.19/£, what is the expected inflation rate for Britain?
   c. If the real risk-free rate is also 3% in Britain, what should be the nominal risk-free rate in Britain?

10. You are considering an investment in stocks of the United Kingdom and France. Information about your expectations is shown below:

	U.K.	France
Domestic Return		
Expected Return	18%	20%
Standard Deviation	30%	35%
Exchange Rate Return		
Expected Return	5%	−4%
Standard Deviation	10%	10%
Correlation with Domestic Return	0.30	0.00

   a. What is the expected return from a foreign investment in each country?
   b. Use the concepts from Chapter 7 to calculate the standard deviation of the foreign return on each country's stocks.

11. The value of the pension portfolio which you manage is $1 billion, and it is all invested in U.S. stocks. Its expected return is 15% and its standard deviation is 25%. Foreign investments are available in other countries; the expected foreign return and the standard deviation of each are 15% and 30%, respectively. The correlation between each foreign return and the U.S. return is 0.30. If you invest the $1 billion equally in the U.S. and in foreign countries, what are the expected return and standard deviation of your portfolio?

12. On January 1 the price of a share of a Japanese stock is 10 yen and the exchange rate is $0.40 per yen. The stock pays no dividends during the year. At the end of the year, the stock is selling for 12 yen and the exchange rate is $0.35 per yen. What was the stock's return to both a Japanese investor and a U.S. investor?

13. A $1 million investment is made in Canadian stocks when the exchange rate is $0.70/ Canadian dollars. At that time, the six-month forward exchange rate is $0.72. The expected six-month domestic return is 9%. The U.S. expected inflation rate for the next six months is 5%.
   a. What is the expected inflation rate in Canada?
   b. What is the expected exchange rate for six months ahead?
   c. Is the value of the dollar expected to increase or decrease? Why?
   d. What is the expected foreign return? Without a hedge, what factors create uncertainty about this return?
   e. Assume that a hedge is used, that the actual exchange rate is $0.68/Canadian dollar in six months, and that the domestic Canadian return is 12%. What foreign return is earned and what were it causes?

14. Identify the characteristics of real estate which make it distinctively different from a normal common stock investment.

15. Published return indexes on real estate equity returns are often criticized. Why? What risk/return biases arise?

16. What are the two principal advantages claimed for the use of real estate equity in an otherwise all stock and bond portfolio? What evidence supports these claims?

DATA ANALYSIS PROBLEMS

Problem 1

The purpose of this problem is to review the performance measures suggested by Sharpe, Treynor, and Jensen on a sample of mutual funds.

Access the MUTLFUND.WK1 worksheet and review the data provided. Note that quarterly returns are provided on a large number of mutual funds together with returns on T-bills, the S&P 500, and the Wilshire 5000.

1. In a separate part of the worksheet, calculate excess returns for each fund, the S&P 500, and the Wilshire 5000. Recall that excess returns are equal to the actual return minus returns on T-bills during the same time period.

2. For each fund, regress its excess returns on the excess returns of first the S&P 500 and then the Wilshire 5000. Interpret the intercept and slope parameters. As each regression is completed, be sure to save the intercept and slope coefficients since they are used later.

3. Calculate the Sharpe and Treynor measures for each fund as well as for the S&P 500 and the Wilshire 5000.

4. Comment on the abilities of these funds to earn consistent excess risk-adjusted returns.

Problem 2

The purpose of this problem is to become familiar with returns on foreign investment which arise from domestic returns versus exchange rate returns.

Access the YRLYINTL.WK1 worksheet and review its contents.

1. What is meant by the captions "pounds to $" and "yen to $"? You can answer this by comparing the returns on British stocks stated in dollars versus those stated in pounds. The same can be done for the Japanese returns.

2. Examine the U.S. dollar returns in 1987. Remember that this was the year during which Black Monday occurred—a year of relatively poor returns on U.S. stocks. Yet the returns to U.S. investors in both Britain and Japan were quite good in 1987. What was the major cause for favorable foreign returns? What does this imply about the value of diversification?

3. Calculate the correlation coefficient between the returns on the S&P 500 and EAFE. (Be sure to use a common set of years for both indexes. The correlation coefficient is the square root of R-squared in a regression equation.) What does this correlation say about the value of international investment?

4. Calculate the returns to a British resident from an investment in the S&P 500.

4 Introduction to Strategy

The previous two parts of the book have: (1) examined concepts which are common to all investment and speculation activities and (2) provided an analysis of the investment and speculative characteristics of the major types of marketable securities. In this part we pull together these concepts and analyses in order to develop an appropriate portfolio strategy.

The lead chapter in this section on strategy focuses on the portfolio investment process of planning, implementation, and monitoring. This is followed by a chapter which examines how the long-run strategic asset allocation might be determined. If one believes in the theory of efficient markets, then the actual portfolio which is held should be an indexed portfolio with asset class weights identical to those specified by the strategic asset allocation.

The two chapters that follow discuss ways in which the strategic asset allocation might be temporarily modified in light of current capital market conditions. Parts of the actual portfolio held would be over- or under-weighted depending on whether that part is believed to be currently under- or overvalued in the markets. Typically, such adjustments to the strategic asset allocation are made at three levels: (1) the allocation to asset classes such as stocks, bonds, cash, etc., (2) the allocation to certain industry groups or sectors within an asset class, and (3) the allocation to individual securities within an industry.

The final chapter discusses issues involved with performance monitoring. These range from problems that arise in calculating returns to problems with our old friend, risk measurement.

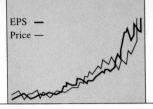

EPS —
Price —

CHAPTER

19 Portfolio Management

With the exception of Chapter 1, prior chapters of this book have focused on *single* aspects of security investment. Topics were "compartmentalized," allowing us to examine each in depth in as efficient a manner as possible. Unfortunately, this approach tends to take us away from the most basic question of all—"How should a security portfolio be managed?" Thus the purposes of this chapter are twofold: (1) to examine the process of portfolio management and (2) to illustrate how various topics covered earlier in the book can be integrated into this process.

The process of portfolio management is, conceptually, quite easy to understand, in that it involves a logical set of steps common to any decision: plan, implement, and monitor. Yet applying this process to actual portfolios can be complex, and opinions are divided on how best to do so. Ideally, investment theory and empirical evidence should provide clear guidelines for each stage of the portfolio-management process, but, unfortunately, this isn't the case. Large gaps exist in current theory, and empirical tests often yield contradictory results. For example, the capital asset pricing model is based on a single-period world in which all individuals have common beliefs and tax rates,[1] a world that exists only in theory. In addition, empirical tests of the CAPM have led to contradictory conclusions. In fact, Roll has suggested that the model can never be truly tested. Another example is portfolio immunization. If a 100% bond portfolio is held, a *nominal* return can be (virtually) guaranteed. Unfortunately, immunization cannot provide a guaranteed *real* return and, when equities are held, considerable uncertainty exists about the total portfolio's duration.

But even though theory and empirical evidence are unable to provide definitive answers, they can at least guide the process of portfolio management. Certain basic principles should be applied to all portfolio decisions:

1. *It is the portfolio that matters*. Individual securities are important only to the extent that they affect the aggregate portfolio. For example, a security's risk should

---

[1]See Chapter 9 for a discussion of these assumptions and their effect on the standard version of the CAPM.

not be based on the uncertainty of a single security's return but, instead, on its contribution to the uncertainty of the total portfolio's return. In addition, assets such as a person's career or home should be considered together with the security portfolio. In short, all decisions should focus on the impact the decision will have on the aggregate portfolio of all assets held.

2. *Larger expected portfolio returns come only with larger portfolio risk.* The most important portfolio decision is the amount of risk which is acceptable, which is determined by the asset allocation within the security portfolio. This is not an easy decision, since it requires that we have some idea of the risks and expected returns available on many different classes of assets. Nonetheless, the risk/return level of the aggregate portfolio should be the first decision any investor makes.

3. *The risk associated with a security type depends on when the investment will be liquidated.* A person who plans to sell in one year will find common stock returns to be more risky than a person who plans to sell in 25 years. Alternatively, the person who plans to sell in 25 years will find one-year maturity bonds to be more risky than the person who plans to sell in one year. Risk is reduced by selecting securities with a payoff close to when the portfolio is to be liquidated.

4. *Diversification works.* Diversification across various securities will reduce a portfolio's risk. If such broad diversification results in an expected portfolio return or risk level which is lower (or higher) than desired, then borrowing (or lending) can be used to achieve the desired level.

5. *Each portfolio should be tailored to the particular needs of its owner.* People have varying tax rates, knowledge, transaction costs, etc. Individuals who are in a high marginal tax bracket should stress portfolio strategies which increase after-tax returns. Individuals who lack strong knowledge of investment alternatives should hire professionals to provide needed counseling. Large pension portfolios should pursue strategies which will reduce brokerage fees associated with moving capital between equity and nonequity managers (for example, by using options on futures). In short, portfolio strategy should be molded to the unique needs and characteristics of the portfolio's owner.

6. *Competition for abnormal returns is extensive.* A large number of people are continuously using a large variety of techniques in an attempt to obtain abnormal returns—returns larger than should be expected given a security's risk. Securities which are believed to be undervalued are bought until the price rises to a proper level, and securities which are believed to be overvalued are sold until the price falls to a proper level. If the actions of these speculators are truly effective, security prices will adjust instantaneously to new information—the efficient market theory will be correct.

The extent to which EMT is correct as well as the extent to which one has unique information determines whether a passive "investment" strategy or an active "speculative" strategy should be used.

THE PORTFOLIO INVESTMENT PROCESS

Overview

The process used to manage a security portfolio is conceptually the same as that used in any managerial decision. One should:

1. Plan
2. Implement the plan
3. Monitor the results

This *portfolio investment process* is displayed schematically in Figure 19-1. Each aspect of the process is discussed in some detail later. For now, however, we will simply give an overview of the complete process.

The aspect of portfolio management most often overlooked is adequate planning, yet this is perhaps the most important element of proper portfolio investment and speculation. In the planning stage, a careful review should be conducted of the inves-

FIGURE 19-1 *The Portfolio Investment Process*

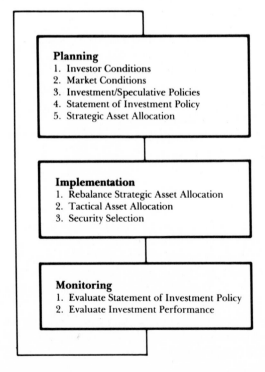

Planning
1. Investor Conditions
2. Market Conditions
3. Investment/Speculative Policies
4. Statement of Investment Policy
5. Strategic Asset Allocation

Implementation
1. Rebalance Strategic Asset Allocation
2. Tactical Asset Allocation
3. Security Selection

Monitoring
1. Evaluate Statement of Investment Policy
2. Evaluate Investment Performance

tor's financial situation and current capital market conditions. Taken together, these will suggest a set of investment and speculative policies to be followed. These policies should then be formally documented in a written *statement of investment policy* (SIP). The SIP will document: (1) the portfolio objective, (2) strategies which may (or may not) be used, and (3) various other investment and speculative constraints. An output of proper planning will be a clearly defined *strategic asset allocation* (SAA). The SAA represents the optimal combination of various asset classes in an efficient market. The SAA is an indexed portfolio which would actually be held if a passive, pure-investment strategy is to be employed. The SAA portfolio might never actually be held, since adjustments in line with various speculative strategies may be made, but it represents the basic pure "investment" portfolio against which actual portfolio returns can be compared in order to determine whether speculative strategies are actually "adding value."

In the *implementation stage*, three decisions need to be made. First, if the percentage holdings of various asset classes are currently different from the desired holdings as stated in the SIP, the portfolio should be rebalanced to the desired SAA. If a pure-investment strategy is required by the statement of investment policy, this is the only thing which is done in the implementation stage. However, many portfolio owners engage in speculative transactions in the belief that such transactions will generate excess risk-adjusted returns. Such speculative transactions are usually classified as "timing" or "selection" decisions. *Timing decisions* over- or underweight various asset classes, industries, or economic sectors from the strategic asset allocation. Such timing decisions have come to be known as *tactical asset allocation* (TAA) decisions. *Selection decisions* deal with securities within a given asset class, industry group, or economic sector and attempt to determine which securities should be over- or underweighted. Tactical asset allocation is discussed in Chapter 21, and security selection is discussed in Chapter 22.

The last stage in the portfolio investment process consists of monitoring portfolio returns in order to determine which speculative decisions seem to be adding value to the portfolio and to ascertain that the portfolio's objective and constraints are being met and have not changed. Portfolio monitoring is discussed in Chapter 23.

Planning

Aspects of the planning stage are shown in Figure 19-2. Investor and capital market conditions are blended in order to determine a set of investment and speculative policies as well as a long-run strategic asset allocation. These are formally expressed in the statement of investment policy.

Investor Conditions. The first question which must be answered is this: "What is the purpose of the security portfolio?" While this question might seem obvious, it is too often overlooked, giving way instead to the excitement of selecting the securities which

FIGURE 19-2 *Portfolio Planning Stage*

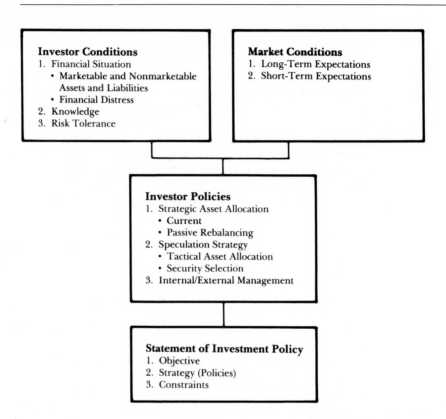

are to be held. Understanding the purpose for trading in financial securities will help to: (1) define the expected portfolio liquidation date, (2) aid in determining an acceptable level of risk, and (3) indicate whether future consumption (liability needs) are to be paid in nominal or real dollars, etc.

For example, a 90-year-old woman with small to moderate savings probably (1) has a short investment horizon, (2) can accept little investment risk, and (3) needs protection against short-term inflation. In contrast, a young couple investing for retirement in 40 years have (1) a very long investment horizon, (2) an ability to accept moderate to large investment risk because they can diversify over time, and (3) a need for protection against long-term inflation. This suggests that the 90-year-old woman should invest solely in low-default-risk money market securities. The young couple could invest in many other asset classes for diversification and accept greater investment risks. In short, knowing the eventual purpose of the portfolio investment makes it possible to begin sketching out appropriate investment/speculative policies.

Next, the *complete* financial status of the investor must be understood. For example, consider the augmented balance sheet for a Mr. Paulson, shown in Table 19-1.

TABLE 19-1 *Hypothetical Present-Value Balance Sheet for Mr. Paulson*

Marketable Assets		*Marketable Liabilities*	
Security Portfolio	$ 100	Short-Term Debt	$ 50
Home	200	Mortgage	140
Personal Possessions	30		
			$ 190
	$ 330		
		Nonmarketable Liabilities	
Nonmarketable Assets		Present Value of Minimum	
Insurance Policies	20	Future Consumption	1,500
Present Value of			
Expected Future Pay:		*Net Worth*	
— Employment	1,000	Marketable Equity	140
— Social Security	500	Nonmarketable Equity	520
— Pension Benefits	500		
	$2,020		660
Total	$2,350	Total	$2,350

Two types of assets and liabilities are defined. Marketable assets and liabilities refer to assets which could be sold now and liabilities which could be paid for now. These represent the assets and liabilities which would be reported by standard accounting procedures, only stated at current market value. Mr. Paulson's current marketable net worth is $140.

Nonmarketable assets are of two types. Insurance policies effectively represent long positions in put options which pay off under certain conditions, for example, physical disability or loss of assets through theft or damage. Although they cannot be sold to other individuals, they represent an asset to Mr. Paulson which has a positive (albeit difficult to determine) value. The second type of nonmarketable asset is the present value of expected future pay. This pay comes in three forms: (1) wage income from employment, (2) retirement income from social security, and (3) retirement income from employment-based pension benefits. The total risk of each of these nonmarketable assets and the extent to which they can be diversified or hedged differ considerably. For example, the $1,000 asset value arising from future wage income is closely tied to the talents of Mr. Paulson and the future fortunes of his employer. This asset cannot be diversified. The only way in which its risk can be reduced would be by taking offsetting hedges in other asset and liability positions. For example, if Mr. Paulson is employed as a computer salesman by IBM, he could hedge his risk by underweighting IBM shares and the shares of other computer companies in his security portfolio. In contrast, the risk inherent in the $500 present value of future pension benefits can be reduced by making sure that the employer has fully funded the pension plan and has invested all pension funds in a well-diversified security portfolio.

How should the $100 marketable security portfolio be invested? This is the critical investment question which Mr. Paulson faces. To answer this question, he should *not* focus on the distribution of returns on the $100 security portfolio itself. Instead, *he should focus on the distribution of his future net worth.*[2]

Portfolio investment and speculation decisions are too often based solely on potential security portfolio payoffs with no attention given to interactions between the security portfolio and other economic assets and liabilities of the individual or investment organization. This is the wrong approach. We saw one example above— the underweighting of computer stocks in Mr. Paulson's security portfolio. Consider another example. If the current value of future consumption is directly correlated with unexpected inflation, assets which hedge against this risk should be weighted more heavily than if little inflation risk were present. Such assets include equities and real estate.

The potential for temporary financial distress must also be considered. The economic net worth of Mr. Paulson might always remain positive. But if cash flows from his wage income are variable, he could find himself unable to pay current debts. For example, as a computer salesman, his compensation might be volatile and tied to economic activity. Thus, it is possible that his employment income might be low at the same time that the value of his security portfolio has fallen in value as a result of poor economic conditions. This suggests that a larger position in low-risk liquid securities such as Treasury bills should be taken.

In short, the total economic position of the individual must be examined. The unique short- and long-term risks inherent in major assets and liabilities must be understood. Although this is difficult to quantify, the problem is important and deserves careful thought.

The investor's knowledge of various securities also has an important impact on the types of security classes which should be held and the speculative strategies employed. The investor must understand that yearly equity returns are quite variable, short-term returns on bonds are sensitive to the bonds' duration, futures require daily mark-to-market, options are leveraged positions, international investment entails considerable exchange rate risk, etc. If the investor does not truly understand the nature and extent of a security's short- and long-term risk, the security should not be held.

Finally, the tolerance which the investor has for investment risk must be considered. This is clearly a difficult aspect of developing a proper investment strategy. Investment theories are largely based on a single future date at which the portfolio will be liquidated; theory speaks to the standard deviation of the security portfolio's value at that date. But this neglects a number of very important practical investment considerations. These include the following:

1. The relationship between investment horizon date payoffs from the marketable security portfolio and payoffs from other assets or liabilities of the investor (both marketable and nonmarketable). Two examples of this were presented above.

---

[2]In previous chapters, we did focus solely on the returns on the underlying asset investments. This implicitly assumed that there were no other assets and no liabilities. Thus, the assets and net worth were identical.

2. The investor's reaction to portfolio results during periods of time which are shorter than the investor's true investment horizon. For example, even though Mr. Paulson is investing for retirement and should be relatively unconcerned about yearly portfolio returns, a year or two with particularly good or bad returns might cause him to make short-term decisions which are not in his best long-term interest — for example, selling stock after it has fallen in value to buy gold at high prices. Long-term investors must be able to bear up to the despair or euphoria that temporary price swings can cause.

3. Although students of investment theory can interpret what the "standard deviation" of returns or wealth means, most investors cannot. Thus, the nature and extent of security risk must be communicated to investors in a way they can truly understand.

Market Conditions. An assessment of potential future returns on various classes or marketable securities must also be made. This is discussed at length in the next chapter and will not be treated here. However, two points need to be made. First, short-term (say, one year) expectations might differ considerably from longer-term expectations. If so, the portfolio's tactical asset allocation will differ from the long-term strategic asset allocation. Both short- and long-term market forecasts must be made *if one has any intent of engaging in tactical asset allocation.* The forecasts might turn out to be identical. But if TAA is allowed, both forecasts should be explicitly made. Second, forecasts should be stated in real dollars if future consumption and liabilities are tied to inflation. If consumption and liabilities are unaffected by inflation, then nominal return forecasts are appropriate.

Strategic Asset Allocation. The most important investment decision which the owner of a portfolio must make is the portfolio's asset allocation. Asset allocation refers to the percentage invested in various security classes. Security classes are simply the type of securities discussed earlier in the text:

1. Money market investment
2. Fixed-income obligations
3. Common stock
4. Real estate investment
5. International securities

Futures and options are not unique asset classes since they are effectively positions in another asset class such as common stock or bonds. Thus, futures and options do not provide any diversification advantages. They simply alter the nondiversifiable risk position in the underlying asset.

A number of studies have shown that 90% or more of a portfolio's rate of return is determined by the portfolio's asset allocation. Of much less importance are the actual securities held. The simple fact that $X\%$ is invested in stocks as a class or $Y\%$ in bonds as a class is *the* dominant force which generates portfolio returns.

Strategic asset allocation represents the asset allocation which would be optimal

FIGURE 19-3 *Hypothetical Efficient Frontiers of Investor Net Worth Return*

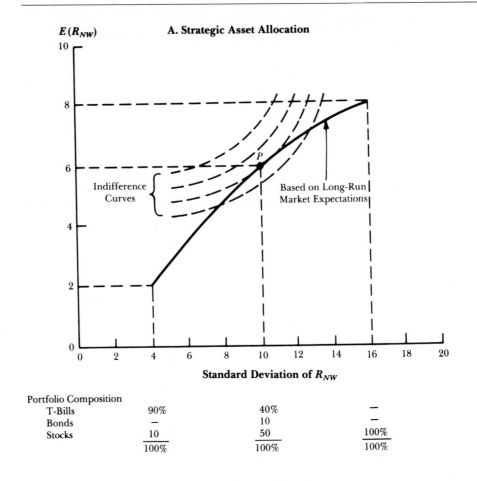

A. Strategic Asset Allocation

$E(R_{NW})$

Standard Deviation of R_{NW}

Portfolio Composition			
T-Bills	90%	40%	—
Bonds	—	10	—
Stocks	10	50	100%
	100%	100%	100%

for the investor if all security prices trade at their long-term equilibrium values—that is, if the markets are efficiently priced.

Consider panel A in Figure 19-3, in which a hypothetical efficient frontier of various asset classes is displayed. Investment portfolio decisions should focus on the investor's *net worth*, not on security investment returns. Therefore, the vertical axis represents the one-year expected returns on net worth due to security portfolio returns, $E(R_{NW})$. The horizontal axis represents end-of-year standard deviations of return on net worth.[3] The dashed curves represent utility indifference curves, the curves to the left representing greater utility. The efficient frontier is shown as the

---

[3]Mathematics and numerical examples are presented in Chapter 20. The discussion here is purely conceptual. Also note that a risk-free security is not shown since we were evaluating real rates of return as opposed to nominal returns. There are no securities which provide risk-free real returns.

FIGURE 19-3 *(continued)*

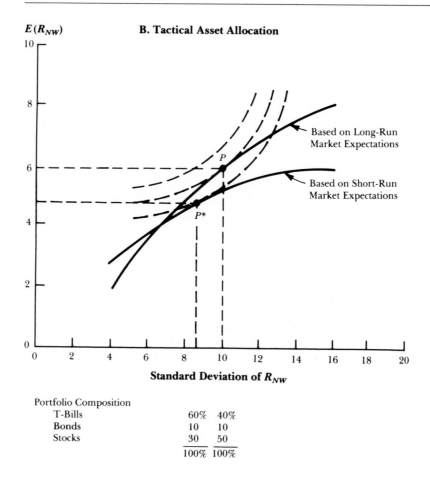

B. Tactical Asset Allocation

$E(R_{NW})$

Based on Long-Run
Market Expectations

Based on Short-Run
Market Expectations

P

*P**

Standard Deviation of R_{NW}

Portfolio Composition		
T-Bills	60%	40%
Bonds	10	10
Stocks	30	50
	100%	100%

solid curve. Clearly, the optimal portfolio is the one which maximizes utility. This is designated as portfolio *P*.

If this efficient frontier is based on the investor's assessment of expected returns, risks, and correlation coefficients *which the investor believes will be true on average in the future*, then portfolio *P* defines the investor's current optimal strategic asset allocation. Based on such long-run expectations, the investor should currently invest 40% in T-bills, 10% in bonds, and 50% in stocks.

If expectations for the short term differ from long-run expectations, it is possible that the current optimal portfolio composition would temporarily differ from the strategic asset allocation. This is illustrated in panel B of Figure 19-3. Two efficient frontiers are shown. One is based on long-run market expectations as in panel A. The other, however, is based on current short-run expectations (say, for the next year). These short-run expectations are clearly more pessimistic about returns on high-risk securities. Given such short-term expectations, portfolio P^* is now optimal since it results in greater utility. The investor should temporarily depart from the strategic mix of 40/10/50 to a tactical mix of 60/10/30 (T-bills/bonds/stocks). This timing decision is called tactical asset allocation. We return to it later in the chapter.

Deciding what the investor's current SAA should be can be a difficult task. In theory, it requires predictions of future return distributions for various security classes, estimates of the major economic risks faced by the investor, and estimates of the extent to which all of these factors are intercorrelated. In practice, however, simple common sense is often the best guide. If the economic situation of the investor is carefully considered together with reasonable estimates of capital market conditions, then commonsense estimates of the current SAA can be made.

In the next chapter, we review how one might develop a strategic asset allocation policy for one of the largest institutional investors in the United States—pension plans. At that time, we will use a number of relatively sophisticated techniques. But regardless of the technical sophistication of the procedure used, the final results must appeal to common sense.

Passive Rebalancing. Few investment strategies are static. They require changes as time passes, as the investor's wealth changes, as security prices change, as the investor's knowledge expands, etc. Thus, the optimal strategic asset allocation will also change. Even if the investor continues to believe that all security prices are fair, the SAA will probably require periodic rebalancing. Such changes are *passive* changes to the portfolio. These are not active changes made in the hopes of earning excess risk-adjusted returns from potential security price disequilibriums. Instead, they represent logical shifts in the investor's strategic asset allocation in response to changes in the investor's condition or (fairly priced) market conditions.

Conceptually, we could think of investors as continuously revising their SAA. Thus, there would be no need to plan for a passive rebalancing strategy. At each moment in time, investors would evaluate their personal investment needs and market expectations to develop a current strategic asset allocation. As a practical matter, however, the costs of doing this are too large. For example, pension funds spend large sums of money and months of effort to develop an SAA. They simply cannot afford to engage in a continuous analysis of what their SAA should be. Individual investors who have much less capital and knowledge face even larger problems. As a result, it makes sense that part of the SAA decision should be a decision about how the SAA is to be changed as certain important economic variables change.

Thus, the strategic asset allocation decision should actually contain two elements: (1) definition of a current SAA and (2) specification of a rebalancing strategy which passively adjusts the current SAA to changes in the investor's situation and security market conditions.

Three passive rebalancing decisions which the investor should make are discussed here. The first is possibly the most important and the easiest to implement. It deals with how the SAA decision should change as time passes. The other two passive rebalancing decisions are associated with shorter time spans. They deal with how the SAA might be affected by (1) changes in the investor's wealth level and (2) changes in the level of stock prices.

FIGURE 19-4 *Investment Risk and the Investment Horizon*

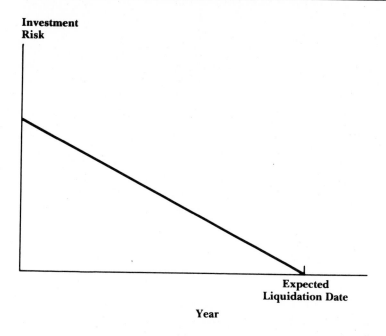

The shift in optimal investment risk as time passes is illustrated in Figure 19-4. Holding all other factors constant, the level of investment risk which will be acceptable to the investor will decline as the final date of portfolio liquidation approaches. For example, consider Rosalind Allen, who has $10,000 to invest and intends to use it to make a down payment on a home in one year. Since the portfolio's liquidation date is near, Rosalind will probably be willing to accept very little investment risk and will invest largely in one-year money market securities (CDs or money market funds). Now consider her husband, Robert Allen, who also has $10,000 to invest but intends to do so for retirement in 40 years. He is able to accept relatively large investment risk and should probably invest in a variety of mutual funds which are diversified across a large variety of common stocks, bonds, real estate, and foreign securities. However, as time passes and he approaches retirement, the amount of investment risk that he will find acceptable will fall.

The reason why the investor's acceptable risk exposure and the investment horizon of the portfolio are so closely tied is simple to understand—time diversification. The longer one has before a portion of the portfolio must be liquidated, the greater the ability for good return years to offset bad return years. We have seen this earlier in the text and will return to it again in the next chapter. A major determinant of an investor's SAA is the portfolio's investment horizon.

The next type of passive rebalancing strategy which should be planned for relates to changes in the investor's *net worth* (wealth). Given the potential variability of security returns over relatively short time spans, a predetermined passive rebalancing strategy would be wise. For example, there have been a number of occasions during this century when a 50/50 investment portfolio in bonds and stocks would have increased or decreased in value by 30% or more during a period of three years or less. Since many investors do not explicitly review their SAA more often than every three years, an interim passive rebalancing strategy should be developed.

The alternatives are basically three, as displayed in Figure 19-5. The amount of investment risk exposure is shown on the vertical axis. For simplicity we have defined this as the percentage invested in stock. At the investor's current level of net worth, the SAA consists of 60% in equities (with the remaining 40% in, say, T-bills). Rebalancing alternative #1 consists of a *constant* rebalancing strategy. Regardless of changes in the investor's wealth, whether due to changes in stock returns or changes in the value of other assets and liabilities the investor might have, the SAA remains constant. Alternative #2 represents an *increasing risk tolerance* strategy. If net worth increases, the amount of investment risk exposure is increased and, if net worth declines, risk exposure is decreased. Alternative #3 represents exactly the opposite case, *decreasing risk tolerance*—the greater the level of net worth, the smaller the amount of risk tolerance.

This strategic rebalancing decision is clearly a difficult one to make. But, given the potential volatility of equity and debt markets over a two- to three-year period, it is a matter which deserves to be explicitly considered.

FIGURE 19-5 *Passive Rebalancing of the SAA for Changes in Net Worth*

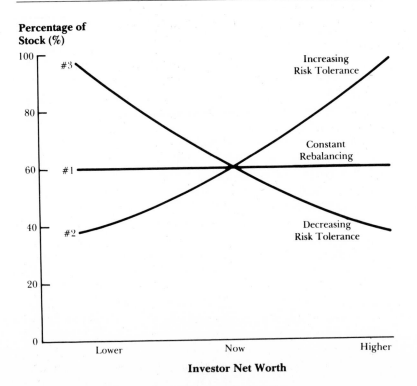

The last type of rebalancing strategy we will consider focuses not on time or on the investor's net worth, but on the level of prices of a given asset class. We illustrate the idea with the level of aggregate stock prices, but the strategy is equally appropriate for other asset classes, particularly bonds.

Consider Figure 19-6. Equity risk exposure is displayed on the vertical axis and the level of aggregate stock prices on the horizontal axis. Given current market conditions, the SAA calls for a 60% investment in equities. Three alternative strategies are shown for changes in the level of stock prices. In alternative A, the commitment to equities remains constant regardless of future changes in equity values. This is a *constant* rebalancing strategy and is used by most investors. If stock values rise, stocks are sold in order to remain at the defined SAA. If stock values fall, more stock is purchased. This constant rebalancing strategy is essentially a neutral strategy.

In contrast, alternatives B and C require passive adjustments to equity risk as stock price levels change. Under alternative B, stock is sold as stock prices fall and purchased as stock prices rise. This policy is analogous to purchasing (some amount of) portfolio insurance! Alternative C is the opposite—the sale of portfolio insurance.

In summary, we have seen three ways in which an initial strategic asset allocation might be rebalanced. The first is associated with a reasonable reduction in investment risk as the portfolio approaches its eventual liquidation date, the investment time ho-

FIGURE 19-6 *Passive Rebalancing of the SAA for Changes in Stock Prices*

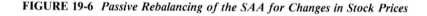

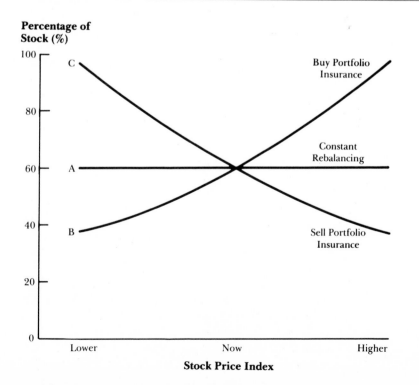

rizon. Such SAA rebalancing strategies are based on the concept of time diversification. The second is associated with changes in the investor's net worth. These decisions are driven by changes in the investor's risk tolerance as his or her wealth changes. The third rebalancing strategy is based on the need for portfolio insurance or the ability to provide it.

Decisions such as these are, indeed, difficult to make. In many cases precisely defined portfolio adjustments may not be possible. Yet they must be thought about — unless the investor intends to stumble blindly into the future.

Speculation Strategy. After the investor has determined a current strategic asset allocation and decided how the allocation should be passively rebalanced as time passes, net worth changes, or stock prices vary, a decision must be made as to the types and amounts of security speculation which will be allowed. Speculative strategies can be classified as either tactical asset allocation (timing) decisions or security selection decisions. They are reviewed below and discussed at length in Chapters 21 and 22.

Internal-External Management. If no speculative strategies are to be used, the management of the portfolio is relatively easy. One simply purchases a number of *index portfolios* which emulate the desired SAA. Small investors can do this by purchasing mutual funds which are indexed to a stock index such as the S&P 500, a bond index such as the Shearson Lehman Hutton Government/Corporate Bond Index, the EAFE Index, etc. Larger investors such as pension funds can also use mutual funds, but many investment organizations create index funds solely for large investors.

If speculative trades are to be allowed, however, one must decide whether the investor will make such decisions or employ an outside professional. Individuals with little investable capital can obtain outside management skills by purchasing shares of actively managed mutual funds. Individuals and organizations with large capital can also employ investment management firms to make their speculative trading decisions. If one wishes to engage in speculative strategies through timing and security selection, outside professional managers are more likely to provide better performance *net of all costs* than investors could by developing their own opinions.

Implementation

In Figure 19-7 the implementation stage is shown schematically. One begins by periodically adjusting the asset mix to the desired mix called for in the SAA. Next, any tactical asset allocation and security selection decisions are made.

Tactical Asset Allocation. If one believes that the price levels of certain asset classes, industries, or economic sectors are temporarily too high or too low, actual portfolio holdings should depart from the asset mix called for in the strategic asset allocation. Such a *timing* decision is referred to as tactical asset allocation. As noted, TAA decisions could be made across aggregate asset classes (stocks, bonds, and T-bills),

FIGURE 19-7 *Portfolio Implementation Stage*

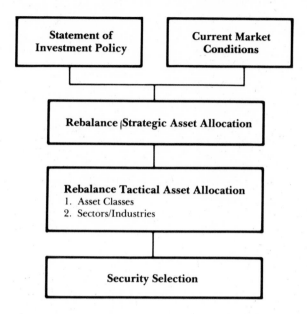

industry classifications (steel, airline, food), or various broad economic sectors (basic manufacturing, interest-sensitive, consumer durables).

Traditionally, most tactical asset allocation has involved timing across aggregate asset classes. For example, if stock prices are believed to be too high, one would reduce the portfolio's equity allocation and increase the allocation to, say, Treasury bills. If one is indeed successful at TAA, the abnormal returns which would be earned are certainly enticing. For example, Table 19-2 presents the results of an analysis conducted by Goldman Sachs and Company which was designed to examine the benefits of *perfect* timing foresight. Columns 1 and 2 list estimates of the proportions of portfolio assets which private pension funds allocated to stocks and cash equivalents between the years 1973 and 1984.[4] Columns 3 and 4 show the yearly returns on the S&P 500 and T-bills in each year. To estimate the benefit of perfect timing foresight, Goldman Sachs assumed that in years in which T-bills had larger returns than the S&P 500, investors doubled the percentage holdings of T-bills shown in column 2. In years in which the S&P 500 had the greater return, the investment in stocks was set at 100%. Column 5 shows the return on the timing-adjusted portfolio, and column 6 shows the actual portfolio return without timing foresight. Finally, column 7 indicates the excess yearly return gained by perfect timing foresight. The normal portfolio would have had an average yearly return of 8.2%, while the perfect foresight model

---

[4]Portfolio holdings were split between cash and stocks. When the term "cash" is used, it is implicit that the investment is really T-bills. Use of the term cash, or cash equivalents, is a common way of referring to T-bill holdings.

TABLE 19-2 *The Potential Benefit of the Asset-Allocation Decision for Equity-Only Private Pension Funds*

Year	Estimated Allocation to Stocks (1)	Cash (2)	S&P 500 (3)	Total Return on T-Bills (4)	Adjusted Portfolio (5)	Normal Portfolio (6)	Potential Benefit of Asset-Allocation Decision (7)
1973	89%	11%	(14.8)%	6.9%	(10.1)%	(12.5)%	2.4%
1974	82	18	(26.4)	8.0	(14.1)	(20.3)	6.2
1975	86	14	37.2	5.8	37.2	32.7	4.5
1976	90	10	23.6	5.1	23.6	21.8	1.8
1977	87	13	(7.4)	5.2	(4.3)	(5.8)	1.6
1978	83	17	6.4	7.4	6.7	6.5	0.2
1979	82	18	18.2	9.5	18.2	16.6	1.6
1980	82	18	32.3	11.4	32.3	28.6	3.7
1981	83	17	(5.0)	14.2	1.5	(1.7)	3.3
1982	83	17	21.4	11.4	21.4	19.7	1.7
1983	86	14	22.4	8.8	22.4	20.5	1.9
1984	85	15	6.1	10.0	7.3	6.7	0.6
Average			7.8	8.6	10.7	8.2	2.5

Source: *Portfolio Strategy*, Goldman Sachs and Company, March 1985.

would have had a return of 10.7%. The extra 2.5% per year is not insignificant. Equity managers that outdistanced the S&P 500 by 2.5% over this time period would have ranked in the top 5% of all equity managers.

Security Selection. The second type of active speculation involves the selection of securities within a given asset class, industry, or economic sector. The strategic asset allocation policy would call for broad diversification through an indexed holding of virtually all securities in the asset class. For example, if the total market value of XYZ Corp. shares currently represents 1% of all outstanding stock, then 1% of the investor's portfolio allocated to equity would be held in XYZ Corp. shares. The only reason to overweight or underweight particular securities in the SAA would be to offset risks the investor faces in other assets and liabilities outside the marketable security portfolio. Security selection, however, actively overweights and underweights holdings of particular securities in the belief that they are temporarily mispriced.

To measure the potential effect of stock selection, Goldman Sachs conducted another simple study, as shown in Table 19-3. The allocations to equities and cash were held equal to the actual percentages shown in columns 1 and 2. Then it was assumed that all stocks in the S&P 500 with returns greater than the average were overweighted by 10% and all stocks with returns less than the average were underweighted by 10%. Column 5 reports the returns from such a stock-selection model, and column 6 shows the returns without timing or selection. Again, perfect foresight resulted in a return improvement which cannot be considered minor. The benefit of stock selection was less than that of timing foresight, but this could be due to the construc-

TABLE 19-3 *The Potential Benefit of the Stock-Selection Decision for Equity-Only Private Pension Funds*

Year	Estimated Allocation to Stocks (1)	Cash (2)	Total Return on S&P 500 (3)	T-Bills (4)	Adjusted Portfolio (5)	Normal Portfolio (6)	Potential Benefit of Asset-Allocation Decision (7)
1973	89%	11%	(14.8)%	6.9%	(10.9)%	(12.5)%	1.6%
1974	82	18	(26.4)	8.0	(19.2)	(20.3)	1.1
1975	86	14	37.2	5.8	34.7	32.7	2.0
1976	90	10	23.6	5.1	23.3	21.8	1.5
1977	87	13	(7.4)	5.2	(4.8)	(5.8)	1.0
1978	83	17	6.4	7.4	7.6	6.5	1.0
1979	82	18	18.2	9.5	18.4	16.6	1.8
1980	82	18	32.3	11.4	30.8	28.6	2.2
1981	83	17	(5.0)	14.2	(0.3)	(1.7)	1.5
1982	83	17	21.4	11.4	22.0	19.7	2.3
1983	86	14	22.4	8.8	21.8	20.5	1.3
1984	85	15	6.1	10.0	7.8	6.7	1.1
Average			7.8	8.6	9.7	8.2	1.5

SOURCE: *Portfolio Strategy*, Goldman Sachs and Company, March 1985.

tion of each test. The important point is that the rewards from active timing and selection speculation can be substantial — *if one is good at it.*

Is anyone good at it? Many claim to be. In fact, it's a rare investment manager who doesn't claim that he or she can substantially "beat the market" through some combination of timing and selection. But remember that during any given time period, one half of all portfolios will have returns greater than the average. Above-average returns are not proof that a manager has speculative skills.

Portfolio performance is a product of (1) the investment risk accepted, (2) chance, and (3) speculative abilities. We have seen in earlier chapters that virtually all of a portfolio's return is due to its investment risk.[5] In addition, chance alone seems to explain above- or below-average risk-adjusted returns, indicating that there is little relationship between a manager's performance in one period and his or her future performance. Much the same conclusion is reached in Chapter 23, when we look closely at the historical returns of investment managers and their ability to generate abnormal returns through timing and selection. The evidence in support of speculative profits is weak at best.

Yet the question is unresolved. Empirical tests conducted to date often rely on return-generating models such as the CAPM and APT, which are the subject of considerable debate. In addition, it could be that the procedures used to test for speculative profits simply are not powerful enough to capture such profits if they are small. A few studies, in fact, claim to have found evidence of speculative profits.

---

[5] See the discussion of efficient market theory in Chapter 10.

Investment theory and empirical evidence cannot provide definitive rules for how actively a security portfolio should be managed. However, both provide a general guide. If speculative profits can be obtained through active management, they are, on average, small. However, active management involves transaction costs which could more than offset any speculative returns. If a portfolio is managed by its owner, these costs consist of brokerage fees (about 1% on each trade) and the opportunity cost of the time spent identifying speculative trades. If the portfolio is a mutual fund managed by a professional manager, transaction costs consist of the load to buy the fund (from 0% to 9%), brokerage fees which the manager incurs (less than 1% because of the size of managed trades), and the manager's fee (1% of portfolio value is common). It is easy to see how transaction costs could easily exceed timing and selection returns.

Portfolio Monitoring

The portfolio monitoring stage is shown schematically in Figure 19-8. There are three aspects to this monitoring. First, the actual portfolio held should be examined to ascertain that it is in compliance with the statement of investment policy and to determine whether any passive rebalancing of the asset mix is required. Second, investment performance should be reviewed. This should consist of a review of returns on (1) the aggregate portfolio, (2) each asset class and investment manager, and (3) the returns from any speculative strategies employed. Finally, adjustments to the SIP and investment managers should be made if necessary. Performance monitoring is the subject of Chapter 23.

FIGURE 19-8 *Portfolio Monitoring Stage*

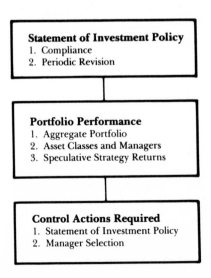

THE STATEMENT OF INVESTMENT POLICY

The portfolio objective, constraints, and strategy should always be stated explicitly in a written document. This is not a nicety which only large portfolios need — it is a necessity for all portfolios. This statement of investment policy (or whatever one elects to call it) can be amended periodically as economic conditions or the portfolio owner's needs change. In fact, the statement of policy should probably include the requirement that the statement itself be reviewed at least every two to three years.

There are at least four advantages to having a written statement of policy:

1. Requiring that a written document be prepared forces the investor to make difficult decisions which might otherwise be set aside.
2. A well-thought-out SIP can add discipline and stability to the long-run management of the portfolio, reducing whipsaw reactions to temporary price swings. By acting as documentation and education for why particular decisions were made, it should reduce capricious changes in investment strategies.
3. A well-drafted SIP defines the investor's strategic asset allocation and passive rebalancing strategies.
4. Future performance evaluation is simply impossible without a clear benchmark against which a comparison can be made. The strategic asset allocation serves as the benchmark.

In a sense, the statement of investment policy is the constitution under which the investor's assets are to be managed. As such, it should be prepared only after the investor has fully investigated all major aspects of managing an investment portfolio.

Examples of two statements of policy are shown in Appendixes 19A and 19B. The example in Appendix 19A was prepared by the trustees of a medium-size pension plan ($25 million in assets) and focuses on the equity portion of the pension's portfolio. In contrast, Appendix 19B was prepared by the trustees of a larger pension plan ($250 million) and applies to the total portfolio. Since the needs and expectations of investors differ, neither statement of policy is intended to reflect an ideal approach. Instead, they are intended to reflect the types of policy statements which are used in practice.

The Portfolio Objective. The portfolio objective should represent the single most important requirement of the portfolio owner. Often this is stated to be the maximization of portfolio returns for the risk level inherent in the portfolio. Such an objective is consistent with portfolio theory as presented in Part 2 of this book. Yet many people prefer a more precise statement of the objective. As an example, many statements of policy will specify a desired long-run real rate of return of, say, 4% per year. Others will specify a relative nominal return, such as an average return 100 basis points greater than that of the S&P 500 Composite Index. Some will give no specified return rate but, instead, state that the preservation of capital value is desired.

Any objective is valid as long as it is legal. But, in truth, most objectives turn out to be closely related to the theoretical objective of maximizing return for the level of risk inherent in the portfolio. For example, the objective of a 4% real return is usually followed by a constraint that the portfolio be invested X% in a broadly diversified portfolio of a common stock and $1-X$% in a broadly diversified portfolio of high-grade corporate bonds. Taken together, this is a statement of the desired return for a given level of portfolio risk. Along the same lines, the objective of a return 100 basis points better than the S&P 500 Composite Index is usually followed by a constraint that the portfolio consist solely of stocks with characteristics similar to those in the S&P 500. Again, a desired return for a given risk level is being stated. Even the objective of capital preservation implies a *real* risk-free rate (at least 0%) and very little risk tolerance.

The manner in which a portfolio's objective is actually expressed should (1) communicate the portfolio owner's major desire, (2) be easily understood by the portfolio's owner, and (3) be easily understood by others who are involved in the portfolio's management. In practice, objectives usually are related to achieving the greatest return for a given risk level — exactly what theory would suggest.

Constraints. Any constraint can, of course, reduce the chances of achieving the portfolio objective. For example, it would be virtually impossible to earn a 4% yearly real return if the portfolio is constrained to holdings of short-term Treasury obligations, since in the past, nominal returns on such securities have barely offset inflation. Common sense dictates that there be a reasonable relationship between the objective and the constraints. Typical constraints included in a statement of policy pertain to:

1. *Portfolio risk level.* If the objective is stated in terms of a desired rate of return, the most important constraint should be the acceptable risk of the portfolio. In theory, the risk level could be expressed as a portfolio beta or the standard deviation of portfolio returns. In practice, such quantitative measures are not commonly used at present. Whether this is due to a lack of investment education, imprecision in measuring the variables, or conceptual flaws in the use of beta or standard deviations as risk measures is unclear. Some combination of the three is probably close to the truth.

   In practice, aggregate portfolio risk is usually defined in terms of the percentage of the portfolio allocated to various security types. For example, a 60/40 equity/fixed-income asset allocation is a common constraint of many large pension portfolios. Actually, such an approach is a fairly good way to identify allowable portfolio risk as long as the types of securities included in each group are well defined.

2. *Allowed securities.* All parties to the management of the portfolio should have a clear understanding of the types of securities which may be purchased. For example, if 40% of all assets are to be invested in fixed-income securities, the intended duration, default risk, callability, tax features, etc., should be clearly identified.

   More often than not the owner of a portfolio will entrust actual purchase and sale decisions to another party. Small investors, for example, can do this by purchasing mutual fund shares. Larger investors employ professional investment managers known as separate account managers. If a mutual fund is to be used, the statement of policy should clearly specify the principal investment characteristics of the types of funds which may be purchased—for example, the mutual fund beta, S&P quality, and dividend yield. If a separate account manager is to be used, a precise statement of what types of securities the manager may purchase should be prepared and given to the manager. This is commonly known as a manager assignment statement.[6]

3. *Diversification.* Regardless of whether the portfolio owner, a mutual fund, a separate account manager, or some other party will be making purchase and sale decisions, some statement should be made about the extent of diversification desired. This can be done by specifying (1) the minimum number of securities to be held, (2) the maximum percentage of the portfolio which may be held in a given security, (3) the maximum percentage of the portfolio which may be held in a given industry, (4) the R^2 obtained when portfolio returns are regressed against some market index such as the S&P 500, etc.

   If more than one mutual fund or separate account manager is to be given money to invest, the diversification restrictions required from each can be less stringent than required for the portfolio as a whole. Nonetheless, the greater the diversification of the aggregate portfolio, the less its risk.

4. *Tax and liquidity.* Consideration should be given to both the tax and liquidity requirements of the portfolio. Investors in a high marginal tax bracket are faced with complex portfolio decisions which only professional financial consultants trained in taxation can address. If taxes are an important factor, however, the principle that it is the total portfolio of all invested assets that matters is particularly critical. Marketable securities and real asset investments must be considered together in order to increase total after-tax portfolio returns.[7] Investors that do not pay taxes, such as pension funds, may wish to exclude the purchase of securities which are priced in large part for their tax advantages. An example would be low-coupon bonds. Investors with average marginal tax rates may wish to include a statement that the portfolio be reviewed periodically during the course of a year in order to identify possible tax swaps.

   Liquidity needs vary considerably among investors. Liquidity can be obtained in two principal ways: (1) by allocating an appropriate percentage of the portfolio to short-term securities or money market managers, or (2) by requiring that the bonds and equities purchased be highly marketable. Which of the two approaches is the more reasonable depends on why liquidity is needed. If quick access to cash is needed in order to make scheduled withdrawals from the portfolio (for bills, vacations, retirement, etc.), the first approach reduces transaction costs. However, if liquidity is desired to enable active speculation, the second approach may be more effective in reducing transaction costs.

5. *Social investing.* A growing concern of the 1980s has been the extent to which an investment portfolio should be constrained by social issues. In the mid-1980s, the

---

[6]A manager assignment statement is not intended to tell the manager precisely what securities are to be purchased. Instead, it should provide general guidelines as to the types of securities to be purchased. Examples include low dividend yield versus high dividend yield, low beta versus high beta, etc.

[7]Because of the complexity and ever-changing nature of tax laws, we will not review them in the book.

major issue was investment in U.S. corporations doing business in South Africa. But even prior to that many portfolios were restricted from purchasing securities of firms engaged in alcohol or tobacco sales. There is no doubt that such restrictions reduce the diversification potential of the portfolio. How much so depends, of course, on the number of securities which are restricted. In the case of South Africa, the author has seen lists of restricted securities ranging from 30 to more than 200. The elimination of 30 securities probably would have minimal impact on diversification (although some of the 30 were large firms such as IBM). In contrast, the elimination of 200 securities could do severe damage to the ability to diversify.

6. *Strategy.* Finally, the statement of policy should discuss the forms of active speculation which will be allowed. In the broadest sense, speculative transactions can be related to either *timing* or *selection*.

In *timing*-related speculation, a given asset class is over- or underweighted in comparison to the proportion called for in the baseline investment portfolio. For example, if the baseline portfolio calls for a 40/60 bond/equity mix, and the portfolio owner elects to temporarily use a 50/50 mix in the belief that stocks are currently overvalued relative to bonds, this is a timing decision. To date, there is little evidence that professional investment advisers are able to consistently earn abnormal profits from speculative timing decisions. In addition, considerable care must be given to adjustments to the portfolio's asset allocation between bonds, stocks, etc., since it is this allocation which has the greatest impact on the portfolio's risk position. Both factors cause many investors to restrict the amount of timing which will be allowed in the portfolio.

In *selection*-related speculation, an individual security is over- or underweighted in comparison to the proportion called for in the baseline investment portfolio. For example, if the baseline equity portfolio is similar to the S&P 500 Composite and IBM represents 3% of the total value of the S&P Composite, then a decision to place 10% of all equity into IBM is a selection decision to overweight IBM. Whether speculative selection decisions can consistently lead to abnormal profits is unclear. Efficient market theory would suggest not, but empirical tests have failed to provide conclusive evidence that this is true.

Based on one's belief in the usefulness of timing and selection speculation, the statement of policy should identify the extent to which they may be used.

PORTFOLIO TYPES AND THEIR NEEDS

Security portfolios are owned by individuals and organizations having dramatically different objectives and constraints. To illustrate how the portfolio investment process applies to different situations, we will briefly examine four different groups:

1. Individuals
2. Pension funds
3. Endowment funds
4. Financial intermediaries

Individuals

The range of portfolio objectives, constraints, and strategies varies more among individual investors than among any other group of portfolio owners. As a result, we can provide only an overview of the major issues which most individual investors face.

Considerations in Setting the Objective. The most likely objective of a person's security portfolio is to provide a supplement to social security and pension benefits during the individual's retirement. Other needs, such as saving for a house, vacation, child's education, etc., are also common, of course. But the pervasive need is to increase income during retirement. As a result, an individual's age has a significant effect on the perceived riskiness of various types of securities. For example, a person who is 25 years from retirement can ride through the inevitable good and bad years of stock returns, whereas someone in retirement will be immediately affected by such movements since portions of the portfolio will have to be liquidated to meet current consumption needs. All other things held equal, the amount of equity risk inherent in a portfolio should decrease as an individual draws closer to retirement. As we have learned, this equity risk can be decreased in one of two ways: (1) by holding the same stocks but reducing the proportion of the portfolio committed to stocks and increasing the commitment to high-grade, short-term debt instruments, or (2) by changing the types of equities held from high-beta, high-growth stocks to lower-beta, high-dividend-yield stocks. The first approach is conceptually better since it provides the greater diversification potential (and probably involves lower transaction costs).

In addition to the individual's age, his or her other assets should be considered. Particular attention should be given to any real estate holdings and the nature of the person's career. In order to ensure the greatest possible diversification, the individual should probably underweight securities whose returns are highly correlated with returns on such existing assets. For example, the security portfolio should probably underweight equity securities issued by its owner's employer, bonds issued by local governments, etc. This might appear disloyal, and the employer and local government may make strong cases for overweighting such securities, but the individual's risk is increased if such securities are not underweighted.[8]

Finally, the individual's level of investment knowledge can affect the portfolio's constraints and strategy. Unfortunately, there is often a big difference between what should be done conceptually and what is done in practice. Because most individual investors lack investment expertise, they should attempt to diversify broadly (say, by purchasing a mutual fund), minimize costs (trade little and only in no-load mutual funds), and avoid active speculation and complex securities (such as options and futures). In practice, however, a major portion of the security information that individuals receive comes from brokers, who are paid only if their customers trade.

---

[8]One example of this lack of diversification often occurs in pension plans when pension assets are heavily invested in the securities of the corporation having the pension plan. Employees covered by such pensions incur two risks which are almost perfectly correlated: (1) that jobs will be lost because of poor company performance and (2) that the value of pension assets will fall for the same reason.

Consequently, many individuals own security portfolios which are poorly diversified, invest in load mutual funds, trade actively on broker recommendations, and use complex securities such as options and futures to gain speculative profits. Many brokers and brokerage firms sincerely try to provide general investment counseling. However, as a rule, such efforts are meager in comparison with the efforts devoted to persuading the customer to trade.

In sum, three factors are important in determining the individual investor's portfolio constraints and strategy:

1. A focus on retirement benefits
2. Other assets owned
3. Level of investment knowledge

Constraints. With this as background, various constraints can be considered. Among the most common are the following:

1. *Risk level.* This is a decision which the individual should make after reviewing information about the risks and expected returns from various asset mixes. Later in the chapter we will examine how this might be done. All other things held equal, the equity portion should decrease as the person approaches retirement.
2. *Strategy.* The investor's knowledge should largely determine what can be held. People with little knowledge should minimize holdings of complex instruments, such as options and futures, and instruments which require close monitoring, such as bonds with above-average default risk.
3. *Diversification.* Consideration should be given to the nature of other assets owned so the securities portfolio can underweight similar investments. No-load mutual funds and bank trust accounts are reasonable ways of achieving a diversified portfolio.
4. *Taxes and liquidity.* Investors in high tax brackets should seek professional advice. In general, they will find that municipal bonds, low-coupon bonds, and low-dividend-yield stocks provide larger after-tax returns. Investors in lower tax brackets should own taxable bonds with high coupons and dividend yields. Liquidity requirements depend on the individual's age and desire to speculate.
5. *Speculation.* In general, individual investors do not have the training and rapid access to new information necessary to successfully engage in speculative trades. They should follow a passive investment approach.

Pension Funds

The growth of employee retirement-benefit plans has been one of the dominant forces affecting the security markets since the mid-1900s. Since the early 1960s, of all institutional investors, pension funds have owned the largest amount of common stocks, and their relative importance continues to grow. For example, in 1960 noninsured pension funds owned 5% of the market value of all stocks listed on the NYSE. By the late 1980s, their ownership interest had increased to about 25%.[9]

There are two basic forms of employee benefit plans: (1) *defined contribution plans* and (2) *defined benefit plans*.[10] Defined contribution plans specify the amount which the employer will contribute to an employee's retirement plan. The contribution could be a flat dollar amount, a percentage of the employee's pay, or a specified share of corporate profits (a profit-sharing plan). Once the contribution has been made, all investment risk is borne by the employee. If the investment portfolio has performed better than expected, when an employee begins to withdraw pension benefits his or her payments will be larger than expected. If investment performance has been lower than expected, the employee's benefits will also be lower than expected. Again, all the investment risk of a defined contribution plan is borne by the employee. Consequently, employees covered by such a plan should be given considerable say in how their funds are invested.

In contrast, defined benefit plans specify a contractual benefit which will be paid to the employee after retirement. The size of the retirement benefit is calculated in a variety of ways. Examples of benefit formulas include: (1) a percentage of earnings (say, 50% of an employee's average salary during the last three years of employment), (2) an amount per year of service (say, $300 times the number of years of service), and (3) a percentage of earnings per year of service (say, 1% of the sum of all yearly earnings). Regardless of the precise formula used, defined benefit plans provide a contractual retirement benefit to the employee. All investment risk is borne by the employer. As such, the employer should have the strongest say in how plan assets are invested. For the rest of this chapter, we will restrict our discussion of pension funds to defined benefit plans.

Funding a Defined Benefit Plan. Under a defined benefit plan, the employer has a legal obligation to pay employees a contractually agreed-upon retirement benefit. The sole purpose of having a pension investment portfolio is to be able to meet these obligations in the future.

To help understand the various forces which determine the objective, constraints, and strategy of a pension portfolio, it is necessary that we understand the general process by which benefit liabilities are "funded." We will not delve too deeply into the details of pension funding here, since they are discussed more fully in Chapter 20. However, the general process of pension funding is relatively easy to understand. In fact, the pension-funding decision is no more than an application of time-value-of-money concepts.

Assume that you are the owner of a business which has 100 employees, each of whom now receives compensation of $20,000 a year. You have signed a pension agreement with the employees promising to pay a yearly individual pension benefit

---

[9]Many people believe that, by the year 2000, domestic U.S. pension assets will account for more than one-half the market value of all U.S. securities.

[10]We will not discuss Keogh plans or Individual Retirement Accounts (IRAs), which allow employees to place a limited amount of their earnings in a tax-deferred retirement plan.

equal to 30% of the retiring employee's compensation during his or her last year of employment. This retirement benefit will be paid at year-end during each year of the employee's retirement until the employee dies. A pension investment portfolio has been set up to help pay these future benefits. At present, the portfolio has a market value of $1 million.

You face two interrelated questions:

1. What are the *expected benefit payments*?
   a. In what years?
   b. In what dollar amounts?
2. What *contributions* should be made to the pension portfolio to ensure that the expected benefit payments will be met?

In order to calculate the expected benefit payments and required contributions, a number of assumptions need to be made:

1. Salary growth—Merit: 1.0% per year
                 Inflation: 5.0% per year

                     Total: 6.0% per year

2. Mortality rate—Preretirement: None
                  Postretirement: All employees live 15 years after retirement
3. Termination rate: No one leaves employment until retirement in 25 years
4. Years to retirement: Everyone will retire in 25 years
5. Postretirement benefit increases: None (no cost-of-living adjustment)
6. Investment returns—Real: 4% per year
                    Inflation: 5% per year

                        Total: 9% per year

7. Funding method: Annual annuity sufficient to fully fund by retirement

Estimated retirement benefits and required contributions are calculated in Table 19-4. Consider first the estimated benefits. Current salaries total $2 million. Since no employees are expected to leave employment because of death or termination, and since all employees are expected to retire in 25 years from now, the retirement benefit is based on the expected total salary payout in 25 years. Yearly salary growth consists of a merit increase and an inflation component, which sum to 6% per year. Growing at 6%, the current $2 million salary base will be $8.58 million in 25 years. Since employees have a right to yearly benefits equal to 30% of this total and all are expected to live for 15 years after retirement, the retirement benefits will be a 15-year annuity of $2,575,122 (30% × $8.58 million).

Now let's calculate the contributions which are required in order to pay these benefits. The yearly contribution will depend on two things: (1) the return we expect to earn on portfolio investments and (2) the funding method chosen. The expected investment return is 9% per year, consisting of a 4% real return and a 5% inflation

TABLE 19-4 *Estimated Pension Benefit Payments and Contributions*

Estimated Benefits	Years of Employment		Years of Retirement			
	0	*25*	*26*	*...*	*39*	*40*
Current Salary	$2,000,000	—				
Salary at Retirement: $2,000,000 × 1.06^{25}	—	$ 8,583,741				
Retirement Benefits: $8,583,741 × 30%	—	—	$2,575,122	...	$2,575,122	$2,575,122
Estimated Level Contributions						
P.V. of Benefits at Retirement: $2,575,122 × $\sum_{t=1}^{15} \dfrac{1}{1.09^t}$	—	$20,757,286				
Future Value of Current Portfolio: $1,000,000 × 1.09^{25}	—	$ 8,623,081	—		—	—
Deficiency		$12,134,205				
Level Annuity Contribution Required to Meet Deficiency: $12,134,205 ÷ $\sum_{t=1}^{25} 1.09^{t-1}$	$143,260	... $143,260				

component (the same inflation rate used for salary growth). The funding method requires that all benefit liabilities be "fully funded" by the retirement date (end of year 25) and that any contributions necessary to fully fund the portfolio be made in annual annuity installments.[11] The present value at the end of year 25 of the $2.57 million, 15-year-benefit annuity at a 9% investment rate is $20.76 million. Thus, if the pension portfolio has a value of $20.76 million at the end of year 25 and earns 9% each year, it will be able to exactly meet the yearly $2.57 million benefit liability. Unfortunately, the current $1 million portfolio growing at 9% per year will be worth only $8.62 million in 25 years. A deficiency of $12.13 million exists. To meet this deficiency a 25-year contribution annuity of $143,260 is necessary. Given the assumptions we have made, a level $143,260 yearly contribution to the pension portfolio is required. If any of the assumptions were to change, so would the contribution requirement. For example, what would happen if we increased the assumed inflation rate? First, the yearly benefit liability would rise because the employees' ending salaries would be larger. However, the investment return would also rise and, all other things

---

[11] In practice, contributions are typically not calculated as level-dollar annuities but, instead, as a level percentage of expected future salary.

being equal, cause required contributions to fall. Taking into account both effects, contributions would fall since the inflation rate increases the investment return for the full 40-year period of the portfolio's accumulation and liquidation, whereas the salary growth is affected for only the 25-year employment period. Increasing the assumed inflation rate without allowing for cost-of-living adjustments to benefits during the employees' retirement harms the employees and provides a gain to the employer in the form of lower contributions. We will not examine other possible modifications to our assumptions. But two things are clear. First, the analysis can quickly become quite complicated as we move from our simple example to more realistic cases. Second, the assumed investment return is only one of many components that determine a pension fund's contribution requirement.

ERISA. Retirement-benefit plans of corporations are subject to the legal requirements of the Employee Retirement Income Security Act — ERISA. Prior to ERISA, pension sponsors were legally responsible for their actions under a somewhat loose common-law principle known as the *Prudent Man Rule*. Historically, the Prudent Man Rule evaluated the risk of a security in isolation from other securities held in the portfolio and required that professional fiduciaries purchase only securities with low enough risks that a "prudent man" would also own them. In 1974 Congress enacted ERISA, the first nationwide statutory law to regulate the management of corporate pension funds. In many ways, the intent of ERISA was similar to the Prudent Man Rule. However, it differs in two important aspects. First, the risk of a security is now considered in the context of the total portfolio. Thus, a very risky security may now be purchased (although it may not have been allowed under the Prudent Man Rule) if its risk is offset by other securities in the portfolio. Second, ERISA explicitly requires that sponsors diversify "the investments of the plan so as to minimize the risk of large losses, unless under the circumstances it is clearly prudent not to do so."[12] In short, ERISA is a legislated version of what modern portfolio theory says the Prudent Man Rule should be.

Only corporate pension funds must follow ERISA requirements. All other professional fiduciaries are still subject to the common-law Prudent Man Rule. However, if logic prevails, legal interpretation of the Prudent Man Rule will move more closely towards the risk and diversification concepts inherent in ERISA.

PBGC. At the same time that Congress enacted ERISA, it created a governmental agency which guarantees certain minimum benefit payments to employees belonging to defined benefit plans. This agency is the Pension Benefit Guarantee Corporation — PBGC. It plays a role analogous to that of the Federal Deposit Insurance Corporation and the Federal Savings & Loan Insurance Corporation, which guarantee deposits in national banks and savings and loans. PBGC, however, guarantees pension benefits to employees of corporations which default on their pension promises — usually through firm bankruptcy. All firms that fall under ERISA are required to pay a yearly

---

[12]From section 404 (a) (1) (c) of the Employee Retirement Income Security Act of 1974.

insurance fee to the PBGC for each member of their defined benefit plans. Since governmental pension plans do not fall under ERISA, their future benefits are not guaranteed by the PBGC.

Considerations in Setting Objectives and Constraints. Sponsors of defined benefit plans are interested, of course, in the risk/reward characteristics of their investment portfolios. But this is solely because a portfolio's expected return and risk directly affect both expected contributions and uncertainty about such contributions. *The objective of a defined benefit plan sponsor is to minimize expected contribution costs without accepting undue risk.* Portfolio risk and return must be viewed in this context—as one of a number of factors which influence expected contribution levels and uncertainty.

The statement of policy for an investment portfolio should be prepared with this in mind. Careful attention should be given to the other variables which interact with portfolio returns in determining future contributions. In the next section of this chapter we will look at various ways of doing this. For now it is sufficient to say that the statement of policy should be drafted only after investment decisions have been considered in light of the current portfolio's value and actuarial estimates of benefit liabilities. In addition, corporate pension sponsors must give careful attention to the requirements of ERISA.

In view of this, let's examine the constraints we've discussed before:

1. *Risk level.* Again, this depends on the circumstances facing the pension sponsor as well as the sponsor's tolerance for risk. For example, consider a plan which is underfunded, fairly mature, and unable to draw large contributions from the sponsoring corporation or governing body. Such a plan will have to be exposed to larger investment risk in the hopes of greater returns than otherwise. An opposite example would be a plan which is fully funded today even using a relatively risk-free assumed investment return. Sponsors of this second plan would probably accept less return (and risk) than they would in other circumstances.[13] In short, the risk level a pension plan selects will depend on both the sponsor's risk tolerance and the financial circumstances facing the plan.

2. *Allowable securities.* Because of their large size, most pension funds have the financial ability and investment sophistication to hold a diverse group of different asset classes. For example, direct and indirect investment in real estate equity, international investment, venture capital pools, etc., are widely used. However, a close monitoring of how these securities affect the aggregate portfolio risk level is necessary.

---

[13]The sponsor of a plan which is more than fully funded might ask another party, such as an insurance company, to assume the pension's liabilities. The sponsor would pay the insurance firm an amount equal to the actuarial value of the liabilities and sell off the assets of the plan. Since the plan is overfunded, excess cash will be received from the sale of assets over the actuarial liability. This excess cash will then be used by the corporation as it wishes—to buy a new plant, retire debt, etc. During the middle 1980s such pension-plan terminations were common.

For instance, assume that pension sponsors have stated that a 60/40 equity/ T-bill mix will be maintained in order to achieve a desired risk/return tradeoff. Also assume that this is now being accomplished by assigning $600 million to various equity managers and $400 million to various money market managers. If options and futures trading were to be added, they could significantly change the effective stock/T-bill mix. Writing calls, for example, would have the effect of reducing the amount of equity risk in the total portfolio.

In short, the size and sophistication of many pension plans enable them to hold a wide variety of different security types. But active monitoring is necessary to ensure that the desired portfolio risk level is not violated.

3. *Diversification*. Again, because of their size and investment sophistication, pension plans can purchase a wide variety of asset types in order to increase portfolio diversification. Examples were mentioned above and include real estate, foreign investment, and venture capital projects.

4. *Taxes and liquidity*. Pensions do not pay taxes on investment income. As a result, holdings of securities which provide major tax advantages need to be closely evaluated. For example, municipal bonds and preferred stock are rarely purchased. Similarly, much of the return on equity investment in depreciable real estate comes in the form of tax advantages which the pension cannot realize.

   With rare exceptions the benefit liabilities of pension funds are long term in nature. As a result, there is little need for liquidity and immediate cash flow.

5. *Speculation*. Sponsors of pension plans have access to the best information available through myriad investment consultants. As a result, they are usually aware of the arguments in favor of or against active speculation. Many pension funds have, in fact, concluded that the best approach is to index—to purchase money market, bond, and equity index funds as well as to immunize via dedicated portfolios. Most pension funds, however, have not given up the search for speculative profits. Nonetheless, they maintain close control of the risks which their managers are able to accept. Managers are usually assigned specific roles. For example, an equity manager may be told to invest only in high-quality, low-beta securities and a bond manager might be told to guarantee a return via contingent immunization. In short, to the extent speculation is allowed, the sponsor will maintain active control over total portfolio risk.

Endowment Funds

An endowment fund is a portfolio of assets which is managed to help pay for a specific social or cultural need. Such funds are created by donations to educational institutions, religious organizations, and cultural organizations such as museums and orchestras, hospitals, and private foundations.

Historically, the investment management of endowment funds was somewhat lax because the funds tended to be run by individuals with limited investment training who gave little attention to appropriate long-run risk/return positions. Currently, however, professional investment management and the application of modern portfolio concepts are becoming more widespread. One reason for this shift may be the difficulties most endowment funds suffered during the 1970s. With managers who were untrained and quite risk-averse, most endowment assets were held in intermediate- to long-term bonds, and any equities were in the form of high-dividend stocks such as public utilities. This was a disastrous position to be in when the inflation of the 1970s hit. The value of endowment assets fell at the same time that inflation was increasing the funds' needs for cash. Although this is certainly not the only reason for the active attention now being given to proper portfolio management, it did wake up the management of many endowment funds.

Five factors largely determine the objective and constraints of an endowment portfolio:

1. Income versus growth
2. Supplemental cash flows
3. Management knowledge
4. Taxes
5. Social issues

Income Versus Growth. All endowment funds are organized to help provide cash for a specific need. Sometimes this need is temporary in nature, such as the construction of a hospital. In such cases, portfolio management is straightforward—invest in fixed-income securities whose average duration matches the time contractor payments are due. In most cases, however, the endowment fund is expected to provide a continuous cash flow sufficient to meet both current and growing long-run expenses. The apparent conflict between desires for large current cash flows versus long-run growth in cash flows represents what many people believe to be the fundamental investment problem faced by endowment funds. At one extreme, current cash flow could be increased by investing solely in high-coupon bonds and high-dividend stocks—a policy that sacrifices future growth in cash flows. At the other extreme, investments in growth-oriented equities provide growth at the sacrifice of current cash.

In truth, such funds face exactly the same investment dilemma that we have returned to so often—what is an acceptable portfolio risk level? In the case of endowment funds we speak in terms of the ability to meet cash flow needs. In the general case, we speak in terms of uncertain rates of return. But it is easy to see that the two are the same once you recognize that the endowment's expenses don't have to be paid solely from dividend and interest income. Expenses can also be met by the sale of securities. This is an important point, too often overlooked, so let's stay with it for a moment.

Consider an endowment fund which now has $1,000 to be invested. Next year the endowment's expenses are expected to be $50. Management is examining two portfolios which are *identical in expected return and risk*. Portfolio *A*, however, has a flow of interest and dividends which is exactly $50. Portfolio *B* has a current yield of only $20. Clearly, portfolio *A* is the more "income-oriented" portfolio, whereas portfolio *B* is the more "growth-oriented."

Assume that a year goes by and both portfolios have incurred a negative 10% return. The situation which the endowment fund will find itself in with either portfolio is:

	Portfolio A	*Portfolio B*
Rate of Return	$\dfrac{850 + 50}{1,000} - 1$	$\dfrac{880 + 20}{1,000} - 1$
	$= -10\%$	$= -10\%$
To Cover Cash Outflows		
Interest and Dividends	$ 50	$ 20
Sale of Assets	0	30
Total	$ 50	$ 50
End-of-Year Portfolio Value		
Prior to Sale of Assets	$850	$880
Sale of Assets	0	(30)
Total	$850	$850

In both cases, the $50 cash outflow is met. And, in both cases, the portfolio is worth $850. Whether the cash outflow comes solely in the form of interest and dividends or in combination with the sale of securities is unimportant. The relevant consideration is uncertainty about each portfolio's return. And whether the return comes in the form of cash or changes in market value is also unimportant. In sum, there is no reason to require, as many funds do, that interest and dividends be the only source for meeting cash-outflow requirements.

The income-growth concern is really a concern about an acceptable level of portfolio risk. In the next section of this chapter we examine various ways to determine an acceptable risk level. Most of the discussion will be based on the decisions of a pension fund, but much of the analysis can be applied to endowment funds. The income-growth concern is better thought of as a concern about the life of the endowment fund. In particular, the duration of fund outflows should be a major consideration in selecting the optimal mix of securities. For example, a longer duration of fund outflows leads to lower risk for common stocks and greater risk for money market instruments. Conversely, a shorter duration of fund outflows leads to greater risk for common stocks and lower risk for money market instruments.[14]

Supplemental Cash Flow. In some cases, the endowment portfolio is the only source of cash outflows. If this is true, the risk level which can be tolerated is lower than otherwise. For example, an endowment set up to meet the needs of a small symphony orchestra might be the prime source of cash flows and, thus, would have to be invested at a lower risk level than if the orchestra were large and able to attract sizable paying audiences. If other sources are available to supplement necessary cash outflows, greater investment risk can be accepted.

---

[14]See Chapters 11 and 12 for a review of duration and its importance.

Management Knowledge. Those in the top management of most endowment organizations are selected for their knowledge of the goals for which the endowment was formed, not for their investment expertise. For this reason, they should seek independent professional counseling to help guide investment policy, but unfortunately they often don't. As a result, some endowments have embarrassingly liquidated their equities at a market bottom only to repurchase after sizable market advances. If efficient market theory is correct, no one is expected to be a consistent loser (or winner). Yet the transaction costs associated with trying to time the market are large, and the volatility of portfolio returns is likely to increase. This runs counter to the desire of most endowments to minimize portfolio expenses and obtain a relatively stable investment return.

Tax and Social Concerns. With the exception of private foundations, endowment funds are not taxed.[15] As a result, tax-advantaged securities such as municipal bonds and preferred stock are usually not held.

A number of endowments, particularly those developed by religious and certain educational organizations, tailor their investment constraints and strategies to various social issues. For example, many religious endowments forbid the ownership of tobacco and liquor stocks. Others restrict ownership of securities issued by companies involved in certain aspects of defense contracting. Most recently, many endowments have stated that they will not purchase securities of firms engaged in trade with South Africa until the South African policy of apartheid is abolished.

Financial Intermediaries

A financial intermediary is simply an organization that obtains cash from individual savers and then lends the cash to individual borrowers. The terms *lending* and *borrowing* should be construed in the broadest scope to include both equity and debt purchases or sales. In truth, pension funds and endowment funds are financial intermediaries, since they obtain cash from one party and allocate it to another. However, the term *financial intermediary* is commonly used to mean a commercial bank, a life insurance company, or a casualty insurance company.

The portfolio constraints and strategies of financial intermediaries differ, since each portfolio must be tailored to the particular characteristics of each business. However, three common themes have affected their investment strategies. First, each intermediary faces significant *regulations* regarding allowed investment practices. Second, the nature of the banking and insurance business has been dramatically affected by the *inflation* of the 1970s and the resulting increased volatility of interest rates. In addition, a movement towards increased *competition* both within each industry and across the three industries has altered the traditional types of portfolio securities which each holds.

---

[15]Investment income of private foundations is taxed at a rate of 2%.

Commercial Banks. The commercial banking system epitomizes the operations of a financial intermediary. Banks obtain cash from depositors or the sale of bank obligations and disburse the cash by making commercial loans, consumer loans, real estate loans, etc., or by purchasing government and corporate securities. Their profit arises from the yield spread between the rate at which they borrow and the rate at which they lend.

The investment posture of commercial banks is designed to have relatively little risk. The banks' shareholders, of course, may wish to earn the larger returns which can be expected by assuming greater risk. But it is public policy that the risk of bank operations be minimized.

There are two fundamental reasons for this policy. First, the commercial banking network is at the heart of our financial system. If a few large banks were to fail, many people believe that the public would lose confidence in the system as a whole, causing a breakdown in our financial markets. Second, the banking network is highly leveraged both within individual banks (where, on average, about $1 of equity is used to support $10 in assets) and through the fractional reserve system across the full banking system. A continuing conflict revolves around the proper risk level, with bank management seeking greater risk and returns and bank regulators restricting risk. The *precise* level of investment risk which should be allowed is widely debated, but, relative to other investment portfolios such as pension and endowment funds, there is no doubt that bank investment portfolios must be much less risky.

The risk position of a commercial bank is basically determined by two factors: (1) the default risk of its loans and securities, and (2) the extent to which the durations of assets and liabilities are not matched. Default risk should be a concern, of course, and has been the cause of many bank failures in recent years. But it can be easily managed by insisting that most loans and security purchases be made only in very high-grade "paper." Mismatching the duration of assets and liabilities is, however, equally important, if not more so.

Banks provide a classic illustration of how portfolio immunization can be used to minimize investment risk. Their liabilities are largely paid in nominal, as opposed to real, dollars. Thus, conceptually, immunization should work. In addition, their liabilities are very short term. Since there are numerous short-term assets available, immunization should also work in practice. (This contrasts with, say, a defined benefit pension fund whose liabilities are in real dollars and have a longer duration than most available securities.) Immunization against interest rate risk has become a dominant concern to bank management. Numerous consulting services and models are actively used by bank management to track exposure to interest rate risk. Some banks attempt to truly immunize their assets and liabilities. Others will slightly mismatch in an attempt to speculate on expected changes in interest rates. But virtually all major banks have an investment policy which is closely integrated with an asset/liability duration model. Since most of their liabilities are short term, so too are their security investments.

Banks are perhaps the most actively regulated of all financial intermediaries. At the federal level, they must meet the requirements of the Federal Reserve Board, the Federal Deposit Insurance Corporation, and the Comptroller of Currency. In addition, numerous laws have been enacted which restrict their activities. An example is the Glass-Steagall Act, which prohibits commercial banks from engaging in many of the activities now performed by investment banking houses. At the state level, banks are subject to a variety of regulatory agencies and legislation.

During the 1970s and early 1980s, various regulations and laws began to severely hurt the competitive position of commercial banks. A major difficulty was Regulation Q, which placed a limit on the maximum interest rate which banks could pay to depositors. As interest rates rose in the 1970s and 1980s, banks were unable to compete against the higher yields paid by money market funds, and disintermediation became severe.[16] At the same time, usury laws in many states limited the interest rate which banks could charge on their loans. These and other regulations caused many banks to pursue a more aggressive investment strategy by purchasing higher-risk securities and by mismatching asset/liability durations in an attempt to speculate on interest rate moves. Today, many of the most severe regulations have been lifted. For example, Regulation Q no longer limits interest rates on deposits, usury laws have been changed, and many banks offer their own money market funds.

Inflation and the associated volatility of interest rates have also affected bank investment strategies by making it very clear that proper management of asset and liability durations is critical. Since the duration of liabilities is very short, so too is the duration of average asset investments. The manager of security investments might fine-tune portfolio selection by looking for quality swaps, higher yields in various economic sectors, etc. But the dominant security investment will be in high-quality, short-term securities. In addition, security portfolio decisions will be fully integrated into loan portfolio decisions. For example, if the duration of the loan portfolio is lengthened, the security portfolio's duration should be shortened.

Life Insurance Companies. The portfolio strategies of life insurance firms are also affected by regulation, inflation, and competition. Because their liabilities are very predictable and are often in nominal dollars, portfolio immunization plays an important role.

The regulation of life insurance firms is extensive. In the United States, all regulation is at the state level. Among states, similar approaches to the regulation of investment, accounting rules, financial statement presentation, etc., are achieved through the National Association of Insurance Commissioners. These regulations are a principal determinant of investment policy. State laws determine the asset classes in which insurance firms may invest and place limits on the proportion held in each class. For example, many states constrain the *cost* value of common stock holdings to 10% of total assets. State laws also define quality standards within each asset class that must be met before a particular security can be held. For example, bonds usually have to meet a specified interest coverage ratio. In short, regulation significantly reduces the investment flexibility of life insurance firms.

Inflation has also had an effect on life insurance investment strategies. Historically, life insurance companies have provided two services when they sell a "straight life" policy: (1) death benefits and (2) the ability to borrow against the cash value of a pol-

---

[16]Disintermediation means the withdrawal of deposits from commercial banks.

icy at a rate of interest which is statutorily fixed. As interest rates rose during the 1970s in response to increased inflation expectations, policy holders began to borrow extensively at contractual rates of 4% to 5%. The profit implications of this are obvious. But, in addition, the increasing interest rates caused a decline in sales of straight life policies and an increase in sales of term policies. This occurred because term policies were cheaper and people could use the cost differentials to invest at higher rates than the insurance company could legally offer. Finally, the rise in interest rates caused major declines in security portfolio values, since most portfolios were invested heavily in long-term bonds.

The net result was a scramble for new profitable products—in particular, investment annuities, guaranteed investment contracts (GICs), and universal life policies. Each of these changed the cash liability structure of the life insurance business. Immunization of various segments of the investment portfolio became important, and the duration of investments was generally shortened in line with each of the new products' cash liabilities. In addition, investments in real estate and common stock were increased in an attempt to hedge against future inflation.

Casualty Insurance Firms. Casualty insurance firms provide health, property, marine, workers' compensation, and liability insurance. Because their benefit liability stream is much shorter and less predictable than that of a life insurance firm, they have significantly different investment needs. For example, immunization is less workable because of the unpredictability of liability claims. Regulatory restrictions are also fewer and are measured primarily as a required ratio of premiums to equity capital. Usually, $1 of equity capital is required for each $2 to $3 of insurance premiums. In order to provide liquidity and safety to meet casualty claims, a portfolio of high-grade, short- to intermediate-term bonds is held. The remainder of the portfolio is held in equities in the hope that they will, on average, provide the fastest growth in equity capital which, in turn, will provide the ability to increase premium revenue. The precise allocation between fixed income and equity securities is not regulated, but left instead to the risk tolerance of shareholders.

SUMMARY

The portfolio investment process consists of three logical stages:

1. *Planning.* The needs, knowledge, and risk tolerance of the investor are brought together with long-run capital market expectations to define the investor's long-run strategic asset allocation (SAA). The SAA decision should consist of two subdecisions: (*a*) what the current SAA should be and (*b*) how the SAA should be passively rebalanced as time passes, as the investor's wealth changes, or as stock prices change. The portfolio objective, constraints, and all speculative strategies which are to be allowed should be formally documented in a written statement of investment policy.

2. *Implementation.* Once the strategic asset allocation has been determined, various speculative strategies can be considered. Such strategies fall into two broad approaches: timing and selection. Timing decisions over- and underweight various asset classes, industries, or economic sectors in an attempt to earn excess risk-adjusted returns. Such timing decisions are referred to as tactical asset allocation decisions. Security selection speculation consists of over- or underweighting individual securities within a given asset class. If timing and selection strategies are not used, then the investor's portfolio should consist of index funds which are held in proportions consistent with the SAA. If security prices are efficiently priced, timing and selection decisions will result in a loss of value because of transaction costs.

3. *Monitoring.* The portfolio should be periodically monitored to ensure that all constraints of the statement of investment policy are being met and to monitor returns from asset allocation and speculative strategies.

REVIEW PROBLEM

You are examining the financial condition and investment policies of two defined benefit pension plans, Yung Technology and Auld Land Signs. Information about each is given below:

	Yung	*Auld*
Current Investment Portfolio Value	$5.0 million	$60.0 million
Employee Information		
Number of employees	1,000	1,000
Average current salary	$20,000	$30,000
Benefit payments as % of final salary	25%	25%
Average years to retirement	30	15
Actuarial Assumptions		
Annual salary growth	4%	4%
Mortality rate prior to retirement	0%	0%
Employee termination preretirement	0%	0%
Retirement cost-of-living increases	0%	0%
Average years of retirement	15 years	15 years
Investment Portfolio Assumptions		
Desired stock/bond mix	70%–30%	30%–70%
Expected nominal stock return (per year)	10%	10%
Expected nominal bond return (per year)	4%	4%
Funding Policy	Year-end annuity to fully fund requirements by end of last employment year	

a. What are the basic differences in the benefit liabilities of each firm?

b. Both Yung and Auld desire that the value of their investment portfolios be sufficient to meet the retirement benefits of their employees. Specifically, their goals are to have portfolio values on the last day of an average person's employment equal to the present value of expected future benefit liabilities. What is this desired portfolio value for each firm?

c. Given the asset allocation chosen by each firm, is the current portfolio value sufficient to meet the needs of part b above?

d. If Yung wishes to make year-end level-dollar (annuity) contributions to its investment portfolio, what must the contribution be?

Solution

a. The plans differ principally in their maturities. The Yung pension plan has an employee base with an average of 30 years to retirement. In contrast, the Auld pension plan's employees will retire on average in 15 years. All other things being equal, Yung can accept greater investment risk.

b. *Present Value of Benefit Liabilities at Average Retirement Date*

Benefit Annuity	*Yung*	*Auld*
Current Salary Base	$20.000 million	$30.000 million
Compound Rate of Growth to Average Retirement	1.04^{30}	1.04^{15}
Retirement Salary Base	$64.868 million	$54.028 million
Benefit Payment Rate	0.25	0.25
15-Year Benefit Annuity	$16.217 million	$13.507 million
Actuarial Investment Return		
Stock Return (0.7 × 10%)	7.0%	
(0.3 × 10%)		3.0%
Bond Return (0.3 × 4%)	1.2%	
(0.7 × 4%)		2.8%
Expected Portfolio Return	8.2%	5.8%

Present Value Factor of a 15-Year Annuity

$$\sum_{t=1}^{15} \frac{1}{1.082^t} \qquad\qquad \sum_{t=1}^{15} \frac{1}{1.058^t}$$

$$= \frac{1}{0.082}\left(1 - \frac{1}{1.082^{15}}\right) \qquad = \frac{1}{0.058}\left(1 - \frac{1}{0.058^{15}}\right)$$

$$= 8.4559 \qquad\qquad = 9.8404$$

Present Value of Annuity
(8.4559 × $16.217) $137.129 million

(9.8404 × $13.507) $132.914 million

c. *Growth of Current Portfolio with No Contributions*

	Yung	*Auld*
Current Portfolio Value	$ 5.0 million	$ 60.0 million
Compound Rate of Growth	1.082^{30}	1.058^{15}
Expected Portfolio Value	$53.18 million	$139.78 million

The Auld pension plan has assets which are expected to grow to more than necessary to meet future benefit liabilities. It is overfunded slightly. Management could either reduce the investment risk exposure by investing less in stocks or withdraw some of the assets from the portfolio. Regardless of any such decisions, future contributions are not expected to be needed.

Since the Yung pension plan does not have sufficient current portfolio assets to meet expected benefit liabilities, Yung will have to provide future contributions and may wish to increase its commitments to stocks in order to increase the expected investment returns.

d. Future value annuity factor with interest $= 8.2\%$ and period $= 30$ years is:

$$\sum_{t=0}^{29} 1.082^t = 117.524$$

Value of Liability at Retirement	$= \$137.129$ million
Expected Current Portfolio Value	$= \quad 53.180$ million
Deficiency	$= \$ \ 83.949$ million
Required Annual Contribution	$= 83.949 \div 117.524$
	$= \$ \quad 0.714$ million

QUESTIONS AND PROBLEMS

1. Consider the data given in the Review Problem for Yung Technology. Discuss the interrelationship between (a) the expected contribution level and its uncertainty and (b) the asset-allocation decision.

2. (CFA Exam Question)
You are being interviewed for a job as a portfolio manager at an investment counseling partnership. As part of the interview, you are asked to demonstrate your ability to develop investment portfolio policy statements for the clients listed below:
   a. A pension fund that is described as a mature defined benefit plan, with the work force having an average age of 54. There are no unfunded pension liabilities, and wage-cost increases are forecast at 9% annually.
   b. A university endowment fund that is described as conservative, with investment returns being utilized along with gifts and donations to meet current expenses. The spending rate is 5% per year and inflation in costs is expected at 8% annually.
   c. A life insurance company that is described as specializing in annuities. Policy premium rates are based on a minimum annual accumulation rate of 14% in the first year of the policy and a 10% minimum annual accumulation rate in the next five years.

   List and discuss the objective and constraints that will determine the portfolio policy that you would recommend for each client.

3. (CFA Exam Question)
John Smalle, an associate in your firm, has asked you to help him establish a financial plan for his family's future. John is 27 years old and has been with your firm for two years. Anne, his 26-year-old wife, is employed as a psychologist for the local school district. They are childless now but may have children in a few years. John and Anne have accumulated $10,000 in savings and recently inherited $50,000 in cash. They believe they can save at least $5,000 yearly. They are currently in a 25% income tax bracket and both have excellent

career opportunities. They are eager to develop a financial plan and understand that it will need to be periodically adjusted as their circumstances change. You tell John that you would be happy to meet with Anne and him to discuss their financial plans.

a. Identify and describe an appropriate investment objective and investment constraints for the Smalles and prepare a comprehensive investment policy statement that is based on the objective and constraints.

b. State and explain your asset-allocation recommendations for the Smalles based on the policy statement you developed in part a.

4. (CFA Exam Question)

Jason Robertson is a successful business executive who voluntarily retired at age 63 after 40 years of service with a privately owned firm of which he was a shareholder. He is married and has three adult children who are married and self-supporting. At time of retirement Mr. Robertson owned his own home free and clear of mortgages, held $25,000 in life insurance, and had savings and a miscellaneous list of good-quality bonds and stocks aggregating $50,000 in value. He is also entitled to a yearly pension of $30,000, which is fully funded and has survivor's benefits to his wife of $17,000. Upon retirement, he liquidated the preferred and common shares acquired in his company over a span of 25 years under a stock purchase plan and realized cash of $170,000 (net, after provision for capital gains taxes). As a retirement benefit, Mr. Robertson and his wife are also entitled to the protection of a major medical group health insurance program fully subsidized by his firm.

As he reviews his financial position at retirement, Mr. Robertson considers himself quite well off, but he believes he should obtain some professional advice about the proper management of his capital resources at this stage of his life. Accordingly, he makes an appointment with you as an investment counselor to discuss his financial affairs. During an initial conversation, you learn that he requires an annual pretax income of $45,000 to $50,000 to maintain his present standard of living, and he would like to leave as large an estate as possible for his three children. He is concerned about the effects that inflation and taxation may have on his desired income and asset objectives.

a. Discuss the general investment policy Mr. Robertson should follow to attain his financial objectives.

b. Exhibit A indicates various categories of securities available, assumed yields, and three portfolios that have been constructed for the $220,000 Mr. Robertson has available for investment. Select and justify the portfolio that you think is most appropriate for Mr. Robertson to achieve his investment objectives.

5. (CFA Exam Question)

A pension fund sponsor has established a simplified baseline portfolio to serve as a benchmark for the fixed-income portfolio. By mutual agreement with the sponsor, the manager retains complete discretion to implement strategic changes in the composition of the actual portfolio. For example, if she is bearish on bonds, she may hold as much of the portfolio in short maturities as she considers advantageous. The fund's baseline portfolio is:

	Maturity	*Percent*
Short-Term	(Up to 1 Year)	10%
Intermediate-Term	(1 to 10 Years)	40
Long-Term	(More than 10 Years)	50
Total Baseline Portfolio		100%

a. Briefly discuss the steps involved in determining the composition of a baseline portfolio.

EXHIBIT A *Three Portfolio Alternatives*

Category of Security	Recent Market Yield	Portfolio No. 1	Portfolio No. 2	Portfolio No. 3
Money Market Securities	9.50%	$ 10,000	$ 10,000	$ 10,000
Government Bonds				
Short-Term	8.98			20,000
Intermediate-Term	9.57		10,000	30,000
Long-Term	10.06			50,000
Long-Term Corporate Bonds				
AAA Rated	9.26			50,000
AA Rated	9.46			
A Rated	9.62		30,000	
BBB Rated	10.10		20,000	
Tax-Exempt Municipal Bonds	6.30	80,000	20,000	
Preferred Stocks	8.86			20,000
Transportation Common Stocks	4.95			
Utility Common Stocks	8.95	10,000	30,000	20,000
Financial Common Stocks	5.30	10,000	20,000	
Industrial Common Stocks	5.00	110,000	80,000	20,000
Total		$220,000	$220,000	$220,000

    b. If the manager retains complete discretion to alter the composition of the actual portfolio (as in this case), discuss the probable impact of the baseline portfolio on the manager's investment strategy.

    c. Given this baseline portfolio, describe the procedure for measuring the manager's actual performance.

    d. Suppose that at a particular point in time, the average maturity of the portfolio increases from 10 years to 11 years. At the same time, the duration of the portfolio declines.

      (1) Explain how this could happen.

      (2) Other things being equal, explain what an increase in average maturity, but a decline in duration, would suggest concerning the riskiness of the portfolio.

6. (CFA Exam Question)

Shelia John is Director of Employee Benefits for XYZ Corporation, which has a $50 million pension fund managed by five money management organizations. She has had this assignment for two years and has identified some of the more troublesome problems that have arisen during this period. At the conclusion of the formal part of your quarterly presentation, she asks you to respond to the following:

    a. The fundamental question of asset allocation has really not been addressed clearly by the fund managers or the sponsor. Identify the relevant factors that should be considered and state briefly how these factors would apply to each of the three major investment categories — liquid reserves, bonds, and stocks.

    b. The conventional wisdom is that the performance of an investment manager should be measured over a "full market cycle." State and support three good reasons for disagreeing with this view.

    c. Describe four factors in portfolio strategy that you would expect the portfolio managers of the pension fund to be following.

    d. Describe four portfolio practices that may support dismissal of a manager regardless of his or her record of investment performance.

    e. Identify three advantages and three disadvantages of passively investing a substantial portion of the equity sector of the fund.

7. (CFA Exam Question)

You are the chief investment officer for your company's pension fund and are preparing for the next meeting of the Investment Committee. Several committee members are interested in reviewing and updating past discussions relating to the use of index funds for your pension fund, which utilizes both internal management and multiple external managers. Prepare brief answers to the following requests from committee members:

    a. Cite and explain four reasons why consideration should be given to using an index fund.

    b. Cite two decisions which are part of the investment process and which should have priority over the decision about whether or not to use an index fund.

    c. Cite and explain four strategies and/or operating features that could cause an index fund portfolio to have a different return from the index itself.

    d. Explain why the following are, or are not, suitable indexes on which to base an index fund:

        (1) The Dow Jones Industrial Average

        (2) Standard & Poor's 500 Stock Index

8. (CFA Exam Question)

You are a portfolio manager and Senior Executive Vice President of Advisory Securities Selection, Inc. Your firm has been invited to meet with the trustees of the Wood Museum Endowment Fund. Wood Museum is a privately endowed charitable institution that is dependent on the investment return from a $25 million endowment fund to balance the budget. The treasurer of the museum has recently completed a study that indicates a need for cash flows from the endowment fund of $3.0 million in 1982, $3.2 million in 1983, and $3.5 million in 1984 in order to balance the budget. At the present time, the entire endowment portfolio is invested in Treasury bills and money market funds because the trustees fear a financial crisis. The trustees do not anticipate any further capital contributions to the fund. The trustees are all successful businessmen, and they have been critical of the fund's previous investment advisers for not following a logical decision-making process. In fact, several previous managers have been dismissed because of their inability to communicate with the trustees and their preoccupation with the fund's relative performance rather than the cash flow needs.

Advisory Securities Selection, Inc., has been contacted by the trustees because of its reputation for understanding and relating to its clients' needs. The trustees have specifically asked to meet with you because of your recent article in a professional journal outlining the decision-making process of your firm. In the letter of invitation addressed to you, the trustees have included the flow chart in Exhibit B and the following quotations from a speech by Professor William F. Sharpe that were included in the article:

> It is important to understand that, even if the market were perfectly efficient with every security plotting right on the plane, the investment management process would still require sophisticated procedures. In particular, it would require the tailoring of portfolios to meet clients' attitudes toward risk and clients' attitudes toward yield vis-à-vis gains.
>
> One important part of this exercise [modern portolio theory] is finding out what the client is all about—where one client differs from another.

EXHIBIT B *The Portfolio Management Process*

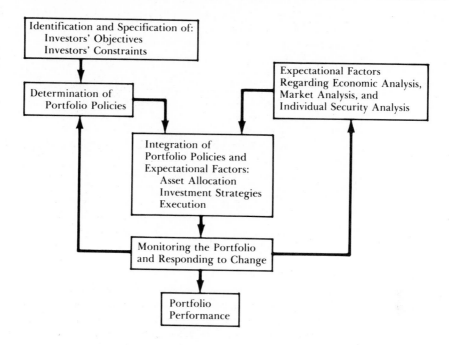

The Trustees have asked you, as a prospective portfolio manager for the Wood Museum Endowment Fund, to prepare a written report in response to the following questions. Your report will be circulated to the trustees prior to the initial interview on June 15, 1981.

a. Explain in detail how *each* of the following relates to the determination of either investor objectives or investor constraints that can be used to determine the portfolio policies for this three-year period for the Wood Museum Endowment Fund:

- Liquidity requirements
- Return requirements
- Risk tolerance
- Time horizon
- Tax considerations
- Regulatory and legal considerations
- Unique needs and circumstances

b. Interest rate futures, common stock options, immunization, and international diversification are investment strategies that can be used as modifiers of portfolio risk.
  (1) Explain how *each* of these four investment strategies can be used to modify portfolio risk.
  (2) Identify and explain which one of these four strategies is *most* suitable for the Wood Museum Endowment Fund.

9. (CFA Exam Question)

   You have been named as investment adviser to a foundation established by Dr. Walter Jones with an original contribution consisting entirely of the common stock of Jomedco, Inc. Founded by Dr. Jones, Jomedco manufactures and markets medical devices invented by the doctor and collects royalties on other patented innovations.

   All of the shares which made up the initial contribution to the foundation were sold at a public offering of Jomedco common stock and the $5 million proceeds will be delivered to the foundation within the next week. At the same time, Mrs. Jones will receive $5 million in proceeds from the sale of her stock in Jomedco.

   Dr. Jones' purpose in establishing the Jones Foundation was to "offset the effect of inflation on medical school tuition for the maximum number of worthy students."

   You are preparing for a meeting with the foundation trustees to discuss investment policy and asset allocation.

   a. Define and give examples that show the differences between an investment objective, an investment constraint, and an investment policy.

   b. Identify and describe an appropriate investment objective and set of investment constraints for the Jones Foundation.

   c. Based on the investment objective and constraints identified in part b, prepare a comprehensive investment policy statement for the Jones Foundation to be recommended for adoption by the trustees.

   d. Discuss the issues involved in determining whether or not the investment adviser should make the asset-allocation decision for the Jones Foundation investment portfolio.

   e. Identify and describe the critical capital market variables required for a two-asset allocation model for the Jones Foundation.

   f. Discuss the difficulties associated with using historical information in making estimates of each of the critical variables enumerated in part e.

   g. Using the data in Exhibit C and your own assumptions for other critical variables, state the optimal asset allocation that you would recommend for the Jones Foundation for the coming annual holding period and explain how you determined that asset mix.

10. (CFA Exam Question)

    Harvey Bowles, CFA, recently joined Perennial Trust Company, a firm specializing in financial management for wealthy families. Bowles's first assignment is the Allen family, a new client who came to Perennial upon the death of Charles A. Allen. Bowles soon will be meeting with the late Mr. Allen's widow, Emily Allen, and son, George Allen. To familiarize himself with the Allens' situation, he reads the following memorandum prepared by Perennial's new business officer:

    > Mrs. Emily Allen, age 84, lives simply on the income from a trust created by her husband, the Charles A. Allen Trust for Emily Allen. The *present* status of this trust is

EXHIBIT C *Expected Returns for Major Asset Categories over the Next 12 Months*

	Expected Return
Treasury Bills (90 days)	11%
Long Treasury Bonds	14%
Common Stock	15%

SOURCE: Investment Management, Ltd.

EXHIBIT D *Investment Assets (6/1/86)*
Charles A. Allen Trust for Emily Allen

	Cost	Market Value	After-Tax Yields
Short-Term Reserves (Tax-Exempt)	$ 3,000,000	$ 3,000,000	4%
Growth Stocks	500,000	1,000,000	1
Cyclical Stocks	1,000,000	1,000,000	2
Defensive Stocks	3,000,000	4,000,000	2
Tax-Exempt Bonds	4,000,000	4,500,000	7
Equity Real Estate*	1,000,000	2,000,000	6
Totals	$12,500,000	$15,500,000	

*Exclusive of personal residence.

shown in Exhibit D. Mrs. Allen is the trust's only income beneficiary; on her death, the assets go to her son, George, free of taxes (which were paid at Charles A. Allen's death). Mrs. Allen contributes her excess income to various charities, and occasionally makes gifts to George and members of his family. She feels George is somewhat irresponsible, although a good son, father, and husband. Mrs. Allen lived through the Depression, is not comfortable in the present-day financial environment, and has often said, "We saw great companies and great fortunes destroyed. We were terrified, we suffered great hardship, yet my husband was able to build our fortune by investing wisely over the years." The Allen Trust's only investment restriction is a requirement that George Allen be consulted, as a courtesy, before any investment action is taken.

George Allen, age 54, is married and has three children, all sons, one in prep school and two in college. Mr. Allen is not employed, but volunteers his services to a variety of civic and charitable organizations. Neither he nor his wife, a homemaker, seem to be financially sophisticated, although Mr. Allen is a strong believer in free investment markets and free enterprise. He feels that "smart investors can double their money every five years" and looks forward to financing businesses for his sons as they graduate from college. The George Allens' living style and family needs require an annual income of $100,000. This now is derived from investment income and occasional gifts from his mother. Mr. Allen's *current* investment portfolio is shown in Exhibit E.

Before his meeting with the Allens, Bowles reviews Perennial's latest investment return projections, dated June 1, 1986. His firm believes that continued prosperity is the most likely outlook for the next three to five years, but is mindful of the possibility of two disturbing alternatives: first, a return to high inflation, or, second, a drift into deflation/depression. Exhibit F presents the details of Perennial's projections.

a. Treating the Allen family as an entity, *create* an investment policy statement to fit their combined situation.

b. Based on your answer to part a, *recommend* and *justify* a new asset allocation strategy for *each* of the existing Allen portfolios. Your allocation must sum to 100% for each portfolio.

c. Assume that Emily Allen dies suddenly. *Revise* your allocation strategy for George Allen. Your allocation must sum to 100%.

11. (CFA Exam Question)
Jack Quick and Heidi Bronson have been discussing the CFA Level I study materials as they relate to the determination of portfolio policies for different types of investors. Quick

EXHIBIT E *Investment Assets (6/1/86)*
George Allen

	Cost	Market Value	After-Tax Yields
Money Market Checking	$ 50,000	$ 50,000	3%
Growth Stocks	150,000	300,000	1
Cyclical Stocks	200,000	250,000	2
Defensive Stocks	300,000	400,000	2
Venture Cap. Fund	100,000	100,000	0
Tax-Exempt Bonds	300,000	400,000	7
Equity Real Estate*	200,000	300,000	6
Totals	$1,300,000	$1,800,000	

*Exclusive of personal residence.

EXHIBIT F *Perennial Trust Company*
Three- to Five-Year Expected Annual Investment Returns (as of 6/1/86)

Continued Prosperity (60% Probability)	Expected Annual Total Return	Expected Total Return Range	Expected Income Component of Total Return
Short-Term Reserves (Tax-Exempt)	5%	4 to 6%	5%
Stocks (S&P 500 Index)	14	0 to 28	4
Tax-Exempt Bonds	7	2 to 12	7
Equity Real Estate	9	6 to 12	6
High Inflation Scenario (20% Probability)			
Short-Term Reserves (Tax-Exempt)	9%	6 to 12%	9%
Stocks (S&P 500 Index)	16	−6 to 38	5
Tax-Exempt Bonds	2	−8 to 12	7
Equity Real Estate	14	9 to 19	6
Deflation/Depression Scenario (20% Probability)			
Short-Term Reserves (Tax-Exempt)	2%	0 to 4%	2%
Stocks (S&P 500 Index)	−5	−20 to 10	2
Tax-Exempt Bonds	15	10 to 20	7
Equity Real Estate	−3	−10 to 5	3

remembers reading that behind all investment portfolios are investors, each of whom is unique, and that there is literally a different set of portfolio management opportunities, needs, and circumstances for every investor. Because of this diversity of investor situations, Quick has concluded that it is impossible to generalize about portfolio policy determination—everything must be done on a case-by-case basis. Bronson agrees in terms of specific portfolio construction but reminds Quick that there is a *framework* illustrated in the readings through which portfolio policies can be established for even the broadest range of investor types and interests.

a. Outline a broadly applicable *framework* for establishing portfolio policies, incorporating objectives and constraints, such as the one that Bronson has recalled.

b. Bronson is working on a defined benefit retirement portfolio for a sizable and growing corporation with a young work force. Quick is working on a modest personal portfolio now providing essential income to a 70-year-old widow whose assets pass on her death to her children. *Apply* your part a *framework* to each of the above investment situations, taking into account all of the relevant *framework* elements. (You may find it helpful to use a matrix format for this answer.)

APPENDIX 19A: SAMPLE STATEMENT OF POLICY FOR A MEDIUM-SIZE PENSION PLAN

Equity Pension Funds Policy Guidelines and Performance Evaluation

Introduction

Legal constraints have been placed upon all pension fund investments of the City and should be strictly adhered to by any investment manager. This statement is designed to expand upon these minimum legal requirements in order to (1) provide equity advisers with a more accurate understanding of the City's equity investment objective and constraints, (2) contribute to a long-run consistency in management style, and (3) indicate the criteria by which investment-manager performance will be evaluated.

Equity Fund Objective

The equity manager shall seek a return over a three- to five-year interval in excess of the return on the Standard & Poor's 500 Index. But this objective must be subject to a prudent regard for legal considerations, safety of capital, and volatility of returns as outlined below.

Equity

1. *Complete investment in equities.* The equity manager should hold only equity securities. Fixed-income securities are being separately managed. Use of commercial paper and other money market instruments should not exceed 15% of the market value of funds being managed. It is the intention of the City that the manager be fully invested.

Since the City does not wish to unduly restrict the effectiveness of the portfolio manager, temporary cash balances which exceed the 15% limitation will be tolerated for unforeseen events such as large deposits to the manager's account or large volume sales without the ability for immediate reinvestment. However, the portfolio manager must inform the City in a timely manner of the reasons for these excessive cash balances.

2. *Diversification.* No fewer than 20 different equity securities will be held. No more than 10% of the market value of an equity manager's portfolio will be held in one security. A minimum of five industry groups must be represented by the various equity securities. No more than 25% of the portfolio may be held in any one of the major industry groups.

3. *Investment types.* Equity managers may invest in common stocks, convertible preferred stocks, and convertible debentures. Investments in the latter two are expected to be a total return play on the respective underlying equities and are not to be made primarily on the basis of yield. Stocks of firms with inactive trading markets will not be held.

4. *Exceptions from constraints.* Equity managers are expected to follow these constraints. In cases where managers believe it will be profitable to violate a constraint, except with regard to cash balances, they will do so only after approval by the Board of

Trustees. The Deputy City Manager for Management and Financial Services will be notified of a requested exception and present the request to the Pension Review Committee, which will then forward the request to the Board of Trustees.

Performance Evaluation

1. *Reporting.* Each quarter the investment manager will provide the Deputy City Manager for Management and Financial Services any data and reports which the Pension Review Committee requests in advance.

2. *Meetings with the Pension Review Committee.* Each six months the investment manager will meet with the Pension Review Committee to discuss the status of the account. The Board of Trustees will be notified of the meeting. The presentation should be limited to an hour and a half and must include an adequate written report which highlights and graphically illustrates your verbal comments. This report should be distributed to those in attendance at the meeting. Approximately ten (10) copies will be needed. The specific topics which are to be addressed are:

   a. Portfolio performance during the prior quarter as compared with the standard index specified in the managerial contract.

   b. Portfolio performance since inception as compared to the standard index.

   c. Conformance with the guidelines and constraints.

d. Economic review as related to the performance of the portfolio.

e. Economic preview and anticipated moves in relation to the forecast.

f. Commentary on any other relevant facts.

3. *Performance reviews.* Performance will be tracked on a quarterly basis. However, the Board of Trustees believes that a three-year interval is generally needed to properly assess a manager's performance. Thus, decisions to replace managers will normally be made using at least a three-year performance history. However, the Board does reserve the right to change managers under unforeseen events.

4. *Performance criteria.* The following types of factors will be considered in reviewing the manager's performance:

   a. Average rates of return (adjusted for contributions and withdrawals) compared with equivalent returns on:

      • The S&P Composite Index

      • Other managers as published by SEI

   b. Degree of risk compared with the S&P Composite Index based on cross-sectional portfolio betas over time.

   c. The extent to which the manager fulfills the fund objectives and objectives noted above.

APPENDIX 19B: SAMPLE STATEMENT OF POLICY FOR A LARGE-SIZE PENSION PLAN

Foreword to Statement of Investment Policy

The investment policy of the _____ has been developed from a comprehensive study, evaluation, and investigation of many alternatives. The primary objective of this policy is to implement a plan of action which will result in the highest probability of maximum investment return from the Fund's assets available for investment.

The cornerstone of our policy rests upon the proposition that there is a direct correlation between risk and return for any investment alternative. While such a proposition is reasonable in logic, it is also provable in empirical investigations. Additionally, it is appropriate to review investment return in real terms, net of inflation, and to take into consideration the probability of investment return occurrence in the decision-making process, as well as to monitor the value added to the Fund.

Because of inflation, it is essential that the value added by the Fund's investment management be appropriate not only to meet inflationary effects but also to provide additional returns above inflation to meet the investment goals of the Fund. Meeting the Fund's investment goals finances an optimal package of retirement benefits for _____ and maximizes the utilization of the _____ contributions and the tax dollars of the citizens of _____ .

In order to achieve maximum returns the policy of the Board is to diversify between various investments including common stocks, bonds, real estate, short-term cash instruments, and other investments deemed suitable. [Note: The strategic asset allocation chosen for this pension fund is shown in Table 19B-1.]

Summary

1. *Systematic risk control.* Prior to 1980 the Board had not implemented a systematic risk-control plan for pension fund assets—that is, no clear delineation between debt and equity ratios had been structured by the Board. Such decisions had formerly rested in the hands of outside investment advisers. The Board conducted an investigation to determine the impact of various expected rates of return upon pension fund costs. The results of this study led the Board to conclude that the debt/equity ratio should be determined by the Board rather than left to chance. Currently, the Board believes that a 70% equity/30% debt ratio will produce an ex-

pected real rate of return of approximately 4%. This return is slightly in excess of the expected rate of return of 4% actuarially assumed for the pension fund.

2. *Nonsystematic risk control.* Prior to 1980 the Board had not analyzed the significance of non-systematic risk control—that is, risk over and above the market itself. Such risk involves concentration of securities in one particular sector of the market. Since there has been no long-term history of commensurate return expectation for incurring such risk, the Board has concluded that all efforts to diversify investment sectors should be undertaken. This has resulted in the investment of new contributions, and realignment of present capital, to advisers with different risk characteristics.

3. *Contra-funding techniques.* Some pension funds have historically funded annual contributions to the investment advisers in approximately equal amounts. Other pension funds have tended to fund their new contributions to advisers whose recent results would appear to have been based on superior management techniques. However, deeper studies into the subject indicate that recent positive results may or may not be attributable to superior management techniques. Consequently, the Board is implementing a program whereby new contributions will be funded to those managers whose secu-

TABLE 19B-1 *Investment Strategy Portfolio Structure*

Investment Medium/Style	Percent of Assets		
Real Estate			5.0%
Fixed-Income Securities			25.0
Equities			70.0
High-Quality Growth	35.0%	(50.0)%	
Secondary Growth	10.5	(15.0)	
Growth/Income	14.0	(20.0)	
Income	10.5	(15.0)	
Specialized			
	70.0%		100.0%

Equity Investment Style Parameters	Quality	P/E	Yield
High-Quality Growth	7.3–9.5	1.25	2–4%
Secondary Growth	6.1–7.71	1.25	1.2–3
Growth/Income	7.0–8.5	.85–1.10	5.5
Income	6.5–8.0	.60– .85	5.5

rities' characteristics have recently been out of favor with investors.

4. *Manager-selection techniques.* When the Board embarked upon a manager-selection review, it retained a professional consultant to assist in this effort. This consulting firm will produce for the Board the records as well as the risk characteristics of the pooled accounts of various investment management organizations. The Board will screen these results and select various investment managers with different risk/return characteristics to implement the long-term policy of the Board. This strategy allows the Board to analyze the continuation trend of superior existing records rather than experiment with investment advisers.

5. *Value added by management analyses.* The Board has implemented the strategic aspects of the investment policy, and the Board and its consultant will continually review and analyze both the value added by managers and the best probabilities for new contribution alternatives. Second, the Board will continue to monitor the "expected rate of return" trend in order to assess realistic investment assumptions. Finally, the Board and its consultant will implement procedures for rebalancing the risk/return model when market advances and contractions impact upon the asset mix.

I. Statement of Investment Policy

1. The Board will employ strategies to maximize the advantages of diversification for optimal capital protection and to implement appropriate risk-acceptance strategies for optimal return on investment.

2. The Board may retain independent professional investment consultants to assist in implementation of investment policy.

3. The Board will establish a ratio between various forms of investment instruments which are calculated to satisfy the requirements of the investment policy.

4. The Board may review and change the investment ratios at any time; however, the Board will review and confirm or change the investment ratios annually.

5. The Board will continually evaluate the trend of investment results in relationship to investment expectations.

6. The Board will evaluate results on a total rate of return basis.

7. The Board will attempt to utilize investment managers whose demonstrated results are a matter of public record.

8. The Board will evaluate each investment manager's value added to the fund as compared to other investment managers of the same investment style or philosophy.

9. The Board will evaluate each of the fund's investment manager's style for compliance with the fund's investment objectives.

10. The Board may amend the statement of policy and the statement of strategy after discussion at two regular meetings by the Board of Trustees.

II. Statement of Investment Strategy

1. The Board will structure its present investment strategy to achieve an expected total long-range real rate of return (net of inflation) of 4%.

2. For purposes of determining investment return, the Consumer Price Index for All Urban Consumers (CPI-U) will be utilized as the inflation factor.

3. The fund's actuarial real rate of return (net of inflation) of 4% will constitute a minimum goal for investment return.

4. The Board will maintain an active investment strategy for the fund. This will be accomplished by implementing a mechanical decision rule which increases the equity portion of the fund when the risk premium in the stock market is moderately priced relative to its book value and, conversely, reduces the equity portion of the fund when the available risk premium is being overvalued relative to the book value of the S&P 400. The purpose of the active approach is to reduce the volatility of the fund; the rate of return expectations remains unchanged.

Market/Book Value Range of the S&P 400		Equity/Fixed Income Ratio
Below Book	1.2	80/20
	1.2–1.5	70/30
	1.5–1.7	60/40
	1.7–1.8	50/50
	1.8–1.9	40/60
	1.9–2.0	30/70
Above 2× Book		20/80

The Board must approve any liquidation of assets of the portfolio to maintain the above equity/fixed income ratio.

5. To structure the fund's portfolio for maximum investment-style diversification and to achieve expected investment return results, the Board:

   • Will retain separate fixed-income portfolio managers
   Fixed-income investments will constitute a portion of the fund's asset investment to primarily reduce the risk volatility of the total portfolio in addition to providing low-risk total returns. The total return concept as it applies to this portion of the fund means interest income plus realized and unrealized capital appreciation.

   • May retain a separate real estate portfolio manager
   Real estate investments may constitute a portion of the fund's assets to provide long-term income and/or capital appreciation. Investment in this type of asset is deemed prudent for purposes of reduction of total portfolio volatility.

   • May retain a specialized asset manager

6. The Board will prepare and transmit written guidelines and expectations to the fund's existing and potential investment managers.

7. The Board will evaluate each investment manager for the following measures of performance on at least a quarterly basis:

   • Value-added production
   • Style characteristics based upon portfolio quality, relative P/E to S&P 500, and yield
   • Investment effectiveness on a total rate of return basis
   • Compliance to the fund's investment objectives and guidelines

   Since the Board will be intensively monitoring the investment managers as to style and performance, the practice of requesting meetings with the managers will be discontinued. Meetings with managers in the future will be at the Board's discretion and ordinarily will be for a reason deemed important to the Board.

8. The Board may direct new contributions to portfolio managers to maintain the desired percentage of assets in each investment medium.

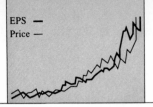

CHAPTER

20 Strategic Asset Allocation

The strategic asset allocation an investor chooses is clearly the most important decision he or she must make. It will be *the* prime force driving future portfolio returns, both average returns and the volatility of returns. As noted in the preceding chapter, many studies have shown that 90% or more of the returns earned on most portfolios were the result of allocation of assets across various classes.

In this chapter we examine a number of ways in which a strategic asset allocation might be developed. Two basic methodologies are presented. The first focuses on potential return payoffs from the *security portfolio* itself. Little or no attempt is made to integrate such payoffs with other assets and liabilities of the investor. The second focuses on how returns from the security portfolio affect the investor's future *net worth* (or wealth). As a result, this approach explicitly considers other assets and liabilities of the investor. Although the second approach is clearly better, it is still in an early stage of development. Thus, many thorny problems remain unanswered.

In many of the examples, we relate the approaches to the situation faced by defined benefit pension plans, which, because of their size, need state-of-the-art methodologies and can afford to use them. In fact, most of the recent advances in asset-allocation theory have come from analysis of the problems faced by such pension plans. By the end of this chapter, you should be moderately expert in your knowledge of pension plans.

An important point should be made before we proceed. The final asset-allocation decision should be made by the owner of the portfolio. While professional investment counselors can aid in making a well-informed decision, it is the portfolio owner who will be directly affected by the portfolio's returns and volatility over time. Only the owner can truly assess his or her personal tolerance for risk.

A FOCUS ON PORTFOLIO PAYOFFS

Let's begin by examining three relatively simple ways of approaching the problem of asset allocation. Each suffers from conceptual weaknesses, but all are used in practice. Perhaps the major weakness of each of these techniques is that they focus solely on the return payoffs from the security portfolio. They do not focus directly on the investor's wealth.

Cash Flow Requirements

Perhaps the most naive approach attempts to develop an asset mix that will provide interest and dividend cash flow to match the cash needs of the portfolio owner. For example, assume that a $10 million endowment fund has anticipated cash outflows of $600,000 for the next year. Current yields on U.S. Treasury bonds are 11%, and the Standard & Poor's Composite has a dividend yield of 4%. If interest and dividend receipts are to be equal to $600,000, 71.43% of the portfolio should be invested in stocks and 28.57% invested in bonds:

	Dollar Investment	×	Current Yield	=	Cash Inflow
Stocks	$ 7,143,000	×	4%	=	$285,720
Bonds	2,857,000	×	11%	=	314,270
	$10,000,000				$599,990

The only advantage of this approach is its simplicity. Apart from that, it is wrong. For example, it makes no provision for required future growth in cash outflows. To illustrate, assume that the endowment's cash outflows will grow at a 9% annual rate. If the growth rate associated with the common stocks being evaluated is 11% and the growth rate of bonds is 0%, then the 71.43%/28.57% stock/bond allocation will provide a portfolio growth rate of only 7.8% (11% × 0.7143). The artificial requirement that interest and dividends be the sole source of required cash outflows leads to poor decisions.

But the conceptual fault of this approach is even more fundamental—it ignores the risks associated with portfolios being evaluated. There are numerous stock/bond portfolios which provide expected returns large enough to cover the current and future cash flow needs of this investor. However, they differ considerably in risk. Any asset-allocation decision should explicitly consider both the risks and the expected returns associated with the allocation.

Historical Risk/Return Tables

One commonly used way to communicate the risks and returns associated with various asset mixes is to provide tabled values of historical returns. An example is shown in Table 20-1. Two asset classes are evaluated: (1) a GIC (guaranteed investment contract) which is assumed to provide a guaranteed real return (after inflation) and (2) common stocks as proxied by the annual real returns on the S&P Composite Index between 1926 and 1987. Returns are shown for six portfolios ranging from 100% invested in a GIC to 100% in the S&P Composite. The expected return column shows the portfolio return which should be expected if the future is the same as the past and if the investor holds the portfolio for a one-year period. For example, if the future is the same as the 1926–1987 period, the expected return on a stock portfolio which is held for one year and which is similar to the S&P 500 is 8.8%. Columns to the left and right of the expected return show the rate of return for various probabilities. For example, if 100% is held in stock, there is a 10% chance that the annual return will

TABLE 20-1 *Annualized Real Returns for a One-Year Holding Period*

Portfolio	Asset Mix		Downside Risk*			Upside Potential†	
	GIC	S&P 500	10%	25%	Expected	25%	10%
A	100%	0%	1.0%	1.0%	1.0%	1.0%	1.0%
B	80	20	−3.0	−0.4	2.6	5.5	8.1
C	60	40	−7.0	−1.7	4.1	10.0	15.2
D	40	60	−10.9	−3.1	5.7	14.5	22.4
E	20	80	−14.9	−4.4	7.2	19.0	29.5
F	0	100	−18.9	−5.8	8.8	23.5	36.6

Based on S&P 500 real returns, 1926–1987. GIC is a guaranteed investment contract.
*Probability that the annualized return will be less than (or equal to) the return shown.
†Probability that the return will be greater than the return shown.

be less than (or equal to) −18.9%. Similarly, there is a 10% chance that the return will be greater than 36.6%. Since many people find it difficult to interpret standard deviations, historical return tables such as this are used by professional investment counselors to communicate the manner in which asset allocation determines both expected portfolio returns and risks.

The tables can also be used to illustrate how the length of the holding period affects risk. The longer a portfolio is held before being liquidated, the lower the uncertainty about the average annualized rate of return. For example, Tables 20-2 and 20-3 provide the same data as Table 20-1 but for holding periods of five and ten years, respectively. Note that as the holding period lengthens, the range of potential return outcomes narrows. A graphic approach to presenting historical data such as this is shown in Figure 20-1.

Figures and tables such as these are invaluable tools for expressing the returns and risks associated with various asset mixes. They communicate useful information to portfolio owners who are unfamiliar with statistics such as variance and covariance. But they do have weaknesses. These include the following:

TABLE 20-2 *Annualized Real Returns for a Five-Year Holding Period*

Portfolio	Asset Mix		Downside Risk*			Upside Potential†	
	GIC	S&P 500	10%	25%	Expected	25%	10%
A	100%	0%	1.0%	1.0%	1.0%	1.0%	1.0%
B	80	20	0.4	1.4	2.4	3.5	4.5
C	60	40	−0.2	1.7	3.9	6.0	7.9
D	40	60	−0.7	2.1	5.3	8.5	11.4
E	20	80	−1.3	2.4	6.8	11.0	14.8
F	0	100	−1.9	2.8	8.2	13.5	18.3

Based on S&P 500 real returns, 1926–1987. GIC is a guaranteed investment contract.
*Probability that the annualized return will be less than (or equal to) the return shown.
†Probability that the return will be greater than the return shown.

TABLE 20-3 *Annualized Real Returns for a Ten-Year Holding Period*

Portfolio	Asset Mix		Downside Risk*		Expected	Upside Potential†	
	GIC	S&P 500	10%	25%		25%	10%
A	100%	0%	1.0%	1.0%	1.0%	1.0%	1.0%
B	80	20	1.0	1.7	2.4	3.2	3.9
C	60	40	1.0	2.4	3.9	5.4	6.8
D	40	60	1.1	3.1	5.3	7.6	9.6
E	20	80	1.1	3.8	6.8	9.8	12.5
F	0	100	1.1	4.5	8.2	12.0	15.4

Based on S&P 500 real returns, 1926–1987. GIC is a guaranteed investment contract.
*Probability that the annualized return will be less than (or equal to) the return shown.
†Probability that the return will be greater than the return shown.

1. The data are very sensitive to the time period chosen. It is not unusual that the inclusion or exclusion of a few years of returns will result in figures which differ by more than 150 basis points. As such, the data should not be interpreted too strictly. Instead, they should be viewed as illustrative of the potential return and risk levels.

2. Many asset classes simply do not have a history of returns which can be trusted. Examples include real estate and international assets.

3. When more than two asset classes are being considered, tabled values become unwieldy to use.

4. Many people believe that the distribution of past returns is not a good proxy for potential future returns.

5. This approach illustrates risks and average returns on arbitrarily selected portfolio combinations. There is no attempt to isolate efficient portfolios for various risk levels.

Asset Pricing Models

Two major theories exist which attempt to define risk and explain the market value of any asset: the capital asset pricing model and arbitrage pricing theory. Both have implications for an investor's decision on strategic asset allocation.

The Capital Asset Pricing Model. As discussed in Chapters 8 and 9, the capital asset pricing model has a great deal to say about the optimal portfolio of risky assets for any investor. In particular, the CAPM implies that people should own *all* risky assets in proportions which depend on the total market values of each asset. For example, if U.S. corporate bonds represent 15% of the value of all risky securities, then 15% of everyone's risky security portfolio should consist of U.S. corporate bonds. Once such a risky portfolio has been acquired, there are no further diversification benefits to be gained. If this portfolio is too risky, it can be held in combination with

FIGURE 20-1 *Distributions of Possible Rates of Return, Comparing One- and Ten-Year Periods for Different Investment Policies*

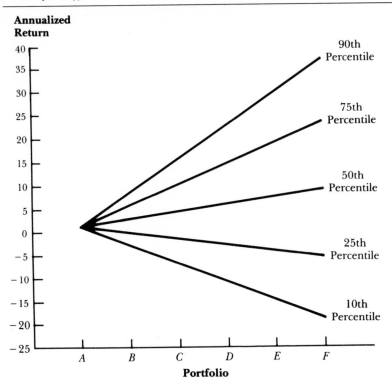

| Port. | Asset Mix | | Downside Risk* | | | Upside Potential† | |
	GIC	S&P 500	10%	25%	Expected	25%	10%
A	100%	0%	1.0%	1.0%	1.0%	1.0%	1.0%
B	80	20	−3.0	−0.4	2.6	5.5	8.1
C	60	40	−7.0	−1.7	4.1	10.0	15.2
D	40	60	−10.9	−3.1	5.7	14.5	22.4
E	20	80	−14.9	−4.4	7.2	19.0	29.5
F	0	100	−18.9	−5.8	8.8	23.5	36.6

| Downside Risk* | | | Upside Potential† | |
10%	25%	Expected	25%	10%
1.0%	1.0%	1.0%	1.0%	1.0%
1.0	1.7	2.4	3.2	3.9
1.0	2.4	3.9	5.4	6.8
1.1	3.1	5.3	7.6	9.6
1.1	3.8	6.8	9.8	12.5
1.1	4.5	8.2	12.0	15.4

S&P 500 real returns based on 1926–1987. GIC is a Guaranteed Investment Contract.

*Probability that the annualized return will be less than (or equal to) the return shown.

†Probability that the return will be greater than the return shown.

FIGURE 20-1 *(continued)*

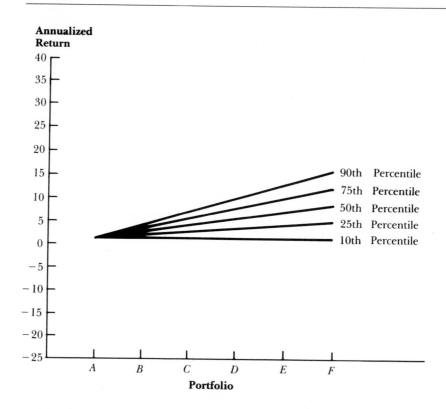

a risk-free security. If it is not risky enough, then the investor should borrow (at the risk-free rate) and invest the borrowings. In short, the CAPM suggests that the optimal risky asset portfolio is the market portfolio of all risky assets.

Although the CAPM is a profound conceptual tool, its practical implications should not be interpreted too strictly. People have differing investment horizons, tax rates, transaction costs, etc. — each causing different optimal asset mixes. Investment concepts such as the value of diversification and the importance of systematic risk needn't be abandoned. However, the optimal allocation of different classes of assets must consider the unique needs of each portfolio. The CAPM should be used only as a theoretical starting point from which actual portfolios are created which better fulfill the needs of the portfolio owner.

Arbitrage Pricing Theory. In contrast to the CAPM, arbitrage pricing theory does not give any special importance to the market portfolio of all risky assets. It suggests that a variety of economic risks might be nondiversifiable. As a result, investors will demand a risk premium to accept such risks. Examples of such "priced" risk factors would include inflation, industrial production, default risk, and the slope of the yield curve. If you subscribe to the notion of APT, the first thing you should do is eliminate the non-priced, diversifiable risks by broad diversification. Next, you should specify the priced factors on which you wish to place your bets or to hedge against. For example, if you wish to hold a portfolio which is neutral to all factors, the portfolio sensitivity to each factor should be 1.0. This would result in a risky security portfolio virtually identical to the market portfolio of CAPM. A fully diversified portfolio would have a beta of 1.0 on each nondiversifiable factor risk.

The potential advantage of APT over CAPM lies in the ability to hedge risks in assets and liabilities which the investor incurs outside the marketable security portfolio. For example, assume that the investor is the sponsor of a defined benefit pension plan whose business is heavily influenced by unexpected changes in inflation. To partially hedge this risk, securities with large sensitivities to an inflation factor would be underweighted.

As with the CAPM, there are substantial problems in basing a strategic asset allocation on the principles of APT. Most important, we don't know what the priced APT factors are! Various consulting firms have *assumed* a variety of potential return factors, but there is little evidence that such factors indeed exist. APT remains an important way to think about problems. But its quantitative application is questionable.

Efficient Asset Allocation

Existing investment theory does not provide models of optimal security selection under the real-world conditions faced by investors. There are two basic problems with current theory: (1) it does not integrate security selection with other (marketable and nonmarketable) assets and liabilities the investor might have, and (2) it doesn't adequately address the multiperiod nature of cash inflows and outflows to the portfolio. The first problem is addressed in the next section. For now, however, we will assume that the investor has no other assets or liabilities to consider. This leaves us with the problem of multiperiod decisions.

Only in the very limited case of a single-period decision (I have cash to invest today and will withdraw all of it at a single known date in the future) does theory provide various methodologies which result in clearly optimal decisions. The most widely known single-period approach is the concept of a mean-variance efficient frontier first suggested by Harry Markowitz three decades ago.[1] If an investor faces a single-period decision, the mean-variance approach to security selection can be used. In fact, it can easily be fancied up to include transaction costs, taxes, nonexistence of a risk-free rate, etc. And there is no particular constraint on the length of the period. Investor A with a one-month investment horizon and investor B with a ten-year investment horizon are both conceptually correct in using the model to identify optimal security portfolios. But the mean-variance approach remains conceptually valid only if we are dealing with a single-period decision. If an investor intends to contribute and withdraw unknown amounts of cash at a series of unknown future time periods, there simply are no optimal decision models which are on firm theoretical ground. Investment theory offers only a little help with multiperiod problems.

---

[1] See Chapter 7 for a review of the Markowitz model.

But practicing investment managers must make decisions. As a result, a number of ad hoc techniques have been developed. In this section, we will integrate a number of these approaches. The process which is suggested consists of the following four steps:

1. Segment portfolio needs.
2. Select asset types.
3. Develop market expectations.
4. Evaluate the efficient frontier for a desired horizon date.

1. Segment Portfolio Needs. Often the investment portfolio is intended to meet a variety of needs. For example, pension fund portfolios are expected to provide investment returns to help pay benefits to two distinct groups of individuals: (*a*) past employees who are currently receiving pension benefits, and (*b*) present employees who will receive benefits at a distant future date. The nature of the liability to each group can be quite different. In the case of "retired lives," the liability is relatively short-term, virtually known with certainty, and often in the form of nominal dollars. Thus the retired-lives portion of the pension plan is ideal for some form of bond immunization. In contrast, the nonretired-lives portion of a pension's liability stream is long-term, is difficult to predict with precision, and usually varies directly with inflation. As such, it is much less suitable for immunization techniques.

There are a number of other ways in which pension liabilities can be segmented which we will not review. The same is true, of course, for portfolios held by individuals, endowments, commercial banks, etc. In each case, it can be helpful to categorize the distinctly different needs which the portfolio is intended to serve and to handle them one at a time.

Segmentation of the portfolio will not always aid in determining a proper asset allocation, however. In fact, at times it will simply delay critical decisions. For example, the immunization of retired lives does not solve the fundamental question of the proper risk level for the aggregate pension fund—it simply delays it until that portion of the portfolio devoted to current employees is analyzed. Nonetheless, segmentation can at least provide organization to the decision-making framework and clarify the variety of differing needs which must be addressed.

2. Select Asset Classes. Why shouldn't we simply select one asset class, say, common stocks similar to the Dow Jones industrials, and invest in it? The answer is certainly not because the DJIA has too much, or too little, risk. There are other asset classes, such as preferred stocks, bonds, and T-bills, which could be purchased at lower risk. Similarly, other asset classes, such as OTC stocks, real estate equity, and even international equities, could be purchased at higher risk. We don't consider the ownership of a variety of asset classes because they enable us to shift the risk level of the portfolio. This can be accomplished very simply by owning only one asset class. So, again the question—why consider investment in a variety of asset classes?

We do it to *diversify*—to obtain an equivalent expected return at lower risk than is available from investing in a single asset class.

When asset classes are defined, they should be as distinctly different from each

TABLE 20-4 *Average Correlation Coefficient and Standard Deviation of Selected Asset Classes (Real Returns, 1969–1987)*

	Correlation Coefficient						
	T-Bills	Govt. Bonds	Corp. Bonds	S&P 500	Small Company	PRISA	EAFE
T-Bills	1.00						
Govt. Bonds	0.66	1.00					
Corp. Bonds	0.65	0.97	1.00				
S&P 500	0.39	0.52	0.59	1.00			
Small Company	0.14	0.25	0.32	0.78	1.00		
PRISA	0.28	0.05	0.04	0.37	0.49	1.00	
EAFE	0.32	0.40	0.38	0.69	0.43	0.30	1.00
	Yearly Real Return						
Average	1.13%	1.92%	2.33%	4.10%	7.67%	2.84%	11.07%
Standard Deviation	3.19	14.49	15.30	18.02	27.85	6.40	25.14

other as possible in order to provide the greatest potential for diversification. For example, there is little to be gained by adding a "call option group" to a portfolio which otherwise consists of T-bills and common stock. This is because a call option is essentially a long position in a given stock and a short position in T-bills. In the same fashion, returns on Treasury note financial futures are highly correlated with spot Treasury notes and bonds. In short, there is little value associated with including asset classes which are highly correlated.

Many asset classes, however, have returns which are relatively uncorrelated. For example, Table 20-4 presents correlation coefficients on a number of asset classes using annual real returns (after inflation) for the period 1969–1987. Returns prior to 1969 were not available for PRISA and the EAFE indexes.[2]

The number of different asset classes which an investor should consider depends in large part on the size of the portfolio and the knowledge of the investor. Once we move from well-known asset classes such as T-bills, government/corporate bonds, and common equities into less-known asset classes such as real estate, international equities, and venture capital, there is a greater need for professional expertise. Yet there are no hard and fast rules relating portfolio size to classes of assets selected. The trade-off between potential diversification gains and increased information costs is a decision which is unique to each portfolio.

To illustrate the value gained from diversification, the historical data in Table 20-4 were used in a computer program to find two ex post efficient frontiers. These are displayed in Figure 20-2. The frontier to the right consists of holdings of Treasury bills, corporate bonds, government bonds, the S&P 500 (a proxy for large firms), and small company stocks. These have traditionally been the security classes used in stra-

---

[2]PRISA is a commingled equity real estate portfolio managed by Prudential Insurance. It is used here as a proxy for real estate equity investment returns. The Europe, Australia, Far East (EAFE) Index is a proxy for international investment.

FIGURE 20-2 *Historical Efficient Frontiers (Annual Real Returns, 1969–1987)*

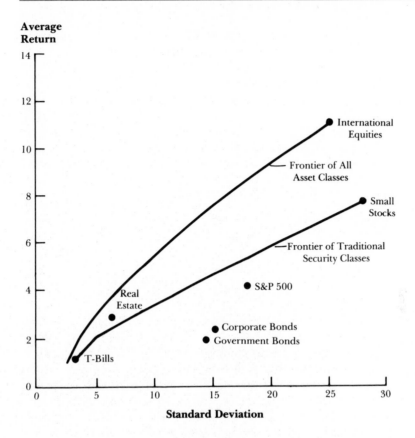

tegic asset allocation decisions. Note that the efficient frontier of these five asset classes provides a greater average return for each level of standard deviation than would have been obtained by holding any one of the five asset classes. This is the benefit of diversification.

The higher efficient frontier adds two asset classes to the traditional group: real estate and international equities. Again, the benefits of diversification are clear. Although the composition of ex post efficient frontiers will depend on the time period evaluated, holding many asset classes always dominates holding one asset class.[3] Diversification works!

3. Develop Market Expectations. In order to develop Markowitz efficient frontiers, estimates must be made of the *expected* returns and covariances of returns on each asset class being evaluated. It is at this point that two difficult problems must be

---

[3]The greatest-return portfolio is an exception. It consists of a 100% investment in the asset class with the greatest return.

faced. First, how can the concept of a single-period efficient frontier be used in the context of a multiperiod decision? Second, how does one develop the expected returns and covariances which are used as inputs to the model?

A reasonable approach to solving the multiperiod problem is to estimate an *average date* at which there will be net cash outflows. This is done in much the same way that we calculate the duration of the cash inflows for a bond. For example, consider the following simplified example.

Assume that a pension plan will have three equal cash outflows of $100 at the end of years 1, 2, and 3. In addition, the U.S. Treasury yield curve is flat at a yield to maturity of 10%. Note that the cash outflows to the pension plan are, in fact, cash inflows to the pension beneficiaries. In essence, the beneficiaries own a bond which promises to pay $100 at each year-end for three years. The duration of this bond is 1.9 years:

Year-End	Cash Flow	Present Value at 10%	Percent of Total	Weighted Duration
1	$100	90.91%	36.66%	0.3666
2	100	82.64	33.33	0.6666
3	100	75.13	30.30	0.9090
Total		247.96		1.9422

If beneficiaries are correct in considering their benefits as having a 1.9-year duration, then the pension sponsors are also correct in considering their future liability stream as having the same duration.

By using the notion of duration, a multiperiod pension liability stream can be stated in terms of a single-period cash outflow. And the length of this single-period cash outflow can then be used as the horizon date in the Markowitz model. For example, in our example, the pension sponsor would evaluate expected returns and covariances on various asset groups *assuming that they are to be held for 1.9 years*.

There are difficulties with this technique of reducing a multiperiod problem (for which theory provides no answers) to a single-period problem (for which the Markowitz model works). The liability stream is not known with certainty, the covariance between future benefits and security returns isn't considered, and the appropriate interest rate for calculating the duration is unclear. But until investment theory can offer something better, the calculation of benefit duration is a reasonable way to restate a multiperiod problem to fit the single-period asset-selection model.

Although the precision of this approach can be questioned, one thing is clear: The risk associated with owning various classes of assets depends upon how long one intends to own the assets. Many investors, particularly pension funds, are long-term investors. As such, it is inappropriate for them to evaluate the risk inherent in, say, common stocks by the volatility of one-year common stock returns. Some attempt must be made to evaluate the risk of a security class over the anticipated holding period.

Let's move now to the difficulties inherent in estimating expected returns and covariances for each asset class. Ideally, these are *informed* opinions held by the *port-*

folio owner (pension sponsor) about the likely returns and uncertainty of each asset class. But where do these opinions come from? How can one estimate the required inputs?

In practice, four major approaches are widely used:

1. Historical data
2. Econometric simulations
3. Existing market prices
4. Personal opinion

Historical Data. Historical returns are available on many security classes. A widely used source for such returns is published papers and monographs periodically updated by Roger Ibbotson and various coauthors. They present a series of monthly returns on T-bills, U.S. government and corporate bonds, and the S&P 500 extending back to January 1926. They have also prepared (less precise) historical estimates of returns on forms of real estate and international investments. Each of these has been reviewed in earlier chapters.

Historical returns are certainly the place to begin. But some care must be taken. For example:

1. Many knowledgeable people believe that the future which investors face in the late twentieth century is fundamentally different from the events which shaped the 1920s through 1980s. If this is true, the past will be a poor predictor of the future.
2. Some asset classes, such as international investments, have a very short history of past returns. And during the time periods for which such data are available, a few major economic events shaped the pattern of returns. For example, the returns on international securities were swamped by the deterioration of the U.S. foreign exchange rate during the 1970s and hit by a dramatic reversal in the 1980s.
3. Some historical return estimates are very imprecise. Estimates of real estate returns, in particular, are usually based on appraised market values instead of actual market trading prices. This tends to smooth out returns and make real estate investment appear to be less risky than it is.

In addition, the information obtained from historical data can be sensitive to the time period examined. For example, consider the panels in Figure 20-3. In panel A, average yearly real returns are plotted for various 20-year periods. Each point in the panel represents the average return for the 20 years ended at the date of the point. It is obvious that average yearly returns, even over relatively long time spans, are quite volatile. In panel B, standard deviations of yearly returns based on a 20-year return series are shown. Although standard deviations are less sensitive to the time period chosen than are average returns, they are also dependent on the period evaluated. All efficient frontier data estimates which are based on historical data are sensitive to the historical time period evaluated. This, of course, is simply a result of the basic problem that we are trying to deal with — risk.

Econometric Simulations. Econometric simulations are also available from a variety of consulting firms. These simulations are based on empirically tested economic rela-

FIGURE 20-3 *Historical Average Returns and Standard Deviations over Various Time Periods (Real Returns, 1926–1986)*

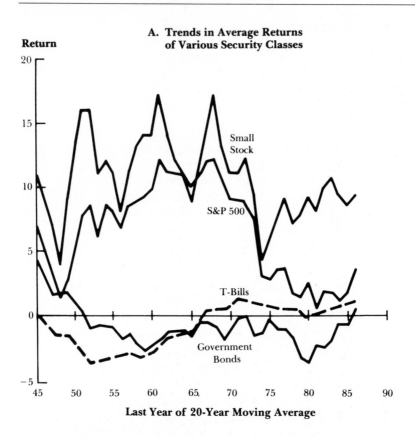

tionships which tie various sectors of the economy together. For example, Figure 20-4 illustrates a structure which could describe the manner in which corporate security returns are determined. Similar structures could be developed for real estate returns, government bond returns, etc., and each sector of the model could be integrated with the others. Underlying the final model structure would be a number of driving variables. For example, in Figure 20-4 the variables would probably be such factors as government expenditures and taxes, labor productivity, technological changes, and money growth. An expected level of each variable would be forecast together with the potential dispersion of each (perhaps by a standard deviation). Once all input variables are specified, a computer simulation of the model can be run. Output typically includes rates of return on various security classes for a number of years into the future. Since the driving variables are usually distributions of possible outcomes, a distribution of returns is obtained for each year.

The data may be summarized in a number of ways. A common approach is illus-

FIGURE 20-3 *(continued)*

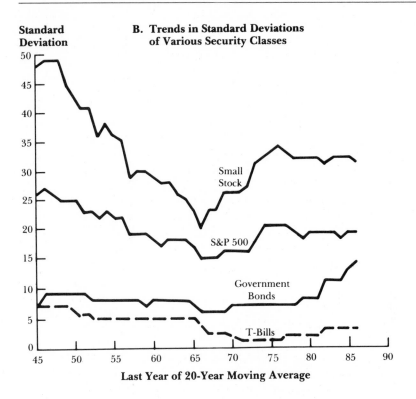

B. Trends in Standard Deviations of Various Security Classes

trated in Table 20-5. The output consists of the yearly rates of return which are possible on a portfolio consisting of 65% stocks, 25% long-term corporate bonds, and 10% cash equivalents (T-bills). Three hundred iterations were performed for each year. Returns by percentile rank are displayed. For example, in the year 2000 the model forecast that 30% of the time portfolio returns would be less than 5.48% and greater than 24.62%.

Portfolio simulations provide at least three principal aids to the analyst. First, developing and understanding the internal structure of the model forces analysts to be explicit in their opinions about the process generating security returns over time. Second, a large variety of alternative strategies can be experimented with to determine the ranges of potential returns during future years. Finally, input variables may be altered in an attempt to determine how sensitive the output is to various input factors. Naturally, the quality of the output is only as good as the quality of the model structure.

Existing Market Prices. Some people use existing market prices to estimate necessary efficient frontier inputs. For example, security analysts at Wells Fargo Bank forecast future dividend growth rates for a large number of stocks and then use these estimates

FIGURE 20-4 *Model of Corporate Security Returns*

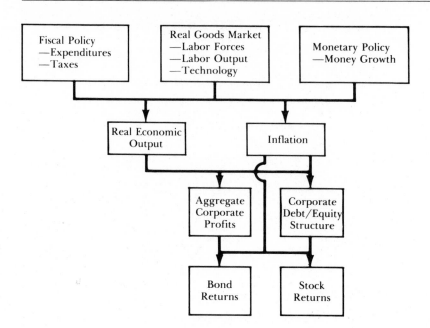

together with each stock's *existing* market price to estimate expected rates of return. This procedure was discussed in Chapter 14. In addition, we saw in Chapter 16 that current call option prices can be used to estimate the variance of a given common stock's future return. Similarly, Chapters 6 and 11 showed how existing yields to maturity (or yields to a given duration) can be used to estimate both current and expected future bond returns. In short, many of the needed inputs can be inferred from prevailing market prices.

Unfortunately, this is a very difficult task for many classes of assets, real estate and international equities in particular. In addition, none of these procedures is able to estimate the correlation coefficient between returns on alternative assets.

Personal Opinion. Certainly one can, and should, examine historical data, econometric simulations, and prevailing market prices. But, in the end, it should be the personal opinion of the portfolio owner that determines the expected returns, standard deviations, and correlation coefficients necessary to determine an efficient frontier.

4. Evaluate the Efficient Frontier for the Desired Horizon Date. Once the needed inputs are available, it is a simple matter of finding a computer package that can compute a Markowitz efficient frontier. A number of such programs have been developed and are available at low cost.

Assume that after a thorough review of historical returns and expected long-run economic conditions, we develop the return distribution assumptions shown in Ta-

TABLE 20-5 *Econometric Simulation — Possible Rates of Return on a Sample Portfolio*

	10th	30th	50th	70th	90th
1990	−4.41	2.74	13.16	24.61	39.18
1991	−6.74	8.03	14.53	25.54	43.19
1992	−16.42	2.38	11.19	19.76	28.30
1993	−9.98	4.38	11.43	20.97	37.76
1994	−7.94	4.30	14.91	23.05	37.79
1995	−22.53	6.03	14.60	22.77	40.38
1996	−9.94	2.89	11.37	27.08	36.05
1997	−9.57	1.60	14.43	23.94	42.96
1998	−15.47	0.41	13.92	22.84	45.06
1999	−8.02	3.45	14.70	32.49	45.33
2000	−12.79	5.48	11.47	24.62	43.80

Display Information:
Variable(s): 11-Annual Fund Return (Percent)

			Asset Mix (%)					
Simulation	Policy	Simulation	Stock	G Bond	C Bond	Cash	Foreign	Real M/GIC
A3	A	S	65	0	25	10	0	0 0

Portfolio Simulation for a $20 Million City Pension Fund

ble 20-6. These represent our beliefs about the one-year return payoffs which we expect to prevail in the long run. Thus, they are the return distribution data on which the strategic asset allocation decision should be made. They are not necessarily equal to forecasts we might make for the coming year. Such shorter-term forecasts should be used in developing the tactical asset allocation.[4]

The efficient frontier which results from these forecasts is shown in Figure 20-5. The composition of five efficient portfolios is shown at the bottom of the figure. Note that portfolio *A* is dominated by holdings of Treasury bills. But even such low-risk portfolios include small amounts of other asset classes—in this case the S&P 500 and real estate—in order to obtain the benefits of diversification.

If an investor has a one-year investment horizon, then the one-year return payoffs shown in Figure 20-5 can be used to determine an appropriate strategic asset allocation. Rarely, however, will the investment horizon be as short as one year. And, if it were, it is doubtful that forecasts of returns on international equities, corporate bonds, stocks, etc., would be necessary, since the strategic asset allocation would probably be obvious: invest primarily in one-year, low-default-risk money market instruments. In most cases, we need to determine the return outcomes of various one-year efficient portfolios over longer investment horizons.

In Table 20-7, the payoffs of portfolio *C* (shown in Figure 20-5) are displayed for

[4]You might find it useful to compare the ex ante estimates in Table 20-6 with the ex post values in Table 20-4. Do you agree with the differences between the tables? Why or why not? By answering such questions you are beginning to develop the ability to make ex ante forecasts.

TABLE 20-6 *Hypothetical Ex Ante Return Distribution Assumptions About One-Year Returns Expected over the Long Run*

	Correlation Coefficients						
	T-Bills	*Govt. Bonds*	*Corp. Bonds*	*S&P 500*	*Small Company*	*Real Estate*	*Int'l Equity*
T-Bills	1.00						
Govt. Bonds	0.60	1.00					
Corp. Bonds	0.60	0.95	1.00				
S&P 500	0.20	0.30	0.30	1.00			
Small Company	0.12	0.20	0.20	0.80	1.00		
PRISA	0.25	0.05	0.05	0.35	0.40	1.00	
EAFE	0.30	0.40	0.40	0.60	0.40	0.30	1.00

	Yearly Real Return						
Average	1.5%	2.5%	3.5%	8.5%	14.0%	5.0%	11.0%
Standard Deviation	4.0	10.0	11.0	20.0	40.0	15.0	30.0

various investment horizon dates. We will not review the mathematics underlying the projections since they are relatively complex and are not needed for the purpose of our discussion.[5]

Table 20-7 has two parts. In the top part, terminal wealth percentiles from initially investing $1 are shown. For example, if $1 is invested in portfolio *C*, there is a 1% chance that the portfolio will be worth less than $0.81 or more than $1.39 *after one year.* If the investment horizon is one year, there is a significant probability that the portfolio will decline in value! In contrast, consider the 30-year investment horizon. At that point, there is a 1% chance that the portfolio will be worth less than $1.30 or more than $25.28. With a 30-year investment horizon, there is little chance that the portfolio's value will be less than the initial investment. This, of course, is due to the benefits of time diversification.

Two comments about these terminal wealth forecasts need to be made. First, note that terminal wealth is skewed towards higher wealth levels and that this skewness increases as the investment horizon increases. Consider the 30-year horizon. The 50th percentile is $5.74; that is, there is a 50% chance that wealth will be less than $5.74 or greater than $5.74. At the lower end, there is a 1% chance of the portfolio's value being lower than $1.30, a spread of $4.44 from the 50th percentile. But at the upper end, there is a 1% chance of the portfolio's value being greater than $25.28, a spread of $19.54 from the 50th percentile. Clearly the terminal wealth distribution is skewed "to the right." Second, terminal wealth is displayed in percentile fashion instead of

---

[5]The discrete returns of Figure 20-5 are expressed as continuous returns. For example, portfolio *C*'s 6.0% discrete expected return is expressed as a 5.823% continuous return. Normally distributed continuous returns are used since they result in lognormally distributed portfolio values. This assures that the portfolio will never have a negative value. If normally distributed discrete returns are used, there is a probability that the portfolio will have a negative value in the future. But this is clearly impossible!

FIGURE 20-5 *Estimated Efficient Frontier Based on Annual Real Returns*

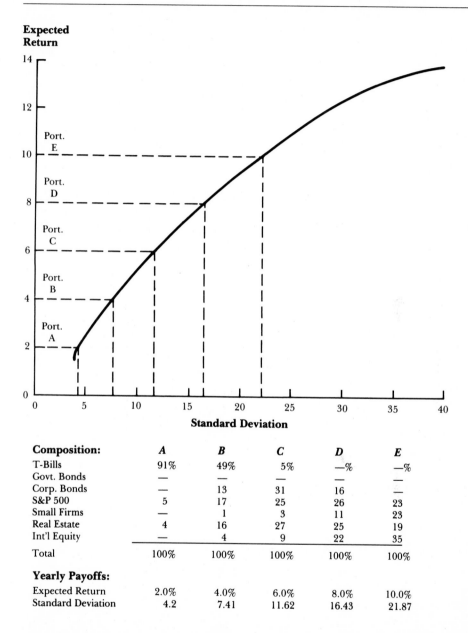

Composition:	*A*	*B*	*C*	*D*	*E*
T-Bills	91%	49%	5%	—%	—%
Govt. Bonds	—	—	—	—	—
Corp. Bonds	—	13	31	16	—
S&P 500	5	17	25	26	23
Small Firms	—	1	3	11	23
Real Estate	4	16	27	25	19
Int'l Equity	—	4	9	22	35
Total	100%	100%	100%	100%	100%

Yearly Payoffs:					
Expected Return	2.0%	4.0%	6.0%	8.0%	10.0%
Standard Deviation	4.2	7.41	11.62	16.43	21.87

in terms of standard deviations. Because of the skewness of portfolio values, the standard deviation becomes a less meaningful measure of risk. In addition, most investors are able to interpret percentile distributions more easily than statistical measures such as standard deviation and skewness.

TABLE 20-7 *Investment Payoffs of Portfolio C*

Investment Horizon (Years)	Terminal Portfolio Wealth Percentiles								
	.01	.05	.10	.25	.50	.75	.90	.95	.99
1	0.81	0.88	0.91	0.98	1.06	1.15	1.23	1.28	1.39
2	0.77	0.86	0.91	1.01	1.12	1.26	1.39	1.47	1.65
3	0.75	0.86	0.92	1.04	1.19	1.36	1.54	1.66	1.90
4	0.73	0.86	0.94	1.08	1.26	1.48	1.70	1.85	2.17
5	0.73	0.87	0.96	1.12	1.34	1.59	1.87	2.05	2.45
10	0.76	0.98	1.12	1.40	1.79	2.29	2.87	3.28	4.21
15	0.84	1.14	1.35	1.77	2.40	3.24	4.26	5.02	6.83
20	0.95	1.36	1.65	2.26	3.20	4.55	6.24	7.53	10.76
30	1.30	2.01	2.54	3.74	5.74	8.81	12.97	16.34	25.28

	Geometric Return Percentiles								
	.01	.05	.10	.25	.50	.75	.90	.95	.99
1	−19.1	−12.45	−8.67	−1.99	6.00	14.63	23.02	28.32	38.95
2	−12.5	−7.40	−4.60	0.28	6.00	12.03	17.77	21.34	28.36
3	−9.3	−5.08	−2.74	1.31	6.00	10.90	15.51	18.36	23.93
4	−7.4	−3.67	−1.61	1.92	6.00	10.23	14.19	16.63	21.36
5	−6.1	−2.69	−0.83	2.35	6.00	9.78	13.30	15.46	19.64
10	−2.7	−0.2	1.1	3.4	6.00	8.7	11.1	12.6	15.5
15	−1.2	−0.55	0.86	3.26	6.00	8.80	11.39	12.97	16.01
20	−0.2	1.6	2.5	4.2	6.00	7.9	9.6	10.6	12.6
30	0.9	2.4	3.2	4.5	6.00	7.5	8.9	9.8	11.4

Input Assumptions: Portfolio *C*

Mean Continuous Return:	5.823
Standard Deviation:	11.620
Serial Correlation Assumptions:	
Serial Correlation:	0.000
Current Return Level:	3.540

SOURCE: Courtesy of PI Analytics, Inc.

In the second part of Table 20-7, percentile distributions are shown for the geometric returns underlying each of the terminal wealth levels above. For example, consider the $5.74 terminal wealth at year 30. This translates into a geometric return of 6% per year:

$$\$1.00\,(1 + G)^{30} = \$5.74$$

$$G = (\$5.74/\$1.00)^{1/30} - 1.0$$

$$G = 6.00\%$$

Geometric return percentiles are often used in strategic asset allocation studies because investors are able to interpret them more readily than terminal wealth outcomes.

Before we move into the next section of this chapter, the data in Table 20-7 provide an opportunity to hit on a critical investment concept once again—time diversification. Five of the geometric return percentiles from Table 20-7 are plotted in

FIGURE 20-6 *Time Diversification, Portfolio C*

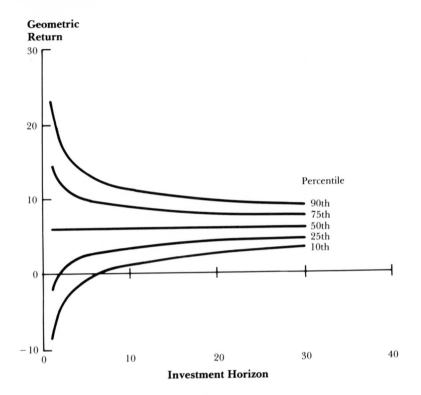

Figure 20-6. The visual conclusion is one we have seen before but which is important enough to make again: The longer the investor's time horizon, the smaller the uncertainty about (geometric) average annual returns. Investors with long investment horizons can accept greater amounts of short-term investment risk than can investors with short investment horizons. The investor's time horizon is a critical determinant of his or her strategic asset allocation.

A FOCUS ON INVESTOR WEALTH

Each of the approaches discussed in the prior section focused exclusively on the investor's security portfolio. They did not consider any interaction of security portfolio returns with returns on other assets and liabilities the investor might have. Thus, they did not directly examine the net worth—that is, the wealth position—of the investor.[6]

_____

[6]The exception is the unrealistic case in which all of the investor's assets consist of the security portfolio and the investor has no liabilities.

In this section, we examine the strategic asset allocation implications of considering the security investment portfolio as only one component of many other assets and liabilities which the investor has. To help illustrate the concept, we examine the situation facing a defined benefit pension plan.

Pension Plan Basics

Strategic asset allocation for a defined *contribution* pension plan is relatively straightforward. Since the assets of the plan belong to the employee, and the employer makes no promises as to the plan's future value, the employee bears all investment risk. Thus, employees should be allowed full investment discretion over how their portion of the plan is invested.

In a defined benefit plan, on the other hand, the pension sponsor promises a future benefit level and, thus, bears (much of) the investment risk.[7] If asset values decline, the sponsor will have to make larger than expected contributions to the pension fund so that employees can receive their promised benefits. Thus, the sponsor of a defined benefit plan has a vital interest in the strategic asset allocation chosen.

There are actually three parties to defined benefit plans covered by ERISA (Employee Retirement Income Security Act). These include the sponsor (employer), the beneficiary (employee), and the PBGC (Pension Benefit Guarantee Corporation). Their relationship is shown in Figure 20-7. In the center is the pension plan itself, consisting of escrowed pension assets, the sponsor's liability to beneficiaries, and any surplus (if plan assets exceed liabilities) or deficit (if liabilities exceed assets).

The sponsor's position is shown at the top of the figure. The sponsor can be thought of as owning the plan assets and owing the plan liability. If assets exceed the liability, the sponsor's net position is equal to the value of the surplus. Usually, any current surplus will be used to reduce future contributions by the sponsor until plan assets are equal to the plan liability. Under certain conditions, however, the sponsor can also terminate the pension plan and return any surplus assets to the sponsoring corporation. This is known as an asset revision.[8] The sponsor also has an effective ownership of another asset—a put on the pension assets sold to the sponsor by the PBGC. If the assets of the plan are substantially below the plan's liability to employees, the sponsor can terminate the plan and turn over all plan assets to the Pension Benefit Guarantee Corporation. Although the PBGC is allowed a legal claim on a major portion of the sponsor's corporate net worth, corporate net worth might be negligible. Thus, the "pension put" owned by the sponsor might represent an asset which partially offsets any deficit caused by excess liabilities.

The position of the PBGC consists of asset investments and a short position in the pension put. The asset investments represent the accumulation of yearly insurance fees

---

[7]We will see below that corporate sponsors do not bear all investment risk if their pension plans are covered by the Pension Benefit Guarantee Corporation.

[8]Surplus assets reverted to the sponsoring corporation are subject to excise taxes and other possible penalties.

FIGURE 20-7 *The Parties to a Defined Benefit Pension Plan (Guaranteed by PBGC)*

Sponsor's Position in Pension	
Debit	Credit
Plan Assets	Plan Liability
Deficit *or*	Surplus
Put to PBGC	

Escrowed Pension Plan	
Debit	Credit
Assets	Liability
Deficit *or*	Surplus

Pension Benefit Guarantee Corporation	
Debit	Credit
Insurance Fees	Put to Sponsor

Employees	
Debit	Credit
Plan Liability	None

paid to the PBGC by corporations which have defined benefit plans. The pension put represents the PBGC's legal obligation to buy the assets of a given sponsor's plan at a price equal to the value of the plan's liability. For example, if plan assets have a market value of $80 million but the liability is $100 million, the sponsor can turn over both assets and liabilities to the PBGC. In this case, the PBGC would effectively be paying $100 million for assets worth only $80 million.[9]

Each employee has an asset equal to the present value of future benefits that the pension will pay to the employee—the sponsor's liability. This will be paid by either the sponsor or the PBGC.

Fundamental Pension Decisions. There are three fundamental decisions which must be made in any defined benefit pension plan:

1. *Benefits.* The sponsor and employees must agree on the promised level of future benefits. There are a large number of ways in which such benefits can be determined. In our examples, we will use a technique which is widely used in practice. It is based on the employee's *final salary* and accumulated *benefit rate*. For exam-

---

[9]Conceptually, the PBGC has a legal claim on 100% of the sponsor's net worth. This claim has the effect of decreasing the put's effective exercise price. Thus, the effective exercise price will not be equal to the sponsor's liability to employees. The extent of any difference will depend on the financial health of the sponsoring firm.

ple, assume that an employee accumulates a benefit rate equal to 2% of his or her salary for each year of employment with the sponsor. If an employee has worked 20 years and has a final salary of \$40,000, the promised yearly pension benefit would be \$16,000:

$$\$40,000 \ (0.02 \times 20) = \$16,000$$

2. *Funding ratio.* The funding ratio (FR) is equal to the market value of assets divided by the present value of future benefits. For example, if assets are worth \$500 million and the present value liability is equal to \$450, the FR is 1.11.

   The funding ratio is directly under the control of the sponsoring firm. If the ratio falls, the sponsor can increase it by contributing cash from the corporation to the escrowed pension fund. If the ratio increases, the sponsor can reduce it by decreasing contributions.

   However, having direct control over the funding ratio does not give the sponsor full discretion over what it will be. The employees and the PBGC have indirect control. For example, if the sponsor allows the funding ratio to fall substantially below 1.0, employees will probably take this as a negative signal regarding the sponsor's true intent to pay promised benefits. This will result in decreased worker morale, productivity, and, in turn, corporate profitability. Similarly, if the PBGC observes low funding ratios, it can either insist on increased contributions to the plan or require that the sponsor pay larger insurance fees to the PBGC.

3. *Strategic asset allocation.* Given a promised benefit level and current funding ratio, a strategic asset allocation decision must be made. ERISA requires that all plans covered by the PBGC (governmental plans are not covered) must be invested solely in the interest of plan participants for the exclusive purpose of providing future benefits. Taken at face value, this implies that the pension plan should be thought of as a *financial institution managed independently of the sponsoring corporation.* We will refer to this view as the *traditional* approach.

   But a close examination of Figure 20-7 suggests that the pension plan is not truly independent of risks faced by the sponsoring firm. For example, even if the current funding ratio is 1.0, future decreases in the corporation's earning power will affect the firm's ability to meet its obligations for benefits which accrue over time. Thus, if the sponsor's earning power is highly dependent on oil prices, the pension fund should probably underweight oil investments. *Sponsor risk does affect pension risk.* We will refer to this as the *integrated approach.*

   Another view of the pension plan is known as the *corporate* approach. It adds the pension assets and liabilities to the corporation's balance sheet and makes SAA decisions whch *maximize shareholder wealth.* Not only is this in violation of ERISA, but (as we will see later) it leads to some rather strange SAA prescriptions.

Before we can proceed with a further discussion of either an optimal funding ratio or an optimal strategic asset allocation, we need to understand the nature of the pension liability. It turns out that the sponsor has a number of liabilities. These have implications for a given pension's optimal funding ratio and strategic asset allocation.

Pension Liabilities

As noted in Chapter 19, the first question that needs to be asked in any evaluation of a proper SAA is: "What is the purpose of the security portfolio?" In the case of a defined benefit pension plan, it is to pay future benefit liabilities to employees. Thus, it is important that we understand the nature of these liabilities. At any point in time, the sponsor of a defined benefit pension plan has three liabilities to pension beneficiaries:

1. *The accrued benefit obligation* (ABO) is the present value of future benefits which employees have *accrued to date* based on *current wage levels*.

2. *The projected benefit obligation* (PBO) is the present value of future benefits which employees have *accrued to date* based on *expected wages at retirement*.

3. *The total benefit obligation* (TBO) is the PBO plus the present value of benefits which current employees are expected to earn from *future service*. Employees have not yet earned a claim to the difference between the TBO and the PBO. But it can be useful to know what the level of the TBO is when deciding on an appropriate funding ratio and strategic asset allocation.

To illustrate how each of these liabilities is calculated, the following hypothetical data are used. AmerTech Corp. is a medium-size firm engaged in designing and manufacturing telecommunication equipment such as satellites and satellite dishes. The firm has a defined benefit plan which provides a yearly pension benefit equal to a 2% benefit rate for each year of employment times the employee's final salary. Although employees accumulate benefits for each year they work, they must work for Amer-Tech at least seven years in order to obtain the benefit. If they leave employment prior to seven years of service, they receive no benefits. If they leave employment after seven years, they receive *during the years of their retirement* a yearly pension benefit based on their salary at termination. Employees with more than seven years of service are referred to as being *vested*. Those with less than seven years are *nonvested*.

Employees are also classified as active or inactive. Active employees are still working for the firm. Inactive employees are either retired or have terminated their employment prior to retirement, usually to accept a job with another firm.

Table 20-8 provides basic information about each type of employee. For example, there are 100 retired employees who have a right to pension benefits because they were vested when they retired. Each retired employee had a final salary of $20,000 and had worked 20 years with AmerTech. Finally, each retired employee is expected to draw benefits in retirement for 20 years after today.

In order to calculate present values and yearly pension costs, two interest rates are needed. The first is the yield to maturity on low-default-risk bonds having a duration similar to the duration of the benefit claims. Often referred to as a *settlement rate*, it represents the risk-free interest rate which could be earned if the pension plan were terminated—or settled—today. It is used to find the present value of future benefits. In addition, an interest rate reflecting what the pension assets are expected to earn is required in order to determine a portion of the yearly total pension expense. This

TABLE 20-8 *Hypothetical AmerTech Corp. Employee Data*

Employee Category	Number	Years of Service	Current or Final Salary	Years to Retirement	Years in Retirement
Vested:					
Retired	100	20	$20,000	0	20
Terminated	50	10	20,000	15	20
Active	100	10	20,000	15	20
Nonvested:					
Active	25	5	20,000	15	20

return on assets will be larger than the settlement rate if any assets with investment risk are owned—real estate, U.S. equities, international equities, etc. We will assume a settlement rate of 8% and an expected return on assets of 12%.

Accrued Benefit Obligation. The ABO is the present value of future benefits which employees have accrued to date based on *current wage levels*. Accrued benefits are discounted at the settlement rate to find the present-value liability. The ABO is composed of both vested accrued benefits and nonvested accrued benefits.

Table 20-9 illustrates the calculation of the vested and nonvested ABO. The calculations are relatively straightforward. For example, consider the liability for vested active employees. The current salary (or wage) of such employees is $20,000. Each active vested employee has worked for 10 years with AmerTech and, thus, has a retirement annuity claim equal to 20% of current salary, or $4,000 per year during retirement. Since there are 100 such employees, AmerTech is obligated to pay $400,000 to these employees each year in their retirement. Given our assumptions, the $400,000 annuity will extend from the end of year 16 through the end of year 35. Discounting at the risk-free settlement rate, AmerTech's present-value liability to vested, active employees is $1.238 million.

The shaded portions of panels A and B in Figure 20-8 represent AmerTech's vested and total accrued benefit obligation. The unshaded portions are additional liabilities which are discussed below.

Four important aspects of the ABO have to do with the firm's *current legal obligation* to employees. If the pension plan were to be terminated today, employees would have a legal right to future cash flows having a present worth of $9.866 million.[10] If the plan were underfunded and transferred to the PBGC, employees would continue to have a present-value claim of $9.866 million—for which the PBGC would be legally obligated. If the plan were overfunded and terminated by AmerTech in order to revert surplus assets to the corporation, employees would still have a present-value legal claim of $9.866 million. In the case of an asset reversion, AmerTech would probably purchase annuity contracts from an insurance company. The annuities would be constructed to exactly pay off employees' future benefit claims. Employees

---

[10]In plan terminations by the employer, nonvested active employees are automatically vested.

TABLE 20-9 *Calculation of the Accrued Benefit Obligation*

		Retired	*Terminated*	*Active*
Vested:				
I.	Yearly Accrued Benefit Annuity			
	Final Salary	$ 20,000	$ 20,000	$ 20,000
	Years of Service	× 20	× 10	× 10
	Benefit Rate	× 0.02	× 0.02	× 0.02
	Per Employee	$ 8,000	$ 4,000	$ 4,000
	Number of Employees	× 100	× 50	× 100
	Total Annuity	$ 800,000	$200,000	$ 400,000
II.	Present Value			
	$\sum_{1}^{20} 1/1.08^t$	× 9.8181		
	$\left(\sum_{1}^{20} 1/1.08^t\right)\Big/1.08^{15}$		× 3.0951	× 3.0951
III.	Accrued Benefit Obligation	$7,854,480	$619,015	$1,238,030
IV.	Total	$9,711,525		
Nonvested:				
	Active	154,754*		
Accrued Benefit Obligation		$9,866,279		

*($20,000(5)(.02)(9.8181)/1.08^{15})25 = $154,754.

have a legal right to the accrued benefit obligation and will receive it either from the employer or the PBGC.

Second, the ABO is a *nominal dollar liability*. As is the case with most plans, AmerTech has not tied its accrued benefit obligation to future inflation. It is determined solely by *current* salaries. If the plan were to be terminated today, future benefit payments would be known with certainty—they would not vary with inflation. And, if the plan were terminated, a total of $9.866 million invested in nominally risk-free securities yielding 8% per year would be sufficient to exactly pay off all ABO claims.

Third, the accrued benefit obligation will change as time passes, current salaries change, etc. The only way AmerTech can lock in its current ABO is to terminate the plan! That is why the accrued benefit obligation is often referred to as the *termination liability*. Termination does not mean that the firm has defaulted on its promise to pay any accrued benefits. It simply means that such benefits are frozen. Any future increase in benefits will have to come from a newly formed pension plan. Unless the plan is terminated, the ABO will change over time.

Fourth, an important cause of changes in the ABO is changes in the settlement rate. If the interest rate used to discount future benefit payments increases, the ABO

FIGURE 20-8 *The Pension Liability*

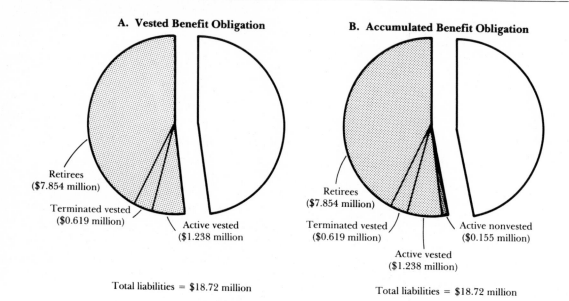

A. Vested Benefit Obligation

Retirees
($7.854 million)

Terminated vested
($0.619 million)

Active vested
($1.238 million

Total liabilities = $18.72 million

B. Accumulated Benefit Obligation

Retirees
($7.854 million)

Terminated vested
($0.619 million)

Active nonvested
($0.155 million)

Active vested
($1.238 million)

Total liabilities = $18.72 million

will fall. If the discount rate decreases, the ABO will rise. Even if the value of asset investments remains unchanged, the surplus inherent in the plan will vary over time as changes in interest rates cause inverse changes in the ABO liability. This fact has gained considerable attention in recent years. We will return to it later when we examine the concept of surplus management.

To summarize, the accrued benefit obligation is (*a*) based on current salaries; (*b*) a legal obligation of the firm if the plan were to be terminated today; and (*c*) a nominal dollar liability which changes as interest rates change.

Projected Benefit Obligation. The PBO is the present value of future benefits which employees have accrued to date based on *expected wages at retirement*. It differs from the ABO in only one respect—it uses projected wages at retirement instead of current wages. The logic underlying the PBO is as follows. Employees realize that they have a current claim to pension benefits only to the extent to which they have accrued past employment service with the firm. But, *if they expect that the pension plan will not be terminated prior to their retirement, they see their benefit claims as claims to prior service applied to wages expected to be earned just prior to retirement.*[11]

The projected benefit obligation for AmerTech is shown in Table 20-10, in which salaries are forecast to grow at a compound rate of 7% per year. The retirement an-

---

[11]Actuaries will make adjustments to the PBO for expanded employee terminations prior to retirement. For simplicity, we neglect such adjustments.

TABLE 20-10 *Projected Benefit Obligation*

	Active Employees	
	Vested	Nonvested
I. Projected Benefit Annuity to Active Employees:		
Current Salary	$ 20,000	$ 20,000
Growth Rate	$\times 1.07^{15}$	$\times 1.07^{15}$
Projected Final Salary	$ 55,181	$ 55,181
Years of Service	$\times 10$	$\times 5$
Benefit Rate	$\times 0.02$	$\times 0.02$
Per Employee	$ 11,036	$ 5,518
Number of Employees	$\times 100$	$\times 25$
	$ 1,103,600	$137,950
II. Present Value	$\times 9.8181/1.08^{5}$	$\times 9.8181/1.08^{5}$
	$ 3,415,724	$426,966
III. Projected Benefit Obligation		
Active Employees	$ 3,842,690	
Inactive Employees	8,473,495	
Total PBO	$12,316,185	

nuity which would be paid to active employees (based on their accrued service and projected salaries at retirement) is calculated first. Using a discount rate of 8%, the present value of this annuity is $3.843 million. The accrued liability to inactive employees (retired and terminated) of $8.473 million is then added to obtain the total projected benefit obligation of $12.316 million.

If the pension plan is not terminated in the future, employers see the plan as having a present-value obligation to employees equal to $12.316 million. In Figure 20-9, the shaded portion represents the projected benefit obligation portion of the plan's total liability.

There are two important economic differences between the APO and the PBO. First, the ABO is based on the liability the firm would owe if the pension plan were to be terminated immediately. It is the minimum legal obligation which employees have a claim to. In contrast, the PBO is based on the assumption that the pension plan will not be prematurely terminated. Thus, the PBO embodies an *implicit contract* between employer and employee that future salary increases will be credited for current accrued service.

This implicit contract has a clear dollar value that an employee would lose if the plan were to be terminated prior to the employee's retirement. To see what the value of this implicit contract is, consider the retirement benefits an active, vested employee of AmerTech would receive if:

FIGURE 20-9 *Projected Benefit Obligation*

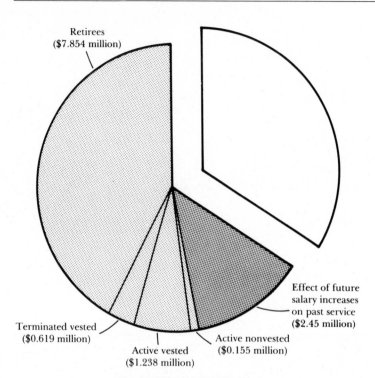

Retirees
($7.854 million)

Effect of future
salary increases
on past service
($2.45 million)

Terminated vested
($0.619 million)

Active vested
($1.238 million)

Active nonvested
($0.155 million)

Total liabilities = $18.72 million

1. the plan is not terminated *versus*

2. the plan is terminated today and immediately replaced with an identical new plan.

If the plan is not terminated, each active vested employee will receive a yearly retirement annuity of $27,590:

$$\$20,000(1.07^{15})(0.02)(10 \text{ years} + 15 \text{ years}) = \$27,590$$

If the plan is terminated and replaced with an identical new plan, the yearly retirement annuity would be only $20,554:

Original Plan:	$20,000(0.01)(10 \text{ years})$	$= \$\ 4,000$
New Plan:	$20,000(1.07^{15})(0.02)(15 \text{ years}) =$	$16,554$
Total		$\$20,554$

Thus, if the plan is terminated immediately and replaced by an identical new plan, the employee's yearly pension annuity is $7,036 smaller. This occurs because the employee's current 10 years of accrued service is applied to current salary and *not* to retirement salary.

The present value of this loss from plan termination is equal to $21,776.94 per employee:

Annuity Lost in Retirement	$ 7,036.00
Present Value of a $1 Annuity for 20 Years at 8%	× 9.8181
Present Value at End of Year 15	$69,080.15
Present Value of a $1 Lump Sum at End of Year 15 at 8%	0.3152417
Present Value of Loss	$21,776.94

This $21,776.94 is the difference between the PBO and the ABO per employee. For example, from the data in Table 20-10, the PBO per employee (active and vested) is $34,157.24. And from Table 20-9, the ABO per employee is $12,380.30. The difference of $21,776.94 represents the value lost by each active, vested employee if the plan is terminated:

	Per Employee
PBO	$34,157.24
Less ABO	12,380.30
Potential Termination Loss	$21,776.94

Clearly, employees have a significant economic incentive to see that the plan is not prematurely terminated. Later we will discuss how this should affect the pension's funding ratio and strategic asset allocation.

As we have seen, the first economic difference between the projected and the accrued benefit obligations is that the PBO allows the employee's past accrued service to be credited against projected salary at retirement, whereas the ABO credits past service only against current salary. The difference between the two represents the loss active employees would suffer if the plan were to be terminated. The difference represents the value of an implicit contract between employees and employer that the pension plan will be an *ongoing plan*. Therefore, AmerTech's pension liabilities consist of:

Accrued Benefit Liability	$ 9,866,279
Implicit Ongoing Plan Liability	2,449,906
Projected Benefit Liability	$12,316,185

The second difference between the ABO and the PBO is that the ABO is a nominal dollar liability, whereas much of the PBO is a real dollar liability. If the plan is terminated, the sponsor has an obligation to pay a sequence of future *nominal dollar* benefits to both active and inactive employees. The absolute size of such benefits can be forecast with considerable precision and will not vary with inflation. Even if the sponsor does not terminate the plan, benefit payments to inactive employees are fixed *nominal dollar* claims. But if the pension sponsor intends to continue the plan,

TABLE 20-11 *Nominal and Real Benefit Obligations of AmerTech Corp. (in thousands)*

Year	Nominal Dollar Benefits			Real Dollar Benefits			Grand Total
	Retired	Terminated	Total	Vested	Nonvested	Total	
1	$ 800.00		$ 800.00				$ 800.00
2	800.00		800.00				800.00
3	800.00		800.00				800.00
4	800.00		800.00				800.00
5	800.00		800.00				800.00
6	800.00		800.00				800.00
7	800.00		800.00				800.00
8	800.00		800.00				800.00
9	800.00		800.00				800.00
10	800.00		800.00				800.00
11	800.00		800.00				800.00
12	800.00		800.00				800.00
13	800.00		800.00				800.00
14	800.00		800.00				800.00
15	800.00		800.00				800.00
16	800.00	$200.00	1,000.00	$1,103.60	$137.95	$1,241.55	2,241.55
17	800.00	200.00	1,000.00	1,103.60	137.95	1,241.55	2,241.55
18	800.00	200.00	1,000.00	1,103.60	137.95	1,241.55	2,241.55
19	800.00	200.00	1,000.00	1,103.60	137.95	1,241.55	2,241.55
20	800.00	200.00	1,000.00	1,103.60	137.95	1,241.55	2,241.55
21		200.00	200.00	1,103.60	137.95	1,241.55	1,441.55
22		200.00	200.00	1,103.60	137.95	1,241.55	1,441.55
23		200.00	200.00	1,103.60	137.95	1,241.55	1,441.55
24		200.00	200.00	1,103.60	137.95	1,241.55	1,441.55
25		200.00	200.00	1,103.60	137.95	1,241.55	1,441.55
26		200.00	200.00	1,103.60	137.95	1,241.55	1,441.55
27		200.00	200.00	1,103.60	137.95	1,241.55	1,441.55
28		200.00	200.00	1,103.60	137.95	1,241.55	1,441.55
29		200.00	200.00	1,103.60	137.95	1,241.55	1,441.55
30		200.00	200.00	1,103.60	137.95	1,241.55	1,441.55
31		200.00	200.00	1,103.60	137.95	1,241.55	1,441.55
32		200.00	200.00	1,103.60	137.95	1,241.55	1,441.55
33		200.00	200.00	1,103.60	137.95	1,241.55	1,441.55
34		200.00	200.00	1,103.60	137.95	1,241.55	1,441.55
35		200.00	200.00	1,103.60	137.95	1,241.55	1,441.55

Present Value at 8%

	$7,854.48	$619.01	$8,473.49	$3,415.72	$426.97	$3,842.69	$12,316.18

benefit obligations to active employees are *real dollar* obligations. Since future benefits to active employees are tied to salary, and salary is tied to worker productivity and inflation, the stream of benefits to active employees is also tied to productivity and inflation.

As an example, Table 20-11 shows the nominal and real dollar benefit claims against AmerTech. During years 1–20, the firm owes retired workers a nominal dollar payment equal to $800,000 per year. Nominal dollar payments are also due terminated employees in years 16–35 in an amount equal to $200,000 per year. In contrast, active employees have a real dollar claim in years 16–35 equal to $1,241.55 per year. The size of this claim will vary with worker productivity and, probably more important, with inflation. In terms of present values, the claims are:

	(in thousands)
Nominal Dollar Obligation	$ 8,473.49
Real Dollar Obligation	3,842.69
Projected Benefit Obligation	$12,361.18

The strategic asset allocation implications are obvious. If the pension sponsor does not intend to provide inactive employees (often referred to as "retired lives") with cost-of-living adjustments, their liability can be immunized. A risk-free investment strategy can be implemented consisting of the purchase of default and call-free bonds having a duration equal to the duration of the nominal dollar obligation. However, if cost-of-living adjustments are to be provided, a risk-free strategy is not possible. This is certainly true for the real dollar liability to active employees. For active employees, securities that provide at least a partial hedge against productivity and inflation are clearly less risky than long-term bonds that provide no hedge against either risk.

APO or PBO? So, which is the true economic liability of the sponsor and asset to the employee—the ABO or the PBO? Actually, the answer is left up to the sponsor. Employees have a legal right to the ABO and no more. But the only way the sponsor can actually realize this minimum legal obligation is to terminate the plan. There *are* rational reasons for plan termination. Assets might be so much smaller than the ABO that the sponsor would choose to terminate the plan and turn both assets and liabilities over to the PBGC. Alternatively, assets might be so much larger than the ABO that the sponsor would choose to terminate the plan in order to return excess assets to the sponsoring firm. In either case, however, employees are harmed in that the sponsor has defaulted on the firm's implicit contract liability—the differences between the PBO and the ABO. This is likely to cause morale problems and reductions in employee productivity. So, whether the pension liability is the ABO or the PBO depends on the sponsor's intent and actions. If the plan is to be terminated, the liability is the ABO. If the plan is to be an ongoing plan, the liability is the PBO.[12]

Total Benefit Obligation. The ABO and the PBO treat only the service that employees have accrued from past employment. But, if the sponsor does not intend to terminate the plan, future service will also be accrued as time passes. Since future service accruals can be sizable, it is often useful to examine their relative size. Calculations for AmerTech are shown in Table 20-12.

---

[12]The sponsoring firm owns an option allowing the sponsor to decide what the pension liability will be. The exercise price of the option is the lost employee productivity, and thus profits, caused by the default on the implicit contract liability. If the present value of lost profits is less than the value of the implicit contract liability, the sponsor will exercise the option to terminate the plan.

TABLE 20-12 *Total Benefit Obligation of AmerTech Corp.*

	Active Employees		
	Vested	*Nonvested*	*Total*
I. Retirement Benefit Annuity			
A. Current Salary	$ 20,000	$ 20,000	
B. Salary Growth	$\times 1.07^{15}$	$\times 1.07^{15}$	
C. Retirement Salary	$ 55,181	$ 55,181	
D. Benefit Rate	$\times 0.02$	$\times 0.02$	
E. Total Years of Service	$\times (10 + 15)$	$\times (5 + 15)$	
Benefit Per Employee	$ 27,590	$ 22,072	
F. Total Employees	$\times 100$	$\times 25$	
Total Benefits	$2,759,000	$ 551,800	$ 3,310,800
II. Present Value at 8%			
Active Employees	$8,539,311	$1,707,862	$10,247,173
Inactive Employees			
—Retired			7,854,480
—Terminated			619,015
Total			$18,720,668

The firm's total benefit obligation is displayed in Figure 20-10 and consists of the following:

Accrued Service and Salary:

Retirees	$ 7,854,480
Terminated Vested	619,015
Active Vested	1,238,030
Active Nonvested	154,754
Total ABO	$ 9,866,279
Effect of Future Salary	2,449,906
Total PBO	$12,316,185
Effect of Future Service	6,404,483
Total Benefit Obligation	$18,720,668

The importance of looking at the total benefit obligation can be seen by examining the forecast yearly benefits to active employees. Based on accrued service, these benefits are expected to be $1.24 million per year (from Table 20-11). But if the plan is not terminated, total payments to active employees are actually expected to increase to $3.31 million (from Table 20-12). Clearly, benefit payments will be much larger than implied by service accrued to date.

FIGURE 20-10 *Total Pension Liabilities*

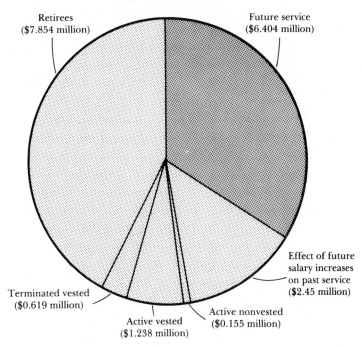

Retirees
($7.854 million)

Future service
($6.404 million)

Effect of future
salary increases
on past service
($2.45 million)

Terminated vested
($0.619 million)

Active vested
($1.238 million)

Active nonvested
($0.155 million)

Total liabilities = $18.72 million

Yearly Pension Expense. The yearly pension expense which pension sponsors incur consists of three elements:

1. *Accrued service cost* — the increase in the PBO during the course of the past year.
2. *Net interest cost* — interest due employees on the PBO less the expected return on plan assets.
3. *Amortization cost* — amortization of any unfunded liability (PBO minus the value of assets) over the expected future service life of active employees.

For example, consider the pension expense of AmerTech Corp. During the next year active employees will accrue additional benefit payments having a present value of $461,127:

$$= \frac{(\$20,000 \times 1.07^{15} \times 0.02 \times 1 \text{ year})(125 \text{ employees}) \sum_{1}^{20} (1/1.08^t)}{1.08^{14}}$$

$$= \frac{(\$1,103.61)(125)(9.8181)}{1.08^{14}}$$

$$= \frac{(\$137,951.25)(9.8181)}{1.08^{14}}$$

$$= \$461,127$$

In addition, the PBO at the start of the year was $12,316,135. Since this is a liability which the sponsor owes to employees, the employees should be allowed to earn an interest return. At an 8% rate, the employer would incur a $985,295 interest cost ($12.316 million × 0.08). However, AmerTech will have accumulated a pool of marketable pension assets on which a rate of return will be expected. Earlier we assumed that the expected return on assets would be 12%. In addition, we will assume that the market value of assets at the start of the year was $10 million. Thus the expected return on assets would be $1.2 million ($10 million × 0.12). This results in a net interest cost of a negative $214,705:

Interest Cost on PBO Liability	$ 985,295
Expected Return on Assets	− 1,200,000
Net Interest Cost	−$ 214,705

The final component of pension expense is the linear amortization of any unfunded liability. Assume that, at the end of the year, the PBO is $12,962,607 and the value of assets is $11 million. The unfunded liability would be $1,962,607.[13] At that time, employees have an expected service life of 14 years. Thus, the amortization of the unfunded liability would represent an expense of $140,186 ($1,962,607/14). Note that the amortization of any unfunded liability will, over time, account for actual asset returns which might differ from the expected return on assets. If actual asset returns are greater (smaller) than expected, pension expense will be smaller (greater) than expected.

In total, AmerTech's pension expense would be:

Normal Service Cost	$461,127
Net Interest Cost	− 214,705
Amortization of Unfunded Liability	140,186
Pension Expense	$386,608

FAS 87. In late 1985, the Financial Accounting Standards Board issued Financial Accounting Statement #87. Based on economic concepts virtually identical to those discussed above, the statement was designed to standardize and improve corporate pension accounting. Prior to FAS 87, firms had considerable latitude in the manner in which pension expense and benefit obligations were calculated. For example, many firms tied their pension expense to contributions made to the plan. In addition, there was no standard discount rate applied to future benefit obligations, and the discount

---

[13]In practice, the actual market value of pension assets might not be used to calculate the unfunded liability. Instead, a moving average of, say, the past five years could be used.

rate chosen was infrequently changed. Under FAS 87, detailed guidelines were given for the calculation of pension expense, and the discount rate was defined as the "settlement rate." As a result, the pension expense of many firms changed dramatically. Some firms incurred much larger expense, but most companies initially had decreased expense.

Since the discount rate is specified as a *prevailing* market rate of interest, many people are concerned that pension expense will become more volatile in the future. In addition, if the market value of pension assets is less than the accrued benefit obligation, a net liability must be shown on the sponsoring firm's balance sheet.

FAS 87 has had ramifications for pension investment decisions. For example, many plan sponsors became so worried about the potential volatility of their pension asset market values that they reduced asset investment risk exposure and bought portfolio insurance. In fact, FAS 87 was a principal motivation for the growth of portfolio insurance strategies. Perhaps the most important investment result of FAS 87 is that it forced sponsors to consider simultaneously both the assets and the liabilities of their plans. No longer is attention focused solely on investment returns. Instead, strategic asset allocation decisions are now focused on pension surplus – the combination of asset and liability payoffs.

The Optimal Funding Ratio

The major topic of this chapter is strategic asset allocation. We have chosen to illustrate the considerations involved in developing an optimal SAA by using the situation faced by defined benefit pension plans, since their situation is complex and involves large cash flows. However, by selecting defined benefits plans, we are forced to address a decision which must be made prior to the strategic asset allocation decision. What should be the funding ratio of the plan?

The funding ratio (FR) is equal to the market value of plan assets divided by the plan's liability. Two FRs are commonly calculated, one based on the ABO and another on the PBO. For example, if the market value of AmerTech's pension assets is $10 million, the two funding ratios would be:

$$\text{Accrued Benefit Obligation} = \$10/\$9.866$$

$$= 1.014$$

$$\text{Projected Benefit Obligation} = \$10/\$12.316$$

$$= 0.812$$

The funding ratio will change as (*a*) the value of assets varies over time, (*b*) the value of the liability varies over time (with changes in the settlement discount rate and increases in accrued benefits), (*c*) the sponsor makes additional contributions to the plan, and (*d*) benefit payments are made. Increases in accrued benefits and benefit payments can be predicted with reasonable accuracy, at least for intermediate time intervals. Thus, the major determinant of the current funding ratio will be the speed with which adjustments are made to the sponsor's contribution rate in response to changes in asset and liability values.

Practitioners and scholars have given little serious thought to what the optimal funding ratio might be. In fact, the two major approaches developed to date yield prescriptions which are exactly the opposite of each other. However, a logical case can be made that the FR should usually be based on the accrued benefit obligation and be equal to 1.0.

Tax Shelter Hypothesis. In the mid-1970s Fischer Black suggested that the sponsor of a defined benefit pension plan should overfund the plan in order to take advantage of a possible tax shelter.

The tax shelter argument is quite simple in concept. First, the corporation sells bonds to the public. The proceeds are then contributed to the pension plan, and a tax deduction is taken on the contribution. Finally, the pension plan buys the bonds that the company had initially issued. If investors view the assets of the pension as belonging to the corporation, the firm's net position in the bonds is zero. But it has reduced its taxes. A tax shield has been created.

The implications of this strategy are that the pension plan should be overfunded as much as possible in order to create the largest possible tax shield, and that high-taxed (and thus low-risk) securities such as bonds should be held by the pension fund.

There are a number of problems with such a tax strategy. For example, it is doubtful that the IRS would allow firms to create such tax shelters to any significant degree. In addition, even if the IRS raised no objections, the strategy offers no advice to sponsors of pension funds who do not pay taxes—governmental bodies especially. Finally, it doesn't describe reality. Pension funds simply do not act this way!

The Pension Put. In the mid-1980s Sharpe suggested that funding decisions could be influenced by management actions to maximize the value of its "pension put." Recall that when ERISA was enacted, the Pension Benefit Guarantee Corporation was formed to guarantee that employees would receive the accrued benefit obligation even if the sponsoring firm defaulted. To protect the PBGC, each corporate sponsor paid a yearly insurance fee to the PBGC. But these fees were initially fixed—they did not depend on the plan's funding ratio, the investment risk, or the financial health of the sponsoring firm.

The insurance provided by the PBGC effectively provided the sponsoring corporation with a long position in a put on the pension assets. At the sponsor's option, pension assets could be turned over to the PBGC, and the sponsor would be free of its pension liability. The sponsor had the right to sell the assets at a price equal to the plan's ABO. In effect, the sponsor owned a pension put whose cost was not related to the probability of exercise.

Sharpe suggested that, under these conditions, the sponsor should maximize the value of the long put position by underfunding the plan and buying very risky securities. After all, with the way PBGC insurance was structured, the sponsor (presumably) had nothing to lose and could only gain by placing the pension plan in a maximum risk position. To maximize the value of the firm's pension put, management should underfund the plan as much as possible and purchase risky securities with any funds held by the plan.

Recent legislation and regulations have been designed to reduce management's ability to extract wealth from the PBGC and transfer it to the corporation. Insurance fees charged by the PBGC now depend on each plan's financial condition. In addition, the Omnibus Budget Reconciliation Act of 1987 allowed the PBGC a legal claim on as much as 100% of a corporation's net worth. Thus, the value of any pension put has been significantly reduced, if not eliminated.

To date, these are the only well-developed theories which attempt to identify an optimal funding ratio. Yet they call for completely different strategies. The tax shelter argument suggests large overfunding and low-risk securities. The pension put argument suggests large underfunding and high-risk securities. In fact, when Harrison and Sharpe considered the two theories together, they concluded that one argument would always dominate the other. For some firms the pension put would create more value than the tax shelter, and in other firms the tax shelter would be dominant. But only extreme funding ratios would be optimal.[14]

Employee Productivity. Employees receive compensation from their employer in three forms: (1) a current wage or salary income, (2) a guaranteed retirement benefit based on current wage or salary income (ABO), and (3) an additional implicit retirement benefit based on a projected wage or salary at retirement (PBO). For example, a vested employee of AmerTech Corp. currently receives a salary of $20,000 per year, has a claim to an accrued benefit obligation of $12,380.30, and has an implicit claim to a projected benefit obligation worth $21,776.94 more than the ABO. Changes in the $20,000 salary will be determined by the employee's productivity and inflation. The $12,380.30 ABO is guaranteed by the PBGC, but the $21,776.94 is totally dependent on whether the pension plan is terminated or is an ongoing plan. Thus, employees have a strong interest in seeing that management will not terminate the plan.

As shown in panel A of Figure 20-11, the probability that the employer will terminate the pension is a direct function of how overfunded or underfunded the plan is. If assets are smaller than the accrued benefit obligation, plan termination would be caused by sponsor default and assignment of the pension to the PBGC. If assets are larger than the accrued benefit obligation, plan termination would be caused by the sponsor's returning surplus pension assets to the corporation. But regardless of the cause, the probability of plan termination increases whenever plan assets depart substantially from the ABO.

In panel B of Figure 20-11, the probability that the employee will receive the full PBO is shown as an inverse function of how overfunded or underfunded the plan is. As the ABO funding ratio departs from 1.0, the probability that the incremental value inherent in the projected benefit obligation will be received decreases. This is due to

---

[14]Bicksler and Chen have shown that various implicit costs incurred with either strategy *might* result in an optimal funding ratio between the extremes suggested by the pension put and tax shelter arguments. To some extent, their suggestions are similar to the employee productivity argument presented here.

FIGURE 20-11 *Impacts of the ABO Funding Ratio*

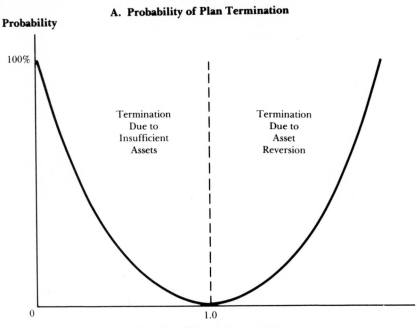

A. Probability of Plan Termination

Probability

100%

Termination
Due to
Insufficient
Assets

Termination
Due to
Asset
Reversion

0   1.0

Funding Ratio (Assets/ABO)

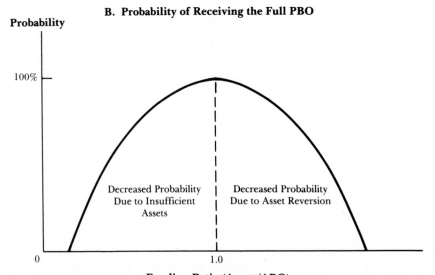

B. Probability of Receiving the Full PBO

Probability

100%

Decreased Probability
Due to Insufficient
Assets

Decreased Probability
Due to Asset Reversion

0   1.0

Funding Ratio (Assets/ABO)

the increased probability of plan termination. Employees have a strong motive to see that the employer maintain an ABO funding ratio close to 1.0.

Note that the funding ratio above is based on the ABO, not the PBO. From the employee's viewpoint, any asset movement away from the ABO is potentially detrimental. For example, AmerTech's ABO and PBO were calculated to be $9.8 million and $12.3 million, respectively. If the funding ratio based on the PBO were 1.0, assets would be worth $12.3 million. In this case, employees would face the risk that the employer would terminate the plan and return the $2.5 million ($12.3 − $9.8) in excess assets to the firm. Only at an ABO funding ratio of 1.0 is the employee's risk of premature termination minimized. Thus, from the perspective of the employee, the optimal funding ratio should be based on the ABO and be equal to 1.0.

It can be argued that, from the employer's perspective, the optimal funding ratio is also 1.0. Neglecting any possible value from a pension put or tax shelters created by contributions, the only way that shareholder wealth can be affected by changes in the funding ratio is through its effects on worker productivity.

Consider first the case of a plan in which assets are less than the ABO. The corporation has a clear legal and economic liability which it will eventually *have to pay* (again, neglecting the pension put or bankruptcy). The question is, who should be the owner of the liability—employees or outside parties? If the funding ratio remains below 1.0, employees are effectively investors in the firm's debt.

If the funding ratio is increased to 1.0 by new financing, then outsiders own the debt. If the debt were held by employees, it would not be marketable and would contain risks which the employee could not easily diversify. In contrast, if the unfunded liability is financed by new outside financing, the debt could be marketable and its risks more easily diversified. As a result, the effective interest costs of an unfunded ABO liability are likely to be larger than if outside investors were to finance the unfunded liability. The firm would pay such costs in the form of reduced worker productivity. In short, an unfunded ABO liability is a costly form of corporate financing.

Consider now the case of an overfunded plan, one in which assets exceed the accrued benefit obligation. Assume that at the start of a year the ABO funding ratio is 1.0 but that by year-end, returns on security investments are much larger than expected such that the year-end funding ratio is greater than 1.0. Should management take actions to restore the ratio to 1.0 immediately? The answer depends on what such actions might be.

If the funding ratio can be brought back to 1.0 by reduced contributions, it probably should be. At funding ratios greater than 1.0, employee productivity would probably decrease because of the increased probability of plan termination.[15] In addition, if assets are greater than the ABO, employees will often attempt to negotiate for larger benefits. This is referred to as *surplus sharing*.

But what if reduced short-term contributions are insufficient to bring the funding ratio back to 1.0—that is, that the only way to set FR equal to 1.0 is to terminate the

---

[15]Moderate FRs above 1.0 are likely to be unimportant to employees. However, if contributions are not decreased, FRs moderately above 1.0 can grow to sizable differences in a time span of a few years.

pension plan? In this case, the sponsor must determine whether the plan should, in fact, be terminated. If the plan is terminated, employees will lose the value of the implicit contract that the plan is an ongoing plan. In the case of AmerTech, this was worth $21,776.94 per employee (PBO minus ABO). As a result, employee productivity will decrease if the plan is terminated and excess assets are returned to the firm. If the present value of this decreased productivity is greater than the implicit contract's value, the plan *should not* be terminated. In this case, the sponsoring firm should announce to employees that it has no intention of terminating the plan and intends to reduce contributions so that the funding ratio will approach 1.0 over time. If the present value of decreased productivity is less than the implicit contract's value, however, the employer will terminate the plan.

In short, both employees and employers have a financial incentive to see that the ABO funding ratio is approximately 1.0.

Optimal Strategic Asset Allocation

The strategic asset allocation decision of a pension plan (or of any organization or individual) should be focused on how the decision will affect the surplus of the plan (or wealth of the investor) at the expected date of portfolio liquidation. It should not be focused solely on asset investment returns, since asset returns will interact with returns on other assets and liabilities of the pension (or individual).

The security portfolio is only a part of the total position of the pension. To illustrate, hypothetical balance sheets for AmerTech's pension plan are shown in Table 20-13. Let's first review each item in the balance sheet for the ongoing plan, starting with the liabilities. The ABO is $9.866 million. This is the employee's current legal claim, the present value of retirement benefits if the plan were to be terminated today. The implicit contract liability of $2.450 million represents the present value of incremental retirement benefits if the plan is never terminated. These incremental benefits come from the crediting of service accrued to date against future wages or salary increases. The pension's current *projected* benefit obligation is based on *past* employee service. Finally, the present value of incremental benefits that will be paid for *future* employee service is $6.404 million.

Three assets are identified in this balance sheet. The first is a marketable security portfolio now worth $10.000 million. It is the strategic asset allocation of this portfolio that we must determine. The other two assets are effectively nonmarketable promissory notes issued to the pension plan by the sponsoring corporation. They are occasionally referred to as "shadow assets." The $2.316 million employer note for past service is equal to the difference between the $10.000 million in marketable assets and the $12.316 million PBO. The $6.404 million employer note for future service is equal to the future service liability.

If the plan is terminated, the balance sheet is much simpler. Assets are worth $10.000 million, and the only liability is the ABO of $9.866 million. Surplus assets of $133,721 would be returned to AmerTech.

TABLE 20-13 *Balance Sheets for AmerTech Pension Plan*

	Ongoing Plan	

Assets		*Liabilities and Supplies*	
Marketable Securities	$10,000,000	Accrued Benefit Obligation (Termination Liability)	$ 9,866,279
Present Value of Future Contributions:		Implicit Contract Liability	2,449,906
— For Past Service	2,316,185	Total Projected Benefit Obligation	$12,316,185
— For Future Service	6,404,483	Future Service Liability	6,404,483
		Total Benefit Obligation	$18,720,668
		Surplus	0
Total	$18,720,668		$18,720,668

	Terminated Plan	

Assets			
Marketable Securities	$10,000,000	Accrued Benefit Obligation	$ 9,866,297
		Surplus (to be returned to employer)	133,721
Total	$10,000,000		$10,000,000

In deciding what the SAA should be for the $10.000 million security portfolio, we are faced with a complex situation. If AmerTech elects to terminate the pension plan, we must decide how to invest any remaining assets in a manner which will *guarantee* future payment of employee benefits inherent in the $9.866 million ABO. If Amer-Tech does not terminate the plan, the interactions between marketable security returns and returns on each of the other assets and liabilities must be considered.

Plan Termination. Strategic asset allocation in a plan termination is straightforward. Since each employee's past service, wage or salary, and retirement date are known, benefit claims are known with certainty. The only uncertainty relates to the employee's date of death, but in large groups, uncertainty about the group total is small. In addition, the present value of the retirement benefit stream is *nominal* dollar liability. The investment strategy should be one which guarantees that employees will receive their known nominal dollar retirement benefits.

The optimal asset allocation is obvious. The security portfolio should be nominally risk-free. It should consist of default and call-free bonds having an average duration equal to the duration of the retirement benefits. Ideally, it would be a cash-dedicated portfolio in which future cash inflows exactly match future retirement benefits in both amount and timing.

Strategic Asset Allocation of an Ongoing Plan

If the pension plan is not terminated, the SAA decision is more complex. To date, no conceptual models have been developed which treat all the questions that need to be addressed. One must rely, instead, on common sense. In this section we examine four basic issues:

1. In whose interests should the SAA decision be made—those of the sponsoring firm or those of the pension beneficiaries?

2. Given that we have an answer to the question above, what should be the objective of the SAA, and how should risk be measured?

3. How does the presence of the pension liabilities affect the SAA decision and our concept of a risk-free security?

4. Given that cash inflows and outflows will extend over a long time horizon, to what extent should short-term security price volatility affect the SAA?

In Whose Interests Should the SAA Decision Be Made? There are three parties to any pension plan covered by ERISA: the Pension Benefit Guarantee Corporation, the employee, and the employer. Few people, if any, would argue that the SAA decision should be made in the interests of the PBGC. However, it is much less clear whether employees, as a group, should be allowed to determine the SAA or whether the employer should be allowed full discretion over the SAA.

When Congress enacted ERISA, its intentions were clear. ERISA states that pension investment decisions must be made in the sole interests of pension beneficiaries—employees! In essence, Congress viewed pension plans as financial institutions which are legally independent of the sponsoring firm and which must consider only the interests of pension beneficiaries in setting the SAA. If one were to make SAA decisions based solely on ERISA's stated legal requirements, it is clear that the interests of employees should come first.

A problem with this is that employees might be more risk-averse than shareholders of the sponsoring firm. As a result, employees might select lower-risk asset allocations than shareholders would select. Since investment risk is inversely related to future contributions the sponsor expects to make, an SAA decision made by employees could lead to larger expected contributions than the sponsor would desire.[16]

To obtain full discretion over the SAA of marketable pension assets, the employer could share with employees some of the gains obtained from smaller expected con-

---

[16]Many people believe that employees delegate their rights to make the SAA to the employer because the employer is somehow able to make better decisions. This might be true. The employer is often more familiar with proper decision methodology and financial markets and can speak with one voice. However, it should be noted that most pension sponsors employ pension consultants to aid in their decisions (employees could do so also), and that employers have a potential conflict of interest when they are asked to work for both employees and shareholders of the firm.

tributions in the form of greater pension benefits. In short, if employees are more risk-averse than the employer, employees can obtain greater retirement benefits if the employer is given the right to control the SAA.

If the employer is given complete discretion over pension asset allocation, however, employees do face the possibility of lower retirement benefits, since management might take investment actions which turn out to be harmful to employees. For example, large investments in stocks and bonds of the employer corporation (to create tax shelters, as defenses against corporate takeovers, etc.) are not in the employees' interests. To reduce such risks, employees can insist on an ABO funding ratio of (about) 1.0, the right to review all SAA decisions by having employee representatives on the SAA committee, investment constraints in the pension contract, etc.[17] In practice, employees rarely (if ever) have full control over the SAA of their defined benefit pension plan. Instead, the decision is left solely to the sponsoring firm or a committee composed of employer and employee representatives.

We will assume that the sponsor has been given the right to determine the SAA, either explicitly or implicitly. In addition, we will assume that sufficient controls have been set up to ensure that the sponsor does not take positions in the pension portfolio which aid the sponsor at the expense of the employee.

SAA Objective and Risk Measurement. Earlier in the discussion, the objective of the strategic asset allocation was to maximize the expected dollar value of the investor's wealth at some future portfolio liquidation date. Risk was measured as the variability of potential wealth at the liquidation date. The problem now is somewhat different. The pension sponsor (who, by assumption, determines the SAA) does not own the pension assets but acts as an investing agent for the actual owner—the employee. The employer shares in the value of the portfolio only to the extent that investment returns larger (smaller) than expected result in smaller (larger) than expected employer contributions. In addition, there is no single portfolio liquidation date but, instead, a sequence of many contribution dates which could extend over the remaining life of active employees.

The employer's position in an ongoing pension is best thought of as a sequence of future required contributions to the pension. Thus, the sponsor's SAA objective will be to minimize the level of expected future contributions. Risk is now related to the uncertainty of future contributions.

Given the multiperiod nature of the problem, there are two dimensions to investment risk. The first dimension focuses on *long-run* contribution levels and the second on *short-term* volatility of contributions.

Assume that we are exploring the long-run return/risk characteristics of a given

---

[17]When the employer has discretion over the SAA decision, the employee faces what is called a "principal-agent" moral hazard risk. The employee is the principal who faces the risk that his or her investing agent—the employer—will take actions which are to the employer's advantage but to the employee's harm.

asset mix. A simulation model would probably be used to calculate a sequence of possible yearly contributions for, say, the next 20 years. To assess the long-run contribution rate associated with the asset mix, the 20-year average contribution rate or the contribution rate in a "typical year" could be used. But the results of one simulation of future contributions represent only one of many possible future outcomes. In order to more fully determine the risk/return payoffs of the asset mix, the simulation would be repeated for, say, 100 times. After completing the simulations, the average yearly contribution rate (or the typical year rate) would be examined to determine the probability that the contribution would be greater or lower than a certain rate.

An example of this procedure using the "typical year" approach is shown in Figure 20-12. On the vertical axis, the sponsor's contribution as a percentage of employee pay during 1995 is shown. Five asset mixes are shown on the horizontal axis. For each, various percentile contribution rates are shown. Portfolio 1 is clearly the least risky, since it has the least uncertainty about contribution rates in 1995. But its contribution rate at the 50th percentile is also the largest. In contrast, portfolio 5 is the most risky but has the lowest 50th-percentile contribution rate. Note that the percentile distributions shown in the figure are not symmetric. Much of the value of the risky portfolio comes from the 10% chance that no contribution will be needed in 1995. This will occur if long-term risky portfolio values are skewed to the right.

The second risk dimension occurs only in the multiperiod case and arises from the

FIGURE 20-12 *Range of Contributions as a Percentage of Pay (Projection Period: 1995)*

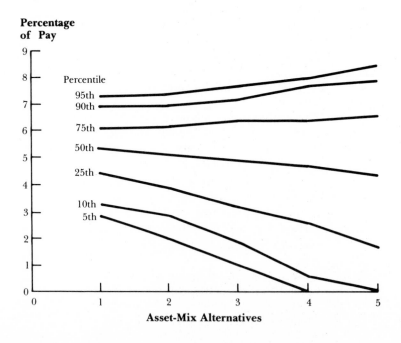

potential volatility in the contribution rate from year to year.[18] Even though the long-run risk inherent in a given portfolio might be acceptable, its potential short-run volatility might not be. Thus, the variability of year-to-year changes in the contribution rate should be examined.

Investment Risk and the Pension Liability. The balance sheet of AmerTech's pension plan (shown in Table 20-13) is summarized below:

	$ Million		$ Million
Marketable Securities	$10.0	PBO Liability	$12.3
Implicit AmerTech		Future Service Liability	6.4
Promissory Notes			
—Past Service	2.3		
—Future Service	6.4		
Total	$18.7	Total	$18.7

The pension plan can be thought of as a financial institution, legally separate from the employer and the employee. It is an escrowed fund which accumulates contributions from the employer to pay a stream of retirement benefits to employees. It can be terminated at the employer's option (through default or asset reversion) or allowed to remain "alive."

If an internal administrator of this plan were to make the SAA in the interests of employees, the administrator would probably consider the extent to which the marketable security portfolio is correlated with returns on the two promissory notes issued to the plan by AmerTech Corp. as well as changes in the PBO and future service liabilities. However, SAA decisions are not usually made solely from the perspective of the employee. Instead, the corporate sponsor is usually given the right to determine the plan's strategic asset allocation. If the corporate sponsor is less risk-averse than employees, the employer would be willing to provide larger employee benefits in return for the right to determine the SAA.

From the viewpoint of the sponsor, the two implicit promissory notes owned by the pension plan wash out. If added to the sponsor's balance sheet they are both a liability and an asset. The only items which would directly transfer to the sponsor's economic balance sheet are the $10.0 million in securities and the $12.3 million PBO liability. We will return to the importance of the implied promissory notes later. For now, however, we will concentrate solely on the relationship between the marketable securities and the PBO liability.

When deciding what the SAA should be, the interrelationship between asset returns and potential changes in the liability must be well understood. For example, AmerTech Corp. shows a projected benefit obligation of $12.3 million. However, this is not the firm's true liability—it is simply the present value of the expected benefit pay-

---

[18]Individual investors also face a similar risk if they intend to make contributions to or withdrawals from the portfolio over time.

ments discounted at the current risk-free long-term interest rate. *The true liability is the sequence of future benefit payments—which are unknown today.*

It is better to think of the liability as an unknown future cash outflow than as an estimated present value. When we focus on the true future liability, our concept of what a risk-free security consists of changes. For example, Treasury bills are often said to be risk-free. But in the context of a long-term, unknown pension benefit stream, T-bills are not risk-free. They guarantee a return over the life of one T-bill, but not over the course of 20 or more years. How about Treasury bonds? Would they represent a risk-free security when placed into an ongoing pension fund? No. Although they might promise to pay a long-run known rate of interest, their returns are not related to changes in the future stream of benefit payments. If Treasury bonds (or any long-term bonds) are bought, the contributions required by a sponsor to eventually meet all future benefit payments are uncertain. Although Treasury bills and Treasury bonds promise known rates of return, they are not risk-free assets in the context of an ongoing pension plan.

A risk-free security to the sponsor of a pension plan is one whose payoffs are perfectly correlated with changes in future benefit payments. If benefit payments increase as a result of unanticipated inflation, cash flows from the risk-free security should increase equally. If benefit payments increase as a result of unanticipated improvements in worker productivity, cash flows from the risk-free security should increase equally. In short, a risk-free security to the sponsor of a pension plan is one which perfectly hedges the risks inherent in the benefit payment stream.

As implied above, two forces are the major cause of uncertain benefit payments— inflation and worker productivity. For an ongoing plan, a perfectly risk-free position does not exist, since no securities are available which perfectly hedge against unanticipated changes in worker productivity and inflation. Yet assets such as common stocks and real estate equity provide a better hedge against such forces than Treasury bills or Treasury bonds.

Finally, if the sponsor's objective is to minimize future contributions subject to an acceptable level of uncertainty about contribution levels, the following data are necessary:

Asset Investment Return Data

1. Expected returns on each asset class
2. Standard deviations of asset class returns
3. Correlation coefficients between asset class returns

Benefit Payment Liability Data

4. Expected level of benefit payments (by year)
5. Standard deviation of benefit payments (by year)
6. Correlation coefficients between asset class returns and changes in benefit payments

The first three variables are traditional inputs to portfolio selection. The last three are needed when assets are integrated with liabilities—when the goal is to manage contribution levels instead of investment payoffs alone.

Other Hedges. Risks other than pension liability risks might also be considered when an SAA decision is being made.

From the employer's perspective, the pension plan holds two shadow assets in the form of implicit promissory notes issued by the sponsoring firm. In the case of the AmerTech pension plan, one note worth $2.3 million is a promise to pay for past employee service, and another note worth $6.4 million is a promise to pay for future service. When these are considered to be pension assets, about 46% of all plan assets are tied to securities issued by the sponsor—that is, the plan is heavily tied to the risks of the sponsor. To reduce their risk exposure, employees should insist that hedges be taken in the types of securities held in the pension's marketable security portfolio. At the least, securities with economic risks similar to those of the sponsoring firm should be underweighted.

A similar story can be told from the employer's perspective. The sponsor would also wish to underweight securities which have economic risks similar to those of the firm. Ideally, the value of pension assets would be inversely correlated with cash flows from the firm's operations. If this were possible, large (small) contributions would be made in years in which cash flows from operations are high (low). Realistically, perfect inverse relationships are not possible, but economic risks similar to those faced by the sponsoring firm can, at least, be underweighted in pension assets.

SUMMARY

The strategic asset allocation decision is the most important investment decision the investor must make. In this chapter, we have examined two ways in which alternative asset allocations could be evaluated.

The first approach focuses on asset investment payoffs at a single future date. Estimates of expected returns, return standard deviations, and return correlations for various asset classes are developed under the assumption that security markets are fairly priced. A computer model is then used to identify a frontier of efficient portfolios—various combinations of the asset classes which have the least risk for any level of feasible expected return. Typically the returns used in this analysis are expressed as annualized values. If the date at which the investor expects to liquidate the portfolio is longer than one year, the annualized data are extrapolated to an appropriate number of years.

The second approach focuses on the investor's future wealth. If no other assets are owned and if the investor has no liabilities, the two approaches are identical. This, of course, will rarely occur. Virtually all individuals and organizations have assets and liabilities to consider beyond those of the security portfolio. Thus, an analysis which focuses on investor wealth must include a consideration of the risks and correlations between the security portfolio, non-security assets, and liabilities of the investor.

The asset-allocation decision faced by a defined benefit pension plan illustrates the complex nature of the decision. If the pension is not terminated, future benefit payments (which are tied to employee productivity and inflation) are uncertain. Thus, there is no truly risk-free security. And securities such as equities and real estate are less risky than usually perceived, whereas T-bills and long-term bonds are more risky than usually perceived. To date, an asset-allocation model which quantitatively integrates all of the forces faced by pension plans has not been developed.

REVIEW PROBLEM

Microfix Corp. is a small firm founded in 1975 to design, produce, and market hardware for microcomputers. The firm has 50 employees who are participants in the firm's defined benefit pension plan. The average employee has worked for the firm for 10 years and earns a salary of $25,000. The average employee is expected to remain with the firm until retirement 20 years from now. Once in retirement, employees will draw pension benefits until death, say, 20 years after retirement equal to 1½ times the number of years of active service times their final salary. Salaries are expected to grow at a compound rate of 6% per year. All current employees are vested, and there are no retired or terminated employees with vested benefits.

Pension assets have a market value of $1.0 million and are expected to earn a long-run return of 12% per year. The current settlement discount rate is 5%.

a. What is the yearly retirement benefit which each employee
   — has a legal right to, based on current salary?
   — is projected to receive, based on past service and projected salary at retirement?

b. What are the ABO and the PBO of the plan?

c. What is the present value of the total plan liability to current employees if the plan is never terminated?

d. Show the pension plan's current balance sheet assuming that it is an ongoing plan. (Hint: Review Table 20-13.)

e. Estimate the pension expense for next year.

f. Assuming that the plan is ongoing, why are Treasury bills not a risk-free security to this pension plan?

g. Assuming that the plan is ongoing, why are Treasury bonds not a risk-free security to this pension plan?

h. Why would employees be unhappy if the management of Microfix Corp. were to announce that the current plan is to be terminated in order to return excess assets to the firm, but that a new plan with identical terms will be created?

Solution

a. Based on current salary:

$$(\$25,000)(0.015)(10) = \$3,750$$
$$(\$25,000)(1.06^{20})(0.015)(10) = \$12,027$$

b.

	ABO	*PBO*
Benefit per Employee	$ 3,750	$ 12,027
Number of Employees	50	50
Total Yearly Annuity	$ 187,500	$ 601,350
20-Year Annuity Factor at 5%	12.4622	12.4622
Liability at End of Year 20	$2,336,662	$7,494,144
20-Year Present-Value Factor	0.3769	0.3769
Present Value of Liability	$ 880,688	$2,824,543

c. TPO = ($25,000)$(1.06^{20})$(0.015)(50)(10 + 20)(12.4622)(0.3769)

   = $8,473,458

d.

Marketable Securities	$1,000,000	ABO	$ 880,688
Present Value of Future Contributions		Implicit Contract	1,943,855
— Past Service	1,824,543		
— Future Service	5,648,915	PBO	2,824,543
		Future Service	5,648,915
		Surplus	0
Total	$8,473,458	Total	$8,473,458

e. Interest on PBO (0.05)($2,824,543)   = $141,227

   Expected Asset Return (0.12)($1,000,000) = −120,000

   Amortization of Unfunded Liability

   ($1,824,543/20)   91,227

   Pension Expense $112,454

f. T-bills promise a short-term known return. The long-term return, however, is unknown.

g. Treasury bonds provide a known nominal long-term return. But such returns are not indexed to uncertain worker productivity and inflation.

h. Employees would lose the $1,943,855 value in the PBO which is not in the ABO. The difference arises because current years of service are credited against an employee's final salary in the PBO. If the plan is terminated, current years of service are credited only against the current salary.

QUESTIONS AND PROBLEMS

1. In the chapter, two broad approaches for determining a strategic asset allocation were presented. How do they differ and what are their advantages and disadvantages?

2. The capital asset pricing model and arbitrage pricing theory are two conceptual approaches to defining risk and determining how securities are priced. Discuss the implications each has on the SAA decision.

3. One approach to determining the SAA for an individual (or an organization such as a pension plan) begins by estimating an efficient frontier of expected returns and risks on various classes of securities.

   a. What inputs are needed to do this?

   b. How might you develop such inputs?

   c. Why might such "efficient portfolios" not be the best for an individual or organization such as a pension fund?

4. "Thou shalt diversify!" Explain why.

5. "Thou shalt diversify investments in marketable securities—but not totally!" Explain why.

6. What is the difference between a defined contribution and a defined benefit pension plan? What are the implications on who should decide on the strategic asset allocation of the investment portfolio?

7. The strategic asset allocation decision should not focus on the risks and returns inherent in the marketable security portfolio. Instead, it should focus on the investor's net worth. What does this mean? Provide an example of why a focus on investor wealth might lead to better SAA decisions.

8. Florox Corp. is a medium-size producer of chemical products. The firm has 100 retired employees who will receive $1.0 million in retirement benefits next year. These benefits are not indexed to changes in the cost of living. For simplicity, assume that benefit payments to retired workers will extend for another 20 years. There are no terminated employees with vested benefits.

   Information about active employees is shown below. Their pension contract does not require that the sponsor provide cost-of-living adjustments to benefits in retirement.

	Nonvested	Vested
Total Employees	100	100
Years of Service	5	10
Years of Retirement	20	20
Current Salary (per employee)	$20,000	$25,000
Assumed Salary Growth		
—Productivity	1.9	1.9
—Inflation	3.0%	3.0%
Compound Total	5.0%	5.0%
Expected Years in Retirement	20	20

The current yield to maturity on long-term default and call-free bonds is 6.0%.

   a. Calculate the ABO.
   b. Calculate the PBO.
   c. How much money would be required to terminate the pension plan today?
   d. If the sponsor does terminate the plan today, what is the present value loss to employees?
   e. Assume that the market value of assets in the plan is identical to the accrued benefit obligation and that management has no intention of terminating the plan. Prepare the ongoing pension plan's current balance sheet analogous to the one in Table 20-13. Discuss what the "shadow assets" represent.

9. The chapter presented three theories which attempt to explain what the optimal funding ratio should be in an ongoing pension. Explain the rationale of each.

10. Why would employees allow the employer to decide the SAA of pension securities?

11. Indexed equity portfolios have been available to pension funds for about 20 years. In recent years, however, specialty index funds have been created which underweight portfolio holdings in economic sectors in which the sponsoring firm does business.

     a. Explain the rationale for such specialty index funds.

     b. What problems do you see in its implementation?

12. When FAS 87 was implemented, many sponsors of defined benefit pension plans had a pension surplus—the market value of assets was greater than the pension's existing ABO. Many investment consultants suggested that, to protect such surplus assets against changes in the ABO due to interest rate shifts, the duration of assets should be set equal to the duration of the ABO liability. Thus, if interest rates fell, for example, the market value of assets would increase by the same dollar amount as the increase in the ABO—the surplus would be maintained. Comment on the logic of this approach for an ongoing pension plan.

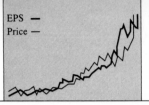
EPS —
Price —

CHAPTER

21 Tactical Asset Allocation

The strategic asset allocation (SAA), based as it is on the investor's expectations of long-term risks and returns associated with various asset classes, will be the portfolio which, on average, should be held. However, short-term investment expectations may occasionally be different from expectations about the long term. If so, the actual portfolio which is held should be different from the SAA. Such temporary changes in the portfolio's composition are commonly referred to as tactical asset allocation (TAA).

The conceptual difference between SAA and TAA is illustrated in Figure 21-1. Two efficient frontiers are shown in the figure. One is based on risks and returns expected on three asset classes over the long run. Together with the investor's risk tolerance, it is used to identify an SAA—in this case, portfolio *P*, which consists of 40% in T-bills, 10% in bonds, and 50% in stocks. The other efficient frontier is based on short-term expectations. As displayed in the figure, short-term expected returns on high-risk securities are considerably lower than long-run expectations. Thus, the optimal portfolio called for by the tactical asset allocation decision is portfolio *P**, which consists of a temporary underweighting of stocks and overweighting of T-bills.

For tactical asset allocation strategies to work, one must be able to distinguish between long-run versus short-term risks and expected rewards on various asset classes. That is, one must be able to correctly *time* the purchase and sale of aggregate asset classes.

There are many ways of defining an asset class and even more ways to evaluate whether the class should be over- or underweighted relative to the strategic asset allocation. In the United States, speculators have traditionally timed between stocks and T-bills (known as market timing) or long-term bonds and T-bills (interest rate timing). Recently, however, TAA decisions have been expanded to include real estate, international equities, positions in individual countries, foreign currency, etc.

In this chapter we will explore two areas of tactical asset allocation: aggregate equity market timing and industry timing. The techniques discussed are based largely on fundamental analysis.

FIGURE 21-1 *SAA Versus TAA*

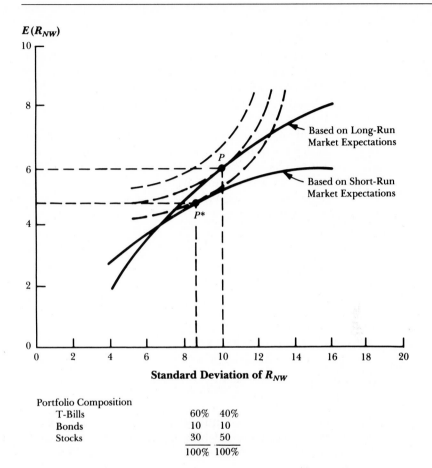

Portfolio Composition

T-Bills	60%	40%
Bonds	10	10
Stocks	30	50
	100%	100%

EQUITY MARKET VALUATION

The decision to overweight or underweight the portfolio investment in domestic equities can be made by answering any of the following three questions:

1. Given my expectations of long-run dividends and required rate of return on domestic equities, *is the current level of aggregate stock prices correct?*

2. Given my expectations of long-run dividends and the current level of aggregate stock prices, *is the return from investing in stocks equal to the return I require?*

3. Given my required rate of return and the current level of aggregate stock prices, *is the implied growth rate of dividends equal to my expectations of future dividend growth?*

In each case, two variables are specified and the third variable is calculated. These three questions are simply different ways to view the same issue.

To determine whether aggregate equity markets are currently priced according to long-run return and risk expectations, one has to use a stock index as a proxy of aggregate stock prices. Throughout our examples we will use the S&P 500 Index as this proxy. In truth, the S&P 500 reflects the values of large, mature U.S. corporations. It might not always capture the value of smaller firms traded on listed exchanges or in the OTC market. Nonetheless, it is a widely used index on which considerable past data are available.

The value of any financial asset (or index) should be the present value of expected future cash flows discounted at an appropriate risk-adjusted discount rate. Thus, we must answer two basic questions if we wish to assess the economic worth of the asset: (1) What do we expect future dividends to be? (2) What is an appropriate discount rate? Since we can never answer either question with absolute certainty, it is wise to use a variety of approaches.

Expected Dividend Growth

Three approaches are commonly used to estimate future dividend growth on stock indexes such as the S&P 500:

1. Historical growth
2. Sustainable internal growth
3. Long-run growth of the total economy

Calculating Historical Growth Rates. In Table 21-1, the nominal and real dividends on the S&P 500 Index are shown for the period 1926–1988. Real dividends are stated in 1988 dollars. For example, the nominal dividend of $0.69 in 1926 is the equivalent of $4.76 in 1988.

Two approaches can be used to calculate a historical *compound annual growth rate* (*CAGR*). The easier approach simply finds the annual rate of growth associated with a beginning value and a terminal value. For example, the *CAGR* associated with the nominal dividend of $0.69 in 1926 and $10.25 62 years later is 4.45%:

$$\$0.69 \ (1 + CAGR)^{62} = \$10.25$$

$$CAGR = (\$10.25/\$0.69)^{1/62} - 1.0$$

$$= 0.04448$$

The problem with this approach is that it neglects all values between the beginning and terminal values. This can be overcome by using a *CAGR* calculated from a *log-least-squares regression analysis*. In this case, the log-natural of yearly dividends per share (*DPS*) is calculated and regressed against a year identifier as follows:

TABLE 21-1 *Historical Dividends on the S&P 500 Index*

	Nominal		Real			Nominal		Real	
Year	DPS	ln(DPS)	DPS	ln(DPS)	Year	DPS	ln(DPS)	DPS	ln(DPS)
1926	0.69	−0.37	4.76	1.56	1958	1.75	0.56	7.28	1.99
1927	0.77	−0.26	5.42	1.69	1959	1.83	0.60	7.50	2.01
1928	0.85	−0.16	6.04	1.80	1960	1.95	0.67	7.87	2.06
1929	0.97	−0.03	6.88	1.93	1961	2.02	0.70	8.10	2.09
1930	0.98	−0.02	7.40	2.00	1962	2.13	0.76	8.44	2.13
1931	0.82	−0.20	6.84	1.92	1963	2.28	0.82	8.89	2.18
1932	0.50	−0.69	4.65	1.54	1964	2.50	0.92	9.63	2.26
1933	0.44	−0.82	4.07	1.40	1965	2.72	1.00	10.28	2.33
1934	0.45	−0.80	4.08	1.41	1966	2.87	1.05	10.49	2.35
1935	0.47	−0.76	4.14	1.42	1967	2.92	1.07	10.36	2.34
1936	0.72	−0.33	6.26	1.83	1968	3.07	1.12	10.40	2.34
1937	0.80	−0.22	6.75	1.91	1969	3.16	1.15	10.09	2.31
1938	0.51	−0.67	4.43	1.49	1970	3.14	1.14	9.51	2.25
1939	0.62	−0.48	5.41	1.69	1971	3.07	1.12	8.99	2.20
1940	0.67	−0.40	5.79	1.76	1972	3.15	1.15	8.92	2.19
1941	0.71	−0.34	5.59	1.72	1973	3.38	1.22	8.80	2.17
1942	0.59	−0.53	4.25	1.45	1974	3.60	1.28	8.36	2.12
1943	0.61	−0.49	4.26	1.45	1975	3.68	1.30	7.98	2.08
1944	0.64	−0.45	4.37	1.48	1976	4.05	1.40	8.38	2.13
1945	0.66	−0.42	4.41	1.48	1977	4.67	1.54	9.05	2.20
1946	0.71	−0.34	4.02	1.39	1978	5.07	1.62	9.01	2.20
1947	0.84	−0.17	4.36	1.47	1979	5.65	1.73	8.86	2.18
1948	0.93	−0.07	4.70	1.55	1980	6.16	1.82	8.60	2.15
1949	1.14	0.13	5.81	1.76	1981	6.63	1.89	8.49	2.14
1950	1.47	0.39	7.08	1.96	1982	6.87	1.93	8.47	2.14
1951	1.41	0.34	6.41	1.86	1983	7.09	1.96	8.42	2.13
1952	1.41	0.34	6.36	1.85	1984	7.53	2.02	8.60	2.15
1953	1.45	0.37	6.50	1.87	1985	7.90	2.07	8.69	2.16
1954	1.54	0.43	6.93	1.94	1986	8.28	2.11	9.01	2.20
1955	1.64	0.49	7.36	2.00	1987	8.81	2.18	9.20	2.22
1956	1.74	0.55	7.59	2.03	1988	10.25(E)	2.33	10.25(E)	2.33
1957	1.79	0.58	7.58	2.03					

E = estimated in early 1989.

Log-Least-Squares CAGR

$$\ln(DPS_t) = a + b \ (\text{Year}_t) + e_t \tag{21.1}$$

Here $\ln(DPS_t)$ is the random dependent variable (the natural log of dividends per share in year t) and Year_t could be 1926, 1927, . . . , 1988 or 1, 2, . . . , 62. As long as successive values of Year are incremented by 1.0, the absolute scale of Year affects only the constant term a, a term which is unimportant. The e_t values are random error terms.

In Figure 21-2, the natural logs of nominal and real S&P 500 dividends are plotted on the vertical axis, and each year is plotted on the horizontal axis. The slope of regression equation 21.1 is shown by the solid line. The slope of this line represents the *CAGR based on the log–least-squares methodology* and the *b* coefficient in the following regression equations:

Nominal CAGR of S&P 500 Dividends (1926–1988)

$$\ln(DPS_t) = -91.7791 + 0.047197 \,(\text{Year}_t) \qquad R^2 = 91.9\%$$

Real CAGR of S&P 500 Dividends (1926–1988)

$$\ln(\text{Real } DPS_t) = -22.4206 + 0.012449 \,(\text{Year}_t) \qquad R^2 = 59.9\%$$

Consider the nominal dividend regression output. The constant term of -91.7791 represents the log-natural of dividends when the year number is equal to 0. In a regression of this sort, the term is meaningless and no attention is paid to it. The more important regression term is the slope coefficient *b*. This slope term represents the unit change in log-natural of dividends for each 1.0 unit change in time—one year. *Because one full unit change in the log-natural of dividends is 100%*, the 0.047197 value is interpreted as an average compound annual growth rate of 4.7197%. The R^2 term is the percentage of variation in log-natural dividends associated with variation in time. *R*-squared can range from 0% to 100%, where 0% indicates no relationship be-

FIGURE 21-2 *Log–Least-Squares Growth of S&P 500 Dividends*

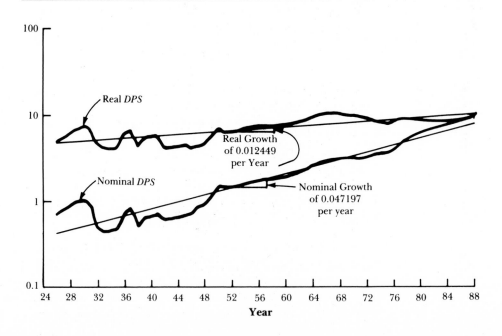

TABLE 21-2 *Log–Least-Squares Compound Annual Growth Rates of S&P 500 Dividends*

Period	Nominal		Real	
	CAGR	R^2	CAGR	R^2
1926–1988	4.72%	91.9%	1.24%	59.9%
1926–1945	−1.23	93.2	−1.34	15.2
1946–1988	5.39	97.72	1.24	49.3
1971–1988	7.17	98.4	0.37	13.8

tween the two regression variables and 100% indicates perfect correlation. *R*-squared is simply the correlation coefficient squared.

In Table 21-2, *CAGR*s based on log–least-squares regressions are shown for a variety of periods. Except in the 1920s and early 1930s, nominal growth in S&P 500 dividends has been relatively stable, certainly more stable than real dividend growth. Over the full 62-year period, nominal dividend growth was 4.72% per year. However, in the post–World War II era, dividend growth has averaged between 5 and 7%, depending on the time period chosen.

Sustainable Internal Growth. If the return on equity (*ROE*) and dividend retention rates (*B*) are constant in the future, then internal corporate growth can sustain a growth rate in dividends (*G*) equal to:[1]

$$G = ROE \times B \qquad (21.2)$$

For example, if you believe that the S&P 500 Index will have a long-run *ROE* of, say, 12% and a dividend retention rate of 55%, this implies that future dividend growth will be 6.6%:

$$12\% \times 0.55 = 6.6\%$$

Returns on equity and retention rates could be estimated using historical averages. For example, Table 21-3 provides data on the reported *ROE* and profit-retention rates of firms in the S&P 500 between 1946 and 1988. There are at least two related problems in using past data, though. First, the past is not necessarily a good predictor of the future. As can be seen, growth estimates varied widely, depending on the time span chosen. Unpredictable events such as unexpected inflation, natural disasters, and wars can have significant effects upon any one year's results. Probably more important is the implicit assumption that equity returns and retention rates are related and that growth rates for the average firm are determined by $B \times ROE$. The assumption is that corporations can increase dividend growth rates simply by retaining larger amounts of profits. Given an *ROE* of 15%, growth will be 10% if two thirds of profits are retained and 7.5% if one half of profits are retained. This implies that ag-

---

[1]The concept of sustainable internal growth is discussed at more length in Chapters 13 and 22.

TABLE 21-3 *S&P Sustainable Growth Estimates Based on Past Data*

Year	ROE	Retention Rate	Sustainable Growth
1946	8.22%	28.26%	2.32%
1947	12.73	48.43	6.16
1948	16.04	60.94	9.77
1949	15.95	52.89	8.44
1950	17.47	47.78	8.35
1951	13.67	43.14	5.89
1952	12.21	41.46	5.06
1953	12.48	43.24	5.39
1954	13.08	45.67	5.98
1955	15.07	55.56	8.37
1956	13.40	49.58	6.64
1957	11.89	47.43	5.64
1958	9.62	39.32	3.78
1959	10.94	46.18	5.05
1960	10.05	41.00	4.12
1961	9.67	38.28	3.70
1962	10.64	43.15	4.59
1963	11.11	43.87	4.87
1964	12.01	46.17	5.54
1965	12.67	48.28	6.11
1966	12.92	49.41	6.38
1967	11.85	46.82	5.55
1968	12.25	48.29	5.92
1969	11.93	47.00	5.61
1970	10.31	40.33	4.16
1971	10.89	47.18	5.14
1972	11.71	52.86	6.19
1973	14.10	60.72	8.56
1974	14.29	61.61	8.80
1975	12.07	55.79	6.73
1976	14.00	60.21	8.43
1977	14.07	57.13	8.04
1978	14.62	59.22	8.66
1979	16.42	63.11	10.36
1980	14.89	59.39	8.85
1981	14.38	58.08	8.35
1982	11.14	45.65	5.08
1983	12.04	49.97	6.02
1984	14.58	58.68	8.56
1985	12.14	49.35	5.99
1986	11.57	43.51	5.03
1987	16.23	57.22	9.29
1988	NA	61.97	NA

gregate dividend growth is determined solely by management—that it is not *constrained by economic opportunities.*

Over lengthy periods of time this simply isn't true. The growth of corporate profits and dividends is constrained by the growth in aggregate economic activity. It is difficult to envision a situation in which for long periods of time dividends grow more rapidly than the GNP. As a result, a better approach to estimating profit and dividend growth may be to start with a long-run estimate of aggregate economic growth and back into likely dividend growth.

Long-Run Economic Growth. To use the long-run economic growth approach to valuation:

1. Estimate expected long-run *real* growth in GNP together with optimistic and pessimistic ranges.
2. Estimate the relationship which is likely to exist between *real* dividend growth and real GNP growth and use this to estimate dividend growth rates and ranges.
3. Estimate long-run rates of *inflation* and their impacts on nominal dividend growth rates.
4. Estimate reasonable required rates of return and ranges.
5. Estimate market values.

Figure 21-3 plots real levels of GNP, S&P 500 earnings per share (*EPS*), and S&P 500 dividends per share (*DPS*) from 1946 to 1987. (Values are reported in constant 1988 dollars.) During this time span, real GNP exhibited some volatility caused by

FIGURE 21-3 *Real GNP, EPS, and DPS*

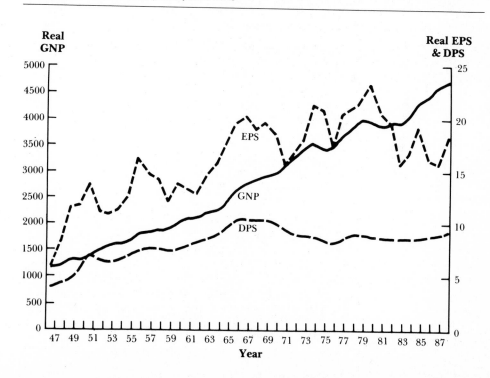

various business cycles, but its long-run growth rate was reasonably stable and equal to a compound annual growth rate of 3.4%. This compares favorably with estimates made by Denison of 3.33% between 1929 and 1969 and 3.85% between 1948 and 1969. Based simply on these results, one would expect future real GNP growth to be between 3 and 4%. However, since a 3% growth versus a 4% growth can result in substantially different values for the S&P 500 Index, one should attempt to make an explicit forecast of future real growth. Table 21-4 provides just such a forecast based on Denison's approach to determining real economic growth. Legitimate arguments could, of course, be raised about each of the forecast values, but they are designed

TABLE 21-4 *Estimates of Real Economic Growth*

		Pessimistic	Expected	Optimistic
I.	*Factor Inputs*			
	A. Employment Population growth rates will slow down and proportion of the retired population will increase.	0.95%	1.0 %	1.15%
	B. Hours Hours worked will continue a slight decline as people continue to move out of the farm sector into the nonfarm sector. Slight changes will be caused by unionization, increased standard of living, smaller families, and leisure alternatives.	−0.22	−0.21	−0.20
	C. Age/Sex Composition Historical negative effects were caused mainly by the movement of women into teaching areas. A reversal is forecast as they gain increased responsibility within the business sector.	0.00	0.10	0.13
	D. Education Major advantages of increased worker education have probably been seen in the past 50 years. However, as better-trained women and minorities enter the work force, education will continue to play a positive role.	0.30	0.35	0.40
	E. Other Use 1929–1969 average.	0.09	0.09	0.09
	Total Labor	1.12%	1.33%	1.57%
	F. Total Capital Major increases in capital will occur as the United States retools to meet international competition and growth in postwar household formations.	0.70	0.90	1.00
	Total Factor Input	1.82%	2.23%	2.57%

TABLE 21-4 *(continued)*

	Pessimistic	Expected	Optimistic
II. Output Per Unit of Input			
A. Advances in Knowledge	1.00%	1.20%	1.30%
Not only is this a difficult factor to measure, it seems to be one of the more volatile. There does not seem to be any significant slowdown in scientific knowledge, but, instead, major discoveries in organic chemistry, microcircuitry, power generation, etc.			
B. Improved Resource Allocation	0.20	0.25	0.30
This is another difficult factor to forecast. A major pro is the development of international human and natural resources, and a major con is the depletion of scarce resources.			
C. Economies of Scale	0.35	0.35	0.35
Historical value for 1929–1969			
D. Other	−0.05	−0.05	−0.05
Historical value for 1929–1969			
Total	1.50%	1.75%	1.90%
Total Annual Growth in GNP	3.32%	3.98%	4.47%

to illustrate the types of factors which should be considered. The three real GNP growth rates are:

	Future Compound Annual Growth Real GNP
Pessimistic	3.32%
Expected	3.98%
Optimistic	4.47%

Projected real GNP levels are shown in Figure 21-3 as the dashed lines.

We turn now to dividend growth. While real GNP grew at a compound annual rate of 3.4% from 1946 to 1987, real growth in dividends per share grew only 1.24% per year. Obviously, in order to determine whether the past will be repeated, we need to know why this happened. Two basic forces were at work. First, profit-retention rates were much higher in the 1970s and early 1980s than they had historically been. Second, real earnings per share grew at a less rapid rate (1.71% per year) than real GNP.

A number of reasons have been offered to explain the increased retention rates and lower profit growth of the 1970s and early 1980s. First, as inflation ran into double digits, effective personal tax rates rose and personal tax management became more important. Recognizing this, corporate managements began to retain larger portions of profits so that investors could take their profits by selling shares and thus pay capital gains taxes, as opposed to taking profits in the form of cash dividends and paying the higher ordinary tax rates. Second, inflation affected the real earnings of corporations also. The data displayed in Figure 21-3 do not truly reflect the *economic* earnings per share of the S&P 500. The earnings series shown is simply the reported accounting earnings per share adjusted for changes in the Consumer Price Index during the year. Unfortunately, accounting earnings can be seriously overstated during periods of rapid inflation. For example, generally accepted accounting principles required that depreciation charges be based on historical cost even though current replacement costs were substantially larger. The same was true for inventories. Cost of goods sold was based on historical inventory cost even though inventory replacement costs were larger. The artificially high earnings figures increased the effective corporate tax rate and required that management retain larger portions of reported profits simply to replace existing fixed assets and inventories. Another force which has kept the S&P 500 earnings growth lower than GNP growth is increased competition, both by smaller domestic firms and by international firms attempting to enter the major markets covered by the S&P 500 firms.

What the future holds is difficult to foresee. Although we may have reasonable confidence in our estimates of real GNP growth, when we move to S&P earnings and dividends the uncertainty expands. The major depressant on earnings growth seems to have been inflation, but a growing number of analysts believe that firms have begun to learn how to handle inflation and that corporate profits are likely to be much less affected by future inflation. In sympathy with this view, we will forecast future S&P 500 earnings growth to be only slightly less than real GNP growth:

	Future Compound Annual Growth	
	Real Earnings	*Real GNP*
Pessimistic	3.00%	3.32%
Expected	3.50	3.98
Optimistic	4.00	4.47

Finally, we turn to a dividend growth forecast. Between 1946 and 1988 real earnings of the S&P 500 grew at a *CAGR* of 1.71%, but dividends grew at a rate of only 1.24%. Applying this 1.24/1.71 relationship to the real earnings forecasts above, we obtain the following growth rates for real dividends:

	Future Real CAGR		
	Dividends	*Earnings*	*GNP*
Pessimistic	2.17%	3.00%	3.32%
Expected	2.54	3.50	3.98
Optimistic	2.90	4.00	4.47

The translation from real growth to nominal growth can require a complex analysis. However, consider the following approach. As of December 1988, long-term Treasury bonds were selling to yield 9.0% to maturity. Assuming investors desire a

3.0% real return and assuming zero liquidity premiums, this implies a long-run expected inflation rate of about 6% per year. By adding this 6% inflation rate to each of the real growth rates, we obtain nominal growth rates:

	Future Nominal Dividend Growth		
	Real	*Inflation*	*Nominal*
Pessimistic	2.17%	+6.0%	8.17%
Expected	2.54	+6.0	8.54
Optimistic	2.90	+6.0	8.90

Selecting an Appropriate Discount Rate

The discount rate reflects the return the investor requires in order to accept the investment risks of the security. We have seen in previous chapters that the standard deviation of yearly returns on the S&P 500 depends on the time period examined, but has generally been between 15% and 20%. The *average* return earned for bearing risk, however, is much more volatile. For example, 20-year average annual outcomes have ranged between 1.0% to 12%, and over the 1926–1988 period the S&P 500 Index had a real return about 8.5% greater than that of Treasury bills and Treasury bonds. We have also seen in Chapter 10 that there is growing empirical evidence suggesting that investor risk premiums vary as economic conditions change.

Perhaps the best strategy is to use a variety of risk premiums which appear to be reasonable in light of past returns and current conditions. In December 1988, the risk-free return on long-term bonds was 9.0%. Applying risk premiums of 4% to 7% results in discount rates ranging from 13% to 16%.

Valuation of the S&P 500 at Year-End 1988. The value of any stock or stock index should be the present value of expected future dividends, as shown in Equation 21.3:

Dividend Valuation Model

$$P_0 = \sum_{t=1}^{D} D_t / (1 + K)^t \tag{21.3}$$

D_t is our expected dividend in year t, K is the required return, and P_0 is the present value of expected future dividends (our estimate of the security's fair value).

If dividends are expected to grow at a constant annual rate of G, Equation 21.3 can be simplified as follows:

Constant Dividend Growth Model

$$P_0 = \frac{D_0(1 + G)}{K - G} \tag{21.4}$$

For individual stocks, the assumption of constant dividend growth is usually too naive. The dividend growth rates of individual firms go through various stages as the firm goes through various stages of its life cycle. However, for an index of large, mature firms such as the S&P 500, the assumption of constant growth is often reasonable. At the end of 1988, the economy did not appear to be at the peak of a business expansion or at the trough of a recession. Although future dividends would clearly be volatile, the best estimate of future S&P 500 dividend growth was a constant growth. Thus, we use the constant growth model of Equation 21.4.

Early in the chapter, we developed a variety of possible dividend growth rates and a range of possible required returns. Assume that after reviewing these estimates, we decide to use a $G = 6\%$ and a $K = 14.5\%$. At December 31, 1988, the S&P 500 Index closed at $277.72, and total dividends paid during 1988 were $10.25. We can estimate whether S&P 500 short-term returns are likely to be consistent with our long-term expectations in three ways.

First, is the price of $277.72 equal to the present value of expected future dividends? Using the constant growth model and the estimates of G and K, the fair value of the S&P 500 would have been $127.82!

$$\frac{\$10.25(1.06)}{0.145 - 0.06} = \$127.82$$

Clearly this implies that the value of domestic equities was too high and that portfolio commitments to equities should have been underweighted.

Alternatively, we could estimate the long-run return we expect to earn on the S&P 500 if we buy at $277.72 and hold the equities for many years with a dividend growth of 6% per year. Using the constant growth model, the expected long-run return from buying at $277.72 would be 9.91%:

$$K = \frac{D_0(1 + G)}{P_0} + G$$

$$0.0991 = \frac{\$10.25(1.06)}{\$277.72} + 0.06$$

Given a required return of 14.5%, the expected long-run return on the S&P 500 Index would have been inadequate. The tactical asset allocation decision would have called for reduced equity holdings.

Finally, we can calculate the long-run dividend growth rate implicit in prevailing prices. Using the discount rate of 14.5%, this implied growth rate was 10.424%:

$$\frac{\$10.25(1.10424)}{0.145 - 0.10424} = \$277.72$$

Again, the tactical asset allocation decision would have called for reduced equity exposure.

The estimates calculated above can be quite sensitive to input assumptions. Therefore, it is wise to consider the results of a variety of assumptions ranging from pessimistic to optimistic. An example is shown in Table 21-5. In the left column, various nominal dividend growth rates are shown. The most pessimistic rate, 4.5%, is only 20 basis points below the 1926–1988 historical S&P 500 dividend growth rate. The most optimistic rate, 9.0%, is 10 basis points above the optimistic nominal dividend growth rate calculated using the long-run economic forecast approach. The top row

TABLE 21-5 *S&P 500 Fair Values for Various G and K Assumptions*

G Values	K Values				
	12.0%	13.0%	14.0%	15.0%	16.0%
4.5%	142.82	126.01	112.75	102.01	93.14
6.0%	181.08	155.21	135.81	120.72	108.65
7.0%	219.35	182.79	156.68	137.09	121.86
8.0%	276.75	221.40	184.50	158.14	138.38
9.0%	372.42	279.31	223.45	186.21	159.61

$D_0 = \$10.25$
S&P 500 Actual Value = $277.72 (December 31, 1988)

shows various discount rates ranging from 12.0% to 16.0%. Given a 9.0% yield to maturity on U.S. Treasury bonds at the end of 1988, these represent equity risk premiums between 3.0% and 7.0%.

Entries in the matrix represent fair values of the S&P 500 using Equation 21.4. Note that fair values are in excess of $277.72 only at low required returns and optimistic growth rates. For example, even if you required only a 3.0% risk premium ($K = 12.0\%$), you would have to believe that G would be 8.0% or more to calculate a fair value of $277.77 or more.

Relative Value Measures. Two relative value measures are commonly used by practitioners. These are the price-to-earnings (P/E) and price-to-book-value (P/B) ratios. The P/E ratio is the current market price of a stock (or index) divided by last year's or next year's earnings per share. The P/B ratio is the current market price of a stock (or index) divided by last year's book value per share. (Book value per share is equal to total shareholder equity divided by outstanding shares.)

Both ratios are plotted for the S&P 500 in Figure 21-4. At the end of 1988, the P/E ratio was close to its historical average and would have suggested to many practitioners that the S&P 500 was not mispriced. The P/B ratio, however, was at a historical high and would have suggested to other practitioners that the index was overvalued.

Considerable care must be taken in interpreting P/E and P/B ratios. For example, there is no reason to believe that current levels of each will necessarily return to historical averages. The value of the ratios should and does change in response to changes in market consensus estimates of K and G. There is some slight evidence that P/B ratios have a slight predictive power, but no evidence that market P/E ratios can predict future returns.

Changing Market Risk Premiums. Recall from Chapter 10 the discussion of potential stock market overreaction. When actual future dividends are discounted back to previous periods in order to calculate what stock index prices should have been if in-

FIGURE 21-4 *Historical S&P 500 Relative Value Measures*

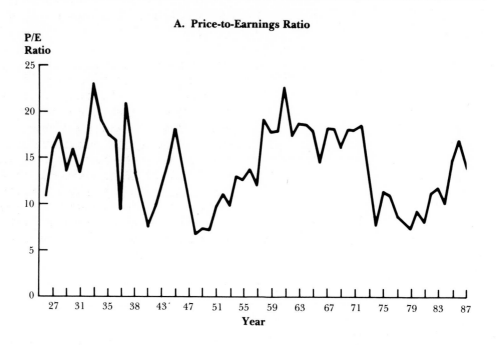

A. Price-to-Earnings Ratio

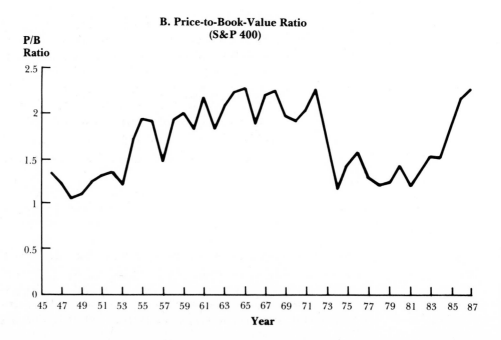

B. Price-to-Book-Value Ratio
(S&P 400)

vestors had been able to correctly forecast future dividends, a relatively stable series of stock prices results. This stable series of prices contrasts dramatically with the large volatility of actual prices. Actual stock prices depart substantially from a rational ex post valuation for *relatively long periods of time*. The results of one study are shown in Figure 21-5. The stable dashed line represents the ex post rational valuation of a stock index. The solid line represents the actual (detrended) index.

The cause of this apparent excess volatility is not fully understood. One possible explanation is that market participants do not price stocks (either implicitly or explicitly) using a long-term dividend valuation model. If this is true, tactical asset allocation decisions based on fundamental dividend models should provide excess returns over the long run. Alternatively, the market could be using a dividend discount approach with highly volatile estimates of G and K. Given the stable increase in past

FIGURE 21-5 *Shiller's Detrended Estimates of Perfect Foresight Stock Index Versus Actual Index (DJIA)*

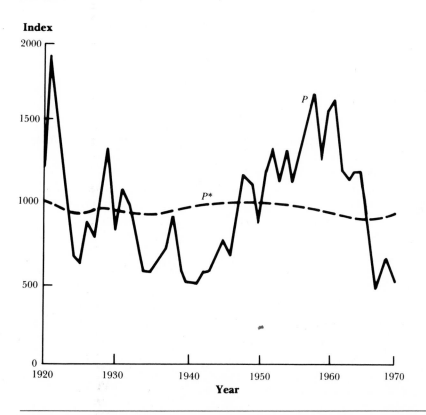

Source: Shiller, R. "Do Stock Prices Move Too Much to Be Justified by Subsequent Changes in Dividend?" *The American Economic Review* 71, no. 3 (June 1981).

nominal dividend growth, many scholars have claimed that variability in K is the cause. According to this view, market participants are constantly changing the risk premium they require on stocks.

If stock price volatility is due to changes in the market's consensus of K, then stock prices are, strictly speaking, always efficiently priced. But even if this view of market efficiency is taken, individuals with more-stable values of K will find periods of time during which stocks should be overweighted or underweighted relative to their SAA. Figure 21-5 suggests, however, that periods of over- and underweighting can last as long as a decade!

Does Tactical Allocation of Equities Work? Most rigorous studies of market timing suggest that the short-term benefits of equity timing decisions are doubtful. Over periods of approximately ten years or less, the quarterly return series of investment managers who time are, on average, no different from those of managers who do not time. However, no studies have examined equity market timing over longer time periods. This is unfortunate, since Figure 21-5 suggests that, if equity timing is to work, it will occur primarily over lengthy periods.

We return to statistical tests of timing in Chapter 23.

INDUSTRY TIMING

Although the variability of aggregate market returns explains a large portion of the variability of individual stock returns, it is also clear that industry effects exist. For example, King's study (discussed in Chapter 13) suggested that between 1952 and 1960 approximately 12% of the variability in a typical stock's returns was associated with industry-wide events. Of course, the relative importance of such an industry factor does vary from industry to industry. For example, King observed that 20% of oil stock variability seemed to be industry related, whereas only 8% of the variability of metal stocks was industry related. Since similar results have been observed by other researchers, most analysts believe that a thorough industry analysis should be an integral part of any fundamental security analysis.

The main purpose of an industry analysis is to become intimately familiar with the history and basic economic forces underlying the industry's past growth so that intelligent forecasts can be made of:

1. Outcomes of *present* problems (and potentials) facing the industry.
2. Identification of possible *future* problems (and potentials) which the industry might encounter.
3. Both short- and long-term growth in assets, sales, profits, and dividends.
4. Economic structure of the industry: Will there be a few large, dominant firms or a large number of smaller firms?
5. The fair value of an industry stock index.
6. Whether the industry should be over-, under- or market-value-weighted in the portfolio.

Table 21-6 illustrates an outline one might follow when performing an industry analysis. Although we will follow this outline in the discussion below, there are any number of other ways to go about it. The keys to any good analysis are really quite simple: (*a*) constantly ask the questions "Why?" and "So what?"; (*b*) be creative; and (*c*) distinguish the important from the trivial.[2]

Defining the Industry

In some cases a clear definition of the industry can be the most critical phase of the analysis. The analyst should be open-minded about the true nature of the product or service being investigated. For example, if you are evaluating commercial banking, the services are potentially much more diverse than simply obtaining funds from demand and time deposits for investment in commercial and installment loans. Instead, the product might be better defined as providing general "financial services." Although the types of funds banks may raise and the areas in which they may invest are legally constrained, these constraints are rapidly disappearing in an attempt to allow increased competition among all forms of financial intermediaries. To a large extent commercial banks want to provide many of the services now provided by savings and loans, insurance companies, security brokers, investment bankers, etc. In the same fashion, each of these institutions wants to offer many of the services now offered by commercial banks. As a result, an analysis of commercial banks should give particular attention to potential regulatory and legal changes which would broaden the services offered by all types of financial institutions.

In a similar vein, should oil companies be viewed strictly as producers and distributors of oil products, or should they be more broadly viewed as energy stocks or even resource stocks? Should IBM be viewed narrowly as a computer manufacturer or more broadly as an information processing and communication firm? We could continue with many other examples, but the point is clear. While profit forecasts for the next few years may not depend on how one decides to classify the industry, longer-run forecasts can be substantially affected. Be aware of what the product or service really is!

Product Life Cycle

Once the nature of the product or service has been defined, many analysts find it helpful to examine historical sales growth in the context of the so-called product life cycle. The concept of a product life cycle, illustrated in Figure 21-6, can be thought of as consisting of three stages:

1. *Introduction and pioneering.* During this stage basic research and development of a new product occurs and the product is initially marketed. Customer demand

---

[2]Easy to say—extremely hard to do.

TABLE 21-6 *Industry Analysis Checklist*

I.   Measure past sales growth
  A. Proper industry definition
       1. Nature of product or service
       2. Source of competition
  B. Product life cycle
       1. Problems inherent in the concept
            a. Need not follow typical pattern
            b. Means little in value determination
       2. Potentials of concept
            a. Capital expenditure needs
            b. Profit margin analysis
            c. Price competition
  C. Calculating growth rates
       1. Compound annual growth rates
       2. Semilog analysis
       3. Explanation of outliers
  D. Relationship with GNP
       1. Lead, lag, coincident
       2. Degree of correlation

II.   Conceptual determinants of sales growth
  A. Shifts in long-run demand-supply curves
       1. Demand curve shifts
            a. Tastes
            b. Income and wealth
            c. Prices of related goods
            d. Size of consumer base
       2. Supply curve shifts (costs)
            a. Labor
            b. Raw material
            c. Technology
            d. Governmental influence
            e. Foreign competition and wealth
            f. Patents
            g. Risk
       3. Elasticity
  B. Adjustment of supply to long-run equilibrium — market saturation analysis
  C. Inflation
  D. Input-output analysis

III. Quantitative determinants of sales growth
  A. Simultaneous solution of demand and supply
  B. Specification of logical model form
  C. Interpretation of regression results
  D. Forecasting with better models
  E. Examination for statistical weaknesses

FIGURE 21-6 *The Product Life Cycle*

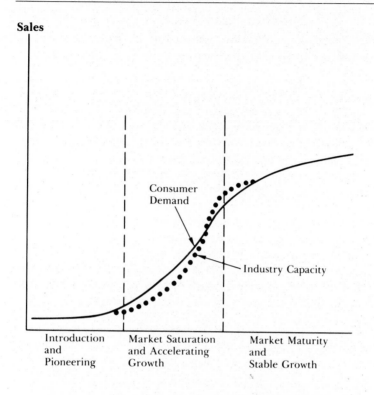

Sales

Consumer
Demand

Industry Capacity

| Introduction and Pioneering | Market Saturation and Accelerating Growth | Market Maturity and Stable Growth |

tends to be small because of uncertainties about the product's reliability and hoped-for technological improvement. Examples would be computers in the 1950s, color television in the late 1950s, TV video machines in the middle 1970s, and satellite communication in the 1980s.

2. *Market saturation and accelerating growth.* During the early part of this stage, a technically viable product is introduced to the market and demand increases dramatically. Often market demand will increase more rapidly than industry capacity and result in not only rapid sales growth but also large profit margins. In turn, a large number of firms are attracted to the industry in hopes of obtaining a share of the market. The color TV market seemed to go through this stage in the early 1960s and the computer industry in the middle 1950s and early 1960s. During the later part of this stage, increased competition can result in excess capacity, extensive price competition, lower profit margins, and numerous business failures. For example, during the late 1960s many of the firms which had entered the computer industry suffered large losses and had to discontinue their computer operations. Much of the sales growth in this stage arises from an increase in market saturation as opposed to growth in the size of the underlying market.

3. *Market maturity and stable growth.* During this phase the potential market is largely saturated—that is, all potential customers have been satisfied. As a result, growth rates decline and future growth comes mainly from either shifts in the demand curve (increased consumer base, changes in customer taste, etc.) or shifts in the supply curve (changes in the industry's cost structure).

Dangers. A number of dangers are associated with applying the product-life-cycle concept to fundamental security selection. For one, there is no reason, of course, to believe that a product's growth rate will actually go through each stage of the cycle. Innumerable products never get beyond the pioneering stage. In addition, the speed with which a product goes through each stage can vary dramatically. For example, the computer industry was probably in a market-saturation stage for more than a decade, whereas the mobile home industry saturated the potential market within four to six years.

Another danger is that some investment advisers may overemphasize growth: "Find a growth stock in stage 2 and you've got a good buy." Although it is true that stocks experiencing accelerating sales growth may also have substantial increases in share prices from year to year, this does not mean that such so-called growth stocks are good buys.[3] For example, assume you develop the following estimates on two stocks. Stock *S* is a stable, mature firm which will likely show only moderate dividend and share price growth. Stock *G*, on the other hand, is experiencing rapid sales and dividend growth rates which are likely to continue for many years. Which stock is the better candidate for purchase?

	Stock G	Stock S
Current Market Price	$44	$10
Last Dividend Per Share	$ 2	$ 2
Required Return	15%	15%
Expected Constant Dividend Growth	10%	3%

This question can be answered by comparing an estimate of each stock's fair value with its current market price. Estimated fair values can be found using the constant dividend growth model as follows:

$$P_G = \frac{\$2(1.10)}{0.15 - 0.10} = \$44.00$$

$$P_S = \frac{\$2(1.03)}{0.15 - 0.03} = \$17.17$$

---

[3]It should be remembered from Chapter 13 that a stock can exhibit great price growth over time for one of two reasons. First, high profit-retention rates have the effect of reducing the portion of return coming in the form of dividends and increasing the portion coming from stock price increases. Second, firms which can earn a higher return on equity investments than shareholders desire will automatically increase share values by increasing the retention rate. This second type of stock is more appropriately referred to as a true growth stock. However, as the text points out, market prices in both cases may be fair. Simply finding a growth stock does not mean one has found a good buy.

Stock *G* appears to be fairly valued even though we expect it to show the greater yearly dividend growth. Stock *S*, however, appears to be a good purchase candidate even though it has low expected dividend growth. Although there is nothing inherently wrong with seeking out so-called growth stocks to add to one's portfolio, this should be done more for tax reasons than out of a belief that growth stocks are usually good buys.

A final danger in using the life-cycle concept is that the analyst may become too enamored with simply describing past growth instead of asking the more critical questions "Why?" and "So what?" For example, if one were to examine the historical sales pattern of the mobile home industry, it would appear that the industry went through a lengthy stage 1 period only to dramatically break out into stage 2 in the early 1960s. An insightful analyst would ask, "Why did the industry's sales rise so rapidly in the early 1960s and not before?" It turns out that the answer is quite simple. Prior to the early 1960s, mobile homes wider than 8 feet or longer than 40 feet could not be moved on the highways. Few people were interested in living in such cramped quarters. However, as various state and federal laws were changed to allow wider and longer vehicles, the industry could begin to build and transfer units which were more acceptable to the public. The fact that mobile home sales rose only after restrictive legislation was changed is important to know because it identifies an area of potential future harm (or aid) to the industry—regulation—which the analyst should examine closely.

Advantages. There are, however, a number of possible benefits to utilizing the life-cycle concept. In particular, it forces one to think explicitly about pricing practices, likely capital expansion, and profit margins by focusing attention on gaps between current levels of market demand and available capacity. If potential demand exceeds available capacity, a situation of excess demand exists which will force selling prices, profit margins, and profits up. This will, in turn, attract new competitors and capital expansion. Typically, a situation of excess demand occurs during the early years of the market-saturation stage. The extent to which stock prices should be affected by the profit increases created by the excess demand depends upon how long it will take before capacity catches up with demand. The longer the period of excess demand and related high profits, the higher stock prices should be. Conversely, if the excess demand is likely to be quickly met by rapid capital expansion, stock prices should be little affected. For example, in the early years of the computer industry's dramatic growth, considerable excess demand existed and led to large profits. Because of the large set-up costs of entering the business, it took a number of years before effective competition eliminated the excess demand. As a result, the price of IBM common stock was heavily influenced by the excess profits earned during the saturation stage. Conversely, initial excess demand in the mobile home industry was rapidly met because of the ease with which new competitors could enter the industry. Whereas entry into the computer industry required uniquely qualified personnel, specialized production facilities, and a product credibility which could take years to establish, entry into the mobile home industry could be achieved almost overnight. All that was needed was a large, flat space for production, a production schedule, and a number of unskilled assembly workers.

Calculating Growth Rates

Historical growth rates of sales, profits, assets, and any other variable which might be important should be calculated. Unfortunately, a number of dangers are associated with calculating past growth rates. Some can be easily overcome; others can't. To avoid problems:

1. Growth rates should be stated on an annual basis. The statement "Sales growth averaged 10% per year between 1975 and 1982" is much easier to interpret than the equivalent statement "Sales were 195% higher in 1982 than in 1975."
2. When comparing the growth rates of two or more variables, a similar time span should be used to measure the growth of each variable.
3. Compound growth rates are more meaningful than simple average growth rates.
4. Growth rates can be very sensitive to the beginning and ending dates chosen. If a major change occurred in the industry at a known point in time, compound annual growth rates should be calculated for both the period before the change and the period after the change. In addition, growth should not be eliminated using beginning and terminal values only. Instead, *CAGR*s using log–least-squares regression should be calculated.
5. If possible, both real and nominal growth rates should be calculated. For example, if sales growth is being analyzed during a period of increasing selling prices, the nominal growth of dollar sales will overstate the real growth of unit sales. Unfortunately, unit selling price data are often not available.
6. A determination of how stable the growth rate was from year to year should be made. Usually, the more volatile the growth rate, the riskier the industry.

In Table 21-7 estimates are shown for historical beer sales. By applying the log–least-squares regression model to find the compound annual growth rate, we find:

$$\ln(\text{Industry Sales}) = -163.78 + 0.0873 \text{ (year)}$$

$$R^2 = 99.05\%$$

During this time period, industry sales grew at a compound annual growth rate of 8.73%. The *R*-squared value of 99.05% indicates that the growth was very stable.

TABLE 21-7 *Estimates of Historical Beer Sales (in millions)*

Year	Sales	Year	Sales	Year	Sales
1969	$3,420	1976	$ 6,020	1982	$11,190
1970	3,820	1977	6,650	1983	11,775
1971	4,140	1978	7,540	1984	12,305
1972	4,050	1979	8,350	1985	13,207
1973	4,340	1980	9,360	1986	14,205
1974	5,050	1981	10,180	1987	15,180
1975	5,640				

Future sales can also be estimated from the regression model. For example, if estimated sales in 1995 were desired, we first would insert "1995" into the model to estimate log-natural sales in 1995 as follows:

$$\ln(\text{Sales in 1995}) = -163.781 + 0.0873 \ (1995)$$

$$= 10.3825$$

Next, we would calculate the antilog of this number. This results in the estimate of 1995 sales:

$$\text{Sales in 1995} = e^{10.3825}$$

$$= \$32,289$$

Actual versus predicted sales are shown in Figure 21-7. Note that the actual value of beer sales rarely equals the predicted value. Major differences between actual and predicted values are referred to as *outliers*, and the analyst should attempt to determine their cause ("Why?") as well as their potential future impact on the industry ("So what?"). For example, the lower than predicted sales of beer products in the late 1980s were explained by increased consumer concern over excessive alcohol consumption and heightened awareness of drunken driving. Clearly, the analyst would want to form an opinion about any long-term trends which may result.

Calculations of the *CAGR* by means of log–least-squares procedures have become

FIGURE 21-7 *Actual Versus Predicted Beer Sales (in millions)*

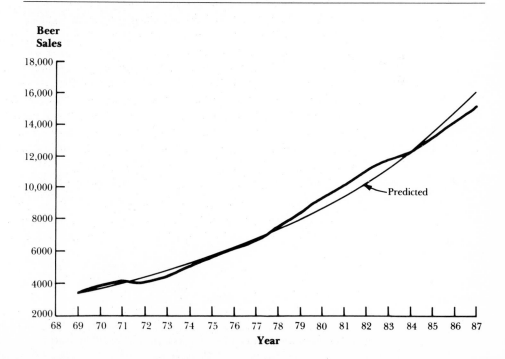

quite common in security analysis because they overcome many of the dangers inherent in measuring growth listed earlier. Although the results are sensitive to the starting and ending dates chosen, this is partially offset by the fact that all data points are used. The major improvement we could make in our example of beer sales growth would be to estimate real sales growth by extracting the effects of selling price increases. Unfortunately, an index of beer selling prices does not exist.[4]

Relationship with GNP

An understanding of the relationship of industry sales and profits to the GNP can be useful for at least two reasons. First, it is helpful to understand how sensitive the industry is to changes in aggregate economic output. Presumably, more-sensitive industries would be more risky. Second, when making short-term industry profit projections, the analyst should know whether the industry tends to lead, lag, or move coincident with aggregate economic activity. Again, regression analysis is helpful in identifying the extent of an industry's sensitivity to the business cycle and any lead-lag relationships. While a number of different types of models could be examined, the following three capture the essence of what is involved:

GNP as a Determinant of Sales

$$(\% \ \Delta \ \text{Sales})_t = a + b(\% \ \Delta \ \text{GNP})_t \tag{21.5}$$

$$(\% \ \Delta \ \text{Sales})_{t+1} = a + b(\% \ \Delta \ \text{GNP})_t \tag{21.6}$$

$$(\% \ \Delta \ \text{Sales})_{t-1} = a + b(\% \ \Delta \ \text{GNP})_t \tag{21.7}$$

Equation 21.5 examines the sensitivity of percentage sales changes to percentage GNP changes *within the same time period*. The estimate of the slope parameter b could be used as a contemporaneous sensitivity measure. If b equals 1.0, industry sales are as volatile as current changes in GNP. If b is less than (more than) 1.0, industry sales are less (more) volatile than current changes in GNP. Equation 21.6 also examines sensitivity through the b term, but this equation tests for a *lagged* relationship between sales changes and GNP changes. Equation 21.7 tests for the possibility that the industry *leads* GNP.

When these regressions are estimated, the following results are obtained:

$$(\% \ \Delta \ \text{Sales})_t = 11.26\% - \underset{(0.46)}{0.24} \ (\% \ \Delta \ \text{GNP})_t \quad \begin{array}{l} R^2 = 2.06\% \\ SEE = 4.53 \end{array} \tag{21.8}$$

$$(\% \ \Delta \ \text{Sales})_{t+1} = 0.49 + \underset{(0.40)}{0.88} \ (\% \ \Delta \ \text{GNP})_t \quad \begin{array}{l} R^2 = 28.63\% \\ SEE = 3.96 \end{array} \tag{21.9}$$

$$(\% \ \Delta \ \text{Sales})_{t-1} = 12.25 - \underset{(0.51)}{0.28} \ (\% \ \Delta \ \text{GNP})_t \quad \begin{array}{l} R^2 = 2.46\% \\ SEE = 4.51 \end{array} \tag{21.10}$$

---

[4]Adjusting dollar sales volume by means of a broad price index such as the CPI would not be appropriate because increases in beer prices do not closely follow CPI increases.

The estimates of Equation 21.8 suggest a constant yearly percentage change in industry sales of 11.26% regardless of the percentage changes in GNP during the same year. The slope term of −0.24 suggests a negative coincident relationship between GNP changes and beer sales. When GNP increases 1%, beer sales fall by 0.24%. The number shown in parentheses below the slope term is the standard deviation of the slope term estimate and can be used to calculate confidence limits on the estimate of each slope term. Throughout the book we have created 95% confidence limits by adding to and subtracting from the slope estimate 1.96 standard deviations.[5] For example, in Equation 21.8 our 95% confidence interval on the slope estimate of −0.24 would be −1.14 to 0.66 (−0.24 ± 1.96 × 0.46). Since this confidence interval includes a value of 0.0, we *cannot* say that current changes in GNP are statistically related to current changes in beer sales. The true value of b in Equation 21.8 could well be 0.0. The R^2 value of 2.06% in Equation 21.8 indicates that only a minor portion (in fact, a statistically insignificant portion, since the slope term is not significant) of percentage sales changes are affected by % Δ GNP in the same year. We will discuss the meaning of the *SEE* statistic later in the chapter.

A review of these equations indicates that there is a slight tendency for beer sales to *lag* percentage changes in GNP. A 1% change in GNP in one year is, on average, associated with a 28.63% change in beer sales in the following year. The relationship is barely statistically significant, however, and only 28.63% of the variation in beer sales is associated with variation in GNP in the prior year. Overall, percentage changes in beer sales do not appear to be closely related to changes in GNP levels.

CONCEPTUAL DETERMINANTS OF SALES GROWTH

After gathering a set of basic data which describe the historical pattern of an industry's growth, the analyst should conceptually attempt to determine the character of the industry's demand and supply curves. For example, has most of the past growth arisen from continued increases in the long-run demand curve which the industry has had no difficulty in supplying? Or has the sales growth arisen from a fairly stable long-run demand to which the industry has been adjusting through steady increases in capacity? Similarly, is long-run demand very sensitive to price reductions caused by lower production costs? Or is long-run demand insensitive to price reductions? In addition, does the cost structure of the industry suggest that it is a natural oligopoly in which only a few dominant firms will survive? Or should the industry structure consist of a large number of highly competitive firms?

A conceptual understanding of the industry's long-run demand and supply conditions is important because it indicates areas the analyst should focus on. Although thorough discussion of the study of microeconomics is beyond the scope of this book,

---

[5]In a small sample such as this, a 95% confidence level actually requires a value greater than 1.96. However, a thorough discussion of the use of regression analysis lies beyond the scope of this text. Throughout the text we will assume large-sample (30 or more observations) statistics are appropriate, even though the example data clearly show this isn't true.

we will briefly review a few basic concepts as they apply to security analysis. In particular, changes in industry sales volume can be thought of as arising from a mixture of three basic causes:

1. Shifts in the long-run equilibrium between demand and supply
2. Short-run adjustments of supply to changes in this long-run equilibrium
3. Inflationary increases in prices

Demand/Supply Curve Shifts

Figure 21-8 illustrates a hypothetical long-run demand/supply curve for the brewing industry. If the industry is currently at a point of equilibrium, sales volume will be 4 billion barrels, and the price will be $2.00 per barrel. Industry revenue will be $8 billion. Future sales changes will come from shifts in either the demand curve or the supply curve.

The demand curve is a function of four factors: (1) the size of the consumer base, (2) income and wealth levels, (3) prices of related goods, and (4) tastes. For example, a large part of the historical growth of beer sales has probably come from the first and last of these factors. The number of people old enough to legally consume beer has been increasing during the past decade, and the variety of beer products has been expanded in order to attract a larger number of people with differing tastes (for example, light beer and premium brands). The supply curve is a function of the industry's cost structure. At any level of output, selling prices must cover wage and salary expenses, raw material expenses, distribution expenses, energy costs, etc., as well as provide a fair return on all asset investments. If any of these factors changes over time, the supply curve will shift and result in a change in industry sales volume.

FIGURE 21-8 *Hypothetical Brewing Industry Demand and Supply*

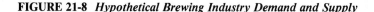

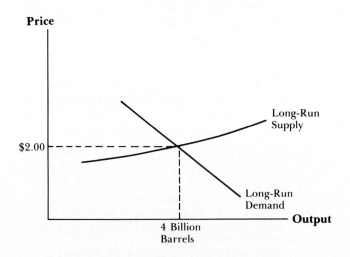

Elasticity. The extent to which shifts in the demand or supply curve affect industry sales depends upon the elasticity of demand and supply to changes in price levels. For example, a decrease in the supply curve caused by, say, an improved production process will have dramatic effects on quantities purchased in some industries but very little impact in other industries. *Price elasticity of demand* is measured as the percentage change in quantity purchased that results from a 1% change in price. For example, if a 1% decrease in beer prices results in a 0.5% increase in consumption, demand elasticity is 0.5. The most important determinant of demand price elasticity is the number and closeness of substitute products available. If beer consumers believe the product has few substitutes (for example, they don't perceive wine, liquor, or soft drinks to be viable substitutes), the demand price elasticity of beer will be small. Conversely, if beer consumers have a large number of alternative substitutes, quantity demanded will be quite sensitive to price changes. Supply curves also are price elastic. Industries which are able to provide large increases in production at only minimal increases in costs will be highly price elastic. Conversely, in industries where costs change dramatically for small shifts in output, a change in prices will have only minor effects upon output (elasticity will be small).

To illustrate the importance of price elasticity, consider panels A and B in Figure 21-9. Assume that panel A depicts the opinions of analyst A about the brewing industry: supply is highly price elastic, but demand is rather inelastic. Analyst's B perceptions are shown in panel B, in which both supply and demand are quite price elastic. Finally, assume that both analysts believe the long-run supply curve will soon fall to the level shown by the dashed line because of improved technology. As can be seen, each analyst has a different belief about how the supply shift will affect industry revenues. Analyst A believes there will be a modest increase in output and a large drop in prices, resulting in a *decrease* in total revenue. Analyst B, however, believes there will be a large increase in revenue caused by the substantial increase in output. Clearly, opinions about the character of an industry's long-run demand and supply curves can have a major effect on beliefs about future sales growth.[6]

Adjustment of Supply to Long-Run Equilibrium

In many cases, the growth of sales within an industry may not reflect so much a shift in *long-run* demand or supply curves as an adjustment of *short-run* supply conditions towards the equilibrium. For example, after state and federal regulations covering the transportation of mobile homes were liberalized, long-run consumer demand increased dramatically. While a number of mobile home manufacturers existed at the time, their production capacity could not begin to meet potential market demand. As a result, the growth of industry sales during the 1960s and early 1970s was more a function of saturating a latent market demand than it was of increasing demand. The

---

[6]Remember, however, that sales growth is not necessarily related to security values. It would be wrong to conclude from this example that the common stocks characterized by panel A should be sold and those in panel B purchased.

FIGURE 21-9 *Impacts of Price Elasticity on Forecasts*

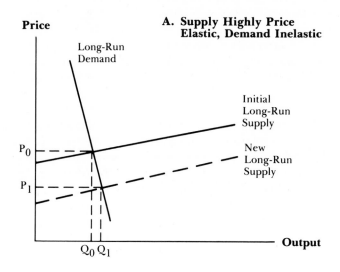

A. Supply Highly Price Elastic, Demand Inelastic

Price

Long-Run Demand

Initial Long-Run Supply

New Long-Run Supply

P_0

P_1

Output

$Q_0 Q_1$

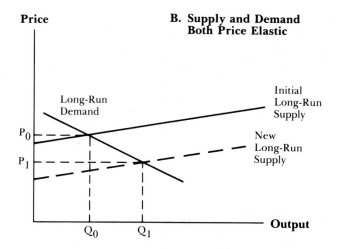

B. Supply and Demand Both Price Elastic

Price

Long-Run Demand

Initial Long-Run Supply

New Long-Run Supply

P_0

P_1

Output

Q_0 Q_1

same is true of the cable television industry. During the late 1970s, changes in telecommunication technology and federal regulations allowed the creation of a product with a large market demand. But again it took a number of years before cable firms could enter all consumer markets and meet the excess demand. As a result, most of the sales growth of the cable industry in the late 1970s was due more to meeting an excess market demand than it was to increases in the long-run demand for cable services.

Analysts should attempt to determine whether the historical growth rate of industry sales was due to fundamental shifts in long-run demand and supply or to market saturation. If the growth is due to market saturation, estimates should be made of (1) the time it will take before long-run demand and supply are in equilibrium, (2) yearly growth rates during this period, (3) the market structure of the industry once equilibrium is achieved (competitive, oligopolistic, monopoly), and (4) potential growth rates thereafter. One technique which can be helpful in evaluating the existing status quo is a plot of market saturation. *Market saturation* is simply the number of customers actually supplied divided by the number of potential customers. For example, in the cable television industry, markets could be broken down into two types: those now receiving two or fewer direct channels and all others. If there are 25 million households in the first market and 70% could be expected to desire cable services, potential demand in this market would be 17.5 million households. Similarly, if there are 30 million households in the second market with a potential market of 40%, potential demand there would be 12 million households. In total, 29.5 million households may eventually be serviced. If only 15 million now receive cable service, the market saturation would be 51%. Plots of historical saturation and knowledge of how long it takes to build a new cable system would aid in determining the speed at which the cable market may be saturated.

Industry Price Inflation

The discussion so far has focused on growth in *real* sales volume. Of course, to estimate nominal sales growth the analyst must add an inflation effect. For the average product the rate would be the long-run inflation rate expected for the economy as a whole. In industries with temporary excess capacity the inflation rate would probably be lower, and in industries with temporary excess demand the rate would probably be higher.

Quantitative Determinants of Sales Growth

After some thought has been given to what the conceptual determinants of past sales growth might have been, econometric tests of these variables can be conducted. The benefits of performing such statistical tests are threefold. First, econometric techniques force the analyst to explicitly state the factors which are believed to have contributed to past sales growth as well as the believed interrelationship between these variables. Second, the statistical procedures allow the analyst to evaluate which factors were the most important contributors to growth. Finally, if a reasonably good model of past sales growth can be found, it can be used to estimate future sales growth. In this section we briefly review the procedures and statistics used as well as some of the problems encountered.

Simultaneous Solution of Supply and Demand. Econometric models can be used to statistically identify the determinants of historical demand and supply curves. In practice, this can be an extremely difficult task. For example, consider Figure 21-10, which plots hypothetical demand and supply curves for the brewing industry over a three-year time interval. Both the demand curves (D_1, D_2, and D_3) and the supply curves

FIGURE 21-10 *Hypothetical Beer Demand and Supply*

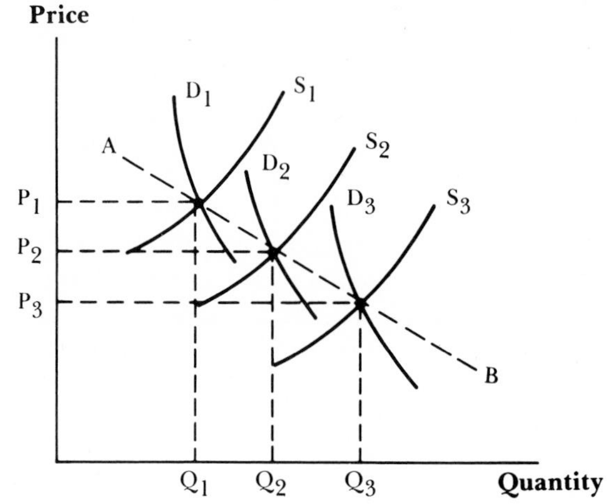

$(S_1, S_2,$ and $S_3)$ shift over time and result in different equilibrium prices $(P_1, P_2,$ and $P_3)$ in each year. If one were to simply plot beer prices against quantities of beer sold in each of the last three years, line AB might be mistaken as the demand curve for beer. Of course, line AB is simply the path of equilibrium relationships between the actual (but unobserved) demand and supply curves. The demand and supply curves have shifted over time with changes in nonprice variables which affect each. For example, increases in the number of consumers or increases in consumers' income levels could explain the shifting demand curves. Similarly, new and more-efficient production processes could result in the shifting supply curve. Of more importance to the analyst than the line AB are the underlying demand and supply curves.

Misinterpreting line AB as the demand curve can lead to serious forecasting errors. For example, assume we believe that production processes used to brew beer will continue to be improved in year 4 (that is, we forecast a continued shift in the supply curve to the right in Figure 21-10). If line AB is taken to be the demand curve, the lower production costs would be expected to increase beer consumption dramatically. However, actual demand will be dictated by demand curve D_3 (assuming no shift in demand) and result in a much smaller increase in consumption.

Ideally, the analyst would like to use historical data to measure the *actual* demand and supply curves over time. Basically, such procedures estimate demand and supply curves simultaneously. For example, if we believe that demand for beer (Q_t) in any period t is determined by its price (P_t) and the income of consumers (I_t), whereas the supply of beer (Q_t) is determined by its price and the price of grain (G_t), then a simultaneous demand-and-supply system such as the following would be estimated using one of a number of econometric techniques:

Demand Curve $\qquad\qquad\qquad Q_t = C_1 + b_1 P_t + b_2 I_t + e_1$ $\qquad\qquad$ **(21.11)**

Supply Curve $\qquad\qquad\qquad Q_t = C_2 + b_3 P_t + b_4 G_t + u_t$ $\qquad\qquad$ **(21.12)**

Equation 21.11 specifies the hypothesized demand curve relationship, where C_1 is a constant demand quantity, b_1 and b_2 represent the impacts of beer price levels and consumer income levels on consumption, and e_1 is a random error term. Equation 21.12 specifies the hypothesized supply curve, where C_2 is a constant supplied quantity, b_3 and b_4 represent the impacts of beer prices and grain prices on supply, and u_t is a random error term. Econometric techniques would be used to simultaneously estimate the regression parameters of both models. Unfortunately, a discussion of such techniques is too complex to be covered here. Instead, we will discuss the more commonly used procedure of estimating a single equation. Some care should be taken when interpreting the results of a single equation, however, because there is no guarantee that the interaction between demand and supply has been satisfactorily handled.

Specifying a Model. The model to be tested should make economic sense—not simply "fit the data" well. Essentially, we wish to find an economically sound and statistically significant cause/effect relationship. For example, population levels, income levels, advertising campaigns, and the like, may *cause* the level of an industry's sales, whereas other variables may only be coincidentally correlated with sales. Including a variable simply because it is highly correlated with sales can create an artificial precision in the model. For example, it is hard to understand why changes in industrial production would directly lead to increased beer consumption, even though the two variables may be highly correlated over time. As such, industrial production should not be included in a beer-consumption model. Instead, a little thought about the determinants of beer consumption would probably lead to a list of causal variables such as the following:

1. Price of the product—*PRC*, average price per barrel of beer
2. Size of the consumer base—*POP*, number of people 18 years and older
3. Income levels—*PCI*, per capita income measured in constant dollars
4. Prices of related goods—assumed to be unmeasurable
5. Consumer tastes—*WTH*, weather, as measured by the difference between the summer's average daily temperature and the long-run national average, and *ADV*, total dollars of beer advertising (in constant dollars)

If we denote the number of barrels consumed during any given year as *BRLS*, then our conceptual model is:

$$BRLS = f(PRC, POP, PCI, WTH, ADV) \tag{21.13}$$

There are a number of ways to express this relationship as an explicit equation. The most common approach is the linear function:

Additive Regression
$$BRLS_t = C_0 + b_1(PRC_t) + b_2(POP_t) + b_3(PCI_t) \\ + b_4(WTH_t) + \beta_5(ADV_t) + e_1 \tag{21.14}$$

The constant level of *BRLS* when population, etc., is zero is C_0. The slope terms (b_1 through b_5) reflect the relative impacts of each independent variable (population, etc.) on the dependent variable (*BRLS*). Finally, the e_t term is a random error term. This linear equation states that any change in each causal variable has an *independent and additive effect* on barrels of consumption.

The second most commonly used equation is the multiplicative form:

Multiplicative Regression

$$BRLS_t = a(PRC_t)^b (POP_t)^c (PCT_t)^d (WTH_t)^f (ADV_t)^g + e_t \quad (21.15)$$

A multiplicative form is most appropriate when the marginal effects of each causal variable are not *independent of the other variables in the equation*. For example, the effects of a change in advertising may depend on the size of the population, income levels, etc. When a multiplicative model is hypothesized, it is usually transformed into a linear model by using the natural log of each variable. For example, Equation 21.15 would be transformed into the following equation:

Transformed Multiplication Regression

$$\ln(BRLS_t) = \ln(a) + b\ln(PRC_t) + c\ln(POP_t) + d\ln(PCI_t)$$
$$+ f\ln(WTH_t) + g\ln(ADV_t) + e_t \quad (21.16)$$

Equation 21.16 is linear in logarithms, and the parameters (*a, b, c, d, f*, and *g*) can be estimated by least-squares regression procedures.

A useful feature of the multiplicative relationship of Equation 21.16 is the fact that regression parameters (*b* through *g*) can be interpreted as elasticity measures. For example, assume that we estimate the parameters of Equation 21.16 and that this results in estimates of $b = -0.3$ and $d = 0.5$. This can be interpreted to mean that a 1% reduction in price is expected to result in a 0.3% increase in barrels of consumption or that a 1% increase in real per capita income is expected to result in a 0.5% increase in barrels of consumption.

The algebraic form of the model chosen should always fit one's conceptual economic model. If a multiplicative relationship between the variables is believed to exist, then a version similar to Equation 21.16 should be used. In practice, however, there may not be any particular reason to select one form over another. In such cases a variety of algebraic forms are used, and the one which best fits the data is selected as the one most likely to mirror reality.

Interpreting the Results. Assume that various versions of Equations 21.14 and 21.16 are estimated using a least-squares regression package to arrive at the results shown in Table 21-8. Two additive models and two multiplicative models are (hypothetically) estimated using 40 years of data. When a variable is assumed not to have been included in a particular model, this is denoted by a line under the entry for the estimated parameter. Model 1 is known as a *simple linear regression* since it includes only one independent variable. All the other models are known as *multiple regressions* since they include more than one independent variable. Estimated standard deviations of each regression parameter are shown in parentheses below the parameter estimate.

The Explanatory Power of a Model. As we have noted before, R^2 is a statistical measure of how well a regression equation predicts the actual values of some depen-

TABLE 21-8 *Hypothetical Regression Results, Dependent Variable = Barrels of Beer Consumed*

Model Number	Constant a	Regression Parameter Estimates							Number of Observations
		PRC	POP	PCI	WTH	ADV	R^2	SEE	
ADDITIVE MODELS (Arithmetic Variables)									
1	20,000	—	1.05	—	—	—	86%	10,000,000	40
	(7,000)		(0.07)						
2	7,000	−1,550	1.02	−200	2,000,000	0.07	89%	5,000,000	40
	(3,000)	(900)	(0.05)	(0.90)	(800,000)	(0.04)			
MULTIPLICATIVE MODELS (Log-Natural Variables)									
3	1.83	−0.50	0.97	0.01	—	0.10	94%	15.4	40
	(0.70)	(0.18)	(0.06)	(0.01)		(0.18)			
4	1.85	−0.62	1.03	—	—	—	92%	15.5	40
	(0.70)	(0.25)	(0.07)						

dent variable—in our example, total barrels of beer consumed in the United States during a given year. R^2, known as the *coefficient of determination*, indicates the percentage of the variation in the dependent variable accounted for by the variation in the set of independent (causal) variables. Ideally, we would wish the model's R^2 to be close to 100%. In practice, however, an R^2 of 80% or better is usually considered acceptable if the model is to be used for forecasting purposes. All four models in Table 21-8 have R^2 values of 85% or better.

Besides providing an intuitive understanding of how well the model fits the data, R^2 can be used to test whether the model *as a whole* is statistically significant—that is, whether the regression parameters in total are statistically different from zero. To do this, an F statistic is first calculated as follows:

The F Statistic
$$F_c = \frac{R^2}{1 - R^2}\left(\frac{T - k - 1}{k}\right)$$
(21.17)

where F_c = the calculated F statistic, R^2 = the percentage of variation in the dependent variable explained by the set of independent variables, T = the number of observations, and k = the number of independent variables considered.

For example, model 2 in Table 21-8 has an R^2 of 89%, 40 yearly observations, and 5 independent variables. As such, the calculated F statistic is 55.02:

$$F_c = \frac{0.89}{1 - 0.89}\left(\frac{40 - 5 - 1}{5}\right) = 55.02$$

The calculated F statistic is then compared with a theoretical F statistic for a given confidence level. If the calculated F statistic is greater than the theoretical F statistic, the model *as a whole* is said to be statistically significant; that is, the *set* of independent variables is statistically related to the dependent variable. Theoretical F statistics can be found by consulting most intermediate statistics tests. In our example the theoretical F statistic at a 95% confidence level with 40 observations and 5 independent variables is 2.49. As such, the model as a whole is statistically significant.

Evaluation of Individual Variables. Typically, an analyst is more concerned with the relative importance of each independent variable than with the model as a whole. First, the algebraic sign and size of each variable should be examined. For example, in model 1 the regression parameter on population has been estimated as +1.05. The positive sign is reasonable, since we would expect population and beer consumption to be positively related. The parameter estimate of 1.05 implies that, as the population (of people 18 years or older) increases by one person, beer consumption increases by 1.05 barrels.

One of the more confusing problems in interpreting regression parameters can arise when some of the data are rounded. For example, in model 2 the regression parameter which measures the impact of advertising expenditures upon barrel consumption was estimated using *total* barrel sales and total advertising expenditures. As such, the parameter estimate of 0.07 implies that an additional dollar of advertising results in 0.07 new barrel sales. However, if advertising expenditures had been rounded to millions and barrel consumption left unrounded, the parameter estimate would have been 70,000. Thus, some care is needed when interpreting parameter estimates.

Finally, the interpretation given to parameter estimates depends on the functional form of the model being examined. For example, parameter estimates related to *PRC* (price per barrel) in models 2 and 3 differ since model 2 is an arithmetic model whereas model 3 is a multiplicative model. In model 2 the −1,550 estimate should be interpreted to mean that a $1 price increase results in a decline in consumption of 1,550 barrels. In model 3, however, the −0.50 parameter estimate is interpreted to mean that a 1% increase in price results in a 0.5 percent decrease in barrels of consumption.

As noted earlier, we can test whether any single parameter estimate is statistically different from zero by dividing the regression estimate by its standard deviation. For example, in model 1 the population parameter is 15.0 standard deviations away from zero (1.05 ÷ 0.07). Using a 95% confidence level, a parameter estimate is statistically different from zero if the estimate is more than 1.96 standard deviations away from zero. Alternatively, we could add and subtract 1.96 standard deviations to the parameter estimate to obtain a 95% confidence level on the value of the parameter.

In many regression models we would expect the constant term to be zero when, in fact, it turns out to be statistically different from zero. For example, in model 1 it is hard to conceive of a positive level of beer consumption when population is zero. But the constant term in model 1 is statistically different from zero and implies an expected barrel consumption of 20,000 units when population is zero. Figure 21-11 illustrates how this could occur. In reality a curvilinear relationship between beer consumption and population may exist. But if the model is estimated using only a few population data points (as shown by the data), the linear regression may suggest a positive intercept term. This would create only a minor problem if forecasts are made using population levels close to those used in estimating the model. However, if longer-term population values are used, the prediction error can be more serious.

FIGURE 21-11 *Explanation of a Positive Intercept*

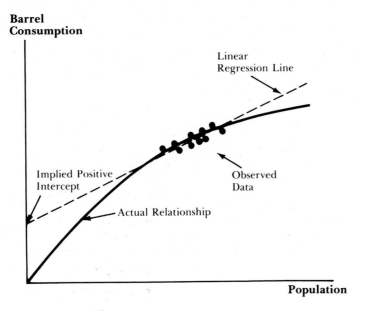

Barrel
Consumption

Linear
Regression Line

Implied Positive
Intercept

Observed
Data

Actual Relationship

Population

Standard Error of the Estimate. The standard error of the estimate (*SEE*) is the standard deviation of the dependent variable *given* the estimated regression line as illustrated in Figure 21-12. In our example we attempted to explain the *actual* levels of beer consumption using 40 years of data. However, none of the models was able to totally predict each year's consumption level. For example, in Figure 21-12 the line *AP* represents the prediction error for a single year. These errors are represented in our models by the error term e_t. The standard error of the estimate is simply the standard deviation of these error terms. Typically, the smaller the *SEE*, the larger the R^2. As such, one would prefer small *SEE* terms.

Example Summary. All four of the hypothetical models in Table 21-8 have reasonably high R^2 values. Model 1 is a simple linear regression and has the lowest R^2, although it is still large enough to be useful for forecasting purposes. The coefficient on population implies that each person over 18 year of age consumes, on average, 1.05 barrels of beer per year (about 29 gallons).

Model 2 has a higher R^2 and lower *SEE*, but the results have a couple of disturbing aspects. For one, although the sign on the price variable is negative (as would be expected), the regression estimate of $-1,550$ is not statistically different from zero (1.72 standard deviations). It is possible, of course, that price has only minimal or no impact on beer consumption, but this runs counter to intuition. More likely the lack of statistical significance has arisen from either a poorly specified model or little change in beer prices over time. The second disturbing aspect of model 2 is the negative sign associated with per capita income. This is particularly bothersome, since

FIGURE 21-12 *Illustration of the SEE*

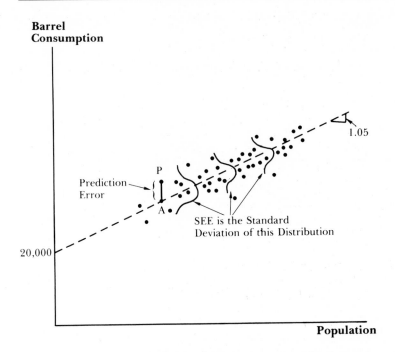

the estimate is statistically significant. Finally, there is some question whether an arithmetic model is most appropriate. For example, it is hard to envision a world in which impacts of changes in per capita income are independent of the level of population.

Models 3 and 4 are multiplicative models which allow the impacts of changes in one independent variable to depend on the level of each of the other variables. Estimates are interpreted as percentage changes in barrels of consumption for each percentage change in the independent variable (except for the constant term). For example, the 0.97 estimate on population in model 3 implies that a 1% change in population leads to a 0.97% change in consumption. Models 3 and 4 are virtually identical except for the deletion of *PCI* and *ADV* in model 4. All signs on the estimates are reasonable, and price now has a statistically significant impact. Overall, it appears that models 3 and 4 are superior to 1 and 2.

Forecasting

Regression analyses are helpful in that they provide a way to rigorously examine which causal variables are the most important in contributing to the level of some dependent variable. Once the analyst has been able to determine the relative importance of various factors, attention can be given to the more important variables. For example, according to models 3 and 4 the most crucial determinants of beer consumption appear to be price and population. Given this finding, analysts should spend more time forecasting beer prices and population trends than forecasting per capita income and advertising expenditures.

Once reasonable estimates of future levels of independent variables are developed, they can be inserted in the model to forecast future levels of the dependent variable. For example, assume that we have decided to use models 1 and 4 to forecast total beer consumption five years hence and have made the following forecasts:

Variable	Expected Value 5 Years Hence
Price Per Barrel	$ 45
Population	170 million

Forecast barrels of consumption per model 1 would be:

$$\text{Barrels} \quad = 20{,}000 + 1.05(\text{Population})$$

$$178{,}520{,}000 = 20{,}000 + 1.05(170{,}000{,}000)$$

Model 4 is a little more complex since it requires the use of natural logs and antilogs as follows:

$$\ln(\text{Barrels}) = 1.85 - 0.62\ln(\text{Price}) + 1.03\ln(\text{Population})$$

$$= 1.85 - 1.62\ln(45) + 1.03\ln(170{,}000{,}000)$$

$$= 1.85 - 0.62(3.81) + 1.03(18.95)$$

$$= 19.0063$$

Converting to forecast barrels of consumption:

$$\text{Barrels} = \text{antilog of } \ln(\text{Barrels})$$

$$= e^{19.0063}$$

$$= 179{,}610{,}289$$

These two forecasts are quite close. Unfortunately, in many situations the forecasts will vary considerably and the analyst must subjectively decide which estimate (or combination of estimates) is best.

Finally, an industry sales figure can be calculated by multiplying forecast barrels of consumption by forecast price per barrel. For example, averaging the two forecasts above results in a forecast consumption of about 179 million barrels. At $45 per barrel, this implies industry revenues of about $8,055 million. If current revenues are $5,482 million, this implies a growth rate over the next five years of about 8%.

Concluding Comments

A large part of this chapter has been devoted to the quantitative measurement of industry growth. Ideally, these quantitative procedures should add precision and rigor to an analyst's evaluation of the industry's past growth as well as provide reasonable estimates of potential future growth. But the tools should not be used without considerable caution and common sense. As we saw earlier, supply-and-demand-curve relationships often can't be measured independently of each other. Instead, supply and demand curves often must be estimated simultaneously, a procedure which lies beyond the scope of this book. In addition, numerous statistical pitfalls can beset the novice.[7] Like so many other topics in investment analysis, a good understanding of regression analysis requires considerable study of that topic alone. Regression results should be compared with qualitative forecasts which rely on the analyst's unique experience, judgment, and common sense.

Many empirical studies have shown that past industry growth rates are extremely poor predictors of future growth rates. Thus, one should be wary of simply extrapolating the past into the future. While much of the variability in these growth rates over time can be captured by the sensitivity of industry sales to changes in basic causal variables through regression procedures, there is no reason to believe that this sensitivity (as captured by the regression slope parameters) won't change also. For example, the sensitivity of beer consumption to changes in beer prices and population levels may be quite different in the 1990s from that during the 1970s and 1980s. Again, the regression results must be interpreted with care and common sense. The analyst must be thoroughly familiar with recent developments and potential future developments which could significantly alter the historical relationships found in the regression analysis.

After an expected industry sales growth has been established, detailed projections of the expected future dividend stream should be prepared. Once expected industry dividends are discounted at an appropriate required return, the resulting fair market value can be compared with the actual industry market value and a decision made to overweight, underweight, or value-weight one's portfolio holdings in the industry. This process of getting from sales growth rates to a fair industry market value is similar to that used for individual stocks and will be discussed in the next chapter.

SUMMARY

This chapter has examined various procedures which might be used in deciding whether a portfolio's tactical asset allocation should be different from its strategic asset allocation. Both aggregate equity allocation and industry weightings were considered.

The intrinsic value of the aggregate stock market is equal to the present value of expected future dividends discounted at an appropriate risk-adjusted interest rate. If

---

[7]The three major statistical problems which can be encountered include multicollinearity (a situation in which various independent variables are highly correlated with one another) heteroskedasticity (the distribution of the error term, e_t, is not constant), and autocorrelation (error terms in one observation are correlated with error terms in other observations). These are discussed in any econometric textbook.

the actual market prices of equity indexes are greater than (lower than) the intrinsic values, then portfolio commitments to such equities should be underweighted (overweighted) relative to the strategic asset allocation. If you are able to develop relatively accurate estimates of the equity market's intrinsic value (and if market prices move towards your estimates), then TAA decisions will generate better risk-adjusted performance than strict adherence to the SAA.

The success of tactical asset allocation decisions is debatable. The returns generated by investment managers who engage in *market timing* are usually not statistically different from the returns of managers who do not time. And even though there are some market timers whose return performance appears to be statistically better than that of non-timers, they are so few in number that their favorable performance could be due solely to chance.

This chapter also discussed the procedures used in examining historical and expected industry sales growth. The first step consists of calculating historical compound annual growth rates ($CAGR$). While a number of techniques can be used to calculate historical $CAGR$s, the log–least-squares procedure is usually best. Once growth rate statistics have been calculated, the analyst should attempt to identify the major determinants of both the average growth rate and the variability in growth over time. Usually, it is helpful to return to basic economic principles and give some thought to the nature of the industry's demand and supply curves. The long-run demand curve is a function of (1) the size of the consumer base, (2) the price of the product relative to other products, (3) real consumer income, and (4) consumer tastes. Which of these seem to have been more important in explaining past growth? The long-run supply curve is a function of the long-run cost of producing the product. Any changes in the industry's cost structure should be evaluated for their relative importance. For example, how important are the influences of labor contracts, technology, raw material, and governmental regulations on the industry's production costs? In addition, some thought should be given to the elasticity of demand (and supply) to changes in prices (and costs). Finally, a clear distinction should be made between growth which has arisen from shifts in the long-run demand or supply curves versus temporary increases in market saturation or inflation.

Once the analyst has formed a set of opinions about why industry sales have grown as they have, they can be statistically tested via least-squares regression analysis. Regression analysis is useful in at least three ways. First, it forces the analyst to be very explicit about which determinants have caused past sales growth and the way in which these determinants are interrelated. Second, regression procedures allow the analyst to estimate the relative importance and statistical significance of each likely determinant. Finally, many regression equations can be used to develop forecasts of expected future sales levels. Yet regression techniques are not a panacea. Considerable care and common sense should be used in evaluating the results.

At the end of the industry analysis, one should step back and explicitly identify the *greatest* potentials and weaknesses inherent in future industry growth. A clear understanding of the major economic forces operating within an industry is much more important than an ability to recite numerous statistical facts.

You have created your own index of common stock prices which you call the EMP Index (Equity Market Portfolio Index). At present the economy is in a slump, resulting in depressed dividend levels. Dividends per share on your EMP Index over the past 10 years have been as follows:

Year	Dividends	Year	Dividends
1981	$1.39	1986	$2.45
1982	1.39	1987	2.60
1983	1.45	1988	2.65
1984	1.62	1989	2.67
1985	2.00	1990	2.68

You run a log–least-squares regression on the data and get:

$$\ln(DPS) = -181.186 + 0.09161(\text{Time}) \qquad R^2 = 89.85\%$$

a. What has been the compound annual growth rate in dividends per share?

b. If you use the regression trend line, what is your expected dividend two years from now (1992)? (Assume dividend levels return to their overall trend level by then.)

c. The 1990 dividend was just $2.68. If you believe dividends will increase in 1991 and 1992 by equal dollar increments to the trend line value in part b, what is 1991's dividend expected to be?

d. Beyond 1992 you are unable to identify the impacts of any business cycles. Nonetheless, starting after 1992 you forecast growth rates equal to the historic average in part a. If you require a return of 15% on an investment in the EMP Index, what fair value would you place on the index as of the end of 1990?

e. If the EMP Index is $55.00 at the end of 1990, how would you adjust your stock/bond ratio?

Solution

a. 9.161% — the slope of the log-natural regression.

b. $3.67 = antilog $[-181.186 + 0.09161 (1992)]$

c. $\dfrac{\$3.67 - \$2.68}{2} = \$0.495$ per year

1991 dividend = $2.68 + $0.495 = $3.175

d. This requires a nonconstant dividend growth model:

$$P = \frac{D_{91}}{1 + k} + \frac{D_{92}}{(1 + K)^2} + \frac{D_{92}(1 + G)}{K - G} \; \frac{1}{(1 + k)^2}$$

$$= \frac{\$3.175}{1.15} + \frac{\$3.67}{1.15^2} + \frac{\$3.67(1.09161)}{0.15 - 0.09161} \; [1/(1.15^2)]$$

$$= \$57.42$$

e. The estimated intrinsic value of the index is slightly higher than the actual value. Thus, slightly increase the actual equity holding compared with the baseline investment portfolio.

QUESTIONS AND PROBLEMS

1. As of year-end the DJIA is selling at 1,000. To evaluate whether this is a fair value, you have developed the following data:

DJIA Estimates	Pessimistic	Expected	Optimistic
Long-Run *ROE*	14.50%	15.00%	16.00%
Profit Retention Rate	50.00%	56.67%	60.00%
Current T-Bond *YTM*	8.00%	8.00%	8.00%
Fair Risk Premium	5.00%	5.50%	6.00%
Year 0 Earnings per Share	$100.00	$106.35	$110.00

   a. Develop pessimistic, expected, and optimistic valuations of the DJIA.
   b. As the investment adviser for a $20.0 million pension fund, you believe that a long-run stock/bond ratio of 50/50 should be maintained. However, you are willing to alter the ratio temporarily to take advantage of perceived price imbalances. Based upon your answer to part a, would you make such an adjustment now?

2. Suppose you have made the following estimates:

	Pessimistic	Expected	Optimistic
Long-Run GNP Growth—Real			
Employment	0.9%	1.0%	1.1%
Work Hours	−0.2	−0.2	−0.2
Age/Sex Composition	0.0	0.0	0.1
Education	0.2	0.3	0.3
Other	0.0	0.0	0.0
Capital	0.6	0.7	0.8
Advances in Knowledge	0.9	1.0	1.1
Resource Allocation	0.2	0.2	0.3
Economics of Scale	0.4	0.4	0.4
Other Output	0.0	0.0	0.0
Long-Run Dividend Growth—Real			
60% of GNP Growth			
Other Information			
Long-Run Inflation per Year	8.00%	7.25%	6.50%
Current Dividends per Share on S&P 500	$5.70	$5.70	$5.70
Current S&P 500 Value	107	107	107

   The required return is 15%. Would you adjust your stock/bond mix?

3. Drawing solely upon your current knowledge of the following industries, identify what are likely to have been the major determinants of each's sales growth during the past decade. Assuming that your opinions are correct, how would you use this information in conducting a thorough analysis of the following industries?
   a. Air transport
   b. Fast-food chains
   c. Health care and hospital supply
   d. Machine tools
   e. Telecommunications

4. a. Which stage of the life cycle is the most favorable from an investment standpoint?
   b. How can the life-cycle concept be used to aid the industry analyst?

5. Why is it important to distinguish between market saturation and market growth?

6. You have been asked to prepare an analysis of the orange juice industry. You have concluded that the dominant supply of juice oranges comes from the central Florida area because of favorable soil conditions which create a sweet-tasting orange. While oranges are grown in other parts of the world, no other location has the same soil makeup as central Florida. Thus, this area is likely to remain the most important source. Unfortunately, available producing land is increasingly being used to support new housing and tourist activities. Juice production and distribution costs are reasonably constant over different levels of output. Sales have grown steadily over the past decade with population growth in the northeastern and midwestern United States, increased advertising, and improved quality of both concentrated and nonconcentrated juice.

   a. Draw conceptual demand and supply curves for orange juice.
   b. Interpret how shifts (both in the near and long term) in both demand and supply are likely to affect industry growth.
   c. What implications could you draw from your comments in part b?

7. (CFA Exam Question)
   In the course of preparing yourself for a field trip to Beckman Instruments, you have been working with your programmable calculator to estimate financial requirements and have come up with the following historical data and regression analysis results:

Fiscal Year	Sales (millions)	Year-End Inventories (millions)	Regression Statistics
1978	$338	$106	$I = 31.6 + 0.204\,(S)$
1977	286	85	Where:
1976	242	75	I = Inventories
1975	229	78	S = Sales
1974	196	78	$R = 0.89$
			Standard Error of the Estimate = 6.7

   a. Draw a chart showing the regression line (as a solid line) and indicate the range within which you would expect 68% of the figures to fall (using dashed lines). Also indicate the actual data for sales and inventories by marking small x's on the chart. Be sure to label the axes and identify the intercept.
   b. Using the regression equation:
      (1) Calculate an estimate of the fiscal 1979 year-end inventory level if fiscal 1979 sales are $400 million.
      (2) Calculate the range for inventories that you would expect to cover about 68% of the probable variation.

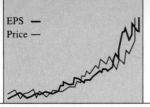

EPS —
Price —

CHAPTER

22 Company Analysis

For many people proper security selection simply means choosing a few good stocks. It is not that simple, of course. Before individual stocks are selected, a number of other decisions need to be made which are often more crucial to long-run performance. For example: (1) How much diversification is needed in the portfolio? (2) *What* should the stock/bond mix be to achieve a desired level of market risk? (3) Should one speculate on movements in aggregate stock and bond prices by departing from the investment portfolio's ideal stock/bond mix? (4) Should particular industries be over- or underweighted relative to their proportions in a pure investment portfolio? (5) Should options, futures, or other sophisticated instruments be used? Only after these more basic questions are answered should one turn to the question of which stocks should be owned and in what proportions. Individual stock selection should be one of the last steps taken in creating good investment or speculative portfolios.

Individual stock selection for investment portfolios is a fairly straightforward task: select enough stocks to provide the desired level of diversification and those stocks which best match one's particular tax and liquidity needs. Stock selection for speculative purposes is more involved. In order to identify mispriced stocks and earn speculative profits, one must hold some unique information about the stock. Ideally, one would like to know everything other traders know—plus something more. Therefore, the analyst should first be totally familiar with the opinions expressed in past analyses and then search for some *new* insights about the firm's earnings prospects and risks. Anything that might provide information about the firm should be analyzed and integrated. At the least, this entails a thorough reading of any corporate reports,[1] other analysts' reports, trade publications, addresses by corporate officers, and government forecasts of industry demand such as the *U.S. Industrial Outlook*. In addition, other sources should be examined, depending on the nature of the company. For example, congressional hearings on factors important to the industry may be examined, an independent marketing survey of customer attitudes may be conducted, or the analyst may find it useful to speak with union members to determine their attitudes about the firm. The keynotes of a good individual security analysis are the same

---

[1] Relevant corporate reports include the annual and quarterly reports to shareholders, 10-K reports filed with the SEC, and any recent prospectuses.

as they are for an industry or market analysis: attempt to find unique information by being creative, ask "Why?" and "So what?" and distinguish the important from the trivial.

The fair value of a stock is positively related to the level and growth of its earnings per share (*EPS*) and negatively related to the risks associated with owning the stock. Therefore, a full section of this chapter is devoted to an analysis of past and future *EPS* growth, and another full section is devoted to risk evaluation and estimation of fair value. In addition, because management actions can have a major effect on a firm's earnings and risks, an additional section is devoted to evaluating management.

ANALYSIS OF *EPS* GROWTH

A General Model

In earlier chapters we noted that the intrinsic growth rate of a firm's earnings (*G*) is a function of the firm's return on equity (*ROE*) multiplied by its earnings retention rate (*B*); that is:

Intrinsic Growth Rate of Earnings

$$G = ROE \times B \qquad (22.1)$$

The logic of this relationship is easy to see. Suppose a firm is able to earn 20% per year on each dollar of equity invested. If half of all profits are retained, the equity balance increases by 10% at each year-end. In subsequent years the larger equity base continues to earn a 20% *ROE*, resulting in 10% higher profits (and dividends). Thus, the two basic forces contributing to both past and future earnings growth are the returns a firm is able to earn on its equity balance and the proportion of profits retained within the firm.

When examining trends in a firm's *EPS* growth rate over time, it is often useful to expand Equation 22.1 in a manner which explicitly highlights the relative importance of changes in the firm's (1) sales-generating ability, (2) expense control, (3) debt utilization, and (4) type of equity financing. This can be done by using the following equation:

$$
\begin{array}{c}
\underline{\text{Year-to-Year Relative Changes}} \\[4pt]
G_1 = \dfrac{\dfrac{TS_1}{TA_1}}{\dfrac{TS_0}{TA_0}} \times \dfrac{\dfrac{NI_1}{TS_1}}{\dfrac{NI_0}{TS_0}} \times \dfrac{\dfrac{TA_1}{NW_1}}{\dfrac{TA_0}{NW_0}} \times \left(\dfrac{BV_1}{BV_0}\right) - 1.0
\end{array}
\qquad (22.2)
$$

Earnings per Share Growth in Year 1 $\quad$ Sales Generation $\times$ Expense Control $\times$ Debt Utilization $\times$ Stock Financing $- 1.0$

where G_1 = percentage growth rate in earnings per share from year 0 to year 1, $TS_t =$ total sales in year t (when $t = 1$, we are referring to this year and when $t = 0$, we are referring to last year), TA_t = total assets in year t, NI_t = net income in year t, NW_t = net worth in year t, and BV_t = book value per share in year t (total net worth in t divided by the number of shares outstanding in t).

Any time one of the terms is greater than 1.0, this factor contributed to a positive *EPS* growth. Alternatively, if a term is less than 1.0, the factor tended to reduce *EPS*. When equal to 1.0, the factor had no impact upon *EPS* growth. Consider each term individually.

For example, the sales-generation term is calculated by dividing the year 1 asset turnover ratio by the year 0 turnover ratio. If, during year 1, the firm is able to generate a larger sales volume on the assets invested than it was able to generate in year 0, the term will be greater than 1.0. In such a case we can say that improved asset efficiency tended to lead to a positive growth in earnings per share. On the other hand, if the term is less than 1.0, a reduction in the year-to-year asset efficiency tended to reduce *EPS* (even though other factors might have offset the decline and resulted in higher *EPS*).

The second term examines the relative change in the firm's net profit margin from year to year. If the net profit margin in year 1 is higher than in year 0, the term will be greater than 1.0, suggesting that an improvement in expense control had a positive effect on earnings growth. Conversely, if the term is less than 1.0, the decline in the net profit margin tended to reduce the level of *EPS*.

The third term is the ratio of total assets in year 1 to net worth in year 1 divided by the equivalent ratio for year 0. Since the year 1 ratio could increase only if a larger proportion of assets were being financed with debt, this term reflects changes in the relative use of debt financing between the two years. If this debt-utilization term is greater than 1.0, the firm relied more heavily on debt financing in year 1, which resulted in a positive impact on *EPS* growth.[2] Finally, the ratio of the firm's book value per share in year 1 and year 0 reflects impacts which various equity-financing decisions have had on *EPS* growth. Book value per share can change with either the issuance of new stock or the retention of profits. We will see later how each of these two factors may have different impacts on *EPS* growth and why it is necessary to identify the relative importance of each in explaining *EPS* growth.

As an example of how Equation 22.2 is calculated, consider the balance sheet and income statement data of Anheuser-Busch, Inc. (A-B), shown in Tables 22-1 and 22-2. Details of Equation 22.2 would be calculated as follows:

Year-to-Year Relative Changes

$$\frac{\text{1987 EPS}}{\text{Growth}} = \frac{\text{Sales}}{\text{Generation}} \times \frac{\text{Expense}}{\text{Control}} \times \frac{\text{Debt}}{\text{Utilization}} \times \frac{\text{Stock}}{\text{Financing}} - 1.0$$

$$G_{87} = \frac{\dfrac{8{,}258.4}{6{,}491.6}}{\dfrac{7{,}677.2}{5{,}833.8}} \times \frac{\dfrac{614.7}{8{,}258.4}}{\dfrac{518.0}{7{,}677.2}} \times \frac{\dfrac{6{,}491.6}{2{,}892.2}}{\dfrac{5{,}833.8}{2{,}313.7}} \times \frac{9.598}{7.549} - 1.0$$

---

[2] This assumes, of course, that the firm's return on assets is sufficient to cover "imbedded" (existing) debt costs. If this is not true, then increases in debt utilization reduce *EPS* growth.

TABLE 22-1 *Consolidated Balance Sheet, Anheuser-Busch Companies, Inc., and Subsidiaries*

Assets (in millions)

December 31,	1987	1986
Current Assets:		
Cash and marketable securities (marketable securities of $78.0 in 1987 and $13.2 in 1986 at cost, which approximates market)	$ 111.3	$ 69.4
Accounts and notes receivable, less allowance for doubtful accounts of $3.8 in 1987 and $3.4 in 1986	382.5	373.0
Inventories—		
Raw materials and supplies	305.0	294.2
Work in process	85.7	84.6
Finished goods	61.2	49.0
Total inventories	451.9	427.8
Other current assets	179.6	150.4
Total current assets	1,125.3	1,020.6
Investments and Other Assets:		
Investments in and advances to unconsolidated subsidiaries	146.6	99.7
Investment properties	13.9	16.5
Deferred charges and other non-current assets	171.3	131.6
Excess of cost over net assets of acquired businesses, net	120.4	137.8
	452.2	385.6
Plant and Equipment:		
Land	109.6	102.3
Buildings	1,829.3	1,715.9
Machinery and equipment	4,160.4	3,804.2
Construction in progress	717.3	466.9
	6,816.6	6,099.3
Less accumulated depreciation	1,902.5	1,671.7
	$6,491.6	$5,833.8

$$= \frac{1.272}{1.316} \times \frac{0.0744}{0.0675} \times \frac{2.244}{2.521} \times 1.271$$

$$= 0.967 \times 1.103 \times 0.890 \times 1.271$$

$$= 0.207$$

$$= 20.7\%$$

Looking at the details of these results, we can see that three variables contributed to most of the 20.7% earnings growth in 1987. First, expense control improved, as seen by the increase in the net profit margin from 6.75% in 1986 to 7.44% in 1987. Second, the use of debt decreased. In 1986 each dollar of equity supported $2.521 in total assets—or $1.521 of debt. During 1987 each dollar of equity supported only $2.244 of assets—or $1.244 of debt. Although the difference is not dramatic, this decreased

TABLE 22-1 *(continued)*

Liabilities and Shareholders Equity (in millions)

December 31,	1987	1986
Current Liabilities:		
Short-term debt	$ .9	$ 34.7
Accounts payable	539.6	491.7
Accrued salaries, wages, and benefits	194.8	180.0
Accrued interest payable	39.2	31.0
Due to customers for returnable containers	38.4	34.0
Accrued taxes, other than income taxes	61.5	63.7
Estimated income taxes	45.5	71.8
Other current liabilities	122.5	108.7
Total current liabilities	1,042.4	1,015.6
Long-Term Debt	1,396.5	1,126.8
Deferred Income Taxes	1,160.5	1,090.8
Convertible Redeemable Preferred Stock	–	286.9
Shareholders Equity:		
Common stock, $1.00 par value, authorized 400,000,000 shares in 1987 and 1986 and 200,000,000 shares in 1985	326.9	295.3
Capital in excess of par value	332.4	6.1
Retained earnings	2,917.6	2,472.2
Foreign currency translation adjustment	10.8	.9
	3,587.7	2,774.5
Less cost of treasury stock	695.5	460.8
	2,892.2	2,313.7
Commitments and Contingencies	–	–
	$6,491.6	$5,833.8

use of debt financing resulted in lower earnings growth. Finally, the ratio of book value per share rose substantially during the year. We review the causes of this later.

To understand how well or poorly a firm has fared in the past, we should compare it with other firms in the same industry class. Starting in the late 1970s, the domestic U.S. brewing industry underwent a transformation which is continuing today. A major competitive struggle took place for increased market share, primarily through extensive marketing campaigns but also through price reductions. As a result, many smaller brewing firms faced declining profits and had to be merged into larger, more profitable firms. Two problems faced the small brewers: (1) lack of marketing expertise and (2) the fact that small size itself precluded economies of sale.

A major competitor of A-B is Miller Brewing. Unfortunately, direct financial comparisons between the two are impossible since Miller is a wholly owned subsidiary of Philip Morris. In place of Miller, we will compare A-B with G. Heileman and Adolph Coors, two major competitors.

TABLE 22-2 *Consolidated Statement of Income, Anheuser-Busch Companies, Inc., and Subsidiaries*

(In millions, except per share data)

Year ended December 31,	1987	1986	1985
Sales	$9,019.1	$8,401.7	$7,683.3
Less federal and state excise taxes	760.7	724.5	683.0
Net Sales	8,258.4	7,677.2	7,000.3
Cost of products sold	5,310.3	4,969.2	4,676.1
Gross Profit	2,948.1	2,708.0	2,324.2
Marketing, administrative, and research expenses	1,819.0	1,702.9	1,491.9
Operating Income	1,129.1	1,005.1	832.3
Other Income and Expenses:			
Interest expense	(124.4)	(96.9)	(93.4)
Interest capitalized	40.3	33.2	37.2
Interest income	12.8	9.6	21.3
Other expense, net	(1.7)	(9.8)	(16.9)
Income Before Income Taxes	1,056.1	941.2	780.5
Provision for Income Taxes:			
Current	360.9	291.2	130.1
Deferred	80.5	132.0	206.7
	441.4	423.2	336.8
Net Income	$ 614.7	$ 518.0	$ 443.7
Earnings per Share	$ 2.04	$ 1.69	$ 1.42

Table 22-3 shows the results of Equation 22.2 for A-B, Heileman, and Coors. Over the 1980–87 period, A-B increased its earnings per share by 223.8% owing in large part to retention of profits (stock financing) and improved profit margins. In contrast, both Coors and Heileman suffered declines in earnings per share owing to reduced sales generation for each dollar of asset investment and to declines in profit margins. These are areas which need careful examination.

Sales Generation

Product Line and Market Share. Clearly, the first place to start a company analysis is with the firm's product line. Virtually all firms sell a wide variety of products to a large number of customers. Although the characteristics of each product are different, the analyst should group the products into reasonably segmented categories. For example, Anheuser-Busch, Inc., sells not only a wide variety of beers but also various yeast and corn products to other manufacturers, operates a number of public entertainment parks, develops residential property, repairs railroad cars, and owns the St. Louis Cardinals baseball team. Ideally, each major product segment should

TABLE 22-3 *Details of EPS Growth Components*

Period	EPS Growth	=	Sales Generation	×	Expense Control	×	Debt Use	×	Stock Financing
Anheuser-Busch									
80–87	2.238		0.945		1.428		0.951		2.524
80–81	0.270		0.995		1.084		1.009		1.167
81–82	0.163		0.876		1.059		1.073		1.167
82–83	0.161		1.188		0.963		0.959		1.058
83–84	0.148		1.031		1.044		0.946		1.127
84–85	0.145		0.951		1.053		1.016		1.126
85–86	0.190		0.963		1.065		1.070		1.085
86–87	0.207		0.967		1.103		0.890		1.272
Adolph Coors									
80–87	−0.290		0.938		0.487		1.119		1.388
80–81	−0.204		0.984		0.764		1.006		1.053
81–82	−0.223		0.934		0.785		1.014		1.045
82–83	1.217		1.058		1.833		1.044		1.095
83–84	−0.498		0.970		0.491		1.015		1.037
84–85	0.188		1.060		1.056		1.015		1.045
85–86	0.086		0.953		1.083		1.012		1.039
86–87	−0.200		0.984		0.789		1.007		1.022
Heileman Brewing									
80–86	−0.376		0.661		0.825		1.040		1.099
80–81	0.053		1.014		1.038		0.882		1.135
81–82	−0.308		0.690		1.052		1.279		0.745
82–83	−0.169		1.251		0.944		0.857		0.821
83–84	0.411		1.036		0.790		0.876		1.968
84–85	−0.185		0.797		0.947		1.127		0.958
85–86	−0.055		0.927		1.111		0.961		0.954

be analyzed separately. Unfortunately, most firms provide only sketchy data about the revenues and costs of each segment.[3] In the case of A-B virtually all revenues, assets, and income are derived from the brewing operations. Consequently, we won't analyze the numerous other subsidiaries in any depth.

In addition, the analyst should have a clear understanding of the nature of the firm's customers. Do a few customers dominate total sales? Is the customer base largely located in one geographic area? Are the sales of the firm's customers made, in turn, to a few customers or a geographically limited area? For example, a machine tool company may sell its products to a large number of different firms, but if they, in turn, sell their products solely to the U.S. Department of Defense, then the machine tool company has only one eventual customer, the U.S. federal government.

---

[3]In FAS 14 the Financial Accounting Standards Board has specified the types of product segment information required and under what conditions the information is necessary.

Once various product segments have been identified, it is useful to examine the firm's relative industry market share. Usually, it is wise to calculate market shares based on units of product sold as opposed to dollar sales volume because this eliminates any differences due to different product-pricing strategies which might arise between firms. In Table 22-4, percentage market shares are shown for the major U.S. brewers for the years 1970–1986. Throughout this period A-B gained substantially larger market shares at the expense of most of the smaller brewers. By 1986 A-B had about 40% of the market, whereas it had controlled only 29% in 1980. A large part of this change in relative market shares can be traced to the acquisition of Miller Brewing by Philip Morris and the intensive competition Philip Morris created in the industry at that time.

This competition was most prevalent in three areas. First, advertising and general marketing expenditures were increased dramatically. While Miller's initial advertising thrust hurt, Anheuser quickly recovered and was able to increase its market share along with Miller. Smaller competitors responded with inadequate and, at times, even disastrous advertising campaigns. Second, a large number of new brands were introduced in an effort to attract new beer drinkers—in particular, new light beers and premium brands. Miller, A-B, and, to an extent, Coors and Heileman were able to introduce new brands which the public accepted more rapidly than those of other firms.

Finally, price competition between brands occurred at various times. From this evidence it appears that the managements of A-B, Miller, and Stroh were best able to respond to changing public desires and capture larger market shares. Whether this will continue into the long term is debatable. There is nothing unique about a firm's ability to attract and hold good management. Management is free to move from firm to firm in response to higher compensation packages, or good management can be developed internally. Thus, it's possible that at some time in the future any remaining brewers (small regional brewers) may be able to compete more effectively with A-B, Miller,

TABLE 22-4 *Leading U.S. Brewers' Domestic Beer Market Share (in percent)*

Brewer	1970	1980	1983	1984	1985	1986
Anheuser-Busch	18.2	28.9	34.1	35.9	38.2	39.8
Miller Brewing (Philip Morris)	4.2	21.5	22.3	21.1	20.8	21.3
Stroh Brewing	2.7	3.6	13.7	13.4	13.1	12.6
G. Heileman Brewing	2.5	7.7	9.9	9.4	9.1	8.8
Adolph Coors	6.0	8.0	7.7	7.4	8.3	8.4
Pabst Brewing	8.6	8.7	7.2	6.5	5.0	4.0
Genesee Brewing	1.2	2.1	1.8	1.7	1.7	1.7
Christian Schmidt	2.5	2.1	1.8	1.4	1.2	1.0
Falstaff Brewing	5.4	2.3	1.5	1.3	1.1	1.1
Pittsburgh Brewing	—	0.6	0.6	0.5	0.5	0.5
Other	48.7	14.7	0.6	1.4	1.4	0.9
Total[1]	100.0	100.0	100.0	100.0	100.0	100.0

[1]Addition of columns may not agree because of rounding.

Source: Various issues of *Standard & Poor's Industry Surveys.*

TABLE 22-5 *Log–Least-Squares Regression of Growth in Sales*

ln ($ Sales) = Constant + CAGR (Year) (1978–1987)

	Constant	*CAGR*	R^2
Anheuser-Busch	−284.73	0.1479	96.9%
Adolph Coors	−156.21	0.0822	94.4
G. Heileman	−278.14	0.1437	82.9

and Stroh as they learn from their past mistakes. Of course, many of the firms which lost market shares in the late 1980s may go out of business or merge with others. But there is no strong reason to believe that over the *long run* smaller firms won't be able to regain a portion of their lost market shares.[4]

Exactly how long a firm should be able to maintain its market share is difficult to estimate. Certainly the simple fact that one firm appears to have a better management group is worth something. And yet new blood can enter most businesses quite easily: witness the major change in competition when Philip Morris entered the brewing industry by acquiring Miller's. Having good management today is certainly no lock on future market share. Nonetheless, in some industries a firm may be able to effectively lock in its market share for a lengthy period by means of patent protection or maintaining an R&D group which is able to consistently stay ahead of the competition.

Sales Growth and Variability. Compound annual growth rates in sales and R^2 values are shown in Table 22-5 using log–least-squares regression analysis. (Note that Miller is not included.) The results are much as one would expect having seen the market share statistics presented in Table 22-4. Between 1978 and the end of 1987, A-B's dollar sales grew at a compound annual growth rate (*CAGR*) of 14.8%, while Heileman had a 14.4% *CAGR*. For A-B, this growth was reasonably stable, as evidenced by the R^2 values of around 97%. Heileman's growth was somewhat more erratic (and slowed substantially after 1984). Coors' lower growth of 8.2% was due to the relative lack of market acceptance for its product.

Asset Efficiency. After the analyst becomes familiar with trends in market shares, sales growth rates, and the implications these may have on future sales growth, the firm's asset efficiency ratios can be interpreted. By asset efficiency we mean the firm's ability to generate sales from a given level of asset investment. Table 22-6 presents asset efficiency ratios for A-B, Coors, and Heileman. Accounting policies often differ among firms, causing difficulties in comparing such ratios. Most brewers use fairly

---

[4]An example of how good management can successfully defend market share for an extended period of time but eventually lose a part of it through more effective competition is General Motors. Throughout the 1950s and the 1960s the management of GM was well recognized as premier in the auto business. Because of less-effective management at Ford, AMC, and Chrysler, General Motors was able to hold or increase its market share. Yet eventually more effective competition arose from foreign manufacturers, and GM lost a major part of its market.

TABLE 22-6 *Brewer Asset Efficiency Ratios*

	1981	1982	1983	1984	1985	1986	1987
Total Asset Turnover							
Anheuser-Busch	1.33	1.17	1.39	1.44	1.37	1.32	1.27
Coors	0.97	0.91	0.96	0.93	0.99	0.94	0.93
Heileman	2.51	1.73	2.17	2.25	1.79	1.66	NA
Plant Turnover							
Anheuser-Busch	1.70	1.53	1.88	1.85	1.80	1.73	1.68
Coors	1.43	1.30	1.42	1.36	1.55	1.45	1.38
Heileman	5.02	5.20	3.38	3.39	3.30	3.14	NA
Accounts Receivable Turnover							
Anheuser-Busch	26.00	19.00	21.00	24.00	23.00	21.00	21.00
Coors	14.00	14.00	15.00	15.00	15.70	13.00	12.00
Heileman	35.00	29.00	31.00	33.00	35.00	25.00	NA
Collection Period (Days)							
Anheuser-Busch	14.00	19.00	17.00	15.00	16.00	17.00	17.00
Coors	26.00	26.00	24.00	24.00	23.00	28.00	30.00
Heileman	10.00	13.00	12.00	11.00	10.00	14.40	NA
Inventory Turnover (on Sales)							
Anheuser-Busch	16.80	14.90	20.20	20.60	20.70	17.90	18.30
Coors	8.00	7.70	8.60	8.70	8.90	8.40	8.70
Heileman	11.90	12.40	10.20	12.00	11.90	12.20	NA
Inventory Turnover (on Cost of Sales)							
Anheuser-Busch	13.00	10.80	13.80	14.00	13.80	11.60	11.70
Coors	5.70	5.60	5.60	6.20	6.04	5.40	5.70
Heileman	8.70	8.90	7.30	8.70	8.50	8.50	NA
Days of Inventory on Hand							
Anheuser-Busch	28.00	34.00	27.00	26.00	26.00	32.00	31.00
Coors	64.00	66.00	65.00	59.00	60.00	66.00	63.00
Heileman	42.00	41.00	50.00	42.00	42.00	42.00	NA

equivalent accounting procedures, however, so we do not have a comparability problem here. In addition, if a firm has experienced major changes in certain balance sheet accounts from year to year, it is wise to calculate the various ratios based on average year-to-year balance sheet values. Since major changes in the brewing company balance sheets didn't occur, the ratios shown in Table 22-6 are based on year-end values.

A review of Table 22-6 indicates that:

1. Heileman consistently had the greatest sales generation per dollar of asset investment. However, this was quite volatile.

2. Each brewer shows a decrease in asset turnover after 1984, suggesting that sales growth was not keeping pace with asset expansion.

3. Plant turnover tells the same story.

4. The accounts receivable turnover (and collection period) of Heileman is the best. The receivables of A-B are reasonable and appear to be well managed.

5. The inventory control at A-B appears to be the best and without any apparent trends.

Care should be taken when interpreting these ratios, since they can vary with product differences, marketing strategies, or management effectiveness.

EXPENSE CONTROL

The best place to start an analysis of a firm's ability to maintain reasonable control over expenses is with a percentage income statement. Such a statement is shown in Table 22-7. A percentage income statement simply expresses each item reported on the firm's published income statement as a percentage of net sales. In many industries gross sales are virtually identical to net sales. In the brewing industry, however, fairly large excise taxes are charged by various states and the federal government. Table 22-7 shows that A-B's profit margin was between 5.7% and 7.4% of net sales, better than both Coors and Heileman. A-B does appear to have an edge in managerial control of expenses.

Although there were no accounting-based "extraordinary items" during the years shown in Table 22-7, they can often distort calculations of net profit margins. For

TABLE 22-7 *Percentage Income Statement*

Anheuser-Busch	*1981*	*1982*	*1983*	*1984*	*1985*	*1986*	*1987*
Sales	114.6	113.3	110.3	110.1	109.7	109.4	109.2
Less Excise Taxes	−14.6	−13.3	−10.3	−10.1	−9.7	−9.4	−9.2
Net Sales	100.0	100.0	100.0	100.0	100.0	100.0	100.0
Cost of Goods Sold	−77.3	−72.8	−68.2	−67.9	−66.8	−64.7	−64.3
Gross Profit	22.7	27.2	31.8	32.1	33.2	35.3	35.7
Marketing and Administrative Costs	−13.4	−16.4	−20.2	−20.5	−21.3	−22.2	−22.0
Operating Profit Before Tax	9.3	10.8	11.6	11.6	11.9	13.1	13.7
Interest Income	0.2	0.4	0.2	0.4	0.3	0.1	0.1
Interest Capitalized					0.5	0.4	0.5
Interest Expense	−2.3	−1.9	−1.8	−1.6	−1.3	−1.3	−1.5
Other Income or Expense	1.3	1.1	0.2	0.2	−0.2	−0.1	0.0
Income Before Taxes	8.5	10.4	10.2	10.6	9.5	12.2	12.8
Taxes	−2.8	−4.1	−4.4	−4.6	−4.8	−5.5	−5.3
Net Income	5.7	6.3	5.8	6.0	6.3	6.7	7.4
Net Profit Margins							
Anheuser-Busch	5.7	6.3	5.8	6.0	6.3	6.7	7.4
Coors	5.6	4.4	8.0	4.0	4.2	4.5	3.6
Heileman	5.0	5.2	5.0	3.9	3.7	4.1	NA

example, in 1979 Anheuser-Busch had switched from "normalizing" investment tax credits to a procedure known as "flow-through" accounting. This accounting adjustment had no effect at all on the firm's true economic income but did cause reported accounting earnings per share to be 36% higher than they would have been without the accounting change.[5]

As many details as possible should be obtained about a firm's expenses. Since the basic income statement presented in annual reports is often quite sketchy, this forces the analyst to read statement footnotes and 10-K reports closely, to obtain independent data on raw material and labor costs, and to look for anything that might provide a better breakdown of expenses. For example, management's discussion of yearly operations for A-B typically provides data on wage, salary, pension, and insurance costs. Similarly, the footnotes provide information on depreciation and leasing costs. In addition, outside data can be evaluated to determine trends in the cost of raw materials. Remember that only by knowing more about a firm than others do can one make better judgments about the fair value of its stock.

In the case of A-B it is likely that the profit margin of 7.4% (or slightly above) is a maximum for some years to come; most likely it will decline somewhat. Competition has been stiff and has forced selling prices to remain fairly stable. Depreciation expenses are likely to rise because of new and more costly plant additions. Advertising costs are clearly going to rise in response to the continuing intra-industry battle for market share. So, over the period 1988–1995, profit margins (before extraordinary items) on the order of 5.5% to 6.0% are likely.

Debt Utilization

The use of debt financing has a number of impacts on a firm's financial condition which must be understood by the analyst. In particular, debt financing affects (1) reported returns on equity, (2) reported earnings per share, and (3) risk.

Reported *ROE* and *EPS*. Earlier we mentioned that the accounting return on equity (*ROE*) is equal to the return on assets (*ROA*) multiplied by the ratio of total assets to net worth (*TA* ÷ *NW*); that is:

Return on Equity $$ROE = (ROA)(TA/NW) \qquad (22.3)$$

This is true, however, only if one measures *ROA* as being equal to net income after taxes *and interest expense* divided by total assets. For example, referring to A-B's financial statements in Tables 22-1 and 22-2, the 1987 return on equity (*ROE*) would be 21.25%:

---

[5]Reported *EPS* were $4.34 in 1979, whereas they would have been $3.19 if the accounting change to flow-through had not occurred. Flow-through accounting is discussed in Chapter 23.

$$ROE = \frac{\$614.7}{\$6,491.6} \times \frac{\$6,491.6}{\$2,892.2}$$

$$= 0.0947 \times 2.244 = 0.2125$$

Note that the net income of $614.7 million is shown *after* interest expense.

Since interest expense is determined not by the level of total assets or the profits which flow from the assets but, instead, by an independent financing decision made by management, a better definition of *ROA* is needed. In particular, *ROA* should be measured as *net operating income* after tax divided by total assets. Referring again to Table 22-2, we see that 1987 net operating income before tax was $1,129.1 million. In addition, interest income (+$12.8 million) and other expenses (−$1.7 million) totaled +$11.1 million. While these two items are not technically "operating items," they are reasonably small and can be expected to continue in the future. So they will be added to the $1,129.1 figure to obtain a revised pretax operating profit of $1,140.2. The tax rate can be estimated by dividing total taxes by taxable income: $441.4/ $1,056.1 = 0.42. Using these values, we can estimate the revised *ROA* (denoted as ROA^*) as follows:

$$ROA^* = \frac{\$1,140.2(1 - 0.42)}{\$6,491.6}$$

$$= 10.22\% \text{ (off slightly due to rounding of tax rate)}$$

Using this revised version of ROA^*, we can now examine how a firm's debt structure influences its accounting *ROE* and *EPS*. We define the following terms:

ROA^* = our revised (and more accurate) measure of return on assets

K_D = interest cost of debt (pretax)

TR = the firm's tax rate

D = the firm's total debt level

NW = the firm's total net worth

TA = $D + NW$

BV = the book value of stock (*NW* divided by the number of shares outstanding)

Then we can derive the following relationships:

Determinants of *ROE*	$ROE = ROA^* + D/NW[ROA^* - K_D(1 - TR)]$	**(22.4)**
Determinants of *EPS*	$EPS = ROE \times BV$	**(22.5)**

The 1987 values for A-B would be:[6]

---

[6]The numbers are off slightly because of rounding. The number of shares was calculated by dividing net income of $614.7 by *EPS* of $2.04.

$$ROE = 0.1022 + 1.244 \ [0.1022 - 0.0234 \ (1 - 0.42)]$$

$$= 0.2125$$

$$EPS = 0.2125 \ (\$2,892.2/301.324 \ \text{shares})$$

$$= \$2.04$$

Armed with Equations 22.4 and 22.5, we can now discuss how debt financing affects a firm's *ROE* and *EPS*. Using Equation 22.4 first, we can see that *an increase in the debt-to-equity ratio will always increase the firm's reported ROE* if marginal after-tax debt costs are less than marginal after-tax asset returns. For example, A-B's average after-tax debt cost was about 1.36% in 1987, and its average return on assets was 10.22%. While additional assets could probably be acquired to yield a 10.22% marginal return, it is unlikely that new debt would be available at an after-tax cost of 1.36%. Assume that an increase in the debt-to-equity ratio to 1.6 would require new debt costs of 5.0% after tax. Since the marginal *ROA* (10.2%) is greater than the marginal debt cost (5.0%), the *ROE* would rise. Table 22-8 continues with this example and shows how different levels of debt financing influence a firm's *ROE*. As seen, once the marginal return on assets is less than the marginal cost of debt, the *ROE* falls. However, for most firms the debt ratio must be very large before new debt costs begin to reduce *ROE*. In most cases returns on equity will rise as the level of debt financing increases. Only in rare cases will increased use of debt result in a lower *ROE*.

Turning to Equation 22.5 and the impact of debt on reported earnings per share, we find much the same thing. As long as marginal after-tax debt costs are lower than marginal asset returns, increased debt levels result in higher *EPS*. The only potential caveat to this statement is the requirement that common share book values not change as the debt levels change.

From the analyst's viewpoint, it is important to clearly recognize the implications of these results. Increased debt levels will usually result in higher *ROE* and *EPS* levels. Even if management is *unable* to improve its market share, asset efficiency, or expense control, the firm will show higher *ROE* levels and growth in *EPS* simply because it relies more heavily on debt financing. However, any growth that results solely

TABLE 22-8 *Example of How Marginal Debt Costs and ROA* Affect ROE*

D/NW	Marginal After-Tax Debt Cost	Total Interest Expense Old + New = Total	ROA*	ROE[1]
0	—	—	0.102	0.102
1.24	1.36%	$1.24 × 0.0136 = $0.01686	0.102	0.102
1.60	5.00%	$0.01686 + $0.36 × 0.05 = $0.03486	0.102	0.231
2.00	8.00%	$0.03486 + $0.40 × 0.08 = $0.06686	0.102	0.239
2.50	12.00%	$0.06686 + $0.5 × 0.12 = $0.1269	0.102	0.230

[1]Calculated using Equation 22.4.

from debt changes is likely to be a one-time effect (one cannot continually use additional debt to increase *EPS*) and result in greater default risk on the debt and systematic market risk to the equity. Analysts should take care not to praise management for earnings growth and *ROE* levels which arise solely from changes in debt financing. Any management team can play with debt structure. Instead, asset returns should receive the most attention, and pats on the back should be given for good asset efficiency and expense control.

Debt and Systematic Risk. A common stock's beta is directly related to the extent of debt financing used by the firm. The risk that debt adds to equity ownership is all nondiversifiable. Hamada has shown that a reasonably close approximation to this relationship is:

$$B_E = B_A \left[1 + \frac{D}{NW} (1 - TR) \right] \tag{22.6}$$

where B_E = beta of the equity, B_A = beta of the assets, D/NW = the debt-to-net-worth ratio (calculated using market values, not book values), and TR = the firm's tax rate. Later in the chapter we will have occasion to use this model to adjust A-B's stock beta for the recent increase in debt financing.

Evaluation of Anheuser-Busch's Default Risk. Table 22-9 presents various default risk ratios for A-B. From A-B's favorable ROA^* and *ROE* and the fundamental stability of industry demand, it seems fair to conclude that default risk is minor.

Stock Financing

The final term to be examined in Equation 22.2 is the book value ratio. As the book value per share increases over time, so do earnings per share. This is only a logical consequence of the fact that accounting returns to equity holders are defined as *EPS* earned per dollar of book value invested ($ROE = EPS \div BV$). Thus, if *ROE* is constant, higher equity book values will yield higher *EPS*. Changes in book value per

TABLE 22-9 *Historical Analysis of Anheuser-Busch's Default Risk*

Ratio	1981	1983	1985	1986	1987
Times Interest Covered					
Earnings	4.6	6.6	8.9	10.4	9.2
Cash Flow	5.8	8.2	11.5	13.2	11.7
Debt to Equity	1.38	1.11	1.35	1.52	1.24
Long-Term Debt to Equity	0.68	0.47	0.5	0.53	0.48
Short-Term Debt to Total Debt	0.51	0.58	0.5	0.47	0.43
Current Ratio	1.09	1.24	1.2	1	1.08
Quick Ratio	0.19	0.3	0.6	0.58	0.64

share can be attributed to two fundamental causes: (1) the retention of profits and (2) the sale of new stock (or the repurchase of outstanding stock). For example, if the details of A-B's 1986 and 1987 statements are analyzed, the change in common shares outstanding, total net worth, and book value per share can be organized as follows:

	Total Net Worth (Millions)	Average Shares (Millions)	Effect on Book Value
Start of 1987	$2,313.7	306.509	$7.55
Net Shares Bought	+ 132.30	−5.186	0.59
Retained Profit	496.2	—	1.46
End of 1987	$2,892.2	301.323	$9.60

In this case, the major part of book value growth can be traced to the retention of profits.

Retention of Profits. The larger the retention rate of profits, the greater the increase in per-share book values and the greater the growth in *EPS*. This is simply a restatement of our earlier definition of earnings growth, which said that sustainable growth is equal to *ROE* multiplied by the retention rate. Figure 22-1 plots the retention rates of A-B and various competitors between 1970 and 1987. Of the three firms, A-B consistently had the lowest retention rate. This was probably due in large part to Heileman's and Coors' attempts to grow as rapidly as possible in order to obtain economies of scale and compete with Miller and A-B on a national scale. In recent years A-B has had a fairly consistent profit-retention rate equal to about 70% of profits.

Stock Financing. The extent to which a firm engages in external stock financing and the per-share price of such financing have an impact on the reported growth of earnings per share and the fair value of the firm's stock. In our discussion of new stock financing we will first concentrate on reported *EPS* growth and then on stock values. The two are not necessarily interrelated, because *EPS* growth can often arise from accounting conventions which have little to do with changes in the economic value of a firm's stock. Yet there are situations in which stock financings do have real economic impacts on the income levels available to current shareholders. If real economic effects of future stock financings *are anticipated* by existing shareholders before the events occur, they should have no effect on share values when they actually occur. However, if these new stock financings are unexpected and have a real economic impact on the *EPS* available to current shareholders, they will affect stock prices only when they occur. These relationships are somewhat complex, and the reader should pay close attention.

The percentage *EPS* growth model of Equation 22.2 states that:

$$\text{Percentage Change in } EPS \text{ During Year 1} = \left(\frac{ROE_1}{ROE_0}\right)\left(\frac{BV_1}{BV_0}\right) - 1.0$$

New stock financing can have two effects on the reported gain in *EPS*. First, the return on equity during period 1 may be different from that in period 0 if the return

FIGURE 22-1 *Comparative Profit-Retention Rates*

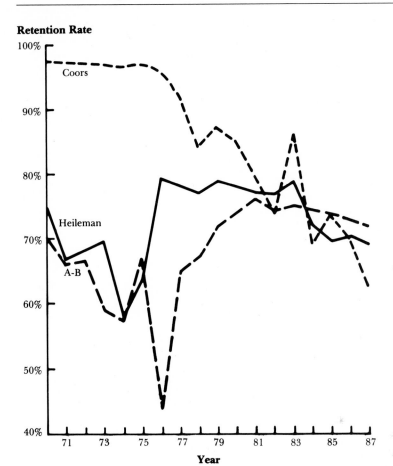

Retention Rate

earned on new investment is different from that earned on old investment ($ROE_1 \neq ROE_0$). Second, if the new shares are not sold at current book values, the per-share book value will change ($BV_1 \neq BV_0$). The net results of these two changes can be expressed as follows:[7]

$$\text{Percentage Change in } EPS \text{ During Year 1} = \frac{N_0}{N_0 + n}\left[1 + \frac{n}{N_0}\left(\frac{P}{BV_0}\right)\left(\frac{ROE^1}{ROE}\right)\right] - 1.0 \qquad (22.7)$$

where N_0 = the end-of-period-0 shares outstanding, n = the new shares sold during year 1, P = the price at which new shares are sold, BV_0 = the book value per share

---

[7]This model assumes that all earnings are paid out as dividends. Results for retention of profits are similar but more complex.

of old shares at year 0, ROE^1 = the return earned on new share investment (the marginal return on new investment), and ROE = the return earned on old share investment (the average return on old investment). For example, assume that at period 0 a firm has 1,000 shares outstanding with a book value of $10 and an ROE of 20%. At the start of year 1 the firm sells 1,000 new shares for $20 each, which can be invested at a marginal return of 20%. Details of the year-to-year EPS gain are shown in the top half of Table 22-10. As seen in the table, the percentage earnings gain is equal to 50%:

$$\frac{1,000}{1,000 + 1,000} \left[1 + \left(\frac{1,000}{1,000}\right)\left(\frac{\$20}{\$10}\right)\left(\frac{0.20}{0.20}\right)\right] - 1.0 = 50\%$$

In this case, the 50% EPS growth arose from selling stock at a price above book value. Returns on equity weren't changed. Even if ROEs are unaffected, the sale of stock above (or below) book value will increase (or decrease) reported EPS. The bottom half of Table 22-10 illustrates a slightly different situation, one in which new stock is sold at book value but at a higher marginal rate of return than previously earned. As expected, EPS increases. Per Equation 22.7:

$$\frac{1,000}{2,000} \left[1 + \left(\frac{1,000}{1,000}\right)\left(\frac{\$10}{\$10}\right)\left(\frac{0.30}{0.20}\right)\right] - 1.0 = 25\%$$

TABLE 22-10 *Effect on EPS on New Stock Sale*

	Period 0	Start of Period 1		End of Period 1
Net Worth	$10,000	+ 1,000 × $20	=	$30,000
Shares Outstanding	1,000	+ 1,000	=	2,000
BV Per Share	$10			$15
Net Income	$2,000			$2,000 + (0.2)(20,000)
ROE	20%			20%
EPS	$2			$3
Price of Stock	$20			NA

$$\text{Percentage Gain in } EPS = \frac{\$3.00 - \$2.00}{\$2.00} = 50\%$$

	Period 0	Start of Period 1		End of Period 1
Net Worth	$10,000	+ 1,000 × $10	=	$20,000
Shares Outstanding	1,000	+ 1,000	=	2,000
BV Per Share	$10			$10
Net Income	$2,000			$2,000 + (0.3)(10,000)
ROE	20%			25%
EPS	$2			$2.50
Price of Stock	$10			NA

$$\text{Percentage Gain in } EPS = \frac{\$2.50 - \$2.00}{\$2.00} = 25\%$$

If price/book ratios are 1.0, the sale of stock to be invested at a higher (or lower) return than is earned on current equity will increase (or decrease) *EPS*.

Whether stock prices should be affected by the automatic *EPS* growth which can arise out of new stock sales depends on whether the sale was expected or unexpected. If shareholders at date 0 expect the firm to report higher *EPS* because of new stock financing, the higher *EPS* for period 1 will already have been discounted in the stock's price. However, *unexpected EPS* growth would affect prices at the time of an earnings announcement, not before. But regardless of whether the automatic growth in *EPS* arising from new stock financings is expected or unexpected, analysts must recognize the cause of the growth for what it is. Unless *ROE* improves, the growth does not arise from management's ability to use assets efficiently or control operating costs. If the growth arises solely from a difference in market/book ratios, it stems closely from an accounting convention. As in the case of automatic growth in *EPS* resulting from the use of larger debt levels, the analyst should be wary about giving management any undue praise for an *EPS* gain associated with selling stock above book value.

An effect analogous to this is the (short-term) locked-in *EPS* growth which results when a firm with a high P/E ratio acquires another firm with a lower P/E ratio. As an example of this, consider the data provided in Table 22-11 on firms *A* and *B*. If Firm *A* acquires Firm *B* at *B*'s outstanding market value, then Firm *A*'s *EPS* will show an immediate increase, due simply to the fact that *A* has a higher P/E ratio than *B*. Since Firm *B* has a total market value of $80 million ($40 × 2 million) and Firm

TABLE 22-11 *EPS Growth Resulting from Acquiring a Firm with a Lower P/E Ratio*

	Premerger	
	Firm A	*Firm B*
Net Worth	$200 million	$80 million
Shares Outstanding	5 million	2 million
BV Per Share	$40.00	$40.00
Net Income	$20 million	$8 million
ROE	10.0%	10.0%
EPS	$4.00	$4.00
Price of Stock	$60.00	$40.00
P/E Ratio	15×	10×

	Postmerger
Net Worth	$280 million (200 million + 80 million)
Shares Outstanding	6⅓ million (5 million + 1⅓ million)
BV Per Share	$44.21
Net Income	$28 million
ROE	10.0%
EPS	$4.42

$$\text{Percentage Growth in } EPS = \frac{\$4.42 - \$4.00}{\$4.00} = 10.5\%$$

A stock is valued at $60 per share, Firm A will issue 1⅓ million new shares ($80 million ÷ $60) to current shareholders of Firm B. Combining each firm's net income results in total merged income of $28 million and an *EPS* after the merger of $4.42 [$28 ÷ (5 + 1⅓)]. *EPS* has grown from $4.00 to $4.42, or 10.53%. In terms of Equation 22.7, 1⅓ million new shares were issued on top of the 5 million outstanding at a price of $60 per share. In turn, total earnings rose $8 million, which, on an investment of $80 million ($60 × 1⅓ million), represents a marginal accounting return on new investment of 10% ($8 ÷ $80). Using Equation 22.7:

$$\frac{5}{5 + 1\frac{1}{3}} \left[1 + \left(\frac{1\frac{1}{3}}{5}\right) \left(\frac{\$60}{\$40}\right) \left(\frac{0.10}{0.10}\right) \right] - 1.0 = 10.53\%$$

Again, the sole reason for the *EPS* to rise was that Firm A acquired a firm with a *lower P/E ratio*.

What effect should this merger have on the price of Firm A's shares? Before the merger, investors believed the total value of Firm A was equal to $300 million (5 million × $60) and the total value of Firm B was equal to $80 million (2 million × $40). Unless some form of economic synergy results from a merger of the two, their total value together should be the sum of their values apart—$380 million.[8] Since 6⅓ million shares would be outstanding, each postmerger share price should be worth $60, the same as Firm A's premerger share price. Therefore, unless economic synergies result from combining the two firms, share prices should not be affected. Then how should we reconcile the fact that *EPS* rises but share prices remain unchanged? The answer to this lies in understanding why Firm A's and Firm B's share prices aren't equal. Ignoring any potential difference in the market risk of each, Firm A's higher P/E ratio can be explained only by higher expected *EPS* growth. Investors perceived a higher *EPS* growth rate for Firm A than they did for Firm B. But once A acquires B, its expected growth rate will be lowered by the inclusion of B's slower growth. The net results can be seen in Figure 22-2. Before the merger, A's current *EPS* was low but expected to increase rapidly. The present value of the low current *EPS* plus the high future *EPS* was judged to be worth $60 per share. After the merger, current earnings rise but at the expense of having lower future earnings levels. The current *EPS* advantage is exactly offset by eventually lower *EPS*, and the stock is still worth $60 per share.[9]

MANAGEMENT EVALUATION

In the long run a firm's profit level and risks are determined by the actions of the firm's management. In the short run external forces such as governmental policies, international events, weather, and business cycles can have impacts on profits and

---

[8] Examples of economic synergies are using A's marketing channels to increase B's sales, using economies of scale to reduce both firm's total costs, etc. Anything that would increase the firm's combined economic income is an economic synergy.

[9] Our discussion of merger analysis stops here. Interested readers should consult Van Horne, Brealey and Myers, Larson and Gonedes, Scott, and Mandelker for a sound start.

FIGURE 22-2 *Effect of Mergers on Long-Run EPS Growth*

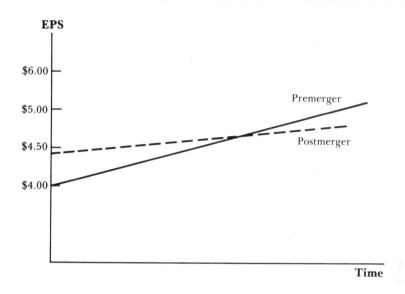

risks which are largely beyond management's control. But even in the short run management can exercise considerable control over how the firm reacts to these outside influences by adhering to an objective of improving the average level of profits and reducing risks. In fact, management is probably *the* most important factor which differentiates firms within the same industry. For example, within a steadily growing industry such as the brewing industry, some firms have been able to maintain or improve their market share and profit growth while others have experienced dramatic declines in market share and profits. Some people would argue that this is due to the taste of the firm's product or the power of the larger firms. However, Miller beer had never enjoyed nearly the market share it was able to achieve once it was acquired by Philip Morris. Brewers weren't forced to sell only their traditional brands but could switch to new brands, and even small firms such as Heileman and Coors were able to gain substantial growth in market share in the face of heavy competition by the dominant firms. The major differentiating factor between firms within a given industry is usually management.

While it is clear that management has a decisive effect on a firm's future performance, it is much less clear how to go about evaluating management's ability. Probably the best guide is the historical record. Relative to other firms in the same industry, to what extent have managerial actions contributed to the firm's pattern of earnings growth? The ability to maintain asset turnover ratios and profit margins in the face of an economic recession when other firms show declining turnovers and margins is fairly strong evidence of good management. In the same manner the ability to limit the effects of labor strikes, hedge variability in raw-material prices, minimize the required current tax costs, etc., also indicates good management. On the other hand, there are other actions management can take to increase profits for which they don't really deserve a pat on the back. For example, increasing the use of debt financing to promote the automatic growth of *EPS* or acquiring firms with lower price/earnings ratios results in higher reported accounting profits. But events like these are often simply due to the vagaries of accounting practices, or they expose shareholders to increased risk in return for the increased profit. So although the historical record is an obvious place to begin, some care should be taken in how the record is evaluated.

Beyond historical ratio analysis, what can the analyst do? This is an extremely difficult question to answer. In fact, there is no reasonably sure procedure. Instead, the analyst is usually forced to develop a general impression based on a variety of creative observations. Some of these are discussed below.

A Few Approaches to Evaluating Management

Some techniques and considerations of management evaluation include the following:

1. *Anticipatory management.* How accurately did management foresee major changes in the industry and position the firm to take full advantage? For example, in the brewing industry, which firms were leaders in expanding the variety of beers available (low-calorie and premium beers) and advertising campaigns?

2. *Extent and reliability of information provided to the public.* Does management provide a thorough review of the firm's financial status and prospects, or is minimal information given, and only begrudgingly? How accurately does the information provided to the public seem to reflect the actual situation?

3. *Clarity of ability and goals.* Has management clearly defined the nature of its comparative advantages and then focused only on ventures in which these advantages can be put to best use? For example, IBM management clearly has a comparative advantage in computer design and services. The firm has not used temporary excess cash flows to invest in car leasing or hamburger chains. Instead, each of IBM's products makes sense, in that it builds on or enhances the other products. Diversification isn't undertaken for its own sake.

4. *Focus of top management.* Does top management spend its time addressing the issues which can lead to increased economic value, such as asset efficiency, expense control, and capital expenditures? Or is a large part of the time devoted to less important factors, such as accounting techniques, expansion of *EPS* via mergers, engaging in share sales, and repurchases in response to beliefs that share prices are over- or undervalued?

5. *Management depth.* Are there a number of top managers who could move into the president's position, or is the firm dominated by one or two key managers? Similarly, are all levels of management equally strong, or is just the upper level strong, with weak middle or lower levels?

6. *Employee morale.* Even the best management team can do little unless employees are satisfied with their jobs and eager to help the firm.

7. *Opinions of competitors.* A good key to the abilities of a firm's management is the opinions of other firms. Usually a good management team will distinguish itself in the industry and gain widespread respect.

Much has been written about how to distinguish between good and mediocre management. Unfortunately, most of the conclusions don't hold up under close scrutiny. For example, is decentralized management better than centralized management? We really don't know. It may depend on the firm's product line and the nature of management's comparative advantage. Is a larger R & D budget indicative of good management? Not if it doesn't pay off. Does the fact that management is willing to take greater risks indicate good management? Not really. Does rapid sales growth indicate good management? Not if the growth is obtained simply by retaining a larger portion of profits or if new ventures are undertaken for growth alone, with little attention to profitability. There is no simple technique to evaluate management quality. Rather, the analyst is forced to rely on a blend of personal creativity, logic, and intuition.

Inside Information

An analyst is able to identify an over- or undervalued stock only by having better information than other people. The *sources* of this information can be categorized as follows:

1. *Direct* information provided by *employees* of the firm — for example, the president's projection of *EPS* or a clerk's statement about unfilled orders.

2. *Direct* information provided by *nonemployees* — for example, a government attorney's private statement that the firm is to be indicted for bribery or a public statement that the Department of Defense has placed a $100 million order with the firm.

3. *Inferential information* developed by examining a large amount of data and drawing conclusions about it — for example, concluding that a new law may have dramatic effects on a firm's profits and growth. Or that potential debt structure and foreign competition could seriously increase the firm's default risk.

Under Rule 10-5b of the Securities Exchange Act, transactions based on direct information provided by employees which has not been made available to the general public are illegal, and any profits earned must be returned to the original shareholders. For example, in the 1960s Texas Gulf Sulphur discovered a rich new oil field, and various officers of the firm, plus some outsiders, traded on information about how productive the discovery — which had not yet been made public — would be. Under Rule 10-5b, a large portion of these inside profits was taken away. Similarly, when a security analyst learned from a former employee of Equity Funding that something was amiss within the firm, he discussed the matter with various institutional clients of his firm. They then sold shares before the information became widely known among the general public and before share prices fell dramatically. The analyst was charged with violating Rule 10-5b.

The most recent insider trading scandal erupted when the SEC charged Ivan Boesky with a wide variety of insider trades. The common denominator in most of his trades involved privileged information about potential corporate mergers. Boesky obtained tips from individuals who worked for the investment banking firms which were putting the mergers together. The indictment and conviction of Boesky have made most market participants very sensitive to illegal insider trading.

Trading on direct information provided by nonemployees (which is not yet publicly available) may or may not be illegal. It depends on the situation. However, trades based on inferential information developed by the analyst as a result of analyzing data in a unique manner are not illegal.

Analysts should be wary of suggesting trades on any *material nonpublic* information. If such information is offered by employees of the firm, the analyst (or the firm) should make a public announcement before suggesting trades for specific clients.

ANALYSIS OF EQUITY RISK AND VALUE

Identification of Uncertainties

The first step in evaluating a stock's risk is to specify explicitly the major uncertainties involved in estimating its value. For example, in early 1985 the major uncertainties associated with the value of Anheuser-Busch stock appeared to be the following:

1. *Effects of intra-industry competition on the pattern of future profit growth.* How large would marketing costs become, and could Anheuser's marketing campaigns remain as effective as they had been in the early 1980s? How soon would new, regional brands gain consumer acceptance and reduce A-B's market share? Might the introduction of new foreign brands reduce A-B's market share?
2. *Labor and raw-material costs.* Over time labor costs should increase with inflation. However, the record shows that labor strikes can have a strong, although temporary, effect on A-B's profit. A-B was particularly vulnerable to strikes because of its dominance in the industry and high profitability relative to other brewers. Raw-material costs can be quite volatile from year to year as a result of unforeseen weather conditions, international events, etc.
3. *Financial leverage.* To maintain (and potentially increase) its market share, A-B had undertaken an aggressive plant expansion in the early 1980s when industry competition was severe and other brewers were reducing capacity. A large percentage of this expansion was being financed by debt. At the time, the firm was able to meet its higher financial burden without any severe strain. However, the higher debt ratio certainly would increase the sensitivity of shareholder returns to future events in the industry—both favorable *and* unfavorable.
4. *Long-term industry growth.* Historically, the growth of industry-wide sales had been reasonably stable and not very sensitive to the business cycle. And at the end

of 1977 there was nothing to suggest that this would soon change. Nonetheless, as the character of the population changes over time, it is possible that consumer tastes could change — switching, for example, from beer to wine.

Next, the analyst should attempt to ascertain which risks appear to be nondiversifiable and which are diversifiable. In fact, large parts of the four risks listed above are diversifiable. Much of the risk associated with intra-industry competition can be diversified away by holding a number of brewing stocks. Market-share losses to Anheuser-Busch would be gains to its competitors. The same is true of uncertain labor strikes, since lost sales to A-B during a strike would largely be picked up as sales gains to competitors. Similarly, some of the uncertainty associated with grain costs could be eliminated by holding shares in large farming ventures. Finally, a portion of the uncertain industry growth could be reduced by holding shares in firms producing wine and liquor. While *all* risks could not be eliminated through creative diversification, most could. It is the nondiversifiable component of risk which should affect the return required on A-B stock. Of these nondiversifiable risks, the firm's expected level of financial leverage is perhaps the most important.

Forecasts of Profits and Dividends

Once the major uncertainties are stated explicitly, the analyst can specify various *scenarios* of events which might affect the firm. For example, Table 22-12 presents three possible scenarios under which forecasts could be developed. Of course, an infinite number of such scenarios could be dreamed up. However, three different choices are usually adequate to indicate how variable profit flows are likely to be. Subjective probabilities should be assigned to each.

Using each scenario, the analyst should make detailed forecasts of *both* future income statements and future sources-and-uses-of-funds statements. Both are needed because they are intimately related. For example, interest expenses can't be forecast until the volume of new debt financing is known. Similarly, dividends per share can't be forecast until the profit-retention rate and new share forecasts are made. A summary of such statements prepared for a "most likely" scenario is shown in Table 22-13. As many details as possible should be forecast in order to reduce *EPS* and *DPS* forecast errors. Even though forecasts of items within the statements are uncertain and are likely to differ from the actual values incurred, such errors tend to offset one another so that final *EPS* and *DPS* forecast errors are minimized. In recent years computer simulation models have been used increasingly to develop such forecasts.

Equity Risk Measurement

The final step necessary to value a stock is to identify what a fair expected return on the stock should be. According to the traditional version of the capital asset pricing model, the only risk relevant to security ownership is systematic market risk, which

TABLE 22-12 *Sample Scenarios for the Future of Anheuser-Busch*

Pessimistic	Most Likely	Optimistic
Probability = 20%	*Probability = 60%*	*Probability = 20%*
1. Foreign brands and regionals engage in effective competition reducing A-B's market share to 30% by the year 2000	1. Market share increases slightly to 45% by 2000 and levels off afterwards	1. Market share increases to 50% by 2000 and levels off afterwards
2. Labor strikes every 5 years reduce sales by 20% in such years	2. No labor strikes	2. No labor strikes
3. Raw-material costs rise 5% per year	3. Raw-material costs rise with general inflation rate	3. Raw-material costs rise by ½ the inflation rate
4. Government deficits cause interest rates to rise	4. Interest rates remain stable	4. Interest rates fall
5. Industry growth declines to 5%	5. Industry growth is 8% per year	5. Industry growth is 10% per year

TABLE 22-13 *Forecasts Using a Most Likely Scenario for A-B*

	1988	1989	1990	1991	1992	1993
Net Sales[1]	$9,415	$10,733	$12,235	$13,948	$15,901	$18,127
Profit Margin	0.075	0.070	0.070	0.070	0.065	0.060
Net Income[1]	$ 706.1	$ 751.3	$ 856.5	$ 976.4	$ 1,033.6	$ 1,087.6
Shares Outstanding[1]	310.03	319.33	328.91	338.78	348.94	359.41
EPS	$ 2.28	$ 2.35	$ 2.60	$ 2.88	$ 2.96	$ 3.03
Payout Ratio	0.30	0.30	0.30	0.30	0.30	0.30
DPS	$ 0.68	$ 0.71	$ 0.78	$ 0.86	$ 0.89	$ 0.91

[1]In millions.

can be measured as the security's beta. Total risk, as measured by the security's standard deviation, is unimportant, since the CAPM suggests that large portfolios be held. In this case the diversifiable components of a security's standard deviation are offset by the diversifiable returns on the numerous other stocks in the portfolio. Although recent theoretical and empirical work has cast serious doubt on the extent to which the traditional CAPM is valid, most knowledgeable people believe market betas should be evaluated. Despite its deficiencies, the traditional CAPM is the basis of virtually all current models of security price determination, and market-related betas play an important role in each model. Even within the arbitrage pricing model, a term quite similar to a market beta is important.

Ex Ante Beta Estimate. Beta is a future-oriented concept, measured as the *expected* standard deviation of a stock's one-period rate of return multiplied by the *expected* correlation of the stock's return with the return on the aggregate market divided by the *expected* standard deviation of the market's one-period return:

$$B_i = \frac{\sigma_i}{\sigma_m} r_{im} \tag{22.8}$$

where B_i = the beta of security i, σ_i = the expected one-period standard deviation of stock i, σ_m = the expected one-period standard deviation of the market portfolio of all securities, and r_{im} = the expected correlation coefficient of stock i returns and market returns.

One way to pull these three elements together is to estimate, say, one-year rates of return under differing "states of nature." Current prices are known with certainty. For example, on December 31, 1988, A-B common shares were selling at $31.50 and the S&P Composite Index (our market proxy) was $277. Suppose we define three possible states of nature for the year 1989 and assign equal odds to them as follows:

- State 1: Declining economic growth with likely recession and rising interest rates in the near future
- State 2: Continuing moderate economic growth
- State 3: Improvement in economic growth and decreased interest rates

Also assume the following price and dividend estimates for each state:

	State of Nature		
	1	*2*	*3*
Probability	⅓	⅓	⅓
S&P Composite			
December 31, 1989, Price	$266.50	$307.00	$350.87
1989 Dividends	$ 10.50	$ 11.50	$ 12.00
1989 Rate of Return	0.0%	15.0%	31.0%
Expected Return		15.3%	
Anheuser-Busch			
December 31, 1989, Price	$ 33.15	$ 35.75	$ 43.25
1989 Dividends	$ 0.65	$ 0.71	$ 0.73
1989 Rate of Return	7.3%	15.7%	39.6%
Expected Return		20.9%	

Standard deviations of the one-year rates of return would be:

$$\sigma_{SP} = [⅓(0.0 - 0.153)^2 + ⅓(0.150 - 0.153)^2 + ⅓(0.31 - 0.153)^2]^{1/2}$$

$$= 12.66\%$$

$$\sigma_{AB} = [\frac{1}{3}(0.073 - 0.209)^2 + \frac{1}{3}(0.157 - 0.209)^2 + \frac{1}{3}(0.396 - 0.209)^2]^{1/2}$$

$$= 13.68\%$$

And the correlation coefficient would be:

$$r_{SP,AB} = \frac{\left(\begin{array}{c} \frac{1}{3}(0.0 - 0.153)(0.073 - 0.209) \\ + \frac{1}{3}(0.15 - 0.153)(0.157 - 0.209) \\ + \frac{1}{3}(0.31 - 0.153)(0.396 - 0.209) \end{array}\right)}{(0.1266)(0.1368)}$$

$$= 0.97$$

Therefore, our ex ante beta estimate for Anheuser-Busch would be:

$$B_{AB} = \frac{13.68\%}{12.66\%}(0.97) = 1.05$$

The problem with this approach is that it requires us to estimate next year's stock value, which itself should be a function of the stock's beta — the very thing we are attempting to estimate. Typically, this problem is handled by estimating historical beta values and then subjectively revising them for known changes in the firm's financial condition.

Judging Betas Using Ex Post Data. One way of estimating a stock's future beta relies on historical regression estimates of beta which are then subjectively amended for known (or expected) changes in the nature of the firm. For example, we might calculate a regression beta to be 1.0 but subjectively revise it upward because of expected increases in the firm's use of debt financing. To illustrate this approach, assume that the monthly rates of return on the common stock of A-B were regressed against monthly returns of the S&P Composite for the period January 1, 1984–December 31, 1988, and resulted in the following:

$$R_{AB,t} = 3.0\% + 1.06(R_{SP,t})$$
Standard Deviation   (1.0)   (0.3)

The historical estimate of beta is 1.06. However, this must be amended for known and expected changes in the firm's product line and financial structure that may affect the future beta. Although A-B is expected to change its product line over time, none of these changes should have a major effect on how sensitive A-B's asset returns are to macroeconomic shocks. Changes in product mix should have little effect on the beta of Anheuser-Busch.[10] However, A-B stated that it planned to decrease its use of debt. As a result, the sensitivity of equity returns and beta should decrease. Using a predebt-change "equity beta" of 1.06, a marginal tax rate of 48%, and a historical

---

[10]In contrast, if A-B were expected to increase its investment in more cyclical ventures (such as its investment in Busch Gardens or its investment in residential development), the beta estimates should increase.

debt-to-equity ratio of 1.00, we could use Equation 22.6 to estimate A-B's asset beta as being about 0.7:

$$B_E = B_A \left[1 + \frac{D}{NW} (1 - TR) \right]$$

$$= 0.7 [1 + 1.00(0.52)] = 1.06$$

Assuming a debt-to-equity ratio in the early 1990s to be 0.8, our future-oriented equity beta estimate would be:

$$0.7 [1 + 0.8(0.52)] = 0.99$$

Care must be taken to avoid assigning an unwarranted degree of precision to beta estimates. Past empirical studies have shown that about 30% of the variability in future regression beta estimates is associated with past regression beta estimates. Although portfolio beta estimates are quite predictable, single-stock beta estimates are not. In addition, various assumptions of the capital asset pricing model are clearly violated, and these could conceivably have major effects on required security returns. Beta values should be subjectively evaluated by the analyst using all information available. A good fundamental analyst will consider all information available and decide what a reasonable rate of return would be. Regression beta estimates should provide only general guidelines.

Valuation

Table 22-13 (page 956) provided forecasts of dividends per share under the expected scenario between 1989 and 1993. Assume we believe under this scenario that after 1993, *DPS* growth will be reasonably constant and equal to 8%. In addition, assume the following *DPS* forecasts were developed under the other two scenarios:

Year	Pessimistic	Expected	Optimistic
	Dividends Per Share Under Scenario		
1989	$0.67	$0.71	$0.74
1990	0.70	0.78	0.81
1991	0.73	0.86	0.90
1992	0.76	0.89	0.99
1993	0.80	0.91	1.10
Growth Rate Beyond 1990	5.0%	8.0%	10.0%

As of December 1988, the promised yield to maturity on long-term U.S. Treasury bonds was about 9.0%. Using a beta estimate of 1.0 and a market risk premium of 5.0%, the required return on A-B stock would be 14.0% in December 1988. Discounting the *DPS* streams under each scenario results in the following estimated intrinsic fair values:

Scenario	Intrinsic Value
Pessimistic	$ 7.33
Most Likely	11.31
Optimistic	18.75

At the end of 1988, common shares of A-B were trading in the low $30 range. Thus, based on our assumptions, the shares were overvalued in the market and should have been underweighted in the baseline investment portfolio.[11]

SUMMARY

Evaluation of individual stocks must rely on detailed market and industry analyses. Consequently, individual stock analysis should be the last step taken in any program designed to find speculative opportunities in the market. In fact, many decisions associated with creating investment or speculative portfolios are clearly more important than the selection of individual securities.

In order to earn speculative profits from identifying mispriced stocks, one must know more about the stock's dividend prospects than other people do. This knowledge can be gained from creative insights, hard work, or inside information. Since trading on inside information is illegal, one must be more creative than others or work harder. Reasons for historical trends in a firm's profit growth should be clearly understood. Many factors of historical growth will persist into the future, whereas others are only temporary or associated with economic events that are unlikely to be repeated. Some earnings growth will be due to effective management, but growth can also be obtained simply by increasing the debt level, selling stock above book value, changing accounting policies, etc. The intelligent analyst will identify exactly why earnings per share have grown and draw out the implications for potential future profit levels.

Forecasts of both income statements and flow-of-funds statements should be made using as many years and as much detail as possible. Preferably, a number of forecasts will be made, with each keyed to a particular economic scenario that the firm could experience. We can estimate the stock's fair value for each scenario by discounting the dividends per share at a reasonable rate of return. When these prices are multiplied by the subjective probability of each scenario's occurrence and summed over all scenarios, we derive a final estimate of the stock's economic value. Reasonable rates of return can be estimated using the traditional CAPM. Beta estimates are generally obtained by subjectively adjusting historical regression betas for any known (or expected) changes in the firm's product line and financial leverage.

---

[11]For the $30 price to be justified at a required return of 14%, a constant growth rate of about 11.36% is needed. This is not out of line with the firm's experience in the 1980–87 period. Our estimates, however, are based on eventual leveling off of A-B's increasing market share.

REVIEW PROBLEM

Assume that you agree with all of this chapter's forecasts for Anheuser-Busch except that you would make the following changes:

- The beta of A-B is only 0.8.
- The constant long-run *ROE* will be about 18%.
- The long-run retention rate will be 66.67%.

a. What is the revised required return using the security market line?

b. What is the forecast sustainable internal growth rate of dividends per share?

c. Estimate the intrinsic value of A-B stock assuming a current *DPS* of $0.68.

Solution

a. $9\% + 0.8(5\%) = 13\%$

b. $18\%(\tfrac{2}{3}) = 12\%$

c. $\dfrac{\$0.68(1.12)}{0.13 - 0.12} = \$76.16$

QUESTIONS AND PROBLEMS

1. Evaluate the reasonableness of the following hypothetical statements:

a. "Most analysts of the office-equipment industry are forecasting a substantial increase over prior years in the earnings per share of Amdahl Corporation and Burroughs Corporation. As a result, they are suggesting active purchasing of common shares of both firms."

b. "Yesterday's announcement by the management of Wang Labs that back orders are continuing to increase is causing many analysts to revise upward their forecasts of Wang Labs' earnings. Yet the market price of the firm's stock doesn't seem to have fully discounted the likely earnings revision. We suggest active buying of these shares at levels below $20."

2. Basic financial data on Pioneer Corporation is provided below.

	19X1	*19X0*
Asset Turnover	1.2	1.0
Net Profit Margin	8⅓%	10%
Total Debt to Net Worth	1.0	0.5
Share Book Value	$50	$45

a. Analyze the various causes of the firm's *EPS* growth in 19X1.

b. Estimate 19X1 and 19X0 *EPS* values.

c. Given this information, what was the firm's profit-retention rate in 19X1? (Assume no new shares were issued.)

3. Company X has engaged in an aggressive program of acquiring other companies through exchange of common stock. Explain briefly how an acquisition may contribute to the rate of growth in earnings per share of company X.

4. There is a great deal of confusion about interrelationships among accounting returns on equity (ROE), desired market returns on equity (K_e), accounting book values per share (BV), and market prices per share (P). Utilizing the constant growth model:

   a. Derive the mathematical function which determines the market-to-book ratio. (Hint: Use the notion that $G = B \times ROE$ and the constant growth model.)

   b. If ROE equals K_e, what is the market/book ratio equal to? When is the market/book ratio greater (or less) than 1.0?

   c. How may changes in expected inflation rates affect the market/book ratio? (Consider all angles.)

5. Using five years of monthly returns, you have estimated the historical equity beta of Marine Products Corporation to be 1.0. During this time span the firm's debt structure was reasonably stable, with the total debt-to-total-asset ratio averaging 0.40. The firm's tax rate was 46%.

   a. Estimate the historical asset beta.

   b. If the firm's total debt-to-total-asset ratio is expected to increase to 0.70, what is a reasonable estimate of the future beta?

6. (CFA Exam Question)

   Knight-Ridder Newspapers, Inc. (KRN), and The Times Mirror Company (TMC) are two of the largest newspaper companies in the U.S. Knight-Ridder was formed in 1977 by the merger of the Knight and Ridder groups. The company owns a number of newspapers, with the following accounting for the indicated percentage of operating revenues in 1983:

Philadelphia Inquirer and *Philadelphia Daily News*	21%
Miami Herald	17
San Jose Mercury News	10
Detroit Free Press	9
Charlotte Observer News	5
St. Paul Pioneer Press and Dispatch	4
Akron Beacon Journal	4
Other Newspapers	21
Nonnewspaper Operation	9
	100%

   KRN's nonnewspaper revenues come from broadcasting (a unit formed in 1978 with the acquisition of three TV stations and the subsequent purchase of two additional stations) and business information services (BIS) (including Commodity News Service, Unicom News, the *Journal of Commerce*, and VW/TEXT). Times Mirror is a large, diversified media company, but it remains heavily dependent on its newspaper operations. Revenue breakdown was as follows in 1983:

Newspapers	48%
Newsprint and Forest Products	13
Book Publishing	11
Information Services	10
Broadcast TV	4
Cable TV	6
Other	8
	100%

TMC's principal newspaper properties are the *Los Angeles Times*, *Newsday*, the *Dallas Times Herald*, the *Denver Post*, and the *Hartford Courant*. The newsprint operations are in support of TMC's own requirements, but the company does sell lumber and newsprint to third parties. Books are principally artistic, legal, and medical in nature. The company has 7 broadcast TV stations and 16 cable systems. The newspaper industry derives the bulk of its revenues (about 70%) from the sale of advertising linage, with most of the remainder coming from circulation income.

a. Using the information in Exhibit A, compare the growth and volatility of (1) the newspaper industry and (2) both KRN and TMC to the growth and volatility of the economy over the 1974–83 period. Show the comparisons in both nominal and real terms.

b. Drawing on the information provided above, in Exhibit A, and in the comparisons developed in answering part a, list and briefly comment on four conclusions that could have significant applicability to an investment evaluation of both KRN and TMC.

c. Using the ratios in Exhibit B, calculate for both KRN and TMC:
   (1) The net return on common equity for 1978 and 1983
   (2) The estimated sustainable growth rate as of 1978 and 1983

EXHIBIT A *The Economy, Industry, and Companies*

Year	U.S. GNP ($ Billions)				Advertising Revenues ($ Billions)			
	Nominal	% Change	Real	% Change	Total	% Change	Newspaper	% Change
1974	$1,434	— %	$1,246	— %	$26.8	— %	$ 7.8	— %
1975	1,549	8.0	1,232	(1.1)	28.2	5.2	8.2	5.1
1976	1,718	10.9	1,298	5.4	33.7	19.5	9.6	17.1
1977	1,918	11.6	1,370	5.5	37.9	12.5	10.8	12.5
1978	2,164	12.8	1,439	5.0	43.3	14.2	12.2	13.0
1979	2,418	11.7	1,479	2.8	48.8	12.7	13.9	13.9
1980	2,632	8.9	1,475	(0.3)	53.6	9.8	14.8	6.5
1981	2,954	12.2	1,514	2.6	60.4	12.7	16.5	11.5
1982	3,073	4.0	1,485	(1.9)	66.7	10.4	17.7	7.2
1983	3,310	7.7	1,535	3.4	75.9	13.8	20.6	16.4

Year	Newspaper Advertising Price Index		Company Revenues ($ Billions)			
	Index	% Change	TMC	% Change	KRN	% Change
1974	113	— %	$ 735	— %	$ 565	— %
1975	128	13.2	800	8.8	593	5.0
1976	140	9.4	965	20.6	678	14.3
1977	153	9.3	1,130	17.1	752	10.9
1978	166	8.5	1,411	24.9	879	16.9
1979	182	9.6	1,639	16.2	980	11.5
1980	201	10.4	1,857	13.3	1,099	12.1
1981	224	11.4	2,131	14.8	1,237	12.6
1982	251	12.1	2,200	3.2	1,328	7.4
1983	276	10.0	2,479	12.7	1,473	10.9

EXHIBIT B *Selected Financial Ratios*

	Sales ÷ Assets		Pretax Profit ÷ Sales		Tax Rate		Assets ÷ Equity		Dividends ÷ Earnings	
	TMC	KRN	TMC	KRN	TMC	KRN	TMC	KRN	TMC	KRN
1983	1.10×	1.32×	14.5%	15.1%	44.6%	45.3%	2.14×	1.42×	36.1%	31.7%
1982	1.09	1.30	11.3	13.8	43.9	42.7	2.13	1.41	48.8	29.0
1981	1.17	1.34	12.1	15.5	41.5	46.5	2.10	1.45	40.7	27.5
1980	1.20	1.37	12.4	15.9	39.4	45.6	1.98	1.41	37.0	25.9
1979	1.39	1.39	15.5	16.3	42.3	44.7	1.73	1.37	29.3	24.9
1978	1.53	1.43	18.9	16.7	46.5	47.5	1.57	1.35	25.2	27.5

EXHIBIT C *Selected Stock Data*

	Per Common Share	
	TMC	KRN
Current Price	$39.00	$27.75
Annual Dividend	$ 1.10	$ 0.62
1983 *EPS*	$ 2.90	$ 1.80
1984 *EPS*	$ 3.30	$ 2.15
1979–83 Average P/E High	13.0×	13.6×
Low	8.3×	8.8×
Value Line Beta	1.05	0.95
Expected Rate of Return	14.9%	12.8%

Other Market Data		
Risk-Free Rate of Return		10.0%
Expected Market Return		15.0%

EXHIBIT D *Selected Financial Statistics ($ Millions Except Per-Share Data)*

	1978	1979	1980	1981	1982	1983
Times Mirror						
Sales	$1,411	$1,639	$1,857	$2,131	$2,200	$2,479
Pretax Income	266	254	230	257	250	360
Taxes	124	108	91	107	110	160
Net Income	142	146	139	150	140	200
EPS	$ 2.07	$ 2.16	$ 2.04	$ 2.20	$ 2.05	$ 2.90
Knight-Ridder						
Sales	$ 879	$ 980	$1,099	$1,237	$1,328	$1,473
Pretax Income	147	160	174	192	183	222
Taxes	70	72	81	92	80	103
Net Income	77	88	93	100	103	119
EPS	$ 1.17	$ 1.35	$ 1.44	$ 1.55	$ 1.57	$ 1.80

d. State the factors that account for the differences in the level of return on equity between KRN and TMC for the two years 1978 and 1983. Comment on the trends and the components of return on equity for each of the two companies over the 1978–83 period.

e. The newspaper industry has the following characteristics:

- An increasing number of cities with only one newspaper
- An increasing number of advertising media alternatives to newspapers, such as cable and broadcast TV and direct mail

How could these trends affect your analysis?

f. Construct a graph showing the security market line (SML) and the position of KRN and TMC relative to the SML.

g. Calculate the required rates of return on the two securities. Identify which security is more attractive. Justify your selection and show your calculations.

h. Using information from Exhibits A through D, list and briefly comment on three additional factors that should be considered in selecting either KRN or TMC as the more attractive investment opportunity.

CHAPTER

23

Performance Monitoring

The last step in the portfolio investment process is to monitor the portfolio over time and make any changes which appear appropriate in light of:

1. Changes in expected future asset returns and risks
2. Changes in the financial needs of the portfolio owner
3. Unacceptable portfolio performance

Changes in expected asset returns and risks could require a modification of the baseline investment portfolio's optimal asset allocation. For example, if the risk of equity ownership increases, the portfolio commitment to equities would probably be reduced. Changes in the financial needs of the portfolio owner would probably require a change in the statement of investment policy as well as in the definition of the baseline investment portfolio. For example, the pension plan of a corporation currently facing unexpected competition and declining profits may have to redefine its portfolio objectives and constraints as well as its baseline investment portfolio. Both events, however, can be handled by simply repeating the planning stage of the portfolio process, which was discussed in Chapter 19. In this chapter, we focus solely on the third reason for portfolio monitoring—to detect unacceptable performance.

The title of this chapter was carefully chosen. Performance measurement is the commonly used term, but we have chosen the term performance monitoring instead because *measurement* connotes a degree of precision which is simply not possible in the evaluation of investment performance. Throughout this chapter, we will encounter the problems that arise whenever we attempt to evaluate the past risk/return performance of a portfolio. For example, though there are many (quite valid) ways of measuring returns, there is no truly acceptable way to measure investment risk. In addition, all performance analyses examine relatively short historical time periods when it is usually long-term future performance that matters. We are simply unable to accurately *measure* performance.

But a number of reasonable approaches exist which allow us to *monitor* the level of historical performance of an investment compared with that of other investments of similar risk. Precise evaluation of portfolio performance is impossible, but broad yardsticks are available which can detect clearly superior or inferior performance. Regardless of the techniques used to monitor performance, three things should be remembered:

1. *It is the total portfolio that matters.* If multiple managers are used, their individual performances are secondary to the performance of the aggregate portfolio. While data on individual managers have to be accumulated in order to determine aggregate portfolio performance, the actual performance analysis should proceed in a top-down fashion. The aggregate portfolio should be evaluated first, followed by an evaluation of each individual manager.[1]

2. *Any performance analysis must examine both returns and risk.* An examination of past returns provides little information about performance unless the returns are related to the risk level incurred.[2]

3. *An attempt should be made to determine why a particular performance level occurred.* If an understanding of why the performance was bad (or good) can be gained, proper steps to improve (or continue) can be taken. Knowing why performance was poor is much more important than knowing simply that performance was poor.

CALCULATING RETURNS

The basis of any performance analysis must be the rate of return earned during past time periods. The risk associated with these returns is clearly important and we will examine it soon. First, however, we need to understand several refinements used in calculating returns.

Compound Versus Simple Interest Returns

Assume that you have calculated yearly portfolio rates of return for each of the past five years as shown in Table 23-1. The question you would like to answer is: "What has been the average yearly return?"

Two approaches could be used: (1) a simple interest return and (2) a compound interest return (referred to as the geometric return in Chapter 4).

The simple interest approach calculates an *arithmetic* average return by adding the individual returns and dividing the sum by the number of returns available. Letting:

---

[1]As obvious as this point might seem to be, many performance services provide little or no information about aggregate portfolio performance. Instead, they concentrate solely on individual managers.

[2]Again the point is obvious but often not followed in practice. For example, some performance services compare the returns on a governmental pension fund with those on other governmental pensions. Since pension funds have substantially different asset holdings and risk exposure, such a comparison may be meaningless.

TABLE 23-1 *Compound Versus Simple Interest Returns*

Year	Portfolio Return
1	11.3%
2	20.0
3	0.0
4	−11.1
5	−15.8

$$\text{Average Simple Interest Return} \quad = \frac{11.3\% + 20.0\% + \ldots + (-15.8\%)}{5}$$

$$= 0.88\%$$

$$\text{Average Compound Interest Return} = [(1.113)(1.200) \ldots (0.842)]^{1/5} - 1.0$$

$$= 0.00\%$$

Growth of $100

Date	0		1		2		3		4		5
Value	$100.00		$111.30		$133.56		$133.56		$118.73		$100.00
Return		11.3%		20.0%		0.0%		−11.1%		−15.8%	

R_t = the rate of return in period t

N = the number of periods

$\bar{R}_s$ = the average simple interest return

Then:

Average Simple Interest Return
$$\bar{R}_s = \left(\sum_{t=1}^{N} R_t \right) \div N \qquad (23.1)$$

As shown in Table 23-1, $\bar{R}_s$ was 0.88%. While not particularly large, the calculated $\bar{R}_s$ suggests that the average yearly return was positive at least.

The compound interest approach calculates a geometric average of (1.0 plus each yearly return). Letting:

$\bar{R}_c$ = the average compound interest return

Then:

Average Compound Interest Return
$$\bar{R}_c = \left[\prod_{t=1}^{N} (1 + R_t) \right]^{1/N} - 1.0 \qquad (23.2)$$

As shown in Table 23-1 and below, $\bar{R}_c$ was 0.00%. The compound interest return indicates that the average yearly return was precisely zero:

$$\bar{R}_c = [(1.113)(1.2)(1.0)(0.889)(0.842)]^{1/5} - 1.0$$

$$= 0.0$$

This is not the first time we have encountered the different results obtained from using arithmetic, simple interest averages versus geometric, compound interest averages. For example, when effective yearly returns on T-bills were discussed in Chapter 2, both measures were presented. Similarly, when historical returns earned on the major security indexes were discussed in Chapter 4, a distinction had to be made between these two approaches in calculating average returns.

Virtually always, the more appropriate measure to use is the compound interest return. To illustrate why this is true, consider the case of a person who invests $100 and then experiences the sequence of five yearly returns as shown in Table 23-1. By the end of the first year the $100 investment has grown to $111.30 ($100 × 1.113). Unfortunately, years 3 through 5 provide zero or negative returns, so that, by the end of year 5, the portfolio is worth exactly $100—no more or less than the initial investment:

$$\frac{\text{Year 5}}{\text{Value}} = \frac{\text{Initial}}{\text{Value}} \times \frac{\text{Compound by Each}}{\text{Yearly Return}}$$

$$\$100 = \$100 \times (1.113)(1.20)(1.0)(0.889)(0.842)$$

Clearly, the average yearly return was equal to 0.0%.

The reason why the arithmetic average return overstates the compound average return is not hard to understand. Arithmetic average calculations assume that a specific percentage *increase* in the portfolio's value is equivalent to the same percentage *decrease* in value. This is not true. For example, consider the portfolio above, which had an initial value of $100. A 10% positive return would increase the portfolio's value by $10 to $110. However, if this is followed by a 10% negative return, the portfolio would decrease in value by $11 ($110 × 0.10) to $99. A 10% positive return followed by a 10% negative return is not a 0.0% average return. Similarly, an initial 10% negative return ($100 to $90) followed by a 10% positive return ($90 to $99) is also not a 0.0% average return.

The arithmetic average *simple interest* return treats equal positive and negative returns as having identical impacts on portfolio values. This is incorrect. In contrast, the geometric average return explicitly accounts for the compounding of portfolio values at various rates of return. Compound interest procedures should be used whenever average return statistics are calculated.

Dollar-Weighted Versus Time-Weighted Returns

The Problem. Consider a portfolio owner, Mr. A, and an investment manager, Ms. B, who manages all of Mr. A's portfolio assets. There can be a difference between the net rate of return earned by Ms. B on the portfolio assets entrusted to her (that is, after all transaction costs and advisory fees) and the rate of return Mr. A actually receives. This occurs if the portfolio owner makes cash contributions or withdrawals to the portfolio over time.

A simple example should make the problem apparent. Assume that Mr. A has a portfolio worth $100 on January 1 and has given Ms. B full discretion over its management. By January 15 the $100 has increased to a value of $150. Seeing the marvelous return of 50%, Mr. A contributes an additional $100 to the portfolio on January 15, increasing the portfolio value to $250. Unfortunately, by month-end the portfolio is worth only $166.66.

Note that Mr. A started with a $100 portfolio value to which he contributed an additional $100. However, by month-end the portfolio's value was only $166.66. Clearly Mr. A had a negative rate of return during the month.

But Ms. B can claim that her rate of return was exactly 0.0% and she'd be correct. During the first half of the month, her return was 50%, ($150 − $100) ÷ $100. During the second half her return was −33.33%, ($166.66 − $250) ÷ $250. Thus her compounded monthly return was 0.0%:

$$(1.0 + 0.50)(1.0 - 0.3333) - 1.0 = 0.0$$

The difference between what Mr. A earned and what Ms. B earned is clearly due to the contribution made in mid-January, just before the large negative return. Ms. B had no control over the receipt of the contribution and thus she should not be charged with the losses on it. Returns earned by the manager of a portfolio should be calculated as if no contributions or withdrawals had been made. Rates of return which are culled of all contributions and withdrawals are known as *time-weighted returns*. In contrast, Mr. A did indeed suffer a negative return because he was unfortunate enough to time his contribution poorly. Returns earned by the owner of a portfolio should include the impacts of contributions and withdrawals. Rates of return which include the impacts of contributions and withdrawals are known as *dollar-weighted returns*.

An Illustration. Table 23-2 presents data and calculations for an actual case encountered by a moderately large pension fund. On April 30, the pension owned 71,478.893 shares of the Axe-Houghton mutual fund. On that day the net asset value (NAV) of Axe-Houghton was $8.14. Thus the pension's investment in this manager was $581,838.19. On May 13, a $250,000 contribution was made (when the NAV was $8.36). By month-end the value of the investment in Axe-Houghton was $772.539.98.

Two rates of return are appropriate to this case: (1) the dollar-weighted return earned by the pension fund and (2) the time-weighted return earned by Axe-Houghton.

The dollar-weighted return calculation is shown in panel A. It focuses solely on cash inflows and outflows. As such, the dollar-weighted return is simply another name for the internal rate of return widely used in corporate finance. The cash flows consist of the following:

Period	Cash Flow
0	−$581,838.19
1	−$250,000.00
2	+$772,539.98

TABLE 23-2 *Dollar-Weighted and Time-Weighted Returns Based on May Contributions to Axe-Houghton*

	A. Dollar-Weighted Return		
	April 30	*Midmonth*	*May 31*
Cash Flow	−$581,838.19	−$250,000.00	+$772,539.98

15-Day IRR = −4.269%

Monthly IRR = $(1.0 - 0.04269)^2 - 1 = -8.36\%$

	B. Time-Weighted Return		
	April 30	*Precontribution*	*Postcontribution*	*May 31*
Shares	71,478.893	71,478.893	101,383.199	101,383.199
NAV	$ 8.14	$ 8.36	$ 8.36	$ 7.62
Value	$581,838.19	$597,563.55	$847,563.55	$772,539.98

$1 + R_1 = 1.027027025$

$1 + R_2 = 0.91148325$

Monthly Time-Weighted Return = $(1.027027025)(0.911473247) - 1.0$

$= -6.39\%$

The 15-day internal rate of return is −4.269%. To express this 15-day return as a full-month return, it is compounded for two 15-day periods. This results in a dollar-weighted monthly return of −8.36%.

The time-weighted return calculation is shown in panel B. First, the rate of return is calculated for the period immediately prior to the contribution. This was 2.70%. Second, the return is calculated for the period starting immediately after the contribution through month-end. This was −8.85%. Finally, these two returns are compounded to obtain the full-month time-weighted return of −6.39%.

The two returns differ. In particular, the dollar-weighted return is lower because the $250,000 contribution was made immediately prior to the negative return in the second half of the month. Both, however, are valid return measures although their interpretations are different. The dollar-weighted return expresses the return earned by the portfolio owner. The time-weighted return expresses the return generated by an investment manager. When calculating returns with the intent of measuring a specific manager's performance, time-weighted returns should be used. In contrast, when calculating returns with the intent of evaluating the portfolio owner's performance, dollar-weighted returns should be used.[3]

[3]Time-weighted returns require a knowledge of the portfolio value at each date of a contribution or withdrawal. For dates other than month-ends, such information is often not available. (Mutual funds are rare in that they state portfolio values each day.) If intramonth contributions and withdrawals are made when portfolio values are unknown, the internal rate of return must be used as an approximation of the true time-weighted return.

MONITORING EQUITY PERFORMANCE

Performance Within Investment Style

Performance monitoring consists of a comparison of historical returns against the risks associated with such returns. A number of methods can be used to evaluate risk. We have already discussed three methods based on the capital asset pricing model in Chapter 8 (the Sharpe, Treynor, and Jensen methods) and will expand on them later in this chapter. However, perhaps the most common approach to dealing with risk is to assign managers to various *styles* of investing and then compare one manager's returns against those of other managers having a similar style.

The investment styles used vary considerably. As an example, Figure 23-1 provides the style definitions used by Merrill Lynch, Pierce, Fenner and Smith, Inc., in their performance-evaluation service. They define seven style groups based on qualitative judgments of each manager's investment approach. Other performance-monitoring organizations use sophisticated statistical procedures to categorize managers into groups with similar characteristics and evaluate the probability of a manager's belonging to one or another of various investment styles. An example of such an analysis is shown in Figure 23-2 for Putnam Voyager mutual fund. In the figure, four styles are used and a statistical procedure known as discriminant analysis is used to evaluate the probability of the fund's being in each style for various quarter-ends.[4]

Figure 23-3 presents an example of how styled returns are often compared. The figure reports on Putnam Voyager's historical time-weighted returns. In Figure 23-2, the mutual fund was consistently styled as an aggressive-growth-oriented fund. Therefore, in Figure 23-3, its returns are compared against those of other managers also styled as aggressive growth. Return information is presented in both graphical and tabular formats. The tabular data represent compound annualized rates of return for one to ten years prior to March 31, 1989. Returns are shown for Putnam Voyager, the S&P 500, and various percentiles within the aggressive-growth style. The graphical data display these returns in percentile form with 0 as the poorest performer and 100 the best. Putnam Voyager, the S&P 500, and various aggressive-growth-style percentiles are ranked against all other equity managers. The following interpretations can be made from the figure:

1. During the 1980s, the S&P 500 outperformed most equity managers.
2. The median aggressive-growth manager performed almost the opposite of the S&P 500. From periods in the 1970s to March 1989 the median aggressive-growth manager had a return at about the 60th percentile of all managers.
3. Putnam Voyager has consistently had returns above the 50th percentile, and its past 10-year returns are close to the 90th percentile.

---

[4]Data used in this discriminant analysis consisted of average stock characteristics such as beta, dividend yield, price/earnings ratio, market capitalization, etc. Thus style probabilities are determined by the types of equity securities owned at each quarter-end.

FIGURE 23-1 *Illustrative Style Definitions*

Style Definition

1. Income: Primary purpose in security selection is to achieve a current yield significantly higher than the S&P 500.

2. Value: Primary selection motivation is to buy securities based on *known* information, and then compare this data to other historical information. Value managers, although sometimes giving some weight to earnings *projections*, rarely buy securities on this basis alone.

3. Core/Growth: These terms, although not having identical meanings, are used here synonymously. They tend to be managers who do *not* buy overly aggressive stocks but do rely heavily on earnings forecasts. This style is characterized as one devoid of extremes, not too much income and not too much risk. One might say that if you were going to place all of your retirement fund assets with one manager, this style would represent the one.

4. Timers: This management style places more emphasis on asset allocation than on stock selection. The primary decision is to own or not to own stocks, and to what extent the total portfolio should be committed.

5. Contrarians: Primarily motivated to purchase stocks that are currently out of favor with investors. These are usually stocks of companies that are cyclically out of favor while still being leaders in their industries. Some contrarians will, however, very automatically purchase stocks on the "New Low List" regardless of industry leadership or quality.

6. Rotators: Their primary emphasis is on finding industries that for some time will outperform the market as a whole. When they perceive a change in an industry's dynamics, they then rotate from the weaker industry to the stronger industry. Their selection process is a top-down, macro approach. It begins with estimates of the economy then focuses on the industries expected to perform best in this economic environment. Lastly, the industry categories are filled with the individual stocks believed to be the strongest in these industries.

7. Aggressive Growth/Small Caps: As the name suggests, these managers tend to buy stocks that have a high degree of price volatility. This style of management is bottom-up in that the primary motivation for buying a stock is inherent in the stock itself. These are the "stock pickers." There may or may not be any similarity in the methods used by one of these "stock pickers" versus another. Some will buy based on price momentum, or earnings momentum, or, but not limited to, changes in company perceptions.

SOURCE: Courtesy of Merrill Lynch, Pierce, Fenner & Smith, Inc.

Monitoring Based on the CAPM

Comparing a manager's past returns against returns of managers with equivalent investment styles is a reasonable way to begin an evaluation of the returns earned for the risks incurred. Such comparisons, however, are often not as precise as could be desired and certainly don't address *why* a particular risk/return performance level occurred. In order to obtain more precise risk/return calculations and to examine why a specific performance level occurred, more precise estimates of risk are needed. To date, the most widely used approaches are based on the capital asset pricing model.

Three general approaches are used:

FIGURE 23-2 *Analysis of Historical Style Probabilities, Putnam Voyager*

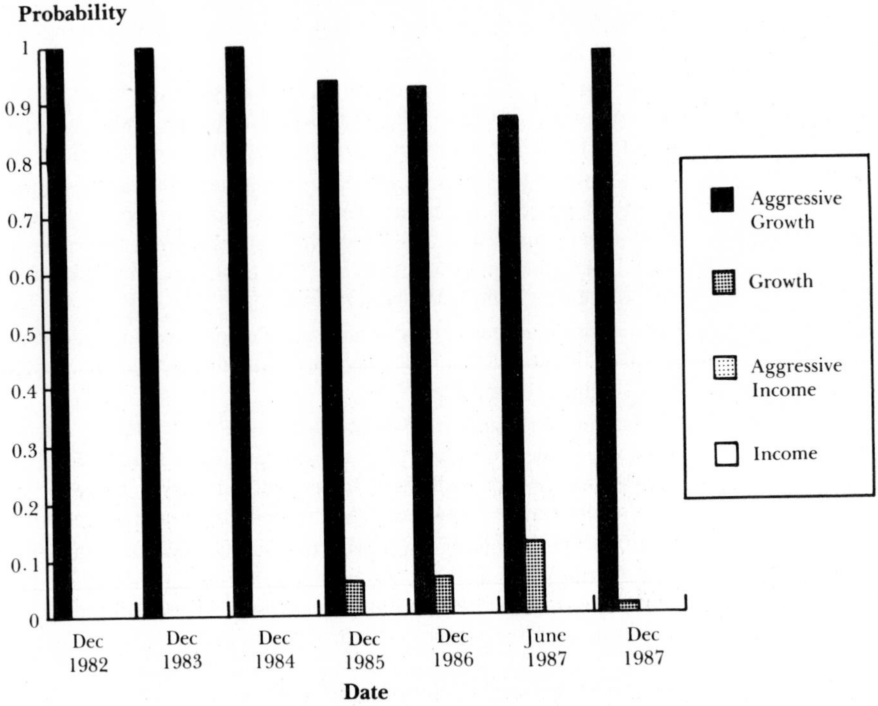

SOURCE: Courtesy of Eppler, Guerin & Turner Pension Consulting.

1. The Sharpe performance index:

$$S_p = (\bar{R}_p - \overline{RF}) \div \sigma_p \qquad (23.3)$$

2. The Treynor performance index:

$$T_p = (\bar{R}_p - \overline{RF}) \div B_p \qquad (23.4)$$

3. The Jensen performance index (alpha in the following regression):

$$\tilde{R}_{pt} - \widetilde{RF}_t = A_p + B_p(\tilde{R}_{mt} - \widetilde{RF}_t) + \tilde{E}_{pt} \qquad (23.5)$$

where:

$\bar{R}_p$	= the (arithmetic) average return on the portfolio
$\overline{RF}$	= the average risk-free return
σ_p	= the standard deviation of portfolio returns

FIGURE 23-3 *Putnam Voyager, Aggressive Growth Return Summary*

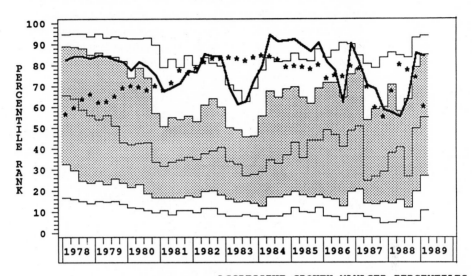

PRIOR	FUND	S&P 500 COMPOSITE	AGGRESSIVE GROWTH MANAGER PERCENTILES				
			10TH PERCT	25TH PERCT	MEDIAN	75TH PERCT	90TH PERCT
10 YEARS	18.52%	16.27%	11.44%	13.13%	15.60%	18.56%	19.65%
9 YEARS	18.84%	17.45%	10.63%	12.92%	14.91%	18.63%	20.59%
8 YEARS	14.54%	14.92%	5.25%	6.97%	10.67%	12.53%	15.97%
7 YEARS	20.30%	19.56%	10.37%	11.92%	14.90%	17.47%	19.89%
6 YEARS	12.73%	15.92%	2.86%	4.99%	9.18%	11.29%	13.51%
5 YEARS	19.64%	17.41%	3.50%	8.24%	12.18%	15.25%	17.30%
4 YEARS	18.73%	17.09%	5.39%	7.89%	11.75%	15.25%	17.45%
3 YEARS	11.43%	10.97%	-0.36%	2.60%	7.17%	10.53%	13.67%
2 YEARS	4.07%	4.05%	-9.74%	-6.60%	-2.49%	1.71%	5.70%
YEAR	13.43%	18.09%	-2.46%	4.04%	11.28%	13.90%	18.75%
QUARTER	9.30%	7.03%	2.09%	4.45%	6.56%	9.33%	11.92%

SOURCE: Courtesy of Eppler, Guerin & Turner Pension Consulting.

B_p = the estimated beta of the portfolio

$\tilde{R}_{pt}, \tilde{R}_{mt}, \widetilde{RF}_t$ = the return in period t on the portfolio, the market portfolio, and the risk-free rate

$\tilde{E}_{pt}$ = the unexpected return on the portfolio in period t

Since each of these was first discussed in Chapter 8 and then used in Chapter 18 to evaluate the historical performance of mutual funds, we will not review them again at this point. Instead, we will use the CAPM concept on which they are based to develop a procedure which allows us to identify why a given level of performance occurred. Basically, this approach separates the return a manager has in a given period into three major components: (1) a benchmark return, (2) a return due to market timing, and (3) a return due to stock selection.

Analysis of Timing and Selection. The procedure that identifies a benchmark as well as timing and selection returns is based on the security market line (SML), which relates returns earned on a portfolio (or security) to its nondiversifiable risk.[5] In Chapter 8, we defined the SML as follows:

Security Market Line
$$E(R_i) = RF + B_i[E(R_m) - RF] \tag{23.6}$$

where:

$E(R_i)$ = the expected return on portfolio (or security) i

B_i = the beta of portfolio (security) i

$E(R_m)$ = the expected return on the market portfolio of all risky assets

Its ex post form can be written as:

Ex Post SML
$$E(R_{it}) = RF_t + B_{it}(R_{mt} - RF_t) \tag{23.7}$$

where:

$E(R_{it})$ = the expected return on portfolio i during period t

RF_t = the risk-free rate associated with period t

B_{it} = the estimated beta of portfolio i during period t

R_{mt} = the actual return on the market portfolio during period t

For example, during the quarter ended September 30, the return on the S&P 500 (our proxy for the market portfolio) was, say, 9.68% and the return on T-bills (our proxy for the risk-free rate) was 2.50%. Thus the relationship between the *expected* return on an investment portfolio and its estimated beta for the quarter would be:

September 30 Ex Post SML
$$\begin{aligned} E(R_{it}) &= 2.50\% + B_{it}(9.68\% - 2.50\%) \\ &= 2.50\% + B_{it}(7.18\%) \end{aligned} \tag{23.8}$$

During that quarter Twentieth Century Growth mutual fund had an estimated beta of 0.94. Thus, the return we would have expected it to earn was 9.25%:

$$2.50\% + 0.94(7.18\%) = 9.25\%$$

---

[5]The procedure presented here was first presented by Eugene Fama in "Components of Investment Performance," *Journal of Finance* 17 (June 1977): 551–67.

FIGURE 23-4 *Twentieth Century Growth, Analysis of Return*

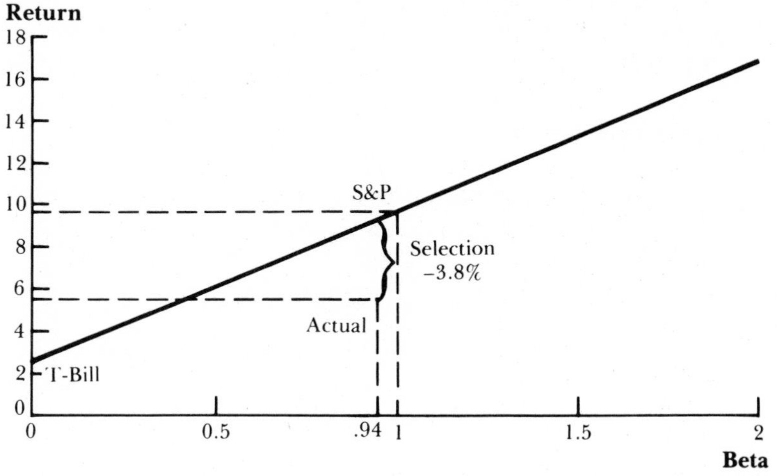

If Twentieth Century Growth's *actual* return during the quarter was 5.45%, its return was 3.8% lower than we would have expected given its estimated beta. These results are shown graphically in Figure 23-4. The difference between the return which was expected *given a portfolio's current beta risk* and the actual return is referred to as the *return from stock selection*. Given the portfolio's current beta risk, Twentieth Century Growth would be expected to earn 9.25%. Since it earned only 5.45%, the difference is attributed to poor stock selection.[6]

We move now to timing and benchmark returns. Many investment managers attempt to time equity market returns by adjusting their stock/nonstock mix and by adjusting the beta level of the stocks held. Their goal, of course, is to reduce (or increase) equity holdings and betas prior to poor (or good) stock market returns.

Twentieth Century Growth appears to be no exception. Although the mutual fund made only minor commitments to nonequities, it shifted its beta level considerably. Assume that over the preceding five years, the fund had an average beta estimate of 1.30. We will refer to the fund's intended long-run beta as its *target beta* and use the historical average as a proxy for the target beta.

If the fund had been at its target beta of 1.3 during the September 30 quarter, we would have expected it to earn 11.83%:

$$2.50\% + 1.3(7.18\%) = 11.83\%$$

This expected return given its target beta is referred to as its *benchmark return*. However, the fund had actually reduced its estimated beta to 0.94, a level at which we would expect a 9.25% return. The difference between the return expected given its

---

[6]Selection returns are closely related to the measure of performance suggested by Jensen—the alpha term in Equation 23.5. In fact, Jensen's alpha is the average of many periodic security-selection returns.

current beta and the return expected at its target beta (the benchmark return) represents the measure of *timing* return. For Twentieth Century Growth, this timing return was a negative 2.58%.

Figure 23-5 summarizes the analysis. Given the estimated target beta (b_{iT}), the benchmark return was 11.83%:

Benchmark Return
$$RF_t + b_{iT}(R_{mt} - RF_t) =$$
$$2.50\% + 1.30(9.68\% - 2.50\%) = 11.83\%$$
(23.9)

The timing return represents the difference between the current fund beta and the target beta multiplied by the excess return on the market portfolio. For Twentieth Century Growth this was −2.58%:

Timing Return
$$(B_{it} - b_{iT})(R_{mt} - RF_t) =$$
$$(0.94 - 1.30)(9.68\% - 2.50\%) = -2.58\%$$
(23.10)

Finally, the selection return represents the difference between the actual return (R_{it}) and the return expected given the current beta estimate. For Twentieth Century Growth, this was −3.8%:

Selection Return
$$R_{it} - [RF_t + b_{it}(R_{mt} - RF_t)] =$$
$$5.45 - [2.50\% + 0.94(9.68\% - 2.50\%)] = -3.8\%$$
(23.11)

To summarize these relationships:

$$\frac{\text{Actual}}{\text{Return}} = \frac{\text{Benchmark}}{\text{Return}} + \frac{\text{Timing}}{\text{Return}} + \frac{\text{Selection}}{\text{Return}}$$

$$5.45\% = 11.83\% + (-2.58\%) + (-3.80\%)$$

FIGURE 23-5 *Twentieth Century Growth, Analysis of Return*

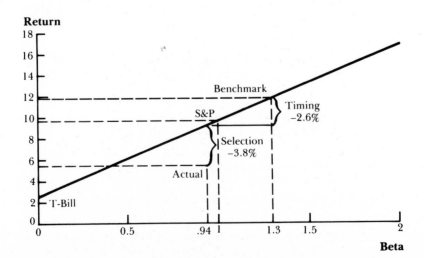

FIGURE 23-6 *Pioneer II Return Analysis*

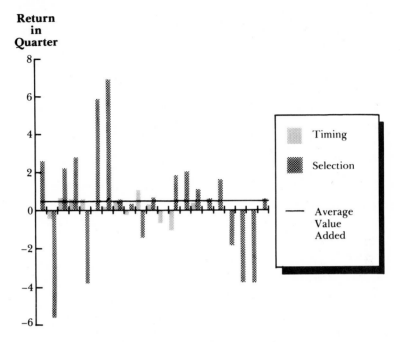

Quarter End

			Average Quarterly Returns (Ending December 31)		
	Actual	*Benchmark*	*Value Added*		
Prior	*Return*	*Return*	*Total*	*Timing*	*Selection*
Quarter	2.32%	1.70%	0.62%	0.00%	0.62%
1 Year	−0.67	1.55	−2.22	−0.01	−2.21
2 Years	3.17	3.56	−0.39	0.03	−0.42
3 Years	4.06	4.26	−0.20	0.00	−0.20
4 Years	3.60	2.85	0.75	0.03	0.72
5 Years	4.30	3.85	0.45	0.09	0.36

Figure 23-6 shows benchmark, timing, and selection returns for a five-year period ending December 1984 for Pioneer II mutual fund.[7] A common practice is to add the timing and selection returns and refer to this as *value added* by the manager's active speculation. In the context of the CAPM, this value added represents an excess risk-adjusted return. Over the five-year period shown in the figure, Pioneer II had an average quarterly value added of 0.45%. This translates to 1.81% on an annual

[7]We consistently use mutual funds in illustrations since their returns are public record. The techniques are applicable to all investment managers.

TABLE 23-3 *Sample Timing and Selection Returns for the Five Years Ending December 30, 1984*

	Actual Return	=	Benchmark	+	Timing	+	Selection
American Capital Comstock	4.87%		3.71%		0.06%		1.10%
American Mutual Fund	4.47		3.68		0.04		0.74
Bank 1	3.13		3.83		−0.01		−0.69
Bank 2	2.15		2.83		−0.29		−0.44
Bank 3	1.26		2.93		−0.03		−1.64
Bank 4	3.57		3.83		−0.36		0.05
Bank 5	4.36		3.65		0.13		0.57
Fidelity Equity Income	5.21		3.49		0.22		1.50
Investment Company of America	4.01		3.77		0.10		0.13
Kemper Summit	3.26		2.62		−0.08		0.72
Mathers	3.37		3.86		−0.03		−0.46
Morgan (W.L.)	3.95		3.71		0.13		0.11
Pioneer II	4.30		3.85		0.09		0.36
Price New Horizon	3.48		3.57		0.07		−0.16
Putnam Investors	3.90		3.98		−0.26		0.17
Putnam Voyager	4.21		4.02		0.07		0.12

basis.[8] Note that virtually all of the value added came from stock selection and that much of this stock selection occurred in the first two quarters of 1981.

There are two advantages to a return analysis such as that in Figure 23-6. First, a more precise estimate of risk-adjusted performance can be made than is possible with a performance analysis based on style. For example, specific estimates are made of the manager's value added, and the sources are traced to speculative returns from timing or selection. In fact, it is possible to calculate the statistical significance of each. Second, the analysis shown in Figure 23-6 can be used to determine why a manager had a particular performance. For example: (1) What portion was due to timing and selection? (2) Do only a few periods account for the net results? and (3) If a few periods are dominating, what was the cause, and is this likely to be reversed in the future?

In Table 23-3, benchmark, timing, and selection returns are shown for twelve well-known mutual funds and five bank managers. The data represent quarterly averages for the five years ending December 1984. On the whole, benchmark returns are quite close to actual managers' returns. And, to the extent that they differ, selection returns are the major cause, most likely a result of both poor timing ability and limited attempts at timing. We will return to the timing and selection ability of investment managers later in the chapter, when some recent empirical studies are reviewed.

Single-Manager Portfolios. When our timing and selection return analysis is applied to individual managers, the results are correct from the manager's perspective. Whether

---

[8] $1.00045^4 − 1.0 = 1.81\%$.

they are also correct from the perspective of a portfolio owner depends on whether the manager is one of many or is the sole manager of the portfolio assets.[9] The reason for this is very simple. When many managers are used, the relevant risk is each manager's nondiversifiable risk as captured by beta. Diversifiable manager risk is of little concern to the portfolio owner if many managers are used, because such risk is diversified away. However, if a single manager is used, the portfolio owner should be concerned with measuring both nondiversifiable and diversifiable risk. Since the previous analysis is based on only nondiversifiable manager risk, an adjustment must be made when the portfolio owner is evaluating a single manager or one of many managers.

Let's consider again the case of Twentieth Century Growth mutual fund. But now we will assume that the fund is the only asset held in the portfolio. Thus, the fund's diversifiable and nondiversifiable risks are *both* important.

Earlier we saw that the fund's estimated beta for the September 1984 quarter was 0.94. If the correlation coefficient between the fund's returns and the market portfolio's returns is +1.0, the fund would have zero diversifiable risk. Beta would be an accurate measure of the fund's nondiversifiable risk as well as its total risk (diversifiable plus nondiversifiable).

However, if the correlation coefficient is less than +1.0, beta would not properly reflect the total risk of the fund. Some diversifiable risk would remain which the fund's beta does not capture. Since a portfolio owner who uses a single manager is principally interested in the manager's (thus the portfolio's) total risk, we need to have some way of accounting for such total risk.

This is done by finding what the beta would be on a portfolio which (1) is perfectly correlated with market portfolio returns and (2) has the same total risk as the manager being evaluated. For example, assume that Twentieth Century Growth's beta estimate of 0.94 is determined as follows:[10]

$$b_{it} = \frac{\sigma_i}{\sigma_m} \ (r_{im})$$

$$0.94 = \frac{21.12\%}{20.00\%} \ (0.89)$$

(23.12)

where:

σ_i = the standard deviation of portfolio returns at period t

σ_m = the standard deviation of market portfolio returns

r_{im} = the correlation coefficient between portfolio and market returns

A portfolio that has a +1.0 correlation coefficient with market returns and the same total risk ($\sigma_p = 21.12\%$) as Twentieth Century Growth's would have a beta of 1.056:

---

[9]The validity of the approach also depends on how diversified a sole investment manager is. We will see shortly that the approach requires no modification for single-manager portfolios if the manager is broadly diversified.

[10]The beta equation 23.12 was initially developed in Chapter 8 and shown in Equation 8.10.

$$\frac{21.12\%}{20.00\%} (1.0) = 1.056$$

We will refer to this adjusted beta as the *perfectly diversified beta equivalent*, b_{it}^*.

Perfectly Diversified Beta Equivalent

$$b_{it}^* = \frac{\sigma_i}{\sigma_m} (1.0) \tag{23.13a}$$

or

$$b_{it}^* = b_{it} \div r_{im} \tag{23.13b}$$

To the owner of a portfolio fully invested in Twentieth Century Growth, the true selection return should be based on this perfectly diversified beta equivalent, b_{it}^*, not on the original beta estimate for the quarter, b_{it}. This is because b_{it}^* more correctly measures the portfolio owner's risk exposure when a single manager is used. Thus the original selection return, as calculated in Equation 23.11, now consists of a *net selection return* plus a return associated with the less than perfect diversification. Specifically:

$$\underbrace{\left[\frac{R_{it}}{-RF_t} - b_{it}(R_{mt} - RF_t) \right]}_{\text{Original Selection Return}} = \underbrace{\left[\frac{R_{it}}{-RF_t} - b_{it}^*(R_{mt} - RF_t) \right]}_{\text{Net Selection}} + \underbrace{[(b_{it}^* - b_{it})(R_{mt} - RF_t)]}_{\substack{\text{Effect of} \\ \text{Lack of Diversification}}}$$

For Twentieth Century Growth:

$$-3.8\% = \left[\begin{array}{c} 5.45\% \\ -2.50\% - 1.056 \times \\ (9.68\% - 2.50\%) \end{array} \right] + \left[\begin{array}{c} (1.056 - 0.94) \times \\ (9.68\% - 2.50\%) \end{array} \right]$$

$$-3.8\% = -4.63\% + 0.83\%$$

Figure 23-7 summarizes the return analysis under the assumption that Twentieth Century Growth is the sole portfolio manager. First, the target beta is still 1.3. Given this beta, we would have expected to earn 11.83% — that is, the *benchmark return is 11.83%*. Next, the return we would have expected given a perfectly diversified beta equivalent to Twentieth Century Growth was 10.08%. This is found by knowing RF_t, R_{mt}, and the beta estimate of the equivalent portfolio, b_{it}^*.

$$2.50\% + 1.056(9.68\% - 2.50\%) = 10.08\%$$

Given that the actual portfolio earned 5.45%, the *net selection return was −4.63%* (5.45% − 10.08%). Finally, we need to evaluate the impact of Twentieth Century Growth's lack of perfect diversification. Although the fund's beta was 0.94, the beta of the perfectly diversified equivalent portfolio was 1.056, or 0.116 larger. Since this

FIGURE 23-7 *Twentieth Century Growth, Analysis of Timing, Selection, and Diversification Inputs*

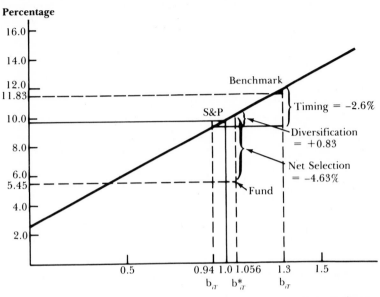

occurred during a period when $R_{mt} - RF_t$ was positive, the return associated with the *lack of diversification was positive and equal to 0.83%*.[11]

To summarize, if Twentieth Century Growth mutual fund had been the only investment of a portfolio owner during the September 1984 quarter, the performance of the fund would have been evaluated as follows:

$$\frac{\text{Actual}}{\text{Return}} = \frac{\text{Benchmark}}{\text{Return}} + \frac{\text{Timing}}{\text{Return}} + \frac{\text{Net Selection}}{\text{Return}} + \frac{\text{Diversification}}{\text{Impact}}$$

$$5.45\% = 11.83\% + (-2.58\%) + (-4.63\%) + 0.83\%$$

Problems in Application. Calculation of these performance statistics requires access to considerable data. In particular, a realistic estimate of the manager's *current* beta is needed to determine both timing and selection returns. This can be accomplished only if the analyst knows the current portfolio holdings and has an estimate of the beta for each holding. If, for example, 30 stocks are held, the beta on each is first es-

---

[11] It is better to think of the gain from the lack of perfect diversification as an adjustment to the manager's selection return. Without this adjustment, the selection return of Twentieth Century Growth was −3.87. With the adjustment, the selection return was −4.63%.

timated using the market model (see Chapter 8), and the market-value-weighted average of these is used as an estimate of b_{it}. Such b_{it} values are constantly updated as stocks are sold and replaced by new stocks. Note that this procedure differs from the approach commonly used to estimate a portfolio beta that applies the market model to *total portfolio returns* over some past time interval. This second approach is certainly easier to calculate, but it cannot be used to evaluate a quarter-by-quarter portfolio beta. In fact, this approach is at best an estimate of the *average* beta position of a manager over many time periods in the past.

If a sequence of b_{it} values cannot be obtained from portfolio inventory listings, a detailed period-by-period analysis of timing and selection cannot be conducted. Some methods are discussed in the next section which allow estimates of average timing and selection abilities over a large number of periods. But these techniques do not allow for a period-by-period analysis and thus cannot investigate why timing or selection was particularly good (or bad) in a given period.

A more formidable problem arises when attempting to examine the effects of the lack of perfect diversification. Recall from Equation 23.13 that either σ_i and σ_m (the standard deviations of portfolio i and the market portfolio) or r_{im} (the correlation between returns on portfolio i and the market portfolio) must be known in order to translate b_{it} into b_{it}^*. Unfortunately, the only way to estimate either is by subjective estimate. The use of b_{it}^* is so rare that the author has seen it only in textbooks and in Fama's original paper, where the idea was first presented. Perhaps new statistical techniques will be developed to allow for the use of b_{it}^*. To date they don't exist.

Average Estimates of Timing and Selection. Usually a sequence of past total portfolio returns is all that's available for measuring portfolio performance. In this case, two variants of the traditional characteristic line can be used to evaluate a manager's *average* timing and selection abilities.

Consider the characteristic line shown in panel A of Figure 23-8. The vertical axis is used to plot excess returns on the portfolio (portfolio returns in period t minus the risk-free rate in period t). The horizontal axis is used to plot excess returns on the market portfolio. The *traditional* characteristic line is shown as the best-fit linear relationship and is found by the following regression equation:

$$\widetilde{ER}_{it} = a_i + b_i(\widetilde{ER}_{mt}) + \tilde{e}_{it} \tag{23.15}$$

where:

$\widetilde{ER}_{it}$ = the excess return on portfolio i in period t

$\tilde{e}_{it}$ = the residual excess return on portfolio i in period t

a_i = the constant excess return on portfolio i

b_i = the systematic risk (estimated beta) of portfolio i

As shown in panel A, the positive a_i suggests that the portfolio manager had a constant excess return. This, of course, is Jensen's alpha, which we discussed in previous chapters. In this chapter we will interpret it as the average level of *security selec-*

FIGURE 23-8 *Timing and Selection Analysis Using Characteristic Line Analysis*

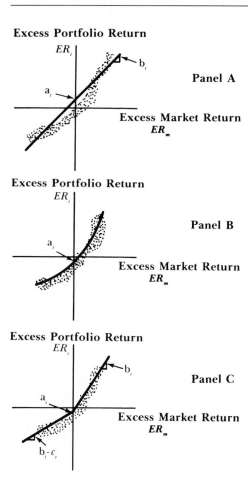

Excess Portfolio Return

Panel A

Excess Market Return

Excess Portfolio Return

Panel B

Excess Market Return

Excess Portfolio Return

Panel C

Excess Market Return

tion earned by the portfolio manager.[12] But this linear characteristic line is unable to tell us anything about the timing ability of the manager—even though there appears to be some evidence of timing from the pattern of the points around the line.

Two approaches have been suggested which attempt to capture both timing and selection ability. The first approach is attributed to Treynor and Mazuy. They suggested that a quadratic regression be examined as follows:

$$\widetilde{ER}_{it} = a_i + b_i(ER_{mt}) + c(ER_{mt})^2 + \tilde{e}_{it} \tag{23.16}$$

---

[12] A positive or negative value of a_i must be statistically significant, of course, before it can be interpreted as evidence of good or bad performance. See Chapters 8 and 18.

Such a quadratic curve is displayed in panel B. A positive value of c would suggest that portfolio returns are more sensitive to large positive market returns than to large negative market returns. This, of course, would be indicative of good market timing. The intercept term, a_i, would still represent an estimate of security-selection ability. Panel B suggests a positive market-timing ability and a zero (or perhaps negative) selection ability.

A second approach for examining market timing was suggested more recently by Henriksson and Merton. They suggest that two straight lines be fit to the excess returns as shown in panel C and in the regression equation below:

$$\widetilde{ER}_{it} = a_i + b_i(\widetilde{ER}_{mt}) - c_i(\tilde{Z}_t) + \tilde{e}_{it} \tag{23.17}$$

The new term reflects whether the market is rising or falling and takes on the following values with the resulting regression equations:

If	*Then*	*Implied Regression Relationship*
$ER_{mt} > 0$	$Z_t = 0$	$ER_i = a_i + b_i(ER_m)$
$ER_{mt} = 0$	$Z_t = 0$	$ER_i = a_i$
$ER_{mt} < 0$	$Z_t = ER_{mt}$	$ER_i = a_i + (b_i - c_i)(ER_m)$

Clearly b_i is the slope of the characteristic line when the market is rising and $(b_i - c_i)$ is the slope when the market is falling. The value of c_i reflects the extent of market timing ability. If c_i is statistically greater (or less) than 0.0, there is evidence of positive (or negative) market-timing ability. If c_i is not statistically different from zero, no evidence of market timing is present. As before, a_i represents the average security-selection ability.

Later in the chapter we will examine empirical tests of Equation 23.17.

Performance Attribution. Some performance-monitoring firms attribute portfolio returns to (1) over- or underweighting of various economic sectors within the portfolio, and (2) above- or below-average returns within the sectors. The first is similar to previous measures of timing, and the second is similar to the approach used in security selection.

To illustrate, assume that the market portfolio consists of three economic sectors with the following average stock returns in each sector during the past quarter:

The Market Portfolio

Sector	Percentage of Total	Previous Quarter's Return	Product
A	20%	−10%	−2.0%
B	50%	5%	2.5%
C	30%	10%	3.0%
	100%	Average Return	3.5%

Now consider portfolio *XYZ*, which had the following weighting and returns during the same quarter:

Portfolio XYZ

Sector	Percentage of Total	Previous Quarter's Return	Product
A	10%	−10%	−1.0%
B	60%	8%	4.8%
C	30%	12%	3.6%
	100%	Average Return	7.4%

The 7.4% return of portfolio *XYZ* is explained as a function of (1) the 3.5% market return, (2) a return associated with over- or underweighting various market sectors, and (3) a return associated with performance within the market sectors.

The return associated with over- or underweighting sectors is equal to 1.5% and is calculated below. The difference between the percentage which each sector represents of the total market and the portfolio weighting given to a sector is multiplied by the *market* return of the sector. When summed across all sectors, we have a measure of the portfolio's return which is attributable to over- or underweighting sectors. In concept this is similar to the measures of timing which we discussed earlier:

Sector	Sector Weighting Portfolio	−	Market	=	Difference	Market Sector Return	Product
A	0.10	−	0.20	=	−0.10	−10%	1.0%
B	0.60	−	0.50	=	0.10	5%	0.5%
C	0.30	−	0.30	=	0.00	10%	0.0%
						Sector-Weighting Return	1.5%

The performance within sectors is calculated by multiplying the portfolio's percentage weight in a sector by the difference between the portfolio's return within the sector and the market's sector return. In our example, this within-sector return is 2.4%:

Sector	Portfolio Weighting	Return During Quarter Portfolio	−	Market	=	Difference	Product
A	0.10	−10%	−	(−10%)		0.0%	0.0%
B	0.60	8%	−	5%		3.0%	1.8%
C	0.30	12%	−	10%		2.0%	0.6%
	1.00	Within-Sector Return					2.4%

In sum, the portfolio's return is composed as follows:

$$\frac{\text{Portfolio}}{\text{Return}} = \frac{\text{Market}}{\text{Return}} + \frac{\text{Sector}}{\text{Weighting}} + \frac{\text{Within}}{\text{Sector}}$$

$$7.4\% = 3.5\% + 1.5\% + 2.4\%$$

As noted earlier, such an analysis results in measures similar to those used in timing and selection returns. The difficulties with the procedure are basically pragmatic: a

TABLE 23-4 *Illustration of Return Attribution for the Quarter Ended March 31, 1983*

	S&P 500		Market Timer		Variance		
Sector	A PCT of Market Value	B Rate of Return*	C PCT of Market Value	D Rate of Return	Selection	Weighting	Total
Technology	15.13	12.28	12.09	28.90	2.01	−0.07	1.94
Capital Goods	4.90	11.00	5.24	38.89	1.45	0.00	1.45
Consumer Durables	3.99	−0.07	0.00	−	−	0.41	0.41
Energy	17.47	7.93	0.00	−	−	0.38	0.38
Transportation	2.46	11.33	0.00	−	−	−0.03	−0.03
Consumer Non-Durables	27.39	10.01	46.12	9.84	−0.09	−0.01	−0.10
Materials and Services	10.57	11.12	0.00	−	−	−0.11	−0.11
Finance	6.30	16.73	0.00	−	−	−0.42	−0.42
Utilities	11.80	8.22	36.55	2.70	−2.01	−0.46	−2.47
Total	100.00	10.04	100.00	11.06	1.36	−0.35	1.01
Latest Year		43.88		62.73	11.12	7.73	18.85
Cumulative Returns Annualized**		13.90		17.06	4.93	−1.77	3.17

*Buy and hold statistics
**Calculated with 10 quarters of data

Selection = C × (D − B)/100
Weighting = (C − A) × (B − Total Index Return)/100

SOURCE: Courtesy of Wilshire Associates.

great deal of data is needed. At the least, the analyst needs end-of-period inventory figures in order to determine sector weightings and returns. But if the analysis is to be truly accurate, the date of every security trade within a period is also needed. Only then can a correct sector-return attribution be conducted.

An illustration of return attribution as conducted by Wilshire Associates is shown in Table 23-4. Although calculation of the sector-weighting return is slightly different from that shown above, the general process and analytic intent are identical. In this case a market timer is being evaluated. Nine different sectors are used, and returns are analyzed for the prior quarter, prior year, and cumulative ten quarters. During the quarter, the manager's return was 11.06%, compared with 10.04% for the S&P 500. The excess is attributed to excess within-sector returns of 1.36% (selection) and excess sector weighting at −0.35% (timing).

MONITORING BOND PERFORMANCE

The procedures used in monitoring the performance of bond managers are often different from those applied to equity managers. This is because bonds are distinctly different securities (having fixed lives and specified promised cash flows) and because the capital asset pricing model just doesn't work well with bonds.

A large variety of techniques are used in monitoring bond performance and, of course, we can examine only a few. But a common theme runs through virtually all approaches: the critical importance of the baseline bond investment portfolio. Most monitoring systems examine bond managers' actual returns against a baseline portfolio and attempt to analyze why the two differ.

The Importance of the Baseline Bond Investment Portfolio

Most security portfolios are held in order to provide future benefits at a relatively distant date. Pension funds, for example, generally will have net cash inflows to the portfolio for 20 to 30 years before net cash withdrawals are necessary. The same is true for many individuals saving for retirement. Performance monitoring, on the other hand, focuses on relatively short time intervals. If a bond portfolio manager relies too heavily on short-term performance, it is quite possible that long-term performance will suffer. Bond strategies that increase short-term risk/return performance often conflict with the long-term needs of the owner as specified by the baseline bond investment portfolio.

For example, consider the case of a typical defined benefit pension fund. Usually, the bond portion of such a pension is intended to provide long-run nominal cash inflows which are relatively free of risk. A reasonable baseline investment portfolio for such a situation would consist of long-term, high-grade bonds which are unlikely to be called. U.S. Treasury bonds with a market price low enough that the bonds are unlikely to be called (that is, a low coupon) are reasonable candidates. If such securities are held to their maturities and then reinvested in new bonds of an appropriate maturity, they should fulfill the desire for long-run, relatively riskless cash flows to the portfolio. However, over short periods of time the risk/return performance of such bonds may look quite dismal.

To see why this is true, consider Figure 23-9. In panel A the potential short-term returns are shown for three different bond strategies: (1) purchase a one-year T-bill, (2) purchase a long-term bond portfolio which is not protected against calls, and (3) purchase the baseline bond investment portfolio. The vertical axis plots actual rates of return over a given one-year period, and the horizontal axis indicates what happens to the generalized level of yields to maturity during the year in which performance is evaluated. If the yield curve does not move, the actual return on both long-term bond strategies will be about equal and somewhat greater than the T-bill return. However, note the considerable range of potential return outcomes from both long-term strategies compared with the certain return associated with T-bills. When performance is viewed from a one-year perspective, T-bills appear the least risky. In addition, the callable bond strategy appears to be somewhat less risky than the baseline bond investment portfolio.[13]

---

[13]If interest rates fall, bonds will be called. This would provide a call premium which is either partially or totally offset by lower reinvestment returns. If interest rates rise, the bonds subject to potential call will probably not rise as much as those unlikely to be called. This can occur simply because of differences in likely coupon rates on the two types of issues. Bonds subject to potential call will carry larger coupons and thus be less sensitive to interest-rate changes.

FIGURE 23-9 *Short-Term Versus Long-Term Bond Return and Risk*

Panel A. Return Profiles Over Short Term Horizons

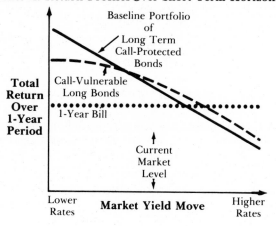

Panel B. Return Profiles Over Long Term Horizons

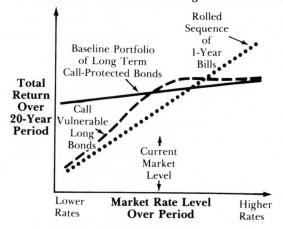

SOURCE: Martin L. Leibowitz, *Total Return Management: A Goal-Oriented Framework for Bond Portfolio Strategy* (Salomon Brothers, 1979).

Panel B, however, examines the long-term return outcomes for various future shifts of the yield curve. Now the story is reversed. The most uncertain strategy is that of investing in T-bills, because its return is directly tied to interest-rate changes. The call-vulnerable strategy suffers low returns if rates drop as a result of the decreased rate of return at which the principal value of called bonds would be reinvested. The least risky strategy is that of the baseline bond investment portfolio. (In fact, that is exactly why the strategy *is* the baseline portfolio.) Although the reinvestment rate applied to coupon interest is unknown with the baseline portfolio, this risk is clearly less than the risk incurred with other strategies.

TABLE 23-5 *Illustrative Simple Bond-Performance Review*

	Rate of Return			Duration		Quality	
Prior	*Baseline Portfolio*	*Actual Portfolio*	*Excess*	*Baseline Portfolio*	*Actual Portfolio*	*Baseline Portfolio*	*Actual Portfolio*
Quarter	5.3%	5.0%	−0.3%	8.0	3.2	90	88
1 Year	15.0	15.6	0.6	8.0	4.1	90	95
2 Years	9.3	10.2	0.9	8.0	7.4	90	83
3 Years	16.2	17.9	1.7	8.0	6.9	90	74
5 Years	14.0	17.2	3.2	8.0	6.8	90	80
Standard Deviation of 5-Year Quarterly Rates of Return:	8.0%	10.3%	—				

Two important conclusions should be drawn:

1. Performance monitoring over short time intervals can be misleading.
2. Performance monitoring should always include a comparison of the actual portfolio against a baseline investment portfolio.

These conclusions apply equally to equity performance and bond performance. They are simply easier to see in the context of bonds. Performance analyses should always keep the long-term objective of the portfolio in mind and be compared with a clearly defined baseline investment portfolio.[14]

Simple Bond Performance

Once a baseline bond investment portfolio has been identified, the performance of the actual bond portfolio can be compared against it. As an example, Table 23-5 illustrates the types of information which may be contained in a bond-performance review. Rates of return are shown for a variety of time periods for both the baseline and the actual portfolio. Clearly, long-run returns are the most important, and, in this case, the five-year returns on the actual portfolio were in excess of the baseline. However, this was accomplished by investing in shorter-duration and lower-quality bonds than called for by the baseline portfolio.

Timing and Selection

As is the case for equity portfolios, any excess returns earned from active management of a bond portfolio will result from either timing or selection activities. In practice, however, the relative emphasis given to each differs. Most equity managers place

---

[14]The baseline portfolio was not explicitly discussed in the foregoing review of equity performance. However, since equity performance is usually based on the CAPM, the market portfolio of all stocks is the implied baseline.

more emphasis on stock selection than on timing, whereas most bond managers place more emphasis on timing.

A number of techniques can be used to estimate timing and selection bond returns. We will examine only one. Assume that the baseline bond investment portfolio is a diversified portfolio of U.S. Treasuries with a duration of six years. Also assume that the yield curve at the start of the period for which performance is being evaluated is shown by the solid curve in Figure 23-10. At the start of the period, the yield to duration is 8.0%, as represented by point A_0. The actual portfolio, however, has a three-year duration and is invested in securities with a 2% yield spread above U.S. Treasuries. The initial actual portfolio, shown as point B_0, has a yield to duration of 9%. Apparently the bond manager expects (1) that interest rates will rise and has thus shortened the duration, and (2) that the yield spread of 3% on lower-quality bonds will narrow and has thus overweighted such instruments.

The yield curve, say, one month later, is shown as the dotted curve, and the positions of the baseline and actual portfolios are shown by points A_1 and B_1. At the baseline portfolio's duration of six years, the yield curve has increased by 100 basis points. Thus, from Equation 12.3, the rate of return expected on the baseline bond investment portfolio would be -5.55%:

**Expected
Benchmark Return**
$$-6.0\left(\frac{1.09 - 1.08}{1.08}\right) = -5.55\% \qquad \textbf{(23.18)}$$

As noted, we will call this the benchmark return. The yield to duration of the actual portfolio, however, has increased from 9% to 10%. Thus, the actual return earned will be -2.75%:

FIGURE 23-10 *Evaluation of Bond Manager Performance*

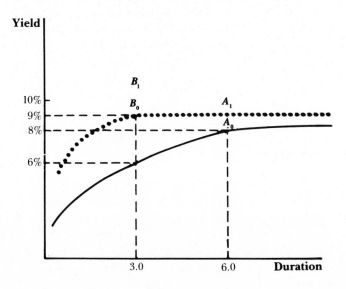

Actual Return $\qquad -3.0\left(\dfrac{1.10 - 1.09}{1.09}\right) = -2.75\%$ $\qquad$ **(23.19)**

The difference of $+2.80\%$ between the actual and the benchmark return is due to a combination of timing and selection returns.

Let's first consider the timing return. If the bond manager had initially invested in Treasuries with a three-year duration, the yield curve would have increased from 6.0% to 9.0%. The return from this portion of the manager's strategy would have been -8.49%:

Expected Return at Actual Duration $\qquad -3.0\left(\dfrac{1.09 - 1.06}{1.06}\right) = -8.49\%$ $\qquad$ **(23.20)**

Since the return on the six-year-duration benchmark was -5.55%, a negative timing return of -2.94% was earned:

$$\dfrac{\text{Expected Return at}}{\text{Actual Duration}} - \dfrac{\text{Expected Return at}}{\text{Benchmark Duration}} = \dfrac{\text{Timing}}{\text{Return}}$$

$$-8.49\% \quad - \quad (-5.55\%) \quad = \quad -2.94\%$$

(23.21)

Note that the bond manager was correct in anticipating increases in interest rates but did not foresee the much larger increase in three-year-duration yields compared to the six-year-duration Treasuries. Some people who evaluate bond performance actually split this net timing return into two components: one due to parallel shifts in the yield curve and the other due to changes in the shape of the yield curve.

The selection return arises from changes in the yield spread between actual securities held and those of the benchmark portfolio at the duration selected by the manager. In our example, this yield spread fell from 3% to 1% and, thus, a positive return from selection was earned. The value of this selection return is simply an amount which balances the bond portfolio's actual return with its benchmark, timing, and selection components. In our example, the selection return would be 5.74%.

To summarize:

$$\dfrac{\text{Benchmark}}{\text{Return}} + \dfrac{\text{Timing}}{\text{Return}} + \dfrac{\text{Selection}}{\text{Return}} = \dfrac{\text{Actual}}{\text{Return}}$$

$$-5.55\% \quad + \quad (-2.94\%) \quad + \quad 5.74\% \quad = \quad -2.75\%$$

AGGREGATE PORTFOLIO PERFORMANCE

We began this chapter by stating that it is the performance of the aggregate portfolio which is most important. The performance of the individual manager is secondary. And yet all of our discussions so far have dealt with the evaluation of a single manager. The reason for this is simply that we need to know how individual equity and bond managers can be evaluated before we can accumulate their performances across the portfolio as a whole.

There are technical problems involved in actually accumulating managers' performances, but conceptually the performance of each manager is weighted by the proportion of the total portfolio managed. For example, assume there are two managers, a bond manager who invested 25% of portfolio assets at the start of the quarter being evaluated and a stock manager who was responsible for the remaining 75% of the assets. If their performances were as shown below, the benchmark total portfolio return would be 7.48%, and the manager value added from timing and selection would be −2.69% and −1.41%, respectively:

	Return	Percentage Holding	Product
Bond Manager			
Benchmark	− 5.55%	0.25	−1.39%
Timing	− 2.94	0.25	−0.74
Selection	5.74	0.25	1.44
Stock Manager			
Benchmark	11.83%	0.75	8.87%
Timing	− 2.60	0.75	−1.95
Selection	− 3.80	0.75	−2.85
Portfolio Benchmark	= −1.39% + 8.87% = 7.48%		
Portfolio Timing	= −0.74% − 1.95% = −2.69%		
Portfolio Selection	= 1.44% − 2.85% = −1.41%		

These returns could then be compared with the actual dollar-weighted return on the portfolio in an exhibit similar to Table 23-6. Note that the actual portfolio return is stated as a dollar-weighted return since this is the true return earned by the portfolio owner. In contrast, the returns used to evaluate the individual managers' performances are time-weighted returns since these are the best measures of the managers' returns. In order for the sum of time-weighted returns to balance with the

TABLE 23-6 *Illustration of Total Portfolio Returns*

Prior	Return*	=	Analysis of Total Portfolio Returns†				
			Sponsor Decisions		+	Manager Value Added	
			Benchmark	*Timing*		*Timing*	*Selection*
Quarter	4.13%		7.48%	0.75%		−2.69%	−1.41%
1 Year	2.62		2.30	0.60		−0.70	0.42
2 Years	20.38		20.11	0.20		−0.10	0.17
3 Years	10.06		10.00	−0.60		0.50	0.16
5 Years	15.00		15.00	−0.60		0.60	0.00

*Dollar-weighted
†Time-weighted

dollar-weighted return, a balancing figure is needed. This is shown in Table 23-6 as the portfolio sponsor's timing return. This is correct because the portfolio sponsor decides when contributions and withdrawals will be made to individual managers. Any difference between dollar-weighted and time-weighted returns should be charged to the portfolio owner and not to the individual managers.

EMPIRICAL EVIDENCE OF TIMING AND SELECTION

There have been few rigorous empirical studies of whether investment managers consistently earn market-timing and selection returns. The reasons are probably twofold: (1) a lack of precise estimates of beta targets and temporary beta departures from the targets, and (2) a conceptual concern with the use of CAPM-based measurement techniques. In this section, we will review two of the more recent studies of stock timing and selection.[15]

Selection

Recall that stock-selection returns represent the difference between the actual portfolio return in a given time period and the return which would be expected given the portfolio's actual beta during the period. From Equation 23.11:

$$\text{Selection Return} = R_{it} - [RF_t + b_{it}(R_{mt} - RF_t)] \qquad (23.11)$$

In order to estimate selection returns, beta estimates for each time period (b_{it}) are necessary. In practice, such an estimate is difficult to determine. It requires that the manager hold only common stocks (no cash equivalents or bonds) and that the analyst have the end-of-period inventory listing of these stocks for all time periods for which performance is being evaluated.

Recently Kon and Jen have suggested a statistical procedure which simplifies the data requirements.[16] They provide a way to use only total portfolio returns to derive one, two, etc., beta estimates. When Kon applied this "switching regression" methodology to the returns on 37 mutual funds, he concluded that 25 of the funds could be said to have used two distinct beta levels and that the remaining 12 used three beta levels. Based on such changing beta estimates, he evaluated both selection and timing returns.

Of the 37 funds examined, 25 had positive estimated selectivity, of which 5 were statistically significant at a 95% confidence level. In addition, across the total sam-

---

[15]Equivalent studies of fixed-income managers have not been conducted to date.

[16]See S. Kon and F. Jen, "The Investment Performance of Mutual Funds: An Empirical Investigation of Timing, Selectivity and Market Efficiency," *Journal of Business* 52 (1979): 263–89, and S. Kon, "The Market-Timing Performance of Mutual Fund Managers," *Journal of Business* 56 (1983): 323–47.

ple, there was evidence that the funds as a group exhibited an ability to generate positive selection performance.[17] Both findings are, of course, contrary to the strong-form version of efficient market theory.

Timing

Kon also evaluated the timing ability of the mutual funds. Of the 37 funds, 14 had overall timing performance estimates which were positive, but none was statistically significant (at 95% confidence). He concluded that mutual fund managers should stress their skills of stock selection and not try to time the market.

Another recent study of timing, conducted by Henriksson, was based on the regression model in Equation 23.17:[18]

$$\widetilde{ER}_{it} = a_i + b_i(\widetilde{ER}_{mt}) - c_i(\tilde{Z}_t) + \tilde{e}_{it} \qquad (23.17)$$

where:

$\widetilde{ER}_{it}$ = the excess return (above the risk-free rate) on fund i during period t

$\widetilde{ER}_{mt}$ = the excess return on the market portfolio in period t

$\tilde{e}_{it}$ = residual return in period t

$\tilde{Z}_t = \begin{cases} 0 \text{ if } ER_{mt} \geqq 0 \\ ER_{mt} \text{ if } ER_{mt} < 0 \end{cases}$

The parameter a_i measures net selectivity over the time period examined. The parameter b_i is the slope of the regression in rising markets, and c_i reflects the extent of market-timing ability. If c_i is statistically greater than zero, there is evidence of market timing ability.

Results of Henriksson's tests are shown in Table 23-7. Monthly returns on 116 mutual funds were used for the period February 1968 through May 1980. Looking first at the measure of timing (c_i), the study simply did not find any evidence of a consistent timing ability. Of the 116 funds over the full time interval tested, only 3 had statistically significant positive estimates of timing ability. In contrast, 9 funds had negative timing estimates which were statistically significant.

Kon also conducted a nonparametric test of the funds' timing abilities with similar results. Mutual funds did not exhibit any ability to consistently time equity market moves.

---

[17]Because of the lack of normality in the data, Kon expressed some concern about the true statistical significance of the results.

[18]See R. Henriksson, "Market Timing and Mutual Fund Performance: An Empirical Investigation," *Journal of Business* 54 (1984): 73–96.

TABLE 23-7 *Market-Timing Test Results*

	$\widetilde{ER}_{it} = a_i + b_i(\widetilde{ER}_{mt}) + c_i(\tilde{Z}_t) + \tilde{e}_{it}$	
Period	*Feb. 1968–June 1980*	*May 1974–June 1980*
Average Estimate of		
a_i	0.0007	0.0022
b_i	0.92	0.86
c_i	−0.07	−0.08
Number of Funds with*		
$a_i > 0$	11	21
$a_i < 0$	8	5
$c_i > 0$	3	2
$c_i < 0$	9	3

*At 95% confidence.

SUMMARY

Investment performance should be actively monitored for two principal reasons: (1) to determine whether the objective of the baseline investment portfolio is being achieved, and (2) if the objective is not being achieved, to understand why this is the case so that proper action can be taken.

Performance information on individual investment advisers must be calculated, of course, in order to evaluate the reasons for the performance of the portfolio as a whole. But the analyst should never forget that it is the aggregate portfolio which is most important and which should receive the most attention. After all calculations have been completed, the actual analysis of returns should proceed in a logical, top-down manner, starting with the aggregate portfolio, then the aggregate equity and fixed-income portfolios, and, last, the individual managers within the equity and fixed-income portfolios.

Considerable care should also be given to risk adjustments. The returns on an actual portfolio should be compared only against those on a benchmark portfolio with equivalent risk. The security market line is a widely used tool for equity performance monitoring. When it is used, the benchmark portfolio consists of an estimated beta-adjusted stock market index such as the S&P 500. When fixed-income performance is monitored, benchmarks are often specifically designed which have similar duration, call risk, and default risk to those called for in the baseline bond investment portfolio. The accuracy of a portfolio's risk-adjusted performance depends heavily on the benchmark used. Therefore, a great deal of thought should go into its determination.

Finally, an examination of why particular performance was obtained should be conducted, if possible. This usually involves the calculation of timing and selection returns.

REVIEW PROBLEM

Peter Nielson's only investment holdings for the past five years have been shares of ABC Mutual Fund. The management of ABC Mutual Fund has stated that they intend to maintain virtually a 100% equity position in stocks with prospects of above-average price growth. The purpose of this problem is to review the historical performance of ABC Mutual Fund and Mr. Nielson's investment in the fund.

a. As of November 30, 1990, Mr. Nielson owned 1,000 shares having a net asset value of $40 per share. On December 15, he bought 120 additional shares at an NAV of $42 per share. On December 31, the fund's NAV was $39. What were the dollar- and time-weighted December returns?

b. Why do these two returns vary?

c. During the months of October and November 1990, ABC Mutual Fund had time-weighted returns of 10.0% and 0.50%. What was the total quarterly return ended December 31, 1990?

d. ABC's estimated beta during this quarter was 1.3. In the past they have had an average beta of 1.0. The return on a market portfolio proxy was 12.0% and the return on T-bills was 2.0%. Estimate the fund's benchmark return and returns from timing and selection.

Solution

a. Dollar-weighted return:

	11/31	12/15	12/31
Cash Flow	−$40,000	−$5,040	+$43,680

15-Day IRR = −1.61%
December Dollar-Weighted Return = $(1.0 - 0.0161)^2 - 1.0 = -3.20\%$

Time-weighted return:

	11/31	Precontribution	Postcontribution	12/31
Shares	1,000	1,000	1,120	1,120
NAV	$ 40	$ 42	$ 42	$ 39
Value	$40,000	$42,000	$47,040	$43,680
Return		5%	−7.14%	

December Time-Weighted Return = $(1.0 + 0.05)(1.0 - 0.0714) - 1.0 = -2.50\%$

b. The dollar-weighted return includes the positive or negative results for the portfolio owner due to timing of contributions and withdrawals, whereas the time-weighted return represents solely the performance of the investment manager. In this case the dollar-weighted return is smaller since Mr. Nielson made a contribution just before ABC declined in value.

c. $(1.1)(1.005)(0.975) - 1.0 = 7.79\%$

d. Benchmark = 2.5% + 1.0(12.0% − 2.5%) = 12.0%
Timing = (1.3 − 1.0)(12.0% − 2.5%) = 2.85%
Selection = 7.79% − [2.5% + 1.3(12.0% − 2.5%)] = −7.06%

Benchmark	+	Timing	+	Selection	=	Actual
12.0%	+	2.85%	+	(−7.06%)	=	7.79%

QUESTIONS AND PROBLEMS

1. In the chapter, three important points were mentioned which any performance-monitoring system should include. What were these?

2. Mr. Curphey has experienced the following annual return on his portfolio during the past four years. You are asked to calculate an estimate of the average yearly return. Do so and justify your answer.

Year	1	2	3	4
Return	20%	−12%	15%	3%

3. Ms. Jane Tear invested $10,000 in a mutual fund two years ago. Since then she has regularly made an additional investment of $1,000 at each quarter-end. Today, just after her eighth and last contribution, her portfolio is worth $25,000. What was her *annualized* rate of return? The mutual fund reported an annualized return for this two-year period of 20%. Why is there a difference?

4. Mr. Morgan's only security investment is in the shares of a mutual fund called Hightech Fund. During the month of June the following transpired:

Date	Transaction	Net Asset Value	Total Shares	Portfolio Value
May 30	Beginning-of-Month Balance	$15.00	1,000	$15,000.00
June 15	Invested an Additional $10,000	$10.00	2,000	$20,000.00
June 30	Dividends Worth $360 Received and Reinvested	$18.00	2,020	$36,360.00

a. Calculate the time-weighted rate of return for June.

b. Will the dollar-weighted rate of return be higher or lower than the time-weighted return in this case? Why?

5. Performance analyses are often made on the basis of investment styles. State what you believe to be the pros and cons of evaluating performance by categorizing investment managers according to their various styles.

6. Mr. Hope has just reviewed a report on the returns of an endowment fund for which he is a trustee. The report compared his endowment portfolio returns with a large number of other endowment funds. Can you suggest what critical analysis may be missing from this report?

7. Ms. A. Davis is an investment performance analyst for a major investment advisory firm. She has before her the following information about the performance of Investech Advisers for the past quarter:

$$
\begin{aligned}
\text{Benchmark Return} &= 8.5\% \\
\text{Timing Return} &= 1.0\% \\
\text{Selection Return} &= -1.5\% \\
\hline
\text{Actual Return} &= 8.0\%
\end{aligned}
$$

Market Return = 8%, Risk-Free Rate = 3%

What were the actual and target betas of Investech Advisers during this quarter?

REFERENCES

Chapter 1
Overview of the Investment Process

BREALEY, R. A. *An Introduction to Risk and Return from Common Stocks.* Cambridge, Mass.: MIT Press, 1983.

MALKIEL, B. *A Random Walk down Wall Street.* New York: W. W. Norton, 1981.

Mutual Fund Values. Chicago: Morningstar, Inc., published biweekly.

Chapter 2
Overview of Security Types

COOK, T., and B. SUMMERS. *Instruments of the Money Market*, 5th ed. Richmond, Va.: Federal Reserve Bank of Richmond, 1981.

GASTINEAU, G. *The Stock Options Manual.* New York: McGraw-Hill, 1975.

GOLD, G. *Modern Commodity Futures Trading.* New York: Commodity Research Bureau, 1968.

GOSS, B. A., and B. S. YAMEY, eds. *The Economics of Futures Trading.* London: Macmillan, 1976.

Handbook of Securities of the United States Government and Federal Agencies. Boston: First Boston Corporation, published biannually.

Investment Companies. New York: Wiesenberger Financial Services, published annually.

STIGUM, M. *The Money Market: Myth, Reality and Practice.* Homewood, Ill.: Dow Jones-Irwin, 1978.

———. *The Money Market*, rev. ed. Homewood, Ill.: Dow Jones-Irwin, 1983.

TEWELES, R., C. HARLOW, and H. STONE. *The Commodity Futures Game.* New York: McGraw-Hill, 1977.

Chapter 3
Overview of the Security Markets

BLACK, F. "Toward a Fully Automated Stock Exchange." *Financial Analysts Journal*, July-August 1971 and November-December 1971.

DANN, L. Y., D. MAYERS, and R. J. RAAB, JR. "Trading Rules, Large Blocks, and the Speed of Price Adjustments." *Journal of Financial Economics*, January 1977.

DEMSETZ, H. "The Cost of Transacting." *Quarterly Journal of Economics*, February 1968.

EDWARDS, F. "Does Futures Trading Increase Stock Market Volatility?" *Financial Analysts Journal*, January-February 1988.

FARRAR, D. E. "Toward a Central Market System: Wall Street's Slow Retreat into the Future." *Journal of Financial and Quantitative Analysis*, November 1974.

GROSSMAN, S. "Program Trading and Market Volatility: A Report on Interday Relationships." *Financial Analysts Journal*, July-August 1988.

HAMILTON, J. L. "Competition, Scale Economies, and Transaction Cost in the Stock Market." *Journal of Financial and Quantitative Analysis*, December 1976.

IBBOTSON, R. "Price Performance of Common Stock New Issues." *Journal of Financial Economics*, September 1975.

KRAUS, A., and H. R. STOLL. "Price Impact of Block Trading on the New York Stock Exchange." *Journal of Finance*, June 1972.

LINDVALL, J. "New Issue Corporate Bonds, Seasoned Market Efficiency and Yield Spreads." *Journal of Finance*, September 1977.

MALKIEL, B. "The Brady Commission Report: A Critique." *Journal of Portfolio Management*, Summer 1988.

MENDELSON, M. *From Automated Quotes to Automated Trading: Restructuring the Stock Market in the U.S.* Bulletin of the Institute of Finance, Graduate School of Business Administration, New York University, March 1972.

ROLL, R. "The International Crash of October 1987." *Financial Analysts Journal*, September-October 1988.

ROSS, S. "Institutional Markets, Financial Marketing, and Financial Innovation." *Journal of Finance*, July 1989.

RUBINSTEIN, M. "Portfolio Insurance and the Market Crash." *Financial Analysts Journal*, January-February 1988.

SCHOLES, M. S. "The Market for Securities: Substitution Versus Price-Pressure and the Effects of Information on Share Prices." *Journal of Business*, April 1972.

SMIDT, S. "Which Road to an Efficient Stock Market: Free Competition or a Regulated Monopoly?" *Financial Analysts Journal*, September-October 1971.

SOBEL, R. *The Big Board.* New York: The Free Press, 1965.

STOLL, H. R. "Dealer Inventory Behavior: An Empirical Investigation of NASDAQ Stocks." *Journal of Financial and Quantitative Analysis*, September 1976.

TOSINI, P. "Stock Index Futures and Stock Market Activity in October 1987." *Financial Analysts Journal*, January-February 1988.

TREYNOR, J. "The Economics of the Dealer Function." *Financial Analysts Journal*, November-December 1987.

WELLES, C. "The Shutdown over Rule 390." *Institutional Investor*, December 1977.

WEST, R. R. "Institutional Trading and the Changing Stock Market." *Financial Analysts Journal*, May-June 1971.

———. "On the Difference Between Internal and External Market Efficiency." *Financial Analysts Journal*, November-December 1975.

Chapter 4
Market Indexes and Returns

CARTER, E. E., and K. J. COHEN. "Bias in the DJIA Caused by Stock Splits." *Financial Analysts Journal*, December 1966.

FISHER, L., and J. LORIE. "Rates of Return on Investments in Common Stock." *Journal of Business*, January 1984, pp. 1-9.

———. "Some Studies of Variability of Returns on Investments in Common Stocks." *Journal of Business*, April 1970, pp. 99-134.

IBBOTSON, R., and R. SINQUEFIELD. *Stocks, Bonds, Bills, and Inflation: The Past and the Future.* Charlottesville, Va.: The Financial Analysts Foundation, 1982.

JONES, C., and J. WILSON. "Stocks, Bonds, Paper, and Inflation: 1870-1985." *Journal of Portfolio Management*, Fall 1987.

LATANÉ, H. A., D. L. TUTTLE, and W. E. YOUNG. "Market Indexes and Their Implications for Portfolio Management." *Financial Analysts Journal*, September-October 1971.

MILNE, P. D. "The Dow Jones Industrial Average Re-Examined." *Financial Analysts Journal*, December 1966.

SCHOOMER, B. A., JR. "The American Stock Exchange Index System." *Financial Analysts Journal*, May–June 1967.

WEST, S., and N. MILLER. "Why the New NYSE Common Stock Indexes?" *Financial Analysts Journal*, May–June 1967.

Chapter 5
The Economic Roles of Security Markets

ARROW, K. "The Role of Securities in the Optimal Allocation of Risk Taking." *Review of Economic Studies*, 1964, pp. 91–96.

DARBY, M. R. "The Financial and Tax Effects of Monetary Policy on Interest Rates." *Economic Inquiry*, June 1975.

DYL, E., and M. JOEHNK. "Competitive Versus Negotiated Underwriting of Public Utility Debt." *Bell Journal of Economics*, Autumn 1976.

FAMA, E. F. "Short-Term Interest Rates as Predictors of Inflation." *American Economic Review*, June 1975.

FELDSTEIN, M., and O. ECKSTEIN. "The Fundamental Determinants of the Interest Rate." *Review of Economics and Statistics*, November 1970.

FISHER, IRVING. "Appreciation and Interest." *Publications of the American Economics Association*, XI, August 1896, pp. 1–100.

———. *The Theory of Interest*. New York: Macmillan, 1930.

FRIEDMAN, M., and A. J. SCHWARTZ. *A Monetary History of the United States, 1867–1960*. New York: National Bureau of Economic Research, 1963.

GIBSON, W. E. "Interest Rates and Inflationary Expectations: New Evidence." *American Economic Review*, December 1972.

———. "Price Expectation Effects on Interest Rates." *Journal of Finance*, March 1970.

HENDERSHOTT, P. H., and J. C. VAN HORNE. "Expected Inflation Implied by Capital Market Rates." *Journal of Finance*, May 1973.

KEYNES, J. M. *A Treatise on Money*. New York: Macmillan, 1930.

LEVI, M. D., and J. H. MAKIN. "Anticipated Inflation and Interest Rates: Further Interpretation of Findings on the Fisher Equation." *American Economic Review*, December 1978.

LINDVALL, J. "New Issue Corporate Bonds, Seasoned Market Efficiency and Yield Spreads." *Journal of Finance*, September 1977.

MUNDELL, R. "Inflation and Real Interest." *Journal of Political Economy*, June 1963.

NELSON, C. R., and G. W. SCHWERT. "On Testing the Hypothesis That the Real Rate of Interest Is Constant." *American Economic Review*, June 1977.

ROSE, A. "Is the Real Interest Rate Stable?" *Journal of Finance*, December 1988.

YOHE, W. P., and D. S. KARNOSKY. "Interest Rates and Price Level Changes, 1952–1968." *Review*, Federal Reserve Bank of St. Louis, December 1969.

Chapter 6
Term Structure

COX, J. C., J. E. INGERSOLL, and S. A. ROSS. "A Reexamination of Traditional Hypotheses About the Term Structure of Interest Rates." *Journal of Finance* 36(1981): 769–99.

CULBERTSON, J. M. "The Term Structure of Interest Rates." *Quarterly Journal of Economics*, November 1957.

DOBSON, S. W., R. C. SUTCH, and D. E. VANDERFORD. "An Evaluation of Alternative Empirical Models of the Term Structure of Interest Rates." *Journal of Finance*, September 1976.

ELLIOT, J. W., and M. E. ECHOLS. "Market Segmentation, Speculative Behavior and the Term Structure of Interest Rates." *Review of Economics and Statistics*, February 1976.

ELLIOT, J. W., and R. B. JEROME. "Econometric Models and Current Interest Rates: How Well Do They Predict Future Rates?" *Journal of Finance*, September 1979, pp. 975–86.

FAMA, E. F. "Forward Rates as Predictors of Future Spot Rates." *Journal of Financial Economics* 3(1976): 361–77.

———. "Inflation Uncertainty and Expected Returns on Treasury Bills." *Journal of Political Economy* 84(1976): 427–48.

———. "The Information in the Term Structure." *Journal of Financial Economics* 13(1984): 509–46.

———. "Term Premiums in Bond Returns." *Journal of Financial Economics* 13(1984): 529–46.

FROOT, K. "New Hope for the Expectations Hypothesis of the Term Structure of Interest Rates." *Journal of Finance*, June 1989.

HICKS, J. R. *Value and Capital*, 2d ed. London: Oxford University Press, 1946.

KESSEL, R. H. *The Cyclical Behavior of the Term Structure of Interest Rates*. New York: National Bureau of Economic Research, 1965.

LEE, W., T. MANESS, and D. TUTTLE. "Nonspeculative Behavior and the Term Structure." *Journal of Financial and Quantitative Analysis*, March 1980.

LUTZ, F. A. "The Structure of Interest Rates." *Quarterly Journal of Economics*, November 1940.

MALKIEL, B. G. "Expectations, Bond Prices, and the Term Structure of Interest Rates." *Quarterly Journal of Economics*, May 1962.

McCULLOCH, J. H. "An Estimate of the Liquidity Premium." *Journal of Political Economy*, January–February 1975.

MEISELMAN, D. *The Term Structure of Interest Rates*. New York: Intext Educational Publishers, 1973.

MODIGLIANI, R., and R. SUTCH. "Debt Management and the Term Structure of Interest Rates: An Empirical Analysis of Recent Experience." *Journal of Political Economy*, Supplement, August 1967.

NELSON, C. R. *The Term Structure of Interest Rates*. New York: Basic Books, 1972.

ROLL, R. *The Behavior of Interest Rates: An Application of the Efficient Market Model to U.S. Treasury Bills*. New York: Basic Books, 1970.

SANTOMERO, A. M. "The Error Learning Hypothesis and the Term Structure of Interest Rates in Eurodollars." *Journal of Finance*, June 1975.

SARGENT, T. J. "Rational Expectations and the Term Structure of Interest Rates." *Journal of Money, Credit, and Banking*, February 1972.

SHOME, D., S. SMITH, and J. PINKERTON. "The Purchasing Power of Money and Nominal Interest Rates: A Re-Examination." *Journal of Finance*, December 1988.

TESLER, L. G. "A Critique of Some Recent Empirical Research on the Explanation of the Term Structure of Interest Rates." *Journal of Political Economy*, Supplement, August 1967.

VANDERHOOF, I. T. "The Interest Rate Assumption and the Maturity Structure of the Assets of a Life Insurance Company." *Transactions of the Society of Actuaries*, May–June 1972.

VAN HORNE, J. "Interest-Rate Expectations, the Shape of the Yield Curve, and Monetary Policy." *Review of Economics and Statistics*, May 1966.

Chapter 7
Risk and Diversification

ARDITTI, F. "Risk and the Required Return on Equity." *Journal of Finance*, March 1967.

BODIE, Z. "Common Stocks as a Hedge Against Inflation." *Journal of Finance*, May 1976.

BRENNAN, M. J. "The Optimal Number of Securities in a Risky Asset Portfolio Where There Are Fixed Costs of Transacting: Theory and Some Empirical Results." *Journal of Financial and Quantitative Analysis*, September 1975.

CHEN, A. H., F. C. JEN, and S. ZIONTS. "The Optimal Portfolio Revision Policy." *Journal of Business*, January 1971.

COHEN, K. J., and G. A. POGUE. "An Empirical Evaluation of Alternative Portfolio Selection Models." *Journal of Business*, April 1967.

COPELAND, T., and J. F. WESTON. *Financial Theory and Corporate Policy*. Reading, Mass.: Addison-Wesley, 1979.

DUSAK, K. "Futures Trading and Investor Returns: An Investigation of Commodity Market Risk Premiums." *Journal of Political Economy*, November–December 1973.

ELTON, E. J., M. J. GRUBER, and M. W. PADBERG. "Simple Criteria for Optimal Portfolio Selection: Tracing Out the Efficient Frontier." *Journal of Finance*, March 1978.

EVANS, J., and S. H. ARCHER. "Diversification and the Reduction of Dispersion: An Empirical Analysis." *Journal of Finance*, December 1968.

FAMA, E. F. "The Behavior of Stock Market Prices." *Journal of Business*, January 1965.

FAMA, E. F., and M. MILLER. *The Theory of Finance*. New York: Holt, Rinehart & Winston, 1972.

FARRAR, D. E. *The Investment Decision Under Uncertainty*. Englewood Cliffs, N.J.: Prentice-Hall, 1962.

FISHER, L., and J. H. LORIE. "Some Studies of the Variability of Returns on Investments in Common Stocks." *Journal of Business*, April 1970.

FOGLER, R., and R. RADCLIFFE. "A Note on the Measurement of Skewness." *Journal of Financial and Quantitative Analysis*, June 1974.

FRIEDMAN, M., and L. SAVAGE. "The Utility Analysis of Choices Involving Risk." *Journal of Political Economy*, August 1948.

JEAN, W. H. "The Extension of Portfolio Analysis to Three or More Parameters." *Journal of Financial and Quantitative Analysis*, January 1974.

KLEMKOSKY, R. C., and J. D. MARTIN. "The Effects of Market Risk on Portfolio Diversification." *Journal of Finance*, March 1975.

KROLL, Y., and H. LEVY. "Stochastic Dominance with a Riskless Asset: An Imperfect Market." *Journal of Financial and Quantitative Analysis*, June 1979.

———. "Stochastic Dominance: A Review and Some New Evidence." *Research in Finance* 2(1980).

LEVY, H., and H. M. MARKOWITZ. "Approximating Expected Utility by a Function of Mean and Variance." *American Economic Review*, June 1979.

MARKOWITZ, H. M. "Portfolio Selection." *Journal of Finance*, March 1952.

———. *Portfolio Selection: Efficient Diversification of Investment*. Cowles Foundation Monograph 16. New Haven: Yale University Press, 1959.

MODIGLIANI, F., and G. POGUE. "An Introduction to Risk and Return: Concepts and Evidence." *Financial Analysts Journal*, March–April and May–June 1974.

PORTER, R. B. "An Empirical Comparison of Stochastic Dominance and Mean-Variance Choice Criteria." *Journal of Financial and Quantitative Analysis* 8: 587–608.

PRATT, J. W. "Risk Aversion in the Small and in the Large." *Econometrica*, January–April 1964.

REILLY, F. K., G. L. JOHNSON, and R. E. SMITH. "Inflation, Inflation Hedges, and Common Stocks." *Financial Analysts Journal*, January–February 1970.

———. "A Correction and Update Regarding Individual Common Stocks as Inflation Hedges." *Journal of Financial and Quantitative Analysis*, December 1975.

RENTZ, W. F., and R. B. WESTIN. "A Note on First-Degree Stochastic Dominance and Portfolio Composition." *Management Science*, December 1975.

RUBINSTEIN, M. E. "A Mean-Variance Synthesis of Corporate Financial Theory." *Journal of Finance*, March 1973.

SHARPE, W. F. "Risk, Market Sensitivity, and Diversification." *Financial Analysts Journal*, January–February 1972.

———. "A Simplified Model for Portfolio Analysis." *Management Science*, January 1963.

SMITH, K. "Stock Prices and Economic Indexes for Generating Efficient Portfolios." *Journal of Business*, July 1969.

TOBIN, J. "Liquidity Preference as Behavior Towards Risk." *Review of Economic Studies*, February 1958.

WAGNER, W., and S. LAU. "The Effect of Diversification on Risk." *Financial Analysts Journal*, November–December 1971.

WINKLER, R. L., and C. B. BARRY. "A Bayesian Model for Portfolio Selection and Revision." *Journal of Finance*, March 1975.

Chapter 8
Capital Asset Pricing Theory

See Chapter 9 references.

Chapter 9
Capital Asset Pricing Extensions

BARRY, C. B. "Effects of Uncertain and Non-Stationary Parameters upon Capital Market Equilibrium Conditions." *Journal of Financial and Quantitative Analysis*, September 1978.

BARRY, C. B., and R. C. RADCLIFFE. "Bayesian Modeling of Alternative Specifications in Portfolio Analysis." *Journal of Economics and Business*, Spring–Summer 1979.

BARRY, C. B., and R. L. WINKLER. "Nonstationarity and Portfolio Choice." *Journal of Financial and Quantitative Analysis*, June 1976.

BLACK, F. "Capital Market Equilibrium with Restricted Borrowing." *Journal of Business*, July 1972.

BLACK, F., M. JENSEN, and M. SCHOLES. "The Capital Asset Pricing Model: Some Empirical Tests." In M. JENSEN, ed., *Studies in the Theory of Capital Markets*. New York: Praeger, 1972.

BLACK, F., and M. SCHOLES. "The Effects of Dividend Yield and Dividend Policy on Common Stock Prices and Returns." *Journal of Financial Economics*, May 1974.

BLUME, M. E. "Betas and Their Regression Tendencies: Some Further Evidence." *Journal of Finance*, March 1979.

BLUME, M. E., and I. FRIEND. "The Asset Structure of Individual Portfolios and Some Implications for Utility Functions." *Journal of Finance*, May 1975.

BREEDEN, D. T. "An Intertemporal Asset Pricing Model with Stochastic Consumption and Investment Opportunities." *Journal of Financial Economics*, June 1979.

BREEDEN, D., M. GIBBONS, and R. LITZENBERGER. "Empirical Tests of the Consumption-Oriented CAPM." *Journal of Finance*, June 1989.

BRENNAN, M. J. "Capital Market Equilibrium with Divergent Borrowing and Lending Rates." *Journal of Financial and Quantitative Analysis*, December 1971.

_____. "Taxes, Market Valuation, and Corporation Financial Policy." *National Tax Journal*, December 1970.

BROWN, S.J., and M. I. WEINSTEIN. "A New Approach to Testing Asset Pricing Models: The Bilinear Paradigm." *Journal of Finance*, June 1983.

CHAN, K., and N. CHEN. "An Unconditional Asset Pricing Test and the Role of Firm Size as an Instrumental Variable for Risk." *Journal of Finance*, June 1988.

CHEN, N. F. "Measuring Security Price Performance." *Journal of Finance*, December 1983.

CHEN, N. F., and J. WARNER. "Measuring Security Price Performance." *Journal of Financial Economics*, 1980.

CHEN, N. F., R. ROLL, and S. ROSS. "Economic Forces and the Stock Market." Unpublished manuscript, Yale University, New Haven, Conn., 1983.

CHO, D. C., E. J. ELTON, and M. I. GRUBER. "On the Robustness of the Roll and Ross APT Methodology." *Journal of Financial and Quantitative Analysis*, March 1984.

DHRYMES, P., I. FRIEND, and N. GULTEKIN. "A Critical Reexamination of the Empirical Evidence on the Arbitrage Pricing Theory." *Journal of Finance*, June 1984.

_____. "New Tests of the APT and Their Implications." *Journal of Finance*, July 1985.

DOUGLAS, G. "Risk in the Equity Markets: An Empirical Appraisal of Market Efficiency." *Yale Economic Essays*, no. 9, 1969.

DYBVIG, P. H. "An Explicit Bound on Individual Assets Deviations from APT Pricing in a Finite Economy." *Journal of Financial Economics*, December 1983.

DYBVIG, P. H., and S. ROSS. "Yes, the APT Is Testable." *Journal of Finance*, September 1985.

FAMA, E. F. "Multi-Period Consumption-Investment Decision." *American Review*, March 1970.

_____. "Portfolio Analysis in a Stable Paretian Analysis." *Management Science*, January 1965.

_____. "Tests on the Multiperiod Two-Parameter Model." *Journal of Financial Economics*, May 1974.

FAMA, E. F., and J. MACBETH. "Risk, Return and Equilibrium: Empirical Tests." *Journal of Political Economy*, May–June 1973.

FAMA, E. F., and G. SCHWERT. "Human Capital and Capital Market Equilibrium." *Journal of Financial Economics*, January 1977.

FERSON, W., S. KANDEL, and R. STAMBAUGH. "Tests of Asset Pricing with Time-Varying Expected Risk Premiums and Market Betas." *Journal of Finance*, June 1987.

FRENCH, K., W. SCHWERT, and R. STAMBAUGH. "Expected Stock Returns and Volatility." *Journal of Financial Economics* 19(1987).

FRIEND, I., and M. BLUME. "Measurement of Portfolio Performance Under Uncertainty." *American Economic Review*, September 1970.

GRINBLATT, M., and S. TITMAN. "Factor Pricing in a Finite Economy." *Journal of Financial Economics*, December 1983.

GULTEKIN, M., and B. GULTEKIN. "Stock Return Anomalies and the Tests of the APT." *Journal of Finance*, December 1987.

HAKANSSON, N. "Capital Growth and the Mean-Variance Approach to

Portfolio Selection." *Journal of Financial and Quantitative Analysis*, January 1971.

HUBERMAN, G. "A Simple Approach to Arbitrage Pricing Theory." *Journal of Economic Theory*, October 1982.

INGERSOLL, J. "Some Results in the Theory of Arbitrage Pricing." Working paper, University of Chicago, 1982.

JEAN, N. "The Extension of Portfolio Analysis to Three or More Parameters." *Journal of Financial and Quantitative Analysis*, January 1971.

JENSEN, M. C. "The Performance of Mutual Funds in the Period 1945–1964." *Journal of Finance*, May 1968.

_____. *Studies in the Theory of Capital Markets.* New York: Praeger, 1972.

JOBSON, J. D. "A Multivariate Linear Regression Test for the Arbitrage Pricing Theory." *Journal of Finance*, September 1982.

KAZEMI, H. "An Alternative Testable Form of Consumption CAPM." *Journal of Finance*, March 1988.

KRYZANOWSKI, L., and T. CHAU. "General Factor Models and the Structure of Security Returns." *Journal of Financial and Quantitative Analysis*, March 1983.

LATANÉ, H. "Criteria for Choice Among Risky Ventures." *Journal of Political Economy*, April 1959.

_____. "The Aggregation of Investors' Diverse Judgment and Preferences in Purely Competitive Securities Markets." *Journal of Financial and Quantitative Analysis*, December 1969.

_____. "Security Prices, Risk, and Maximal Gains from Diversification." *Journal of Finance*, December 1965.

LEVY, H. "The Capital Asset Pricing Model: Theory and Empiricism." *The Economic Journal*, March 1983.

_____. "Stochastic Dominance Efficiency Criteria and Efficient Portfolios: The Multi-Period Case." *American Economic Review* 63: 986–94.

_____. "Multi-Period Consumption Decisions Under Conditions of Uncertainty." *Management Science* 22: 1258–67.

LITZENBERGER, R., and K. RAMASWAMY. "The Effect of Personal Taxes and Dividends on Capital Asset Prices." *Journal of Financial Economics*, June 1979.

LONG, J., JR. "Efficient Portfolio Choice with Differential Taxation of Dividends and Capital Gains." *Journal of Financial Economics*, August 1977.

MARKOWITZ, H. *Portfolio Selection: Efficient Diversification of Investment.* Cowles Foundation Monograph 16. New Haven: Yale University Press, 1959.

MAYERS, D. "Nonmarketable Assets and the Determination of Capital Asset Prices in the Absence of a Riskless Asset." *Journal of Business*, April 1973.

MAYERS, D., and E. RICE. "Measuring Portfolio Performance and the Empirical Content of Asset Pricing Models." *Journal of Financial Economics*, March 1979.

MERTON, R. "A Simple Model of Capital Market Equilibrium with Incomplete Information." *Journal of Finance*, July 1987.

_____. "An Intertemporal Capital Asset Pricing Model." *Econometrica*, September 1973.

_____. "Optimum Consumption and Portfolio Rules in a Continuous Time Model." *Journal of Economic Theory*, 1971.

MILLER, M. H., and M. S. SCHOLES. "Dividends and Taxes." *Journal of Financial Economics*, December 1985.

_____. "Rates of Return in Relation to Risk: A Reexamination of Some Recent Findings." In M. JENSEN, ed., *Studies in the Theory of Capital Markets.* New York: Praeger, 1972.

MODIGLIANI, F., and G. POGUE. "An Introduction to Risk and Return:

Concepts and Evidence." *Financial Analysts Journal*, March–April and May–June 1974.

MOSSIN, J. "Equilibrium in a Capital Asset Market." *Econometrica*, October 1966.

_____. "Security Pricing and Investment Criteria in Competitive Markets." *American Economic Review*, December 1969.

REINGANUM, M. R. "The Arbitrage Pricing Theory: Some Empirical Results." *Journal of Finance*, May 1981.

ROLL, R. "Ambiguity When Performance Is Measured by the Securities Market Line." *Journal of Finance*, September 1978.

_____. "A Critique of the Asset Pricing Theory's Test." *Journal of Financial Economics*, March 1977.

_____. "Evidence on the 'Growth Optimum' Model." *Journal of Finance*, June 1979.

ROLL, R., and S. A. ROSS. "An Empirical Investigation of the Arbitrage Pricing Theory." *Journal of Finance*, December 1980.

_____. "A Critical Reexamination of the Empirical Evidence on the Arbitrage Pricing Theory: A Reply." *Journal of Finance*, June 1984.

ROSS, S. A. "The Arbitrage Theory of Capital Asset Pricing." *Journal of Economic Theory*, December 1976.

_____. "The Current Status of the Capital Asset Pricing Model (CAPM)." *Journal of Finance*, June 1978.

_____. "Return, Risk, and Arbitrage." In I. FRIEND and J. L. BICKSLER, eds., *Risk and Return in Finance*. Cambridge, Mass.: Ballinger, 1977.

ROY, A. "Safety First and the Holding of Assets." *Econometrica*, July 1952.

SHANKEN, J. "The Arbitrage Pricing Theory: Is It Testable?" *Journal of Finance*, December 1982.

SHARPE, W. F. "Capital Asset Prices: A Theory of Market Equilibrium Under Conditions of Risk." *Journal of Finance*, September 1964.

_____. "Mutual Fund Performance." *Journal of Business*, Supplement on Security Prices, January 1966.

_____. "Portfolio Analysis." *Journal of Financial and Quantitative Analysis*, June 1967.

TOBIN, J. "Liquidity Preference as Behavior Towards Risk." *Review of Economic Studies*, February 1958.

TREYNOR, J. L. "How to Rate Management of Investment Funds." *Harvard Business Review*, January–February 1965.

Chapter 10
An Efficient Market

ABDEL-KHALIK, A. R., and J. McKEOWN. "Understanding Accounting Changes in an Efficient Market: Evidence of Differential Reaction." *Accounting Review*, October 1978.

ALEXANDER, S. "Price Movements in Speculative Markets: Trends or Random Walks." *Industrial Management Review*, May 1961.

ALLVINE, F. C., and D. E. O'NEILL. "Stock Market Returns and the Presidential Election Cycle: Implications for Market Efficiency." *Financial Analysts Journal*, September–October 1980.

BACHELIER, L. "Theory Speculation." *Ann. Sci. Ecole Norm.* Suppl. 3, no. 1081 (Paris: Gauther-Villars, 1900). Reprinted in P. COOTNER, *The Random Character of Stock Market Prices*. Cambridge, Mass.: MIT Press, 1964.

BAESEL, J., and G. R. STEIN. "The Value of Information Inferences from the Profitability of Insider Tradings." *Journal of Financial and Quantitative Analysis*, September 1979.

BANZ, R. W. "The Relationship Between Return and Market Value of Common Stocks." *Journal of Financial Economics*, March 1981.

BARON, D. P. "Information, Investment Behavior, and Efficient Portfolios." *Journal of Financial and Quantitative Analysis*, September 1974.

BASU, S. "The Investment Performance of Common Stocks in Relation to Their Price-Earnings Ratios." *Journal of Financial Economics*, June 1983.

_____. "Investment Performance of Common Stocks in Relation to Their Price-Earnings Ratios: A Test of the Efficient Market Hypothesis." *Journal of Finance*, June 1977.

BJERRING, J. H., J. LAKONISHOK, and T. VERMAELON. "Stock Prices and Financial Analysts' Recommendations." *Journal of Finance* 38 (March 1983).

BLACK, F. "Random Walk and Portfolio Management." *Financial Analysts Journal*, March–April 1971.

_____. "Yes, Virginia, There Is Hope: Tests of the Value Line Ranking System." Paper presented at a seminar of the Center for Research in Security Prices, Graduate School of Business, University of Chicago, May 1971.

BRANCH, B. "A Tax Loss Trading Rule." *Journal of Business*, April 1977.

BRENNER, M. "The Effect of Model Misspecification on Tests of the Efficient Market Hypothesis." *Journal of Finance*, March 1977.

BROWN, D. "The Implications of Nonmarketable Income for Consumption-Based Models of Asset Pricing." *Journal of Finance*, September 1988.

BROWN, P., and R. BALL. "An Empirical Evaluation of Accounting Income Numbers." *Journal of Accounting Research*, Autumn 1968.

BROWN, P., and J. KENNELLY. "The Informational Content of Quarterly Earnings: An Extension and Some Further Evidence." *Journal of Business*, July 1972.

BROWN, P., A. W. KLEIDON, and T. A. MARSH. "New Evidence of the Nature of Size-Related Anomalies in Stock Prices." *Journal of Financial Economics*, June 1983.

BROWN, S. "Earnings Changes, Stock Prices, and Market Efficiency." *Journal of Finance*, March 1978.

CAMPBELL, J., and R. SHILLER. "The Dividend-Price Ratio and Expectations of Future Dividends and Discount Factors." *The Review of Financial Studies*, Fall 1988.

CHANG, E., and M. PINEGAR. "Does the Market Reward Risk in Non-January Months?" *Journal of Portfolio Management*, Fall 1988.

CHIRAS, D., and S. MANASTER. "The Information Content of Option Prices and a Test of Market Efficiency." *Journal of Financial Economics*, June–September 1978.

COOPER, R. "Efficient Capital Markets and the Quantity Theory of Money." *Journal of Finance*, June 1974.

COOTNER, P. H. *The Random Character of Stock Market Prices*. Cambridge, Mass.: MIT Press, 1964.

COPELAND, T. E., and D. MAYERS. "The Value Line Enigma (1965–1978): A Case Study of Performance Evaluation Issues." *Journal of Financial Economics*, November 1982.

CORHAY, A., G. HAWAWINI, and P. MICHEL. "Seasonality in the Risk-Return Relationship: Some International Evidence." *Journal of Finance*, March 1987.

DANN, L. Y., D. MAYERS, and R. J. RAAB. "Trading Rules, Large Blocks, and the Speed of Price Adjustment." *Journal of Financial Economics*, January 1977.

DAVIES, P., and M. CANES. "Stock Prices and the Publication of Second-Hand Information." *Journal of Business*, January 1978.

DeBONDT, W., and R. THALER. "Does the Stock Market Overreact?" *Journal of Finance*, July 1985.

_____. "Further Evidence on Investor Overreaction and Stock Market Seasonality." *Journal of Finance*, July 1987.

DeLong, B., A. Shleifer, L. Summers, and R. Waldmann. "The Size and Incidence of the Losses from Noise Trading." *Journal of Finance*, July 1989.

Diefenbach, R. "How Good Is Institutional Research?" *Financial Analysts Journal*, January–February 1972.

Fama, E. F. "The Behavior of Stock Market Prices." *Journal of Business*, January 1965.

_____. "Efficient Capital Markets: A Review of Theory and Empirical Work." *Journal of Finance*, May 1970.

Fama, E., and M. Blume. "Filter Rules and Stock Market Trading." *Journal of Business*, January 1966.

Fama, E., and K. French. "Permanent and Temporary Components of Stock Prices." *Journal of Political Economy* 96(April 1988).

_____. "Dividend Yields and Expected Stock Returns." *Journal of Financial Economics* 22(October 1988).

Fama, E., L. Fisher, M. Jensen, and R. Roll. "The Adjustment of Stock Prices to New Information." *International Economic Review*, February 1969.

Finnerty, J. E. "Insiders' Activity and Inside Information." *Journal of Financial and Quantitative Analysis*, June 1976.

Flavin, M. "Excess Volatility in the Financial Markets: A Reassessment of the Empirical Evidence." *Journal of Political Economy* 91, no. 6.

Foster, G. "Stock Market Reaction to Estimates of Earnings per Share by Company Officials." *Journal of Accounting Research*, Spring 1973.

French, K. R. "Stock Returns and the Weekend Effect." *Journal of Financial Economics*, March 1980.

French, K., W. Schwert, and R. Stambaugh. "Expected Stock Returns and Volatility." *Journal of Financial Economics* 19(1987).

Gibbons, M. R., and P. Hess. "Day of the Week Effects and Asset Returns." *Journal of Business*, October 1981.

Grossman, S. J. "On the Efficiency of Competitive Stock Markets Where Traders Have Diverse Information." *Journal of Finance*, May 1976.

Grossman, S., and R. Shiller. "The Determinants of the Variability of Stock Market Prices." *AEA Papers and Proceedings*, May 1989.

Grossman, S., and J. Stiglitz. "On the Impossibility of Informationally Efficient Markets." *American Economic Review*, June 1980.

Groth, J., W. Lewellen, G. Schlarbaum, and R. Lease. "Security Analysts: Some Are More Equal." *Journal of Portfolio Management*, Spring 1978.

Gultekin, M. N., and B. N. Gultekin. "Stock Market Seasonality: International Evidence." *Journal of Financial Economics*, December 1983.

Ibbotson, R. "Price Performance of Common Stock New Issues." *Journal of Financial Economics*, September 1975.

Jaffe, J. "Special Information and Insider Trading." *Journal of Business*, July 1974.

Jaffe, J., and R. Westerfield. "The Weekend Effect in Common Stock Returns: The International Evidence." *Journal of Finance* 40 (June 1985).

Jensen, M. C. "The Performance of Mutual Funds in the Period 1945–64." *Journal of Finance*, May 1968.

Jensen, M. C., and G. Bennington. "Random Walks and Technical Theories: Some Additional Evidence." *Journal of Finance*, May 1970.

Joy, M., R. Litzenberger, and R. McEnally. "The Adjustment of Stock Prices to Announcements of Unanticipated Changes in Quarterly Earnings." *Journal of Accounting Research*, Autumn 1977.

Kaplan, R., and R. Roll. "Investor Evaluation of Accounting Information: Some Empirical Evidence." *Journal of Business*, April 1972.

Katz, S. "The Price Adjustment Process of Bonds to Rating Reclassifications: A Test of Bond Market Efficiency." *Journal of Finance*, May 1974.

Keim, D. "Dividend Yields and Stock Returns." *Journal of Financial Economics*, no. 14, pp. 473–89.

_____. "Size-Related Anomalies and Stock Return Seasonality: Further Empirical Evidence." *Journal of Financial Economics*, June 1983.

Keim, D., and R. Stambaugh. "Predicting Returns in the Stock and Bond Markets." *Journal of Financial Economics*, no. 17, pp. 357–90.

Kendall, M. "The Analysis of Economic Time Series, Part I." *Journal of the Royal Statistical Society* 96 (1953).

Kon, S. J., and F. C. Jen. "Investment Performance of Mutual Funds: An Empirical Investigation of Timing, Selectivity, and Market Efficiency." *Journal of Business*, April 1979.

Kraus, A., and M. Smith. "Market-Created Risk." *Journal of Finance*, July 1989.

Kraus, A., and H. Stoll. "Price Impacts of Block Trading on the New York Stock Exchange." *Journal of Finance*, June 1972.

Lakonishok, J., and S. Smidt. "Are Seasonal Anomalies Real? A Ninety-Year Perspective." *The Review of Financial Studies*, Winter 1988.

Levy, R. "Relative Strength as a Criterion for Investment Selection." *Journal of Finance*, December 1967.

Lo, A., and A. C. MacKinlay. "Stock Market Prices Do Not Follow Random Walks: Evidence from a Simple Specification Test." *The Review of Financial Studies*, Spring 1988.

Logue, D., and D. Tuttle. "Brokerage House Investment Advice." *Financial Review*, 1974.

Lorie, J., and V. Niederhoffer. "Predictive and Statistical Properties of Insider Trading." *Journal of Law and Economics*, April 1978.

Mankiw, G., D. Romer, and M. Shapiro. "An Unbiased Reexamination of Stock Market Volatility." *Journal of Finance*, July 1985.

McConnell, J., and G. Sanger. "The Puzzle in Post-Listing Common Stock Return." *Journal of Finance*, March 1987.

Pettit, R. "Dividend Announcements, Security Performance, and Capital Market Efficiency." *Journal of Finance*, December 1972.

Reinganum, M. R. "Misspecification of Capital Asset Pricing: Empirical Anomalies Based on Earnings Yields and Market Values." *Journal of Financial Economics*, March 1981.

Rendleman, R. J., and C. E. Carabini. "Efficiency of the Treasury Bill Futures Market." *Journal of Finance*, September 1979.

Rendleman, R. J., C. P. Jones, and H. A. Latané. "Empirical Anomalies Based on Unexpected Earnings and the Importance of Risk Adjustments." *Journal of Financial Economics*, November 1982.

Ritter, J. "The Buying and Selling Behavior of Individual Investors at the Turn of the Year." *Journal of Finance*, July 1988.

Ritter, J., and N. Chopra. "Portfolio Rebalancing and the Turn-of-the-Year Effect." *Journal of Finance*, March 1989.

Roberts, H. V. "Stock Market 'Patterns' and Financial Analysis: Some Methodological Suggestions." *Journal of Finance*, March 1959, pp. 1–10.

Rogalski, R., and J. Vinso. "Stock Returns, Money Supply, and the Direction of Causality." *Journal of Finance*, September 1977.

Roll, R. "A Critique of the Asset Pricing Theory's Tests." *Journal of Financial Economics*, March 1977.

_____. "R-Squared." *Journal of Finance*, July 1988.

ROZEFF, J. S., and W. R. KINNER. "Capital Market Seasonality: The Case of Stock Returns." *Journal of Financial Economics*, November 1976.

ROZEFF, M. "Money and Stock Prices: Market Efficiency and the Lag Effect of Monetary Policy." *Journal of Financial Economics*, September 1974.

SAMUELSON, P. A. "Proof That Properly Anticipated Prices Fluctuate Randomly." *Industrial Management Review*, Spring 1965.

SCHOLES, M. "The Market for Securities: Substitution Versus Price Pressure and the Effects of Information on Share Prices." *Journal of Business*, April 1972.

SCHWERT, G. W. "Adjustment of Stock Prices to Information About Inflation." *Journal of Finance*, March 1981.

————. "Size and Stock Returns, and Other Empirical Regularities." *Journal of Financial Economics*, June 1983.

SEELENFREUND, A., G. PARKER, and J. VAN HORNE. "Stock Price Behavior and Trading." *Journal of Financial and Quantitative Analysis*, September 1968.

SHILLER, R. "Comovements in Stock Prices and Comovements in Dividends." *Journal of Finance*, July 1989.

————. "The Volatility of Long-Term Interest Rates and Expectations Models of the Term Structure." *Journal of Political Economy* 87, no. 6.

STOLL, H. R., and R. E. WHALEY. "Transactions Costs and the Small Firm Effect." *Journal of Financial Economics*, June 1983.

SUNDER, S. "Stock Price and Risk Related to Accounting Changes in Inventory Valuation." *Accounting Review*, April 1975.

TREYNOR, J. "Market Efficiency and the Bean Jar Experiment." *Financial Analysts Journal*, May–June 1987.

VERRECCHIA, R. E. "Consensus Beliefs, Information Acquisition, and Market Information Efficiency." *American Economic Review*, December 1980.

WATTS, R. "The Information Content of Dividends." *Journal of Business*, April 1973.

Chapter 11
Bond Fundamentals

AHEARN, D. S. "The Strategic Role of Fixed Income Securities." *Journal of Portfolio Management*, Spring 1975.

ATKINSON, T. R. *Trends in Corporate Bond Quality*. New York: National Bureau of Economic Research, 1967.

BOARDMAN, C. M., and R. W. McENALLY. "Factors Affecting Seasoned Corporate Bond Prices." *Journal of Financial and Quantitative Analysis* 16, no. 2(1981): 207–26.

BOQUIST, J. A., G. RACETTE, and G. SCHLARBAUM. "Duration and Risk Assessment for Bonds and Common Stock." *Journal of Finance*, December 1975.

BULLINGTON, R. A. "How Corporate Debt Issues Are Rated." *Financial Executive*, September 1974.

COHAN, A. B. *The Risk Structure of Interest Rates*. Morristown, N. J.

DUNETZ, M., and J. MAHONEY. "Using Duration and Convexity in the Analysis of Callable Bonds." *Financial Analysts Journal*, May–June 1988.

EDERINGTON, L. H. "The Yield Spread of New Issues of Corporate Bonds." *Journal of Finance*, December 1974.

FAIR, R. C., and B. G. MALKIEL. "The Determination of Yield Differentials Between Debt Instruments of the Same Maturity." *Journal of Money, Credit and Banking*, November 1971.

FISHER, L. "Determinants of Risk Premiums on Corporate Bonds." *Journal of Political Economy*, June 1959.

FISHER, L., and R. L. WEIL. "Coping with the Risk of Interest-Rate Fluctuations: Returns to Bondholders from Naive and Optimal Strategies." *Journal of Business*, October 1971.

FONS, J. "The Default Premium and Corporate Bond Experience." *Journal of Finance*, March 1987.

FRAINE, H. G., and R. MILLS. "Effects of Defaults and Credit Deterioration on Yields of Corporate Bonds." *Journal of Finance*, September 1961.

GRIER, P., and S. KATZ. "The Differential Effects of Bond Rating Changes Among Industrial and Public Utility Bonds by Maturity." *Journal of Business*, April 1976.

HEMPEL, G. H. *The Postwar Quality of State and Local Debt*. New York: National Bureau of Economic Research, 1971.

HICKMAN, W. B. *Corporate Bond Quality and Investor Experience*. New York: National Bureau of Economic Research, 1958.

HOMER, S. "The Historical Evolution of Today's Bond Market." *Journal of Portfolio Management*, Spring 1975.

HOMER, S., and M. L. LEIBOWITZ. *Inside the Yield Book*. Englewood Cliffs, N.J.: Prentice-Hall, 1972.

HOPEWELL, M. H., and G. G. KAUFMAN. "Bond Price Volatility and Term to Maturity: A Generalized Specification." *American Economic Review*, September 1973.

IBBOTSON, R., and R. SINQUEFIELD. "Stocks, Bonds, Bills, and Inflation: Update." *Financial Analysts Journal*, July–August 1979.

JAFFEE, D. M. "Cyclical Variations in the Risk Structure of Interest Rates." *Journal of Monetary Economics*, July 1975.

JARROW, R. A. "The Relationship Between Yield, Risk, and Return of Corporate Bonds." *Journal of Finance*, September 1978.

JEN, F., and J. WERT. "The Effect of Sinking Fund Provisions on Corporate Bond Yields." *Financial Analysts Journal*, March–April 1967.

————. "The Effect of Call Risk on Corporate Bond Yields." *Journal of Finance*, December 1967.

JOHNSON, R. E. "Term Structures of Corporate Bond Yields as a Function of Risk of Default." *Journal of Finance*, May 1967.

LIVINGSTON, M. "Bond Taxation and the Shape of the Yield-to-Maturity Curve." *Journal of Finance*, March 1979.

————. "Duration and Risk Assessment for Bonds and Common Stock: A Note." *Journal of Finance*, March 1978.

————. "The Pricing of Premium Bonds." *Journal of Financial and Quantitative Analysis*, September 1979.

MACAULAY, F. R. *The Movement of Interest Rates, Bond Yields, and Stock Prices in the United States Since 1856*. New York: National Bureau of Economic Research, 1938.

McINISH, T. H. "Behavior of Municipal Bond Default-Risk Premiums by Maturity." *Journal of Business Research* 8(1980): 413-18

MERTON, R. C. "On the Pricing of Corporate Debt: The Risk Structure of Interest Rates." *Journal of Finance*, May 1974.

PINCHES, G. E., and K. A. MINGO. "A Multivariate Analysis of Industrial Bond Ratings." *Journal of Finance*, March 1973.

POGUE, F., and R. M. SOLDOFSKY. "What's in a Bond Rating?" *Journal of Financial and Quantitative Analysis*, June 1969.

PYE, G. "Gauging the Default Premium." *Financial Analysts Journal*, January–February 1974.

SHARPE, W. F. "Bonds vs. Stocks: Some Lessons from Capital Market Theory." *Financial Analysts Journal*, November–December 1973.

SILVERS, J. B. "An Alternative to the Yield Spread as a Measure of Risk." *Journal of Finance*, September 1973.

VAN HORNE, J. C. "Behavior of Default-Risk Premiums for Corporate Bonds and Commercial Paper." *Journal of Business Research* 7(December 1979): 310-13.

_____. *Financial Market Rates and Flows*. Englewood Cliffs, N.J.: Prentice-Hall, 1978.

WEIL, R. L. "Macaulay's Duration: An Appreciation." *Journal of Business*, October 1973.

WEINSTEIN, M. "The Effect of a Rating Change Announcement on Bond Prices." *Journal of Financial Economics*, December 1977.

WEST, R. R. "Bond Ratings, Bond Yields, and Financial Regulations: Some Findings." *Journal of Law and Economics*, April 1973.

Chapter 12
Bond Trading

BIERWAG, G., and G. KAUFMAN. "Coping with the Risk of Interest Rate Fluctuations: A Note." *Journal of Business*, July 1977.

COX, J., J. INGERSOLL, and S. ROSS. "Duration and the Measurement of Basis Risk." *Journal of Business*, January 1979.

IBBOTSON, R., and R. SINQUEFIELD. "Stocks, Bonds, Bills, and Inflation: Update." *Financial Analysts Journal*, July–August 1979.

LEIBOWITZ, M. "Horizon Analysis: A New Analytic Framework for Management of Bond Portfolios." *Journal of Portfolio Management*, Spring 1975.

_____. *A New Approach to Yield Curve Analysis*. New York: Salomon Brothers, 1977.

LIVINGSTON, M. "Duration and Risk Assessment for Bonds and Common Stocks: A Note." *Journal of Finance*, March 1978.

MACAULEY, F. *Some Theoretical Problems Suggested by the Movement of Interest Rates, Bond Yields and Stock Prices in the United States Since 1856*. National Bureau of Economic Research. New York: Columbia, 1938.

McENALLY, R. "Duration as a Practical Tool in Bond Management." *Journal of Portfolio Management*, Summer 1977.

McENALLY, R., and C. BOARDMAN. "Aspects of Corporate Bond Portfolio Diversification." *Journal of Financial Research*, Spring 1979.

REILLY, F., and R. SIDHU. "The Many Uses of Bond Duration." *Financial Analysts Journal*, July–August 1980.

TRAINER, F., J. YAWITZ, and W. MARSHALL. "Holding Period Is the Key to Risk Threshold." *Journal of Portfolio Management*, Winter 1979.

Chapter 13
Stock Fundamentals

BALL, R., and P. BROWN. "An Empirical Evaluation of Accounting Income Numbers." *Journal of Accounting Research*, Autumn 1968.

BENORE, C. *A Survey of Investor Attitudes Toward the Electric Power Industry*. Paine Webber Mitchell Hutchins, September 1979.

BERNSTEIN, P. L. "Growth Companies vs. Growth Stocks." *Harvard Business Review*, September-October 1956.

BLACK, F., and M. SCHOLES. "The Effects of Dividend Yields and Dividend Policy on Common Stock Prices and Returns." *Journal of Financial Economics*, May 1974.

BOWER, R., and D. BOWER. "Risk and Valuation of Common Stock." *Journal of Finance*, September 1957.

BREALEY, R. *An Introduction to Risk and Return from Common Stocks*. Cambridge, Mass.: MIT Press, 1969.

BRIGHAM, E., D. SHOME, and S. VINSON. "The Risk Premium Approach to Measuring a Utility's Cost of Equity." *Financial Management Journal*, Spring 1985.

CRAGG, J., and B. MALKIEL. "The Consensus and Accuracy of Some Predictions of the Growth of Corporate Earnings." *Journal of Finance*, March 1968.

DURAND, D. "Growth Stocks and the Petersburg Paradox." *Journal of Finance*, September 1957.

FAMA, E. "The Empirical Relationship Between the Dividend and Investment Decisions of Firms." *American Economic Review*, June 1974.

FARRELL, J. "Homogeneous Stock Groupings: Implications for Portfolio Management." *Financial Analysts Journal*, May–June 1975.

FISHER, L., and J. H. LORIE. "Rates of Return on Investments in Common Stock: The Year-by-Year Record, 1927–1965." *Journal of Business*, July 1968.

_____. "Some Studies of the Variability of Returns on Investments in Common Stocks." *Journal of Business*, April 1970.

FRIEND, I., and M. PUCKETT. "Dividends and Stock Prices." *American Economic Review*, September 1954.

GORDON, M. *The Investment, Financing, and Valuation of the Corporation*. Homewood, Ill.: Irwin, 1962.

HAMADA, R. "The Effects of the Firm's Capital Structure on the Systematic Risk of Common Stock." *Journal of Finance*, May 1972.

HOLT, C. "The Influence of Growth Duration on Share Prices." *Journal of Finance*, September 1962.

IBBOTSON, R., and R. SINQUEFIELD. "Stocks, Bonds, Bills, and Inflation: Update." *Financial Analysts Journal*, July–August 1979.

KING, B. "Market and Industry Factors in Stock Price Behavior." *Journal of Business*, January 1966.

MALKIEL, B. G. "The Capital Formation Problem in the United States." *Journal of Finance*, May 1979.

_____. "Equity Yields, Growth, and the Structure of Share Prices." *American Economic Review*, December 1963.

_____. "Expectations, Bond Prices, and the Term Structure of Interest." *Quarterly Journal of Economics*, May 1962.

MAO, J. "The Valuation of Growth Stocks: The Investments Opportunity Approach." *Journal of Finance*, March 1966.

MILLER, M., and F. MODIGLIANI. "Dividend Policy, Growth, and the Valuation of Shares." *Journal of Business*, October 1966.

OFFICER, R. "The Variability of the Market Factor of the New York Stock Exchange." *Journal of Business*, July 1973.

WENDT, P. "Current Growth Stock Valuation Methods." *Financial Analysts Journal*, March–April 1965.

WESTON, F. "A Test of Cost of Capital Propositions." *Southern Economic Journal*, October 1963.

YOHE, W. P., and D. S. KARNOSKY. "Interest Rates and Price Level Changes, 1952–1968." *Review*, Federal Reserve Bank of St. Louis, December 1969.

Chapter 14
Stock Trading

BEAVER, W., and D. MORSE. "What Determines Price Earnings Ratios?" *Financial Analysts Journal*, July–August 1978.

BLACK, F., and M. SCHOLES. "The Effects of Dividend Yield and Dividend Policy on Common Stock Prices and Returns." *Journal of Financial Economics*, May 1974.

BOQUIST, J. A., G. RACETTE, and G. SCHLARBAUM. "Duration and Risk Assessment for Bonds and Common Stocks." *Journal of Finance*, December 1975.

FRUHEN, W. "Lessons from Levitz: Creating Share Values." *Financial Analysts Journal*, April–May 1980.

GROTH, J., W. LEWELLEN, G. SCHLARBAUM, and R. LEASE. "Security Analysts: Some Are More Equal." *Journal of Portfolio Management*, Spring 1978.

HAUGEN, R. "Do Common Stock Quality Ratings Predict Risk?" *Financial Analysts Journal*, March–April 1979.

LARGAY, J., and C. STICKNEY. "Cash Flows, Ratio Analysis, and the W. T. Grant Company Bankruptcy." *Financial Analysts Journal*, July–August 1980.

LITZENBERGER, R., and K. RAMASWAMY. "The Effect of Personal Taxes and Dividends on Capital Asset Prices: Theory and Empirical Evidence." *Journal of Financial Economics*, March 1979.

MODIGLIANI, M., and R. COHN. "Inflation, Rational Valuation, and the Market." *Financial Analysts Journal*, March–April 1979.

OSBORNE, M. "Periodic Structure in the Brownian Motion of Stock Prices." *Operations Research*, May–June 1962.

PORTER, M. "Industry Structure and Competitive Strategy: Keys to Profitability." *Financial Analysts Journal*, July–August 1980.

WRIGHT, F. "Monetary Policy and the Stock Market." *Financial Analysts Journal*, May–June 1976.

Chapters 15 and 16
Option Fundamentals and Option Trading

ARDITTI, F., and K. JOHN. "Spanning the State Space with Options." *Journal of Financial and Quantitative Analysis*, March 1980.

BAUMOL, W., B. MALKIEL, and R. QUANDT. "The Valuation of Convertible Securities." *Quarterly Journal of Economics*, February 1966.

BHATTACHARYA, M. "Empirical Properties of the Black-Scholes Formula Under Ideal Conditions." *Journal of Financial and Quantitative Analysis*, December 1980.

BLACK, F. "Fact and Fantasy in the Use of Options." *Financial Analysts Journal*, July–August 1975.

————. "The Valuation of Option Contracts and a Test of Market Efficiency." *Journal of Finance*, May 1972.

BLACK, F., and M. SCHOLES. "The Pricing of Options and Corporate Liabilities." *Journal of Political Economy*, May–June 1973.

BRENNAN, M. "The Pricing of Contingent Claims in Discrete Time Models." *Journal of Finance*, March 1979.

BRENNER, M., G. COURTADON, and M. SUBRAHMANYAM. "Options on the Spot and Options on Futures." *Journal of Finance*, December 1985.

BRIGHAM, E. "An Analysis of Convertible Debentures: Theory and Some Empirical Evidence." *Journal of Finance*, March 1966.

CHIRAS, D., and S. MANASTER. "The Information Content of Option Prices and a Test of Market Efficiency." *Journal of Financial Economics*, June–September 1978.

COX, J., and S. ROSS. "The Valuation of Options for Alternative Stochastic Processes." *Journal of Financial Economics*, January–March 1976.

COX, J., and M. RUBINSTEIN. "Option Pricing: A Simplified Approach." *Journal of Financial Economics*, September 1979.

FRENCH, K., W. SCHWERT, and R. STAMBAUGH. "Expected Stock Returns and Volatility." *Journal of Financial Economics* 19(1987).

GALAI, D., and R. GESKE. "Option Performance Measurement." *Journal of Portfolio Management*, May 1977.

————. "Tests of Market Efficiency of the Chicago Board Options Exchange." *Journal of Business*, 1977.

GALAI, D., and R. MASULIS. "The Option Pricing Model and the Risk Factor of Stock." *Journal of Financial Economics*, 1976.

GALAI, D. and M. SCHNELLER. "Pricing of Warrants and the Value of the Firm." *Journal of Finance*, December 1978.

GARMAN, M. "The Pricing of the Supershares." *Journal of Financial Economics*, March 1978.

GASTINEAU, G. *The Stock Options Manual*. New York: McGraw-Hill, 1975.

GESKE, R. "The Valuation of Compound Options." *Journal of Financial Economics*, March 1979.

GOULD, J., and D. GALAI. "Transaction Costs and the Relationship Between Put and Call Prices." *Journal of Financial Economics*, July 1974.

HAKANSSON, N. "The Superfund: Efficient Paths Toward Efficient Capital Markets in Large and Small Countries." In H. LEVY and M. SARNAT, eds., *Financial Decision Making Under Uncertainty*. New York: Academic Press, 1977.

INGERSOLL, J. "A Contingent-Claims Valuation of Convertible Securities." *Journal of Financial Economics*, May 1977.

————. "A Theoretical and Empirical Investigation of the Dual Purpose Funds: An Application of Contingent Claims Analysis." *Journal of Financial Economics*, March 1976.

KLEMKOSKY, R., and T. MANESS. "The Impact of Options on Underlying Securities." *Journal of Portfolio Management*, Winter 1980.

KLEMKOSKY, R., and B. RESNICK. "Put-Call Parity and Market Efficiency." *Journal of Finance*, forthcoming.

LATANÉ, H., and R. RENDLEMAN. "Standard Deviations of Stock Prices Ratios Implied in Option Prices." *Journal of Finance*, May 1976.

MacBETH, J., and L. MERVILLE. "Tests of the Black-Scholes and Cox Call Option Valuation Models." *Journal of Finance*, May 1980.

MERTON, R. "Option Pricing When Underlying Stock Returns Are Discontinuous." *Journal of Financial Economics*, January–March 1976.

————. "The Relationship Between Put and Call Option Prices: Comment." *Journal of Finance*, March 1973.

————. "Theory of Rational Option Pricing." *Bell Journal of Economics*, August 1973.

O'BRIEN, T. "Portfolio Insurance Mechanics." *Journal of Portfolio Management*, Spring 1988.

REBACK, R. "Risk and Return in CBOE and AMEX Option Trading." *Financial Analysts Journal*, July–August 1975.

ROLL, R. "An Analytic Valuation Formula for Unprotected American Call Options on Stocks with Known Dividends." *Journal of Financial Economics*, November 1977.

ROSS, S. "Options and Efficiency." *Quarterly Journal of Economics*, February 1976.

RUBINSTEIN, M. "Nonparametric Tests of Alternative Option Models Using All Reported Trades and Quotes on the 30 Most Active CBOE Option Classes from August 23, 1976, Through August 31, 1978." *Journal of Finance*, June 1985.

————. "The Valuation of Uncertain Income Streams and the Pricing of Options." *Bell Journal of Economics*, August 1976.

RUBINSTEIN, M., and J. COX. *Options Markets*. Englewood Cliffs, N.J.: Prentice-Hall, 1985.

SCHWARTZ, E. "The Valuation of Warrants: Implementing a New Approach." *Journal of Financial Economics*, January 1977.

SMITH, C. "Option Pricing: A Review." *Journal of Financial Economics*, January–March 1976.

————. "Applications of Option Pricing Analysis." In J. BICKSLER, ed., *Handbook of Financial Economics*. New York: North-Holland Publishing Co., 1979.

STOLL, H. "The Relationship Between Put and Call Option Prices." *Journal of Finance*, December 1969.

WEIL, R., J. SEGALL, and D. GREEN. "Premiums on Convertible Bonds." *Journal of Finance*, June 1968.

WHALEY, R. "On the Valuation of American Call Options on Stocks with Known Dividends." *Journal of Financial Economics*, June 1981.

Chapter 17
Futures

ANDERSON, R., and J. DANTHINE. "Time Pattern of Hedging and the Volatility of Futures Prices." *Review of Economic Studies*, April 1983.

ARAK, M., and C. McCURDY. "Interest Rate Futures." *Quarterly Review*, Federal Reserve Bank of New York, Winter 1979-1980.

BACON, P., and R. WILLIAMS. "Interest Rate Futures: New Tool for the Financial Manager." *Financial Management*, Spring 1976.

BAESEL, J., and D. GRANT. "Optimal Sequential Futures Trading." *Journal of Financial and Quantitative Analysis*, December 1982.

BLACK, F. "The Pricing of Commodity Options." *Journal of Financial Economics*, January–March 1976.

BRENNAN, M. "The Supply of Storage." *American Economic Review*, March 1958.

BURGER, A., R. LANG, and R. RASCHE. "The Treasury Bill Futures Market and Market Expectations of Interest Rates." *Review*, Federal Reserve Bank of St. Louis, June 1977.

COOTNER, P. "Returns to Speculators: Telser Versus Keynes." *Journal of Political Economy*, August 1960.

CORNELL, B. "Spot Rates, Forward Rates, and Exchange Market Efficiency." *Journal of Financial Economics*, August 1977.

———. "Taxes and the Pricing of Treasury Bill Futures Contracts: A Note." *Journal of Finance*, December 1981.

COX, C. "Futures Trading and Market Information." *Journal of Political Economy*, December 1976.

DUSAK, K. "Futures Trading and Investor Returns: An Investigation of Commodity Market Risk Premiums." *Journal of Political Economy*, November–December 1973.

EINZIG, P. *The Dynamic Theory of Forward Exchange*, 2d ed. London: Macmillan, 1967.

ELTON, E., M. GRUBER, and J. RENTELER. "Intra-Day Tests of the Efficiency of the Treasury Bill Futures Market." *Review of Economics and Statistics*, February 1984.

FIGLEWSKI, S. "Hedging Performance and Basis Risk in Stock Index Futures." *Journal of Finance*, July 1984.

FRENCH, K. "A Comparison of Futures and Forward Prices." *Journal of Financial Economics*, November 1983.

GARBADE, K., and W. SILBER. "Price Movements and Price Discovery in Futures and Cash Markets." *Review of Economics and Statistics*, May 1983.

GAY, G., R. KOLB, and R. CHIANG. "Interest Rate Hedging: An Empirical Test of Alternative Strategies." *The Journal of Financial Research*, Fall 1983.

GOLD, G. *Modern Commodity Futures Trading*. New York: Commodity Research Bureau, 1968.

GOSS, B. A., and B. YAMEY, eds. *The Economics of Futures Trading*. London: Macmillan, 1976.

GRAY, R. "Risk Management in Commodity and Financial Markets." *American Journal of Agricultural Economics*, 1976.

———. "The Search for a Risk Premium." *Journal of Political Economy*, June 1961.

HARRIS, L. "The October 1987 S&P 500 Stock-Futures Basis." *Journal of Finance*, March 1989.

HIERONYMUS, T. *Economics of Futures Trading for Commercial and Personal Profit*. New York: Commodity Research Bureau, 1971.

HOUTHAKKER, H. "Can Speculators Forecast Prices?" *Review of Economics and Statistics*, May 1957.

JARROW, R., and G. OLDFIELD. "Forward Contracts and Futures Contracts." *Journal of Financial Economics*, December 1981.

JOHNSON, L. "The Theory of Hedging and Speculation in Commodity Futures." *Review of Economic Studies*, June 1960.

KALDOR, N. "Speculation and Economic Stability." *Essays in Economic Stability and Growth*. New York: Macmillan, 1960.

KILCOLLIN, T. "Tandem T-Bill and CD Spreads." *Journal of Futures Markets*, Spring 1982.

KOLB, R. *Understanding Futures Markets*. Glenview, Ill.: Scott, Foresman, 1985.

KOLB, R., and R. CHIANG. "Duration, Immunization, and Hedging with Interest Rate Futures." *Journal of Financial Research*, Summer 1982.

KOLB, R., G. GAY, and J. JORDAN. "Are There Arbitrage Opportunities in the Treasury-Bond Futures Market?" *The Journal of Futures Markets*, Fall 1982.

LANG, R., and R. RASCHE. "A Comparison of Yields on Futures Contracts and Implied Forward Rates." *Review*, Federal Reserve Bank of St. Louis, December 1978.

LIVINGSTON, M. "The Cheapest Deliverable Bond for the CBT Treasury Bond Futures Contract." *The Journal of Futures Markets*, Summer 1984.

O'BRIEN, T. "Portfolio Insurance Mechanics." *Journal of Portfolio Management*, Spring 1988.

PECK, A. *Selected Writings of Holbrook Working*. Chicago: Chicago Board of Trade, 1977.

———, ed. *Selected Writings on Futures Markets*, vol. 2. Chicago: Chicago Board of Trade, 1977.

POULE, W. "Using T-Bill Futures to Gauge Interest Rate Expectations." *Economic Review*, Federal Reserve Bank of San Francisco, Spring 1978.

POWERS, M. *Inside the Financial Futures Markets*, 2d ed. New York: John Wiley & Sons, 1984.

PUGLISI, D. "Is the Futures Market for Treasury Bills Efficient?" *Journal of Portfolio Management*, Winter 1978.

RENDLEMAN, R., and C. CARABINI. "The Efficiency of the Treasury Bill Futures Market." *Journal of Finance*, September 1979.

RENDLEMAN, R., and R. McENALLY. "Assessing the Costs of Portfolio Insurance." *Financial Analysts Journal*, May–June 1987.

ROCKWELL, C. "Normal Backwardation, Forecasting, and the Returns to Commodity Futures Traders." *Food Research Institute Studies*, Supplement, 1967.

RODRIQUEZ, R., and E. CARTER. *International Financial Management*. Englewood Cliffs, N.J.: Prentice-Hall, 1976.

SANDOR, R. "Trading Mortgage Interest Rate Futures." *Journal of Federal Home Loan Bank Board*, September 1975.

SILBER, W. "Market Behavior in an Auction Market: An Analysis of Scalpers in Futures Markets." *Journal of Finance*, September 1983.

SOLNIK, B. "An Equilibrium Model for the International Capital Market." *Journal of Economic Theory*, August 1974.

———. "International Pricing of Risk: An Empirical Investigation of the World Capital Market Structure." *Journal of Finance*, May 1974.

STEIN, J. "The Simultaneous Determination of Spot and Futures Prices." *American Economic Review*, December 1961.

TELSER, L. G. "Returns to Speculators: Telser Versus Keynes, Reply." *Journal of Political Economy*, August 1960.

TEWELES, R., C. HARLOW, and H. STONE. *The Commodity Futures Game*. New York: McGraw-Hill, 1977.

WORKING, H. "Price Effects of Futures Trading." *Food Research Institute Studies*, February 1960.

———. "Theory of the Inverse Carrying Charge in Futures Markets." *Journal of Farm Economics*, January 1948.

Chapter 18
Other Investment Alternatives

ABRAMS, R. K., and D. V. KIMBALL. "U.S. Investment in Foreign Equity Markets." *Economic Review*, Federal Reserve Bank of Kansas City, April 1981.

ARDITTI, F. "Skewness and Investors' Decisions: A Reply." *Journal of Financial and Quantitative Analysis*, March 1975.

BERGSTRAND, J. H. "Selected Views of Exchange Rate Determination After a Decade of 'Floating.'" *New England Economic Review*, May–June 1983.

BRANCH, B. "Common Stock Performance and Inflation: An International Comparison." *Journal of Business*, January 1973.

BRAUER, G. "Closed-End Fund Shares' Abnormal Returns and the Information Content of Discounts and Premiums." *Journal of Finance*, March 1988.

BRUEGGEMAN, W. B., A. H. CHEN, and T. G. THIBODEAU. "Real Estate Investment Funds: Performance and Portfolio Considerations." *AREUEA Journal* 12, no. 3 (1984).

CARLSON, R. S. "Aggregate Performance of Mutual Funds 1948–1967." *Journal of Finance and Quantitative Analysis*, March 1970.

COOPER, J. C. B. "World Stock Markets: Some Random Walk Tests." *Applied Economics*, October 1982.

FIELITZ, B. D. "Indirect Versus Direct Diversification." *Financial Management*, Winter 1974.

FRIEND, I., M. BLUME, and J. CROCKETT. *Mutual Funds and Other Institutional Investors*. New York: McGraw-Hill, 1970.

GENTRY, J. A., and J. R. PIKE. "Dual Funds Revisited." *Financial Analysts Journal*, March–April 1968.

GRUBEL, H., and K. FADNER. "The Interdependence of International Equity Markets." *Journal of Finance*, March 1971.

HILLIARD, J. E. "Relationship Between Equity Indices on World Exchanges." *Journal of Finance* 24, no. 1(March 1979).

HUANG, R. "Expectations of Exchange Rates and Differential Inflation Rates: Further Evidence on Purchasing Power Parity in Efficient Markets." *Journal of Finance*, March 1987.

IBBOTSON, R. G., R. C. CARR, and A. W. ROBINSON. "International Equity and Bond Returns." *Financial Analysts Journal*, July–August 1982.

IBBOTSON, R. G., and L. B. SIEGEL. "Real Estate Returns: A Comparison with Other Investments." *AREUEA Journal* 12, no. 3(1984).

———. "The World Market Wealth Portfolio." *Journal of Portfolio Management*, Winter 1983.

IBBOTSON, R., L. SIEGEL, and K. LOVE. "World Wealth, Market Values, and Returns." *Journal of Portfolio Management*, Fall 1985.

INGERSOLL, J. "A Theoretical and Empirical Investigation of the Dual-Purpose Funds: An Application of Contingent Claims Analysis." *Journal of Financial Economics*, March 1976.

Investment Companies 1980. Wiesenberger Financial Services, published annually.

JACQUILLAT, B., and B. SOLNIK. "Multinationals Are Poor Tools for Diversification." *Journal of Portfolio Management*, Winter 1978.

JENSEN, M. C. "The Performance of Mutual Funds in the Period 1945–1964." *Journal of Finance*, May 1968.

LESSARD, D. "World, Country, and Industry Relationships in Equity Returns: Implications for Risk Reduction Through International Diversification." *Financial Analysts Journal*, January–February 1976.

———. "World, Country, and Industry Relationships in Equity Returns: Implications for Risk Reduction Through International Diversification." *Financial Analysts Journal*, January–February 1978, pp. 2–8.

LEVY, H., and Z. LERMAN. "The Benefits of International Diversification in Bonds." *Financial Analysts Journal*, September–October 1988.

LEVY, H., and M. SARNAT. "International Diversification of Investment Portfolios." *American Economic Review*, September 1970.

LITZENBERGER, R. H. "The Theory of Recapitalizations and the Evidence of Dual Purpose Funds." *Journal of Finance*, December 1977.

LITZENBERGER, R. H., and H. B. SOSIN. "The Performance and Potential of Dual Purpose Funds." *Journal of Portfolio Management*, Spring 1978.

LOGUE, D. E. "An Experiment in International Diversification." *Journal of Portfolio Management*, Fall 1982.

MAINS, N. E. "Risk, the Pricing of Capital Assets, and the Evaluation of Investment Portfolios: Comment." *Journal of Business*, July 1977.

McDONALD, J. "French Mutual Fund Performance: Evaluation of Internationally Diversified Portfolios." *Journal of Finance*, December 1973.

———. "Objectives and Performance of Mutual Funds, 1960–1969." *Journal of Financial and Quantitative Analysis*, June 1974.

MILES, M., and T. McCUE. "Commercial Real Estate Returns." *AREUEA Journal* 12, no. 3(1984).

ROLL, R. "A Critique of the Asset Pricing Theory's Tests." *Journal of Financial Economics*, March 1977.

ROLL, R., and B. SOLNIK. "A Pure Foreign Exchange Asset Pricing Model." *Journal of International Economics* 7(1977).

RUGMAN, A. M. "International Diversification by Financial and Direct Investment." *Journal of Economics and Business*, 1975.

SHARPE, W. F. "Mutual Fund Performance." *Journal of Business*, Supplement on Security Prices, January 1966.

SIRMANS, S., and C. SIRMANS. "The Historical Perspective of Real Estate Returns." *Journal of Portfolio Management*, Spring 1987.

SOLNIK, B. "Testing International Asset Pricing: Some Pessimistic Views." *Journal of Finance* 23, no. 1(May 1977).

———. "Why Not Diversify Internationally?" *Financial Analysts Journal*, July–August 1974.

———. "Why Not Diversify Internationally Rather Than Domestically?" *Financial Analysts Journal*, July–August 1974, pp. 48–54.

SOLNIK, B., and B. NOETZLIN. "Optimal International Asset Allocation." *Journal of Portfolio Management*, Fall 1982.

SUBRAHMANYAN, M. G. "On the Optimality of International Capital Market Integration." *Journal of Financial Economics*, 1975, pp. 3–28.

TREYNOR, J. L. "How to Rate Management of Investment Funds." *Harvard Business Review*, January–February 1965.

TREYNOR, J. L., and K. K. MAZUY. "Can Mutual Funds Outguess the Market?" *Harvard Business Review*, July–August 1966.

WILLIAMSON, P. J. "Measuring Mutual Fund Performance." *Financial Analysts Journal*, November–December 1972.

ZERBST, R. H., and B. R. CAMBON. "Real Estate: Historical Returns and Risks." *Journal of Portfolio Management*, Spring 1984.

Chapters 19 and 20
Portfolio Management and Strategic Asset Allocation

BARRY, C. B., and L. T. STARKS. "Investment Management and Risk Sharing with Multiple Managers." *Journal of Finance* 34, no. 1 (June 1984).

BLACK, F. "The Tax Consequences of Long-Run Pension Policy." *Financial Analysts Journal*, Winter 1980.

BLACK, F., and M. P. DEWHURST. "A New Investment Strategy for Pension Funds." *Journal of Portfolio Management*, Summer 1981.

BOOKSTABER, R., and J. GOLD. "In Search of the Liability Asset." *Financial Analysts Journal*, January–February 1988.

BOSTOCK, P., P. WOOLEY, and M. DUFFY. "Duration-Based Asset Allocation." *Financial Analysts Journal*, January–February 1989.

CONDON, K. A., W. L. FOUSE, and M. P. KRITZMAN. *Asset Allocation Decisions in Portfolio Management*. Charlottesville, Va.: The Institute of Chartered Financial Analysts, 1982.

CLARKSON, G. P. *Portfolio Selection: A Simulation of Trust Investment*. Englewood Cliffs, N.J.: Prentice-Hall, 1962.

EZRA, D. "Economic Values: A Pension Pentateuch." *Financial Analysts Journal*, March–April 1980.

FISHER, L., and J. H. LORIE. "Some Studies of the Variability of Returns on Investments in Common Stocks." *Journal of Business*, April 1970.

FONG, G. "An Asset Allocation Framework." *Journal of Portfolio Management*, Winter 1980.

GROPPER, D. H. "The Boom in Asset-Liability Models." *Institutional Investor*, August 1985.

A Guide to Developing a Written Bank Investment Policy. Washington, D.C.: American Bankers Association, 1977.

LEIBOWITZ, M. "Pension Asset Allocation Through Surplus Management." *Financial Analysts Journal*, March–April 1987.

LEIBOWITZ, M., and R. HENRIKSSON. "Portfolio Optimization Within a Surplus Framework." *Financial Analysts Journal*, March–April 1988.

PEROLD, A., and W. SHARPE. "Dynamic Strategies for Asset Allocation." *Financial Analysts Journal*, January–February 1988.

SHARPE, W. "Integrated Asset Allocation." *Financial Analysts Journal*, September–October 1987.

TEPPER, I. "Risk vs. Return in Pension Fund Investment." *Harvard Business Review*, March–April 1977.

WAGNER, W. "The Many Dimensions of Risk." *Journal of Portfolio Management*, Winter 1988.

Chapter 21
Tactical Asset Allocation

BONHAM, H. "The Use of Input-Output Economics in Common Stock Analysis." *Financial Analysts Journal*, January–February 1967.

BRIGHAM, E., and J. PAPPAS. "Rates of Return on Common Stock." *Journal of Business*, July 1969.

BRIGHAM, E., D. SHOME, and S. VINSON. "The Risk Premium Approach to Measuring a Utility's Cost of Equity." *Financial Management Journal*, Spring 1985.

DENISON, E. *Accounting for United States Economic Growth 1929–1969*. Washington, D.C.: The Brookings Institution, 1974.

FAMA, E., L. FISHER, M. JENSEN, and R. ROLL. "The Adjustment of Stock Prices to New Information." *International Economic Review*, February 1969.

FISHER, L. "Outcomes for 'Random' Investments in Common Stock Listed on the New York Stock Exchange." *Journal of Business*, April 1965.

———. "Some New Stock Market Indexes." *Journal of Business*, January 1966 Supplement.

GAUMNITZ, J. "The Influence of Industry Factors in Stock Price Movements." Paper presented at the Southern Finance Association Meeting, October 1970.

GRAHAM, B., D. DODD, and S. COTTLE. *Security Analysis: Principles and Technique*, 4th ed. New York: McGraw-Hill, 1962.

"Input-Output Structure of the U.S. Economy." *Survey of Current Business Conditions*, November 1969.

KELEJIAN, H., and W. OATES. *Introduction to Econometrics: Principles and Applications*, 2d ed. New York: Harper & Row, 1981.

KING, B. "Market and Industry Factors in Stock Price Behavior." *Journal of Business*, January 1966.

LATANÉ, H. A., and D. L. TUTTLE. "Industry Analysis Framework for Forming Probability Beliefs." *Financial Analysts Journal*, July–August 1968.

LEONTIEF, W., et al. *Studies in the Structure of the American Economy*. New York: Oxford University Press, 1953.

LIVINGSTON, M. "Industry Movements of Common Stocks." *Journal of Finance*, June 1977.

MALKIEL, B. G. "The Capital Formation Problem in the United States." *Journal of Finance*, May 1979.

MEYERS, S. L. "A Re-Examination of Market and Industry Factors in Stock Price Behavior." *Journal of Finance*, June 1973.

SHARPE, W. F. "Likely Gains from Market Timing." *Financial Analysts Journal*, March–April 1975.

TYSSELAND, M. "Further Tests of the Validity of the Industry Approach to Investment Analysis." *Journal of Financial and Quantitative Analysis*, March 1971.

Chapter 22
Company Analysis

ABDEL-KHALIK, A. R. "The Efficient Market Hypothesis and Accounting Data: A Point of View." *Accounting Review*, October 1972.

ALTMAN, E. "Financial Ratios, Discriminant Analysis, and the Prediction of Corporate Bankruptcy." *Journal of Finance*, March 1968.

ALTMAN, E., R. HALDEMAN, and P. NARAYANAN. "Beta Analysis: A New Method to Identify Bankruptcy Risk of Corporations." *Journal of Banking and Finance*, June 1977.

BEAVER, W. "Financial Ratios as Predictors of Failure." *Empirical Research in Accounting: Selected Studies, 1966*. Supplement to *Journal of Accounting Research*.

BENSTON, G. "Published Corporate Accounting Data and Stock Price." *Empirical Research in Accounting: Selected Studies, 1967*. Supplement to *Journal of Accounting Research*.

BERNSTEIN, L. *The Analysis of Financial Statements*. Homewood, Ill.: Dow Jones-Irwin, 1978.

———. *Financial Statement Analysis: Theory, Application, and Integration*. Homewood, Ill.: R. D. Irwin, 1978.

BLUME, M. "Betas and Their Regression Tendencies." *Journal of Finance*, June 1975.

BREALEY, R., and S. MYERS. *Principles of Corporate Finance*. New York: McGraw-Hill, 1981.

BRIGHAM, E., and J. PAPPAS. "Duration of Growth, Change in Growth Rates, and Corporate Share Prices." *Financial Analysts Journal*, May–June 1966.

COHN, R., and D. LESSARD. "The Effect of Inflation on Stock Prices: International Evidence." *Journal of Finance*, May 1981, pp. 277–89.

CRAGG, J., and B. G. MALKIEL. "The Consensus and Accuracy of Some Predictions of the Growth of Corporate Earnings." *Journal of Finance*, March 1968.

DONALDSON, G. *Corporate Debt Capacity*. Boston: Division of Research, Harvard Business School, 1961.

DUKES, R. *An Empirical Investigation of the Effects of Statement of Financial Accounting Standards No. 8 on Security Return Behavior*. Stamford, Conn.: FASB, 1978.

EDMINSTER, R. "An Empirical Test of Financial Ratio Analysis for Small Business Failure Prediction." *Journal of Financial and Quantitative Analysis*, March 1972.

ESKEW, R., and W. WRIGHT. "An Empirical Analysis of Differential Capital Market Reaction to Extraordinary Items." *Journal of Finance*, May 1976.

FOSTER, T., III, and D. VICKREY. "The Incremental Information Content of the 10-K." *Accounting Review*, October 1978.

GLEIM, I., and P. DELANEY. *CPA Examination of Review, Volumes I and 2*, 7th ed. Somerset, N.J.: John Wiley & Sons, 1980.

GRAHAM, B., D. DODD, and S. COTTLE. *Security Analysis: Principles and Technique*, 4th ed. New York: McGraw-Hill, 1962.

HAGERMAN, R. "A Test of Government Regulation of Accounting Principles." *Accounting Review*, October 1975.

HAMADA, R. "The Effect of the Firm's Capital Structure on the Systematic Risk of Common Stock." *Journal of Finance*, May 1972.

HARRISON, T. "Different Market Reactions to Discretionary and Nondiscretionary Accounting Changes." *Journal of Accounting Research*, Spring 1977.

HARRISON, W., JR. "Accounting Changes in Principles and Estimates: How Different Are They?" *Economic Consequences of Financial Accounting Standards: Selected Studies*, FASB, July 1978.

HORWITZ, B., and R. KOLODYN. "Line of Business Reporting and Security Prices: An Analysis of an SEC Disclosure Rule." *Bell Journal of Economics*, Spring 1977.

JOY, M., and J. TOLLEFSON. "On the Financial Applications of Discriminant Analysis." *Journal of Finance and Quantitative Analysis*, December 1975.

KAPLAN, R. "The Information Content of Financial Accounting Numbers: A Survey of Empirical Evidence." In A. R. ABDEL-KHALIK

and T. KELLER, eds., *The Impact of Accounting Research on Practice and Disclosure*. Durham, N.C.: Duke University Press, 1978.

LARSON, L., and N. GONEDES. "Business Combinations: An Exchange-Ratio Determination Model." *Accounting Review*, October 1969.

LEVY, R. "On the Short-Term Stationarity of Beta Coefficients." *Financial Analysts Journal*, November–December 1971.

MANDELKER, G. "Risk and Return: The Case of Merging Firms." *Journal of Financial Economics*, December 1974.

RO, B. "The Disclosure of Capitalized Lease Information and Stock Prices." *Journal of Accounting Research*, Autumn 1978.

ROGALSKI, R. J., and J. D. VINSO. "Stock Returns, Money Supply, and the Direction of Causality." *Journal of Finance*, September 1977, pp. 1017–30.

SCOTT, J. "On the Theory of Conglomerate Mergers." *Journal of Finance*, September 1977.

SUNDER, S. "Stock Price and Risk Related to Accounting Changes in Inventory Valuation." *Accounting Review*, April 1975.

VAN HORNE, J. C. *Financial Management and Policy*, 5th ed. Englewood Cliffs, N.J.: Prentice-Hall, 1980.

Chapter 23
Performance Monitoring

ANG, J. S., and J. H. CHUA. "Composite Measures for the Evaluation of Investment Performance." *Journal of Financial and Quantitative Analysis*, June 1979.

ARDITTI, F. D. "Another Look at Mutual Fund Performance." *Journal of Financial and Quantitative Analysis*, June 1971.

BOWER, R. D., and R. F. WIPPERN. "Risk-Return Measurement in Portfolio Selection and Performance Appraisal Models: Progress Report." *Journal of Financial and Quantitative Analysis*, December 1969.

CARLSON, S. "Aggregate Performance of Mutual Funds: 1948–1967." *Journal of Financial and Quantitative Analysis*, March 1970.

CHEN, N. F., T. E. COPELAND, and D. MAYERS. "A Comparison of APM, CAPM, and Market-Model Portfolio Performance Methodologies: The Value Line Case (1965–1978)." Working paper, University of Chicago, University of California, Los Angeles, 1983.

COPELAND, T. E., and D. MAYERS. "The Value Line Enigma (1965–1978): A Case Study of Performance Evaluation Issues." *Journal of Financial Economics*, November 1982.

CORNELL, B. "Asymmetric Information and Portfolio Performance Measurement." *Journal of Financial Economics* 7(1979).

DIETS, P. O. "Components of a Measurement Model, Rate of Return, Risk, and Timing." *Journal of Finance*, May 1968.

DYBVIG, P. H., and S. A. ROSS. "Performance Measurement Using Differential Information and a Security Market Line." *Journal of Finance* 40(June 1985).

———. "The Analytics of Performance Measurement Using a Security Market Line." *Journal of Finance* 40(June 1985).

FAMA, E. F. "Components of Investment Performance." *Journal of Finance*, June 1970.

FRIEND, I., and M. BLUME. "Measurements of Portfolio Performance Under Uncertainty." *American Economic Review*, September 1970.

HENRIKSSON, R. D., and R. C. MERTON. "On Market Timing and Investment Performance, II. Statistical Procedures for Evaluating Forecasting Skills." *Journal of Business*, October 1981.

JENSEN, M. C. "Problems in Selection of Security Portfolios: The Performance of Mutual Funds in the Period 1945-1964." *Journal of Business*, May 1968.

_____. "Risk, the Pricing of Capital Assets, and the Evaluation of Investment Portfolios." *Journal of Finance*, April 1969.

JOY, M. O., and R. B. PORTER. "Stochastic Dominance and Mutual Fund Performance." *Journal of Financial and Quantitative Analysis*, January 1974.

KLEMKOSKY, R. C. "The Bias in Composite Performance Measures." *Journal of Financial and Quantitative Analysis*, June 1973.

KON, S. J. "The Investment Performance of Mutual Funds: An Empirical Investigation of Timing Selectivity and Market Efficiency." *Journal of Business*, April 1979.

KON, S. J., and F. D. JEN. "Estimation of Time-Varying Systematic Risk and Performance for Mutual Fund Portfolios: An Application of Switching Regression." *Journal of Finance*, May 1978.

LEHMANN, B., and D. MODEST. "Mutual Fund Performance Evaluation: A Comparison of Benchmarks and Benchmark Comparisons." *Journal of Finance*, June 1987.

MAYERS, D., and E. RICE. "Increasing Portfolio Performance and the Empirical Content of Asset Pricing Models." *Journal of Financial Economics* 7(1979).

MERTON, R. C. "On Market Timing and Investment Performance, I. An Equilibrium Theory of Value for Market Forecasts." *Journal of Business*, July 1981.

ROLL, R. "Ambiguity When Performance Is Measured by the Security Market Line." *Journal of Finance*, September 1978.

SCHLARBAUM, G. G. "The Investment Performance of the Common Stock Portfolios of Property-Liability Insurance Companies." *Journal of Financial and Quantitative Analysis*, January 1974.

SCHLARBAUM, G. G., W. G. LEWELLEN, and R. C. LEASE. "The Common Stock Portfolio Performance Record of Individual Investors: 1964-1970." *Journal of Finance*, May 1978.

SHARPE, W. F. "Mutual Fund Performance." *Journal of Business*, January 1966.

TREYNOR, J. L. "How to Rate Management Investment Funds." *Harvard Business Review*, January–February 1965.

TREYNOR, J. L., and K. MAZUY. "Can Mutual Funds Outguess the Market?" *Harvard Business Review*, July–August 1966.

VERRECCHIA, R. "The Mayers-Rice Conjecture: A Counter-example." *Journal of Financial Economics* 8(1980).

WILLIAMSON, P. F. "Measuring Mutual Fund Performance." *Financial Analysts Journal*, December 1972.

Chapter 1

6. a. Mgr A = $2 ÷ $5 = 40% per year
Mgr B = $6 ÷ $8 = 75% per year

   b. Mgr A = 1.0 ÷ 0.40 = 2.5 years
Mgr B = 1.0 ÷ 0.75 = 1.3 years

7. a. Stock return = (55.0 − 50.0 + 2.5) ÷ 50.0 = 15%
Bond return = (51.0 − 50.0 + 4.0) ÷ 50.0 = 10%

   b. Dividend yield = 2.5 ÷ 50.0 = 5%
Current yield = 4.0 ÷ 50.0 = 8%

   c. Portfolio return = (106.0 − 100.0 + 6.5) ÷ 100.0 = 12.5%

   or

   = 0.5(15%) + 0.5(10%)
= 12.5%

8. a. $E(R) = (33.0 − 30.0 + 1.5) ÷ 30.0 = 15\%$

   b. Fair return = 9.0% + 1.5(6.0%) = 18%

   c. No. Expected return is less than should be earned given the stock's risk.

10. a.

	1975	1976	1977	1978	1979	1980	1981	1982	1983	1984	1985	1986	1987
AMF price	8.09	10.16	9.51	9.82	10.89	12.48	12.37	13.56	15.41	14.94	17.74	17.99	17.05
AMF div	NA	0.62	0.81	0.84	0.94	1.06	1.02	1.92	1.24	1.34	1.42	2.82	1.77
Return	NA	33.3%	1.6%	12.1%	20.5%	24.3%	7.3%	25.1%	22.8%	5.6%	28.2%	17.3%	4.6%
Harris price	8.594	14.750	23.312	28.750	32.875	52.125	41.125	37.000	40.125	27.125	26.125	29.750	26.000
Harris div	NA	0.36	0.45	0.55	0.66	0.76	0.84	0.88	0.88	0.88	0.88	0.88	0.88
Return	NA	75.8%	61.1%	25.7%	16.6%	60.9%	−19.5%	−7.9%	10.8%	−30.2%	−0.4%	17.2%	−9.6%

   b.

	Average	Std. Dev.
AMF	16.90%	9.98%
Harris	16.71%	32.45%

   AMF is a portfolio of many securities. Thus it is more diversified than Harris.

   c. Portfolio of the two stocks (50% in each):

1976	1977	1978	1979	1980	1981	1982	1983	1984	1985	1986	1987
54.5%	31.3%	18.9%	18.6%	42.6%	−6.1%	8.6%	16.8%	−12.3%	13.9%	17.3%	−2.5%

   Average = 16.80%
Std. dev. = 18.55%

   The standard deviation of the 50/50 portfolio is not the average of the two stocks' standard deviations since the stock returns are not perfectly correlated.

   e.

	1975	1976	1977	1978	1979	1980	1981	1982	1983	1984	1985	1986	1987
T-bill return	NA	5.08%	5.13%	7.16%	10.38%	11.25%	14.70%	10.55%	8.51%	10.14%	7.78%	6.07%	5.13%
T-bill/AMF	NA	19.17	3.35	9.63	15.42	17.79	11.00	17.85	15.65	7.89	18.01	11.69	4.87

	Average	Std. Dev.
T-bill	8.49%	2.87%
T-bill/AMF	12.69%	5.19%

Chapter 2

1. a. Buy price $= 100 - 100(0.087)\dfrac{14}{360}$

   $= 99.6617\%$ of par

   Sell price $= 100 - 100(0.09)\dfrac{14}{360}$

   $= 99.6500\%$ of par

   b. Days to maturity = Jan. + Feb. + March
73   = 30 + 28 + 15

Buy price $= 100 - 100(0.0879)\dfrac{73}{360}$

$= 98.2176\%$ of par

Sell price $= 100 - 100(0.0912)\dfrac{73}{360}$

$= 98.1507\%$ of par

c. $r = \dfrac{(365)(0.0879)}{360 - (0.0879)(73)} = 9.074\%$

d. Sell price $= 100 - 100(0.0885)\dfrac{59}{360}$

$= 98.54958\%$ of par or $9,854,958

Less purchase price $\underline{(9,821,758)}$

Profit $\underline{\$\quad 33,200}$

2. Price of 1 BP $= \$1,000,000(0.0001)\dfrac{91}{360} = \$25.28$

3. **a.** Buy price $= 100 - 100(0.088)\dfrac{29}{360}$

$= 99.291111\%$ of par

For $1 million par $= \$992,911.11$

b. Price quotations are shown assuming 360-day maturity.

Bid	Asked
91.00	91.20

c. $r = \left[\dfrac{100.00}{99.291111} - 1.0\right]\dfrac{365}{29} = 8.986\%$

$r' = \left[\dfrac{100.00}{99.291111}\right]^{365/29} - 1.0 = 9.367\%$

d. Sell price $= 100 - 100(0.095)\dfrac{19}{360}$

$= 99.498611\%$ of par

$r = \left[\dfrac{99.498611}{99.291111} - 1.0\right]\dfrac{365}{9} = 8.475\%$

$r' = \left[\dfrac{99.498611}{99.291111}\right]^{365/9} - 1.0 = 8.835\%$

4. Competitive bids accepted

(A) Discount	(B) Dollars	(C) % of Total	(A) × (C)
8.50%	$ 200	13.3333	1.133333
8.55	400	26.6666	2.280000
8.56	600	40.0000	3.424000
8.58	300	20.0000	1.716000
	$1,500	100.0	8.553333%

Noncompetitive bidders receive the weighted average competitive discount accepted $= 8.553\%$

Price to noncompetitive $= 100 - 100(0.085533)\dfrac{91}{360}$

$= 97.837907$

$r = \left[\dfrac{100.00}{99.837907} - 1.0\right]\dfrac{365}{91} = 8.864\%$

$r' = \left[\dfrac{100.00}{99.837907}\right]^{365/91} - 1.0 = 9.163\%$

8. **a.** FM shares $= \$1,000 \div \$34.40 = 29.0698$ shares

PNH shares $= \$1,000 \div \$12.88 = 77.6398$ shares

b. FM load $= (\$34.40 - \$33.37) \div \$33.37 = 3.09\%$

PNH load $=$ none

9. **a.** $(\$500 - \$10) \div 7 = \$70$ NAV

b. $\$10,000 \div \$70 = 142.857$ shares

10. **a.** 12

b. $16

c. Immediate value $= \$16 - \$15$ $= \$1.00$

Extra paid in hope of stock price increase $= \underline{\$1.00}$

Call premium $\underline{\$2.00}$

d. The November put with $20 exercise has an immediate value of $4. The put should sell for at least $4.

e. You hope stock price will fall so that you can exercise the put and keep premium of $1 received from selling the call.

f. Initial cost of:

	Cash (out) in
Buy put	($3.75)
Sell call	1.00
Total cost	($2.75)

At May exercise date:	
Exercise put (sell)	$20.00
Buy stock	(15.00)
Profit on exercise	$ 5.00
Net profit	$ 2.25

11. **a.** Buy call, sell put

b. Sell call, buy put

c.

Stock Price	Net Profit from Buying: 1.0 Call	Net Profit from Buying: 1.0 Put
$35	−5	5 − 2 = 3
38	−5	2 − 2 = 0
40	−5	−2
43	3 − 5 = −2	−2
45	5 − 5 = 0	−2
48	8 − 5 = 3	−2

12. b. Sell future

   c. The ownership of a T-bill maturing in June 1986.

   d. Price of June index:

$$P = 100 - 100(0.0966)\,\frac{90}{360} = 97.585\% \text{ of par}$$

   e. If purchased from someone who is selling for the first time, open interest increases one unit.
If purchased from someone who had owned the contract, open interest is unchanged.

13. After-tax return on:
Pref. stk. $= 9.2\% - 9.2\%(0.15)(0.45) = 8.58\%$
Corp. bond $= 11.0\% - 11.0\%(0.45) = 6.05\%$

14. Simpson after-tax returns
Pref. stk. $= 9.2\% - 9.2\%(0.0) = 9.2\%$
Corp. bond $= 11.0\% - 11.0\%(0.0) = 11.0\%$ (Best)
Biller after-tax returns
Pref. stk. $= 9.2\% - 9.2\%(0.6) = 3.68\%$
Corp. bond $= 11.0\% - 11.0\%(0.6) = 4.40\%$ (Best)

15. a. Corporate bond $= 8\%(1 - 0.3) = 5.6\%$
This is better than 5.0% on the municipal bond.

   b. $8\%(1 - X) = 5\%$
          $X = 0.375$

Chapter 3

	Per Share
5. a. Underwriter spread	$2.50
Out-of-pocket = $37,500 ÷ 50,000	0.75
Price concession to first buyer	2.00
Total	$5.25

7. a. Total position value = TPV

$$= (500)\,\$40 = \$20,000$$

Margin = Equity = 0.6($20,000) = 12,000

Loan = TPV − Equity $ 8,000

   b. $0.40 = \dfrac{\text{Price} \times 500 - 8{,}000}{\text{Price} \times 500}$

   Price = $26.67

   c. $0.4 = \dfrac{\$20(500) - 8{,}000 + \$New}{\$20(500) + \$New}$

   $New = $3,333.33

   d. $0.4 = \dfrac{\$20(500 - N) - (\$8{,}000 - \$20N)}{\$20(500 - N)}$

   $N = 250$ shares

9.

Transactions today	$ Flow Today	$ Flow Delivery
Buy futures	—	($290.00)
Sell stock	$300.00	
Buy T-bills	($300.00)	

Transactions at delivery		
Sell futures at x dollars		
Buy stock at x dollars		
T-bills mature ($300 × 1.02)		$306.00
Net cash flows	$0.00	$ 6.00

Chapter 4

6. a. through **c.**

From year-end:	EAFE	Small Stocks	S&P 500	Corp. Bonds	Govt. Bonds	T-Bills
1925	NA	12.72%	9.90%	4.89%	4.27%	3.48%
1962	NA	15.55	9.90	6.23	5.77	6.71
1970	17.70%	14.75	10.64	8.49	8.27	7.66

7. a.

Year	Return	UV	Calculation
1978	12.61%	1.1261	1.0 × 1.1261
1979	21.46	1.3678	1.1261 × 1.2146
1980	25.36	1.7146	.
1981	7.76	1.8477	.
1982	29.64	2.3953	.
1983	24.12	2.9731	.
1984	6.43	3.1643	.
1985	30.12	4.1173	.
1986	18.43	4.8762	4.1173 × 1.1843
1987	4.61	5.1009	4.8762 × 1.0461

   b.

	Average
Arithmetic	18.05%
Geometric	17.70%

8. $(1.0 + \text{Return to June 7}) = (17.3 + 0.5) \div 17.0 = 1.04706$
$1.0 + \text{Return from June 7 to June 30} = (17.15 \div 17.3)$
$$= 0.99133$$

$$1 + \text{Total return} = (1.04706)(0.99133)$$
$$= 1.03798$$

June return   3.798%

Return assuming month-end dividend

$$= \frac{17.15 + 0.50}{17.00} - 1.0 = 3.824\%$$

Chapter 5

6. a. Purchase price $= 100 - 100(0.11)\dfrac{50}{360} = 98.4722$

50-day nominal return $= (100 \div 98.4722) - 1.0$
$= 1.5515\%$

Annual nominal return:

Simple interest $= 1.5515\% \left(\dfrac{365}{50}\right) = 11.326\%$

Compound interest $= (1.015515)^{365/50} - 1.0$
$= 11.895\%$

b. 50-day real return $= (0.015515 - 0.01) \div 1.01$
$= 0.546\%$

Annual real return:

Simple interest $= 0.546 \left(\dfrac{365}{50}\right) = 3.986\%$

Compound interest $= (1.00546)^{365/50} - 1.0 = 4.055$

c. 50-day real return $= (0.015515 - 0.02) \div 1.02$
$= -0.4397\%$

Annual real return:
Simple interest $= -3.21\%$
Compound interest $= -3.17\%$

7.

Maturity	Pure Rate	+	Expected Inflation	+	Inter. Term	=	Required Nominal Return	Actual Yield Curve
1	0.02		0.12		(0.02)(0.12)		0.1424	0.14
2	0.02		0.10		(0.02)(0.10)		0.1220	0.10
3	0.02		0.09		(0.02)(0.09)		0.1118	0.12

Don't buy the 1-year maturity (short sell perhaps).
Don't buy the 2-year maturity (short sell perhaps).
Buy the 3-year maturity.

Chapter 6

2. a. $P_A = \$922.30 = \sum\limits_{t=1}^{5} \dfrac{70}{(1 + YTM)^t} + \dfrac{1,000}{(1 + YTM)^5}$

$YTM_A = 9.0\%$ (rounded)
Solved in the same fashion:
$YTM_B = 7.0\%$
$YTM_C = 7.0\%$

b. Bond C has lower coupon — thus lower effective tax rate. This would lead (all other things equal) to a lower before-tax YTM.

c. Bond C — longest maturity and lowest coupon

d. Bond C — lower coupon

e.

Bond	Price
A	$ 960.07
B	$1,294.41
C	$ 852.80

10. $f_{1,5} = 1.09^6 \div 1.087^5 - 1.0 = 10.51\%$

11. a. $f_{1,5} = 1.09^6 \div 1.08^5 - 1.0 = 14.14\%$

b. $f_{2,5} = (1.095^7 \div 1.08^5)^{1/2} - 1.0 = 13.34\%$

12. $f_{15,4} = (1.08^{20} \div 1.085^5)^{1/15} - 1.0 = 7.83\%$

		Date	
Transaction	0	5	20
Buy 1.0 20-year $= 1,000 \div 1.08^{20}$	$(214.548)	—	+1,000.00
Short sell 0.3226 5-year $= 214.548 \div 665.045$	+214.548	(322.60)	
Net	0	(322.60)	+1,000.00

$$\text{Return} = \left[\dfrac{1,000.00}{322.60}\right]^{1/15} - 1.0$$
$$= 7.83\%$$

13. a.

		Date	
Transaction	0	1	2
Buy 1.0 2-year	(873)		1,000.00
Sell 0.94 1-year	873	(942.76)	
$873 \div 926 = 0.94276$			
	0	(942.76)	1,000.00

$$\text{Return} = \dfrac{1,000.00}{942.76} - 1.0$$
$$= 6.07\%$$

b. $YTM_2 = (1,000 \div 873)^{1/2} - 1.0 = 7.0269\%$
$YTM_1 = 1,000 \div 926 - 1.0 = 7.9914\%$
$f_{1,2} = 1.070269^2 \div 1.079914 - 1.0 = 6.07\%$

c. Sell short the 2-year and buy equal dollar amount of the 1-year.

d. UET says your estimate of 8% is wrong — that the market consensus of 6.07% is an unbiased expectation of what 1-year rates should be at the start of year 2.

14.

Year	Forward Rate	$= r^*$	+	$E(I)$	+	$(r^*)E(I)$
1	0.0710	= 0.02	+	0.05	+	(0.02)(0.05)
2	0.0812	= 0.02	+	0.06	+	(0.02)(0.06)
3	0.0914	= 0.02	+	0.07	+	(0.02)(0.07)
4	0.0710	= 0.02	+	0.05	+	(0.02)(0.05)

Year	YTM	Calculation
1	7.10%	$= 1.0710 - 1.0$
2	7.61	$= [(1.071)(1.0812)]^{1/2} - 1.0$
3	8.12	$= [(1.071)(1.0812)(1.0914)]^{1/3} - 1.0$
4	7.86	$= [(1.071)(1.0812)(1.0914)(1.071)]^{1/4} - 1.0$

Chapter 7

10. a.

Year	Return	Year	Return
1	15.00%	6	4.61%
2	−4.54	7	12.69
3	−4.00	8	−17.14
4	34.44	9	33.18
5	16.52	10	11.79

b. $\bar{R} = (15.00 - 4.54 \ldots + 33.18 + 11.79) \div 10$
$= 10.25\%$

$\sigma = [(15 - 10.25)^2 + \ldots + (11.79 - 10.25)^2] \div 10^{1/2}$
$= 15.44\%$

11. a.

Probable	0.1	0.2	0.4	0.2	0.1
Return	−10	0	10	20	30

$E(R) = 0.1(-10) + 0.2(0) + 0.4(10) + 0.2(20)$
$\qquad + 0.1(30) = 10\%$

b. $\sigma = [0.1(-10 - 10)^2 + 0.2(0 - 10)^2 + \ldots$
$\qquad + 0.1(30 - 10)^2]^{1/2}$
$= 10.95\%$

14. a. No effect. Risk and return of country B are the same as those of country A and the correlation co-efficient is 1.0, so there is no diversification gain.

b. Return would remain at 7% but risk would fall to zero since $r = -1.0$.

c. Invest 50/50 in countries A and C.

15. a. $\sigma^2 = (0.5^2)(8^2) + (0.5^2)(10^2)$
$\qquad + 2(0.5)(0.5)(8)(10)(0.5)$
$= 61$
$\sigma = 61^{1/2} = 7.81\%$

b. $\sigma^2 = (1/3^2)(8^2) + (1/3^2)(10^2) + (1/3^2)(12^2)$
$\qquad + 2(1/3)(1/3)(8)(10)(0.5)$
$\qquad + 2(1/3)(1/3)(8)(12)(0.5)$
$\qquad + 2(1/3)(1/3)(10)(12)(-1.0)$
$= 27.11$
$\sigma = 27.11^{1/2} = 5.21\%$

d. $0 = (X_2)^2 100 + (1 - X_2)^2 144$
$\qquad + 2(X_2)(1 - X_2)(10)(12)(-1.0)$
$X_2 = 54.5454\%$
$X_3 = 1 - X_2$

16. $\sigma^2 = (0.25^2)100 + (0.4^2)144 + (0.35^2)225$
$\qquad + 2(0.25)(0.4)(10)(12)(0.3)$
$\qquad + 2(0.25)(0.35)(10)(15)(0.4)$
$\qquad + 2(0.4)(0.35)(12)(15)(0.6)$
$= 104.7925$
$\sigma = 104.7925^{1/2} = 10.24\%$

17. Beta for Ms. D. = $(20 \div 11)0.8 = 1.45$
Beta for Mr. C. = $(20 \div 16)0.2 = 0.25$

Chapter 8

5. $E(R_m) = 0.4(16) + 0.4(12) + 0.2(3) = 11.8\%$
$E(R_{XYZ}) = 0.4(20) + 0.4(13) + 0.2(-5) = 12.2\%$
$\sigma_m^2 = 0.4(16 - 11.8)^2 + 0.4(12 - 11.8)^2 + 0.2(3 - 11.8)^2$
$\qquad = 22.56$
$\sigma_m = 22.56^{1/2} = 4.75$
$\sigma_{XYZ}^2 = 0.4(20 - 12.2)^2 + 0.4(13 - 12.2)^2$
$\qquad + 0.2(-5 - 12.2)^2$
$\qquad = 83.76$
$\sigma_{XYZ} = 83.76^{1/2} = 9.15$
Covariance between m and XYZ:
$0.4(16 - 11.8)(20 - 12.2) + 0.4(12 - 11.8)(13 - 12.2)$
$\qquad + 0.2(3 - 11.8)(-5 - 12.2)$
$\qquad = 43.44$

$r_{m,XYZ} = \dfrac{43.44}{(4.75)(9.15)} = 1.0$

$\text{Beta}_{XYZ} = \dfrac{9.15}{4.75}(1.0) = 1.93$

Fair return = $7\% + 1.93(11.8 - 7)$
$\qquad = 16.26\%$

Since this is larger than the expected 12.2% return, don't buy.

6. Portfolio 1:
$\sigma_1 = 0.7(10\%) = 7\%$
Portfolio 2:
$\sigma_2^2 = B_2^2 \sigma_m^2 + 0.0$
$\sigma_2^2 = (1.5^2)(10^2) + 0.0$
$\sigma_2 = 15\%$

7. a.

Portfolio	$(E(R) - RF) \div \sigma$
1	$(8 - 6) \div 3 = 0.67$
2	$(10 - 6) \div 6 = 0.67$
3	$(13 - 6) \div 8 = 0.875$
4	$(17 - 6) \div 13 = 0.846$
5	$(20 - 6) \div 18 = 0.778$

Portfolio 3 is the optimal portfolio.

b. A standard deviation of 4% results in an expected return of only 9.5%:

$9.5\% = 6\% + 4\%(0.875)$

c. $E(R) = 6\% + 12\%(0.875)$
$\qquad = 16.5\%$
Borrow $0.50 for each $1.00 equity.
$\sigma_p = 1.5(8\%)$
$\qquad = 12\%$

9. $B_X = \dfrac{40}{20}(-0.3)$
$\qquad = -0.60$

$E(R) = 5\% + (-0.60)(5\%)$
$\quad\quad\;\; = 2\%$
$P_0 = (\$70 + \$4) \div 1.02$
$\quad\;\; = \$72.55$

10. a.

Security	Beta
Mesa	$(14.7 \div 4.3)(0.48) = 1.64$
Anheuser	$(6.3 \div 4.3)(0.25)\; = 0.37$
Teledyne	$(11.3 \div 4.3)(0.51) = 1.34$
XYZ	$(5.2 \div 4.3)(0.95)\; = 1.15$
Index	$(4.3 \div 4.3)(1.00)\; = 1.0$

b. Beta estimates smaller than 1.0 will probably increase towards 1.0. Beta estimates larger than 1.0 will probably decrease towards 1.0.

c.

Security	$E(R)$
Mesa	$20.48 = 9 + 1.64(7)$
Anheuser	$11.59 = 9 + 0.37(7)$
Teledyne	$18.38 = 9 + 1.34(7)$
XYZ	$17.05 = 9 + 1.15(7)$
Index	$16.00 = 9 + 1.00(7)$

d.

Security	$E(R)$
Mesa	$32.93 = 9 + 14.7(7 \div 4.3)$
Anheuser	$19.26 = 9 + \;\;6.3(7 \div 4.3)$
Teledyne	$27.40 = 9 + 11.3(7 \div 4.3)$
XYZ	$17.46 = 9 + \;\;5.2(7 \div 4.3)$
Index	$16.00 = 9 + \;\;4.3(7 \div 4.3)$

e. $\beta_p = 0.25(1.64) + 0.25(0.37) + 0.25(1.34)$
$\quad\quad\quad + 0.25(1.15)$
$\quad\;\; = 1.125$

11. a.

Stock	Expected Excess Return	+	RF	=	$E(R)$
i	$1.0 + 1.5(5)$	+	8	=	16.5%
j	$4.0 + 1.0(5)$	+	8	=	17.0%

b.

i	$1.0 + 1.5(2)$	+	8	=	12.0%
j	$4.0 + 1.0(2)$	+	8	=	14.0%

c.

i	$15 - 12 = 3.0\%$
j	$11 - 14 = -3.0\%$

d. Residual errors net out (approach zero) in diversified portfolios.

e. $20^2 = 1.5^2\sigma_m^2 + 10^2$
$\quad\sigma_m = 11.55\%$

12. a.

Plan	Beta
1	$0.0(0.0) + 1.0(1.0) = 1.0$
2	$0.2(0.0) + 0.8(1.0) = 0.8$
3	$0.3(0.0) + 0.7(1.0) = 0.7$

Plan 1 has the greatest market risk—beta.

13. a. Fund 4—the highest R^2.

b. Fund 2—the highest beta.

c. Fund 2—the highest beta and std. dev. of E

d. and e.

Fund	Alpha	"t-value" from one	Rank
1	0.98	0.98	3
2	2.18	1.45	2
3	2.18	2.91	1
4	-0.04	-0.08	4

f.

Fund	Annualized Alpha (Compound)
1	$3.98\% = 1.0098^4 - 1.0$
2	$9.01\;\;\; = 1.0218^4 - 1.0$
3	$9.01\;\;\; = 1.0218^4 - 1.0$
4	$-0.16\;\; = 0.9996^4 - 1.0$

Chapter 9

11. a. Factors 2 and 3 are best thought of as firm-unique factors in this example. In a broadly diversified portfolio the positive and negative values net to zero.

b. Per APT, expected returns *should* be:
$E(R_1) = 6.0(3) = 18.0\%$
$E(R_2) = 1.5(3) = 4.5\%$
Per actual market conditions, expected returns are:
$E(R_1) = (45 \div 40) - 1.0 = 12.5\%$
$E(R_2) = (10.70 \div 10) - 1.0 = 7.0\%$
Stock 1 is overvalued. Stock 2 is undervalued.

Transaction	$	Factor Score
Sell 1.0 Stk 1	$ 40	(6)
Buy 4.0 Stk 2	(40)	6
Net	$ 0	0

13. a.

Transaction	$	Factor Score
Sell 1.0 Stk X	$(50)	+3
Buy 2.0 Stk Y	50	-3
Net	$ 0	0

b. They appear to be diversifiable, firm-unique factors.

c. $P_x = \$58 \div 1.12 = \$51.79$
$P_y = \$26 \div 1.06 = \$24.53$

d. $R_x = 3.0(6) - 1.0(2) + 0.0(4) = 16.0\%$
$R_y = 1.5(6) + 0.0(2) + 0.3(4) = 10.2\%$

Chapter 11

1. a.
$$P_A = \sum_{t=1}^{5} \frac{\$80}{1.1^t} + \frac{\$1,000}{1.1^5} = \$924.16$$

$$P_B = \sum_{t=1}^{20} \frac{\$50}{1.08^t} + \frac{\$1,000}{1.08^{20}} = \$705.41$$

$$P_C = \sum_{t=1}^{20} \frac{\$80}{1.08^t} + \frac{\$1,000}{1.08^{20}} = \$1,000.00$$

b. $P_A = \$906.43$
   $P_B = \$668.78$
   $P_C = \$952.68$

c.

Bond	% Price Change	Rank	Reason
A	−1.92%	Least	Shorter maturity
B	−5.19%	Most	Long maturity, lower coupon than C
C	−4.73%	Middle	

2. $\$880 = \sum_{t=1}^{3} \dfrac{\$70}{(1 + YTM)^t} + \dfrac{\$1,000}{(1 + YTM)^3}$

   $YTM = 12\%$

   $\$1,083 = \sum_{t=1}^{3} \dfrac{\$70}{(1 + YTM)^t} + \dfrac{\$1,000}{(1 + YTM)^3}$

   $YTM = 4\%$

3. a. $P_2 = \sum_{t=1}^{16} \dfrac{\$50}{1.04^t} + \dfrac{\$1,000}{1.04^{16}} = \$1,116.52$

b. $P_2 = \sum_{t=1}^{16} \dfrac{\$50}{1.06^t} + \dfrac{\$1,000}{1.06^{16}} = \$898.84$

c. $1.04^2 - 1.0 = 8.16\%$
   $1.06^2 - 1.0 = 12.36\%$

4. First, find purchase price:

   $\text{Purchase} = \sum_{t=1}^{10} \dfrac{\$90}{1.1^t} + \dfrac{\$1,000}{1.1^{10}} = \$938.55$

Next, find end-of-year-3 value of position:

End-of-Year Coupon	1	2	3	End-of-Year-3 Value
3			$90	$ 90.000
2		90	× (1.08)	97.200
1	90 × (1.08²)			104.976

   Price in year 3 $= \sum_{t=1}^{7} \dfrac{\$90}{1.08^t} + \dfrac{\$1,000}{1.08^7} = \underline{\$1,052.06}$

   Total End-of-Year-3 Value $\underline{\underline{\$1,344.236}}$

Finally, find ARR:
   $ARR = (1,344.236 \div 938.55)^{1/3} - 1.0$
   $\qquad = 12.72\%$

Price risk was most important because the bond was sold before its maturity (more precisely, before its duration).

5. $\$1,000(1.1)(1.08)(1.08) = \$1,283.04$
   $ARR = 1.28304^{1/3} - 1.0$
   $\qquad = 8.66\%$

The ARR was lower than original 10% YTM because reinvestments were made at 8%. The risk in this prob-

lem was reinvestment risk since the securities purchased had a maturity (duration) shorter than the eventual liquidation date.

Students should contrast the results in problem 4 and this problem. Notice the negative correlation between price risk and reinvestment risk.

6. a.   Bond 1's Duration Calculations

Year	$	PV	%	× Yr.#	=	Product
1	40	$ 37.04	4.27	× 1	=	0.0427
2	40	34.29	3.95	× 2	=	0.0790
3	40	31.75	3.66	× 3	=	0.1098
4	1,040	764.43	88.12	× 4	=	3.5248
		$867.51	100.00			

Duration 3.7563 years

   $D_2 = 3.6603$ years
   $D_3 = 4.4392$ years
   $D_4 = 3.7500$ years

15. a. $\$1,120 = \sum_{t=1}^{6} \dfrac{120}{(1 + IRR)^t} + \dfrac{1,000}{(1 + IRR)^6}$

   $IRR = 9.3\%$

b. Yes, issue bonds at 8% and save 9.3%.

c. For years 1–4 you earn 12% on your investment of $1,000. In years 5–10 you earn 8%. In addition, you receive $120 in call premium which earns 8% in years 5–10. Thus, your end-of-year-10 portfolio value would be:

$\$1,000(1.12^4)(1.08^6)$ $= \$2,496.97$
$+ \$120(1.08^6)$ $= \underline{\quad 190.42}$
End-of-year-10 value $= \underline{\underline{\$2,687.39}}$

   $ARR = 2.68739^{1/10} - 1.0 = 10.39\%$

Chapter 12

1. a. $P_A = \$1,000.00$
   $P_B = \$1,013.76$

b. Short sell bond B and buy equal dollar value of bond A.

c. Bond A:

Price in one year	$1,000.00
First coupon $40(1.04)	41.60
Second coupon	40.00
Value	$1,081.60

   $ARR = 1.0816 - 1.0 = 8.16\%$

   Bond B:
   $ARR = (1,081.60 \div 1,013.76) - 1.0 = 6.69\%$
   Since she is short this bond, the 6.69% is a cost to her.

4.

Period	$	PV	%	× Period	= Product
1	40	$ 38.10	4.07 ×	1	= 0.0407
2	40	36.28	3.88 ×	2	= 0.0776
3	40	34.55	3.69 ×	3	= 0.1107
4	40	32.91	3.52 ×	4	= 0.1408
5	40	31.34	3.35 ×	5	= 0.1675
6	40	29.85	3.19 ×	6	= 0.1914
7	40	28.43	3.04 ×	7	= 0.2128
8	1,040	703.91	75.25 ×	8	= 6.0200

Price $935.37

Total 100.00

Duration in ½ year 6.9615

Duration in years = 6.9615 ÷ 2 = 3.481 years

5. $-7.3\left(\dfrac{1.11 - 1.12}{1.12}\right) = -6.52\%$

7. a. $D_P = 0.1(1) + 0.2(3) + 0.1(5) + 0.2(7) + 0.4(12)$
$= 7.4$ years

b. $-7.4\left(\dfrac{1.10 - 1.09}{1.09}\right) = -6.79\%$

c. No, $HD = D$.

d. If interest rates rise, the portfolio duration will fall. To remain immunized after the rate increase, duration will have to be increased.

11. a. Required end-of-year-4 value:
$50 million × 1.1^4 = $73.205 million

Present worth of $73.205 at the available immunized rate:
$73.205 ÷ 1.115^4 = $47.3632 million

Maximum immediate loss and still be able to provide $73.205:
$50.0000 − $47.3632   = $2.6368 million

b. $60(1.11^3) = 82.0578

Since the future value if we did immunize is greater than the $73.205 required, we are not forced to immunize.

c. Depends on duration of bonds held.
If $D > 4$ years, unfavorable
If $D < 4$ years, favorable

d. A portfolio of $50 million initially immunized at 11.5% would have grown to:

$50(1.115^4) = $77.28 million$

Yes, you have "added value."

Chapter 13

4. a.

	Expected Return on:		
	A	B	C
Return on Equity	14%	12%	15%
× Retention Rate	0.50	0.39	0.31
= Growth	7.00%	4.68%	4.65%
+ Dividend Yield	3.70%	4.00%	4.35%
Expected Returns	10.70%	8.68%	9.00%

↑
Buy

b.

	Fair Market Price		
	A	B	C
Fair Price	$\dfrac{\$1.00}{0.1 - 0.07}$	$\dfrac{\$1.00}{0.1 - 0.0468}$	$\dfrac{\$1.00}{0.1 - 0.0465}$
	= $33.33	= $18.80	= $18.69

5. a. Growth in dividends = $(5.00 \div 2.54)^{1/10} - 1.0 = 7.00\%$
$K = 6\% + 1.5(4\%) = 12\%$

$$P_{JJ} = \frac{\$5.00(1.07)}{0.12 - 0.07} = \$107.00$$

b. $DY = (5.35 \div 107.00) = 5.00\%$
$G = 12\% - 5\% = 7.00\%$

6. $G = 0.60(10\%)(1.25) = 7.5\%$
$K = 8\% + 1.3(5\%) = 14.5\%$

$$P = \frac{\$2.50(1.075)}{0.145 - 0.075} = \$38.39$$

Sell the stock since actual market price = $45.

7. a. $ROE = (4)(2\%)(2.0) = 16\%$

b. $G = 16\%(0.25) = 4\%$

c. $K = 8\% + 1.5(6\%) = 17\%$

$$P_0 = \frac{\$3(1.04)}{0.17 - 0.04} = \$24$$

8. Use current price and required return to solve for implicit G in today's price.
$K = 8\% + 0.9(5\%) = 12.5\%$

$$\$40 = \frac{\$2.00}{0.125 - G}$$

$G = 7.5\%$

Since you think growth will be 8% and only 7.5% is implied in the stock's price, buy.

9. $\$35 = \dfrac{\$2.00(1.06)}{K - 0.06}$

$K = 12.06\%$

10. a. $P = \dfrac{\$3.60}{1.18} + \dfrac{\$4.32}{1.18^2} + \dfrac{\$5.184}{1.18^3}$

$+ \dfrac{\$5.184(0.95)}{0.18 - (-0.05)} \dfrac{1}{1.18^3} = \$22.34$

b. $P_3 = \dfrac{5.184(0.95)}{0.18 - (-0.05)} = \$21.41$

$P_4 = \dfrac{5.184(0.95)(0.95)}{0.18 - (-0.05)} = \$20.34$

c. $P_2 = (\$21.41 + \$5.184) \div 1.18 = \$22.54$

$DY = (\$5.184 \div \$22.54) = 23\%$

This is 5% larger than K because of negative dividend growth.

14. a. Current prices:

$P_A = \$1.00 \div (0.2 - 0.14) = \$16.67$

$P_B = \$2.33 \div (0.2 - 0.06) = \$16.64$

If K increases to 21%:

$P_A = \$1.00 \div (0.21 - 0.14) = \$14.29$
(a 14.3% decline in price)

$P_B = \$2.33 \div (0.21 - 0.06) = \$15.53$
(a 6.67% decline in price)

In general, the smaller the value of $K - G$, the more price sensitivity. Higher G implies more of the dividends are "packed into" the future—a higher G implies a longer duration.

b. Neither stock is a true "growth stock" when $K = 20\% = ROE$

Chapter 14

3. a. $D_A = 1.0 \div (0.14 - 0.09) = 20.0$

$D_B = 1.0 \div (0.12 - 0.06) = 16.67$

$D_C > D_B$ since stock C has more rapid growth for 6 years followed by identical growth thereafter.

b. Stock A has largest beta as evidenced by the largest required return (14%).

Chapter 15

1. a. through **d.**

| | Stock Prices | | | | |
	$40	$45	$50	$55	$60
	Expiration date cash flows				
Buy 1.0 call	0	0	0	−50	−50
Write 1.0 call	0	0	0	50	50
Buy 1.0 put	50	50	0	0	0
Write 1.0 put	−50	−50	0	0	0

	Expiration date investment values				
Buy 1.0 call	0	0	0	5	10
Write 1.0 call	0	0	0	−5	−10
Buy 1.0 put	10	5	0	0	0
Write 1.0 put	−10	−5	0	0	0

	Expiration date net profits				
Buy 1.0 call	−8	−8	−8	−3	2
Write 1.0 call	8	8	8	3	−2
Buy 1.0 put	9	4	−1	−1	−1
Write 1.0 put	−9	−4	1	1	1

5.

Write a call option for	$ 8
Buy the stock for	$−65
Hold option open for exercise and receive	$70
Net arbitrage profit	$13

The value of this call should be zero since it is the expiration date and the stock price is less than the exercise price.

7. a. $P_c = P_s - \dfrac{P_x}{1 + RF} + P_p$

$= \$74 - \dfrac{\$65}{1.1} + \$5.09 = \$20.00$

b. Identical to being long the stock:
  –Buy call at P_c
  –Buy debt worth $P_x \div (1 + RF)$
  –Sell the put at P_p

Short the stock:
  –Opposite of the above

c. Identical to writing one put:
  –Buy the call
  –Sell short the stock
  –Buy debt worth $P_x \div (1 + RF)$

8.

Buy the warehouse	($1,100,000.0)
Obtain a loan	$917,431.2 (*PV* of $1 million at 9%)
Purchase insurance	($10,000.0)
Net cost of the synthetic call	($192,568.8)

9.

	Value at Expiration		
	High	Low	Range
1.0 share	$80	$50	$30
1.0 call	20	0	20

For each 1.0 call sold, buy ⅔ share of stock

⅔ share	$53.33	$33.33
1.0 call (written)	(20.00)	0
Net	$33.33	$33.33

So:

$$(\tfrac{2}{3})\,\$60 - \$10.23 = \frac{\$33.33}{1 + RF}$$

$$RF = 11.96\%$$

12. a. For call A:

$$d_1 = (0.13353 + 0.075) \div 0.3 = 0.70$$
$$N_{d1} = 0.7580$$
$$d_2 = (0.13353 - 0.015) \div 0.3 = 0.40$$
$$N_{d2} = 0.6554$$
$$P_c = \$80(0.7580) - \frac{\$70}{e^{(0.12)(0.25)}}\,(0.6554)$$
$$= \$16.12$$

For call B:

$$d_1 = (0.0 + 0.075) \div 0.3 = 0.25$$
$$N_{d1} = 0.5987$$
$$d_2 = (0.0 - 0.015) \div 0.3 = -0.05$$
$$N_{d2} = 0.48$$
$$P_c = \$80(0.5987) - \frac{\$80}{e^{(0.12)(0.25)}}\,(0.48)$$
$$= \$10.62$$

For call C:

$$d_1 = (-0.11778 + 0.075) \div 0.3 = -0.14$$
$$N_{d1} = 0.4443$$
$$d_2 = (-0.11778 - 0.015) \div 0.3 = -0.44$$
$$N_{d2} = 0.33$$
$$P_c = \$80(0.4443) - \frac{\$90}{e^{(0.12)(0.25)}}\,(0.33)$$
$$= \$6.72$$

For call D;

$$d_1 = (-0.11778 + 0.015) \div 0.4243 = 0.08$$
$$N_{d1} = 0.5319$$
$$d_2 = (-0.11778 - 0.03) \div 0.4243 = -0.35$$
$$N_{d2} = 0.3632$$
$$P_c = \$80(0.5319) - \frac{\$90}{e^{(0.12)(0.25)}}\,(0.3632)$$
$$= \$11.77$$

14. a. First, find present value of dividends:

$$PV = \frac{\$1}{e^{(0.12)(0.25)}} + \frac{\$1}{e^{(0.12)(0.5)}}$$
$$= \$0.9704 + \$0.9418 = \$1.9122$$

Next, subtract this from current stock price:

$$P' = \$65 - \$1.9122 = \$63.0878$$

Next, find d_1, d_2, N_{d1}, and N_{d2}:

$$d_1 = \frac{\ln\!\left(\dfrac{63.09}{60.00}\right) + 0.5\left(0.12 + \dfrac{0.16}{2}\right)}{(0.04)(0.7071)} = 0.53$$

$$d_2 = \frac{\ln\!\left(\dfrac{63.09}{60.00}\right) + 0.5\left(0.12 - \dfrac{0.16}{2}\right)}{(0.04)(0.7071)} = 0.25$$

$$N_{d1} = 0.7019$$
$$N_{d2} = 0.5987$$

Finally, find price of call:

$$P_c = \$63.09(0.7019) - \frac{\$60}{e^{(0.12)(0.5)}}\,(0.5987)$$

$$= \$10.45$$

Chapter 16

1.

Period	Discrete Returns	Continuous Returns	Difference from Mean Squared
1	5.00%	4.88%	0.000204
2	15.00	13.98	0.011078
3	2.00	1.98	0.000216
4	−8.00	−8.34	0.013898
5	1.00	1.00	0.000603
6	−4.00	−4.08	0.005675
7	20.00	18.23	0.021849
8	5.00	4.88	0.000204
9	−8.00	−8.34	0.013898
10	10.00	9.53	0.003697
11	8.00	7.70	0.001802
12	0.00	0.00	0.001191

Average: 3.83%   3.45%

Sum of squared differences: 0.074315
Sum divided by $n-1$:   0.006756
Square root = std. dev.   8.22%

2. The calls should have the same *ISD* values. Since call A has the smaller *ISD*, its price is undervalued relative to call B. Buy 1.0 call A and write 0.80 call B (40%/50%).

4. Sell T-bills, which have a par value of $20,833,333.

5.

Transaction	Today	$P_s < P_x$	$P_s > P_x$
		Expiration Date	
Buy 1.0 stock	$-P_s$	$P_s + D$	$P_s + D$
Buy 1.0 put	$-P_p$	$P_x - P_s$	$-$
Write 1.0 call	P_c	$-$	$-(P_s - P_x)$
Net	$-(P_s + P_p - P_c)$	$P_x + D$	$P_x + D$

Thus, $P_c - P_p = P_s - (P_x + D)/(1 + RF)$

6. a. This uses the put-call relationship derived in problem 5 above.

In theory:

$$P_c - P_p = P_s - (P_x + D)/(1 + RF)$$

$$= \$300 - (\$280 + \$3)/(1.1^{0.5})$$

$$= \$30.17$$

In the markets:

$$P_c - P_p = \$35 - \$5$$

$$= \$30$$

Thus, put-call parity is virtually working, but the call is slightly overvalued.

b. Let N = number of puts to own

$N (\$300 + \$5) \times 100 = \$30$ million

$N = 983.606557$

P_s	Stock Value*	Dividends†	Put‡	Total
\$200	\$19,672,131	\$295,082	\$7,868,852	\$27,836,065
250	24,590,164	295,082	2,950,820	27,836,065
300	29,508,197	295,082	0	29,803,278
350	34,426,229	295,082	0	34,721,311

*$N \times P_s \times 100$
†$N \times (\$300 \times 100) \times 0.01$
‡$N \times (P_x - P_s) \times 100$ if $P_x > P_s$

c. Buy T-bills with a par value of $27,836,065.
Price of one T-bill = $1 million/(1.1^{0.5})$
$$= \$953,462.59$$
Cost of T-bills = $953,462.59 \times 27.836065$
$$= \$26,540,647$$
$$\text{Number of calls} = \frac{(\$30,000,000 - \$26,540,647)}{\$3,500}$$
$$= 988.386677$$

P_s	T-Bills	Calls	Total
\$200	\$27,836,065	0	\$27,836,065
250	27,836,065	0	27,836,065
300	27,836,065	\$1,976,773	29,812,838
350	27,836,065	6,918,707	34,754,772

The result of using calls is slightly better since the call was slightly undervalued in the put-call parity model.

18. Beta of S&P 100 call = $(\$250/\$15)(1.0)(0.75) = 12.5$

a. $0 = (0.5)1.0 + (\$ \text{ calls}/\$100 \text{ million})12.5 + 0$
$\$$ calls $= -\$4,000,000$
\# calls = 2,666⅔ calls written

b. $1.0 = 0.5(1.0) + (\$ \text{ calls}/\$100 \text{ million})12.5 + 0$
$\$$ calls $= \$4,000,000$
\# calls = $\$4,000,000/(\$15 \times 100)$
$$= 2,666⅔ \text{ calls bought}$$

c. \# calls = 533⅓

Chapter 17

4. a. Pay $977,875 per contract (or $4,889,375 for 5 contracts) in late June.

$$P = \$1.0 \text{ million} - \$1.0 \text{ million} (0.0885)\frac{90}{360}$$

$$= \$977,875$$

b. $2,000 per contract × 5 contracts = $10,000

c. Maintenance margin = $1,500 per contract. Thus you may lose $500 per contract before a margin call is made. At $25 per basis point, this means discounts can rise by 20 (500 ÷ 25) basis points. Discount at which maintenance margin is reached:

$8.85\% + 20 \text{ BP} = 9.05$

d. Sell price = $1.0 million − $1.0 million $(0.0895)\dfrac{90}{360}$

$$= \$977,625$$

Purchase price = $977,875

Loss $= \$\ \ \ \ \ 250 = 10 \text{ BP} \times \$25$

e. Expected profit will equal zero. Gains or losses on the futures will exactly be offset by losses or gains on spot T-bills. For example, assume $d = 9.00\%$ at delivery:

Per Contract		
Futures:		
Sell	\$977,500	\$1.0 mill − \$1.0 mill$(0.09)\frac{90}{360}$
Buy	977,875	From part a
Loss	\$ 375	
Spot:		
Buy	\$977,500	
Loss above	375	
Net price	\$977,875	

f. First, find equivalent 90-day yield = R_{90}

$R_{90} = (100 \div 97.785) - 1.0 = 2.26\%$

Next, this is a 90-day T-bill, so dollar duration will be:

$$0.2466 \left(\frac{0.0326 - 0.0226}{1.0226}\right) \$4,889,375 = \$11,790$$

5. Note: The prices in this question are assumed to be quoted as a percent of par, not as 1/32s.

Futures:		Spot:	
Sell futures	\$99.25	Buy	\$99.75
Buy futures	95.25	Less gain	−4.00
Gain	\$ 4.00	Net price	\$95.75

8. 90-day forward rate on T-bills starting in 30 days:
$1 + R_{180} = 100 \div 98.5 = 1.015228$
$1 + R_{90} = 100 \div 99.25 = 1.007557$
$F = (1.015228 \div 1.007557) - 1.0 = 0.7613\%$

90-day return on T-bill future:
$R_F = (100 \div 99) - 1.0 = 1.0101\%$

Arbitrage: Buy futures, sell 180-day T-bill, buy 90-day T-bill. Do this in quantities so that the initial cash flow is zero and the amount received on the spot T-bills on day 30 is equal to the value of futures purchased.

9. a. 8.00% – since they are maturing, they should sell at a price identical to spot T-bills.

b. Forward rate in spot market between 270 and 360:

$$P_{270} = 100 - 100(0.084)\frac{270}{360} = 93.70$$

$P_{360} = 100 - 100(0.086)1.0 = 91.40$
$1 + R_{270} = 100 \div 93.70 = 1.06724$
$1 + R_{360} = 100 \div 91.40 = 1.09409$
$F_{270-360} = (1.09409 \div 1.06724) - 0.02516$

Price of futures maturing in 270 days:
$100 \div 1.02516 = 97.5457$

Discount quote for futures maturing in 270 days:
D_{90} day $= 100 - 97.5457 = 2.4543$

$$D_{360} \text{ day} = 2.4543\left(\frac{360}{90}\right) = 9.817\%$$

c. There is a risk associated with daily marking to market which is not considered in the arbitrage relationships used above to price the futures.

d. If we buy 1.0 of the 90-day and the 180-day futures, this would provide a return between day 90 and 270 of:
P_{90} future $= 100 - 100(0.08)\ 90/360 = 98.00$
P_{180} future $= 100 - 100(0.9)\ 90/360 = 97.75$
$1 + $ Return on 90-day future $= (100 \div 98)$
$\qquad = 1.020408$
$1 + $ Return on 180-day future $= (100 \div 97.75)$
$\qquad = 1.023018$

Compound return on sequence of both futures:
$(1.020408)(1.023018) - 1.0 = 4.3896\%$

Next, find the 180-day forward return on spot T-bills between day 90 and day 270:
Price spot 90 = 98.00
Price spot 270 = 93.70
$1 + $ Return spot 90 $= (100 \div 98) = 1.020408$
$1 + $ Return spot 270 $= (100 \div 93.70) = 1.06724$
Forward rate 90–27 $= (1.06724 \div 1.020408) - 1.0$
$\qquad = 4.5895\%$

Arbitrage: Buy 270-day spot and sell 90-day spot. Sell the futures deliverable in 90 and 180 days.

13. $\dfrac{\text{Realized Future}}{\text{Trading Price}} = \dfrac{\text{Initial}}{\text{Spot}} + \text{Initial Basis} - \dfrac{\text{Cover}}{\text{Basis}}$

$\qquad 973.75 \quad = 978.75 + (1,025 - 978.75) - 51.25$

Gain or Loss:
Sell spot	973.75
−Buy spot	−978.75
Loss	−5.00 Per $1,000 par

or −$5.00 (5,000 par bonds) = −$25,000 total

18. $Q_F^* = Q_s(\sigma_s \div \sigma_F)r_{sF}$
$\quad = \$100 \text{ million } (3 \div 2)0.7 = \$105 \text{ million}$
Sell $105 million of the T-bill futures.

21. a. Dollar duration of portfolio addition:

$$6.0\left(\frac{0.11 - 0.10}{1.10}\right)\$100 \text{ million} = \$5.454545 \text{ million}$$

Dollar duration of cheapest to deliver:

$$(6.5 \div 0.9)\left(\frac{0.11 - 0.10}{1.1}\right)\$100,000 = \$6,565.66$$

Number of T-bond futures to buy:
$\$5,454,545 \div \$6,565.66 = 830.77$ contracts

b. Desired dollar duration:

$$4.0\left(\frac{0.11 - 0.10}{1.10}\right)\$700 \text{ million} = \$25.454545 \text{ million}$$

Current dollar duration:

$$6.0\left(\frac{0.11 - 0.10}{1.10}\right)\$700 \text{ million} = \$38.181818 \text{ million}$$

Change in dollar duration:
$38,181,818 - 25,454,545 = \$12,727,273$
Number of contracts to sell:
$\$12,727,273 \div \$6,565.66 = 1,938.46$

25. $\quad F = S(1 + RF) - D$
$\qquad = 167.24(1.0428) - 3.70 = 170.70$
The futures appear to be overvalued.

Chapter 18

5. a.

Year	Fund A		
1	$\dfrac{12.0 - 10.0 + 6.0}{10.0}$	=	80.0%
2	$\dfrac{10.0 - 12.0 + 4.0}{12.0}$	=	16.7%

3 $\dfrac{10.5 - 10.0 - 5.5}{10.0}$ = 60.0%

4 $\dfrac{11.5 - 10.5 + 6.0}{10.5}$ = 66.7%

Year	Fund B	
1	$\dfrac{13.0 - 10.0 + 5.0}{10.0}$	= 80.0%
2	$\dfrac{11.25 - 13.0 + 3.75}{13.0}$	= 15.4%
3	$\dfrac{12.5 - 11.25 + 4.75}{11.25}$	= 53.3%
4	$\dfrac{14.5 - 12.5 + 5.0}{12.5}$	= 56.0%

Pre-Tax	A	B
Mean return	55.8%	51.2%
Standard deviation	23.7%	23.1%

b. Both funds had similar risk, but fund A had slightly greater return.

c.

Fund A				
	1	2	3	4
Dividends	$6,000	$4,000	$5,500	$6,000
Ord. tax	(1,600)	(1,400)	(1,600)	(1,600)
C.G. tax	(400)	(100)	(300)	(400)
Net	$4,000	$2,500	$3,600	$4,000
Change in NAV*	2,000	−2,000	500	1,000
$ Profit	6,000	500	4,100	5,000
After-tax return	60.0%	4.2%	41.0%	47.6%

*Assuming shares are not sold and thus not taxed.

Fund B				
	1	2	3	4
After-tax return	62.0%	4.2%	37.8%	41.6%

After Tax	A	B
Mean	38.2%	36.4%
Std. dev.	20.8%	20.7%

Some of fund A's pretax greater performance disappears when taxes are considered. Yet it still has slightly better performance.

8. a. Hartwell is riskier than Acorn as evidenced by the beta and standard deviation of excess returns.

b. Evergreen and Hartwell are probably aggressive growth funds given their high betas.

Scudder is probably a low-risk, income fund given its low beta.

c.

Fund	S_p
Acorn	$3.82 \div 11.02 = 0.35$
Chemical	$0.68 \div 8.59 = 0.08$
Evergreen	$4.93 \div 13.03 = 0.38$
Hartwell	$4.10 \div 13.41 = 0.31$
Scudder	$0.55 \div 6.54 = 0.08$

Fund	T_p	Alpha
Acorn	$3.82 \div 1.13 = 3.38$	1.40%
Chemical	$0.68 \div 0.93 = 0.73$	−1.31%
Evergreen	$4.93 \div 1.33 = 3.71$	2.09%
Hartwell	$4.10 \div 1.58 = 2.59$	0.44%
Scudder	$0.55 \div 0.54 = 1.02$	−0.61%

d.

Fund	Alpha ÷ σ of alpha	
A	$1.40 \div 0.74 = 1.89$	
C	$-1.31 \div 0.38 = -3.45$	Underperformed
E	$2.09 \div 0.93 = 2.25$	Overperformed
H	$0.44 \div 1.46 = 0.30$	
S	$-0.61 \div 0.73 = -0.84$	

e. Purchase some of each fund using as broad a diversification as possible but being sure that the average portfolio beta is about 1.0.

9. a. $0.0815 = 0.03 + I + 0.031$
$I = 5\%$

b. $\$1.19/\pounds = \$1.25/\pounds \dfrac{1.05}{1 + IB}$

$IB = 10.29\%$

c. $0.03 + 0.1029 + (0.03)0.1029 = 13.60\%$

10. a. $E(R_{UK}) = (1.18)(1.05) - 1.0 = 23.9\%$
$E(R_F) = (1.20)(0.96) - 1.0 = 15.2\%$

b. $\sigma_{UK}^2 = 1.0(30^2) + 1.0(10^2) + 2(30)(10)(0.30)$
$\qquad = 1,180$
$\sigma_{UK} = 34.35$
$\sigma_F^2 = 1.0(35^2) + 1.0(10^2) + 2(35)(10)(0.0)$
$\qquad = 1,325$
$\sigma_F = 36.40$

12. Return to Japanese investor:
$R_J = (12 \div 10) - 1.0 = 20\%$
Return to U.S. investor:

Period 0	$4.00	$\xrightarrow[\text{in}]{\text{invested}}$	10 yen
			↓
			grows to
			↓
Period 1	$4.20	$\xleftarrow[\text{dollars}]{\text{returns}}$	12 yen

$R_{US} = (4.20 \div 4.00) - 1.0 = (1.2)(0.35 \div 0.40) - 1.0$
$\qquad = 5\%$

13. a. $0.72 = 0.70 \dfrac{1.05}{1 + IC}$

$IC = 2.0833333\%$

b. 0.72, the forward exchange rate

c. Decrease, because more rapid inflation in U.S. than in Canada.

d. $R_{US} = (1.09)(0.72 \div 0.7) - 1.0 = 12.11$

Uncertainty is caused by any uncertain returns in Canada and uncertain exchange rates.

Chapter 21

1. a.

	P	E	O
Growth:			
ROE	14.50%	15.00%	16.00%
Retention rate	0.5	0.5667	0.6
G	7.25%	8.50%	9.60%
Required return:			
RF	8.00%	8.00%	8.00%
RP	5.00	5.50	6.00
K	13.00%	13.50%	14.00%
Next dividend:			
EPS_0	$100.00	$106.35	$110.00
Payout	0.50	0.4333	0.40
D_0	$50.00	$46.08	$44.00
1 + G	1.0725	1.085	1.096
D_1	$53.63	$50.00	$48.22

	P	E	O
Price	$\dfrac{\$53.63}{0.13 - 0.0725}$	$\dfrac{\$50.00}{0.135 - 0.085}$	$\dfrac{\$48.22}{0.14 - 0.096}$
=	$932.69	$1,000.00	$1,095.90

b. No adjustment is necessary. The index is selling for the expected value calculated in parts.

7. b. $I = 31.6 + 0.204(400) = 113.2$

Range $= 113.2 \pm 1.0(6.7) = 106.5$ to 119.9

Chapter 22

2. a.

$$\dfrac{EPS}{Growth} = \dfrac{Sales}{Generation} \times \dfrac{Expense}{Control} \times \dfrac{Debt}{Use} \times \dfrac{Stock}{Finance} - 1.0$$

$$= \dfrac{1.2}{1.0} \times \dfrac{0.083}{0.100} \times \dfrac{2.0}{1.5} \times \dfrac{50}{45} - 1.0$$

$$48.15\% = 1.2 \times 0.833 \times 1.333 \times 1.111 - 1.0$$

–improved sales generation

–increased debt

–increased equity financing offset partially by poorer expense control

b.

Year	EPS	=	ROE	×	BV
0	$ 6.75	=	15%	×	$45
1	$10.00	=	20%	×	$50

5. a. $1.0 = B_A[1.0 + 0.667(1.0 - 0.46)]$

$B_A = 0.735$

b. $B_E = 0.735[1.0 + 2.333(1.0 - 0.46)]$

$= 1.66$

Chapter 23

2. $\bar{R}_s = (20 - 12 + 15 + 3)/4 = 6.5\%$

$\bar{R}_c = (1.2)(0.88)(1.15)(1.03^{1/4}) - 1.0 = 5.75\%$

For long-term investors, $\bar{R}_c$ is better.

3. Find R in:

$$\$10,000 = \sum_{t=1}^{8} \dfrac{-\$1,000}{(1 + R)^t} + \dfrac{\$25,000}{(1 + R)^8}$$

$R = 5.455\%$ per quarter

or

$R = (1.05455^4) - 1.0 = 23.67\%$ per year

The 23.67% is a dollar-weighted return, whereas the 20.00% would be a time-weighted return.

4. a. Time-weighted return:

Period	(1 + R)
May 30–June 15	$10 \div 15 = 0.6666$
June 15–June 30	$36,360 \div 20,000 = 1.818$
Full month	$= (0.6666)(1.818) - 1.0$
	$= 21.19\%$

b. Dollar-weighted return:

Find 15-day return:

$$15,000 = \dfrac{-10,000}{(1 + R)} + \dfrac{36,360}{(1 + R)^2}$$

$R = 25.89\%$ per 15-day interval

or

$R = (1.2589^2) - 1.0 = 58.48\%$ per month

7. $8.5\% = 3.0\% + B_T(8.0\% - 3.0\%)$

$B_T = 1.1$

$(B_a - 1.1)(8.0\% - 3.0\%) = 1.0\%$

$B_a = 1.3$

73 Figure 3-3 reprinted by permission of Moody's Investors Service. **118** Figure 4-1 reprinted by permission of Morgan Stanley & Company, Inc. **159** Figure 5-8 reprinted by permission of Shearson Lehman Hutton. **164–65** Figure 5-10 adapted from *Stocks, Bonds, Bills, and Inflation: Historical Returns (1926–1978)*, by Roger G. Ibbotson and Rex A. Sinquefield. Copyright © 1979 by Roger G. Ibbotson and Rex A. Sinquefield. Reprinted by permission. **205** Table 6A-1 from D. Meiselman, *The Term Structure of Interest Rates*. Reprinted by permission of the copyright holder, David I. Meiselman. **305** Table 8A-3 from M. Blume, "Betas and Their Regression Tendencies," *Journal of Finance* 10, no. 3(June 1975): 785–96; Table 8A-4 from M. Blume, "On the Assessment of Risk," *Journal of Finance* 6, no. 1(March 1971): 1–10. Copyright © 1975, 1971 by the American Finance Association. Reprinted by permission. **318** Table 9-1 from G. Douglas, "Risk in the Equity Markets: An Empirical Appraisal of Market Efficiency," *Yale Economic Essays* 9, no. 1(1969). Reprinted by permission of R. C. Levin, Chairman, Department of Economics, Yale University, New Haven, Conn. **319,320** Figures 9-4 and 9-5 from Figures 9-1 and 9-2 in *Studies in the Theory of Capital Markets*, edited by Michael C. Jensen, copyright © 1972 by Holt, Rinehart and Winston, Inc., reprinted by permission of the publisher. **363** Table 10-3 from "Stock Price Behavior and Trading," by A. Seelenfreund, G. G. C. Parker, and J. Van Horne, in *Journal of Financial and Quantitative Analysis* (September 1968): 263–81. Reprinted by permission of the Journal of Financial and Quantitative Analysis. **364** Table 10-4 from "Random Walks: Reality or Myth," by M. Jensen, in *Financial Analysts Journal* 23, no. 6(November/December 1967): 79. Copyright © 1967 by the Financial Analysts Journal. Reprinted by permission. **365** Table 10-5 from S. Basu, "Investment Performance of Common Stocks in Relation to Their Price-Earnings Ratios: A Test of the Efficient Market Hypothesis," *Journal of Finance* 32(June 1977): 667. Copyright © 1977 by the American Finance Association. Reprinted by permission. **367** Tables 10-6 and 10-7 adapted from S. Basu, "The Relationship Between Earnings Yield, Market Value, and Return for NYSE Common Stocks: Further Evidence," *Journal of Financial Economics* 12, no. 1(1983). Reprinted by permission of Elsevier Science Publishers, Physical Sciences and Engineering Division, publishers of the *Journal of Financial Economics*. **369** Table 10-8 from R. Roll, "A Possible Explanation of the Small-Firm Effect," *Journal of Finance* 36(September 1981): 879–88. Copyright © 1981 by the American Finance Association. Reprinted by permission. **373,374** Figures 10-6 and 10-7 from "The Adjustment of Stock Prices to New Information," by E. Fama, L. Fisher, M. Jensen, and R. Roll, *International Economic Review*, February 1969. Reprinted by permission of the International Economic Review and E. Fama. **376** Figure 10-8 from "An Empirical Evaluation of Accounting Income Numbers," by R. Ball and P. Brown, in *Journal of Accounting Research* 6(Autumn 1968): 169. Reprinted by permission of the Journal of Accounting Research. **377** Figure 10-9 from "Empirical Anomalies Based on Unexpected Earnings and Importance of the Risk Adjustments," by R. Rendleman, C. Jones, and H. Latane, in *Journal of Financial Economics* 3(November 1982): 285. Reprinted by permission of Elsevier Science Publishers, Physical Sciences and Engineering Division, publishers of the *Journal of Financial Economics*. **379** Figure 10-10 (panel A) from S. Sunder, "Relationship Between Accounting Changes and Stock Prices: Problems of Measurement and Some Empirical Evidence," *Journal of Accounting Research* (Supplement 1973): 1–45. Reprinted by permission of the Institute of Professional Accounting, Graduate School of Business, University of Chicago. **381** Figure 10-11 from A. Kraus and H. Stoll, "Price Impacts of Block Trading on the New York Stock Exchange," *Journal of Finance* 27, no. 3(June 1972): 569–88. Copyright © 1972 by the American Finance Association. Reprinted by permission. **384,385** Figures 10-12 and 10-13 from R. Shiller, "Do Stock Prices Move Too Much to Be Justified by Subsequent Changes in Dividend?" *The American Economic Review* 71, no. 3(June 1981), reprinted by permission of the American Economic Association. **387** Figure 10-14 from W. DeBondt and R. Thaler, "Does the Stock Market Overreact?" *Journal of Finance* 11, no. 3(July 1985). Copyright © 1985 by the American Finance Association. Reprinted by permission. **419** Table 11-2 from T. R. Atkinson, *Trends in Corporate Bond Quality* (New York: National Bureau of Economic Research, 1967). Reprinted by permission of the National Bureau of Economic Research. **420** Table 11-3 adapted from Standard & Poor's *Bond Guide* and Moody's *Bond Record* by permission of Standard & Poor's Corporation and Moody's Investors Service. **421** Unnumbered table and "Hickman" column in Table 11-4 from W. B. Hickman, *Corporate Bond Quality and Investor Experience*, 1958, reprinted by permission of the National Bureau of Economic Research; "Fraine/Mills" column in Table 11-4 from H. Fraine and R. Mills, "The Effect of Defaults and Credit Deterioration on Yields of Corporate Bonds," *Journal of Finance* 16, no. 3(September 1961). Copyright © 1961 by the American Finance Association. Reprinted by permission. **425** Table 11-6 from L. Fisher, "Determinants of Risk Premiums on Corporate Bonds," *Journal of Political Economy* 67, no. 3(June 1959): 217–37, reprinted by permission of the University of Chicago Press. Copyright © 1959 by the University of Chicago. All rights reserved. **428** Figure 11-5 from F. Jen and J. Wert, "The Effect of Call Risk on Corporate Bond Yield," *Journal of Finance* 4(December 1967): 646. Copyright © 1967 by the American Finance Association. Reprinted by permission. **448** Figure 12-4 from "Aspects of Corporate Bond Portfolio Diversification," by R. McEnally and C. Boardman, in *The Journal of Financial Research*, Spring 1979. Reprinted by permission of the Journal of Financial Research. **462** Figure 12-8 from "Managing Bond Portfolios with Combination Active/Passive Strategies," by K. Meyer, in *Techniques for Managing Bond Portfolios*, edited by D. Tuttle. Copyright © 1983 by the Institute of Chartered Financial Analysts. Reprinted by permission. **509** Figure 13-5 from Charles Benore, "A Survey of Investor Attitudes Toward the Electric Power Industry," September 25, 1979. Reprinted by permission of Paine Webber Mitchell Hutchins, Inc. **510,511** Figures 13-6 and 13-7 adapted from E. F. Brigham, D. K. Shome, and S. R. Vinson, "The Risk Premium Approach to Measuring a Utility's Cost of Equity," *Financial Management Journal* (Spring 1987): 33–45. Reprinted by permission of the Financial Management Journal and Eugene F. Brigham. **515** Figure 13-11 adapted from "An Empirical Evaluation of Accounting Income Numbers," by R. Ball and P. Brown, in *Journal of Accounting Resarch* 6(Autumn 1968): 169. Reprinted by permission of the Journal of Accounting Research. **517** Table 13-6 from B. King, "Market and Industry Factors in Stock Price Behavior," *Journal of Business* 39(January 1966): 139–90, adapted by permission of the University of Chicago Press. Copyright © 1966 by the University of Chicago. All rights reserved. **530,531** Tables 14-1 and 14-2 from *Portfolio Strategy*, September 1980, January 1985, and January 1989. Copyright © 1980, 1985, and 1989 by Goldman, Sachs & Company. Reprinted by permission. **532** Table 14-3 from "Do Common Stock Quality Ratings Predict Risk?" by R. Haugen, in *Financial Analysts Journal* (March–April 1979): 68–71. Copyright © 1979 by the Financial Analysts Journal. Reprinted by permission. **539** Table 14-4 from *Predicasts Basebook*; copyright © 1988 Predicasts, Cleveland, Ohio. Reprinted by permission. **541** Table 14-6 based on various issues of Value Line Investment Survey, 1978–1985 (New York: Arnold Bernhard & Co.). Copyright © 1989 by Value Line, Inc.; used by permission. **611** Figure 15-13 adapted from J. MacBeth and L. Merville, "Tests of the Black-Scholes and Cox Call Option Valuation Models," *Journal of Finance*, May 1976. Copyright © 1976 by the American Finance Association. Reprinted by permission. **623** Figure 16-1 from K. French, G. Schwert, and R. Stambaugh, "Expected Stock Returns and Volatility," *Journal of Financial Economics* 19(1987). Reprinted by permission of Kenneth R. French, G. William Schwert, Robert F. Stambaugh, and Elsevier Science Publishers, Physical Sciences and Engineering Division, publishers of the *Journal of Financial Economics*. **655,656,657** Figures 16-14, 16-15, and 16-16 reprinted from T. O'Brien, "The Mechanics of Portfolio Insurance," *Journal of Portfolio Management*, Spring 1988, by permission of Institutional Investor Systems, Inc. **694** Table 17-3 from *Trading and Hedging with Short-Term Interest Futures*. Reprinted by permission of the Chicago Mercantile Exchange. **755,756,769** Figures 18-5, 18-6, and 18-9 reprinted from R. Ibbotson, L. Siegel, and K. Love, "World Wealth: Market Values and Returns," *Journal of Portfolio Management*, Fall 1985, by permission of Institutional Investor Systems, Inc. **757** Figure 18-7 from "Why Not Diversify Internationally Rather Than Domestically? *Financial Analysts Journal* (July–August 1974): 48–54. Copyright © 1974 by the Financial Analysts Journal. Reprinted by permission. **758** Table 18-5 reprinted from B. Solnik and B. Noetzlin, "Optimal International Asset Allocation," *Journal of Portfolio Management* (Fall 1982): 11–21, by permission of Institutional Investor Systems, Inc. **772,773** Tables 18-9 and 18-10 from Ibbotson and Siegel, "Real Estate Returns: A Comparison with Other Investments," and Miles and McCue, "Commercial Real Estate Returns," *AREUEA Journal* 12, no. 3(1984). Copyright © 1984 by the American Real Estate and Urban Economics Association. Reprinted by permission. **800,801** Tables 19-2 and 19-3 from *Portfolio Strategy*, March 1985. Copyright © 1985 by Goldman, Sachs & Company. Reprinted by permission. **903** Figure 21-5 from R. Shiller, "Do Stock Prices Move Too Much to Be Justified by Subsequent Changes in Dividend?" *The American*

Economic Review 71, no. 3(June 1981), reprinted by permission of the American Economic Association. **934–35,936** Tables 22-1 and 22-2 reprinted by permission of Anheuser-Busch Companies, Inc., and Subsidiaries. **938** Table 22-4 reprinted from various issues of *Standard & Poor's Industry Surveys* by permission of Standard & Poor's Corporation. **990** Figure 23-9 from *Total Return Management: A Goal-Oriented Framework for Bond Portfolio Strategy*, by Martin L. Leibowitz. Copyright © 1979 by Salomon Brothers, Inc. Reprinted by permission.

Selected questions from the Chartered Financial Analysts Examination appear in the end-of-chapter Questions and Problems. Reprinted by permission of the Institute of Chartered Financial Analysts.